MW01554032

PIONEERING STUDIES
IN SOCIONOMICS

PIONEERING STUDIES IN SOCIONOMICS

Socionomics — The Science of Social Prediction
Volume 2

by

Robert R. Prechter, Jr.

Pioneering Studies
in Socionomics

Copyright © 2003 by Robert Rougelot Prechter, Jr.

Printed in the United States of America

For information, address the publishers:
New Classics Library
Post Office Box 1618
Gainesville, Georgia 30503 USA
Phone: 800-336-1618, 770-536-0309
Fax: 770-536-2514
E-mail address for products: customerservice@elliottwave.com
E-mail address for comments: bb@elliottwave.com
Web site: www.elliottwave.com

New Classics Library is the book publishing division of
Elliott Wave International, Inc.

ISBN: 0-932750-56-7
Library of Congress Catalog Control Number: 2002117628

This book is dedicated to Robert Prechter, Sr., Barbara Prechter, Douglas Rumble, Margaret O. Bynum, Marilyn Hopkins, Jim Futral, David Larkin, Gretchen Mieszkowski, Irving Janis, Marty Kugell, Creighton Hooker, Phil Roth, Bob Nurock, Dick Diamond, Bob Meier, Liebe Geft, Hernan Cortes and John Casti.

Acknowledgments

I would like to acknowledge invaluable assistance from Dave Allman, Leigh Tipton, Angie Barringer, Rachel Webb and Sally Webb. The jacket design is by Darrell King and Roberta Machcinski. Thanks especially to the brave souls who are this book's guest contributors.

Note: For this book, the original essays have been lightly edited for grammar, clarity and precision.

CONTENTS

✓ Protecting Investors (Not.) - J. Notsinger + K. Kim 221

Toward a Revolution in Macroeconomics

Science and the Wave Principle

Controversy and Validation

Socionomics and Quantum Physics

Miscellaneous Articles, Letters, Speeches and Observations

Appendix: **Toward Quantifying Sociometers Other Than the Stock Market**

Foreword: A Socionomic Manifesto

Men have tried for millennia to forecast human events. In the long history of social forecasting, the chronic propensity for immense error has resulted from linear thinking, the extrapolation of current trends into the future. This nearly ubiquitous approach is a result of the assumption that laws governing billiard ball behavior apply to human behavior. Simply stated, most people, including economists, are social mechanists. They believe that markets and societies share the property of an object in motion, which will continue along a calculable path until some new outside influence — a force or an obstruction — alters its trajectory. It remains a source of amazement to me how often I am asked what events will cause (or, in modified form, what "catalyst" will "precipitate") a change in the direction of the market, politics or the economy, a query which has as its basis the unquestioned assumption that the record of human history is somehow at the mercy of random outside influences. Usually the question is not asked in the context of truly outside influences, such as earthquakes, volcanoes and floods but with regard to one presumed social influence over another presumed social effect. Yet social forces cannot be "outside influences" because they reside within the human social experience, in which all elements are interrelated. The general assumption of outside causality nevertheless persists and has as its result the continuing bizarre state of affairs in which most people involved in areas of life where the future is important waste hours debating the various potential "causes" of the trends they hope to predict. They usually conclude that forecasting with any reliability is impossible, yet they persist in the exercise anyway! Successful anticipation of future events *is* possible. However, it is possible only with the knowledge that human behavior changes as a result not of external forces but of internal ones.

Generally speaking, the human mind has two aspects, which impel two types of actions. Rational, conscious mental processes can induce actions that create airplanes, computers and skyscrapers. Unconscious mental processes do not produce goods and services but rather generate hard-wired emotional signals that trigger impulsive actions. These emotional signals developed through eons of evolution, which is why they impel all kinds of actions with respect to concerns that are common to lower animals, such as territorialism, fighting, fleeing and sex. (The production of art probably involves both mental aspects, which is why it provides the richest experiences.) One of the unconscious mind's occupations is increasing the chances of survival through mimicking, which is reflected in the herding impulse, a fact that provides a biological and psychological basis for socionomics.

Conventional economists have been mired in the error that trends in finance result from the exercise of the first type of thinking: the rational and the conscious. It is a false premise, which has just begun to be undermined. In twenty years, academic economists have gone from believing that markets are rational, efficient calculators of intrinsic value — and therefore random — to believing that psychology occasionally might have something to do with extremes in short term financial valuation. Someday, a large segment of the profession will surely come to understand that a mix of randomness and psychology is not the answer to overall financial market behavior. At the forefront of the new understanding is the Chairman of Psychiatry at Metro West Medical Center (Boston), Dr. John Schott, who is also an instructor at Harvard and Tufts medical schools and a successful money manager. Even on the subject of practical investing for the individual, he states unequivocally, "Emotions are central; they are the entire ball game."[†] Emotions are certainly the entire ball game for many individuals, so that as a rare few investors' individually informed and rational decisions cancel each other out, what remains on the stock market graph is a record of the trends of shared emotion, the mood of the herd.

It is not in the social nature of mankind to accept and be content with stasis. If there is one constant regarding social mood, it is its continuous flux. However, the fact that social mood is ever-changing is not, as many would assume, an impediment to forecasting; it is the key to it. Investigation by R.N. Elliott in the 1930s and 1940s yielded the crucial knowledge that social behavior changes not randomly but according to a pattern. Social mood *does* have constancy, but it is a dynamic one. While the extents of social mood, experiences and conditions vary from time to time and place to place, the patterns of behavior that lead to a reversal in trend do not. In order successfully to anticipate changes in society reliably, one must understand the consistent pattern of society's internal dynamics.

[†] Schott, John W. and Arbeiter, Jean S. (1998). *Mind Over Money*. Boston: Little Brown & Co., p.3.

Social mood trends apparently result from forces endogenous to the process of collective mental interaction. These forces are not rational but impulsive, probably deriving from herding behavior governed by the basal ganglia and the limbic system, which are pre-rational portions of the brain. This dynamic creates social *attitudes*, which are manifest instantaneously in investment trends, political sentiment, the character of popular cultural symbols and other such immediately expressible outlets for the prevailing social mood. These attitudes fluctuate according to the Wave Principle, which is a robust fractal governed by Fibonacci mathematics.

Because the naturally patterned interaction of individual limbic systems governs the dynamics of social mood, it ultimately compels the consciously undertaken collective social actions that are generally considered historically significant. *Non-social* yet significant events, such as natural disasters, clearly do not affect the patterned sociological dynamic and are irrelevant to it. On the other hand, *social* actions temporally follow *and* are in sympathy with the patterned sociological dynamic. The conclusion best fitting these data is that the dynamic itself shapes human social action and is its primary stylistic motivator.

Social action comes in two types. The first is *collective action*, which is group-based action, such as a labor strike. It takes purposeful cooperation and a majority decision by a group or a group's leader(s) to effect a group-based action. The second type is *aggregate action*, a summation of individual actions, such as trends in cigarette smoking. Both types follow Elliott waves because they have the same basis. In each case, people's decisions to act are based not primarily upon independent reason but upon substantial influence from others. Interaction and communication with others leads to a shared attitude, or "social mood," which prompts collectively shared opinions, which prompts and shapes social actions.

All economic, political and cultural developments are shaped and guided by the Wave Principle of human social behavior. It is the engine of everything from popular fads and fashions to the events of collective action that make history. Because the social mood dynamic unfolds according to a principle governed by *phi* (the Fibonacci, or "golden," ratio), which is the basis for many processes of growth and decay, expansion and contraction, and progress and regress in nature, we can see that humanity's social experience reflects an essential aspect of the processes of life and the universe in general.

Once you understand the fundamentality of social mood change, you approach the socionomic insight. The socionomic insight is that conventional assumptions about the direction of social causality are not only incorrect but opposite to what actually occurs. Social events do not compel social mood, as is widely supposed; rather, the patterns of social mood impel social events. For example, the state of the economy does not underlie social mood; social mood underlies the state of the economy. Politics do not affect social mood; social mood affects politics. Demographics do not determine stock market trends; the social mood that determines stock market trends determines demographics. Rising stock trends do not improve people's mood; people's improving mood makes stock prices rise. Styles of popular art and entertainment do not affect social mood; social mood determines the popularity of various styles of popular art and entertainment. War does not impact stock trends; the mood that governs stock trends determines the propensity for war. And so on.

The sociological dynamic unfolds regardless of whether humans create a gauge of it for observation and reaction, but when a gauge (such as the Dow Jones Industrial Average) is created and widely observed, people incorporate the gauge itself into the process of mental interaction. It is a conscious reference point for the individual participants and an unconscious reference point for the social dynamic. Consciously rendered changes in the components of the gauge (such as occasionally replacing one or two of the stocks in the Dow), then, are irrelevant to the more important fact that the unconscious dynamic uses the gauge as a reference regardless of its components.

People do not notice the operation of the sociological dynamic because they're not looking. Indeed, given the opportunity, they typically reject the idea outright because such dynamics are contrary to the natural assumptions that people make about how societies (and more narrowly, markets) progress and regress. That these processes must be unknown to or rejected by virtually all is a prerequisite for their operation. Only people who are blind to the principles that govern the social dynamic can behave so as to produce it, because only then can they be passionate, active participants in it.

An individual who can rise above the social trends that sweep along his fellows so that he can observe their operation has an incalculable advantage over all those who do not. He has a basis upon which to anticipate the future, not every time and not perfectly, but well enough to have immense value. Anticipating the social future has always appeared to be a gift unavailable to humanity. That has been true until now not because the task is impossible but because it requires detailed knowledge of the patterns of social behavior and an ability to think and act in a fashion contrary to that impelled by unenlightened human nature as directed by the primitive brain stem and limbic system. Armed with the knowledge of patterned social behavior, a wise individual can train his reasoning cerebral cortex to recognize his emotionally driven thought processes and thus observe the activity of groups and societies calmly from Olympus. He cannot avoid human society and thus cannot avoid the social dynamic. However, he can make conscious, rational decisions to benefit his prosperity, and at times even his survival, while others, who participate fully in the dynamic unconsciously, use rationalization to justify emotional decisions, never once seeing the forest for the trees and, sadly, without even knowing there's a forest to be seen.

Merely to accept the fact of social flux is to be prepared for the future in a way that no linear thinker can be. Even at this primitive level of understanding, a forecaster will have a much better chance of avoiding the mistakes of the crowd in chasing one investment fad after another, in taking on debt at the peak of an economic expansion, in selling his productive assets at the bottom of a depression or in getting caught up in the latest political trend or rushing off to war. Conversely, when linear thinkers live as if today's conditions are the way the world will always be, they commit exactly the error that causes a buildup of excesses, thus resulting in the very cyclicality that they deny or of which they are unaware.

Successful social forecasting is possible only on the basis of probabilities. Often, when knowledge is sufficient, one can say with certainty what those probabilities are. In the long run, acting in accordance with the most probable future conditions will result in a more successful life. Unfortunately, people tend to demand certainty in forecasting, and if they cannot get it, they do not change their behavior. This has been, and will continue to be, a recipe for personal disaster. In 1929, it was those who were entirely unprepared for the crash and Great Depression, those who were mortgaged to the hilt betting on further expansion, those who had become convinced that a "new era" had dawned, who ended up in bread lines or jumping out of windows. In 1980, it was those who were entirely unprepared for an era of prosperity, those who were invested to the hilt in gold and silver and Swiss francs, those who had become convinced that recovery was impossible, who ended up losing much of their fortunes and missing out on two decades of productive success. Today is perhaps one of the best times ever to be socionomically aware, but the vast majority of people are again unprepared for yet another major sea change.

At the very least, *psychological* preparation for changes in the social and economic climate should be considered a worthwhile goal. Financial and physical preparation for downturns, even if the downturns do not occur, should be considered a reasonable cost of insurance. On the other hand, when events *do* occur along the lines of the greatest probability, whether in the case of emerging uptrends or downtrends, your preparedness will be worth its weight in gold to you, your family and perhaps even your progeny.

This book is about using socionomics to evaluate social conditions and make social predictions. Predictions involve two levels of complexity: the *general character* of coming events and the specific events themselves. The primary aspects of the social dynamic are its formological imperative, which governs the former, and its chaotic process, which governs the latter.

A formological system is one within which the essential cause of events is an imperative of form rather than of preceding events or conditions or of outside influences. (For a discussion of this term, see *The Wave Principle of Human Social Behavior and the New Science of Socionomics*, pp. 17, 399-400.) Social mood trends are, and must be, independent of social-event causality because their primary register — the record of aggregate stock prices — is patterned as the Wave Principle. Social mood trends, and therefore trends in the *character* of social action, are thus determined formologically, not by antecedent events.

Socionomics recognizes that *specific* social events, which are among the results of social mood trends, have specific antecedents and derive from the chaotic aspect of social activity. As an example of the difference, trends of social goodwill vs. bellicosity are formologically determined, but the specific manifestations of those impulses — which peace treaties will be proposed or signed and which leaders will take adversaries into war, and so on — result from the workings of chaos with antecedents in prior events.

Formological developments are far more deterministic and predictable than chaotic ones. Nevertheless, such developments provide the context within which specific events occur and so aid in the attempt to anticipate various specifics as well. Predicting trends and changes in the character of social behavior is an ability available only to those who fully incorporate the socionomic insight. Those who hold this insight are also therefore better equipped to predict trends and changes in specific social circumstances as well.

Before diving into these essays, you should at least be familiar with the basics of the Wave Principle, as presented in Chapter 1 of *The Wave*

Principle of Human Social Behavior. The rest of that volume provides the proper grounding fully to appreciate the studies collected here. On the other hand, there is some adventure in following along "blind" as we developed and applied our ideas in the early days.

This book primarily chronicles the sociological studies and forecasts that Pete Kendall and I conducted between 1985 and 2002, covering not only various formological aspects of the real-time social present and future but also some of their specific manifestations. I have also included a few guest editorials. As the human experience, particularly in the aggregate, is a stew of joy, pain, wisdom and folly, many of these studies make for lively reading. We hope you enjoy reading these pages as much as we did writing them.

—Robert R. Prechter, Jr., December 2002

POPULAR CULTURE

Prechter

The Elliott Wave Theorist
August 3, 1979

[This commentary accompanied the display of a multi-year symmetrical wave pattern with certain mathematical properties. The full report is reprinted in *Market Analysis for the New Millennium* (2002).]

What's Going On?

[The] wave structure I have shown here unfolded its pattern quite clearly regardless of wars, energy crises, speeches, assassinations, Watergates, Peanutgates, jawboning or the weather. To a phenomenal extent, the DJIA appeared to know exactly where it was, exactly where it had been, and exactly where it was going. But *why* is an average of thirty [major industrial] stocks so reliable in exhibiting over and over again these phenomena of construction? For a hundred years, investors have noticed that events external to the market often seem to have no effect on the market's progress. With the knowledge that the market continuously unfolds in waves that are related to each other through *form* and *ratio*, we can see why there is little connection. *The market has a life of its own.* Now what ultimately *causes* that particular pattern of the market's life is open to debate. It can be surmised, though, that it is *mass human psychology* that is registering its changes in the barometer known as the DJIA. This idea helps to explain the cause of future events: changes in the mass emotional outlook. That's what comes first. The market is a mirror of the forces, whatever they may be, which are affecting humanity both *in* and *out* of the market arena. The market doesn't "see into the future" as the discounting idea suggests; it reflects the causes of the future. Increasingly optimistic people expand business; increasingly depressed people contract their businesses. The *results* show up later as a "discounted" future. It's not the politicians who gallantly "save" a bear market by returning to policies of economic sanity, it's the mass emotional environment, as reflected by the market, which forces them at some critical point to do it. Events do not shape the forces of the market; it is the forces behind the market that shape events.

Prechter

The Elliott Wave Theorist
August 1985

Popular Culture
and the Stock Market

Most people believe that stock market movement is caused by fundamental economic and political conditions and events. Experienced stock market watchers have recognized that such events "cast their shadow before," on the stock exchange. However, the assumption even among veteran market students is that the stock market foreshadows events because "smart money" is correctly guessing future events. This report is an attempt to lend some justification[†] to an alternate explanation. The reasoning is as follows:

1) Popular art, fashion and mores are a reflection of the dominant public mood.

2) Because the stock market changes direction in step with these expressions of mood, it is another coincident register of the dominant public mood and changes in it.

3) Because a substantial change in mood in a positive or negative direction foreshadows the character of what are generally considered to be historically important events, mood changes must be considered as possibly, if not probably, being the basic cause of ensuing events.

Both a study of the stock market and a study of trends in popular attitudes support the conclusion that the movement of aggregate stock prices is a direct recording of mood and mood change within the investment community, and by extension, within the society at large. It is

---

[†] *This report is designed as a rough introduction to an idea, not a final statement. My intention is to indicate a field of study that others may wish to pursue. All facts presented herein were checked, most with first-hand sources but some with second-hand sources (particularly in the pre-1950s data), which may have produced errors. I would appreciate notice of any errors, which will be corrected in any future printing(s).*

clear that extremes in popular cultural trends coincide with extremes in stock prices, since they peak and trough coincidentally in their reflection of the popular mood. The stock market is the best place to study mood change because it is the only field of mass behavior where specific, detailed and voluminous numerical data exists. It was only with such data that R.N. Elliott was able to discover the Wave Principle, which reveals that mass mood changes are natural, rhythmic and precise. The stock market is literally a drawing of how the scales of mass mood are tipping. A decline indicates an increasing "negative" mood on balance, and an advance indicates an increasing "positive" mood on balance.

Major historic events which are often considered important to the future (i.e., economic activity, lawmaking, war) are not causes of change; they are the result of mass mood changes that have already occurred. The reason that such events are lagging indicators of mood change is that it takes a good deal of time and an extensive swing in mood throughout the populace for the shared mood change to result in such events. For instance, to motivate a society or a body which represents the society to undertake a collective action such as creating a sweeping new law, electing a new regime or starting a war, the new mood must have taken root throughout much of the society and reached extreme proportions.

In some cases, extremes in mood permit actions that impose a structural (usually political) rigidity on the society. The effects of this institutionalization may continue to be felt for a long period because it takes time to mobilize machinery and play out the consequences of the actions initially taken at the extreme point of mass mood. As an example, the collective mood in Germany in 1933 was so negative that its expression resulted in the granting of power to Adolf Hitler. Although the underlying public mood was changing toward the less negative from that date forward, the consequences of that popular action took twelve years to play out because the representatives of the negative popular mood at the low gained such great political power. The collective mood in the United States also reached a negative extreme in 1933, the year the depression hit its depths. As one manifestation, enrollment in and disruptive activity by the Communist Party in the United States peaked in the 1930s. In contrast to the German experience, however, those forces never achieved political control, so the improving mood was allowed to express itself in the years that followed.

Any activity that by its nature quickly reflects a change in how people in general feel is a coincident indicator of mood change and thus an advance indicator of important social events. A person communicates his mood when he puts on a record, chooses a movie, decides what sporting event to see or chooses a book to read. Many people, as is obvious from the swings in elections, base their votes on their then-current mood rather than on rational thought. The availability in a free society of numerous books, records, styles, entertainment events and candidates to choose from is a requisite for the attainment of reliable, detailed data. The relative popularity of the styles available then reflects the dominant mood. It should be stressed that the record of these overall societal changes says nothing necessarily about how an individual or a specific group might feel or act, but it is an indication of the "net" mood of the society at large (and apparently at times of humanity at large). For the overall change in mood to express itself, all that is required is for *some* particularly susceptible people to undergo a *substantial* change in mood and/or for *most* people to undergo *some* change in mood. The latter explanation is more convincing to this writer, after ten years of watching individuals' behavior as the stock market ebbs and flows. In this case, those individuals whose state of mind placed them closest to taking action in the direction of the changing trend can be stirred to action as a result of just a slight change in mood, which pushes them past the threshold. The further the swing in public mood carries, the larger will be the number of people stirred to action.

If mass mood change is indeed the cause, and its manifestation a visible indicator, of coming social events, then evidence of mood change is the single most important area of discovery for those who wish to peek into the future of social events. In the world of popular culture, "trendsetters" and the avant-garde must be carefully observed since their ideas are often an expression of the leading edge of public mood.

Trends in music, movies, fashion, literature, television, popular philosophy, sports, dance, automobile styling, mores, sexual identity,[1] family life, campus activities, politics and poetry all reflect the prevailing mood, sometimes in subtle ways. Noticeable changes in slower-moving mediums such as the movie industry more readily reveal changes in larger degrees of trend, such as the Cycle. More sensitive mediums such as television change quickly enough to reflect changes in the Primary trends of popular mood. Intermediate and Minor trends are likely paralleled by current song hits, which can rush up and down

Direction of Mood Trend

Cultural Manifestation

AREA OF CULTURE	RISING TRANSITION	PEAK POSITIVE MOOD	FALLING TRANSITION	PEAK NEGATIVE MOOD
CAMPUS TRENDS	Work hard, have fun	Positive-minded save-the-world social concern	Rebellious, angry social concern	From riots to sudden quiet
CREATIVITY	Positive mood creativity	Positive mood creative trend fully realized	Negative mood creativity; lack of creativity	Negative mood creative trend fully realized; destruction
DANCE	Partners together, tempo speeds up, partners separate	Partners apart, fast tempo	Partners come back together; tempos slow down	Partners together
FAMILY LIFE	Babies popular, family orientation, marriage	Trend reaches extreme	Children a negative value, divorce, "single" life preferred	Trend reaches extreme
FASHION (color)	Colors emerge	Bright colors dominate	Drabness emerges	Drab colors dominate
FASHION (covering)	Men's ties narrow	Bodies exposed, short skirts, bikinis for women, tight pants for men	Men's ties widen	Bodies covered; floor-length dresses, baggy pants
FASHION (style)	"Correctness" stressed	Flamboyant individuality for men and women	Anti-fashion fashions	Conservative dress returns
FITNESS/HEALTH	Healthy lifestyle, physical fitness practiced, encouraged	Body admired. Body-building peaks. Smoking, "junk" foods taboo	Fitness fanaticism wanes rapidly. Social concern replaces concern with self	"Working out" is out of fashion.
GOOD vs. EVIL	Bad guys vs. good guys (movies, pro wrestling). Heroes celebrated	Everybody's a good guy	There are no bad guys and no good guys. Heroes trashed	Everybody's a bad guy
JUDGMENTS	Answers are black and white	There is good in all	Who's to judge?	There is evil in all
MOVIES/TV/LITERATURE	"G" rated themes, adventure	Celebrate life; upbeat, entertaining themes	Social concern, symbolism, heaviness, anti-heroes	Horror, dead-end themes
NOSTALGIA	Nostalgia for black-and-white values	Focus on now	Nostalgia for mythical simpler times (back to the earth)	Focus on now
POETRY	Structured	Lyrical	Anarchic	Ugly

AREA OF CULTURE	RISING TRANSITION	PEAK POSITIVE MOOD	FALLING TRANSITION	PEAK NEGATIVE MOOD
POLITICIANS (perceptions of)	Strengths magnified, weaknesses overlooked, forgiven	Politicians revered (Camelot, "Teflon")	Weaknesses magnified, strengths overlooked or denied	Politicians hated or deified
POLITICS	Relative stability	Desire to maintain status quo	Old styles fail	Radical parties and solutions
POP ART	Structured, traditional	Colorful, wild, "alive"	Anarchic --anything goes	Deliberately ugly, heavy, sedate
POP MUSIC (Arrangement)	Simplicity peaks, complexity returns		Complexity peaks, simplicity returns	
POP MUSIC (Image)	Dirty, happy	Clean, happy	Clean, angry	Dirty, angry
POP MUSIC (Lyrics)	Any non-negative theme OK	Joyous celebration and love songs	Anxious, socially conscious themes emerge	Songs of despair, hate, violence; also happy denial
POP MUSIC (Melody)	Melody emerges as a key ingredient	Lilting, complex, inventive melodies and harmony	Melody is eclipsed by various elements: rhythm, arrangement	Little melody or chord structure
POP MUSIC (Mood)	Upbeat, major keys	Upbeat, major and minor keys	Minor keys, downbeat, arty	Distorted sounds, atonality, dissonance
POP PHILOSOPHY	Achievement is possible and desirable	Love will save the world	Achievement is a waste of time	Hate and destruction will give the world what it deserves
RELIGION	Conservative religion but increasingly subdominant	Religious tolerance and inclusiveness	Religion is openly questioned and passionately reintroduced	Powerful fundamentalist religions and cults
SEXUAL IMAGES	"Masculine" men and "feminine" women	Heterosexual images peak	"Feminine" caring men; "masculine", liberated women	Focus on alternative sexual styles
SPORTS	Clean "good guy" sports		Rough "bad guy" sports	
STOCK MARKET (popular valuation of productive enterprise)	Rising	Topping	Falling or correcting	Bottoming
WAR	Old wars fought and concluded	Little conflict	More conflict; new wars begin	New wars begin or intensify

the sales charts as people change moods. Of course, *all* of these media of expression are influenced by mood changes of all degrees (i.e. extents and time spans). The net impression communicated is a result of the *mix and dominance* of the forces in all these areas at any given moment.

Forecasting the mood changes themselves can best be accomplished through a knowledge of the Wave Principle[2] and a study of the record of the relative strength of "positive mood" and "negative mood"[3] manifestations at all degrees of trend. Although the stock market would probably remain the single best indicator because of its reliably precise measurement of mood and mood change, other social phenomena *could* be detailed, numericized and studied, and used to forecast social events and even changes in the mood trends themselves when extremes are achieved. If reliable data on social activities other than stock valuation were available, we could undoubtedly graph and interpret them with a similar degree of reliability. The main difficulty in assessing indicators of mood other than stock prices is the woeful lack of precise numerical data produced by social "scientists." A precise, measurable detailing of sporting event attendance figures, the number of notes and note changes in popular melodies, the lyrical content of popular songs, story content in popular books, hemline lengths, tie widths, heel heights, the prominence of various fashion and pop art colors, the angularity vs. roundness of automobile styling, the construction of various architectural styles and a host of other reflections of the popular mood, all weighted according to volume of sales, would allow us to read graphs of the public mood in the same way we read graphs of aggregate stock prices now. By comparing the evidence to stock price movement, their implications could be assessed and the general hypothesis presented here could be tested. It is highly likely that plots of the net existence and dominance of these various popular cultural elements on a daily basis would parallel those of aggregate stock prices and reflect the Wave Principle. It would take a multi-year research project to gather such data, so for now some general observations will have to suffice.

Fashion

Stock broker Ralph Rotnem observed, rather casually, that the long-term trends of stock prices and of the hemlines on women's skirts appear to be in concert. Skirt heights rose to mini-skirt brevity in the 1920s and in the 1960s, peaking with stock prices both times. Floor-length fashions appeared in the 1930s and 1970s (the Maxi), bottoming with stock prices. This is not likely a frivolous observation. In my judgment, it is not unreasonable to hypothesize that a rise in both hemlines and stock prices reflects a general increase in friskiness and daring among the population, and a decline in both, a decrease. Because skirt lengths have limits (the floor and the upper thigh, respectively), the reaching of a limit would imply that a maximum of positive or negative mood had been achieved.

Similar changes appear in fashion *colors*. Bright colors are associated with market tops and dull, dark colors with bottoms. It is not coincidence, then, that, generally speaking, the smaller the skirt or swimsuit, the brighter the color(s). Floor-length fashions, in turn, are more often associated with dull, dark colors such as brown, black and gray. These fashion elements reflect the same general mood. Tie width, heel height, pants leg style, and flamboyance or conservatism in men's fashions (remember London's Carnaby Street, which peaked in influence when the Value Line topped in 1968?) also fit the trends in the stock market.

The idea that outside events could cause a rising trend in skirt heights would appear ridiculous on the surface of it. Skirts' hemlines didn't suddenly jump to above the knee because Lyndon Johnson created ebullience by announcing the formation of the Great Society. Skirt heights had been rising for years and merely continued along the established trend, as did the trends toward brightly colored clothes and bikinis. The announcement of the Great Society programs was merely an expression of how far the ebullient mood had carried in the previous 20 years, so far that the public representatives wanted it institutionalized. In the same way, isn't it ridiculous to assume that outside events would cause a rise in the stock market? It appears more sensible to recognize that the mood reflected by rising stock prices is the impetus for later grand-scale events.

Popular Art

The late 1960s produced Peter Max, who specialized in adorning objects for public consumption with bright primary colors. The brightness of color peaked with Day-Glo poster art, which sported shimmering alive colors when showered with ultraviolet light. The irony of Day-Glo art was that it was intended to be viewed in pitch darkness, a curious mixture of experience (the brightest possible colors in the darkest possible surroundings). Fittingly, it occurred during the transition phase from peak positive mood to bear market that took place from 1966 to 1969. 1970s' pop art, produced during the long bear market from 1969-1982, generally consisted of massive hunks of dark or heavy sculpture, much of which was detested for its ugliness and later removed. In both cases, a common question was, "Is it really art?" The avant-garde is always questioned (properly so), but our concern is not whether it is art, but whether it expresses a light, bright, positive mood or a heavy, dark, negative one. The former is found in bull markets and in extremes at market tops; the latter is found in bear markets and in extremes at market bottoms. (Perhaps an upcoming peak will be accompanied by brightly colored laser art.)

Movies

While musicals, adventures, and comedies weave into the pattern, one particularly clear example of correlation with the stock market is provided by horror movies. Horror movies descended upon the American scene in 1930-1933, the years the Dow Jones Industrials collapsed. Five classic horror films were all produced in less than three short years. *Frankenstein* and *Dracula* premiered in 1931, in the middle of the great bear market. *Dr. Jekyll and Mr. Hyde* played in 1932, the bear market bottom year and the only year that a horror film actor was ever granted an Oscar. *The Mummy* and *King Kong* hit the screen in 1933, on the double bottom. These are *the* classic horror films of all time, along with the new breed in the 1970s, and they all sold big. The message appeared to be that people had an inhuman, horrible side to them. Just to prove the vision correct, Hitler was placed in power in 1933 (an expression of the darkest public mood in decades) and fulfilled it. For thirteen years, lasting only slightly past the stock market bottom of 1942, films continued to feature Frankenstein monsters, vampires, werewolves and undead mummies. Ironically, Hollywood tried to introduce a new monster in 1935 during a bull market, but *Werewolf of London* was a flop. When film makers tried again in 1941, in the depths of a bear market, *The Wolf Man* was a smash hit.

Shortly after the bull market in stocks resumed in 1942, films abandoned dark, foreboding horror in the most sure-fire way: by laughing at it. When Abbott and Costello met Frankenstein, horror had no power. That decade treated moviegoers to patriotic war films and love themes. The 1950s gave us sci-fi adventures in a celebration of man's abilities;

all the while, the bull market in stocks raged on. The early 1960s introduced exciting James Bond adventures and happy musicals. The milder horror styles of the bull market years and the limited extent of their popularity stand in stark contrast to those of the bear market years.

Then a change hit. Just about the time the stock market was peaking, film makers became introspective, doubting and cynical. How far the change in cinematic mood had carried didn't become fully clear until 1969-1970, when *Night of the Living Dead* and *The Texas Chainsaw Massacre* debuted. Just look at the chart of the Dow and you'll see the crash in mood that inspired those movies. The trend was set for the 1970s, as slice-and-dice horror hit the screen. There also appeared a rash of re-makes of the old Dracula and Frankenstein stories, but as a dominant theme, Frankenstein couldn't cut it; we weren't afraid of him any more. Hollywood had to horrify us to satisfy us, and

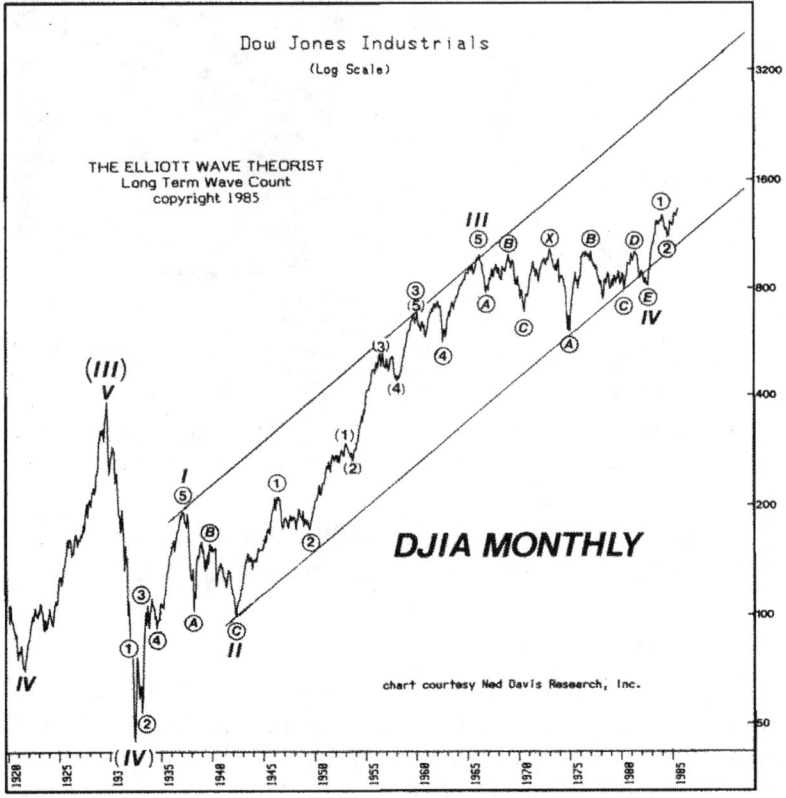

it did. The bloody slasher-on-the-loose movies were shocking versions of the '30s' monster shows, while the equally gory zombie films had a modern twist. In the 1930s, Dracula was a fitting allegory for the perceived fear of the day, that the aristocrat was sucking the blood of the common people. In the 1970s, horror was perpetrated by a *group* eating people alive, not an individual monster. An army of dead-but-moving flesh-eating zombies devouring every living person in sight was a fitting allegory for the new horror of the day, voracious government and the welfare state, and the pressures that most people felt as a result. The nature of late '70s'

warfare ultimately reflected the mass-devouring visions, with the destruction of internal populations in Cambodia and China.

Popular Music

Pop music has been virtually in lock step with the Dow Jones Industrial Average as well. The remainder of this report will focus on details of this phenomenon in order to clarify the extent to which the relationship (and, by extension, the others discussed above) exists.

As a 78-rpm record collector put it in a recent *Wall Street Journal* article, music reflects "every fiber of life" in the U.S. The timing of the careers of dominant youth-oriented (since the young are quickest to adopt new fashions) pop musicians has been perfectly in line with the peaks and troughs in the stock market. At turns in prices (and therefore mood), the dominant popular singers and groups of the time have faded quickly into obscurity and were replaced by styles that reflected the newly emerging mood.

The 1920s' bull market gave us hyper-fast dance music and jazz. The 1930s' bear years brought folk music laments ("Buddy, Can You Spare a Dime?"), and mellow ballroom dance music. The 1932-1937 bull market brought lively "swing" music. 1937 ushered in the Andrews Sisters, who enjoyed their greatest success during the corrective years of 1937-1942 ("girl groups" may be a corrective wave phenomenon; more on that later). The 1940s featured uptempo big band music, which dominated until the market peaked in 1945-46. The ensuing late-1940s' stock market correction featured "cool jazz" and mellow love ballad crooners, both male and female, whose styles reflected the dampened public mood.

The post-war bull market's initial advancing wave, wave (1) from 1949 through 1953, brought a flood of new grassroots-style music to the charts. During that period, 49 Country or Western music titles suddenly sold over a million copies each, and "race" music sold strongly enough to require its own sales charts in the industry's trade magazines. Interest in the more powerful black music by whites grew so strong during the early years of the bull market that Cleveland disc jockey Alan Freed arranged a "Rock and Roll Party" show in March 1953. Ironically, the show was canceled due to the chaos resulting from 30,000 people (two-thirds of whom were white) demanding to sit in a 10,000-seat arena. It was not re-staged until the exact month in the fall that kicked off wave (3) of ③, an upside acceleration, in the stock market's wave structure.

From that point on, the emerging excitement of an improving public mood could no longer be contained. The grassroots styles of music began to merge, and high energy rock 'n' roll exploded on the scene. Within a few years, the trendsetters were jitterbugging like crazy to work off their collective emotional high. By the late '50s, some of the doo-wop song tempos were so fast that the singers and musicians could

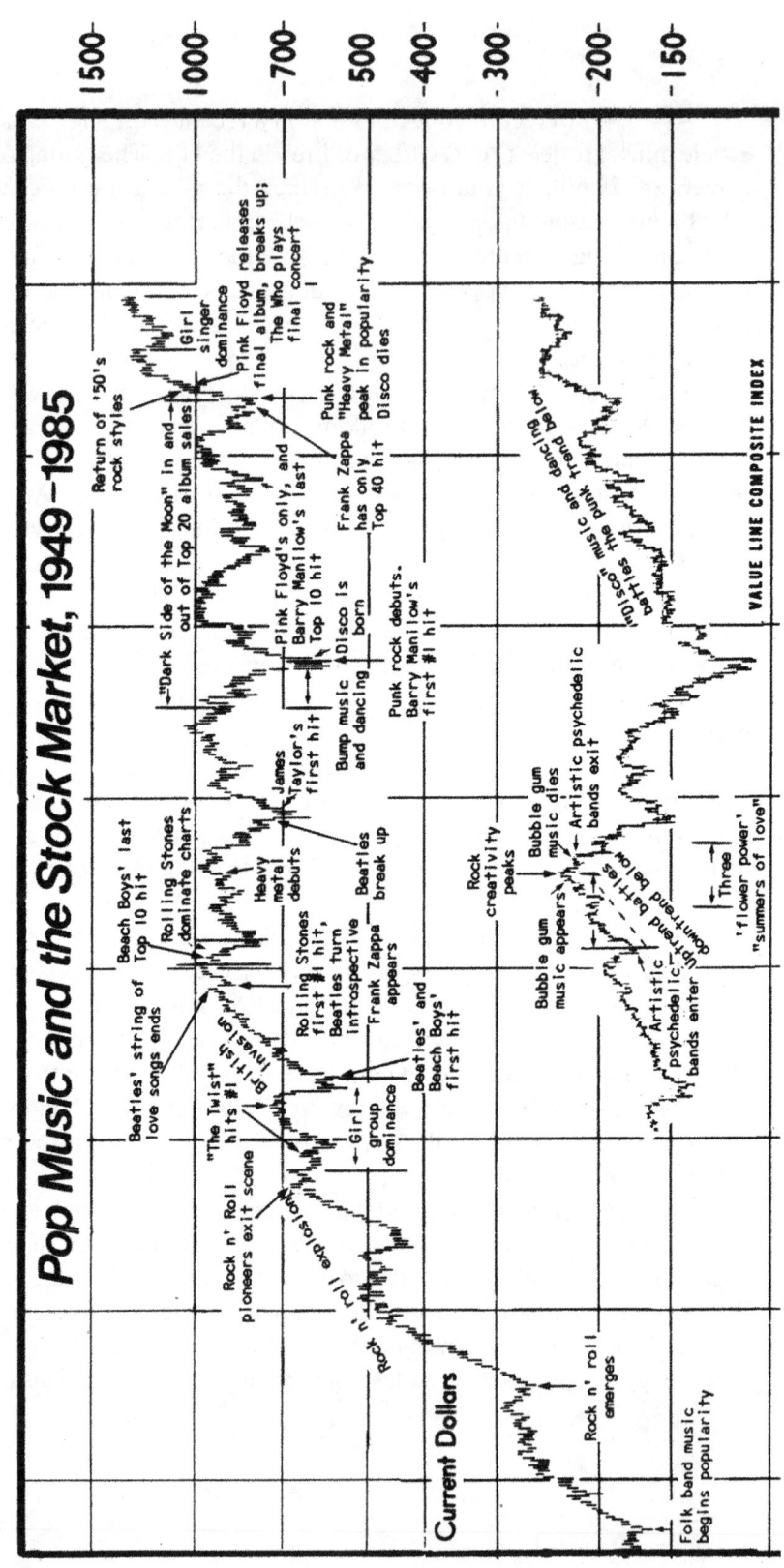

Pop Music and the Stock Market, 1949–1985

Current Dollars

VALUE LINE COMPOSITE INDEX

- Folk band music begins popularity
- Rock n' roll emerges
- Rock n' roll explosion
- Rock n' Roll pioneers exit scene
- "The Twist" hits #1
- Girl group dominance
- British invasion
- Beatles' string of last love songs ends
- Beach Boys' last love songs ends
- Rolling Stones dominate charts
- Beatles' and Beach Boys' first hit
- Frank Zappa appears
- Rolling Stones first hit, Beatles Introspective
- Heavy metal debuts
- Beatles break up
- James Taylor's first hit
- Bump music and dancing
- Punk rock debuts. Barry Manilow's first #1 hit
- Rock creativity peaks
- Bubble gum music appears
- Bubble gum music dies
- Artistic psychedelic bands enter
- Artistic psychedelic bands exit
- Three "flower power" "summers of love"
- Uptrend/downtrend battles below
- "Disco" music and dancing below the punk trend
- Pink Floyd's only, and out of Top 20 album sales
- "Dark Side of the Moon" in and out of Top 20 album sales
- Disco is born
- Barry Manilow's last Top 10 hit
- Frank Zappa has only Top 40 hit
- Punk rock and "Heavy Metal" peak in popularity
- Disco dies
- Return of '50's rock styles
- Girl singer dominance
- Pink Floyd releases final album, breaks up; The Who plays final concert

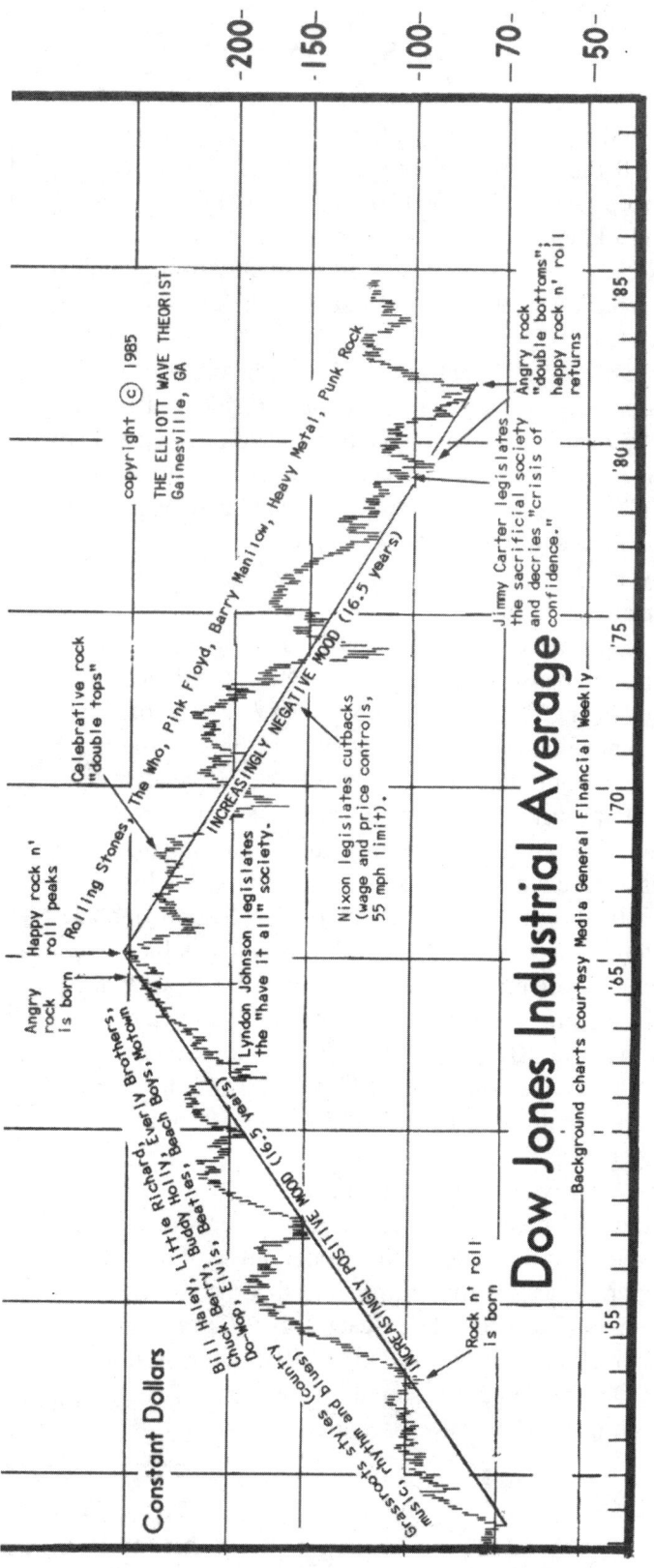

Dow Jones Industrial Average

Constant Dollars

Background charts courtesy Media General Financial Weekly

THE ELLIOTT WAVE THEORIST
Gainesville, GA

copyright © 1985

Angry rock is born

Happy rock n' roll peaks

Rolling Stones

Celebrative rock "double tops"

The Who, Pink Floyd, Barry Manilow, Heavy Metal, Punk Rock

"INCREASINGLY NEGATIVE MOOD (16.5 years)

Bill Haley, Little Richard, Everly Brothers, Buddy Holly, Beach Boys, Motown Chuck Berry, Elvis, Beatles, Do-wop,

Lyndon Johnson legislates the "have it all" society.

Nixon legislates cutbacks (wage and price controls, 55 mph limit).

Jimmy Carter legislates the sacrificial society and decries "crisis of confidence."

Angry rock "double bottoms"; happy rock n' roll returns

"INCREASINGLY POSITIVE MOOD (16.5 years)

Grassroots styles music: rhythm and blues) (country)

Rock n' roll is born

barely keep up with the pace. 1959 was the year that wave ③ peaked and the year that all the joyous, celebrative rock 'n' rollers' careers came to a sudden stop. They either died (Buddy Holly, Eddie Cochran, Ritchie Valens, and J.P. Richardson), were drafted (Elvis Presley), quit the scene (Little Richard, Chuck Berry) or faded quickly from popularity (Bo Diddley, Jerry Lee Lewis and a hundred Northeast doo-wop groups).

Popular music went into what rock 'n' roll historians consider somewhat of a stagnancy (producing many great songs, but little innovation) between 1959 and 1962, which just happens to be the period of the wave ④ stock market correction.[4] The correction in stock prices and the "correction" in popular musical innovation coincided precisely. This phase was marked by three phenomena in the realm of pop music and dance: phony made-by-the-record-company "stars," who were marketed on the basis of a handsome face or TV popularity and who copycatted rather than innovated, the emergence of "girl groups" on the charts and a basic change in social dance with the advent of the Twist (more on that later). Twist king Chubby Checker (a record-company-created star whose name was borrowed from Fats Domino and whose hit was stolen from Hank Ballard) and other copycats topped the charts from 1960 through 1962, then abruptly lost their dominance.[5] During these years, Chubby Checker's popularity was so strong that his hit, "The Twist," reached the #1 position on Billboard's list *twice*, once in August 1960 and again in November 1961, a feat not achieved by any record before or since. If you study the Dow Jones Industrials, you'll see that each of these months was the exact month of the peak of a "B" wave within the Primary wave ④ correction. As readers of *Elliott Wave Principle* know, "B" waves reflect excitability, and the Twist let people express it. Checker's last Top 10 hit peaked on the charts in September 1962, one month prior to the orthodox bottom of the 3-year stock market correction.

The energetic, positive emotions that Primary wave ③ exhibited up to 1959 turned out to be only a warm-up for the euphoric joy expressed by the Beatles and the melodic, harmonic music of the "British Invasion" and American bands that dominated the charts during Primary wave ⑤ from 1962 to 1966. The Beach Boys' first hit made the charts in September 1962. The Beatles' first hit was released almost simultaneously in October 1962, the month of the orthodox bottom in stocks. It wasn't until the Beatles' next release in January 1963 that they zoomed to #1 status in Britain and began moving toward their dominance of the pop-music world. That same month, Chubby Checker's final Top Ten hit began dropping from the charts. (Try as he did over the ensuing years, his message was "out," and the public would no longer buy it.) Three months later, the Beach Boys scored their first Top Ten hit and soared in popularity in the States. During the acceleration phase, wave (3) (not shown on the chart) of ⑤, the "fun music" phenomenon exploded as had rock 'n' roll's itself in wave (3) of ③. In January 1964, Britain's happy music flooded into the U.S. In February, the Beatles accounted for 60% of U.S. record sales and in March, *Meet the Beatles* became the biggest selling album in history. During the entirety of Primary wave ⑤, the public wanted upbeat, joyous high-energy songs about love and fun, and for three years, they got them, from the Beatles (12 of their 16 hits of 1964 had the word "love" in the lyrics), the Beach Boys (whose hit songs included "Dance, Dance, Dance" and "Fun, Fun, Fun"), various "British Invasion" bands, Motown artists, Frat Party bands and others. That mood ended promptly with the bull market.

The first #1 hit by the Rolling Stones appeared in June 1965, the exact month of the correction low that preceded the final run to new highs in stocks. After trying for more than a year, the Stones finally began gaining the upper hand as avant-garde expressors of the popular mood. Their message was one initially of dissatisfaction and impatience, about the most strongly negative attitudes the public was willing to experience. The same month marked a dramatic style change for the Beatles, separating their three-year "innocent love song" period from their introspective period, introduced by "Help" and "Yesterday" in August and October 1965 respectively.[6] Precisely these same months ushered in three years of hard-edged "soul" music by blacks[7] and turned even Bob Dylan's electrified taunts into hit material. These events foreshadowed the bull market top just months later in January 1966. In 1966, the Rolling Stones suddenly outdid the Beatles in the number of Top Ten hits, with themes of drugs, mental breakdown, crying and death, with their final hit of the year coming in October. Look at the crash in stock prices from January to October 1966 and see how precisely it reflected the new mass mood. By mid-1966, says Philip Norman in *Shout*, "The latter-day Mersey groups had all gone home to settle down as pork butchers and damp-course engineers." The same thing happened to other happy-music bands who did not change musical direction, such as the Beach Boys, Herman's Hermits, Gary Lewis & the Playboys, etc., whose strings of Top Ten hits ended abruptly in 1966.[8] The public was now looking for something else and found it in the Stones, Bob Dylan (who had sung prophetically, "The Times, They Are A-Changin'"), soul music, the more worldly British and San Francisco bands and others. Coincidentally, the name for rhythmic popular music changed, from "rock and roll" to just plain "rock," a name that correctly suggested the hardness of the new musical style.

The Beatles, who remained innovators, did not yet retire, but changed precisely in line with the times. In August 1966, two months before that year's crash bottom in stocks, they announced their retirement from live performing and released an album cover featuring dismembered toy dolls and bloody joints of meat. The public's mood had changed so dramatically that the Beatles as a group suffered a worldwide hate campaign (the stated reasons are irrelevant) even as they adapted to the new mood. Not coincidentally, as a bull market returned in late 1966, the "butcher" album cover (now a collector's item) was quickly recalled and replaced with a bland photo. In June 1967, the Beatles "committed suicide," announcing their reincarnation as a new band (Sargent Pepper's Lonely Hearts Club Band) with a complex identity reflecting both the peace/love sentiments of the emerging psychedelic "flower power" era and the more worldly style that had been expressed on their previous two albums. This mood mixture precisely reflected the bull market/bear market battle that was raging on Wall Street, with the secondary indexes heading for new highs against the Dow Industrials, which had made their orthodox top in January 1966 and were already declining, particularly in real-dollar terms. In a reflection of the rich sea change in mood that was taking place in those years, rock music became consciously artistic and flowered in terms of innovation, creativity, subtlety and complexity, as exemplified by the compositions and arrangements of Jimi Hendrix, Chicago, Santana, Quicksilver, Jefferson Airplane, Big Brother, Cream, The Who, Spirit, The Grateful Dead, Blood Sweat & Tears and a host of other bands.

Then in the fall of 1968, as the secondary stock bull market was preparing to enter its top, "heavy metal" music entered the scene, as hits by Iron Butterfly, Deep Purple and Steppenwolf all entered the charts concurrently. The sudden popularity of this new style at the bottom of the correction preceding the final peak foreshadowed the stock market top in December 1968 just as the Rolling Stones' two #1 hits in the second half of 1965 had foreshadowed the peak of January 1966.

The peace-love sentiments of the psychedelic era coincided with the last hurrah in the stock market, which peaked in a speculative frenzy with new all-time highs in the Value Line index (representing the dominance of secondary stocks). The good intentions found generally in bull market music peaked at the same time, with a string of studio-manufactured "Bubble Gum" hits, a sickly-sweet extreme in trend. Despite their agility in navigating the newest change in mood, the Beatles were apparently still a "bull market" band.[9] In January 1969, just as stock prices turned down and the bear market began to take firm hold, George Harrison walked out of the tension-filled *Let It Be* sessions, foreshadowing the final breakup of the band. Their final recordings, which had already been in the making, were released later that year.

Innovation, musical creativity and complexity in rock peaked at the same time, as the flood of ground-breaking bands came to an abrupt halt. Releases of the new music continued into the new year, and the momentum carried just long enough to produce the Woodstock festival that summer, the general disarray of which came off like the celebration of a bear market rally. As a New York ABC radio personality flatly said later in a front page *Wall Street Journal* article, "Rock peaked in 1969."

The Beatles themselves fought throughout the following year, with the final split coming in April 1970, as the stock market crashed toward its multi-year low. *Let It Be*,[10] a movie that chronicled the group's frictions (in dramatic contrast to their good-natured 1964 and 1965 movies), premiered on May 20, 1970, days from the crash bottom in stocks and the shootings of students at Kent State University. During the same period, the pop-music groups and stars that had shaped the topping phase abruptly fell from popularity, quit, broke up, or died in droves (Jimi Hendrix, Cass Elliot, Janis Joplin, Jim Morrison, Duane Allman).

A distinct change in rhythm occurred in the 1970s; it was as if someone had thrown a bucket of sludge into the pop music machine. Many songs were presented in a half-speed tempo (i.e., a backbeat every four beats instead of every two, "The Night They Drove Old Dixie Down," "I Shot the Sheriff," "Lonely People," for example). Some former hits were re-recorded at dramatically slower tempos ("Breaking Up Is Hard to Do," "Handy Man," "Higher and Higher," for example). Ballads were sung an octave lower than the previous average or pounded out at an agonizingly plodding pace as if the musicians were exhausted (James Taylor and Barry Manilow, for example). The timing of these artists' appearances followed immediately upon the exit of the "topping phase" bands. James Taylor (who, ironically, was discovered by the Beatles and recorded by Apple) had his first hit, "Fire and Rain," on the heels of the 1970 crash bottom in stocks, just a few months after the Beatles' breakup. (As with so many of the "negative mood" artists, his last hit was in 1981, near the end of the negative-mood period.) Barry Manilow's first dirge-like hit soared to #1 on the exact week of the major stock market bottom in December 1974, ending a crash in mood that expressed itself partly in a general blinding hatred of Richard Nixon, who had been forced from office in a sea of scandal. (Manilow's last Top Ten hit fell from the charts in late March, 1980 as the last of the stock market "massacres" bottomed; he remained in the lower areas of the charts into 1983.) Dance music also suddenly became slower in 1974, the year of the crash bottom. That year, a phenomenon known as "bump" music performed the function of bringing dance couples back together again. It was with only a tentative fanny-bump, but it paved the way for the later emergence of "disco" dance, which required fully cooperating partners, a typical occurrence near the end of corrective waves.

While the ballad buyers and dancers felt depressed, the kids felt angry. The bear market dating from 1966 that accelerated in 1969 supported bands whose accent was on the negative. The Rolling Stones thrived on themes of war, sex and the devil. Heavy metal bands, which had originally been satisfied to present merely a noisy, foreboding sound, adopted a calculated theatrical approach to their recordings and performances and sported names such as Black Sabbath, Blue Oyster Cult, Queen, AC/DC, The Scorpions and Kiss, suggesting darkness, sexual ambiguity and general nastiness. In a related development, early psychedelic "garage bands" gave way to groups that specialized in long, hypnotic compositions with negative-mood themes. The most accomplished and successful of these was Pink Floyd, which formed shortly after the onset of the wave IV bear market and which eventually became the strongest selling group in "downer theme" history, singing songs about self-destruction, axe murderers, money grubbing, war and alienation, all to a comfortably numbing or gratingly distorted soundtrack. Their classic album *Dark Side of the Moon* floated continually into the Top 20 album sales charts during the years from 1973 to 1982 (the final bear market year in real terms), when the group's popularity began to wane.

The most extreme musical development of the mid-1970s was the emergence of punk rock. The lyrics of these bands' compositions, as pointed out by Tom Landess, associate editor of *The Southern Partisan*, resemble T.S. Eliot's classic poem "The Waste Land," which was written during the 'teens, when the *last* Cycle wave IV correction was in force (a time when the worldwide negative mood allowed the communists to take power in Russia). The attendant music was as anti-"musical" (i.e., non-melodic, relying on one or two chords and two or three melody notes, screaming vocals, no vocal harmony, dissonance and noise), as were Bartok's compositions from the 1930s. It wasn't just that the performers of punk rock would suffer a heart attack if called upon to change chords or sing more than two notes on the musical scale, it was that they made it a *point* to be non-musical minimalists and to create ugliness, as artists. The early punk rockers from England and Canada conveyed an even more threatening image than did the heavy metal bands because they abandoned all the trappings of theatre and presented their message as reality, preaching violence and anarchy while brandishing swastikas. Their names — Johnny Rotten, Sid Vicious, Nazi Dog, The Damned, The Viletones, etc. — and their song titles and lyrics — "Anarchy in the U.K.," "Auschwitz Jerk," "The Blitzkrieg Bop," "You say you've solved all our problems? You're the problem! You're the problem!" and "There's no future! no future! no future!" — were reactionary lashings out at the stultifying welfare statism of England and their doom to life on the dole, similar to the Nazis' backlash answer to a situation of unrest in 1920s and 1930s Germany. Actually, of course, it didn't matter what conditions were attacked. The most negative mood since the 1930s (as implied by stock market action) required release, period. These bands took bad-natured sentiment to the same extreme that the pop groups of the mid-1960s had taken good-natured sentiment.[11] The public at that time felt joy, benevolence, fearlessness and love, and they demanded it on the airwaves. The public in the late 1970s felt misery, anger, fear and hate, and they got exactly what they wanted to hear. (Luckily, the hate that punk rockers' reflected was not institutionalized, but then, this was only a Cycle wave low, not a Supercycle wave low as in 1932.) The speed of the songs was usually breakneck, as the negative mood fell into its depths, just as the breakneck speed of doo-wop music from the late 1950s marked the peak of the energetic mood of wave ③. Ironically, even the punk rock audience had its way of re-introducing a

"partners touching" style of dance in a unique frenzied frontal ram-
ming-together of each other's bodies called "slam dancing." (One way
or another, bear market bottoms bring couples back together!) These
bands' domination of the airwaves lasted until the early 1980s, when
Cycle wave IV, the great bear market that began in 1966, ended.[12]

In summary, an "I feel good and I love you" sentiment in music
paralleled a bull market in stocks, while an amorphous, euphoric "Oh,
wow, I feel great and I love *everybody*" sentiment (such as in the late
'60s) was a major sell signal for mood and therefore for stocks. Conversely, an "I'm depressed and I hate you" sentiment in music reflected
a bear market, while an amorphous tortured "Argh! I'm in agony and I
hate *everybody*" sentiment (such as in the late '70s) was a major buy
signal.[13]

Leading Up to Today

Just as the beginning of Cycle wave IV was a sloppy process with
two peaks (January 1966 and December 1968), its end was as well,
with two bottoms (December 1974 and August 1982[14]). The music scene
between the two *tops* resembled a complex battle between good and
evil, which, in a sense, it was. The music scene between the two bottoms was schizophrenic as well, with disco music doing its best to affirm
the happy positive and punk rock and heavy metal asserting the dominance of the angry negative. In the early 1980s, the negative mood
manifestations reached extremes that signaled a major bottom, while
truly positive forces (excluding disco itself, which, like the Twist, was
only a transition-phase phenomenon), one by one, began claiming major victories in turning the tide.

The first big victory for the positive-mood forces in general was
the public adoption of "bootstrap" psychology. It was as if people had
tired of the negative and were determined to pull themselves, each as
an individual, out of that mood. The first hint was the jogging fad,
which turned into a full-blown craze for physical self-improvement.
The 1980 method for spreading the craze was through video. Guess
what was popular in that very analogous year (more on that later), 1920:
workout *audio*. The new-fangled technology of *that* period gave us
phonograph records to do exercises by. There was a new energy building
in the early 1980s, and humans had to express it by running, lifting and
jumping up and down. This was a coincident indicator of an *emerging*

bull market for stocks. (Few embraced exercise in 1970.) This same "I'm sick of hearing the negative!" psychology was reflected in the blockbusting popularity of the film, *Rocky*, which expressed the new mood that "you can succeed (or at least avoid the natural state of failure) if you try like hell and push yourself to the limit." Four years later, a "bootstrap" president was elected.

The next big hint of change was the emergence of the nostalgia craze. All of a sudden, the social scene changed, and 1950s styles in just about everything were adopted. The country witnessed the return of family values, Disney movies, Ray-Ban sunglasses, campus rest, Boy Scout popularity, baseball popularity, etiquette, macho men, westerns, marriage and babies. Even nerds became "cool," and science began replacing sociology as the study of preference. '50s' pop music performers began touring again for "oldie" concerts and showing up, dead or alive, on TV programs (Jerry Lee Lewis, Elvis, Chuck Berry, Carl Perkins, etc.). New bands which flatly copied the styles of the 1950s became popular (Stray Cats), and performers who powerfully resembled stylists of the 1950s (always with an '80s' twist) became stars (Michael Jackson echoed Elvis Presley's breathy vocals and girl-melting physical movement; Prince echoed Little Richard's combination of wildness and overt sexual lyrics). 1983 in particular witnessed a flood of articles on fashion, art and culture that reflected "conservative" times reminiscent of the 1950s or early 1920s, when bull markets were young.

At the same time, Christian rock music (Amy Grant, etc.) burst upon the scene and rose quickly in popularity. Sound tracks by "techno-pop" bands reflected the herky-jerky computer age while greatly mellowing the jagged edges of the still-remaining punk influence. Even the heavy metal band Kiss removed its horror-theatre makeup in the early 1980s. Melody hadn't yet returned to a dominant role in pop music, but the hate element was dissipating.

There was also a discernible shift in the sentiment of popular song lyrics in the early '80s. With "All we are is dust in the wind..." still echoing from Kansas' hit of February 1978, the month of an intermediate stock market bottom,[15] John Lennon[16] in late 1980 remained on the cutting edge of the newest mood by releasing an immensely popular album of sweet love songs to his family. October 1982 actually brought a social-commentary style hit that was upbeat, optimistic, and celebrated the computer and transportation revolution, concluding, "What a beautiful world this will be; What a glorious time to be free," with a favorable mention of the "Stars and Stripes" thrown in for good measure. The love song returned as an acceptable, if not dominant, theme for pop hits as the bull market of 1982-1983 took off. Even Lou Reed, an early leader in '70s' "downer theme" music, emerged from obscurity singing, "I Love You, Suzanne"! In 1983, Pink Floyd, after ten years of popularity, released its last album and broke up as a band. The Who, an aggressively toned and relatively anarchic rock group whose music remained a strong seller from the exact start of the negative-mood trend (having achieved notice originally with an auto-destructive stage act that included smashing guitars, amps and drums and releasing smoke bombs), played its last concert and disbanded. [They both reunited briefly for tours and live albums in subsequent years. —Ed.] Both of these groups, as well as numerous punk bands, exhausted themselves under the pressure of the new trend, as happened to the "fun" bands in 1966 and the Beatles in 1970.

After Primary wave ① peaked in 1983, the '50s' craze in music began to wane. The 1950s' styles, while still very much in evidence, yielded dominance to those of the early 1960s, specifically the years 1960-1962, which were transition years prior to the next big bull market advance in stocks. In the dance and music fields, the main trends that took over in 1984 were break dancing, girl groups and cutesy copycat rockers.

After ten years of "partners touching" disco dancing,[17] the new style, once again having taken hold despite the warnings of doctors and the dismay of parents, was "break dancing," the new "Twist." In 1960, the Twist was a major event, a basic change in dance style from a partners-touching style of dance to a partners-separate style. It was as if each dancer had so much energy that to stay together was just too dangerous. The Twist was denounced by doctors as potentially damaging to the sacroiliac, but the dancers loved it anyway. In the recent transition, it was "break dancing" that pushed partners apart from the partners-touching disco dancing convention and turned each into a whirling dervish impervious to his doctor's warnings. Again, everybody "on the scene" loved it, to the extent that several break dancing movies became box office hits. The dancing seen on prime time TV programs today is almost all partners-separate again, as opposed to the myriad partners-touching disco programs of the late 1970s. The girl-group phenomenon hardly needs elaboration. Female pop singers have returned in droves, successfully invading the traditionally male idiom

WANT SOMETHING FULL OF PEP THAT COMES IN A FIVE-PACK AND MAKES YOU SMILE? TRY NEW EDITION

Chief, I think I've found someone for the new bubble-gum campaign. I know you wanted the Jacksons, but let's face it, they're going to be pricey. So how about New Edition? It's a five-kid group from Boston's Roxbury ghetto, and their music is known as—get this—bubble-gum soul. Perfecto, no?

The kids sign, sing, and poppo! zoom to No. 1 on the black-singles chart. Sure, the lyrics are kind of drippy—*You look so sweet/You're a special treat*—but they might be just the thing for the TV spots, eh, chief? But here's the capper: These kids

are *nice*. They come from working-class families, don't do drugs ("We were raised differently," says Ralph) and even travel with a tutor. In fact, our only problem might be that they're *too* popular right now. Some 5,000 fans showed up for an October autograph-

Life in fast lane: USA ignores 55 mph

More motorists are ignoring the 55-mph speed limit

U.S. Department of Transportation surveys show an average of 42 percent of us drove faster than 55 last year. On rural interstates, 3 of 4 sped.

"People are driving faster.

There's no doubt about it," said DOT spokesman Bob Beasley. "Interstates are designed for 70 miles an hour. People get on 'em and go like hell," said Bob Sherman, aide to Vermont Gov. Madeleine Kunin.

Sweaters set wi... daring

NEW
Bold &
son's sw
tradition
signs sh
patterns
out geo
squiggle
bounty o
tinues th
and brill
ing yello

Deregulating Stock Credit

For more than 50 years Federal regulators have told stockbrokers how much credit they can extend to their customers to purchase stock, a practice known as buying on margin. Under the rules in effect since the Depression, investors had to post at least 40 percent, using the stock as collateral for the balance.

The Federal Reserve Board suggested last week that changes in the market had rendered those rules obsolete. The board wants to turn over responsibility for regulating credit to the stock exchanges, and Treasury Secretary Donald T. Regan suggested they should consider abolishing requirements completely.

Congress restricted the purchase of stock on margin in 1934 partly in an effort to control dramatic fluctua-

SEC Approves Increased Limits On Option Positions

WASHINGTON—The Securities and Exchange Commission gave four exchange approval to increase their limits on option positions, enabling investors to hold m options contracts.

The new position limits will
—8,000 contracts on stocks with a s month trading volume of 40 million sha or a 30 million-share volume and a put float of 120 million shares outstanding
—5,500 contracts on stocks with a s month volume of 20 million shares or a million-share volume and 40 million shal outstanding.
—3,000 contracts on less active stoc

Katrina and crew really 'Walking on Sunshine'

"I think the timing was just right," she says. "People are ready for a good band singing down-to-earth pop songs, and people are in the mood for summer."

"It's going to be in the same vein," Miss Leskanich says. "Maybe a bit more rocked up, but we're going to keep the innocent, honest, band-next-door approach.

"I like to think we come off sounding friendly — like we're nice people. Even if that might get us labeled a pop band — which some people think is a derogatory status — success is success." June 8, 1985

'Silly Love Songs' Sweep the Country

If you turn your radio dial carelessly these days, you may well come across a station that promises you "Love Songs — Nothing but Love Songs." Like fast food and other forms of mush, the "love song" format that has emerged recently is a uniquely American invention. Although it is aimed at the age 25-49 market, the explosion of love-song programming suggests some interesting trends in popular music. At the very moment when West European rock music is becoming more and more political, American pop has become dominated by love songs that are increasingly banal.

*In the Silicon Valley,
L'Enfant Terrible Is*

Also L'Enfant Riche

SCOTTS VALLEY, Calif.—The spotlight shivers on a fuming wall of dry ice. A drum roll sounds, the crowded ballroom falls silent. Even the guest ripping slabs of meat from the whole roast pig on the buffet turn to watch.

Eventually, the night's host glides into center stage, his considerable girth draped in a purple and gold tent—er, toga—and a wreath of grape leaves on his head. "All hail Bacchus," someone bellows. He hoists his saxophone in salute and begins to play.

The saxophonist and host is Philippe Kahn, the founder and owner of Borland International and the self-appointed court jester of Silicon Valley. Even here, where extravagant indulgence and eccentricity are commonplace, the expansive software publisher has become a legend within two years of his arrival from his native France.

His toga party is costing him $45,000, with a gluttonous mob of 600 on hand, including an ersatz satyr wearing little more than a sheepskin loincloth and a pair of horns. A trapeze artist performs, and merrymakers pelt one another with balloons filled with shaving cream.

A local newspaper subsequently calls the affair "a drunken orgy." Mr. Kahn replies, with a melodramatic sigh, "I can't quarrel with the drunken part. I only wish I remembered the orgy."

"I have all the money I need," he says. "Now, I dedicate myself to fun."

When Inflation Rate Is 116,000%, Prices Change by the Hour

Bolivians aren't yet lugging their money about in wheelbarrows, as the Germans did during the legendary hyperinflation of the Weimar Republic in the 1920s, when prices increased 10 billionfold. But Bolivia seems headed in that direction.

"This isn't even good as toilet paper," says pharmacist Ruth Aranda, holding up a 100-peso bill. Indeed, she points out, admission to a public toilet costs 300 pesos.

Three years ago, she says, she bought a new luxury Toyota auto for what she now sells three boxes of aspirin for.

"We're headed for the garbage can."

tions in the market. The sale of stock on credit with only a fraction of the price paid in advance was widely blamed for having inflated prices during the unregulated days of the 1920's. A slight decline in value could wipe out a customer's investment, with his collateral for the balance (the stock) declining as well. A crash, as occurred in 1929, could break thousands of investors and leave the creditors to collect only a few cents on the dollar.

In a study of margin requirements released last week, the board argued that the market had largely outgrown the dangers of these leveraged purchases.

"My concern is that the exchanges might compete on margins," said Nicholas Giordano, president of the Philadelphia Stock Exchange. "Traders would like to have no margin at all, and it puts us in a difficult position. The stock exchanges are competing with the options and financial futures markets, so they could be pressured to go to the lowest common denominator so they can compete."

Pop rockers Wham!

Wham! Just like that, they've got the No. 1 record in the USA.

How did an obscure British dance band manage to push past such heavyweights as Prince and Stevie Wonder?

It's simple, says the band's lead singer. "We're cute," explains George Michael, who, along with guitarist Andrew Ridgeley, turned *Wake Me Up Before You Go-Go* into one of the most lightweight, but infectious, pop hits of the year.

"You have to have a strong rhythm track to make a hit pop record. *Wake Me Up* has a lightweight, sing-along melody but it also has an intense rhythm track. …

Michael, who produces, arranges and writes the music, feels Wham! has a formula for success. "Our songs may seem familiar because we've used as our foundation some of the great commercial artists, especially the Motown sound. The melodies we have are very simple and easy to hum."

TWILIGHT ZONE

USA TODAY · THURSDAY, APRIL 4, 1985

HOLLYWOOD — This fall, the mystery anthology format is back big.

Out of favor since the glory days of *Alfred Hitchcock Presents* and *The Twilight Zone* and off the tube entirely since ABC's *Darkroom* in 1982, the style will enjoy a rebirth with CBS' *Twilight Zone* and Steven Spielberg's *Amazing Stories* on NBC.

Compared to the old series, "some things have changed and some haven't," he says.

Of the first shows, all the segments are new stories except two remakes:

■ "Night of the Week." A 1960 Rod Serling teleplay featuring Art Carney as a drunken department store Santa Claus who "enters a strange kind of North Pole ...part of the magic that can only be found in the *Twilight Zone*."

■ "Dead Man's Shoes." In 1962, Warren Stevens played a bum who steals shoes from a dead gangster, puts them on and becomes the gangster. In the new version, the bum will have his gender changed to a brunette.

---

fall fashion scene

Thursday, August 1, 1985

designs and color

YORK, N.Y. —

...raphics make this sea... ...eaters stand out from the ...al crowd of the past. De... ...ow a new daring with ...that range brom blocked ...metrics, to new wave ...tapestry mosaics and a ...f fancy florals. Color con... ...e emphasis on boldness ...ance. Electric blue, jolt... ...w, fiery red and stark

black and white add to the vivid appeal of this year's sweater set.

One clear winner, *Seventeen's* fashion editors predict, will be an updated Aztec graphic in the attention-getting color combination of black, white and grey zapped with bright yellow. Worn with a white and yellow striped cotton shirt and stop-light yellow mini skirt, the look is sure to end up in the fashion spotlight.

Guys get familiar with fashion

1925...1962...1985?

Much to the surprise of the store — which expected the avant-garde look to have limit...

...ex-
...res
...ons
...re

...be-
...ix-
...res
...lic

...ix-

...ed appeal — the $125 sweater by designer Andrew Fezza immediately sold out.

Other USA stores — such as Marshall Field's in Chicago and Macy's in New York — also report that the most fashion-forward men's looks are selling faster than traditional ones. Men, it seems, are beginning to cotton to clothes like never before.

Boot lovers go gaga over go-go — again

By Elizabeth Sporkin
USA TODAY

NEW YORK — With miniskirts and lace stockings reviving 1960s style, can go-go boots be far behind?

on Broadway in March. DeMora snapped up eight pairs for the opening number; dancers will wear them with miniskirts and midriff tops.

"They should never have gone away," says deMora of

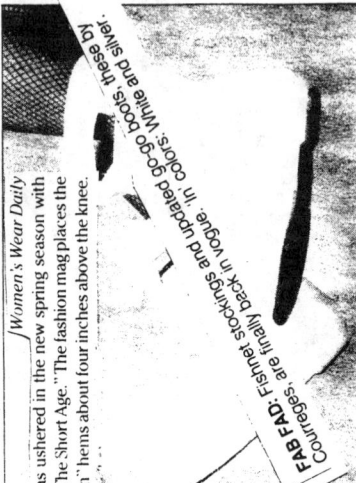

FAB FAD: Fishnet stockings and updated go-go boots, these by Courreges, are finally back in vogue. In colors: white and silver.

"There's definitely an upswing" in interest in white boots, says Lois Kopf of Courreges, the Paris design house that first introduced the mid-calf-high go-go boot in 1964.

This year, Courreges has brought back restyled versions — in white and silver, with cutouts at the tops — to some of its 15 USA boutiques. "They're selling like crazy in Beverly Hills and there has been growing interest in New York," Kopf reports.

One customer was Bob deMora, costume designer for *Leader of the Pack!*, a musical set in the 1960s that will open the boots.

Shoe manufacturer Two City Kids also will bring out updated go-go boots with a punch-out design that allows stockings to show through.

"Fashion is cyclical and things do repeat themselves," says avant-garde shoe designer Kenneth Cole, who late this spring will bring out a new version of the go-go boot: short white boots that are tight around the ankle. Some have high heels; some are flat.

"I think miniskirts call for something that comes up the foot," he says. "It just feels right again."

Women's Wear Daily

has ushered in the new spring season with "The Short Age." The fashion mag places the "in" hems about four inches above the knee.

"Anything dabbled in by women is now dabbled in by men. Men are much more experimental with fabrics, silhouettes and color," says Howard Sussman, Macy's men's fashion coordinator. "There's never been a time like this in men's fashion."

Two-piece swimsuits resurface on beaches

By Elizabeth Sporkin
USA TODAY

NEW YORK — 1985's most stylish swimmers will shun the long-popular maillot for a splash from the past: the two-piece.

Not a teeny bikini, mind you, but a suit that covers a little more hip, thigh and stomach.

"There's a whole generation of women who have never seen these suits before," says Doug Arbetman, spokesman for Cole of California, which offers a style that can be rolled up or down for more or less coverage. "They really have a fun fashion look."

After three years of one-piece predominance. "This is a natural evolution," says designer Norma Kamali.

By MICHAEL POLLOCK
Press Staff Writer

OCEAN CITY — They were a product of the late 1950s and 1960s, a time of prosperity and two-car garages. The stock market appeared to be a bull market that would ride forever and small investors wanted to ride the bull in their own tiny herds.

Investment clubs were chic and novel, as popular as outdoor barbecues and "The Donna Reed Show."

There may not be as many investment clubs around today as there were in the 1960s, but there are still a reported 25,000 such clubs active in the United States.

Investment clubs are gatherings of people with a common interest: investing in the stock market.

The National Association of Investment Clubs, based in Royal Oak, Mich., reports that the average member invests $43 a month. The entire association, representing 115,000 investors in 5,900 clubs, invests $4.4 million a month.

"It's not a get-rich-quick program," warned Thomas O'Hara, association chairman and co-founder. "It's an accumulation program."

O'Hara credited the bull market which began in August 1982 with renewing much of the interest in investment clubs. The NAIC, which had nearly 14,000 members in 1969, was down to fewer than 4,000 in 1980.

Family life is 'in,' 1950's return

Parents renew an emphasis on etiquette

FRIDAY, FEBRUARY 8, 1986 · USA TODAY

For some children, learning to say "please" and "thank you" is as difficult as learning to eat with a knife and fork — and about as much fun. When parents nag them to do or say things "correctly," they are hard pressed to understand what all the fuss is about.

Today, parents are making more of a fuss over manners — the art of doing things correctly — than they did during the free-for-all 1960s.

Respect for age, wisdom and the establishment are back, and an emphasis on good manners is part of this return to more traditional values.

Casual sex on campus declines

PALM SPRINGS, Calif.

Scouting is 75 yrs. today and growing

From a peak of 4.9 million in 1972, BSA's youth membership fell by more than a third to a low of just 3.3 million in 1979. The number of adult volunteers also dropped dramatically. "It was the tenor of the times," Chief Scout Executive Ben H. Love said. "There was rebellion against anything that had traditional values. Some of the things we believe in — patriotism, duty to God — were being challenged."

In the past five years, the organization has managed to reverse its slide. Preliminary 1984 figures show youth membership at nearly 3.7 million, a 2.5 percent increase over 1983. Scouting is benefiting, Love said, from what he sees as a return to "basic values and basic beliefs." (Scouts, after all, still take an oath to be "physically strong, mentally awake and morally straight.")

Funicello at 41: Back to basics with Disney

Some things never change. The sun rises in the East. April showers bring May flowers. And Annette Funicello exudes as much exuberance about life at 41 as she did in her Mouseketeer years —

"When I heard the name Disney, I jumped at the chance," says Funicello. Her last Disney film was *Monkey's Uncle*, nearly 20 years ago.

"I have the kids that watched the Mickey Mouse Club that are now my age, the kids that watched the

Ron Kirchoff, a real estate agent here, started his club five years ago "just to be sociable, to have fun. We're not trying to make a killing."

The club, which began in June 1983 with five members, "just looks for anything that looks half-decent." Kirchoff said. "We're down, to be honest with you."

Explode

with the rebirth of Westerns

Macho

May 19, 1985

College students today are less likely to engage in casual sex than they were a decade ago and they feel more guilty about their sexual behavior, suggests a new study to be released here Saturday.

In 1974 and 1984, researchers surveyed 100 students at Northern Iowa University in Cedar Falls on their sexual attitudes and practices. The study will be presented at the annual meeting of the Society for the Scientific Study of Sex.

"The changes in sexual behavior just go along with the conservative shift in our society's values over the past 10 years," says Marilyn Story, a family studies professor at Northern Iowa.

"Sexual guilt, for example, correlates with being religious and a more conservative political orientation. That's what we're seeing on campuses and in society at large."

beach pictures that are now young adults, and the little kids who are now watching the Skippy (peanut butter) commercials."

Jane Pauley: 'new father' is a myth

RAMBO

strides back

12 states move to cut taxes

Dick, Wall St. hit highs

By Richard Benedetto
USA TODAY

Dear Ann: Hugs beat sex

JANUARY 15, 1985—USA TODAY

72%

DICK'S HAMBURGERS, is a startup outfit (with experienced management) that plans to open drive-in fast-food restaurants that resemble those that were popular in the 1950s. JUNE 4, 1985

"Our reports show everybody likes it," says an ecstatic Jerry Esbin, Tri-Star vice president. "What this film really is doing is saying we're coming out of the closet as far as Vietnam is concerned."

"Phil Donahue is an endangered species," says Arthur Cooper, editor of *Gentlemen's Quarterly* magazine. "For a while, men were defining themselves in terms of their reactions to the feminist movement. Now, they've said, 'Enough

"I see it as a healthy antidote to *Strawberry Fields Forever* and all the peace-love junk of the '60s," says Art Murphy, an industry analyst for *Variety* and University of Southern California film professor.

already.' They don't want to see themselves as Jimmy Cagney, but they're not silent sobbers either. *Masculine* is what's happening."

5-19-85

I may be wrong, but there seems to be a mood in America at the moment which is reflected in the kind of television that America produces. And something of the spirit of that is reflected in this miniseries."

And what mood is that? "A sort of patriotism." he said. "A feeling that there is hope. that one can press forward and achieve. Above anything else, Christopher Columbus was a great achiever. And there's great respect, I think, in America for the achiever, for the man who brooks no obstacle and is determined to achieve his end. And I think that's something that American audiences will relate to."

Fashions a-go-go for '60s look

By Betsa Marsh
USA TODAY

Skirts are short, pants are pegged and shoes are pointed.

The time is now, but the look is unmistakably 1960s.

Twenty years and one generation after fishnet stockings, miniskirts and turtleneck dickeys blasted onto the fashion scene, they're back — thanks to the sons and daughters of the men and women who wore them the first time around.

Teens and college students are scouring the secondhand shops for '60s garb and completing the look with dramatic eye makeup, teased hair and flashy sunglasses.

"Most of the kids are 16 to 18," says Jon Bok of Cowboys and Poodles boutique in Los Angeles, where the '60s fashion fad seems to be hottest.

For several months, he says, $20 paisley shirts and $20 miniskirts — unused clothing from manufacturers' and retailers' overstocked warehouses — have been selling out.

"The kids are into '60s music, like the Monkees and the Shangri-Las," Bok says, "and that sort of led them into the clothes."

Until last summer, sales were roughly 80 percent from '50s clothes and 20 percent from '60s styles. Bok says. The '60s sales "skyrocketed" when school was out. Now, '60s clothes are 80 percent of the sales.

Especially popular are Beatles boots, polka dots, op-art designs, go-go boots and oversized jewelry in Day-Glo colors.

In New York, the '60s fad has been "definitely there, but it a major influence," says R J Goodman of Trash and deville.

AUGUST 18, 1985

Unless you have been sequestered in a cave for the past few months, you must know that stirrup pants are the latest trousers for young fashionables to sport on the streets. Slim and narrow, they bring the legs into focus, with an emphasis on fit. Stirrups first sauntered onto the fashion scene for skiing in the early '20s, boasting jodhpur-type legs. Gradually the legs got slimmer and sleeker, thanks to innovations in fabrics, especially of the stretch variety.

During the '40s, noted Italian fashion designer Emilio Pucci brought out sleek-looking stirrup pants, according to Sol Kent, Rich's fashion director, who to this day doesn't have much use for them. "At that time, everyone looked like hookers in these pants," he said, "wearing them with high-heeled mules. Ellen Melinkoff quoted several women who wore stretch stirrups during the '60s. One said, "I remember hating ski pants or stretch pants even though I wore them.

However, women clung to these pants and by 1961, they made their first general appearance in the stores for street wear. Called stretch pants —

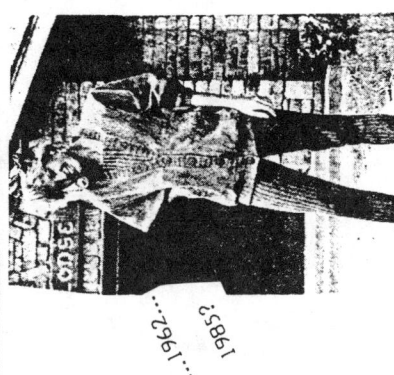

1923...1962...

1985?

By Barb Kinney, USA TODAY

PAST IS PRESENT: A dickey, pegged pants for him; a minidress, fishnet stockings for her. Classic Clothing, Washington, D.C.

Break dancing fever hits Germany

West Germany (AP) — Break dancing, the street sensation of the South Bronx, has boogied across the Atlantic to Germany.

West German youngsters are doing the supple falls, gyrations and gymnastics of break dancing for tips in shopping malls, and some department stores are luring customers with break dance exhibitions. Cinemas, television and magazines also are featuring the acrobatic steps.

Dancers dazzle onlookers with their spins and struts in Frankfurt's main shopping district, and earn about $78 a day in small change.

A local disco called the No Name holds weekly break dance competitions. The winner gets a prize of $196. "It's like a fever right now," said Peter Boehm, 32, who works at the City Music store in downtown Frankfurt.

Break dancing is the latest fad in a country where successive generations of teen-agers since World War II have been quick to adopt American styles in music, dance and clothes.

The West German Dance Teachers' Association estimates that 360,-000 young Germans are caught up in the craze.

London goes prim in the age of punk

LONDON—Punk is passé. Prim is in.

That's the message London's young, trendy women are sending out these days.

Outrageous outfits are giving way to grown-up gowns. Suddenly young women have taken to looking like their moms: Elbow-length gloves, black cocktail dresses, high heels, severe hairdos, lots of costume jewelry, bright lipstick, heavy mascara.

Nowhere is the new look more evident than at Hyper Hyper, the market-stall designer hall opened a year ago as a showcase for young English designers.

Some 70 of these stalls are found in Hyper Hyper, which is much larger and more sophisticated than the Kensington Market, another designer market across the street. Kensington, which got its start in the 1960s, faded in the 1970s and is currently undergoing a revival.

Spring fling: Short skirts

When it comes to skirts for spring, the thigh's the limit.

After a winter of sidewalk-sweeping hemlines, "It's time to see a little bit of leg," says designer Perry Ellis. His spring 1985 collection features above-the-knee skirts after four years of predominantly long styles. "Suddenly, the short skirts and soft shapes look refreshingly feminine."

Other USA designers shortening skirts (and showing leg-revealing shorts): Calvin Klein, Ralph Lauren, Willi Smith and Norma Kamali, who unveil their collections Oct. 29-Nov. 9 in New York.

Will they sell? "I think they're real cute as long as they're not too short, and as long as they look good on you," says Edwina Richard, 21, a model from Tucson, Ariz.

■ Europe also goes short, 3D

Short skirts, shorts reign at Paris show

PARIS (AP) — Short skirts got the nod at Karl Lagerfeld's summer ready-to-wear show Saturday, and designer Claude Montana unveiled hot pants and micro-skirts from beneath long duster coats.

There were even white cuffed shorts in Lagerfeld's bridal wear.

Lagerfeld also showed some long pleated skirts, but his clear preference was for leg-revealing minis and micros.

once again. Some of the biggest sensations of the pop-music world recently have been women, including the Go-Go's, the Pointer Sisters, Madonna, Cyndi Lauper, Tina Turner, Pat Benatar and others. They own the airwaves, as they did in the early 1960s. As a final parallel with the early '60s, lightweight copycat rockers Wham! (like Bobby Vee and others in 1960-1962) sold records and cavorted on video wearing "Choose Life" T-shirts. Can it be just coincidence that after all these years, the Everly Brothers staged a packed-house "reunion" concert and Chubby Checker is touring again?

Where Are We Now?

What may be important for signaling another mood change is that the dominance of women in pop music appears to have reached an extreme this year. Cyndi Lauper graced the March 4 cover of *Newsweek*, which featured the lead article, "Rock and Roll: Woman Power." In January, *USA Today* quoted Patti LaBelle (who had her first "girl group" hit herself in 1962) as saying "We (women) are taking over." On May 27, Madonna made the cover of *Time*. As Paul Montgomery's studies of magazine covers would indicate, this year must mark the peak of girl-group popularity.

Now let's move up to the present. *Playboy* and *Penthouse* magazines, trying to cash in on the girl-singer craze, hoped to sell out their August issues with nude pictures of Madonna. An interesting thing happened. Sales were brisk, but not as good as hoped. Remember those headlines about the one-day crash in Utility stocks on July 29th? "Worst Day For Utilities in 23 Years," they read, referring to May 28, 1962, one month before the price low in the wave ④ correction in stocks and five months before the orthodox bottom. And as if to seal the fate of the "available female" as a pop image, Madonna got married last Friday night (August 16). Meanwhile, the upbeat love-song trend that began in 1980 and has been flashing in and out of style is again picking up steam. Even the Beach Boys have been touring again.[18] From late 1982 to the present, there has been an undercurrent of happy pop music that, according to this model, should be about to explode on the scene as the dominant style, featuring melody, harmony and relative creativity. The message from the state of today's popular music is that the uncertain, corrective phase is nearing its end and that a full-fledged speculative bull market in mood is preparing to emerge.

Rarely have so many women performing rock had so many hit records on the charts. Never have so many women with such strong images so dominated the music videos shown on MTV, the rock-and-roll cable network (page 54). Madonna's new album, "Like a Virgin" (Sire), recently No. 1 for three weeks, is already "triple platinum." In 14 weeks it's sold some 3.5 million copies—a staggering amount, particularly since her first tour doesn't start until April. Turner, the Pointer Sisters, Pat Benatar and Chaka Khan all have current albums that have topped the million mark. And after 63 weeks, Cyndi Lauper's album, "She's So Unusual" (Portrait), is still charted in the Top 30, with nearly 4 million copies sold. Lauper's recordings have earned five Grammy nominations and her album has produced four Top Five singles—a new record for female singers.

The first big break for women in rock came in the early '60s, with girl groups like the Shirelles, the Ronettes and the Crystals. The songs the girls sang, like "Be My Baby" and "(Today I Met) The Boy I'm Gonna Marry," may have given marriage a false glow of paradise. But their bee-hive hairdos and stiletto heels gave the game away. The boy they wanted to marry was probably a biker.

Some insiders point to Madonna's steamy image and argue that little has really changed for women in rock and roll since the days of "girl groups" like the Ronettes.

"I get so much bad press for being overtly sexual," sighs Madonna. "When someone like Prince, Elvis or Jagger does the same thing, they are being honest, sensual human beings. But when I do it: 'Oh, please. Madonna, you're setting the women's movement back a million years'." Lauper agrees: "How can you criticize a woman for having a sexuality that women for years and years have been singing about nothing else? She's just doing her thing. My thing happens to be different. Women have a sexuality that shouldn't be suppressed."

Rodgers, her current producer, concocted a relentless rhythm track for "Like a Virgin" that suggests a bright, major-key version of Michael Jackson's "Billie Jean." The lyrics—all about how true love makes a girl feel "shiny and new, just like a virgin"—fit like a glove. So does Madonna's vocal. Her singing evokes the pie-eyed kid in "Bobby's Girl," the pert Marcie Blane hit of 1962. But when Madonna summons a nervous, fey hiccup on the chorus, she sounds more like the giddy vixen of the video version. It's a perfect pop epiphany—pure erotic fluff.

Even Madonna's staunchest fans would not claim that their idol is a radical ground-breaker. Indeed, the most beguiling aspect of Madonna is the way in which she is a throwback to interesting "girl" vocalists of years past.

LaBelle started singing in a more innocent era. In the early '60s, she led Patti LaBelle and the Bluebells in her native Philadelphia. The combo, which included former Supreme Cindy Birdsong, scored its first hit in 1962 with I Sold My Heart to the Junkman.

In the '70s, Patti and Bluebells Nona Hendryx and Sarah Dash transformed themselves into Labelle. A blazing fusion of sexy space-funk, raw rock power and provocative social commentary, Labelle was ahead of its time — and paid the price for it.

"It was something too different; something nobody was willing to accept," says LaBelle. "There was no category for three outrageous women at the time.... We were saying things that women were afraid to say — sexual, political, whatever we felt."

When the group split up in 1977, LaBelle's solo career was launched. She's pleased with the changes that have come for women over the years: "We're takin' over the charts," she jokes. And she's still carrying the hot stuff — right onto Broadway.

A "fundamental" (i.e., outside of the market itself, but seemingly related) event that is akin to a bad earnings report after the stock has declined is the sudden new insistence that popular music albums utilize a rating system. If lyrics have gotten so disgusting that people are finally reacting, the peak in negative lyrics has passed. This fundamental event is not unlike Congress's move during the 1973-1974 bear market to institutionalize the nation's depressed pace by mandating a 55-mph speed limit nationwide. Laws like this merely signal that an extreme has been reached and therefore that the trend is about to change. They certainly can't, short of iron military enforcement (which *is* an option), stop a trend that is aching to express itself.

This month, another fascinating event occurred, the release of a movie entitled, *Return of the Living Dead*, billed as a *spoof* of the zombie horror movies. In other words, it's Abbott & Costello meet the Zombies. The power of horror is dying right now, strongly suggesting that *Halloween, Part 17* and *Friday the 13th, Part 32* will never be made.[19] The newest trend in movie themes is that science and brains are not nerdy but cool. Films such as *Weird Science, My Science Project, Real Genius* and computer-oriented adventure stories are coinciding with kids' new desire to run computers and manipulate technology, in stark contrast to the values of the late 1960s and 1970s. These are all hints that better times lie ahead.

As with music and movies, it is still too early to characterize the fashion trends as typical of a major top. Fashion designers keep trying to re-introduce mini-skirts, but as yet, the public hasn't rushed to buy them. On the longer-term trend, women have been slowly raising hemlines, but as one article puts it, "Will they [shorter skirts] sell? 'I think they're real cute as long as they're *not too short*,' says a model from Tucson." No, it's not the *late* '20s or '60s yet! Two-piece bathing suits are making a comeback, but skimpy bikinis are still worn only by a minority at the beaches. "Daring colors" are being introduced by some fashion designers, while reactionaries are trying to re-introduce the Maxi-skirt as the stock market corrects. The bright colors and shorter hemlines should win this battle, but while it is still a battle, and until the newly introduced styles make the covers of *Time* and *Newsweek* and are seen everywhere at the shopping malls, the bull market should have more to go.

The years 1921 through 1929 experienced a *fifth* Cycle-degree wave in stocks, the same wave label and degree of the current bull market, which dates from August 1982 in the Dow Industrials. The parallels today with the mid-1920s (a period similar to the early 1960s) are becoming more and more obvious. There have been a number of parallel economic phenomena occurring in recent years, including the end of inflation in 1980, which corresponds to the inflationary peak of 1920, the end of the constant-dollar Dow's bear market in 1982, which corresponds to the same event in 1921, the current runaway inflation in South America, which corresponds to the same phenomenon in 1923 Germany, and the proposal to eliminate legal margin requirements for stock purchases, a widely recognized prerequisite for the speculative heights achieved in the bull market of the 1920s. More to the point, however, is that the *social* scene of today is beginning to resemble that of the mid-1920s, with advertisements for "Great Gatsby" parties and articles about computer business multi-millionaires whose new-found goal is to party all night long. As yet, however, evidence that the party-crazed mini-skirted *late* '20s have arrived is not to be found. By the time Cycle wave V is over, the trendsetters should have reached that point, living life in a new version of the late '20s and mid-to-late '60s.

There are many indications that Cycle wave V is a nostalgia wave that is doing its best to re-create the glories of the past. (I don't know whether the 1920s exhibited a similar tendency.) In stocks, it should end with the old-line Dow Industrials providing the final run. In politics, the longing to return to "old-time values" elected a president. In fashion, nostalgia has its hand on the helm, and the speeded-up replay of the fashions of Cycle wave III should continue right into a re-creation of the mini-skirted, foppish, frenzied peak of the late 1960s. "There's definitely a '60s' inspiration in today's hair fashions," says a representative of Vidal Sassoon on TV, "not a copying, but a creative inspiration...." The pop-music world is rushing through a re-creation of the trends in the 1940s (Linda Ronstadt's prom-queen music revival), 1950s and 1960s. In fact, re-formations of groups from the 1960s and small-scale tours and TV appearances are beginning already.

What is the implication of nostalgia as a driving cultural force? One of the observations revealed by a study of the Wave Principle is that third waves are accompanied by increasingly favorable "fundamental" news events, while fifth waves' fundamentals are less impressive by comparison. In a similar way, '50s' & '60s' music, produced during a third wave, was a strong step forward because it was *innovative*, while '80s' music is less impressive because it's *derivative*. (The great symphonic music was undoubtedly produced during the latter stages of a third wave of Supercycle and/or Grand Supercycle degree.) For those who lived through the 1950s and 1960s, the modern echo has been hollow, in the same way that the bull market in stocks has lacked the solid breadth (percentage of stocks advancing) of the bull market of 1942-1966. In other words, all indications are that the advance in mood which began in 1982 *is* a fifth (Cycle wave V), and that ultimately, this wave, in all its manifestations, is doomed to usher in another collapse in stocks and in mood. In the meantime, enjoy it, profit from it, and don't sell it short too soon.

NOTES

[1] Men are more "masculine" during bull markets, and women more "feminine." "Feminism" gains power during corrections, as it did in the 1850s during Supercycle wave (II), around World War I during Cycle wave IV of (III), and again in the 1970s, during Cycle wave IV of (V).

[2] History suggests that creativity in all fields (entrepreneurial, philosophic, literary, scientific, musical, etc.) peaks with third waves.

[3] Evidence of these directional forces lends support to the idea of Yin and Yang in Eastern philosophy. It will take the approach of a Western frame of mind, however, to gather and interpret the specific data to substantiate the concept.

[4] Artists such as Ricky Nelson, Bobby Vee and the Everly Brothers took over. Their sweet melodies and harmonies kept them popular through the 1959-1962 correction. Their consecutive string of hits ended in 1962 in both cases.

[5] "Girl groups" continued to produce hits into 1964 until the Beatles took over, and on a lesser scale right into the orthodox top in January 1966; after that time, the only women who could make it in rock music were the ones who could act rougher than men, such as Grace Slick and Janis Joplin.

[6] In "Help!", John Lennon sang, "Help me if you can, I'm feeling down; Help me get my feet back on the ground; Won't you please, please help me?" In "Yesterday", Paul McCartney sang, "Yesterday all my troubles seemed so far away; Now it looks as though they're here to stay...."

[7] Soul music singers went out of style in 1969, so their reign covered the period of the double top in stocks.

[8] These bands' appearance at lower levels on the charts continued until late 1968-early 1969, ending abruptly with the second top in the bull market. Brian Wilson, leader of the Beach Boys, went into seclusion and suffered psychological problems.

[9] Paul McCartney, particularly, kept in tune with the last gasp of the bull market that had carried to new highs in the secondary stock indexes. John Lennon, on the other hand, switched immediately and powerfully into the new mood. His post-1965 song contributions became darker and darker until his input on the White Album in 1968 prompted these (admiring) liner notes:

The harshness of the imagery is, if anything, even harsher;
'The eagle picks my eye/The worm he locks my bone.' Black

birds, black clouds, broken wings, lizards, destruction. And, most grotesque of all, there is a terrifying track just called 'Revolution 9,' which comprises sound effects, overheard gossip, backwards-tapes, janglings from the subconscious memories of a floundering civilisation. Cruel, paranoiac, burning, agonised, hopeless, it is given shape by an anonymous bingo voice which just goes on repeating 'Number nine, number nine, number nine'—until you want to scream.

As a trend setter, Lennon, whose popular career began in 1962 with (effectively) the simple emphatic announcement, "the bull market is on!" was saying simply and increasingly emphatically, "the bear market is on," a statement that began with "Help!" in August 1965.

[10] The Beatles' last album, of the same title, was labeled not with a green apple symbol but with a red one. This simple statement not only indicated that they knew, unlike many groups who self-destructed, exactly "where they were" but that they understood on some level the importance of their band's demise.

[11] A number of socially conscious people have attacked negative-sentiment movies, rock music, literature and art as *causing* a pervasive negative psychology, an inversion of the relationship. One wonders if they give the same styles of artistic expression the credit for causing *good* feelings in the 1950s and early 1960s. The only reason the underlying sentiments are manifested is that Western culture enjoys freedom of expression. To remove that would remove the manifestation but not the reality behind it, which would merely be vented via other avenues. A case could be made that musical, artistic, literary and sports expression of negative sentiments is a healthy release, as opposed to some possible alternatives. Negative-mood music and sports, for instance, do not exist to make the listener or watcher feel bad. If that were so, it wouldn't sell. On the contrary, it makes people feel good because it mirrors their feelings. Hearing a happy song when you feel angry is an annoyance. It can actually make you feel worse. An angry song says, "Go ahead and feel your anger," which probably helps dissipate it. Imagine how you would feel in a rigid society which only allowed elevator music. Would you really walk around all day with a bland smile on your face, or would you eventually want to lash out, screaming?

[12] One of the last gasp punk (renamed "new wave" in the U.S., whose music buyers didn't feel as angry as their British cousins) groups managed to put out this record two years ago, apparently misspelling its own name:

> **Fibonnaccis**, *Fibonnaccis* (Enigma): The country's most obscure cult band releases a three-song, 12-inch 45 rpm record.

[13] The sexual progression in pop music from 1954 to 1974 which appears to be beginning again as of the early 1980s, is, Men: "I'm a man!"; Women: "I'm cute and available — come and get me!" (speeding up the dance); Men: "I love you!" Men: "Enough happiness; I need thrills!" Men and Women: "Let's get D-I-V-O-R-C-E-D." Men and Women: "Let's kiss, make up, and have a slow dance."

[14] A climax of sorts also seems to have occurred in early 1980, coinciding with the last of three yearly stock market "massacres," the lowest recorded value for the Dow Jones Industrials since early in the rise off the 1974 low, and the lowest value for stocks in terms of gold since 1932.

[15] Intermediate highs and lows also correlate with hit songs. Paul McCartney's "Silly Love Songs" (which implored, "Some people want to fill the world with silly love songs — what's wrong with that?") was the biggest hit of 1976, the year of an important intermediate-term top in the Dow.

[16] Lennon's early '70s' music fit into the hard-edged sound with *grating protest songs* and long recordings of his wife's distinctive caterwauling. After a five-year hibernation in the late '70s, he again burst on the scene in 1980 with "(Just Like) Starting Over," effectively announcing, earlier than the crowd, the start of another bull market. He was murdered a month later by someone who was still caught in the grip of the slowly dying bear, which didn't breathe its last until a year and a half later.

[17] Linda Ronstadt engineered a brief revival among older people of crooning ballads and partners-touching ballroom dancing in 1984, around the Primary wave ② low.

[18] Remember James Watt's embarrassment when he canceled the Beach Boys concert in Washington, D.C. in 1983 to keep out "undesirable elements"? Everyone laughed because the Beach Boys don't attract undesirable elements — they're a bull market band.

[19] An even more horrible slew of movies and songs will undoubtedly be released at the bottom of the next Supercycle (and perhaps Grand Supercycle) crash, due in the 1990s. [2000s. — Ed.] There are many straws in the wind of very bad things to come. The appearance of AIDS, for instance, is the most serious plague-like threat since the Dark Ages.

A Few Examples of Applied Social Observation
(Reprinted from Robert Prechter's *Elliott Wave Theorist*)

February 7, 1983

What's the social scene like these days? Roaring '20s' parties, '30s' style gangland "hits," tramp camps for the unemployed, falling prices, conservative values, increasing religion, a move to "clean up 42nd Street" and fashion from the '20s and '50s. All are part of the typical social background in the early stages of a long bull market.

Get out circle skirts, pedal pushers; '50s come sashaying back into style

And what is the venerable Hemline Theory saying? The split skirt, a perfect symbol for the split market of the late '70s, is "out." Conservative dress is "in," and minis are still nowhere to be seen. Remember, rising hemlines, not high hemlines, coincide with healthy bull markets. If the mini-skirt returns, it may signal the approaching peak of a bull market (the last mini came out in 1967 in England and hit the U.S. in 1968). In other words, the social and mass psychological extremes occur together. So be happy if the move back to minis takes awhile.

August 18, 1983

The position of the market under the Wave Principle is a direct reflection of how people feel about the future. Wave positions analogous to those that have occurred in the past are often accompanied by similar attitudes among the public and therefore similar phenomena in the art and fashion worlds, which are highly responsive to the shifting winds of public sentiment. The current wave position has some things in common with the early 1920s, since that was also the beginning stage of a fifth wave of Cycle degree, with the mid-1930s, since wave V should be similar in time, extent and construction to wave I, and with the 1940s and 1950s since that was the early stage of the most recent wave of Cycle degree. The social scene should reflect those similarities, and I think it does (see collage, next page). By the top, however, the nostalgic conservatism of the current social scene should give way to a wild abandon characteristic of the late 1920s and late 1960s.

Rockabilly: It's all the rage

Old and new

Delta's 6,000 flight attendants will be wearing new styling — more structured uniforms in that respect, the new fashions are similar to those worn by Delta's first attendants in 1940 (above). Although the new uniforms will be all-season clothes, they are the same color as the winter version of the '40 style: navy blue. Both men and with a touch of propeller-age styling — starting March 1. After a decade during which Delta looked like sportswear, Delta has decided to return to age uniforms — what mostly ants of major airlines were attired in

Chloé suit, Calvin Klein dress: Tailored '20s chic, '50s flair

1950s rock '83 teen fashions

Clothes for today's young Gidgets are rolling out of the 1950s to rock around the 1980s — at least around spring '83.

Teenyboppers can choose from all the former groovy favorites: Bobby sox, pedal pushers, cropped tops, shorts, bowling skirts, bandstand skirts, sorority sweater sets and more.

Some trends stores have even set up special departments to house these 1950s fashion reincarnations. And don't be surprised to see Marilyn Monroe shops featuring adaptations of the sexy lady's clothes — Bloomingdale's in New York has one.

Ronstadt swings into an older era

Linda Ronstadt is kicking off her rock 'n' roll shoes come summer's end.

Ronstadt, rock's leading female vocalist for the past decade, will release an album of Sinatra-style pop standards next month and will follow it up with September performances on both coasts in which she will be backed by a full orchestra.

"It's a period that's really fascinated me ever since I was a kid," says Ronstadt of the 1930s, '40s and '50s tunes she features on the new album.

CROONER: Linda Ronstadt is releasing Sinatra-style album.

Goin' All the Way

A giggle-jiggle film, aimed at those who pigged-out on "Porky's." As the title suggests, the plot concerns the efforts of a high school senior to get his girlfriend into bed. The '80s are sounding more like the '50s every day. *Omni.*

Old is new!

Update '80s styles back to '50s chic

By PATRICIA WEISS
Times/Gannett News Service

Maybe it's just a fad, this obsession with Marilyn Monroe, pedal pushers, poodle skirts and fabulous '50s chic.

Long-lived or not, the latest fashion craze is a revival, not something new. That means economical dressing — turning castaways from your closet or the thrift shop into high-fashion finds.

Perhaps you don't still fit into your red tulle and taffeta prom dress from 1955. But surely you have a cardigan sweater to wear buttoned up the back. The problem is not finding the basic necessities, but knowing how to put them together.

To this end, Susan McGraw is traveling around the nation to promote the "deja vu" concept of dressing.

NEWSWEEK/JUNE 27, 1983

If some influential high-fashion designers—led by Karl Lagerfeld of Chanel and Chloé—have revived the long-line, tailored silhouettes of the '20s, complete with luxurious accessories like gloves and brimmed hats, some designers are also bringing back the look of the '50s: returning to herringbone patterns, circle skirts, nipped-in waists, wide belts and strapless cocktail dresses.

At the heart of this revival, of both the '20s and the '50s, is an inventive, freewheeling geometry inspired by the original modern movement.

The Elliott Wave Theory, says Prechter, holds that mass psychology creates waves of optimism and pessimism in the economy, which determine — rather than result from — prevailing economic indicators. Gold prices, stock market averages and hemlines all are measures of that confidence.

"When people are feeling more optimistic, friskier and more energetic, men wear louder ties and women let their hemlines rise," Prechter pointed out.

"Gold is very reflective of how human beings feel about the future, it's virtually a barometer. I don't know the mechanism for it, why people change, but they do.

Neil Young's latest rock rolls back the clock to '50s

EAST TROY, Wis. — Like a magician possessed, Neil Young continues to pull rabbits out of his amazing career. The latest surprising phase for the veteran rocker is mid-'50s rock 'n' roll, as represented by Bobby Freeman's *Betty Lou's Got a New Pair of Shoes* and *Do You Want to Dance?* and such early Elvis Presley hits as *It's All Right, Mama.*

* * *

The SEC proposes to temporarily limit exchanges to trading only two new stock-index option instruments. The limit is designed to prevent the new instruments from multiplying more quickly than they can be handled by brokers.

From Elvis to the Stray Cats

Pop music periodically recycles itself, drawing on the styles of earlier periods for musical as well as sartorial inspiration. Until recently, the latest stratum to be excavated in detail was the 1950's, which provided the original models for pop phenomena as disparate as the current rockabilly revival and the ascension to television-rerun valhalla of the Fonz and "Happy Days." But the 1960's are next on the agenda. In fact, though it may seem a bit premature, a 1960's revival is already upon us.

Teens cut drug use

In Pop, a 1960's Revival Has Already Begun

August 6, 1984

The social scene still reflects the assumed position of the market within the overall wave structure. If the January high were a 1929 or 1968 type of top with a monstrous bear market having just begun, then social behavior would probably be similar to that of the wild and happy late 1920s or late 1960s. Those were great times, and judging from personal experiences (at least as far as '60s go!), we're not there yet. Today's fun and fashion is still typical of conservative times (see collage, next page).

November 4, 1985

Unfortunately, there isn't room in *The Elliott Wave Theorist* each month to point out the continuingly revealing evidence that trends in popular culture parallel the trends in the stock market. However, I would like to take the space to clear up a misconception among many who wrote in August and September worrying about the appearance of various expressions of negative mood. The point made in my Special Report was not that cultural fads precede changes in psychology, but that they are a direct reflection of it, as is the position and trend of the market. Expressions of popular mood are not a leading indicator of stock trends but a *coincident* one. In other words, the widespread popularity of mini-skirts doesn't forecast a top, it *is* the top. Therefore, this summer's appearance of dark fashion colors (notably offset by pink tennis shoes among the trendsetters, just to show they're not that serious about sporting black), long skirts, negative-theme books on the *New York Times* book review, etc., *is not bearish*. It is merely a cultural reflection of the mood correction that also showed up on Wall Street with falling prices and record put buying. The only forecasting value in these phenomena currently is that observations of popular cultural trends clearly indicate that the public mood, and therefore the market, is not at a major top of historic proportion. Thus, although a decline is possible on that evidence, a 1929-style collapse is highly improbable. It's the only implication about the future one can draw, but it is knowledge of some value.

I can't resist making one observation. While the public at large reflects a cautious mood, some possible trendsetters may be seeing through the curtain. Mick Jagger of the Rolling Stones at the 1968 top shouted angrily, "The time is right for fighting in the street." His current

Tradition registers high Oldies but goodies revived on newlyweds' wish lists as ad execs remember when

By Elizabeth Sporkin
USA TODAY

Never mind the age or background of the bride. When it comes to setting up house, tradition has come back," says *Bride's* magazine editor Barbara Tober. "Everybody wants more elegance."

The pot-luck suppers of the 1960s and '70s have given way to more formal dinners at home, Tober says, and brides want to host them in style. So woks and fondue pots, while still on wish lists, have been eclipsed by formal serving pieces, tableware and linens.

Hats Are Back

That's especially true in California. "Even little women there wear brims out to their shoulders. They look something like toadstool," he chuckles. Californians also go to hat heaven, cabbage roses and ostrich plumes, like in the good old hat days of the 1950s.

Easter may be the celebration of everlasting life, but one thing associated with it, the Easter bonnet, almost expired permanently.

Almost, that is. But fitting to the season, it is a style that is being resurrected.

ADVERTISING
& MARKETING

BY ROBERT
GARFIELD

After years of selling Comet cleanser on TV, Josephine the Plumber finally piped down in 1973. If you thought she'd not be heard from again, you were sadly mistaken.

Bert and Harry, the beer-selling Piel brothers, were a popular success — and a marketing flop — in the mid-60s. They were retired — but not forever.

Speedy, Alka-Seltzer left the advertising scene in 1963. Was he all fizzled out? Hardly. Ad-

vertising is not like real life. The qualifications for resurrection are modest.

A parallel case: the famous Hathaway man. After serving as the persona of C.F. Hathaway & Co. dress shirts since 1951, the man with the eye patch vanished in the mid-1970s. After two aborted revivals, he seems to be back.

Ray Bans: We've got it made in '50s shades

By Richard David Story
USA TODAY

Ray Ban Wayfarers — popularized by Buddy Holly in the '50s, favored by the late blues singer Muddy Waters, and donned by jaunty Tom Cruise in the summer smash *Risky Business* — are once again the rage.

The dark glasses, designed by Bausch & Lomb in the '50s, have seen waves of popularity. (John) Belushi and (Dan) Aykroyd wore them in their Blues Brothers skits, says Lee Hill of Bausch & Lomb.

were all sold in 1981; so far in 1983, more than 250,000. Next spring, watch for the Wayfarer Woody, timed to coincide with the '60s wood-paneled station wagon.

18,000 Wayfarers

Fine points of etiquette aren't passe

Once again, boys and girls are learning the right way to walk, talk, eat and dress

By Ellen Brown
USA TODAY

OCONOMOWOC, Wis. — This classroom is a luncheon table. And served with the soup is a lesson on the proper way to eat it: From the center of the bowl, lift the spoon up and away from you, then bring it to the lips. Never, ever, lean toward the bowl.

Jenny Hepp, 14, from Plymouth, Wis., and 15-year-old Julie Pekar of Cudahy, Wis., listen while Janet Sherkow, an instructor for Menars Studios at the Olympia Spa here, details tried-and-true table manners at the four-day, $600 Teen Finishing course — a 4-month-old program born from a rising interest across the USA in teaching manners to the young.

"For a few decades people dropped what they thought wasn't important at the time," says Sherkow. "You can always eat a hamburger at McDonald's, but you'll feel more confident if you know which is the fish fork, and the proper way to gracefully eat a Napoleon."

■ Last month, 14 young gentlemen in the making and six budding young ladies, ages 8 to 14, attended the first Emily Post Summer Camp at the posh Breakers Hotel in Palm Beach, Fla. They learned telephone and thank-you-note manners, "dressing for the occasion," and ballroom dancing.

Fraternities back — and in trouble

AMHERST MAN: Keith Dawson 'devastated.'

By Barbara Palmer
and Richard Price
USA TODAY

Social fraternities and sororities, which faded from campus life in the early 1970s, are enjoying a big comeback — and stirring controversy again, too.

The latest battleground: Amherst, Mass., where G. Armour Craig, acting president of Amherst College, was booed Monday during a chapel assembly as he tried to explain why the board of trustees has voted to abolish the school's coeducational frats.

hit, in un-Jagger-like fashion, proclaims, "The time is right for dancing in the street!" As Peter Kendall of the *OTC Stock Journal* asks, could Mick be talking about Wall Street?

August 10, 1987

The most important popular cultural event is occurring not in the U.S. but in Russia. The USSR is typically about 30 years behind the West in popular culture (wasn't it about 30 years ago that they officially accepted jazz?). Now glasnost may have bitten off more than it can chew. Allowing private taxis and tailors is one thing. But now that the Soviets have let rock 'n' roll get a foot in the door, there will be no easy turning back from the desire for greater knowledge of the tempting joys of the freedom-loving West. This terrifically written article by Edna Gundersen of *USA Today*, reproduced on the next page, says it all. It sounds like a scene from 1957 in the U.S....

Joel rocks 'em back in the U.S.S.R.

MOSCOW — The man at the piano spoke in broken Russian: "Hi, my name is Billy Joel. I'm nervous."

He had reason to be. Sunday night's 2½-hour concert at the Olympic Sports Complex began sluggishly. About 20,000 Soviets sat politely in silence as the first USA rock star to tour the U.S.S.R. energetically belted out one hit after another.

But an hour into the show, Joel pointedly invited the audience to join him at the stage, and the night was transformed. Thousands streamed from the stands to stomp and cheer and whistle and — flouting house rules — dance with abandon.

The performance grew more dramatic and surprising with each slickly performed tune. During *Angry Young Man*, a Soviet boy in Adidas high-top sneakers raised a USA flag. Others quickly joined him. Joel prompted roars of approval when he dedicated *Honesty* to the late Vladimir Vysotsky — the Soviet Bob Dylan — a balladeer revered for his brazen social commentary.

(Saturday, Joel visited Vysotsky's gravesite, along with 4,000 Muscovites. "It touched me deeply that a man that suc-

cessful could find the time to see my son's grave," said Maximava Vysotsky after Sunday's concert.)

But most of the show's notes were joyous. The barbershop harmonies of *For the Longest Time* set the crowd clapping, and the hard-rocking treatment of *A Matter of Trust* brought even stern-faced parents to their feet.

Joel was a tornado of vitality. He introduced songs with earnest jokes and bittersweet speeches, explaining the inspiration behind the distinctly back-home *Allentown* and *Goodnight Saigon.*

Sweat streaming down his neck, he twirled and strutted, at one point leaping into the throng to grasp the hands of startled onlookers.

Gradually, the shell-shocked Soviets answered the call to rock 'n' roll. Girls shimmied; boys stood on their feet and shouted.

And when the band let loose with a full-throttled *Still Rock and Roll to Me*, starch-collared crowd-control soldiers clapped and danced, throwing caution to the sudden wind of change. Even the military guards who had first attempted to blockade the stampede surrendered to

Joel's spell with toe-tapping and rare smiles.

Though Joel earlier complained of a sore throat brought on by an unplanned jam session in Tbilisi, he sang with dizzying passion and bravado. His grinning musicians rocked with unstoppable glee. Crowd-wowing saxophonist Mark Rivera and drummer Liberty DeVitto were especially luminous.

Joel's wife, Christie Brinkley, also was flushed with pride. Wearing a ruffled denim miniskirt and white sneakers, she snaked through crowded aisles unescorted, a video camera on her shoulder.

The one sobering snag in this intoxicating conquest came when Joel said goodnight and the audience, unschooled in the art of commanding encores, obediently shuffled to the exits. Joel returned anyway, and perplexed fans scurried back for roof-raising renditions of *Back in the U.S.S.R.* and *Big Shot.*

By Edna Gundersen
USA TODAY

Magic in Moscow

Roll over Beethoven, tell Tchaikovsky the news: Billy Joel has Moscow rockin'.

■ Vladislav Besnin, 20, a soldier assigned to crowd control, was quaking. "It was so energetic. This rock 'n' roll — it's beautiful."

■ Sergei, 24, another soldier, was afraid to give his last name, but said: "I'm not bothered they (Soviet fans) are waving the American flag. I like the spirit, the freedom and, most of all, the possibilities to dance."

■ Student Dina Pavlinkova, 18, was overwhelmed. "We're not allowed to dance at rock concerts, but when Billy invited us, that made it easier. I've never seen such dancing in my life!"

■ Moscow rock journalist Andrei Orlov said the rush to the stage was "instantaneous. And the volume! People have never heard anything this loud."

■ Moscow rock critic Artyom Troitsky called the concert "a big achievement. Musically, it is exactly what Soviet cultural authorities can accept and appreciate: smooth and safe."

Prechter

The Elliott Wave Theorist
October 27, 1995

Reflections of Social Mood in Religion

Religious events and trends reflect a social emotional high. Headlines have noted that Pope John Paul II's "mass appeal" extends beyond denomination. Throngs filled Aqueduct Race Track in New York City and Giant Stadium in New Jersey and sat mesmerized with joy, undaunted by hours of rain. One typical fan was quoted as saying she could not describe how "exuberant and exhilarated" she felt. With rifts between the Pope and Catholic advocates of women in the priesthood, birth control, pre-and extra-marital sex, divorce, gay rights and abortion, *Time* magazine asks "Why are these Catholics so happy?" Only the top in social mood explains it, showing once again that for societies, events do not determine mood. In the past, jubilant receptions of the Pope in New York City have been quickly followed by big declines on Wall Street. The first Pope to visit the New World was Pope Paul VI, who spoke to four million people. That was in October 1965, four months before the Cycle Wave III high of February 1966. In October 1979, an outpouring of emotion greeted Pope John Paul on his first American visit, and the stock market immediately began one of its famous October "massacres." John Paul's next visit took place in September 1987, less than a month before that year's infamous crash. Followers were ecstatic then as well, but the current state of euphoria, to judge from the news reports, is even greater.

October 22, 1995

HOLY LAUGHTER

Some other denominations, also caught up in the spirit of the times, are, say newspapers, "giggling before God." Worshippers lie down on church floors to receive the holy spirit, thereby engaging in uncontrollable "holy laughter." The phenomenon originated in Toronto right before the January 31, 1994 stock market high and has spread to congregations throughout North America. *Christianity Today* reports that in addition to laughing, worshippers bark like dogs, roar like lions, peck like chickens and get so staggeringly "drunk in the spirit" that some churches have to appoint designated drivers.

This activity is the polar opposite of what took place in 1348, which *The Elliott Wave Theorist* has previously identified as the likely end of a Millennium-degree bear market. In that year, the bubonic plague reached its zenith and the Flagellant Movement swept parts of Europe. As in 1995, the Flagellants would lie down on church floors to receive what many believed to be divinely inspired impulses, but they were not laughing. *The Black Death* by Robert Gottfried (1983, The Free Press), recounts that from 1348 to 1350, the celebrants were "literally whipping themselves into a frenzy," tearing their own flesh to appease what they presumed must be an angry God. At times, they drove spikes so deeply into their bodies that they could only be pulled out with a wrench.

These manifestations of mass mood in the field of religion, 6½ centuries apart, are exquisitely reflective of the position of the long term Elliott wave structure and the collective emotional conditions it has implied. Today, religious groups, like other social groups, are reveling in the emotional good feeling of a topping social mood trend of Grand Supercycle degree. At the next Grand Supercycle bottom, ideally due decades hence (see *At the Crest of the Tidal Wave*), religious groups — along with many others — will once again act out a tortured social mood.

2002 Addition:

There is also some evidence that religion becomes more important to people as bear markets progress and less important as bull markets progress. At the stock market low of wave (II) in 1857, 22 years after the peak of wave (I) in 1835, newspapers reported that people in New York City were lined up for blocks to join churches for the first time. In contrast, it was in the late 1960s, near a multi-decade stock market top, that a national magazine asked on its cover, "Is God Dead?" In extended periods of social depression, such as the Dark Ages, religion is generally a central aspect of people's lives. In long periods of social ebullience, religion plays a secondary role. Thus, social mood trends appear to affect not only the style of religious practices, but also the very importance of religion itself. We can see both aspects of this influence in the dramatic rise of fundamentalism in the form of terrorist activities by radical Muslims and efforts by Baptists to get stories in Genesis taught as science, both having emerged since the stock market peaked in 2000. Both *At the Crest of the Tidal Wave* (Chapter 21) and *The Wave Principle of Human Social Behavior* (Chapter 14) anticipated the character of these events.

Kendall

The Elliott Wave Theorist
March 27, 1998

A Socionomic Study of Restaurants

Munching on Evidence of a Grand Supercycle Peak

When people feel good, they like to get out, be seen, eat well and drink socially. This makes restaurants a focal point for the expression of a bull market mood. In our town, chain restaurants now seem to spring up a row at a time, which led us to dig up the following highlights in the history of the restaurant industry.

Data show that the urge to eat out has been synonymous with the urge to buy stock for the duration of the Grand Supercycle bull market. The first true restaurant was the Grande Taverne de Londres, which was established in Paris around 1782, approximately the year that we believe Supercycle wave (I) began. Delmonico's, the first American restaurant, was established during the final leg of Supercycle wave (I). Between its establishment and the stock top of 1835, the Delmonico brothers and two other proprietors became the first to "operate multiple restaurants which functioned as a complex organism — the use of the same name, almost duplicate menus, and similar genetic consistencies to create clones," according to the book, *From Boarding House to Bistro*. Through the middle of the 19th century, restaurants became more common, but the choppy stock market conditions were reflected in a high failure rate. Of the 497 different addresses in New York City from 1850 to 1860, only 11, or 2%, were open under the same proprietor in both years. True chains appeared after the Civil War, as Supercycle wave (III) began its steady advance. In 1875, in the middle of wave (III), the Harvey House, which ultimately grew to a highly standardized family of 50 restaurants, revolutionized the industry. "Like the Delmonicos, Fred Harvey was at the right spot at the right time," records *America Eats Out*, a history of the restaurant business. "[His] effect was immediate, populist, and spread through the entire country, [setting] the course of culinary history." In the bull market of the 1920s, cafeterias, speakeasies and White Castle hamburger joints spread rapidly across the country. Howard Johnson, Marriott Corp. and countless other "white box" hamburger stands tapped into the mass appeal that White Castle had uncovered. The next "revolution" was called "fast food," which *From Boarding House to Bistro* dates to 1949, the exact year of the start of Supercycle wave (V) in inflation-adjusted stock prices, when the McDonald brothers established a walk-up hamburger stand. In many ways, "McDonald's story was a re-enactment of the [White Castle system] in the 1920s." In 1954, as the "third of the third wave" entered its acceleration phase, Ray Kroc bought the franchise rights, capturing what may be America's No.1 brand name by introducing speed, efficiency and mass marketing to the industry. McDonald's capped off a decade of rapid growth with the first major offering of a restaurant stock in 1965, a few months before the wave III peak.

Through the first 200 years of the Grand Supercycle bull market, the relatively fragmented and faddish nature of the industry kept most eateries from being listed on the stock exchange. McDonald's still makes up almost 80% of the S&P restaurant index because it remains one of just four well-established restaurant-chain stocks. Appropriately, however, in this final decade of the advance, the public has assumed much of the risk that is inherent in catering literally to tastes. In the 1990s, the number of restaurant stock offerings has mushroomed into the 100s, financing an unprecedented boom in restaurant-industry growth. Almost 45% of the money spent on food now is spent in restaurants. In some multi-purpose establishments, dining has been upgraded to a full-sensory experience known as "eatertainment." At the Rainforest Café, patrons are treated to an "environmentally conscious 'family adventure' featuring live tropical birds, simulated nature sounds, waterfalls, aromatic scents and a gift shop retail area." Planet Hollywood packages its fare around the aura of celebrities from movies, sports and music. Both are publicly traded.

The stock market is an advance-warning device, so it is of interest that the stocks of these two companies have fallen substantially. In fact, it's hard to find a restaurant stock that is still participating in the bull market. Even McDonald's is struggling to regain "it's golden touch." Over the last two years, McDonald's shares have been flat versus a 70% gain in the S&P. Suddenly, "the company that once seemed a half-step ahead of pop culture" cannot even "construct an appealing new lunch sandwich." Our view is that McDonald's and the restaurant business are powerful reflections of a positive social mood. The quantity, diversity and increasing complexity of restaurants reflect the same aspects of the bull market. The inability of their stock prices to match the bull market hints of a coming retrenchment in the industry. That, in turn, portends an end to the long term economic uptrend that has supported their success.

Kendall

The Elliott Wave Financial Forecast
March 31, 2000

Broadstreet

The following chart of annual gross revenues for Broadway theaters paints a revealing portrait of the correlation between a rising social mood and the demand for popular stage shows. Over the last half century,

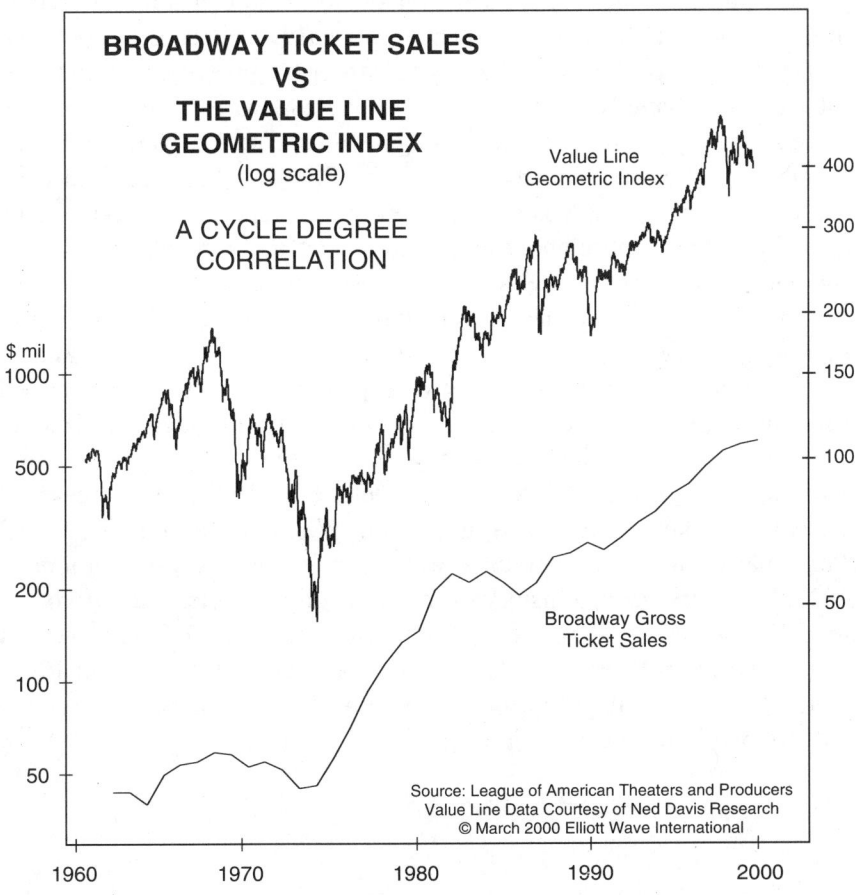

**BROADWAY TICKET SALES
VS
THE VALUE LINE
GEOMETRIC INDEX**
(log scale)

A CYCLE DEGREE
CORRELATION

Value Line
Geometric Index

Broadway Gross
Ticket Sales

Source: League of American Theaters and Producers
Value Line Data Courtesy of Ned Davis Research
© March 2000 Elliott Wave International

Broadway's box office performance has ebbed and flowed with the Cycle-degree trends in the stock market. Just like stocks, ticket sales had a long rise to a double top in 1966 and 1968 (attendance topped in 1966 and revenues in 1968), a major bottom in 1974 and another long advance through the end of the 1990s. Broadway's recent take suggests that a trend change is at hand. Projections for the year ending May 31 call for little more than a slight increase of $1 million. This slowing would fit our Elliott wave case for stock market downturn of at least Cycle degree.

Lending support to this quantitative assessment is the more qualitative analysis that appeared in the August 1997 issue of *The Elliott Wave Theorist*. A study of New York City's theater district at past peaks revealed a clear tendency to finish long advances with a flourish of activity and showmanship. "Entertainment industry histories covering the Supercycle peaks of 1835 and 1929 show that flashy but shallow drama is a recurrent theme in fifth waves of Cycle degree." The same word, "spectacles," continually surfaces in descriptions of Broadway's earlier fifth wave peaks and its latest era. "You have two kinds of shows on Broadway — revivals and the same kind of musicals over and over again, all spectacles," laments Stephen Sondheim, who was recently tabbed "the Broadway musical's last great artist." "Broadway today is more than ever about spectacle than real drama or real emotions, more about giving audiences an 'experience.'" Like the figures for Broadway ticket sales, this more subjective confirmation of a fifth wave also carries a clear sign its impending demise. "*Cats*, the longest running production in Broadway history will close June 25," says *The New York Times*. "*Cats* fundamentally reshaped the Broadway landscape by ushering in the era of the megamusicals: big flashy spectacles that required little theatrical sophistication or knowledge of the English language to appreciate." *Cats* came to Broadway on October 7, 1982, a few weeks after the stock market's upturn in August 1982. When the curtain falls June 25, *Cats'* many critics will undoubtedly applaud, but probably not for long. "In 1930," *Times Square*, a history of the NYC district notes, "the frivolity of the 1920s gave way to a serious, if not grim tone." By 1932 only six shows were playing on Broadway. That compares to an all-time high in 1928 of 294! The show will go on, but not without drastic changes in tone and reductions in number.

SOCIAL CAUSALITY

Prechter

The Elliott Wave Theorist
November 1999

Socionomics in a Nutshell

Understanding socionomics requires comprehending the contrast between two postulations:

(1)   The standard presumption: Social mood is buffeted by economic, political and cultural trends and events. News of such events affects the social mood, which in turn affects people's penchant for investing.

(2)   The socionomic hypothesis: Social mood is a natural product of human interaction and is patterned according to the Wave Principle. Its trends and extent determine the character of social action, including the economic, political and cultural.

The contrast between these two positions comes down to this: The standard presumption is that in the social setting, *events govern mood*; the socionomic hypothesis is that *mood governs events*. In both cases, the stock market is seen as an efficient mechanism. In the first instance, it presumably revalues stocks continually and rationally in reaction to events; in the second, it revalues stocks continually and impulsively as the independent social mood changes. We will now investigate five presumed "outside forces" to see which of these views their relationship to the stock market supports.

The Economy

The standard presumption is that the state of the economy is a key determinant of the stock market's trends. All day long on financial television and year after year in financial print media, investors debate the state of the economy for clues to the future course of the stock market. If this presumed causal relationship actually existed, then there would be some evidence that the economy leads the stock market. On the contrary, for

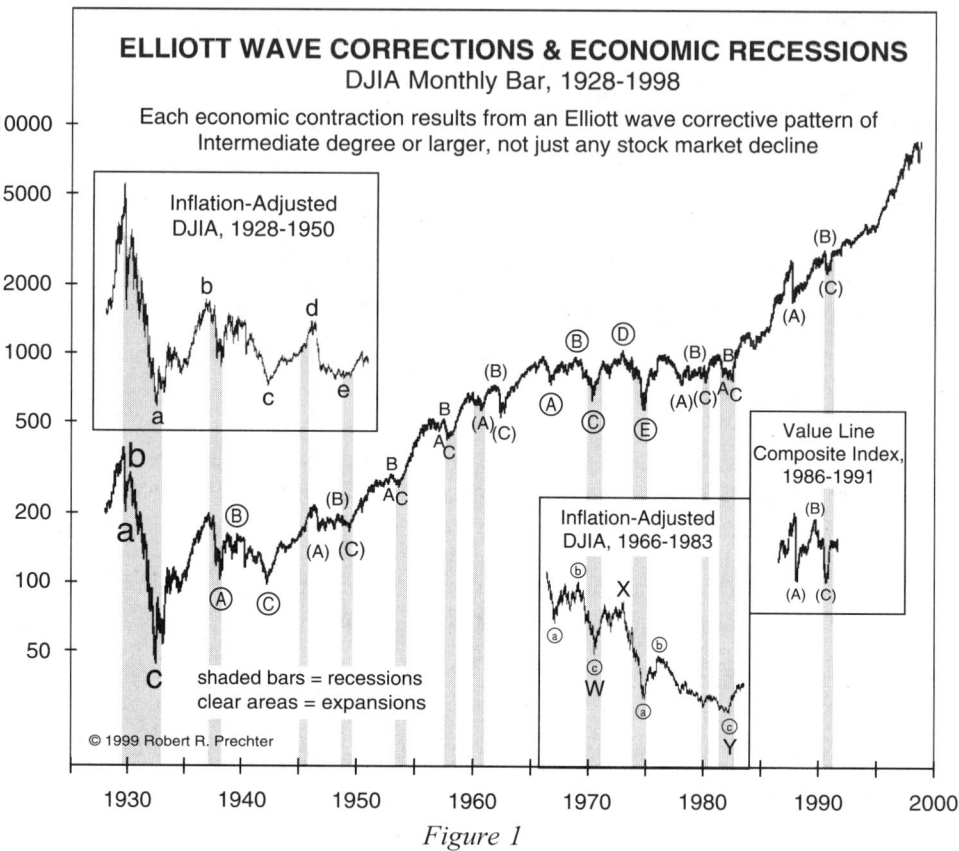

ELLIOTT WAVE CORRECTIONS & ECONOMIC RECESSIONS
DJIA Monthly Bar, 1928-1998

Each economic contraction results from an Elliott wave corrective pattern of Intermediate degree or larger, not just any stock market decline

Inflation-Adjusted DJIA, 1928-1950

Value Line Composite Index, 1986-1991

Inflation-Adjusted DJIA, 1966-1983

shaded bars = recessions
clear areas = expansions

© 1999 Robert R. Prechter

Figure 1

decades, the Commerce Department of the federal government has identified the stock market as a leading indicator of the economy, which is indeed the case.

If the standard presumption were true, then changes in the economy would coincide with or *precede* trend changes in aggregate stock prices. However, a study of Figure 1 will show that changes in the economy coincide with or *follow* trend changes in aggregate stock prices. Except for the timing of the recession of 1946 (which supports neither case), all economic *contractions* came upon or after a *downturn* in aggregate stock prices, and all economic *recoveries* came upon or after an *upturn* in aggregate stock prices.[1] In *not one case* did a contraction or recovery precede a like change in aggregate stock prices, which would repeatedly be the case if investors in fact *reacted* to economic trends and events. This chronology persists back into the nineteenth century as far as the data goes.

The socionomic hypothesis explains the data. Changes in the stock market immediately reflect the changes in endogenous social mood. As social mood becomes increasingly positive, productive activity increases; as social mood becomes increasingly negative, productive activity decreases. These results show up in lagging economic statistics as expansions and recessions. The standard presumption has no explanation for the relative timing of these two phenomena.

Politics

The standard presumption is that political trends are a key determinant of the stock market's trends. As an election approaches, commentators debate the effect that its outcome will have on stock prices. Investors argue over which candidate would likely influence the market to go up or down. "If so-and-so gets elected, it will be good/bad for the market," we often hear. If this causal relationship were valid, then there would be evidence that a change in power from one party's leader to another affects the stock market. There would also be evidence that certain political parties or policies reliably produced bull or bear markets. To the contrary, there is no study that shows any such connection.

A socionomist, on the other hand, can show the opposite causality at work. Examine Figure 2 and observe that strong and persistent trends in the stock market determine whether an incumbent president will be re-elected in a landslide or defeated in one. In all cases where an incumbent remained in office in a landslide, the stock market's trend was up. In all cases where an incumbent was rejected by a landslide, the stock market's trend was down.[2] In *not one case* did an incumbent win re-election despite a deeply falling stock market or lose in a landslide despite a strongly rising stock market.[3]

The socionomic conclusion is this: When social mood waxes positive, as reflected by persistently rising stock prices, voters desire to retain the leader who symbolizes their upbeat feelings and who they presume helped cause the conditions attending them. When the social mood becomes more negative, as reflected by persistently falling stock prices, voters decide to throw out the incumbent who symbolizes their downbeat feelings and who they presume helped cause the conditions attending them. *The political policies of the incumbent and his challenger are irrelevant to this dynamic.* The key is a desire for change *per se*, not any particular type of change. The standard presumption has no explanation for reconciling the relationship between these phenomena.

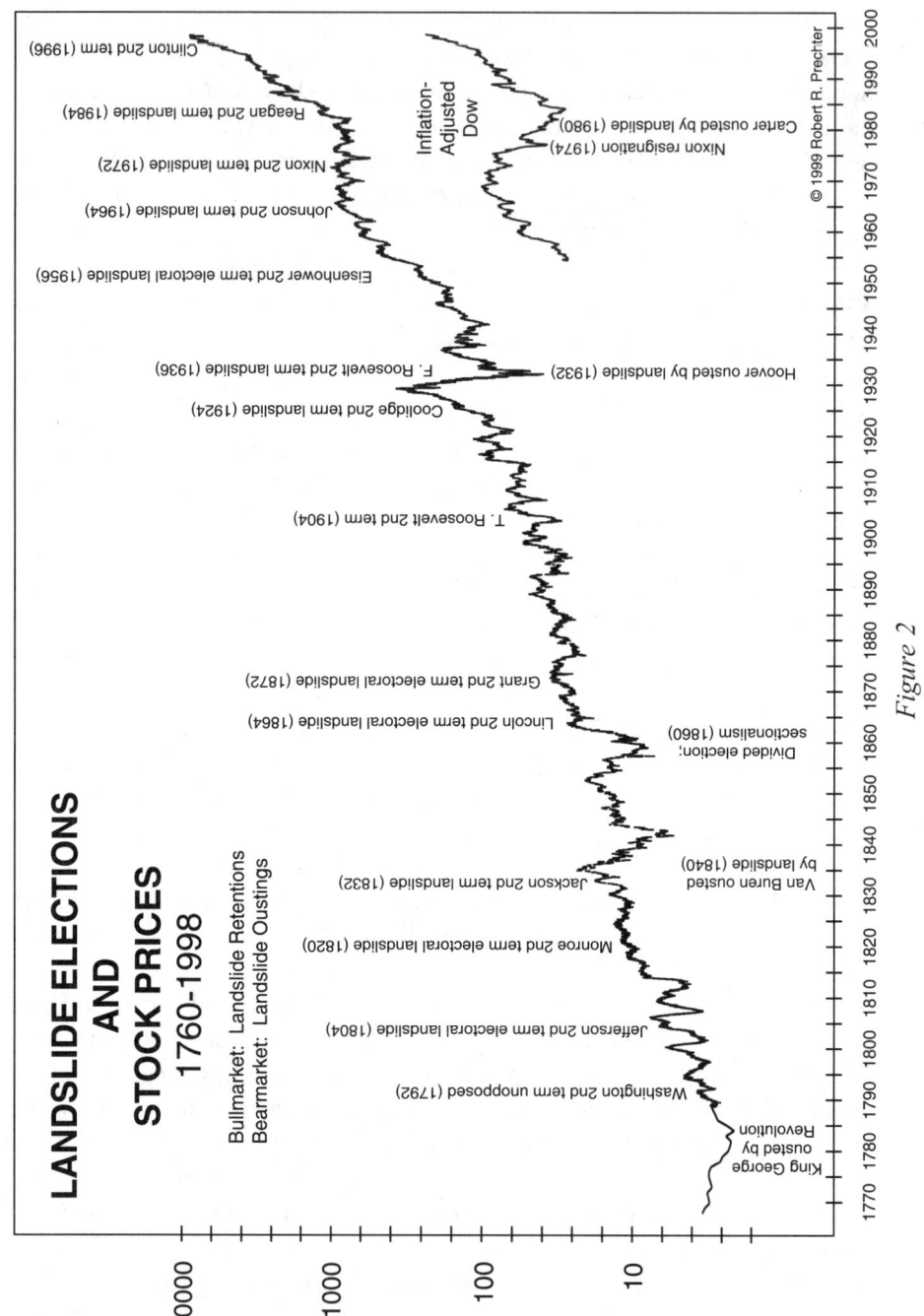

Figure 2

Peace & War

"Surely," says the supporter of the conventional view, "if war broke out, that would affect social mood and the stock market." Such a comment would be, and is, an utter assumption. It is unsupported by argument or history. As to argument, many people assume that war is a dangerous enterprise that would cause concerned investors to sell. Many historians, on the other hand, argue that war is good for the economy, which by conventional logic would make it good for the stock market. As this reasoning is contradictory, so is the historical record. The Revolutionary War took place entirely during a falling stock market in England. The Civil War took place entirely during a rising stock market in the U.S. World War I saw the stock market rise in the first half and fall in the second half. World War II saw the opposite, as the stock market fell in the first half and rose in the second half. During the Vietnam War, it went up, down, up, down and up, finishing about unchanged. In sum, there is no data to support the conventional view, and all the data taken together contradict it.

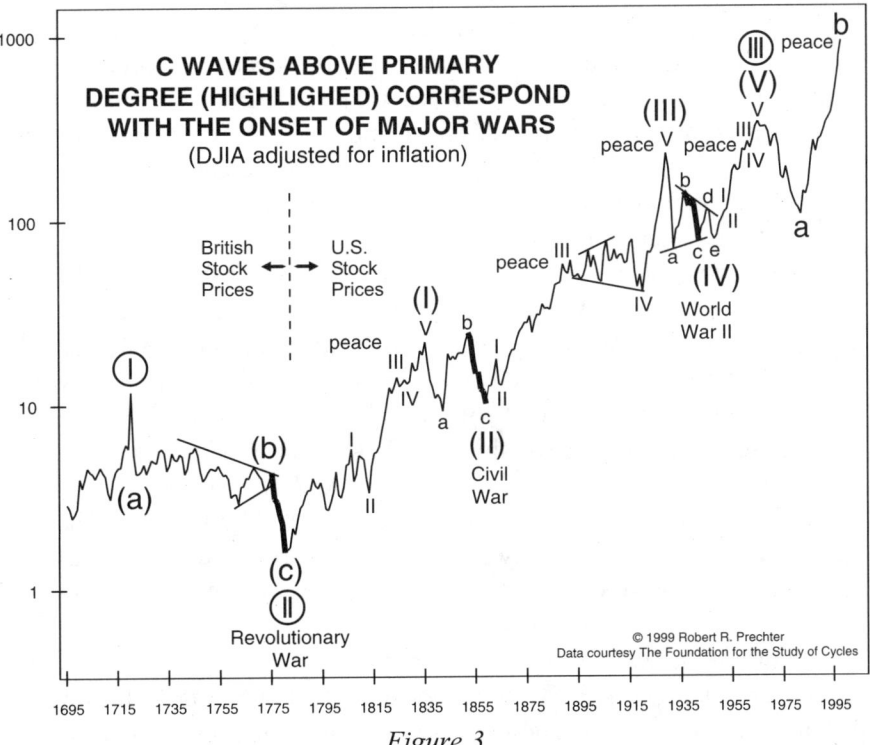

Figure 3

Socionomics, in contrast, points out a *consistent* correlation with a *consistent* rationale. Because social mood governs the character of social activity, a persistently *rising* stock market, reflecting feelings of increasing goodwill and social harmony, should consistently produce peace, and a persistently *falling* stock market, reflecting feelings of increasing ill will and social conflict, should consistently produce war. Figure 3 bears out this expectation. Long rises in the stock market unerringly result in climates of peace. Similarly, we find that major wars virtually always erupt during or immediately following "C" waves of Elliott wave corrections above Cycle degree. The Revolutionary War took place during wave (c) of the Grand Supercycle bear market from 1720 to 1784. The Civil War broke out shortly after the end of wave c of the Supercycle bear market from 1835 to 1959. World War II started during wave c of the Supercycle bear market (in inflation-adjusted terms) from 1929 to 1949. In every case, a rising social mood eventually brought an end to the war.[4]

Demographics

Currently fashionable is the idea that demographics determine stock market trends. It was discovered, when sliding birth data around on top of a chart of the stock market, that there is a four-decade correlation when birth data are moved forward 46-49 years. The explanation for this correlation, roughly stated, is that people spend and invest more when in their 40s, so the stock market will go up and down with the percentage of people in their 40s. It seems so sensible to the conventional mindset that people across the country have embraced this thesis.

The first problem with this case is that when data may be moved around at will, apparent correlations appear often. I can find three different multi-decade periods of correlation between immigration data and the stock market when I am allowed to slide the two series around until they fit. The second problem with this case is that the available data prior to the mid-1950s diverges so significantly from this postulation that it disproves any causality. At least four studies[5, 6, 7, 8] have debunked the assertion.

What is the socionomic position on demographic causality? Think about it for a minute. We have already seen that social mood determines the trends of the economy, politics, and the conditions for peace and war. Might social mood also determine demographics?

Figure 4 shows that demographic data line up almost perfectly with the stock market, particularly when it is expressed in terms of the advance-decline line, which reflects how many stocks are going up or down. The a-d

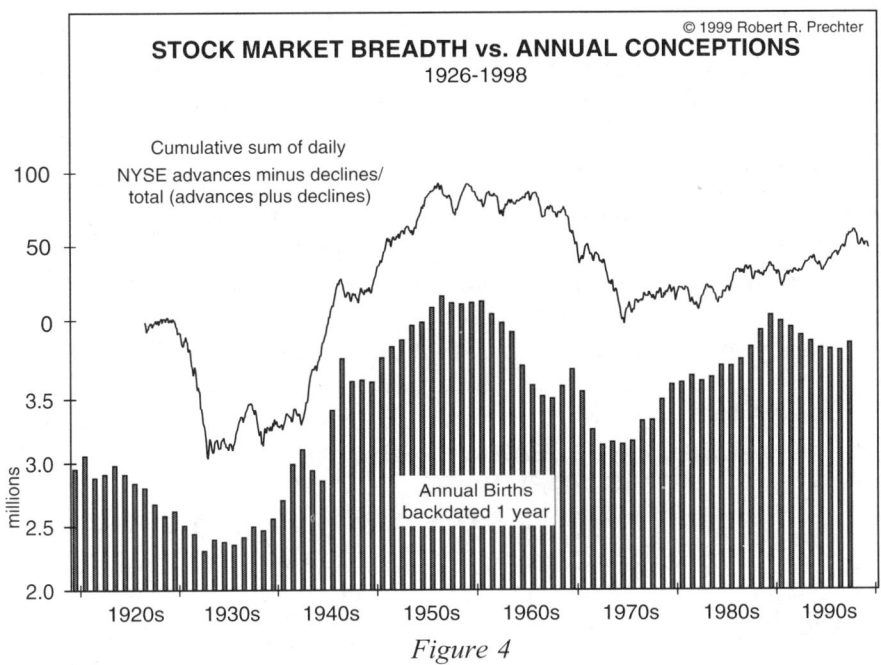

Figure 4

line is a broad measure, and therefore is more useful to compare and contrast with the full population's participation in national demographics (as opposed to data on the economy, which can be propelled by a narrow list of industry leaders). The data shown in bars is annual birth data, lagged by one year to reflect (within three months) the number of annual *conceptions*. The major stock market lows of 1932 and 1974 coincide exactly with the major nadirs in procreational activity. The peaks in procreational activity correspond to peaks in the a-d line.

There is not enough data to be certain of a causal relationship, but it is nearly twice as long a correlation as the one that convinces so many people of the "demographics determine stock prices" case. More important, and in contrast to the aforementioned case, this correlation holds *throughout all the available data*, which dates from 1908 for conceptions and 1926 for the a-d line. No data contradict it. The socionomic hypothesis can account for this correlation. As people in general feel more energetic, confident and happy, they have more children. Conversely, as people in general feel more sluggish, fearful and unhappy, they have fewer children. Thus, social mood determines aggregate procreational activity. Once again, the hypothesis is simple and elegant and explains the data.

Nuclear Explosions

"O.K., Bob," a skeptic might say, "Maybe I can accept the idea that social mood determines the economy, politics, peace and war, and maybe even the birth rate. But you can't claim, as you appear to be doing, that no outside forces affect the stock market. I mean, what if, out of the blue, somebody detonated a nuclear bomb in a major city? You can't say that wouldn't affect people's mood or the stock market!" Clearly, this person has yet to incorporate fully the socionomic point of view. What does he mean, "out of the blue"? This is the same fictional "out of the blue" that we have already debunked in economics, politics, peace, war and demographics.

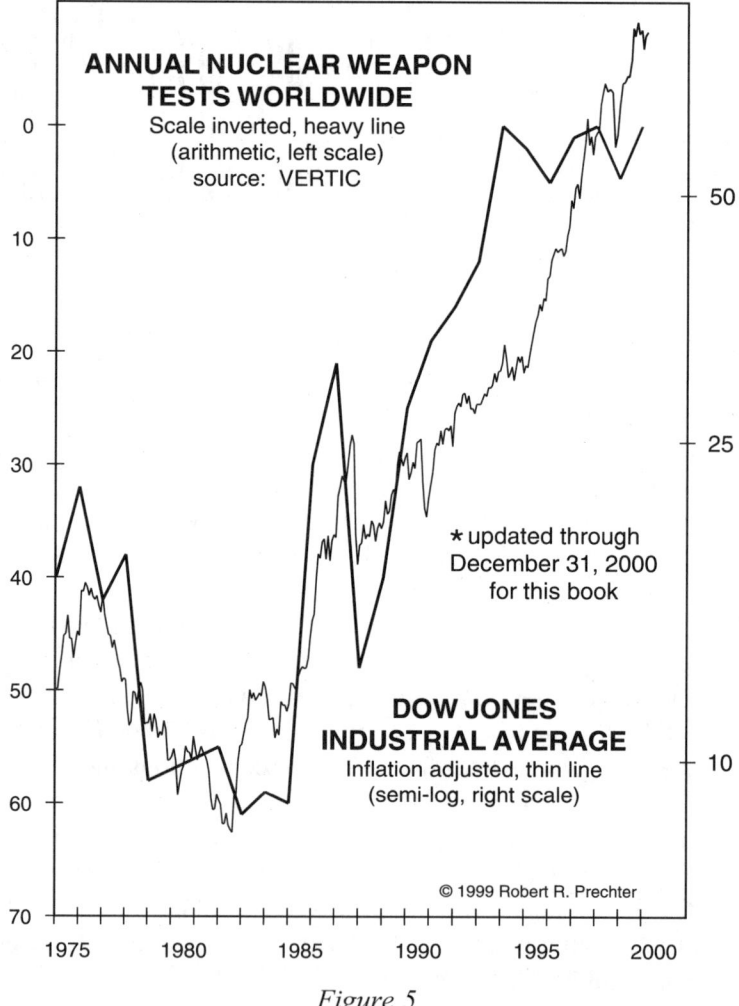

Figure 5

Every social act has an antecedent in mood, so nuclear explosions are unlikely to be an exception. Not only do I claim, based on the fact that social mood is patterned, that the detonation of a nuclear bomb would have no effect on social mood, but also once again, the causality is the other way around: *Social mood determines the penchant for exploding nuclear devices.*

Figure 5 demonstrates that the socionomic hypothesis governs even here. As you can see, the stock market (adjusted for inflation), which is a direct reflection of social mood, correlates almost perfectly with the rate at which governments detonate nuclear bombs. The reason is this: As social mood becomes more positive, people become more confident, trusting and content. They feel little need to prepare a defensive or offensive force. As social mood becomes more negative, people become more fearful, distrusting and angry. They are impelled to prepare to defend themselves or attack an enemy. As in politics and economics, if you would like a view to the future in this area, just watch our most responsive and precise reflector of social mood, the stock market. Its trends will tell you when to expect more or fewer nuclear explosions, and whether they are more likely to be deployed defensively or offensively.[9] The blackest moods of this century occurred in 1932 and 1942, the latter time providing the social impetus to develop the nuclear bomb in the first place.

The Degree of Mood Change Determines the Degree of the Results

The socionomic hypothesis suggests that the extremity of social behavior should be directly proportional to the extremity of the social mood swing. This is indeed the case. The longer, further and more broadly the stock market rises, reflecting a waxing positive mood, the more consistently the economy expands, the more citizens vote to "stay the course," the more children people produce and the more broadly peaceful is the resulting social climate. The longer, further and more broadly the stock market falls, reflecting a greater swing toward negative mood, the more deeply the economy contracts, the more citizens vote to "throw the bums out," the fewer children people produce and the greater is the resulting social tension and conflict. Small stock market corrections beget recessions, mild defeats at the polls and minor wars. For example, the Primary degree correction of 1959-1962 led to a mild recession in 1960 and the Cuban Missile Crisis of 1962, a near minor war. (Had 1962 been an election year, the incumbent would have lost.) The Primary-degree correction of 1987-1990 led to the moderate Gulf War in 1990 and a brief recession in 1991. In 1992, the incumbent lost the election by a small margin. The larger

Cycle degree correction of 1966-1974, in contrast, led to two major recessions (in 1970 and 1974), the ousting of a president by resignation and the comparatively severe Vietnam War. Larger stock market corrections, such as those highlighted in Figure 3, beget depressions, political upheaval and all-out war. Corrections of Millennium degree, such as the Dark Ages, destroy economies, political systems and entire nations, and warring becomes chronic. Conversely, small uptrends produce moderate benefits, while uptrends of the highest degree produce the greatest social achievements of mankind such as the Renaissance, the Industrial Revolution and the Information Age.

Summary

As social mood becomes more positive, people buy more stocks, behave more productively, vote for more incumbents, have more children, blow off fewer bombs and act peacefully toward their neighbors. Conversely, as social mood becomes more negative, people sell more stocks, behave less productively, vote for more challengers, have fewer children, blow off more bombs and act belligerently toward their neighbors. All this correlation is consistent with the idea that all these activities have a common engine, which is social mood. Of course, social mood dynamics produce countless other manifestations, such as trends in art, music, entertainment, mores and fashion, to name but a few.

Because social mood change, as revealed by stock market's form, is patterned according to the Wave Principle, we can propose a larger socionomic hypothesis, that the Wave Principle ultimately shapes the dynamics underlying the character of all human social activity. The Wave Principle, in brief, is the engine of history.

NOTES

[1] We may also say that every downturn in aggregate stock prices of at least Primary degree produced an economic contraction, as long as we define "downturn in aggregate stock prices" as the onset of an Elliott wave correction (see letter labels in Figure 1). Thereafter, the resulting recession may occur in wave A, C or both.

[2] To this summary we may add Richard Nixon, who, after being re-elected on a landslide as the DJIA rose to an all-time high, was forced to resign during the 1973-1974 bear market.

[3] Narrowly contested elections sometimes hinge on near-term market trends and/or the lagging performance of the economy, as in the cases of Truman and Bush.

[4] This is where historians get the bizarre notion that war is good for the economy. Actually, each war is triggered by an extreme low in mood, typically in the climate of economic depression. The social mood then reverses naturally and brings about both increased productivity and, eventually, peace.

[5] *Bank Credit Analyst*. (1997, January and 1999, March). Toronto.

[6] Holt, Derek. (1997, June 20). Royal Bank of Canada, as quoted on Bloomberg.

[7] Poterba, James M. (1998, October). "Population age structure and asset returns: An empirical investigation." Cambridge: Massachusetts Institute of Technology.

[8] Prechter, Robert R., Jr. (1999, September 17). Debate with Harry S. Dent, presented by Bill Good Marketing, Chateau Elan, Braselton, GA.

[9] In the last two decades, there has been no Elliott wave correction large enough to induce anything beyond nuclear weapons *testing*. The next "C" wave of larger than Cycle degree will undoubtedly impel the use of nuclear weapons for offensive purposes.

The Elliott Wave Theorist
September 1999

A Socionomic View of Demographic Trends
or
Stocks & Sex

Most people think that the economy is a key determinant of stock market behavior. Pages 260 through 264 of *The Wave Principle of Human Social Behavior and the New Science of Socionomics*[1] demonstrate that actually, social mood trends, as reflected by the trends of the stock market, determine the direction of economic activity. Most people think that politics affect the stock market. Pages 272 through 282 in the book show that the social mood, as reflected by the stock market, controls the selection of leaders and therefore the direction and outcome of politics. Most people think that peace and war mightily affect the valuation of stocks. Pages 265 through 270 show that aggregate mood trends, as reflected by stock prices, determine social climates that are conducive to peace or war. The fundamental observation of the new science of socionomics is that social mood, which is patterned according to the Wave Principle, is the generator of social action, be it economic, political or cultural. The key insight of socionomics is that the *direction of causality* between social mood and social action is precisely the opposite of that which is almost universally presumed; the former dictates the character of the latter, not vice versa.

Most people who attempt to relate demographics to the stock market operate under the standard presumption that, if there is any relationship at all, demographic changes (like changes in politics, economics, cultural events, and so on) would be causal to the trends of the stock market. In reviewing related studies, one finds full agreement on that starting point and utter disagreement thereafter. Of course, in any instance when there is a paucity of data and a researcher has the option of sliding two series around until he finds a fit, it is quite easy to find confluence somewhere.[2] With respect to demographics and the stock market, one study, based on a cycle theory, postulates a 20-year lag in the stock market's reaction to the number of births.[3] Another, based on the hypothesis that people in their forties spend and invest more than those in other age groups, shows a 44-to-49-year lag between birth rates and stock price trends from 1956 to the present.[4,5] Another researcher disputes this claim, pointing out that the number of 44-to-49-year olds "kept rising right through the 1929[-1932] crash, [which] calls the reliability of 'the spending wave' as a stock market indicator into question." To improve the correlation, he constructs a five-year moving average of the rate of change of a "saver/spender ratio" (in this case, the number of 40-to-49-year-olds divided by the number of 25-to-34-year-olds) that correlates with broad stock trends in the U.S. and Japan since 1948 and 1965 respectively, but not well beforehand.[6] At least three studies, including one from academia, argue that there is too little data, too little cross-cultural correspondence and far too much divergence in pre-1956 data to suggest any relationship at all between the stock market and lagged birth trends.[7,8,9] It is clear from the disagreement among the proponent studies and the statistical analysis in the opponent studies that there is in fact, as the latter conclude, little or no basis for proposing that there is a causal relationship between demographic trends and later stock market trends. However, that is as far as these studies go, because social researchers cannot imagine a basis for investigating any other correlation.

What all of these studies have in common, despite their wide differences, is the presumption that if there is any causality at all, it is demographics that would be causal to the stock market's trends. This stance reflects the standard misconception of causality, i.e., the idea that social mood, and therefore the stock market, is a slave to "outside" influences. The socionomist understands that this view with respect to demographics, as with every other major social phenomenon, is precisely backwards; the *premise* is false. Naturally, this false presumption has led, as it has with studies relating stocks to economic or political causation, to utter chaos in the aggregated conclusions, as the wide disagreements catalogued above reveal.

How may we state the correct premise for the purposes of testing its validity? We must start from the socionomic perspective on social causality. We know that social mood, as reflected by the stock market, determines the expansions and contractions in the economy. We know that extremes in social mood, as reflected by extremes the stock market, determine whether a landslide election will favor the incumbent or the challenger. We know that the direction and extent of social mood change, as reflected by the stock market, determine the extent of peace or whether there is a social mindset conducive to the outbreak of war. Is it possible to imagine that social mood also determines demographics? Most people would never pose such a question; I hope to suggest an answer.

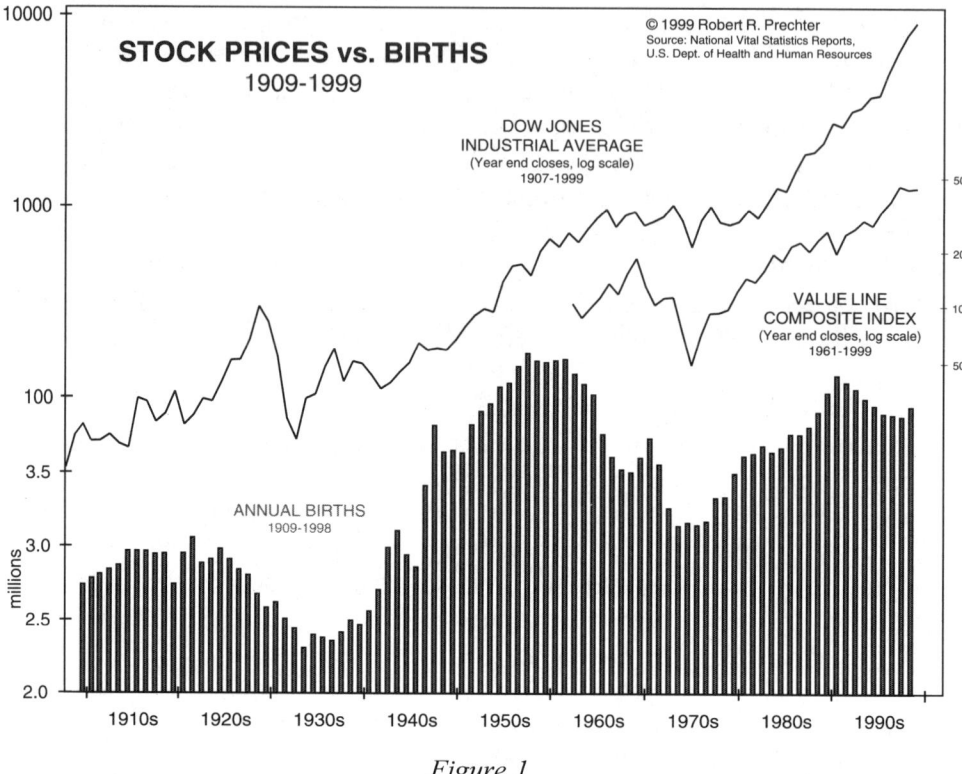

Figure 1

Figure 1 shows stock market prices plotted against birth rates from 1909 to the present. The data is shown with *no lag*. The first thing to notice is that there is a fairly noticeable correlation between the two sets of data.

Why would births and the stock market trend together, if they do at all? Sometimes answers can be found in subtleties. Notice that the deepest low in births this century came in 1933, the year after the deepest low in the stock market this century. Notice that the second most important low in births occurred again in 1975, one year after the second most important stock market low of this century. Why would there be a one-year lag? Well, can you think of any activity that always precedes a birth by about a year? If so, could this activity be correlated directly with people's moods and therefore the trend and level of the stock market? Chapter 14 of *The Wave Principle of Human Social Behavior* characterizes a rising social mood trend as correlating, among other things, with "friskiness, daring and confidence," a falling trend with "somberness, defensiveness and fear." We now have a tenuous basis for a socionomic hypothesis regarding demographic trends. When aggregate feelings of friskiness, daring and confidence wax, people engage in more sexual activity with the aim of having children. When these feelings wane, so does the desire for generating offspring. It takes about nine months between the procreative impulse and a child's birth, which is why, at least at market bottoms, annual data on births lag annual data on the stock market by one year. Figure 2 shows the same data, lagged by one year to reflect conceptions. The result is not an extrapolation or theory, nor is it the result of elaborate exercises in data fitting, as we find so often with hypotheses that demographics drive the economy. We *know* that a procreative decision or impulse is required nine months prior to a birth, so there is no theoretical presumption in repositioning and renaming this data.[10] Now the two major lows line up exactly.

Let's investigate the relationship at market tops. As you can see from the slash marks imposed upon Figure 2, the rate of procreation has declined prior to major tops in the Dow Jones Industrial Average. This is precisely the same behavior exhibited by indicators of market breath and rates of

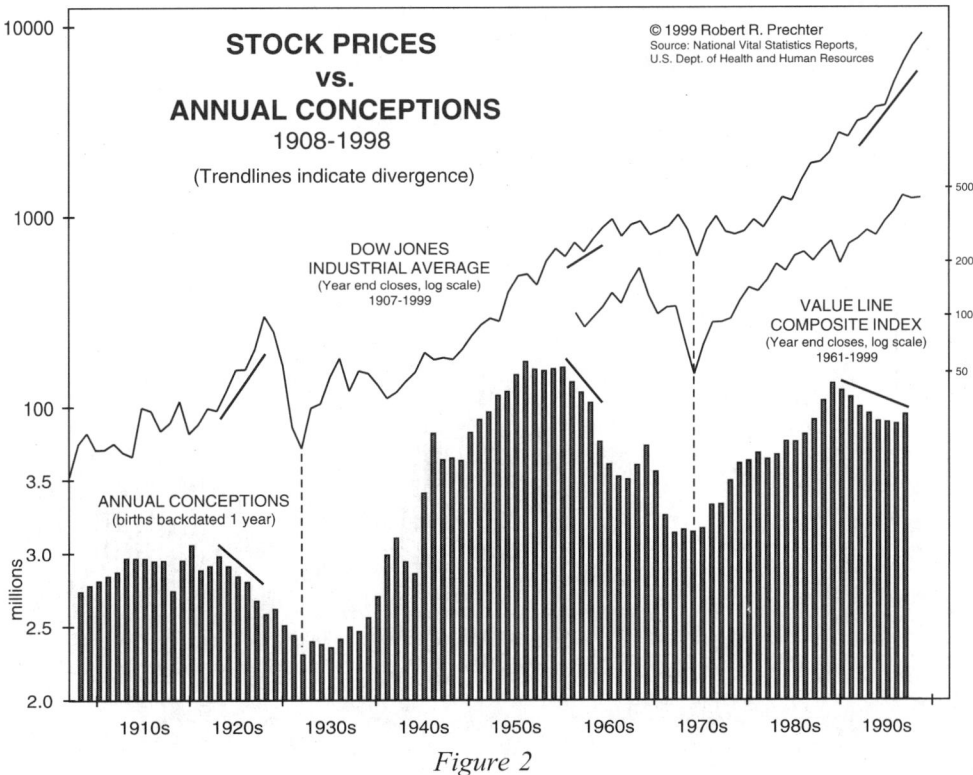

Figure 2

change for stock averages, which always peak and begin declining before the major blue-chip averages top out. To visualize the similarity, let's graph the relationship between procreative activity and the success of the broad stock market, not just the blue chips.

A stock market indicator known as the advance-decline line records the cumulative trading activity of *all* stocks on the New York Stock Exchange that have advanced and declined each day. It reflects trends of stock prices throughout the country, even down to smaller local companies. In other words, it reflects, more deeply and broadly than the DJIA, the breadth of overall corporate success and thus the overall mood, which is the engine of buying and selling among all stocks. Presumably, the a-d line would therefore better reflect the mood of a broad segment of the population that might be tempted to a procreative decision, not just the mood of people who influence the trend of advancing blue chip stocks. Figure 3 shows the same procreation data plotted against the advance-decline line. As you can see, this correlation is far tighter. In light of this relationship, one might be excused for concluding that during the twentieth century, the stock market's

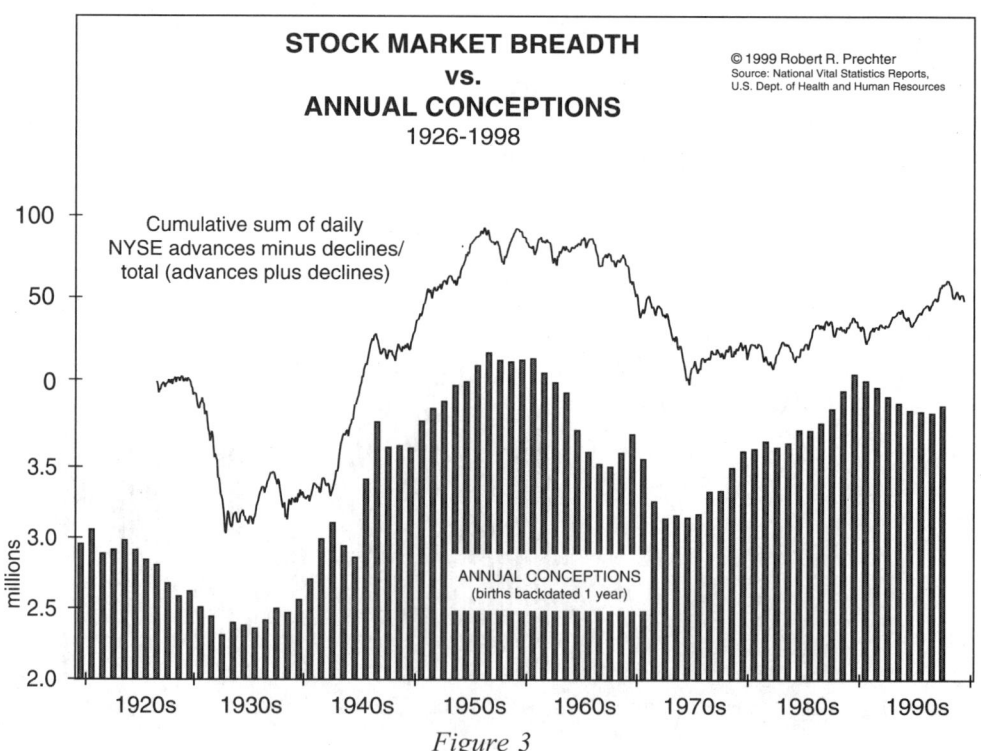

Figure 3

advance-decline line (despite its imperfections in this role) has been a fairly accurate ongoing real-time reflection of the number of U.S. couples that are engaging in procreation.

This contemporaneous relationship holds for all of the available data in both series, which is far more time than the lagged data: 73 years as opposed to only 43 years. Thus, there is a stronger correlation between these two sets of data than there is in any argument involving a multi-decade lag. Therefore, if you think that the popular "spenders" correlation is valid simply by how it looks when graphed from 1956 to the present, then you must accord this relationship nearly twice the validity on longevity alone. What's more, its expression is restricted only by a lack of breadth data prior to 1926 and of birth data prior to 1909, *not* a glaring divergence from the hypothesis as is encountered with the lagged data prior to the 1950s. Thus, unlike the demographics-as-first-cause argument, all available data supports the socionomic conclusion, and none contradicts it.

It is at least possible to suggest, based on this limited evidence, that human social mood, the engine that drives the stock market, also regulates aggregate impulses to procreate. This engine is fired by the interactive limbic systems of people, which are impulsively driven. *If there is any connection between demographics and the stock market, then, it is that social mood, as reflected by stock market trends and levels, determines demographics, not the other way around.* Like all socionomic observations, this one reveals the proper direction of causality, which is the opposite of the one that forms the false premise and foundation of most economic and sociological study.

Demographics and the Socionomic Hypothesis

Socionomics differs from conventional economics and sociology in one crucial aspect: It recognizes that social causality is precisely the opposite of the standard presumption. Most researchers begin with the presumption that the economy, politics, peace and war, demographics, and all kinds of other cultural events and situations influence people's thinking, and therefore the social mood, and therefore the trend of the stock market. Socionomics recognizes that the social mood is endogenous and patterned, the result of cooperating impulsive human limbic systems. The result is a patterned series of waves of human social mood, which in turn determine the character of social and cultural events, including economics, politics, demographics, peace, war, fashion and culture. When the socionomic premise is adopted, the proper correlation among various cultural and societal trends becomes readily apparent. For the first time, the various products of human interaction make sense together. This result is in dramatic contrast to the chaotic sea of uncertainty and cross-inapplicability that pervades the fields of economics and sociology today.

The demographic data presented here, while they are too limited for a firm conclusion, are nevertheless undeniably compatible with the socionomic hypothesis. Humans inherited a primitive pre-rational portion of their brains that engages in impulsive mentation[11] and controls activities crucial to animal survival such as herding, the selection of leaders, fighting and *mating*. Because of the demonstrated commonality among all these activities in our graphs of economic, political and cultural activity, it appears that this portion of the brain actually generates a single mood-regulating impulse, which is the basis for unity in the trends and aggregate character of these activities. Since the stock market is the most accurate sociometer we have, one need hardly be surprised that these data show a tight correlation between its trends and the procreative impulse. If further studies show that the demographic correlation described in Figure 3 holds over the centuries and throughout cultures, they will strengthen our socionomic hypothesis that social mood trends are the genesis of demographic trends.

While the procreative impulse appears to result from feelings of "daring, friskiness and confidence," one must not presume that the latter term rests upon rationality regarding the wisdom of having children. The key word is *feelings*, which originate in the limbic system. It might seem attractive to argue that people have fewer children because when the economy contracts, they restrain themselves due to poverty and the cost of child rearing. If this thought entered your mind, you were exercising (probably in seconds; am I right?) the conventional style of rationalization. We should not be surprised that sociologists rationalize the practicality factor *in the opposite way* when they declare that people in poor countries must be having many children in the quest to produce more family workers or have someone around to take care of them in their old age. On one hand, they opine that poverty induces people to restrict child-bearing, and on the other, they say that it induces people to expand it. Needless to say, contradiction has never halted conventional theorizing about social causality. Traditional thinking makes people naturally offer such event-causal arguments. They are, however, anti-socionomic and assuredly wrong.

Is it reasonable that people *respond* to a contracting economy by having fewer children? First, as you can see in Figure 2, rises and falls in the conception rate coincide with rises and falls in the advance-decline line, which is a register of social mood. This correlation means that trends in conceptions significantly *precede* expansions and contractions in the economy, which lag the a-d line, usually by years. Most noticeably, the lows in procreation coincide with *stock market lows, not economic lows*, which follow shortly thereafter. For example, procreative activity bottomed in 1932 with the stock market, *not* in 1933 with the economy. This chronology contradicts the conventional explanation. Second, as it happens, we have some data on the subject of procreative causality. In ancient Rome, Augustus Caesar tried to make couples poorer if they *refused* to produce the desired number of children. Here is the result:

> In 18 B.C., Augustus passed a series of laws that are often referred to as his "social" or "moral" reforms, in which he regulated, or tried to regulate, marriage and procreation. These laws made adultery a criminal offence for the first time.... He also passed laws encouraging couples to have children, mainly through *large tax penalties* on those who did not. These laws...*didn't work*...the divorce rate did not notably go down, *the birth rate did not notably go up*....[12]

In other words, practicality for the couples involved has little to do with decisions for or against procreation. Such responses support my case that impulsion has everything to do with it.

   In the social aggregate, increasing procreation results from increasing *feelings* of confidence more so than with actual family economics. In the aggregate, procreative decisions, like stock-buying decisions and leader selection, are more commonly impulsive/emotional than meditative/rational. In the case of procreation, they are the result of couples in a state of excitement agreeing either, "Let's have a baby!" or "Let's risk sex that could lead to conception!" Any associated discussion by prospective parents is undertaken mostly to rationalize an impulsive desire that they cannot actually explain.

   There also exists an offset correlation between aggregate procreation and aggregate prosperity *per se* because prosperity results from the shared feelings of increasing confidence that also spur the procreative impulse. This socionomic perspective reveals why the trends of the economy *lag* trends in both the stock market and procreation. As is the case with all socionomic observations, one must realize that the economy is not an isolated outside force that independently influences procreative decisions. Like interest rates, politics and war, the economy is the result of human interaction; it is an intimately intertwined element of the human social experience, not an isolated outside cause.

Trend Divergence and Practical Application

As you can see in Figure 2, conceptions fell persistently against rising stock market averages in 1920-1929 and again in 1956-1966, i.e., in the ten years prior to the top of waves V of (III) and III of (V) respectively, the two biggest tops of this century. After each of those periods, aggregate stock prices rapidly joined the trend of procreation on the downside. We might be tempted to suggest cavalierly that, like waning market breadth and velocity, waning procreative activity is a sentiment-based "sell signal" for the stock market because only the extremity of bullishness at an approaching major market top could make people more interested in stocks than in sex. It's a good line for speeches, anyway. However, I believe, based on our graphs relating stock trends to political trends as well as Figure 3, that it is more accurate to postulate *an intimate and contemporaneous relationship between the limbic system's impulses both to procreate and to herd.*[13] In relating sociometers, it is important to compare apples to apples; national procreation rates track the broad public's mood, which is better reflected by the a-d line than by the much narrower Dow. These two trends rarely diverge. Regardless of our hypothesis, *the same type of trend divergence that occurred prior to previous major market tops is again in evidence from 1989 to 1999*, portending a social mood reversal of like magnitude.

NOTES

[1] Prechter, Robert R., Jr. (1999). *The wave principle of human social behavior and the new science of socionomics*. Gainesville, GA: New Classics Library.

[2] With 180 years of data, I can slide graphs of the U.S. immigration rate and aggregate inflation-adjusted stock prices to show a tight 100-year period of correlation with a 20-year lead, a 35-year period of correlation with a 2-year lead, a 90-year period of correlation with a 20-year lag, and a 67-year period of correlation with an 80-year lag. One can construct a plausible "theory" to go with at least three of them.

[3] Berry, Brian. (1991). *Long wave rhythms in economic development and political behavior*. Baltimore: Johns Hopkins University Press.

[4] Dent, Harry S. (1993). *The great boom ahead*. New York: Hyperion.

[5] Dent, Harry S. (1998). *The roaring 2000s*. New York: Simon & Schuster.

[6] Carder, John. (1997, September). *Encyclopedia of historical charts*. Boulder, CO: Topline Graphics.

[7] *Bank Credit Analyst*. (1997, January and 1999, March). Toronto.

[8] Holt, Derek. (1997, June 20). Royal Bank of Canada, as quoted on Bloomberg.

[9] Poterba, James M. (1998, October). "Population age structure and asset returns: An empirical investigation." Cambridge: Massachusetts Institute of Technology.

[10] Obviously this extrapolation does not account for multiple births (twins, triplets, etc.), which would slightly reduce the conception numbers, or abortions, which would increase them. Abortions are not *necessarily* a factor, as sexual activity risking unwanted conception might increase *because* abortions are legally available, so the sum of aborted fetuses might equal the sum of conceptions that would not otherwise have taken place. Anyone who wants to take the time to refine the birth data to more precisely reflect procreative decisions is welcome to do so.

[11] MacLean, Paul. (1990). *The triune brain in evolution*. New York: Plenum Press.

[12] Vandiver, Elizabeth. (n.d.) "The *Aeneid* of Virgil." Course Number 303, Lecture 3, The Teaching Company audio tape.

[13] Indeed, procreation may be seen as herding in the sense that it increases the size of the herd. Further, because procreation undergoes long social trends, engaging in it or refraining from it may be an expression of herding for many people, who may be spurred to action or non-action by the spectacle of increasing or decreasing childbirths among their relatives, neighbors and friends.

The Elliott Wave Theorist
February 27, 1998

Rationalizing Optimism with Demographics

In January, a *Barron's* headline boldly claimed: "Demography is Destiny." We were regaled yet again with the argument that stocks will continue higher for at least another decade as 9.7 million Americans turn 45 between now and 2008. Paul Montgomery (*Universal Economics*, Legg Mason Wood Walker, Newport News, VA) responded in a letter to the editor, noting that the $146 billion this segment is expected to bring to the market is nothing compared to the $450 billion the market took away in just one day last fall. Instead of calculating what boomers can do for the stock market, Montgomery concluded, boomers should consider "what the market can do to them." Proponents volleyed back with another *Barron's* feature ("Triple Play") on February 16. A long-time advocate of the demographics theory discovered another $25 *trillion* in inevitable stock market flows. The author's new study, "The Big Shift — Barely Begun," asserts that the stock market will triple again over the next 15 years simply by assuming that it will rise at a historical growth rate of 8% a year. We point out that if GDP were simultaneously to maintain its comparatively meager historical growth rate of 2.5% a year, it would bring stock market valuation to 500% of GDP. The figure as of September was 125%, 50% higher than the old record set in August 1929. Are we to be concerned with such things? "With an air of satisfaction," the article notes, "The nice thing about demographics is that you're not wrong unless there's a plague." So to some, the proposed relationship of demographics to the stock market is not a theory but a law of nature: the bull market as manifest destiny. We have discussed the flaws in this case before, in *At the Crest of the Tidal Wave* and in *The Elliott Wave Theorist*. Recent statistics show that baby boomers are not saving much, but they are saving differently. What used to go into the bank or a second home now goes right into the stock market. We think this change in behavior illustrates Montgomery's point: Investment is based on emotional, not mechanical, decision-making. We think that the demographics theory will ultimately prove to have been a rationalization of an emotional state.

Prechter

The Elliott Wave Theorist
July 2002

A Socionomic View of
Central-Bank Causality

Both supporters and critics of the Federal Reserve System agree that the first cause of paper money inflation and credit expansion in the U.S. since 1913 is the Fed. How does a socionomist respond to this assertion?

Conventional statements about social causality always treat the purported cause as an isolated force, as if it appeared from nowhere, with no antecedent causes of its own. Likewise, the Fed is taken as akin to the Law of Gravity, and all consequences flow therefrom.

Certainly the Fed is the primary *engine* of inflation via money creation and the fostering of easy credit through the banking system. But an engine and a first cause are different things. The motor of an automobile is the engine of locomotion but it is not the cause of it. Somebody built the motor *in order that locomotion could occur*. Likewise, people built the Fed in order that credit could be made easy.

The socionomic insight provides a principle of social causation that requires an inversion of conventional statements of causality. To reverse the presumed direction of causality expressed in the first paragraph of this report, we may conclude that the proper reformulation is as follows: The Fed is not the root cause of money and credit inflation; the desire for money and credit inflation is the root cause of the Fed.

If this re-statement is true, then a socionomist should be able to find evidence of it in the record of the formal structure of social mood fluctuation, which is best manifest in the fluctuations of aggregate stock prices. As we shall see, a review of that record suggests that the Fed did not appear out of nowhere at a random time but in fact was a product of social mood forces desiring an engine of credit inflation. We come to this conclusion because in three out of four instances, central-bank formation occurred at almost exactly the same place in wave structure, i.e., in the progression of social psychology.

Credit Engines as Products of Fourth and Fifth-Wave Psychology

Figure 1 shows the stock-price record from its beginning in 1695 in England. I would be remiss as a socionomist if I neglected to mention that the very appearance of reported stock prices was itself a symptom of fourth and fifth-wave social psychology, just as the appearance of financial network television was in the early 1980s. In other words, minds were turning to finance, and these outcomes were simply manifestations of that orientation.[1]

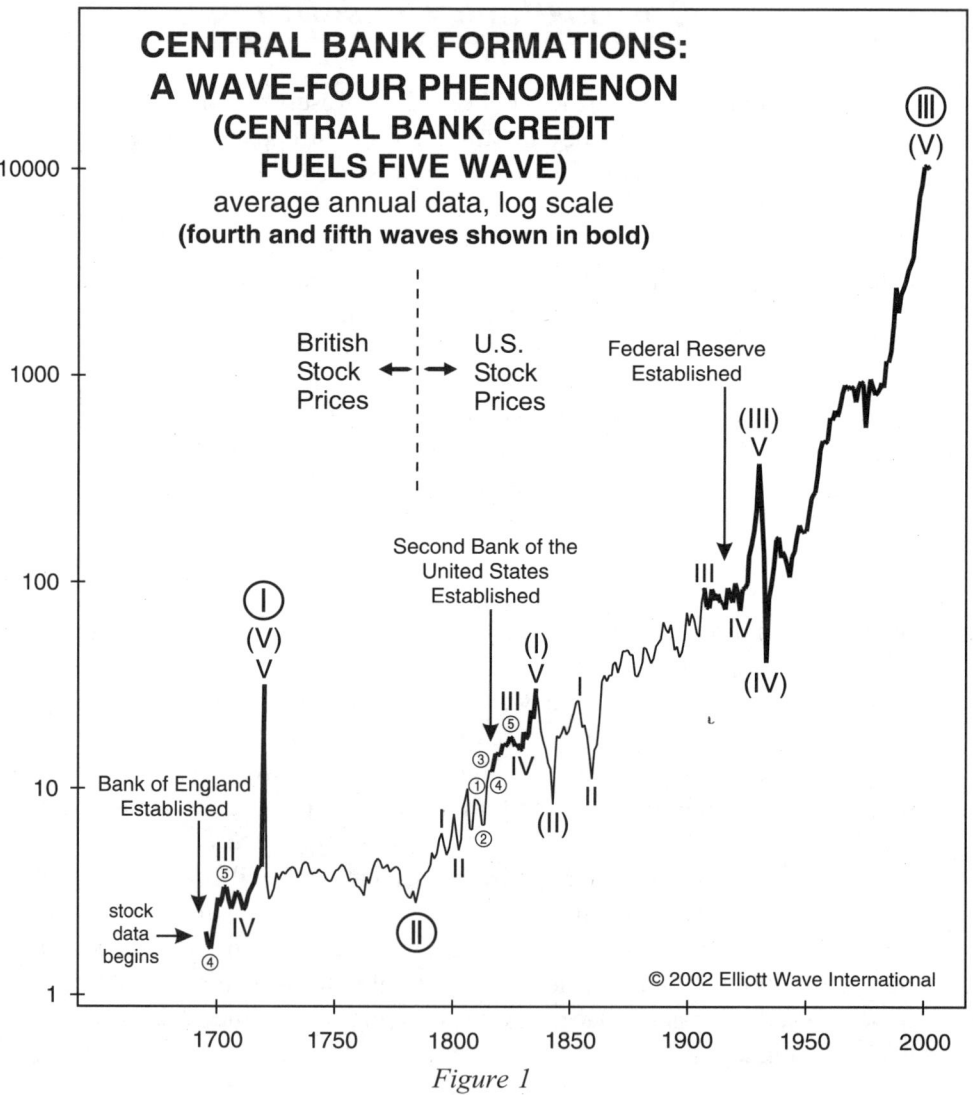

Figure 1

In Figure 1, the points of three central-bank formations are marked with arrows. The ensuing period that encompassed fourth and fifth waves are traced with a bold line. By the way, the labels on the graph are *not* retrofitted to this discussion. For over twenty years, publications of Elliott Wave International have labeled the wave structure consistently as shown.

Observe that there is a remarkable correlation between the wave position and central bank creation. These central banks all came into being during *fourth* waves of large degree:

— The first modern central bank was the Bank of England, constituted in 1694. **It appeared during wave ④ of III, just prior to wave IV of (V).**

— The second American experiment with central banking was the second Bank of the United States, chartered in 1816. **It appeared during wave ④ of III, just prior to wave IV of (I).**

— The latest incarnation of central banking in the U.S. is the Federal Reserve System, which was signed into law in 1913. **It appeared during wave IV of (III).**

In each of these three cases, government constituted the central bank in time to provide credit for the excesses of a Cycle-degree fourth wave and the ensuing Cycle-degree fifth wave. The Bank of England financed the ongoing Nine Years' War (also known as King Williams' War and the War of the Grand Alliance) with France during wave IV and then the South Sea Bubble, wave V. The second Bank of the United States created the credit to finance the War of 1812's debt legacy and then wave V, the Era of Good Feeling. The Federal Reserve System created credit to finance World War I during wave IV and then the Roaring Twenties, wave V. Probably because the next major correction was itself a fourth wave, wave (IV), the Fed remained in operation to finance the New Deal of wave (IV) in constant-dollar terms and the major expansion of wave (V), which culminated in wave V of (V), the Great Asset Mania of the 1980s and 1990s. So the Fed has accompanied not only a fourth and fifth wave of Cycle degree but also a fourth and fifth wave of Supercycle degree.

The second Bank of the United States was an object of political controversy. The presidential campaign of 1832 between Jackson and Clay was fought largely over the issue of re-chartering the second bank. Clay, who supported the bank, lost the election. The bank operated just long enough to finance waves IV and V of (I). In 1836, the first down year after the top, its 20-year charter was allowed to expire.

There is little question that the Federal Reserve System was a product of a certain necessary social psychology as well, because it came into being only after decades of political opposition to the idea of a central bank. In the 77 years following the expiration of the second Bank, promoters of central banking in the United States lost all of their political battles. In 1913, during a major fourth wave, resistance melted away, and proponents got their central bank.

An Exception

There is one exception in our period of record. The *first* Bank of the United States, which Alexander Hamilton guided to formation in 1791, did not appear in the same wave position as the other three examples. It was formed in the midst of an economic depression substantially to finance Revolutionary War debts that had already been incurred. Thus, while we may postulate that the social psychology of fourth and fifth waves is conducive to facilitating the formation of a credit-expansion engine, such engines may come into being and operate at other times as well. It is probably pertinent that after the debts were paid, Congress closed the bank in 1811. Until we get evidence to the contrary, we might suggest that central banks formed in fourth waves will continue to operate through the ensuing fifth wave. Those formed at other times, such as the first Bank of the United States, will be discontinued fairly quickly because they have no fourth and fifth-wave social imperative to keep them going.

First Cause

The chronology we have explored supports the socionomic premise that psychology is the first cause of the credit excesses of fifth waves. I conclude, then, that governments have formed central banks to facilitate credit in response to the psychological demands of major fourth and fifth waves. Fourth waves induce society to build the credit engine, and then fifth waves are propelled by it.

Because the Wave Principle is the first cause of the tenor of social events, we should properly conclude that had the specific event not occurred, had the Federal government not authorized a central bank, then during the terminal waves **V** of (III) and **(V)**, other banks and financial institutions would have exploited credit anyway, through their own ingenious methods and with much of the public happily participating throughout the process. Major fourth and fifth waves, we may safely postulate, encourage and thrive on easy credit no matter what the mechanism.

A Moral Question

If this thesis is true, then is there any reason to object to central banking monopolies? Yes, because a free market in money and banking would allow prudent banks to operate independently from the incautious majority. They would advertise their safety services, and prudent people would have the opportunity to protect themselves with sound banks. Then only those choosing to take risk would get hurt. Under central banking, the innocent suffer the most.

Future Prospects

Regarding this topic, what might we postulate with respect to the fact that at Grand Supercycle degree, the stock market is in wave (IV), with wave (V) due thereafter? Clearly, if a credit engine generally appears during major fourth waves to finance their attendant social profligacies and conflicts and then to accommodate the desire for speculation typical of fifth waves, and if fourth and fifth waves of immense degree are due, then we might anticipate the emergence of an unprecedented credit engine for waves (IV) and (V) over the next two or three centuries. Some economists, such as Charles Kindleberger in the appendix to his book, *Manias, Panics, and Crashes*, advocate a "lender of last resort" to stave off deflation, in other words, a global super-Fed. This is like advocating crack smoking to save a cocaine addict, but sense has no force against the formological imperative. The existence of such a lender provides an excuse allowing people to abandon prudence under the assumption of safety, thus fueling the society-wide extension of credit to ever-weaker debtors. Such a proposal would forestall the next deflation only by generating an even greater credit expansion than has been accomplished by any previous monetary experiment. The ensuing crash and deflation would then be the largest ever.

Given the imperative of Grand Supercycle waves (IV) and (V), I suggest that authorities will embrace the "lender of last resort" proposal, or something like it, some time in the next hundred years as wave (IV) progresses. Wave (V) will be the most spectacular credit inflation in the history of man and lead to the greatest credit bust in the history of man. After that experience, the wave position suggests that fiat-money central banking will go out of style for a millennium or so.

NOTES

[1] As Marshall McLuhan said, "The medium is the message." That financial news networks came into being is far more important than their content. When (if) they go off the air in response to public disinterest, it will be in the vicinity of a major bottom in stock prices.

SPORTS

The Elliott Wave Theorist
July 31, 1992

An Elliott Wave in Olympic Participation

If you were to graph the number of nations competing in the Olympics since their renaissance in 1896, what picture would you see? Since it would track human behavior, you might expect to see an Elliott wave.[1]

Figure 1, on arithmetic scale, is reproduced from the newspaper, and Figure 2 shows the same data on semi-log scale. The new high in worldwide participation is one socionomic effect of a waxing positive social mood, which always engenders harmonious cooperation.

Notice that wave 4 pulled back approximately to the fourth subwave of wave 3, following the guidelines of impulse wave development. That was the year that the Olympics were held in Moscow and Russian troops were in Afghanistan. Why did the Olympic committee choose to hold the event in Moscow at such an emotional time? The "why" is elusive, but the decision fulfilled Elliott wave guidelines for how people *do* act. In 1916, 1940 and 1944, the Olympics were canceled due to war.

The wave structure suggests that among the next three Olympics scheduled, at least one will be canceled and/or

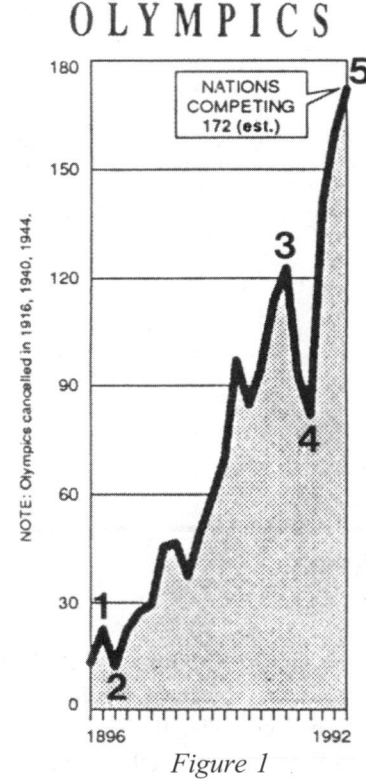

Figure 1

will have fewer than 120 nations (the top of the previous fourth wave) competing, despite the larger number of nations now in the world resulting from the breakup of the Soviet Union.

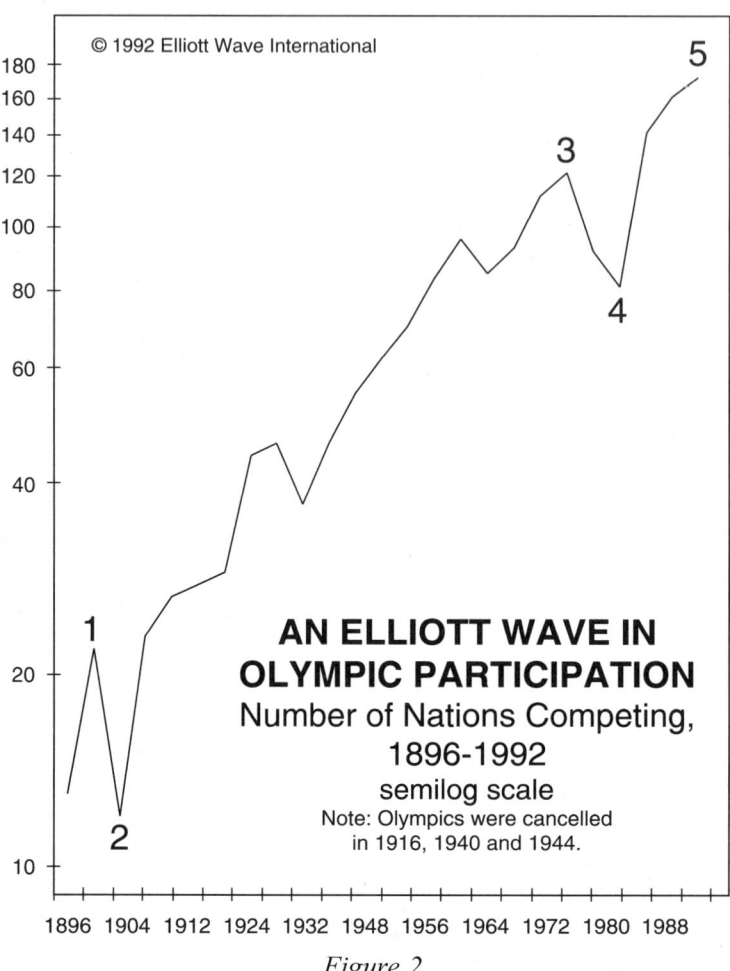

Figure 2

NOTES

[1] Wave 2 in these data ends lower than the start of wave 1, which does not occur in ongoing Elliott waves. The extension in the advance labeled wave 3 is typical of third waves, however, which justifies the labeling as shown. I consider the starting point of a brand new wave such as this to be zero. The same thing happened in gold in 1971. Wave II bottomed at $34.50, which is .50 below the fixed price of $35 that had held for decades. That lower low did not violate the Wave Principle because prior to wave I's burst upward, *there had been no market*. That is in essence what we have in these data, too.

Prechter

As published in
The Elliott Wave Theorist
on the dates shown

A Historic Extreme in Baseball Emotions

November 1, 1991

Sports can provide a background for extreme emotions socially expressed. Long time readers will remember that in the August 1985 Special Report, "Popular Culture and the Stock Market," football was listed as flourishing in bear markets, baseball in bull markets. In the early 1980s, at the end of the 16-year bear market pattern and the low for stocks in constant dollars, baseball bottomed in its slump at a low point that saw players on strike. Since then, baseball has been on a powerful "comeback" trend that has continued right through to this year. In fact, baseball players' salaries constitute one of the few speculative markets that have hit new all time highs this late in the 1987-to-present topping phase. The attention toward baseball this year has been nothing short of tremendous. What makes the story even more interesting is the party atmosphere and intense fan activity of the crowds attending the league playoffs and the World Series. Listen to baseball analyst Don Sutton, being interviewed before Game 3 of the NL playoffs:

> *Reporter*: "You normally see these kinds of crowds at college football games in the Southeast. It's hard to believe this is baseball and to see *this sort of enthusiasm*."

> *Sutton*: "Atlanta has become a very unusual baseball city. You normally see this *outflow of emotion* in a city like Chicago, negatively in cities like New York and Philadelphia. If you go to ball games in San Francisco or Los Angeles...you don't see this kind of *emotional outpouring*. And most of the time when people are really revved up and into it, it is from a negative standpoint, and not from a positive standpoint. In 28 years of being around baseball, *it has been the most remarkable phenomenon I've seen in baseball*."

"I have never seen anything more dramatic than what's happening in Atlanta today."

"It was great, super. We feel good. We feel happy. It's amazing."
— Quotes from fans, *The Atlanta Journal-Constitution*
October 1991

The "tomahawk chop," the "Indian war chant" and "homer hankies" were continually displayed in unison by *tens of thousands of people at a time*. 40 year olds acted like 20 year olds. Drums beat for weeks, game or no game. People showed up hours early at the ballpark to soak up the supercharged atmosphere of the crowd. These upbeat social rituals directly involved hundreds of thousands of people. Millions were involved indirectly via television. Victory celebrations in Atlanta and Minneapolis (despite sleet) attracted 760,000 people. The victory parade in Atlanta, with floats and 16 bands, attracted *the largest crowd ever to flood downtown for any event*. As one observer said on TV prior to a game, "*It's the Woodstock of sports*."

October 30, 1992

A Top in Baseball?

The first World Series game was held in 1903. This year was the Fibonacci *89th* World Series. The *emotion* surrounding the 88th and 89th World Series games was huge. The 1991 series was widely described as "the best World Series ever." It brought together two "worst-to-first" teams, a battle of underdogs (who are always popular). Fans were chanting and "tomahawk chopping" like college fraternity lunatics. The games attracted a high 24.0 share of TV viewers. The teams were greeted by throngs totaling nearly a million people at post-series hometown parades. The 1992 series was similarly emotional, particularly in Canada, as the Toronto Blue Jays took on the symbolism of national pride. Indeed, the Atlanta Braves were the only team ever to have been magically groomed for such a setting by a decade of billing as "America's Team." It was the first nationalistic World Series ever.

Among a list of overpriced items of the 1980s, most have fallen in value. Baseball players' salaries, as well as baseball cards and other memorabilia, are an exception. There is reason to believe these prices have just made a "spike top" along with fans' emotions. Here is a list of subtle hints that a major disaffection with baseball is in the offing.

1) The 1992 World Series had the *second lowest U.S. viewership ever*. (Experts say that the fact that one team was from out of the country was a minor factor.)

2) This year following the World Series, the Atlanta Braves were feted by *97% fewer* people than last year (24,000 vs. 750,000, according to newspapers).

3) CBS will have lost *half a billion dollars* broadcasting the World Series by the time its contract ends in *1993*.

4) On October 17, a 1937 jersey owned by the famed Lou Gehrig *failed to sell* at a Christie's auction. A Mickey Mantle card sold below expectations.

5) Veteran announcers and writers are griping on the air and in print about baseball's "selling out" to commercialism, evidenced by the World Series' nighttime TV scheduling, inflated salaries and players team-hopping for extra money. As one writer put it, "a unique event in our national life has been reduced to just another prime time special," too late for kids to watch, too late for dads to take them to the game and forty minutes longer due to commercials. "A leisurely and timeless event...is now about ratings and money." The national pastime is suddenly not *perceived* the same as it was. *This is a major change in the fans' emotional orientation toward baseball*, from the euphoric to the cynical.

6) While making money is certainly a virtue, baseball may be earning big dollars partly because today's adults enjoyed it as kids. If today's kids grow up without baseball, the money will disappear. In other words, baseball may be short sightedly living high off its capital base and not replacing it.

7) You may recall that our "Popular Culture" Special Report of 1985 concluded that baseball is a *bull market sport* (good guys are the good guys) and football a bear market sport (bad guys are the good guys). When the first World Series was played in October 1903, the Dow was making a low at 43. It was never lower during another World Series, enjoying an 89-year net uptrend. If stocks are topping in a major way as the Wave Principle argues, so is the uptrend in baseball's popularity. Here is corroborating evidence of a top. Atlanta acquired the Braves when it felt rich in 1966, the exact year of the top of Supercycle wave III (and the all time inflation-adjusted peak) in stocks. After all this time, the city has now decided that it can afford a new

$207 million state-of-the-art stadium, to begin construction in 1993. This decision qualifies as further evidence that the top of Supercycle wave V is upon us.

8) In the past few years, Hollywood has idolized baseball in *Field of Dreams*, *The Babe* and *A League of Their Own*. The widespread popularity of such sentiment toward a subject often coincides with a peak in interest among the population.

Could baseball be in for a 55-year period of decline in public favor? Signs of a turn are there. If you're an investor, take profits on baseball cards. If you're a player, sign a long term contract. If you're an owner, sell your club. Kids will soon be trading in their bats for helmets (or hockey pucks, soccer balls, or equipment for a more violent sport yet to come). If you're a real fan, you'll still find yourself griping about baseball some time in the 1990s.

January 29, 1993

The Elliott Wave Theorist presented a full page of detailed discussion in the October 30 issue arguing that after 89 years, the trend of increasing popularity of baseball had given eight major signs of topping. (Immediately thereafter in the post-season, team owners signed 34 players to contracts guaranteeing $258 million. Barry Bonds will make over $45,000 a *game*, more than former top heroes made in a *year*; talk about locking in "Bond" yield....) That write-up apparently came at the top of a spike, just before a dramatic reversal. Here's a hot-off-the-press assessment of what's happened since.

Baseball-card stocks were hit by news that market leader Topps Co. will report its first quarterly loss in more than a decade.

Topps – which experienced strong insider selling last year – sank 31% to $8.50 from $12.25, on seven times its usual volume.

The announcement sent shares of several other companies in the sports-memorabilia business south yesterday. Among them was Marvel Entertainment group, the comic-book giant that purchased card manufacturer Fleer Corp. last September. Shares of Marvel, which according to analysts get roughly half its revenue from Fleer, slid $3.25, or 11.5%, to $24.875.

"The speculative bubble has burst in the new cards," said....

—*The Wall Street Journal*, January 27, 1993

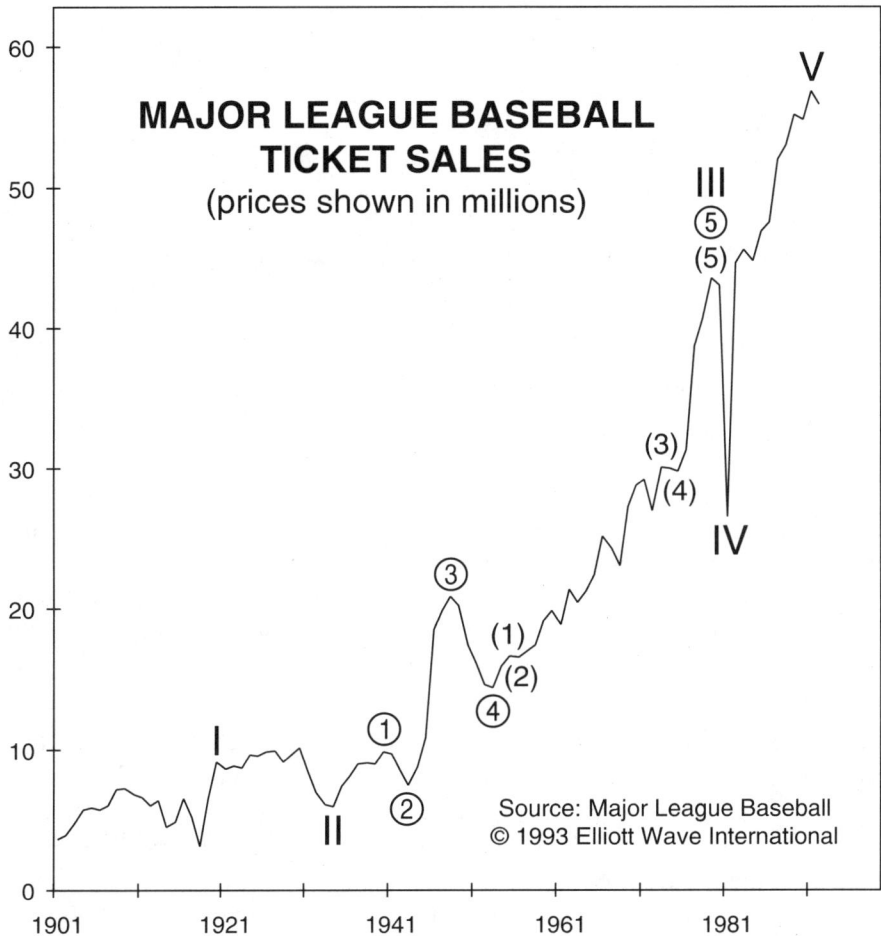

MAJOR LEAGUE BASEBALL
TICKET SALES
(prices shown in millions)

Source: Major League Baseball
© 1993 Elliott Wave International

Pete Kendall has just obtained the data on baseball attendance during this century. As you can see by the chart, the figures appear to have traced out an exceptional Elliott wave, ending with the 1991 season. Notice that the 1981 strike brought attendance back to the preceding fourth wave, just as it was scheduled to do. When the data is plotted on semilog scale (not shown), the entire rise from the World War I low in 1916 forms a wedge, which has bearish implications. At minimum, then, *baseball faces its largest percentage drop in attendance since it became the national sport*. At junctures such as this, it is even appropriate to consider that it may fall far enough out of favor in coming years to cease *being* the premier national sport.

The Elliott Wave Theorist Special Report
September 29, 1994

Sports, Markets and Forecasting

> *"Baseball faces its largest percentage drop in attendance since it became the national sport."*
> — *The Elliott Wave Theorist*, January 29, 1993

The forecast cited above was based entirely on technical [socionomic] analysis, including (1) the Elliott wave pattern in baseball attendance figures, (2) Fibonacci time sequences, (3) the cultural connection between baseball popularity and bull markets in stocks, and (4) an extreme psychology, which included record attendance and revenue, record baseball card prices among collectors and "investors," record player salaries, highly emotional World Series in 1991 and 1992, and a period of production of numerous baseball movies. In other words, when baseball was at its all-time healthiest "fundamentally," that was the time to turn bearish.

The 1993 season was the biggest ever in terms of attendance, and that rise on the chart finished the "fifth of the fifth" wave from 1918. Bear market emotions were running high early in the 1994 season, as an amazing total of seven "bench-clearing brawls" had occurred in this gentleman's game before even two months had passed (ending near the May bottom in mood and the stock market). The 1994 season nevertheless promised a new home run record, a "first" in consecutive pitching awards, and a modern record for a batting average, keeping interest at fever pitch. The final sign of an exhaustive "blowoff" in national baseball psychology came with the production of Ken Burns' 18 1/2-hour PBS documentary, *Baseball*, which was completed literally days before the 1994 strike was called and therefore right at the peak of the long term trend. One observation by Burns is a loud echo of what *The Elliott Wave Theorist* has been saying, both in a specific and general sense: "We can measure our health as a country," says Burns, "by the health of the game itself." Burns' documentary divides baseball history into nine "innings," one for each decade. Is the game over?

As you can see by the chart, baseball's 1994 attendance figure has already resulted in the largest numerical drop in annual attendance in the history of baseball, thanks to a nationwide players' strike. This is a fitting start to what is expected to be the largest *percentage* drop in history. The 1995 season is reported to be in question, and if there is no season or a truncated season next year, the forecast will be fulfilled. However, corrective waves are often complex, so from now on, no particular year is crucial. The overall trend for many years should continue toward lower popularity, lower attendance (though a brief slight new high is possible within the corrective pattern) and more frustrating obstacles to success in resuming the old uptrend. As EWT postulated a year and a half ago, "At junctures such as this, it is even appropriate to consider that [baseball] may fall far

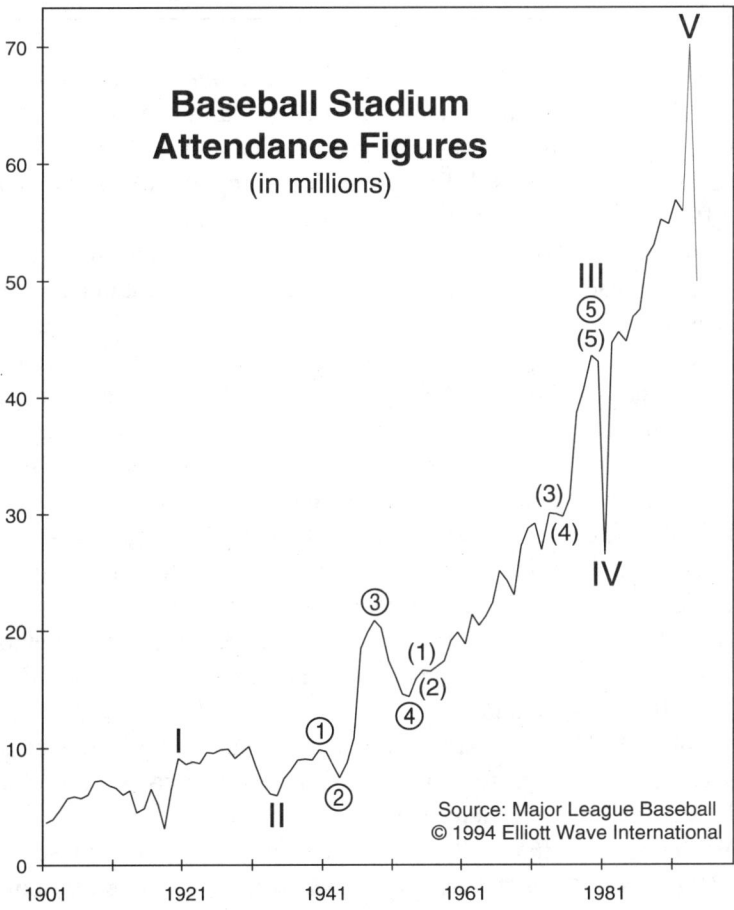

Baseball Stadium Attendance Figures
(in millions)

Source: Major League Baseball
© 1994 Elliott Wave International

Is baseball on road to ruin?

Fallen Classic: no Series in '94

Baseball season over with no end in sight to historical work stoppage

Baseball's season is over, sending the national pastime down a black hole

Wednesday, on the 34rd day of the second-longest work stoppage in major league history, acting baseball commissioner and owner of the Milwaukee Brewers Bud Selig canceled the remainder of the 1994 season.

And baseball fans have hit bottom.   SEPTEMBER 15, 1994

R.I.P. ... Baseball died in 1994. Oh, it'll be reinvented, but it'll never be the same and the game we all grew up with and loved is gone.

'95 in doubt

The Shortest Season

owners, union refuse to budge

Styles of Confrontation Made A Bad Situation Worse;

a sad day for baseball

---

enough out of favor in coming years to cease *being* the premier national sport." That thought, unthinkable at the time and outrageous today, still pertains. Certainly this warning from October 1992 has proved valid: "If you're a real fan, you'll still find yourself griping about baseball some time in the 1990s." The enormity of the trend change can be observed by the fact that only one other World Series was ever canceled, and that was in 1904.

For Fibonacci fans, it is worth noting that the remainder of the baseball season was canceled on the **34th** day of the players' strike. For stock market observers, it is worth noting that the players' union was *formed* in 1966, the year of the Grand Supercycle top in U.S. stocks, measured in constant dollars. Union activity, being exclusionary and confrontational, is a bear market phenomenon. The bear market in stocks and mood that should last a decade will undoubtedly wreak havoc on Major League Baseball, and will almost certainly result in an end to Major League Baseball's antitrust law exemption and its absolute dominance of the profession. As *The Elliott Wave Theorist* said in October 1992, fans will begin turning to rougher sports, such as football, hockey, soccer "or a more violent sport yet to come." Since then, "gladiator" sports have become big on TV and no-rules boxing is back and selling tickets.

While EWT's forecast was one season early, the Fibonacci analysis employed actually therefore pertains to an even greater degree. The first World Series game was held in 1903, and there was none played in 1904, so EWT concluded that 1992 was the Fibonacci 89th World Series. However, 1993 was the 89th *consecutive* World Series, apparently completing the Supercycle uptrend after an uninterrupted Fibonacci duration of 89 years. 1903's games were simply a false start. It was the 89th consecutive *season*, 1991, that produced the most emotionally charged playoffs ever (see description in November 1991 EWT), ending with what was widely called "the best World Series ever." 1991 and 1993, then, created a sort of a "double top," balancing, *each after 89 years*, the double beginning of 1903 and 1905.

The forecast cited at the start of this section was more important than most people realize, given its seemingly trivial subject. The first reason is that every successful forecast of this type serves further to demonstrate the breadth of application of the Wave Principle and technical analysis [socionomics]. Second, success in predicting social events *outside* markets serves to support the case in "Popular Culture and the Stock Market" (1985) that market trends and social trends are simply manifestations of deeper sociological trends. Third, it validates the specific conclusion in that essay that baseball, a "clean, good-guy sport," thrives in bull markets and suffers in bear markets when "rough, bad-guy sports" capture the fervor of the fans. Basketball is a bull market sport as well, and after coming from near bankruptcy at the end of Cycle wave IV and a roaring fifteen years of increasing success during wave V, it, too, now faces a players' strike. (In contrast, football should be on the verge of a surge in success.) Fourth is the practical value of such forecasts for people involved in a related industry. EWT was specific in its advice on October 30, 1992: "If you're an investor, take profits on baseball cards. If you're a player, sign a long term contract. If you're an owner, sell your club." Prices for collectible baseball cards peaked very near that time, and by April 1993, articles announced that "the market is crumbling." The stock of The Topps Company, Inc., maker of baseball cards, was at 16 at the time, and has now fallen 68% from its January 1992 record high of 20 1/4 (following the record-emotional 1991 season) to 6 1/2 today. The 1993 season, which set all-time attendance records, was the ideal time for any club owner to sell and the ideal time for a player to lock in a high salary, which many players did. Finally, correct forecasting of social trends increases the probability that our *market* forecasts will be accurate. As noted in the November 1992 EWT, "When the first World Series was played in October 1903, the Dow was making a low at 43. It was never lower during another World Series." The long term peak in baseball's fortunes is mirroring a peak in the long term value of stocks.

Kendall

The Elliott Wave Theorist Special Report
December 16, 1996

Basketball and the Bull Market

Introduction

R.N. Elliott's discovery of the Wave Principle was derived from empirical evidence, in stock prices. Elliott soon realized, however, that the only possible explanation for the market's "rhythmical bias" was a mass psychological condition that went beyond Wall Street. In *The Wave Principle* (his first treatise on the subject in 1938), Elliott asserted that he had found a natural law that shapes "all social-economic processes." Until his death in 1947, Elliott focused almost exclusively on the stock market because it furnished an "abundance of reliable data," and it was the field where the predictive value of his work could be most practically applied. Elliott's greatest contribution in this regard was the use of his discovery to describe a bull market in stocks that is only now concluding. But if Elliott was right about the Wave Principle, the bull market that he predicted implied changes in other human endeavors along the same line of progress. Indeed, on a Grand Supercycle basis, the bull market is more than 200 years old, so the over-arching impact of this positive social mood trend must have created some uniquely bullish institutions, endeavors and achievements. Over the years, *The Elliott Wave Theorist* has identified many of these manifestations.

This report focuses on one more: the game of basketball. As a seasonal activity that is played far less frequently and observed by fewer people than the stock market, basketball has its limitations as a register of mass mood. But basketball has a long history and is an intensely competitive enterprise. It is a field where performance is closely monitored and recorded. This examination of that history shows the dominant influence of social mood on an American sport. Basketball is a coincident reflection of the fluctuating but net-rising mood behind the bull market of the last century. The game's structure, rules and fortunes have developed in a manner that is totally consistent with the ebb and flow of the bull market in stocks.

By linking the peaks and troughs of this professional game to the same junctures in the stock market, this analysis will shed light on the way a bull market operates in the cultural realm.

When the market is rising, optimism is growing and people express that emotion by attending basketball games. Owners express it by starting teams and leagues. This report also reveals surprising consistencies in the play itself by exploring the sport's propensity to crown the greatest teams and heroes at the most explosive points in the bull market as well as its regression to violence and chaos in bear markets. We will also speculate on just what it is about basketball that keeps it in time with the rhythm of the stock market. In the final analysis, we return to Elliott's original intent and examine ways in which this application of the Wave Principle can be profitably employed.

Basketbull

In 1985, when *The Elliott Wave Theorist* presented the first in-depth dissertation on the link between cultural behavior and the direction of stock prices, included was a descriptive chart showing the "cultural manifestations" that could be expected at four different phases of "mood trend." In the box for the field of sports in a "rising mood," we associated bull markets with "clean, good guy sports." At the time, the current bull market was unfolding and baseball was still the undisputed national pastime, so baseball was labeled "supreme." The next box, for a sports manifestation of a "peak positive mood," was left blank. With the biggest stock market peak in history behind us, or very nearly so, we can now fill in that blank. Basketball is the ultimate bull market game. Its dependence on speed, height and jumping ability are all physical expressions of a bull market; its use of "fouls" to minimize contact make it the epitome of a "clean, good guy sport."

The game's long rise to prominence supports the case well. Professional basketball was born in 1896, the same year as the Dow Jones Industrial Average. In that year, the Dow put in a low of 26.08, which has never been challenged. Over the last 100 years, the basketball season has correlated precisely with what is on average the best seasonal 6-month stretch for stock prices. The November to April period, pro basketball's regular season, coincides with an average stock-market gain of 2.6%, almost twice the average semi-annual gain of 1.34% since 1896. Basketball's off-season is among the worst for stocks. Over the last century, May to October has produced a gain of just 0.5%.

The status of the game in the 1990s is the final indication of its status as the premier bull-market sport. As of 1993, *Professional Sports Team Histories* declared that professional basketball "had risen to the pre-eminent sport in America. ...Much to the distress of baseball and football, basketball was now the favorite sport of American children." Basketball cards are the fastest growing sector of the card market. Six of the top eight U.S. sports spokesmen are NBA players or former players. Michael Jordan and Shaquille O'Neal, with $38 and $23 million in endorsements, respectively, are the two most valuable names in sports. Jordan is the most valuable celebrity spokesman, period.

Attendance

Figure 1 shows how NBA attendance from 1968 through the first half of 1996 has generally tracked the Dow. Its steady growth was interrupted by consolidation in the mid-1970s and early 1990s. The only major divergence from the Dow came in the 1970s, when attendance slowed only briefly in the early part of the decade, then expanded through a devastating bear market in 1974. In real terms, however, the market did not hit bottom until 1982, foreshadowing the NBA's attendance boom of the 1980s by a year. The Dow's correction of 1990 was followed by a season of falling ticket sales in 1990-91. Today, football is off 2% from 1995 and baseball attendance is down 14%, but basketball attendance has continued to rise with the bull market. In 1995-96, the NBA sold a record total of 21 million tickets.

The Basketball Expansion

In its earliest days, professional basketball was far less organized than it is today. Every pro player was a free agent who jumped from one team to the next, sometimes on a game-by-game basis. There were 12 different pro leagues in the East up through the 1920s, but none gained any national recognition. They paid according to minutes played: $1 per minute for "good" players. According to *The Pro Basketball Encyclopedia*, it took the signing of the original Celtics to exclusive contracts in 1922 to "bring order out of chaos in basketball." That signing took place months after the end of a multi-year net-sideways period of chaotic movements in stock prices. In 1925, during the Roaring Twenties bull market, basketball's first major league, the American Basketball League (#2 in Figure 2), was formed. By all accounts, the economic disruption that followed the stock market crash

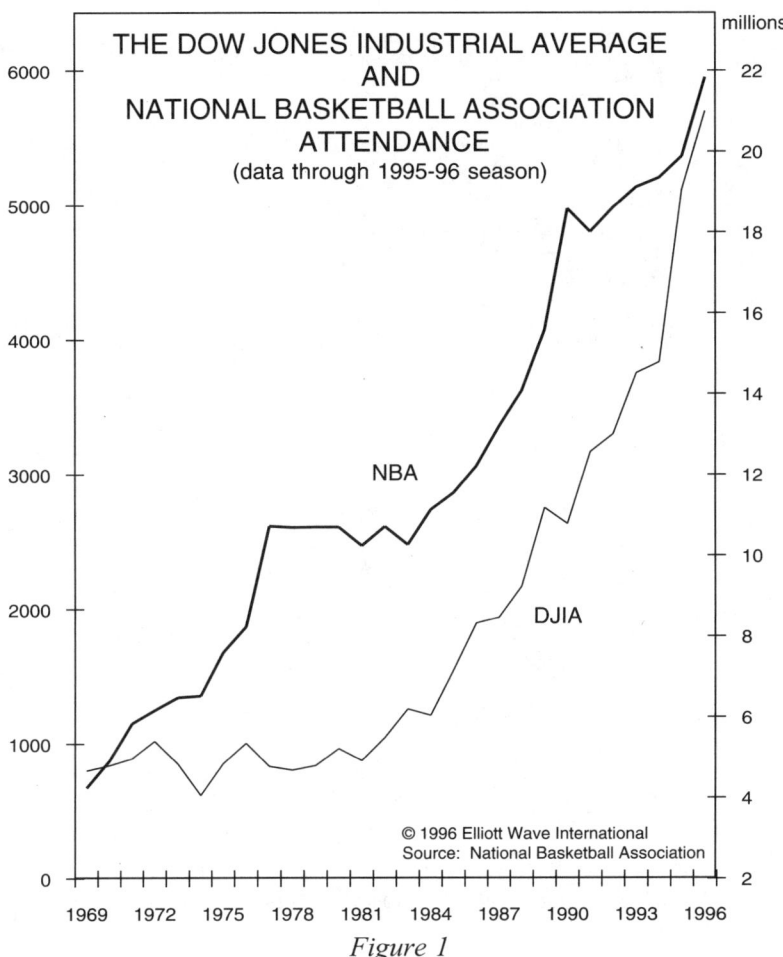

Figure 1

of 1929 led to an immediate reversal of fortune for pro basketball. The league went out of business after the 1930-31 season (#3). During the Great Depression, pro basketball slipped back into a hodgepodge of industrial leagues and traveling squads that would go from city to city to get up a game.

Basketball history shows that the psychology of team owners is strikingly similar to that of stockholders. They can be counted on to lay their money on the line at the worst possible moment. Even more remarkable is that these errors of enthusiasm infect both the game and the stock market at precisely the same times. In 1937, the year of the Depression-era high in the Dow Jones Industrial Average, pro basketball formed a new league. Of

1. First professional basketball game, 1896
2. ABL, basketball's first major league, formed
3. ABL folds
4. 13-team NBL formed
5. NBL consolidates into 4-teams
6. Rival BAA formed bringing total number of teams to 23
7. NBL and BAA consolidate to form NBA
8. ABL formed
9. ABL folds
10. ABA formed, NBA adds 8 teams in 5 years
11. ABA/NBA merge
12. NBA expands by four teams
    (two in 1988-89 and two in 1989-90)
13. NBA expands to a record 29 pro teams
14. ABL and WNBA formed

© 1996 Elliott Wave International

1896 1904 1912 1921 1929 1937 1946 1954 1962 1971 1979 1987 1996

Figure 2

course, by the time the National Basketball League (#4) was up and running, the Dow was back in a downtrend. The Dow slumped to a Cycle degree bottom at the still-unbroken low of 1942 (#5), and the number of pro basketball teams hit a simultaneous 54-year low of four. In 1946, the Dow hit another important peak, and basketball owners bought in at the top. The number of major league basketball teams increased to a new high of 22 with the formation of a rival league, the Basketball Association of America (#6). After the 1948-49 season, the owners of the two leagues consolidated to form the National Basketball Association (#7). Again, pro basketball reflected the correction in social mood perfectly, as this retrenchment came at a major bottom. In fact, on an inflation-adjusted basis, it was the end of a Supercycle correction from 1929 (see dashed lines in Figure 2). This bottom led directly to the relentless third wave rise in stock prices and the game's revolution from "an elbows out, feet-on-the-floor game" to the high-scoring, high-flying affair we know today.

After further consolidation in the early 1950s, the eight-team NBA enjoyed an era of unprecedented stability. The next expansion didn't come until 1961, when a minor rival league was formed. The American Basketball League (#8) concluded its first and last season with the Dow at all-time highs. The following autumn brought the "Cuban Missile Crisis" low in stocks and, apparently, enough of a washout in bullish sentiment to ground the ABL (#9). The larger degree of the Cycle degree top of 1966 was reflected by the ebullient mood of pro basketball owners. Starting with the Bulls in 1966, the NBA added 8 teams through 1971. The expansion mirrored the big top in stocks, as the Dow got within 5% of 1000 five times during that span. In 1968, at a major speculative peak in stock prices, the American Basketball Association (#10) was launched. Initially, the ABA expressed the festive mood of the time. With it came a red, white and blue ball and a wide-open offensive game that featured the three-point shot. It was the only serious challenge to the NBA. Ultimately, the ABA came to be viewed as a negative influence on the game. The new league divided fan loyalties while creating a fierce competition for talent that drove up team cost structures. By 1974, the expansion had diluted the overall level of play and fostered a style that focused more on individuals than the team game that characterized the Boston Celtics of the 1950s and 1960s and the Minneapolis Lakers before them. Unlike its predecessors, the ABA actually survived the bear market of 1974, but not by much. News articles later revealed that even established NBA teams were losing money by 1974. The ABA was consolidating by 1974 and finally shut down in 1976. Four of its teams survived in the NBA.

Despite the box office rebound in the 1980s, the NBA was hesitant to add new franchises, just as it was in its initial heyday, the late 1950s and early 1960s. By 1987, however, owners could not contain their optimism. They were confident enough to schedule the addition of four franchises. Two were added for the 1988-89 season and two more for the 1989-90 season, in time to catch the correction of 1990 (which featured a deep decline in the Value Line index and a 50% drop in the Dow Jones Transports) and the game's own recession in 1990. The last two teams were added in 1995-96 to create a record total of 29 major league basketball franchises. Like the most recent leg of the bull market, pro basketball's current expansion lacks the breadth of its predecessors, but it is unprecedented in terms of duration. Just as there has been no bear market in stocks since 1974, the number of major league basketball teams has not declined since 1976. Also, two new leagues of professional women players have been formed. The American Basketball League started in October 1996 and the Women's NBA will initiate play in 1997.

Rules and Mores

Another big clue to the bullish essence of basketball has been the century-long evolution in how the game is played. Early on, the character and rules of the game had more bear-market characteristics. The tempo was slow. A score of 20-15 would be considered a fantastic total. In its earliest days, basketball was referred to as "basket football" or "football in a gym." A goal was called a "touchdown," and players wore padded clothing that resembled early football uniforms. When young children play basketball, observers have noted the resemblance to a rugby scrum. Photos of the early game played on dirt fields suggest that this may be a fair approximation of what basketball was like initially. The amount of physical contact was clearly closer to hockey or rugby than a modern NBA game. By Rule 5 of Naismith's original 13 Rules of Basketball, contact was not actually allowed, but referees seldom blew the whistle.

"When you were fouled, it was a real one," remembered Joe Lapchick, an early pro. "With only one referee, the guy who did the fouling usually got away with it. So you belted him back. Players practically tore their opponents' shorts and pants off when playing defense. Players were geared for almost any indignity." Not just from the opposing team. Fans' favored form of expression was open hostility. "Spectators invariably got into the act," Lapchick added. "A common annoyance in highly industrialized cities was the practice of 'fans' who would flip stove bolts at the 'out-of-towners.'"

Also missing from the modern game: the cage. Originally, pro basketball was played behind a wire enclosure. The cages came down in 1929, the year the Dow hit its great peak of 381. A second referee was also added that year.

After pro basketball crashed with the market, its first step toward rebuilding came in 1932, which is the same year the Dow hit its low of 41. One of the game's big problems was that instead of advancing toward the goal, outmanned teams would simply use the whole length of the court to keep the ball out of the other team's hands. The 10-second rule was established to prevent this stalling. Although the pro game was still unable to organize effectively, there were some signs of underlying strength. From 1932 to 1937, the market rallied and, as it did, the "faster, cleaner amateur game" swept the nation. By 1937, Madison Square Garden was featuring regular, highly popular college double headers and tournaments. "The greatest year for rule changes" was 1937, the year of the Dow's recovery high and the return of the pro game. The changes emphasized offense. They included the elimination of the center jump after each basket, the legalization of the laceless ball and a rule making it illegal for defensive players to touch the ball when it was on the rim of the basket.

The college game continued to flourish in the 1940s. Pro basketball gained momentum after the 1942 low, but it would not shed its "image as a slow sluggish sport until the 1950s," which is when the stock market emerged from its slow, sluggish sideways correction of the 1940s. Until that decade, fans still wanted a game that was more like a bear market sport, hockey. In fact, pro hockey at the time was a more established sport that served as a model for pro basketball owners. The National Hockey League was established 10 years before the first pro basketball league, and it survived the Depression when pro basketball fell into chaos. "Owners knew from their experience with hockey that a little fight now and then was good for business. Rough stuff was quietly encouraged." Fights were still common in the first half of the 1950s, and into the later half of the decade many teams still employed "enforcers," tough, lesser talents who were used to intimidate opponents, as is common in hockey.

The basketball establishment has generally displayed a willingness to experiment at the outset of a big move in the Dow. At the beginning of Cycle wave III, pro basketball really began to change following a 19-18 game in November 1950, the lowest scoring game in NBA history, one year after the end of a 20-year correction and two years after the smallest DJIA annual range in history up to that time. After this game, stalling, once again, came to be viewed as a problem, particularly in the fourth quarter, when fouling was also common. Teams would get a small lead, foul, get the ball back and play keep away until the final buzzer. A series of rule changes followed. Among the remedies attempted was a jump ball after every foul shot in the last 10 minutes. But this backfired when teams contrived ways to get their best leapers in on the jump ball.

The speed and scoring that typify the modern game came in 1954 as the 24-second clock was adopted. The shot clock, which was instituted at the top of Intermediate (3) of Primary ③ of Cycle III, the powerful mid-point of the Supercycle from 1932, accelerated the energy and excitement of the game by forcing teams to shoot the ball within 24 seconds of taking possession. In this third-of-a-third wave up, the shot clock did for basket-ball what the electric guitar did for popular music, and at the same time.

Rule changes since the 1950s have all been minor by comparison. Perhaps the most significant were the addition of a third referee and the three-point shot. Both continued the long tradition of reducing the level of physical contact and opening the game up for more offense. They came in the late 1970s, when the Dow had put in its lows and was slowly building a base for the bull market of the 1980s and 1990s. Perhaps the most signifi-cant change was to the tone of the game, in the late 1950s and early 1960s. The trademark soaring of Michael Jordan would never have happened if certain conventions restricting the defender from undercutting opponents near the basket did not become standard operating procedure during this period. Basketball is still a contact sport, but nothing like the early game or even that of the early NBA. Crowds don't throw things at players, fights are rare and the game basically moves too fast for lead-footed bruisers to keep up. These days "touch" fouls are called frequently, especially if the person being touched is one of the league's stars.

The Dynasties, the Heroes and Their Magic

To an amazing degree, pro basketball has greeted every major stock market advance since the 1920s with "blue chip" talents. In the 1920s, the original Celtics were the first heroes of the hardwood. Like all the great bull market basketball powers, the Celtics took the game to a new level with a series of innovations. The original Celtics introduced the give-and-go, switching man-to-man defense, and the pivot play. In the pivot play, the ball is thrown to a taller post player who turns and shoots or passes it to an open man cutting to the basket. The Celtics effective introduction of the play foreshadowed the era of the great centers in Cycle wave III of the next Supercycle. In fact, it wasn't until the 1920s that height was even consid-ered an important trait in players. The first tall talent was Francis Meehan, 6-foot-7 center who came into the game in 1919 as the Dow was nearing its run to 381 in 1929. Meehan earned the fantastic total of $100 a game in the 1920s. Joe Lapchick was considered the best of the new breed. At 6-foot-6, the Celtics star said he was considered something of a freak.

In the early 1930s, when the Dow collapsed, the pro game fell so hard that there were *no* champions during that decade. Still, the amateur game prospered. On the court, the big breakthrough was the one-handed shot. Hank Luseitti of Stanford University first awed the Madison Square Garden crowd at the stock market high in 1937. Joe Fulks introduced the jump shot at the next stock market high, in 1946. Fulks led his Philadelphia team to a title with a scoring average of 23.2 points per game. With this new weapon, opponents considered Fulks "unstoppable." But Fulks' performance was only a glimpse of the talent to come. At .305, Fulks' shooting percentage was half that of modern-day league leaders.

From the low of 1949 until 1954, George Mikan and the Lakers won five out of six championships. At 6-foot-10, Mikan was the first to approach the height of modern-day big men and became the NBA's first great center of attention. After his retirement in 1954, both the league and the stock market hit a four-year plateau. From the spring of 1955 to 1958, four different teams won the NBA title. Over the same span, the Dow gained just 30 points, a cumulative gain of 6% in a decade of otherwise steady advances. From 1958 to the Cycle wave III high in 1966, the Dow doubled and the Boston Celtics owned the NBA, with eight straight championships. In keeping with the market's move to a higher plane, the Celtics raised the skills of the game to a whole new level. They brought a combination of size, speed, dribbling ability and shooting that was previously unknown to the NBA.

Their perfection of the fast break helped lift scoring leaguewide. Scoring averages rose from 79 to a league record of 107 in the early 1960s. The introduction of a shot clock was only one reason for the scoring outburst. Others ranged from better shoes and balls to the jump shot's replacement of the two-hand set shot as the standard method of scoring from the outside. The Celtics star was Bill Russell, the first in a long line of athletic giants that would become the league's hallmark. Wilt Chamberlain followed Russell by three years. Chamberlain was the first 7-footer, and, by many accounts, the greatest player ever to play the game. Clearly, Chamberlain delivered the game's greatest all-around individual performances. All of them came during the stock market's waves ④ and ⑤, ending at Dow 1000. From 1959 to 1966, Chamberlain won seven straight scoring titles (1959-66). He also hauled in most of his record total of 24,000 rebounds. In 1961-62, he averaged 25.7 rebounds and 50.4 points per game. On March 2, 1962, at a major psychological peak in the stock market immediately preceding the 1962 crash, Chamberlain scored 100 points in a single game.

More than any other event, Chamberlain's rivalry with Russell and the Celtics drove the NBA to its new standing as the most popular winter sport. The clashes continued until Russell's retirement in 1969, five months after a 13-year high in the Value Line Composite index. The year also marked the official end of the Celtics' glory years, as the Russell-coached Celtics won just one more title.

On the court and in the market, the 1970s were a mixed bag. While basketball's talent pool was as deep as ever, the bear market in social mood manifested itself in another period of shifting fortunes at the top. During the decade, not one NBA champion team managed to defend its title successfully. After the arrival of Kareem Abdul Jabbar in 1969, 7-footers became more routine and overall player heights approached their peak. In 1968, the former Celtic and pro coach, Joe Lapchick, noted that players had nearly perfected the required skills.

By the most definitive measure, higher stock prices, the fifth and final wave of the Supercycle bull market began in December 1974. The fifth-wave character of the advance manifested itself as more of a refinement in the style of play than the introduction of any fundamentally different skills or techniques. All it took was a liberation of sentiment for the game to literally take off near the lows of 1974. The high-flying slam dunks of Julius Erving revealed the new mood. "My game is in the air," Erving said. Or, as one of his first coaches said, Erving "was the first to fly; he did things with a basketball nobody else had ever done."

Few of the earliest players were even capable of dunking the ball. In the 1940s, many were able, but few did. "Back then it was showing a guy up," explained Alex Hannum, a player and coach who came into pro ball in 1948. "Today it's showtime." The dunk shot was popular in the 1950s and 1960s, but until Erving came along, it was an efficient way to score rather than a gravity-defying display. In the 1960s, players never took to the air with abandon. That era's greatest play maker, Oscar Robertson, displayed a more cautious approach. He urged players "never to go up in the air unless they knew what they were going to do with the ball."

In the later part of 1970s, however, a basketball writer noted that more and more young players were "choosing the pleasure and uncertainty of going up in the air to create a situation, deciding what to do when in full flight." After outlawing the dunk in 1967, the college game permitted it again in 1976.

As the constant-dollar Dow approached a 16-year low in 1982, basketball hit some rough spots. Basketball purists did not embrace the new freer style. The new trend toward "slam dunking," for instance, was considered a side effect of the consolidation with the ABA and not a particularly positive influence. "Although it showcased a player's pure athletic skill and made for some great highlight film clips, this wide-open individual play was antithetical to the structured team play" that had characterized the great teams of the past. A 1978 headline in a *Sports Illustrated* read, "There's An Ill Wind Blowing For the NBA." Television had "focused attention on spectacular slam dunks, the epitome of playground ball, running replay after replay of them and eschewing explanations of the intricacies of team play." In *Professional Sports Team Histories*, the second half of the 1970s is recorded as a period of "serious trouble" for the NBA. The problems were classic cultural manifestations of a bear market: "rampant selfishness," "violence" and "drugs." In 1980-81, 16 of 23 NBA teams lost money, and attendance fell by 1 million.

Julius Erving's rise as a basketball icon personified the slow emergence of the bull market. He entered pro ball during the 1971-72 season with a relatively obscure Virginia franchise in the less established ABA. 1972 was the year the Dow closed above 1000 for the first time. In 1976, when the Dow surpassed 1000 for the second time, Erving won a title for the ABA's New York franchise and then raised his profile to a higher orbit with the NBA/ABA merger and a move to the Philadelphia 76ers, an established NBA franchise. "We got the Babe Ruth of basketball," said the 76ers general manager. During the entire 1980-81 season, the Dow moved back and forth across the 1000 barrier and Erving won his first and only NBA MVP award. At the outset of the 1982-83 season, the Dow penetrated 1000 for good and Erving went on to his first and last NBA championship.

The dominance of the two major stars of the 1980s, by contrast, was apparent from the start, just like the bull market. Larry Bird and Magic Johnson graduated to the pros in 1979. While their rivalry "never approached" Russell/Chamberlain "for intensity and ferociousness," it is sometimes credited with saving the NBA. Here again, however, it seems to have taken a clear uptrend in social mood, as reflected in stock prices, to get momentum really going on the court. Three months after the Dow touched a low of 729 in March 1980, which is still intact, the Johnson-led L.A. Lakers won their first title. Bird's Celtics won in 1981. After the Lakers won again in early 1982, Erving had his title. On the professional level, the Bird-Johnson rivalry was not officially consummated until the conclusion of the 1983-84 season, when the Lakers and Celtics, the two powers of the 1950s and 1960s, met in the finals for the first time since the glory days of the Celtics. The initial big-league showdown between Larry Bird and Magic Johnson drew the largest television audience in NBA history and defined the game in the 1980s. At 6-foot-10 and 6-foot-8, respectively, Bird and Johnson were the best passing big men in the history of the game. "One of the reasons Bird and Magic made such a difference to the league was the breadth of their abilities. They could score as well as dish the ball in ways once done only by the Harlem Globetrotters against patsy teams in exhibitions." From 1980 to 1988, the Lakers and Celtics won 8 titles (3 by Boston, 5 by the Lakers). The Lakers ultimately emerged as the team of the decade when they defeated the Celtics in the 1987 finals. That's when the "'showtime' game hit its peak," with the Lakers "playing the finest example of fast-paced Western Conference basketball the league had ever seen," according to *Team Histories*.

The stock market crash of 1987 was coincident with the emergence of a new force in the league, the "Bad Boys" of Detroit. The Pistons "played a rough physical game of basketball that harkened back to the old days." *Team Histories* describes a contrast in play that was as stark as the difference in the Dow in the five years before August 1987 and the three-and-a-quarter years thereafter (a 250% rise versus a 15% decline). "This rivalry between Magic and Bird and their teams had revitalized the game. Never ugly or bitter, the two teams battled with skill and brilliance and consistently displayed the sport at its best. The Pistons, however, displayed, to many, the sport at its worst." In 1988, Los Angeles beat the Pistons by three points in the final game of a grueling seven-game series. The following year, the Laker reign ended as the team fell in four straight. The "Bad Boys" ruled through the stock market correction of that year with another championship in 1990. The Pistons' reign effectively ended with the bottom in October.

The rising star of the Chicago Bulls eclipsed all others at the outset of the 1990-91 season. The Bulls finished the year 10 games ahead of Detroit and then swept to a 4-0 victory in the playoffs. In 1991, 1992 and 1993, the Bulls won all three championships, the first team to win three in a row since the Celtics' string of eight through 1966. (The only other team to win three championships was the Minneapolis Lakers. Their streak was through 1954, the year the Dow finally surpassed the 1929 high.) In the spring of 1996, the Bulls seemed to match the Dow point for point as they won at a record rate and ended the season with 72 victories, the most ever. The old record of 69 was set by the Lakers in 1972, also a year leading to new highs for the Dow.

For whatever reason, in every period of substantial and continuous new highs in the Dow, there has been a pro basketball power that has thrived on the high ebb of social mood. The Bulls' reign in the last great wave of the Supercycle degree bull market from 1932 shows how deep the link between basketball and the stock market goes. The very name, which has caused big red snorting bulls to be stamped on caps, t-shirts and bumpers across America, is a vibrant and ubiquitous symbol of the connection. Skeptics may say it is just another coincidence, but the history of pro basketball in Chicago suggests more than an arbitrary symbol. In the early 1960s, Chicago's NBA franchise was called the Packers. The team struggled, and the owners tried to repair fan apathy with a new name. The Zephyrs didn't last a season. In 1966, the year of the great Dow peak, the NBA returned to Chicago. As the *Bulls*, pro basketball finally survived there. Few, if any, fans see any relationship between their devotion to both the Bulls and their mutual fund portfolios. This is how it is with a collective psychological state: too pervasive — perhaps even poetic — to be recognized by most people.

Michael in Microcosm

To put an even finer point on the athletic expression of social mood, consider the professional history of Michael Jordan. Jordan first entered the cultural consciousness in 1982, the year of the bull market's blast-off. As a freshman at North Carolina, he hit a shot in the last 16 seconds to win the NCAA college championship. In 1984, he joined the Bulls and was named Rookie of the Year. In 1987, the year of a substantial Dow high at 2723, he won his first MVP award and had a single-season scoring average of 37 points per game, which remains the highest since Wilt Chamberlain. His lifetime scoring average of just over 30 points per game is the highest ever.

As the highest-paid athlete in the world and Madison Avenue's most prolific endorser, Jordan's image is also locked to the stock market. In Figure 3, notice how the two fortunes expand and recede together. Plagued by gambling accusations and the death of his father, Jordan retired before the 1993-94 season. The sabbatical coincided perfectly with a correction in the market. Jordan came out of retirement in March 1995 and accompanied the Dow past 5000. The stinging personal attacks that drove Jordan from the game two years ago have all but disappeared. It's not that Jordan is perfect; he's still accused of various shortcomings, but "criticism of Jordan doesn't stick," *Sports Illustrated* noted in a recent profile. Why? Because Jordan enjoys a "devotion that criticism can't touch." In the fall of 1996, as the

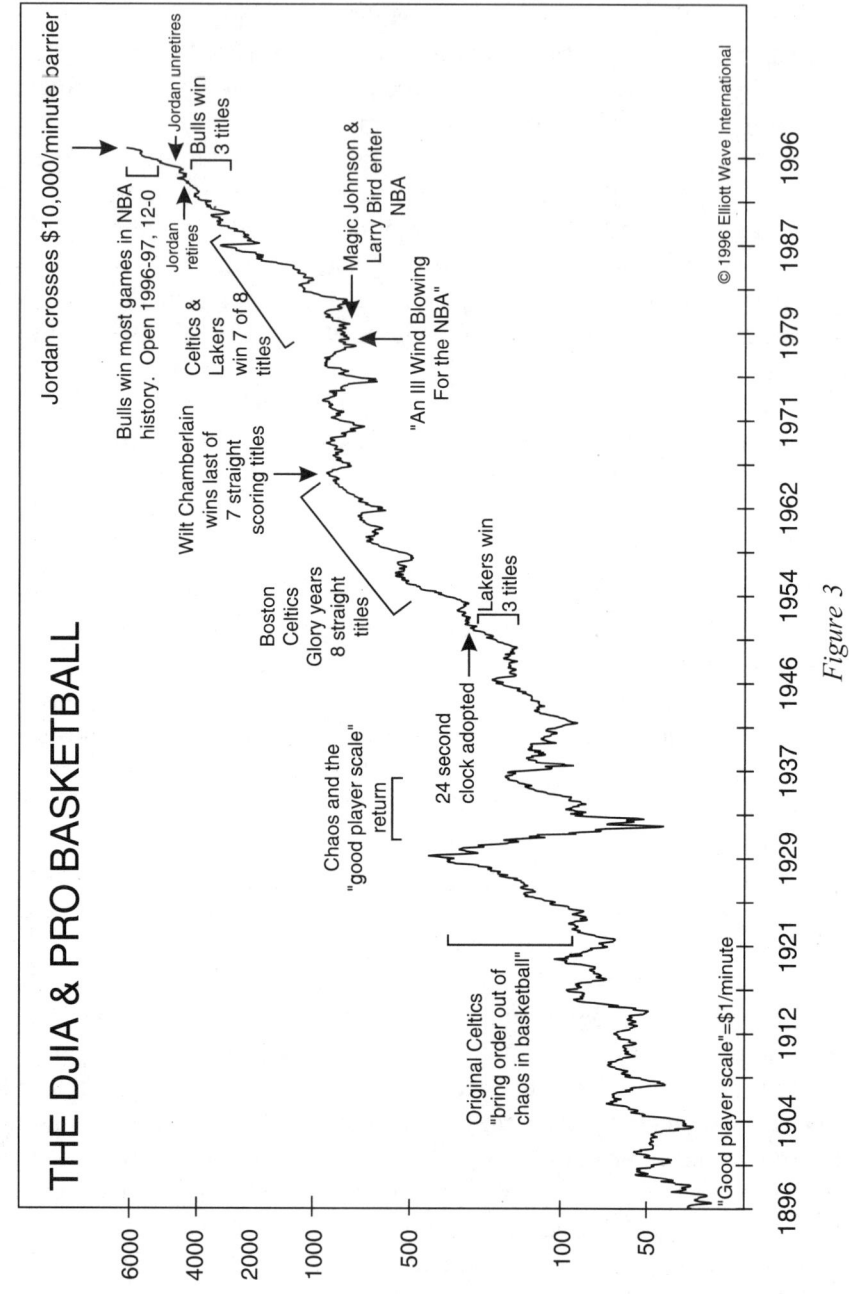

Figure 3

Dow pushed past 6000 in a relentless succession of new highs, Jordan drove the Bulls to their best start ever, unveiled a new perfume and premiered as the star in a feature film that *The Wall Street Journal* calls the "ultimate commercial movie." "Michael is superman, plain and simple," concludes *Sports Illustrated*. "Dab on a little Michael Jordan and you're dabbing on the scent of success," claims a news article headlined "Smell Like Mike." Smell like a sweaty athlete? Only the hero factor can explain the depth of Jordan's popularity. *The Elliott Wave Theorist* has observed a cultural preference for heroes in bull markets. As the game's greatest hero, Jordan personifies the happiness and energy of the bull market just as George Mikan did in the early 1950s, Bill Russell in the 1960s and Magic Johnson in the 1980s, bull markets all.

Waves and Means

How does a wave of mass emotion express itself in the performance of a single individual? As the center for the Boston Celtics in the 1960s, Bill Russell was the most valuable player on the best team in basketball history. In his autobiography, he offers some observations that might explain how a bull market game might manifest itself in the actions of solitary participants. He describes the atmosphere of a big game as a kind of "spell" that "surrounded" fans, coaches, opposing players and "even the referees." "To me, the key was that both teams had to be playing at their peaks, and they had to be competitive. The Celtics could not do it alone...That mystical feeling usually came with the better teams in the league that were challenging us for the championship...It usually began when three or four of the ten guys on the floor would heat up; they would be catalysts, and they were almost always the stars in the league. If we were playing the Lakers, for example, (Jerry) West and (Elgin) Baylor and (Bob) Cousy or Sam (Jones) and I would be enough. The feeling would spread to the other guys and we'd all levitate. Then the game would just take off, and there'd be a natural ebb and flow that reminded you how rhythmic and musical basketball is supposed to be."

Russell says he never admitted it to his teammates, but, at such times, winning itself didn't matter to him as much as reaching that higher plane. "On the five or ten occasions when the game ended at that special level, I literally did not care who had won."

Players at substantially lower levels of play have reported similar sensations. Essayist and schoolyard ballplayer John Boe wrote, "It is popular to talk about rhythm and flow in basketball. And when playing basketball, you indeed feel the rhythm, flow with the group mind. I play basketball in order to experience those moments when I feel in rhythm, and it is more a matter of the rhythm having me than of my having the rhythm."

The structure of the game produces a "dance of ascendancy," wrote George Kovacs in *Hoops Zen*. "The obvious advantages of basketball over other sports as a medium of spiritual self-development is the idea — the ideal — of *upward striving*...(an) unrestrained yet disciplined challenge of the mortal entity against gravity and other oppressive earthbound limitations. James Naismith's notion of hanging a peach basket 10 feet off the ground to taunt and tantalize athletic pretenders was a stroke of genius in forcing hoopsters to elevate their endeavors and objectives as well. Thanks in considerable measure to 'upward striving,' no other sport, no other athletic activity — perhaps no other human activity — allows, encourages, enhances, necessitates the poetry, the poetic movement of the human body like hoops." That ideal of upward striving, we contend, derives from social mood and is manifest also in rising stock prices.

Another element in basketball's bullish essence may be the central importance of the ball. Boe once noted how newspaper photos of basketball games capture the ball frozen above the rim with the eyes of players and fans fixed upon it. "When the game is on TV, there are millions of eyes focused upon the same ball. This is a collective spiritual experience; the group consciousness is united by a single thing, the ball. The ball acts like the mandala of Tibetan systems of concentration and meditation, focusing the psyche of the individual, uniting the consciousness of the group."

According to the Wave Principle, we've been in a bull market at Grand Supercycle degree for more than 200 years, so it's hard to imagine what a bear market sport would be like. We envision something along the lines of boxing, where it's man against man. There is no ball to displace man's natural aggression and no hoop to make us focus on any loftier ambition than survival. As Russell tells us, basketball at its highest level doesn't pit men against each other. It's about technique and intelligence and working together to place a rubber ball through a round goal that is out of reach. Of a true bear market game, we suspect that it could never be said that winning didn't matter, as Russell said of his sport at its peak. Ball games have had their place in North American culture since before Columbus arrived. Various tribes played different games with round rubber balls. Black Elk, an Ogala Sioux priest, described a rite called "The Throwing of the Ball." He says it was born when a sacred ball was offered to the six directions — "North, South, East, West, *Up* and *Down*." The ball is a spirit that is "at every direction and is everywhere in the world." A buffalo calf then nudged the ball to a man and said, "This universe really belongs to the two leggeds, for we four legged people cannot play with a ball...It is the two legged men alone who, if they purify and humiliate themselves, may become one with — or may know" the ball.

The Bottom Line

One of the great benefits of the Wave Principle is that it inspires such universal questions. Another is that none of them have to be answered for the speculator to take advantage of changes in social mood.

In November 1992, for instance, *The Elliott Wave Theorist* illustrated how cultural studies can be profitably pursued with the help of the Wave Principle, saying, "There is reason to believe that [baseball card] prices have just made a 'spike top' along with fans' emotions." Within three months, shares of The Topps Co., a producer of baseball cards, were halved, and the great baseball card bust of the 1990s was on. A July 1996 *Sports Illustrated* report on the card market described a textbook investment bubble. On the way up "there was this notion that sports cards were scarce," "the secondary market exploded" and "demand appeared insatiable." Next, "dozens of manufacturers sprouted, and hobby shops spread like pollen." A combination of oversupply, Wall Street hype and "greed by the leagues" are said to have pushed the market over the edge. Eventually, there came a "selling frenzy" and "a shake-out" of dealers across the country. "Crash is not too strong a word to describe what has happened."

This article and others through the fall of 1996 contend that baseball and the card market are bouncing back. They cite a rebound in baseball attendance, a new all-time high contract amount for a baseball player, the record purchase of a baseball card for $645,000 and a new labor agreement for Major League Baseball. While these items do reflect the continuing influence of the bull market, the top is behind us in the big picture. The November issue of *The Elliott Wave Theorist* noted that 1996 baseball attendance was still 14% lower than the all time high of 1993. In 1993, we showed a 90-year chart of baseball attendance and noted the completion of a clear five-wave structure. This pattern means that baseball's three-year-old high in popularity will not be exceeded by any substantial margin. Basketball's bull market, on the other hand, is still in force. *Sports*

Illustrated's anticipation of a turnaround in the card market was based partially on the fact that "basketball cards are the fastest growing sector." The evidence in this report suggests the opposite of the article's implication. Basketball, not the market for trading cards, is likely to reverse course, and in the other direction.

To paraphrase our advice to baseball interests in November 1992: If you're an investor, take profits on basketball cards. If you're a player, sign a long term contract. If you're an owner, sell your club. If you're a fan, prepare to gripe increasingly about the game of basketball after the stock market reverses to the downside.

The NBA's expansion to an all-time high of 29 teams, the addition of two new professional leagues, the total dominance and worldwide popularity of the Olympic Dream Team, the Bulls settlement of a suit with the NBA that will make "record numbers of Bulls games available on free television," the inauguration of a women's NBA, the likelihood of a long term peak in stock prices and the overall euphoria for the sport all say that a peak in basketball is at hand.

The elation surrounding basketball's brightest star is particularly telling. Last May, the aura of giddy excitement that encircled Jordan as the Bulls completed the greatest season in basketball history and sailed through the playoffs was exceeded only by that surrounding a small selection of NASDAQ stocks. A June 19 *USA Today* article was headlined "Michael Jordan's bigger than basketball: he's a pop icon." A sports sociologist said fans "worship Michael Jordan with much the same intensity as they worship religious figures." Another author invoked the name of the hero of Cycle wave III, calling Jordan a "black Elvis with wings." In the past, *The Elliott Wave Theorist* has successfully used milestone contracts (like Michael Jackson's March 1991 deal with Sony) to pinpoint a major trend change in the recipient's popularity. Jordan's $30 million contract for 1996 is the highest ever. Jordan negotiated the deal over the phone in a half hour. It pays him $5.8 million more than other teams are allowed to pay *all* their players and 10,417 times the original good-player scale of $1 per minute. Throw in $40 million more in endorsements, his top billing (over Bugs Bunny) in a $95 million movie and a $20 million investment in the new Michael Jordan "aroma," and the unrivaled extreme in popularity that Jordan represents is unmistakable and historic. Two other players recently signed long-term contracts valued at more than $100 million. History suggests that pro basketball's next consolidation could lag a Dow decline, but not by much. Salaries, attendance and the number of teams will unquestionably accompany the market down as people's attention moves away from this "bull market sport" and toward more violent fare.

This report on basketball is valuable from another perspective: Throughout this century, when enthusiasm for the sport has been unbridled, the stock market has fallen on hard times. "Top" signals in the sport are top signals for stocks.

As in the stock market, the euphoric sentiment for the sport masks signs of underlying fundamental weakness. They include the aging of the league's stars, a sudden decline in scoring and a crash in shooting percentages to 44.4% for so far this year, the lowest total in at least eight years. In another development that has baffled long-time observers, NBA referees are suddenly making the traveling call. A player travels by taking more than one step without dribbling. "For years, traveling in the NBA was like jaywalking — illegal but generally accepted. Not anymore. ...Even the unwritten rule that allowed superstars more liberty in regard to traveling no longer exists." The enforcement of this original rule is a subtle but profound change from the trend that began with the 10-second rule in 1932. It violates the long tradition of opening the game up by *restricting* rather than abetting the scorer. Others have observed a decline in the level of play. Expansion and the entry of players at younger and younger ages have thinned the talent pool appreciably. As one star, Charles Barkley, said recently, "There are only five good teams in the league. The rest are terrible." Finally, there has been a decline of gate receipts through the first 22 games of the 1996 season.

Non-fans should not dismiss these developments as trivial. The bull market in stocks has run so long that there are many outward examples of basketball's and the stock market's co-dependence on a rising social mood. One example was an editorial in *Pension & Investment* magazine urging Jordan to endorse a family of mutual funds that teaches kids how to invest in stocks. P&I suggested that Jordan entice children into the market by explaining that they could use the proceeds from their stock investments to purchase Nike sneakers. This spoon-feeding of the mania for stocks with the mania of basketball is based on the mistaken belief that the rising mood is a permanent fact of life. Fortunately for investors, it is so deeply entrenched that it has provided the means to profit by taking the hints of basketball's coming decline. First, it is a signal that an overall bear market in stock prices is not far off, a warning that could prove very valuable.

More specifically, one might consider the implication for shares of Nike Inc. The firm recently paid $40 million for the rights to rookie golfer, Tiger Woods. It did so after a decade-long increase of more than 50 fold in its stock price, an increase that was built on the exploits of Jordan and other heroes of the bull market. Woods' contract represents an unprecedented willingness to *speculate* on the *next* bull market hero. "Air" Nike is a fiscal incorporation of the psychology of expanding expectations. When the bubble breaks, the next big profit will fall to the Nike short sellers.

The Coming Changes in Trend

The Grand Supercycle degree of the current trend change in social mood suggests a big retracement in basketball. The game will probably survive the bear market, but not without regressing back toward its roots. The first and most noticeable sign of the trend change will occur when Michael Jordan and a host of other longtime stars retire or become less effective. Based on *The Elliott Wave Theorist's* observation of a rising demand for anti-heroes in bear markets, Dennis Rodman rather than Jordan is the role model for the NBA's immediate future. Rodman is not a scorer. His special talent is getting fouled by his opponents as they try to score. He sports fluorescent hair, tattoos and a penchant for cross-dressing and antagonizing opponents. Whereas Michael Jordan saves the NBA with teamwork in his new cartoon movie, Rodman's credo is that "individuality is the most important thing in life." After this season, clean-cut team players will be remembered as the heroes of a bygone era. Shortly thereafter, football, hockey, soccer or some other rough game will replace basketball as the No. 1 sport. Eventually, fans will turn hostile, and fights will be common. Ultimately, salaries will crash and player heights will fall. Finally, when the new leagues have consolidated or shut down and falling attendance and TV ratings have caused several NBA owners to fold or move, Michael Jordan's true heir will appear. As he rises, history says, the stock market won't be far behind.

REFERENCES

Hill, Bob. (1988). *The amazing basketball book: The first 100 years.* Louisville, KY: Devyn Press.

Kovacs, George. (1968). *Hoops zen: The spiritual beauty of basketball.* Lewiston, NY: Edwin Mellen Press.

Lapchick, Joe. (1968). *50 years of basketball.* Englewood Cliffs, NJ: Prentice Hall.

Neft, David and Cohen, Richard M. (1989). *The NBA's official encyclopedia 1891-1989: Pro basketball.* New York: St. Martin's Press.

Pluto, Terry. (1992). *Tall tales.* New York: Simon & Schuster.

Rudman, Daniel. (1980). *Take it to the hoop.* Richmond, CA: North Atlantic Books.

Salzberg, Charles. (1987). *From set shot to slam dunk: The glory days of basketball in the words of those who played it.* New York: Dell-Dutton.

Kendall

The Elliott Wave Theorist
April 30, 1999

Fibonacci Glory Days for Sports Heroes

It's striking that within a few weeks of each other, the giant, singular figures of three major sports — basketball's Michael Jordan, hockey's Wayne Gretzky, and football's John Elway — have retired. Only pro baseball was left out of this remarkable trend. Or was it? Baseball's Joe DiMaggio died in recent weeks and was eulogized as a legend among legends, a man of singular grace and style, the "classiest" player of them all. [Note: Ted Williams died with similar accolades in 2002. — Ed.] It's remarkable that this pattern is playing out now, with the stock market also suggesting the "glory days" are pretty much over.
— EWT subscriber Rick Peterson

This gentleman has learned a lot from reading *The Elliott Wave Theorist*, where we argue that these trends are not coincidence, but intimately related. These men and their stature are products of bull market social forces.

Getting out on top and *at* the top will not be the feat for which these heroes are remembered, but it may be the one that goes the furthest toward preserving their bright legacies. These guys played exactly the right number of seasons. For Jordan and DiMaggio, it was 13, and for Gretzky it was 21. Is the perfect career length a Fibonacci number? To come closer to an answer, we investigated the duration of other all-time greats in their respective sports and found a clear tendency for the number of years played to cluster around Fibonacci numbers. In baseball, for instance, the all-time top ten players (as identified by the *Sporting News*) had an average career length of 21.3 years. In hockey, Wayne Gretzky broke the scoring records of Gordie Howe, who played 35 seasons, one more than a Fibonacci 34. The career of the sport's other undisputed great, Bobby Orr, spanned 13 years. The all-time leading goaltender (in victories and shutouts) was Charlie Sawchuk, who played 21 NHL seasons. When Jordan retired, *USA Today* issued a list of the greatest basketball players. It showed that, plus or minus one year, all played a Fibonacci number of seasons. In order of greatness, they were Michael Jordan (13), Wilt Chamberlain (14), Bill Russell (13), Kareem Abdul-Jabbar (20), Larry Bird (13), Earvin "Magic" Johnson (13), Oscar Robertson (14) and Jerry West (14).

For the record, we found no strong Fibonacci correlations among the greatest football players other than a 13-year career by Walter Payton, the game's all-time leading rusher. EWT opined in 1985 that unlike baseball and basketball, football is a "bear market" sport. Therein may lie a reason for the difference.

Viewed against their productivity, some of the best athletes reveal an all-too human tendency to overstay their greatness. Babe Ruth is a prime example. After a Fibonacci 21 brilliant seasons with the Red Sox and Yankees, he jumped to the National League, where he had 6 homers and hit a measly .181 for the Braves in 1935. Hank Aaron broke Babe Ruth's home run record in his 21st season as a Brave. After that, he had two forgettable seasons with the Milwaukee Brewers. Willie Mays, who played 22 seasons with the Giants, is ranked right behind Ruth as the second best player on the all-time list. But the papers are still talking about what happened when he went back to New York and the Mets in his final season. "It was gut wrenching to see Willie Mays misplay flyballs in the 1973 World Series," said the April 26 issue of *USA Today*. This evidence indicates that when a great player chooses to play past his Fibonacci time, his abilities deteriorate rapidly, driving him to quit a year later.

Quitting at the top is the best move one can make. It may not seem as Herculean a feat as their scoring records, but Jordan and Gretzky wisely turned down enormous incentives to play one more season. Jordan's retirement cost the Chicago Bulls all hope of contention, the city of Chicago an estimated $1 billion and his heirs well over $30 million. Gretzky's own wife was reportedly trying to convince him to play one more season. The ability of so many of these heroes to resist such pressures is another display of the classic form that made them the great men that they are. (For guidance on how *you* can time your big exit, read pages 316-318 of *The Wave Principle of Human Social Behavior*.)

[*Note: Jack Welch retired from General Electric in his 34th year with the company and in his 21st year as CEO. The Beatles made hit recordings for 8 years, then broke up. Our observation with respect to Fibonacci durations for basketball celebrities, we suspect, probably extends to "bull market" celebrities of all types. –Ed.*]

Kendall

The Elliott Wave Financial Forecast
August 27, 1999

Another Home-Run Year

For the first time since 1986 and 1987, the two seasons leading to the 1987 crash, a new record for the total number of homers (5,064 last year) is likely to be set in consecutive years. Home runs are running 11.1% ahead of last year's pace. On top of that, Mark McGwire and Sammy Sosa are replaying last year's home run race. But "there is no home run mania sweeping the nation — decidedly *unlike* last summer." "The homer has become commonplace," laments Bob Costas. The other day, when people barely even noticed that McGwire had "set yet another incredible" record by hitting his 50th homer for a fourth straight year, the papers even came up with a name for it, "chronic milestone fatigue. "Too many baseball records are falling in too short a period of time to keep the national interest." This is another cultural manifestation of the diverging social mood covered in the Cultural Trends section of the April *Elliott Wave Theorist*. This divergence actually extends back to 1992-1993, when we called for a reversal in baseball's attendance based on a five-wave, century-long pattern in attendance figures. On a per game basis, the highs of 1993 have not been exceeded.

The following graphic from *USA Today*'s cover story on the fans' "ho-hum" reaction to the greatest home-run display in history suggests that performance will eventually catch up to the slowly developing bear market in fan interest. It shows that measured in 10-year spans, the bull market in home runs has traced out a five-wave pattern of its own. The fact that the multiple from high to low is 2.618 strengthens the case for a peak this decade.

As we have said before, in the cultural realm, the completion of five waves leads to changes in style and performance simply because "it's time." Sluggers will tire and stop hitting home runs just as fans become tired of watching them. In April, EWT noted that the greatest athletes seem to have internal clocks that reflect mass changes in social mood to an almost uncanny degree. That's why they keep getting "out on top and *at* the top."

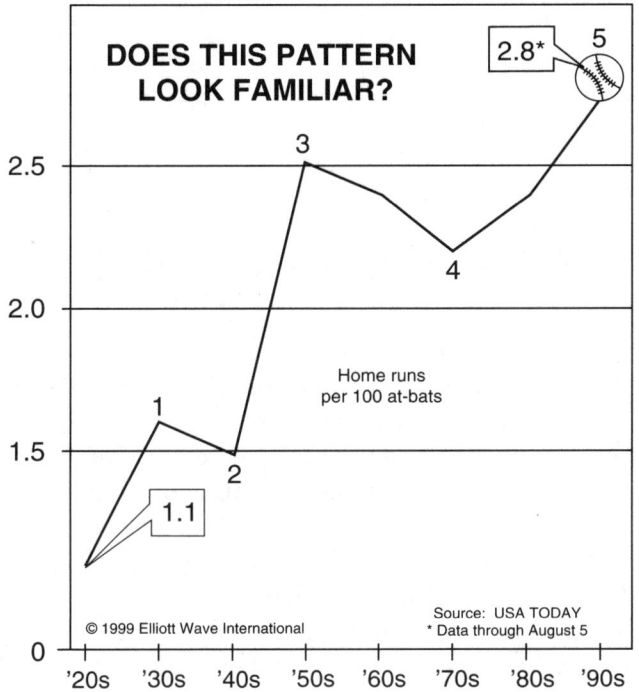

DOES THIS PATTERN LOOK FAMILIAR?

Home runs per 100 at-bats

© 1999 Elliott Wave International

Source: USA TODAY
* Data through August 5

August brought two additions to our list of retiring greats. Detroit Lions running back Barry Sanders and tennis champion Steffi Graf (easily one of the greatest female tennis players in history) "shocked" the sports world by calling it quits. Sanders retired even though he could have become the pro game's all-time rushing leader this year. Graf's decision came just two months after she had won her 22nd major tournament in May. Like Michael Jordan, Graf had turned pro in 1982 at the lift-off of the bull market and emerged as a dominant force in 1987 when she won her first major tournament. She was also ranked as the sport's No. 1 women's player for a Fibonacci 377 weeks, a record. But "when the fun stopped, Steffi Graf did what so many superstars have done in recent months. She said goodbye. 'I just feel the time is right to move on.'"

[*Just as sports achievements reach new heights in bull markets, so sports failures set records in bear markets. For example, the all-time record for hits against one pitcher occurred in a 17-inning game in which a hapless hurler gave up a whopping 29 hits. The time was July 1932, the month of the bottom in the biggest bear market in U.S. history to date. — Ed.*]

Kendall

The Elliott Wave Financial Forecast
February 4, 2000

Pro Wrestling and the Bull Market

The February 7 *Newsweek* cover story asks *why* professional wrestling is "No. 1 in Cable, Videos, Toys & Books." *The Elliott Wave Theorist* answered this question fifteen years ago. Back in 1985, EWT explained that pro wrestling, "with its well-defined representatives of good and evil," is popular in bull markets. Definitive morals and heroes accompany a bull market; blurred morals and mixed heroes accompany a bear market. Indeed, the history of the World Wrestling Federation, as described by *Newsweek*, parallels that of the bull market.

The modern era began in 1982 (the year of the low in inflation-adjusted stock prices), when Vince McMahon took control of the company and started its expansion. "In the mid-1980s, it grew more popular than ever. For a 1987 show at the Pontiac Silverdome, the company sold 93,000 tickets. Then trouble struck." It lasted a little past the stock market's correction in 1990. Since 1996, "wrestle mania" and the stock mania have actually be indistinguishable in some ways. "Wrestle mania," with its good guys and bad guys, has exploded to become the dominant form of cable television entertainment, while the stock mania has exploded to become a dominant form of network television entertainment, with its "good guys" (bulls) and "bad guys" (bears). Combining the two trends, the WWF is now a publicly traded stock with a market capitalization of $1 billion.

On February 5, WWF president McMahon appeared on CNBC and in announcing a new plan to expand into professional football said, "I don't think we can fail." "Performers can make $5 million, plus stock options," *Newsweek* reported. In one insightful, behind-the-scenes note, *Newsweek* quoted a veteran wrestler boasting about his investment performance. Another wrestler, who plays the lovable Mankind and the redneck psychopath Cactus Jack, said, "When a new guy comes in, I try to give him financial tips." He has also written a book, which is No. 3 on *The New York Times* nonfiction list. His nemesis, the Rock, has a book, too, and it hit No. 1 on January 30. As Paul Montgomery (*Universal Economics*, Legg Mason Wood Walker, Newport News, VA) has noted, the standing of these books indicates "that public interest in pro wrestling could not get any greater than it is right now." That sentiment precisely reflects the stock market's level of popularity as well.

Kendall

The Elliott Wave Financial Forecast
March 3, 2000

Top Tick for Basketball

In December 1996, *The Elliott Wave Theorist* released a Special Report, "Basketball and The Bull Market," which asserted, "Basketball is the ultimate bull market game." The largest part of that report was a four-page section called, "The Dynasties, The Heroes and Their Magic." It began, "To an amazing degree, pro basketball has greeted every major stock-market advance since the 1920s with "blue chip" talents." It traced out a 75-year history of precise correlations and ended with a long paragraph on Michael Jordan. "To put an even finer point on the athletic expression of social mood, consider the professional history of Michael Jordan. Jordan first entered the cultural consciousness in 1982, the year of the bull market's blast off." From that moment when he hit the game-winning shot to become a national champion, his career has kept an uncanny rhythm with the bull market.

On January 14, 2000, the very day of the all-time high in the Dow, Jordan added a final, perfect distinction to his unparalleled legacy as personal embodiment of "the happiness and energy of the bull market." He became a team owner. The world's greatest Bull is now the head Wizard, with complete control over the NBA's Washington franchise. In an analogy to today's stock market, Jordan may be a blue chip that is making a personal new high while the broader group is sinking. TV ratings are down 15% from strike-stunted levels a year ago. The first NBA all-star game without Jordan saw a 35% ratings decline. Apparently, blue-chip athletes, like blue-chip stocks, are the last to fall in with a downturn in social mood. Fall he will, though, and tying his fortune to a team will probably end up being a mistake.

The underlying trend in basketball's fortunes has been deteriorating for some time. The chart of Nike's stock on the next page tells the story. As we said in the "Bottom Line" of our 1996 basketball special, "'Air' Nike is a fiscal incorporation of the psychology of expanding expectations." Our recommendation at that time is shown on the chart. Despite a decline in

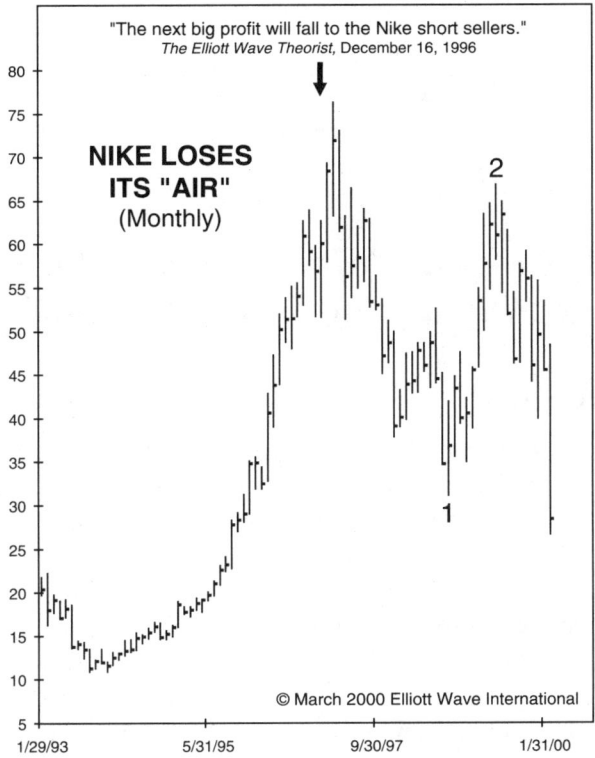

"The next big profit will fall to the Nike short sellers."
The Elliott Wave Theorist, December 16, 1996

NIKE LOSES ITS "AIR" (Monthly)

© March 2000 Elliott Wave International

price of more than 50%, Nike stock appears to be in a third wave down, which means that it still has much further to fall. "People have kind of OD'd on big-name athletes, and there's definitely a trend to get away from them," says a sporting goods industry official. Shoe contracts have "always been the bellwether endorsement" for star basketball players. Still, the media and the players themselves seem merely puzzled by their fall from grace. They should be seriously concerned, because the chart of Nike actually understates what their sport is up against. Converse, Inc., the maker of Chuck Taylor All-Star canvas sneakers, is a better indicator because it is more of a pure play in the sport, and it has a deeper history with it. In the 1950s and 1960s, Chuck Taylors were "worn by 99% of NBA players." In the 1980s, its ads featured Larry Bird and Julius Erving, the brightest stars in the game, singing the praises of Converse shoes as "limousines for the feet." Converse stock reached its high of 28 two months after our special report. Since then it has declined an amazing 97%. This is a forewarning of the coming fortunes of professional basketball.

Kendall

The Elliott Wave Theorist
April 2001

Evidence of a Major Downturn in Social Mood: Plummeting Interest in Ballgames

A Baseball Forecast

In 1985, *The Elliott Wave Theorist*'s original study on "Pop Culture and the Stock Market" asserted, "Trends in sports reflect the prevailing mood." The emergence of a bull market produces an escalating energy level that is physically embodied in the organization of athletic competitions. As the rise in social mood progresses, people share the optimism of the time by heading out to the ball park in larger numbers and constructing elaborate events. The leagues and their champions become increasingly sophisticated and revered. Eventually, massive stadiums are constructed to house the widespread public obsession with sports. EWT theorized that a reversal by a dominant bull market sport like baseball could be "an advance indicator of important fundamental events." In late 1992, EWT put this theory to the test by publishing the following forecast for baseball:

A Top in Baseball?

> Signs of a turn are there. If you're an investor, take profits on baseball. If you're a player, sign a long-term contract. If you're an owner, sell your club.

In early 1993, we counted a five-wave rise in total baseball ticket sales since 1901 and concluded, "At minimum, baseball faces its largest percentage drop in attendance since it became the national sport." The wave count from 1993 is displayed in Figure 1 with an updated version in Figure 2 showing that total ticket sales collapsed in 1994 then rebounded to a B-wave high. At 73.4 million, the 2000 total is slightly higher than the total for 1993, but it is labeled a bear market rally for several reasons. The key factor is that the implied attendance growth is illusory. First, observe in

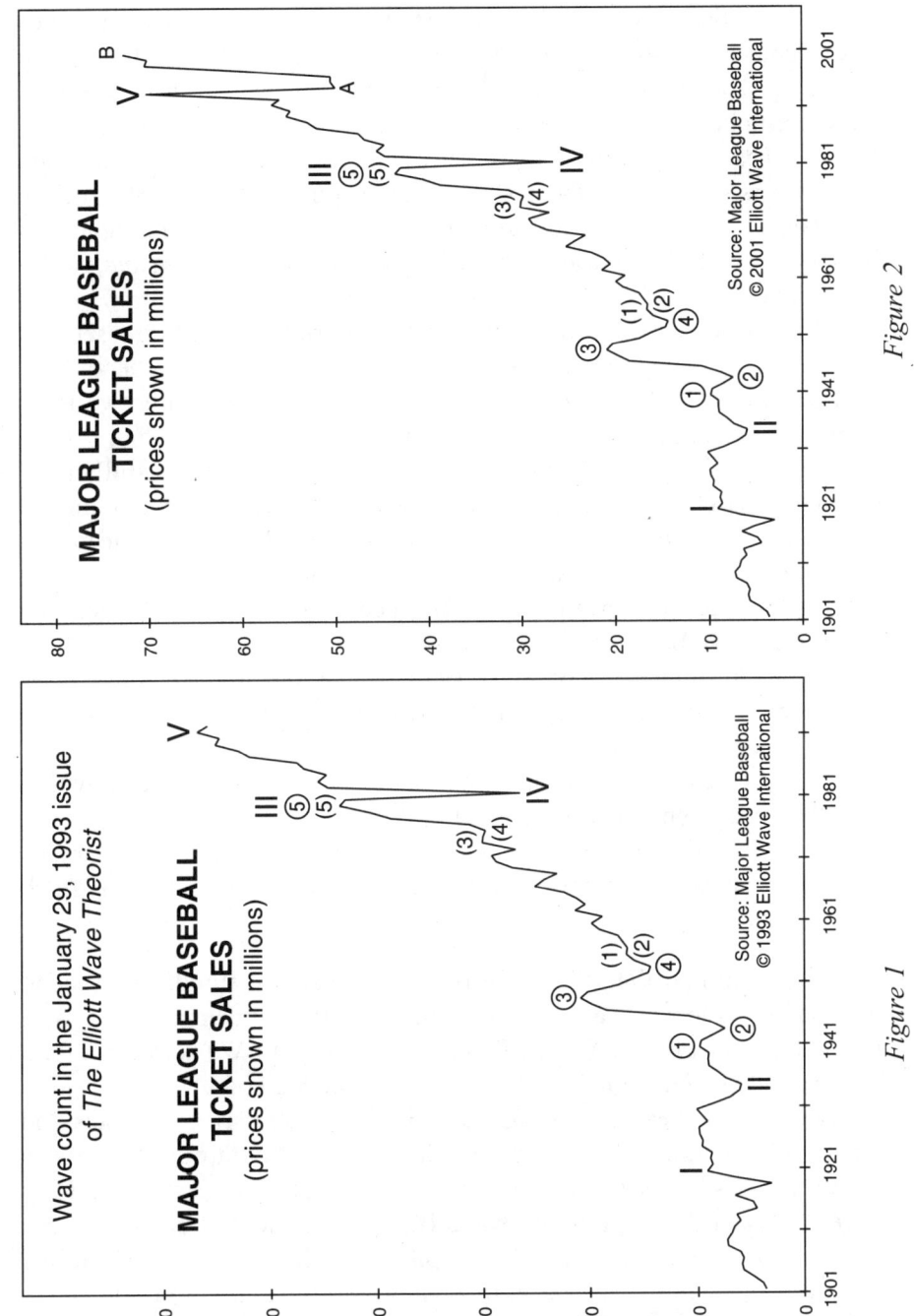

Figure 2

Figure 1

Figure 3 the lack of a new high in the *per-team* ticket sales. The number of tickets sold in the average major league city peaked in 1993, the season following EWT's forecast. Further, the sales totals shown in these charts represent tickets sold, *not actual attendance*. Brokers report that demand for seats has plunged. In fact, so many season tickets are not being used that scalpers sell some of the best seats in the house at "60% to 80% below face value." So in terms of reflecting popularity, the new high in Figure 2 is illusory and typical of B-wave personality (see *Elliott Wave Principle*, pp.79-81).

Another clue to the major change in the primary trend in baseball's fortunes is the plunge in television ratings for the All-Star game and the World Series. The total number of fans tuning in to baseball's two most important annual events actually topped the year before baseball's 1993 attendance peak, the same year as EWT's forecast. After successfully fore-shadowing baseball's initial decline in ticket sales, TV ratings have continued to contradict a slight new high in total sales with a decline to their lowest level in history. This is a bearish non-confirmation of the new high in total ticket sales. The five-wave pattern of this decade-long trend announces the onset of a major bear market.

An interesting aspect of our forecasts is that they involve both classes of socionomic forecasting. *The Wave Principle of Human Social Behavior* defined the two types as:

1) predicting trends in social phenomena based upon waves within the phenomena themselves, and

2) predicting economic, political, social, cultural and other trends based upon the wave position of overall social mood such as the stock market.

We identified the 1992/1993 peak by the first method. The second method points to a B-wave high in 2000 or 2001, coinciding closely with the peak in stock prices. So, the B-wave rally has put EWT's forecast for a major trend change on track by both socionomic methods.

Two other measures of baseball's bull market, player contracts and team values, continued to climb with the stock market through the 1990s. These are less direct registers of grassroots demand for the game. They have continued higher through wave B, much as the "nifty fifty" stocks made new all-time highs in 1973 despite lower highs in breadth and the inflation-adjusted averages. Figure 4, showing the value of the top player contract per year since 1980 suggests a sharp reversal immediately ahead.

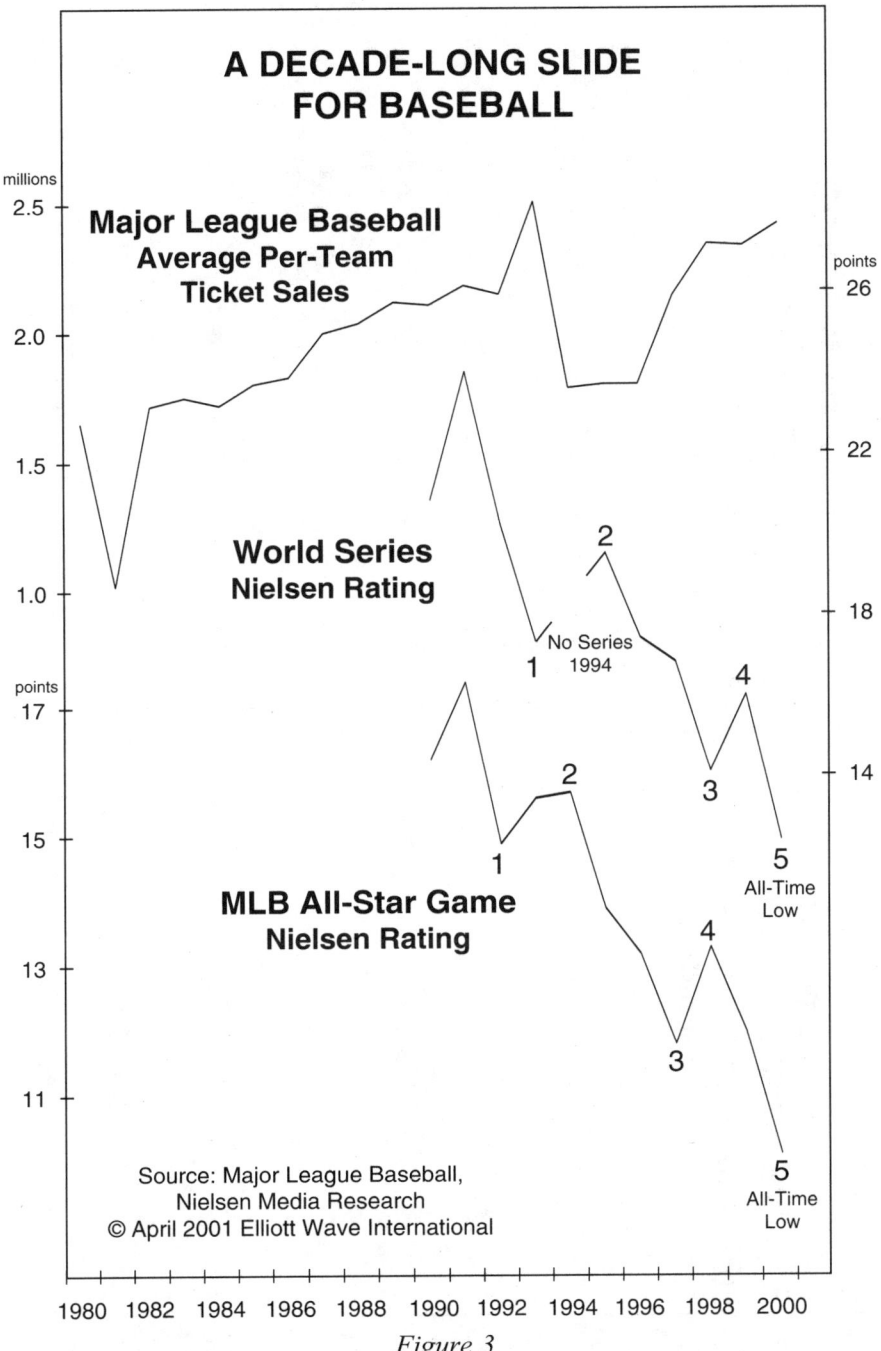

A DECADE-LONG SLIDE FOR BASEBALL

Major League Baseball
Average Per-Team
Ticket Sales

World Series
Nielsen Rating

No Series
1994

MLB All-Star Game
Nielsen Rating

All-Time
Low

All-Time
Low

Source: Major League Baseball,
Nielsen Media Research
© April 2001 Elliott Wave International

Figure 3

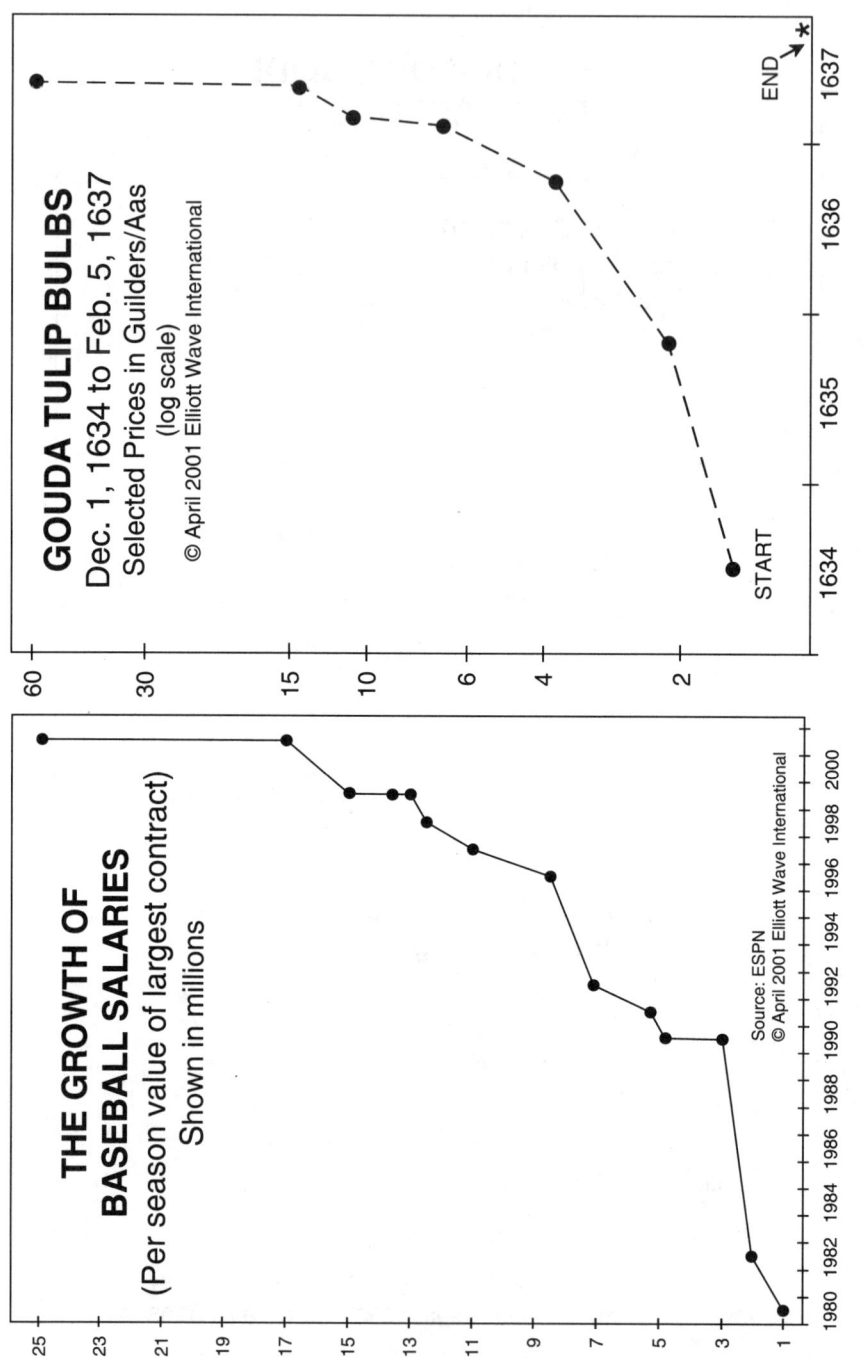

Figure 5

Figure 4

Notice the similarity to the run up in tulip bulb prices from 1634 to 1637 in Figure 5. The *Elliott Wave Theorist* has made very effective use of this simple "investment mania" pattern in recent months. The Texas Rangers added the last point on the chart when they signed shortstop Alex Rodriguez to the richest contract in the history of sports. The $252 million contract maintains a parabolic rise since 1980. Salaries of top players have now outstripped public demand for their services to an extent reminiscent of the Internet stock runup of 1999. If the classic pattern holds, the reversal in top salaries should be even more drastic than the drop in ticket sales. Based on the full retracement of past manias, a decline below the starting point of $1 million per year should follow.

A Basketball Forecast

In 1996, *The Elliott Wave Theorist* relied on the second type of socionomic forecasting to anticipate the future of professional basketball. The correlation between the stock market and professional basketball identified basketball as "the ultimate bull market game." EWT's 11-page examination of basketball's history began, "The game's structure, rules and fortunes have developed in a manner that is totally consistent with the ebb and flow of the bull market in stocks." EWT noted that pro basketball and the bull market were born in the same year, 1896. Ticket sales, franchise growth and even the tempo of play have traversed a path that was virtually identical to the century-long expansion in stock prices. Using another socionomic forecasting tool, calling for reversals based on extremes in the fortunes of public icons (see *The Wave Principle of Human Social Behavior*, p. 314), EWT pinpointed the event that would mark the peak for basketball. The following excerpt is from a section on "The Heroes and Their Magic," which illustrated the sport's rich history of epitomizing each bull market era with very specific sets of idols:

> For whatever reason, in every period of substantial and continuous new highs in the Dow, there has been a pro basketball power that has thrived on the high ebb of social mood. The [Chicago] Bulls' reign in the last great wave of the bull market from 1932 shows how deep the link between basketball and the stock market goes. The very name, which has caused big red snorting bulls to be stamped on caps, t-shirts and bumpers across America, is a vibrant and ubiquitous symbol of the connection. To put an even finer point on the athletic expression of social mood, consider the professional history of [Bulls' star] Michael Jordan. Jordan first entered the cultural consciousness in 1982, the year of the bull

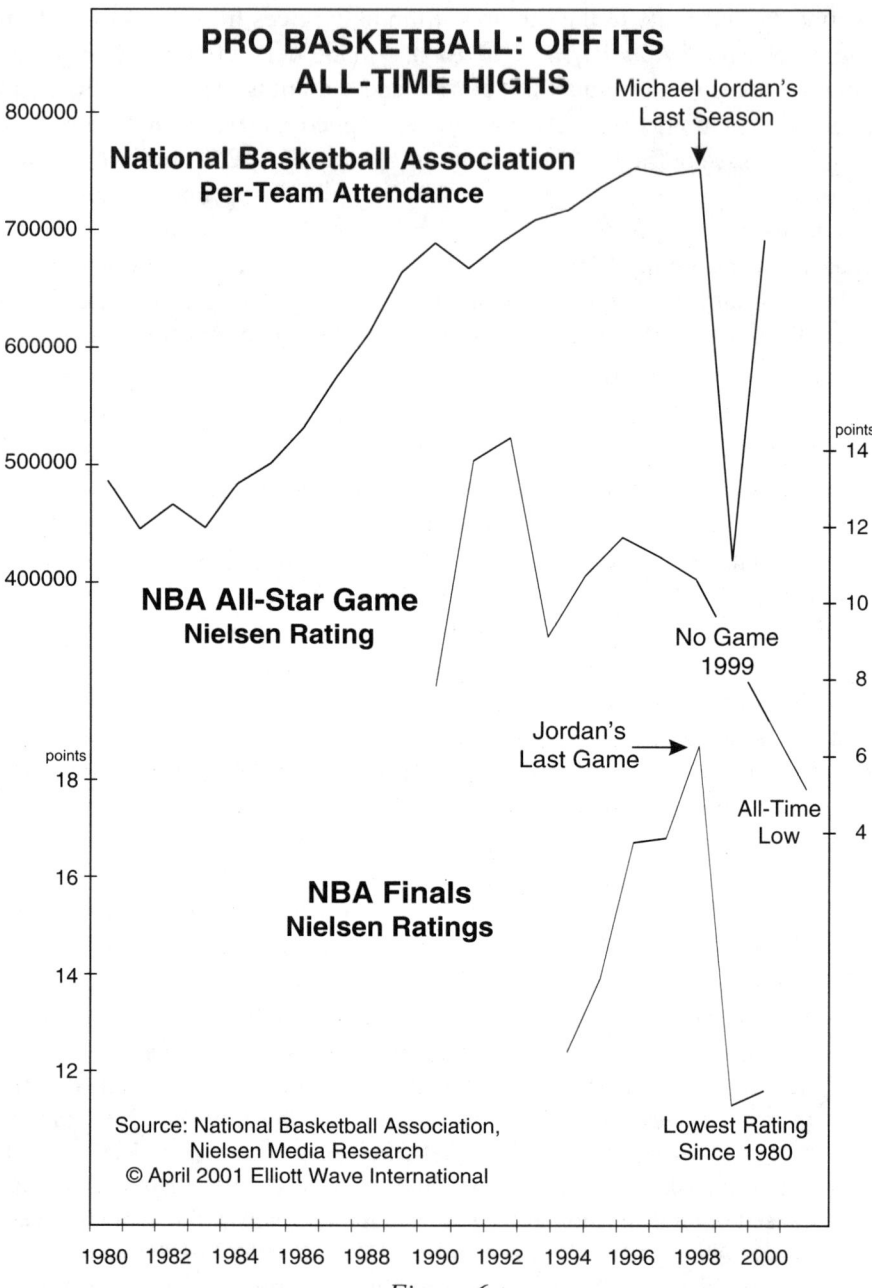

Figure 6

market's blast off. In 1987, the year of a substantial Dow high at 2723, he won his first MVP award. In the fall of 1996, as the Dow pushed past 6000, Jordan unveiled a new perfume and premiered as the star in a feature film. "Michael is superman," concludes *Sports Illustrated.* Only the hero factor can explain the depth of Jordan's popularity. As the game's greatest hero, Jordan personifies the happiness and energy of the bull market just as Bill Russell did in the 1960s and Magic Johnson in the 1980s.

EWT concluded, "the most noticeable sign of the trend change" would occur when Michael Jordan retired. Jordan retired in June of 1998. The euphoria of the moment was captured by a climactic NBA final in which Jordan made a last second shot to win the last game of the season and his last NBA title. Jordan's great finish marks the pinnacle of TV ratings for the National Basketball Association finals (see the bottom of Figure 6). A *Wall Street Journal* editorial said, "We were allowed up to Olympus." This Olympic peak was followed by the huge break in per-team attendance, as you can see at the top of Figure 6.

Taking the socionomic implication a step further, EWT added, "Top signals in the sport are top signals for stocks." The trend change clearly reflects the performance of the stock market, as it came just two months after the peak of a 24-year rise in the advance/decline line and thus the average NYSE stock, as shown in Figure 7.

Over the course of the last two years, every major index has followed suit, and the Chicago Bulls' dynasty has completely unraveled. Every single player from the championship era has left the team. Like the NASDAQ, the Bulls had the worst record in their history in 2000-2001. Back in 1996, EWT said, "Few, if any, fans see any relationship between their devotion to both the Bulls and their mutual fund portfolios." Now they feel as disgusted *at both* as they were elated during the mania, and they are no more aware of the principle that guides their collective emotional outlook than they were before. As we noted in 1996, this is the hallmark of "a collective psychological state — too pervasive to be recognized by most people."

The Depth and Breadth of the Decline in Team Sports Viewership

The *extent* of the ratings plunge for televised sports is as enlightening as the timing. Ratings for the NBA's February all-star game were the lowest *ever*, plunging 17% from 2000, which was also an all-time low. Since the start of the NBA season in November, regular-season NBA television

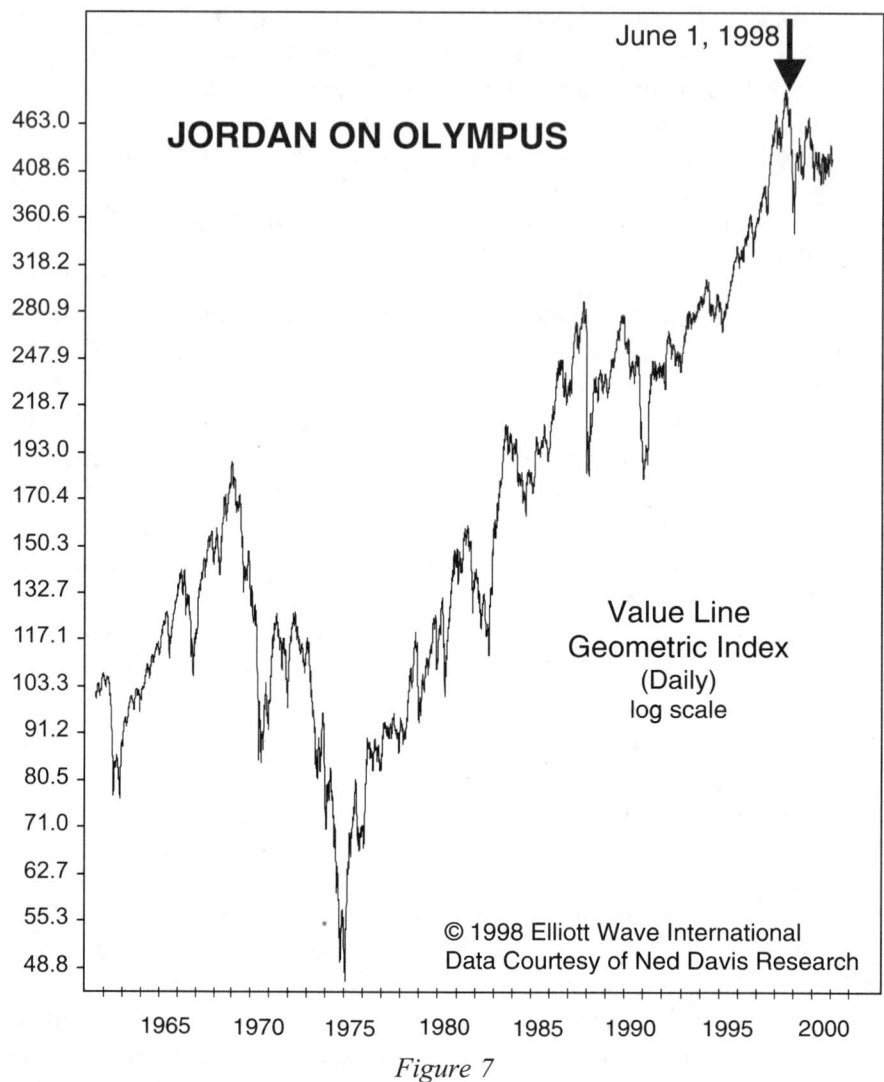

Figure 7

ratings are down 28% from low levels in 2000. College basketball ratings
have also fallen hard. As the NASDAQ broke from its all-time high in
March, 2000, viewership for tournament games fell 20% to an all-time low.
Ratings for this year's NCAA tournament were down still more.

Ratings for another highly organized athletic endeavor, the Olympic
Games (which *The Elliott Wave Theorist* also linked to the long advance

from 1896), fell off the table in 2000. Here again, the ratings were *never* lower. In fact, 2000 marked a clean sweep for the bear market in social mood, as every major sport experienced ratings declines. On April 23, *The Wall Street Journal* called the XFL, a new football league, "one of the biggest flops in television history." The breadth of the decline confirms that the long topping process that started with baseball ratings in the early 1990s has given way to a full-scale bear market in team sports viewership. (With a Grand Supercycle bear market in force, we should perhaps prepare for a prolonged fall from favor in team sports *per se*, which themselves may reflect the harmonious social relations typical of bull market.)

Ticket brokers report that the slack demand for seats extends to virtually every major sport. Another sign of exhaustion is that pent-up demand in many markets that were without teams, like Vancouver, Tampa and Miami, has been tapped as the big leagues expanded into just about every major geographic region. With the addition of new stadiums to most markets, sports in the 1990s attracted more marginal fans just as the stock market attracted more novice investors. The slumping per-team attendance figures shown at the top of Figures 3 and 6 show that the novelty is wearing off.

Bull Market Sports on the Ropes: Expectations vs. Results

As in the stock market, the raised *expectations* engendered by the preceding bull market have persisted through the first phase of collapse. Despite waning fan interest, values based upon *expectations*, such as salaries, stadium construction, the value of stadium naming rights and forward-sold advertising fees, continued to increase through 2000. Even new all-time lows in television ratings throughout 2000 could not dent the bullish expectations of participants. Table 1 shows how elevated official hopes have been on the eve of each recent sports event. The second headline shows that, in every case, a poor showing took television networks and sports authorities by surprise.

EWT has noted several times over the years that government is "the ultimate crowd." "It is always acting on the *last* trend, the one that is already over," it said in 1994. The following excerpt from the March 2001 issue of *Building Design & Construction* shows that the government commitment to the development of new stadiums is so deep that builders regard the spiraling growth in the costs and amenities of modern-day facilities to be a permanent condition.

HIGH HOPES vs. THE NEW BEAR MARKET REALITY
Despite one disappointing result after another, the media reflected bullish expectation
for baseball, basketball, and the Olympics in 2000.
© April 2001 Elliott Wave International

Bull Market Expectations	Bear Market Result
NCAA Tournament March 20, 2000 **CBS expects "improved ratings"**	April 5, 2000 **NCAA Tournament Ratings Hit an** **All-Time Low**
NBA Finals June 7, 2000 **NBC Expects Ratings Bump for Finals**	June 9, 2000 **NBA Finals Ratings Hit Low Point**
Baseball All-Star Game July 10, 2000 **Baseball Banks on All-Star Game Ratings**	July 13, 2000 **NBC's Coverage Draws Lowest Numbers** **Ever For All-Star Game**
Olympics September 14, 2000 **NBC Expects Good Ratings, Good Profits**	September 20, 2000 **NBC's Ratings For Olympics Are** **Worst Ever**
World Series October 20, 2000 **Fox Sports Aims For Big Series Ratings**	October 28, 2000 **A Dubious Honor: Lowest Ratings Ever**

Sports Projects on the Dole

While building projects in many commercial sectors face uncertain futures, the sports niche is as robust as ever. Fueled by a mix of technology, ebullient fans — and government support — the momentum of sports construction is like that of the public sector: There is never a recession. Part of the reason is the use of public funds and new taxes and bonds to pay for these projects.

Local and state authorities have taken on enormous financial obligations to preserve the "major league status" that is on the cusp of its biggest devaluation in history. Eventually, a public fury over the stadium projects is inevitable. As the public thirst for ball games dissipates, funds available for the real dole will be squeezed, and many will cry, "What were they thinking?!" At this point, however, most are still blinded by the emotional attachment to the erstwhile bull market. Like governments, TV networks remain institutionally bound to the old trend. Despite losses dating back to the early 1990s on contracts with pro leagues, they continue to make long-term commitments based on false hopes of a quick return to growth. After losing $40 million on the 1998 World Series and suffering through the worst ratings period in the history of baseball, Fox entered into a new contract that will nearly quadruple its yearly payout to the sport! The new contract runs through 2006 and will certainly cause Fox to lose a fortune.

Home To Roost

2001 has produced the first inkling of the potential for a prolonged decline in the popularity of professional sports. In February, the record NBA all-star game ratings plunge joined a 45% decline for football's Pro Bowl and a 37% drop for the all-star hockey game. Fallout from the developing bear market was so pronounced that the media finally took notice. The first hint of recognition was signaled by headlines like this one from the *Detroit Free Press*:

Are We Tired Of Sports?
Early Sign Suggest Fans
Are Losing Interest

"Early sign?" The true early sign was the Elliott wave count nine years ago. Now people are noticing the results. The press labeled the trend a "bedeviling, sociological change" and revealed that participation in most team sports fell through the 1990s. *Newsweek* disclosed on February 19 that after captivating America and verging on "global conquest" at the end of the 1990s, pro basketball "appears to have lost its magic." CNN Moneyline reports that one-time high-flying financial and technology firms that spent millions acquiring the naming rights to new professional sports facilities would love to get their names off these grand edifices. The problem is that no one wants the naming rights, at least not for the price they paid. An investigation of ticket prices by *The Wall Street Journal* found "enough to send a chill down the spine of the sports industry. Sports analysts say the industry could be sitting on a time bomb. The main reason fans don't renew their seats isn't the price or even the team's performance – but the number of times their tickets go to waste." An April 13 *USA Today* story reports that 25 of 30 major league teams lost money last year, and "teams are going deeply in debt to pay [player] salaries." "Baseball is in a golden era right now, but underneath all that is this huge problem," admitted the game's commissioner. Everything hinges on attendance and ratings growth that

has been waning for a full decade. "It's insane," says the general manager of the Cleveland Indians. Well, someone is insane, all right, but is it the fan, or is it the owner who signed the record high contract, or the banker who lent money to the team, or the government body that pledged taxpayers' millions for a stadium?

Into the Teeth of the Bear

Most sports consultants say that fans are not tiring of sports; the prices of tickets and hot dogs just got a little too high. When prices come down, sports industry insiders insist that people will head back to the ballpark. But it does not cost anything to watch the World Series on television or to play baseball and basketball. A more reasonable explanation for the fallen interest is that the bull market in social mood has given way, just as *The Elliott Wave Theorist* predicted it would at the end of the Grand Supercycle bull market. The result is a reversal of the bull market trend described at the outset of this report. As the bear market emerges, a declining energy level has reduced participation and fan interest.

Eventually, more developed expressions of the long rise will unravel. In addition to the attendance shrinkage that EWT initially called for in 1993, the bear market should produce a retracement in every other aspect of these endeavors. The number of teams, leagues and viewers, the level of salaries and even the physical attributes and abilities of players should shrink substantially over the next few years. On and off the field, the games should be characterized by an increasingly rough tone. Player-on-player, fan-on-player, and fan-on-fan violence should continue a rise that has already begun. Formerly silent opponents will come forward to charge that sports are too violent, too commercial, sexist, racist or a corporate leech on communities. As the downturn in social mood accelerates, look for more revelations about the loss of passion on the part of sports fans everywhere.

To date, the lost interest in bull market sports and the psychology that surrounds them certainly support our case for an unprecedented downturn in social mood. These changes reveal the immense value of the Wave Principle and the concept of socionomics, which describe the psychology of crowd behavior. As we continue to demonstrate, these ideas allow for true forecasting at important junctures, when others' expectations are all pointed the opposite way.

The Pittsfield Gazette
May 24, 2001

Elliott Wave Analysis: Baseball Stadiums Now a Risky Investment

by Edward J. Baptiste

The Wave Principle is a tool of unique value, whose most striking characteristics are its generality and its accuracy. Its generality gives market perspective most of the time and its accuracy in pointing changes in direction is at times almost unbelievable. Many areas of human activity also tend to follow the Wave Principle, but it is best associated with stock market analysis. Wave analysis is useful in gauging markets from a longer-term perspective.

For example, Elliott wave analysis recognized the worthiness of gold at $35 an ounce, followed its move to $200, its correction to $101 in 1976, and then to its eventual climax in January 1980 to $875. By then, it was conventionally correct to own gold. The dollar was under attack, there was an oil crisis, Russian troops invaded Afghanistan and the gnomes of Zurich even had fears of their crossing over the Swiss Alps. Arab OPEC nations who sold their crude for years at $2 a barrel saw their earnings buying less in exchange value of other goods and services, reacted hawkishly. Amid rising commodity prices and concern over inflation, Elliotticians such as I clearly saw completion of a major wave movement and advised total liquidation of gold. Bullion within two months dropped to the $450 area and has since in this 20-year span been as low as $255.

Its most recent success was indicating a top of significance for the Dow Jones Industrials in January 2000, yet its signals for the Nasdaq were a trifle premature, as that index topped later in March of that year. Nevertheless, investors who listened to those signals were well served by avoiding the bubble collapse that followed. The Nasdaq 100 Index has dropped from 4816 to 1348. It has paid to heed Elliott wave analysis.

Now for wave analysis' relevance to baseball, stadiums and Pittsfield. Elliotticians see clear signals of a top in baseball and sports in general. We do not pontificate about such an observation and conclusion, nor do we rejoice in it. Had our conclusions indicated a major surge in baseball, it would have been reported as such.

My friends at Elliott Wave International in Gainesville, GA, in a piece dated April 30, 2001, have sounded the alarm for baseball in a seven-page single spaced report. This follows another report dated 12/16/96, "Basketball and the Bull Market." Both reports are available at elliottwave.com or 800-336-1618.

They wrote in 1993: "A Top in Baseball? If you're an investor, take profits on baseball. If you're a player, sign a long-term contract. If you're an owner, sell your club." Rest assured that baseball will survive, but prices change, as in gold. From 1901, there appears to be a clear five waves up in baseball game attendance, which has immediate implications for a correction or downturn of secular proportions. A sharp drop in ticket sales is foreseen over the next few years, concomitant with a collapse in inflated baseball salaries. Such salaries (measured on a per season value of the largest contract in millions of dollars) have risen from $1 million in 1980 to an exponential $25 million currently. The Texas Rangers probably capped this bubble with signing of shortstop Alex Rodriguez to the richest contract in the history of sports akin to the Tulip Bubble in Holland of the 1630s. Succinctly put, salaries of top players have now out-stripped public demand for their services to an extent reminiscent of the Internet run-up of 1999. Supporting these conclusions are a sharp drop in World Series Neilsen Ratings since the early 1990s and ratings for the All Star game plunging to new lows. The total number of fans tuning into baseball's two most important annual events actually topped the year before baseball's 1993 attendance peak.

The five-wave pattern of this decade-long trend announces the onset of a major bear market. Nevertheless, two other measures of baseball's bull market have held firm, i.e., player contracts and team values, which continued to climb with stock markets of 1999 and early 2000. Fundamentals tell a different story. Growth in fan attendance and TV ratings both have been waning for a full decade, explaining why 25 of 30 major league teams lost money last year. The fact is that teams are going deeply into debt in order to pay higher and higher team salaries!

As EWI puts it,. quoting the manager of the Cleveland Indians, "It's insane." They go on: "Well, someone is insane, all right, but is it the fan, or is it the owner who signed the record high contract, or the banker who lent money to the team, or the government body who pledged taxpayers' millions for a stadium?"

This change in social behavior can be replicated in what is happening to the NBA, Olympic Games and even the NCAA College March Madness finals, of which I am a devotee, having graduated from Duke. It is further exemplified by a *Wall Street Journal* article of April 23, which described the new XFL football league as one of the biggest flops in TV history!

This is as in stock market tops, where the majority of people buy just prior to and certainly after the peak. This is "Crowd Psychology" at its best. Elliott Wave International has noted several times over the years that government is the "ultimate crowd" as it is always acting on the LAST trend.

I leave the issue of eminent domain to others, location of stadium to still others. But I offer a genuine caveat to all concerned: The likelihood of a no-win, no-profit situation for baseball, challenging the idea of its being an economic engine for Pittsfield, is all too real.

CORPORATIONS, LEGISLATION AND SOCIAL CONFLICT

Kendall

The Elliott Financial Forecast
December 3, 1999

A Dow-Stock Case Study: Coca-Cola

What is it about Coca-Cola? Is it the cola nut? The coca extract? The sugar? The answer, of course, is none of the above. In 1993's *For God, Country and Coca-Cola*, Mark Pendergrast actually published Coca-Cola's coveted 107-year-old secret formula. Since then, no one has cooked it up and successfully sold a reasonable facsimile of The Real Thing. In fact, Pendergrast reports that when he was researching his history, the company literally handed him the recipe. Coca-Cola executives were not concerned because they know full well that it is not the drink their customers are buying. As one put it, "We're selling smoke. They're drinking the image, not the product."

It is plain old sugar water, yet some call it the "essence of capitalism." How can it be? The answer appears on page 168 of *The Wave Principle of Human Social Behavior*. In a section called "Social Visioning as an Aspect of Herding," Prechter explains how social moods find expression in "shared fantasy images." As the chart of Coke from 1957 shows, it is a "social vision" that conforms nicely to the dictates of the Wave Principle. While Coke can stray from the Dow, it always finds its way back to the main trend.

The corporate history behind Coke's long rise shows that the company's old jingle is actually pretty accurate. *Things* really do go better with Coke. Unless, of course, the thing is a bear market. At such times, things don't go so well, not even for Coke. The firm's history is a living illustration of this passage from page 168: "Trends based upon subjective mental imagery undergo violent reversals when the imagery dissolves." Like the Dow Jones Industrial Average, Coca-Cola took off in the mid-1890s when its founders realized that there was more future in the beverage as refreshment than as medicine. "We found we were advertising to the few when we ought to advertise to the masses," said one of the firm's original leaders. By the turn of the century, the company was burrowing deep into the public psyche as it "pioneered celebrity endorsements" to become "not simply a soft drink,

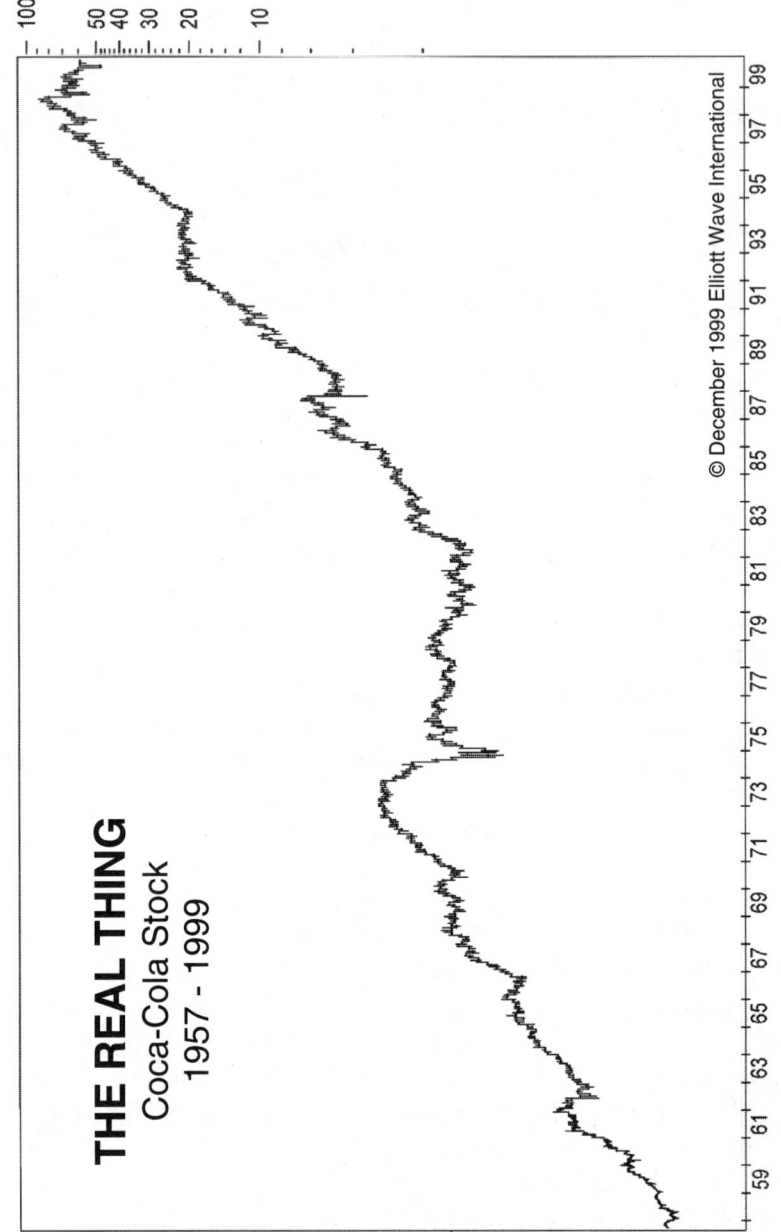

THE REAL THING
Coca-Cola Stock
1957 - 1999

© December 1999 Elliott Wave International

but a phenomenon." The first big setback for Coke was the passage of the Pure Food and Drugs Act. Its date of passage was June 1906, five months after a Dow high that would not be materially exceeded until the 1920s. At the outset, Coca-Cola loyalists referred to proponents of the "pure food movement" as "cranks" and "misguided fanatics," but they had far more clout and staying power than expected. Their leader was Harvey Wiley, a man Pendergrast calls the Ralph Nader of the early 1900s. In 1907, Wiley took aim at Coca-Cola with the formation of a new "Poison Squad." Coke's annual report of 1907 reflected a coincident downturn in the company's prospects. As the bear market dragged on, Coca-Cola was beset by woes. In 1908, the U.S. government filed suit over its labeling and employment practices. "Even though Coca-Cola won the case in 1912, the publicity hurt the drink. D.W. Griffith put out an anti-Coca-Cola epic in which the inventor of 'DOPOKOKE' watched his son fall prey to the drink's cocaine. 'The drink no longer satisfies,' read one caption as the young man went on to hypodermic injections." Through the end of the 1910s, Coke was riled by rocketing sugar prices and a "civil war" for control of the company. After a "disastrous" year in 1920, as stock prices fell, Coca-Cola finally righted itself in 1922, a year after the Dow bottomed.

Pendergrast dates the start of Coca-Cola's "golden age" to 1923. With a push into global markets and a new age of mass media, Coke soared to heights of wealth generation previously unimagined for a maker of a 5-cent item. The real "secret," of course, was the company's primitive but powerful understanding of its underlying attractiveness. Ad man Archie Lee, "one of the first to realize that a product's image was more important than the product itself," came up with the "Pause that Refreshes" campaign in 1929. It is to that moment that anthropologist Clifford Geertz dates Coca-Cola's crossover from a soda fountain and syrup making company to "a system of symbols which acts to establish powerful, pervasive and long-lasting moods." The company "promotes a particular, satisfying, all-inclusive world view espousing perennial values such as love, peace and universal brotherhood. As a sacred symbol, Coca-Cola induces varying 'worshipful' moods, ranging from exaltation to pensive solitude, from near-orgasmic togetherness to playful games of chase."

With the help of its "social vision" and Prohibition, Coke held up better than most firms in the early 1930s, but by 1949, the end of the bear market in inflation-adjusted terms, it was experiencing the same anti-Coca Cola sentiment that had pulled it down in the 1910s. In Paris, mobs overturned Coke trucks, and "the level of hysteria reached such a pitch" that the wife of Coca-Cola's French president worried that her house might be bombed. "Coca-Cola faced similar threats and rumors at mid-century around the world." In Japan, the drink was said to sterilize women.

In the 1950s, the drink got back on track with the bull market. "Consumer behavior was often irrational, based on subconscious psychological motives," Pendergrast writes. "For the first time, the company attempted to plumb the depths of the subconscious mind." Coca-Cola was soon riding high again. In 1966, the end of Cycle wave III in the Dow and a long advance for Coke, the company "suddenly became a hot political topic" and nearly lost the Jewish market by refusing to grant an Israeli bottling franchise. The crisis was forestalled until late 1968 when the Dow topped and the resulting Arab boycott went into effect. In 1969, Ralph Nader himself surfaced with attacks in a hearing before the Select Committee on Nutrition and Human Needs. Shortly thereafter, "the Food and Drug Administration sounded another theme of the approaching seventies by revealing alarming results of tests on cyclamates." Coke's "perfect harmony" ad campaign of the early 1970s helped carry it to a final high with the Dow in 1973, but after that, it was all downhill as the company lost its long battle with the FTC, internal morale fell to an all-time low and "cozy relationships with dictators blew up one after the other." "No one would have guessed that a hopeful new era was about to commence." No one but a socionomist.

By 1995, Coca-Cola was the world's best known brand, with nearly half of the worldwide soft-drink market. The perfection with which the "peace and harmony" of its commercials reflected the public mindset is captured in the stock's price climb from 1982 to 1998.

Since its peak in July 1998, however, things have changed in ways reminiscent of past stock market tops. Coke has been shaken by a continuous stream of mysterious corporate crises that range from mold scares to the French government's rejection of its bid to buy Orangina to an assortment of unfavorable court rulings. In one case, the Belgian government successfully forced Coke to stop selling its beverages at a discount. In another, its own employees won the right to internal documents that they will use to mount a major discrimination case. As *The New York Times* said, the troubles have "revealed a different Coca-Cola," one that somehow manages to make unfortunate situations "even worse."

The true nature of Coke's problems is revealed by another recent snafu, an outbreak in which several Belgian school students reported feeling bad after buying Coca-Cola from a vending machine. Some were hospitalized, but no medical problems were ever diagnosed. Even though the company analysis showed "consumers were generally limited to subjective symptoms," massive recalls followed in Belgium and then France. "The pattern of this epidemic is consistent with a clinical entity which has been described as 'mass sociogenic illness.'" In socionomic terminology, this translates to "We're in a bear market."

Food Fights and the Seattle Mob

As in 1906 and 1968, much of Coca-Cola's turmoil is rooted in emotional fears about food. The campaign against genetically engineered "Frankenfoods," which people have been consuming for years with no evidence of harmful side effects, started in Europe and has spread to the U.S. in recent weeks. As in 1908 and 1969, government hearings have been called to discuss the health risk in food. "The second of three FDA hearings on the safety and regulation of biotech foods is expected to be as contentious as the first meeting [on] November 18." "Growing resistance to new technology" has prompted the public forums. At the World Trade Organization conference in Seattle, protestors attacked a McDonalds, smashing its windows and unfurling a banner protesting the genetic engineering of food. Nobody seems to know what triggered the wave of irrational fears, but many are taking action. "Once Quick Converts, Farmers Begin To Lose Faith In Biotech Crops." Even when the "customer is wrong, the customer is right," says a farmer who has decided not to plant genetically modified seed next year.

In the middle of the unexpectedly explosive world-trade summit, Ralph Nader himself resurfaced and grabbed more public notice than at any time since the Naders' Raiders days. In countless other ways, the events of Seattle over the last few days have provided clear signs of a reversal in the long-term trend in social mood. What was supposed to be an inclusionistic *tour de force*, the biggest free-trade meeting in history, has been all but shut down by a well-organized amalgam of eco-terrorists, union agitators, food phobes, students and protectionists. With tear gas hovering over crowded streets, a call out for the National Guard, law-and-order types decrying the "mob tactics" of their adversaries, and the sudden labor unrest, a whole host of long-dormant cultural manifestations of a bear market have emerged. The National Association of Manufacturers tried to head off the demonstrators by calling an army of Fortune 500 CEOs to the front. Before the WTO meetings even started, however, it was obvious that the world's corporate heroes would be powerless against the protestors. "We're never going to compete with thousands of Naderites rappelling and chanting," said a NAM spokesman. This is what happens in a bear market; the emotional forces of the crowd simply overwhelm the established order.

Kendall

The Elliott Wave Financial Forecast
April 2000

Is the Break in the Big Brand Names a Warning for the Overall Market?

Three months ago, the concept of the "old economy" barely existed. Now, it is the focus of daily speculation on the strength or weakness in the stock market. When the Dow falls, it is because the "bastions of safety are crumbling under this new economy." When the Dow rises, it's a "New Bull Market for [the] Old Economy." The chart below shows, however, that in lumping everything in the "old economy" into a single group, observers are missing an important distinction that could hold the key to the direction of the overall market. Figure 1 breaks the "old economy" into two distinct

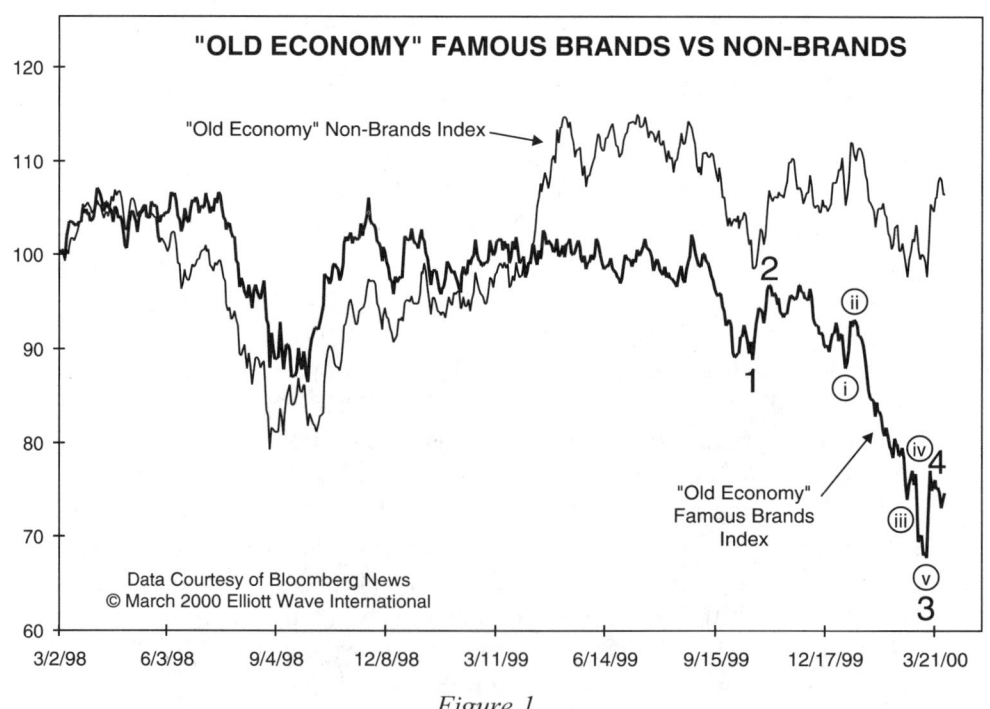

Figure 1

sectors: companies that rely heavily on famous brand names and those that do not. Our Famous Brands Index consists of 21 stocks that generate their business from well-established brand names. It encompasses hundreds of different products that have built identities as major American brands dating as far back as the mid-1800s. Table 1 lists some of their key products and their year of establishment. Our Non-Brands Index consists of the 35 "old economy" stocks from the S&P 100 that are *not* dependent on branded products. Its membership includes established firms like Bethlehem Steel, Boeing and Columbia Healthcare.

Company Name	Key Product(s) & Year Established	Date of Peak	Decline Through March 10
1) Kellogg	Corn Flakes 1906 Rice Krispies 1928	01/01/98	68%
2) Campbell Soup	condensed soup 1897	03/23/98	53%
3) Brunswick	recreational products 1874	03/25/98	56%
4) Mattel	Barbie 1959	03/31/98	80%
5) Sara Lee	cheescake 1949	04/07/98	54%
6) Hershey	chocolate 1894	04/09/98	49%
7) Fruit of the Loom	textiles 1856 underwear 1938	04/21/98	97%
8) Disney	films 1923 theme parks 1955	05/04/98	17%
9) Ralston Purina	cereal 1898 Purina Dog Chow 1957	06/30/98	37%
10) Coca-Cola	Coke 1886	07/15/98	50%
11) H.J. Heinz	ketchup 1876	11/17/98	48%
12) Unilever	laundry soap 1885 Lipton Tea 1937	01/06/99	55%
13) Gillette	Safety Razor 1903	03/26/99	53%
14) Avon	perfume 1886 beauty products 1950	04/19/99	55%
15) RJR Nabisco	Fig Newtons 1891 Oreo 1912	06/11/99	60%
16) Anheuser-Busch	Budweiser 1876	09/08/99	33%
17) McDonald's	fast food 1954	11/11/99	39%
18) Quaker Oats	oatmeal 1901	11/12/99	35%
19) Johnson & Johnson	BAND-AID 1921 Tylenol 1960	11/17/99	33%
20) Procter & Gamble	Ivory 1879 Tide 1946	01/12/00	54%
21) Colgate Palmolive	toothpaste 1873	01/13/00	39%

Table 1

Without the drag of issues that rely heavily on brand names, stocks in the Non-Brands Index went to a new high in 1999. In recent days, this brand-free group also moved back above its high of April 1998. In contrast, the Famous Brands Index never exceeded its April 1998 peak and is now down more than 30% from that point. In the years preceding its all-time high, the index kept pace with the bull market, as you can see in Figure 2. One by one, however, each of these stocks has decoupled from the rising trend of the averages. Through March 10, the date of the NASDAQ's all-time high, all 21 had suffered serious declines. The numbers on the chart correlate to Table 1 to show the steady progression. Procter & Gamble, the granddaddy of American brand marketing, was one of the last to drop. It turned down two days before the Dow's January peak and has since lost 51%.

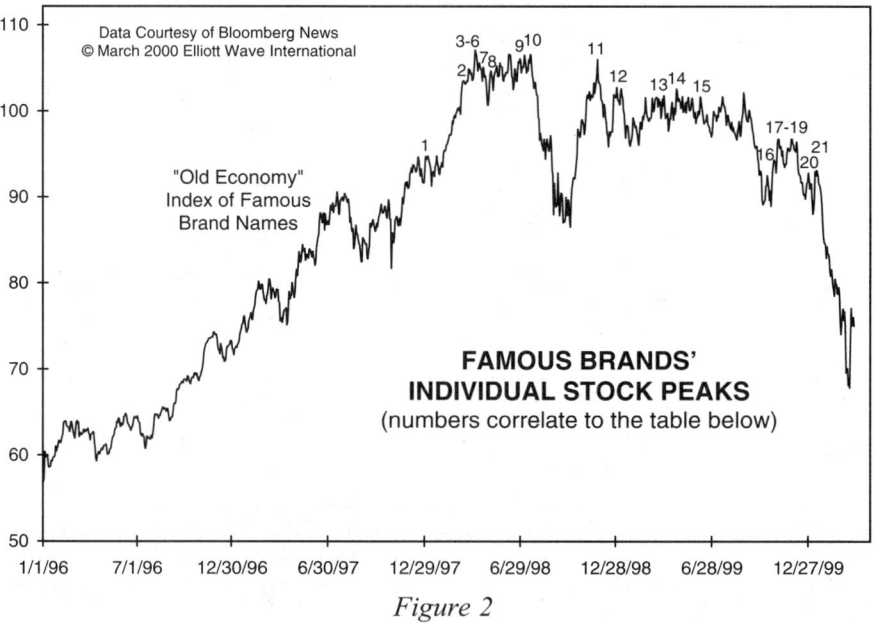

Figure 2

The exciting news is that the break in the brand stocks has established ideal conditions for a real-time test of a socionomic theory discussed in the chapter on "Impulsivity and Herding" in Prechter's book, *The Wave Principle of Human Social Behavior*. According to the idea of "social visioning," which Bob proposed on the basis of studies and observations from a host of social theorists (see Chapter 9), "it may be that shared fantasy images are an *intermediate step* between mood change and resulting action." When these images dissolve, he added, the trends they are "based upon undergo violent reversals." They may even "reflect mood quite immediately, before the public could mobilize itself enough to act in the economic and political arenas." This study takes the question to the market itself. Can a basket of equities backed by a broad cross-section of commercial fantasy images developed over the course of a bull market reflect the end of that bull market ahead of other major indexes? Since companies with major brands represent near-total investments in the techniques of crafting and maintaining icons that are amenable to the long uptrend in social mood, it seems quite possible. Their shares should be extremely sensitive to any loss of potency in the symbols, sayings, jingles, tastes or subliminal appeals they have created over the course of a long bull market. At downturns of lesser degree, EWFF's case study of Coca Cola (see EWFF December issue) showed how readily the complex and highly subjective process of building a business around a bull market icon can break down.

Only the market can answer, of course. But at this point, we can make an initial confirmation of "the intermediate step" described in the book because it also describes the form that social visioning must take. "Herding people feel a certain way and can express themselves *impulsively* to reflect those feelings," it says. "If social visioning is an intermediate step between social mood and social action, the dynamics of its manifestation would have to follow the Wave Principle, which governs its cause." The decline from mid-1999 does, in fact, bear the trademark of an Elliott impulse wave. Notice wave 3 on Figure 1. It is a clear five waves down within the larger five. The rally off that low went to a fourth wave of one lesser degree and then stopped cold even as the Dow rocketed higher and the Non-Brand Index moved back above its April 1998 high. What we are saying is that the Famous Brands Index has taken on a character of its own.

This character reflects the two sides of a major, major peak. The media have not noticed that the brand-name issues of the old economy have been rolling over one after another since the peak of the advance/decline line in April 1998. At the same time, the *idea* of branding has actually grown bigger than ever as the rationale for tolerating losses in the *new* economy. Rivers of red ink at Internet companies are not just tolerated but in fact *demanded* by investors who insist that "new economy" companies "need large marketing expenditures to build brand awareness." Proof of this assertion is that stocks of Internet companies that generate losses to build brand names have consistently outperformed stocks of Internet companies that turn a profit. Another indication that a historic extreme in brand awareness has reached its zenith is that in recent months, even individuals have become brand names. A number of them, including Dick Clark, Donna Karan, Tommy Hilfiger, Ralph Lauren, Martha Stewart and C. Everett Koop, have become publicly traded companies. All are down substantially from their closes on their first days of trading, but the effort literally to buy heroes continues to spread. The latest development is at the venture capital level, where numerous promoters are busily launching Internet investment funds with superstar athletes because "athletes have tremendous brand presence." Many venture capitalists and investors expect to get in on the ground floor of the "new paradigm," but the elevator is actually on the penthouse floor and starting down. If the bull market is topping as we assert, then these are the final death throes of brand name imaging *per se*.

The Elliott Wave Theorist
May 2000

A Socionomic Perspective on the Microsoft Case

How would you answer the question, "What effect will the Justice Department's antitrust lawsuit against Microsoft have on the overall stock market?" A fundamental analyst might write a thesis about it, pointing out the market's behavior after past antitrust actions and discussing why this time might be the same or different. He would remind us that we can draw no useful conclusions without knowing more about upcoming events. Many technical analysts would say that the market, digesting advance knowledge of the event, probably factored most of its impact into stock prices prior to the action. He would assure us that further events will be similarly discounted in advance. Again, though, we would be reminded that there are no useful conclusions to draw without anticipating upcoming events. Despite their differences, these responders would agree that events are causal to the stock market's behavior. The socionomic perspective is otherwise.

The report, "Socionomics in a Nutshell" (December 1999), demonstrated in brief that in the realm of economics, politics, demographics, war and even the threat of nuclear destruction, events are *not* causal to social mood and stock market trends. In every case, the direction of causality is the opposite of that generally assumed. The performance of the economy does not govern the stock market; the social mood as reflected by stock market trends governs economic performance. Politics do not govern the stock market; the social mood as reflected by stock market trends governs politics. Demographics do not govern the stock market; the social mood as reflected by the stock market regulates the overall rate of procreation. Changes in the threat of nuclear destruction do not affect stock prices; the social mood as reflected by the stock market affects the level of the threat. In each instance, social mood trends as reflected by stock market trends dictate the character of events, not the other way around. How, then, would a socionomist respond to the question posed at the start of this report? Before answering, let's explore some data.

The Timing of Attacks on Successful Corporations

In 1890, a year after a new all-time peak in stock prices that would last a full decade, Congress passed the Sherman Act, which in vague language outlawed "trusts," which in fact means companies that service a large market without significant competition. Take a look at the comments above the graph of stock prices in Figure 1. Observe that the government's antitrust suits against U.S. corporations, particularly the landmark suits that make the history books, consistently come near stock market peaks, usually slightly afterward. Often the correlation is so close as to be within weeks of a major top that leads to declines in the averages of 50% or more.

Railroads were arguably the most successful U.S. industry in the late 19th century. On the run-up to the stock market peak of June 1901, the stock of Great Northern Pacific railroad, which later became part of Northern Securities Co., increased more than ten fold in less than a month. Shortly thereafter, the government sued Northern Securities Co. in the first major application of the Sherman Act. In 1906, the year of a peak that was not exceeded for ten years, President Theodore Roosevelt filed his famous suit against the country's largest company, Standard Oil. During the Panic of 1907, the President offered no objection to a merger involving U.S. Steel when asked to do so and explicitly directed his attorney general not to bring an antitrust action against International Harvester. In 1911 and 1912, after stock prices had recovered, President Taft's antitrust division filed suit against both companies. A month after the all-time high of 1929 and before the crash, the U.S. attorney general announced that the Justice Department would deal "vigorously with every violation of the antitrust law." In 1930, the Justice Department filed suit against one of the biggest success stories of the 1920s bull market, RCA. In 1937, the year of a major top in stock prices, the government sued aluminum maker Alcoa. The antitrust movement saw little action throughout the nearly two-decade long bull market of 1949-1966/68 until the very end, when the stock market reached a top of the same Elliott wave degree as that of 1937. In 1967, the government ordered Proctor & Gamble to divest itself of Clorox, and in January 1969, a single month after the most speculative bull market peak since 1929, the Justice Department sued the country's most successful company, IBM. From 1982, antitrust activity again virtually disappeared during nearly two decades of bull market. On May 18, 1998, just one month after the final high in the advance-decline line and the Value Line geometric index, both of which had risen for 24 years, the Justice Department sued the world's most successful company, Microsoft. On April 3, 2000, a single week after

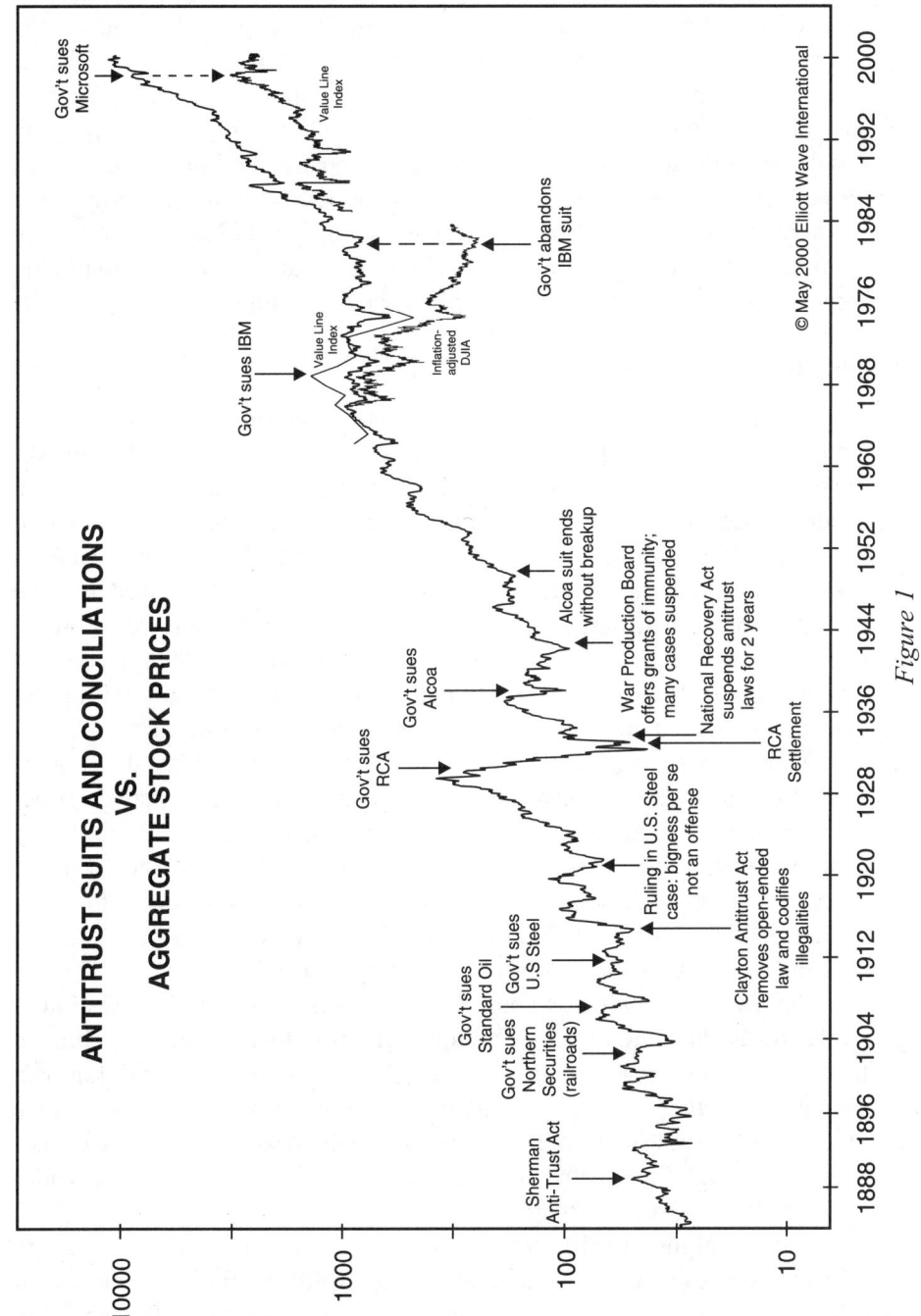

**ANTITRUST SUITS AND CONCILIATIONS
VS.
AGGREGATE STOCK PRICES**

Gov't sues Microsoft

Value Line Index

Gov't abandons IBM suit

Value Line Index

Gov't sues IBM

Inflation-adjusted DJIA

Alcoa suit ends without breakup

Gov't sues Alcoa

War Production Board offers grants of immunity; many cases suspended

National Recovery Act suspends antitrust laws for 2 years

RCA Settlement

Gov't sues RCA

Ruling in U.S. Steel case: bigness per se not an offense

Gov't sues Standard Oil

Gov't sues U.S Steel

Clayton Antitrust Act removes open-ended law and codifies illegalities

Gov't sues Northern Securities (railroads)

Sherman Anti-Trust Act

1888 1896 1904 1912 1920 1928 1936 1944 1952 1960 1968 1976 1984 1992 2000

10000   1000   100   10

© May 2000 Elliott Wave International

Figure 1

the closing high in the NASDAQ 100 index, the court sided with the U.S. Justice Department in ruling that Microsoft had unlawfully violated the Sherman Act. Like his predecessors at prior historic turns, U.S. District Court Judge Thomas Penfield Jackson, representing "the people," has pursued and denigrated Microsoft with a fervor that borders on the evangelical. His desire to break up the most successful company of all time as measured by percentage gain in value per year is a passion born of the passing of a social mood peak of even higher degree than that of 1929. As you can see from this century-long history, major antitrust suits coincide remarkably consistently with the passing of major stock market tops.

Direction of Causality

A conventional analyst would surely conclude from this evidence that antitrust suits *cause* stock market declines. This response does not answer the question of why the entire economy would be affected by a single suit, an idea bordering on the preposterous. Presumably, competitors would benefit as the target suffered, neutralizing any broad effect. The erroneous conclusion, moreover, is utterly negated by the fact that the target of the latest suit, Microsoft, saw its stock *triple in price* after the suit was brought. In fact, the last doubling took place after the November 1999 "finding of fact" in which Penfield ruled, "Microsoft Corp. is a monopoly with practices that wounded competition and consumers and hurt innovation."

More important, and typical of conventional explanations, the suggestion of a causative link between antitrust actions and falling stock prices goes against the assumptions of many other conventional analysts. Many economists believe (mistakenly) that "trust-busting" is good for the economy. If they were correct, and if their assumption that economic performance dictates stock market trends were correct, then stock prices should *rise* after an attack on a presumed monopoly, not fall.

Finally, this conclusion about causality fails to answer the question of why antitrust suits are typically brought after the stock market has climbed for years or even decades to a state of overvaluation in a climate of rampant speculation *rather than at any other time*. For the most part, the Justice Department leaves successful corporations alone near the end of bear markets and through 90%-100% of bull markets, even if it has to wait decades to do so. What is really going on?

The social mood shift that occurs at the transition from bull market to bear includes a change in general attitudes toward the financial success of others. Society moves from a feeling of support toward one of resentment.

During a bull market, the social mood is directed toward rewarding achievement; during a bear market, it is directed toward punishing it. The bear market mood begins to creep into collective thinking late in a bull market. Democratic governments are instruments of egalitarianism. At some point, their representatives cannot stand watching some companies succeed wildly more than most others. When the bull market reaches exhaustion, the old supportive mood begins to crumble, and the new punitive mood bursts forth. One result of this metamorphosis in social character is governmental attacks against highly successful enterprises. In fact, they typically start with a major attack against *the* most successful enterprise of the time.

This socionomic perspective, moreover, is quite comfortable with the fact that Microsoft stock tripled after the suit was announced. The environment of stock market tops is one of rampant speculation fueled by a manic psychology. Reason and outside-event causality are not part of this landscape. Bullish fever among speculators and righteous anger among egalitarians can coexist for brief periods as major social mood tops are being formed, thus producing the anomaly of a soaring stock price for a company that is being attacked in court by its own government.

The Timing of Permissiveness with Respect to Successful Corporations

Antitrust action typically continues throughout most of a bear market. As each bear market comes to an end, the old mood of resentment evaporates. The timing of this correlation is just as remarkable as that for tops, as demonstrated by the comments underneath the graph of stock prices in Figure 1.

At the 1914 low, the Clayton Anti-Trust Act reined in the broadness of the Sherman Act. In 1920, as the market was approaching the low from which the bull market of the Roaring Twenties would erupt, the Supreme Court "rejected the challenge to Andrew Carnegie and J.P. Morgan's formation of U.S. Steel, saying "mere size" is no offense. Near the 1932-1933 lows, the government settled its case against RCA, and the National Recovery Act suspended antitrust law for two years. Near the 1942 low, the War Production Board offered grants of immunity from antitrust action, and the government suspended many of its antitrust cases. A year after the 1949 low, the government settled its suit against Alcoa without achieving its objective of breaking up the company. In 1982, after a sixteen-year decline in real stock prices, the Justice Department abandoned its suit against IBM.

Like its attacks, the government's major acts of reconciliation and permissiveness typically occur within weeks or months of a major turn in the stock market, this time to the upside. In both cases, its acts are in response to, and part of, the changing social mood.

One could try to argue that once a stock market decline goes far enough, corporate fortunes in general are so poor that there is no longer any need to punish trusts. However, if the government's theory of monopoly power were correct, a contracting business environment would have no effect on a company's relative position. Further, this view does not explain why in some cases the government pulls back after stock prices fall 50% and the economy is in recession and in other cases after stock prices fall 90% and the economy is in depression. There is no mathematical "magic level" at which governments stop their attacks. *They stop when the social mood reaches bottom, wherever that may be.* The exact timing and level of *that* event are determined not by extent or time but by *form* as revealed by the wave pattern.

A Socionomist's Response

With regard to the question posed at the outset, then, the answer from a socionomic perspective is this: The Justice Department's antitrust action against Microsoft has had, and will have, no effect whatsoever on the overall trend of the stock market (just as it had no effect on the price of Microsoft stock itself). The causality is the other way around: The exhaustion of an extremely positive social mood trend, as reflected by stock market statistics, affected the Justice Department's emotional mindset and caused it to capitulate to a desire to attack the most successful corporation it could identify, which was Microsoft.

Forecasting

In contrast to the predictive uselessness of conventional assumptions about the direction of causality between social events and mood (see opening paragraph), the socionomic perspective allows a basis for at least some limited probabilistic forecasting. With a knowledge of the Wave Principle, we can roughly anticipate the timing of major antitrust actions and later, their resolutions. For example, we can predict that no major government attacks on corporate success are likely from the time of a stock market bottom of Cycle degree or larger through most of the ensuing bull market. We can also predict continual government attacks on corporate success from the time of a stock market top of Cycle degree or larger through most of the ensuing bear market (the later attacks typically being of lesser import than the first one). We can state further that when a major antitrust action takes place after a long period of non-action, it is a sign that the social mood trend of at least Cycle degree is likely changing from bull to bear. We can also state that when a major antitrust action is resolved after a long period of conflict, it is a sign that the social mood trend of at least Cycle degree is likely changing from bear to bull. We can say these things because antitrust actions and resolutions do not occur randomly; they occur at *specific times* in response to a psychological environment involving a major extreme in social mood and its reversal.

The Timing of Attacks on Monopolies

First, we must define our terms. A monopoly is an entity that holds an economically preferential position due primarily to the use of force. Monopolies are maintained by the force of the state in favor of selected individuals, guilds, companies or state enterprises. European monarchs routinely granted monopolies on specific markets to individuals. Guilds successfully barred competition when the power of the state was behind them. Corporations and state enterprises such as the U.S. Postal Service, the Federal Reserve System and the U.S. Mint enjoy monopoly privileges. Persons attempting to provide services in competition with entities such as these are aggressively punished by fines and imprisonment.

A monopoly differs from an especially successful company in that the latter is *always* at the risk of competition. Monopolies have survived for *centuries* despite bad products and services. On the other hand, every non-monopoly company is subject to collapse if its products or services deteriorate, if it misses the next innovative trend in its field, or if the very field it is in becomes passé. Some people claim that an especially successful company can become a monopoly simply because its success gives it "power" to destroy the competition. It is true that immense success can allow a company to make deals with other businesses to induce them to deal with it exclusively. This condition is different from monopoly power, however, because the dealings are voluntary. Another business can always refuse to cooperate if it so chooses; there is no gun behind the deal. Further, such "power" is temporary. To the extent that any successful business engages in elaborate restrictive schemes, it will, in the long run, drain its resources and weaken itself, allowing future competitors to gain an edge. Competition, moreover, is not fixed to any number of firms existing at a particular time. A successful company frets as much over *potential* competition as over actual competition. It knows that the slightest slip in top quality goods and services will endanger it immensely. No matter how hard it may try, no company can keep a premier position forever. The natural order of things eventually reduces the relative success of every exceptional enterprise.

This distinction between actual monopolies and purported monopolies that are not is important for the purposes of our socionomic thesis regarding "trust busting." It allows us to see the essence of the commonality between the *suspension* of government's actions against successful *non-monopoly* corporations near stock market bottoms (shown below the graph in Figure 1) and its simultaneous *initiation* of attacks on *actual* monopolies.

Figure 2 shows times when the U.S. government has acted to limit or break apart the monopoly power of the original U.S. phone company, AT&T. Under the Communications Act of 1934, the U.S. government dubbed AT&T a natural monopoly and allowed the communications carrier to operate without competitive forces. In 1949, the year that a 20-year bear market pattern in real stock prices (not shown) ended, the U.S. Justice Department cited AT&T for "maintaining a monopoly" that violated the Sherman Act. On November 20, 1974, the month between the final lows in all the stock market averages following declines of 45% to 74%, the Justice Department sued AT&T for monopolizing the telecommunications industry. In 1982, the year that real stock prices bottomed, AT&T was ordered to divest itself of all seven of its local operating companies and cease offering local phone service, which it did in 1984. As a result of that action, the monopoly no longer existed, and the telecommunications industry exploded with innovation so dramatically that in just 16 years, many of the most successful and entrepreneurial companies on earth are those associated with telecommunications.

The more entrenched monopoly power of the U.S. Post Office survived the bear market of the 1970s, but it might not have if the decline had been one degree larger. In 1970, the two-century old U.S. Post Office was transformed from an agency of the executive branch of the U.S. government to a "quasi-independent postal corporation" modeled after a private-sector firm. At the same time, notes a "History of the Postal Monopoly in the United States" from the *Journal of Law and Economics,* the governors of the new U.S. Postal Service established a regulation allowing them "to surrender bits and pieces of their exclusive grant to preserve the substance of the monopoly." It adopted this policy to head off a rising chorus of public attacks on the Postal Service monopoly. As the law journal

**U.S. GOV'T
VS.
MONOPOLY
POWERS**

U.S. Postal Service
converted to a
quasi-private enterprise

Gov't sues AT&T
for monopolizing U.S.
telecommunications
&
effects a limited suspension of
prohibition on private
mail carriage

AT&T ordered to
divest Baby Bells

Gov't finds AT&T
in violation of the
Sherman Act

© May 2000 Elliott Wave International

Figure 2

history notes, the attacks themselves "are extraordinary because ever since its original colonial times, the postal monopoly has seemed inviolable." In 1973, the House of Representatives convened hearings on mail delivery restrictions that had been in place for more than 150 years. In October 1974, the very month of the bottom in the S&P, the first official suspension of prohibitions on private carriage were put into effect for certain items. As a result, Federal Express, UPS and even the Postal Service itself brought a burst of innovation to the delivery industry. Congress was still debating a number of bills calling for the privatization of mail delivery as late as June 1982, two months before the final low of a 16-year decline in real stock prices. Things changed when the social mood trend turned up. In October 1982, as the Dow made its first decisive rise above 1000, the Reagan administration "decided for now to de-emphasize its opposition to the U.S. Postal Service's mail monopoly."

Monopoly privileges stifle innovation, so when monopoly power is removed, an industry is allowed to develop. In contrast, upon every single antitrust action against successful *non*-monopoly corporations (see Figure 1), innovation did *not* immediately burst forth. The reason is that each of these successful companies, in a climate of free competition, was precisely the one responsible for the immense innovation that had already occurred. These disparate results confirm the difference between the two types of entities.

We can now see that the principle behind the government's actions with respect to these disparate entities is the same: At tops, the government *initiates* force to stifle free competition and success; at bottoms, it *removes* force that has stifled free competition and success. This latter impetus takes two forms: withdrawing antitrust actions against successful non-monopoly companies and dissolving actual monopolies. With this knowledge, we again have the ability to do some limited probabilistic forecasting both in terms of predicting actions against monopolies and predicting major social mood changes when those actions occur.

The Timing of Bailouts

In the past three decades, the U.S. government has taken to bailing out losing enterprises. These actions derive from the same egalitarian impulse behind its attacks on successful companies at major social mood tops. Rather than acting to prevent *success*, though, the government acts to prevent *failure*. The overall economic result is still destructive, as saving one enterprise endangers its competitors and wastes both productive resources and tax money at the same time, but this fact is irrelevant to the socionomic observation that impulsive social mood is the engine of these actions.

When do bailouts occur? Bailouts occur near stock market lows, when the mood is the opposite of that near peaks. As you can see in Figure 3, Lockheed Aircraft and Penn Central Railroad applied for aid in March and May 1970, as the stock market was crashing into its biggest low in 28 years. (Aid was approved in December 1970 and August 1971.) In another

Figure 3

bailout of Penn Central and several other northeastern railroads, Congress created Conrail in 1974, the final year of the biggest bear market since 1937-1942. (It took two separate "federal investments" of $2.1 billion in 1976 and $1.2 billion in 1980, as real stock prices continued falling, to keep Conrail on track.) The government's initial rescue of Continental Illinois bank came in May 1984, at the bottom of a fear-laden "wave two" stock market correction. (It was completed with a $4.5 billion FDIC package in late July.) Following the 1987 crash and the sluggish, mostly sideways year of 1988, Congress established the Resolution Trust Corporation on February 6, 1989 to bailout a slew of failed savings and loan institutions. Its creation marked the beginning of the biggest financial bailout in U.S. history. The crisis lasted through the 1990 bear market (which brought the Value Line index down to its 1987 low and cut the Transportation Average in half) and abated by mid-1993, when the RTC had liquidated or paid off the debts of 90% of the failed institutions it had taken over.

Although a bailout involves the use of force — taking tax money and using it to shore up an enterprise that no one will support voluntarily — it is *psychologically* the opposite of an attack. While free competition in fact requires allowing failure, the force wielded by the government is *intended*, however erroneously, to benefit competition by keeping the number of competitors in the marketplace higher than it would be otherwise. These actions, therefore, are consistent with the socionomic hypothesis that their origin is psychological.

A Comment on the Breadth of Mood Causality with Respect to Pro- and Anti-Corporate Sentiment

Although the data available for this report pertain to government actions, results of social mood change with respect to the treatment of corporations are not confined to acts of the state. The changes in social mood that govern antitrust action are broadly experienced by the populace and have other effects.

During a major topping and declining mood trend, all kinds of sociological forces work against corporations that are visibly successful. Exactly which companies may be affected by the social mood change from bull to bear is probably unpredictable, but the mood will have its way with *some* entities or other.

For example, in the bear market environment of the early 1970s, countless people were apoplectic over an irrational fear that ITT (the International Telephone and Telegraph company), which had begun a program of taking over smaller companies, would "take over the world." It was considered an immense threat. College students fretted over it, and talk show hosts discussed it continually. ITT must have been mystified. In the end, it never threatened anyone but its own employees, as its fortunes flagged and its business focus narrowed to hotels and casinos. In 1998, ITT itself was taken over by a relatively obscure REIT.

As another example, in the past twelve months, Coca-Cola has experienced both widespread panic in Europe over a supposedly tainted product and protest marches in the United States over purported discriminatory hiring practices. The panic proved to be based primarily upon fantasy, and the hiring practices under protest have been in place throughout the bull market without similar consequence.

Evidence that mood change alone has compelled these actions in each case is the fact that they were based on *nothing new that was tangible*. The waxing negative social *mood* generated negative social *action*. ITT and Coke just happened to become targets. The stated reasons for public dissatisfaction were not actually *reasons* but *rationalizations* by frantic neocortexes that found themselves thrust into the position of having to objectify a mood that was forcing its way out of their hosts' limbic systems. (For more on this mechanism, see Chapter 8 of *The Wave Principle of Human Social Behavior*.)

When social mood is early in a positive trend, the same thing happens, but in reverse. Can anyone really justify the deeply sentimental mood with which flavored sugar water has managed to become associated in the minds of people around the world? (For a case study on the Coca-Cola phenomenon, see the December 1999 issue of *The Elliott Wave Financial Forecast*.) A socionomist recognizes that the waxing benevolent mood trend associated with the bull market appears first. The objects of its focus (whether it be pop drinks or pop stars) find themselves in the right place at the right time and exploit it.

Practical Value in the Socionomic Perspective

Imagine the value of a knowledge of socionomics to enterprises designed *consciously* to harness the social mood trend. Even the one small observation presented in this paper would help the typical company. It would have a handle on when to increase its public presence and when to hold back. It would know when to push products and services attuned to the bull market mood and when to push products and services attuned to the bear market mood.

Let's try a practical application in our own small way. Now that we know the implication of major antitrust actions for the position of the social mood trend, we can anticipate that two to five years from now, the stock market is likely to be much lower than it is today. Conversely, when today's antitrust acrimony dissolves, the next bull market will be just around the corner. If we arrange our financial affairs to take advantage of this high probability, we stand an excellent chance of benefiting from it.

Kendall

The Elliott Wave Financial Forecast
July 20, 2000

New Assault on U.S. Corporations Confirms Microsoft Sell Signal

In May, *The Elliott Wave Theorist* analyzed more than a century of U.S. antitrust activity and found the government's case against Microsoft to be a socionomic confirmation of a significant stock market peak. Figure 1 in our "Socionomic Perspective on the Microsoft Case" shows the succession of antitrust actions at the start of major bear markets since 1889. The report explains that at the onset of a market top of Cycle degree or larger, a "new punitive mood bursts forth. One result of this metamorphosis in social character is governmental attack against the most successful enterprises. In fact, they typically start with a major attack against *the* most successful enterprise of the time." Within days of publication, Judge Thomas Penfield Jackson brought "the harshest penalty possible" against Microsoft, the dominant firm in the fastest growing segment of the U.S. economy. By ordering a break-up of the software giant, he "rubber-stamped" every aspect of the U.S. Justice Department's proposed penalty and issued one of history's most definitive long term stock market sell signals. The fact that the judge is a conservative Reagan appointee shows the power of social mood even over ideology.

In addition to signaling the start of a bear market, initial major antitrust cases mark a re-awakening in the antitrust movement as a whole. That's one reason that our May issue called for "continual government attacks on corporate success from the time of a stock market top." At this point, we should begin seeing an extension of the attack beyond Microsoft, and that is exactly what has been happening. Recent headlines have unveiled the gathering of anti-business forces in a wide range of social realms. In politics, the Vice President of the United States and Democratic candidate for President has adopted a "strategy of turning big business into [the] boogeyman" by launching a succession of attacks against drug, gun, HMO and oil companies. For the first time, a jury has reached "a reasoned and unanimous conviction to punish the tobacco industry." The $145 billion judgment is 30 times greater than the previous record and well beyond the companies' capacity to pay. The foreman explained the verdict as a matter of attitude and emotion. "It was insulting. It's just the tobacco industry's mentality, that they are beyond challenge. No one has ever challenged them and won." In another break from the former bull market mood, anti-trust authorities have set their sights on the electronic frontier. European and U.S. authorities have decided to scrutinize the "growing number of Internet business-to-business exchanges" for illegally colluding on prices and sharing purchasing services. The credit card industry has seen yet another milestone. The government is taking on card giants Visa and Mastercard for "collusion" in their control of 75% of the market. According to the U.S. Justice Department suit, the consortium of 7,000 banks that shares ownership of both groups is a "duality" that stifles competition. As *The Elliott Wave Theorist* noted with regard to recent attacks on Coca-Cola, this is further evidence of a waxing negative social mood because it is based on absolutely "nothing new that is tangible." According to the earliest market share data that we could find (from the Credit Card Management newsletter), Visa and Mastercard had the same 75% share of the industry in 1986. In fact, as the dominant credit card issuers since the 1970s, Visa and Mastercard have been the backbone of the consumer credit economy since the inception of Cycle wave V in 1974.

Mergers and Mood

One way legal historians have quantified progress and regress in the U.S. antitrust movement is the amount of merger activity. Many have documented an inverse relationship whereby as antitrust activity rises, mergers "disappear." In our research for the May issue, we found the data on mergers for Figures 1 through 3 in a book on federal antitrust policy. The data for the most recent bull market is updated from the February issue of *The Elliott Wave Financial Forecast*. If you put each of these charts up against Figure 1 from the May *Elliott Wave Theorist* depicting antitrust suits and conciliations, you will see how beautifully they fill in the blank spots, i.e. the major bull markets.

In light of this century-long correlation between the number of mergers and rising stock prices, another major confirmation of a reversal in social mood is a recent outbreak of anti-merger fever. Within the last few weeks, the U.S. authorities have blocked WorldCom's purchase of Sprint, H.J. Heinz's purchase of BeechNut Nutrition and the $6 billion combination of the Burlington Northern Santa Fe and the Canadian National Railway, which

NUMBER OF U.S. CORPORATE MERGERS AGAINST THE DOW
© July 2000 Elliott Wave International

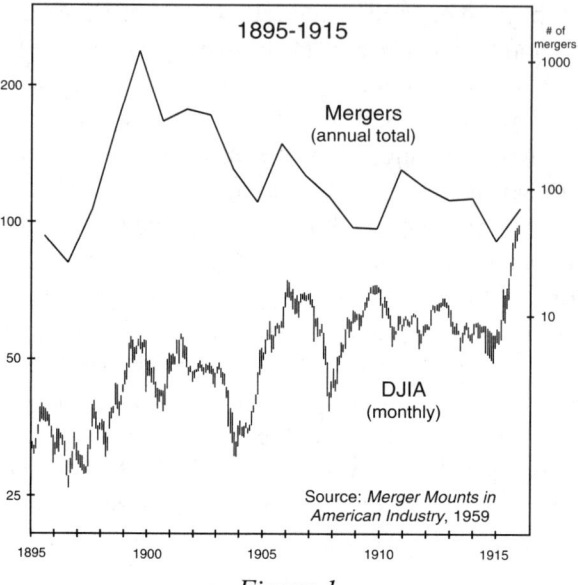

Figure 1

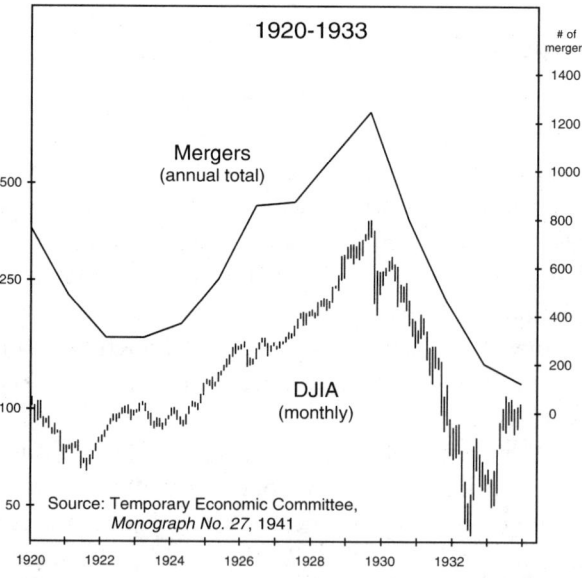

Figure 2

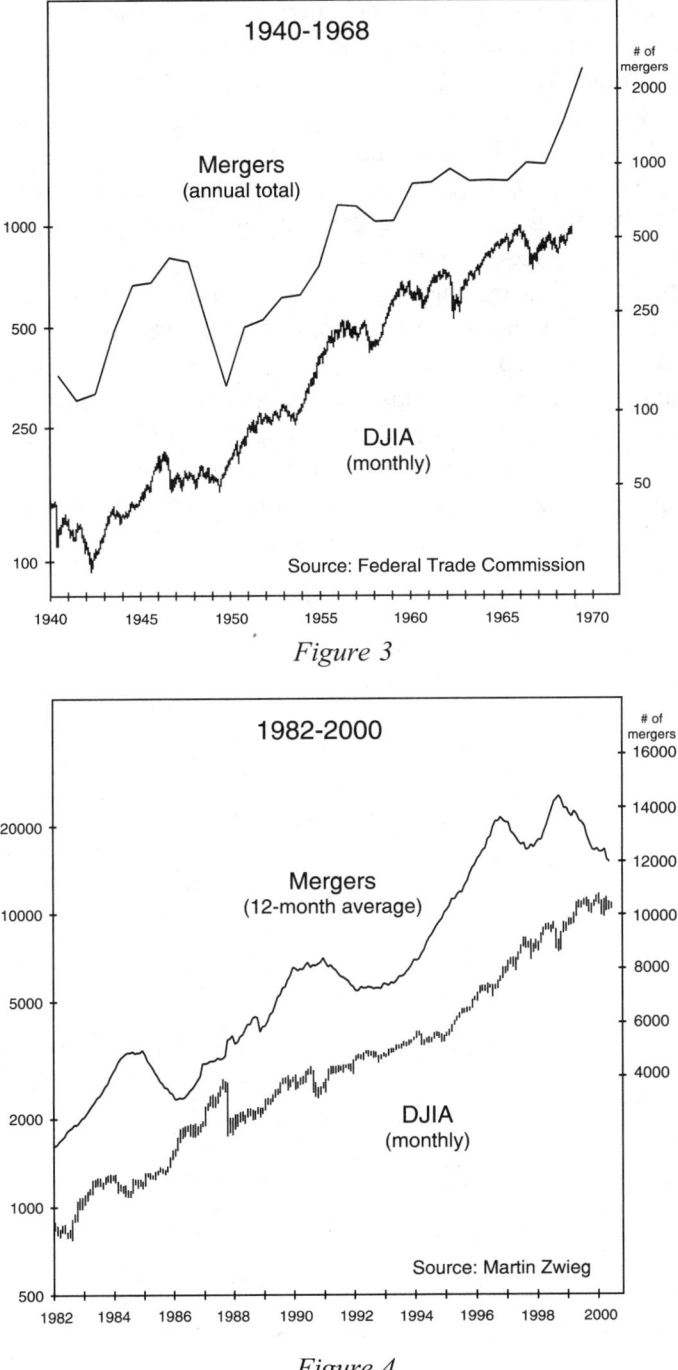

Figure 3

Figure 4

would have been the biggest railroad combination in history. Several other deals that would have met with no resistance in the late 1980s and 1990s, including United Airlines' buyout of US Air, AOL's merger with Time Warner and Bell Atlantic's bid for GTE, are now being challenged by various federal agencies. The SEC and Federal Accounting Standards Board have undermined the potential for *any* more record breaking deals with an attack on the "pooling of interest" accounting method that has allowed countless firms to make acquisitions with their inflated stock rather than with cash or debt. "During the topping and declining mood trend, all kinds of sociological forces work against corporations that are visibly successful," EWT said in May. Support, cooperation and synthesis give way to divisiveness and resentment. In the last two months, the speed and scope of this social change has clearly accelerated. Once the judge threw the book at Microsoft, it was as if he had declared "open season" on mergers and cooperative business relationships. This massive social change in attitude is consistent with the transition to a bear market in stocks.

The Elliott Wave Financial Forecast
June 2001

The Land of Flint and Steel

Global conflict is a product of a downturn in social mood. The inescapable tensions between nations and distinct social groups that arise at such times is best illustrated by our long term chart of the "Political Results of Social Sentiment" (see page 337 of *The Wave Principle of Human Social Behavior* or the June, 2000 issue of *The Elliott Wave Financial Forecast*), which shows Hitler's rise to power, World War II, the Holocaust and the dropping of two atomic bombs on Japan between the bear market lows of 1932, 1942 and 1949.

Social clashes take myriad forms, but one bellwether rift that has an almost perfect record of erupting into open hostility right at the onset of major downturns is in the Mideast. Figure 1 shows that relations between Jews and Arabs in Israel (or Palestine before 1948) have been particularly responsive to the onset of important bear markets since 1929. In that year, says *The Year of the Great Crash*, "All hell had broken loose in Palestine. At the end of August, a series of relatively inconsequential disputes concerning the privileges of worship for Jews and Muslims erupted into an orgy of bloodletting." The violence came a few days before the Dow's final high.

If major hostilities are defined as wars or mob violence that result in mass killings, each of the headlines on the graph marks a significant outbreak. All were preceded by periods of easing tension (or at least an absence of bloodshed) and followed by further clashes. The greatest stretch of peaceful cooperation between the two sides is shown in the Era of Good Feelings table at the bottom of Figure 1. It started on September 13, 1993 with the famous handshake between the Prime Minister of Israel and the Chairman of the Palestine Liberation Organization. Historians said the handshake was a symbol of "a major breakthrough after a century of conflict." *The Elliott Wave Theorist* identified it as a product of the century-long advance in stock prices that would mark a long-term top rather than a great new era for Palestinian and Israeli relations. The next seven years of bull market yielded

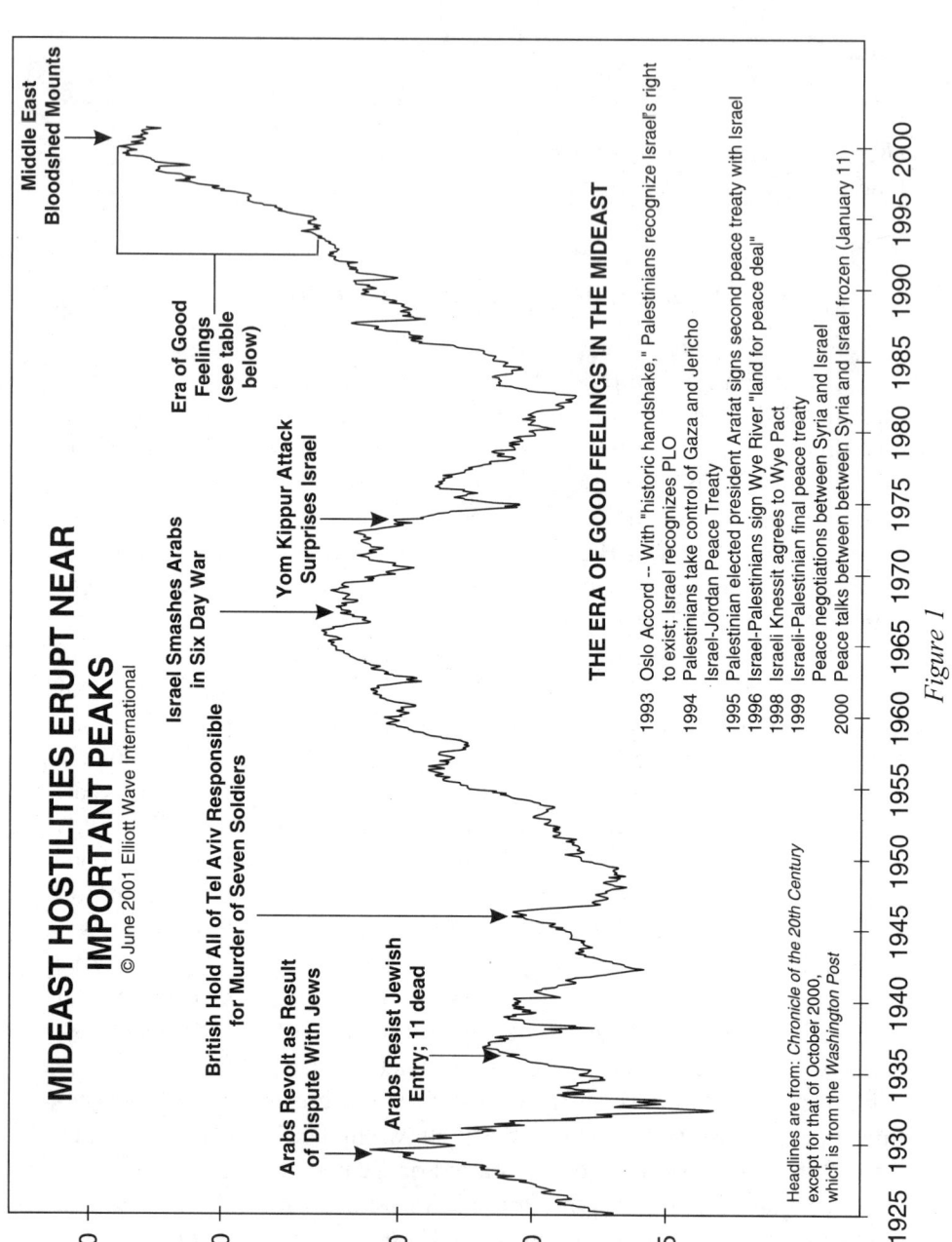

Figure 1

productive talks but no lasting peace. As late as January 30, 2000, the *Houston Chronicle* reported that the "tide of history" was moving the "Mideast toward peace."

In reality, however, the tide had already reversed. In July 2000, the same paper would mark the moment by reporting, "Syrian-Israeli peace negotiations have been frozen since mid-January." The exact date of the freeze was January 11, *three days before the Dow's all-time high*. By last summer, the anxiety level was clearly rising fast as the Palestinians threatened to declare statehood and another peace conference failed to produce a breakthrough for the first time since 1993. As stocks entered their September-October swoon, Palestinian sections of Israel exploded in a continuous wave of rioting. In December, this headline evidenced the depth of anger: "As Arafat Embraces Revolt, His Sagging Popularity Rises." Israel responded with the election of hardliner Ariel Sharon. In the first half of May 2001, the situation bordered on open warfare. "Is It War Yet?" asked one headline on May 20. On May 21, the Bush administration criticized Israel for using U.S. supplied warplanes against Palestinians for the first time since the 1967 war, which was a year after the peak of Cycle III. Finally, on May 22, the day of the Dow's secondary high, there was a "glimmer of hope" as Sharon talked of compromise and ordered Israeli forces "only to return fire if shot at."

Past signals have usually come at and after long term turns, although the 1967 outbreak was followed by a run that almost made a new high in 1968. Given that precedent, perhaps the unfolding crisis in the Mideast does not preclude a new high in the Dow. If the Dow goes to a new high, the conflict may ease briefly, but a historic sell signal for the stock market has clearly been issued by the open warfare. The Mideast's record as an *early* register of negative social mood suggests that a major bear market and thus the trend toward global hostility has only just begun.

Prechter

The Elliott Wave Theorist
September 11, 2001

Elliott Waves and Social Reality

*We here at EWI have lost dear friends in the World Trade Center attack.
We grieve for them and for those of you who have suffered the loss of
loved ones.*

As terrible as today's tragedy is, we must pause to point out another
tragedy, which is that so few understand why it happened, what will happen next and what they can do about it. This issue of *The Elliott Wave
Theorist* will try to present an unemotional account of these issues.

Sometimes it takes an appalling drama to stir people from lethargy
and make them pay attention to matters of grave importance. If your friends
and family have yet to wake up to the Wave Principle's crucial message,
please do your part to help them realize where we are in the social cycle
and why it matters. For this issue, we will suspend our ban against re-
transmission so that you may distribute it to others as you see fit.

Comfort and safety come from *understanding.* If you can see the big
picture clearly, both past and future, you will be able to make fruitful decisions calmly.

As this issue is being composed and issued in a single day, please
excuse any passages that appear rough or incautious.

Understanding the Engine of Social Trends

The radical thesis of *The Wave Principle of Human Social Behavior
and the New Science of Socionomics* (New Classics Library, 1999) was
unmistakably manifest in the raucous social comedy of the 1990s, and now
it is playing out in the first act of a developing worldwide social tragedy
that will last years. The primary thesis of this book is that *changes in social
mood **cause** and therefore **precede** changes in the character of social events*.
In contrast to this idea, most people erroneously try to divine the implications of events in attempts to forecast financial markets and people's
collective feelings. Their approach *cannot* work because *markets are driven*

by natural trends in mass psychology, and events resulting from those psychological trends come *afterward*. It is the changes in such trends, as indicated by turns in the stock market, that signal a coming change in the tenor of social events.

An equally radical thesis underlying socionomics is that *social mood is patterned, and it is patterned according to the Wave Principle*. Since these patterned mood trends precipitate social events, you can *forecast the character of social events* by tracking the trends and patterns in the primary meter of social mood, the stock market.

The Wave Principle of Human Social Behavior explained why global atrocities *followed* the 1929-1932 crash and continued during most of the rest of the bear market pattern, which ended in 1949. It also explained why the worldwide peace initiatives and unprecedented acts of reconciliation of the 1990s *followed* nearly half a century of social mood uptrend. The dramatic, historic pictures shown in Chapter 18 of that book convey the power of these moods were not placed there simply for academic purposes. This is real life we're talking about. You have to live near those events to sense that fact.

Forecasting the Tenor of Social Events

Such observations have not simply been reflections on the past. In 1982, *The Elliott Wave Theorist* forecast a rising stock market, boom times and "no war for at least ten years."[1]

At the Crest of the Tidal Wave (1995) then forecast the next major change, saying in no uncertain terms that severe social unrest would follow the onset of what was then the approaching — and is now the developing — Grand Supercycle bear market. Here is the book's introduction to that topic:

SOCIAL IMPLICATIONS [excerpted from *At the Crest of the Tidal Wave*, pp.432-433]

While the Wave Principle is the single best method for anticipating the behavior of markets, its value at times goes way beyond even that great benefit. As explained in Chapter 12, the effects that a change in market trend will have on society are not in evidence at the start of the trend. They become intensely manifest by the time of its termination. Is it too early to begin projecting events that will result from the approaching bear market in social mood? To be sure, this book contains dozens of very specific financial forecasts, which are at root social phenomena. Forecasting social events outside that realm, however, is an even more complex and less exact science. Nevertheless, a few observations appear suited to the limited scope of this book.

A long term trend toward a positive social mood always leads to times of peace and political cooperation, such as we enjoy today. An extreme trend change in social mood toward the negative always leads to calamities. The average level of conflict during the bear market will be far greater than it was during the bull market and will lead to periods of turmoil, not just in financial markets, but in society. Indeed, the trends now implied by long term market patterns have *always* produced dramatic social upheaval. The last time a bear market of the currently projected magnitude took place was 1720 to 1784, a period that began with a market crash, ended with the Revolutionary War, and led to a deep and global five-year depression.

The coming trend of negative social psychology will be characterized primarily by polarization between and among various perceived groups, whether political, ideological, religious, geographical, racial or economic. The result will be a net trend toward anger, fear, intolerance, disagreement and exclusion, as opposed to the bull market years, whose net trend has been toward benevolence, confidence, tolerance, agreement and inclusion. Such a sentiment change typically brings conflict in many forms, and evidence of it will be visible in all types of social organizations. Political manifestations will include protectionism in trade matters, a polarized and vocal electorate, separatist movements, xenophobia, citizen-government clashes, the dissolution of old alliances and parties, and the emergence of radical new ones. Tariffs will become popular, regardless of the fact that virtually everyone knows they are dangerous and wrong, because they are a consequence of an increasingly negative psychology involving fear, envy and a misguided attempt at self-defense. Xenophobia will be practiced regardless of people's generally good intentions, because fear and hatred become pervasive in major bear markets regardless of whether or not they are justified. There will also be a danger that governments will impose police-state type controls as a consequence of the bear market. Such periods often end with emotional political oustings, whether by vote, resignation, impeachment, coup or revolution.

The worst economic and social programs are years away, but advance planning is incalculably better than trying to react when it is too late.

Predicting Wave Form

At the Crest detailed a number of specific forecasts with respect to the bear market, including the expected pattern of the entire wave, the likely years for the end of each wave, downside price targets in the Dow, etc. (For a diagram, see Figure 5-12 in the book.) One of the most specific predictions was this one, showing the exact form that the first wave down would take:

How the Pattern Will Start [excerpted from *At the Crest*, p.82]
Regardless of which specific long-term pattern ultimately unfolds at Grand Supercycle degree, there is no question that the first (or only, under the milder scenario) Supercycle degree decline will be of the *zigzag* family. It will be composed of *three* waves, to be labeled A-B-C or W-X-Y. **Every initial decline through Primary degree** (the "first" waves), and probably through Cycle degree (wave A), **will be composed of *five* waves in order to be compatible with the larger trend.** The declines of 1929 and 1937-1938 were "A" waves within Supercycle and Cycle degree bear markets respectively. Figures 5-8 and 5-9 show pictures of what these first declining waves looked like. **Expect the first major decline of the coming bear market to reflect the form of these waves.**

Figures 1 and 2 reproduce these illustrations, and Figures 3 and 4 show the recent development of S&P and NASDAQ price change from those indexes' all-time highs in the first quarter of 2000. Can you see that they are the same Elliott wave form? And it was *predictable*.

Wave Form as the Key to More Specific Timing in Social Forecasting

An Elliott wave analyst can even put a fine point on when the best and worst social times will occur. The *Human Social Behavior* book explains that wars always erupt during or immediately after "C" waves in bear markets of Cycle degree or larger. More important, *the bigger the corrective process, the bigger the war*. We are in only wave (a) of the Grand Supercycle bear market, which will have to do mostly with *financial* destruction. So shocking though they may be, events to date are in fact correspondingly and comparatively mild, like Hitler's takeover of Czechoslovakia was to ensuing events within Supercycle wave (IV). Within wave (a), wave **c**, which should unfold from 2002 to 2004, will bring greater acts of conflict and instances of physical danger. Yet as *At the Crest* explained, the worst global horrors — and this is good news for now — will not occur until

Examples of "How the Pattern Will Start," as shown in At the Crest of the Tidal Wave (1995)

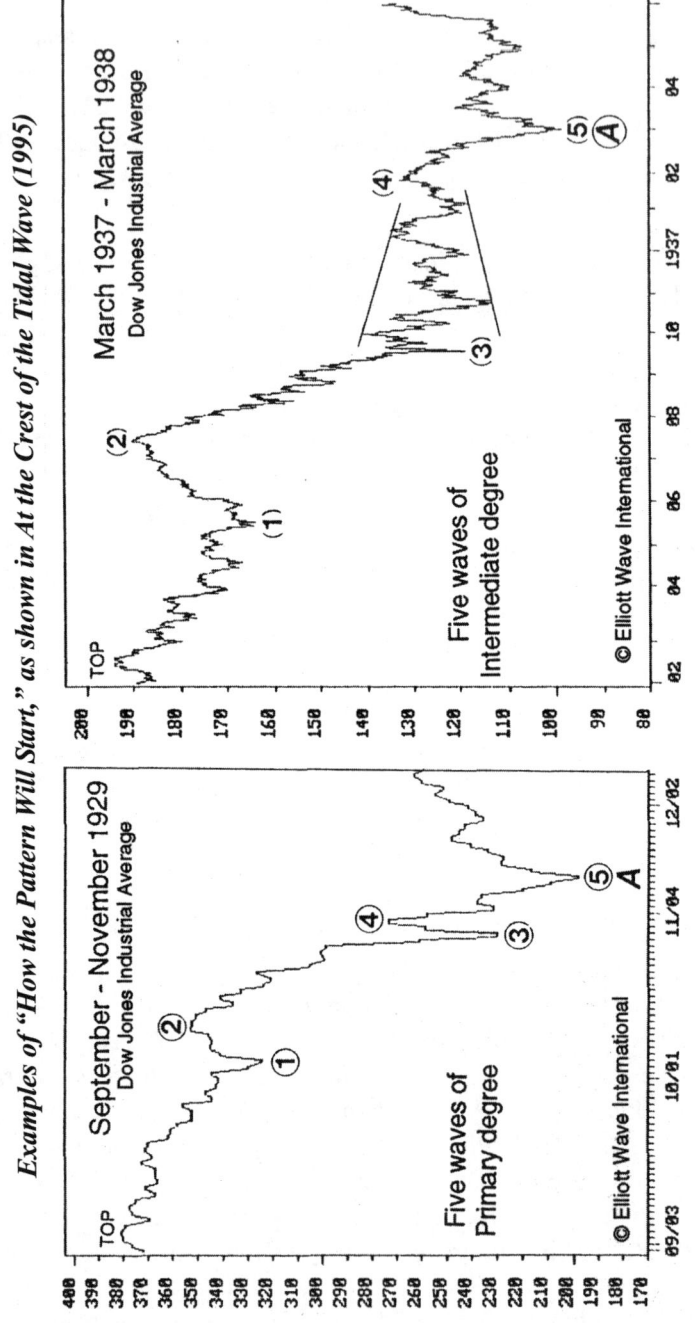

Figure 2

Figure 1

Initial pattern nearly fulfilled in five waves of Primary degree since 1Q 2000:
(Data through 9/11/01)

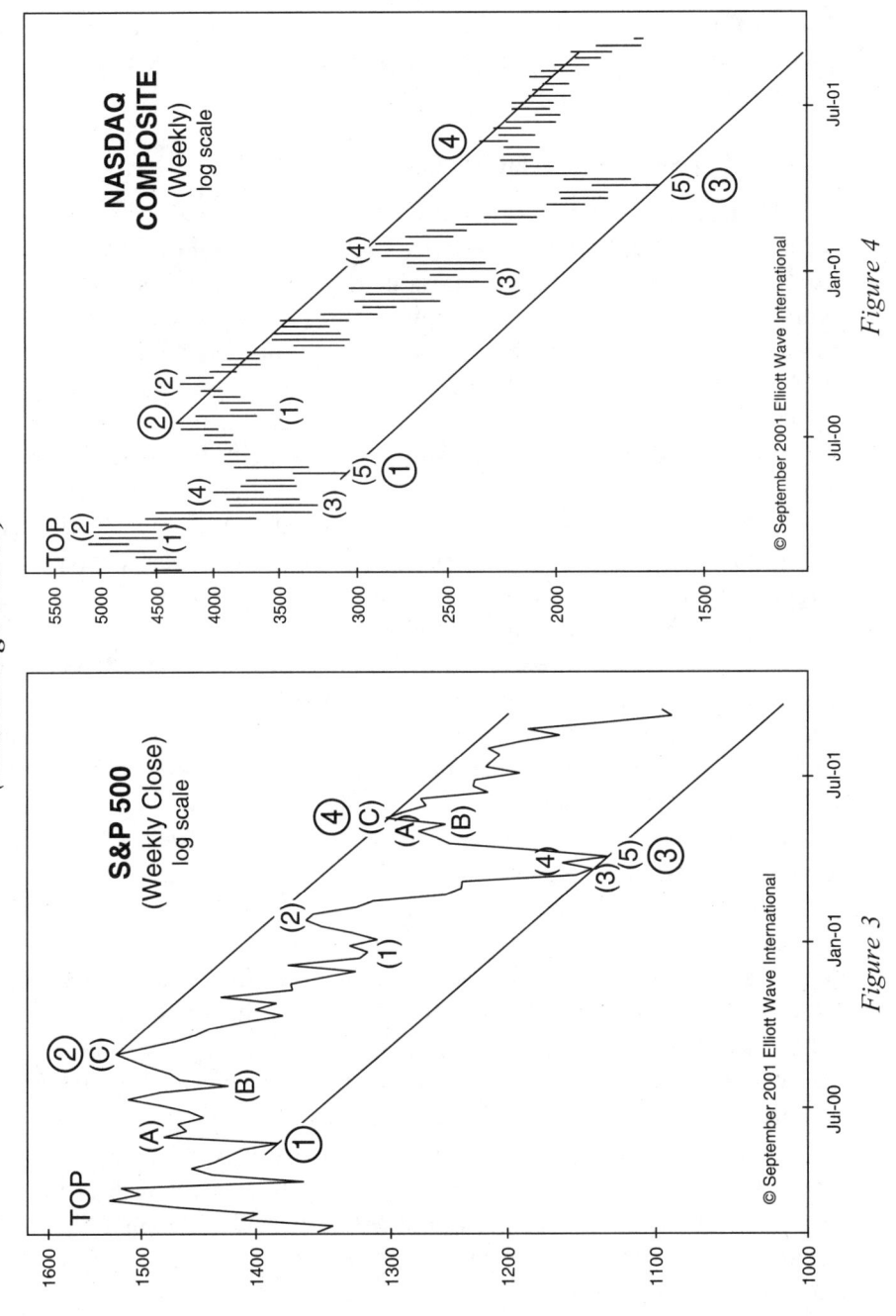

Figure 3

Figure 4

wave (c) of the entire Grand Supercycle, which is not due for several decades. The diagram in Figure 5 shows in detail what I consider a likely
pattern for Grand Supercycle wave Ⓘ.

Forecasting Styles of Social Events

Here is another esoteric point but one of great value. A section on
"Nuances" in Chapter 15 of *The Wave Principle of Human Social Behavior*
explains that negative social themes due to appear in any approaching bear
market first express themselves in milder form in the preceding fourth wave
of one lesser degree. Stop for a minute until you get this idea. Here is a
more detailed explanation: Social mood repeatedly traces out five waves
up followed by three waves down. The negative themes in "wave four"
within the "fives waves up" presage those that will dominate, *more dramatically and on a much bigger scale*, in the ensuing "three waves down."

This is true of the styles of cultural trends. For example, *Psycho* came
out in 1962, at the end of a fourth wave correction of Primary degree. In the
larger bear market of 1966-1982, slasher films (the *Halloween* and *Friday
the 13th* series) were a dominant theme.

It is also true of the character of social events. In an earlier fourth
wave from 1916 to 1921, collectivists took over Russia. In the larger fourth
wave that followed, from 1929 to 1949, collectivists took over nearly half
of the earth's population, in Germany, Italy, Eastern Europe and China.

In the current case, the most recent fourth wave of Cycle degree or
higher took place from 1966 to 1982, roughly, "the '70s." Aside from a
slew of terrorist incidents in the 1910s,[2] a decade dominated by a long bear
market in stocks, *the idea of "terrorism" as a social force began with the
1966-1982 bear market*. A 10-volume chronology of American social history over the last 100 years (*American Decades*, Manly, Inc.) lists *no* acts
of terrorism in the 1920s, 1930s, 1940s, 1950s or the 1960s. In early 1970,
when the Dow was in year four and the Value Line Composite in year two
of a Cycle-degree bear market, the age of terrorism began. An Arab terrorist strike killed one person and injured 23 in Munich. On February 21,
1970, another group of suspected Arab terrorists hijacked a Swissair flight
and crashed it. On September 6-9, 1970, Palestinian terrorists hijacked five
planes and blew up three. Unlike the earlier period of "scattered terrorist
bombings" in the 1910s, this era was distinguished by the frequency, extent and organization behind the attacks. As the bear market continued, the
events grew in size and complexity. The increasing sophistication of terrorist tactics and their rising political power is revealed by the progression

from the scattered strikes in 1970 to the PLO raid on the Olympic Village in Munich in 1972 and eventually to a state-sponsored takeover of the U.S. embassy in Iran in 1979. The worst of it ended approximately when the bear market did, as Iran finally released its U.S. hostages in January 1981. In those first terrorist acts committed against the United States, we caught a glimpse of the style of conflicts that we would have to endure when the bear market of next bigger size arrived, which it certainly has.

Neither is this point made only in retrospect. Our recent publications have speculated as to specific social actions that will take place during Grand Supercycle wave ⒾⓋ, and *The Wave Principle of Human Social Behavior* listed events typically associated with major bull and bear markets. Two excerpted comments summarize the scene that has just come to pass:

> "Foreigners will commit terrorist acts on U.S. soil...."
> — *At the Crest of the Tidal Wave* (1995)
> Chapter 21, p.435

> "The impulse to build shows up in the construction of record-break-ing skyscraper buildings at social-mood peaks. At troughs, few buildings are built, and many of those already in place may be burned or bombed out of existence."
> — *The Wave Principle of Human Social Behavior and the New Science of Socionomics* (1999)
> Chapter 14, pp.229-230

Here is a summary of today's event, which truly is "more dramatic and on much bigger scale" than those that occurred during the previous fourth wave of the 1970s:

> New York, Sept. 11 (Bloomberg) — The attacks on the World Trade Center and Pentagon today are the worst acts of terrorism ever on U.S. soil and change the scope of foreign policy, experts say.

> Never before has a large-scale terrorist attack on the U.S. been co-ordinated successfully in more than one U.S. city. At this point, no organization has taken responsibility.

> "It's just an attack of extraordinarily sophisticated planning," said Michael R. Fischbach, a professor of history specializing in the Middle East at Randolph-Macon College in Ashland, Virginia. "The world that we know has now changed."

> "Americans' whole attitude about daily life, about foreign policy will be forever changed," Fischbach said.

"The world that we know has changed" is a correct statement, but it did not change "now." It changed between January 14 and March 24, 2000, a two-month period during which the three major U.S. stock indexes signaled the end of a Grand Supercycle uptrend that had been in force for *216 years*. We are only now beginning to feel the lagging results of that change.

The 1966-1982 period had many other unfortunate characteristics that we will see again to a larger extent in the current bear market. At *Grand Supercycle degree*, however, the "preceding fourth wave" actually refers to 1929-1949. As the Grand Supercycle bear market pattern unfolds over the next few generations, eventually it will bring on the kinds of conflicts that ruled *that* correction.

Do you recognize the value of this information? Most people understandably fret over whether or not an action is "a one-time event" and speculate on whether "the worst is over" without *any idea* of how to answer these questions. Socionomics can answer them, and it does. Right now, we can say with confidence, *we are at the beginning of a long period of social unrest, and while it will wax and wane with the waves, overall it will intensify*. The best time to prepare was two years ago, but it is *not too late* to do so now.

Symbols as the Focus of Anger

During the 1990s, we studied the history of skyscraper construction and issued several reports on the correlation between the erection of tall buildings and the late stages of positive long-term social mood trends. As EWT stated in April 1996, "Of all the cultural relationships we consider here, the link between stock prices and the tallest buildings is one of the most fascinating because it is literally etched in stone." We concluded that skyscrapers are "monuments to peaking social mood." Some people take such studies as frivolous. They are not. Now that we are in a negative social mood trend of greater magnitude than any since the construction of the first skyscrapers in the 1890s, we should hardly be shocked that the forces expressing the emerging downtrend in mood have aimed their sights at these towering structures, symbols of the productive optimism of Grand Supercycle wave ⒾⒾⒾ.

Why Now?/What's Next?

Generally speaking, the most shocking news in the social context comes in two places: in declining *fifth* waves and in declining *C* waves. The stock market is not in a *C* wave. Since the all-time high, it has been in wave **a** of what will eventually be an **a-b-c** decline. *Within* wave **a**, it is almost certainly in wave 5, as you can see in Figures 3, 4 and 5.

If the stock market is indeed in wave 5 down, then this wave will end within days or weeks and lead to a substantial A-B-C rally (or perhaps a triangle) for wave **b**. Then wave **c** down will begin. If this assessment proves correct, it is good news for the short term. If instead, the "big crash" is upon us, we should know shortly after the markets' reopening. Rest assured that *The Elliott Wave Financial Forecast* (perhaps with an Interim Report) and the *Short Term Update* (to be published next on Wednesday night, whether markets are open or not) will keep you abreast of all our conclusions regarding the stock market, and bonds, gold and the U.S. dollar as well.

What To Do

We have already discussed in detail what you should do with respect to your finances. A full list of useful and necessary services is in the back of *At the Crest*. You can still study and act on our "Bear Market Strategies" page, which we composed a couple of years ago and have updated continually, in our "subscribers only" section at http://www.elliottwave.com/subscribers/subsonly.htm. [Note: These recommendations were expanded and published in *Conquer the Crash*. — Ed.]

What to do about your physical safety is a more difficult problem for most people. Obviously, living in a populous area or near a military or important infrastructural site is dangerous in times of social unrest. If you are tied to a job site, decisions are even more difficult. We will try to keep an eye on the world's social trends for you in coming issues of EWT, but I have no pretensions of being expert on physical safety. At best, we will try to direct you to those who are.

A Long Term Development

Today's terrorist focus on the United States is *not* an isolated, inexplicable situation. The founding fathers, notably George Washington and John Adams, warned our new country against foreign entanglements. They begged us, in Washington's words, "in regard to foreign nations...to have with them as little *political* connection as possible." (Source: http://www.virginia.edu/gwpapers/farewell/transcript.html.) Contrary to this advice, many U.S. presidents of the twentieth century, usually citing altruistic motives, have insinuated our government into foreign hives to such an ex-

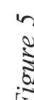

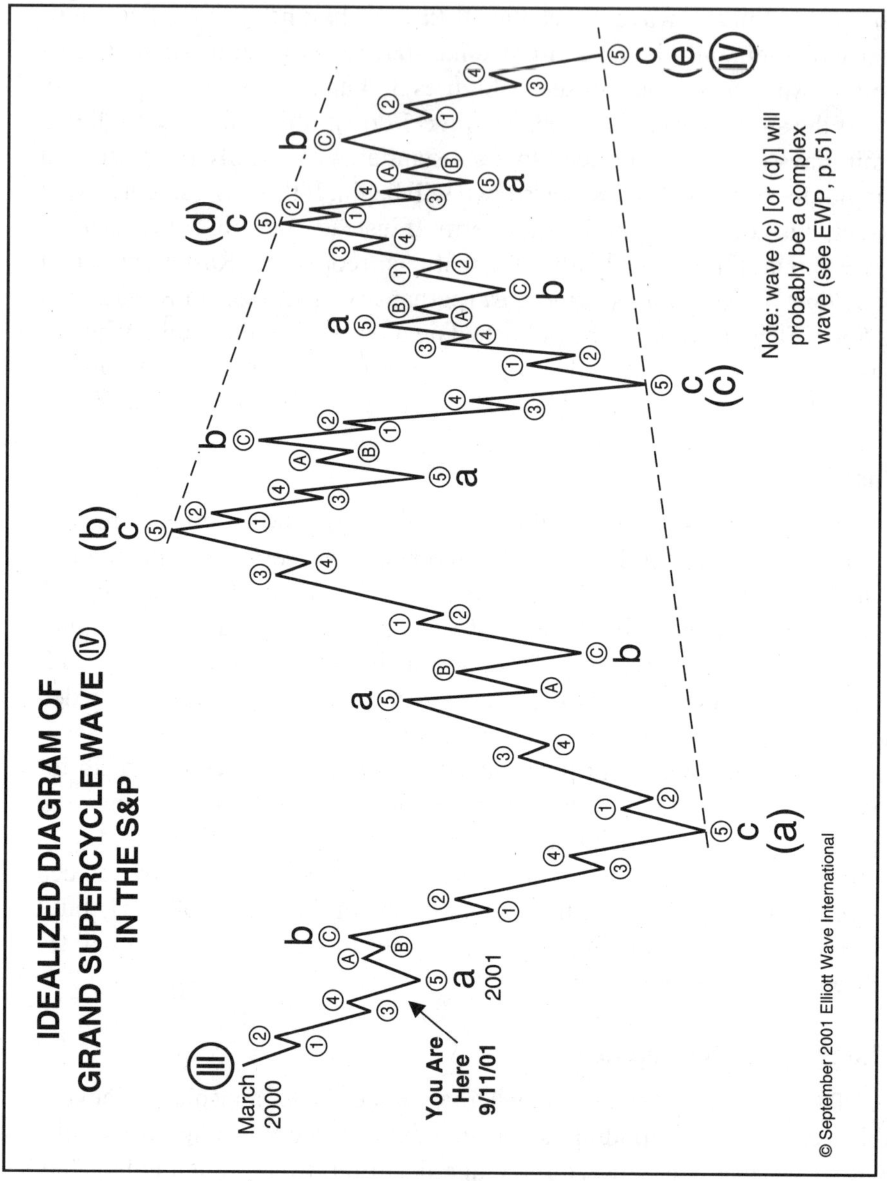
IDEALIZED DIAGRAM OF
GRAND SUPERCYCLE WAVE Ⓘⓥ
IN THE S&P
March
2000
You Are
Here
9/11/01
2001
Note: wave (c) [or (d)] will
probably be a complex
wave (see EWP, p.51)
© September 2001 Elliott Wave International

Figure 5

tent that we have finally stirred one set of bees into reacting. Though no one has yet "taken credit" for today's atrocities, the actions of the perpetrators are surely irrational, perhaps based on dreams of global domination or the hope of a glorious reward in the next world. That is, generally speaking, what the founding fathers feared: the mire of foreign political irrationality. The environment in which we are currently beginning to suffer results from decades of redirected government policy, and the underlying cause of *that* change is the initially brave but ultimately reckless set of shared emotions underlying the magnificent ascent of Grand Supercycle wave Ⅲ. This is not to affix blame on "us." Many everyday Americans have decried our "police the world" policies, and our leaders' penchant for well intentioned meddling has just been part of the social pattern. Its outcome was therefore predictable. Tens of times during the past decade, we at EWI cringed as our president issued yet another threatening ultimatum to various other countries' governments (at least seven, which we documented in EWT at the time). We thought, *"Does he know what this attitude will lead to, how many Americans it will ultimately endanger?"* All the while, and in keeping with the waxing mood of invincibility, our "fundamentals" — in terms of national intelligence, security and military preparedness — were going to seed. Don't let anyone tell you that these attacks and our lack of preparation are a surprise. They are the result of feelings of complacency and overconfidence born of the final decades of GS Ⅲ. Ironic as it may seem, the suffering in bear markets is greatly the consequence of cavalier policies adopted late in bull markets.

The Utility of Socionomics

Are Elliott waves and socionomics purely academic toys? They are not. Like good philosophy, they are not just *theoretically* correct; they are *practical* and useful in everyday life. At major junctures, understanding the change at hand can mean the difference between success and failure, life and death. The people who started successful businesses in 1949 and 1982 or went bankrupt in 1933 and 1975 understand the first point. The people who got out of Europe in 1938, or who stayed there, would understand the second.

In coming months and years, others will be repeatedly shocked over "surprising" single events, which they do not understand as being part of a larger pattern. At least you will know *that* we are in a pattern and even, most of the time, *where* we are in it. From that, you can make important decisions that will guide your life.

Getting the Word Out

In response to a question about how EWT's long-term stock market forecast would be remembered, the February 2000 issue responded as follows:

> "Most people will not be paying as much attention to the stock market after it falls, so in a few years, *most of today's investors will not care who predicted what. Their focus will be on other things.*"

People have also asked me in the past two years why I have stayed off television. Forecasting unrest during good times is like singing to rocks. Nobody's listening. Then once the unrest begins, you can't be heard over the cacophony. Everyone's singing, and most of it is off key. Besides, you cannot communicate a book like *At the Crest*, much less *The Wave Principle of Human Social Behavior*, in 2½ minutes. You have to sit down and read them.

If anyone asks you why these things are happening, just give them one short answer: *"Read Prechter's socionomics book."* This is not an ad for the sake of selling books; we don't make much money on book sales. The point is to help people understand an important aspect of life and perhaps save their own. Tell anyone you know that they can have it for half price, if they mention this issue of *The Elliott Wave Theorist*. Then tell them, "Yes, you should have read it two years ago. But better late than never."

NOTES

[1] Prechter, Robert R. (1982, October 6). *The Elliott Wave Theorist*

[2] The first act of terrorism listed in *American Decades* is the explosion of the Los Angeles Times Building in October 1910, which was linked to organized labor. The last one of note was a bomb that rocked Wall Street on September 16, 1920. The scars of that blast can still be seen in the façade of 23 Wall Street, then as now the offices of J.P. Morgan Inc. The financial attack centered on Wall Street became physically manifest. Almost the same thing has happened today.

The Elliott Wave Theorist
October 2001

World Peace, World War, Fibonacci and Elliott

U.S. President George W. Bush made two statements that, taken together, may turn out to be meaningful to history. He called the September 11 attacks "an act of war" and, speaking to all the governments of the world, said, "You are either with us, or you're with the terrorists." Taken together, these statements conjure the image of world war. Will this inference prove to be hyperbole or reality?

The 20th century was one of the most violent and deadly in history. Most of the deaths were not due to war, however; they were due to governments slaughtering their own people, primarily in the Soviet Union, Germany, China, and Cambodia (in that order). Nevertheless, the mortality rate in the 20th century's two world wars was substantial and dwarfed that of most previous wars. The last time that a war was as deadly for Americans as World War II was the Civil War. These wars followed the bottoms of Supercycle bear markets, waves (IV) and (II) respectively. (See Chapters 16 and 18 *The Wave Principle of Human Social Behavior*.)

Many are saying that the attack on the World Trade Center and the Pentagon is analogous to the Japanese attack on Pearl Harbor in 1941. If so, it is alike not only in the element of surprise but perhaps also in terms of sparking a world war. One significant difference between these two attacks is that this latest one was three times as deadly as that on Pearl Harbor.

So is the world headed for war, and if so, has it begun? This issue will explore a time progression that suggests that a world war has begun. It will also give reasons, based on the history of wars and their usual position in the Elliott wave pattern, for believing that the greater risk lies several decades in the future.

A Fibonacci Progression in War and Peace over the Past Century

As detailed in *The Wave Principle of Human Social Behavior*, the Fibonacci sequence governs many of the forms and processes within animate objects. It also governs aspects of aggregate human interaction, as indicated by the patterns of the Wave Principle. A growing body of evidence suggests that the *timing* of social change is governed to some degree by the Fibonacci sequence as well.

A Fibonacci number of days or years often separates major turning points in the stock market. Such durations are often tempered, slightly exceeding or falling short of precise Fibonacci numbers. Any difference is only one unit in durations up to 55 and expands thereafter accordingly. For example, the advance from the lowest point of Supercycle wave (II) in 1842 to the high of Supercycle wave (III) in 1929 took 87 years, which is **89** (-2) years. Within those parameters, the periods of world war and periods of relative world peace since 1914 seem to be governed by a Fibonacci progression, as detailed in Figure 1.

The assassination of Archduke Ferdinand of Austria in 1914 sparked World War I. World War II began when Hitler seized Austria in 1938 (but was not officially declared until 1939 upon the invasion of Poland). From their sparking points, these two wars lasted four years and seven years respectively, which are a Fibonacci **3** (+1) years and **8** (-1) years. The periods of world-scale peace that followed these wars lasted twenty years and fifty-six years (so far) respectively, which are a Fibonacci **21** (-1) years and **55** (+1) years. As shown in Figure 1, the two world-war durations skip a Fibonacci number (5), and the two peace durations (to date) skip a Fibonacci number as well (34).

Notice that each set of numbers alternates between +1 and -1 in the war durations and -1 and +1 in the peace durations. These differences cancel each other out in a sense, so that an idealized progression arrives at the same year, 2001. To illustrate, *if* the following durations had occurred, we would have ended up at the same point from 1914: World War I lasting **3** years to 1917, peace lasting **21** years to 1938, World War II lasting **8** years to 1946 and peace lasting **55** years to 2001. In other words, the Fibonacci progression 3+21+8+55 covers the ground from 1914 to 2001. The turn dates in history were off by one year each time, alternating between "long" and "short" periods.

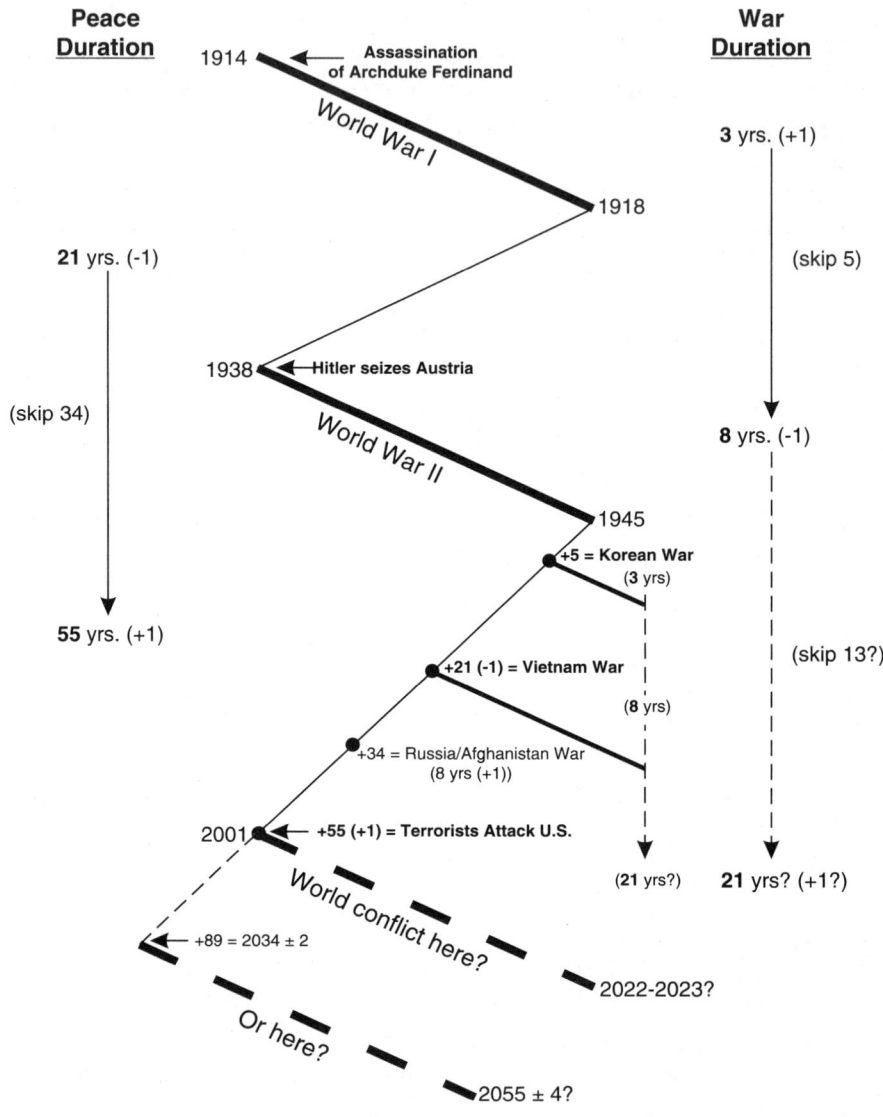

Figure 1

Subordinate Fibonacci Progressions in War Since 1945

The long period of relative worldwide peace from 1945 to 2001 was hardly benign. Lesser conflicts erupted that involved the United States. As you can see beside the "bullet" points in Figure 1, those conflicts occurred on a Fibonacci progression from 1945. The Korean War began **5** years after 1945, and the U.S. sent troops to begin the Vietnam War **21** (-1) years after 1945. (Also, the Indochina War began **1** year after 1945 and was a precursor to the Vietnam War. Russia invaded Afghanistan **34** years after 1945, which is a precursor of the current conflict.) Now after **55** years, a "War on Terrorism" may have begun.

Notice that the progression of U.S. involvement in important wars skips some of the Fibonacci numbers in this sequence. U.S. involvement begins with the Korean War after **5** years, skips 8 and 13, returns with the Vietnam War after **21** (-1) years, skips 34 and returns again with last month's terrorist attack after **55** (+1) years. Conflicts that did *not* fall on the Fibonacci progression, such as the Cuban Missile Crisis, the war in Grenada and the Persian Gulf War, caused very few U.S. casualties.

There is another progression. Each of these interim wars involving the U.S. lasted a Fibonacci number of years (+ or − 1). The Korean War lasted **3** years, and the U.S. fought the Vietnam War for **8** years. (Russia also fought Afghanistan for **8** (+1) years.) Notice that these durations — **3** and **8** — are the same as those for World Wars I and II. Like the first progression, this one also implies a **21**-year duration for the next global conflict.

The Combined Picture

As you can see, the attack that took place in September 2001 is doubly significant in terms of Fibonacci time progressions. It occurred at the culmination of a Fibonacci progression of peace durations from 1918 and a Fibonacci progression of war commencement from 1945. The smaller progression implies that 2001 is a year to be concerned about the onset of U.S. involvement in a war. The larger progression implies that 2001 is a year to be concerned about the onset of U.S. involvement in a *world* war.

The Presumed Outlook from Figure 1

First, let's note that the suspected Fibonacci progressions are hardly extensive enough to demonstrate statistically that they are real. The larger progression does not extend back into the 19th century. These progressions could be no more than an imposed construct.

If these Fibonacci progressions continue, then a significant war has begun. *If* the progression on the left of Figure 1 is valid, then a *world* war has begun. Regarding its duration, *if* the skipping of Fibonacci durations continues, as implied by *both* progressions of "war duration," then one would expect the current conflict to last twenty-one years. *If* the progression of plus and minus one year continues, that duration would last an extra year. 2001 + 21-22 years comes out to 2022-2023.

Given the fact that the genesis of the current conflict is less the product of the designs of political states and more the product of radical elements within a religion that has millions of adherents in numerous countries around the world, the suggested worldwide scope and extended duration of struggle should not be lightly dismissed.

The Wave Pattern Says That Now Is *Not* the Start of the Largest War of this Century

There is a very good reason to believe that the world war implied by the left column in Figure 1 either will not take place or will not meet our worst fears, at least not in the earlier projected time span. Chapter 16 of *The Wave Principle of Human Social Behavior* demonstrates that wars have consistently developed in "C" waves of corrections of Cycle degree and higher, whereas "A" waves are usually far less violent and often relatively peaceful, being confined to financial debacle. (This trait does *not* extend to any of the countless "C" *sub*waves of the main waves in the correction.) As explained in the book, the greatest physical danger for the U.S. is therefore likely to occur closer to the middle of the current century rather than in its early decades. Today, the stock market is in wave (a) of the Grand Supercycle bear market, as you can see in Figure 2. Therefore, a truly devastating world war is more likely to begin decades from now, during or immediately after wave (c).

If the guideline for timing wars holds true, it will mean one of two things about the present situation. Either the apparent current threat of world war will not materialize, deferring war until wave (c), or it *will* materialize in mild form and be followed by a *worse* conflict during wave (c), much as World War II broke out two decades after World War I ended. If Figure 1 means anything, perhaps it is telling us to be alert for the latter development.

When might the more serious world conflict begin? A continuation of the Fibonacci progression of Figure 1 to 89 years after 1945 would carry to

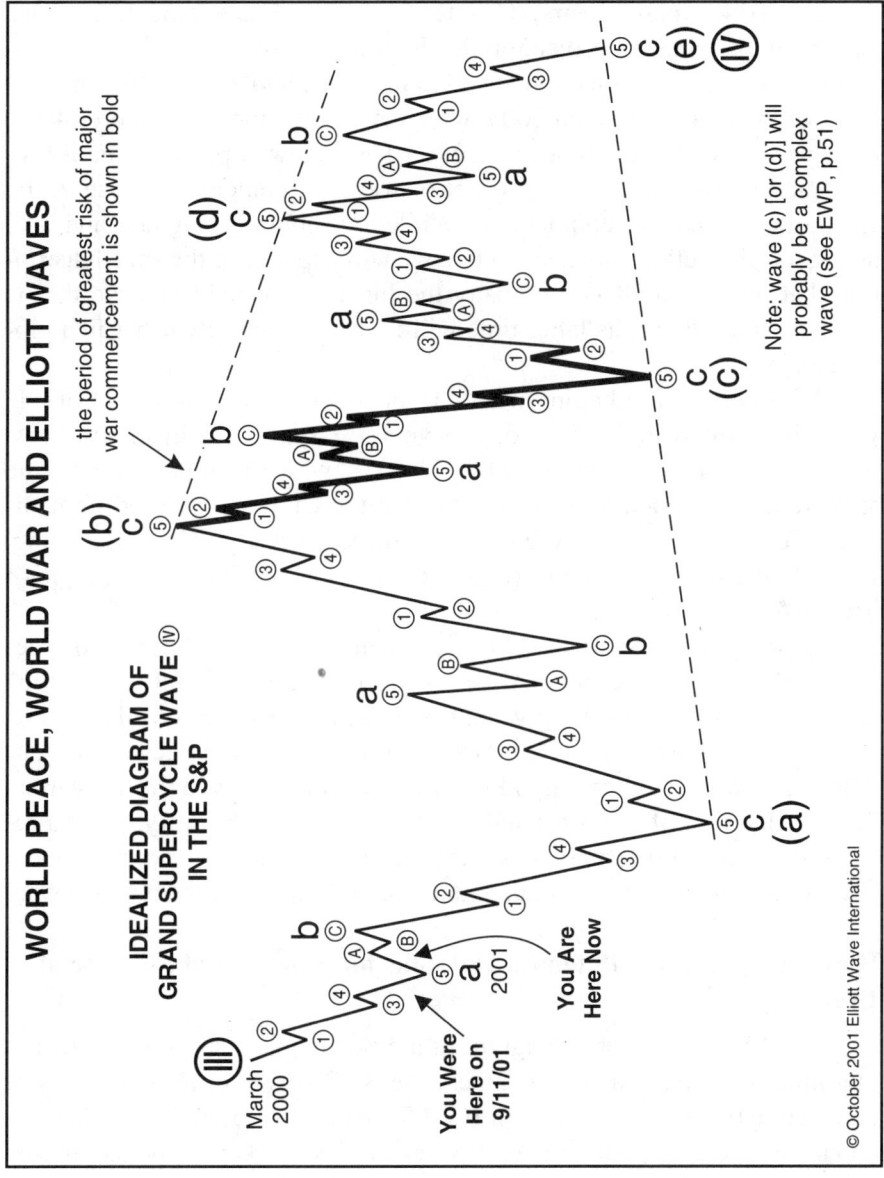

Figure 2

the year 2034 (+ or – 2 years). Chapter 5 of *At the Crest of the Tidal Wave* gave a highly tentative projection for the peak of wave (b) as 2037 (+ or – 2 years). These two projections overlap in **2035-2036**. (If the stock market bottoms in 2004 rather than 2003, which is looking more and more likely, these periods will overlap only in **2036**.) Thus, the war progression of Figure 1 and a time target for the onset of wave (c) coincide in those years, creating a compatible conjunction. While we should be vigilant and take necessary precautions now, and while we will experience the social disruption that will assuredly accompany the historic financial debacle that is currently unfolding, this latter time will far more assuredly usher in a global conflict.

Note that if a war begins in 2034 (+ or – 2 years) and lasts 21 (+ or – 1) years, it will end in 2055 (+ or – 3 years). Figure 5-12 in *At the Crest* projected the end of wave (c) for 2053-2058, which is almost exactly the same range. We should keep in mind that the Civil War started immediately *after* a C wave ended. While our Fibonacci work is perhaps a plaything, wave structures are not. Wave (c) will bring social danger whether or not it occurs when we surmise.

Despite our hopes, it would be prudent to adopt the "wave (c)" scenario only after we are satisfied that the risk implied in Figure 1 for 2001 and the immediately ensuing years has passed. At least as of this writing, that has not happened. The U.S. and its allies may win a decisive victory quickly, which would be a good sign. Yet even if so, given the substantial 22-year duration of the projected conflict, we should be wary about a resumption of hostilities for quite some time into the first period of risk before abandoning the concerns that the attack of 2001 has sparked a world war.

How the Near-Term Potential Outlooks for Stocks Might Fit Social Events

The "You Are Here" diagram in the September issue showed that at the time of the September 11 attack, the S&P was late in the process of completing five waves down from 1Q 2000, with wave ⑤ of that progression about half over. Sure enough, in the week that the market re-opened, selling brought the S&P right down to its lower channel line, completing the fifth wave depicted in that diagram (reproduced in Figure 2). This resolution calls for a significant A-B-C (up-down-up) countertrend rally. Supporting this potential, the NASDAQ also shows five waves down, the DJIA on September 28 stopped right on its Cycle degree uptrend line dating all the way back to 1980, and the Dow Transports stopped precisely on their lowest possible long-term support line. If the stock market stages a multi-month rally, then the chances will increase that the attack of September 2001 will have a happy resolution, *perhaps* finally but at least initially.

If before any such recovery the Dow breaks its Cycle degree uptrend line, if in coming days the market accelerates on the downside in terms of breadth and daily percentage loss, if the lower channel line of the S&P (see October EWFF) is penetrated significantly, the potential for a significant rally will be eliminated, and the crash will be immediately upon us. If the market plays out this way, then the odds of an early resolution to the world's war against terrorism will drop, and you should dig in your heels for a long fight.

[*Note: The Dow rallied for six months following the September low, tracing out an Ⓐ - Ⓑ - Ⓒ rally. During that time, the trend of the conflict turned in favor of the United States, and no foreigners committed terrorist acts on U.S. soil. — Ed.*]

Prechter

The Elliott Wave Theorist
June 1, 2002

The Socionomic Insight vs.
The Assumption of Event Causality
The Enron Scandal: A Case in Point

The Socionomic Insight

The socionomic insight is that the conventional assumption about the direction of causality between social mood and social action is not only incorrect but the opposite of what actually occurs. Socionomics is based on a principle developed by deduction from the existence of the Wave Principle and by induction from the chronology of market behavior and other social actions. The principle is that *social mood determines the character of social events.*

As previous studies demonstrate, rising stock trends do not improve the public mood; an improving social mood makes stock prices rise. Economics do not underlie social mood; social mood underlies economics. Stock trends do not follow corporate earnings; corporate earnings follow stock trends. Politics do not affect social mood; social mood affects politics. Demographics do not determine stock market trends; the social mood that determines stock market trends determines demographics. Styles of popular art and entertainment do not affect the social mood; the social mood determines the popularity of various styles of art and entertainment. War does not impact stock market trends; the mood that governs stock market trends determines the propensity for war. And so on. All economic, political and cultural developments are shaped and guided by the Wave Principle of human social behavior. It is the engine of everything from popular fads and fashions to the events of collective action that make history.

Conventional belief is the opposite of the above insight. It is solidly entrenched and pervasive almost to the point of ubiquity. It is deeply intuitive and utterly wrong.

The conventional mind sees social events as causes of social mood. Few ever ask the causes of the events themselves. Those who do simply assign the causes to other events.

The Counter-Intuity of the Socionomic Insight

I continually marvel at how counter-intuitive the socionomic insight is. For the entire time of my professional career, I have been comfortable with the central implication of technical analysis, which is the primacy of market form over extramarket events such as economics and politics. (I eventually discovered to my dismay that technicians rarely accept this implication and believe that various random, unpredictable "fundamentals" are behind the market's patterns, which is a contradiction.) Yet even I find myself upon occasion having to work hard at dispelling old contradictory thought patterns in order to re-establish mental integrity on the more difficult challenges of the socionomic insight. My first real challenge came from the claim that "demographics" determined stock price trends. I knew the claim had to be incorrect, and it took only a few days of research to debunk it. But it was only during the course of that pursuit that I began to formulate the proper response: that if indeed there were any correlation at all, *the causality had to be in the other direction*. The result was the 1999 study, *Stocks and Sex*, which shows exactly that. My latest — and greatest — challenge to date has been the proper conception of the Federal Reserve Bank's role in the causality of monetary trends, which I will discuss in an upcoming report. [See July issue on page 77. — Ed.]

The average person's resistance to the socionomic insight is so formidable that it compares to having one's view of existence challenged. I believe that the reason for this resistance is the easy naturalness of the idea of event causality: It works in physics, so people assume that it must operate in sociology. This deeply rooted assumption is stronger than piles of evidence to the contrary.

Let me give you an example of how strong this resistance is. On April 25, 2002, I was pleased to address the Sixth Congress of the Psychology of Investing, sponsored by the Massachusetts Mental Health Center, which is a major teaching hospital of Harvard Medical School. Attendance ran the gamut from academics and psychiatrists to Wall Street professionals and private investors. After presenting the Wave Principle and explaining its social effects, I was told by numerous attendees that the presentation had changed their perspective on markets and social causality.

The following day, I attended the afternoon's final half hour, in which attendees were given the opportunity to ask questions of that day's panel. The final question was, "The Enron scandal has deeply discouraged investors; when can we hope that this black cloud hanging over the stock market will go away?"

Several respondents — both from the panel and the audience — answered the question as if it were valid. Not a soul in the room challenged the questioner's assumption.

A week later, *USA Today* and doubtless countless other newspapers and magazines were trumpeting the same theme. "Scandals Shred Investors' Faith," declared a front-page headline. Begins the article, "A drumbeat of corporate misdeeds has helped crush stock prices and eviscerate pension plans."[1]

If you recognize the socionomic insight as a *principle*, you need know nothing about the details of the situation. You can formulate the proper response immediately. Before reading further, would you like to give it a try? Remember, the socionomic insight is that the conventional assumption about the direction of social mood vs. event causality is the *opposite* of what actually occurs. I will make your task easy by re-stating the assumption that the questioner held: "The Enron scandal discouraged investors." Can you state its opposite in terms of causality?

The Significance of the Enron Scandal

Did the Enron scandal discourage investors? *No, discouraged investors precipitated the Enron scandal.*

Many readers undoubtedly will balk at accepting the principle behind this formulation without their own tedious process of induction via repeated examples. To aid in that process once again, we must disprove the questioner's and media's false premise and demonstrate the validity of the socionomic stance.

First, let us define scandal not as misdeeds themselves, which can occur in secret. Scandal is the recognition of misdeeds, the outcry of recrimination and the public display of interest and outrage.

The premise is revealed as utterly false when we observe, despite virtually everyone's *feelings* to the contrary, that (1) investors in general knew nothing about Enron's malpractice prior to or anytime during the stock market's decline, and (2) *throughout the drama of the Enron scandal, the market advanced, and related psychological indicators improved.* Figure

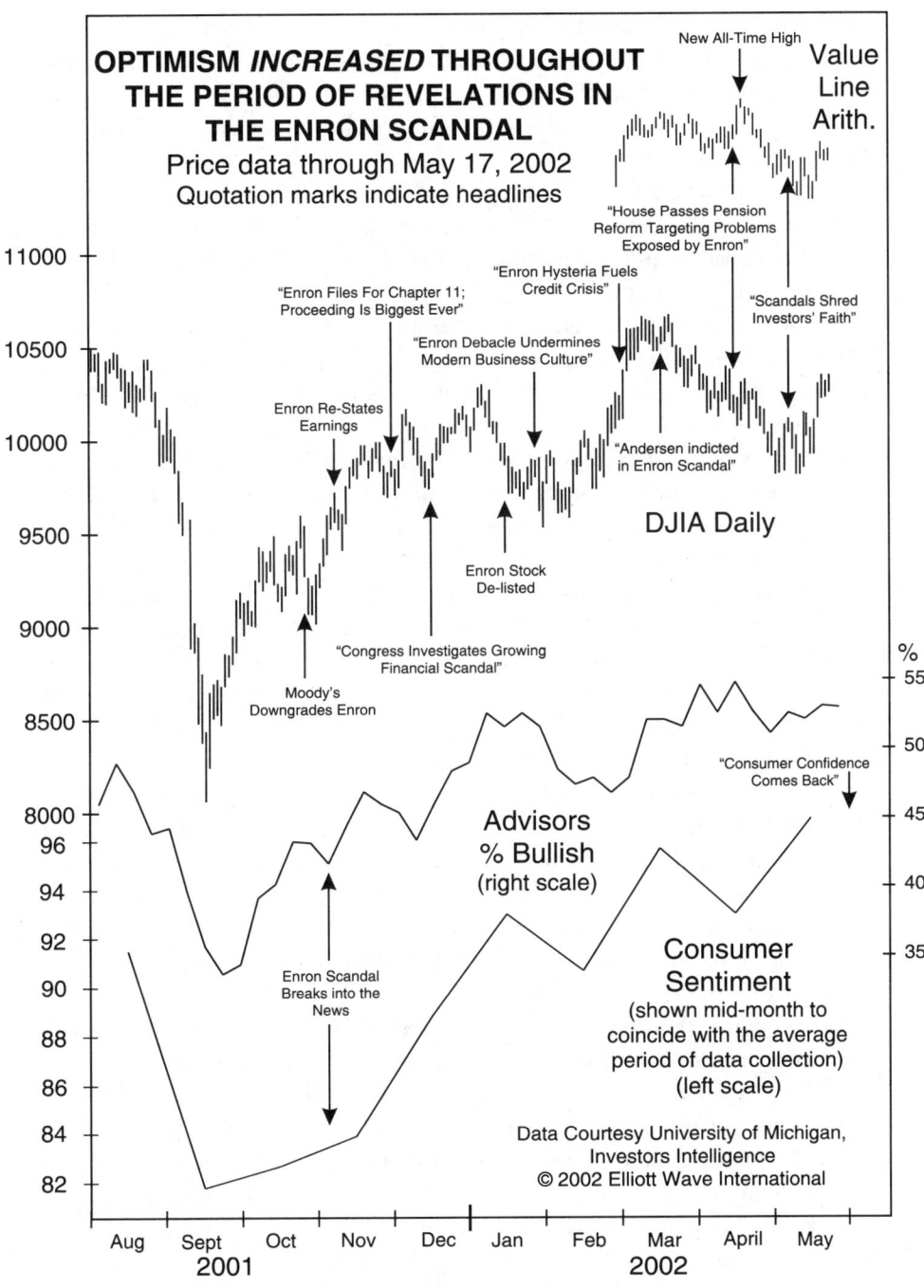

Figure 1

1 shows the stock market's progress, two measures of optimism and the key events surrounding the Enron scandal. It is abundantly clear that as the Enron scandal developed, *investor and consumer psychology improved, and stock prices rose.* Therefore, it is utterly false that the Enron scandal "discouraged investors."

Anyone who posits event causality in this instance is boxed into a corner. Given the facts before our eyes, he has no choice but to conclude that the Enron scandal was bullish for stock prices and that it caused investors' mood to improve![2]

I would like to proceed directly to what would seem to be an obvious statement: that such a conclusion is ridiculous. Incredibly, though, I cannot say it. Why? Because conventional analysts *actually proceed directly to such absurd conclusions repeatedly as a matter of course.* For example, *The Wave Principle of Human Social Behavior* relates a news report of an analyst who watched the stock market rally despite revelations of President Clinton's misbehavior and came to the conclusion that presidential sex scandals are bullish! Economists have reviewed the temporal proximity of war and economic recovery, and they assert, almost to a man, that war is good for the economy. If economists can argue that the most destructive activity of man is a positive force for economic well being, then conventional thinkers will have no trouble devising an argument as to why financial scandals are bullish. I can do it myself; such rationalization is easy.

The only antidote to such perversity is the socionomic insight. War is not causal to any aspect of social mood; it is a *result* of a deeply negative social mood. Likewise, the Enron scandal was not causal to any aspect of social mood whatsoever; it was a *result* of a change in social mood.[3]

Figure 2 demonstrates the chronology that supports this statement. As you can see, the stock market fell for many months prior to the scandal breaking. This meter of social mood showed increasing negativity — involving conservatism, suspicion, fear, anger and defensiveness — all of which went into precipitating the Enron scandal. As the CEO later explained, increasing conservatism affected the company's derivative positions, bear markets triggered "exit clauses" that allowed partners to their deals to withdraw their funds, and increasing fear and suspicion prompted them to do it. Throughout 2001, the company's stock retreated, removing support for financing. The house of cards built upon confidence collapsed.

By the time the *results* of that negative mood trend brought the Enron scandal to light, the negative mood trend was already over. The S&P 500 completed five waves down on September 21, and it was time for the largest

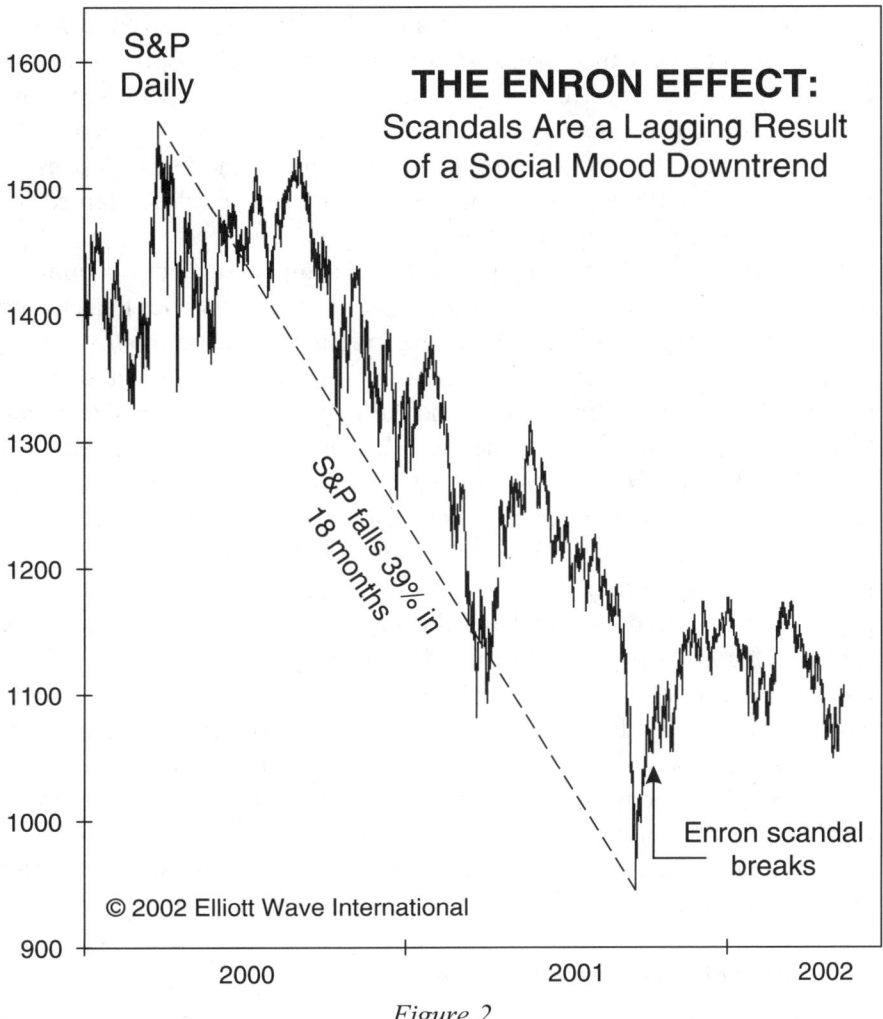

Figure 2

rally since the high in March 2000 (as forecast in *The Elliott Wave Theorist* on September 11). During that rally, these particular consequences of the downward mood trend became manifest.[4]

Now we know for sure: The Enron scandal did not "discourage investors" or "shred investors' faith" *one bit*. Their level of faith *rose* during the scandals. It did not "crush stock prices and eviscerate pension plans," either. Stock prices *rose* during the scandals. All the hand wringing and ink spilling on this presumption has been a waste of time and energy.

To make a subtler point, "corporate misdeeds" are not even to blame for the bear market that *preceded* the eruption of the Enron scandal. Corporate misdeeds were in full flower throughout the 1990s, yet no scandals erupted. In fact, those very misdeeds — Ponzi-like accounting practices — could be credited with *raising* stock prices and *fattening* pension plans during the 1990s to the same extent that they could be blamed for crushing and eviscerating them now.

Yet the proper amount of credit to assign to suspect accounting practices for both trends in stock prices is zero. The credit goes to a change in mass psychology. Various accounting irregularities were an *effect* of the psychological environment. They were in place for years, and they were reported from time to time, sometimes in major journals, *but during the bull market, few cared*. Corporate *misbehavior* persisted for a decade, but there was no *scandal* until well after the trend changed. While the trend was up, people ignored the phony accounting; when the trend turned down, they began to investigate it. When the trend was up, psychology supported both actual and illusory corporate health; when the trend turned down, psychology caused both actual and illusory corporate health to deteriorate rapidly. Again, the formulation of causality is the opposite of the conventional belief: Corporate misdeeds did not crush stock prices; crushed stock prices finally drew back the curtain on corporate misdeeds. What, then, caused corporate misdeeds to expand so greatly in the first place? The mass psychology of the stock mania, which was unskeptical to an extreme, invited and even rewarded companies for "creative accounting." It was the psychological environment of the bull market that led companies to dare to mislead investors in the first place.

The Power of Socionomic Prediction

Figure 2 at least sets the chronology of the true cause and effect with respect to the Enron scandal. It falls short of proving it, of course, as the other option regarding causality is that the two events (and all the others we have explored) are unrelated. Let's see if we can dismiss that hypothesis.

An important aspect of science is the ability of a hypothesis to *predict*. Using the socionomic insight, could anyone have predicted the flood of accounting and corporate scandals that has so far climaxed with the revelations regarding Enron?

The answer is yes. Moreover, someone did.

At the height of the stock mania and during the months thereafter, Peter Kendall of Elliott Wave International went on record in *The Elliott*

Wave Theorist and *The Elliott Wave Financial Forecast* identifying the end of the line for what we dubbed "bull market accounting standards" and forecasting a climate of scandal and recrimination. As we now know, that emerging climate decimated images of all kinds of heroes, from corporate CEOs to economists to brokerage firm analysts to accountants, to name just a few. The ensuing commentary[5] shows the predictive advantage of the socionomic perspective in the area of corporate scandal (emphases added):

September 16, 1998

The discovery of "fictitious revenue" at Cendant Corp. [first reported just 13 days after the all-time peak in the advance-decline line on April 3, 1998] is part of a slow awakening to the realization that the fundamentals of many companies, weak as they have become, are not even what they purport to be. Financial improprieties at Sunbeam, Oxford Health, Green Tree Financial, Boston Chicken and Mercury Financial have also been reported.... The emerging shift in social mood is beginning to shatter the collective financial delusion. *These stories can "now be told" because people are disposed to listen to them. As the bear market unfolds, many more "scandalous" cases will be revealed.*

October 1, 1999

Accounting standards have eroded as the bull market has aged. The flip side of these papered-over cracks in the fundamentals is that in a bear market they will be an enormous weight on growth. Combined with the unprecedented global economic dependence on a rising U.S. stock market, the likelihood is that they will exert their drag with stunning speed.

February 25, 2000

The bull market's attendant accounting gimmicks will get a lot more ink as the blinding light of the new era gives way to sober reflection and recrimination.

May 26, 2000

Financial Shenanigans Coming to Light: Some of the lame excuses for optimism are being outed. As *The Elliott Wave Theorist* noted in our 1998 Special Report on the relative weakness of the fundamentals in Cycle V vs. Cycle III, "*the enduring psychological coercion of the bull market*" has compensated for Cycle V's obvious fundamental shortcomings with the general acceptance of accounting standards that overstate the quality of companies' financial performance. The exposure of fallacious bull-market bookkeeping has been a subject of ongoing discussion in EWFF. For our purposes, the importance is not the transgressions themselves but the timing of their discovery and repudiation. This process has accelerated in the wake of the NASDAQ's retreat. There is now "growing concern among accounting professionals that many companies are relying on financial alchemy to burnish their results." Instead of peripheral corporate players and outright fraud, the charges of "financial engineering" are now being leveled against stalwarts like Microsoft, Dell and Cisco Systems *for accounting practices that have been known to be in place for years.* Less than a month after Cisco was tabbed as the new stock-market bellwether, its aggressive acquisition strategy was profiled as a "modern house of cards" in *Barron's*. Days later, Cisco's reported earnings, which surpassed analysts' expectations by one cent for the 12th straight quarter, failed to produce the usual upside pop.

June 30, 2000

Last month, we reported that the exposure of slack bull market accounting standards and outright frauds was worth watching as an indication that the "return to sobriety" was gaining ground.... It turns out that *Cendant's accounting shenanigans date all the way back to its initial public offering in 1983.* As columnist Floyd Norris notes, "For investors, the most interesting question is not whether [the firm's founder] will go to jail. It is how this fraud managed to go on so long." The answer, according to a professor of accounting who has studied a report on Cendant's bookkeeping practices, is that *"auditors were fooled because, in some measure at least, they wanted to be fooled." This, at bottom, is the thesis of socionomics. The social mood dictates how people treat real data. From 1983 through 1999, public mood was in a bull market. This year, it all changed, and so has the socially perceived reality.*

A steady stream of big-time financial scams gave the world its first hard look at the scale of financial fraud that bull market psychology had refused to expose. On June 15, reports revealed the "largest securities fraud sting in history," as the FBI arrested 120 people and broke up "a ring of organized crime on Wall Street" that has been operating for *five years*. When the Royal Bank of Canada was charged with stock manipulation, a Toronto paper said, the "practice of manipulating stock prices and pension fund performance *has been suspected for so long*, the only real surprise is that Canada's largest bank got caught first." *This acceleration in the size and scope of fraud exposure is exactly what* The Elliott Wave Theorist *has said we should expect in a post-mania environment.*

September 1, 2000

Many of the bull-market accounting gimmicks that we have covered in recent issues of EWFF are also alternate forms of financial leverage…. The trend poses "systemic, long-term risk" to companies' debt ratings, says one specialist. *All it took was a two-month decline of 16% in the Dow to expose this weakness. The same practices that goosed the numbers on the way up will drag them down in a bear market.*

December 1, 2000

It turns out that GE massages its numbers. *Money* magazine even reported in November that GE's earnings consistency is "a charade." Even "fans" are asking about the "confusing but apparently legal gimmicks" GE has used "to achieve its vaunted consistency." As *The Elliott Wave Theorist* pointed out in September 1998, this "discovery" of questionable bull market accounting standards is exactly what we should expect in the early stages of the bear market. In reaching GE, the last of the original Dow companies, *the emerging financial skepticism goes a long way toward confirming that the stock market's long-term topping process is behind us.*

March 28, 2001

Considering the size of the NASDAQ's bubble and its inexorable, year-long decline, the attacks on Greenspan, CNBC and Wall Street analysts constitute a relatively serene response so far. Ironically, a rally might never be accomplished by an escalation in the attacks. The preliminary breaks from the mania in 1997 and 1998 illustrate how this delayed response works. In 1997, many emerging markets actually peaked in the first half of the year and fell out of bed in October as the U.S. market joined in. Once the bottom was actually in, the IMF became the focal point of an international backlash. On December 2, 1997, *The Wall Street Journal* reported on a sweeping wave of "resentment." "From Thailand to South Korea, casualties of the region's market meltdowns are casting blame far and wide." In October 1998, after the worst of another selling wave was over, we were treated to criticism over the bailout of Long-Term Capital Management and a Congress that roiled with demands for the regulation of hedge funds. As the market rallied on, the storm dissipated. [Perhaps one] reason for the delay is that the economy lags the stock market, and people don't reach their peak of anger until they are buffeted by the economy. [*Note: This is the same chronology that attended the Enron scandal, as revealed in Figure 1. — Ed.*]

June 29, 2001

The Witch Hunt Takes Flight: In matters of survival, particularly those that are defined by highly subjective human interactions, the rational faculties of the neocortex are no match for the emotionally based survival instincts that inhabit the limbic system. The expanding controversy over accounting standards is a perfect example of the same brains later taking the opposite of a previous view in response to the demands of survival. As of late 1990, many thousands of analysts altered the tenets of the profession to a point where book value, dividends, profits and total earnings *did not matter*. Contending otherwise was grounds for dismissal; in fact, some analysts lost their jobs because they refused to adopt the new standard. Now, however, succeeding in the same job requires a single-minded devotion to judging earnings. The change revolves around a very specific event at a very specific time. On March 10, 2000, the direction of the NASDAQ switched from up to down, and the influence of social mood on millions of limbic systems reversed. On the approach to that high, the accountants themselves were consumed with hope and denial. Afterward, the essence of the job became to doubt the numbers. *USA Today*'s June 22 story notes, "accounting experts, analysts and academics" all agree, "companies are twisting the numbers to show better results." Numerous bull market instruments, like corporate stock buybacks, splits and stock options, which EWFF and *The Elliott Wave Theorist* said would have "an equal and opposite effect in a downtrend," are now getting all sorts of bad press (see March 1999 EWT and May and June 2000 issues of EWFF). Within the last few weeks, newspapers report, "Share Buybacks Hit a Wall of Fear," and stock options have "turned the investing world upside down." In an unexpected twist, "repricings" have created "a perverse incentive" for employees to "hold stock prices down."

It is no coincidence that as the backlash gathers steam, analysts and other economic thinkers are a special point of focus. In 1999, economists — scratch that; we mean *bullish* economists — emerged as the new "superstars of academia." Now a *Newsweek* column calls economics "the illusion of knowledge" and reveals, "Economists are clueless." In June, Congressional hearings were conducted to dissect the inaccurate opinions of securities analysts. A team of professors from four major California universities produced a paper showing that the stocks analysts liked the most fell 31% in 2000, while their least favorable recommendations rose 49%! The detailed analysis calls into question the "usefulness of analysts' stock recommendations." As we said months ago, this is not news. Has there has ever been a time when *average* Wall Street analysis has been useful as anything more than a contrary indicator? The news is how much of the academic and media firepower that supported Wall Street notions is now directed against Wall Street. This defrocking appears to be an inevitable response to the reversal of a mania. As *The Wave Principle of Human Social Behavior* points out, people tend to "live in the limbic system, particularly with respect to fields such as investing where so few are knowledgeable and the tendency toward dependence is pervasive." This was at least doubly true in the mania, as even the most highly developed neocortex was at a loss for prior experience to draw upon. The failed images of the previously bullish social mood now induce jilted investors to destroy the advisors upon whom they have grown so dependent. It is fascinating to see how much sense the neocortexes of the attackers can make as this limbic-based process plays itself out.

November 30, 2001

Enron Corp.'s imminent [bankruptcy] will easily be the largest bankruptcy ever, topping the old record (Texaco in 1987) by almost 70%. The "forensic accountants" have been called in to sort out a mess that will lead on to a *seemingly endless series of financial catastrophes.*

February 1, 2002

All Enron, All the Time: "Twenty minutes ago, the only topics on the nation's radar screen were Afghanistan and terrorism. Now there's Enron," says a *USA Today* column on "How Enron Stole Center Stage." One of the big mysteries is why the public suddenly cannot get enough dirt on Enron. "*A few years ago, it would hardly have seemed possible,*" *Business Week* notes. "The nation's attention, from the halls of Congress to Main Street, has been riveted on an accounting scandal, a subject so abstruse it rarely makes the front page." *But there it is on page 1, day after day after day.* The Enron scandal and its recent "spread to other large, complex companies" shows that *investors are waking up to what they did not want to know during the bull market.*

March 1, 2002

What's Beyond Enron: Last month, we showed how perfectly the Enron scandal fits the blueprint for a Grand Supercycle-degree bear market. This month, the river of recriminations broke its banks. The potential for a flood of Enron-style revelations into virtually any sector of the economy is signaled by word that the Federal Reserve is "stepping up" its scrutiny of securitized credit-card debt and mortgages as well as a *Fortune* expose that offers investors "More Reasons to Get Riled Up." *Fortune* points out that Enron's $63 billion in market losses is nothing compared to the $155 to $423 billion in market cap that disappeared from 10 other firms. "*Let's get mad at them, too,*" says the magazine. "Let's put *our anger and righteous outrage* in all the places they belong."

Meanwhile, Enron has evolved into what one Washington attorney called "an eerie financial witch hunt" that is comparable to the Salem witch trials. The still-expanding demand for dirt on Enron is apparent by its arrival on the cover of the *National Enquirer*. The tabloid claims to have the "untold story" in its latest issue. When it comes to Enron, however, the only story the media has left untold is what's driving the fascination.

Mr. Kendall thus predicted in no uncertain terms that the consequences of the approaching — and then the developing — bear market would result in accounting scandals increasingly hitting the newspapers. (Note that this

is a double forecast: both for a bear market and some of its social results.)
Thus, socionomics once again predicted the character of upcoming events,
events that have since led to dramatic congressional hearings, anguished
public outcry and of course, the classic conventional error in assigning
causality.

Thanks to an intrepid writer of the above-quoted article of May 2,
2002, Kendall was provided space in *USA Today* to summarize the correct
stance on the rash of scandals and recriminations. Here are the relevant
excerpts:

> Peter Kendall, co-editor of newsletter *The Elliott Wave Finan-
> cial Forecast*, says a bear market often reveals the worst excesses of a
> bull market. "Everything that was revered on the upside is a target in a
> bear market." Those excesses have to be corrected before the public
> regains its confidence. Typical features of the so-called recrimination
> phase: reviled CEOs. "Those who had Teflon in the bull market have
> Velcro in the bear market," Kendall says. In 1929, the chief target was
> Richard Whitney, president of the New York Stock Exchange. Ken-
> neth Lay, former CEO of Enron, may be the current target.
>
> Reform and regulation are one step to regaining the public's con-
> fidence. But that often happens well after much of the damage is done
> to investors' trust. "The government takes steps after the horses have
> left the barn," Kendall says.[6]

We socionomists are few in number. Were this a developed science
with many practitioners, an astute socionomist might have listed Enron
specifically as being one of the companies likely to explode in scandal.
One financial ratings firm in April 2001 placed Enron on its "Corporate
Earnings Blacklist" and cited the company as being "highly suspect of
manipulating its earnings reports," so the hints were there.[7] An alert
socionomist who knew, as we did, that corporate accounting scandals were
rising in a flood might have filled in the blanks and anticipated this specific
manifestation of the socionomic dynamic, although certainly not its ultimate
position as the premier poster-child of manipulative accounting.

Toward a New Understanding

People have a tendency to ask questions such as, "Are you saying that
had the trend in social mood *not* changed, the Enron scandal would not
have come to light?" The short answer is yes, but the questioner is missing

an important point. It is crucial to understand that while the precipitation of Enron's financial meltdown and the revelation of its shaky accounting practices were due to forces behind the new negative social-mood trend, the precondition of their very existence was the psychological forces behind the old *positive* social-mood trend. Had the rose-colored glasses of optimism not clouded investors' vision in the first place, no company would have been able to survive practicing such shenanigans. During the 1990s, countless companies practiced them, and they were actually *rewarded* for it.

Socionomists were able to predict the eruption of scandals for three reasons: (1) because we knew that the euphoric optimism of the positive social-mood trend was inducing individuals and corporations to take huge financial risks and simultaneously inducing observers to turn a blind eye to improprieties, (2) because we knew that the qualities of a negative social-mood trend would reverse both of those forces and (3) because, knowing that social mood change would be the determining factor, we researched past major downside reversals in the stock market to glean some of their social characteristics, one of which was the rapid eruption of scandals, recriminations and Congressional investigations into corporate malfeasance. Believers in the conventional assumption of event causality, in contrast, were caught blindsided, as usual.

While the conventional error of thought regarding social mood causality is nearly ubiquitous, a few thinkers in history have derived the correct posture on this question, at least to a limited degree. For instance, Thomas Paine observed, "Panics bring things and men to light, which might have lain forever undiscovered." In other words, panic is causal; scandals are a result. It is time for social scientists to accommodate this view and to embrace the greater socionomic insight that lies behind it.

Corporate accounting scandals are only one area of social behavior among dozens that we at Elliott Wave International have successfully predicted. To cover them all would take several books. While this report details just a single example of what socionomists can do, it also elucidates a principle of social forecasting that anyone can learn to apply. A practiced artisan in this field can predict the headlines in countless areas.

Quiz

You can do this. On May 2, 2002, the same day that newspapers blamed the Enron scandal for shredding investors' faith, another front-page article about arson and a gun battle at the Church of the Nativity in Bethlehem

(West Bank) declared, "Church Battle, Fire Inflame Passions."[8] What is the socionomically inspired, i.e., the causally correct, formulation for that headline?

Now that you have formulated the correct headline, you should be able to see the value of the socionomic perspective not only in understanding what is going on in the world but also in forecasting. Had you been privy to a meter of the local social mood in this instance, you could have predicted the character of the events that resulted.

NOTES

[1] Waggoner, John and Fogarty, Thomas. (2002, May 2). "Scandals shred investors' faith," *USA Today*, p. 1

[2] Any economist who bothers to view the relationship between the U.S. trade deficit and the stock market or the economy faces the same dilemma. The two trends move together in near lock step, opposing the ubiquitous presumption to the contrary. For chart and discussion see Prechter, Robert, *The Wave Principle of Human Social Behavior and the New Science of Socionomics*, pp. 377-380.

[3] Likewise, the social mood downtrend of 1974 forced the Watergate scandal to become a national obsession, crushing President Nixon's approval ratings and causing him to resign. The social mood uptrend of the 1990s, in contrast, allowed President Clinton to maintain his popularity despite lying in court and to the public about an adulterous affair with an intern.

[4] Further evidence of the power of social psychology to rule social events and social visioning is the amazing fact that the aspect of the scandal over which investors and politicians were most enraged was phony. Newspapers reported endlessly that the "big shots" at Enron got out of the stock while the poor employees were "locked in." In truth, employees could have gotten out whenever they wished, except for a brief period of 16 days during which the stock slipped an additional four points from 13 to 9, on its year-long descent from 83 down to 0.57, at which time it was de-listed in January 2002. The restriction, moreover, was not a punitive policy but a technical consequence of the company's turning over management of its pension plan to another firm. Investors in Enron stock, employees included, lost a lot of money because they were imprudent and foolish, just as countless other investors have lost money. The psychological desire of investors to redirect blame for their decision not to sell is stronger than facts.

[5] Prechter, Robert R. (1998, September 16). *The Elliott Wave Theorist* Special Report. Also Hochberg, Steven and Kendall, Peter. (1999, October 1; 2000, February 25, May 26, June 30, September 1, December 1; 2001, March 28, June 29, November 30; 2002, February 1, March 1). *The Elliott Wave Financial Forecast*.

[6] See Endnote 2.

[7] Weiss Ratings, Inc.; www.weissratings.com

[8] Gee, Robert W. (2002, May 2). "Church battle, fire inflame passions." *The Atlanta Journal-Constitution*, p. 1.

Challenging the Conventional Assumption About the Presumed Sociological Effect of Terrorist News

There is probably not one person in a million who would disagree with the conventional view, espoused everywhere, that the attacks of September 11, 2001 and the subsequent deliverance of anthrax-laced letters to individuals shattered the confidence of Americans. Yet that conclusion flies in the face of the facts.

Figure 1 shows every one of those events in the context of stock market behavior, consumer confidence and market psychology. As you can see, social mood and confidence *bottomed* six trading days after the 9/11 attack and continued to improve for months, throughout the reports of anthrax-laden mail deliveries, throughout the spectacles of men covered from head to toe in protective suits testing offices and other facilities for deadly anthrax spores, throughout reports of six deaths by anthrax, throughout the reports that al-Qaeda was running rampant and planning to poison water supplies, blow up bridges, release smallpox into the population and detonate a nuclear bomb in major U.S. cities. The conventional belief, which is an utter assumption, is that these reports would and did cause and instill increased fear and pessimism in society. This belief is the way people think, probably because they assign the type of causality that exists in the world of physics, the realm that humans have greatly learned to manipulate and control, to that of sociology. The facts contradict this notion.

Pundits who make the claim of news causality *never* check the data. Now we can see that social mood actually *improved* throughout the time of the anthrax news reports. Proponents of the conventional view of social causality (i.e., virtually everyone) are now obliged to ignore this fact in order to maintain that incorrect view.

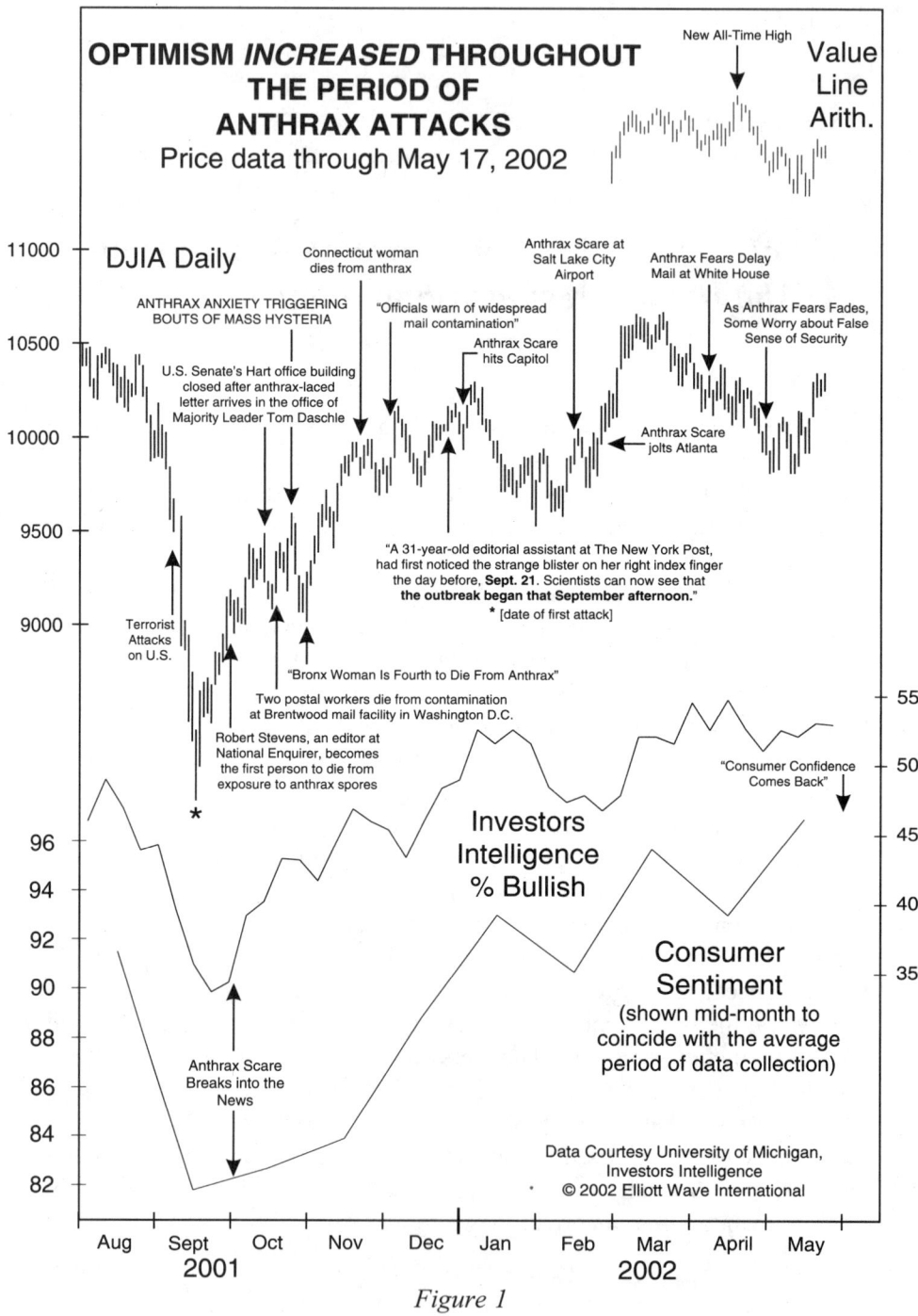

OPTIMISM *INCREASED* THROUGHOUT THE PERIOD OF ANTHRAX ATTACKS
Price data through May 17, 2002

New All-Time High

Value Line Arith.

DJIA Daily

Connecticut woman dies from anthrax

Anthrax Scare at Salt Lake City Airport

Anthrax Fears Delay Mail at White House

ANTHRAX ANXIETY TRIGGERING BOUTS OF MASS HYSTERIA

"Officials warn of widespread mail contamination"

As Anthrax Fears Fades, Some Worry about False Sense of Security

Anthrax Scare hits Capitol

U.S. Senate's Hart office building closed after anthrax-laced letter arrives in the office of Majority Leader Tom Daschle

Anthrax Scare jolts Atlanta

"A 31-year-old editorial assistant at The New York Post, had first noticed the strange blister on her right index finger the day before, **Sept. 21**. Scientists can now see that **the outbreak began that September afternoon.**"
* [date of first attack]

Terrorist Attacks on U.S.

"Bronx Woman Is Fourth to Die From Anthrax"

Two postal workers die from contamination at Brentwood mail facility in Washington D.C.

Robert Stevens, an editor at National Enquirer, becomes the first person to die from exposure to anthrax spores

"Consumer Confidence Comes Back"

Investors Intelligence % Bullish

Consumer Sentiment
(shown mid-month to coincide with the average period of data collection)

Anthrax Scare Breaks into the News

Data Courtesy University of Michigan, Investors Intelligence
© 2002 Elliott Wave International

Aug   Sept   Oct   Nov   Dec   Jan   Feb   Mar   April   May
       2001   2002

Figure 1

Does that mean that social events and mood are random? Is there no causality at all? No, the socionomic hypothesis explains the proper causality. Social mood had deteriorated for eighteen months prior to the outbreak of these attacks. The negative mood permeating society by September 2001 had served to cause government agencies to become sloppy, missing cues to al-Qaeda's plans. It gave al-Qaeda's members the emotional trigger to decide that then was the time to strike. It caused someone either aggressive or unbalanced to choose that time to kill people through the mail and others later to perpetrate anthrax hoaxes.

Now observe the aftermath: A few months after the trend changed toward the positive, as evidenced by all the graphs in Figure 24-1, what happened? *There were no more attacks from al-Qaeda, and the anthrax mailings ceased.* The improving mood supported coordinated efforts to deal with these events and suppressed the forces that triggered them.

Whether or not you accept the idea that the changes in social mood effected these changes in social actions, the fact is that the chronology supports this case while simultaneously *decimating* the conventional view of causality. At minimum, an honest thinker has no choice but to abandon the conventional view. Whether he accepts the socionomic insight is another question, but he may no longer without contradiction espouse the old way of thinking. In fact, any objective person who bothers to check the chronology of various such assertions will be forced to abandon the conventional view.

The Feedback Loop Works Only Within Waves, Not With Actions

I used to think that mood formed a feedback loop with events, which in turn reinforced the mood. I have since seen that this idea is erroneous. Our studies on the Enron scandal and the terrorist attacks demonstrate this point empirically: Events *do not* affect aggregate mood. Theoretically speaking, moreover, it is abundantly clear that events *cannot* affect social mood. If events formed a feedback loop with mood, then social trends would never end. Each new extreme in mood in a particular direction would cause more reinforcing actions, and those actions would reinforce that same mood, and so on forever. This is an untenable idea.

The only feedback loop that occurs is one involving the propagation of Elliott waves through human minds. In order to participate in social Elliott waves, minds must *interact* with others and become synchronized with them. All types of communication media, from face-to-face discussion to satellite television news, serve to effect this interaction.

This interaction produces Elliott waves, and Elliott waves determine the trends of social mood, and those trends stimulate actions, which are reported as events. The actions and events are final end results *with no consequences of their own in terms of the waves*. Events do affect minds to the extent that they often shape specific actions that owners of those minds take, but they do not alter or affect the shared mood trend.

November 2002

The Timing and Character of Investment Legislation

Introduction

Until now, no researcher outside Elliott Wave International and the Socionomics Institute has applied the socionomic insight when investigating relationships in social data. I am proud to say that just prior to the completion of this book, two academics have made a pioneering mark in being the first outside researchers to test and apply the socionomic hypothesis.

Washington State University finance professor Dr. John Nofsinger, an expert on the psychology of investing, and his colleague, Kenneth Kim, have been writing a book characterizing the stock mania of the 1990s. Nofsinger was considering recommending laws to temper investors' behavior to prevent the bubble and crash cycle from repeating. He wondered, for example, whether incentives would work better than regulations.[1] Implied in this line of inquiry was the idea that regulation is causal to investor behavior.

Gordon Graham, Director of the Socionomics Institute, contacted Nofsinger for a discussion. Graham suggested that he consider viewing financial laws not as *causes* of social behavior but as *products* of social behavior. Intrigued by this statement of causality, Nofsinger reviewed all major investment legislation from the 1920s to present. He found that the character of each new investment law reflected the direction of the stock market *prior to* its enactment. Moreover, the relationship held every time; there were no exceptions. As I would hasten to add, these results suggest, per the hypothesis, a process of *cause and effect*.

This is another example of how a socionomic perspective leads one to search for the right relationships. It does not take social actions as "givens" independent of human thought but rather ties preceding thoughts to resulting actions, in this case government legislation related to investing. A simple change in perspective shed the light. Nofsinger's work would support an assertion that the socionomic insight is a prerequisite for understanding the social forces behind the making and unmaking of financial legislation, and their timing. Expansive legislation is a symptom of a maturing or completed positive mood trend, and restrictive legislation is a product of a maturing or completed negative mood trend.

Consider the implications were economists and politicians to take the unlikely path of viewing most legislation primarily as products of social mood. The endless debates about which new policy should be adopted in response to a preceding trend would end. A wiser tone and a longer term perspective would prevail, unleashing resources available for more productive purposes. It would be real progress.

Nofsinger has provided a model for other academic economists to work from. We encourage all to take note and follow his lead in considering the socionomic perspective when investigating social history.

— Robert Prechter

PROTECTING INVESTORS (NOT)

by Dr. John Nofsinger and Kenneth Kim[2]

The government continually tightens and loosens its laws regarding the investment industry just as it continually raises and lowers income taxes. After each major bear market or scandalous period, the government enacts new laws to protect investors. Consider the new laws shown in Table 1.

MAJOR LAWS CREATED TO PROTECT INVESTORS

Act	Purpose	Preceded By
1933 and 1934 Banking Act and Securities Exchange Act	Separates commercial and investment banking, creates SEC as market regulators	Stock market crash of 1929 and ensuing bear market removes nearly 90% of Dow value
1940 Investment Company Act and Investment Advisors Act	Regulates investment companies and advisors	Market decline of 25% from October 1939 to May 1940
1970 Securities Investor Protection Act	Creates Securities Investor Protection Corporation and insurance from broker defaults	Market decline of 30% from April 1969 to June 1970
1974 Employee Retirement Income Security Act	Regulates pension funds	Long bear market from December 1972 to September 1974 takes the Dow down 40%
1988 Insider Trading and Securities Fraud Enforcement Act	Increases penalties and liabilities for insider trading and fraudulent activities	Stock market crash of 1987 takes Dow down over 40%
2002 Public Company Accounting Reform and Investor Protection Act	Increases regulation of auditors, lengthens punishment for white collar crimes, and creates more corporate fraud laws	2½ year bear market reduced Dow by 35%, Nasdaq declines 75%

Excerpts from *Infectious Greed: Restoring Confidence in America's Companies*
By John R. Nofsinger and Kenneth A Kim

Table 1

The securities acts passed in 1933 and 1934 followed the corporate governance problems of the late 1920s, the 1929 stock market crash, and the beginning of the Great Depression. The investment company and advisors acts in 1940 followed a bear market that took 25% of the value of the stock market. The late 1960s experienced a 30% bear market. In 1970, the government created the Securities Investor Protection Corporation (SIPC). Investor protection laws also followed the bear market of the early 1970s and the Black Monday market crash of October 19, 1987. And, of course, the recent corporate scandals combined with the severe stock market decline spawned the 2002 Public Company Accounting Reform and Investor Protection Act.

Unfortunately, the laws that are enacted to protect shareholders and investors are often repealed during times of economic strength and stock market euphoria. The 1920s and the 1990s had many similarities. Both decades experienced strong economic expansions and powerful bull markets. Indeed, investors at the end of each decade could have been called irrationally exuberant. In the middle (or toward the end) of the excitement over stocks, the government changed its laws that protected investors.

REPEALS OF SOME INVESTOR PROTECTION		
Action	Purpose	Preceded By
1927 Government agency policy allowing commercial banks to issue securities	Allows commercial banks into investment banking activities	Stock market rose over 200% from 1925 to 1928
1995 Private Securities Litigation Reform Act	Limits the ability and available damages of investors suing for corporate fraud	Dow increased 60% between 1993 and 1995
1998 Securities Litigation Uniform Standards Act	Precludes plaintiffs from bringing securities actions in state courts	Dow increased 125% from 1996 to 1999
1999 Financial Services Modernization Act	Allows the combining of commercial and investment banking activities	Dow increased 125% from 1996 to 1999

Excerpts from *Infectious Greed: Restoring Confidence in America's Companies*
By John R. Nofsinger and Kenneth A Kim

Table 2

Consider the examples in Table 2. In 1927, the stock market was toward the end of a bull market that increased values over 200%. There were many new companies conducting IPOs that were not really strong enough to be offered to investors. Investors did not seem to care and rushed in to snap them up. The commercial banks were prevented from getting into the investment banking activities to share in the lucrative fees. They lobbied the government to change the rules and succeeded. Commercial banks began helping companies issue securities. Unfortunately, the stock market crash of 1929 left commercial banks with many losses that jeopardized people's bank deposits. The people panicked and demanded their money back. Of course, banks did not have the cash to return all the deposits at once. That cash was loaned out. So, the banks had to close their doors.

Now, examine the three law changes in the 1990s. The Private Securities Litigation Reform Act limited the ability of investors to sue companies and executives for damages due to corporate fraud in federal courts. This law was enacted in the midst of a strong bull market that increased the value of the Dow Jones Industrial Average by 60%. It was followed three years later with a similar act that applied to state courts. The Financial Services Modernization Act allowed commercial banks to associate themselves with investment banks again. This is similar to the 1927 capitulation. Again, this reduction in investor protection occurred toward the end of a market rally that increased the Dow 125%.

Another recent example is not listed in the table. In 1997, the SEC proposed new rules that would have severely limited the ability of shareholders to introduce corporate resolutions. The procedure for the SEC to enact new rules is that the regulator proposes a new rule and then provides a time period in which people can comment on the rule. A consortium of investor activists lobbied strongly against the new rule. In the end, the SEC decided not to enact the new limitations. Even though it was defeated, this is still an example of how investor protections are often reversed or limited during an extended bull market.

Our point is that laws are frequently made to protect shareholders and investors. This usually occurs after people become angry over scandals and a bear market. However, these protections can also be reversed in the midst of good times. A strong economy and good bull market lead to pressure on lawmakers to loosen restrictions on corporate participants. The loosened restrictions have the potential to help push the stock market from a bull market to a bubble market.[3] When a bubble occurs, a crash will inevitably follow. This leads to more scandals and more investor protection laws. We need to avoid this cycle.[4]

Yet, the social mood can be represented by stock prices. The level of the stock market indicates what kind of mood the people are in. This dictates the tone and character of the resulting action by government, regulators, and investors. The relationship we show between how the stock market has performed and the resulting legislation[5] illustrates this point.

EDITOR'S NOTES

[1] This thinking reflects the conventional viewpoint, not the socionomic perspective.

[2] Excerpted from Nofsinger, John and Kenneth Kim, *Infectious Greed: Restoring Confidence in America's Companies*, Financial Times Prentice Hall, forthcoming 2003, January.

[3] Socionomists would maintain that loosened restrictions do not "push the stock market from a bull market to a bubble market" but rather that the shared psychology of a late-stage bull market pushes investors, CEOs and regulators to loosen restrictions.

[4] Bull and bear markets can neither be avoided nor changed. Whether the behavior of lawmakers can change may be open to debate, but we are skeptical.

[5] The August 1, 1997 issue of *The Elliott Wave Theorist* also cited the SEC's adoption of "Rule 144a" in 1990/1992, which loosened reporting laws for restricted securities in order to induce foreign corporations to sell bonds — typically "junk" bonds — to U.S. institutions. *The Wave Principle of Human Social Behavior* cites related legislation, the Monetary Control Act of December 1980, which was enacted in response to the preceding entire decade's accelerating inflation, which had in fact already ended in January of that very year.

A Graphical Summary of Nofsinger's Observations

We always find graphics instructive. Figure 1 summarizes Nofsinger's observations. The upper arrows mark the timing of expansive legislation, and the lower arrows mark the timing of restrictive legislation. Note that the former type occurs late in bull markets, the latter type late in or after bear markets. It should be particularly impressive to Elliotticians that the essentially identical laws of 1927 and 1999 combining commercial and investment banking (see the asterisks on the graph) occurred near the end of a stock mania within a wave V of Cycle degree (labels not shown; see Figure 1 on page 78).

Figure 1

Mr. Graham concurrently expanded upon this theme in response to an article in The New Republic.

The New Republic
October 21, 2002
Letter to the Editor

In the first part of "Busted,"[1] George Soros deftly outlines the nature of boom and bust market behavior. The theory of reflexivity is a step in the right direction, but it misses the big picture. Soros's article sounds like an echo of the sentiments expressed in 1932. Then, as now, many prescriptions for controlling the behavior of market participants were implemented. Indeed, shortly after each bear market dating back to the Depression — 1933, 1934, 1940, 1970, 1974 and 1988 — legislation was introduced to protect investors with the intention of producing a more stable investment environment. What happened?

As stocks broke out of their slump in the early 1980s, an increasingly positive social mood brought forth a new set of "values": market fundamentalism. After the 1987 hiccup, the markets, propelled by social mood, gained a full head of steam, and the "protections" offered in the previous bear markets were altered, ignored and ultimately scoffed at, reflecting the blossoming euphoria and the desire for "financial gain irrespective of how it is achieved."

Bear markets produce regulation in response to the public's demand for protection, and bull markets dissolve them. As Mr. Soros points out, investors in the bull market had put a premium on management's ability to massage the numbers; the euphoria driving outrageous stock valuations drives equally outrageous social events.

From this perspective, the concept of equilibrium seems mighty strange, for the market is in constant flux. Mr. Soros's search for just the right amount of legislation and the proper values hints at "equilibrium seeking." However, no such thing exists in society or has ever existed. The fluctuating patterns of social mood are fundamental and ceaseless. One silver lining of the current bear market may be that it will cause a paradigm shift away from the search for market equilibrium(s) and toward a model that reflects an obvious reality: Social mood is never at "equilibrium," and its constant flux drives social action, including actions designed — futilely — to stop it.

—Gordon Graham
The Socionomics Institute
Gainesville, GA

NOTES

[1] Soros, George. (2002, September 2). "Busted." *The New Republic.* http://www.tnr.com.

TOWARD A REVOLUTION IN MACROECONOMICS

Prechter

The Elliott Wave Theorist
September 2002

Predicting Economic and Monetary Trends

How does one apply socionomic techniques to economic forecasting? A socionomist knows that the stock market is a meter of social mmood, which is the engine of social progress and regress. Therefore, the current-time change in the stock market is an immensely useful indicator of upcoming economic change. With a knowledge of the Wave Principle, a socionomist has two further advantages over conventional approaches. First, he can often anticipate and recognize the *degree* of the trend change and therefore the probable extent and severity of the new trend. Second, he can refine his timing in certain cases with respect to the *label* of the corrective wave, for example expecting only one recession in and (A)-(B)-(C) correction of Primary degree, as a response either to wave (A) or wave (C), as explained in Chapter 16 (p.262) of *The Wave Principle of Human Social Behavior.*

There are three supporting elements to socionomic forecasting: the wave patterns in economic data, the momentum of stock market and economic data (involving rates of change and divergences) and the psychological state of the professionals and the public. These factors provide evidence either that an analyst has correctly interpreted the wave patterns or that he has done so *incorrectly*, forcing a re-examination of his outlook.

Some of what follows in this section may be found in Chapter 17 of *The Wave Principle of Human Social Behavior*, Chapters 13 and 14 of *At the Crest of the Tidal Wave* and Chapters 1 and 5 of *Conquer the Crash*. This seems a good opportunity to chronicle the highlights of the record in one place. It also provides an opportunity to include some recent additions to it. The purpose of this chapter is not to claim a track record for economic forecasting (because I gave it so little thought and effort) but rather to show some ways that a socionomist might approach the task.

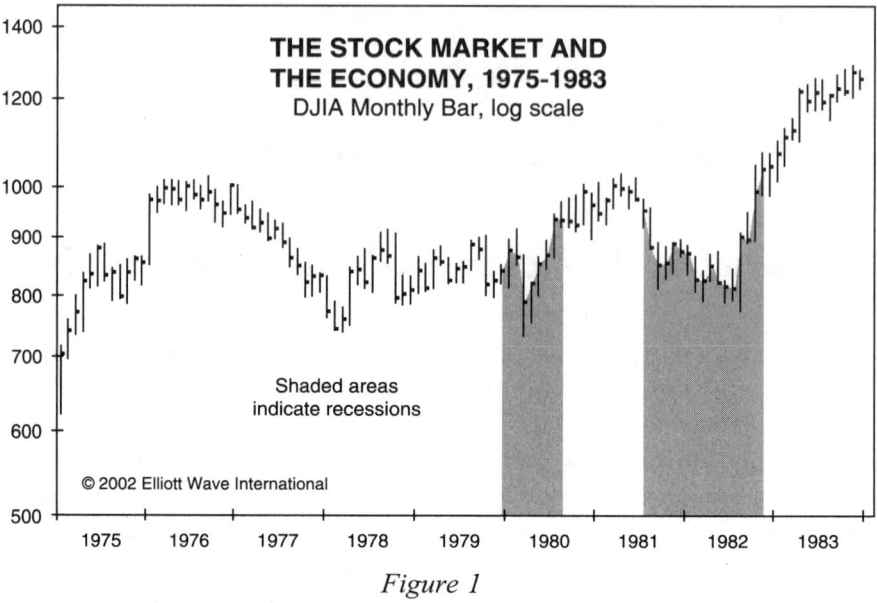

Figure 1

Some Success in Forecasting Near-Term Economic Trends

Figure 1 shows that from 1975 through 1979, the U.S. economy was recession-free. Then it underwent two recessions, which lasted from January through August 1980 and from July 1981 through November 1982, respectively.

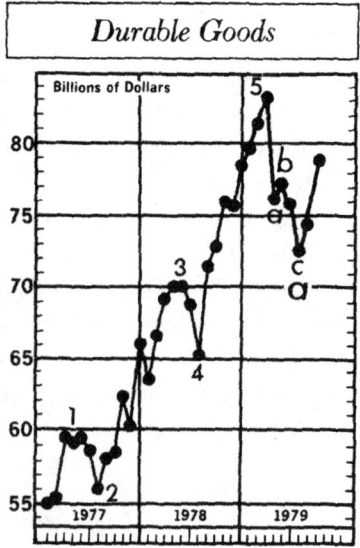

The following quotations show how *The Elliott Wave Theorist* navigated the expansions and the recessions from the publication's inception in April 1979 through 1983's developing boom.

November 4, 1979

> In the September 9 letter, I reproduced from the *Wall Street Journal* a chart of durable goods orders, which then stood at $72b., under the title, "Is the Recession Over?" Here is an updated chart, and as you can see, the a-b-c reaction in mid-1979 has already produced a rebound. A headline on the front page of the Journal on October 31

read, "Surprising Surge — Third Quarter Profits Topped Expectations."
Elliott waves appear to be useful even with fundamental data, as Elliott
claimed.

In a normal wave pattern, the current rise would constitute wave B
upward, to be followed by a downward wave C. If this pattern occurs, a
steeper downturn in the economy
might be expected between now and
early next year.

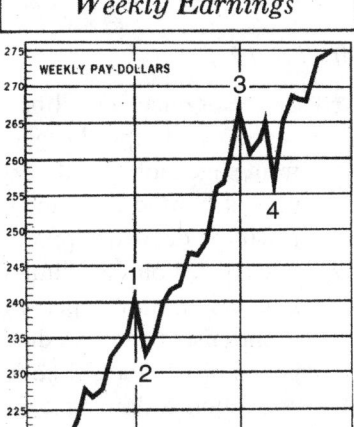

January 6, 1980

The chart of weekly earnings
shows five upward waves separated by
corrections, which follow the rule of
alternation (wave two is simple, wave
four complex). Close scrutiny shows
hints of five wave subdivisions within
each broad upwave. The wave appears
to channel well, also. This chart suggests that, unless an extension is
building, the first quarter of 1980 may
show an a-b-c downswing of greater
proportion than any of the past three
years (see durable goods orders chart
in November issue). Does that mean
stock prices have to come down? Not
if the recession is discounted, and if
you haven't discounted this recession
in your own portfolio, you haven't
been reading the papers for the last
three years....

AVERAGE WEEKLY PAY of factory
workers in November rose to $275.37 from
a revised $274.85 the preceding month, the
Labor Department reports.

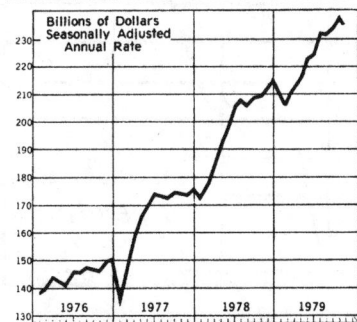

February 9, 1980

In the past several issues, I have
featured charts of fundamental economic data that seem to display an
Elliott pattern. So far, I have included
charts of durable goods orders and
weekly earnings of factory workers,
both of which show five waves upward. Now comes another data series,

SPENDING for construction fell in November to a seasonally adjusted annual
rate of $235.3 billion from a revised $238.5 billion in October, the Commerce Department
reports.

construction spending, which shows exactly the same pattern. Taken together, the charts of the economy suggest a marked slowing of economic activity some time in 1980, unless of course an extension forms. A "slowing" may indeed mean a recession by the official definition, but even if it occurs, it will take a lot more than that to frighten the stock market, since whatever slowing we do get has been more than discounted over the last three years.

April 6, 1980

Not once since I began these letters have I said anything about the economy except "Forget the Recession." Now, as you can see on the front page table, I fully expect one to occur. The reasoning is simple. The market, for the first time since 1973, is predicting a recession. How deep it will be depends upon the severity of the decline in the market..

Based on the Elliott counts of economic data (see previous letters), a recession now appears to have its best excuse for occurring since the economists began predicting one three years ago. This chart of durable goods orders looks like it's right at the top of the "b" wave of an a-b-c correction following a five-wave advance. The "c" wave should carry under the 72 level.

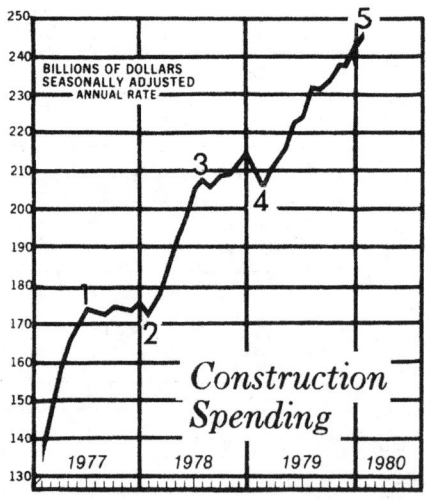
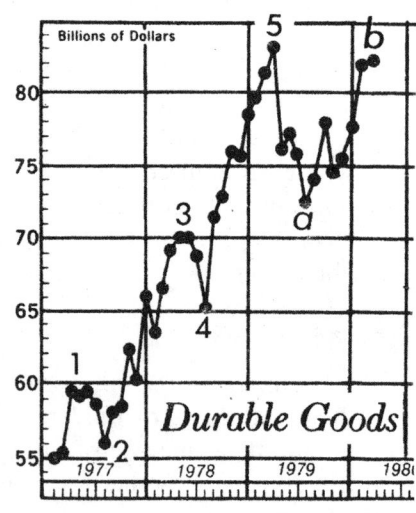

June 10, 1980

From the time I began writing these reports to the March 9, 1980 issue, my front-page conclusion regarding the economy was "Forget the Recession." Since last November, however, I have been displaying all sorts of charts of fundamental economic data that were counting out complete "fives," from the average weekly pay of factory workers to construction spending to durable goods orders to the number of new incorporations. We knew we were close to that recession, but two pieces were missing. The first was the contrary opinion aspect, which finally fell into place when the WSJ headlined: "As the Heralded Slump Still Doesn't Show Up, Firms Disregard Threat — Analysts Explain Mistakes, Now See Mild Recession and Still More Inflation." The other indicator which had yet to "click in" was the stock market, and the performance in March supplied the missing piece. The Elliott conclusion was then clear as crystal: SEVERE RECESSION 1980-1981.

As the two charts below indicate, the economy, which has been weakening ever so slightly, absolutely collapsed in April and May, and may still be collapsing. The leading indicators dropped 4.8% for the month of April, their largest drop since the series began in 1948. That drop compares to a 3% drop in the worst month (September) of the 1974-75 recession. The incredible slide in short term interest rates indicates that the demand for funds is practically zero. The charts of the fundamental data mentioned above are well into their a-b-c declines as well. O.K., score one for Elliott analysis, which not only saw the turn in the economy developing, but recognized "the top" as well.

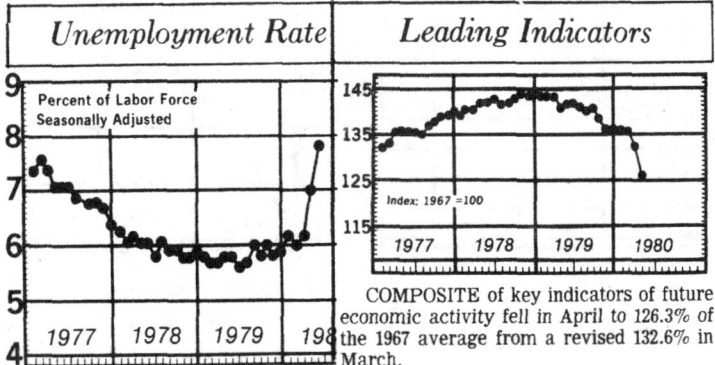

| Unemployment Rate | Leading Indicators |

Percent of Labor Force Seasonally Adjusted

Index: 1967 = 100

COMPOSITE of key indicators of future economic activity fell in April to 126.3% of the 1967 average from a revised 132.6% in March.

July 6, 1980

The economy has remained on its downward course as per expectations. These charts of retail sales, new incorporations, durable goods orders and construction spending illustrate the Elliott influence since 1977.

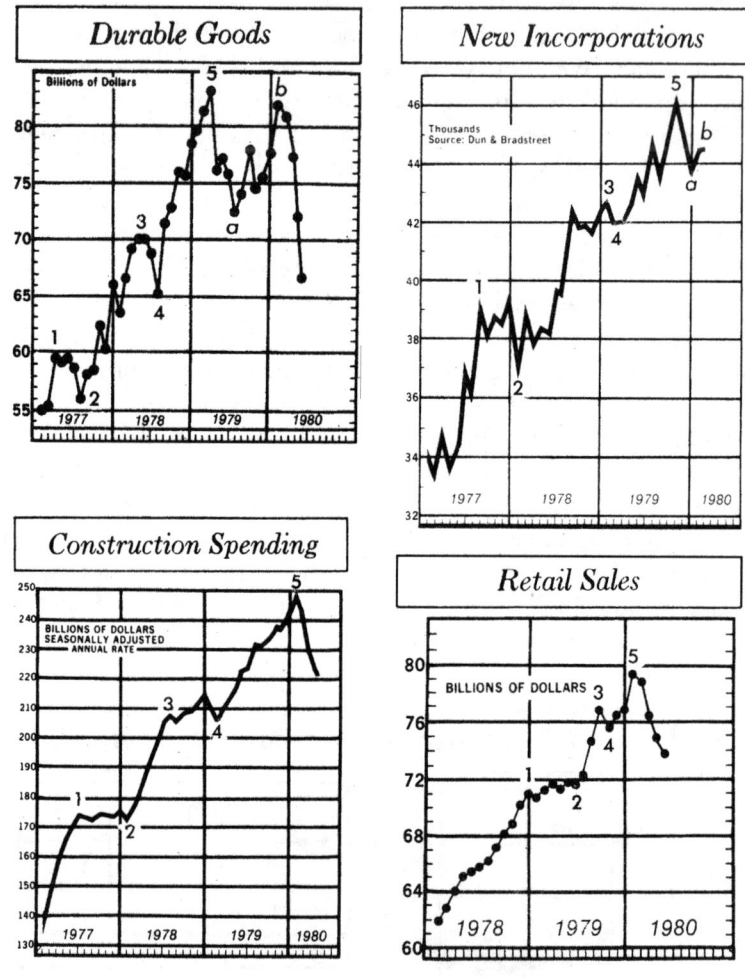

Since the Elliott guideline for a normal bear market is the low of the previous fourth wave of lesser degree (or the second wave of lesser degree when the first wave is extended), we might expect a bottom in the recession quite soon. "Normal" targets for these economic indicators are as follows:

Retail Sales: $71b.
Construction Spending: $207b.
Durable Goods Orders: $65b.
New incorporations: 42,000.

August 10, 1980

Elliott Wave analysis caught the "top" in the economy just weeks before the economic indicators tumbled. Last month I displayed four charts of economic data and commented that based on the normal expectation of wave retracement, "we might expect a bottom in the recession quite soon." I also gave downside targets for the four fundamental factors. The only follow-up data yet available is for durable goods orders, for which a normal Elliott guideline projected a bottom at $65b. The chart at right shows the latest data, and the slowing down in the rate of descent could indicate a bottom right on target.

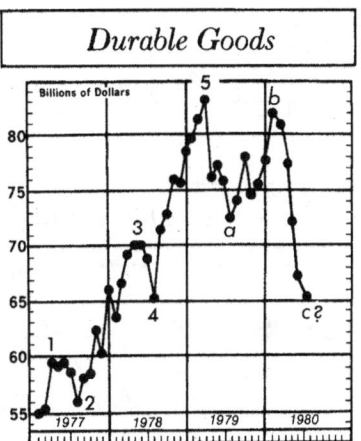

September 9, 1980

In the July 6 letter, I put "RECESSION ENDING" on the front page table and showed charts of four different measures of economic data, with target points for each. As you can see, durable goods orders bottomed at $66b. (target $65b.), while retail sales (target $71b.), construction spending (target $207b.), and new incorporations (target 42,000) appear to have a bit more to go. Based on these charts, we could have a "pullback" (as part of a W pattern) in some areas of the economy, with retail sales the most vulnerable area.

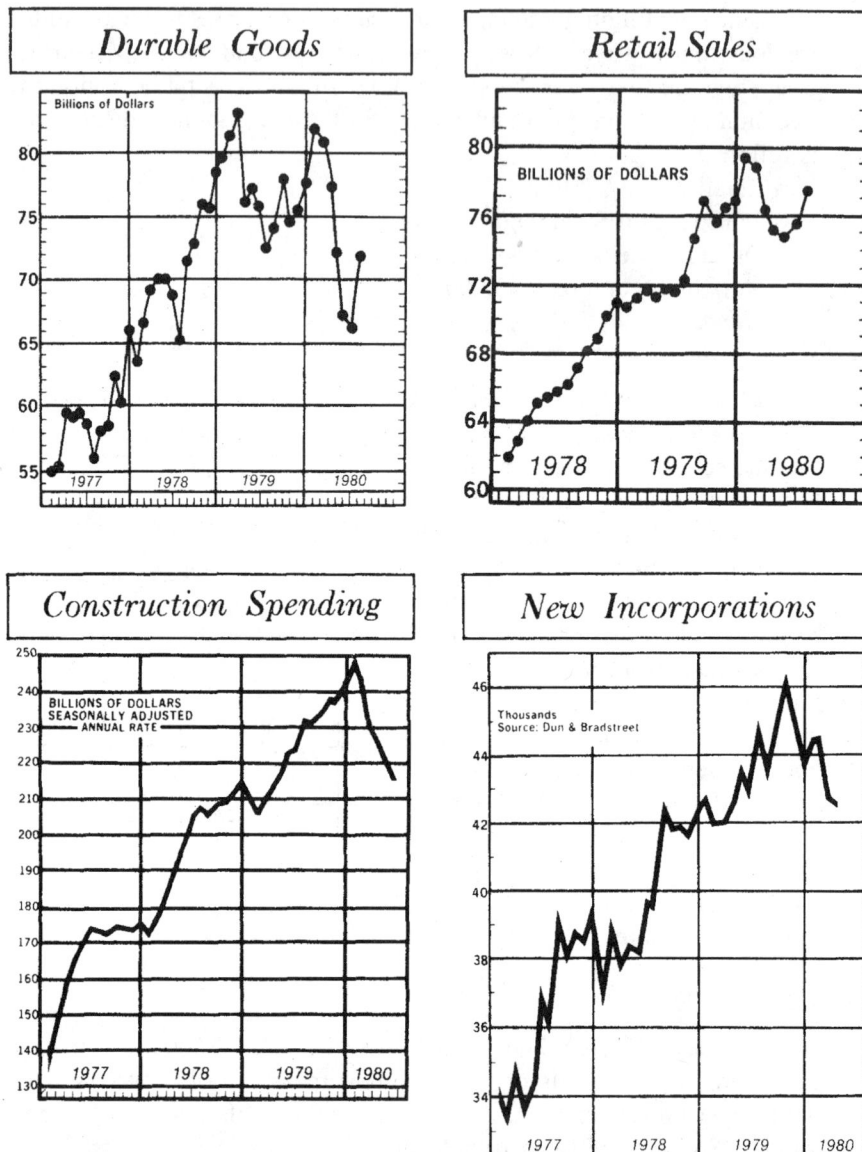

October 3, 1980

July was my first letter marked "RECESSION ENDING." Along with many other economic indicators, the chart of industrial production shows a July low, as you can see from the accompanying chart.

As for the current recovery, I expect that it will peak out in the first quarter of 1981 and show a second dip into the latter half of the year. This projection is based on the Elliott outlook for the stock market and the bond market, as well as an expected tightening of monetary policy after the election no matter who wins.

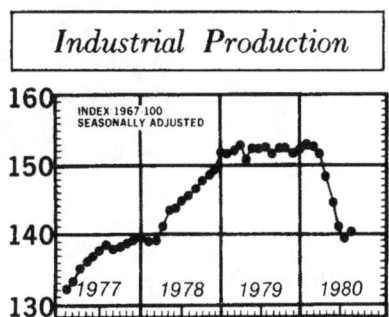

January 9, 1981

The economy rebounded right on schedule from the Elliott-based forecast, as the accompanying chart of industrial production illustrates.

Last month I indicated that I expected a "second dip" some time during 1981. That second dip should not be a full-fledged recession, but only a month or two of weak statistics. The most important point I can make is that I think the "second dip" has been entirely discounted during the corrective wave of the past four months, so it's not something to worry about from a stock market standpoint.

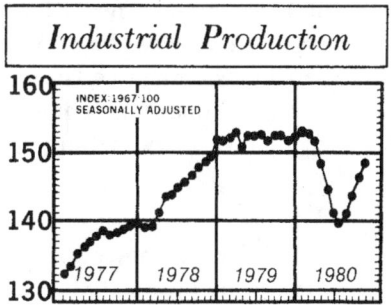

April 12, 1981

Starting on the front page of the December 14 issue of *The Elliott Wave Theorist*, I indicated that the economy should undergo a "SECOND DIP EARLY 1981." This "second dip" was not (and still is not) expected to become a new full-fledged recession. These quotes from the WSJ's front page summarizes what has occurred since the robust economic rebound that began last July started slowing down.

THE ECONOMY slowed in February on the effects of inflation and high interest rates, and new government figures support economists' predictions of sluggish performance this year. Housing starts plunged nearly 25% to an adjusted annual rate of 1,218,000 units, while industrial output fell an adjusted 0.5% after six consecutive gains. Personal income rose an adjusted 0.7%, its smallest gain since June, and the savings rate in January, at 4.4% was the lowest in three decades.

For two years now, I've had excellent success in calling the turns in the economy, and I don't mind revealing my secret. But don't hold your breath; it's one that's been known for decades: If you can define what the stock market is doing, then you can anticipate the economy with a precision as yet unmatched by any other method. A Cycle degree decline precedes a severe recession. A Primary degree decline generally precedes a moderate or short recession. An Intermediate degree correction, such as we have undergone since August, should precede a "softening" in the economy. These "forecasts" are often possible only with a knowledge of the Wave Principle, since many sideways periods might not be defined as corrective "declines" under another method of analysis. Furthermore, one must employ a flexible definition of recession, not the economist's rigid definition of X number of months of decline in GNP.

August 2, 1981

I don't comment on the economy very often because it isn't necessary. In the July 6, 1980 letter the front page comment was "RECESSION ENDING." That changed to "REBOUND IN PROGRESS" until December 1980, when it changed to "SECOND DIP EARLY 1981." Following a marked slowdown in economic activity in the first quarter, I changed the heading in the April 12 letter to "SECOND DIP OCCURRING." The data for April-May-June are now in and show these results:

THE ECONOMY contracted at an adjusted 1.9% annual rate in the second quarter, and many analysts see continued weakness through the fall. They attributed the decline largely to high interest rates. Price increases in the period slowed to a 6% annual rate, down sharply from the 9.8% pace of the preceding quarter.

Durable-goods orders fell 0.8% in June to an adjusted $87.46 billion.

Even though I put very little effort into it, I've had no trouble forecasting the general trend of the economy in these letters. My methods were explained in the April 12, 1981 letter and can be used by anyone who prefers to avoid digesting reams of statistics in order to reach a conclusion. Since no method of forecasting is perfect, one of these days I'm bound to get a false signal, but I expect that the overall record will continue to be highly successful.

September 8, 1981

As these paragraphs from the WSJ indicate, the economy is still on track with a "second dip" in progress. The chart of housing starts displays the double dip profile quite clearly. I fully expect to be changing the front page comment on the economy next month from "SECOND DIP OCCURRING" to "SECOND DIP ENDING." [Note: This change was not made.]

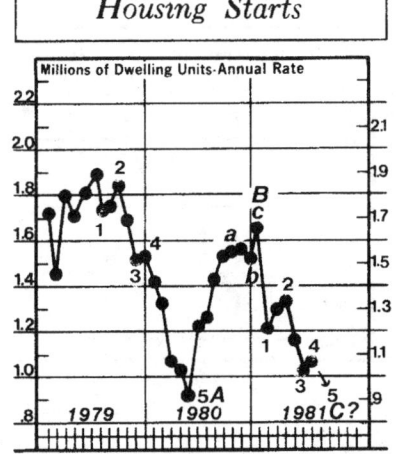

Housing Starts

CORPORATE PROFITS after taxes fell 11.3% in the second quarter, the Commerce Department said, indicating the economy was weaker than had been thought. Gross national product declined at an adjusted 2.4% annual rate after allowing for inflation. The department has estimated the decline at a 1.9% pace.

* * *

The economy deteriorated in July as production, employment and new orders plummeted, according to a survey of purchasing agents.

January 11, 1982 through *October 4, 1982*

"RECESSION IN PROGRESS."

November 8, 1982

I haven't said much about the economy lately, being satisfied to leave "RECESSION IN PROGRESS" on the front page of the letter. Until now, the market had not given an adequate indication that the economy was truly about to turn, so I had no reason to change it. Now it's given a powerful signal: the current very deep recession is ending. Economic recovery will begin soon.

The correlation between the stock market and the economy is so consistent that it is by far the finest tool for forecasting the economy, as long as you don't restrict yourself to "official" definitions of recession. It is extremely instructive to note the precision with which the March-May rally gave an advance indication of the subsequent moderate improvement in some economic indicators. The May-August slide then correctly preceded a "mysterious" backsliding in the economic figures once again. I've waited for the stock market to give an unmistakable major turn signal by roaring ahead before placing "RECOVERY BEGINNING" on the front page of the letter. Now it's done it, and the Elliott counts on economic data (see charts) agree. By waiting for the full signals, I haven't been wrong on the economy since *The Elliott Wave Theorist* began. Let's see how this one works out.

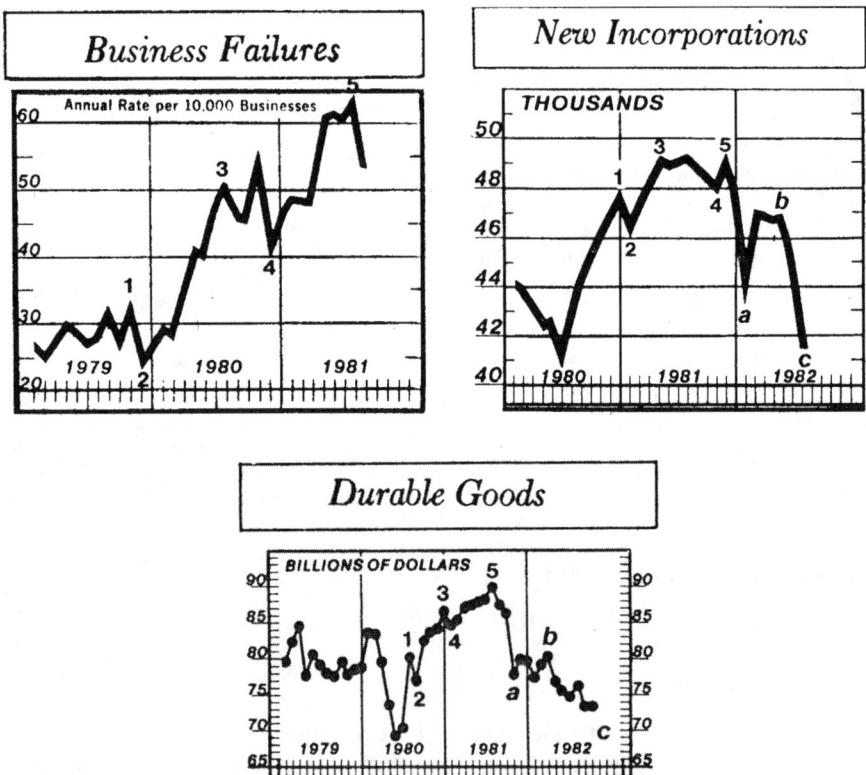

March 7, 1983

Even while administration officials were still sending out gloomy messages as recently as January, the economy has been roaring into life. Finally, as this recent report shows, the data can no longer be ignored.

At this point, I feel it warranted to change "RECOVERY BEGINNING" to "ECONOMIC BOOM" on the front page table. This is somewhat of a change in my thinking regarding the environment for the 1980s. The *monetary* environment should be one of stability, but the economy itself, if my outlook for stocks is correct, really should enter a full-blown boom, similar in many ways to the 1920s. The rise in stocks, the drop in the price of oil and overall monetary stability for the first time in ten years should provide the fuel. By the way, if someone (as *Time* magazine did recently) is still telling you to worry about an imminent banking collapse, you should ask them why bank stocks have just begun to take off on the upside.

T**HE INDEX** of leading economic indicators rose 3.6% in January, the largest one-month gain since July 1950. The increase confirms that the recession has ended. But Commerce Secretary Baldrige warned that the index's strength shouldn't be perceived "as a sign of a coming economic boom."

We checked in with the World Bank the other day and discovered some good news: The bank's earnings are running several hundred million dollars ahead of last year, thanks in large measure to handsome gains in its bond portfolio. In addition, loan requests from the poor countries that the bank is in business to help have fallen off sharply.

August 9, 1983

On the front page of the March 7 issue, I changed the comment on Economic Conditions from "RECOVERY UNDERWAY" to "ECONOMIC BOOM" based entirely on the performance by the single best indicator of economic trends, the stock market. 4 1/2 months later, the news is out. The accompanying comments appeared under the headline, "Economy Surges to 2-Year High":

JULY 22, 1983 – USA TODAY

The economy's growth has hit a two-year high, the government said Thursday, setting a "stunning" 8.7 percent pace that President Reagan called "the surest route to more jobs."

Gross national product — the total output of goods and services — soared by an inflation-adjusted $31.3 billion in the April-June quarter. Consumer spending increased by $23.8 billion.

The surge is much higher than the government's early estimate of 6.6 percent, and higher than virtually all private forecasts.

From that point forward, my interests shifted, and I ceased analyzing economic statistics. Unfortunately, my lack of rigor in this area from that time forward eventually led to numerous premature warnings about the depression that was expected to follow wave V. For an explanation of why I was so early in my concerns, please see Section Two of *View From the Top of the Grand Supercycle.*

"Getting It" from the Point of View of Macroeconomic Causality

Having studied the typical results of Primary degree corrections (see *The Wave Principle of Human Social Behavior*, Chapter 16, p. 262), I was able to make this statement on August 4, 1986:

> Primary wave ④ will precede an outright recession in economic activity, much as Primary wave ④ in 1926 led to the 1926-1927 recession.

This exposition anticipated what did happen, as the final months of the 1987-1990 (1991) wave ④ produced a recession, as you can see in Figure 2.

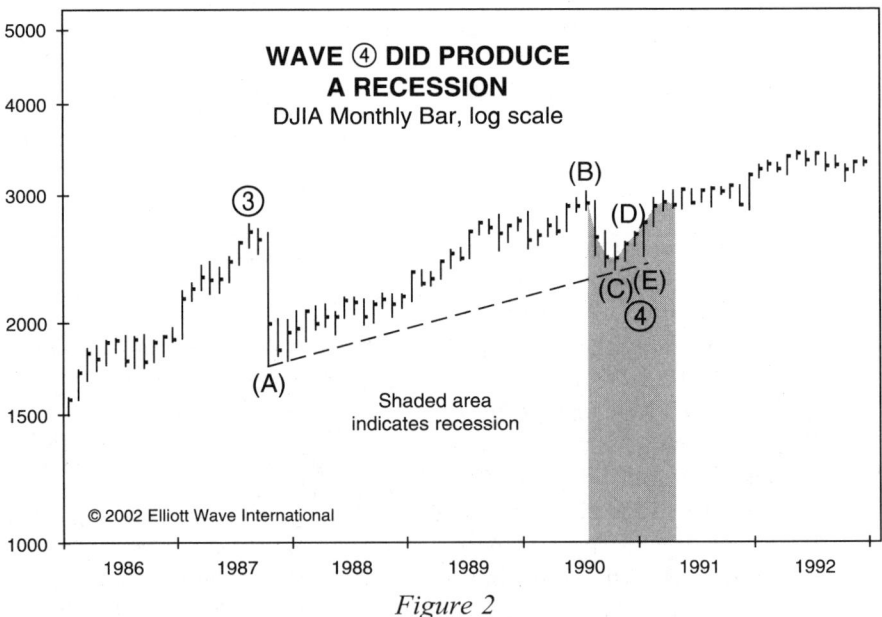

Figure 2

For the record, I did not recognize wave ④ for what it was, and when the time came to announce a new phase of boom, I instead issued this erroneous commentary from July 26, 1991:

There is a lot of talk about the "shape" of the recession. Is it a "V"? Will it be a "W"? A "U"? An "L"? While "W" and "L" shapes are proposed as the worst possibilities, they are too optimistic. The Wave Principle suggests more of a crippled "M", as in the illustration shown here.

you are here

I did gain some equilibrium and occasionally reminded readers that as long as the stock market was rising, the economy would do well, but my continual concerns for an imminent downturn in wave V produced a way-too-bearish near term outlook through most of the 1990s. While the Japanese economy followed the script relentlessly, the U.S. economy sailed through the 1990s unscathed.

Some Success in Forecasting Long-Term Economic Trends

Economic Expansions

Chapter 13 of *At the Crest of the Tidal Wave* tells this story of forecasting a major upturn in the economy based upon socionomics:

The first three years of the 1980s contained the most months of officially recognized economic contraction since the Great Depression bottomed out in March 1933. On November 8, 1982, right at the end of this period, *The Elliott Wave Theorist* announced on its front page, RECOVERY BEGINNING, commenting, "The stock market has given a powerful signal: the current very deep recession is ending." The January 10, 1983 issue announced RECOVERY UNDERWAY, which was amended to ECONOMIC BOOM on March 7. This forecast was based on one thing: an understanding of the *degree* of the upturn in the stock market. The start of a bull market of Cycle degree implied a long period of economic expansion. What indeed began the very next month was the longest uninterrupted economic expansion since 1961-1969.

Economic Contraction

The same book, published in 1995, then went on to anticipate the next major signal:

This book is being published at what I believe is a juncture opposite that of mid-1982. At that time, the long term stock market pattern indicated RECOVERY AHEAD, but the actual start of the recovery was not signaled until stocks advanced on powerful upside momentum in August-October of that year. Today, the long term pattern in the stock market emphatically indicates DEPRESSION AHEAD. When will it arrive? The signal will be the same as that of thirteen years ago: a change in the trend of the stock market, this time in the opposite direction. *The Elliott Wave Theorist* commented on this approach a decade ago, in December 1985:

> We should keep the ultimate probability of an economic crash and financial calamity in mind, but it is still *too early* to prepare for it. Legions of super bears have warned of impending monetary collapse, imminent full-scale banking crises, and so forth for years. Although they continue to warn that such events could occur "out of the blue," "at any time," and "without warning," history shows that a substantial decline in the stock market has always provided an early warning to such conditions. As long as the stock market is trending upward, there is no reason to harbor such fears.

So years ago, the Wave Principle answered concerns about the economy by saying, "Not yet," allowing us to prosper from the very start of the expansion. This approach is in direct contrast to those of the two main groups: the perennial doomsayers, who have for decades predicted another depression "just around the corner," and the far larger contingent of perennial optimists, who have neither the means nor the desire to identify signs of impending trouble.

As the above quotation indicates, the signal for the Grand Supercycle downturn will be given when the stock market begins falling in earnest. Then you will know that a new label will be added to our front page forecast: DEPRESSION BEGINNING.

Wave V took far longer than I thought it would, so in retrospect, it would have been better to refrain from warning of an upcoming turn toward depression for another few years. Because I was so concerned about the implications of the approaching Grand Supercycle degree downturn, I prematurely anticipated economic contraction, leaving PREPARE FOR DEPRESSION on the front page of my publication for much of the 1990s. I should not have made that mistake, because, as indicated in the final paragraph quoted above, socionomics allows plenty of time for the market to change direction *before* we are called upon to make a strong case for economic change. Today, I (and you) now know enough about socionomics never to repeat that mistake. Nevertheless, I believe these words of caution will have saved many individuals and businesses from financial ruin as they positioned themselves for an economic contraction of Grand Supercycle degree.

Since stocks turned down in early 2000, and because I am of the opinion that the turn was of Grand Supercycle degree, I continue to forecast depression. The front page label in *The Elliott Wave Financial Forecast* changed to DEPRESSION UNDERWAY in 2001. In March 2002, I completed a "pop" book on how to protect yourself against bear markets, economic contraction and deflation entitled, *Conquer the Crash — You Can Survive and Prosper in a Deflationary Depression*. The outcome of this forecast remains to be seen.

Forecasting the Relative Strength of an Economic Expansion

Fifth waves are weaker than third waves, both in terms of their breadth of stock participation and their economic results. This simple truth has immense value in macroeconomic forecasting.

The idea that there is a difference in quality between the macroeconomic trends that manifest from a *third* wave and those that manifest from a *fifth* wave has been a part of the Wave Principle for over twenty years. *Elliott Wave Principle* describes third waves as "wonders to behold" as they deliver on the promise of rising stocks with "increasingly favorable fundamentals." In contrast, "the fifth of the fifth [wave] will lack the dynamism that preceded it." This description is useful because contrasting periods of economic performance can confirm or contradict a wave interpretation. However, it can also provide a basis for forecasting the *quality* of economic trends. For example, by labeling the March 1942 to February 1966 bull market wave III, Frost and I in 1978 established the extramarket vitality of the 1950s and early 1960s as a standard that the forecasted wave V bull market would not surpass. *The Elliott Wave Theorist* reiterated the expected relationship between the two periods with this description in the August 1983 report (reprinted in the Appendix to *Elliott Wave Principle*) on the upcoming "superbull market":

> This fifth wave will be built more on unfounded hopes than on soundly improving fundamentals such as the U.S. experienced in the 1950s and early 1960s. And since this fifth wave, wave V, is a fifth within a larger fifth, wave (V) from 1789, the phenomenon should be magnified by the time the peak is reached.

This is an unusually specific forecast. The very idea of commenting on the relative strength of a projected multi-year recovery is so unusual that no economist has ever attempted anything of the kind. Once you understand that economic trends fit the overall Elliott wave structure, you can understand how I could presume to do it. How has this prediction fared?

Each of the two great post-Depression expansions accompanied a bull market in stocks that lasted a quarter-century, from 1942 to 1966 in the first instance and from 1974 to 2000 in the second. The percentage gain in the DJIA during the latter period was nearly *double* what it was during the former (1930 percent vs. 971 percent). On that basis alone, one might assume that wave V should have produced a stronger economy than wave III. On the contrary, an objective contrast of the quality of the macroeconomic and fiscal aspects of waves III and V shows that wave V has been a weaker

Balance Sheet Items at the End of Wave III vs. Wave V
(scales at left)

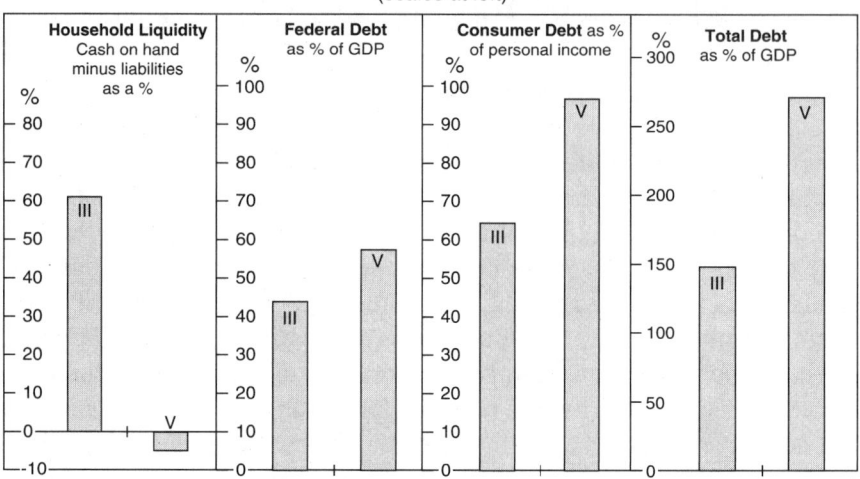

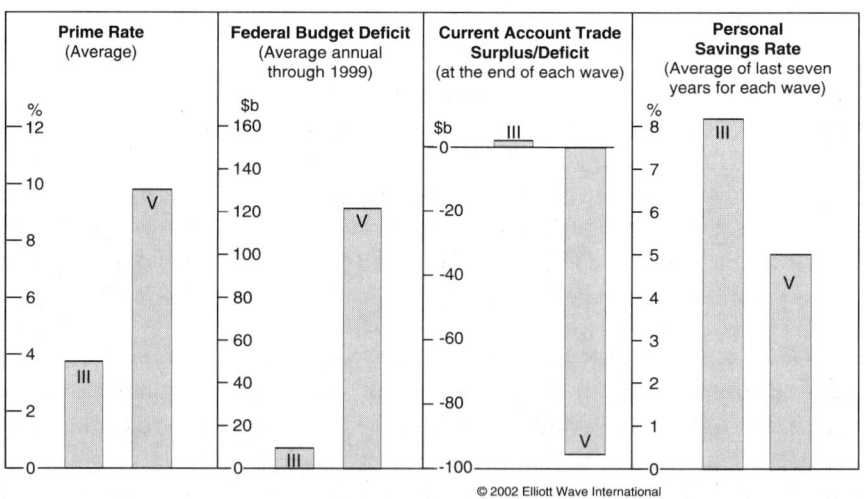

Figure 3

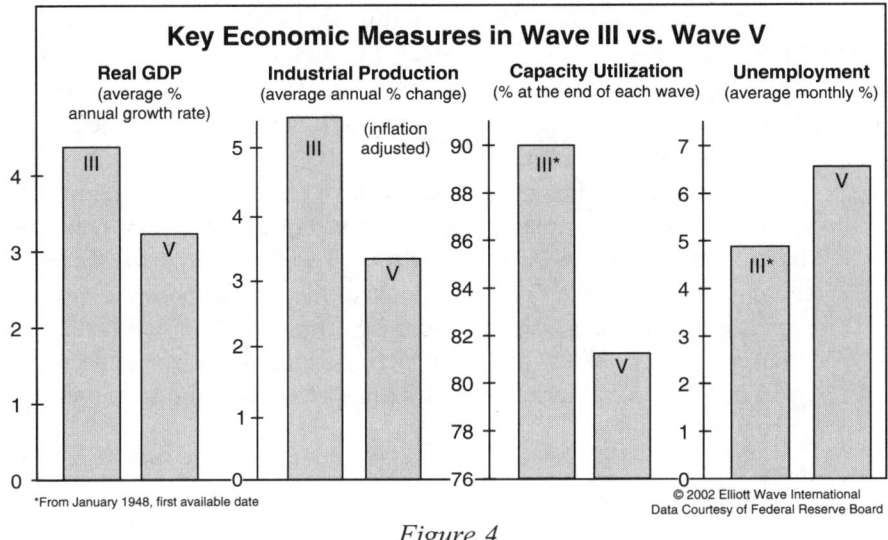

Figure 4

performance in terms of *every relevant measure*, as shown in Figures 3 and 4. Combining the GDP and Industrial Production figures, we may generalize that the economic power of wave V was two-thirds of that of wave III.

The forecast included this phrase: "The phenomenon should be magnified by the time the peak is reached." In other words, the economic expansion would wane even further as wave ⑤ of V progressed and further as wave (5) of ⑤ progressed. True to expectation, the economic expansion slackened further in the latter stages of wave V.

Probably because background conditions in the 1980s and 1990s were so much better than those in the *1970s*, conventional observers miss this very important long-term distinction. In contrast, the Wave Principle provides the basis for a profound insight regarding the relative character of the economic environment of the 1980s and 1990s. What's more, it is available not only as a useful latter-day observation (which even today is utterly lacking in current conventional economic discourse) but as a *prediction*, published four years into the second quarter-century expansion. (Had you been a practicing socionomist at the time, you could have presented that outlook in 1975 or even earlier.)

Picking Up Where We Left Off

When the stock market turned up in September 2001, my associate Peter Kendall and I anticipated a temporary economic respite within the context of a developing depression. Then, in January 2002, we bucked the

mounting euphoria and predicted the end of that respite in an article entitled, "The Big Hook: It's Not a Recovery; It's a Developing Depression."
We submitted it to *Barron's* on January 11, 2002 and to *The Financial
Times* (London) on January 29, 2002, but it was not published. The article
contained this near-term outlook:

> Bear-market rallies in the Nikkei have led to brief one-month in-
> creases in year-to-year real GDP growth in Japan, to 4.7% or better, in
> March 1991, March 1997 and March 2000. *The San Francisco Chronicle*
> records that during the first such bounce, the "entire policy establish-
> ment is congratulating itself for being the first regulators in history to
> deflate an asset bubble without impacting severely on economic activ-
> ity." Yet after each brief recovery, the market headed for new lows and
> the economy followed.
>
> If the sentiment behind the rally in U.S. stocks since September has
> the strength to generate an uptick in some economic indicators in the
> first quarter of 2002, it will likewise prove to be only a "false spring."
> Any such event, ironically, would coincide with the time when 91% of
> economists reporting to the January Blue Chip survey say they expect
> the recession to be over.

The first quarter indeed saw "an uptick in some economic indicators," with
GDP, according to preliminary reports, growing at a six percent annual
rate. As of the second quarter of 2002, economists have celebrated the onset of a new boom, and the consensus outlook is for 2.5 to 6.0 percent
growth for the year.

In the August 30, 2002 *Elliott Wave Financial Forecast*, Mr. Kendall
illustrated and updated the graphs we had reviewed for our article (see Figure 5):

> These charts of the economic data from the last three years show
> that the same impulsive form has left its imprint on the fundamentals
> once again. The big difference is that this time the complete "fives" are
> pointing in the opposite direction[, downward, while the counter-trend
> patterns are on the upside]. These data are particularly relevant now be-
> cause durable goods orders, consumer sentiment, consumer goods orders
> and the home building index are set to resume their respective declines.
> Technically, the corrective patterns can develop into more complicated
> sideways moves, but with the lagging effect of the stock market's fall
> through July 24 still in the pipeline, we do not expect it. The economy
> should enter a more severe contraction in a matter of weeks.

"FIVES" POINT TO A FUNDAMENTAL TREND CHANGE

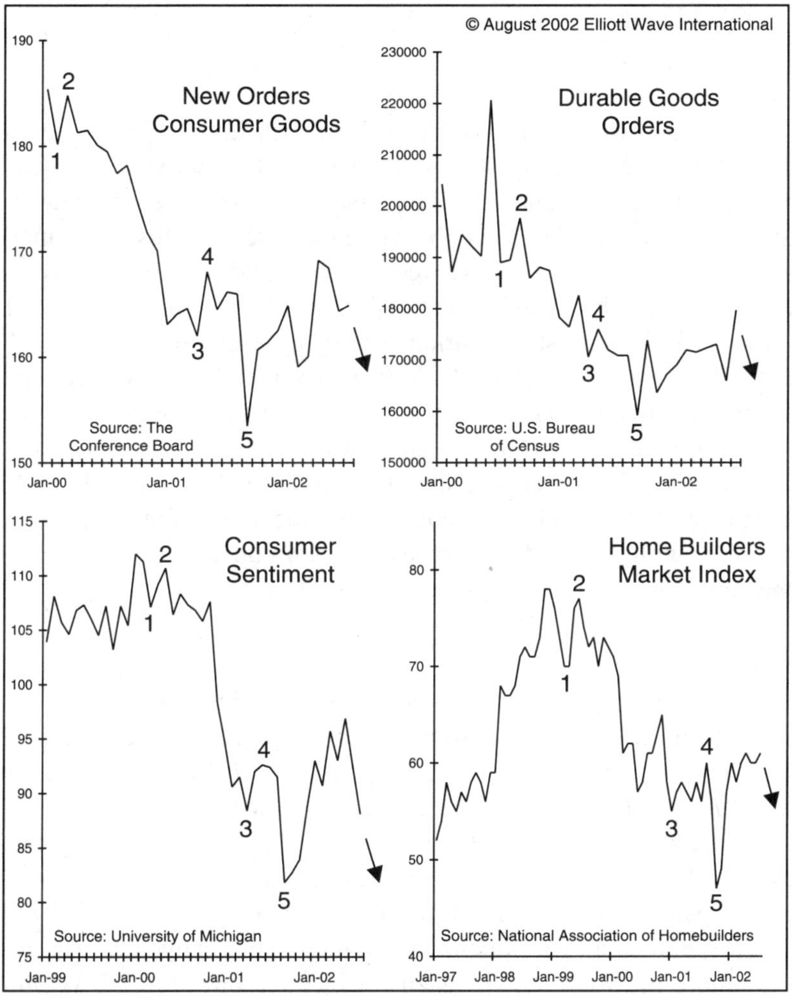

Figure 5

It remains to be seen whether the widely expected long term boom will materialize or whether in fact our anticipated uptick in economic indicators was indeed a "false spring."

Some Success in Forecasting Monetary Trends

Socionomics is hardly a perfect tool for forecasting long-term monetary trends, but in its brief history of application, it is already unparalleled in that role. We have records of successful forecasts of inflation, disinflation and deflation.

Inflation

Because I was young and did not publish until 1976, our evidence here is weak but certainly shows some value compared to conventional approaches to market analysis. The first investment I ever made was in gold stocks in 1972. The Wave Principle indicated a bullish gold market. I bought West Rand and Orange Free State Geduld, but only partly for Elliott wave reasons because I was only just learning about the subject. (From 1976 to 1979, I published market-timing gold commentary for Merrill Lynch.) Figure 6-11 in *Elliott Wave Principle* and the accompanying commentary show that in 1978, despite our bullish outlook for the stock market, Frost and I were open to further gains in gold, particularly given the sizeable "expanded flat correction" that it traced out from 1974 to 1976. So the Wave Principle was useful in recognizing indications of monetary inflation and staying with the trend — or at least accommodating it — until very late in the game, as we are about to see.

Disinflation

Elliott wave analysis has proved useful in forecasting a major trend change from accelerating inflation to disinflation (i.e., decelerating inflation). The story, related in *At the Crest of the Tidal Wave* and briefly in *The Wave Principle of Human Social Behavior*, is hereby retold.

The spiraling inflation dating from 1967, after weathering two setbacks, finally culminated in January 1980 in an atmosphere of long term financial panic. The month before, in December 1979, *The Elliott Wave Theorist* spelled out expectations for the major sea change that was at hand. *Commodities* (now *Futures*) magazine published some of EWT's comments in its January 1980 issue. Here is an excerpt:

> The incredible conjunction of "fives" in different markets [gold, silver, interest rates, bonds, and commodities] all seem to point to the same conclusion: *The world is about to begin a phase of general disinflation.* As I see it, a pattern of several disinflationary years leading to a deflationary trend later on would be a perfect scenario for the Elliott outlook for stocks. A gradual disinflation would create an optimistic mood in the country and lead to the conclusion that we may have finally licked the inflation problem. This sentiment would support a bull market in stocks for several years until the snowballing forces of deflation began

to take over. At that point, a major deflationary crash would be impossible to avert, and the Grand Supercycle correction would be underway.

The inflationary trend that had accelerated for a Fibonacci 13 years ended abruptly, as indicated by gold and silver prices, the very next month. Indeed, the above paragraph spelled out, just weeks before the reversal of trend, the experience of the ensuing two decades.

The onset of the new trend was as exciting as the termination of the old one. The 1980 peak was followed by a brief two-year period of extremely rapid disinflation that shocked the markets. From a peak of $850 per ounce in January 1980, gold collapsed to $296.75 (basis London fix) in June 1982. From its long-time resistance area just above 1000, the Dow fell back to 777 in August 1982, reaching its lowest real value since World War II. The bond market was scraping bottom, having been ravaged by both the inflationary period, which stoked fears of ever-rising interest rates, and the recessions of 1980 to 1982, which kindled default worries. The next monetary event appeared to be anyone's guess. The most popular competing opinions were (1) that inflation would accelerate into hyperinflation, and (2) that deflation and economic contraction would bring about financial collapse. These opinions were so popular that they were called "The Great Debate" at financial conferences, which attracted thousands of people.

In contrast to the two prevailing opinions, the September 13, 1982 issue of *The Elliott Wave Theorist* offered ten points supporting the forecast for the Dow to quintuple to 3885. (For details, see the Appendix to *Elliott Wave Principle*.) Two of those points pertained to the expected monetary environment:

— Fits the idea that the Kondratieff cycle plateau has just begun, [supporting] a period of economic stability and soaring stock prices. Parallel with late 1921.

— Celebrates the end of the inflationary era [and] accompanies a stable reflation.

Specifically, then, *The Elliott Wave Theorist* forecasted a mild *reflation* relative to the crunch of 1980-1982 that would occur within the longer term trend of *disinflation*. Monetary stability was the last thing on most people's forecast list. Yet, the period of stability and reflation began right then. That the Wave Principle could be applied to recognize the onset of such a period was of immense value to investors, particularly in the stock and bond markets, which began historic advances.

Four months later, in January 1983, *The Elliott Wave Theorist* added to its case as follows: "Quietly behind the scenes, despite all the return-of-inflation rhetoric, the utility stocks have scored a major breakout, providing [another] strong foundation for the 'continuing disinflation' argument." That November, EWT further bolstered the case that the slackening in the rate of inflation was not just a brief respite but was of multi-year significance:

> Two years ago, I used the percent change in the PPI to show a massive momentum divergence against new highs in the index in 1980. That lower peak in the rate of change was essentially a "sell signal" on inflation. Since then, the inflation rate has not only declined substantially, but its rate of change has fallen beneath the long term uptrend line from 1949. That break...does seem to support the claim that there has been a change over the last three years that is larger than just a cyclical disinflation due to recession.

In June 1984, as stock prices slipped to an intermediate-term low, *The Wall Street Journal* published a five-page special report on the financial outlook, which included interviews with many distinguished economists and statesmen. The consensus was overwhelming that the country's economic and monetary problems were insurmountable and about to get worse. (Page 128 of *The Wave Principle of Human Social Behavior* provides some details of this report.) Yet the benign disinflationary trend was already underway, supporting the bull markets in stocks and bonds that continued for another decade and a half.

Deflation

As you have read, the forecast for disinflation issued in late 1979 spelled out the expected sequence of events, calling for "several disinflationary years leading to a deflationary trend later," which would resolve with "a major deflationary crash." In 1995, *At the Crest of the Tidal Wave* argued that outright deflation was imminent, worldwide. Japan had been experiencing deflation for five years. Countries in Southeast Asia underwent deflationary crashes in 1997 and 1998. Argentina's deflation hit bottom in 2001. Hints of deflationary pressures have continued to build in the United States and Europe, particularly after early 2000. For more on my outlook for deflation, see *Conquer the Crash*. The outcome of this forecast remains to be seen, but I believe that signs of accelerating, developing or approaching (depending on your locale) deflation are now more legion than ever.

A Basis of Value for Macroeconomic Prediction

There are two ways to look at the performance of conventional economists vs. what socionomists can do. One is to assess how right they both are in terms of a percentage of the time that they make predictions. On that basis, conventional economists do pretty well, being right about whether the economy will expand or contract in the next quarter as much as 70 percent of the time. Their opinions, demonstrably in the aggregate and (based on my observations) in almost every individual case as well, simply lag the actual economy. Thus, after they finally recognize a new trend that has been in force, their extrapolated predictions can be correct for awhile thereafter when the economy trends that way for a long period of time. In terms of time, socionomists would probably do about as well. The second way to assess performance gives a far different result. If one presumes that economists' job is to anticipate change, then they are virtually never right. Economists' views lag the economy, which lags the stock market. Socionomists anticipate the stock market, which anticipates the economy, so they are often way ahead of coming changes. Even when they fail to anticipate the stock market, they can observe the stock market in real time and forecast economic change quite reliably thereby. Most conventional economists get something close to a zero for performance, a lower score than one would get flipping a coin annually to call economic expansions and contractions. Socionomists, on the other hand, can be trained to read the indicators of approaching or concurrent trend reversal, so they can anticipate change correctly fairly often (although there are as yet no data addressing the rate of success). To be sure, sometimes they anticipate changes that do not occur, and sometimes they miss changes that do. Still, they often *do* anticipate change, and conventional macroeconomists do not. On this basis, there is no comparison between the two approaches; socionomics wins hands down.

December 2001

Toward a New Understanding of Growth and Recession, Boom and Depression

by Hernán Cortés Douglas

"This expansion will run forever."[1] So said an MIT Professor of Economics in *The Wall Street Journal*. Think about it. A respected leader in the field comes to a conclusion about economic behavior that defies the entirety of history. Since that article appeared on July 30, 1998, we know that its breathless conclusion also failed to accommodate the future. Nor was this opinion unique at the time. Ninety-eight percent of economists in *The Wall Street Journal's* New Year's poll of 2001 said they expected continued expansion throughout the year.

This type of forecasting error is hardly a first for academic economists. Examples of our profession's failure to anticipate economic contractions are legion and span its entire history. *The Economist* reiterated in its November 29, 2001 issue, "Economists have a dismal record in predicting recession." Some instances have been so glaring and instructive that they beg retelling.

A Brief Review of Major Failures in Economic Forecasting

To most famed and respected economists of the 1920s, the crash that preceded the Great Depression was utterly unexpected. Fourteen days before Black Tuesday, October 29, 1929, Irving Fisher, America's best-known economist and Professor of Economics at Yale University, declared, "In a few months I expect to see the stock market much higher than today." Fisher, a consummate theoretician, a founder of econometrics, and a pioneer in index number analysis, was also a successful capitalist, having invented the c-kardex file system, which he sold for a staggering sum. He had such faith in his economic analysis that he is reported by his son to have lost an estimated 140 million of today's dollars in the crash.[2]

British economist John Maynard Keynes, a renowned father of macroeconomics who had amassed fortunes in the financial markets for both himself and Cambridge University, was caught unprepared, shedding a million of today's pounds sterling of his net worth.[3]

Days after the crash, the Harvard Economic Society reassured subscribers, "A severe depression such as 1920-21 is outside the range of probability. We are not facing a protracted liquidation." In 1932, after a string of failed optimistic forecasts, the Society closed its doors.

New societies — at universities, central banks and independent "think tanks" — have since sprung up. Do they know any more about macroeconomic forecasting than their predecessors?

Since the Great Depression, we have had immense improvements in science and technology. Given seven additional decades of data collection and progress in econometric techniques, one might presume that the forecasting tools of macroeconomics have become vastly more effective than their predecessors of 1929. Yet as recently as 1988, some leading economists went on the record about the profession's lack of progress. Writing in *The American Economic Review*, the journal of the American Economic Association, Kathryn Domínguez, Ray Fair, and Matthew Shapiro reported that a modern economist, armed with the latest and most sophisticated econometric techniques, and even using voluminous data that was unavailable in 1929, would have had no idea in 1929 that the Great Depression lay around the corner.

Real results continue to bear out the implications of this conclusion. For example, as one writer observed, "It is hard to imagine any article with worse timing than, say, 'Asia's Bright Future,'"[4] which appeared in the November/December 1997 issue of *Foreign Affairs*. The article, by two Harvard professors, appeared as East Asian economies were already melting down and as Japan was staggering through one of the three recessions it has suffered in a decade of financial difficulty. Consider its disutility in light of the fact that the year 1974, a full 23 years earlier, would have been the best time for such a forecast, while 1997, *late* 1997 at that, was the worst time since the onset of World War II to have made it.

President Herbert Hoover, reflecting in his Memoirs on economists' consensus prior to the Depression for which the public so often blamed him, complained, "With growing optimism, they gave birth to a foolish idea called the 'New Economic Era'. That notion spread over the whole country. We were assured we were in a new period where the old laws of economics no longer applied." Seven decades later, our MIT professor's prognostications about the "New Economy" echoed those same follies. The justification once again was that we had conquered the business cycle: "As we have the tools to keep the current expansion going," he wrote, "we won't have [a recession.] We have the monetary and fiscal resources to keep one from happening, as well as a policy team that won't hesitate to use them for continued expansion."[5] If that were true, then Japan, with its own dedicated "policy team" of macroeconomists and its world-class kit bag of macroeconomic "tools," would have prevented the prolonged stagnation that was as evident in 1998 as it still is now.

Mysteries Loaded with Suspects

The Minneapolis Fed, in October 2000, invited some sixty noted economists to a conference to present research papers on the Great Depression. The event attracted a number of macroeconomist luminaries, including University of Chicago professor Robert E. Lucas Jr., the 1995 Nobel Laureate, and professors from the University of Minneapolis, UC Berkeley, Princeton, Carnegie Mellon and other top universities. All that talent brought to bear notwithstanding, the report on the conference in the Minneapolis Fed Review, *The Region*, concludes on a rather disappointing note. When economists review the facts surrounding the Depression, it says, they "each time come up with another explanation. The Great Depression is...a mystery that is loaded with suspects and difficult to solve, even when we know the ending." [6]

By and large the explanation of this failure is that economists have been leaning on so-called macroeconomic fundamentals to attempt such predictions. Have they ever succeeded? The historical data say that they *cannot* succeed; financial markets never collapse when things look bad. In fact, quite the contrary is true. Before contractions begin, macroeconomic flows always look fine. That is why the vast majority of economists always proclaim the economy to be in excellent health just before it swoons. Despite these failures, indeed despite repeating almost precisely those failures, economists have continued to pore over the same macroeconomic fundamentals for clues to the future. If the conventional macroeconomic approach is useless even in retrospect, if it cannot explain or understand an outcome *even when we know what it is*, has it a prayer of doing so when the goal is assessing the future?

Apparently not. As Lucas candidly observed years ago, "Economic reasoning will be of no value in cases of uncertainty."[7] We have learned from Nobel laureate Friedrich von Hayek, his mentor, Ludwig von Mises, and from Frank Knight, a Professor of Economics at the University of Chicago who taught several Nobel Laureates, that uncertainty is normal and pervasive. Given that the future is always uncertain, is Lucas saying that "economic reasoning" has no forecasting value whatsoever? Reasoning *per se* is not at fault; more and more, it appears that the flaws reside in the *conventional economic premises* upon which that reasoning is founded. There is a different but correct set of fundamentals.

Toward a New Understanding

What are economists missing? What did they once learn but later forget or neglect? What new studies shed light on the subject? For answers, I suggest looking to the following three subsets of empirical observations that have emerged from disparate sources.

1. Debt drives the business cycle.

Well-known to economists but oddly ignored is the fact that large, sustained increases in money and private sector debt accompany economic booms. Conversely, important contractions in money and private sector debt accompany economic contractions. Fluctuations in private debt levels correlate with stock indices and economic activity in general, especially with respect to trends lasting years or decades. These observations are consistent with the monetary (Milton Friedman) and Austrian (Mises and Hayek) theories of the business cycle, but economists have ceased putting them to practical use. In 1933, Irving Fisher highlighted the correlation in an article in *Econometrica*, "Debt-Deflation Theory of Depressions," which most economists have neglected. Similarly, in a lifetime of work ignored by mainstream economists, post-Keynesian economist Hyman Minsky focused on the financial instability created by expanding indebtedness. In the major boom that ended with the 20th century, private sector debt accumulated at a blistering pace and hit very high levels, especially near the end. Economists again paid scant attention to this phenomenon and again paid the price by missing the reversal.

2. Market indices trace patterned paths.

Ralph N. Elliott, author of *The Wave Principle* in 1938 and succeeding works,[8] established in the mid 1930s that financial markets trend and reverse in recognizable patterns. Their structures are clear and definite in form, although not fixed in time or amplitude. Market movements have different degrees. Patterns of smaller degree link together to form similar patterns at larger degree. Thus, Elliott established that markets are hierarchical. In recent years, physicists who have studied financial markets have discovered aspects of market behavior that are compatible with this insight.[9,10]

For the past three decades, Robert R. Prechter, Jr. has applied and extended these principles to a wide variety of social phenomena.[11] Perhaps most important, his latest book, *The Wave Principle of Human Social Behavior and the New Science of Socionomics*, has established that markets are "robust fractals," (termed quasi-fractals by physicists Arneodo *et al.*[12]). The existence of self-affinity in price patterns at all scales indicates fractal ordering, but if Elliott is right, they are intermediately ordered fractals in contrast to the indefinite fractals described by Mandelbrot. They have "a qualitative specificity of form akin to that of self-identical fractals such as nested squares as well as a quantitative elasticity akin to that of indefinite fractals such as clouds and seacoasts,"[13] says Prechter.

Because of the form specificity of robust fractals, there is an element of predictability in markets, not in spite of, but because of, their complexity. As one recent example, physicists Anders Johansen and Didier Sornette found that markets proceed unabatedly toward a crash, "anticipating [it] in a subtle self-organized and cooperative fashion, releasing precursory fingertips observable in stock market prices."[14] Yet at such times, everything looks rosy to mainstream macroeconomists because stocks have been rising persistently, and output, employment and other standard indicators appear healthy. Economists relying on such "fundamentals" invariably extrapolate the good times into the future ("the crudest form of technical analysis"[15]), rather than recognize their true import in a patterned world.

If we economists are to advance our craft, we will have to abandon the widespread illusion that financial markets are random walks, as many top business schools, unfortunately, continue to preach, against formidable evidence such as that reported by Andrew W. Lo and A. Craig MacKinley.[16] Markets proceed relentlessly according to a robust fractal, whose components or phases Elliott designated as "waves." The new theoreticians and social physicists find themselves in good company with classical analysis: Pythagoras's doctrine called for inquiry into pattern rather than substance to determine the essence of things.[17] Such inquiry is now bearing fruit in the macroeconomic field.

3. Changes in economic variables follow stock market fluctuations according to degree.

Changes in the stock market indices precede — they do not follow — changes in economic fundamentals or news about them. Thus, they are a leading indicator of economic activity. Eight decades ago, Wesley Mitchell and the National Bureau of Economic Research recognized this phenomenon, but an inability to recognize different degrees made the breakthrough less helpful than it might have been.

If the changes in markets are hierarchical, then so are the economic changes that follow. This explains why declines in stock indices of very high degree anticipate depressions, while drops of lesser degree anticipate recessions and milder downturns. Paul A. Samuelson, 1970 Nobel Laureate, famously quipped, "The market has anticipated five out of the last three recessions," completely missing the hierarchical nature of markets. It was a clever but inaccurate remark. Understanding the hierarchy and chronology of stock market and economic events will allow macroeconomists more accuracy in prediction.

A New Basis for Theory and Modeling

Only two academic economists — Friedrich August von Hayek and Ludwig von Mises — correctly forecast the market break of 1929 and the ensuing Depression.[18] Did economists adopt their Austrian theory? Alas, no. They adopted the economics of Keynes, and not the best economics of Keynes.[19]

In a world of uncertainty, expectations are a critical variable in most financial decisions. Some notable economists have acknowledged that the mental variability of human beings in this regard is missing from the conventional model. "It is acutely uncomfortable," 1987 Nobel Laureate Robert M. Solow wrote recently, "to have so much in macroeconomics depend on how one deals with a concept like expectations, for which there is (inevitably?) so little empirical understanding and so much room for invention."[20] If you know where to look, though, you will find a growing body of new work that displays an impressive empirical understanding of aggregate expectations, so its lack is in no way inevitable if we put our minds to it.

As Solow intimates, a solid concept of expectations is crucial. We may be close to that goal. Certainly if stock markets are patterned, so must be the causal forces driving them. Citing the prior work of Paul Montgomery of *Universal Economics* and Paul MacLean of the National Institute of

Mental Health, Prechter presents an intriguing hypothesis regarding the forces behind expectations. He proposes that this key macroeconomic variable may derive from pre-rational thought patterns that drive the fundamental impulse of human social cooperation in a context of uncertainty.[21] The emotions that govern expectations, he says, are essentially a "first cause," generated by impulsive portions of the brain associated with herding. Yale economics professor Robert J. Schiller, a leading voice in the new field of Behavioral Finance, concurs at least to the extent of saying, "Solid psychological research does show that there are patterns of human behavior that suggest anchors for the market that would not be expected if markets worked entirely rationally."[22] If so, consider an alternative to mainstream macroeconomics' idea that each individual is a "representative agent" with rational expectations, responding mechanically to exogenous changes in news about economic fundamentals to create in the aggregate a random walk in the stock market and the economy. Perhaps we should entertain the contrasting assumption that endogenous changes in aggregate expectations — in confidence and mood, in optimism and pessimism — are at least a force, if not *the* driving force, behind stock prices and the economy.[23] The economy expands and contracts not because of random shocks, as suggested by mainstream business-cycle theory, but because optimism and pessimism in societies naturally trend and reverse in the form of a robust fractal.

With this new insight, we may begin to suggest a consistent theory of business cycles: Naturally expanding optimism during a boom stimulates hiring, expansion, investment and speculation. Euphoria in the latter stages encourages excessive credit extension and cavalier financial risk-taking. When optimism reaches a natural extremity, the boom ends and pessimism takes over. Companies lay off employees, investors recall their capital, lenders recall loans, banks tighten credit, bankruptcies accelerate and a major contraction ensues. When pessimism has run its course, debt has been liquidated to low levels, financing has become conservative, the stock market has reached its nadir, the society is ready for recovery.[24] There are no "new eras" or "new economies" and no conditions upon which the patterns of social behavior will disappear.

The indication that a major change is actually beginning comes with a major trend change in the stock market, which is a proxy for a major change in expectations. The model has some predictive value because the necessary precursors for a major change in trend are a state of extremity in the volume of debt and a potentially completed wave pattern of changes in expectations at high degree.

Recall the sweeping certainty of the quotation that begins this article, the guarantee in 1997 of "Asia's Bright Future" and the Harvard Economic Society's assertion in 1929 that "A severe depression such as 1920-21 is *outside the range* of probability" and will "*not*" happen. As it happens, our new model also explains why conventional macroeconomists are so certain just before they are most wrong. Because economists lack useful tools to guide them, they are powerless to resist getting caught up along with everyone else in the optimism at the peak or the pessimism at the bottom. Or, as Prechter asserts, "the prevailing social mood has full rein to affect the tone of their conclusions."[25]

Conclusion

Nobel Laureate James Buchanan, in his "Economics and Its Scientific Neighbors," stated, "Precisely because it has divorced itself from the central proposition relating to human behavior, [Keynesian and Post-Keynesian] macroeconomic theory is really no theory at all."[26] In contrast, the new model provides a consistent theoretical framework with strong predictive implications. For the linear extrapolation of the present commonly used by macroeconomists, it substitutes the nonlinear framework of markets' robust fractal patterns. This framework, in turn, offers compelling evidence that, to a first degree, changes in optimism and pessimism, measured by changes in stock market indices, are exogenous — independent of changes in economic variables, which simply follow. By understanding the nature and hierarchy of stock market changes, we economists can improve our predictions for the economy in terms of form, magnitude and timing.

Hernán Cortés Douglas is Professor of Economics at Catholic University of Chile. He is a former Deputy Research Administrator at the World Bank and Senior Economist at the International Monetary Fund. Professor Cortés Douglas has taught at American, European and Latin American universities. For the 2002-2003 academic year, he will serve as the Luksic Scholar at Harvard.

NOTES

[1] Dornbusch, Rudi. (1998, July 30). "Growth forever." *The Wall Street Journal.*

[2] Based on nominal figures provided by Irving Fisher's son and biographer, Irving Norton Fisher and adjusted by the U.S. CPI.

[3] *Ibid.* Figures provided by Keynes' biographer, Professor Skidelski.

[4] Grabbe, J. Orlin. (n.d.). "And now, financial apocalypse." www.aci.net/kalliste/Apocalyp.htm.

[5] See endnote 1.

[6] "Something unexpected happened." (2000, Dec.). *The Region.* Minneapolis Fed.

[7] Lucas, Robert. (1977). "Understanding business cycles." In K. Brunner and A. H. Meltzer, (Eds.) *Stabilization of the domestic and international economy.* North Holland, p. 15.

[8] Elliott, Ralph N. (1938). *The wave principle.* Reprinted (1980/1994) Robert R. Prechter, Jr. (Ed.) *R.N. Elliott's masterworks.* Gainesville, GA: New Classics Library.

[9] Arneodo, A. *et al.* (1993). "Fibonacci sequences in diffusion-limited aggregation." In J.M. García-Ruiz *et al.* (Eds.) *Growth patterns in physical sciences and biology.* New York: Plenum Press.

[10] Discrete scale invariance, as developed by D. Sornette (1997, October 15). "Generic mechanisms for hierarchies." *InterJournal complex systems,* 127. And (1999). "Discrete scale invariance and complex dimensions." *Physics Reports,* 297.

[11] Prechter, Robert R. (1999). *The wave principle of human social behavior.* And (1995). *At the crest of the tidal wave.* And with Frost, A.J. (1978). *Elliott wave principle.*

[12] Arneodo *et al.* put it this way: "There is room for 'quasi-fractals' between the well-ordered fractal hierarchy of snowflakes and the disordered structure of chaotic or random aggregates."

[13] Prechter, Robert R., email in response to inquiry.

[14] Sornette, Didier and Johansen, Anders. (1997). "Large financial crashes." *Physics A,* 245, 3-4.

[15] Prechter, Robert R. (1999). *The wave principle of human social behavior.* Gainesville, GA: New Classics Library.

[16] Lo, Andrew W. and MacKinlay, A. Craig. (1999). *A non-random walk down wall street.* Princeton University Press.

[17] Bateson, Gregory. (1972). "Form, substance and difference." *Steps to an ecology of mind.* Chandler, p. 449. Also Collingwood, R.G. (1945). *The idea of nature.* Oxford.

[18] Hayek in February 1929 wrote in the *Austrian Institute of Economic Research Report*, "The boom will collapse within the next few months." Mises foresaw a worldwide depression in the 1930s, as reported by Fritz Machlup, Mises' assistant at the time. Mises' wife, Margit, wrote in her husband's biography that, in the summer of 1929, he declined a high-ranking position in Kredit Anstalt, then one of the largest banks in Europe because "a great crash is coming and I do not want my name in any way connected with it." Within two years, Kredit Anstalt was bankrupt.

[19] Keynes' *opus magnum, The General Theory of Employment, Interest and Money*, contains not one but several theories. The profession, unfortunately adopted the Hicks-Samuelson version.

[20] Solow, R. (2000, Winter). "Toward a macroeconomics of the medium run." *Journal of Economic Perspectives*.

[21] See endnote 15.

[22] Schiller, Robert J. (2000). *Irrational exuberance*. Princeton University Press.

[23] Early in the century, some economists were well aware of the importance of these waves of optimism and pessimism. Pigou, Arthur C. (1927). *Industrial fluctuations*. London: Cass; Also (1920). *The economics of welfare*. London: Cass. And, yes, Keynes, John Maynard. (1936). *The general theory of employment, interest and money*. London: Macmillan, chapter 12.

[24] An expanded treatment of this process applied to the present situation appears in Douglas, H. Cortés. (2001, January). "Forewarnings." *processed*, Catholic University of Chile.

[25] See endnote 15.

[26] James, Buchanan. (1979). *What should economists do?* Liberty Press.

SCIENCE AND
THE WAVE PRINCIPLE

Adapted from a speech delivered to the
Market Technicians Association
May 1986

The Fractal Design of Social Progress

While for years some theoreticians have argued that stock price movements are random because all investors make fully informed and rational decisions, those who study the market and its participants know that few investment and trading decisions are based on reason, logic and knowledge gained from comprehensive research. Some decision making is informed and rational, but most apparently reasonable explanations for investors' decisions are merely *rationalizations* of emotionally based decisions.

The primary mover of aggregate stock market prices is mass emotional change. The Wave Principle reveals that aggregate stock price movement, and therefore mass emotional change, is patterned. It is patterned, moreover, independently from concurrent news. Thus, social mood and changes in it must simply be a reflection of the workings of human nature in society. The determinants of the specifics of market action are the naturally occurring direction, speed and extent of social mood changes.

Social mood change does not necessarily affect every individual involved, but in the aggregate, the people participating in markets are acting as a crowd. A pioneer in the study of crowd psychology once made the observation that a very rational and sensible human being, when part of a crowd, becomes a "blockhead." To be more precise, he ceases to think independently and reasonably. Wall Street is certainly a crowd. Every day, investors read the same newspapers, listen to the same TV shows and watch the same market indices go up and down. Millions of people involved in the market watch and hear all the same things. It is almost as if the participants are on a town square, and an orator trying to whip up revolution is standing on a balcony, making the crowd's emotions wax and wane with each change in content, tone and volume. In the case of markets, however, the orator and crowd are usually one and the same. Much of Wall Street's information (such as price level, direction, speed of price change and volume) is self generated, and just like a crowd, Wall Street feeds off its own frenzies. (This process clearly involves the feedback of result back into the system as a new cause, making it a candidate for study under chaos theory.) Because crowds have a nature all their own, and a behavioral style which reflects it, mass emotional change has a fair degree of predictability.

R.N. Elliott's discovery of the Wave Principle fifty years ago was a major breakthrough in sociology. His observations reveal that social psychological dynamics create the same pattern of "waves" in aggregate stock price movement from the smallest to the largest degree of trend (see Figure 1). In fact, there is a new science, the science of fractals, indicating that much of nature is made up of the kind of patterns and relationships that Elliott recognized and described.

The modern pioneer in the concept is Benoit Mandelbrot, a former professor at Harvard, Yale and the Einstein College of Medicine, who wrote a book called *The Fractal Geometry of Nature*. It documents his discovery that many natural forms that scientists had assumed were disorderly are not. In looking at clouds, seacoasts and mountain ranges, for instance, the

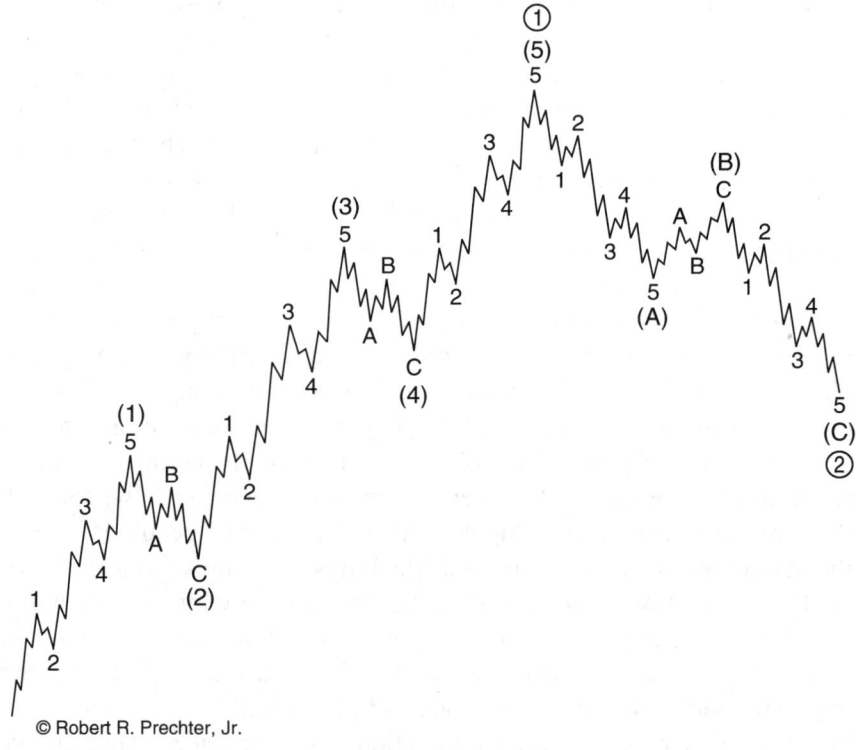

© Robert R. Prechter, Jr.

Figure 1

typical conclusion was that they were governed by no specific geometry. Mandelbrot said that that wasn't true; they display a relational form that scientists hadn't considered.

Here are some excerpts from a *New York Times* article of five months ago [December 1985] about Mandelbrot's ideas on the way nature develops.

> He has invented a new way of describing, calculating and thinking about shapes that are irregular and fragmented, jagged and broken up. A new geometry has emerged, and it turns out to be nature's own.... The interesting feature of a lightning bolt's path, for example, is not the straight line direction, but rather the distribution of its zigs and zags.... A new kind of symmetry has emerged, not of left to right or front to back, but of small scale patterns to patterns on larger and larger scales, the self similarity of a broccoli floret whose tiny bifurcations echo the branching of the stalk as a whole.... Oddly, the mathematical description of them seemed to apply just as well to very different problems, from fluctuating cotton prices since the 19th century to the rising and falling of the Nile River through two millenniums.... In unexpectedly orderly fashion, they have self similarity on different scales.

This description echoes Elliott's observation that stock market movements trace out five waves in the direction of the one larger trend and three waves (or a variation thereof) against that trend at all degrees, or sizes, of trend, producing self similarity on different scales. Daily, hourly and shorter term charts all show the same patterns as do longer term charts. The article continues,

> When you zoom in, looking closer and closer, the irregularities don't smooth out. Rather, they tend to look exactly as irregular as before. Some of Mandelbrot's fractal patterns looked indistinguishable from records of stock market prices. Economists needed to understand the heretical idea that prices don't change in a smooth, continuous flow. [Why an idea that reflects reality may be labeled "heretical" is a question only for academia, not for those who deal intimately with markets. — Ed.] "They can change abruptly in instantaneous jumps. And dam builders, reservoir builders, and risk insurers of all kinds needed to understand that traditional notions of probability were leading them to underestimate the likelihood of the rarest, most catastrophic events.

Similarly, Elliott recognized that big bear markets are no different in basic shape from short-term reactions. They are just of a larger scale and thus occur less often. They do not, however, occur less often *relative to the scale of advances that precede them.* A headline-making market "crash," for instance, is merely a large version of what happens all the time on smaller scales. Likewise, bull markets and minor degree rallies have the same basic shape.

The article continues, "The same question applies to economics. Daily fluctuations are treated one way, while the great changes that bring prosperity or depression are thought to belong to a different order of things. In each case, Mandelbrot said, my attitude is: Let's see what's different from the point of view of geometry. What comes out all seems to fall on a continuum; the mechanisms don't seem to be different." This was precisely one of R.N. Elliott's revolutionary messages.

Just to show one kind of structure produced by Mandelbrot's ideas, Figure 2 presents a line that moves either up or sideways according to a formula employing a fractal dimension. Unfortunately, this particular computer-generated illustration does not include declines, which would have made it look even more like a chart of financial market prices.

Figure 3, though it looks substantially different, brings us nearer to another of R.N. Elliott's revolutionary observations. It shows a computer generated snowflake. In this example, unlike Figure 2, the whole is a replica of its parts, from the largest size component to the next and the next. If your observations were to continue at smaller degrees, you would forever find the same shape. Figure 4 shows a computer generated tree. Notice that when you observe the smaller degrees, it continues to be the same picture, just like the snowflake. These pictures actually more closely reflect what R.N. Elliott said happens in the stock market. The smaller advancing and declining patterns depicted in the illustrative diagram of Figure 1 not only display discontinuity (i.e., size and frequency of internal trend reversals) to the same extent as the larger ones, but they also form component *replicas* of the larger patterns. The entire structure is based on one simple pattern. [*The Wave Principle, like many of nature's fractals (trees for example), is what The Wave Principle of Human Social Behavior identifies as a "robust fractal," which is neither as infinitely indefinite as clouds and seacoasts nor as precisely repetitive as Figures 2 through 4 but rather a definite basic structure with infinite subordinate variability.—Ed.*]

Although Elliott came to his conclusions fifty years before this new science blossomed, he went a great step further than current observers of natural processes. He explained not only that the progress of the market was fractal in nature but discovered and described the component patterns. He catalogued five specific simple pattern units that combine to compose

Figure 2

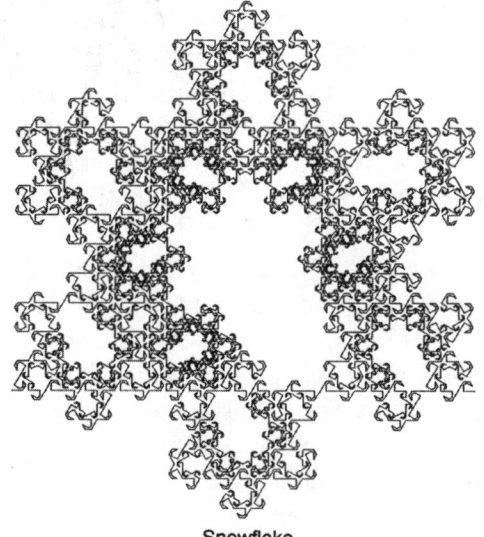

Snowflake

Figure 3

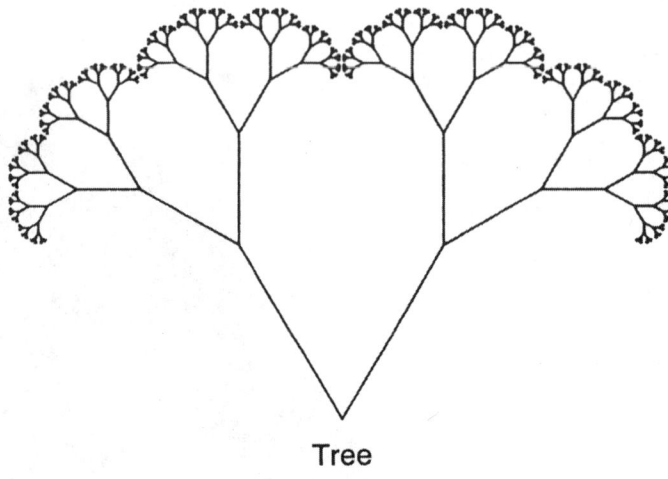

Tree

Figure 4

the stock market's behavior. These five patterns occur over and over, and a combination of them on a small degree will create one of those same shapes on the next larger degree, and so on.

The further time extends, the larger the degrees of trend get, implying a geometric expansion in the size of the advances and retrenchments that form mankind's progress, the entire structure propelled by the ebb and flow of mass mood. The spiraling line in Figure 5 conveys this idea visually by connecting the top of each first wave of increasingly higher degree. While forms such as triangles, squares and circles (and concepts such as "cycles" in markets or human experience) imply stasis or precise repetition, a spiral implies net growth or decay, expansion or contraction. (The largest degree depicted on the chart, of course, would be the first wave up of the *next* larger degree.)

The process, moreover, is not governed by mathematics that are applicable only in this case. As Elliott explained in his final unifying conclusion, the Fibonacci ratio (.618..., 1.618...) governs the number of waves which form in the movement of aggregate stock prices, in an expansion upon the underlying 5:3 relationship. The same ratio governs growth and decay processes found in nature and expanding and contracting phenomena found throughout the universe (see examples, Figure 6). Stock prices are the popular evaluation of productive enterprise, in other words, how people value their ability to produce. Thus, the form of the progress and regress of the

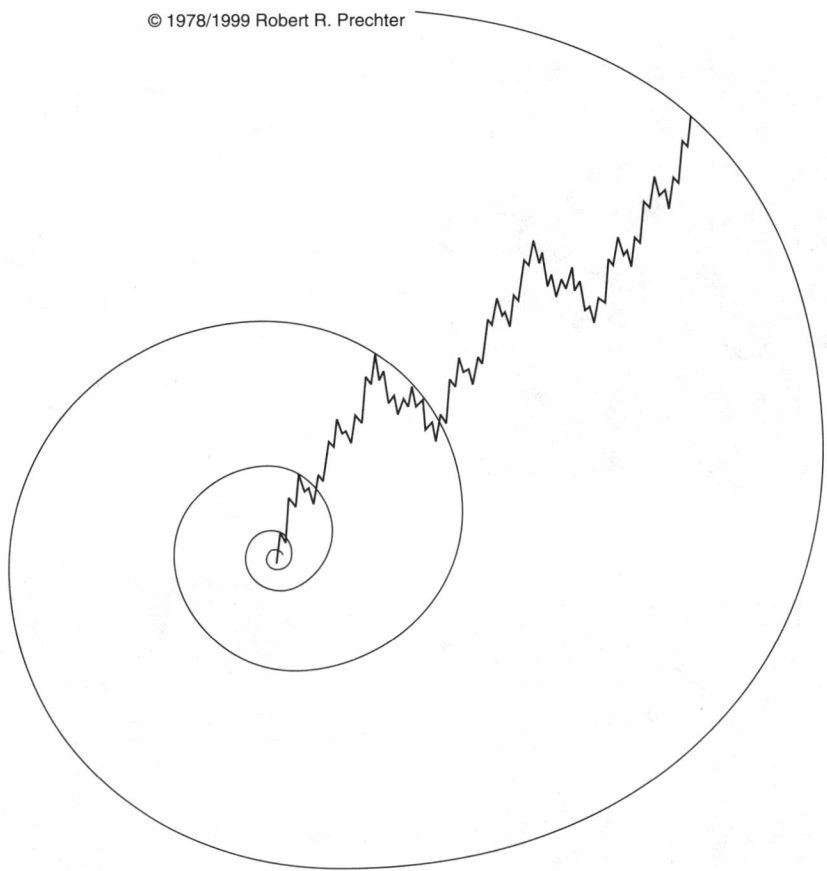

Figure 5

valuation of mankind's productive enterprise through history follows an expansion/contraction pattern that is typical of processes in nature that display patterned growth.

Whether specific component forms and governing ratios also exist for river meanders or seacoasts remains to be discovered, but I would contend that it is a possibility. For now, we must be content to contemplate the simple yet profound idea that on the whole, mankind's progress through history, propelled by the natural ebb and flow of social mood, follows a grand fractal design governed by the Fibonacci ratio, the same ratio that governs patterns of growth and expansion found throughout the universe.

COURTESY HERTA HOGGATT

COURTESY C. CHAPIN

Figure 6

Figure 6 (cont'd)

Illustrations from *Fascinating Fibonaccis* by Trudi H. Garland (1987, Dale Seymour Publications), *1929 Again?* by Terry R. Rudd (1988, Bell Curve Research) and *The Fractal Geometry of Nature* by Benoit Mandelbrot (1988, W.H. Freeman).

The Elliott Wave Theorist
June 7, 1999
Published in the *MTA Journal*, Winter-Spring 2000

Science is Validating the Concept of the Wave Principle

New discoveries in the field of complexity theory, fractal geometry, biology and psychology are rapidly yielding more knowledge bolstering the probability that the Wave Principle is a correct description of financial and social reality. This report provides a cursory overview of some of these advances.

To understand the connection between today's scientific discoveries and the Wave Principle, it is necessary to describe it in modern terms. In the 1930s, Ralph Nelson Elliott (1871-1948), through extensive empirical observation, discovered that price changes in stock market indexes produce a limited number of definable patterns (called "waves") that are variably self-affine[1] at different degrees, or sizes, of trend. As opposed to self-identical fractals, whose parts are precisely the same as the whole except for size (see example in Figure 1), and indefinite fractals, which are self-similar only in that they are similarly irregular at all scales (see example in Figure 2), Elliott proposed a model of intermediate specificity. Though variable, its component forms, within a defined latitude, are replicas of the larger forms. Waves have event-specific *relative* quantitative properties, as do self-identical fractals, but they are unrestricted in absolute quantitative terms, like indefinite fractals. The fact that both waves and (as we shall soon see) natural branching systems are fractals of *intermediate specificity* implies that

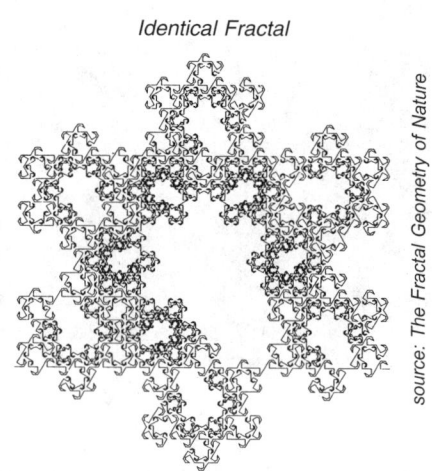

Identical Fractal

source: The Fractal Geometry of Nature

Figure 1

Indefinite Fractal

Figure 2

nature uses this fractal style to pattern systems that require highly adaptive variability in order to flourish. Therefore, I think the best term for this variety of fractal is *robust* fractal. As we shall see, this is a form that living structures typically display.

The essential form of the Wave Principle is five waves generating net progress in the direction of the one larger trend followed by three waves generating net regress against it, producing a three-steps-forward, two-steps-back form of net progress. The 5-3 pattern is *the* minimum requirement for, and therefore the most efficient method of, achieving both *fluctuation* and *progress* in linear movement.

Elliott described how waves at each degree become the components of waves of the next higher degree, and so on, producing a structured progression, as illustrated in Figure 3. The word "degree" has a specific meaning and does not mean "scale." Component waves vary in size, but it always takes a certain number of them to create a wave of the next higher degree. Thus, each degree is identifiable in terms of its relationship to higher and lower degrees. This is unlike the infinite scaling relating to clouds or sea-coasts *and* unlike the discrete scale invariance[2] of simple fractals created by recursive interpolation such as the snowflake in Figure 1. By incorporating features of both, Elliott described a third type of fractal, which we will shortly explore.

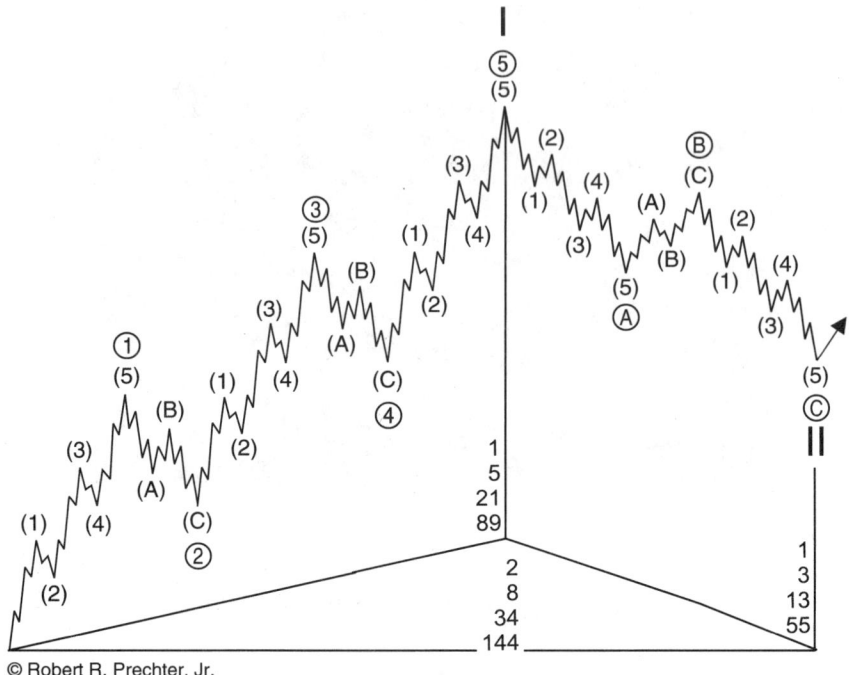

© Robert R. Prechter, Jr.

Figure 3

Benoit Mandelbrot, an IBM researcher and former professor at Harvard, Yale and the Einstein College of Medicine, did pioneering work bringing to light the fact that fractals are everywhere in nature.[3] The term "nature" in this context includes the activities of man, as Mandelbrot began by studying cotton prices[4] and most recently presented a multifractal model of the stock market.[5] This excerpt from a 1985 article in *The New York Times* summarizes his exposition on the subject of financial fractals:

> Daily fluctuations are treated [by economists] one way, while the great changes that bring prosperity or depression are thought to belong to a different order of things. In each case, Mandelbrot said, my attitude is: Let's see what's different from the point of view of geometry. What comes out all seems to fall on a continuum; the mechanisms don't seem to be different.[6]

This is what R.N. Elliott said about the stock market sixty years ago. Some members of the scientific community have recently recognized the connection. Three physicists researched the stock market's log-periodic structures and concluded that R.N. Elliott's model of financial behavior fits their findings. In 1996, France's *Journal of Physics* published the study, "Stock Market Crashes, Precursors and Replicas" by Didier Sornette and Anders Johansen, then of the Laboratoire de Physique de la Matière Condensée at the University of Nice, France, and collaborator Jean-Philippe Bouchaud. The authors make this statement:

> It is intriguing that the log-periodic structures documented here bear some similarity with the "Elliott waves" of technical analysis [citation *Elliott Wave Principle,* Frost & Prechter]. Technical analysis in finance can be broadly defined as the study of financial markets, mainly using graphs of stock prices as a function of time, in the goal of predicting future trends. A lot of effort has been developed in finance both by academic and trading institutions and more recently by physicists (using some of their statistical tools developed to deal with complex times series) to analyze past data to get information on the future. The "Elliott wave" technique is probably the most famous in this field. We speculate that the "Elliott waves"…could be a signature of an underlying critical structure of the stock market.[7]

Mandelbrot's work supports this conclusion. For example, every aspect of Mandelbrot's general model, as presented in *Scientific American,*[8] fits Elliott's specific model, and no aspect of Mandelbrot's general model contradicts Elliott's specific model. Mandelbrot's work in this regard should properly be seen as compatible with, and therefore support for, Elliott's more comprehensive hypothesis of financial market behavior. We must also concede the possibility that Elliott's specific model will be proven false and that financial markets will ultimately be shown to be indefinite fractals, which is as far as Mandelbrot's work goes in this regard. At minimum, though, it may be said that Mandelbrot's studies are among a number of modern discoveries that increase the probability that R.N. Elliott's fractal model of financial markets is true.

A year after the above-referenced Sornette study (one hopes that it was not in *response* to it), Mandelbrot published a brief dismissal of Elliott and his work, deriding his predecessor and taking credit for modeling the stock market as a multifractal. (See "Prechter's Response to Mandelbrot's Dismissal of Elliott" at www.elliottwave.com/response.htm and the May 21 Special Report, reproduced in this book.) Advocates of the Wave Principle are not particularly interested in this controversy *per se* but in the far more important fact that a renowned scientist has decided that at least one implication of Elliott's work is so important that he wants credit for it. Whether that credit is to be taken properly or otherwise is a question for the scientific community decide, but the key point is that this very situation is yet another fact that increases the potential validity of the Wave Principle hypothesis.

The Robust Fractal

It is imperative to understand that R.N. Elliott went far beyond the comparatively simple idea that financial prices form an indefinite multifractal. One of his big achievements was discovering *specific component patterns* within the overall form.[9] Until very recently, it has been generally presumed that there are two types of self-similar forms in nature: (1) *self-identical* fractals, whose parts are precisely the same as the whole, and (2) *indefinite fractals*, which are self-similar only in that they are similarly irregular at all scales. (See Figures 1 and 2.) The literature on natural fractals concludes that nature most commonly produces indefinite fractal forms that are orderly only in the extent of their discontinuity at different scales and otherwise disorderly. Scientific descriptions of natural fractals detail no specific patterns composing such forms. Seacoasts are just "jagged lines," trees are composed simply of "branches," rivers but meander, and heartbeats and earthquakes are merely "events" that differ in frequency. Likewise, financial markets are considered to be self-similarly discontinuous in the relative sizes and frequencies of trend reversals yet otherwise randomly patterned. These conclusions may be due to a shortfall in empirical study rather than a scientific fact.

R.N. Elliott described for financial markets a third type of self-similarity. By meticulously studying the natural world of social man in the form of graphs of stock market prices, Elliott found that there are *specific patterns* to the stock market fractal that are nevertheless *highly variable* within a certain definable latitude. In other words, some aspects of their form are *constant* and others are *variable*. If this is true, then financial markets, and by extension, social systems in general, are not vague, indefinite fractals. Component patterns do not simply display *discontinuity* similar to that of larger patterns, but *they form, with a certain latitude, replicas of them*. Elliott defined waves in terms of those aspects that make them identical, thereby allowing for their variability in other aspects of detail within the scope of those definitions. He was even able to define some of the patterns' variable characteristics in probabilistic terms. Elliott's discovery of *degrees* in pattern formation, i.e., that a certain number of waves of one degree are required to make up a wave of the next higher degree, is vitally important because it links the building-block property of self-identical fractals to the Wave Principle, revealing an aspect of self-identity among waves that indefinite fractals do not possess.

Elliott's discovery of specific hierarchical patterning in the stock market is fundamental. Fractality alone is only a vague comment about that form. *If you can describe the pattern, you have the essence of the object.* The more meticulously you can describe the pattern, the closer you get to knowing what it is.

Although Elliott came to his conclusions fifty years before the new science of fractals blossomed, the very idea that financial markets comprise specific forms and identical (within the scope of their definitions) component forms remains a revolutionary observation because to this day, it has eluded other financial market researchers and chaos scientists. Elliott's work shows that the power-law relationship between sizes and frequencies of financial movements, currently considered a breakthrough discovery, is not the essence, but a by-product, of the fundamentals of financial market patterns.

A group of scientists (see below) has very recently recognized that there is a type of fractal in nature whose self-similarity is intermediate between identical and indefinite. As far as I know, theirs is the only published study on the subject. Before we discuss this new aspect of Wave Principle validation, we first must detour through another of R.N. Elliott's discoveries and understand how it contributes to his grand hypothesis.

The Role of Fibonacci in Robust Fractals

Because the essential form of the Wave Principle's is a repeated 5-3, the numbers of waves at different degrees reflect the Fibonacci sequence. The Fibonacci sequence is 1, 1, 2, 3, 5, 8, 13, 21, 34, 55, and so on. It begins with the number 1, and each new term from there is the sum of the previous two. The limit ratio between the terms is .618034..., an irrational number sometimes called the "golden mean" but in this century more succinctly *phi* (ϕ).

The simplest expression of a falling wave is 1 straight-line decline. The simplest expression of a rising wave is 1 straight-line advance. A complete cycle is 2 lines. At the next degree of complexity, the corresponding numbers are 3, 5 and 8 (see Figure 4). This Fibonacci sequence continues to infinity.

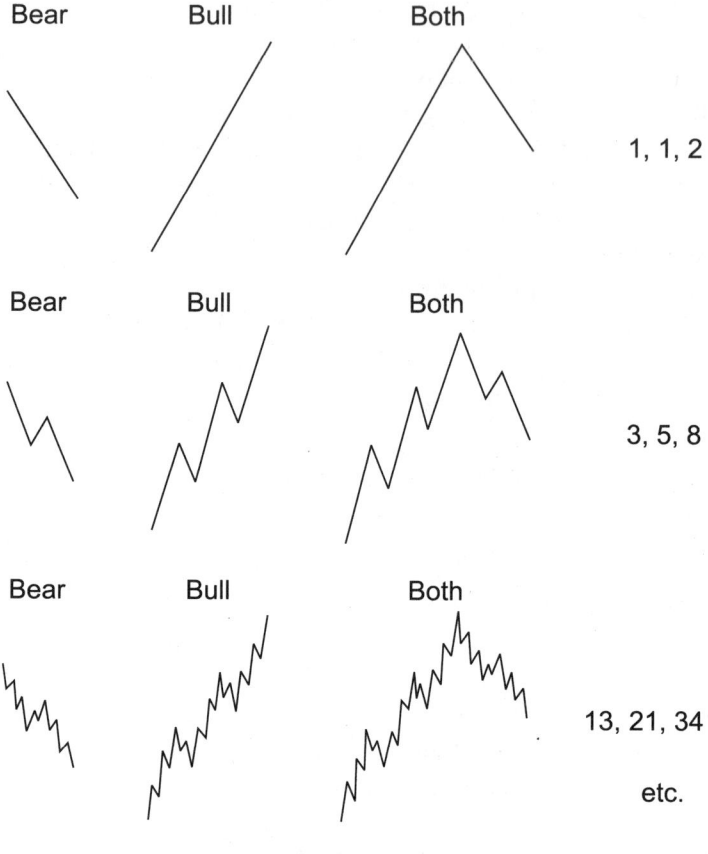

Figure 4

Both the Fibonacci sequence and the Fibonacci ratio appear ubiquitously in natural forms ranging from the geometry of the DNA molecule to the physiology of plants and animals. Figures 5 and 6 show examples. (For more, see Chapters 3 and 11 in *The Wave Principle of Human Social Behavior*.) In the past few years, science has taken a quantum leap in knowledge concerning the universal appearance and fundamental importance of Fibonacci mathematics to nature. Without the benefit of that knowledge, after researching the subject to the small extent possible at the time, Elliott presented the final unifying conclusion of his theory in 1940,[10] explaining that the progress of waves is governed by the Fibonacci sequence and ratio, a mathematical principle that governs so many phenomena of life. From this observation, he concluded — decades ahead of later researchers — that the

Fibonacci subdivisions in the hand

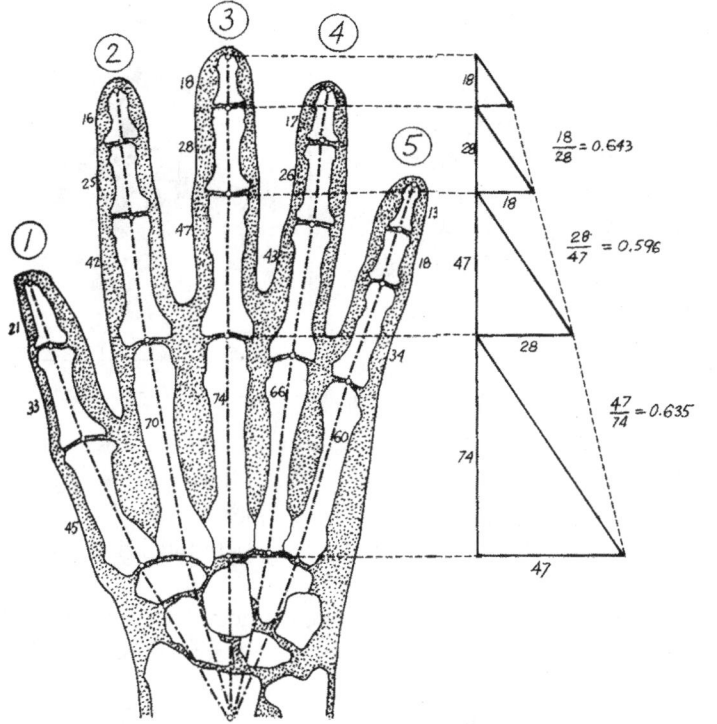

source: The Power of Limits

Figure 5

A SPIRALED FLOWER

The diagram at right reveals the double spiraling of the daisy head. Two opposite sets of rotating spirals are formed by the arrangement of the individual florets in the head. They are also near-perfect equiangular spirals. There are 21 in the clockwise direction and 34 counterclockwise. This 21:34 ratio is composed of two adjacent terms in the mysterious Fibonacci sequence.

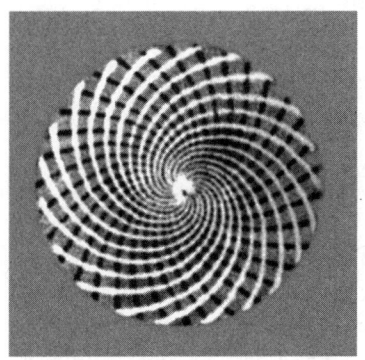

source: Mathematics

Figure 6

progress of mankind is the same type of growth process that we see in so many instances throughout nature.

Modern science is catching up to R.N. Elliott. In 1993, five scientists from the Centre de Recherche Paul Pascal and the Ecole Normale Supeieure in France investigated the diffusion-limited aggregation (DLA) model, which is a set that diffuses via smaller and smaller branches, just like the branching fractals found in nature, such as the circulatory system, bronchial system and trees. Arneodo *et al.*

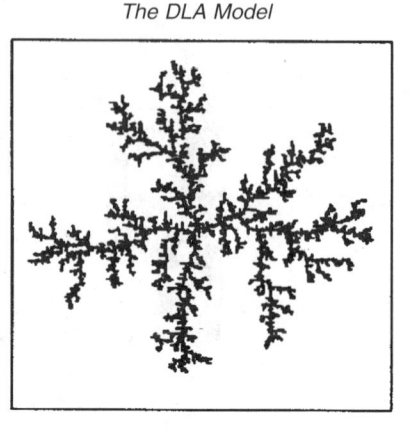

The DLA Model

Figure 7

source: Growth Patterns in Physical Sciences and Biology

state at the outset that it is "an open question whether or not some structural order is hidden in the apparently disordered DLA morphology."[11] To investigate the question, they use a wavelet transform microscope to examine "the intricate fractal geometry of large-mass off-lattice DLA clusters." (See Figure 7.)

What mathematics govern *this* robust fractal? In the first linking (as far as I can discover) of the two concepts of fractals and Fibonacci since Elliott, they demonstrate that their research "reveals the existence of Fibonacci sequences in the internal 'extinct' region of these clusters." The authors find that the branching characteristics of off-lattice DLA clusters "proceed according to the *Fibonacci recursion law*," i.e., they branch in intervals to produce a 1-2-3-5-8-13-etc. progression in the number of branches. The authors of this study, then, have found the Fibonacci sequence in DLA clusters *in the same place that R.N. Elliott found the Fibonacci sequence in the Wave Principle*: in the increasing numbers of subdivisions as the phenomenon progresses.

The authors find even more evidence of Fibonacci. They have discovered that the most commonly occurring "screening angle" between bifurcating branches of these DLA clusters is 36 degrees, which holds *regardless of scale*. (See Figure 8.) This is the ruling angle of geometric phenomena that display Fibonacci properties, from the five-pointed star (Figure 9) to Penrose tiles (Figure 10), a robust filling of plane-space with just two rhombi. The authors elaborate:

> The intimate relationship between regular pentagons and Fibonacci numbers and the golden mean $\phi = 2\cos(\pi/5) = 1.618...$ has been well known for a long time. The proportions of a pentagon approximate the

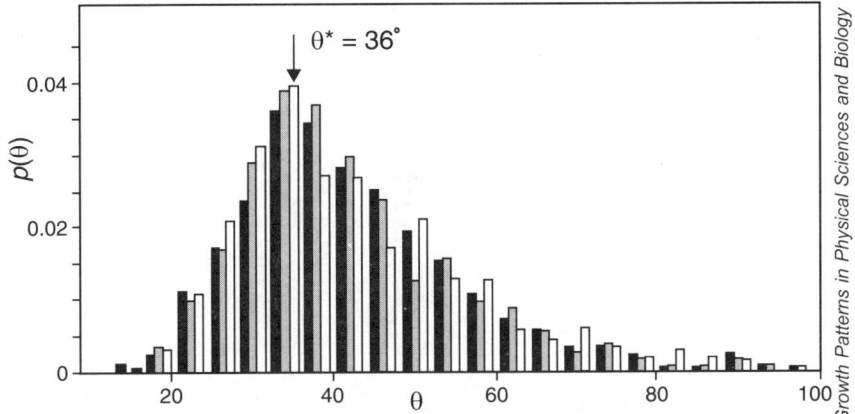

Histogram of screening angle values at the branching bifurcations in the wavelet transform representation of 4 off-lattice DLA clusters; three magnifications a⁻¹ (black), (2.2) ᵃ⁻¹ (grey) and (2.2)² ᵃ⁻¹ (clear) are shown, corresponding respectively to three successive generations of branching. A single maximum is observed for θ ~ 36º.

source: Growth Patterns in Physical Sciences and Biology

Figure 8

proportions between adjacent Fibonacci numbers; the higher the numbers are, the more exact the approximation to the golden mean becomes. The angle defined by the sides of the star and the regular pentagons is $\theta = 36°$, while the ratio of their length is a Fibonacci ratio (F_{n+1}/F_n).

The authors conclude, "The existence of this symmetry *at all scales* is likely to be a clue to a structural hierarchical fractal ordering." Indeed, it is. In a similar way, Elliott found that the price lengths of certain waves are often related by .618, *at all scales*, revealing another, though perhaps less fundamental, Fibonacci aspect of waves.

These mathematics pertain to "apparently randomly branched fractals that bear a striking resemblance to the tenuous tree-like structures observed in viscous fingering, electrodeposition, bacterial growth and neuronal growth," which are "strikingly similar to trees, root systems, algae, blood vessels and the bronchial architecture," i.e., *the typical products of nature*.

This is exciting news, but it concerns a model that *looks* like nature. What do we find when we investigate the *actual* products of nature? We find *phi* again and again. In the early 1960s, Drs. E.R. Weibel and D.M. Gomez meticulously measured the architecture of the lung (see Figure 11) and reported that the mean ratio of short to long tube lengths for the fifth through seventh generations of the bronchial tree is *0.62*, the Fibonacci ratio.[12] Bruce West and Ary Goldberger have found that the diameters of the

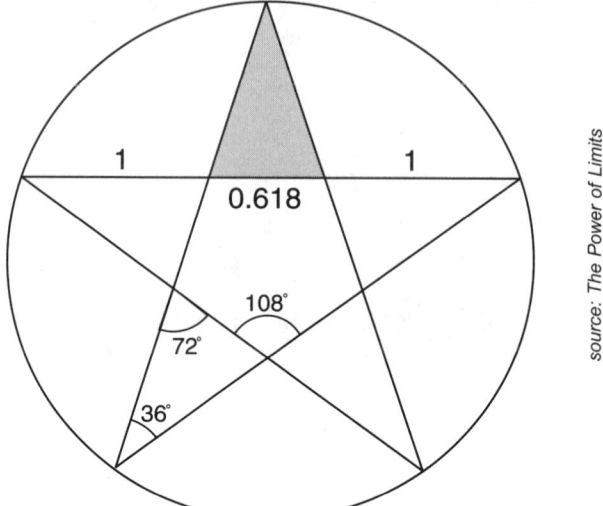

source: The Power of Limits

Fibonacci in the 5-pointed star

Figure 9

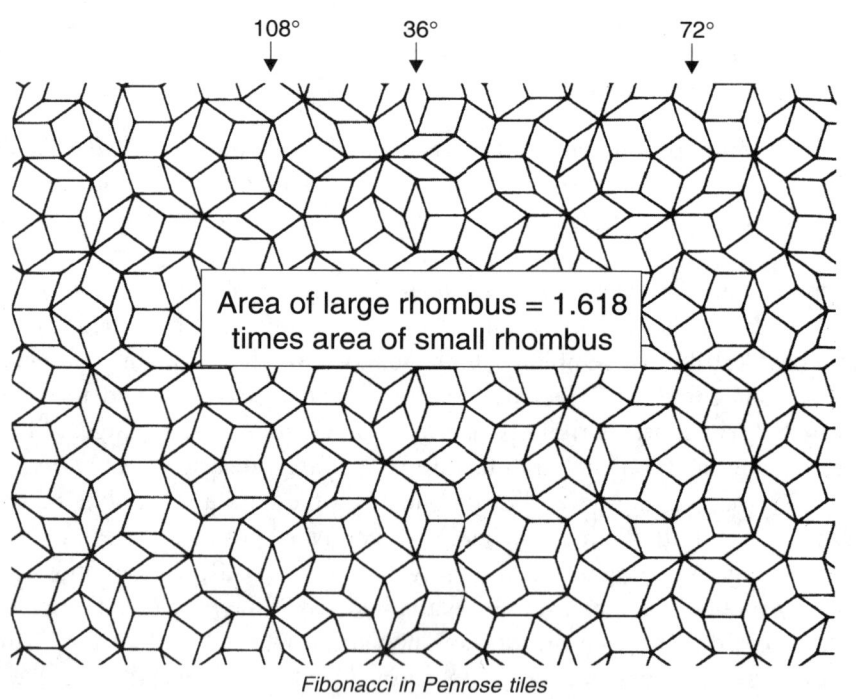

source: Bull. Inst. Math. & its Appl., Vol 10

Fibonacci in Penrose tiles

Figure 10

first seven generations of the bronchial tubes in the lung decrease in Fibonacci proportion.[13] Oxford professor of mathematics Roger Penrose, who shared the Wolf Prize for Physics in 1988 with cosmologist Stephen Hawking, presents this discussion of the smallest components of our nervous system in his 1994 book, *Shadows of the Mind*:

source: Lung Structure

> The organization of mammalian microtubules is interesting from a mathematical point of view. …the skew hexagonal pattern…is made up of 5 right-handed and 8 left-handed helical arrangements…. The number 13 features here in its role as the sum: 5 + 8. It is curious, also, that the double mi-

Robust fractal architecture of the human lung

Figure 11

crotubules that frequently occur seem normally to have a total of 21 columns of tubulin dimers forming the outside boundary of the composite tube — the next Fibonacci number![14] [See Figures 12 and 13.]

Led by Eugene Stanley of Boston University, fifteen researchers from MIT, Harvard and elsewhere recently studied the physiology of neurons (see Figure 14) in the central nervous system with the goal of quantifying the arboration of the neurites, which are the arba of neurons. Taking the ganglion cells of a cat's retina as a model system, they find that the fractal dimension of the cells is "*1.68 + or - 0.15* using the box counting method and *1.66 + or - 0.08* using the correlation method."[15] Although the authors do not mention it, this is quite close to *phi*.

The source of all these biological structures is DNA. Given current best measurements, the length of one DNA cycle is 34 angstroms, and its height is 20 angstroms, very nearly producing the Fibonacci ratio (see Figure 15). Stanley *et al.* note parenthetically in their power-law study, "The DNA walk representation for the rat embryonic skeletal myosin heavy chain gene [has a long range correlation of] *0.63*,"[16] which again — although not mentioned in the study — is quite close to *phi*. A bit of data integration, then, shows that living systems are permeated with *phi*-based structures.

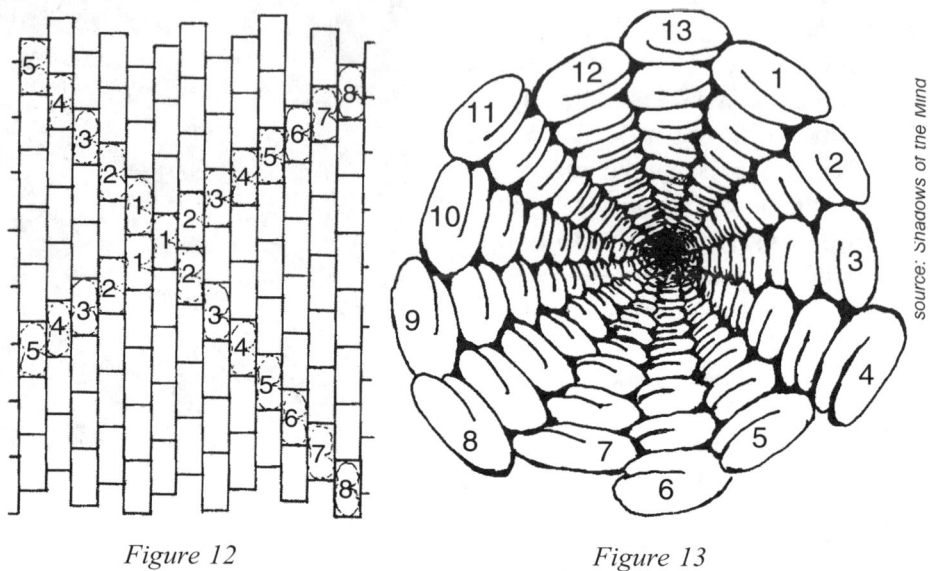

Fibonacci organization of mammalian microtubules

source: Shadows of the Mind

Figure 12   Figure 13

Neurons have a Fibonacci fractal dimension

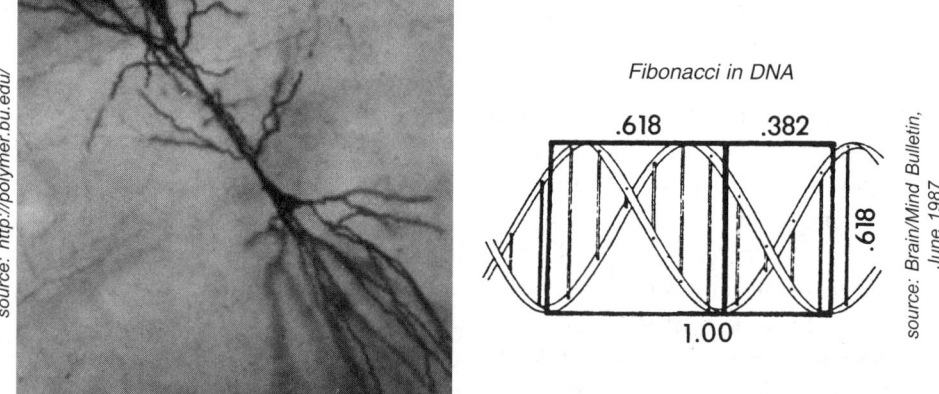

source: http://polymer.bu.edu/

Fibonacci in DNA

source: Brain/Mind Bulletin, June 1987

Figure 14   Figure 15

Recall that each pattern under the Wave Principle has identifiable *rigidities* as well as *tendencies*. This is true not only of Elliott waves but of nature's branching patterns. While the general assumption has been that branching patterns are indefinite fractals, this study shows that these apparently random fractals are in fact *more orderly than previously realized*. Indeed, Arneodo, *et al.* determine that they are working with a type of fractal that scientists had not yet found, an intermediate form between exact self-identity and vague, indefinite self-similarity:

> The intimate relationship between regular pentagons and Fibonacci numbers and the golden mean...has been well known for a long time.... The recent discovery of "quasi-crystals" in solid state physics is a spectacular manifestation of this relationship. This new organization of atoms in solids, *intermediate between perfect order and disorder*, generalizes to the crystalline "forbidden" symmetries, the properties of incommensurate structures. *Similarly, there is room for "quasi-fractals" between the well-ordered fractal hierarchy of snowflakes and the disordered structure of chaotic or random aggregates.*[17]

This is the same type of intermediately ordered fractal that R.N. Elliott described for the stock market. I conclude from these studies and the Wave Principle that fractals that characterize nature's life forms share at least two properties: *robustness* (intermediate orderliness/variability) and *Fibonacci*.

I prefer the term *robust* fractal to quasi-fractal, as its connection to natural, usually living, phenomena indicates that there is nothing quasi about it. I believe that robustness and Fibonacci ordering will prove to be the essence of fractals that matter most in nature.[18]

Conclusion

The latest scientific research is racing headlong toward validating the concept of the Wave Principle, and not just in its simple expression as a financial multifractal. It is also supporting its grander implications that nature's living fractals are robust, that they are governed by Fibonacci, that one of them governs the entire activity of social man, and therefore that the mathematical basis of man's sociocultural progress and of other natural growth systems is the same.

The level of aggregate stock prices is not a mere curiosity but a direct and immediate measure of the popular valuation of man's total productive capability. That this valuation has a *form* is a fact of profound implications that should ultimately revolutionize the social sciences.

NOTES

[1] Fractal objects whose properties are not restricted display self-*similarity*, while those that develop in a direction such as price graphs display self-*affinity*. The term "self-similar" is often employed more generally to convey both ideas.

[2] For more on this topic, see Johansen, A. (1997, December). "Discrete scale invariance and other cooperative phenomena in spatially extended systems with threshold dynamics" (Ph.D. Thesis). Sornette, D. (1998). "Discrete scale invariance and complex dimensions." *Physics Reports* 297, pp. 239-270.

[3] Mandelbrot, B. (1988). *The fractal geometry of nature*. New York: W.H. Freeman.

[4] Mandelbrot, B. (1962). Sur certains prix spéculatifs: faits empiriques et modèle basé sur les processus stables additifs de Paul Lévy. Comptes Rendus (Paris): 254, 3968-3970. And (1963). The variation of certain speculative prices. *Journal of Business*: 36, 394-419. Reprinted in Cootner 1964: 297-337. University of Chicago Press.

[5] Mandelbrot, B. (1999, February). "A multifractal walk down wall street." *Scientific American*, pp. 70-73.

[6] Gleick, J. (1985, December 29). "Unexpected order in chaos." *This World*.

[7] Sornette, D., Johansen, A., and Bouchaud, J.P. (1996). "Stock market crashes, precursors and replicas." *Journal de Physique I France* 6, No.1, pp. 167-175.

[8] See endnote 5.

[9] Elliott, R.N. (1938). *The wave principle*. Republished: (1980/1994). Prechter, Robert R. (Ed.). *R.N. Elliott's masterworks — The definitive collection*. Gainesville, GA: New Classics Library.

[10] Elliott, R.N. (1940, October 1). "The basis of the wave principle." Republished: (1980/1994). *R.N. Elliott's masterworks — The definitive collection*.

[11] Arneodo, A., Argoul, R. Bacry, E., Muzy, J.F. and Tabbard, M. (1993). "Fibonacci sequences in diffusion-limited aggregation." Garcia-Ruiz, J., Louis, E., Meakin, P., and Sander, L.M. (Eds.). *Growth patterns in physical sciences and biology*. New York: Plenum Press.

[12] Weibel, E.R. (1962). "Architecture of the human lung." *Science*, No. 137 and (1963) *Morphometry of the human lung*. Academic Press.

[13] West, B.J. and Goldberger, A.L. (1987, Jul/Aug). "Physiology in fractal dimensions." *American Scientist*, Vol. 75.

[14] Penrose, R. (1994). *Shadows of the mind — A search for the missing science of consciousness.* Oxford University Press.

[15] Stanley, H.E., *et al.* (1993). "Fractal landscapes in physics and biology." Garcia-Ruiz, J.M. *et al.* (Eds.). *Growth patterns in physical sciences and biology.* New York: Plenum Press.

[16] *Ibid.*

[17] See endnote 11.

[18] Clouds and mountains, which are indefinite fractals, have a Hurst exponent near 0.8. Neurons (which grow as branching fractals) and the stock market (which grows as waves) have a Hurst exponent related to *phi*. These studies prompt me to suggest the hypothesis that fractal objects that manifest as branches or waves, i.e., the fractal objects of growth and expansion, will have a Hurst exponent related to *phi*, setting them apart from other fractal objects, which will have other Hurst exponents. What this means is that *robust fractal objects split the difference between two Euclidean dimensions by .618*, while other fractal objects do not. In other words, *phi*-related dimensionality is a property only of robust fractals.

The Elliott Wave Theorist
August 1999
Published in the *MTA Journal*, Summer-Fall 2000

Science is Revealing the Mechanism of the Wave Principle

It is one thing to say that the Wave Principle makes sense in the context of nature and its growth forms. It is another to postulate a hypothesis about its mechanism. The biological and behavioral sciences have produced enough relevant work to make a case that unconscious paleomentational processes produce a herding impulse with Fibonacci-related tendencies in both individuals and collectives. Man's unconscious mind, in conjunction with others, is thus disposed toward producing a pattern having the properties of the Wave Principle.

The Paleomentational Herding Impulse

Over a lifetime of work, Paul MacLean, former head of the Laboratory for Brain Evolution at the National Institute of Mental Health, has developed a mass of evidence supporting the concept of a "triune" brain, i.e., one that is divided into three basic parts. The primitive brain stem, called the basal ganglia, which we share with animal forms as low as reptiles, controls impulses essential to survival. The limbic system, which we share with mammals, controls emotions. The neocortex, which is significantly developed only in humans, is the seat of reason. Thus, we actually have three connected minds: primal, emotional and rational. Figure 1, from MacLean's book, *The Triune Brain in Evolution*,[1] roughly shows their physical locations.

The neocortex is involved in the preservation of the individual by processing ideas using reason. It derives its information from the external world, and its convictions are malleable thereby. In contrast, the styles of mentation outside the cerebral cortex are unreasoning, impulsive and very rigid. The "thinking" done by the brain stem and limbic system is primitive and pre-rational, exactly as in animals that rely exclusively upon them.

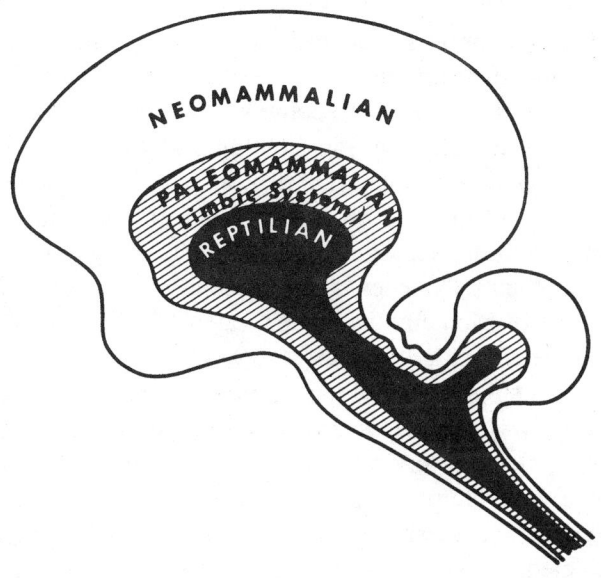

Figure 1

The basal ganglia control brain functions that are often termed instinctive: the desire for security, the reaction to fear, the desire to acquire, the desire for pleasure, fighting, fleeing, territorialism, migration, hoarding, grooming, choosing a mate, breeding, the establishment of social hierarchy and the selection of leaders. More pertinent to our discussion, this bunch of nerves also controls coordinated behavior such as *flocking, schooling* and *herding*. All these brain functions insure life-saving or life-enhancing action under most circumstances and are fundamental to animal motivation. Due to our evolutionary background, they are integral to human motivation as well. In effect, then, portions of the brain are "hardwired for certain emotional and physical patterns of reaction"[2] to insure survival of the species. Presumably, *herding* behavior, which derives from the same primitive portion of the brain, is similarly hardwired and impulsive. As one of its primitive tools of survival, then, emotional impulses from the limbic system impel a desire among individuals to seek signals from others in matters of knowledge and behavior and therefore to align their feelings and convictions with those of the group.

There is not only a *physical* distinction between the neocortex and the primitive brain but a *functional dissociation* between them. The intellect of the neocortex and the emotional mentation of the limbic system are so independent that "the limbic system has the capacity to generate out-of-context, affective feelings of conviction that we attach to our beliefs *regardless of whether they are true or false.*"[3] Feelings of certainty can be so overwhelming that they stand fast in the face of logic and contradiction. They can attach themselves to a political doctrine, a social plan, the verity of a religion, the surety of winning on the next spin of the roulette wheel, the presumed path of a financial market or any other idea.[4] This tendency is so powerful that Robert Thatcher, a neuroscientist at the University of South Florida College of Medicine in Tampa, says, "The limbic system is where we live, and the cortex is basically a slave to that."[5] While this may be an overstatement, a soft version of that depiction, which appears to be a minimum statement of the facts, is that most people live in the limbic system with respect to fields of knowledge and activity about which they lack either expertise or wisdom.

This tendency is marked in financial markets, where most people feel lost and buffeted by forces that they cannot control or foresee. In the 1920s, Cambridge economist A.C. Pigou connected cooperative social dynamics to booms and depression.[6] His idea is that individuals routinely correct their own errors of thought when operating alone but abdicate their responsibility to do so in matters that have strong social agreement, regardless of the egregiousness of the ideational error. In Pigou's words,

> Apart altogether from the financial ties by which different businessmen are bound together, there exists among them a certain measure of *psychological interdependence*. A change of tone in one part of the business world diffuses itself, *in a quite unreasoning manner*, over other and wholly disconnected parts.[7]

"Wall Street" certainly shares aspects of a crowd, and there is abundant evidence that herding behavior exists among stock market participants. Myriad measures of market optimism and pessimism[8] show that in the aggregate, such sentiments among both the public and financial professionals wax and wane concurrently with the trend and level of the market. This tendency is not simply fairly common; it is ubiquitous. Most people get virtually all of their ideas about financial markets from other people, through newspapers, television, tipsters and analysts, without checking a thing. They think, "Who am I to check? These other people are supposed to be experts." The unconscious mind says: You have too little basis upon which to exercise reason; *your only alternative is to assume that the herd knows where it is going.*

In 1987, three researchers from the University of Arizona and Indiana University conducted sixty laboratory market simulations using as few as a dozen volunteers, typically economics students but also, in some experiments, professional businessmen. Despite giving all the participants the same perfect knowledge of coming dividend prospects and then an actual declared dividend at the end of the simulated trading day, which could vary more or less randomly but which would average a certain amount, *the subjects in these experiments repeatedly created a boom-and-bust market profile*. The extremity of that profile was a function of the participants' lack of experience in the speculative arena. Head research economist Vernon L. Smith came to this conclusion: "We find that inexperienced traders never trade consistently near fundamental value, and most commonly generate a boom followed by a crash...."[9] Groups that have experienced one crash "continue to bubble and crash, but at reduced volume. Groups brought back for a third trading session tend to trade near fundamental dividend value." In the real world, "these bubbles and crashes would be a lot less likely if the same traders were in the market all the time," but novices are always entering the market.

While these experiments were conducted as if participants could actually possess true knowledge of coming events and so-called fundamental value, no such knowledge is available in the real world. The fact that participants create a boom-bust pattern *anyway* is overwhelming evidence of the power of the herding impulse.

It is not only novices who fall in line. It is a lesser-known fact that the vast majority of professionals herd just like the naïve majority. Figure 2 shows the percentage of cash held at institutions as it relates to the level of the S&P 500 Composite index. As you can see, the two data series move roughly together, showing that professional fund managers herd right along with the market just as the public does.

Apparent expressions of cold reason by professionals follow herding patterns as well. Finance professor Robert Olsen recently conducted a study of 4000 corporate earnings estimates by company analysts and reached this conclusion:

> Experts' earnings predictions exhibit positive bias and disappointing accuracy. These shortcomings are usually attributed to some combination of incomplete knowledge, incompetence, and/or misrepresentation. This article suggests that the *human desire for consensus* leads to herding behavior among earnings forecasters.[10]

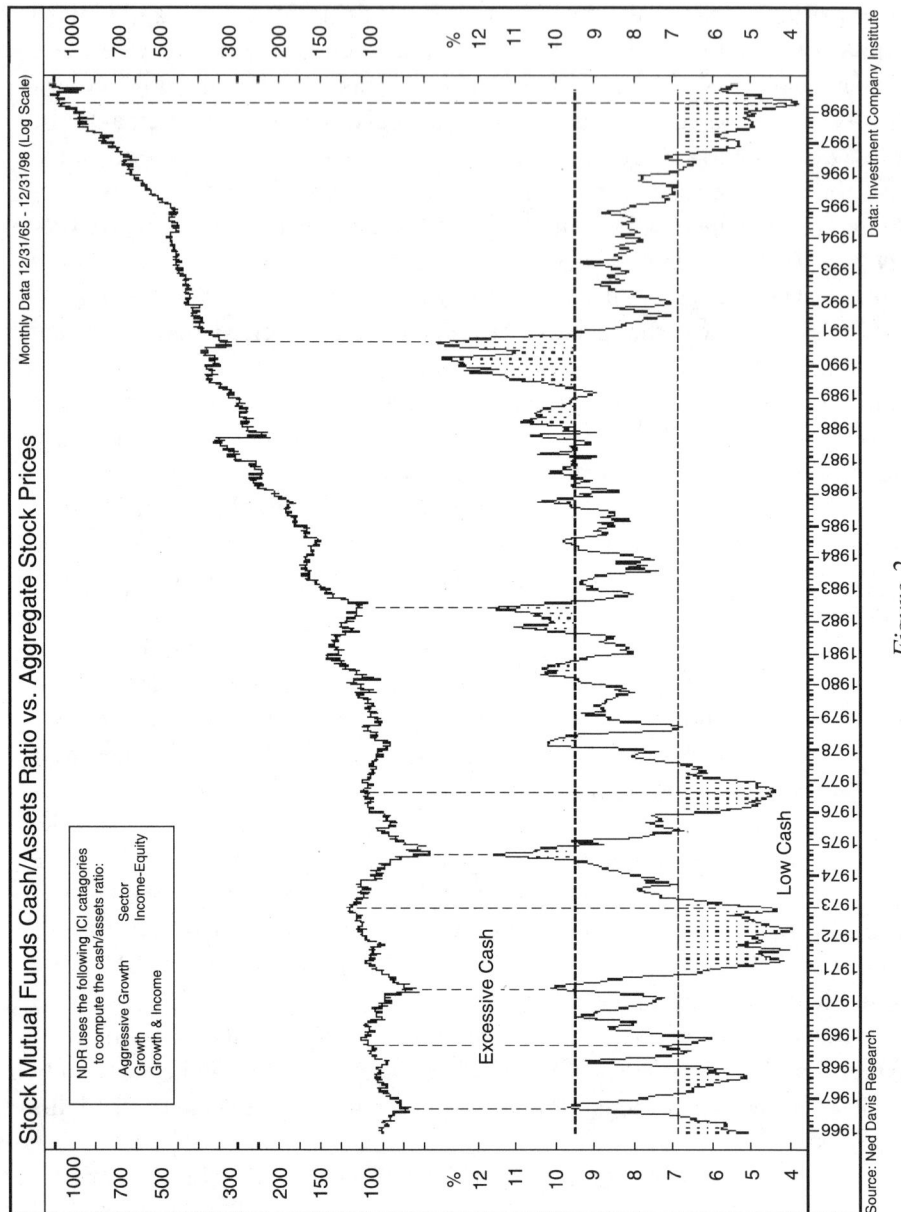

Figure 2

Data: Investment Company Institute

Olsen's study shows that the more analysts are wrong, which is another source of stress, *the more their herding behavior increases.*[11]

How can seemingly rational professionals be so utterly seduced by the opinion of their peers that they will not only hold, but *change* opinions collectively? Recall that the neocortex is to a significant degree functionally dissociated from the limbic system. This means not only that feelings of conviction may attach to utterly contradictory ideas in different people, but that they can do so *in the same person at different times.* In other words, the *same brain* can support *opposite views* with equally intense emotion, depending upon the demands of survival perceived by the limbic system. This fact relates directly to the behavior of financial market participants, who can be flushed with confidence one day and in a state of utter panic the next. As Yale economist Robert Schiller puts it, "You would think enlightened people would not have firm opinions" about markets, "but they do, *and it changes all the time.*"[12] Throughout the herding process, whether the markets are real or simulated, and whether the participants are novices or professionals, the general conviction of the *rightness* of stock valuation at each price level is powerful, emotional and impervious to argument.

Falling into line with others for self-preservation involves not only the pursuit of positive values but also the avoidance of negative values, in which case the reinforcing emotions are even stronger. Reptiles and birds harass strangers. A flock of poultry will peck to death any individual bird that has wounds or blemishes. Likewise, humans can be a threat to each other if there are perceived differences between them. It is an advantage to survival, then, to *avoid rejection by revealing your sameness.* D.C. Gajdusek researched a long-hidden Stone Age tribe that had never seen Western people and soon noticed that they mimicked his behavior; whenever he scratched his head or put his hand on his hip, the whole tribe did the same thing.[13] Says MacLean, "It has been suggested that *such imitation may have some protective value by signifying, 'I am like you.'*" He adds, "This form of behavior is phylogenetically *deeply ingrained.*"[14]

The limbic system bluntly assumes that all expressions of "I am not like you" are infused with danger. Thus, herding and mimicking are preservative behavior. They are powerful because they are impelled, regardless of reasoning, by a primitive system of mentation that, however uninformed, is trying to save your life.

As with so many useful paleomentational tools, herding behavior is counterproductive with respect to success in the world of modern financial speculation. If a financial market is soaring or crashing, the limbic system senses an opportunity or a threat and orders you to join the herd so that your chances for success or survival will improve. The limbic system produces emotions that support those impulses, including hope, euphoria, cautiousness and panic. The actions thus impelled lead one inevitably to the *opposite* of survival and success, which is why the vast majority of people lose when they speculate.[15] In a great number of situations, hoping and herding can contribute to your well-being. Not in financial markets. In many cases, panicking and fleeing when others do cuts your risk. Not in financial markets. The important point with respect to this aspect of financial markets is that for many people, *repeated failure does little to deter the behavior*. If repeated loss and agony cannot overcome the limbic system's impulses, then it certainly must have free rein in comparatively benign social settings.

Regardless of their inappropriateness to financial markets, these impulses are not irrational because they have a purpose, no matter how ill-applied in modern life. Yet neither are they rational, as they are within men's unconscious minds, i.e., their basal ganglia and limbic system, which are equipped to operate without and to override the conscious input of reason. These impulses, then, serve rational general goals but are irrationally applied to too many specific situations.

Phi in the Unconscious Mentational Patterns of Individuals and Groups

At this point, we have identified unconscious, impulsive mental processes in individual human beings that are involved in governing behavior with respect to one's fellows in a social setting. Is it logical to expect such impulses to be patterned? When the unconscious mind operates, it could hardly do so randomly, as that would mean no thought at all. *It must operate in patterns peculiar to it*. Indeed, the limbic systems of individuals produce the same patterns of behavior over and over when those individuals are in groups. The interesting observation is *how* the behavior is patterned. When we investigate statistical and scientific material on the subject, rare as it is, we find that *our Fibonacci-structured neurons and microtubules* (see "Science is Validating the Concept of the Wave Principle") *participate in Fibonacci patterns of mentation.*

Perhaps the most rigorous work in this area has been performed by psychologists in a series of studies on choice. G.A. Kelly proposed in 1955 that every person evaluates the world around him using a system of bipolar constructs.[16] When judging others, for instance, one end of each pole represents a maximum positive trait and the other a maximum negative trait, such as honest/dishonest, strong/weak, etc. Kelly had assumed that average responses in value-neutral situations would be 0.50. He was wrong. Experiments show a human bent toward favor or optimism that results in a response ratio in value-neutral situations of 0.62, which is *phi*. Numerous binary-choice experiments have reproduced this finding, regardless of the type of constructs or the age, nationality or background of the subjects. To name just a few, the ratio of 62/38 results when choosing "and" over "but" to link character traits, when evaluating factors in the work environment, and in the frequency of cooperative choices in the prisoner's dilemma.[17]

Psychologist Vladimir Lefebvre of the School of Social Sciences at the University of California in Irvine and Jack Adams-Webber of Brock University corroborate these findings. When Lefebvre asks subjects to choose between two options about which they have no strong feelings and/ or little knowledge, answers tend to divide into Fibonacci proportion: 62% to 38%. When he asks subjects to sort indistinguishable objects into two piles, they tend to divide them into a 62/38 ratio. When subjects are asked to judge the "lightness" of gray paper against solid white and solid black,

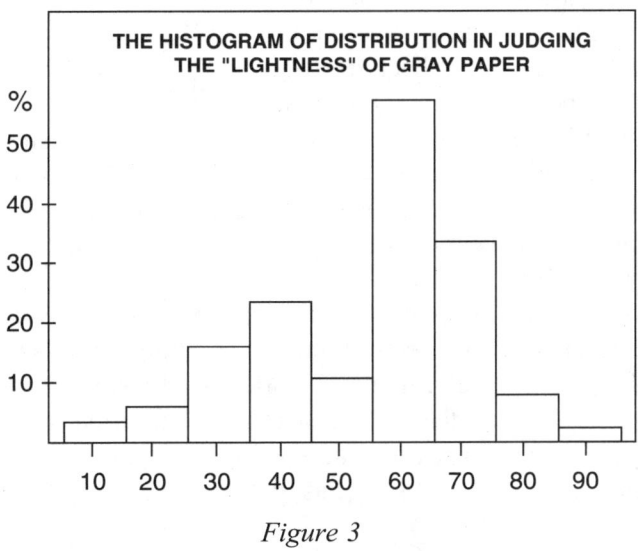

Figure 3

they persistently mark it either 62% or 38% light,[18] favoring the former. (See Figure 3.) When Adams-Webber asks subjects to evaluate their friends and acquaintances in terms of bipolar attributes, they choose the positive pole 62% of the time on average.[19] When he asks a subject to decide how many of his own attributes another shares, the average commonality assigned is 0.625.[20] When subjects are given scenarios that require a moral action and asked what percentage of people would take good actions vs. bad actions, their answers average 62%.[21] "When people say they feel 50/50 on a subject," Lefebvre says, "chances are it's more like 62/38."[22]

Lefebvre concludes from these findings, "We may suppose that in a human being, there is a special algorithm for working with codes *independent of particular objects*."[23] This language fits MacLean's conclusion and LeDoux's confirmation that the limbic system can produce emotions and attitudes that are independent of objective referents in the cortex. If these statistics reveal something about human thought, they suggest that in many, perhaps all, individual humans, and certainly in an aggregate average, *opinion is predisposed to a 62/38 inclination*. With respect to each individual decision, the availability of pertinent data, the influence of prior experiences and/or learned biases can modify that ratio in any given instance. However, *phi is what the mind starts with*. It defaults to *phi* whenever parameters are unclear or information insufficient for an utterly objective assessment.

This is important data because it shows a Fibonacci decision-based mentational tendency in *individuals*. If individual decision-making reflects *phi*, then it is less of a leap to accept that the Wave Principle, which also reflects *phi*, is one of its collective products. To narrow that step even further, we must be satisfied that *phi* appears in *group* mentation in the real world. Does Fibonacci-patterned decision-making mentation in individuals result in a Fibonacci-patterned decision-making mentation in collectives? Data from the 1930s and the 1990s suggests that it does.

Lefebvre and Adams-Webber's experiments show unequivocally that the more individuals' decisions are summed, the smaller is the variance from *phi*. In other words, while individuals may vary somewhat in the *phi*-based bias of their bipolar decision-making, a large sum of such decisions reflects *phi* quite precisely. In a real-world social context, Lefebvre notes by example that the median voting margin in California ballot initiatives over 100 years is 62%. The same ratio holds true in a study of all referenda in America over a decade[24] as well as referenda in Switzerland from 1886 to 1978.[25]

In the early 1930s, before any such experiments were conducted or models proposed, stock market analyst Robert Rhea undertook a statistical study of bull and bear markets from 1896 to 1932. He knew nothing of Fibonacci, as his work in financial markets predated R.N. Elliott's discovery of their Fibonacci connection by eight years. Thankfully, he published the results despite, as he put it, seeing no immediate practical value for the data. Here is his summary:

> Bull markets were in progress 8143 days, while the remaining 4972 days were in bear markets. The relationship between these figures tends to show that bear markets run **61.1 percent** of the time required for bull periods.... The bull market['s]...net advance was 46.40 points. [It] was staged in four primary swings of 14.44, 17.33, 18.97 and 24.48 points respectively. The sum of these advances is 75.22. If the net advance, 46.40, is divided into the sum of advances, 75.22, the result is **1.621**. The total of secondary reactions retraced **62.1 percent** of the net advance.[26]

To generalize his findings, the stock market on average advances by **1s** and retreats by **.618s**, *in both price and time.*

Lefebvre and others' work showing that people have a natural tendency to make choices that are 61.8% *optimistic* and 38.2% *pessimistic* directly reflects Robert Rhea's data indicating that bull markets tend both to move prices and to endure 62% relative to bear markets' 38%. Bull markets and bear markets are the quintessential expressions of optimism and pessimism in an overall net-neutral environment for judgment. Moreover, they are created by a very large number of people, whose individual differences in decision-making style cancel each other out to leave a picture of pure Fibonacci expression, the same result produced in the aggregate in bipolar decision-making experiments. *As rational cogitation would never produce such mathematical consistency, this picture must come from another source, which is likely the impulsive paleomentation of the limbic system, the part of the brain that induces herding.*

While Rhea's data need to be confirmed by more statistical studies, prospects for their confirmation appears bright. For example, in their 1996 study on log-periodic structures in stock market data, Sornette and Johansen investigate successive oscillation periods around the time of the 1987 crash and find that each period (t_n) equals a value (l) to the power of the period's place in the sequence (n), so that $t_n = l^n$. They then state outright the significance of the Fibonacci ratio that they find for l:

> The "Elliott wave" technique...describes the time series of a stock price as made of different "waves." These different waves are in relation

with each other through the Fibonacci series, [whose numbers] converge to a constant (the so-called golden mean, 1.618), implying an approximate geometrical series of time scales in the underlying waves. [This idea is] *compatible with our above estimate for the ratio l @ 1.5-1.7$.*[27]

This phenomenon of *time* is the same as the one that R.N. Elliott described for *price* swings in the 1930-1939 period, as recounted in Chapter 5 of *The Wave Principle of Human Social Behavior*.

In the past three years, modern researchers have conducted experiments that further demonstrate Elliott's observation that *phi* and the stock market are connected. The October 1997 *New Scientist* reports on a study that concludes that the stock market's Hurst exponent,[28] which characterizes its fractal dimension, is *0.65*.[29] This number is quite close to the Fibonacci ratio. However, since that time, the figure for financial auction-market activity has gotten even closer. *Europhysics Letters* has just published the results of a market simulation study by European physicists Caldarelli, Marsili and Zhang. Although the simulation involves only a dozen or so subjects at a time trading a supposed currency relationship, the resulting price fluctuations mimic those in the stock market. Upon measuring the fractal persistence of those patterns, the authors come to this conclusion:

> The scaling behavior of the price "returns"…is very similar to that observed in a real economy. These distributions [of price differences] satisfy the scaling hypothesis…with an exponent of H = *0.62*.[30]

The Hurst exponent of this group dynamic, then, is *0.62*. Although the authors do not mention the fact, this is the Fibonacci ratio. Recall that the fractal dimension of our neurons is *phi*. These two studies show that the fractal dimension of the stock market is related to *phi*. *The stock market, then, has the same fractal dimensional factor as our neurons, and both of them are the Fibonacci ratio.* This is powerful evidence that our neurophysiology is compatible with, and therefore intimately involved in, the generation of the Wave Principle.

Lefebvre explains why scientists are finding *phi* in every aspect of both average individual mentation and collective mentation:

> The golden section results from the iterative process. …Such a process must appear [in mentation] when two conditions are satisfied: (a) alternatives are polarized, that is, one alternative plays the role of the *positive pole* and the other one that of the *negative pole*; and (b) there is no criterion for the utilitarian preference of one alternative over the other.[31]

This description fits people's mental struggle with the stock market, it fits people's participation in social life in general, and it fits the Wave Principle.

It is particularly intriguing that the study by Caldarelli *et al.* purposely excludes all external input of news or "fundamentals." In other words, it purely records "all the infighting and ingenuity of the players in trying to outguess the others."[32] As Lefebvre's work anticipates, participants in such a subjective environment should default to *phi*, which Elliott's model and the latest studies show is exactly the number to which they default in real-world financial markets.

Conclusion

R.N. Elliott discovered *before any of the above was known*, that the form of mankind's evaluation of his own productive enterprise, i.e., the stock market, has Fibonacci properties. These studies and statistics say that the mechanism that generates the Wave Principle, man's unconscious mind, has countless Fibonacci-related properties. These findings are compatible with Elliott's hypothesis.

NOTES

[1] MacLean, P. (1990). *The triune brain in evolution: Role in paleocerebral functions.* New York: Plenum Press.

[2] Scuoteguazza, H. (1997, September/October). "Handling emotional intelligence." *The Objective American.*

[3] MacLean, P. (1990). *The triune brain in evolution,* p. 17.

[4] Chapters 15 through 19 of *The Wave Principle of Human Social Behavior* explore this point further.

[5] Wright, K. (1997, October). "Babies, bonds and brains." *Discover,* p. 78.

[6] Pigou, A.C. (1927). *Industrial fluctuations.* London: F. Cass.

[7] Pigou, A.C. (1920). *The economics of welfare.* London: F. Cass.

[8] Among others, such measures include put and call volume ratios, cash holdings by institutions, index futures premiums, the activity of margined investors, and reports of market opinion from brokers, traders, newsletter writers and investors.

[9] Bishop, J.E. (1987, November 17). "Stock market experiment suggests inevitability of booms and busts." *The Wall Street Journal.*

[10] Olsen, R. (1996, July/August). "Implications of herding behavior for earnings estimtion, risk assessment, and stock returns." *Financial Analysts Journal,* pp. 37-41.

[11] Just about any source of stress can induce a herding response. MacLean humorously references the tendency of governments and universities to respond to tension by forming *ad hoc* committees.

[12] Passell, P. (1989, August 25). "Dow and reason: Distant cousins?" *The New York Times.*

[13] Gajdusek, D.C. (1970). "Physiological and psychological characteristics of stone age man." *Symposium on Biological Bases of Human Behavior, Eng. Sci.* 33, pp. 26-33, 56-62.

[14] MacLean, P. (1990). *The triune brain in evolution,* p. 239.

[15] There is a myth, held by nearly all people outside of back-office employees of brokerage firms and the IRS, that many people do well in financial speculation. Actually, almost everyone loses at the game eventually. The head of a futures brokerage firm once confided to me that never in the firm's history had customers in the aggregate had a winning year. Even in the stock market, when the public or even most professionals win, it is a temporary, albeit sometimes prolonged, phenomenon. The next big bear market usually wipes them out if they live long enough, and if they do not, it wipes out their successors. This is true regardless of today's accepted wisdom that the stock market always goes to new highs eventually and that

today's investors are "wise." Aside from the fact that the "new highs forever" conviction is false (Where was the Roman stock market during the Dark Ages?), what counts is *when people act*, and that is what ruins them.

[16] Kelly, G.A. (1955). *The psychology of personal constructs*, Vols. 1 and 2.

[17] Osgood, C.E., and Richards, M.M. (1973). *Language*, 49, pp. 380-412; Shalit, B. (1960). *British Journal of Psychology*, 71, pp. 39-42; Rapoport, A. and Chammah, A.M. (1965). *Prisoner's dilemma*. University of Michigan Press.

[18] Poulton, E.C., Simmonds, D.C.V. and Warren, R.M. (1968). "Response bias in very first judgments of the reflectance of grays: Numerical versus linear estimates." *Perception and Psychophysics*, Vol. 3, pp. 112-114.

[19] Adams-Webber, J. and Benjafield, J. (1973). "The relation between lexical marking and rating extremity in interpersonal judgment." *Canadian Journal of Behavioral Science*, Vol. 5, pp. 234-241.

[20] Adams-Webber, J. (1997, Winter). "Self-reflexion in evaluating others." *American Journal of Psychology*, Vol. 110, No. 4, pp. 527-541.

[21] McGraw, K.M. (1985). "Subjective probabilities and moral judgments." *Journal of Experimental and Biological Structures*, #10, pp. 501-518.

[22] Washburn, J. (1993, March 31). "The human equation." *The Los Angeles Times*.

[23] Lefebvre, V.A. (1987, October). "The fundamental structures of human reflexion." *The Journal of Social Biological Structure*, Vol. 10, pp. 129-175.

[24] Lefebvre, V.A. (1992). *A psychological theory of bipolarity and reflexivity*. Lewinston, NY: The Edwin Mellen Press. And (1997). *The cosmic subject*. Moscow: Russian Academy of Sciences Institute of Psychology Press.

[25] Butler, D. and Ranney, A. (1978). Referendums Washington, D.C., American Enterprise Institute for Public Policy Research.

[26] Rhea, R. (1936). *The story of the averages*: *A retrospective study of the forecasting value of Dow's theory as applied to the daily movements of the Dow-Jones industrial & railroad stock averages*. Republished January 1990. Omnigraphi. (See discussion in Chapter 4 of *Elliott Wave Principle* by Frost and Prechter.)

[27] Sornette, D., Johansen, A., and Bouchaud, J.P. (1996). "Stock market crashes, precursors and replicas." *Journal de Physique I France* 6, No.1, pp. 167-175.

[28] The Hurst exponent (H), named for its developer, Harold Edwin Hurst [ref: Hurst, H.E., *et al.* (1951). *Long term storage: An experimental study*] is related to the fractal, or Hausdorff dimension (D) by the following

formula, where E is the embedding Euclidean dimension (2 in the case of a plane, 3 in the case of a space): $D = E - H$. It may also be stated as $D = E + 1 - H$ if E is the *generating* Euclidean dimension (1 in the case of a line, 2 in the case of a plane). Thus, if the Hurst exponent of a line graph is .38, or ϕ^{-2}, then the fractal dimension is 1.62, or ϕ; if the Hurst exponent is .62, or ϕ^{-1}, then the fractal dimension is 1.38, or $1 + \phi^{-2}$. [source: Schroeder, M. (1991). *Fractals, chaos, power laws: Minutes from an infinite paradise.* New York: W.H. Freeman & Co.] Thus, if H is related to ϕ, so is D.

[29] Brooks, M. (1997, October 18). "Boom to bust." *New Scientist.*

[30] Caldarelli, G., *et al.* (1997). "A prototype model of stock exchange." *Europhysics Letters*, 40 (5), pp. 479-484.

[31] Lefebvre, V.A. (1998, August 18-20). "Sketch of reflexive game theory," from the proceedings of *The Workshop on Multi-Reflexive Models of Agent Behavior* conducted by the Army Research Laboratory.

[32] See endnote 30.

The Elliott Wave Theorist
September 2002

Another Indication of Possible Elliott Wave Tendencies in Physical Phenomena

Chapter 21 of *The Wave Principle of Human Social Behavior* showed a possible Elliott wave in a graph of the infrared light absorbance of cement. Recently, Charles V. Berney forwarded a copy of his 1973 study[1] on the spectroscopy of trifluoroacetic acid (CF_3COOH) and wondered if a similar form was manifest. Included were graphs of the neutron inelastic-scattering spectra of both solid and liquid CF_3COOH.

In the accompanying illustration, I have labeled these graphs with the Wave Principle in mind. These forms are not Elliott waves because, in one instance apiece, they exhibit "overlap" between the values of waves one and four. In social trends, wave four in an impulse does not enter the value territory of wave one. Yet there seems to be a strong hint of an Elliott wave *tendency* in these graphs, as you can see by the labeling.

No one has conducted a comprehensive investigation into the existence of Elliott wave tendencies in non-life phenomena. It would be interesting to know whether nature has such tendencies within certain non-living compounds apart from their participation in life forms.

NOTES

[1] Berney, C.V. (1973.) "Spectroscopy of CF_3COZ Compounds. V. Vibrational Spectra and Structure of Solid Trifluoroacetic Acid," *Journal of the American Chemical Society*, **95**, 708.

Possible Elliott Wave Tendencies
in the Spectroscopy of Trifluoroacetic Acid

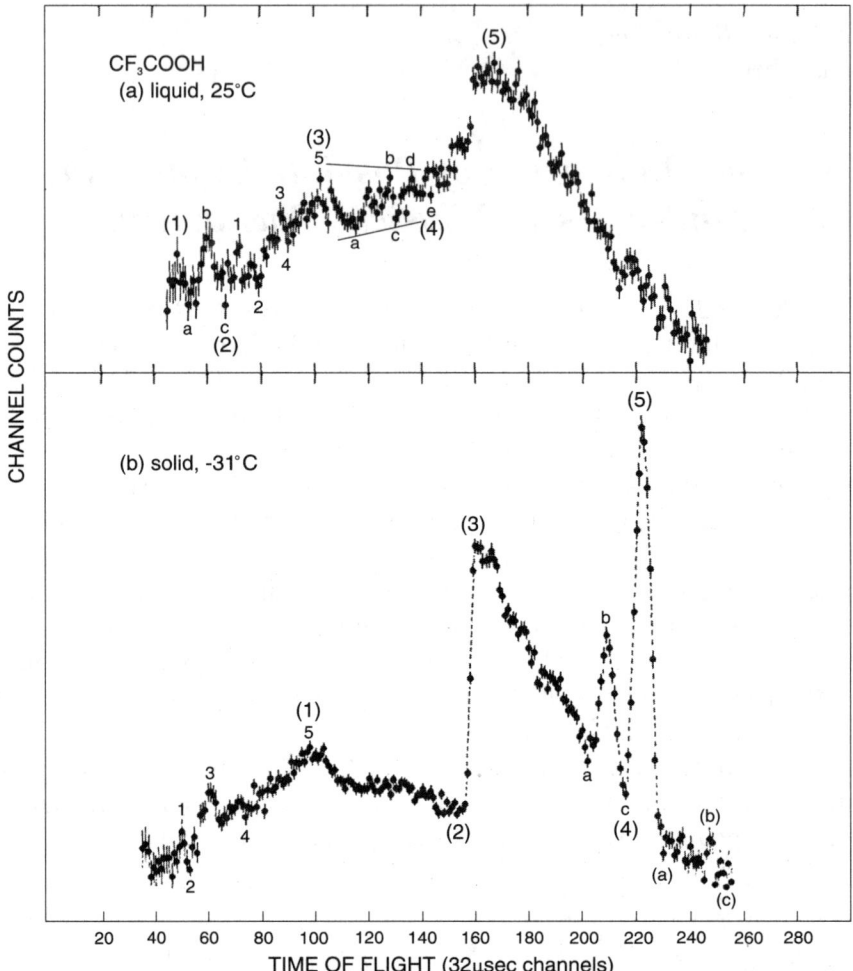

Figure 2. Neutron inelastic-scattering spectra of CF_3COOH. Wave number equivalents of some of the channels are indicated (458. . .27 cm^{-1}). Intense Bragg peaks are observed in the solid for neutron wavelengths of 5.23 and 5.55 Å; they can be interpreted as the 100 and 002 reflections of a monoclinic unit cell with parameters $a = 5.25$, $b = 9.165$, $c = 11.142$ A, and $\beta = 85$.

The Elliott Wave Theorist
July 2002

Another Example of a Link Between Nature's Trees and Waves

Chapter 3 of *The Wave Principle of Human Social Behavior* (1999) proposed the following hypothesis:

> Are nature's developing waves, branching arbora [i.e., trees] and expanding spirals all the same thing? Figures 3-15, 3-16 and 3-2 express the Fibonacci sequence in three different ways: as a *tree*, a *spiral* and a *wave*.... Natural processes express this cross-representational property as well. For example, evolution is a process that makes *waves, spirals and arbora*.... This transformation property may cover other types of fractals as well. For example...a topographic fractal (mountains, hills, hillocks, etc.) [is] also an arborum...when water, snow or flowers fill the cracks. See Figure 3-20.... It is also true that price trends can be graphed in such a way as to reveal not a line but a spiral.... All these pictures resemble many natural expressions of growth and expansion [or recession and decay], from life forms to galaxies. In terms of their essence, then, there may be little difference among nature's progressing forms. The only difference may be the template upon which nature projects them.[1]

The work of a scientist in the field of fractal geometry has allowed us to view another example of this idea. Benoit Mandelbrot's latest book, *Gaussian Self-Affinity and Fractals* (2002) presents an illustration of a highly stylized tree, "a Peano motion in the plane." The illustration may be conceived of as "rivers that flow into the black 'sea'" or as trees with "new layer[s] of shorter branches," which you can see in Figure 1. This is a simple stylized arborum (branching fractal).

The more interesting depiction is Figure 2, which displays "the graph $\mathcal{P}$ of the limit curve," i.e., "the $X(t)$ coordinate function of the Peano motion in Figure 1."[2] The fact that the *tree* in Figure 1 can be shown as a *wave* in Figure 2 supports the observation quoted above from *The Wave Principle of Human Social Behavior*.

Figure 1

The Arborum in Figure 1, Plotted as a Wave

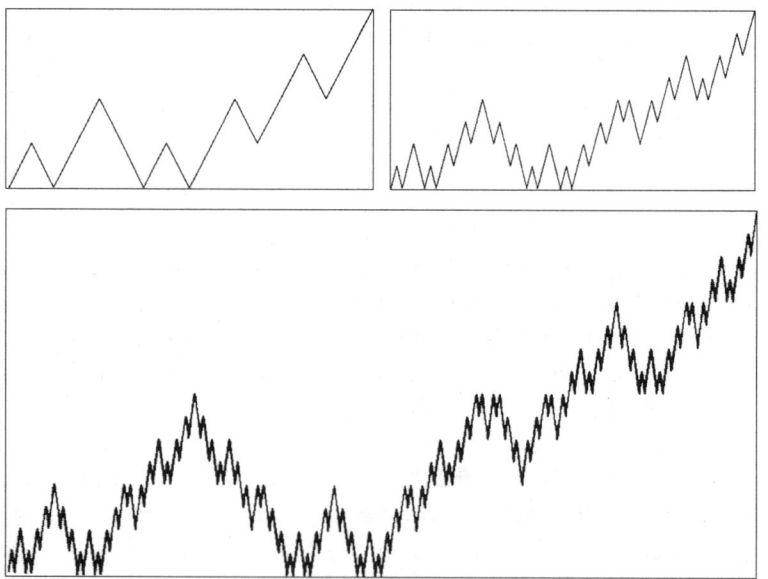

Figure 2

Nearly an Elliott Wave

The details of the result are even more fascinating to a trained eye because as detailed in Figure 3, the self-affine fractal in Figure 2 reflects the 5-3 form of net progress described by R.N. Elliott's Wave Principle. It follows Elliott's observations of market behavior even to the point of including alternation (see *Elliott Wave Principle*, pp. 61-63) between waves two and four. *This stylized tree, then, does not reflect an indiscriminate line fractal but something extremely close to an ideal Elliott wave.*

The pattern's detail is interesting. Corrections bottom at the level of the preceding wave four, as under the Wave Principle. With respect to alternation, it sports a short-long declining pattern in the "wave 2" position and a long-short pattern in the "wave 4" position.

There are two main variations from the rules of Elliott wave construction. The first is that wave four in this pattern continually falls to the level of the peak of wave one, which never happens in financial markets.

The Arborum in Figure 1, Labeled in Elliott Fashion

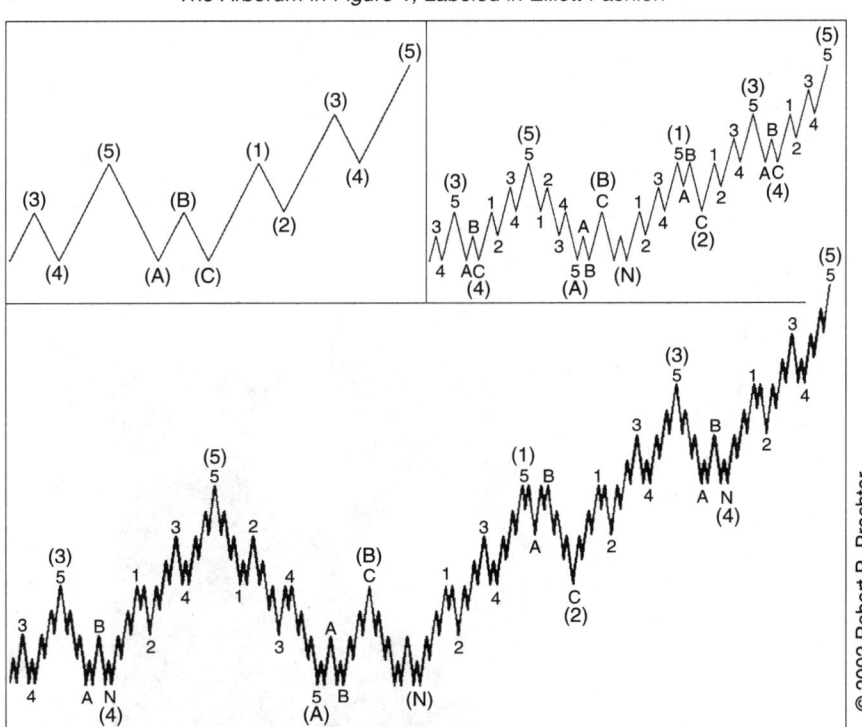

© 2002 Robert R. Prechter

Figure 3

Secondly, what should be wave C under the Wave Principle alternately subdivides into three waves instead of five. (I have labeled this construction "N" in Figure 3.) There are other variations in terms of guidelines. For example, in Figure 3, all advancing subwaves are the same length, which does not typically occur in financial markets or in Elliott's model, which reflects reality.

The Expanded Hypothesis

Since plotting an aspect of a stylized tree produces a stylized Elliott wave, we may reiterate the suspicion that plotting aspects of robust fractals in the form of arbora in nature is likely to produce robust fractals called Elliott waves, with all the natural order and variation that we have come to know from their expressions in financial markets. They should have this property because arbora and Elliott waves both depict aspects of natural growth patterns. Indeed, as shown in *The Wave Principle of Human Social Behavior*, they can depict the *same* natural growth patterns, such as the number of families of fauna produced through evolution.

The Spiral Implied by the Arborum in Figure 1

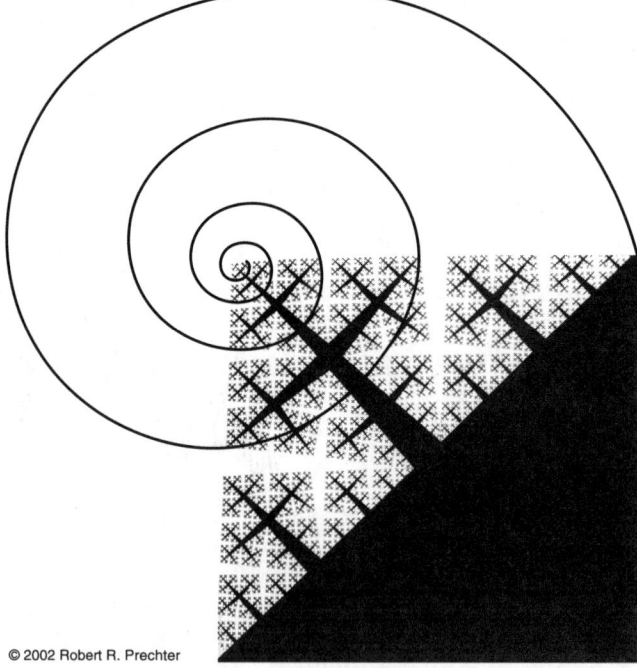

Figure 4

The Spiral Implied by the Wave in Figure 2

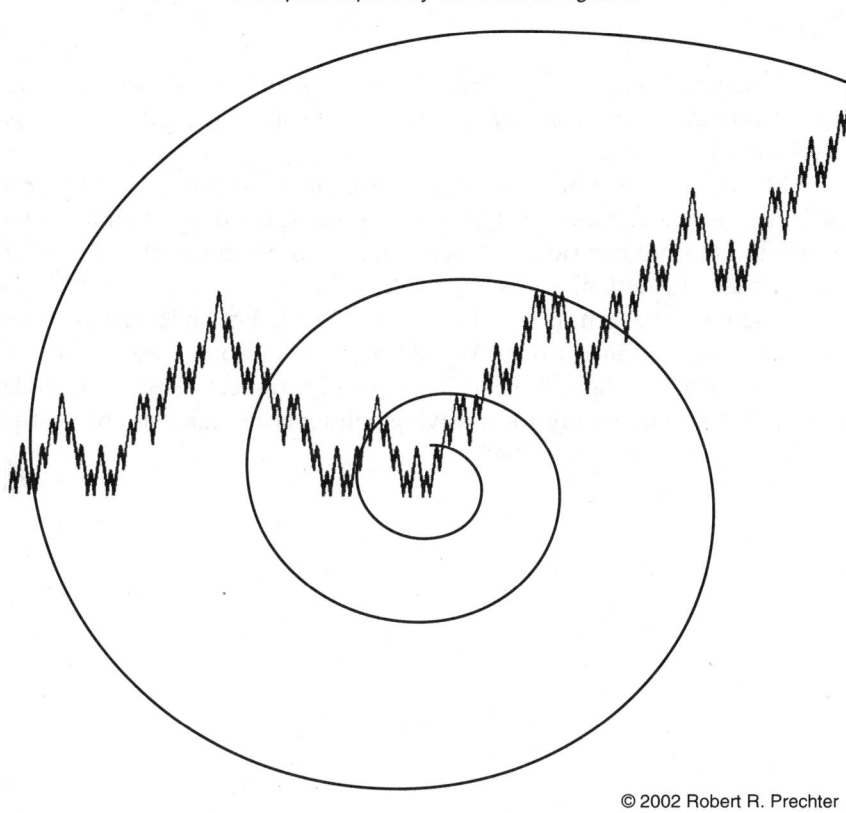

© 2002 Robert R. Prechter

Figure 5

Both the stylized tree in Figure 1 and the stylized advancing wave in Figure 2 may be circumscribed with spirals, as shown in Figures 4 and 5. (See also Figures 2-29 and 3-14 in *The Wave Principle of Human Social Behavior*.) Thus, once again, we have expressions of all three of nature's primary growth forms in a single process.[3]

NOTES

[1] Prechter, Robert R. (1999). *The wave principle of human social behavior and the new science of socionomics*. Gainesville, GA: New Classics Library, pp. 75-82.

[2] Mandelbrot, Benoit B. (2002). *Gaussian self-affinity and fractals*. New York: Springer. Note: As the author explains, the illustration in Figure 1 exaggerates one-dimensional branches into two-dimensional ones for effective visual illustration.

[3] Scientists are getting so close to the Wave Principle that they are within smelling distance of it. An educated nose would prove a useful resource. Ironically, Mandelbrot's aloofness with respect to Elliott's model has provided an opportunity for a wave practitioner to make an observation that otherwise he could have made.

CONTROVERSY
AND
VALIDATION

Mr. Prechter:

If you haven't done it yet, hop on down to the local newsstand and pick up the February 1999 issue of *Scientific American*. Contained therein is an article called "A Multifractal Walk Down Wall Street," by none other than Benoit Mandelbrot. I read this and my jaw dropped — it is very similar to the Wave Principle.

—J. Gregory Wharton, AIA Project Architect
February 1, 1999

Prechter

The Elliott Wave Theorist
March 4, 1999

Controversy

I urge you to obtain the February 1999 issue of *Scientific American*. Its cover article is entitled "A Fractal Walk Down Wall Street." In it, a famous scientist purports to present the "new" idea that financial markets may be modeled as variable hierarchical fractals. Illustrations depict markets as having patterns that subdivide into identical sub-patterns. Credit for this idea belongs to R.N. Elliott. The author of the article knows this, as he took pains to read Elliott's works thoroughly so as to find bits of writing that enabled him to denigrate Elliott in a 1997 book. When you look at the illustrations and read the text of this article, you cannot help but consider the idea that Elliott was ripped off. Get the magazine and make up your own mind.

After you read the article, you might send *Scientific American* a letter to the editor at 415 Madison Ave., New York, NY 10017 or by e-mail at editors@sciamer.com. I have composed a brief response, which the magazine says it will publish probably in its June issue, due out in mid-May. In a coming issue of EWT, I will alert you to a more detailed response, which will be available on our web site.

...and Affirmation

The good news, as we have seen in recent years, is that cutting-edge scientific work is converging toward the Wave Principle. We are coming very close to having Elliott's ideas confirmed and verified by the scientific community. It is in fact evidence of further validation that a renowned scientist has decided that at least one implication of Elliott's work is so important that he wants credit for it (properly or otherwise; we will let the scientific community decide). Proponents of the Wave Principle can take heart that these ideas are rapidly becoming viewed as *important*.

Prechter
Scientific American
June 1999
Letter to the Editor

Fractals and Finance

I am impelled to point out that most of the ideas presented in Benoit B. Mandelbrot's article, "A Multifractal Walk Down Wall Street," [February] originated with Ralph Nelson Elliott, who put them forth more comprehensively and more accurately with respect to real-world markets in his 1938 book, *The Wave Principle.* Figure 1 shows an illustration from Elliott's literature depicting the [hierarchical] multifractal nature of markets; Figure 2 shows Mandelbrot's exposition. Slight differences in the specific pattern used in these diagrams are irrelevant because Mandelbrot is not arguing a specific form, just multifractal self-affinity. For a detailed response to Mandelbrot's article, please visit http://www.elliottwave.com/response.htm on the World Wide Web.

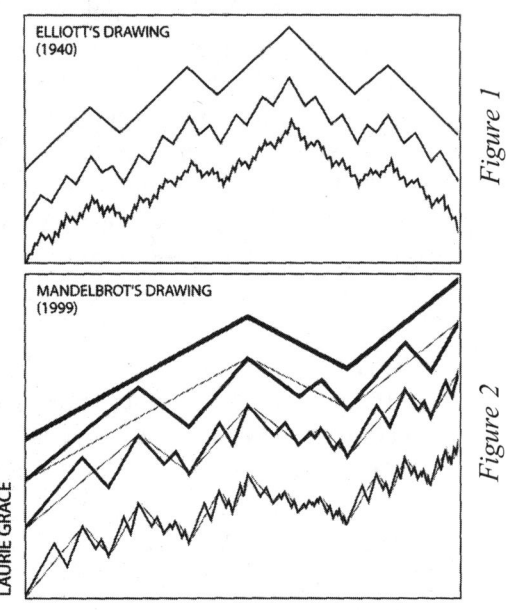

—Robert R. Prechter, Jr.
President, Elliott Wave International
Gainesville, GA

Prechter

The Elliott Wave Theorist[1]
May 1999

Personal Note*: In 1985, it was with pleasure that I watched Benoit
Mandelbrot receive adoring news coverage for his case that fractals
permeate nature. It was in a cooperative spirit that I sent him material
describing R.N. Elliott's original 1938 discovery of the same thing in
finance. He did not respond. Out of deference to a great scientist, I
chose to keep quiet about Mandelbrot's libelous treatment of Elliott in
his 1997 book. However, his claim to a substantial portion of Elliott's
work in the February 1999 issue of* Scientific American *has forced me
to address these issues. If it is a sad day when one's hero falls short of
expectations, then this day for me is grievous. — RP*

Credit Where It Is Due

Benoit Mandelbrot's cover article in *Scientific American* (February
1999, "A Multifractal Walk Down Wall Street")[2] is a good read and contains important knowledge. His only omission is in properly crediting most
of the ideas presented therein to Ralph Nelson Elliott, who put them forth
more comprehensively, and more accurately with respect to real-world
markets, sixty-one years ago in his book, *The Wave Principle*.[3]

A Study in Similarity

Figure 1 shows R.N. Elliott's depictions from 1938 of the fractal nature of markets. Figure 2 shows Mandelbrot's from 1999. Figure 3 shows
an illustration traced directly from Elliott's literature. Figure 4 shows *Scientific American's* depiction of Mandelbrot's thesis, from a figure he
provided.[4] It is important to understand that slight differences in the specific pattern used in these diagrams are irrelevant to the matter of proper
credit because Mandelbrot is not arguing a specific form, just multifractal
self-affinity.

The similarity between these figures is undeniable, yet Mandelbrot
lists only four references for his article: Mandelbrot, Mandelbrot, Mandelbrot and Mandelbrot.[5] His article includes the following self-references:

ELLIOTT'S FRACTAL
GENERATOR MODEL (1938)

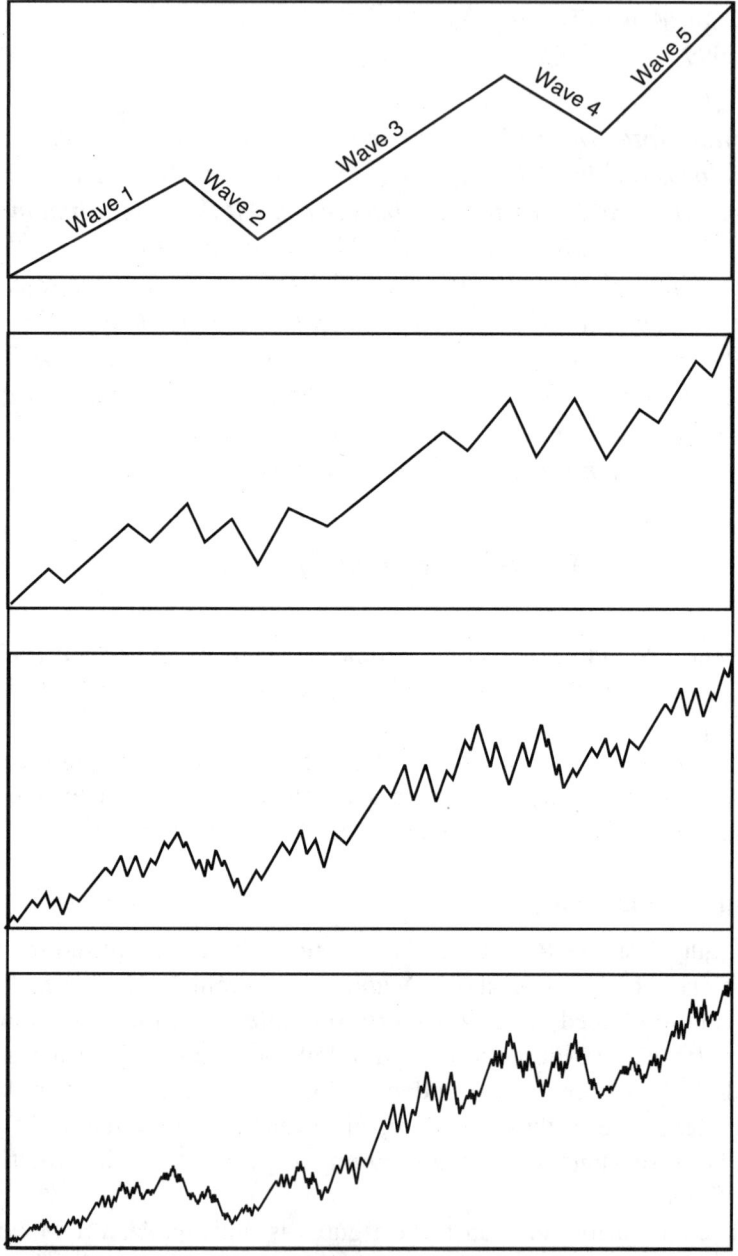

Figure 1

MANDELBROT'S FRACTAL GENERATOR DEPICTION (1999)

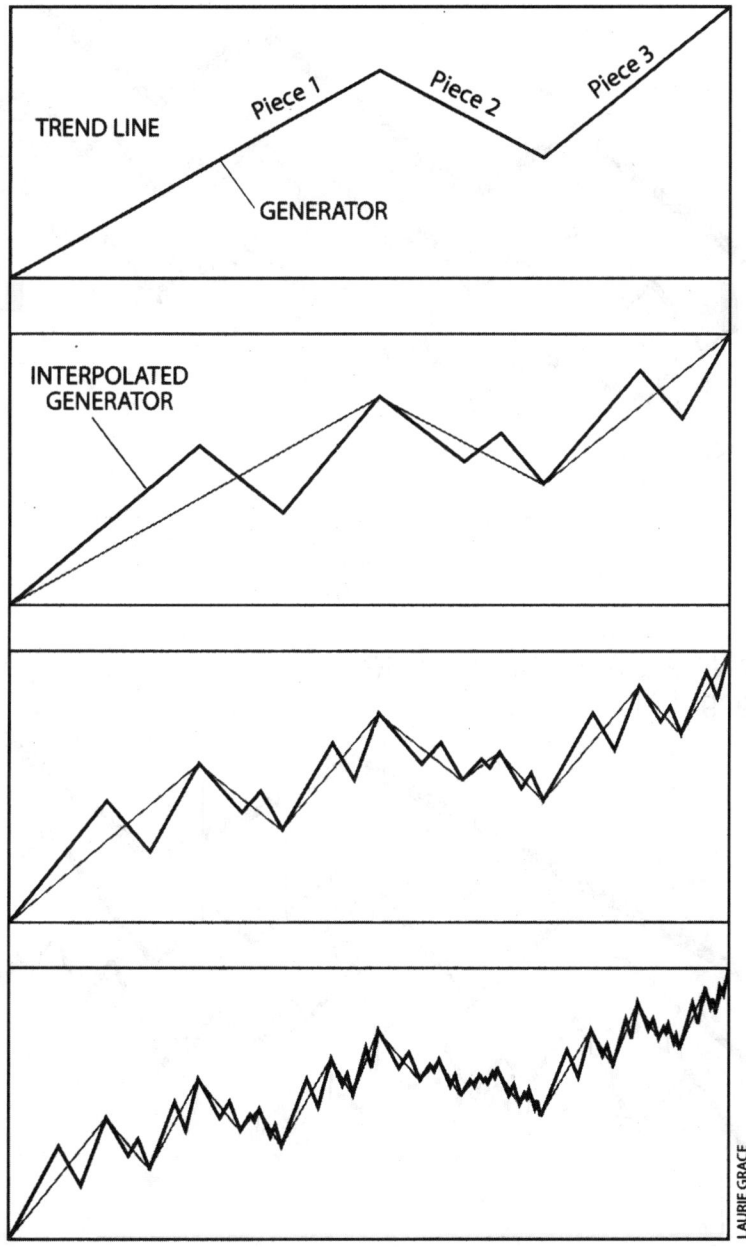

Figure 2

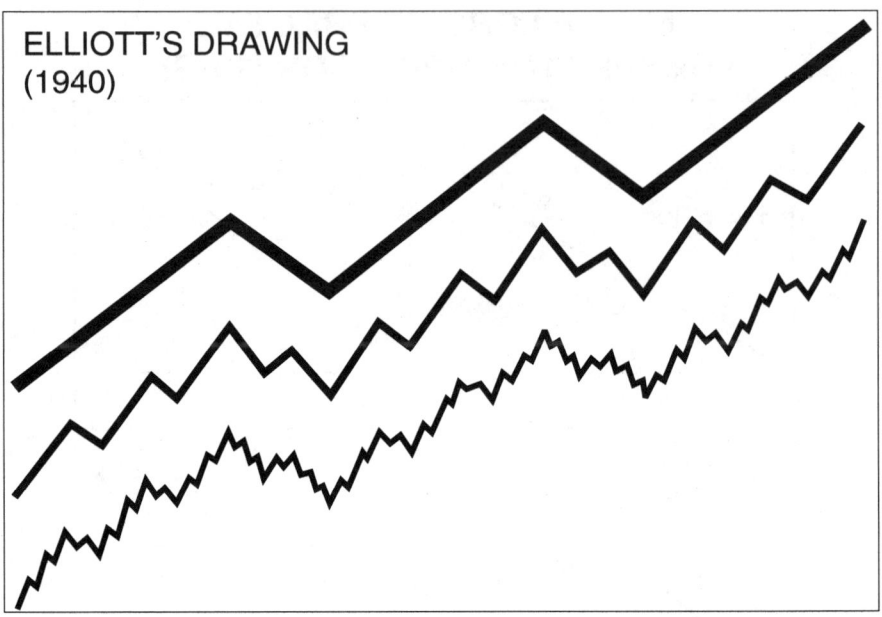

Figure 3

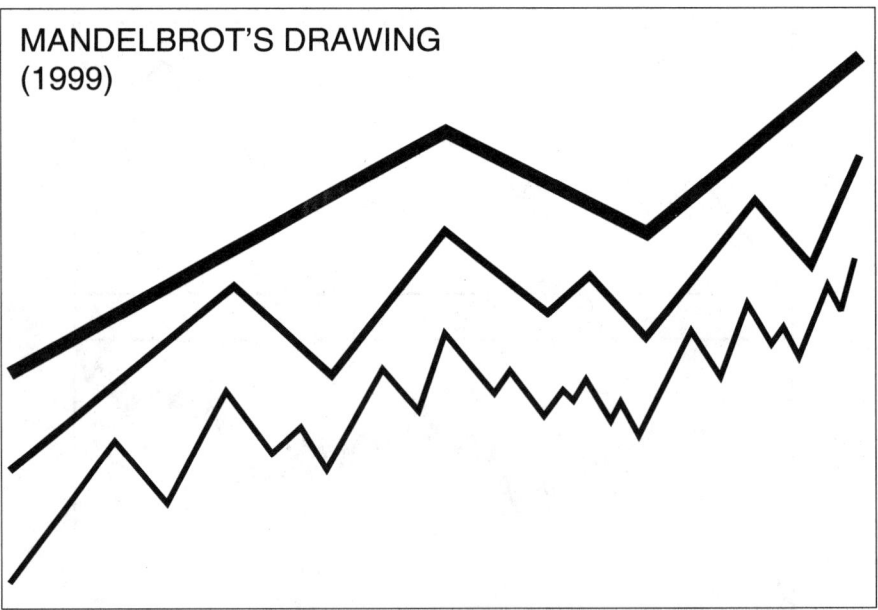

Figure 4

"*I claim* that variations in financial prices can be accounted for by a model derived from *my work* in fractal geometry."

"These…*new modeling techniques* are designed to cast a light of order into the seemingly impenetrable thicket of the financial markets."

"*My own work* [contradicts modern portfolio theory and random walk]."[6]

In fact, it was R.N. Elliott in 1938[7] who meticulously described the fractal self-affinity of market patterns. It was a 1978 book, *Elliott Wave Principle*, that included among the implications of Elliott's discovery that it "challenges the Random Walk theory at every turn."[8]

The modeling technique displayed in Figures 1 through 4 is over six decades old, and Mandelbrot knows it. This is clear because in dismissing Elliott in 1997[9], he quoted from a volume[10] that includes all of Elliott's major work as well as the illustrations contained in Figures 1 and 3.

Mandelbrot's long-delayed response to years of questions about the significance of Elliott's work was to pen a brief condescending dismissal of Elliott's discovery. As you will see in an upcoming discussion, Mandelbrot's summary of Elliott is half *ad hominem* attack and half misrepresentation, the net effect of which is to malign Elliott both by innuendo and omission. Worse than the condescension, however, is that Mandelbrot appears to have effected it, if his *Scientific American* article is any indication, in order to ignore the man and claim his predecessor's breakthrough as his own.

Even in his dismissal, Mandelbrot himself could not avoid stating the obvious truth that "Elliott's diagrams are qualitatively reminiscent of certain self-affine generators [in my book]…."[11] Mandelbrot knew this before he wrote his article for *Scientific American*, yet it still reads, "The *novelty* (and *surprise*) is that these self-affine fractal curves exhibit a wealth of structure — a foundation of both fractal geometry and the theory of chaos."[12] This is no novelty or surprise, but rather an observation with sixty years of history involving six major authors,[13] who have produced a nearly continuous stream of literature on the Wave Principle since 1938. If, as Mandelbrot says, these curves indeed reveal the foundation of both fractal geometry and the theory of chaos, then according to Mandelbrot's own formulation, Elliott deserves the credit for discovering and elucidating it.

Although Mandelbrot's words (and lack thereof) imply that in the scientific world, Elliott is a nonentity, this is not the case. Physicist Didier

Sornette of the Department of Earth and Space Science and the Institute of Geophysics and Planetary Physics at the University of California at Los Angeles, who has been systematically conducting pioneering studies in the fractal nature of markets, along with colleagues Johansen and Bouchaud stated three years ago in their 1996 study, "Stock Market Crashes, Precursors and Replicas," which appeared in France's *Journal de Physique*: "We speculate that the 'Elliott waves'…could be a signature of an underlying critical structure of the stock market."[14,15]

As honorable scientists should, Sornette *et al.* cite a proper reference source (*Elliott Wave Principle*) in this and several other studies. Here is how Mandelbrot phrases his only mention that other knowledge preceded his "new modeling technique":

> …this concept is not a rootless abstraction but a theoretical reformulation of a down-to-earth bit of market folklore — namely, that movements of a stock or currency all look alike when a market chart is enlarged or reduced so that it fits the same time and price scale.[16]

In that statement, Mandelbrot alludes to a supposed real-world foundation for what truly is his otherwise "rootless abstraction" yet omits referring to the empirical work that R.N. Elliott undertook over two decades in order to lay that foundation. Mandelbrot ascribes the empirical foundation he invokes to "market folklore," which it emphatically is not, either in its origin or in the implication that the idea is widely accepted. Folklore is an oral or fable tradition with misty origins, whereas the original source of this idea is on the written record. As for his term's implication that market self-affinity is common knowledge, most economists and even most financiers assign the cause of long term trends to economics and politics and of near term trends to "psychology." They neither espouse nor accept the idea of financial market self-affinity in either cause or appearance. (I have personally fought that lonely battle for 23 years.)

If circumstances were as Mandelbrot describes, then his article would have been mostly superfluous, not the "novelty" it claims to be. Which is it, then, a "novelty" or "down-to-earth market folklore"? In trying to have it two ways, Mandelbrot renders false both sides of his contradictory characterization. It is neither a novelty nor folklore. The truth is that in the financial world, the idea that market movements at all scales look alike has been entirely the domain of the Wave Principle. Elliott recognized the originality of his idea, calling it "a newly discovered phenomenon."[17] He wrote two books, twelve articles and four essential essays on the subject, all of which are contained in the volume from which Mandelbrot quoted. This "folklore" comment, absent any other reference, from someone who knows the true source of the idea, appears to be designed to avoid crediting the man who discovered that financial market patterns are a variable, self-affine, hierarchical fractal.

Regardless of what one thinks of Elliott's occasional unscientific incaution, which gave Mandelbrot ammunition for his dismissal, it does not diminish his achievement. One cannot concede as much to Mandelbrot's incaution. It is one thing to dismiss another's work as valueless. It is another to claim someone else's work as one's own. To combine the two acts is hypocrisy.

Mandelbrot claims in his article to present a "theoretical reformulation" of the idea of market self-affinity, which it is not. It may be a reformulation only of his own thinking, in which case exposure to Elliott's work appears to have prompted it. Allowing for differences in terminology and form, there is nothing in his model "fractal generator" that writers about the Wave Principle have not already proposed, either in the same way or in a better way.

Mandelbrot persistently ignores (and has derided, as we shall soon see) Elliott's seminal discovery of the fractal nature of markets, but in this article he appears specifically to desire credit for the potentiality that the market might be *discretely hierarchical*. In no uncertain terms, Elliott elucidated his conviction in this regard, both as an *actuality* and as a theoretically defensible model. Mandelbrot, in contrast, has never argued that financial markets are anything but indefinite fractals, like clouds and seacoasts. If Mandelbrot has decided that Elliott's model — or a variation of it — *might* be true, it would explain why he attempts to capture this aspect of it for himself via his fractal generator depicted in Figures 2 and 4.

Mandelbrot cites his "new modeling techniques" and states:

On a practical level, this finding suggests that a fractal generator can be developed based on historical market data. The actual model does not simply inspect what the market did yesterday or last week.... The charts created from the generators produced by this model can simulate alternative scenarios based on previous market activity.[18]

This is hardly a "new modeling technique" that can now arise from Mandelbrot's "finding." Developing a "fractal generator based on historical market data" is exactly what Elliott did. Numerous published practitioners have used it to produce "alternative scenarios based on previous market activity" as an ongoing exercise over six decades. Mandelbrot uses virtually the same language employed years earlier in *Elliott Wave Principle*, which specifically describes "ordering the relative probabilities" to develop an "expected scenario" from among the "valid alternatives."[19] In 1986, my firm employed the Lockheed Corporation to begin developing a computerized expert system that applies Elliott's model to the task of stock market forecasting. It considers stock market data going back to the start of the century and ranks alternate counts by the degree to which they fit the ideal model. (For details, see Chapter 4 of *The Wave Principle of Human Social Behavior*.) In other words, we have been *doing* for years what Mandelbrot is simply *proposing*.

In 1993, a correspondent wrote to my firm in response to an article about physicists pursuing chaos in financial markets and said, "Like Alexander King's story of the man in the isolated village in Switzerland who unknowingly reinvented the typewriter, it looks like these people are about to rediscover the Elliott wave."[20] Rediscovery in isolation may be excused. Knowing about a previous discovery and claiming it for oneself may not.

Pattern Recognition

In the latter 1980s, James Gleick made Professor Mandelbrot famous in a glowing *New York Times* article and his national best selling book, *Chaos*. Gleick, an unabashed fan, was nevertheless compelled to include this frank discussion of what fellow scientists saw as a chronic and disturbing propensity of Mandelbrot's:

> Mandelbrot['s]...book...rings with the first person: *I claim...I conceived and developed...and implemented...I have confirmed...I show...I coined...."* Wherever chaos led, Mandelbrot had some basis to claim that he had been there first.... Even an admirer would cry with exasperation, "Mandelbrot didn't have *everybody's* thoughts before they did." [emphasis in the original][21]

Whatever the extent of his proclivity, in this latest article, he has overstepped the bounds of courtesy and honesty by an unforgivable margin. This transgression is particularly glaring given Mandelbrot's own lifelong passion for demanding proper credit when it is warranted. Gleick describes this ardor:

> At the height of his success, he was reviled by some colleagues, who thought he was unnaturally obsessed with his place in history. They said he hectored them about giving due credit.... Sometimes when articles appeared using ideas from fractal geometry he would call or write the authors to complain that no reference was made to him or his book.[22]

Because R.N. Elliott is safely dead,[23] he is unable to exercise the same privilege. It is fortunate for the integrity of the history of scientific discovery that some of us know the facts.

In an inset to his article, Mandelbrot asks us to "pick the fake." This is a tempting invitation that I will avoid answering out of deference to a brilliant mathematician who has given the world so much in advancing the science of fractal geometry. Yet after giving the world so much, is it really necessary that he claim even more? The 1993 book, *Classics on Fractals*,[24] sets the record straight regarding much of the history of work involving fractals. My 1999 book, *The Wave Principle of Human Social Behavior*,[25] which discusses the vast implications of Elliott's work, credits Mandelbrot with his inarguably great achievements. Can he not bring himself to do the same for his predecessor?

Prechter's Response to Mandelbrot's Dismissal of Elliott

Mandelbrot's brief dismissal of R.N. Elliott was emailed to our website in 1998 by a concerned reader, who requested that I respond. I held off in deference to a famous scientist, but because the article in *Scientific American* makes it appear to be part of a larger injustice, I can no longer do so. Here is the citation in full from his book, *Fractals and Scaling in Finance — Discontinuity, Concentration, Risk* (1997):

> Elliott Waves: This section devoted to miscellanea is as good a place as any to mention Ralph N. Elliott (1871-1948). A former peripatetic accountant and expert on cafeteria management, he studied Fibonacci, the Secrets of the Great Pyramid and the prophecies of Melchi-Zedik, and in 1938 announced a great "discovery," a "Wave Principle" that "really forecasts." A claim that he was a precursor of the use of fractals in finance prompted me to scan Elliott [in] 1994. It is true that some of Elliott's diagrams are qualitatively reminiscent of certain self-affine generators of the kind studied in Section 4 of Chapter E6. That is, they embody the wisdom present in Swift's qualitative metaphor quoted earlier in this section, but nothing more. Elliott's work fails the requirements of objectivity and repeatability: in his own words, "considerable experience is required to interpret [it] correctly" and "no interpretation [is] valid unless made by [him or his direct licencees]."[26]

Below are numbered phrases constituting Mandelbrot's full commentary, followed by my responses.

(1) "This section devoted to miscellanea is as good a place as any to mention Ralph N. Elliott (1871-1948). A former peripatetic accountant and expert on cafeteria management..."

This is pure condescension. Elliott is not tangential to Mandelbrot's field but its originator. A grab-bag of *miscellanea* is hardly "as good a place as any" to discuss a pioneer unless one's object is to bury him. Why is Elliott a *former* accountant, because he is dead? Or because after pursuing the accounting profession as a business reorganization expert for four decades, he published a book on the stock market at the age of 67? If Mandelbrot were to publish a book on music at age 67, would he be a *former* mathematician? Mandelbrot's term *peripatetic* implies that Elliott was some kind of itinerant semi-professional who worked out of a suitcase. Elliott was not just an accountant but the chief accountant for several major corporations and national railroads and even administered the finances of Nicaragua as an appointee of the Coolidge administration's State Department during the U.S. occupation. For a brief period of two years, he did author several articles and a book on cafeteria management to cash in on the nationwide tea-room craze of the 1920s (whose counterpart today is the trendy coffee shop). Mandelbrot's subtly precious citation of this aspect of Elliott's entrepreneurship appears designed to characterize him as being beneath the discovery of fractal geometry in finance.[27]

(2) "...he studied Fibonacci, the Secrets of the Great Pyramid and the prophecies of Melchi-Zedik and in 1938 announced a great 'discovery'..."

The fraud behind this calculated composition is appalling. The parts of this phrase that matter are utter invention, extrapolated from a few words on two pages in Elliott's second and final book.[28] Elliott did not study or even cite "secrets" of the Great Pyramid or the prophecies of anybody. What he did was to credit a book with the unfortunate title, *Prophecies of Melchi-Zedik*, as the source of a tidbit of information regarding the height of the Great Pyramid that suggested to him that its builders knew about Fibonacci numbers. In Frost's and my 1978 book *Elliott Wave Principle*, we similarly quote Peter Tompkins, author of *Secrets of the Great Pyramid* (1971), as confirming that the dimensions of the structure are related by *phi*. Our collective point is simply that knowledge of Fibonacci numbers and ratios has been around for a long time. At most, Elliott was (as perhaps we were) guilty of ignorance of scientific sensitivities, but that's all there is to it. While scientists rightfully reject anything that hints of the mystical, Elliott's reference in this regard was not of that nature. More important, this reference, along with two associated comments in all of Elliott's writing that derive from religion, is tangential and conceptually irrelevant to the nearly 300 pages that precede and follow it. Mandelbrot concocts his phrasing to imply that central to Elliott's thought was an error of magical thinking, which is false. What's more, to have located this obscure sentence in a 300-page book makes it clear that Mandelbrot painstakingly searched for any tidbit he could find that would serve to belittle his predecessor, even if doing so required both omissive and commissive misrepresentation.

Mandelbrot further implies by his sentence structure that the "studies" he imputes to Elliott preceded, and therefore were the basis for, Elliott's discovery and its announcement. In fact, Elliott explored Fibonacci mathematics in botany two years after he published the fractal illustrations in his first book. The cited brief reference occurred eight years after the publication of his first book. Given the fact that Mandelbrot possesses Elliott's literature and knows its chronology, his false implication is clearly deliberate.

Mandelbrot's putting the word "discovery" in quotes is more condescension. Mandelbrot credits *himself* — again and again and again — with great discoveries, yet he does not put his self-credits in quotes.

Up to this point, Mandelbrot's introduction reads in the same manner as if he were trying to claim that he had recently concocted the theory of evolution while dismissing Darwin as "an indecisive, wandering globetrotter who suffered from chronic nausea and who could barely be bothered to write about his own incompletely formed ideas." There may be some truth to the words, but as a summary, it is a misrepresentation tinged with obfuscation and meanness.

(3) "...a 'Wave Principle' that 'really forecasts.'"

In the *Scientific American* article, Mandelbrot says this about his model:
These techniques...*provide estimates of the probability of what the market might do and allow one to prepare for the inevitable sea changes*.... The actual model *does not simply inspect what the market did yesterday or last week*[, but] charts created from the generators produced by this model can *simulate alternative scenarios based on previous market activity*.

In other words, he claims in no uncertain terms to have discovered a technique that "really forecasts." He makes the same claim as Elliott, yet he mocks Elliott for it.

Mandelbrot cites no fact to justify his mockery of Elliott's claim to having provided a basis for prediction. Is it true or false? If false, why so? Far worse from a scientific standpoint, Mandelbrot does not describe any method for using his own model to achieve his dramatic claims of "providing estimates of the probability of what the market might do" or allowing one to "simulate alternative scenarios based on previous market activity," much less to "prepare for the inevitable sea changes." These bold assertions are highly misleading, as a close read of the article reveals that all Mandelbrot can offer is a catalogue of past market volatility, which any market student may glean by casually perusing a historical chart. What forecasts can Mandelbrot show to justify his claim to his model's predictive ability? *There are none.* Nor will there ever be, given his model's assumption of specific event randomness, not to mention his proposed generator's unnatural 3-wave-3-wave construction. Mandelbrot's model can simulate only "the same patterns of variability" in the sense of volatility, power laws and indefinite fractals, which offer no basis for forecasting specifics. He coyly demurs, "multifractals do not purport to predict the future with certainty," as if they can predict the future at all. In truth, indefinite fractals cannot be employed to predict any specific future event even to a useful probability. The title of his article, "A Multifractal Walk Down Wall Street," is a play on Burton Malkiel's *A Random Walk Down Wall Street,* but for practical forecasting purposes, it may as well be the same title.

James Gleick confirmed in a 1985 article, "Mandelbrot's mimicking of stock market and river charts *does not help in predicting* particular rallies and floods."[29] That is still true, fourteen years later, because Mandelbrot has mimicked only one very rough aspect of stock market and flooding patterns: the extent of their fractal irregularity. He has not even considered, much less discovered as Elliott did, that their behavior might exhibit forms. While Mandelbrot's claims to forecasting and practical utility stand unsubstantiated either by a forecasting model or by any attempt to predict anything, R.N. Elliott and later writers elucidated how to do exactly these things with the Wave Principle.

Mandelbrot's assertions of predictability appear as a desperate bid to claim Elliott's territory yet without the substance necessary actually to capture it. In contrast, Elliott made some of the most remarkable stock market forecasts ever, and they are on the record.[30] The chief difference between the two men with regard to their claims of forecasting value is that Elliott made good on his claim.

(4) "A claim that he was a precursor of the use of fractals in finance prompted me to scan Elliott in 1994."

Let us first note from this sentence that some observant people *do* recognize that Elliott pioneered "the use of fractals in finance." This very recognition must irritate Mandelbrot to the point of prompting the behavior that is the focus of this discussion. The term *precursor* is misleading and condescending. Elliott did not *predate* the use of fractals in finance; he orginated the idea and developed it in detail. What's more, his model actually did effect — extensively, in fact — "the *use* of fractals in finance," which Mandelbrot's has not and cannot.

Additionally, if Mandelbrot did not "scan Elliott" before 1994, I will eat my hat. Because I sent them to Mandelbrot (to no response), he had in his possession *Elliott Wave Principle* (1978) and my essay, "The Fractal Design of Social Progress," (1986)[31] at least as early as 1986. It is difficult to accept ignorance on the subject of the Wave Principle on the part of someone who has been interested in finance and fractals for his professional lifetime. He could even have known about it prior to 1962 when he first investigated the distribution of cotton prices.[32] The well-known editor of *The Bank Credit Analyst*, A. Hamilton Bolton, who served as president of the Financial Analysts Federation, published widely read "Elliott Wave Principle" supplements annually from 1953 to 1966 from his office in Montreal, Quebec and wrote a book on the subject in 1960 entitled *The Elliott Wave Principle — A Critical Appraisal*, which further popularized the Wave Principle on Wall Street. Gleick says that it was in the same year of 1960 when Mandelbrot first had "...a ghost of an idea, a faint, unfocused image..."[33] that started his search for fractals. This chronology might explain why Mandelbrot's studies of nature's fractals began with the financial markets (specifically the cotton market, to which Elliott referred in his 1946 book as following the Wave Principle) rather than coastlines, mountains or clouds. Alternatively, he should at least have heard about it some time after 1978, when *Elliott Wave Principle* was published and waves in the market began making waves in the press, particularly after 1983.

Now consider Mandelbrot's flip declaration that he bothered to *scan* Elliott. His unearthing of the obscure bits of information quoted in citations

(1), (2), (3) and (8) belie this characterization and reveal that in fact he *scoured* Elliott from cover to cover. Mandelbrot seems to want to present a disinterested front, but that is not what we observe. His meticulous hatchet-job and careful claims for credit show that he is on a mission.

> (5) "It is true that some of Elliott's diagrams are qualitatively reminiscent of certain self-affine generators of the kind studied in Section 4 of Chapter E6."

Well, that is a key concession. Even here, though, Elliott's diagrams cannot be *reminiscent* of generators that *postdated* them. "Reminiscent" also carries connotations of only the vaguest recollective similarity. This carefully selected word thus appears designed to steer the reader's mind into thinking that Elliott was an after-the-fact dabbler. Chronologically speaking, it is some of Mandelbrot's illustrations that look like Elliott's, not the other way around, and that is the way it should be stated if proper credit is to be given.

> (6) "That is, they embody the wisdom present in Swift's qualitative metaphor quoted earlier in this section..."

Here Elliott is depicted as embodying *Jonathan Swift's* wisdom, as if the poet's brief line about fleas had scientific weight or even (in the context of the larger poem) addresses self-affinity at all, which it does not.

> (7) "...but *nothing more*."

Elliott discovered so much more than Mandelbrot (forget Swift) about financial market behavior that the gulf is unbridgeable. If there is any difference between Elliott's and Mandelbrot's formulations of their models, it is the relative richness of the former and the thinness of the latter. Elliott's body of work shows that there is much more to the stock market than general fractality. It details the formal characteristics of the actual financial market fractal, while Mandelbrot's only new offering in the area of modeling is an artificial construct. His main thesis in the article, that financial markets may be modeled as any number of mechanical fractals and multifractals, manipulated along one axis or the other — not by nature but by the modeler — is arbitrary, primitive and random compared to Elliott's robust[34] fractal model, which he uncovered in his meticulous cataloguing of the intricate details of pattern formation.

Elliott spent the better part of a decade studying actual market price movements before coming to a conclusion regarding the essential patterns that repeat at higher scales. He observed that in the real world, rising trends typically subdivide into five waves and falling trends into three. His detailed model is thus consonant with the real world, while Mandelbrot's fractal generator is truly, to use his words, a "rootless abstraction." Mandelbrot proposes no specific pattern while nevertheless being forced to invent one for his depiction. He just draws three lines (he calls them "pieces") in each direction to simulate market fractality. Mandelbrot reveals the arbitrary nature of his model when asking us to "imagine a die on which each side bears the image of one of the six permutations of the pieces of the generator. Before each interpolation, the die is thrown, and then the permutation that comes up is selected." (Then the one chosen is available for infinite manipulation!) The 65-year history[35] of uniquely successful Elliott wave forecasting would not exist if the market fluctuated according to random die-throwing instead of the Wave Principle.

Mandelbrot's multifractal model is, as he says, better than Modern Portfolio Theory, which isn't saying much. The only way that the multifractal model improves on MPT is to add a warning that large or swift moves can occur at any time at any scale, a fact that portfolio managers may just as easily glean from a brief review of market history. Elliott's robust fractal model takes these simple implications of the multifractal model into account. In fact, it does so far better since it elucidates when to expect changes in the slope and rate of ascent or descent in the market and at what degrees to expect them. The market is in fact *not* a multi fractal but a robust one, so while the multifractal model may simulate market *volatility*, it does not simulate the market. Mandelbrot concedes as much when he refers to the actual market as obeying "unknown rules." Whether the Wave Principle correctly reveals those rules is open to debate, but that does not change the fact that Mandelbrot has said nothing novel, and, if the Wave Principle is true, he has modeled the market at a level way beneath Elliott's.

Elliott's fractal generator is also more coherent that Mandelbrot's. Two aspects of human social endeavor are *fluctuation* and *net progress*. Elliott's model accomodates both aspects in a natural way. To achieve fluctuation, a wave model must have at least three waves in each direction, which Mandelbrot recognizes. To achieve net progress, however, it must have, absent additional assumptions, at least two more waves in one direction than the other. Elliott's depiction, then, provides both fluctuation and progress in the simplest possible model, which reflects nature's efficiency in achieving goals. In contrast, Mandelbrot's assignation of three "pieces" in each direction is arbitrary because it omits net progress from its essence. His model entreats one to ask, "Why should the rising lines be longer than the falling ones?" With no theoretical justification for an upward bias, the same number of waves up and down *should* imply a cycle producing no net progress. The only way that Mandelbrot can depict net progress is to lengthen the waves in one of the two directions, which he does without explanation. Mandelbrot does not claim to have done so because the market in *reality* does so, because he disclaims that the market actually follows his fractal generator depiction. Therefore the lengthening of waves in one direction is an *ad hoc* concession to the truth that the stock market — like mankind — makes progress over time. Elliott's alternating 5-3 concept, in immense contrast, is *logical* in terms of more naturally implying progress and *objective* in having been developed from real-world observation.

Mandelbrot has made historic contributions to science: He elucidated fractal dimension, developed the mathematics of measuring roughness, recognized the wealth of variety that fractal rules can produce and discovered that fractals permeate the world. These are seminal achievements. Unfortunately, they are of no use in creating an accurate, practical, predictive model of financial market behavior, so his claim to this territory fails. Elliott's claim, backed by empirics and 65 years of application, is a demonstrable success.

Mandelbrot's belittling of Elliott's hypothesis cannot be born of ignorance, as he possesses the literature. A scientist of financial fractals may attempt to dispute Elliott's work in cataloguing the forms that appear in the real world, but he may not dismiss it or ignore it. If he disagrees with either Elliott's detailed observations or his wider conclusions, he should say so and explain why, not simply mock them as a phony "discovery." I cannot help but wonder if he is *wishing* them away because (at least in my opinion) they are so profound and, if proven true, will dwarf even the great Mandelbrot's contribution to our knowledge of finance.

> (8) "Elliott's work fails the requirements of objectivity and repeatability: in his own words, 'considerable experience is required to interpret [it] correctly' and 'no interpretation [is] valid unless made by [him or his direct licencees].'"

Elliott wrote this "warning" on the title page of his first book so that readers would guard against inept forecasting from opportunists who might wish to make a fast buck without studying the subject. It was simply a business decision meant to establish his planned stock market publication as the authoritative one on the Wave Principle. He never claimed that knowledge of the Wave Principle was proprietary to any one person's brain. In fact, he explained his work repeatedly in two books in 1938 and 1946, a series of 12 articles for *Financial World* magazine in 1939 and even via a course on the subject taught in New York City, information that is covered in the biography published in the very book that Mandelbrot used as his source. These facts, along with the entire remainder of Elliott's writing, contradict Mandelbrot's depiction via this out-of-context quotation. We might ask whether Mandelbrot's own (unsubstantiated) claim to useful probabilistic forecasting can be exploited by someone who lacks "considerable experience" with fractals. If not, will he write that he has proved his own model's non-objectivity and non-repeatability? Of course not; it would be irrelevant.

A man with Mandelbrot's obvious intelligence knows that culling one line from Elliott's books and articles to assert the grand damnation of non-objectivity and non-repeatability shows nothing of the sort. Quoting these few words out of context is a smokescreen that skirts the question. *If Mandelbrot can show that Elliott's work fails the requirements of objectivity and repeatability, then he should do it. Otherwise, he has no business stating it as if it were a fact.* The expression of the Wave Principle is objective, as there are books that spell out the ideas. I, for one, reject subjectivity as having any place in the field. Whether the Wave Principle is true is another question, but Mandelbrot's lifetime work supports the case that it is. Mandelbrot's dismissal is, simply stated, a blanket assertion that is utterly unscientific in failing to address the point at hand and dishonest in pretending that it does.

Elliott on His Discovery

In citation (5), Mandelbrot concedes only that R.N. Elliott's *diagrams* are "reminiscent" [sic] of self-affine generators. He avoids saying that Elliott's *words* on the subject of self-affinity in social processes, which are in the book he quotes, also predate all modern commentary on the subject. Here is some of Elliott's commentary introducing what at the time was a revolutionary concept, derived completely independently of others' influences:

Extensive research in connection with what may be termed human activities indicates that practically all developments which result from our social-economic processes follow a law that causes them to repeat themselves in similar and constantly recurring serials of waves or impulses of definite number and pattern. It is likewise indicated that in their intensity, these waves or impulses bear a consistent relation to one another and to the passage of time.

The expression "human activities" includes such items as stock prices, bond prices, patent (application)s, [the] price of gold, population, movements of citizens from cities to farms and vice versa, commodities prices, government expenditures, production, life insurance [purchases], electric power produced, gasoline consumption, fire losses, price of seats on the stock exchange, epidemics, real estate, business, politics [and] the pursuit of pleasure.[36] It is particularly evident in those free markets where public participation in price movements is extensive.

Those who have attempted to deal with the market's movements have failed to recognize the extent to which the market is a psychological phenomenon. They have not grasped the fact that there is regularity underlying the fluctuations of the market, or, stated otherwise, that price movements in stocks are subject to rhythms, or an ordered sequence. The wild, senseless and apparently uncontrollable changes in prices from year to year, from month to month, or from day to day, link themselves into a law-abiding rhythmic pattern of waves. The same rules apply to the price of stocks, bonds, grains, cotton, coffee and all the other activities previously mentioned.

The student should recognize that there are cycles within cycles. Major waves subdivide into intermediate waves[, which] subdivide into minor waves. One cycle becomes but the starting point of another, or larger, movement that itself is a part of, and subject to the same law as, the lesser movement. This fundamental law cannot be subverted or set aside by statutes or restrictions. Current news and political developments are of only incidental importance, soon forgotten; their presumed influence on market trends is not as weighty as is commonly believed. Underlying this progression, in whatever field, is a fixed and controlling principle, or the master rule under which nature works. This treatise has made use of price movements in stocks to illustrate the phenomenon, but all the principles laid down herein are equally applicable to the wave movement in every field where human endeavor is registered.[37]

—R.N. Elliott, 1938, 1939, 1940, 1946

Clearly, Elliott was fully conscious of the facts, to use Mandelbrot's own words (cited at the outset of this paper) that he had created "a new modeling technique" that "cast a light of order" on market behavior from his own original "work in fractal geometry." Not only did Elliott draw fractal diagrams but he also understood their meaning and implication. That the markets' fractal is robust rather than self-identical or indefinite, along with Elliott's recognition that Fibonacci mathematics govern its behavior, ultimately establishes an intimate kinship between mankind's pattern of progress and countless other growth forms in nature. These observations predate the same implications of Mandelbrot's discovery of the ubiquity of fractals. In fact, it was decades later before words such as those quoted above emerged as a result of studies in fractal geometry. I believe that, especially along with his diagrams, they are more than sufficient to credit Elliott with having introduced the idea that fractal self-affinity governs social processes and is fundamental to nature. Indeed, with his dedicated empiricism, mathematical insights, encompassing hypothesis and universal perspective, I think that Elliott, though a business professional unaccustomed to scientific protocol, was worthy of the title "scientist."

A Bifurcation in the Road

Whenever Mandelbrot knew about Elliott's work, he must have decided to ignore it in hopes that it would go away. It didn't. It seems that by the late 1990s, he could no longer resist or postpone staking his claim to Elliott's territory. Given Mandelbrot's obsession for taking credit, he would have no choice but to avoid depicting a financial market's fractal generator as five waves and three waves because his place in history would then be reduced to confirming and furthering work originated by R.N. Elliott. He came as close as he dared, depicting his financial market fractal "generator" in the same way as Elliott did but with three waves in each direction. In his 2002 book, he asserts that his "newly coined" term, "tile self affinities," provides pictures "of almost every basic fractal or multifractal," presumably thereby including Elliott's Wave Principle.

At least we know, given Mandelbrot's 1997 comments cited above, that he knew of Elliott's work before penning his *Scientific American* article. At an inadequate bare minimum, he should have cited Elliott among his sources, because that's where he got the idea for the illustrations of his fractal generator. But to do so would have been to admit that Elliott invented the idea. He was between a rock and a hard place. In my opinion, morally speaking, which means practically speaking as well, he chose the wrong way out.

Anyone who wishes to make up his own mind on this subject, as well as on the credit Elliott deserves, need only read one of these three volumes:

(1) *R.N. Elliott's Masterworks* (1980/1993), which includes all of Elliott's original books, articles and major essays, as well as a biography.

(2) *Elliott Wave Principle — Key to Market Behavior* (1978/1998) by Frost and Prechter, a concise presentation of Elliott's work.

(3) *The Wave Principle of Human Social Behavior and the New Science of Socionomics* (1999) by Prechter.

These books are published by New Classics Library, which has also published the historical works of every other major practitioner of the Wave Principle. For a list, visit www.elliottwave.com/books or use the following contact information: Address: P.O. Box 1618, Gainesville, GA 30503; phone: 770-536-0309; fax: 770-536-2514; e-mail: customerservice@elliottwave.com.

Postscript

Mandelbrot may also have incorporated and claimed some original ideas and expressions of other Elliott wave practitioners. The preceding pages discuss, for example, the wording of Mandelbrot's claims to his model's forecasting value that mirror expressions appearing in *Elliott Wave Principle*. Perhaps the following quotations will serve further to demonstrate that Mandelbrot has read and absorbed the expressions in that volume. Compare this quote:

> Can we both theorize and observe that the stock market operates on the same mathematical basis as so many natural phenomena? The answer is yes.... *In its broadest sense, the Wave Principle suggests the idea that the same law that shapes living creatures and galaxies is inherent in the spirit and activities of men en masse.*[38]
> —Frost and Prechter, *Elliott Wave Principle,* 1978

with this one, which opens Mandelbrot's article:

> *The geometry that describes the shape of coastlines and the patterns of galaxies also elucidates how stock prices soar and plummet.*[39]

This idea is repeated in the article, as follows:

> *Fractal patterns appear not just in the price changes of securities but in the distribution of galaxies throughout the cosmos* [and] *in the shape of coastlines....*[40]
> —Mandelbrot, "A Multifractal Walk Down Wall Street," 1999

While I am prone to quip that all these lines could be part of the same fractal object, I will leave it to you to judge their similarity.

Cynics have often objected to comments such as the one quoted above from *Elliott Wave Principle* on the grounds that its implications are too grand. As you can see, one of the most renowned scientists in the world is now saying essentially the same thing.

A Market Forecast?

Mandelbrot's article ends with this line: "The new modeling techniques...also recognize the mariner's warning that, as recent events demonstrate, deserves to be heeded: *On even the calmest sea, a gale may be just over the horizon.*" One might take this as simply a general comment about the suddenness of major movements within the financial fractal except that its imagery is specific to market panics. Thus, in conjunction with the magazine's table of contents introduction saying, "When will the Dow top 10,000? When will it crash?", it stands as a sentence that Mandelbrot would probably love to have quoted when the stock market does crash. It would seem so *prescient*. Yet Mandelbrot's method provides no basis for anticipating any such thing. Any implication that it does is false. Only the Wave Principle — or perhaps some other specific market model — can do that. If his closing line is to be accepted as a knowing hint of coming events, as an indication that Mandelbrot was *bearish on the stock market*, then we would have to ask him on what basis he held such an opinion. One hopes that he did not simply purloin Elliott wave analysts' long term stock market outlook, which has received worldwide publicity through countless books and articles.

NOTES

[1] This chapter is an expanded version of the original exposition.

[2] Mandelbrot, Benoit. (1999, February). "A multifractal walk down wall street." *Scientific American*, p.70.

[3] Elliott, Ralph Nelson. (1938). *The wave principle*. Republished: Prechter, Robert (Ed.).(1980/1994). *R.N. Elliott's masterworks — The definitive collection*. Gainesville, GA: New Classics Library.

[4] Mandelbrot projected Figure 4 from a slide during his lecture at Emory University on May 11, 2002.

[5] Mandelbrot, Benoit. (1982). *The fractal geometry of nature*. W.H. Freeman & Co. Also (1997). *Fractals and scaling in finance: Discontinuity, concentration, risk*. Springer-Verlag; And (1997). "The multifractal model of asset returns," discussion papers of the Cowles Foundation for Economics, #1164-1166, Yale University; And (1999). *Multifractals and 1/f noise: Wild self-affinity in physics*. Springer-Verlag.

[6] See endnote 2.

[7] See endnote 3.

[8] Frost, Alfred John, and Prechter, Robert R. (1978). *Elliott wave principle — Key to market behavior*. Gainesville, GA: New Classics Library, p.184.

[9] Mandelbrot, Benoit. (1997). *Fractals and scaling in finance — Discontinuity, concentration, risk*. Springer-Verlag.

[10] Prechter, Jr., Robert Rougelot (ed.) (1980/1994). *R.N. Elliott's masterworks — The definitive collection*. Gainesville, GA: New Classics Library.

[11] See endnote 9.

[12] See endnote 2.

[13] They are R.N. Elliott, Charles J. Collins, A. Hamilton Bolton, A. John Frost, Richard Russell and Robert R. Prechter, Jr.

[14] Sornette, D., Johansen, A., and Bouchaud, J.P. (1996). "Stock market crashes, precursors and replicas." *Journal de Physique I France* 6, No.1, pp. 167-175.

[15] The ellipses in this quotation replace the unfortunate phrase, "...so strongly rooted in the financial analysts' folklore...." Sornette, *et al.* may perhaps be excused for having referred to the Wave Principle in this fashion even though the "folklore" terminology is false because at least they conscientiously credited a *proper source* from which interested parties may glean the truth. Further, Sornette today more accurately refers to the Wave Principle as "a market model hypothesis." No person fully informed of Elliott's orginal work, as Mandelbrot is, may be excused from using the term "folklore."

[16] See endnote 2.

[17] See endnote 3, p. 87.

[18] See endnote 2.

[19] See endnote 8, p. 87.

[20] (1993) Personal letter to R. Prechter from J. Barnes, Wetumpka, Alabama.

[21] Gleick, James. (1987). *Chaos: Making a new science.* New York: Penguin Books, pp. 111-112.

[22] *Ibid.*, p. 111.

[23] This is not the first time a famous researcher has claimed Elliott's work for his own. Edson Gould, writing under the pseudonym Edson Beers, presented a pack of Elliott's original ideas in a *Barron's* article on May 19, 1941, eight months after Elliott published them. Gould, an inventive and rising star in the market forecasting field, apparently recognized the seminal importance of Elliott's work and wished himself into the originator's chair. (Does that sound familiar?) In that instance, Elliott was alive, so he could lodge his own well justified protest. For more on the story, see "A Biography of R.N. Elliott" in *R.N. Elliott's Masterworks.* (1980/1994). Prechter, Jr., Robert Rougelot. (Ed.). Gainesville, GA: New Classics Library.

[24] Edgar, G.A. (ed.) (1993). *Classics on fractals.* Reading, MA: Addison-Wesley.

[25] Prechter, Robert. R. (1999). *The wave principle of human social behavior.* Gainesville, GA: New Classics Library.

[26] See endnote 9.

[27] With multi-million dollar corporations and universities to support him, Mandelbrot, to be sure, has not had to stoop to commerce to make a living. His sniffy attitude on this topic reveals an intense annoyance — fueling what appears to be denial — that someone outside of the scientific world, someone who had to work for a living in the commercial world — originated the idea of fractals in finance and made many of the biggest discoveries in the field. Being miffed is hardly sufficient justification for this ungracious response.

[28] Elliott, R.N. (1946). *Nature's law.* Republished: (1980/1994). *R.N. Elliott's masterworks — The definitive collection.* Prechter, Jr., Robert Rougelot. (Ed.). Gainesville, GA: New Classics Library.

[29] Gleick, J. (1985, December 8)."The man who reshaped geometry." *The New York Times.*

[30] For a good summary, see Chapter 5 of *The Wave Principle of Human Social Behavior.* For Elliott's full record, see *R.N. Elliott's Masterworks* (1980/1994) and *R.N. Elliott's Market Letters* (1993) New Classics Library.

[31] Reprinted in this book on page 269.

[32] Mandelbrot, Benoit. (1962). Sur certains prix spéculatifs: faits empiriques et modèle basé sur les processus stables additifs de Paul Lévy. *Comptes Rendus* (Paris): 254, 3968-3970. And (1963). The variation of certain speculative prices. *Journal of Business*: 36, 394-419. Reprinted in Cootner 1964: 297-337. University of Chicago Press.

[33] See endnote 21, p. 83.

[34] Chapter 3 of *The Wave Principle of Human Social Behavior* explains this term.

[35] Dating from Elliott's first letter to Collins in 1934, in which he made a brief, general market forecast.

[36] Elliott showed graphs of these activities in *The Wave Principle* (1938).

[37] These sentences are collected from pp. 92, 147, 157, 183, 192, 217, 218, 228, 229 of *R.N. Elliott's Masterworks* (1980/1994), which includes *The Wave Principle* (1938), The *Financial World* articles (1939), "The basis of the wave principle" (1940) and *Nature's law* (1946). I have omitted ellipses and one-letter brackets for reading clarity.

[38] See endnote 8. p.114, 121.

[39] See endnote 2.

[40] *Ibid.* p.71.

Reply and Response

Mandelbrot's Reply...

In the June 1999 issue of *Scientific American*, Mandelbrot replied to the storm of response to his article (see next section) as follows:

> At some point Ralph Elliott's "principle" and my cartoon simulations both use recursive interpolation in which each part is a reduced-scale version of the whole. The idea is ancient, but his use and mine stand in absolute contrast. Elliott drew a certain nonrandom "wave" that he claimed "really forecasts" every real-world market; however, this simplistic wave was first stretched, squeezed or otherwise adjusted by hand. In contrast, fractal or multifractal models must follow firm mathematical rules that allow quantitative developments throughout, as mine do. In any event, the random or nonrandom cartoons themselves are of no interest; they serve only to introduce the subtle quantitative properties and tools of my model of price variation — fractional Brownian motion in multifractal time. The rules of this model are not recursive but fully specified mathematically and can be adjusted to fit the historical financial data.[1]

...and Prechter's Response

Prechter posted the following response on the Elliott Wave International website:[2]

> "At some point Ralph Elliott's "principle" and my cartoon simulations both use recursive interpolation in which each part is a reduced-scale version of the whole."

That's our point. It is more accurate to say, though, that Elliott did not *use* recursive interpolation but rather *reported* it in the actual stock market. Mandelbrot condescendingly uses quotes and lower case for "principle," but the model has a *name*, which he knows full well, and the idea is grand enough fully to deserve it.

"The idea is ancient..."

Please. The idea of recursive interpolation (for art and so forth) may be ancient, but the use of it to describe and model the stock market is not. It originated with Elliott.

"...but his use and mine stand in absolute contrast."

That they do.

"Elliott drew a certain nonrandom 'wave' that he claimed 'really forecasts' every real-world market..."

The Wave Principle is indeed substantially non-random. Its specificity is what makes it useful. In probabilistic terms, and with varying degrees of success, it can indeed be employed to forecast most real-world markets.

"...however, this simplistic wave was first stretched, squeezed or otherwise adjusted..."

In this comment we find both error and irony. Elliott did not model the market as a certain simple picture and then stretch, squeeze or adjust it. He was describing reality, and reality itself is diverse. This accusation is akin to saying that someone who sketched pictures of a dozen types of trees and then proposed a composite model to depict tree-ness "started with a simplistic tree model and then stretched, squeezed and otherwise adjusted it." It's backwards.

There is irony in Mandelbrot's depiction because in fact it describes precisely what he himself is doing in creating his "multifractal model." He begins with a simple fractal generator and then *adjusts* it by *stretching* it on the vertical axis and *squeezing* it on the horizontal axis, all quite on an ad hoc basis, as you can clearly see in Figure 1, taken directly from his article.

"...by hand."

Was Elliott supposed to have used a computer? In 1934?

"In contrast, fractal or multifractal models must follow firm mathematical rules that allow quantitative developments throughout, as mine do."

Stretching, Squeezing and Adjusting

(Mandelbrot's fractal model, as shown with attending
commentary in *Scientific American*, February 1999)

MOVING A PIECE of the fractal generator to the left ...

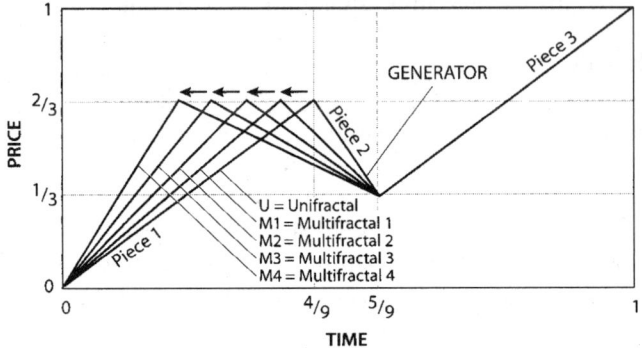

... causes the same amount of market activity in a shorter time interval for the first piece of the generator and the same amount in a
longer interval for the second piece ...

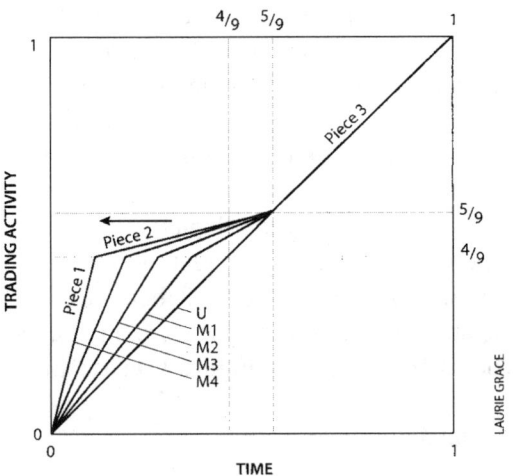

... Movement of the generator to the left causes market
activity to become increasingly volatile.

Figure 1

Must they? It is important to distinguish between a model that we can manipulate precisely and a model of reality. The ability to model with precision requires mathematical rigidity, but a model of reality requires a commitment to truth, which may preclude mathematical rigidity, at least in the model's formative stages when knowledge is limited. This result seems particularly applicable to living systems and even more especially to human behavior. A model with firm mathematical rules that purported to predict your friend Charlie would be absurd, and one that allowed for Charlie to do *anything* would be useless, yet we get both of these things from Mandelbrot's model with respect to financial markets. One could certainly build a useful model of Charlie's past and potential behavior, but it would have neither that basis nor that outcome. Consider the question of whether trees follow "firm mathematical rules." Perhaps they do, but no currently known model using such rules would be useful for forecasting the final outcome of any particular tree. On the other hand, a robust model based on detailed empirics — using mathematical rigidities and probability statements — might help you anticipate much of it. Elliott's model is of this type.

The above discussion is in no way a concession to Mandelbrot's claim that only his model can be described mathematically. Elliott's model *can* be quantified with firm mathematical rules. That is why we were able to create our EWAVES computer program[3] to label data series according to Elliott's rules and guidelines. I have no illusions, though, that the resulting program has captured every possible nuance of market behavior, perfectly assigned its ranges of probability, eliminated all impossible patterns or completely encapsulated the robust Wave Principle model, about which there is surely more to learn.

Neither is this discussion a concession to Mandelbrot's claim to having modeled the stock market in the first place. Although he claims that his model "follow(s) firm mathematical rules," it doesn't follow any *useful* rules of form but rather allows for infinite manipulation. Can you imagine the dismissive response to R.N. Elliott had he claimed that markets can do anything at all as long as they fluctuate up and down? What kind of model is that, and of what practical value are such "firm mathematical rules"? Do you want a model that admits random "quantitative developments throughout" *if that's not what happens in reality?* Random walk theorists can describe their model with mathematical precision, too, but it is not therefore relevant to the stock market. Elliott's model and Mandelbrot's model both allow for an infinite variety of quantitative developments, except that Elliott's model *limits aspects of the variety that may occur*, making it useful in real-world forecasting. Mandelbrot's model eliminates no potential market event (except that prices cannot move backwards in time!). The incorporation of infinite possibilities for price behavior in Mandelbrot's purported model in fact makes it no different from a random walk and thus, for practical purposes, *no model at all.*

> "In any event, the random or nonrandom cartoons themselves are of no interest..."

In his 1997 book, Mandelbrot presents drawings like those in Figures 2 and 4 in the preceding chapter, as well as a few others, that utilize a specific pattern (such as 3-up, 3-down, using certain lengths) in order to display the idea of multifractal self-affinity. He calls these illustrations "cartoons," an apt word in this case, perhaps, because with respect to the actual patterns of financial market behavior that Elliott elucidated, they represent either arbitrary constructs or potentialities, not actualities. As we can see by Mandelbrot's inclusionary use of the term above, he means to include Elliott's drawings among such "cartoons," which may be why he chose such a diminutive word. Elliott's illustrations, however, are no more cartoons than a detailed painting by a realist. Elliott drew aspects of reality, not abstract constructs. For this reason, Elliott's *nonrandom* cartoons are of interest to thousands of people. Indeed, they are fascinating both in their reliable reflection of reality[4] and in their theoretical implications. Mandelbrot's *random* cartoons are of far less interest. (Having seen Paree, I would extend that judgment to his entire model.)

If Elliott's depictions are of no interest to Mandelbrot, that's fine. He has placed this fact on the record to his great detriment if and when the Wave Principle model is vindicated. Yet shouldn't Mandelbrot be thrilled to discover that someone who set out to depict actual stock market behavior recorded a structure that his model accommodates? Apparently, the problem with his recognizing this feat is that Elliott did it decades ago. Had someone come up with this depiction ten years into the future, Mandelbrot could claim that his model, however vaguely, anticipated it. Given the true chronology, admitting Elliott's Wave Principle into the academic discussion places Mandelbrot in the position of being a latecomer who is either giving Elliott's model some added justification or proposing a broader derivative umbrella under which to consider market fractality, which may have theoretical value (though still no practical value) only if Elliott's model is disproved. That must be why to him, the Wave Principle is "of no interest."

If Mandelbrot were to undertake a theoretical modeling of the auto-mobile, he could perhaps take credit for having invented "carness." The mere fact that people have already *built* cars should have no bearing on his claim. He could dismiss them as "non-random cartoons of no interest."

We should further note that Mandelbrot never created any cartoons — or used that term — until *after* he saw R.N. Elliott's illustrations depicting the Wave Principle. Mandelbrot's cartoons and his related commentary may have some value apart from the Wave Principle, but their timing and presentation appear designed at least partly with the hope of enveloping Elliott's model within the scope of his work while simultaneously relegat-ing it to near insignificance. When Elliott's specific observations become accepted in the scientific community, this strategy, if that's what it is, will be revealed as inadequate to the task and turn the tables on the implied relative significance between the contributions to financial market model-ing.

> "...they serve only to introduce the subtle quantitative properties and tools of my model of price variation — fractional Brownian motion in multifractal time."

That's what *Mandelbrot's* cartoons do. Elliott's model does not depict *Brownian* motion; it depicts *stock market* motion. They are very different categories.

> "The rules of this model are not recursive..."

Mandelbrot's model may not be recursive, but his fractal generator is; that's what Figures 2 and 4 imply, and that's what he himself says: "...my cartoon simulations...use recursive interpolation...." If there is no recur-sion, then what is the point of the illustrations other than to muscle in on Elliott's territory? Elliott's model is not *rigidly* recursive; there is great variety within the Wave Principle. Finally, the stock market *is* robustly recursive, so a model that is *not* — like Mandelbrot's — does not capture the essence of the stock market.

> "...but fully specified mathematically and can be adjusted to fit the historical financial data."

To repeat, of what value is a model that is "fully specified mathemati-cally" but whose result is no different from saying, "The stock market can do anything"? Elliott's model describes what aspects of stock market movement are certain *and which are not*, and therein lies much of its value.

Mandelbrot says proudly that his model *"can be adjusted* to fit the historical data." Did we not just read a few sentences ago that Elliott's model is a joke because it was *"adjusted"* to fit actual market behavior, i.e., historical data? Aside from noting the hypocrisy, observe this crucial difference: Elliott *derived* his model from "historical financial data." People applying it do not have to *adjust* it to fit new data. Indeed, his model is adequate for anticipating *future* financial data.

Regardless of one's opinion on these matters, *Mandelbrot's claim to full mathematical specification is utterly inadequate to the goal of discrediting or dismissing Elliott's discovery*. That there is a difference between their models does not reduce Elliott's achievement, much less obliterate him from the scene. So what if Elliott did not work out all the mathematics of his model? Darwin did not work out any of the mathematics of evolution. At least Elliott worked out an important portion of the math, for example the crucial governance by Fibonacci, which Mandelbrot has yet to discover or acknowledge. Because Darwin's model of evolution — a fractal process after all — did not include "firm mathematical rules," was it therefore unimportant or not a model? No. His model made a quantum leap in our understanding of reality. Does a successor to Darwin get credit for *originating the idea of evolution* because he figured out some of the math involved? No. The credit goes to the person who had the groundbreaking insight that all others had missed. With respect to social behavior, that man is R.N. Elliott, who uncovered the fundamental truth that group behavior creates a fractal dynamic of waves. Does a successor to Darwin get credit for modeling evolution because he invented a mathematical construct that can't predict a single evolutionary trend? No. The credit goes to the person whose model can anticipate events in reality. It was R.N. Elliott who described the Wave Principle and formulated rules and guidelines for anticipating coming trends. Both of these achievements are on the record for all to see. Readers of *Scientific American* were right to recoil at Mandelbrot's glaring omission, and I am right to challenge his derogation of Elliott's achievement.

NOTES

[1] Mandelbrot, Benoit. (1999, June). Letters to the Editor. *Scientific American*, p.6.

[2] The original text has been lost, so I have re-created it to the best of my recollection. I would appreciate hearing from anyone who downloaded the original comments.

[3] See Chapter 4 of *The Wave Principle of Human Social Behavior*.

[4] This email from a professional portfolio manager, who began following the market closely in 2002 after learning the Wave Principle, arrived yesterday: "I'm a born again waver!!!! Seriously, this is the most amazing tool I've ever seen. I sit on the board of the James Madison College at Michigan State University, a liberal arts school that encourages students to read all the great works of western thought. I'd like to get some of the professors acclimated to the Wave Principle." I get messages like this all the time because the Wave Principle does model reality, and it does it well.

The June 1999 issue of Scientific American *begins, "Benoit B. Mandelbrot's article 'A Multifractal Walk Down Wall Street' in the February issue elicited myriad responses from readers." Among those addressing the Elliott question, only Prechter's letter was published. Fortunately, a few of the many letters not published in the magazine were cc'd to our web site's Bulletin Board, so we can reproduce them here.*

Letters to the Editor of Scientific American

Today, I read Benoit Mandelbrot's article, "A Multifractal Walk Down Wall Street." In it, he does a good job of arguing against the prevailing assumptions at the heart of Modern Portfolio Theory. (Those assumptions remain dear to the heart of academic economists even though the person on the trading floor knows them to be false.) He also furthers the understanding of stock prices as fractals with his method for modeling them. Unfortunately, the model bears a large number of similarities to work that precedes his by years, even decades. Mandelbrot's model borrows heavily from R.N. Elliott's work during the 1930s. This work has since been refined by Robert Prechter and A.J. Frost. The similarity becomes very striking when comparing Mandelbrot's article side-by-side with previously published work. For example, Mandelbrot's Figure 1 is little more than a simplified version of Figures 1-2 to 1-4 in Frost and Prechter's *Elliott Wave Principle*, published in 1978. That's twenty-one years ago! In 1978, Frost and Prechter did not yet refer to market prices or the wave model that describes them as fractals. The term fractal was still new, and fractal methods and concepts were still too arcane. However, now writers, investors and analysts such as Prechter, Bill Williams and others have understood, discussed and published on the fractal nature of the market and waves for over a decade. Yet nothing is mentioned in Mandelbrot's article, and ALL items in the further reading refer to his work and his work ALONE. I never anticipated referring to a genius of Mandelbrot's caliber as unprofessional, but I find the need now. Had a graduate student of mine written a paper that only referred to his own work, he would quickly find himself sent to do more research in the library! I look forward to Mandelbrot's future work, which should add greater mathematical rigor to our understanding of the fractal nature of market prices and the tendency of markets to trend with waves of various duration. It will help advance the field. But it will advance a field that already exists, whether he acknowledges it or not. I know that I can respect the integrity of *Scientific American*. I look forward to an editorial comment in a future issue correcting the false impressions left by an otherwise useful article.

— James J. Donovan, PhD
February 15, 1999

This message is about the article "A Multifractal Walk Down Wall Street" by Benoit B. Mandelbrot in the February 1999 issue of *Scientific American*. I am sending this message for two reasons: (1) To say well done for putting the above article on your cover and (2) To protest that Mandelbrot did not give credit to R.N. Elliott as the first person who modeled financial markets using multifractals. It is appropriate that in these times of a high profile to the stock market that a scientific point of view is published. Mandelbrot is right in saying that the current models do not perform well and that better models are required. His fairly simple model of markets using fractals quickly shows how fractals model the market much more closely than modern portfolio theory. His article and reputation bring much needed credibility to this fascinating area of investigation. However, while Mandelbrot is providing this benefit to financial modeling, he is subtracting from his own integrity. Mandelbrot states on the second page of his article the following: "I claim that variations in financial prices can be accounted for by a model derived from my work in fractal geometry." Notice how Mandelbrot states, "my work in fractal geometry." The reader can imply that Mandelbrot is the first to use fractals to model financial prices. It is true that the model Mandelbrot uses can model the variations in financial prices, but it is NOT true that Mandelbrot was the first to do so.

Mandelbrot should have been scientifically honest enough to cite R.N. Elliott as being the first person to publish a fractal approach to analyzing financial markets — way back in the 1930s. The word "fractal" was not coined at that time, but it is clearly the contribution that Elliott made. Even the diagrams that Mandelbrot shows in illustration 1 in the article are strikingly similar to many diagrams published in Elliott's writings. Examples of Elliott's diagrams are Figures 3 and 4 in *The Wave Principle* (1938) and Figures 5 to 13 in *Nature's Law* (1946). Elliott's publications are still available in *R.N. Elliott's Masterworks*, published by New Classics Library, which contains these and other Elliott publications. Mandelbrot has published a book that criticizes Elliott, so we know Mandelbrot is aware of Elliott's work. The book is *Fractals and Scaling in Finance: Discontinuity, Concentration, Risk* — listed under "Further Reading" in the article — so Mandelbrot cannot excuse himself out of ignorance. Mr. Mandelbrot is deservedly famous for his work on fractals and chaos but is less than professional in his attitude to Elliott's contribution.

Scientific American has a valuable opportunity to further its contribution to science by pursuing this debate further. Scientific debate is always healthy, especially when it affects something at the foundations of our way of life — money. Your magazine could publish an article about R.N. Elliott to present a balanced view. Mr. Robert Prechter Jr. who heads Elliott Wave International in Gainesville, Georgia is appropriately knowledgeable about Elliott to provide such an article.

— Eugene Morrow, Sydney, Australia
April 4, 1999

Down Wall Street again!

An investor's principal question is: "How can I make money tomorrow?" In "A Multifractal Walk Down Wall Street," Benoit Mandelbrot has woven a chaotic pattern of claims and self-defeating counterclaims. There is an incorrect implication that, by employing the principles of fractal geometry, the investor's question has been answered. In the process he has borrowed generously without citations and incurred the ire of many proponents of Elliott's Wave Principle. Perhaps the same is true of supporters of Burton Malkiel, one of his colleagues at my old Alma Mater, who authored *A Random Walk Down Wall Street*. One is hard-pressed to succinctly unscramble such a tangle of short threads.

Mandelbrot labors to force his multifractals to resemble a specific period of price history. With that as his only guiding rule, unfortunately, any other technique, including a kid drawing freehand with a crayon, should accomplish the same minimum noise result. Logically, he first reasons that stock price fluctuations are governed by rules which he does not know. He demonstrates that he can replicate a period of reality from a stock chart using a sequence of 3 vectors divided into multiply nested 3-vector offspring. But then he incorrectly assumes that the rules of reality automatically apply equally to both representations and that through some magic of fractal geometry, his model somehow contains new and valuable information not contained in the original price chart.

By his own admission, his simulation has essentially no predictive power. In a two-part article entitled "Pseudo Securities for Technical Analysts," which will soon be published in *Technical Analysis of Stocks and Commodities* (www.traders.com), I graphically illustrate a basic problem in modeling to which Mandelbrot's replicas are subject. In essence, one may make numerous radically different mathematical models that over a limited time span appear to accurately mimic reality. However, such models for the investor are valid only if, when allowed to run in time beyond the limits of the analysis span, they continue to accurately mimic both previous history and, more important, the future. The rules of cause and effect still appear to be ignored at one's peril.

His stress test is to compare his "model" to the original data source he copied. There's little surprise that he might subtract the two and get the small difference noise signals in his illustrations, regardless of the degree of volatility involved. It is unclear how a portfolio manager might profitably stress test a portfolio (or a security) by comparing it to a purposely inaccurate approximation of itself over the time span selected.

Finally, Mandelbrot suggests that with further work, his invention may become a useful predictor of future stock prices. Indeed, your readers should be informed that it already has! R.N. Elliott in the 1930s recognized that the markets follow a succession of zig-zag "waves" consisting of a 5-up then 3-down core structure. If, as seems logical, Elliott considered the simpler 3-wave structure, he rejected it as not being valid when he formulated his final model of market behavior. Both Elliott and Mandelbrot recognized that the basic patterns in real life are fractals, being composed of smaller repetitions of themselves, and multiples of themselves being the building blocks for larger look-alike structures. The word fractal had, of course, not been coined in Elliott's time. The Elliott Wave Principle subsequently has been widely studied and applied, somewhat refined, and made available in several software applications that run on a modern home computer.

Elliott's fundamental approach was exactly opposite that of Mandelbrot's. His theory, with its hundreds of rules and guidelines, was developed from a meticulous combing of historical records to find the real basis for the bits and pieces of the fractals and to determine painstakingly the myriad ways the market fits them together. That's just what Mandelbrot hopes to accomplish in the future.

—Charles E. Miller, Carlisle MA
March 5, 1999

I purchased a copy of *Scientific American* today and read the article. I find it interesting, especially in light of the fact that Mandelbrot wrote about Elliott's discoveries in 1997, that he gave no credit [to him] at all. I also found it interesting that the article gives a hint of how "multifractals" might be used to approximate action in the financial markets, but it is very frustrating to attempt to make much sense out of his graphs and relate them to real-world events.

— Andy MacKenzie
February 16, 1999

I read the February article, "A Multifractal Walk Down Wall Street," by Benoit Mandelbrot, with interest, amusement and disappointment. I found the topic interesting and timely since the U.S. stock market has been in a historic bull trend that has become of manic proportion recently. I was amused because Mandelbrot acts as if he has discovered something new. In fact, the essence of his thesis has been known and described for years. R.N. Elliott talked about market patterns of this type from observations he made and published in the 1930s and 1940s. I was somewhat disappointed by Mandelbrot's failure to credit Elliott for his work but hugely disappointed that Mandelbrot didn't prove his hypothesis with examples and discussion. I don't think his examples prove a thing, and his description of them is inadequate.

But there is good news for those who might want to pursue this line of reasoning and actually apply it to present day financial markets. The works of R.N. Elliott have been collected and published by Elliott Wave International, easily contacted at www.elliottwave.com or 1-800-336-1618. In fact, Elliott Wave International has developed summary and detailed descriptions of the Elliott patterns (free) and prints daily and monthly newsletters (for a fee) that interpret and predict United States and world market movements on the basis of them.

A short list of pertinent titles that Mandelbrot might have quoted include the following:

R.N. Elliott's works:
The Wave Principle (1938)
The *Financial World* articles (1939)
Nature's Law — The Secret of the Universe (1946)

Elliott Wave Principle — Key to Market Behavior
by A.J. Frost and Robert R. Prechter (1978, revised 1998)

At the Crest of the Tidal Wave — A Forecast for the Great Bear Market
by Robert R. Prechter, Jr. (1995)

— Jay Ham, MD
February 4, 1999

To a person with a deep interest in financial theory, just reading the title of Mr. Mandelbrot's paper indicates that it must have something to do with the Elliott Wave Principle first described almost 70 years ago. But as the reading continues, curiosity and enjoyment begin yielding to astonishment, which turns into outright dismay at the end of the paper: No mention of R.N. Elliott, Robert Prechter, A.J. Frost and others? How can that be? Is Mr. Mandelbrot so arrogant that he believes nobody else matters, or is he so ignorant that he has never heard of the books and papers in which others described the fractal geometry of financial markets? As it's hard to imagine that Mr. Mandelbrot would be unaware of these other contributions, one arrives at the conclusion that arrogance may be the engine at work. Mr. Mandelbrot's attitude to acknowledge the work of nobody and to recommend only himself for "further reading" appears to be an ego trip that lies outside the standard deviation of decent scientific behavior. It seems that scientific self-centeredness can run away in a manic pattern, just as the behavior of market participants occasionally bursts out in "irrational exuberance." Mr. Mandelbrot is not the first scientist who fell deeply in love with himself. The knowledge of this phenomenon prompts raising another question: Does *Scientific American* have something like a peer review? If the answer is no, then maybe the magazine should learn from this experience and consider establishing such a system — just to protect its own reputation. If the answer is yes, and if Mr. Mandelbrot's paper was indeed reviewed, shouldn't a flag have gone up at the realization that all recommended "Further Reading" bears the author's name? Credentialism is a perpetually recurring and non-eradicable quirk in the realm of investment, where the misdirection of capital to those "who have done it before" recently pushed the world to the brink of a financial meltdown. Credentialism in the scientific field may be less hazardous to the general population, but it is no less upsetting to the few who are affected by it. More likely than not, credentialism was the mechanism that prompted the rubber stamping of Mr. Mandelbrot's paper: If the theme has something to do with fractal geometry, can anybody dare lecture the man who wrote the book about fractals? To be a good reviewer, it is not enough to have an in-depth understanding of the pertinent field of science. One must also be able to understand that even the most accomplished individuals, be they scientists, artists, statesmen or whatever, remain humans and can frequently not conquer to the most basic human instincts and emotions. Consequently, good reviewers must be able to stand up to the big names of their field when ego, pride and other ingredients of human nature threaten to overwhelm the established rules of decent scientific demeanor.

— Eduard J. Botz
February 16, 1999

Your article on Benoit Mandelbrot's "discovery" that markets exhibit fractal like price behavior prompts a sharp response, since Professor Mandelbrot's insight was predated by decades by R.N. Elliott. His "Wave Principle" has been in the public domain since the 1940s and has been used with enormous success by such high profile market operators as Edson Gould.

Long disparaged by mainstream investment theory and academia, Elliotticians within the broad discipline of technical analysis could have told Professor Mandelbrot how to apply his mathematics to the marketplace. Technical analysts generally welcome academics' growing awareness that the skilled use of tools within our trade produce a level of success in forecasting market movements. However, it seems rather ironic that having derided technical analysis and Elliott in particular, that the academic establishment should suddenly decide that it works and take credit for it.

I write to you as a practitioner using Elliott's theories to forecast daily movements in the interest rate and currency markets. With a consistently high degree of accuracy in my daily work for major institutional clients, I can assure you that I have known and used Professor Mandelbrot's so-called insight for years. His assertion of novelty is ludicrous. Should you wish to take a balanced view in the matter, I suggest you inquire with Robert Prechter of Elliott Wave International. Bob is the foremost Elliottician in the world and since the 1970s has been the torch bearer of Elliott's work to the next generation of market analysts.

> — Nina G. Cooper, President, Pendragon Research Inc.
> February 22, 1999

In the February 1999 issue of *Scientific American,* you included an article by the above author entitled "A Multifractal Walk Down Wall Street." You probably need to know that your inclusion of that article has worked to tarnish the image of *Scientific American,* as the author, in writing his article, appears to have borrowed heavily from the ideas of others without giving credit where credit is due. In fact, it is rather pathetic that the author has previously chosen to dismiss the work of R.N. Elliott while at the same time borrowing heavily from Elliott's theories about the market. Before including future articles on the same subject, you may want to become familiar with the works of R.N. Elliott and Robert Prechter. It is my hope that you will then be able to ferret out the Elliott-Wannabes like Mr. Mandelbrot or at least force such authors to give credit where credit is due. P.S. Please pass this on to Mr. Mandelbrot, as his ego should not be spared knowledge of the consequences of his actions and inactions.

> — E.L.
> February 16, 1999

Dear Editor, I am appalled that a publication as respected and as well read as *Scientific American* would publish such a blatant piece of plagiarism as was written by Mr. Mandelbrot. It's very surprising to me that a journal such as yours, which I have always immensely enjoyed consuming, would insult all who have studied the Elliott Wave Principle by condoning dishonesty among writers who are supposed scientists in the pursuit of truth. Disappointedly,

> — Dr. Rashid A. Buttar, Emergency Medicine, Preventive Medicine
> February 16, 1999

To the Editors of *Scientific American*: That Dr. Mandelbrot coined his own word for "self-similar" points to an overactive ego. Your February article supports this [conclusion]. It may be impossible to say whether Mandelbrot knew of Ralph Elliott's 1930s discoveries before he verified them in several complex systems, but by now he ought to be objective enough to share credit with his remarkable predecessor. This especially so in an article dealing with Elliott's venue, the financial markets. That you allowed such an omission is an unfortunate collaboration in the mis-writing of history.

— Andrew Robin, Center Sandwich, New Hampshire
February 15, 1999

There's no getting around the insight and brilliance, not to mention just plain truth, embodied in Benoit B. Mandelbrot's piece in the February issue of *Scientific American*. But the omission of any reference to the work of R.N. Elliott, A.J. Frost, and R.R. Prechter, et al. is just too glaring to pass unremarked. Market technicians have used fractal analysis since Elliott introduced it in the 1930s, though to my knowledge the term fractal may have been first [connected to the Wave Principle] in Prechter's 1986 report "The Fractal Design of Social Progress."

Mandelbrot's analysis is best regarded as a refinement of this prior work. This point is strikingly and most graphically brought home by a quick comparison of the four diagrams in illustration 1 with Figs. 1-1 to 1-4 in Frost and Prechter's 1978 book, *Elliott Wave Principle*; see also Prechter's riveting 1995 sequel *At the Crest of the Tidal Wave* (both New Classics Library). These financial classics certainly merit a place on the recommended reading list.

— William E. Terrell, Stafford, VA
January 30, 1999

I find it appalling that R.N. Elliott would plagiarize the work of Professor Mandelbrot decades before Mandelbrot created it.

— Pete Shamlian
May 24, 1999

Follow-Up Correspondence Directed to Elliott Wave International

I am a scientist, and it has always irritated me when "credit is not given where it is due." As I have moved through my career, I have come across scientists who only reference themselves, who will not recognize others' work, and (fortunately only seldom), who steal others' ideas and claim them for their own. As these behaviors are carried out in the public arena, refutation and condemnation should also be carried out there. I urge you to submit the material in your "Special Report" to *Scientific American*. They should be willing to air both sides, I would hope.

— Jodie V. Johnson, Ph.D., Chemistry Department, University of Florida
May 21, 1999

I think this is a non-issue and that no one benefits by the argument. In mathematics, it is the mathematical characterization that counts, so—as Mandelbrot first defined fractals mathematically—Mandelbrot did indeed discover fractals, and fractals in finance. I myself have seen firsthand the hostility accorded Mandelbrot in having done so (in economics departments and in finance).

With respect to Elliott, an analogy with respect to Brownian motion may be illuminating. Brownian motion is named after Robert Brown because he first observed the phenomena in a *general* context in 1827 even though Brown himself cites at least one earlier observation of the phenomena in a specific context of fish eyes.

However, the first mathematical descriptions of Brownian motion were given independently by Louis Bachelier in 1900 and Albert Einstein in 1905. So it might be said the latter two individuals "discovered" Brownian motion. But, of course, the mathematicians wanted a much more rigorous development, which didn't come along until Norbert Wiener in 1923. So maybe Wiener created Brownian motion (the "Wiener process").

In the same spirit as Brown, Elliott clearly observed fractals in financial markets and can be said to have "discovered" financial fractals. But in the same spirit as Bachelier and Einstein, Mandelbrot "discovered" fractals because he defined the term and gave a specific mathematical characterization. It is only because of Mandelbrot that most in an academic environment would pay any attention to Elliott. (This approach to truth may not be justified, but that's the way it goes anyway.)

When I first encountered Robert Prechter (in 1984 on FNN, channel 64 in the Philadelphia area), and then the term "Elliott Wave," I immediately recognized it as a fractal approach to financial markets—although it was an open question in my view whether the structure of these fractals necessarily followed the form specified by Elliott.

So I have no problem with your (Robert Prechter's, whoever's) statement that Elliott discovered fractals in financial markets. Clearly Elliott did. Clearly Prechter was justified in adopting the name "fractal" as a description of Elliott's description. Nor do I have any problem with Mandelbrot's saying he discovered fractals in financial markets, because he created and popularized the entire mathematical concept. If you read Mandelbrot's books, you will see that he goes out of his way to point out predecessors. And if Mandelbrot doesn't think Elliott is that interesting, he—of all people—should be allowed that right. But I think you should feel quite free (and not defensive) about ignoring Mandelbrot on this point.

— J. Orlin Grabbe, Ph.D.
June 11, 1999

Prechter replies: Perhaps it would indeed be a non-issue if it were generally acknowledged that both Elliott and Mandelbrot discovered fractals in markets but with differing amounts of qualification and quantification. The only reason there is a controversy is because Mandelbrot wants it all. I believe that is way *too much credit to give. Look at Figures 1 through 4 again. Can you imagine the howl that would arise were someone today to write an article featuring a replica of the Mandelbrot Set and call it a "novelty," a "surprise" and the result of "my own work"? Mandelbrot has described his multifractal* market model *mathematically, but that is not at all the same thing as having described the* stock market *mathematically. The fact is that he has applied mathematics (brilliantly, to be sure) to only one aspect of the financial market fractal: a measure of its roughness. That is the aspect* he *has pursued and elucidated, but that may be only a small aspect of all there is to say about it. If one describes the circumference of an elephant with mathematical precision, it does not mean he has described the elephant. So it is far too much to say that Mandelbrot has* defined *the financial market fractal. According to Elliott, there is an immense amount of information about its form — its very definition — of which Mandelbrot is unaware. Elliott modeled the financial markets' fractal form in 1938 and in 1940 described the Fibonacci mathematics governing his model and, if the model is accurate, therefore the form of the market. It is unfortunate if others have been hostile to Mandelbrot for his achievements. In this case, though, it is Mandelbrot's hostility that requires a response. Regarding "pointing out predecessors," one scientist's email,[1] listing five sources, says, "Several groups in the world have noticed previously that more precise models of self-affinity and multi-self-affinity (loosely called multifractality by Mandelbrot) can better describe the real stock market." Also, defensiveness is hardly the issue when it is Elliott whom I am defending; ignoring attacks and omissions would be an injustice.*

I haven't spoken to you for many years, but I wish to congratulate you on your response to the *Scientific American* article on Mandelbrot. I have read a number of articles and books written by Mandelbrot over the years, and I endorse your overall rebuttal of his recent article wholeheartedly. I was in fact very lucky to have subscribed in May (having read Mandelbrot's article in the *Scientific American*), not knowing that you would refute his claims but delighted that you took him so head-on. In some of my own research over the years and in business practice in general, I have found a tendency for people to claim all sorts of innovations as their own. This practice is so disturbing to the investigative mind (which of its nature is non-defensive) that your rebuttal is all the more pleasing. In fact, I think that the way you analysed the article and carefully went through each passage was first rate.

— Stephen Barrett
June 11, 1999

Thanks for your well-documented and thorough essays regarding Benoit Mandelbrot's intellectual theft of the ideas, even the principles, of R.N. Elliott's seminal works. I, too, am appalled at the use of perjorative terminology by Mandelbrot, whose only intent can be to denigrate and dismiss the pioneering works that so definitely preceded his "tinkerings." I find it refreshing that someone, anyone, would stand on the principle of "credit-where-credit-is-due," one of many concepts I'd thought had left the planet or at least the small corner in which I reside....

— K. Skinner, pclv.com
May 21, 1999

First and foremost, *Scientific American* is not a scientific journal. I have never submitted anything to this magazine myself, but I believe it does not perform pre-publication peer review. I know of no scientific or mathematical journal which publishes without expert review, nor do I believe a journal would publish any paper accompanied by literature references restricted entirely to the author's prior publications. I have never seen one yet, and I have read and reviewed thousands of physical chemistry papers during the last 60 years. Nor have I ever seen the phrase, "I claim that," used! At the most, one could accept "I propose...." My point is simply that if you have a worthwhile contribution to make, why publish it in *Scientific American*? The answer is that no self-respecting journal would accept it without review. Having been subjected to similar failure to acknowledge (my) prior contributions in chemistry, I can empathise with your disappointment that Mandelbrot failed to recognize Elliott's original work and the developments of it which you and Frost have made.

— Harry Godfrey Oswin
May 31, 1999

He must have studied Elliott quite closely to be able to fabricate this: "2) He studied Fibonacci, the Secrets of the Great Pyramid and the prophecies of Melchi-Zedik and in 1938 announced a great 'discovery.'" I share your outrage.

— Joseph F. Joyce
May 21, 1999

I like Bob's car inventor analogy [posted on the EWI's Bulletin Board and used in the text cited in this chapter], but I have a better analogy. Remember when Vanilla Ice (the rock star) came out with the song, *"Ice Ice Baby"?* It had a real catchy tune (bass riff). It was really good, and became very popular, very quickly. Only thing is, he happened to steal the basic tune from the song by Queen (with David Bowie) called *"Under Pressure"* (it was a music video, also). Well, one day at the height of Vanilla Ice's fame and fortune, he was being interviewed on television (MTV, I think), and he was asked about it. The interviewer came right out and said, "Didn't you steal that from Queen? Do you know what Vanilla (Mandelbrot) Ice said? He said, "No I didn't, mine is an original tune. The tune in Queen's *'Under Pressure'* went like this:" *Doo doo doo...da..da do do...do do...Doo doo doo...da..da do do...do do...* "But mine went like this: "Doo *doo doo... da da do do...do do..... Doo doo doo... da da do do...do do.....*The interviewer looked at him somewhat incredulously, but you know something, Vanilla was serious as could be. He really believed that that infinitesimal little pause [between "doo doo doo" and "da da do do"] actually made that song his. Needless to say, his popularity plummeted over the coming years.

— Rich DeRosa
May 21, 1999

[Regarding] Mandelbrot, I have seen it before. He is ripping Elliott off and knows it.

— Steven W. Poser, President, Global Market Strategies, Inc.
May 14, 1999

I have a comment to make about the controversy surrounding Mandelbrot and R.N. Elliott. I am 16 years old attending Upper Dublin High School in Pennsylvania, and we are studying fractals in math. There is not very much information in our textbook, so our teacher uses programs and recent articles to teach our class about fractals. We have been taught that Mandelbrot was a genius, pioneer and ten steps short of a Mathematical God in the Twentieth Century. I sat down to write a quaint four-page paper on fractals. My unimaginative topic was the history of Mandelbrot and his cotton prices. I am rather busy, and that seemed to be the easiest topic at hand. After finding a nice webpage about Mandelbrot's childhood and a brief history on fractals, I returned to the search engine only to uncover a controversy. I honestly do not know what to think. I have the image of a small Frenchman with Einstein hair and a nice IBM computer smiling maniacally while rewriting Elliott's book for a *Scientific American* article. Can this be true? Certainly not. I understand the need for citing sources. Plagiarism means expulsion from school. I simply cannot understand Mandelbrot's motives, and even fractals cannot clearly represent this man's reality! I am confused, so I hope someone could answer my question. Has Mandelbrot fooled himself into the belief that he "invented the car" seventy years after the inventor made the first model? Or is Mandelbrot actually a genius who compiled these images and predictions using strict mathematical procedure?

— David Wengert
May 25, 1999

Prechter replies: Mandelbrot is certainly one of the mathematical gods of the twentieth century. He discovered the ubiquity of fractals and revealed their mathematics, thereby fundamentally and immeasurably expanding the world of geometry, an accomplishment on a par with Euclid's. So he is indeed a genius; he is just not the only *genius.* **Elliott discovered the hierarchical nature of financial markets, catalogued their quasi-geometric forms, explained their mathematical base, linked the entire process to universal forms, and then developed a fractal model of market progression, all on his own in a decade and a half, after his 60th birthday, without the aid of computers.** *Is that genius, or what?*

Elliott's and Mandelbrot's financial models are different. Elliott claimed (rightly, in my opinion) to have discovered the pattern behind financial markets, which is a specific (robust) fractal. Mandelbrot has not explored pattern but proceeds as if markets are indefinite fractals. Mandelbrot's mathematics do not contradict Elliott's model; they support it.

Mandelbrot derides Elliott the man with obvious bias, as if to head off anyone's exploring the man's work, and summarily dismisses Elliott's pattern model without any contrary evidence or discussion. Regardless of one's views on the specificity of the financial market fractal, Elliott did come first, and Mandelbrot did read his work. Perhaps Mandelbrot (as some colleagues appear to believe) recoils from the possibility that the reverence he enjoys might be partially parceled out to another. If Elliott is wrong, science will tell us. If Elliott is right, his genius is comparable to Mandelbrot's. Were Elliott alive, he would be urging his primacy with vigor, though with far more courtesy than Mandelbrot has shown.

Mr. Prechter, you cleared up my confusion concerning Mr. Mandelbrot, and I ended up writing my paper on financial fractals. I appreciate you taking the time to answer. Thank you.

— Sincerely, David Wengert

NOTES

[1] Several scientists responded with like dismay and emailed us with comments of support. They declined to have their comments published due to their perception of risk in opposing such a renowned figure.

Following Up in 2002

At 4 p.m. on Saturday, May 11, 2002, I attended a lecture by Benoit Mandelbrot in Room 208 of White Hall at Emory University in Atlanta. That evening, the university was to present him with an honorary doctorate. It was a rare opportunity to hear the famous mathematician speak.

Mandelbrot ran through a list of the pioneers of fractals, being careful to point out their shortcomings. For example, he noted with a wry smile that George Cantor, inventor of the Cantor Set, had the "unfortunate fate that his papers were not destroyed," since they reveal that he believed his fractal compositions "had nothing to do with the real world."

Though Mandelbrot cited half a dozen figures in the history of fractals, and despite the response to his *Scientific American* article, he omitted any mention of R.N. Elliott. It is disappointing to discover that this great scientist continues simultaneously to ignore Elliott and to claim territory that belongs to him.

In his lecture, Mandelbrot showed slides of the drawings presented at the start of this chapter as Figures 2 and 4. Figure 2 also appears on page 51 of his new book for 2002, *Gaussian Self-Affinity and Fractals*. In that book, Mandelbrot comments,

> This is a very special family of constructions for which Chapter H2 will propose the (newly coined) term, "tile self-affinities." For many purposes, however, this very restricted family proves to be sufficiently versatile. In particular, it includes – hence relates to one another – special examples that provide "cartoons" of almost every basic fractal or multifractal behavior examined in M 1997E, M 1999N [i.e., his papers], this book, *and elsewhere*.[1]

Presumably, that wide net captures Elliott's "cartoons" as well. As far as Mandelbrot is concerned, that is all that needs to be said.

Injustice should be combatted in every field of human endeavor, particularly in science, where facts matter most. For the record, one thing is clear from Mandelbrot's writing: He does not endorse Elliott's specific model of financial behavior either generally speaking, in terms of its 5-3 wave construction, or specifically speaking, in terms of Elliott's detailed observations about the real-world financial fractal. We should remember his rejection if and when the scientific world finally accepts the validity of the Wave Principle.

Mandelbrot's stance on Elliott's irrelevance places him squarely in the path of a tidal wave of scientific discovery that is pointing to the opposite conclusion. New discoveries in the field of complexity theory as well as natural fractal geometry, particularly in biology (see Parts I and III of *The Wave Principle of Human Social Behavior and the New Science of Socionomics*), are rapidly yielding more and more knowledge bolstering the case that the Wave Principle is a correct description of financial reality. In our opinion, there will be no escaping this juggernaut of discovery. Time and science are on our side. In the end, truth will out, and Elliott will get his due. I call on every concerned scientist to help assure that R.N. Elliott is properly credited with having originated the idea of fractal modeling in finance and pioneering its utility.

NOTES

[1] Mandelbrot, Benoit. (2002). *Gaussian self-affinity and fractals*. New York: Springer, p. 52.

SOCIONOMICS
AND
QUANTUM PHYSICS

November 2002

Parallel Revolutions in the Physical and Social Sciences

Preface

My favorite books are ones that dispel decades, centuries or millennia of misconception in one brilliant stroke. Intricate, long-standing misconceptions are called "error pyramids." Perhaps the greatest error pyramid ever constructed in the hard sciences was the one built around the false premise of a geocentric universe. Some planets appeared to act weirdly as a result of this error, such as Mercury moving "retrograde" with respect to Earth. Astronomers produced complicated calculations and theories to account for the motion of the planets in a perceived geocentric solar system, even to the point of perfect prediction. Yet Copernicus' 1543 book on celestial mechanics, *On the Revolution of the Heavenly Spheres*, wiped away the entire vision. Not atypically, the collective "Oops!" took over a century to occur. I have read only a few books that have accomplished a similar feat, but each one was a pleasure.

One comparable achievement is J. Thomas Looney's *Shakespeare Identified*.[1] This 1920 book attacks the problem of identifying who Shakespeare really was in the manner of an open-minded detective interested in facts and where they lead, not in presumption. It presents a coherent picture of the true author. The collective "Oops!" has taken 80 years so far to play out, but after getting louder every decade, it is now getting louder every year. When the "Stratfordians," who still issue content-free "biographies" of Shakespeare, finally give up, this one insight will have wiped away perhaps a thousand times the print volume that Copernicus' insight did. Encyclopedias will have to be re-written because of Looney.

Another book that may qualify is Iman Wilkens' *Where Troy Once Stood*.[2] While I know enough about Shakespeare to be sure that Looney is correct, I cannot say the same about the *Iliad* and *Odyssey* of Homer. Yet

Wilkens' book so thoroughly wipes away discrepancies between the descriptions in Homer's books and the standard scholars' attempts to locate their battles and voyages in and around the Mediterranean that the reconciliation is stunning. In a nutshell, Wilkens says that the stories are accurate accounts of a Celtic-era war between British and European continental forces and of sea voyages in the Atlantic, with astrological imagery employed to facilitate navigation. As to how the tales got to Homer, you will have to read the book. Unfortunately, that's not so easy to do. Published in 1990, the book is already out of print; you can get it only from used book dealers. This fact seems to bear out Schopenhauer's dictum, "Without exception, every original thinker is surrounded by a conspiracy of silence." Established scholars should take a stand on the book, whether in agreement or disagreement, stating *why*. Some books, to be sure, are rightfully to be ignored, such as New Age tomes. Even in such cases, however, a crafted response can devastate any claim to validity, and it stands for all time. To be silent in the face of a substantial effort, on the other hand, implies stubbornness and fear. Is Wilkens' thesis too challenging to scholars who have published volumes on the traditional interpretation? If so, we have an explanation for the silence. One reviewer anticipates the defense, "Homer wasn't being literal." That's what the Stratfordians say about Shakespeare's intimate descriptions of court life. When the truth, if that's what Wilkens has given us, becomes accepted, then the time-honored attempts at mapping the *Iliad* and the *Odyssey* from a Greek perspective will appear as a fool's errand. They all will have been due to a stubborn premise, born of a reasonable — yet ultimately untenable in the face of contradictory evidence — assumption of a connection between the Greek language of the author and the "Greek" names in the book and the location of its subject matter. This is the same simple-minded deduction that rules Stratfordianism: The name "Shakespeare" is on the cover, so the author must be a guy with that name. (Tell that to Sam Clemens.)

I also include *Stonehenge Decoded*,[3] by Hawkins and White, on my list. In a brief, scholarly volume, Hawkins vaporizes the condescending view of the designers of Stonehenge as a gaggle of mystic Druids and showed us why it was actually a team of intelligent, stone-age astronomers and engineers.

Probably also in this category is *Dr. Atkins' Diet Revolution*,[4] by Robert C. Atkins, MD. His thesis has been updated and expanded in such books as *The Zone*[5] and *Protein Power*.[6] These writers present anthropological and biological evidence that a healthy diet is high in protein, fat and vegetables, and low in starch and sugar. This thesis virtually *inverts* the standard "food pyramid" so widely promoted by nutritionists and the government in the twentieth century. Until recently, one could hardly cite Atkins without being called a crank, but research from Harvard on up is lately validating the diet.

Last is a recent book called *Drunks, Drugs and Debits*,[7] by Doug Thorburn, which might better be titled, *Turmoil — How to Spot the Secret Alcoholic/Addict in Your Life*. Doug draws from myriad sources to contend that people do not become addicts because they suffer from psychological problems, but rather they suffer from psychological problems because they are addicts, by genetic disposition. The symptom and the cause are the reverse of what most people believe. An army of psychologists and psychiatrists has wasted years treating people — sometimes with more drugs — for severe psychological problems that in fact are the symptoms of undetected addiction. Rehabilitation is erroneously focused on symptoms when it should be focused on the cause. A psychoanalyst friend tells me that Doug is not the first to propose this argument, and I have no reason to doubt that to be the case, but if so, the idea has been mostly ignored. Thorburn's book is an independent investigation and a comprehensive tour de force. After reading it, you can diagnose probable addiction not only in people close to you but also from afar based on reports of behavior patterns. If he succeeds in popularizing this information, it will save many lives and billions of dollars. I like the thesis of this book because it posits *a reversal of the presumed order of causality*, which is what I have tried to do with respect to social events and social mood in *The Wave Principle of Human Social Behavior*.

This paper will introduce you to a new book on my list, which has yet to be published: Lewis E. Little's *Theory of Elementary Waves — A Causal Explanation of Quantum Phenomena*.[8] This thesis, in contrast to most of those in the above list, is in the hard sciences, specifically, physics. It is of additional interest because the revolution that the author will ultimately bring about parallels the revolution that I hope socionomics will effect in the social sciences.

Foreword

The path I have taken to get to the point of composing this paper might be of some interest. In college, I switched majors twice because there are some things upon which I refuse to waste my time. For example, after spending a day with philosophy books by Kant and Hegel, I vowed to avoid philosophy courses at all costs. Hegel's obliqueness seemed purposeful, as if the author deliberately chose to make it nearly impossible to follow his trains of thought. Kant's challenge to reality and its perception was a clever mind game but contradictory and false, so there was no point in studying it.

I quickly rejected my first two majors, physics and economics, for similar reasons. In physics, the biggest topic was quantum theory, which sounded absurd. It proposed that a subatomic particle had multiple identities simultaneously when it was not being observed but condensed into one upon its being observed. A famous analogy is that of a cat in a box that is not dead *or* alive but both dead *and* alive simultaneously, the final state to be determined by the action of someone opening the box to look.[9] Broadly speaking, we were told, one's consciousness can change the nature of reality simply by deciding to observe it. People who introduced this idea to you would look at you with a mischievous grin, as if they were supremely clever and your skepticism was sad ignorance. I could not imagine pursuing such ideas as my life's work.

I was interested in economics, so I took an economics course in my freshman year, soon thinking that it would be my major. As we ploughed deeper through Samuelson's *Economics*, though, I began to get discouraged. While the book is scholarly and wide in scope, many of the formulae were too "pat," ignoring the changeability of people, and the book is cavalier on the matters of central banking, forced redistribution of income and other government monopolies and intervention. I saw these things as errors in principle (and evils as well) and was aghast at the intertwining of politics — the use of force — and economics, as if the two belonged together. (Of course, I now realize that the idea of a legitimate intertwining is the dominant view of economists.) In the final week of class, our professor took a deep breath and said, "I have now taught you what I am paid to teach you. But you may be surprised to find out that I don't believe most of this stuff." Five of us — you could tell who we were by glancing around — sat up straight and quickly adopted a state of keen attention. Would he finally dismiss all the errors? Would he deliver us from Keynesianism? "Actually," said the professor, "I'm a Marxist." Five bodies deflated back into their seats. We listened for the rest of the period as he described how each neighborhood should have a mass meeting every Saturday to vote on who would do what jobs and how much they would be paid. I did not take another economics course after that.

After two years of uncertainty, I finally settled on psychology. At least the professors were honest about the subject's shortcomings and its conjectural nature. It was years later before I realized that actually I *had* majored in macroeconomics by majoring in psychology. That path has led me, via R.N. Elliott, to formulate what I believe is a revolutionary idea of macroeconomic causality, so it turned out to be the right path after all. Maybe in a sense, I also took a path parallel to the one I could only have hoped to pursue in quantum physics, our next topic.

What's Wrong with Twentieth Century Quantum Mechanics

Scientists have accurately observed the patterns of sub-atomic particle emission and diffusion, yet they have come to bizarre conclusions about the universe as a result. Here is a highly simplified version of the situation: Sub-atomic particles travel by waves. The intensity of a wave affects the probability that a particle, emitted from a source, will arrive at a detector. The problem is that waves, and thus particles, do not appear to behave as one would initially expect. The famous "double-slit" experiment shows that when particles with multiple trajectories are screened by narrow slits in a barrier, the particles that arrive at various points on the surface of a flat-screen detector on the other side of the barrier create a distribution pattern. Fine. But when the detector is moved forward or back with respect to a fixed source of particles and a fixed slitted barrier, the pattern of particles reaching the detector remains constant not with respect to a straight-line trajectory from the source but *with respect to the surface of the detector*, which means that the trajectory of particles along the waves that carry them changes depending upon the location of the detector.[10] Physicists have had extreme difficulty explaining this phenomenon. Once a particle has left a source, it must go in a straight line, yet the straight line is different depending upon where the detector is placed. So physicists have proposed that reality itself changes to accommodate the observer. Werner Heisenberg, who described quantum mechanics in 1925, formulated in 1927 what has come to be called the "uncertainty principle" or "principle of indeterminacy," in which he postulated, "The 'path' [of a subatomic particle] *comes into existence only when we observe it*."[11] To accommodate this conclusion, physicists have attempted to describe waves and sub-atomic particles not as things but only as co-existing potentials, "wave-particles," that follow all paths corresponding to all possible detector locations simultaneously *as long as they are unobserved*. These non-entities "collapse" into actuality only upon *being* observed, the very act of which literally creates an actual particle. Bingo. The mere act of looking turns an unexplained (and unexplainable) potential into an entity, which shows up on the detector one is using.[12]

The uncertainty principle, which most physicists have accepted since its formulation, states that accurate measurement of quantum behavior is *impossible in principle* because the very existence of sub-atomic particles depends upon the action or non-action of an observer, so the simple act of attempting to observe such particles alters reality, making it impossible to detect and measure any sub-atomic system without disrupting the system and thus altering the measurements.[13] Our mental/visual powers of reality alteration, which operate *whether we want them to or not*, therefore present an insurmountable impediment to truly knowing reality *because there is no constant reality to know*. The inescapable further conclusion is that there is *no direct causality from one physical event to the next*; it all depends upon consciousness, which in turn affects the paths of particles backwards in time.

How atomic particles would behave were there no conscious beings to observe them is not satisfactorily explained. How consciousness can remain constant when its domicile — a brain — is built only from unobserved non-actual potentialities is not satisfactorily explained. How certain conscious entities — we, the observers — can maintain a single identity while entities that make us up — atomic particles — have multiple potential identities whose ultimate actualization is determined by the consciousness of the observer they constitute as well as other observers simultaneously is too complex a question even to have been addressed.

The German philosopher Immanuel Kant proposed that our means of knowledge, i.e., our senses, cannot be trusted to detect any actual reality and in fact create discrete personal realities apart from "real" reality, which is in principle unknowable. Kant's formulation is surely the philosophical origin of the uncertainty principle. Heisenberg challenged the idea that "if we know the present exactly, we can calculate the future" by saying, "it is *not the conclusion that is wrong but the premise*."[14] In other words, even the present is unknowable because reality is inconstant.

Whether stated as philosophy or as quantum physics theory, the idea is just as bogus and contradictory. If there is no constant reality, what is a detector? What is a particle? What are you? What is your mind? None of these things has definition or reality if there is no definition or reality possible. You cannot even discuss your philosophy when you have this belief, because none of your words can be trusted to mean anything. You can imagine the intellectual gymnastics required to hold such a contradictory idea. As George Orwell, an astute observer of the human mind, once observed, "There are some ideas so wrong that only a very intelligent person could believe in them."[15]

It takes no more than common sense to dismiss the resulting concoction, but it takes an objectivist intellectual to recognize the fundamental error in such ideas and to challenge them on principle. Einstein knew that the conclusion of quantum mechanics was wrong because, as he put it, "You believe in a dice-playing God and I in perfect laws in the world of things existing as real objects." In other words, consistent physical causality is a universal principle. He diplomatically stated his opinion that quantum mechanics was therefore "incomplete."[16] As we will soon see, Einstein's view has now been vindicated.

A Parallel Error in Finance

As argued in *The Wave Principle of Human Social Behavior*, accepted "explanations" of social causality likewise begin with a false premise, a pure *assumption*, which the evidence, properly applied, refutes. This false premise, that social events shape social mood, has supported a long-standing error pyramid comprising much of the literature on social causality, which includes macroeconomics, finance and history. This fundamental error has suffused the practice of social forecasting, which is why it has a nearly unblemished record of failure (unlike quantum physics, whose predictions are accurate). This error, one would presume, has been around since the dawn of humanity, which makes it one of the longest-standing errors of human thought. We have explored the magical thinking in conventional quantum mechanics, so let us turn to why some financiers and economists, probably without realizing it, are also using magic to "explain" how things work.

First, we are forced to take a detour because of the miserable state of what passes for knowledge in macroeconomics today. Good economists know that the stock market is the single best leading indicator of the economy, but they are few and far between and rarely quoted in the press. Most economists are so lacking in knowledge about their field that they do not even *realize* that social mood trends precede compatible social actions. All day, newspapers and television present interviews with economists and financial professionals who offer "forecasts" for the stock market by reference to current events or by guessing what future events will cause it to move. They are oblivious to the fact that trends in the stock market, which is an immediate register of shared mood, *precede* events that are compatible with those trends. An analogous situation in physics would be one in which the majority of physicists did not realize that wave trajectory precedes particle detection. They all know that fact because they are scientists who pay attention to details.

As it happens, some financial professionals are indeed observant enough to see that stock market trends precede economic trends. To explain this chronology, they offer the idea that "the stock market discounts the future." In other words, while most economists believe that *current* events are causal to present stock price movements, these financiers believe that *future* events are causal to present stock price movements. The essence of their premise — that social events dictate the trend of the market — is the same; only the chronology is different.

The discounting idea has been around for at least a century, as evidenced in the writings of Charles Dow, founder of *The Wall Street Journal*, who died in 1902. The succeeding Journal editor, William Peter Hamilton, packaged and expanded upon Dow's ideas. In 1911, he wrote,

> The superficial observer is constantly startled to find that the stock market fails to respond to sudden and important developments; while it seems to be guided by impulses too obscure to be traceable. Consciously or unconsciously, the movement of prices reflects not the past but the future. When coming events cast their shadows before, the shadow falls on the New York Stock Exchange.[17]

In Hamilton's 1922 book, *The Stock Market Barometer*, a title that accurately reflects his view, he added, "The price movement represents the aggregate knowledge of Wall Street and, above all, its aggregate knowledge of coming events."[18] Dow Theorist Robert Rhea used similar words in his 1932 book, *The Dow Theory*:

> *The Averages Discount Everything.* Whenever a group of market students get together, some one of them nearly always starts a debate as to whether stock prices, by their action, discount events not foreseen by the individual speculator. Surely all students who have an understanding of the Dow theory *know* this to be a fact.[19]

As market forecaster E. George Schaefer put it,

> Since investors by their very nature constantly scan the news and react either bullishly or bearishly to it, the movements of the averages reflect the sum total of collective investment thought through the

willingness of investors to purchase or sell stocks. As a result, trends in business are usually discounted six months to a year ahead.[20]

This idea is so common that I ran across it again just this week in a magazine, in which an advisor and money manager agrees, "The market is a mechanism for discounting the future, most notably earnings per share for the coming two or three years."[21] If all economists understood the proper chronology between the market and events, this theory of social causality would undoubtedly be as widely accepted as quantum theory is among physicists and even used successfully to forecast macroeconomic trends. The question is whether the theory behind that success would be correct.

I do not wish to deduct anything from the brilliance of the seminal thinkers Dow, Hamilton and Rhea, who remain ahead of their time a century later in many ways. Not the least of these is simply in having observed that movement in the stock averages precedes compatible economic events. Pundits today are routinely "startled to find that the stock market fails to respond to sudden and important developments" because of their entrenched yet erroneous belief that the market reacts to news. Hamilton, moreover, made wise accommodations in saying that the process is "guided by *impulses*" and takes place "consciously *or unconsciously*," phrases that anticipate elements of socionomics. Nevertheless, can we really embrace beliefs that "the movement of prices *reflects* the future," as if the future is a fixed edifice impacting the present, that "stock prices, by their action, discount events not foreseen by the individual speculator," as if a mass of individuals can know what separate individuals cannot, and that "coming events cast their shadows before," i.e., *backwards in time*? Did investors six months ago really divine today's newspaper?

These beliefs are as flatly espoused among certain financiers as conventional quantum theory is among physicists, and they are, to be blunt, just as ridiculous. How can a non-existing social future months or years ahead impress itself upon a mass of presently existing people? The social future must be unknown to the mass of investors because *it hasn't happened yet*. The very idea that investors en masse divine the future is a lazy explanation for the properly observed chronology between stock market trends and parallel economic trends. I seriously doubt that anyone has stopped to think about what he is saying with such a theory. Indeed, I have never seen a convincing attempt to account for it. As a typical example, MIT professor Paul Samuelson's discussion of this idea contains (1) the fundamental error of event causality, (2) the idea that the majority of people can guess the future trend of the economy and (3) the fact that it is impossible for anyone to do so, all in one statement. Here is what he says in his classic textbook:

> To the age-old question, Does the market follow business activity or business activity the market? no simple answer can be given. It is reasonably clear that business activity, national income, and corporate earnings determine stock prices and not vice versa; and also that the psychological effects of market movements no longer have primary importance. But still the market can occasionally *anticipate* changes in national income and total purchasing power. It then appears to be leading them when really it is following what it thinks they will be later.
>
> *How to Invest*: There are no simply stated fool-proof rules for making money out of the stock market. Anyone who can accurately predict the future course of business activity will prosper; but there is no such person.[22]

Notice the irony: No individual can predict anything at all about the social future, but the mass of investors supposedly can and does, all the time.

Rhea's and Schaeffer's explanations attempt to accommodate this contradiction by asserting that individuals can divine their own personal business futures, and the resulting *aggregation* of small divinations creates the stock market's trends, while no one individual can divine the whole process.[23] Clearly, through, if the majority of investors could divine even their own future business success, they would then be correct on the macroeconomic trend, so this proposed dictionary between individual and collective divination is untenable. Further distressing to the theory of individual divination is that the data contradict it. Indicators of market psychology typically reveal aggressive bullishness during and well after market peaks and aggressive bearishness during and after market lows. For a few good examples, see Chapter 11 in *At the Crest* and Chapters 6 and 7 in *Conquer the Crash*. This of course, is as it must be, because investors (aside from socionomists) are necessarily aware only of the events and conditions of the present and the past, not the future. The passage below from *The Wave Principle of Human Social Behavior* addresses this aspect of the "discounting" theory:

Reasoning from Conditions to Markets – in Advance

The belief that news affects the market is the lowest level of misunderstanding, and it is the most common. There is a higher level of misunderstanding, which at least pays tribute to the fact that the market moves ahead of events. Technicians say that the reason earnings lag stock prices is that smart investors anticipate, or "discount," the future, in other words, guess the future correctly.

While this position is a time-honored and valiant attempt to explain why events lag stock prices, I believe it is false. The idea of the mass of investors possessing near-omniscience about the economic future is difficult to defend. Nor does it explain why in 1928 the market foresaw nothing but blue sky, in 1929 very suddenly foresaw depression, and in early 1930 saw a recovery that never happened.

One might try to make a case that smart investors sell stocks when they get a whiff of trouble in their own businesses. If the economy typically turned before or even coincidentally with stocks, this argument might be plausible. But stocks lead the economy, normally by months. Then there is the problem that when you ask investors what they think, they express no inkling of coming economic changes. In fact, in the aggregate, they always erroneously anticipate the opposite of what then happens. At the start of a bull trend, the vast majority is bearish and wrong, and at the start of a bear trend, it is bullish and wrong.[24]

Up to this point, I have taken the time to challenge the two conventional views on non-Elliott-wave grounds, but there is a shortcut to understanding why they are wrong. The fact that the market is patterned according to the Wave Principle establishes the primacy of social mood in financial market valuation and contraindicates the primacy of events. As *The Wave Principle of Human Social Behavior* observes,

Because markets are patterned, the idea of near-perfect collective forecasting must be false. Otherwise, future events would have to be patterned according to the Wave Principle, and the collective would have to anticipate each nuance perfectly. This is an untenable position.[25]

The idea that investors price stocks today according to events in the future parallels one of the great errors in the conventional theory of quantum mechanics. Little states, "[The current theory of] quantum mechanics forces one to conclude that...*events can affect one another backwards in time*...." This is exactly what the current theory of "discounting" espouses with respect to social causality, and it is just as erroneous. "What must one say of a belief in the existence of inexplicable phenomena?" asks Little about his field. "This amounts to a reversion to the ideas of the middle ages — the very ideas supposedly overridden by modern methods."[26] Discounting theory amounts to the same thing. These parallel errors have parallel solutions.

Socionomics Clears Up the Mystery of Apparent Discounting

R.N. Elliott took finance out of the Middle Ages when he said properly, "At best, news is the tardy recognition of forces that have already been at work for some time."[27] Better stated, news is the tardy *manifestation* of those forces. The following passage, edited from *The Wave Principle of Human Social Behavior*, gives the proper explanation for why trends in the stock market precede trends in the economy:

> The truth is that the stock market does not see into the future, as the discounting idea suggests; it reflects instantaneously the causes of the future. Optimistic people buy stocks and decide to expand their businesses; depressed people sell stocks and decide to contract their businesses. The economic results show up later as an apparently "discounted" economic future. The actions of human beings spurred on by an increasingly ebullient or pessimistic social mood cause earnings to rise or fall. Rising earnings are the fruits of a bull market, and falling earnings are the result of a bear.[28]

The socionomic explanation dispenses with reverse-temporal causality. It relies entirely upon chronological cause and effect. In so doing, it dispenses with magic. This is exactly what Little has done in revolutionizing quantum physics.

Lewis E. Little Clears Up the Mystery of Quantum Mechanics

From the beginning, physicist Lewis E. Little thought properly about the problem of explaining quantum mechanics because, like Einstein, he knew that the conventional explanation is contradictory, which means that it is wrong. He did not *wonder* if it was wrong; he *knew* it was wrong, for the same reasons that one cannot properly "wonder" about ghosts, which are impossibly defined as both an entity and a non-entity, both corporeal and non-corporeal, at the same time, just as so-called "wave-particles" are defined today. Conventional attempts to explain quantum mechanics, Little observes, are fundamentally flawed: "Proofs claiming that one couldn't avoid contradictions didn't prove that those contradictions were real. They rather proved that the premises of those proofs already contained a contradiction."[†] The proper orientation to conventional quantum mechanics theory is dismissal on philosophical grounds because metaphysically, reality precedes and is independent of consciousness. To be conscious means to be conscious *of* something and *within* something, each of which must exist and have identity for consciousness to occur.

Understanding the basic error of thought led Little to look for a proper explanation for quantum behavior that did not rely on ghosts and psychokinesis. He began by recognizing that the whole idea that *observation* — mere consciousness — should be credited for the results of measurements of quantum activity is an unwarranted conclusion, because the only thing that physicists have shown to affect the path of sub-atomic particles is *the placement of a physical detector*, which is an entirely different thing from consciousness. By thus isolating the physical cause from the metaphysical conclusion, Little's mind paved the way for a solution.

Little describes 20th century quantum mechanics as the second-biggest error pyramid ever constructed in the hard sciences, and he has taken a deep breath and blown it over with one mighty puff. In 1996, *Physics Essays* published his ground-breaking paper, "The Theory of Elementary Waves." Little's thesis challenges the conventional view of quantum mechanics and presents a new theory that places activity at the sub-atomic level on the same grounds of cause and effect as all other physics. "Bell's theorem," says Little, "coupled with the experiments confirming the associated quantum mechanical predictions, does not 'refute reality,' as is so frequently claimed." Rather, quantum mechanics "can be understood in an objective manner, in which facts are facts, causality is valid, and reality is real."[†] To do this, he has challenged one of quantum physicists' unexamined premises, a pure assumption, which the evidence, properly applied, refutes.

Little's Insight from Elementary Waves:
The Direction of Waves Is Opposite the Conventional Assumption

Here is a summary of what Little says:

Conventional theorists are making a false presumption. Because it seems natural and reasonable, they assume, without evidence (indeed, in contradiction to the evidence), that the waves that carry sub-atomic particles travel in the same direction as the particles. It seems to be a logical assumption, but it leads to a nonsensical theory. In fact, he proposes, *waves actually travel in the opposite direction*. Waves travel *from the particle detector to the particle source*. If the intensity of a wave is strong enough to stimulate the emission of a particle, that particle travels along the path of the stimulating wave back to the detector from which the wave originates. The number of particles emitted depends upon the intensity of the stimulating wave. The qualities of an emitter also affect the number of particles that it will emit in response to a wave. Throughout the universe, waves travel from all points on the surface of all objects (including detectors) in all directions, stimulating countless emissions of particles. Each such particle then travels back to the source of the wave that stimulated its emission. Waves travel endlessly, continually stimulating emissions. Particles exert no influence on the waves that they follow. The direction of initial causation is not from particle source to destination but from destination to source. Everyone else is looking at it backwards.

The Socionomic Insight from Elliott Waves: The Direction of Causality Is Opposite the Conventional Assumption

You can imagine that when I read of Lewis' insight two years ago, I was excited. After all, I had come to the same conclusion about *social* causality, which parallels Little's thesis as follows:

Conventional theorists are making a false presumption. Because it seems natural and reasonable, they assume, without evidence (indeed, in contradiction to the evidence), that any influence that relates social events to social mood carries in the direction from events to mood. It seems to be a logical assumption, but it leads to a nonsensical theory. In fact, I propose, *the influence actually travels in the opposite direction*. Waves *originate in social mood*. If the intensity of a wave is strong enough to stimulate a social action (an "event emission"), that action will be of the same character as the mood that generated it. In collective terms, it "travels back" to impact the society that was the source of the wave. The number of participants in, and the intensity of, social actions depend upon the degree of the stimulating wave. The qualities of an individual affect the extent to which he will undertake social actions in response to a wave. Throughout the world, waves animate various groups in many ways, stimulating countless social actions, which then impact the societies whose waves stimulated their occurrence. Waves develop endlessly, continuously stimulating actions. Actions exert no influence on the waves that generate them. The direction of causation is not from social actions to social mood but from mood to actions. Everyone else is looking at it backwards.

The Two New Theories Correct the Same Type of Errors

Quantum physicists have gotten their mathematics down properly, so they can make probability forecasts of particle appearance at a detector. From that standpoint, their theory appears to "work." Discounting theory is almost never applied to macroeconomic forecasting, but when it is, it also appears to "work." The rare financier who gives the idea more than lip service can watch the stock market and successfully forecast changes in the economy. He assumes that the stock market has a mystical knowledge of the economy's future path, an idea similar to conventional explanations of quantum physics. In contrast, both new theories offer explanations that rely upon direct cause and effect. *Elementary waves precede and stimulate particle emissions; Elliott waves precede and stimulate social actions.*

Physicists cannot predict every particle emission, and a socionomist cannot predict every social event, but we can both make probability statements about the physical and social future, respectively. The socionomic insight brings sociology to the same point as Little's quantum physics in providing a proper theory to account for the fact that certain aspects of the future are predictable, at least to a degree of probability and generalization.

Differences from a Perfect Analogy

Before exploring the striking parallels between the theories of elementary waves and Elliott waves, we should note that they are not precisely analogous. Here are some of the imperfections in that regard, at least in my mind, along with some possible resolutions for them.

(1) According to Little's theory, elementary waves are fundamental, i.e., irreducible to components or causes. Elliott waves are probably fundamental to growth patterns in a universal sense, because evolution for example appears to travel in Elliott waves,[29] and human thought is irrelevant to that process. Elliott waves may further be viewed as the fundamental waves of sociology in that they stimulate actions, much as Little's waves stimulate particle emissions. Without Elliott waves, there might be no social growth or progress, perhaps no social action at all. In human society, though, Elliott waves may be viewed as reducible in having a more fundamental cause, such as the cooperative herding impulse common to all human minds[30] or perhaps some outside physical cause of which we are unaware.[31]

(2) In Little's physics, waves and particles are discrete physical objects. The Wave Principle operates *within* physical entities and effects actions *through* physical entities, but I am not sure whether Elliott waves themselves are physical objects. They are objects in the sense of comprising electrical impulses within brains and nervous systems, but I am inclined to call Elliott waves processes, not objects. At the same time, there is an analogous aspect respecting the manifestations of the two types of waves. We cannot see Elliott waves, but we can plot their various effects — such as decisions about securities prices — on a graph to make them manifest and

thus *see them* as if they were physical objects. Likewise, we cannot see elementary waves with our eyes or even with instruments, but we can plot their effects — such as the patterns of particles reaching a detector — on a graph. That is why Little postulates a *theory* of elementary waves; if we could see them, it would not be a matter of theory. The same is true of Elliott waves and the socionomic hypothesis.

(3) The results of the two types of waves are not identical, but they do seem to be similar: Elementary waves stimulate physical emissions, and Elliott waves stimulate physical actions.

(4) The particles within entities organize environmental elementary waves into mutually coherent elementary waves, which then stimulate particle emissions from *other entities*. Discrete limbic systems in a social setting may similarly organize various individuals' mental waves into mutually coherent Elliott waves, but they then stimulate actions, for the most part, from some of the *same* entities that participated in those waves. One possible exception that would mimic the results of elementary waves would be an Elliott wave among a population stirring action from an individual who had no emotional stake, merely a dispassionate one, in that action (for example, someone who sells beverages at a pep rally or trades markets based on Elliott waves).

(5) In Little's theory, particles on the surface of all objects reflect and organize elementary waves, although only some objects emit particles in response. Elliott waves may be similar: All people participate in the organization of Elliott waves, but only some of them take actions in response to particular Elliott waves. Even then, though, the emitter of a particle in physics is never the same as the source of the wave that stimulates it. Those taking social actions are always among the participants in the Elliott waves that stimulate them.

(6) Little asserts, "One derives the behavior of larger systems from the behavior of the parts. (Even 'emergent' properties can — must — be so derived.) In the elementary waves theory the waves simply exist, with their various properties. They are primary constituents of reality. Thus there is no need to deduce their behavior from anything." We can look at this statement several ways with respect to Elliott waves. (1) Elliott waves are primary, like elementary waves, and need no explanation from the action of constituent parts. (2) Unlike elementary waves, Elliott waves are emergent properties that derive from their primary constituents, i.e., the unconscious mentation of individual participants in social trends. (3) The premise is wrong. In formological[32] systems, the behavior of the whole is a

function of its organizational form, to which smaller parts conform. Human beings, for example, have overall behavioral properties over and above the behavioral properties of the atoms that make them up, as evidenced by the fact that one's atoms change all the time without affecting the organization of the larger system. The behavior of the parts is a function of the behavior of the whole, not the other way around.[33] Elliott waves are a formological system, not a summation of component properties. Economists lament the "butterfly effect" destroying all ability to predict social events when in fact, the system is not only chaotic but also formological, which is why substantial prediction — prediction specifically of the character of social action — is possible. Individuals' rational thinking does not register in an Elliott wave; only impulsive herding behavior does, so the individual property of rationality coexists apart from the Elliott wave dynamic. The herding impulse in an individual limbic system cannot express itself within an Elliott wave without other human beings to mimic, the larger context giving form to the component.

(7) The physical world is fully deterministic. The social world is much less so, and the individual far less than that. As far as limbic system stimuli and responses go, there is substantial collective determinism, because these unconscious mental processes produce Elliott waves. Yet differences in individual knowledge, rationality and free will preclude determinism in individual thinking, and those same differences preclude determinism in both individual actions and specific social actions, the latter of which are akin to chaotic processes subject to the "butterfly effect" in which previous actions and situations affect later ones. Nevertheless, quantum physics still suffers from unpredictability, if not as much as with Elliott waves. Compare these formulations to see the difference:

From Little's paper: "There is some unpredictability, as opposed to indeterminism, in this theory, in that we do not know in advance which wave the source will respond to in emitting a particular particle photon. However, unlike the situation in the usual theory, here the unpredictability can be described as resulting from a random process following an ordinary probability distribution. All the wave states exist as real waves. The source then simply has a constant probability of responding to the intensity of each incident wave. The randomness thus reflects lack of knowledge of the value of some parameters in the source, rather than representing a fundamental indeterminism."

Regarding socionomics: There is both unpredictability and indeterminism in this theory, in that we do not know in advance exactly which people will respond, and precisely how they will respond, to a wave in terms of taking specific actions. All waves have the potential to stimulate actions. People's limbic systems simply have a certain probability of responding to the intensity of each wave. The imperfect predictability of specific individual and social actions reflects a lack of knowledge of individual limbic system parameters as well as the capacity for free will and the variations in understanding that individuals possess. These attributes preclude both specific social event determinism and individual response determinism, which produces unpredictability in those areas.

From Little's paper: "The exact value of the particle momentum is unpredictable. We don't know which wave will lead to the emission of a particle at which time and hence do not know in advance the value of the parameters describing a particular particle. But this is now due solely to ignorance of the value of parameters in the emitting system and not to any fundamental uncertainty."

Regarding socionomics: While waves provide for predictability with respect to the character and intensity of future social action, the exact details of any specific future action in response to a wave is unpredictable. We do not necessarily know which person or social group will respond to a wave at which time. This is due to indeterminism attending human free will and understanding as well as a lack of knowledge of the thresholds of individual human limbic systems.

I may not have expressed all the differences and possible reconciliations between elementary waves and Elliott waves for the purposes of pursuing an analogy. Suffice it to say that the analogy is not perfect or at least that I have not grasped its perfection if it is.

The remainder of this paper will present the details of Little's thesis while exploring parallels between it and socionomics. Because the analogy is not perfect, the pairs of quotations below sometimes fit each other perfectly and other times fit only when one of them is taken out of strict context or implies an otherwise unsupported conjecture about socionomics. I am aware of the expressions with these differences but include them because of their possible compatibility.

Primary Parallels between the Two New "EW" Theories in Physics and Sociology

The parallels between the Theory of Elementary Waves and Elliott waves/socionomic theory are legion and exciting. Here are some key correlations:

(1) Elementary waves and Elliott waves are both fundamentally causal to subsequent actions.

(2) Elementary waves' stimulation of the emission of subatomic particles relates to Elliott waves' stimulation of individual and/or social actions.

(3) Elementary waves do not travel from the emitter to the detector but from the detector to the emitter. Similarly, Elliott waves of shared mood do not "travel" from actions to minds but from minds to actions.

(4) These new theories properly account for why particle direction correlates with the position of a detector (in the first case) and why the character of social action correlates with the trend of social mood (in the second case).

(5) The volume of particle emission varies with the intensity of the elementary waves that stimulate the source of particles. Similarly, the number of participants in and people affected by social actions — and the intensity with which they act and are acted upon — varies with the degree of the Elliott waves that stimulate the source of those actions.

(6) Conventional quantum mechanics divorces cause and effect from the proper chronology, asserting that an observer in the present affects the past path of a particle, which means that an observer in the future can affect the present path of a particle. A conventional view of social behavior, that the stock market discounts the economic future, similarly places the cause in the future and the effect in the present, asserting that an event in the future affects the present mood of investors, which means that an event in the present has already affected the past mood of investors. Elementary waves theory obeys proper chronology, as the demonstrable effect of waves, the emission of particles, occurs in the future. The socionomic hypothesis obeys proper chronology, as the demonstrable effect of Elliott waves, social actions, occur in the future (whether immediately or later, depending upon the nature of the action).

(7) Elliott waves determine the trends of social mood, and those trends stimulate actions, which are reported as events. The actions and events, like particle emissions in physics, are final results *with no consequences of their own in terms of changing or reinforcing the waves that stimulated them.* Events "bombard" minds and thus often shape the *specific* actions that owners of those minds take, but they do not alter or affect the waves of shared mood trend. Likewise, particles bombard detectors and thus effect a specific action at the atomic level, but they do not alter or affect the elementary waves.

(8) In quantum physics, when an observer moves the detector around, he seems to be affecting the future action of particles, *and he is*. Likewise, as observer-participants move the stock market up and down, they seem to be affecting future social actions, *and they are*.

Some Parallel Statements in the Two EW Theories, the Theory of Elementary Waves (TEW) and the Elliott Wave Theory (EWT)

In this section, I take quotations directly from Little's paper and book chapter and cast parallel expressions relating to socionomics. Some of these renditions may be little more than mental exercises; the ones I perceive to be strong and/or important are highlighted at the outset in bold print.

TEW: "Nonlocality [in conventional quantum physics] implies that distant events can affect one another instantaneously by no physical means. But no effect can be produced by no means."

EWT: Conventional discounting theory implies that events distant in time can affect human thinking in the present by no physical means. But no effect can be produced by no means.

TEW: "...it was *simply assumed* that both [the wave and the particle] had to move intromissively, and thus in the same direction as one another. ...Common sense also seems to dictate that the wave is intromissive."

EWT: It is *simply assumed* that causality has to move in the direction from event to mood. Common sense also seems to dictate that it moves in this direction.

TEW: "The essence of the proposed answer is very simple: it is the quantum wave itself that moves in reverse."

EWT: The essence of the proposed answer is very simple: the causality moves forward in time.

TEW: "We know by direct observation that particles move forward... so the only thing left to move in reverse is the quantum wave itself."

EWT: We know by direct observation that actions move forward in time, so the only things left to move in the reverse of the conventional assumption — i.e., in the forward direction — is the causality between thoughts and actions.

TEW: "All of the evidence supporting the hidden variables proofs actually is evidence of the reverse motion."[†]

EWT: All of the evidence supporting the idea of markets discounting the future actually is evidence of the reverse direction of causality.

TEW: "The contradiction involved in the forward wave theory's attempt to explain the double slit — this in any interpretation, conventional, Bohm's, or others — is that of trying to capture the dependence on the screen location without any physical means for that dependence."[†]

EWT: The contradiction involved in the discounting theory's attempt to explain the correspondence of the present (stock prices) with the future (the economy) is that of trying to capture the dependence on the future without any physical means for that dependence.

TEW: "Many of the properties currently assigned to particles will be shown in this work to in fact be properties only of the waves."[†]

EWT: Properties normally assigned to social events, those of affecting shared mood and of causing specific styles of responses, for example, are properties only of the waves.

TEW: "All particle emission in this theory is stimulated by a wave."[†]

EWT: All social action in this theory is stimulated by a wave.

TEW: "If one wishes to validate the [conventional] wave-particle theory, it is thus not enough simply to say that the formulas work. One must also be able to demonstrate, based on empirical evidence, that the further physical hypotheses are correct. Specifically, one must be able to demonstrate that the waves move forward and not in reverse. But this cannot be done for wave-particle theory."

EWT: If one wishes to validate the [conventional] "discounting" theory, it is not enough simply to say that the formulation seems to work. One must also be able to demonstrate, based on empirical evidence, that the further physical hypothesis is correct. Specifically, one must be able to demonstrate that the waves move backward in time and not forward. But this cannot be done for the discounting theory.

TEW: "The test of any hypothesis is this: does the hypothesis fit all the facts with no contradictions? …If one accepts the forward-wave picture of things, one is forced to accept the existence of non-local behavior: interactions over long distances by no physical means. But an interaction by no means is a contradiction."

EWT: The test of any hypothesis is this: does the hypothesis fit all the facts with no contradictions? If one accepts the backward-wave picture of things, one is forced to accept the existence of non-chronological behavior: interactions backward in time by no physical means. But an interaction by no means is a contradiction.

TEW: "Clearly, reverse waves imply a radically different theory. No longer are the waves somehow the particles. Rather, the waves are present in the environment already, and the particles then follow those waves."

EWT: Clearly, forward wave causality implies a radically different theory. No longer are the waves somehow the product of future actions. Rather, the waves are present in the environment already, and actions then follow those waves.

TEW: "The waves were always assumed to move forward, with (or as) the particles. The physical effects caused by the 'information' carried by the reverse waves could only be accounted for through one kind or another of nonlocal interaction."

EWT: The waves (of mood or knowledge) were always assumed to move backward, from future actions. The mental effects caused by the "information" carried backwards in time could only be accounted for through one kind or another of non-chronological interaction.

TEW: "At every point on the screen, the number of particles arriving is proportional to the intensity, at the particle source, of the wave emitted by that point."

EWT: The number of people stirred to and affected by social action is proportional to the degree of the wave in force.

TEW: "The wave is present at all times and not only when the particle is emitted."

EWT: Waves are acting at all times and not only when historic social events result.

TEW: "Waves are waves and particles are particles, and both have an exact state at all times. [Particles are not simultaneously waves.]"

EWT: Waves are waves and actions are actions, and both have their own states. Actions in the future are not simultaneously waves that travel backwards in time to trigger the discounting that anticipates those actions.

TEW: "[In the conventional view,] the act of measuring the state of a particle after it passes through an apparatus appears to affect the earlier process...but of course such reverse-temporal causality is impossible. What we have here is direct experimental evidence of the reverse time sequence."[†]

EWT: In the conventional view, later events appear to affect the earlier process of mood change...but of course such reverse-temporal causality is impossible. What we have here is direct empirical evidence of the forward time sequence.

TEW: "So instead of having the wave emitted as the photon, the photon is simply a particle emitted in response to the already existing 'available state' wave."

EWT: So instead of the wave being emitted with an event, the event is simply emitted in response to the already existing wave.

TEW: "And those available states, in order that they be able to affect an emitting system, must move toward that system, that is, in the direction opposite to that in which the particle will move when it is emitted."

EWT: And those waves, in order that they be able to effect physical actions, must have the same character those actions, that is, move in the same "direction" — positive or negative — as the spirit in which the action will be taken.

TEW: "Now the causality of the process makes sense. The 'weirdness' has been eliminated, but with no change to the mathematics."

EWT: Now the causality makes sense. The "weirdness" has been eliminated but with no change to the temporal sequence.

TEW: "These waves exist independently, in addition to the elementary particles. ...They are primary constituents of reality on the same level as the elementary particles."

EWT: These waves exist independently, in addition to social actions. They are primary constituents of social reality on the same level as actions. Without waves, there would be no actions. Without actions, there would be no social reality to experience.

TEW: "...particulate objects do not actually emit these waves. The waves are present continually and with constant intensity. All that [particulate objects] do is to establish mutual coherence among the waves leaving their vicinity. An organization is imposed on the already existing waves. It is the mutual coherence that then leads to the observed interference effects."

EWT: Individual limbic systems do not actually emit Elliott waves. All that they do is align their impulses into mutual coherence to others with which they come into contact. It is the mutual coherence that then leads to the observed herding behavior.

TEW: "Th[e] wave intensity at the source determines the probability that a particle is emitted by the source in response to the particular wave."†

EWT: Th[e] degree and therefore the intensity of a wave determines the probability that an individual will take social action in response to the particular wave.

TEW: "In current theory the wave-function is not considered to be a real, physical wave, but rather merely part of a 'formalism' which 'works.' …The reverse waves in the new theory are real, physical waves, not merely a formalism that 'works.'"[†]

EWT: In current theory, the reverse-temporal effect of future events is not considered to be a real, physical wave, but rather merely part of a "formalism" that "works." The forward waves in the new theory are real, causal waves, not merely a formalism that "works."

TEW: "All the dynamics of particles are determined by the waves. The particle itself needn't carry any of the 'classical' dynamic quantities generally attributed to particles: mass, momentum, energy, etc. All these properties describe only the waves, with the particle then acting accordingly…. One might say that the particle has mass or momentum or what have you. But the actual numerical quantity is carried by the wave."

EWT: All the dynamics of actions are determined by the waves. The action itself needn't carry any of the "classical" dynamic quantities generally attributed to action: mass, momentum, energy, etc. All these properties describe only the waves, with people then acting accordingly. One might say that the action has mass or momentum or what have you. But the actual numerical quantity is carried by the wave.

TEW: "Particles are emitted in response to waves of particular frequency/momentum. The behavior of the particle then reflects exactly the momentum of the wave."

EWT: Actions are taken in response to waves of particular position, degree and momentum. The style of the action then reflects the position, degree and momentum of the wave.

TEW: "The source responds 'randomly' to the various wave 'pieces' which arrive there. However, that randomness can now be understood in terms of additional variables — the so-called 'hidden variables' — in the source. One simply has a constant probability, proportional to the wave intensity, that the source will respond to each particular wave 'piece.'"[†]

EWT: The limbic system of each unidentified person responds "randomly" to the various wave "pieces" that reach him. However, that randomness can now be understood in terms of additional variables — the so-called "hidden variables" — in each person. One simply has a constant probability, proportional to the wave intensity, that each unidentified person will respond to each particular wave "piece."

Regarding those hidden variables, each individual has his own trigger point with respect to becoming stimulated to act in accordance with a wave. Some people respond early, to mild stimuli; others respond later, to intense stimuli, and some do not respond at all if the wave never reaches beyond their particular threshold of reactivity. This explains why some people buy or sell early or late, or are the first or last to adopt new fads or fashions, or choose not to participate. (It is unlikely that people maintain a constant probability of reacting throughout their lives. Probabilities change as people age and as they experience more of life.)

TEW: "Because the waves exist in their own right, there is no need to somehow obtain the laws of the waves from those of the particles, as is done in the usually canonical quantization procedure. It is from the observed behavior of particles that one determines the fact that the waves exist and what their properties are; but once one knows their properties, one simply says that waves exist."

EWT: Because the waves exist in their own right, there is no need to derive the laws of social waves from those of social actions, as is done in the history books. It is from the observed behavior of actions (for example, buying and selling on the stock exchange) that one determines the fact that the waves exist and what their properties are; but once one knows their properties, one simply says that waves exist.

TEW: "The reverse wave theory thus eliminates all of the physical arguments, based on quantum mechanics, which allege to prove that the nature of reality is somehow intimately tied up with human consciousness."[†]

EWT: The forward wave theory thus eliminates all of the arguments, based on discounting theory, which allege that future social reality is somehow detected by present human consciousness.

TEW: "An object 'emits' only those waves that correspond to particles that it would absorb."

EWT: People participate only in waves that are capable of stimulating actions that it could take in response.

TEW: "The effects of the two waves at the source are, one might say, 'entangled,' that is, the emission of each photon is affected by both waves, but not the waves themselves."

EWT: The effects of two waves (for example a corrective wave of Intermediate degree within a motive wave of Primary degree) at the source of social action are, one might say, "entangled," that is, the potential emission of actions is affected by both wave directions, but the wave itself at any one time is a unity.

TEW: "It is only in the actual stimulation of the emission of particles that there is any issue of interference between waves. Only in the *effect* on the probability of emission is there any cancellation between waves in that interference."[†]

EWT: It is only in the actual stimulation of actions that there is any issue of interference between waves. Only in the effect on the probability of actions being taken is there any cancellation between waves in that interference.

In other words, the wave at any moment is naturally "at ease" with its own place in the overall structure. Only effects are muddled by the occurrence of, for example, a motive wave upward within a corrective wave downward within a motive wave upward.

TEW: "In this theory the reverse wave is present at all times and not only when a particle is following it."[†]

EWT: In this theory, the forward wave is present at all times and not only when it is clear that people are acting in accordance with it.

The waves are first a mental phenomenon, and some individuals may not react to it or may have subtle reactions that go unnoticed or take time to become manifest, such as making a decision tonight to do something tomorrow or next month. Also, sometimes people are acting in accordance with a wave, but because that wave is in a position of calm, the resulting actions are not dramatic enough to impress most people as being the product of shared mood.

TEW: "A particle must always follow an existing wave — the wave by which it was generated; it is that wave that determines the dynamics. If that wave disappears, the photon must jump into 'coherence' with one of the new waves; it cannot remain in its original state because the corresponding wave is gone."

EWT: A social action must always follow an existing wave — the wave by which it was generated; it is that wave that determines the dynamics. If that wave disappears, the action must jump into "coherence" with one of the new waves; it cannot remain in its original state because the corresponding wave is gone.

For example, a rising Elliott wave of major degree may stimulate a peace negotiation and determine its dynamics. If the advancing wave ends and a declining wave begins, the peace process will must ultimately resolve into coherence with the new wave, which means that it will disintegrate, because the mental trend that generated it has reversed. Conversely, a declining Elliott wave of major degree may stimulate a war and determine its dynamics. If the declining wave ends and an advancing wave begins, the war must ultimately resolve into coherence with the new wave, which means that it must end, because the mental trend that generated it has reversed.

TEW: "This is interpreted by Kaiser as implying that the subsequent action — after traversing the interferometer — of narrowing the bandwidth affects the prior bandwidth of the wave packet and hence its coherence length, one of many examples of reverse-temporal causality in current quantum mechanics, which, of course, makes no sense."

EWT: This is interpreted by practitioners in finance as implying that subsequent actions affect the prior state of the wave, including its direction and intensity, the prime example of reverse-temporal causality in current financial theory, which, of course, makes no sense.

TEW: "When all the unnecessary baggage required by the forward wave theory has been eliminated, it will become apparent to the reader that overwhelming empirical evidence of the reverse motion has been staring physicists in the face for decades."[†]

EWT: When all the unnecessary baggage required by the backward wave theory has been eliminated, it will become apparent to the reader that overwhelming empirical evidence of the forward motion of causality has been staring economists and sociologists in the face for decades.

TEW: "What forces one to assign a fundamental uncertainty to particles in current theory is the forward motion of the waves. By assuming that the wave goes from source to detector and that the wave *is* the particle, one is forced to conclude that the particle exists in multiple states simultaneously in order to explain phenomena involving 'widths.'"

EWT: What forces one to assign a fundamental uncertainty to the social future in current theory is the presumed backward motion of the waves. By assuming that the wave goes from future actions to present mood and that the action therefore generates the wave, one is forced to conclude that future actions exist in multiple states simultaneously in order to explain phenomena involving surprise news to which the market briefly reacts as if it were unaware of that future event.

TEW: "Relativistic phenomena alone provide a sufficient basis to deduce the elementary waves theory, at least for photons, provided one maintains the view that facts are facts."

EWT: Chronological phenomena alone provide a sufficient basis to deduce the socionomic hypothesis, for all types of social events, provided one maintains the view that facts are facts.

TEW: "The real waves do not go out of existence when they interfere; only their effects interfere."

EWT: Elliott waves do not go out of existence when they interfere (for example, when an Intermediate uptrend occurs within a Primary downtrend); only their effects interfere, tempering resulting social actions.

TEW: "Once a particle becomes coherent with a wave, it loses the ability to respond to anything other than that wave."

EWT: Once an action coherent with a wave takes place, it cannot be recalled. As social actions proceed in the direction of the wave that stimulated them, they are able to continue along the same path only in response to that wave.

As examples, a stock market advance can continue only as long as the wave continues in a positive direction; if a peace process begins, it can progress only if the Elliott wave that stimulated it continues in the same direction and supports it.

TEW: "There is some degree of 'randomness' in how a particle follows its wave. Internal, 'hidden' parameters in a particle determine which of several mutually coherent waves the particle will respond to at a particular vertex."

EWT: There is some degree of "randomness" in how a particular unknown person will act in response to waves. Internal, "hidden" parameters in individuals determine which of several mutually coherent waves a person will respond to at a particular vertex.

TEW: "But, as before, the randomness is only apparent, due to ignorance regarding the values of the internal parameters. There is no lack of causality."

EWT: But, as before, the randomness is only apparent, due to ignorance regarding the values of the internal parameters of individuals. There is no lack of causality.

Some people may respond to waves sooner vs. later and fully vs. partially vs. not at all. But in the aggregate, Elliott waves appear, so the cause has its effect.

TEW: "The momentum and energy can now be defined in terms of the 'picture' of the waves, without reference to the resulting behavior."

EWT: The momentum and energy in society can now be defined in terms of the "picture" of the waves (showing, for instance, that society is in wave 3 of (3) of 5 of V of (V) of ⑪, which tells you all you need to know), without reference to the resulting behavior.

TEW: "The wave that stimulates the emission of a particle, and which the particle then follows, takes multiple paths between 'detector' and source. So there is interference between the different waves. The entire space through which the waves travel — and not simply the discrete line along which the particle travels — will then affect the probability of the particle process."

EWT: Waves that stimulate an action, and which that action reflects, take multiple paths between the cooperative generating process of those waves and the individuals who may act in response. So there is interference among different waves. The entire social fabric through which the waves travel — and not simply the discrete wave that an action reflects — will affect the probability of individual and social action.

TEW: "The response of the original particle will depend on exactly where it is located when the disturbance occurs. But that in turn will depend on the particular path chosen up to that point, which in turn depends on the particle's inner parameters. The overall motion is thus no longer simply a function of the initial motion of all the particles, as in classical physics. The inner parameters also play a role. One cannot predict the future motion of a system simply from a knowledge of its initial state of motion."

EWT: The specific response of social action will depend on exactly what the configuration of the actors is when the wave affects them. But that in turn will depend on the particular paths that individuals within society have taken up to that point, which in turn depends on society's and individuals' inner parameters. The specific social actions taken are thus not simply a function of the initial impetus from Elliott waves. The inner parameters of individuals also play a role. One cannot predict specific individual and social actions simply from knowledge of the state of current individual and social actions. (We can nevertheless predict the *character* of social action without any such knowledge.)

TEW: "In fact we never directly observe a quantum wave. We only observe the 'quanta' or particles. Any detector, including our eyes, responds to the particles, not the waves. Wave patterns appear only as the result of the observation of numerous individual particles. The particles carry the light signal, not the wave."[†]

EWT: In fact, we never directly observe an Elliott wave. We only observe the actions that it induces. Any detector, including our eyes, responds to the record of those actions, not the waves. Wave patterns appear only as the result of the observation of numerous individual actions. Actions carry the wave signal, not the wave itself.

A stock market graph is a record of human actions (in this case, buying and selling), which take place in response to the waves. It is not a record of the wave itself.

TEW: "The wave does not itself carry any energy or momentum from one location to another; only the particles do that. The wave merely serves as a guide, if you will, for the particle motion."

EWT: The wave does not itself carry any energy or momentum from one location to another; only actions do that. The wave merely serves as a guide, if you will, for actions.

TEW: "Current theory obtains the equations of quantum mechanics by starting with the equations of classical physics and then 'quantizing' them, using the canonical quantization procedure. The premise here is that somehow the classical laws are primary, and quantum mechanics is then derived from them. But this has matters backwards."

EWT: Current theory presumes the properties of social mechanics by starting with the equations of classical physics and then "socializing" them, imposing mathematical equations upon mental processes. The premise here is that somehow the laws of physics are primary in social behavior, and mood is a mechanical response to actions. But this has matters both wrong and backwards. The laws governing unconscious mental processes are different from the laws of physics.

TEW: "In the elementary waves theory all aspects of the mathematics of quantum mechanics correspond to something real. ...In no way are we required to conclude that there is a breach between the real and the observed, between our knowledge and the objects of that knowledge."

EWT: In the Elliott wave theory, all aspects of causal mechanics correspond to reality. In no way are we required to conclude that there is a breach between the real and the observed, between our observations and the forward direction of time or the phenomenon of direct causality.

TEW: "This statement replaces the usual statement of how anti-(wave-) particles are negative frequency (wave-) particles moving backwards in time. Nothing moves backwards in time in elementary waves theory, as, of course, must be true in any theory that purports to represent real objects."

EWT: This statement replaces any attempted statement of how anti-(wave-) actions are negative frequency (wave-) actions moving backwards in time. Nothing moves backwards in time in Elliott wave theory, as, of course, must be true in any theory that purports to represent real processes.

TEW: "All that needs to be modified from the usual treatment is the direction of the wave, the direction of propagation of the 'principle function.' It must be reversed."

EWT: All that needs to be modified from the usual treatment is the direction of the causality, the direction of propagation of the "principle function." It must be reversed.

TEW: "So there is complete causality at every step, both for the particles and the waves."

EWT: So there is complete causality at every step, both for actions and the waves.

TEW: "A theory that results in absurd conclusions is false. Reality does not make mistakes; only physicists do."

EWT: A theory that results in absurd conclusions is false. Reality does not make mistakes; only economists do.

TEW: "Most of what has been accomplished [with elementary waves theory] follows simply from the recognition that the waves move in reverse."

EWT: Most of what has been accomplished with socionomics follows simply from the recognition that causality moves in reverse of the common assumption.

TEW: "Virtually all the principle mysteries of twentieth-century physics disappear as soon as one corrects the one error."

EWT: Virtually all the principle mysteries of conventional macroeconomics and the chronic failures of social prediction disappear as soon as one corrects the one error.

TEW: "All of this is accomplished with a theory that is far simpler than current quantum mechanics. Occam's razor does not say that the simpler theory is correct. But it does say that one cannot validly add further aspects to a theory without additional evidence, evidence going beyond what is explained by the simpler theory."

EWT: All of this is accomplished with a theory that is far simpler than current discounting theory. Occam's razor does not say that the simpler theory is correct. But it does say that one cannot validly add further aspects to a theory without additional evidence, evidence going beyond what is explained by the simpler theory.

TEW: "While the simplicity of the reverse wave theory is certainly beneficial, most significant is the fact that the theory is free of any contradictory, unphysical aspects."[†]

EWT: While the simplicity of the forward wave theory is certainly beneficial, most significant is the fact that the theory is free of any contradictory, non-chronological aspects.

TEW: "Quantum mechanics is indeed an error pyramid — the most gargantuan error pyramid in the history of humankind"[†] (at least in the area of physical science).

EWT: The idea of social event causality with respect to social mood is indeed an error pyramid — the most gargantuan error pyramid in the history of humankind (at least in the area of social science).

TEW: "Clearly, the fact of reverse elementary waves has been demonstrated. Too many things are explained by the one simple hypothesis to conclude otherwise."

EWT: Clearly, the fact of forward socionomic causality has been demonstrated. Too many things are explained by the one simple hypothesis to conclude otherwise.

TEW: "Furthermore, the theory accomplishes what has been sought for many years: a single framework within which all known physical phenomena can be comprehended."

EWT: Furthermore, the theory accomplishes what has been sought for many years: a single framework within which all known social phenomena can be comprehended.

The Two "EW" Theories Explain Special Relativity

The Theory of Elementary Waves explains special relativity neatly and simply and without resorting to contradiction and magic, whereby, for example, objects change shape when an observer moves while simultaneously not changing shape for other observers who do not move.[34] In Little's words:

"The elementary waves theory provides a simple, physical explanation for the fact that light travels at the same velocity c relative to all observers and thus serves to explain the Lorenz transformation.... What we see is the particle photon, not the wave. It is the particle that imparts any energy or momentum to the retina, thus producing a visual effect.... But if the dynamics of the particle photon is determined by a wave that comes from the observer, then it is the observer's frame that determines the velocity. The constancy of c relative to the observer is thereby explained.

"Light, then, does not simply move from object to observer or from observer to object; it does both. Nor is it simply a wave or simply a particle. It consists of a wave from observer to object and a particle from object to observer. ...In the standard derivation it is assumed that the light seen by both observers is physically the same light — the same photons. Space and time are then distorted [by theory] in order to account for the fact that both observers see a spherical pulse. But this is because the light is different, not because of a deformation of space-time. The two observers in two different frames do not see the same photons.

"Objects do indeed appear to change when one moves. But facts are facts; facts do not change because one looks at them differently. So one knows for certain that it is the means of observation that changes when one moves, not the objects observed. But motion of the observer can affect the means of observation only if the means involves something traveling from the observer.

"Given the fact of Lorenz transformations, all the consequences of that transformation occur in the elementary waves theory exactly as in current theory. Moving objects appear shorter, time intervals in moving systems appear dilated, etc. However, none of these apparent changes require any change to the objects themselves. Only their appearance changes, due to the change to light. ...The nature of light as a particle following a wave from the observer dictates that simultaneity is relative. ...It is thus clear that there is no contradiction involved in the fact that two observers in relative motion each see objects as being shorter in the other observer's frame. ...Reality is the same for all observers. It is not the case that 'everything is relative.'

"The fact that the theory which accounts for quantum phenomena also at the same time accounts for special relativity serves as the best evidence I will cite that this theory is correct. Had special relativity not yet been discovered, the reverse wave theory would have predicted it!"[†][this paragraph only]

If economists were as creative as physicists, they would have formulated their own theories of uncertainty and special relativity. They would have observed that when their "detector" of future events, the stock market, moved from one trend and level to the next, the future would change right along with it! They would conclude that even with perfect knowledge, the future would be unknowable. Surely, they would argue, there must be an infinite number of pre-existing future social realities, or "wave-futures," in which the economy is both strong and weak, and cats are both alive and dead, simultaneously. The "observer," i.e., society, can bring any one of these futures into actuality simply by changing its financial position from favoring stocks over cash or vice versa. It would not occur to such "quantum economists" that the observer[35] behind the presumed detector actually *originates* the waves of social mood that *direct* events in the future — the *only* future. A socionomist can also see that social causality has its own naturally produced special relativity. As society undergoes changes of mood, the social future changes right along with them because trends in mood produce trends in actions. In other words, the social future remains constant with respect to the present mood of the observers, who produce it. Now we know why, and the answer requires no magical reversal of temporal causality. Instead, the causality is direct and sensible.

Some Potential Questions and Implications for Socionomics Implied by the Analogy

(1) TEW: "The elementary waves are not actually emitted by the observer, as indicated earlier. The observer merely rearranges the organization of the passing wave." Like elementary waves, are Elliott waves everywhere present, stimulating organized actions by living entities in the universe, or do they originate inside the living entities?

(2) TEW: "Waves corresponding to all possible free-particle states exist at all times. In the absence of particles the waves are 'disorganized.' Particles have the effect of imposing coherent organization on the waves." Like elementary waves, are the waves governing living processes disorganized until living units impose organization upon them, in which case they become Elliott waves? Are life forms essentially organizational? Are people's unconscious minds the organizers of disorganized social waves that exist independently?

(3) TEW: "In the elementary waves theory the waves simply exist, with their various properties. They are primary constituents of reality. Thus there is no need to deduce their behavior from anything." Like elementary

waves, are Elliott waves primary constituents of social reality, or are they products of underlying processes?

(4) In quantum physics, "The intensity of the wave — the absolute value of the amplitude squared — at any point on the screen gives the probability that a particle is observed there."[†] Little corrects this formulation to say, "The square is performed at the source; and it gives the probability of particle emission, not of particle observation."[†] Similarly, the intensity of actions that people take in response to Elliott waves seem to be multiplicative with respect to arithmetic increases in degree. Effects of waves of one degree are often 1.618, 2.618 or 4.236 times those of one lower degree (as examples, aggregate stock valuation extremes and war deaths). Little says, "The key to making sense out of the $\cos^2\theta$ dependence is that the square occurs at the source." A translation into Elliott wave theory would be that the multiplicative intensity in the expression of waves occurs at the source of action and is not a property of the waves themselves, which vary in degree arithmetically.

(5) TEW: "These are not waves in a medium, and the signal is not carried by wave fronts. The notion that any periodic 'thing' must propagate as the result of a field equation is a carryover from classical physics. One can deduce wave equations for classical waves from the physics of the medium through which the wave propagates. This notion was then applied to quantum waves, even though no medium is involved. But this is erroneous." It is difficult to say whether Elliott waves propagate through a medium. Certainly the minds of human beings contain electrical impulses that carry herding directives, but can we say that the coherence of those impulses through the cooperation of many minds is accomplished through a medium? The minds are not physically connected. Further, we have Elliott waves in processes outside human society, such as the Elliott waves that describe the flow and ebb in the number of species on Earth. It seems at least possible to conclude that Elliott waves are external entities, not internal waves in a medium, and that they shape living processes from without, which is why disparate parts conform to the whole. Just as various atoms, molecules and compounds participate in the human body yet a person retains its identity, so various people participate in Elliott waves yet the waves retain their identity. This is what I meant in *The Wave Principle of Human Social Behavior* when I called Elliott waves a formological system, not one of linear or nonlinear causality. Such external waves could serve to "explain" or account for formological systems as being the product of outside forces.

(6) TEW: "If one has indeed reached the most 'elementary' level, one can only describe what exists, not explain it. ...If the waves are primary things, without there being any medium, then one simply describes the waves." I often feel that it is enough simply to describe Elliott waves. They exist; we can see their effects on graphs. Several chapters of *The Wave Principle of Human Social Behavior* attempt to explain where they come from, but ultimately, these explanations describe primarily their media and their ubiquity, not their cause. Elliott waves may be just as elementary as elementary waves. Perhaps, as postulated in Chapter 21 of that book, they are a manifestation of phimation, a force opposing entropy.

(7) TEW: "Each point on the screen [and on all objects] is actually emitting [more accurately, organizing and re-directing] waves of all frequencies corresponding to all possible energies, masses, and other characteristics of particles."[†] "Particles are emitted in response to waves of particular frequency/momentum. The behavior of the particle then reflects exactly the momentum of the wave. ...An object 'emits' only those waves that correspond to particles that it would absorb." People are capable of experiencing all manner of emotions induced by waves, but their minds participate only in those that pertain to them at a time. Whatever waves people participate in then stimulate actions that are in accordance with those waves and only from people whose internal "hidden variables" are constituted so as to respond with action to those waves.

(8) TEW: "The reverse wave theory thus predicts not merely the relative distribution but rather exactly the correct number of particles arriving at any point on the screen." Knowledge of the effects of Elliott waves on populations can allow socionomists roughly to predict the mass and energy of their social effects, for example, the number of people that will be unemployed in an economic contraction of each different degree, or the percentage of Earth's population that will be at peace or war. Already there is evidence that the effects of waves vary according to degree, as illustrated in *The Wave Principle of Human Social Behavior*, Chapters 7 and 16.

Conclusion

Little says succinctly, "A physical theory is acceptable only if it is able to account for all experimental evidence *without any contradictions*."[†] This fact not only damns conventional quantum theory but also conventional assumptions and theory regarding social causality. Conventional macroeconomics is replete with contradiction. For example, economists assert that logically, "Falling interest rates are bullish for stock prices," except that they are not always so; in fact, during deflations, interest rates on sound debt fall to very low levels right along with stock prices. So, the macroeconomic assertion contradicts evidence. Conventional sociologists tell us, "Terrorist attacks and corporate scandals make people less optimistic and more fearful of investing," except that the evidence utterly contradicts this assertion, as our studies of *actual* optimism and investing trends during and after such attacks and scandals demonstrate. The discounting theory of markets, in which effects purportedly move backwards in time, is an even more fundamental contradiction of reality.

"Before one can base an explanation on some aspect of reality," says Little, "one must have evidence — observational evidence — that the aspect in question actually exists. Otherwise one would simply have a fantasy, not a scientific explanation."[†] This is precisely the problem with conventional ideas of social and macroeconomic causality. They are not scientific explanations but *fantasies* based upon a false premise, which is unsupported by the evidence and indeed contradicted by it.

The Theory of Elementary Waves corrects the fundamental error in conventional theories of quantum mechanics. Socionomics corrects the fundamental error in conventional ideas of social causality. They are, in many ways, parallel scientific revolutions.

Appendix

Elliott Wave Influence on the Mental States of Physicists and the Nobel Committee

Figure A provides some anecdotal evidence that Elliott waves stimulate similar actions in people at similar points in wave structure. As you can see, the two Elliott waves shown there are nearly identical in *form* despite a 3-times difference in their absolute quantities of duration and percentage rise.

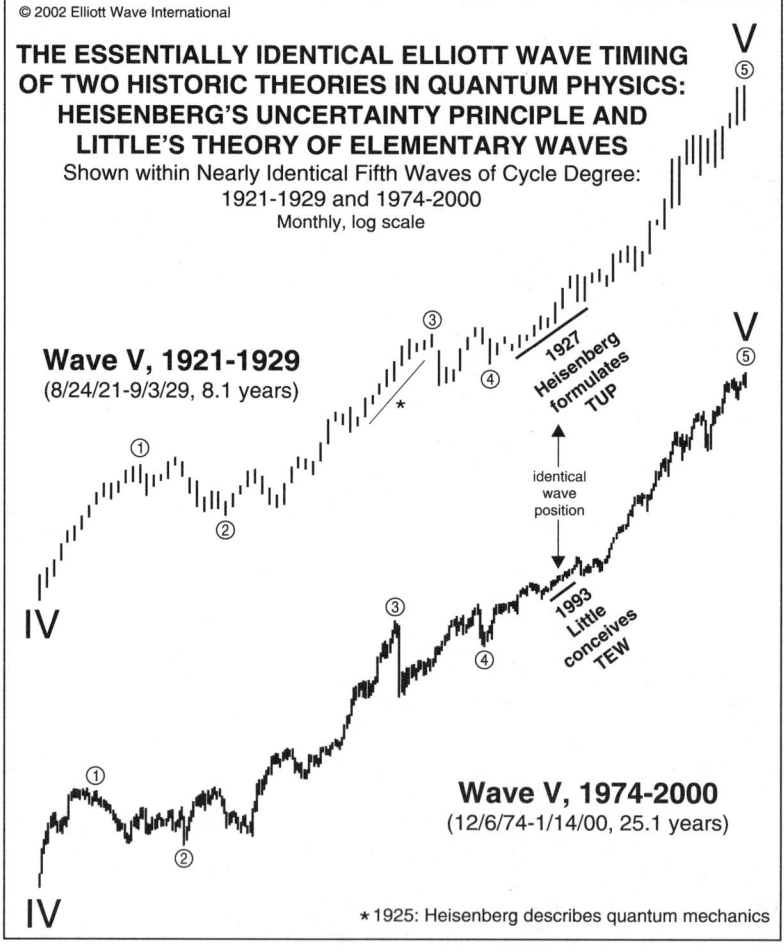

Figure A

Heisenberg formulated his uncertainty principle in 1927, and Little conceived of his theory of elementary waves in 1993. These years are almost precisely analogous in terms of their Elliott wave position. In other words, we may speculate that these Elliott waves coordinated a mental energy that induced historic "aha" experiences in individual quantum physicists at almost the same moment in the progression of Elliott wave form, which is early in Primary wave ⑤ of Cycle wave V in the 1921-1929 and 1974-2000 periods, respectively. From these insights, they formulated grand theories that changed the direction of science.

In all the time in between, physicists dedicated themselves to explaining and elaborating upon Heisenberg's vision. In other words, they were not thinking independently so much as they were herding.

Heisenberg received the Nobel Prize for physics "for the creation of quantum mechanics" not in 1925, 1926, 1927, 1928, 1929, 1930, 1931, 1933 or any year thereafter. He received it in 1932. This timing is unlikely to be coincidence. July 1932 was the bottom of the largest stock market collapse in two centuries, which means that in the aggregate, people (at least in the West) felt more uncertain about their social future than at any other time in that period. It is hardly a surprise that the Nobel prize committee at this time was psychologically primed to embrace an "uncertainty principle" that infected the entire universe.

The socionomic insight was formulated over a period of years from 1985 forward, culminating in 1999 along with the bull market. TEW was formulated in 1993, and its final exposition is still in progress. The two new theories of physics and sociology, then, are not only substantially parallel in their correction of previous thought in their respective areas of science but have also been developed nearly coincidentally. Both gelled into summary expositions in Primary wave ⑤ of Cycle wave V of Supercycle wave (V). This temporal parallelism is probably not coincidence, either.

NOTES

[1] Looney, J. Thomas. (Reprinted 1996). *Shakespeare Identified.* Northampton, MA: The Oxenford Press.

[2] Wilkens, Iman. *Where Troy Once Stood.* 1990, London: Rider Press; 1991, New York: St. Martin's Press.

[3] Hawkins, Gerald S. and White, John B. (1965). *Stonehenge Decoded.* New York: Dell Publishing.

[4] Atkins, Robert C. (1972). *Dr. Atkins' Diet Revolution.* (Republished 2002, M. Evans & Co.)

[5] Sears, Barry, Ph.D and Lawren, Bill. (1995). *Enter the Zone.* New York: Harper Collins.

[6] Eades, Michael R. and Eades, Mary Dan. (1996). *Protein Power.* New York: Bantam Books.

[7] Thorburn, Doug. (2000). *Drunks, Drugs and Debits.* Northridge, CA: Galt Publishing.

[8] Little, Lewis E., *The Theory of Elementary Waves — A Causal Explanation of Quantum Phenomena*; in progress. Chapter 1 published on the Internet at http://www.yankee.us.com/TEW/.

[9] Proposed by E. Schrodinger, *Naturwissenshaften* 23, 807 (1935). I wish I had had Lewis Little's words back then. He says, "The notion that the act of looking at the cat can either kill it or determine that it lives is perhaps the single most absurd prediction of current quantum mechanics. This amounts to a sort of vitalistic psychokinesis."[†]

[10] For a detailed explanation of the "Double-Slit Experiment," please see the paper and chapter posted at Dr. Little's website at http://www.yankee.us.com/TEW/.

[11] Heisenberg, uncertainty principle paper, 1927, as quoted on pages 1 and 2 of http://www.aip.org/history/heisenberg/p08c.htm

[12] This is very like the stance of analysts and reporters when "explaining" the stock market movement of the day. On any typical trading day, all sorts of news is reported, and reporters stand at the ready as if they were applying conventional quantum theory by accepting the fact that all the news has infinite potential causality *until the day is finished*, at which time all those potentials collapse into the *actual* causality. The analysts create reality by looking, and only after looking do they discover which among the myriad potential causes actually pertained to the result! If one were to provide such reporters and analysts with every bit of news for the day *in advance* except the action of the stock market, they would have no hope of determining what the stock market would do because in fact there is no causality of news to mood. (Few people actually investigate history to uncover this fact.) Indeed,

most news events have two contradictory causal arguments attached to them prior to knowledge of what the market actually did that day. As examples, (1) war is bad for consumers' mood, which is *bad* for stocks, and war is good for the economy, which is *good* for stocks, and (2) a decline in interest rates repels investors away from bonds, which is *good* for stocks, or a decline in interest rates indicates a weakening economy, which is *bad* for stocks. And so on.

[13] There is a parallel between Heisenberg's uncertainty principle and an occasionally expressed assumption on the part of financial analysts. They argue emphatically that any attempt publicly to analyze or forecast the market is doomed because as soon as it becomes popular, it affects the behavior of the market, which destroys not only the forecast but also the basis upon which it was made. You can read this argument in any one of a hundred books on the stock market. Once again, the true causality is in the opposite direction. A forecast's popularity does not cause people to change their mood with respect to the stock market, thereby invalidating it; people's moods with respect to the stock market dictate which forecasts are popular, which by definition are ones that will not succeed at that time. The result is the same, but the explanation is wrong, just as with Heisenberg's uncertainty principle.

[14] Heisenberg, in his uncertainty principle paper, 1927, as quoted on page 2 of http://www.aip.org/history/heisenberg/p08c.htm.

[15] I would say the same thing about the conventional idea of social causality, except that common people believe it just as readily as intellectuals, which is not the case for the implications of quantum theory.

[16] As quoted on page 3 of http://www.aip.org/history/heisenberg/p08c.htm

[17] Article in *The Wall Street Journal*, March 27, 1911, as quoted in *The Dow Theory* (1932) by Robert Rhea, p.20.

[18] Hamilton, William Peter. (1922). *The Stock Market Barometer*. Reprinted 1960 by Richard Russell Associates, New York, pp.7-8.

[19] Rhea, Robert. (1932). *The Dow Theory*. Barron's, New York, p.19.

[20] Schaefer, E. George (1960). *How I Helped More Than 10,000 Investors To Profit in Stocks!* Englewood Cliffs, NJ: Prentice-Hall, p.22.

[21] Quickel, Stephen W. (2002, September). "Excessive Stock Prices?" *On Wall Street*.

[22] Samuelson, Paul. (1967). *Economics: An Introductory Analysis*, 7th edition, McGraw-Hill, Inc.

[23] The true dichotomy is the opposite of that espoused by discounting theory: The mass of investors knows nothing accurate about the future, but occasionally an informed individual can apply socionomics to forecast successfully the next trend.

[24] Prechter, Robert. (1999). *The Wave Principle of Human Social Behavior*. Gainesville, GA: New Classics Library, pp.331-332.

[25] *Ibid.*

[26] Little, Lewis E. (1996). "The Theory of Elementary Waves." *Physics Essays*, volume 9, number 1, pp.100-132.

All unmarked quotations attributed to Little in this essay are from this paper. All quotations marked with an endnote style "†" are from Chapter 1 of the book cited in endnote 8.

† See endnote 26.

[27] Elliott, R.N. (1946). *Nature's law: the secret of the universe.* Republished: (1994). *R.N. Elliott's Masterworks — The Definitive Collection.* Prechter, Jr., Robert Rougelot. (Ed.). Gainesville, GA: New Classics Library, p. 277.

[28] See endnote 24.

[29] See Figures 13-1 through 13-3 in *The Wave Principle of Human Social Behavior*.

[30] See Chapter 8 of *The Wave Principle of Human Social Behavior*.

[31] "Astroeconomists" postulate that electromagnetic waves bombarding Earth are regulated by the position of the moon and the planets, and those waves in turn affect humans' aggregate mental states. So correctly or not, some people do propose an outside cause for extremes of shared mood, which would then be an outside cause regulating Elliott waves.

[32] For a discussion of this term, see *The Wave Principle of Human Social Behavior*.

[33] This idea goes back to the ancient Greeks, who viewed form as a primary force of nature.

[34] Little also dispenses with the nonsensical idea that "space" is "curved" or has any properties at all. He explains, "Space, after all, is nothing. Space is merely the place where real objects can be located. What is real are the objects, not the space.... Nothingness cannot have properties.... The elementary waves are curved, not space." His solution is, "The electromagnetic field...is actually itself simply an elementary wave, with particle photons then following the wave."

[35] There is a nuance of difference in this analogy, because in sociology, human thought is causal; in physics, physical action is causal and humans are merely observers.

MISCELLANEOUS ARTICLES, LETTERS, SPEECHES AND OBSERVATIONS

The Elliott Wave Theorist
February 26, 1998

Chapter 13 of The Wave Principle of Human Social Behavior *(p.217) dis-cusses evidence of the Wave Principle in individual life forms. We may have additional evidence along these lines in David Goodman's study of human emotional biorhythms.*

Evidence of the Wave Principle in Human Emotional Biorhythms — A Starting Point for Further Study

The Foundation for the Study of Cycles publishes a magazine called *Cycles*. Volume 46 included a submission by member David Goodman, who recorded his mood swings with great precision for twenty years, from January 1977 through September 1996. Rather than finding a regular cycle, he found that since 1977, the cycle of his mood swings got progressively shorter, from 30 days to 30 *hours*. Now, this might mean nothing; one sample has little value for generalizing, and this is barely a glance at a neglected area of scientific research. However, if this study does prove to reflect an aspect of human psychology, what would be the implications? It might suggest that people's emotional cycles shorten with age, perhaps explaining why people perceive time accelerating as they get older. (My preferred theory is that people experience time as a percentage of their age.) Some clues in the data point to another explanation.

Figure 1 is Goodman's chart, but it is inverted and annotated to reveal a familiar pattern: an Elliott wave, labeled 1 through 5. This picture sug-gests a link between patterns of individual mood and social mood in the production of Elliott waves.

More intriguing is that the one-way longer term trend and the timing of its interruptions are highly reflective of the stock market's concurrent advance, with pauses in the areas of the corrective periods of 1979-1982 and 1987-1991. Notice in Figure 2 that the five-wave sequence reflects the same development in the stock market. This parallelism suggests the possi-bility that *social mood trends are related to the frequency of human mood*

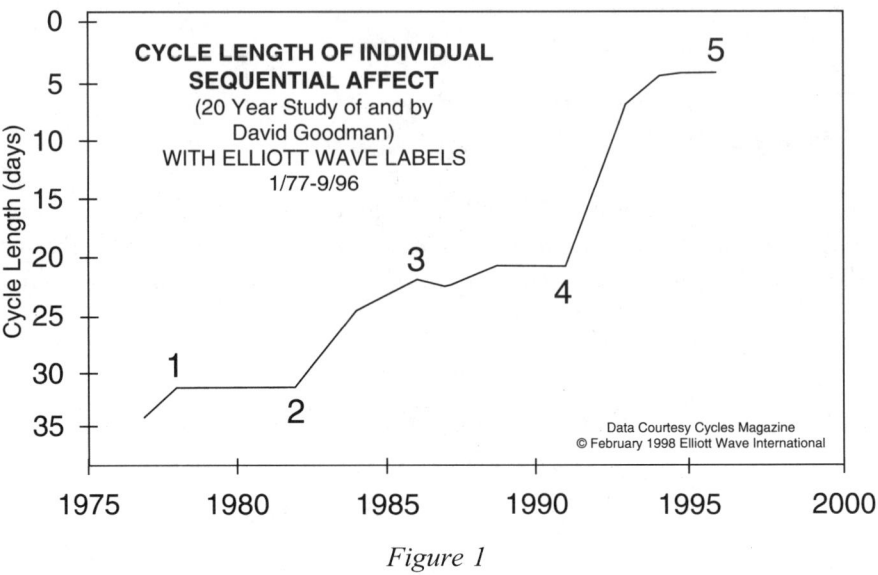

Figure 1

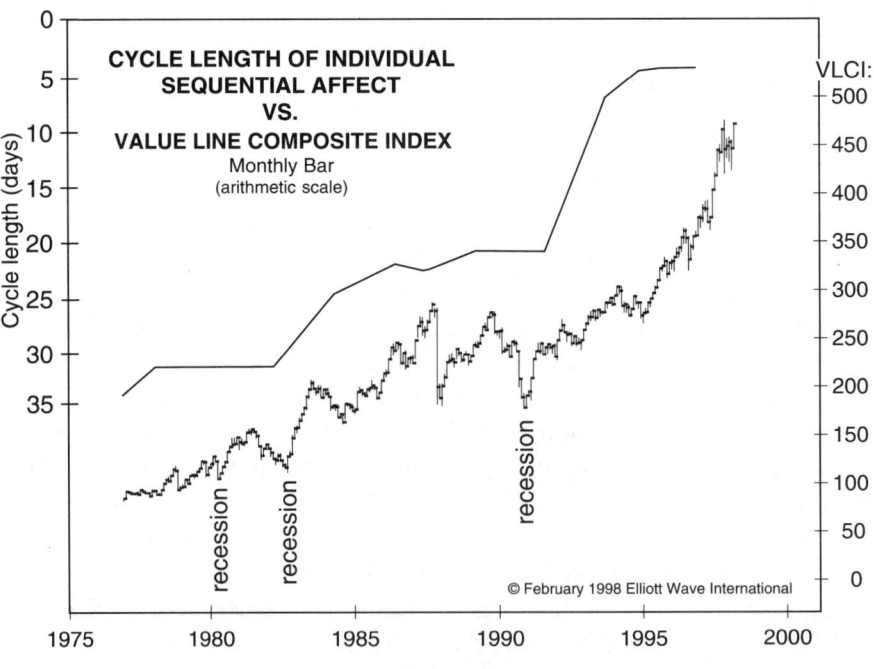

Figure 2

swing. Now observe that concurrently with the upward accelerations in stock prices, the length of Mr. Goodman's emotional cycle fell particularly swiftly after 1982 and again after 1991. These are precisely the times that recessions ended. We already know that the stock market bottoms as or before recessions end, indicating that social mood trends are the engine of aggregate rates of production. Now we might postulate that accelerating biorhythms support an increasingly active sociology that results (among other things) in production and a desire to buy stocks, while decelerating biorhythms bring on a sluggishness that results in retrenchment, conservatism and selling. An increase in the frequency of mood swings might explain why exercise becomes popular in bull markets and unpopular in bear markets. It might also be the reason behind a demonstrable increase in the personal performance of sports stars during bull markets, and vice versa, as revealed in "Basketball and the Bull Market" (1996). Perhaps the frequency of mood swings correlates with preferences for fast-tempo music in bull markets and slow-tempo music in bear markets. In sum, maybe frequency of mood change correlates with direction, which in turn drives the social events that we socionomists observe.

To say that this is conjecture is an understatement, but the potential value of proving such a possibility is so great that this avenue of inquiry should be explored. If a large sample of members of society were found to produce a similar graph, it would add weight to the possibility; if the changes continued along the same lines over several bull and bear cycles, it would become a probability. A proven correlation would add to the predictability of social mood trends and therefore of the timbre of historical events.

It is important to note that Hersey, the originator of the idea of emotional cycles, concluded that for the most part, biorhythms were regular at about a month. However, his studies mostly took place in the 1930s and 1940s, years of a Supercycle degree bear market. Goodman's study shows that cycle lengths can vary from one month to one day. In his experience, the one-month variety occurred near major bear market lows. That is the environment in which Hersey's studies were conducted.

Goodman also lists descriptive terms, based on work by Jung, Pao and Grof, that reflect what he perceives to be four stages of his emotional cycle, as follows:

(1) Calm, contented, friendly, at ease, inventive, imaginative, humorous.
(2) Energetic, happy, affectionate, enthusiastic, successful, influential, loving.
(3) Fatigued, sad, inhibited, fearful, imperiled, distressed, insecure.
(4) Tense, anxious, suspicious, angry, aggressive, hostile, antagonistic.

Read these terms carefully, and you will recognize the moods that *society* progressively projects in the four stages of a stock market cycle: uptrend, top, downtrend and bottom. Roughly speaking, at Cycle degree, the 1920s were (2); the early 1930s were (3); the late 1930s to mid-1940s were (4); the 1950s were (1); the early 1960s were (2); the late 1960s through 1970s were (3) and (4); the 1980s were (1); the 1990s have been (2). You can see that if the majority of investors felt progressively as above, they would buy and sell in such a way as to produce a bull and bear market.

To conclude, the frequency of *bio*rhythmic mood swings may determine the character of *socio*rhythmic moods. Since in most cases, each sociorhythmic cycle would begin from a higher base of retained production value, all that would be necessary for overall progress would be a repeating Elliott wave of biorhythmic frequency. The fractal nature of social mood change may in turn suggest that in the aggregate, biorhythms follow Elliott-wave patterns of frequency and duration, thus generating Elliott waves of human progress and regress.

The Elliott Wave Theorist
March 1998

A Socionomist Looks at Bankruptcies

A correspondent wants to know, "If things are so great in the U.S., why is the bankruptcy rate so high?" Indeed, for the year ended September 1997, there were 1.37 million personal bankruptcies, another new all-time high. It seems logical that bankruptcies would contract in booms and expand in recessions/depressions, doesn't it? Finance is often not so simple. This chart of annual bankruptcy filings from 1930 to 1997 reveals that a rising trend in petitions for relief from creditors is not reliable evidence of economic decline. To the contrary, despite a flurry of debtor-friendly alterations to the bankruptcy code in the 1930s, filings remained flat. Since 1942, bankruptcies have risen along roughly the same path as the stock market, producing an Elliott five-wave advance. Not shown is a similar

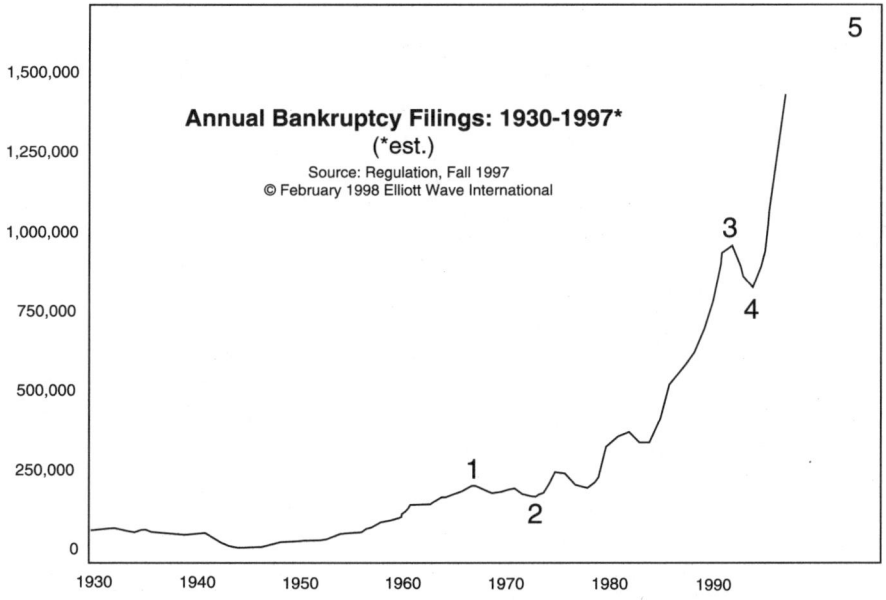

quadrupling in the number of bankruptcies during the booming 1920s. The numbers continued to edge higher to a peak in 1932, when the stock market bottomed, and finally receded in the late 1930s and early 1940s, when conservatism returned to finance.

In the late 1920s, a presidential commission searched for ways to toughen the bankruptcy code. Similarly, today Congress is debating ways to reverse the 1978 law that further loosened creditors' grip.

Why does the trend of bankruptcies go mostly counter to what seems logical? The answer is that bankruptcy rates are a function of lending quality, and lenders are more active when they are more confident, which is in uptrends. Today's record-high bankruptcies reflect lenders' record-high willingness to lend more money to less qualified borrowers, which is a symptom of good times, not bad times. So to answer our subscriber's question, the bankruptcy rate is high *because* things are great. They will stay high through the coming bear market and depression and then recede.

Technically Speaking
(the newsletter of the Market Technicians Association)
June 2000

Seminar Speaker Summary

by Mike Carr

Keynote Address, May 18, 2000

Robert Prechter, CMT, of Elliott Wave International, in a rare public speaking appearance, delivered the keynote address after the Friday evening meal. The topic was "The Wave Principle and the Socionomic Perspective." In it, Prechter promised to provide an answer to what effect the Department of Justice antitrust action against Microsoft will have on the overall market.

First, he shared an insight into the Elliott Wave Principle that idealized wave progressions are contained within a channel. Prechter noticed that if the lower channel line is broken, then the fifth wave should be expected to break the upper channel line. This leads him to believe that we are in the final stages of an extended Wave V, completing the formation that began at the 1932 bottom.

Other technical indicators support his interpretation of the wave structure. He has found that sentiment extremes correlate to waves' peaks and troughs. Using the DJIA dividend yield, sentiment is at a record peak, implying that we are near a Supercycle peak in the market. Wave V is not expected to show the same technical strength as Wave III, and the weakening advance/decline line, which peaked in Wave III, supports this idea.

Economic and financial fundamentals are also expected to be weaker in Wave V. Key economic measures, such as real GDP, industrial production, capacity utilization and unemployment are all, on average, weaker in the current wave than they were in Wave III (1942 to 1966). Financial fundamentals include measures of household liquidity, debt in various sectors of the economy, the prime rate and the current account surplus or deficit. All of these measures are also weaker, on average, in the current wave.

Prechter believes that technicals produce fundamentals, and it is well known that the stock market is a leading indicator of the economy. In fact, eleven of the last twelve recessions occurred after stock market tops. It is the social mood, in Prechter's theory, that is reflected in Elliott waves. It is the social mood of the society that governs the economy.

If this is true, then wars should be expected to result when the social mood is angry. In fact, the major wars our country has fought, from the Revolutionary War through World War II, occurred during or immediately after the completion of C waves, when conditions and the social mood were at their worst.

His work, and the work of academics, finds no correlation between the demographics of 40-year-old "spenders" and the stock market, the commonly touted explanation for the strength of this bull market. However, Prechter does find another correlation between demographics and the market. He sees the decision to conceive as a reflection of positive mood. Shifting the birth rate back one year to reflect the timing of conceptions, he is able to correlate demographics to the stock market. This approach reflects the bottoms in 1932 and 1974. The more popular approach of shifting the birth rate forward by 40 years or more to account for the retirement savings of the Baby Boomers fails to explain these bottoms.

Returning to his original question, Prechter explained that the actual question should be, "What is the social mood of the nation when the government takes antitrust action against the most successful companies?" He has found that this type of action is taken at major peaks, while bailouts occur at bottoms. These peaks correspond to both the social mood and the stock market.

In summary, Prechter concluded that the mood of the market is the real fundamental and that mood is reflected in the charts we study. The Elliott Wave Principle provides an insight into the pattern and progression of the social mood.

Prechter

Private communication
in response to an academic paper
1999

Challenging Another Myth of Market Rationality

I enjoyed your 1999 paper and hope that it triumphs in influence over the [competing] piece. I have one dissenting point. Theory and empirics must agree. If they do not, then one of them is wrong.

The Efficient Market Hypothesis and its reliance on "market rationality" is in the process of destruction. Your work is helping that process along, but your model nevertheless maintains a relic, a key pillar of the argument for randomness, which is market rationality. You propose that when a bubble accelerates, buyers are rationally requesting an increasingly larger return — in terms of capital gain — for the increasing risk of a crash. This idea applies the laws of economics to those of finance. It initially sounds reasonable, being akin to the practice of paying higher fees to stuntmen for riskier movie stunts, which is rational economic behavior. There are several problems with this theory.

First, both the actual and potential return to investors accelerate downward during an accelerating market advance. The actual return via dividends falls as fast as stock prices rise, so the risk of stock ownership is decreasingly compensated in those terms, which are the most reliable terms available. As for potential capital gain, with every tick upward in stock prices, the chances for a higher return diminish in terms of the probability that the price rise will continue. The faster the market's rise, the sooner the inevitable reversal. A truly rational investor would take such factors into account. Buyers in a fast-rising overvalued market either must know that they will be ruined sooner or later, in which case their buying is irrational, or they ignore or are unaware of the fact. Either way, it is like agreeing to play Russian Roulette for more and more money until you shoot yourself dead. This is not economic *or* rational behavior. It is *financial* behavior, which differs by being impulsive.

The empirical problem with your theory is the fact that investors do not report the mindset required by the theory but in fact precisely the *inverse* of it. Statistics on market psychology show a consistent correlation between price rise and complacency. Investors' concern about a market crash *decrease* as prices rise. Poll after poll proves this point. At major market tops, fears of decline are virtually non-existent. Your theory and empirics, then, are at complete odds. Stuntmen will tell you that they charged a higher fee due to higher risk. Investors say the opposite. They perceive less risk and therefore buy with impunity, which is the very reason that prices rise so rapidly. So the theory that an upwardly accelerating market is a rational economic response to buyers' perception of increased risk does not describe new buyers' actual motivation. If what investors actually think does not support what they are expected to think according to the rationality theory, then there must be problems with the theory.

Parabolic-rise-and-crash structures in financial market behavior challenge the idea of rationality. Reason does not lead to these types of patterns. What you are observing is a pattern of paleomentational impulsivity. While such thinking has a rational purpose (survival), it is not based upon reason. The proof is that it leads to failure, and the reason is that the impulse is misapplied by the unconscious mind to finance. The market punishes people for their impulsivity and rewards people for true rationality, which applies only when they understand the market's psychological dynamics.

Then why do markets rise exponentially and then crash? Bubbles accelerate not because people fear a crash *more* but because they fear one increasingly *less* as the market rises. Markets crash not because people think it will do so but because they become *certain that it will not*. When that conviction reaches a critical point (at the end of an Elliott wave) and cannot expand further, the market stops going up. People are out of money and out of room to expand their bullish conviction. As social mood changes and disappointment in the lack of further price rise spreads, a bear market develops.

Your scientific observations are important, but the proposed explanation for them is untenable. Dumping the rationality argument and adopting the unconscious impulsivity argument will strengthen the theoretical foundation of the very real phenomena that you are observing.

Prechter

March 1999

Why Teenagers Lead Fads of Social Expression

Why do teenagers participate so widely and passionately in fads of self-expression? Do they herd less discriminately than adults? Apparently, they do rely more than adults on the primitive portions of the brain, which house the herding impulse. Here is a discussion from the transcript of an ABC News report on the subject of teen vs. adult brain activity:[1]

Are teens really that different from adults? Well, yes, say researchers here at Harvard Medical School's Brain Imaging Center. Here, they put teenagers, and then people my age, into the MRI so they can watch how our brains work. The doctor in charge, Deborah Yurgelun-Todd, says when I and other adults answer questions, we use the rational, thinking part of our brain, the "dorsal lateral prefrontal cortex," and the teenagers use a different part. [DYT]: "Kids use the region behind here called the amygdala." That's the instinctual part of their brain. This may explain their creativity. Some of our better creative work occurs during this time of life because there's not that sense of "I shouldn't do this or I can't do this."

Harvard researchers say that not only are teens more likely to use a part of the brain that may allow for more creativity, they're also less likely to use the part that does critical thinking, that helps people make mature judgments. Teens use the "gut reaction" part of the brain. They're using the more emotional, automatic parts; we smarter adults use our critical thinking. [DYT]: "That's exactly right. You activated more up in this region, and the boys that we saw today activated more down in this region."

NOTES

[1] Stossel, John. (1999, March.) "Teenagers." *20/20*, ABC Network.

Response to a Question from a Renowned Scientist

Question: *What is the essence of your argument that outside causes do not affect the stock market?*

Answer: There are two main arguments for why mood dictates the character of events, not vice versa.

First, if the Wave Principle is true, then the market is hierarchically patterned. The only way to maintain the presumption that outside events move market prices would be to assert that those outside events are perfectly patterned to produce the Wave Principle. This appears to be an untenable position.

Second, whether the Wave Principle is true or not, if you pay attention, you can see that events lag stock market trends. I can always point to the social results of a rise or decline, but economic historians often cannot locate or agree upon the presumed causes of a market move even decades after it occurs. Distinguished attendees at a recent international economic summit admitted that armed retrospectively with the data and the news of 1928-1930, they cannot determine reasons justifying the market's historic crash. (Economist Hernan Cortes wrote a paper on this topic.) On the other hand, you can see its result in the Great Depression without difficulty. Once you understand that a crashing social mood has consequences, understanding the result is easy.

Finally, there is a more subtle and perhaps less compelling point but also valid whether the Wave Principle is true or not: The market is a fractal with a specific dimension, which means that its roughness is about the same at all scales. Even if one were to accept only this fact, it really weakens the "outside causes" argument because one would have to take the position that those outside causes of the market's changes are also a fractal with the same specific fractal dimension! This stance would render useless virtually all economic commentary. The entire cadre of economists who think that the Fed (an "outside cause" in their view) has the market under control would have to close up shop. If the Fed were smoothly controlling the economy, then the market would not be a fractal. The same would be true of every presumed outside force that they would cite. If all forces together are an indefinite fractal, then what's the point in discussing them or forecasting anything? Outside-causality advocates who have integrity would be resigned to mumble, "The market will fluctuate" and leave it at that.

Letter to a Curious Objectivist

Objectivists should definitely be open to the Wave Principle and socio-nomics, which are observations about the workings of mass psychology, as follows:

(1) The desire among many, if not most, individuals to belong to and be accepted by the group, as well as their penchant for second-handedness in epistemology, make their unconscious minds dominate their conscious minds in emotionally charged social settings.

(2) When the unconscious mind dominates, it does not do so randomly (as that would mean no thought at all) but in patterns peculiar to it.

(3) The behavior that results is so repetitive that it is observable as displaying patterns.

(4) Once you perceive patterns of social behavior and understand how they typically develop, you have an objective basis for occasional speculation about probabilities for future courses of social behavior.

(5) The mechanics of the patterns appear to reflect mathematical characteristics of a family of patterns found throughout nature. This fact that gives rise to some speculation about why they might exist and how, biologically and evolutionarily speaking, they arose.

Chronologically, #3 above came first, as it was empirics that got the train of thought going. The Wave Principle *began* with percepts and can be *reduced* to percepts. At bottom, I can point and say, "*Look.*"

Think of a mob in the square listening to a Hitler speech. If the points above make sense to you in that context, then you can see that it makes sense with respect to other highly emotional socially shared experiences such as auctions, which are hotbeds of crowd psychological forces. The stock market is an auction for substantially intangible goods whose attractiveness to general participants increases as prices *rise*. This is a crucial point that makes economic supply/demand/price formulas inapplicable to market analysis, thereby segregating the disciplines of economics and finance.

If you can live with the above five points, then you should have no problem philosophically with the Wave Principle. The only potential problem would be scientific, i.e., whether you could investigate the evidence enough to verify, reject, or dub insufficient the data that suggests that there are patterns in investment behavior.

I believe that socionomics will become the first true social *science*, as opposed to armchair deliberating and theorizing about sociological forces, usually based on whimsy. My arguments are a challenge to the majority of professionals' false premises in this field, so many of them do not wish to investigate them, probably because they don't feel any need to spend mental energy on a challenge to ideas that appear to them as obvious. No negative response is likely to be formidable to me, though, so if you are convinced that a good point in opposition has been scored, I would respond to it. I get far more communication from people who are ecstatic and say they have suspected much of what I contend about markets because their experiences have contradicted what people told them should happen. Objectivists should embrace this new science, as some already have, quite fervently.

One problem that people might rightfully encounter is that, as I mentioned, my books to date are mostly a practical application of what I know, not an exposition of it. Unfortunately, there is no *Atlas* on the Wave Principle, so I cannot point you to a source with that scope or level of integrity. There will not be one until I write it, which will be in my 50s, ten years from now.

If my commentary on socionomic causality does not appear perfectly logical to you despite the sometimes-resulting seeming paradox, then I would certainly want to hear about it. Objectivism contains or implies many seeming paradoxes, as deep truths do. For instance: The worst way to help the poor is to give them something.... If you are truly selfish, you should be kind and benevolent.... The virtue of honesty is contextual.... "Thou shalt not kill" is not a call to virtue.... A society of independent people would be the most harmonious one.... To achieve happiness, you must be disciplined enough to postpone fun and pleasure.... Faith and hope are destructive. People who come across these ideas piecemeal assume you are crazy, and dismiss them. They must "get it" in the broad sense before they can get it in the particulars. They must care enough about the particular *realm* of ideas to bother to do so, which is true of my field as well.

P.S. I am disturbed to see that some Objectivists (two that I know of) are arguing for a "gold standard," which is like arguing in favor of Toyotas. In other words, it is properly a technical preference, not a philosophical one. The philosophical point would be to favor free-market money. What's worse, those saying that the government should adopt a gold standard are in effect arguing that the state should manufacture Toyotas. In such a case you would end up with no real Toyotas (in terms of the quality we originally admired), which is, after time, exactly what you get when a state adopts a gold or silver standard: no standard backed temporarily by a misleading title. Recall what the English "pound" originally meant and how the dollar was originally defined.

Prechter

Contrasting Three Styles of Financial Analysis

In 1983, Jim Grant left *Barron's* to start his own publication, *Grant's Interest Rate Observer*. It also happens that 1983 was the year that subscriptions to *Barron's* peaked, immediately beginning a substantial decline. Now I submit that this fact is highly relevant. But in exactly what way is a question about which there is some debate. Let's look at it as a fundamental analyst, a technical analyst and an Elliott-wave analyst would.

A fundamental analyst would conclude quite logically that the exit of Mr. Grant from the staff of *Barron's* caused such disappointment among *Barron's* readers that thousands of them jumped ship. The numbers in fact show that *Barron's* subscriptions peaked at 299,000 the last year Jim was there and subsequently dropped to 245,000. Armed with these statistics, it would then be obvious to the fundamentalist that *Grant's Interest Rate Observer* has... 54,000 subscribers. Finally, the fundamentalist would point out, with annual subscriptions costing $495, Jim Grant is hauling in $26,730,000 per year.

Now let's look at it from the standpoint of technical analysis. The technical analyst of course also notices that *Barron's* subscriptions peaked when Jim left the magazine, but the technician understands the fact that markets move ahead of fundamental events. His reasoning is that markets discount the future. So, the technician might wonder, were all those subscriptions to *Barron's* pouring in during 1983 on the *anticipation* that Jim would soon be leaving? If so, the conclusion with regard to the current number of subscribers to *Grant's Interest Rate Observer*, and Jim's gross receipts, would be quite different. That does leave a question as to where *Barron's'* 54,000 subscribers went, but undoubtedly they would conclude, it has something to do with hedge funds, derivatives or program trading.

The Elliott wave analyst sees it much more simply: It was time for a change. Jim ended one pattern in his life and started another, right when he should have.

Still, if Jim didn't inherit those missing 54,000 subscribers, why does he toil late into the night week after week to bring us the wit and wisdom for which he is so widely and justly famous? Is it because he has a great message to deliver? Certainly he does. Is it because he's fascinated with markets and history and people? No question about it. However, the central reason I believe, is expressed by a quote from the author Kingsley Amis, who said, "If you can't annoy somebody, there is little point in writing."

Which brings me to the question of why people read *Grant's Interest Rate Observer*. I think the answer lies in another insightful quote, this time from Claude Cockburn, who said, "Never believe anything until it has been officially denied." Jim Grant has that healthy sense of skepticism, that gimlet eye of cold observation, that penchant for questioning the comfortably obvious that makes his articles "must reading." And now, as I am sure we will discover, he is "must listening," too. Will you please welcome our next guest speaker, James Grant.

Miscellaneous Observations

(1988) One of the oldest adages on Wall Street is "use stops." That's great as far as it goes, but the obvious question is, "which ones?" As pointed out numerous times, the Wave Principle is one of the few approaches to market analysis that provides a method for establishing stops objectively. Fundamental approaches use no stops. If you turned bearish in 1982 because the trade deficit was rising, you had no mechanism to force you to change your mind, and presumably stayed short until you were wiped out.

(1992) At the peaks of expansions, most people feel a stronger kinship with animals and trees. The environmental, or ecology, movement, when expressed in terms such as, "let's work together to clean up the environment," is a manifestation of the last stage of the trend toward inclusion. At bottoms of major economic contractions, people care less about the environment and more about survival.

(1998) I would argue against the widespread notion among economists that "wars create jobs." War jobs cost tax money, and the money has to come from the destruction of other jobs. (See *Economics In One Lesson* by Henry Hazlitt.) The latter jobs produced goods and services that the market wanted; war jobs don't. Moreover, war jobs ultimately result in the mass destruction of capital and therefore of the means to create jobs. So on two fronts, the net result is that wars destroy jobs.

(1999) The bull market of the 1950s and 1960s had essentially the same political progression as that of the 1980s and 1990s: from conservative (Eisenhower/Reagan) to moderate (Kennedy/Bush) to liberal (Johnson/Clinton), followed by a big-spending conservative after the top (Nixon/G.W. Bush). In the 1920s, the progression was going in the same direction, but the early timing of the peak curtailed the outcome. It merely went from conservative (Coolidge) to moderate (Hoover). A liberal (Roosevelt) came next anyway, though, because a Democrat had to replace the Republican who rode the crash all the way down. We might postulate that during fairly persistent rising trends, people tend to elect conservatives early on, when they are feeling doubtful; then, as they feel more confident, they elect moderates; when they feel downright expansive, they tend to elect liberals.

(2000) I think there is an important difference between the gambling impulse and the impulse to speculate. The former is a drive to get lucky, to be showered with unearned gain. The latter is a drive to prove you are smarter than everyone else. It's very powerful. Some games — such as poker — involve a combination of both.

(2002) John Stuart Mill asserted, "Panics do not destroy capital; they merely reveal the extent to which it has been previously destroyed." This is close to the truth. Panics do destroy capital, but the *setup* for the destruction occurs beforehand. Dynamite likewise destroys a building, but earlier, someone has to collect the gunpowder, build the stick and light the fuse. Forces accompanying the social mood uptrend *preceding* a panic carry out the equivalent of those activities.

SPI Report (Australia), Issue #667
July 31, 2002

A Craftsman's View

by Adrian Pitt

Even after 20 years of following this market, it never ceases to amaze me just how incredible the Elliott Wave Principle is. These days I get to the point of just casual application as if it's just taken for granted. Not because I apply counts slapdash, but because I've been doing it for so long that much of it just stares right back at me without a lot of thought. There are many occasions, mind you, when deep thought and analysis is required to make sure the most accurate count possible is used, but when you sit back and just look at the wiggles that have occurred since the September 2001 low and how every wave has been perfectly accounted for by the correct wave structure, and market action following the completion of each little pattern has moved exactly as it should have, I don't think anyone can be anything but amazed. I know I am! I can guarantee, there isn't another method that comes close to forecasting moves into the future in time and price, on all levels, whether it be economic or technical.

Technically Speaking
(the newsletter of the Market Technicians Association)
February 2000

Book Review: *The Wave Principle of Human Social Behavior and the New Science of Socionomics*

by Roman Franko

Robert Prechter's new book is unquestionably a ground-breaking work in the development of technical analysis. Its purpose stated at the outset is "to establish the idea that in humans, an unconscious herding impulse impels social mood trends and changes that are specifically patterned according to a natural growth principle and which in turn is the engine of cultural expression and social action." In other words, the book aims to establish that the Wave Principle that flows naturally out of human behavior is the primary cause of social, historical, cultural and economic changes, including market fluctuations.

These audacious arguments can only be described as stunning and revolutionary in intent and scope. They speak broadly for the study of all human efforts and specifically for the place of technical analysis in the study of financial markets. Today, technical analysis is often viewed as a secondary or supplementary form of market analysis. It is supposedly dependent on the study and interpretation of underlying factors that can be accessed only by so-called "fundamental analysis." Prechter explicitly aims to reverse this causal relationship by arguing that the so-called fundamental factors and events are ultimately dependent on the working of the Wave Principle as manifested in social mood and then the financial markets. In short, the form of technical analysis founded on the Wave Principle studies the causal or independent variables while the misleadingly named fundamental analysis studies the dependent financial factors.

The first of the five sections of the book introduces the idea of the Wave Principle. Even here, Prechter goes beyond merely summarizing ground previously covered in his (and Jack Frost's) 1978 *Elliott Wave*

Principle — the five-wave impulse or "motive" and three-wave corrective patterns uncovered by Elliott, as well as the Fibonacci or phi-based (.618... etc.) mathematical relationships underlying these patterns. Rather, the emphasis is on showing how these patterns and relationships are evidence of recurring forms called robust fractals. This form of fractal lies between self-identical and indefinite ones that are similarly irregular at all scales. Robust fractals, which replicate forms within a certain latitude in a branching-like manner, are found not only in the stock market as 5-3 wave patterns but are also being found throughout nature by researchers such as Benoit Mandelbrot. Further, researchers are uncovering that Fibonacci mathematics regulate all fractal branching systems, including the branching characteristics of DLA (not DNA) clusters. "In its broadest sense, then, the Wave Principle communicates the seemingly outrageous idea that the same law that shapes living creatures and galaxies is inherent in the mentation (thinking emanating from both the rational and pre-rational or limbic systems) and activities of men en masse."

Before going on to elaborate upon this claim, Prechter devotes the second part of the book to validating the Wave Principle. First, he demonstrates through the use of rules and modeling that consistency of interpretation under that Principle is possible. He then goes on to review a series of major and astonishingly accurate historical forecasts made by Elliott, Bolton, Collins, and himself between 1941 and 1983 to demonstrate that the Principle is a valid approach to forecasting market behavior. While admitting that these leading Elliotticians have made errors from time to time, he is quite correct in stating that there simply is no other approach to market forecasting which provides a methodological basis or more precisely a rule-based model for such predictions, particularly more than one swing ahead.

The third section is a ground-breaking argument that the Wave Principle is based on biological, psychological and sociological factors. Other technical analysts have previously attempted to explain why, for example, overhanging supply can turn into resistance as money-losing investors begin to sell when a stock rallies back to their buy levels. Prechter, however, attempts to take the analysis of investor behavior to much deeper and causal levels. He provides an explanation of why market participants would collectively act so as to create such overhanging resistance.

His basic thesis is that "the prime mover of aggregate stock market prices is mass emotional change, which itself must be, and demonstrably is, independent of outside influence." While most readers would probably be comfortable with the first half of that thesis, the notion that mass emotional change must be independent of outside influence will undoubtedly elicit more controversy.

To support this thesis, Prechter has assembled and linked together an amazing array of arguments and evidence that will be boiled down to three principal ones. The first step is a discussion of how the limbic part of the human brain that gives rise to emotional responses kicks in quicker than the cerebral cortex that generates rational thought. He then reviews psychological studies that argue that people, including investors, are driven by the interaction of their goal of self-preservation with the emotion-driven limbic system to participate in unconscious herding behavior. "When a herd 'thinks,' the result is not reason but an emotional interpersonal superorganic dynamic that must be the source of waves." Prechter buttresses this idea of unconscious herding behavior with several other processes, all of which help explain investor behavior. The idea of mental contagion, which explains how fads like the slinky, jacks and Pokemon propagate from brain to brain, suggests that individuals in herding mode depend upon the thoughts and actions of others. Feedback mechanisms operate so that investors' decisions make the Dow move in a certain direction and this direction then influences other investors' decisions and so on.

The second step in the argument is that this unconscious herding impulse produces a robust fractal pattern of social interaction. After reviewing robust fractals found in the human body, he concludes "the brain may be disposed to participating in a fractal of collective sentiment because circumstantially it, along with the rest of the human body's structures and function, is of and for fractals in so many ways."

A third step is to provide evidence that unconscious herding is expressed in a Fibonacci form because numerous studies show that individuals' decision making is predisposed to a 62/38 inclination and in the absence of clear parameters tends to default to phi. These far-reaching hypotheses are a testament to Prechter's unequaled ability to weave together emerging evidence into a stunning new model.

The fourth part of the book provides an introduction to 'socionomics.' As Prechter estimates, it will take another ten years to construct a full theory of the components, processes and structure of social mood. He categorizes this initial exposition as observational summaries but not yet a fully-fledged hypothesis. Some might take issue with some of the components of social mood and the cultural trends that he identifies as manifestations of social mood trends. His argument that historical events and economic trends result from social mood trends is certainly thought provoking. As a political scientist by training, I was more than partially persuaded by his argument that "the social psychology that accompanies a bull or bear market is the main determinant not only of how voters select a president but also of how they perceive his performance."

Nonetheless, many readers including myself, will have problems, at least at this early pre-hypothesis, with his flat-out assertion that "Elliott waves, like them or not, are the first cause of history." To his credit, Prechter takes his argument to the logical limit: "As opposed to the traditional mechanistic models of aggregate behavior that are based upon presumptions of multiple exogenous [external] causes and ultimate effects, socionomics recognizes that patterns of aggregate human behavior are endogenous [internally-generated], self-causing, self-regulating, self-reinforcing and, to a far greater degree than has heretofore been imagined, predictable."

Given this perspective, it is not surprising that Prechter spends a good deal of the fifth and final part of his book refuting conventional approaches to financial markets. Even if many technical analysts are not prepared to agree that the Wave Principle is the primary cause of all events, they ought to be able to enjoy his dissection and disproving of the efficient market hypothesis, the presumption that the Federal Reserve Board is able to propel or rein in economic growth through the manipulation of interest rates, and other common chestnuts.

Readers of this review must understand that this is but a cursory exposition of some of Prechter's main hypothesis and observations. This review deliberately avoids most of the new terminology and concepts that Prechter is developing to describe these ideas for it is well nigh impossible to explain even some of them adequately in a relatively short review. It also must be said that some of the evidence, while suggestive, is insufficient to be persuasive and that as Prechter readily admits, much more work will have to be done to flesh out the arguments.

Are Prechter's claims for a new science of socionomics implausible or at least premature? It is certainly not implausible for this reviewer, who has personally witnessed two leading Canadian politics departments both change their names, from political economy in one case and political studies in the other, to political science. These changes were effected to reflect a growing use of quantitative methods but with methods still far short of scientific methods employed in the physical sciences. They were also a reminder of the goal of many of its practitioners to ultimately create a fully-fledged science of politics. As Prechter accurately observes in his introductory comments, "The social sciences today are where the physical sciences were three hundred years ago." However, this has not stopped the social sciences from appropriating the term scientific and it can be very plausibly argued that they are no more so than technical analysis.

For technical analysis to advance at an accelerated rate toward the status of a science, all serious technical analysts ought to first read this book with open minds. Many may object to Prechter's assertion that "the Wave Principle is to sociology and related sciences what Newton's laws were to physics," but there simply are no other approaches to technical analysis that have a basis for even making such a claim. For that matter, this reviewer, after reviewing his not inconsiderable library of key political science books, is unable to find any that are as sweepingly important and have the same potential to bring about a paradigm shift in the study of social events as the book under review.

It must be said that an objective discussion of the merits of these arguments would certainly be enhanced if Prechter, who is so intimately associated with the Elliott Wave approach, would in turn keep an open mind on the markets and reconsider his multi-year belief that the markets are at 'the crest of the tidal wave.' In this book, he applies traditional tools in a questionable manner (see for example the unconventional placement of channel lines on the chart of the DJIA on page 329) [Note: They are conventional for Elliott waves. — Ed.] to continue to advance this argument. Despite good calls in his career, Prechter's bearish outlook on U.S. stocks in the 1990s has generated so much criticism so as to undermine not only his very real and seminal contributions to technical analysis but also allow detractors to dismiss the validity and utility of the Wave Principle altogether.

Having read this book, technical analysts ought to give thoughtful consideration to his hypotheses and realize that it is in our collective self-interest to contribute to their further development. One way to do this is to channel any relevant evidence to Prechter's organization (care of comments @socionomics.org) that contributes to the further elaboration of these arguments. Another way is to critically analyze these hypotheses and supporting evidence at each and every annual conference of IFTA, MTA, CSTA and other national association meetings. The preferred method would be that used by social and natural scientists at their annual nationwide conferences, with a main presentation followed by responses by two discussants. The more these hypotheses are developed and the more persuasive they become, the more technical analysis will be able to assume a rightful position of equality with mainline fundamental analysis.

Let the debate begin, and let it be a constructive one for the advancement of technical analysis!

Roman Franko obtained a Ph.D. in Canadian and Comparative Politics from Queen's University in Kingston, Canada where he taught for several years. He then worked for the Canadian federal government as a policy analyst before moving on to pursue his passion for technical analysis.

2002

A New Paradigm

by Hernán Cortés Douglas

One might ask, 60 years after Elliott and with much data and experience, "Why are there no signs of economists' recognition of the Wave Principle?" The answer is that it is a totally different paradigm. Economics is still in love with the Newtonian physics paradigm, primarily the ideas that the same cause always generates the same effect, and if you know the parts, then you understand the whole.

Elliott is like modern physics. You do not need to understand the parts to understand the whole. Content is not important; form is important. If an alien being 3000 years from now asks what cathedrals were for, he will not get the right answer if he examines the composition of bricks or the coffins of bishops in the cellar. He will need to look at form; therein lies the path to the answer. This approach is alien to economists. They have become enamored with the mathematics and the mechanical causality of Newtonian physics, which are irrelevant to markets and business cycles.

Private correspondence
2002

Why Socionomics Will Be a Tough Sell to the Entrenched Majority of Professionals

by Valeri S. Safonov, PhD

While reading *The Wave Principle of Human Social Behavior*, I realized many times that it was a kind of "this-is-it" stuff. After studying the whole field in terms of what else was available, which distracted my efforts for years to other fields of market analysis, I see quite clearly that, though the Wave Principle is not perfect, it is nothing but the best available alternative to any other theory of market behavior.

Thank God that the Wave Principle is not a religion. Of course, the Wave Principle should be convincing not only to those who blindly accept it but also to sincere skeptics (as opposed to the hostile opposition, which will never be converted for any reason). Friendly seekers should have every opportunity to see that the Wave Principle is based on scientific, consistent and independently verifiable ground. Of course, there is still some work to do to reach this objective. One wonders, though, whether socionomics will even have a chance to succeed. I think it may present too powerful a challenge to the academic and professional status quo.

I would like to answer your question, "Why does the conventional approach remain so entrenched?" (p.385). One of the related questions worth attention is why the Wave Principle so quickly breaks people into "love-it" followers and "hate-it" opposition. I think that both the limbic system and the neocortex are responsible for this result, which clearly shows in the "conventional entrenchment" phenomenon. In general, I see a rather gloomy prospective for the Wave Principle to be appreciated *comme il faut* in the near future, while socionomics does not seem to stand any chance at all.

To explain why, I will not stop at the fact that people do not accept easily any unpleasant truths about themselves. Quite evidently, it is humiliating for a Homo Sapiens — the King of Nature — who has reached the top place in the spiral of evolution, to see himself as a part of a stone-age herd acting impulsively rather than intelligently.

But here is the real problem: You showed with sometimes scary clarity not only that nothing else can be compared to the Wave Principle in its predictive power but also that the whole army of conventional economists, politicians and many others, who pretend that they control the waves, do not deserve their salaries. The Wave Principle makes users of the conventional approach feel that they are not only stupid but also insecure, which is something much, much worse.

In the Statement of Value (p.6), you urge "economists and sociologists" to consider the material of your book seriously. How could they? That would mean one thing for sure: After accepting the thesis of your book, conventional social science would be ashamed of itself. What are they all paid for, and why were they getting Nobel prizes in economics? Mr. Greenspan, what the hell you are doing with taxpayers' money? When are the World Bank and the IMF, with their thousands of employees, going to stop wasting international funds? Sociologists measuring public opinion, trash your assumptions and use this new one!

Those potentially under siege by socionomics must perceive by their limbic systems that it is a clear and present danger to their very existence. Socionomics stands tall against the bulk of the educated world, which keeps on learning conventional ways of seeing things. (Those academics who die of natural causes are immediately replaced by their students.) The same thing goes for political planners and national leaders, who are so erroneously sure of their effectiveness. Socionomics would ruin their professional careers, destroy otherwise impeccable images, establish them as worthless. After what you have done to herds of economists, politicians, central bankers, etc., one should not expect them to worship socionomics. They would prefer stubbornly to express their good-for-nothing "expert views" on television and in newspapers in order to keep playing leading roles in new "tragicomedies of never ending wrongness."

Right now, the *status quo* is closely guarded by all sorts of unconsciously working Freudian defensive mechanisms. No one could ever show that economics or related sciences can take over brilliantly where the Wave Principle or socionomics fails to yield satisfactory results, but no ones cares to admit that inability. The illusionary conventional world is convenient and almost risk-free because "market experts" and "social scientists," unlike traders, are never in immediate financial danger if they are wrong. Thus, it is very smart of the neocortexes of those people to work to prevent their illusionary world from the destruction that you hopelessly call for. Although I like how well you formulated two fundamental principles of success (both "living in harmony" with trends and yet "acting independently" at crucial turning points), for most people, independent thought — much less an actual reversal of opinion — is anathema.

It will probably take generations to replace, in an evolutionary way, the old-guard mentality of conventional minds. Eventually, perhaps Nobel Prize winners will be Elliotticians. The primary hope for a faster evolution is to establish proper university courses on socionomics, with students becoming bachelors, masters and Ph.Ds in this science. In this regard, I have a dream: to establish something like an Institute of Socionomic Research (ISR) in Russia or Latvia. I have just begun to discuss the idea with my friends and colleagues. I, for one, love this theory, and I am eager to learn more of what I am really in love with.

On the Outlook for Socionomics

In discussing the socionomic hypothesis with intellectuals and professionals, I find that some people are receptive — if not passionate — about it once they examine the idea and study a few examples. The main reason why people in general are not initially attracted to the idea is that they presume that outside event causality — a staple of physics — applies to social mood, which it does not. Some economists reject the idea because they do not care to abandon the illusion that their policies can manage macroeconomic trends (an illusion that is easy to hold in uptrends yet which leads to disorientation and panic in downtrends). Hurdles such as these notwithstanding, truth triumphs in the end.

On the way to that triumph, socionomics will not so much ruin old careers as it will make new careers, ones that are valuable, useful and fascinating to pursue. Until 20 years ago, science either ignored the stock market or developed and defended erroneous hypotheses to model it. In the past two decades, it has mostly made progress in re-hashing some of the simpler market observations that practitioners of technical analysis have been making for decades. The exceptions are the fields of fractal geometry, in which the roughness of markets has been measured, and behavioral finance, in which psychology is finally being taken into account. What has been missing until now is a unifying force. I believe that the Wave Principle and the resulting science of socionomics constitute that unifying force.

As for how long it will take for academia to embrace socionomics, Arthur Schopenhauer made this observation:

> "*All truth passes through three stages. First, it is ridiculed. Second, it is violently opposed. Third, it is accepted as being self-evident.*"

I agree with most of that statement, although as Schopenhauer said at another time, radically new ideas are first primarily *ignored*. Ridicule is only one mechanism — employed when a response is unavoidable — that keeps discussion at bay.

The Wave Principle has suffered through the first stage for seven decades. Its recent introduction to the academic world and the inauguration of the Socionomics Institute (www.socionomics.org) should create enough visibility to assure that the second stage — violent opposition — is nigh. Yet I trust that any thinking person who reads this book and its predecessor cover to cover will become thoroughly ensconced in the third stage. We will win eventually, one open mind at a time.

Appendix:

TOWARD QUANTIFYING SOCIOMETERS OTHER THAN THE STOCK MARKET

This section is relegated to an appendix because the studies presented here were developed without benefit of the socionomic insight. They have some value to socionomics nevertheless, which is why they are included.

Quantifying Social Mood in Popular Song Lyrics

My 1985 study, "Popular Culture and the Stock Market," made this observation:

> Although the stock market would probably remain the single best indicator because of its reliably precise measurement of mood and mood change, other social phenomena *could* be detailed, numericized and studied, and used to forecast social events and even changes in mood trends themselves when extremes are achieved. If reliable data on social activities other than stock valuation were available, we could undoubtedly graph and interpret them with a similar degree of reliability. The main difficulty in assessing indicators of mood other than stock prices is the woeful lack of precise numerical data produced by social "scientists." A precise, measurable detailing of sporting event attendance figures, the number of notes and note changes in popular melodies, the lyrical content of popular songs, story content in popular books, hemline lengths, tie widths, heel heights, the prominence of various fashion and pop art colors, the angularity vs. roundness of automobile styling, the construction of various architectural styles and a host of other reflections of the popular mood, all weighted according to volume of sales, would allow us to read graphs of the public mood in the same way we read graphs of aggregate stock prices now. By comparing the evidence to stock price movement, their implications could be assessed and the general hypothesis presented here could be tested. It is highly likely that plots of the net existence and dominance of these various popular cultural elements on a daily basis would parallel those of aggregate stock prices and reflect the Wave Principle.

In fact, I had taken these words to heart many years earlier, quite without understanding where it would all lead. As a 19-year-old sophomore in college, I took a tentative first step in quantifying popular song lyrics and hypothesizing the meaning of the results. Herewith is presented what we might perhaps term a Paleolithic study in socionomics.

An Investigation of Achievement Motive Level as Expressed in the Musical Art Forms Appreciated by Today's Youth, and Implications

by Robert R. Prechter, Jr.
Psychology of Communication/Psychology of the Arts
January 1969

Background

Mass media today provide their listeners with a barrage of different communications for a variety of different purposes. McLuhan (1964) encourages us to look beyond the content of these many different communications to the effects of the communications themselves. In this paper I ask that the reader look beyond the immediate purpose of the content of individual communications to investigate the results, not of each communication separately, but of the collective body over a period of time. With this outlook it is possible to discover a hidden purpose, one which is probably not intended, except in rare cases, but nevertheless has its effect.

Today's popular music communicates to the youth of our society messages which are highly powerful and quite diverse. This medium is one of the most effective means of communication we can experience, for at the same time it both delivers its message and provides entertainment for its audience, thus making its reception an enjoyable and sought-after experience. Moreover, these communications are spoken most often through a youth medium to a youth audience, thus eliminating one of the most difficult psychological barriers that other communicators must continually deal with: that of overcoming boredom, fear, dislike or mistrust of the communicator. In view of these factors, it seems to me appropriate to investigate this medium in order to attain a more adequate conception of the nature of the communications produced by and affecting today's youth, and the consequent expectations we may formulate regarding the future of our society. The aspect of this medium which I have chosen to investigate is the expression of achievement motive level and its implications.

The research conducted for the preparation of this paper is, in essence, an extension of the work of D.C. McClelland (1953, 1961) concerning the correlation of Achievement Motive with the national rate of economic growth. McClelland found that the level of achievement motivation expressed in stories found in children's readers provides a basis for accurate predictions concerning the overall economic growth rate of a nation. Approximately thirty to fifty years after the achievement themes of these stories become widespread, McClelland discovered, the economy of the nation usually reflects their themes. In effect, early childhood training concerning the value of hard work and competition produces high achievement motivation, which in turn is conducive to an entrepreneurial character; when this entrepreneurial character becomes widespread and entrepreneurial roles are filled competently, the result, as may be expected, is positive economic growth. (See Table One.)

One of the most indicative elements of culture reflecting a nation's collective potential for achievement decades before this potential is evidenced in the national economic growth rate is art. These reflections are not proposed as causes for the development of high or low achievement

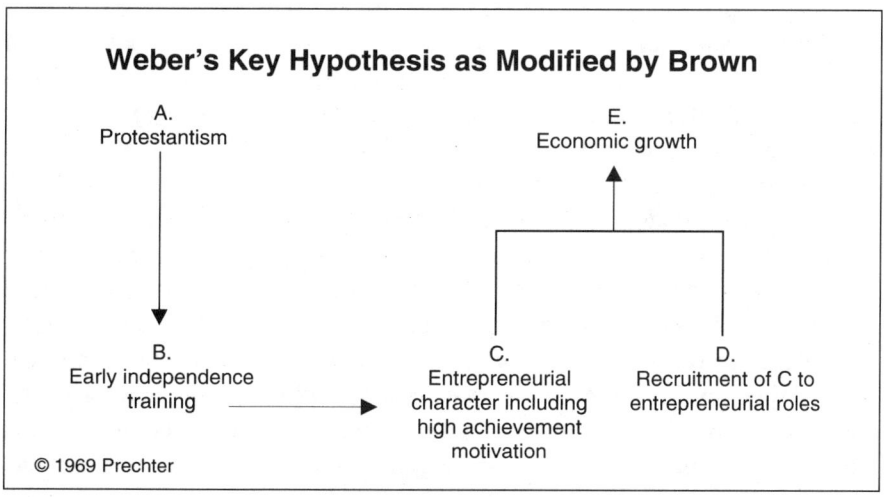

Table 1

motivation in the population but merely as indices for measuring national attitude toward it. In other words, the social environment in which children are raised to regard diligence as a positive or negative good produces at the same time works of art which express this feeling.

Several different art modes can be used to investigate this relationship. Literary art is used both in modern societies, where scholarly attention has been focused upon the stories in standardized children's readers, and in older societies, such as Britain from the 1400s and even as far back as ancient Greece from 900 to l00 B.C. In these older societies, the index used is representative literature from each era, which in turn is correlated with economic development of the country, as measured in a variety of different ways. In ancient Greece, for instance, the size of the area in which large Greek earthenware jars have been found indicates the size of the trade area during different periods of its history. When these jars are carbon-dated, they provide an index for comparison of the relative economic well-being of Greece for these different periods. The visual arts are also used to score level of achievement motivation. Since no written records have survived the civilization of Pre-Incan Peru, investigations were concerned with scoring the achievement level indicated in the choice of characteristics of art work found on Peruvian pottery. Urns dated by carbon-14 calculations were scored for appearances of S-waves and diagonals, characteristic of doodles of high achievers, and multiple waves, characteristic of low achievers. It was discovered that where designs characteristic of high achievement were most abundant, Peru, with an approximate thirty-year lag, entered upon a period of economic growth, as registered by the number and size of public buildings erected during that period. Similarly, drawings characteristic of low achievers preceded periods of low growth rate and even Peruvian conquest by outside forces. This ingenious measure was even used by McClelland to compare thirty modern nations from 1925 to 1950, correlating the achievement motivation level as indicated by their literature with the consequent change in level of kilowatt-hours of electricity produced per capita and the national income in international units per capita.

One important aspect of McClelland's discoveries is that the level of economic growth of a country is characteristically cyclical. The reasons for this phenomenon will be discussed later. However, consider the implications of these cycles upon the future economic outlook for the United States. (See Table Two.) This country has been enjoying healthy economic prosperity for approximately twenty-five years. Is this prosperity to continue,

Cycles Listed by Sorokin Which May be Related to Present Trend Indicated in This Paper

© 1969 Prechter

3 1/2 - 4 years —	Business cycles
7 - 11 years —	Business cycles
15-16 years —	Political life (opinions in government)
30-33 years —	Dominating literary movements and schools, dominating political parties and governmental policy
48-60 years —	Business cycles (accompanied by social phenomena such as revolutions, wars, social and political changes)
300 years —	Great changes: beginning and end of many dynasties and social, religious and political institutions; appearance, development and decline of literary and idealogical systems
500 years —	Approximate period for the growth and decline of some cultures and states

Table 2

or is there reason to expect a decline in relative economic activity in the near future? A strong indication of the answer lies within the art forms appreciated by the younger generation of our culture and the attitudes toward achievement inherent in it. I undertook this research for the reasons that an investigation concerning the economic future of the United States is highly relevant to our times and secondly that the field of music is an art form which to my knowledge has not been utilized in a study of this sort.

My first major assumption, based upon the preceding evidence, is that the music appreciated, listened to, and bought by the younger generation of the past decade will contain evidence of the popular attitude toward the value of achievement and thus, I hope, provide an accurate basis for scoring the achievement motivation level expressed in this material. My second

PIONEERING STUDIES IN SOCIONOMICS

assumption is that music is one of the most, if not the most, important and relevant art forms in the lives of young people today and that therefore this art form would provide the most assurance of a reliable source for investigation. For evidence supporting this assumption, we can refer to the Sunday, November 24, 1968 issue of *The New York Times*, in which an entire section is devoted to "Rock 1968." "In the scant decade and a half of its life," reports recordings editor Theodore Strongin, "rock has become a prime cultural force, one that has captured the attentions and emotions of youth en masse." Never before in history has a society produced in such a short time such a tremendous volume of artistic material which is so expressive of the youth element in a society. With this confidence, I began an investigation of this topic.

Method

My task was to choose in the most random way possible a relatively large number of songs represented by many artists in different fields of recent popular music, score each song for achievement motivation level, and tally the results. I selected a total of seven hundred songs performed by a group of sixty different artists,[1] representing the categories of rock, rhythm and blues, pop, folk and independent singer-songwriters. Most of the songs chosen were single "hits" or from albums highly popular within the last five years. The elements of each song could fall into one or several of nine different categories and in some categories more than once. The two major categories were "Pro-Achievement" and "Non-Achievement," the latter of which was subdivided into "Anti-Achievement" and "Escape." Each of these three categories was further subdivided into three smaller categories, labeled "total theme," "major reference" and "minor reference," depending upon the extent to which the attitude toward achievement was expressed in each song.

Those songs falling into the category of "Pro-Achievement" were those expressive of acceptance of, praise of, or participation successfully in matters concerning economic, social or personal advancement. One example of a work that fell into the "Pro-Achievement—total theme" category is "It's My Life," performed by Eric Burdon and the Animals, with lyrics thus:

> It's a hard world to get a break in
> All the good things have been taken
> But girl there are ways to make certain things pay
> Though I'm dressed in these rags I'll wear sable some day

> ...Hear my command, I'm breakin' loose
> It ain't no use holdin' me down
> You're gonna cry, I'm squeezin' you dry
> Takin' all I can get; no regrets when I openly lie
> And live only money...

(These lyrics may not endorse *honorable* achievement, but they endorse achievement nevertheless.) A typical line meriting entry in the "major reference" category, is "For my baby I work part time/ Down at the neighborhood five and dime," from Stevie Wonder's "Nothing's Too Good For My Baby." An example for "minor reference," from Percy Sledge's "When a Man Loves a Woman," indicates acceptance of the responsibility of achievement; "I couldn't wait to see that little girl of mine/*When I got home from work.*"

On the other side of the scale are the categories, "Anti-Achievement" and "Escape." These are in turn the antitheses of praise of or participation successfully in competitive action, and of acceptance of achievement behavior, respectively. These last two categories were divided in this manner in order to reveal more about the direction that the non-support of achievement was taking. I made this division after pre-testing several songs and noticing this definite division of sentiment. An example of material falling into the category of "Anti-Achievement—total theme," is Donovan's "Writer in the Sun," which concerns the meditations of a man who has wasted his life striving for the "good things": "Too many years I spent in the city/ Playing with Mister Loss and Gain." A line meriting inclusion in the "major reference" category is "Daytime turns me off and I don't mean maybe/ Nine to five ain't takin' me where I'm bound," from Neil Diamond's hit, "Thank the Lord for the Night Time." Deserving inclusion in "minor references" is "Who makes me feel like smiling when the *weary day* is through/ You, baby, you..." from the Mamas and Papas' "You Baby." Finally, we have the "Escape" category, which is characterized by songs which reject responsibility and embrace non-realities or dream worlds. A song scored under "total theme" is "A World of Our Own," by the Seekers, which claims, "We'll build a world of our own that no one else can share/ All our sorrows we'll leave far behind us there/ And I know we will find/ There'll be peace of mind/ When we live in a world of our own." Then, in the category of "major reference," I included from "A Day in the Life," by the Beatles, the reference at the end of the line spoken by a man who has just rushed to work, "Ran upstairs and had a smoke/ Somebody spoke, and I went into a dream...Ahhhhhhh..." Under "minor references" I included such lines as "I've got sunshine on a cloudy day/ When it's cold outside I've got the month of May," from "My Girl," performed by several artists, including the Temptations, the Outsiders and the Mamas and Papas.

Each song could be scored once only in a "total theme" column, and if "total theme" were scored, no other column (either "major" or "minor reference") could be scored under the same major heading (i.e., "Pro-" or "Anti-Achievement" or "Escape"), although the song could score under "major reference" or "minor reference" under a different main heading. If "total theme" were not scored for the song under any of the three main headings, the song could be scored any number of times under any of the "major reference" and "minor reference" categories. This procedure was adopted in order to avoid overweighting a single song by scoring it both under "total theme" and then several times under "major" and/or "minor reference." In this study, no song received more than three checks under a single subheading.

Problems and Potential Objections

Before reporting the results of my research, I would like to mention some of the problems I encountered and answer some of the possible objections to my method. My most egregious problem was that of thematic ambiguity. Some of the songs were often open to two opposing interpretations. For example, "Five Hundred Miles," sung by Sonny and Cher, concerns someone who finds himself penniless after years away from home and feels ashamed to return: "Not a shirt on my back or a penny to my name/ Lord I can't go home this-a-way..." Now, is this to be scored "Pro-Achievement" since the singer regards financial success as a positive value, or "Anti-Achievement" since he has participated in the achievement process and failed, leaving the listener to conclude, "It's no use trying for anything; you never win"? I felt that a score of "Pro-Achievement—total theme" was most consistent with the scale I had constructed. One song I encountered, "Strange Young Girls," by the Mamas and Papas, discouraged the use of LSD. I felt that this was somewhat relevant since it seemed to fit under a heading of "Anti-Escape," which I had not provided for. However, this was the only song which presented this problem, so I decided that since it fit none of my categories concerning achievement motivation I would count it among the "unrelated" songs. Problems of this magnitude, however, were few, and I feel that they have not affected my results significantly.

Other problems included the occasional fine line between "major reference" and "minor reference," and between a score of say, three "major references" as opposed to one "total theme." This problem was one of subjective judgment and one which would have a tendency to compensate for itself on both sides of the spectrum.

As far as major objections to my investigation, I see three. The first concerns the validity of my categorical headings. Why did I not use the scoring method used by McClelland in his evaluations of stories produced by subjects for psychological study (under the pretense that their creativity was being tested)? This point requires rather involved discussion. McClelland's scoring was based upon whether or not his stories "showed concern with competing successfully with some standard of excellence." First, a desire to achieve something does not necessarily mean competition. For example, "Hitch Hike," by Marvin Gaye (and the Rolling Stones), promises, "I'm gonna find that girl if I have to hitch hike 'round the world." There is certainly concern with achieving a goal here, although no competition with a standard or another person is required. Secondly, McClelland's breakdown of points for each interrelated element that may enter into an achievement situation seems somewhat arbitrary, and his concern more for whether or not the story displays achievement imagery and the extent to which it does rather than the opinion expressed by the story concerning the value of such activity leads to the complication that a story scoring 5 could be just as favorable toward achievement as a story scoring 11. Finally, McClelland is dealing with stories, whereas I am testing song material, which is more conducive to direct statements of sentiment rather than a symbolic or representative expression of situation and outcome. Thus, in song lyrics, interpretation by the scorer is at a minimum. The second objection I see is that possibly my category of "Escape" is unrelated to achievement imagery or that a fourth, polar category should have been included, labeled something such as "Acceptance of Involvement." As I have previously mentioned, escape from reality is a rejection of responsibility and thus a rejection of the major prerequisite for achievement. Besides, all songs which do not advocate escape from reality do accept reality and therefore involvement. However, as can be seen in so many examples, one may be involved in reality and still express negative feelings toward achievement. Therefore, the category of "Escape" is merely the antonym of acceptance of achievement as a value, statements of which were scored under the heading of "Pro-Achievement." The third major objection to my research could be that my selection of song material was not random enough and therefore may produce biased results. About ten percent of the songs were chosen randomly from a card file of all the single records owned by radio station WYBC at Yale University. The bulk of the songs were from albums that I chose from libraries of Yale students, including myself, in an attempt to get a wide range of artists included in the scoring process. Although I feel that my choices provide a good representative sample of the more popular recordings of the past five years, the choice was not made by random selection and therefore constitutes a valid criticism.

Results

The results of my research are as follows: from 700 records tested, 134 (approximately 19 percent) contained relevant material. Of these 134 records, there were 36 total "Pro-Achievement" references and themes and 128 total "Non-Achievement" references, with 60 in the "Anti-Achievement" category and 68 under the "Escape" heading. For a breakdown of the scores, refer to Table Three.

It is evident from these results that the general attitude expressed in songs representing today's youth is not favorable toward the values of achievement, competition or diligence. In every subheading, "Anti-Achievement" references top those which are "Pro-Achievement," even up to more than double in the case of "major references." Of the records tested, far more were found to have their total themes concerned with escape from reality and its responsibilities than for the other two categories combined. Strongin (1968) saw an indication of this escape trend in his description of rock music, in which songs "...lend a touch of sadness and a sense of 'being free from the crush of society.'" In fact, of the four instrumentals I encountered on albums used for this research, two of them had escapist titles: "Flying" and "Embryonic Journey." The next highest in total thematic statement is for the "Anti-Achievement" category, suggesting a rebellious, rejecting attitude toward the values of the industrious capitalist. However, the split between pro- and anti-achievement values in entire themes is not very great. The deciding factor is the encouragement for those who wish to escape reality and responsibility and lose themselves in carefree, non-competitive world, thus greatly enlarging the gap between the "Pro-Achievement" and "Non-Achievement" categories. Moreover, upon closer examination of the data, I find that a greater percentage (23 percent as opposed to 6 percent) of those included in the "Pro-Achievement" category are themes dealing with concern about achieving a better love relationship with a member of the opposite sex. These songs usually proposed a plan to better a relationship through means of achieving better economic or social

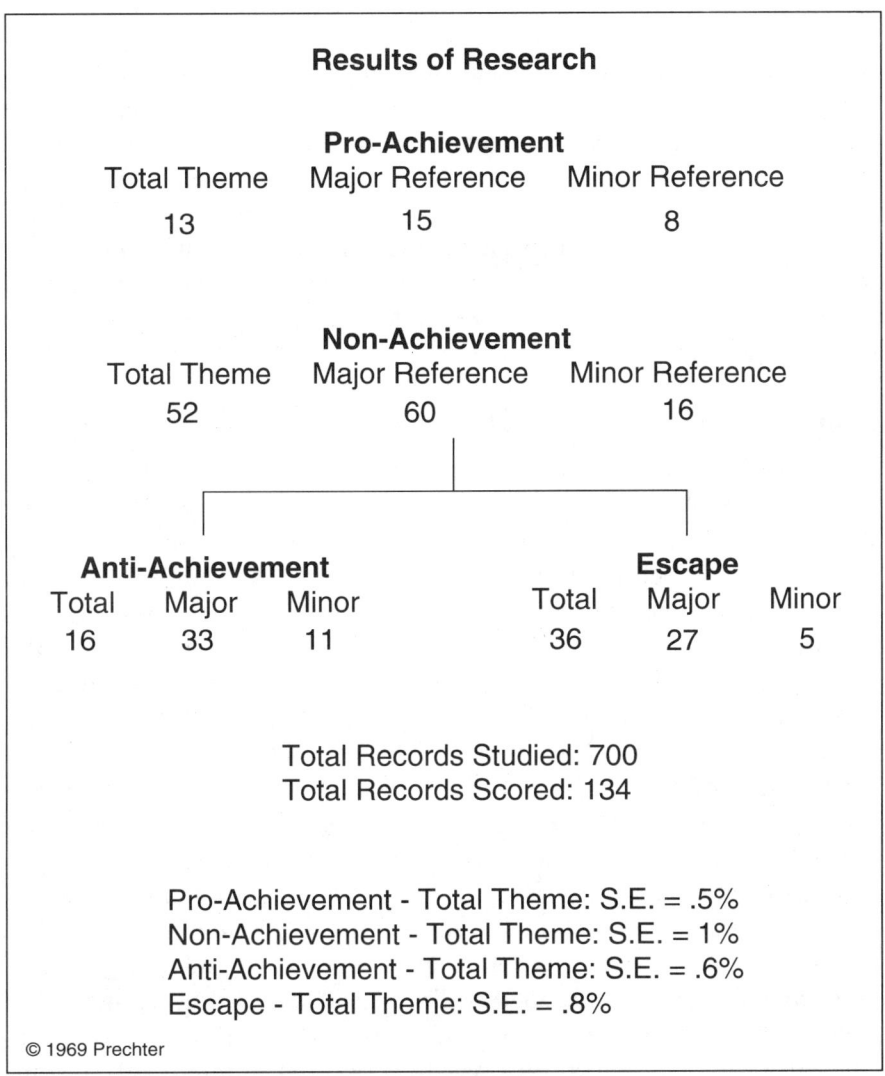

Results of Research

Pro-Achievement

Total Theme	Major Reference	Minor Reference
13	15	8

Non-Achievement

Total Theme	Major Reference	Minor Reference
52	60	16

Anti-Achievement

Total	Major	Minor
16	33	11

Escape

Total	Major	Minor
36	27	5

Total Records Studied: 700
Total Records Scored: 134

Pro-Achievement - Total Theme: S.E. = .5%
Non-Achievement - Total Theme: S.E. = 1%
Anti-Achievement - Total Theme: S.E. = .6%
Escape - Total Theme: S.E. = .8%

Table 3

status. "Do You Love Me?" by the Contours, for instance, concerns a man who returns to ask his girl if she loves him now that he can dance well, giving a positive value to social achievement. "For Your Love," by the Yardbirds and "Hey Gip" by the Animals are both promises of riches to women in return for their love, therefore giving a positive value to economic achievement. On the other hand, most of the entries under the heading of "Anti-Achievement—total theme" are social commentaries. Whether one should consider these entries more relevant or less, however, is questionable.

Forecast

What do these results indicate concerning the future of economic development in the United States? If this measure and these results are to be trusted, one is led to predict a decline in economic growth activity for the United States as a whole in a period of time approximately thirty to fifty years after this tendency began to manifest itself. Since my investigation is not chronological, I cannot speculate upon when this negative attitude toward achievement became so prevalent, although it would seem appropriate to suggest that it was nurtured soon after the emergence of rock music some fifteen years ago.

Possible Psychological Causes of Social Attitudes Toward Achievement

What, we may ask, is the reason for the negative attitude toward achievement? Weber's Key Hypothesis, as modified by Roger Brown (1965), tells half of the story. (See Table One.) An ideological movement, he says, often impels parents to train their children to be independent. An entrepreneurial character is then assumed, the recruitment of which provides for economic growth of a country. But, as Sorokin (1928) and Spengler (1926, 1928, 1932), as well as McClelland, indicate, societies are cyclical. The state of economic growth produces, in its turn, economic prosperity. Thus, an environment of affluence is created which is conducive to child dependency and thus a non-achieving-oriented adult. On a personal psychological level, Erikson (1963) indicates support of McClelland's argument in his discussion of the eight ages of man, in which the development of a dependent child results from lack of independence training by his parents (as Weber implies), which makes difficult or impossible the child's expected act of dissociating himself from his family and embracing roles of productive diligence within society. The crucial stage of development here is under the heading "Industry vs. Inferiority," which, if not resolved successfully, is highly conducive to the development of a non-achievement-oriented adult:

> For before the child, psychologically already a rudimentary parent, can become a biological parent, he must begin to be a worker. With the oncoming latency period, the normally advanced child...learns to win recognition by producing things. He has experienced "a sense of finality regarding the fact that there is no workable future within the womb of his family. He develops a sense of industry...the work principle teaches him the pleasure of work completion by steady attention and persevering diligence.

The child's danger, at this stage, lies in a sense of inadequacy and inferiority. If he despairs of his tools and skills or of his status among his tool partners, he may be discouraged from identification with them and with a section of the tool world. To lose the hope of such "industrial" association may pull him back to the more isolated, less tool-conscious familial rivalry of the oedipal time ...this is socially a most decisive stage, since industry involves doing things beside and with others, a first sense of division of labor and of differential opportunity, that is, a sense of the technological ethos of a culture, develops at this time.[2]

The result of non-resolution of this stage of child development, then, is a lack of willing and diligent entrepreneurs and thus a tendency toward economic decline if the conflict is on a national scale. (See Table Four.) This state of affairs may well be the one in which the United States is situated today. Moreover, the communication of such anti-achievement sentiments is not merely the result of such a feeling or tendency but a cause of it as well, reaffirming and strengthening such sentiments:

"The people of our own age, we are trying to express something," one teenager said recently. "We do it through the music we call rock. It tells our feelings about the way society is today, about war, the system, about relationships today." (Strongin, 1968)

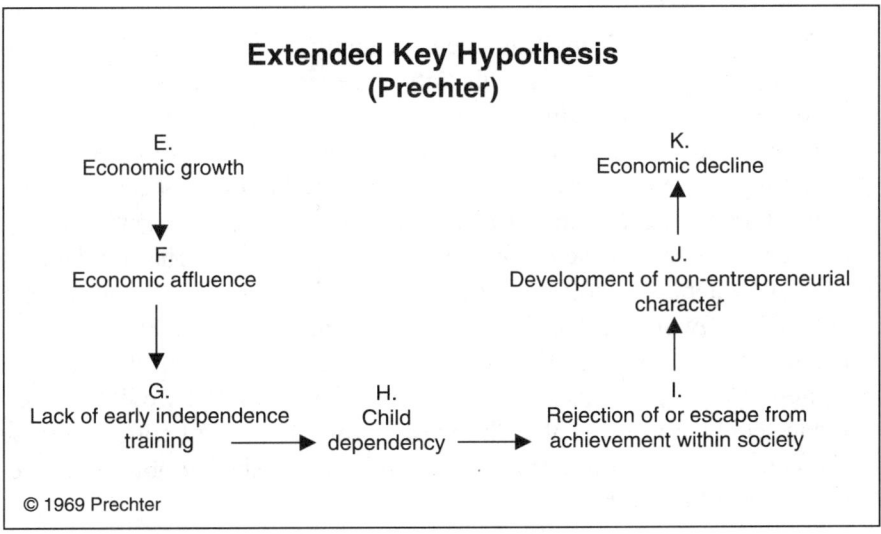

Table 4

Impressions of These Results in Other Social Trends

The conclusions of this research are manifest in other art forms and in other areas of society as well. In the visual arts, "impressionism" has to a great degree replaced the style of true representation, in which the achievement of producing the work of art was of greater importance. Today one doesn't marvel so much at the painstaking task of producing the work of art as he marvels at the effect or impression that it has upon him. The "mind-expanding" drug movement, supported by Barron and Leary, slogans of "turn on, tune in, and drop out," LSD as a religion, and a liking for psychedelia all put emphasis on the experience of the surreal. They are oftentimes merely means of escape from the responsibilities imposed by a world of reality. Even social changes and political movements reflect this anti-achievement tendency. The peace movements and the move to abolish ROTC are rejections of the value of military achievement as a positive good. Student movements at Yale University have changed in the last year and a half no less than five major requirements of students to engage in competition, effecting the abolition of the letter grading system, the abolition of required physical education until judged "fit," the abolition of freshmen course requirements, the reduction of the course credit requirements for graduation and, finally, the abolition of the dean's list.

Looking Forward

The topic I have chosen is open for many more extensive investigations concerning the nature of this anti-achievement sentiment. Is there a difference between the feelings communicated in white rock and black "soul" or rhythm & blues? Research here could lead to discovery of problems confronting these two groups as well as to predictions concerning their relationships with each other. Has the anti-achievement element declined, increased or remained the same in musical expression during the last ten years? A systematic scoring of the "Top 100" songs of each year from 1958 to 1968 would probably answer this question. How about aspects related to achievement motive in the visual arts, such as discreteness vs. fuzziness? Are such terms applicable to musical quality? I would be interested in seeing the results of such investigation, as indeed I am going to be interested to see how these trends continue and whether or not my prediction is realized in the future.[3]

A List of the 134 Songs (Out of 700) Scored For Relevant Content

	Pro-Achievement			Anti-Achiev.			Escape		
	Tot.	Maj.	Min.	Tot.	Maj.	Min.	Tot.	Maj.	Min.
Soul Train						✓			
Crystal Ship							✓		
Time to Dream					✓		✓		
Do You Love Me	✓								
Gimme Some Lovin'					✓	✓			
New Orleans							✓		
California Nights						✓			
Museum							✓		
Sidewalk Surfin'								✓	
Dancing Bear				✓					
England Swings							✓		
People Got to Be Free		✓							
A World of Our Own						✓	✓		
Don't Look Back				✓				✓	
Call Me Lightning		✓							
For Your Love	✓								
Don't Bother Me							✓		
I'll Get You	✓								
Hitch Hike	✓								
Good Times							✓		
One More Try	✓								
Play With Fire					✓✓✓				
19th Nervous Breakdown					✓				
As Tears Go By					✓				
Mother In Law						✓			
Groovin'						✓		✓	
You Baby						✓		✓	
Is It Any Wonder						✓			✓
Let Me Be								✓	
It Ain't Me Babe					✓				
Outside Chance				✓					
You Know What I Mean									✓
With A Little Help/Friends					✓				
A Day In The Life				✓✓	✓		✓		
My Girl									✓✓
King of the Road				✓					
Do You Believe in Magic								✓	
Daydream							✓		
Up Up and Away							✓		
Summer in the City								✓	
Ruby Tuesday								✓	
On a Quiet Night					✓			✓	

Table 5

	Pro-Achievement			Anti-Achiev.			Escape		
	Tot.	Maj.	Min.	Tot.	Maj.	Min.	Tot.	Maj.	Min.
Pretty Ballerina								✓	
Barterers and Their Wives				✓					
Lazy Day					✓				
The Sailing Ship							✓		
In the Café					✓			✓✓	
The Town/Back To					✓		✓		
Up On the Roof					✓		✓		
Mr. Unreliable					✓				
Cobblestone Road				✓					
You've Got to Hide Your Love/					✓				
There's a Place							✓		
Groovy Kind of Love								✓	
Summer Place							✓		
Poor Side of Town		✓							
Michael		✓✓							
The Gypsy Rover					✓				
Tuesday Afternoon								✓	
Early Morning Fantasy								✓	
Turn Down Day					✓✓				
Itchycoo Park					✓		✓		
When a Man Loves a Woman			✓						
We Ain't Gonna Make It					✓				
I Got You Babe					✓				
Flying							✓		
Embryonic Journey							✓		
500 Miles	✓								
Straight Shooter			✓						
California Dreamin'							✓		
No Salt on Her Tail									✓
Sing For Your Supper	✓								
Did You Ever Want to Cry								✓	
Turn Turn Turn		✓✓✓							
Satisfied Mind				✓					
The Times/Changin'			✓✓						
Wait and See	✓								
Mr. Tambourine Man							✓		
All I Really Want to Do						✓			
Don't Doubt Yourself	✓								
It's My Life	✓								
Gonna Send You/Walker			✓						
House of the Rising Sun		✓✓							
We Gotta Get Out/Place					✓✓	✓			
Little Bit O' Soul		✓							
Sugar Town							✓		
Nobody But Me	✓								
Hey Gip	✓								

Table 5 (cont'd)

	Pro-Achievement			Anti-Achiev.			Escape		
	Tot.	Maj.	Min.	Tot.	Maj.	Min.	Tot.	Maj.	Min.
I'm Gonna Make You Love Me	✓								
Let's Live for Today				✓					
Thank the Lord for the Nighttime					✓				
Dock of the Bay					✓				
Papa Was Too					✓✓				
Nothing's Too Good	✓								
Uptight					✓✓				
People Get Ready							✓		
Pushin' Too Hard				✓					
Enchanted Gypsy							✓		
Voyage Into/Screen							✓		
Mandolin Man and His Secret				✓					
Epistle to Derroll					✓				
Skip-a-Long Sam				✓					
There Was a Time		✓							
Land of Doesn't HaveTo Be							✓		
Writer in the Sun				✓					
Guinivere				✓					
The Fat Angel							✓		
Poor Cow								✓	
White Rabbit							✓		
Makin' My Mind Up								✓	
Think I'll Run Away							✓		
Somebody Tell/Name					✓			✓	
Downtown							✓		
Then You Can Tell Me Goodbye			✓						
Alabama Song							✓		
A Girl Like You			✓						
Beautiful Morning			✓						
Flowers Never Bend/Rainfall								✓	
Paint It Black								✓✓	
Flight 505								✓	
Ben Franklin's Almanack							✓		
July							✓		
A Well Respected Man				✓					
Hard Day's Night		✓							
Can't Buy Me Love				✓					
Think for Yourself								✓	
5D							✓		
Mr. Spaceman								✓	
Lear Jet Song							✓		
I Am a Rock							✓		
I Gotta Dream On							✓		
Moody River								✓	
School is Out				✓					
Johnny B. Goode			✓						

Table 5 (cont'd)

NOTES

[1] Here is a sample of some of the artists included: Animals, Association, Beatles, Byrds, Cryan' Shames, Neil Diamond, Donovan, Doors, Fifth Dimension, Herman's Hermits, Jefferson Airplane, Kinks, Left Banke, Lovin' Spoonful, Mamas and Papas, Roger Miller, Outsiders, Rascals, Johnny Rivers, Rolling Stones, Simon and Garfunkel.

[2] The next stage of child development is "Identity vs. Role Confusion," which seems to have been a major problem of the new generation. The question of "finding oneself" is becoming more critically important and more commonly asked and searched out.

[3] Or should I remain unconcerned, a disciple of the Grassroots, who preach, "Live for today/ and don't worry 'bout tomorrow...."

REFERENCES

Brown, Roger. (1965). "The achievement motive." *Social psychology*. New York: The Free Press, pp. 423-476,

Erikson, Erik H. (1963). *Childhood and society*. New York: W.W. Norton & Co., pp. 255-263.

McClelland, D.C., et al. (1953). *The achievement motive*. New York: Appleton-Century.

McClelland, D.C. (1961). *The achieving society*. Princeton: Van Nostrand, 1961.

McLuhan, Marshall. (1964). *Understanding media: The extensions of man*. New York: New American Library.

Sorokin, Pitrom. (1928). *Contemporary sociological theories*. New York: Harper & Brothers, pp. 730-735.

Spengler, Oswald. (1926, 1928, 1932). *Decline of the west*. New York: Alfred A. Knopf.

Strongin, Theodore. (1968, November 24). "Rock 1968." *The New York Times*, section 14.

A Discussion of Outcomes (2002)

Socionomics regards the expression of sentiment in the popular songs of the late 1960s as a *concurrent* expression of social mood. Since the mood of the time was escapist and anti-achievement, it probably accurately reflected the mood of a fledgling bear market, which began in February 1966. That bear market ultimately had economic (and other) consequences.

Whether we should credit the fortunate timing of the author's interest in the subject or the forecasting value of the information, the fact is that the study was just about perfectly timed for the rather dramatic change in trend

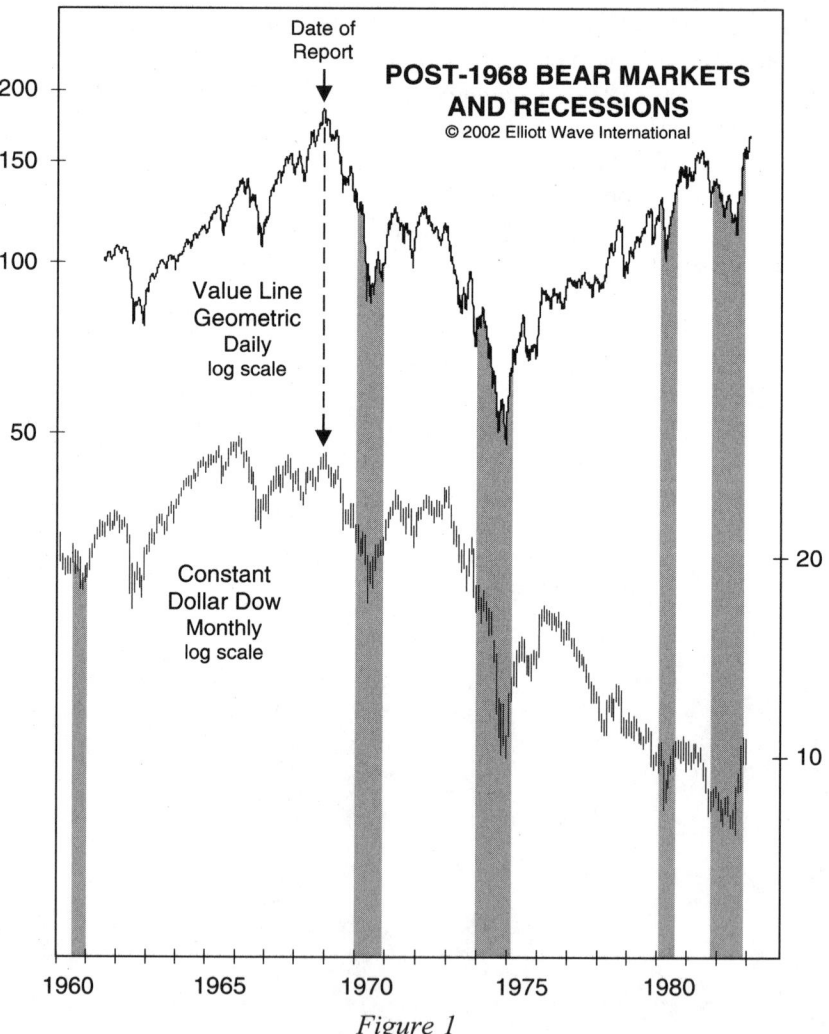

Figure 1

for stocks and the economy that ensued immediately thereafter. The paper was completed in December 1968 and submitted in January 1969, after a period of eight recession-free years, an all-time U.S. record. As you can see in Figure 1, the Value Line geometric average of stock prices reached a speculative top in December 1968 and lost 74 percent of its value over the next six years, ushering in the recessions of December 1969-November 1970 and December 1973-February 1975. In constant-dollar terms, the Dow Jones Industrial Average, which had topped in 1966, continued lower until August 1982, ushering in two more recessions, those of January-August 1980 and August 1981-November 1982. Overall, those fourteen years were the worst comparable period for stock prices and the economy since 1928-1942. In other words, the social mood observed in the study had immediate effects.

The Forecasted Outcome Is Due Now

There is another way to look at the results, which is the way they were construed in the paper: as a harbinger of economic change decades in the future. In the paper, I cited D.C. McClelland's conclusion about timing: "Approximately thirty to fifty years after the achievement themes of these stories become widespread, McClelland discovered, the economy of the nation usually reflects their indications." With nothing else to go on, I gave the conclusion that he would have given: "If this measure is to be trusted, one is led to predict a decline in economic growth activity for the United States as a whole in a period of time approximately thirty to fifty years after this tendency began to manifest itself." Further review leads me to conclude that the trend in popular song lyrics to an anti-achievement theme started in 1965, which would mean, according to McClelland, an economic decline beginning sometime between 1995 and 2015.[1] Whether this delayed effect of the anti-achievement sentiment of the late 1960s will occur in line with McClelland's' theories remains to be seen, but it is certainly compatible with the outlook from an Elliott wave standpoint as expressed in *At the Crest of the Tidal Wave* and *Conquer the Crash*. If the stock market continues to fall and depression ensues, then the onset of economic malaise may turn out to have begun right at the time that the original study said it should.

NOTES

[1] Since the medium of expression was not children's stories but late teenagers' stories, we might today propose an adjustment to the forecasted time reflecting that ten years' difference, producing not a 30- to 50-year range but a 20- to 40-year range for the time before the downturn. Either way, the 30 years that have since elapsed as of the late 1990s represent either the beginning or the center of the range targeted for the start of a period of economic malaise.

Quantifying Pessimistic Rumination in Popular Songs

My 1969 paper cited its own main shortcoming:

> My investigation is not chronological.... Has the anti-achievement element declined, increased or remained the same in musical expression during the last ten years? A systematic scoring of the "Top 100" songs of each year from 1958 to 1968 would probably answer this question.[1]

As if taking a cue from that call to action, in 1990,[2] Harold Zullow of Rutgers University independently undertook to quantify meticulously the degree of "pessimistic rumination in popular songs" over a 34-year period, which was published the following year in the *Journal of Economic Psychology*. For the study, he selected the Top Forty songs of each year from 1955 to 1989 as compiled by *Billboard* magazine and scored them for extent of "rumination," a negative description or evaluation of an event, by the degree of focus and emotion as well as the expressed stability, globality and internality of its cause(s). A chronological table of results is shown on the next page. Here are his primary conclusions:

> Pessimistic rumination in popular music lyrics correlated highly with subsequent values of rumination in *Time* [magazine], the Index of Consumer Sentiment, personal consumption expenditures, and GNP growth. The two-year moving average of pessimistic rumination correlated -.063 (p<0.0002) with the moving average of the year-to-year change in GNP (GNPCHG) in the subsequent two years. In a 2SLS analysis, changes in personal consumption expenditures (PERSCONS) predicted GNPCHG, and the Index of Consumer Sentiment (ICS) in turn predicted PERSCONS. One more step removed, pessimistic rumination and rumination in *Time* predicted consumer sentiment.
>
> Rumination in *Time*, PESSRUM in songs, and its components of pessimism and rumination correlated strongly with: subsequent economic

Pessimism and rumination in popular music and *Time* magazine, 1955–1989.

Year	RUMSONG	PESS SONG	PESSRUM	RUMTIME
1955	24.7%	8.53	−2.30	1.9%
1956	31.7	9.77	0.30	1.9
1957	28.7	8.95	−1.06	1.9
1958	31.7	10.07	0.56	9.7
1959	27.2	8.57	−1.72	9.7
1960	32.0	10.29	0.81	13.2
1961	33.4	10.08	0.93	17.0
1962	25.4	8.83	−1.89	13.5
1963	27.9	8.11	−1.97	7.7
1964	27.4	9.87	−0.55	5.8
1965	23.2	9.14	−2.10	15.1
1966	30.3	10.02	0.21	19.2
1967	32.5	10.81	1.37	19.2
1968	35.3	9.83	1.13	30.8
1969	28.6	11.44	1.07	25.0
1970	27.2	9.26	−1.12	36.5
1971	36.8	10.56	2.09	25.0
1972	34.2	9.58	0.67	19.2
1973	36.9	11.24	2.70	41.5
1974	25.4	8.96	−1.78	48.1
1975	29.0	9.41	−0.60	30.8
1976	17.5	8.79	−3.64	23.1
1977	18.0	10.98	−1.63	25.0
1978	35.1	11.37	2.43	32.7
1979	36.6	10.22	1.75	47.2
1980	28.9	12.59	2.14	42.3
1981	30.6	10.43	0.63	44.2
1982	27.5	11.26	0.68	50.0
1983	25.9	8.17	−2.36	44.2
1984	26.5	10.26	−0.41	28.3
1985	26.9	9.78	−0.74	40.4
1986	29.2	12.40	2.04	34.6
1987	30.3	10.97	1.03	48.1
1988	25.8	10.22	−0.60	30.8
1989	30.7	12.08	2.09	63.5

Note: Higher rumination percentages, pessimism scores, and PessRum scores indicate greater rumination, pessimism, and pessimistic rumination.

from Harold Zullow, *Journal of Economic Psychology* (1991)

growth, the occurrence of a recession year, and the hypothesized mediating variables of consumer optimism and personal consumption expenditures.

Pessimistic rumination in popular songs predicts decreased economic growth with a one- to two-year lead. The hypothesis that this relationship is causal was strengthened by the confirmation by simultaneous equations of a plausible path of influence. The path is that pessimistic rumination in the fantasy-based material of song lyrics predicts changes in the degree to which Americans worry about real-world events. PESSRUM in songs predicts rumination about events on the cover of *Time* magazine and consumer pessimism in nationwide surveys. Consumer pessimism in turn predicts decreased personal consumption expenditures, which strongly predicts decreased GNP growth.

Controlling for psychological variables, current GNP growth did not predict the ICS, rumination in *Time* magazine, or pessimistic rumination in songs.

Pessimistic rumination may aid in forecasting economic recessions and growth with a longer lead time than traditional econometric models because it is an early signal for changes in personal consumption expenditures and GNP one and two years later, a longer lead than many economic variables.

Whatever the cause of the fluctuations, high pessimistic rumination in the lyrics of popular songs and rumination on the cover of *Time* magazine have predicted changes in consumer optimism for the last 35 years.[3,4]

For evidence of these correlations, please see three of Zullow's graphs, reproduced below.

Zullow observes that the overall "pessimism score" reached an optimistic high in 1963 (which not coincidentally in my opinion saw the outbreak of Beatlemania) and a pessimistic low in 1980, which marked the low for stocks priced in gold. He also found substantial pessimism in the final year of his study, 1989. Zullow used his sociometer to make a successful forecast:

Pessimistic rumination in songs in 1989 (especially the second half of 1989) reached one of its highest levels in the last 35 years. Rumination in *Time* magazine in 1989 reached a historic high, in nearly two-thirds of the cover stories, in spite of an auspicious year of economic growth and the demise of Communism in Eastern Europe. This suggests a downturn in consumer optimism in 1990, followed by a recession year in 1991, with the recession beginning as early as later in 1990 — a prediction I first made in May 1990 (Zullow 1990).[5]

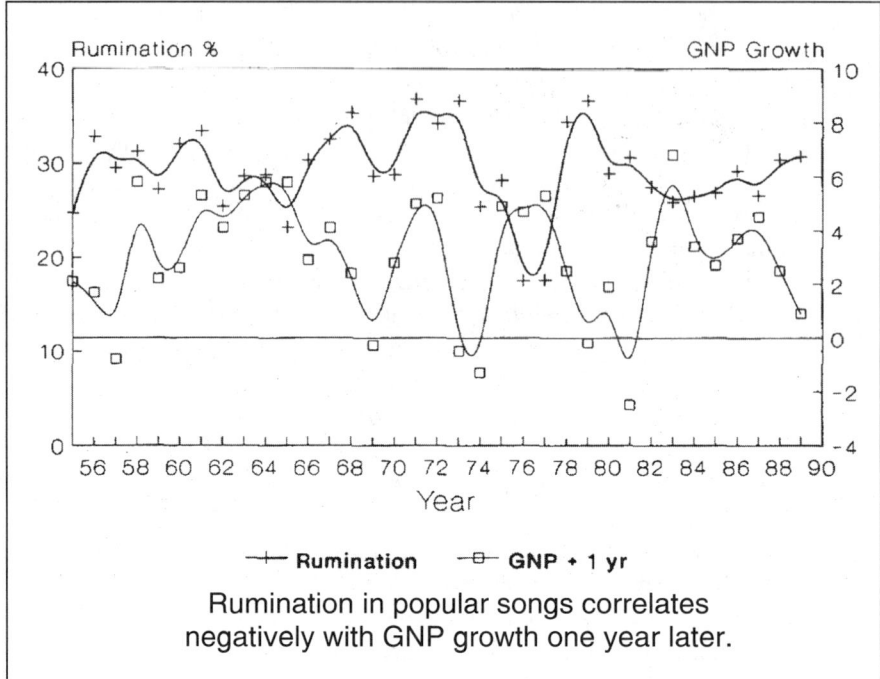

Rumination in popular songs correlates
negatively with GNP growth one year later.

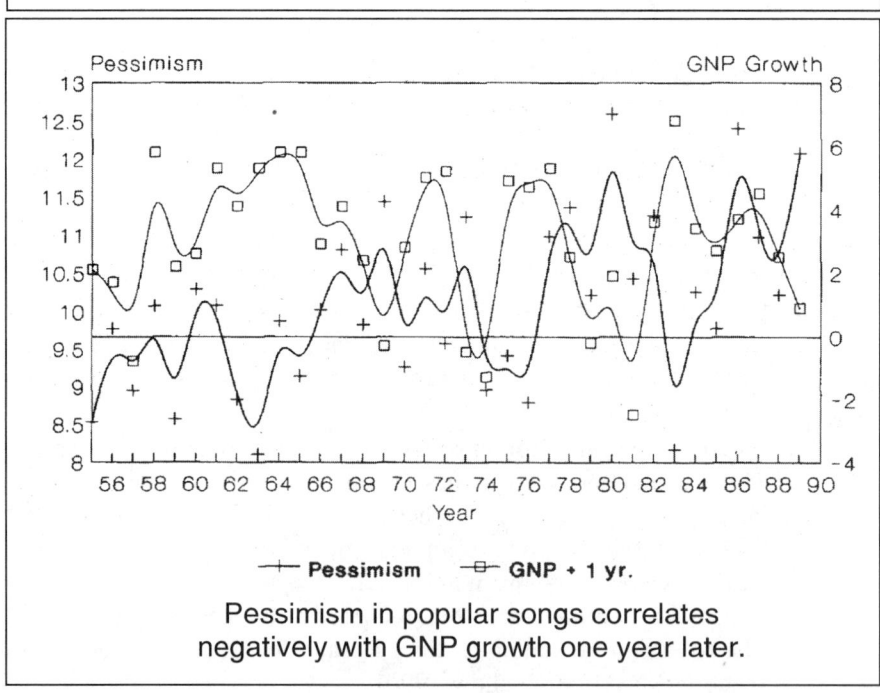

Pessimism in popular songs correlates
negatively with GNP growth one year later.

from Harold Zullow, *Journal of Economic Psychology* (1991)

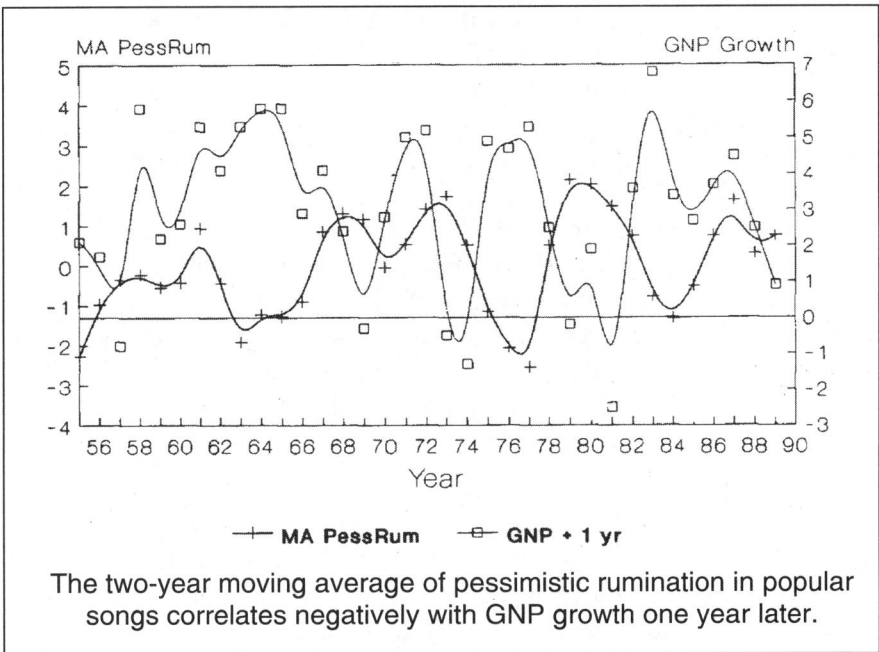

The two-year moving average of pessimistic rumination in popular songs correlates negatively with GNP growth one year later.

from Harold Zullow, *Journal of Economic Psychology* (1991)

Why would pessimistic rumination in popular songs be high in 1989, when the stock market was near an all-time high? The answer is that it was in the middle of an Elliott wave bear market of Primary degree (wave ④), which began in August 1987 and ended in October 1990 at the end of a flat pattern or in January 1991 at the end of a triangle pattern, its social results including recession and war. (For a picture of this corrective wave, see Figure 2 on page 244.) I would surmise that song-lyric pessimism stayed high at least through October 1990. Whatever the trend in rock music lyrics was for the decade of the 1990s, the trend of country music lyrics certainly took a dramatic turn toward optimism as the market resumed its upward path in wave ⑤.

Zullow asks, "Then why do consumer optimism and pessimistic rumination fluctuate?" His tentatively suggested answer naturally assumes an external cause, in this case that bad times might cause people to pursue escapist fantasies and good times might cause them to "expose themselves to negative fantasies in the popular culture." This is similar to one of the assumptions of my paper, as illustrated in Table 4 therein. *His data and mine, however, do not make a strong case that changes in the economy cause changes in mood, opposing or otherwise.* In a footnote, he observes,

"Ordinarily, an economist might model PERSCONS [personal consumption expenditures] as a function of income. However, when GNP [change] is introduced as an independent variable in predicting changes in [personal consumption expenditures], its beta weight is non-significant. Only consumer sentiment was significant...." In other words, social mood, not macroeconomic vibrancy, correlates with personal spending. The tendency for pessimistic rumination to follow boom times and its lack to follow bad times is not causation at work but merely the natural ebb and flow of social mood change. His data do show quite effectively, as he reports, that changes in mood precede changes in the economy. This is exactly what the socionomic insight indicates should be the case. Social mood is endogenous; it *precedes* economic change because it *causes* economic change.

New Directions

To date, the only attempts at creating a sociometer from popular music have involved numericizing lyric content. We each took this path partly because it is easy. I believe, however, that other aspects of popular recordings, such as tempo, melody, harmony, dissonance, noise level and tone of vocal delivery are probably better measures of the mood behind a song than its lyrics. We can *read* the lyrics of "Purple Haze" or "Sunshine of Your Love" and regard them as love songs in a pleasant mood. We can *listen* to their opening notes and their melodies, though, and realize that they are something quite different. Likewise, we can read the lyrics of "Bad Moon Rising" and regard them as a picture of doom, while we can listen to the song's bouncy jump beat and singsong melody and hear something quite benign. Many songs have no ambiguity in any of their aspects and could undoubtedly be rated as utterly positive or negative mood recordings. Until more comprehensive studies are undertaken, we are only scratching the surface.

NOTES

[1] Prechter, Robert. (1969, January). "An investigation of achievement motive level as expressed in the musical art forms appreciated by today's youth, and implications." Paper submitted for Psychology of Communication/Psychology of the Arts, Yale University.

[2] His paper appeared 21 years later and this book 34 years later, which are Fibonacci durations.

[3] Zullow, Harold M. (1991). "Pessimistic rumination in popular songs and news magazines predict economic recession via decreased consumer optimism and spending." *Journal of Economic Psychology* 12, 501-526.

[4] Each paragraph is an excerpt from the larger paper (ellipses omitted).

[5] Zullow, Harold M. (1990, May). "Pessimistic rumination in popular music and news magazines predicts economic recession, 1890-1990." Paper presented at a joint meeting of the American Association for Public Opinion Research and the World Association for Public Opinion Research, Lancaster, PA.

Quantifying Social Mood by Polling

George Katona of the Economic Behavior Program at the University of Michigan apparently made the first successful attempt to quantify a meter of social mood other than the stock market for the conscious purpose of forecasting the economy. To that end, he developed the now widely used Index of Consumer Sentiment. The following account is from Zullow's 1991 paper:

Since Katona and others in the Economic Behavior Program at the University of Michigan began studying consumer optimism in the 1950s, it has become increasingly evident that national mood changes before a recession begins — typically nine months in advance (Katona 1960, 1980). Surveys conducted two to four times a year until 1977, and monthly since 1978, have asked a nationwide sample of Americans about their current and expected financial situation, and that of the economy. Responses are combined into an Index of Consumer Sentiment (ICS), which the U.S. Commerce Department has used since 1978 as a leading indicator of economic activity. The ICS forewarned us of the last seven recessions and sounded one false alarm before the minirecession of 1966-67. The ICS predicts changes in durable goods purchases, such as automobiles, by American consumers. These expenditures reflect the use of discretionary income and provide an advance indicator of turning points in the economy.

These findings have been replicated by continuing surveys in other countries (Katona and Strumpel 1978; Praet 1985; Williams and Defris 1981). A nation's generalized (non-economic) hopes and fears also predict changes in GNP (Noelle-Neumann 1984, 1989).

Does consumer sentiment predict the economy above and beyond traditional macroeconomic variables? Some have found that the ICS can be explained largely by traditional macroeconomic variables: that consumer sentiment reacts to the economy but does not contribute over and above to predicting economic change (Shapiro 1972; Vanden Abeele

1983). In contrast, Katona and others (Adams and Klein 1972; Pickering 1977; Praet 1985; Van Raaij and Gianotten 1990; Williams and Defris 1981) have shown that changes in consumer sentiment are at least in part independent of economic change and contribute to predicting macroeconomic trends.[1]

The Index of Consumer Sentiment has had an excellent record of anticipating recessions, as have corrective Elliott waves in the stock market. In fact, this index moves up and down pretty much with the stock market. That's not the only index that it tracks. Zullow comments:

> PESSRUM, RUMSONG, PESSSONG, and RUMTIME correlated significantly with the annual average of consumer confidence as measured by the Conference Board's nationwide surveys since 1969, providing an independent validation of the predictive relationship between PESSRUM and consumer confidence.[2]

So the stock market, consumer sentiment and the degree of pessimism in popular songs all move up and down roughly together. A socionomist would suggest that the reason for the coincident trends is that changes in mood prompt immediate changes in stock values and the popularity of songs because people can buy or sell stocks and choose to enjoy particular sound recordings almost instantly upon changing moods, while economic actions taken *at the same time* require time to play out and thus have a lagging influence on the economy.

It is pertinent that while some researchers have attempted to bolster the conventional view of social mood causality in purporting to show that consumers are just reacting to present conditions, the bulk of studies to date supports Katona's original observation that changes in consumer sentiment are independent of economic causes and in fact precede trends in the economy. Therefore, the weight of the evidence in this area supports the socionomic insight.

A most important addition to evidence supporting the socionomic insight is that the forecasting ability of public mood is not confined to "consumers" anticipating the economic future. As cited above, Noelle-Neumann (1984, 1989) demonstrates that even the public's general non-economic hopes and fears predict changes in GDP. This is crucial data supporting the case that the limbic system generates changes in general human mood (see Chapter 8 of *The Wave Principle of Human Social Behavior*), which in turn has consequences in *all* areas of social behavior, not just economic behavior.

As useful as the Index of Consumer Sentiment is, it is still not as immediate or detailed an indication of social mood change as the stock market. It takes time to poll the public and publish the results, and the mechanism is not yet there to do weekly, daily, hourly or minute-by-minute polls of public feeling. The stock market, in contrast, stands ever at the ready to register the minutest changes in social mood, instantly, which makes it the ideal sociometer.

NOTES

[1] Zullow, Harold M. (1991). "Pessimistic rumination in popular songs and news magazines predict economic recession via decreased consumer optimism and spending." *Journal of Economic Psychology* 12, 501-526.

[2] *Ibid.*

REFERENCES

Adams, F.G. and Klein, L.R. (1972). "Anticipations variables in macro-econometric models." In: B. Strumpel, J.N. Morgan, and E. Zahn (eds.), *Human behavior in economic affairs: Essays in honor of George Katona*. San Francisco, CA: Jossey-Bass.

Katona, G. (1960). *The powerful consumer: Psychological studies of the American economy*. New York: McGraw-Hill.

Katona, G. (1980). *Essays on behavioral economics*. Ann Arbor, MI: Institute for Social Research.

Katona, G. and B. Strumpel. (1978). *A new economic era*. New York: Elsevier.

Pickering, J.F. (1977). *The acquisition of consumer durables*. London: Associated Business Programmes.

Praet, P. (1985). "Endogenizing consumers' expectations in four major EC countries." *Journal of Economic Psychology* 5, 255-269.

Shapiro, H.T. (1972). "The Index of Consumer Sentiment and economic forecasting — A reappraisal." In. B. Strumpel, J.N. Morgan and E. Zahn (eds.) *Human behavior in economic affairs: Essays in honor of George Katona*. San Francisco, CA: Jossey-Bass.

Vanden Abeele, P. (1983). "The Index of Consumer Sentiment: Predictability and predictive power in the EEC." *Journal of Economic Psychology* 3, 1-17.

Van Raaij, W.F. and Gianotten, H.J. (1990). "Consumer confidence, expenditure, saving, and credit." *Journal of Economic Psychology* 11, 269-290.

Williams, R.A. and Defris, L.V. (1981). "The roles of inflation and consumer sentiment in explaining Australian consumption and savings patterns." *Journal of Economic Psychology* 1, 105-120.

Zullow, Harold M. (1990, May). "Pessimistic rumination in popular music and news magazines predicts economic recession, 1890-1990." Paper presented at a joint meeting of the American Association for Public Opinion Research and the World Association for Public Opinion Research, Lancaster, PA.

Zullow, Harold M. (1991). "Pessimistic rumination in popular songs and news magazines predict economic recession via decreased consumer optimism and spending." *Journal of Economic Psychology* 12, 501-526.

Reviews

"This is unquestionably a ground-breaking work whose audacious arguments can only be described as stunning and revolutionary in intent and scope. These far-reaching hypotheses are a testament to Prechter's unequaled ability to weave together emerging evidence into a stunning new model. After reviewing my not inconsiderable library of key political science books, I am unable to find any books that are as sweepingly important and have the same potential to bring about a paradigm shift in the study of social events."

—Roman Franko, PhD Comparative Politics; market analyst for the *National Post* and Dundee Securities; former lecturer, Queen's University; contributor, Canadian Securities Institute's Technical Analysis course; member, Canadian Society of Technical Analysts.

"I love this theory. *Socionomics* is sure to be a primary reference source for quite some time. The volume and value of analysis that Prechter has conducted is something hard to over-appreciate. There should be university courses and degrees in the science of socionomics and perhaps Nobel Prize winners as well. I recommend many readings of the book to appreciate it in depth."

—Professor Valeri Safonov, PhD Social Psychology, BA Mathematics and Systems Analysis; lecturer, Moscow College of Economics & Linguistics and the Institute of Economics and Culture; former First Secretary of Ministry of External Affairs of USSR and economist with the Russian Embassies in Canada and India.

"A masterpiece of intelligence and ingenuity. Socionomics-grounded thinking will take us over a whole new conceptual threshold in understanding how human sociological and psychological processes are embedded in the behavior of large-scale cultural phenomena."

—Larry R. Vandervert, PhD; founder, the Society for Chaos Theory in Psychology and the Life Sciences; founder, American Nonlinear Systems; Fellow, American Psychological Association; contributor, *Journal of Mind and Behavior*, *CyberEducation: The Future of Long Distance Learning* and *The International Handbook on Innovation*.

"The insights in this book originate with the careful inductive analysis published in the 1930s by Ralph N. Elliott and culminate with the important and breathtaking work that Robert R. Prechter, Jr. has pursued over the last three decades, applying and extending these principles to a wide variety of phenomena."

—Hernán Cortés Douglas, MA, ABD Economics, University of Chicago; Professor of Economics, Catholic University of Chile; Luksic Scholar at the David Rockefeller Center of Latin American Studies, Harvard University; Executive Director and Founder of the Center for Policy Studies; former Deputy Research Administrator at the World Bank and Senior Economist at the International Monetary Fund.

"By examining the bases and patterns of self-organization within society, *Socionomics* establishes a research agenda that places it at the developmental forefront of the newest research methodologies involving patterns, systems, interactive non-linear influences and the pluralism of the sciences. The insights and issues developed by this rich and robust research agenda provide a plethora of fruitful directions for investigation into the nature of social processes."

—Michael K. Green, PhD Philosophy, University of Chicago; Professor of Philosophy, State University of New York at Oneonta.

"The book is beautiful, and I particularly liked your chapters in Parts III-V on herding behavior and social moods. Congratulations for assembling this stimulating and controversial (from the point of view of mainstream research) book."

—Didier Sornette, PhD Statistical Physics; Professor, Institute of Geophysics and Planetary Physics, UCLA; Director of Research, French National Center for Scientific Research; author, *Critical Phenomena in Natural Sciences, Chaos, Fractals, Self-organization and Disorder*; Editor/Associate Editor, *Journal of Quantitative Finance, Nonlinear Processes in Geophysics, Journal de Physique I & II, European Physical Journal B, Journal of Geophysical Research, Synergetics*; referee for the National Science Foundation; winner Science et Defence French National Award, the Risques-Les Echos prize and the Research McDonnell award.

"I have just finished the book — amazing. I hope that you will distribute free copies to experts in the various fields for their comments and suggestions. This is truly a masterwork. It deserves a lot of publicity."

—Arthur A. Merrill MBA Harvard; President, Merrill Analysis, Inc., author *Behavior of Prices* and *Filtered Waves*; recipient, fourth Annual Award of the Market Technicians Association, editor, *Technical Trends*; member New York Society of Security Analysts, Foundation for the Study of Cycles, MTA and Mensa; formerly Secretary of the Society for the Investigation of Recurring Events and Fellow in the Financial Federation.

"Prechter's work in investment psychology is seminal."

—Dr. John Schott, MD; Chairman, Dept. of Psychiatry, MetroWest Medical Center; Instructor, Harvard Medical School; lecturer, Tufts University Medical School; Director and portfolio manager, Steinberg Global Asset Mgmt.; author, *Mind Over Money*; editor, *The Schott Letter*; Director, annual Congress on the Psychology of Investing.

"WOW stuff! Prechter is doing the most creative work that I have seen in my career on Wall Street."

—John R. Greeley, professional market analyst; co-founder, Market Technicians Association

"Learning about socionomics has proven to be one of those rare intellectual epiphanies that results in an absolute change in the direction of my life. So much about the human experience that had mystified me all of my adult life seems so clear now, so understandable — even to the point of being predictable."

—Jack Hobson-Dupont, President, Monadyne Corp.

"Periodic profound shifts in human sentiment affect nearly everything, from financial markets and economies to geopolitics and perhaps much more. These seismic mood changes have been charted by some seminal thinkers, including Bob Prechter, who now transfers his findings from a lifetime of studying financial markets to human

social behavior at large. While social trends and reversals may have root causes apart from Prechter's conjectures, it would be nearly suicidal to ignore the cycles themselves, for there is no other known roadmap to tell us where we are."

—Alfred H. Kingon,
President, Kingon International; Co-Chairman, Council of American Ambassadors; former U.S. Ambassador to the European Union, Assistant to the President and Secretary of the Cabinet (Reagan), Assistant Secretary of the Treasury, Assistant Secretary of Commerce, Editor-in-Chief of *Financial World, Saturday Review* and *Money and Credit* magazines.

"Many may object to Prechter's assertion that 'the Wave Principle is to sociology and related sciences what Newton's laws were to physics,' but there simply are no other approaches to technical analysis that have a basis for even making such a claim."

—*Technically Speaking*
the newsletter of the Market Technicians Association

"This unusual and interesting book combines economics, sociology and psychology to relate human behavior to market actions."

—*Technical Analysis of Stocks & Commodities* magazine

"Bob has inspired me like no other. His work is utterly intriguing. I aggressively contend that his studies provide incredible insight and relevance to the formal study of the social sciences and the nature of life and the universe."

—Brian Patrick Benda

"Congratulations to Robert Prechter for his interesting, insightful and trail-blazing work. Anyone willing to take the time to read this volume will be rewarded with a new understanding of human behavior, markets and events."

—Tom Spradley
retired college mathematics professor

"Spectacular. I was absolutely impressed. A most brilliant work."

—David Johnson, PhD, MD

"I've just read Prechter's *The Wave Principle of Human Social Behavior.*" It's great! I'm sorry I didn't come across it sooner."
—Flavia Cymbalista, PhD, Berkeley CA

"This is cutting edge stuff, certain to make you rethink much of what you think you know."
—Larry Williams, author
President, Commodity Timing.

"A truly staggering accomplishment. I would be hard pressed to identify another work of similar value despite my career in both the natural and social sciences."
—N.F.

"Wonderful book. One of a half dozen I've read in my life that have re-shaped my thinking in a fundamental and profound way."
—D.C.
retired journalist, Dallas

"I just finished Chapter 8 and impulsively returned post-haste to my office in the house to comment. *Chapter 8 was one of the most thought-provoking, dynamic, riveting concepts I have ever encountered.* Now back to my beach chair."
—Allan Harris

"Your book is more than just fascinating, more than just stimulating; it is a treasure trove of ideas. I must congratulate your attempt to structure the Wave Principle with definitions and on your exploratory mindset. It is most stimulating and refreshing to read someone who is truly excited about what he does know but at the same time is not afraid to admit and then speculate about what he has yet to know."
—T.E., Wallingford, PA

"Both the writing and the thought behind it are uncommonly razor sharp."
—J.G.

"I think you have hit on why mainstream or contemporary economics is not just irrelevant but intellectually void."

—W.R.P.

"I am now in my third reading of *The Wave Principle of Human Social Behavior*. I believe this book will become a standard work for thinkers and scientists. History will recall Prechter as a great pioneer who not only reaffirmed the dusty idea that there is unity in all knowledge and purpose in all form but also offered a single perspective that each field of science can use as a frame of reference. Perhaps unknowingly, I think he has also made the face of God more evident in His universe."

—Earl L. Taylor

"We are informing our readers of your masterpiece, *The Wave Principle of Human Social Behavior*, which is a must-read not only for all financial professionals and all social sciences professionals but also for investors and students."

—Tuncer Sengoz, BorsAnaliz.com;
Manager, Technical Analysis Department of a major bank in Turkey

THE WAVE PRINCIPLE OF HUMAN SOCIAL BEHAVIOR AND THE NEW SCIENCE OF SOCIONOMICS

Socionomics — The Science of History
and Social Prediction, Volume 1

by

Robert R. Prechter, Jr.

New Classics Library

The Wave Principle of
Human Social Behavior
and
The New Science of Socionomics

Printed in the United States of America

For information, address the publishers:
New Classics Library
Post Office Box 1618
Gainesville, Georgia 30503 USA
Phone: 800-336-1618, 770-536-0309
Fax: 770-536-2514
E-mail address for products: customerservice@elliottwave.com
E-mail address for comments: bb@elliottwave.com
Web site: www.elliottwave.com

New Classics Library is the book publishing division of
Elliott Wave International, Inc.

ISBN: 0-932750-54-0
Library of Congress Catalog Card Number: 2002108042

This book is dedicated to
Ralph Nelson Elliott,
who deserves to be recognized as
the father of modern social science.

Acknowledgments

My greatest debts go to four groups of people: the scientists who have so rigorously uncovered so many of nature's secrets as detailed herein, the observant subscribers who have so generously alerted me to new developments and sent copies of articles and studies, Paul Montgomery and Didier Sornette, who critiqued the manuscript, and my colleagues at EWI who aided in production, particularly Sally Webb, who handled the bulk of the project, Pam Kimmons, who produced the jacket art, Gay Doles and Pete Kendall, who researched myriad details, Angie Barringer and Dave Allman, who produced charts and illustrations, and Jane Estes, Betsy Forrester, Beth Parks and Rachel Webb, who helped along the way.

TABLE OF CONTENTS

STATEMENT OF VALUE

I hope that readers will forgive a rather advocative opening statement. However, I fear that without it, too few economists and sociologists will seriously consider this material. Therefore, I will state the following unequivocally: The social sciences today are where the physical sciences were three hundred years ago. The Wave Principle is to sociology and related sciences what Newton's laws were to physics. It provides a basis and framework within which to study and quantify social behavior and thus serves as an anchor for the undertaking of true social science. The resulting breakthrough is so profound that it requires a new name for the science it makes possible. I think socionomics is a good term.

Ralph Nelson Elliott's great insight is the idea that financial markets have a specific organizational law of patterned self-similarity that is governed by the Fibonacci sequence, which therefore ties it to the laws of nature. If I have an insight to provide, it is the vast implications of that fact.

I believe that the Wave Principle and socionomics are the most important concepts ever introduced to the field of social science. They *should* change forever the professions of market analysis, economics and sociology. In fear that it might go unread, I make these bold statements in hopes that they will inspire (or annoy) practitioners of social professions enough to prompt some of them to investigate these ideas and reconsider the old assumptions permeating their fields.

APOLOGIA

I think that the Wave Principle and socionomics are stone cold facts. However, I have worked with and developed them for twenty-five years. Only a fraction of what I know about the field is in this book. It does not come close to conveying the full breadth and depth of either the Wave Principle or socionomics. The nuances of patterns, the remarkable precision of expression, and wider social applications are to be found detailed, to the extent currently possible, in other publications, both extant and forthcoming.

The purpose of this book is to make a case for the validity of the Wave Principle and socionomics as they relate to recent scientific discoveries and the current state of related professions. Despite this narrow goal and my best attempt as a layman who spends most of his time on business, this book may not be up to scientific standards. I am aware that no single chap-

ter in this book proves anything. Worse, some parts of this book present information from fields in which I am an utter novice. However, I believe that when I put all this information together and point out the connections, it makes a substantial circumstantial case. I hope that knowledgeable readers will inform me of any errors I have made so that I may make corrections in the next edition of this book.

WHY NOW?

In Manfred Schroeder's new book, *Fractals, Chaos, Power Laws*, the "Scaling in Psychology" section takes up just one page out of 400. With the knowledge of the Wave Principle and the introduction of socionomics, that representative knowledge ratio should change.

> "Ever since his *Principia*, mathematics has been regarded as the most secure form of knowledge. Newton's successful mathematical descriptions of motion transformed human perception of the structure of the universe beyond recognition. Galileo, on whose shoulders Newton stood, once remarked that the 'great book of nature' is written in the language of mathematics."
>
> —Peter Coveney and Roger Highfield in
> *Frontiers of Complexity*, 1995

> "Phenomena of mass action [are] under impulsions and controls which no science has explored."
>
> —Bernard Baruch in the foreword to *Extraordinary Popular Delusions & the Madness of Crowds*, 1932

> "There are no 'Darwin's equations' describing biological evolution in quantitative, mathematical terms."
>
> —Coveney and Highfield in *Frontiers of Complexity*, 1995

> "There exists no branch of science that deals specifically with an explanation of the subjective self and its relation to the internal and external environment....The successive mentational processes have neither been identified nor shown to obey laws that allow predictable conclusions....Because of the untold number of individuals involved, it would be particularly important to understand the...neural mechanisms...that so galvanize the collective human mind that overnight there

is a round-the-globe spread of fashions in dress (e.g., hair styles, Levis), games (e.g., Hula-Hoops) and reading (e.g., Haley's *Roots*) [or of being] it seems suddenly receptive to some particular 'movement' and inclined to mass demonstrations."

—Paul D. MacLean in *The Triune Brain in Evolution*, 1990

"With these decisions, we have what looks very much like the individual actions of people, with very individual reasons. But statistically, we have some routine [.618] number keep appearing. This is evidence that there is at work some machinery, which corresponds to [a Fibonacci] model. I believe that in a couple of decades, there will be a completely new psychology.... The human being is related to some hidden and unknown laws of the universe."

—Vladimir Lefebvre of the University of California, in
The Los Angeles Times, 1993[1]

"I predict — and I am by no means alone — that one of the most exciting growth areas of twenty-first century science will be biomathematics. The next century will witness an explosion of new mathematical concepts, of new *kinds* of mathematics, brought into being by the need to understand the patterns of the living world. Those new ideas will interact with the biological and physical sciences in totally new ways. They will — if they are successful — provide a deep understanding of that strange phenomenon that we call "life": one in which its astonishing abilities are seen to flow *inevitably* from the underlying richness, and the mathematical elegance, of our universe.... A full understanding of life depends upon mathematics. At every level of scale, from molecules to ecosystems, we find mathematical patterns in innumerable aspects of life. *It is time we put the mathematics and the biology together*."

—Dr. Ian Stewart in *Life's Other Secret*, 1998

"Never — I do not think that is too strong a word — have social scientists been able to embed their narratives in the physical realities of human biology and psychology, even though it is surely there.... We know that virtually all of human behavior is transmitted by culture. We also know that biology has an important effect on the origin of culture and its transmission. The question remaining is how biology and culture interact, and in particular how they interact across all societies to create the commonalities of human nature. What, in final analysis, joins the deep,

mostly genetic history of the species as a whole to the more recent cultural histories of its far-flung societies?...It can be stated as a problem to be solved, the central problem of the social sciences and the humanities, and simultaneously one of the great remaining problems of the natural sciences. At the present time no one has a solution."

—Edward O. Wilson in *Consilience*, 1998

For a number of reasons, the time is right for this book. With science on its current path, serious minds are becoming open to concepts such as those presented herein. With the social mood trend about to become volatile (as I believe it is), people generally will find themselves more willing to pay attention to hypotheses of endogenous causes of social change.

Finally, as a subscriber of mine recently wrote in a personal note attached to a story about chaos and finance, "Like Alexander King's story of the man in an isolated village in Switzerland who unknowingly reinvented the typewriter, it looks like these people are about to rediscover the Elliott Wave."[2] Presumably that typewriter maker was forced to admit that his feat had already been accomplished. If someone today rediscovers the Wave Principle, he might not feel so constrained. I want to make sure that R.N. Elliott gets his due.

I would like to discuss so much more that pertains, from the structure of music to the success and failure of industries to the history of philosophy. However, presenting a full case will have to wait until my team and I have the time to gather more data than we have amassed so far. Few people would read a 1000-page presentation on the applicability of socionomics without having first become convinced of its validity, or at least of its possible validity. I hope there is enough herein to make socionomics acceptable as a hypothesis that will intrigue research scientists who will then desire to undertake to prove or disprove the thesis. Fortunately or not, it has fallen upon me to make the presentation. To transmute the old joke, "It's a fun job, but someone's got to do it."

Foreword

Several times in my life, I have come across a grand concept that was so beautiful, logical and compelling from the standpoint of its pattern that I decided almost immediately that it was valid. That is not cautious science. However, I did not stop there, but investigated further, often much further because of my conviction and fascination, to make sure that I had not been misled.

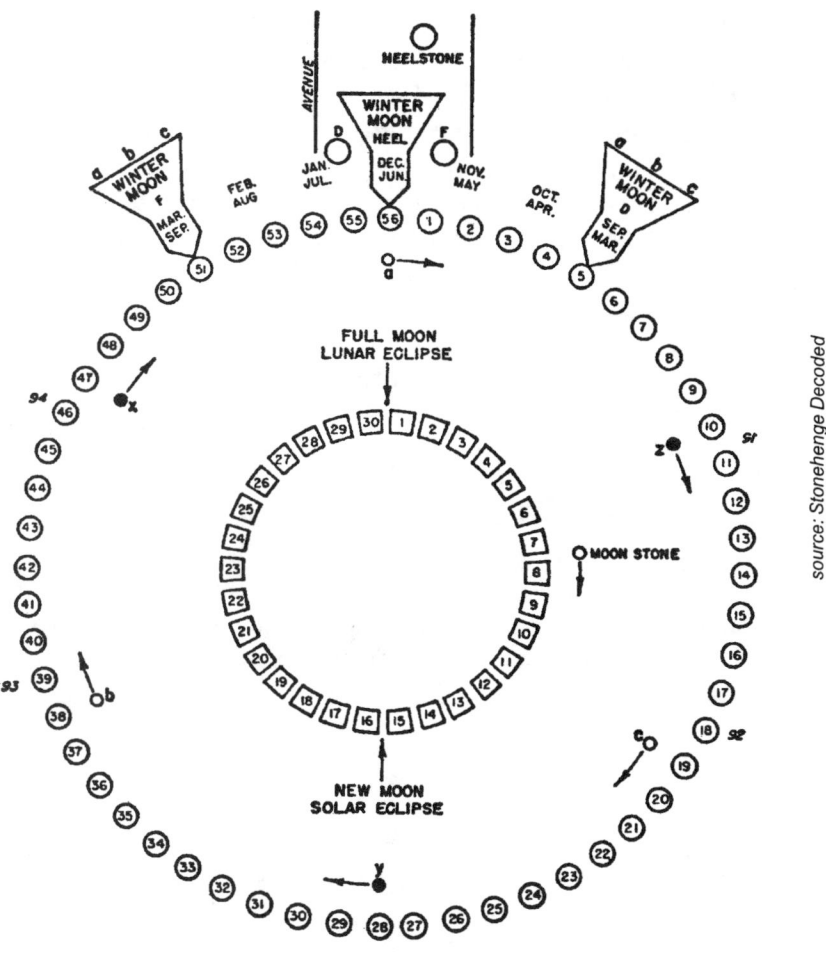

The arrangement at Stonehenge,

per Gerald S. Hawkins

The first such experience I can recall was upon reading the brilliant *Stonehenge Decoded* by professor Gerald S. Hawkins.[3] I was only 17 at the time, but I could see that the pattern of the stones and holes so perfectly matched solar and lunar cycles that thereafter no reasoning person could insist that it was built simply as a chanting ground for druids. When I visited the site the following year, I excitedly mentioned the theory to the official in charge, who had obviously heard about it. "Rubbish!" was his instant reply; "It was a druid temple!" The exquisite coincidence of pattern meant nothing to him.

My next such experience came upon an introduction to the concept of continental drift in a geology course at Yale. The fit among the continents' coastlines is so remarkable and the contour of the ocean floors so compatible with drift that it seemed a compelling deduction at first exposure. It was only a few years ago that I read the story of Alfred Wegener, who postulated the theory in *The Origin of Continents and Oceans* in 1922, and how for decades the profession had not simply challenged but mercilessly derided both him and his idea. The coincidence of pattern meant nothing to them. Then, some forty years later, the concept was quietly slipped into the textbooks by the next generation of experts who, as supporting data accumulated, could see its validity as easily as their predecessors could see its ludicrousness.

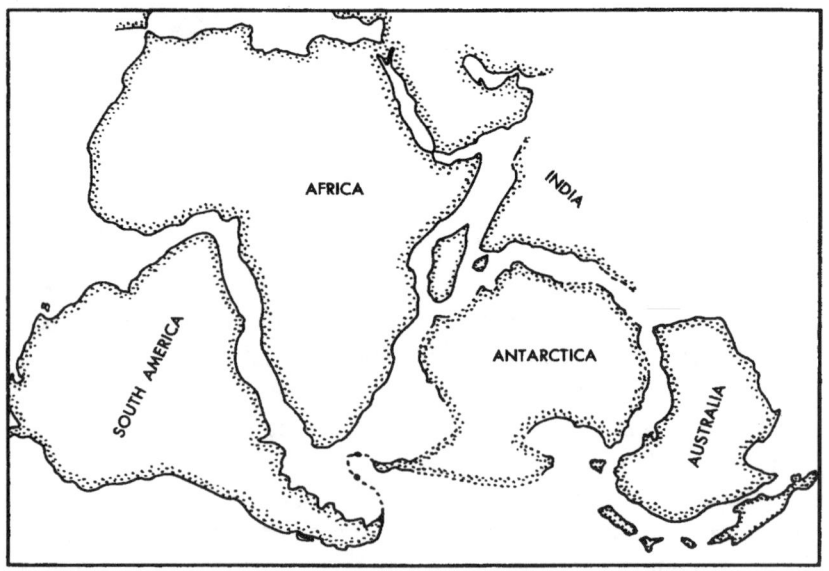

source: Essentials of Earth History

source: The Mysterious William Shakespeare

Edward de Vere, 17th Earl of Oxford

Another time I had this experience was about five years ago upon attending a one-hour speech by Charles Vere, Earl of Burford, about the authorship of the poems and plays written under the pseudonym "Shakespeare." The evidence in favor of the Stratford-Upon-Avon fellow whose name was William Shaksper (as far as anyone can tell, as he was unable to scrawl his own name the same way twice) is essentially nonexistent, and that in favor of Edward de Vere, 17th Earl of Oxford, is so overwhelming as to be definitive. Yet once again, the majority of established scholars, not to mention the tourist trappers in that small town of Stratford, value intricate pattern coincidence between the life and character of an author and the life and character of his plays as naught. In fact, orthodoxy is so bitterly

opposed to admitting a lifelong error that its members denigrate, with vicious *ad hominem* attacks, the intrepid detectives of the author's true identity. They almost never argue the facts because frankly, there are no adequate responses. To experience fully the shallowness and prejudice of the Stratfordians' responses, as well as the richness and genius of the Oxfordians' case, you should read the scholarly *The Mysterious William Shakespeare — The Myth and the Reality* by Harvard alumnus Charlton Ogburn and the work of his predecessors. I am convinced that when the tawdry factoids[4] fostered by the current establishment are finally overwhelmed and replaced by the real story, our children will be reading about de Vere's unique accomplishments and genius, immeasurably enriching the experience of his revolutionary literary output.

Previously, in the early 1970s, I had another such experience with respect to technical methods of stock market analysis. Their basis in recurring patterns (of human behavior, this time) seemed so obviously more valid than the conventional approach that I wasted little time with the latter after comprehending the difference. Needless to say, economists are virtually unanimous in their denigration of technical analysis. The derisive arrogance of some random walk enthusiasts has been so egregious in this regard that it has been satisfying to watch their sacred cow get gored by the new academics who have discovered that the market is not random but apparently governed by nonlinear[5] mathematics, which can produce patterns and thereby provide a basis for technical analysis.[6] Has this breakthrough changed random walkers' minds? Of course not. Max Planck said, "A new scientific truth does not triumph by convincing its opponents and making them see the light, but rather because its opponents eventually die, and a new generation grows up that is familiar with it."[7] As with the Stonehenge curator, the anti-continental drifters and the Stratfordian Shakespeare orthodoxy, random walkers are just going to have to die off to allow the truth to flourish.

My acceptance of the Wave Principle actually came a bit less suddenly. I began trying to apply a rudimentary understanding of it as part of my investigation of technical methods of stock market analysis. By the mid-1970s, I was keeping an hourly chart of the Dow and becoming more fascinated watching the waves unfold as R.N. Elliott described and seeing many of my forecasts on that basis come to pass. In 1976, I read Elliott's original works and was on fire. Here was something not only true but *important*. It just needed some more thought and research.

I will not dwell on the resistance to the idea of the Wave Principle that I have encountered. The good news is that the light of understanding is beginning to shine through the mist. The October 1993 issue of *The Economist* contained a special section called "Frontiers of Finance," which told readers that market prices may not be random; they might reflect nonlinear mathematics. The page 1 sidebar reads, "The idea that a financial market can be predicted is no longer confined to cranks." To me, that is like a 17th century chronicler observing, "The idea that sun lies at the center of the solar system is no longer confined to cranks." In this context, one wishes to be a crank because it means you are a guy who, against a herd of mythologers, came up with the right answer.

Furthermore, many brilliant people have become intrigued with the idea. Dr. John Shea of Memphis's Shea Clinic (who at the age of 30 developed the stapedectomy operation for deafness), arranged for me to join a group of distinguished scientists in addressing "Symmetry in its Various Aspects" at the 21st International Congress on the Unity of the Sciences (ICUS) in Washington, D.C. in 1997. A few months later, I was intrigued to see that two studies of large financial crashes by scientists from the Institute of Geophysics and Planetary Physics at the University of California and the Niels Bohr Institute in Copenhagen use *Elliott Wave Principle* as a reference, a welcome event. (See citations later in this book.) Though work on this book precluded my attendance, I was honored that Daniel Shechtman, the discoverer of quasi-crystals, invited me to address the International Society for the Interdisciplinary Study of Symmetry (ISIS) conference this year in Haifa, Israel. These are marvelous signs of progress in attention paid to the Wave Principle by the scientific community.

I am prepared for backlash from the entrenched old guard of the professional establishment, but I don't care about that. I had my share of both adulation and derision in my "guru" years on Wall Street, times when I could do no wrong in my forecasting and times when I could do little right (that anyone would acknowledge, anyway). Rarely does derision have much real substance, and smart people can see that. I hope I am still young enough to be able to wait, if necessary, for the old guard to die off and to see the new guard start from a fresh perspective. I hope more fervently that upon reading this book and observing the pattern connections, you will experience that same reaction that I have upon occasion and say to yourself, "Yes, of course this is true. How could anyone doubt it?"

SUMMARY

The purpose of this book is to establish the idea that in humans, an unconscious herding impulse impels social mood trends and changes that are specifically patterned according to a natural growth principle and which in turn is the engine of cultural expression and social action. Following is a summary of the main points in this book:

In the 1930s, Ralph Nelson Elliott (1871-1948) discovered that price changes in stock market indexes produce a limited number of definable patterns, or waves, that are robustly self-affine[8] at different degrees, or sizes, of trend. He described how waves at each degree become the components of waves of the next higher degree. Elliott called this phenomenon "The Wave Principle." The essential form is five waves generating net movement in the direction of the one larger trend followed by three waves generating net movement against it, producing a three-steps-forward, two-steps-back form of net progress. Because the basis of the essential form is a repeated 5-3, the numbers of waves at different degrees reflect the Fibonacci sequence. This model has produced a substantial documented success in both accounting for and forecasting stock market trends. Stock market indexes are important because they record man's valuation of his own productive enterprise. The fact that this valuation follows an intricate Fibonacci-based pattern indicates that there is a single essential cause of that valuation, the social mood that underlies it, and the enterprise that results from it.

There is some evidence that the cause of the pattern may be the unconscious herding impulse generated by the brain's limbic system. This impulse determines men's social mood and is independent of outside influence. Fractal, spiral and Fibonacci phenomena in biology and human perception and mentation suggest a biological basis for the phenomenon.

Social mood trends represent changes in human attitudes. Changes in social mood trends precede compatible changes in history and culture, indicating that the former causes the latter. Thus, there is powerful evidence that the pattern of mood change produced by the social interaction of men is the underlying engine of the trends of social progress and regress. This orientation has allowed successful forecasting of financial, economic, political and cultural events. The relationship of the pattern to Fibonacci mathematics suggests that the Wave Principle is another manifestation of a type of growth pattern found throughout nature in processes of growth and decay, expansion and contraction.

DEFINITIONS

The Wave Principle or The Elliott Wave Principle

The Wave Principle is the pattern of progress and regress characteristic of social (and apparently other) phenomena in which progress occurs in specific patterns of five waves and reaction occurs in specific patterns of three waves or combinations thereof.

Elliott wave

An Elliott wave (or *wave*, in context) is any one of the patterns that occurs as a fundamental component of the Wave Principle.

wave

The term "wave" is used as part of the designation of a particular manifestation of an Elliott wave. It is followed by a term describing its position within at least the wave of one larger degree, for example, "wave 1," "wave A," "wave ⓒ of 4," etc.[9] Each wave must allow the movements preceding, following and encompassing it also to be so designated.

From a socionomic perspective, each wave is a unit of social expression and experience.

Elliotter or Elliottician

Using what is becoming conventional terminology, an Elliotter or Elliottician is one who analyzes data series in terms of the Wave Principle.

socionomics

Socionomics is the science of social analysis based upon the socionomic insight.

the socionomic insight

The socionomic insight, as opposed to the conventional belief that social events determine the character of social mood, is the understanding that in fact social mood determines the character of social events.

The mechanism for this causality is as follows: There are biologically based psychological impulses within individuals that relate to human interpersonal dynamics. These dynamics contribute to patterns of fluctuation in collective mood that are *formological* in that they have consistent Fibonacci-based mathematical properties and produce the Wave Principle.[10]

This patterning of social mood creates a *sociological imperative* that mightily guides and influences the character of individual and social behavior. The resulting human actions in turn cause the trends and events of history. The overall process may be termed *historical impulsion*. As opposed to the traditional mechanistic models of aggregate behavior that are based upon presumptions of multiple exogenous causes and ultimate effects, socionomics recognizes that patterns of aggregate human behavior are endogenous, self-causing, self-regulating, self-reinforcing and, to a far greater degree than has heretofore been imagined, predictable.

socionomist

A practical *socionomist* develops and analyzes indicators of social mood in order to forecast the character of social events, occasionally actual social events, and, when possible, the path of social mood itself in light of its following the Wave Principle.

sociometer

A sociometer is a direct reflector of the states and trends of social mood, such as a stock market average. (Other types are proposed in Chapter 15.)

formological system

A *formological system* is neither linear nor nonlinear in terms of event causality because the cause of its processes is not events. A formological system is formologically causal, meaning that the form of the system determines the shape of its process. (For more, see Chapter 20.)

robust fractal

As opposed to self-identical fractals, whose parts are precisely the same as the whole, and indefinite fractals, which are self-similar only in that they are similarly irregular at all scales, a *robust fractal* is one of intermediate specificity. Though variable, its component forms, within a certain defined latitude, are replicas of the larger forms. Both waves and arbora (see below) are robust fractals. (For more, see Chapter 3.)

arborum, etc.

I use the term *arborum* (plural *arbora*) to denote a robust branching fractal common to nature (as opposed to a self-identical or indefinite branching fractal). An *arbum* (plural *arba*) will denote one of the branches of an

arborum. The verb, *to aborate* will denote "to proceed in a robust branching fractal." The process of robustly branching will be termed *arboration*. The adjective *arboral* will mean "having the properties of an arborum." (For more, see Chapter 3.)

Social Mood

I would like to have a single word to stand for "social mood," but have been unable to find one. Words such as "zeitgeist" and "archetype" tend to be stereotyped quickly, and I want to avoid trendiness. The best word I could come up with is *maiesthai*. Maiesthai is the Greek word for "to strive" and is one of the roots of the word "mood," according to Webster's. The combination of mood and striving is a perfect synthesis to express what the Wave Principle governs, so we could make it an English noun. Unfortunately, it is not an easy word to cozy up to. Suggestions are welcome.

Notes on the Definition of Wave

Instead of *Elliott wave*, we could choose always to use the term *wave*, as R.N. Elliott did. However, there are so many types of waves — sine, ocean, light, radio, micro, etc. — that the particular form described as the Wave Principle requires a specific designation. The use of the term wave in the context of a discussion of Elliott waves is no problem. Indeed, the definitions of that and related words in the unabridged *Webster's New International Dictionary* (1976) are remarkable in combining so many of the features of Elliott waves. Here are pertinent excerpts:

As a noun:
- A surge of sensation or emotion.
- An undulating or jagged line constituting a graphic representation.
- One of the vicissitudes of life or fortune.
- A tide of opinion or sentiment carrying many with it: a movement sweeping large numbers in a common direction.
- A disturbance or variation that transfers itself and energy progressively from point to point in a medium or in space in such a way that each particle or element influences the adjacent ones....

As an intransitive verb:[11]
- (Of a crowd): to move in a restless, irregular or fluctuating way likened to that of sea waves.

Waver (the archaic form of which is *wave*):
- To...alternate between...objects [or] conditions (a mood that wavered between uncertain cheer and blackest gloom).
- To vacillate irresolutely between options or attractions.
- To fluctuate in opinion.

NOTES

1 Washburn, J. (1993, March 31). "The human equation." *The Los Angeles Times.*

2 (1993) Personal letter to R. Prechter from J. Barnes, Wetumpka, Alabama.

3 Hawkins, G.S., and White, J. (1965). *Stonehenge decoded.*

4 This useful word originally and properly meant an oft-repeated apparent fact that is false. Journalists have transformed the word to mean "trivial fact," an egregious error that makes their new definition itself a factoid.

5 Actually, I challenge this terminology in Chapter 20.

6 See Brock, W., *et al.* (1992, December). "Simple trading rules and the stochastic properties of stock returns." *Journal of Finance.*

7 Planck, M. (1949). *Scientific autobiography and other papers.*

8 Fractal objects whose properties are not restricted display self-*similarity*, while those that develop in a direction such as price graphs display self-*affinity*. The term "self-similar" is often employed more generally to convey both ideas. In this book, I sometimes use this term in its general sense.

9 See Chapter 1 for a brief discussion of wave notation.

10 See Chapter 3 for a brief discussion of Fibonacci mathematics.

11 It also means "to gesture in greeting." Elliott waves may be nature's way of doing just that. An archaic synonym for wave is *bob*, which I like.

NOTE TO THE READER

I have often added italics in cited quotations to highlight pertinent words and passages. I do not note "emphasis added" after each one.

PART I:

AN INTRODUCTION TO
THE IDEA OF
THE WAVE PRINCIPLE

In the first three parts of this book, I will explain the theory of the Wave Principle, connect it to fractals and spirals, show that it can be modeled and quantified, relate it to indicators of market behavior, demonstrate its utility in forecasting, and then explore its biology, psychology and sociology. Casual readers who are interested only in social-trend forecasting may wish to turn directly to Part IV, beginning with Chapter 14.

Part I is the "bear with me" section. It travels far afield in directions whose relevance may not be immediately apparent but which will be bolstered and clarified as the book progresses.

Chapter 1:

Basic Tenets of the Wave Principle

This chapter provides a succinct overview of the Wave Principle so that those new to the concept can get the idea as quickly as possible. That way, we can move on to address the validity of the concept of the Wave Principle and then discuss its implications and application. Full details are available in *Elliott Wave Principle* (1978/1998). This chapter is necessarily dry as a bone, but I promise that the steam will rise as we move along.

R.N. Elliott's Discovery

In the 1930s, Ralph Nelson Elliott discovered that aggregate stock market prices trend and reverse in recognizable patterns. The patterns he discerned are repetitive in *form*, but not necessarily in time or amplitude. Elliott isolated and defined thirteen patterns, or "waves," that recur in market price data. He named and illustrated the patterns. He then described how they link together to form larger versions of themselves, how they in turn link to form the same patterns at the next larger size, and so on, producing a structured progression. He called this phenomenon The Wave Principle.[1]

Many areas of mass human activity display the Wave Principle, but it is most popularly applied to stock market averages. There is voluminous, meticulously tabulated data on financial markets because people deem them important. Actually, the stock market is far more significant to the human condition than it appears to casual observers and even to those who make their living by it. The level of aggregate stock prices is a direct and immediate measure of the popular valuation of man's total productive capability. That this valuation has a *form* is a fact of profound implications that should ultimately revolutionize the social sciences.

While Elliott progressed to the recognition of patterns and their linkage by a painstaking process of cataloging the minute details of price movement, we will forego such exercises and proceed directly to a description of the overall pattern.

The Five-Wave Pattern

In markets, progress ultimately takes the form of five waves of a specific structure. Waves (1), (3) and (5) in Figure 1-1 actually effect the directional movement. Waves (2) and (4) are countertrend interruptions. The two interruptions are apparently a requisite for overall directional movement to occur.

Elliott noted three consistent aspects of the five-wave form. They are: Wave two never moves beyond the start of wave one, wave three is never the shortest wave,

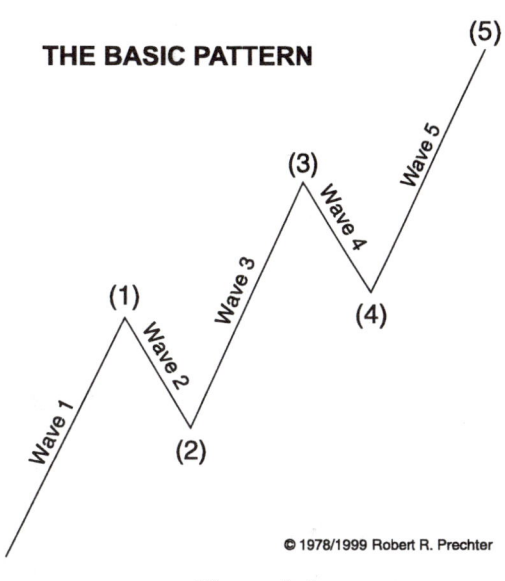

THE BASIC PATTERN

© 1978/1999 Robert R. Prechter

Figure 1-1

and wave four never enters the price territory of wave one. The stock market is always somewhere in the basic five-wave pattern at the largest degree of trend. Because the five-wave pattern is the overriding form of market progress, all other patterns are subsumed by it.

Component Structures

Figure 1-2 shows the first two waves of Figure 1-1 *in greater detail*. Notice the difference in their subdivisions, which reflect the two modes of wave development: *motive* and *corrective*. The two modes are fundamentally different in both their roles and construction.

A motive wave (also called a "five") has a *five*-wave structure. Its subwaves are denoted by numbers (in this case, 1, 2, 3, 4, 5). Both the five-wave pattern of Figure 1-1 and its *same-directional components*, i.e., waves (1), (3) and (5), employ motive mode. Their structures are called "motive" because they powerfully impel the market.

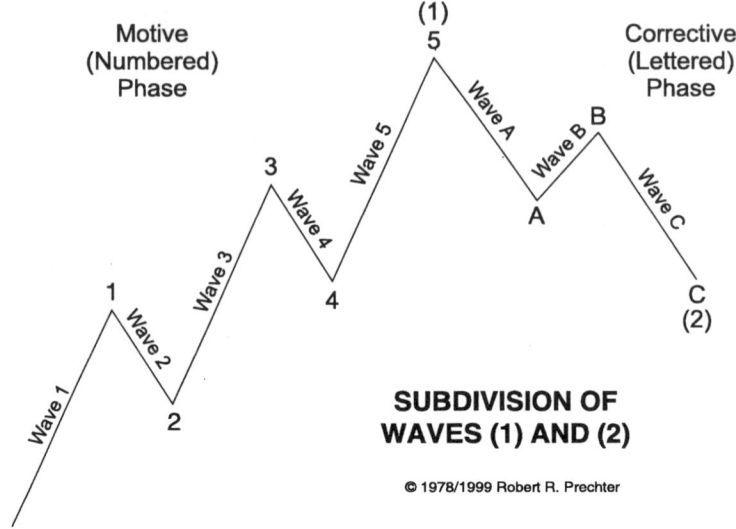

Figure 1-2

A corrective wave (also called a "three") has a *three*-wave structure or a variation thereof. Its subwaves are denoted by letters (in this case, A, B, C). All countertrend interruptions, which include waves (2) and (4) in Figure 1-1, employ corrective mode. Their structures are called "corrective" because each one appears as a response to the preceding motive wave yet accomplishes only a partial retracement of the progress it had achieved, "correcting" its extremity.

Self-Similarity and Degree

When the motive wave in Figure 1-1 ends, a corrective wave of corresponding size follows, so that overall, the result looks like Figure 1-2. Figure 1-3 shows more detail of this development. Observe that the overall form of Figure 1-3 is the same as that of its own subwaves (1) and (2), depicted in Figure 1-2. The only difference is that Figure 1-3 represents a pattern of *one degree* (i.e., relative size) *larger* than the waves of which it is composed.

The word "degree" has a specific meaning and does not mean "scale." Component waves vary in size, but it always takes a certain number of them to create a wave of the next higher degree. Thus, each degree is identifiable in terms of its relationship to higher and lower degrees. This is unlike the infinite scaling relating to say, seacoasts (see Chapter 2).

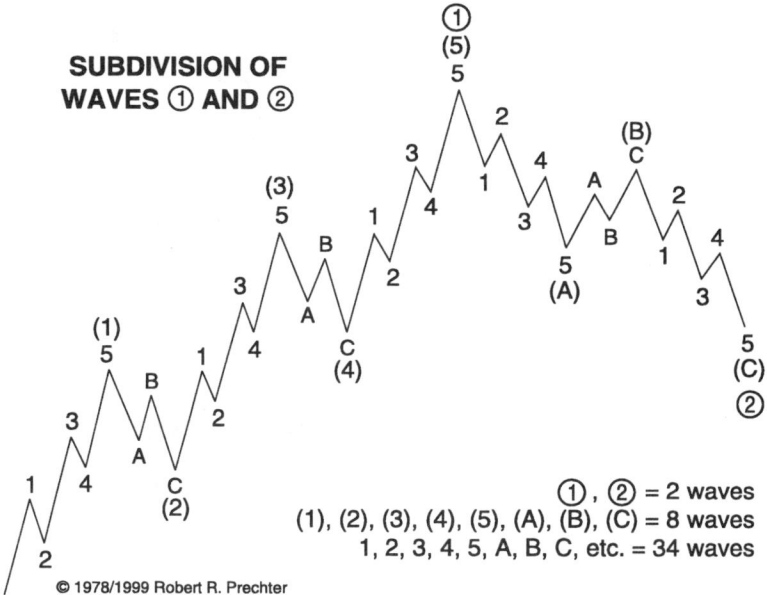

SUBDIVISION OF
WAVES ① AND ②

① , ② = 2 waves
(1), (2), (3), (4), (5), (A), (B), (C) = 8 waves
1, 2, 3, 4, 5, A, B, C, etc. = 34 waves

© 1978/1999 Robert R. Prechter

Figure 1-3

As Figure 1-3 illustrates, then, *each same-direction component of a motive wave* (i.e., wave one, three or five) *and each full-cycle component* (i.e., waves one + two, or waves three + four) *of a complete cycle is a smaller version of itself.*

At this juncture, the significant point to understand is that Figure 1-3 not only illustrates a *larger* version of Figure 1-2, but its pattern also depicts *Figure 1-2 itself,* in greater detail. In Figure 1-2, each subwave 1, 3 and 5 is a motive wave that must subdivide into a "five," and each subwave 2 and 4 is a corrective wave that must subdivide into a "three." Waves 1 and 2 in Figure 1-3, if examined under a "microscope," would take the same form as waves (1) and (2), and in further detail, waves ① and ②. *Regardless of degree, the form is constant.* We can use Figure 1-3 to illustrate two waves, eight waves or thirty-four waves, depending upon the degree to which we are referring.

The Essential Design

Now observe that within the corrective pattern illustrated as wave ② in Figure 1-3, waves (A) and (C), which point downward, are each composed of five waves: 1, 2, 3, 4 and 5. Similarly, wave (B), which points

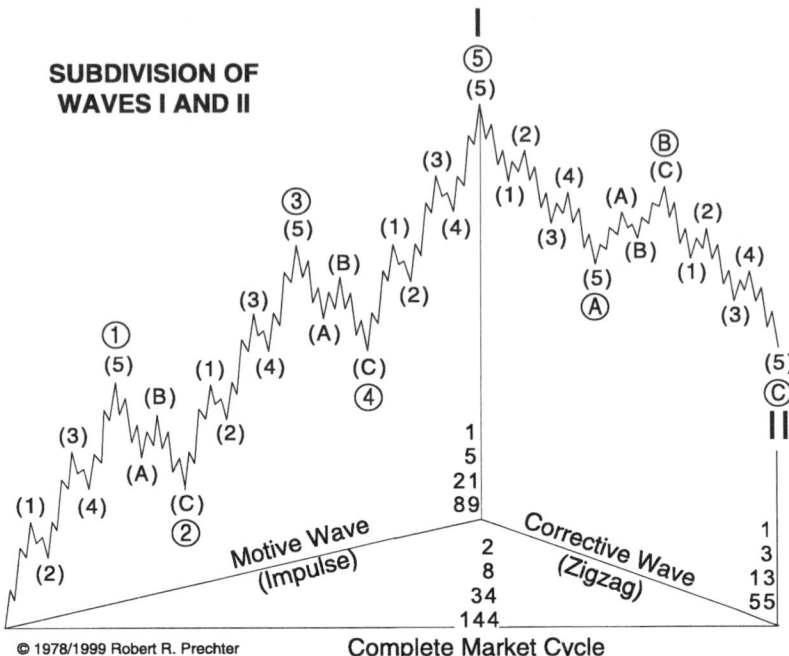

Figure 1-4

upward, is composed of three waves: A, B and C. This construction discloses a crucial point: Motive waves do not always point upward, and corrective waves do not always point downward. The mode of a wave is determined not by its absolute direction but primarily by its *relative* direction. Aside from four specific exceptions, which are discussed in the literature, a wave divides in *motive* mode (five waves) when trending in the *same* direction as the wave of one larger degree of which it is a part, and in *corrective* mode (three waves or a variation) when trending in the *opposite* direction. Waves (A) and (C) are motive, trending in the same direction as wave ②. Wave (B) is corrective because it corrects wave (A) and is countertrend to wave ②. In summary, the essential underlying tendency of the Wave Principle is that *action in the same direction as the one larger trend develops in five waves, while reaction against the one larger trend develops in three waves,* at all degrees of trend.

These phenomena of *form, degree* and *relative direction* are carried one step further in Figure 1-4. This illustration reflects the general principle that in a market cycle, waves will subdivide as shown in the table below.

Number of Waves at Each Degree

	Impulse	+ Correction	= Cycle	
Largest waves	1	1	2	
Largest subdivisions	5	3	8	
Next subdivisions	21	13	34	
Next subdivisions	89	55	144	, etc.

As with Figures 1-2 and 1-3, neither does Figure 1-4 imply finality. Following the form, this larger cycle automatically becomes two subdivisions of the wave of *next* higher degree. As long as progress continues, the process of building to greater degrees continues. The reverse process of subdividing into lesser degrees apparently continues indefinitely as well. As far as we can determine, then, all waves both *have* and *are* (or at the largest degree, *will be*) component waves.

Why 5-3?

Elliott himself never speculated on why the market's essential form was five waves to progress and three waves to regress. He simply noted that it was happening. Does the essential form have to be five waves and three waves? I think so.

First, were there no fluctuation, there would be no progress. A steadily increasing trend of 3% per year, for instance, would be stasis; nothing would ever change. Fluctuation in a net sideways trend, i.e., one with no net change, would also be stasis. Progress must include setbacks *and* net change over time. From the point of view of a participant, *punctuated* progress is the only kind of progress that is possible to perceive.

Second, the 5-3 pattern is *the* minimum requirement for, and therefore the most efficient method of, achieving both *fluctuation* and *progress* in linear movement when the only constraint is that the lengths of odd-numbered waves of each degree be longer than those of the even-numbered ones. One wave does not allow fluctuation. The fewest subdivisions to create fluctuation is three waves. Three waves in both directions do not allow progress. To progress in one direction despite fluctuation, movements in the main trend must be at least five waves, simply to cover more ground than the three waves. While there could be more waves than that, the most efficient form of punctuated progress is 5-3, and nature typically follows the most efficient path.

Notation and Nomenclature

Waves are categorized by degree. The degree of a wave is determined by its size and position *relative to component, adjacent and encompassing waves*. Elliott named nine degrees of waves, from the smallest discernible on a graph of hourly stock prices to the largest he could assume existed from the data then available. He chose the following terms for these degrees, from largest to smallest: Grand Supercycle, Supercycle, Cycle, Primary, Intermediate, Minor, Minute, Minuette, Subminuette. Cycle waves subdivide into Primary waves that subdivide into Intermediate waves that in turn subdivide into Minor waves, and so on. This specific terminology is not critical to the identification of degrees, although out of habit, longtime practitioners have become comfortable with Elliott's nomenclature.

When labeling waves on a graph, some scheme is necessary to differentiate the degrees of waves in the stock market's progression. The most desirable form for a scientist might be 1_1, 1_2, 1_3, 1_4, 1_5, etc., with subscripts denoting degree. We use this form in our computer program (see Chapter 4), although it is difficult to read a large number of such notations on a graph. Elliott Wave International has standardized a sequence of labels involving numbers and letters. The following notations, for instance, denote first waves from Grand Supercycle degree down to Subminuette: (I), (I), I, (1), (1), 1, (i), (i), i. This standard provides for rapid visual orientation.

It is important to understand that these names and labels refer to specifically identifiable degrees of waves. By using a nomenclature, an analyst can identify precisely the position of a wave in the overall progression of the market, much as longitude and latitude are used to identify a geographical location. To say, "The Dow Jones Industrial Average is in Minute wave (v) of Minor wave 1 of Intermediate wave (3) of Primary wave (5) of Cycle wave I of Supercycle wave (V) of the current Grand Supercycle" is to identify a specific point along the progression of stock market history.

Variations on the Basic Theme

The basic model is simple, but reality is a bit more complex, as there are specific variations on the underlying theme that Elliott catalogued in detail. He also noted the important fact that each pattern has identifiable *rigidities* as well as *tendencies*. From these observations, he was able to formulate descriptions of typical wave behavior and therefore *rules* and

A REALISTIC ELLIOTT WAVE

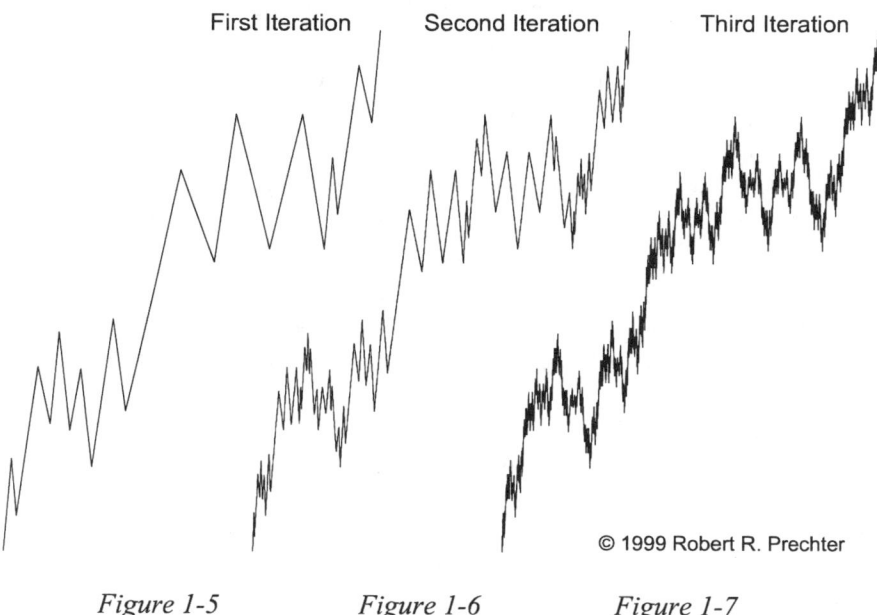

First Iteration   Second Iteration   Third Iteration

© 1999 Robert R. Prechter

Figure 1-5   *Figure 1-6*   *Figure 1-7*

guidelines for proper wave identification. For example, in the five-wave pattern (termed an "impulse"), the middle wave is usually the longest, and the two corrective waves usually alternate in form, the first "sharp," the second "sideways," as shown in Figure 1-5. Figures 1-6 and 1-7 then take this form to two and three iterations respectively.

A thorough understanding of such details is necessary to know what the market can do, and at least as important, what it does not do. However, as the purpose of this chapter is limited to introducing the general hypothesis, a discussion of such nuances is omitted. Chapter 3 will present a highly detailed representative list of wave-formation rules for impulses to give you a flavor of their intricacy. Some readers may wish to peruse a short list of fine points in order to understand more precisely the reasons behind some aspects of the labeling in the historical graphs shown throughout this book. If so, see endnote 2.[2]

Modern Science Comments on the Wave Principle Hypothesis

1996 was an important year for the Wave Principle. In that year, the *Journal of Physics* published a scientific study entitled "Stock Market Crashes, Precursors and Replicas" by Didier Sornette and Anders Johansen,

then of the Laboratoire de Physique de la Matière Condensée at the University of Nice, France, and collaborator Jean-Philippe Bouchaud. The authors make this statement:

> It is intriguing that the log-periodic structures documented here bear some similarity with the "Elliott waves" of technical analysis [citation *Elliott Wave Principle*]. Technical analysis in finance can be broadly defined as the study of financial markets, mainly using graphs of stock prices as a function of time, in the goal of predicting future trends. A lot of effort has been developed in finance both by academic and trading institutions and more recently by physicists (using some of their statistical tools developed to deal with complex times series) to analyze past data to get information on the future. The "Elliott wave" technique is probably the most famous in this field. We speculate that the "Elliott waves"...could be a signature of an underlying critical structure of the stock market.[3]

In this book, I further speculate that the Wave Principle could be a signature of the underlying structures of a whole lot of things. Let us begin our journey.

NOTES

1 Elliott, R.N. (1938). *The wave principle.*

2 **Summary of Additional Technical Aspects**: Additional technical aspects of waves, which are discussed in detail in *Elliott Wave Principle – Key to Market Behavior* by A.J. Frost and Robert R. Prechter, are herewith stated as briefly as possible: Impulses, i.e., five-wave patterns like those shown in Figures 1-1 through 1-7, are typically bound by parallel lines. One wave in an impulse, i.e., 1, 3 *or* 5, is typically extended, i.e., much longer than the other two. In impulses, waves 2 and 4 nearly always alternate in form, where one correction is typically of the zigzag family and the other is not. There are two rare motive variations called diagonal triangles, which are wedge-shaped patterns that appear in one case only at the start (wave 1 or A) and in the other case only at the end (wave 5 or C) of a larger wave. Corrective waves have numerous variations. The main ones are named zigzag (which is the one shown in Figures 1-2, 1-3 and 1-4), flat, and triangle (whose labels include D and E). These three simple corrective patterns can string together to form more complex corrections (the components of which are labeled W, X, Y and Z). Corrections usually terminate within the span of wave 4 of the preceding impulse. Each wave exhibits characteristic volume behavior and a "personality" in terms of attendant momentum and investor sentiment.

3 Sornette, D., Johansen, A., and Bouchaud, J.P. (1996). "Stock market crashes, precursors and replicas." *Journal de Physique I France* 6, No.1, pp. 167-175.

New note: For the record, while Sornette and Johansen have continued to augment their research in areas related to the paper here quoted, Bouchaud participated in a 1998 challenge to "recent claims that financial crashes can be predicted using the idea of log-periodic oscillations or by other methods inspired by the physics of critical phenomena...[i]n particular, the October 1997 correction..." (Laloux et al., "Are Financial Crashes Predictable?" *Condensed Matter* 9804111 v.1, April 9, 1998). I have no specific hope or bias with respect to this claim and counterclaim, as the Wave Principle, while suggestive of occasional log-*amplitudinal* oscillations (see pp. 102-103, as well as Prechter, Robert R., "Packet Waves," *Market Analysis for the New Millennium*, pp.201-228, New Classics Library, 2002 and discussions of corrective triangles in Frost and Prechter, *Elliott Wave Principle*, pp.48-52 and pp.115-116), does not depend upon log periodicity. Physics may not be the proper path to elucidate the Wave Principle, which is a social phenomenon involving human mental states. Nevertheless, I heartily applaud physicists' recent research into financial price phenomena, none of which contradicts and much of which supports the case for the Wave Principle.

Chapter 2:

Universal Forms: Fractals, Power Laws and Spirals in Self-Organizing Systems, and Their Connection to the Wave Principle

Fractals and Their Relationship to the Wave Principle

A fractal is an irregularly shaped object that is nonrandom in the sense that its discontinuities (i.e., fluctuations) at all scales are similarly irregular. For example, if someone were to show you a line representing the indentations of land along a coastline, you would not be able to say, without other evidence, whether the coastal section was 1 mile long, 10 miles long, 100 miles long or 1000 miles long. A fractal displays the property of self-similarity (or self-affinity, depending on its form) at different scales. The jaggedness of a coastline is self-similarly irregular at different scales. So it is with price graphs of financial markets. As R.N. Elliott pointed out in 1938, the patterns of the Wave Principle take a similarly jagged shape whether viewed on an hourly, daily, weekly, monthly or yearly graph.

In 1689, Jakob and Johan Bernoulli were able to "discern the minute in infinity" in a mathematical progression that foreshadowed the discovery of the fractal geometry of nature.[1] Perhaps the first person specifically to advance the idea of self-similarity at different scales in natural forms was the German poet and naturalist, Johann Wolfgang von Goethe, who in 1790 described the self-similarity of parts to the whole of plants.[2] A century later, from 1874 to 1897, mathematician Georg Cantor studied self-similar sets as mathematical phenomena.[3,4]

In 1919, Felix Hausdorff invented the idea of fractional dimensions to describe the plane- or space-filling property of complex fractals.[5] A fractional dimension (called a Hausdorff dimension prior to the 1980s) describes

objects that share properties of two sets of dimensions. For example, if a sheet of paper is considered as a two-dimensional plane, is a partially compressed ball of paper two-dimensional or three-dimensional? It is still a plane, but it has been folded so as to appear to fill space, giving it three-dimensional properties. Its dimension can be measured as a fraction between 2 and 3. In the same way, plots of financial market prices can be considered as a one-dimensional line or as taking up space on a two-dimensional plane.

It is quite certain, since he was careful to name sources that inspired his later ideas, that Elliott never studied Bernoulli, Goethe, Cantor or Hausdorff, so it is acceptable to say that in the 1930s, R.N. Elliott independently rediscovered the idea of self-similarity at different scales. More important, he was unquestionably the first to describe self-affinity as a fundamental property of social phenomena and to recognize its implication for social causality. Here is some of Elliott's commentary that introduced these revolutionary ideas:

Extensive research in connection with what may be termed human activities indicates that practically all developments which result from our social-economic processes follow a law that causes them to repeat themselves in similar and constantly recurring serials of waves or impulses of definite number and pattern. It is likewise indicated that in their intensity, these waves or impulses bear a consistent relation to one another and to the passage of time.

The expression "human activities" includes such items as stock prices, bond prices, patent (application)s, [the] price of gold, population [growth], movements of citizens from cities to farms and vice versa, commodities prices, government expenditures, production, life insurance [purchases], electric power produced, gasoline consumption, fire losses, price of seats on the stock exchange, epidemics, and real estate, business, politics [and] the pursuit of pleasure.[6] It is particularly evident in those free markets where public participation in price movements is extensive.

Those who have attempted to deal with the market's movements have failed to recognize the extent to which the market is a psychological phenomenon. They have not grasped the fact that there is regularity underlying the fluctuations of the market, or, stated otherwise, that price movements in stocks are subject to rhythms, or an ordered sequence. The wild, senseless and apparently uncontrollable changes in prices from year to year, from month to month, or from day to day, link themselves into a law-abiding rhythmic pattern of waves. The same rules apply to the price of stocks, bonds, grains, cotton, coffee and all the other activities previously mentioned.

The student should recognize that there are cycles within cycles. Major waves subdivide into intermediate waves [, which] subdivide into minor waves. One cycle becomes but the starting point of another, or larger, movement that itself is a part of, and subject to the same law as, the lesser movement. This fundamental law cannot be subverted or set aside by statutes or restrictions. Current news and political developments are of only incidental importance, soon forgotten; their presumed influence on market trends is not as weighty as is commonly believed. Underlying this progression, in whatever field, is a fixed and controlling principle, or the master rule under which nature works. This treatise has made use of price movements in stocks to illustrate the phenomenon, but all the principles laid down herein are equally applicable to the wave movement in every field where human endeavor is registered.[7]

It has been decades since similar words, more precisely stated, have emerged as a result of studies in fractal geometry. I believe that, especially along with his pioneering diagrams, they are more than sufficient to credit Elliott with having introduced the idea that self-affinity governs social processes and is fundamental to nature. As these words imply, though, and as we shall see more clearly in Chapter 3, Elliott explained that there is much more to the Wave Principle than mere self-affinity.

Examples of the Basic Pattern from the Lowest Extreme of Available Data Duration to the Highest

Elliott pointed out that the impulse-correction pattern, which subdivides into five waves then three waves, is manifest at all degrees of trend. Figures 2-1 through 2-7 illustrate this observation with real-life examples.

The shortest duration of available data is that which shows every single price change in a financial index. Such changes sometimes register in less than a second and are called "ticks." Figure 2-1 shows a "tick" graph from October 6, 1997.

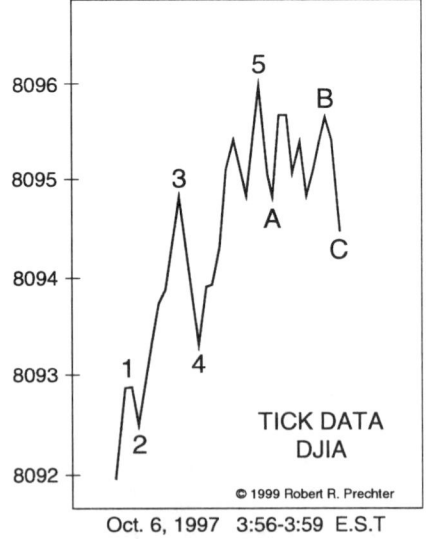

TICK DATA
DJIA

© 1999 Robert R. Prechter

Oct. 6, 1997   3:56-3:59 E.S.T

Figure 2-1

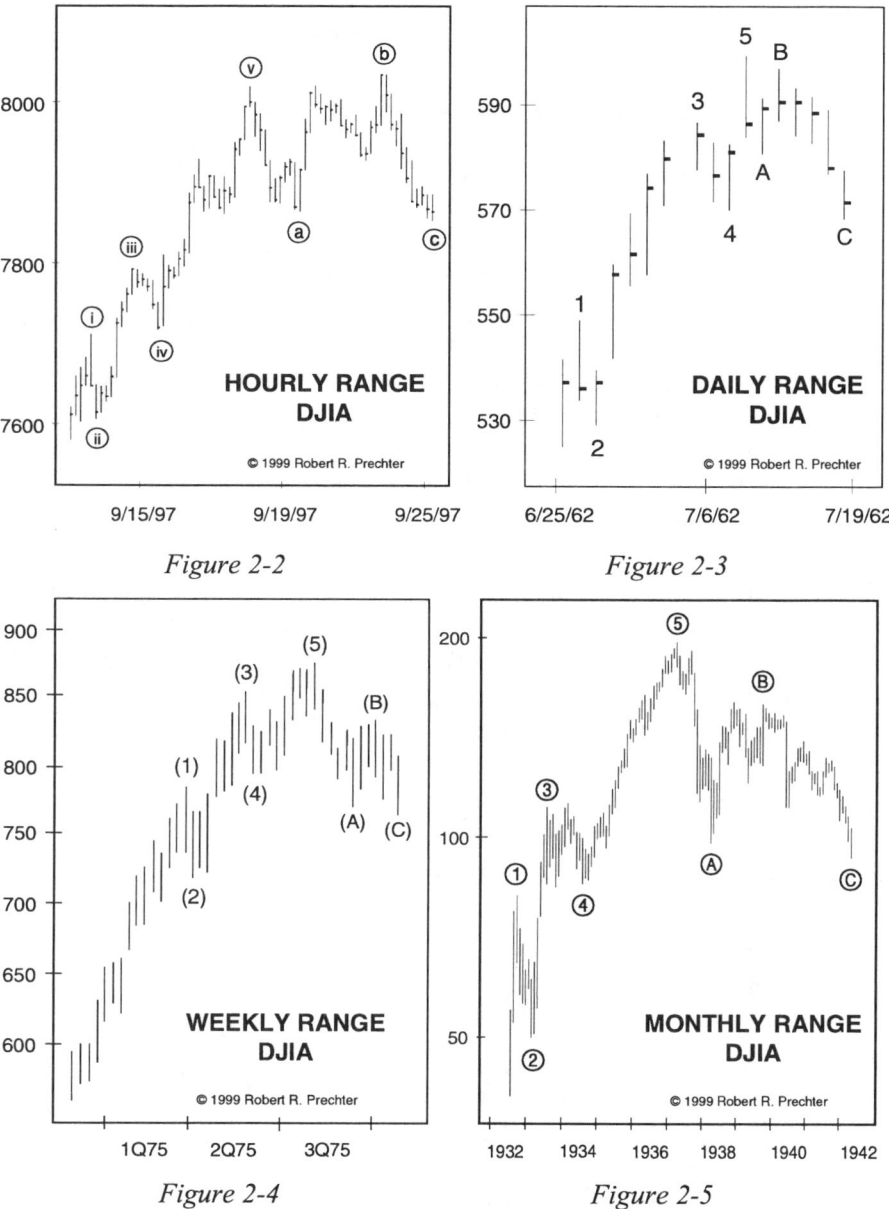

Figure 2-2

Figure 2-3

Figure 2-4

Figure 2-5

Figure 2-2 shows an hourly graph from September 1997. Figure 2-3 is a daily graph from 1962. Figure 2-4 is a weekly graph from 1974-1975. Figure 2-5 is a monthly graph from 1932 to 1942. Figure 2-6 is a yearly graph from 1929 to the present. Figure 2-7 is a decade-by-decade graph from 1700 to the present. There are no data prior to 1690. All these plots show similar patterns of movement despite a difference in time span of over 30 million to 1. The longer-term formulations depicted in Figures 2-6 and 2-7

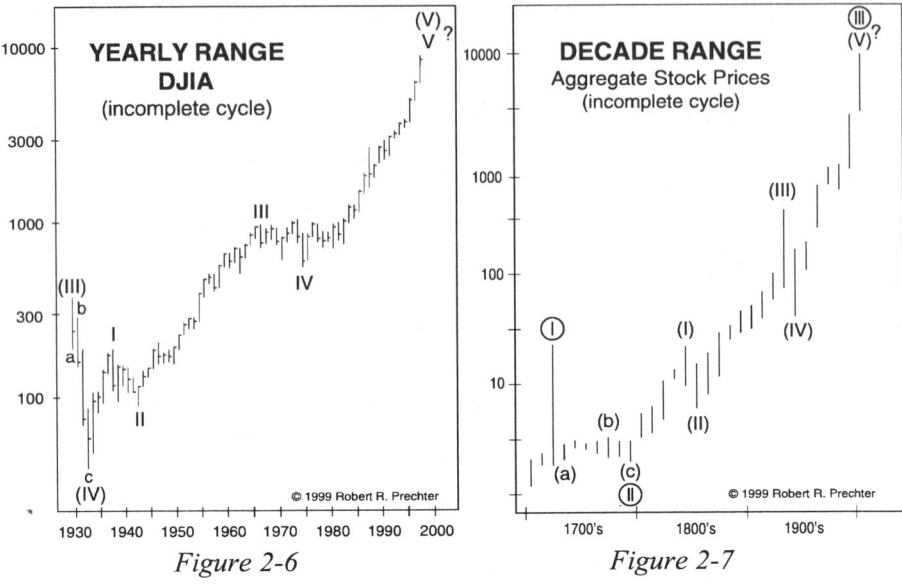

Figure 2-6   *Figure 2-7*

are still unfolding, but to date the pattern is following the same form as the smaller-degree plots.

The Ubiquity of Fractals in Nature

The modern science of fractal geometry reveals that nature is replete with self-similar patterns. The pioneer in the recent furthering of this concept is Benoit Mandelbrot, an IBM researcher and former professor at Harvard, Yale and the Einstein College of Medicine. What Mandelbrot has demonstrated is the *ubiquity* of fractals and self-similarity in nature. This discovery has dispelled the idea of randomness in natural forms. Before Mandelbrot, most scientists had presumed that no single geometry governed clouds, seacoasts, mountain ranges, cotton prices and trees. Mandelbrot said that in fact they display a relational form, an orderliness that comes from the fact that they possess self-similarity at different scales.[8]

Countless natural forms are self-similar. Waves on the ocean range from huge swells hundreds of meters in length that are generated by gravitational fluctuations to so-called capillary waves of about one centimeter in length that are controlled by surface tension.[9] In trees, branches off the trunk look like small versions of the tree, as do the twigs off the branches and the veins in the leaves. River systems look like trees, as they branch from rivers to streams to creeks to runoff ditches. Lightning takes a similar

form. Manganese oxide creates a fractal branching pattern when it undergoes a reaction-diffusion process on the surface of limestone. Bacteria create similar patterns when growing in a petri dish.

It is tempting to begin viewing almost *everything* as a fractal. A house is a box composed of smaller boxes called floors, which have smaller boxes called rooms. All the houses together in a small geographical area make a neighborhood, and all the neighborhoods in a larger geographical area make a city. Reflecting the same idea, a library has rooms that subdivide into racks that subdivide into bookcases that subdivide into bookshelves that subdivide into books that subdivide into chapters that subdivide into paragraphs that subdivide into sentences. Reverse that list, and you can see how the body of human knowledge grows and how it is stored, all the way up to today's largest encapsulation, the Internet. Psychiatrist Montague Ullman suggests that dreams are fractals, wherein the central concern of the dreamer is expressed both in the overall "story" of the dream and separately in its component parts.[10] Figures 2-8 through 2-15 depict three types of fractals. Chapter 3 will explore their differences.

Fractals in Finance

This excerpt from a 1985 article in *The New York Times* summarizing Mandelbrot's exposition brings us closer to the subject of social fractals:

> When you zoom in, looking closer and closer, the irregularities don't smooth out. Rather, they tend to look exactly as irregular as before. Some of Mandelbrot's fractal patterns looked indistinguishable from records of stock market prices. Economists needed to understand the heretical idea that prices don't change in a smooth, continuous flow. They can change abruptly in instantaneous jumps.[11]

Similarly, Elliott contended that major bull markets are no different in shape from short-term rallies, and big bear markets are no different in shape from short-term reactions. They are just of a larger degree and thus occur less often. A headline-making market "crash," for instance, is simply a large version of what happens all the time on smaller scales. The article continues:

> Daily fluctuations are treated [by economists] one way, while the great changes that bring prosperity or depression are thought to belong to a different order of things. In each case, Mandelbrot said, my attitude is: Let's see what's different from the point of view of geometry. What comes out all seems to fall on a continuum; the mechanisms don't seem to be different.

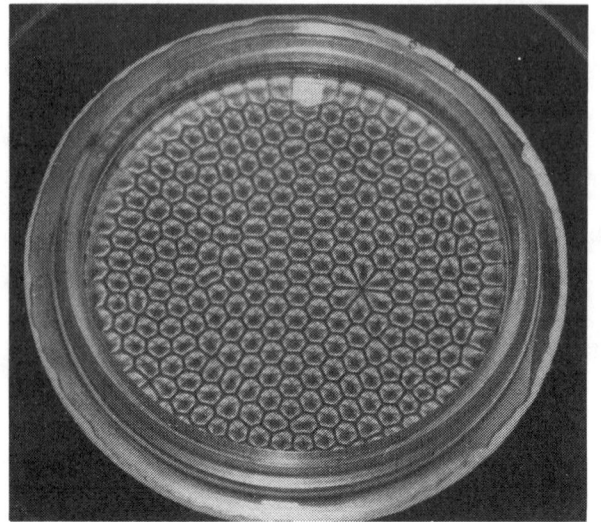

source: Fractals: The Pattern of Chaos

*A self-identical fractal: silicone oil heated to a critical state —
a collection of identical hexagons of increasing size*

Figure 2-8

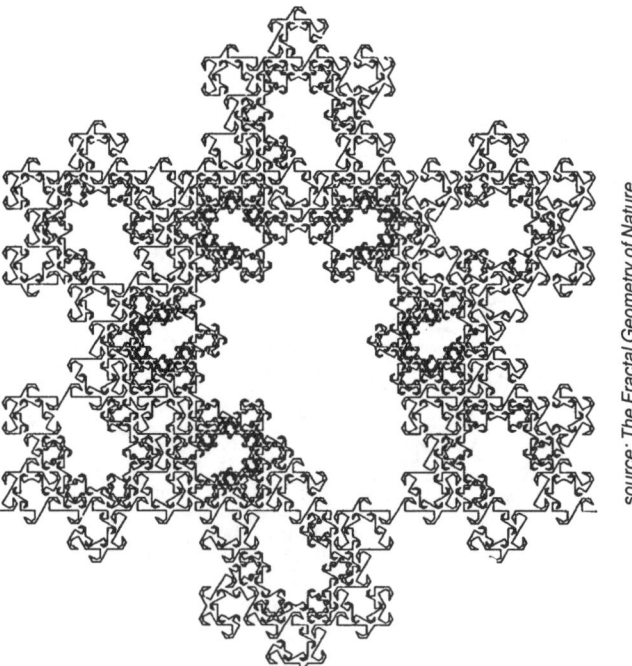

source: The Fractal Geometry of Nature

*A self-identical fractal: computer-generated snowflake —
a collection of identical hexagonal forms of increasing size*

Figure 2-9

A self-identical fractal: line Iteration – repeating patterns of increasing size

Figure 2-10

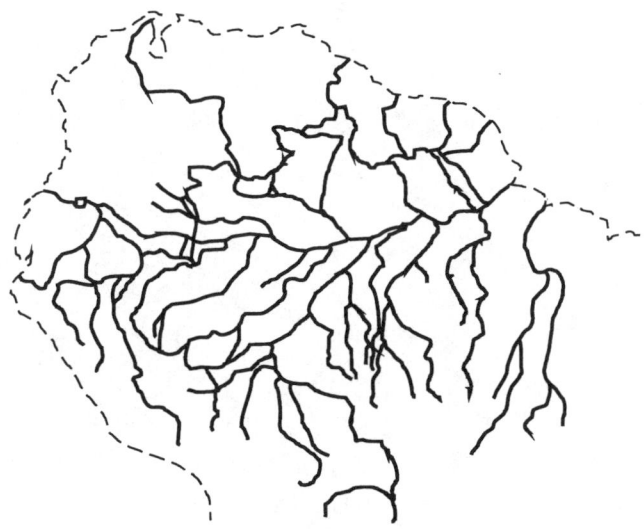

A branching fractal: South American river system

Figure 2-11

A branching fractal: lightning

Figure 2-12

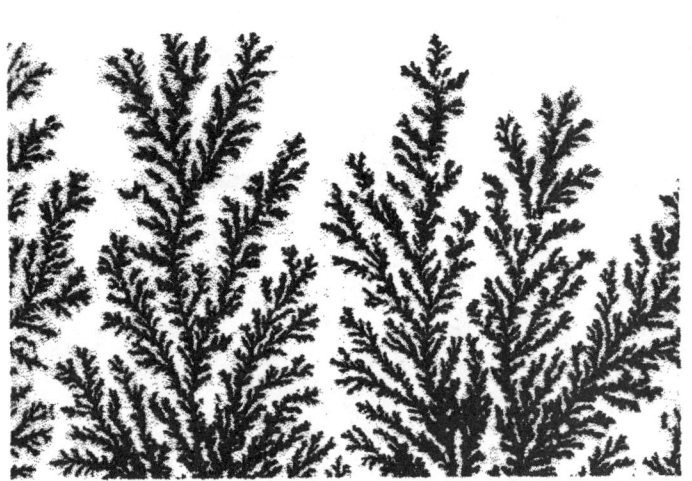

A branching fractal: manganese oxide diffusion

Figure 2-13

source: Growth Patterns in Physical Sciences and Biology

source: http://gordonr.simplenet.com

An indefinite fractal: clouds

Figure 2-14

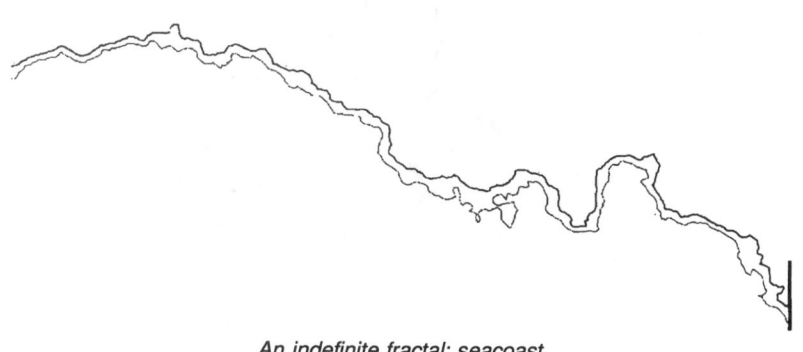

source: The Fractal Geometry of Nature

An indefinite fractal: seacoast

Figure 2-15

This is precisely what R.N. Elliott said about the stock market, and he said it sixty years ago. The following quote, from *Insight* magazine, throws some light on the enormity of Elliott's feat. He discovered all this (and much more; see Chapter 3) in the 1930s using hand-drawn charts of hourly to yearly market data:

> Because of the complexity of the images [scientists] are studying, they use virtually millions of numbers in their calculations. These numbers, says, Quentin Dolecek of Johns Hopkins's Applied Physics Laboratory, would be impossible without computers.[12]

The Ubiquity of Power Laws in Nature

A power law is a formula that when graphed produces a curve whose height is inversely proportional to its distance raised to a power. For instance, with repect to some proportional constant (a), the frequency (f) of earthquakes is inversely related to their energy (e) raised to a power (n), as in the formula $f = ae^{-n}$. In other words, if a logarithm of the number of events is plotted against the logarithm of their energy, the result is a straight line. Power laws have no intrinsic scale, meaning that graphs of such phenomena appear the same regardless of the size of measurements one might take to assess them.

Much has been made of the fact that power laws govern fractals, although the very idea of a fractal seems naturally to imply a power law. Self-similarity *at all scales* implies that the *frequency* of events, fluctuations or patterns in a fractal will vary inversely with their *size*.

The Gutenberg-Richter law, identified a half-century ago, states that the severity of earthquakes as measured by the Richter scale is related to their frequency according to a power law.[13] Also in 1949, G.K. Zipf found that the distribution of wealth throughout a society follows a power law and that the frequency of word usage follows a power law with respect to syllable length.[14] In the 1990s, scientists are discovering that power laws govern an immense number of fractal formations and events, both animate and inanimate, including avalanches, earthquakes, mountain sizes, zigs and zags in the flights of bees, economic fluctuations and financial market fluctuations. Richard Voss of IBM's T.J. Watson Research Center found a power law in the structure of DNA.[15] H. Eugene Stanley of Boston University, says *New Scientist,* has found a power law "in the dynamics of the human heart and lungs."[16] Stephen Wolfram of Wolfram Research in Champaign, Illinois, has developed a computer program, "Mathematica," that applies power-law aspects of complexity theory (see Chapter 20) to

fields as diverse as "designing the bicycle track at the 1996 Olympic games, predicting the flow rates of molecules in commercial shampoos, determining how tidal waves evolve...and 'how biological systems can be constructed.'"[17] Wolfram's research began with a search in the 1980s to investigate "patterns on mollusk shells, the behavior of molecules swirling in a turbulent fluid, and fluctuating prices on the stock market." Norman Packard, an associate who with Wolfram set up the Center for Complex Systems at the University of Illinois, applies the fundamentals of complexity theory "to help Swiss banks play the stock market."[18] Scientists today are studying complex systems to find out how matter can organize itself into more complex forms (Per Bak of the Neils Bohr Institute in Copenhagen), how life originated (Stuart Kauffman at the Santa Fe Institute), and how complex systems, from a collection of bacteria to a group of competing companies, behave (Christopher Langton at the Santa Fe Institute). Power laws are everywhere in such systems, including financial markets.

A Power Law in the Stock Market

R.N. Elliott's depiction of the progress of the stock market unequivocally implied that while larger stock market reactions occur less often than small ones, they do not occur less often *relative to the size of advances that precede them*, but in fact just about as often. In other words, Elliott implied that the stock market follows a power law. In 1995, Boston University physicists Gene Stanley and Rosario Mantegna found that the fluctuations in the Standard & Poor's Composite index of the 500 highest capitalized stocks do follow a power law. This particular power law is a Levy stable law (named after a French mathematician of the early 20th century), which produces a bell curve with "extended wings," indicating that far-from-normal fluctuations in terms of size occur a bit more often than they would if they followed a one-to-one relationship to the duration of the data sample. Figure 2-16, from Mantegna and Stanley's article in *Nature,* demonstrates that the S&P's fluctuations are quite uniform throughout the time scale, from 1 minute to 1000 minutes.[19] This finding is consistent with the Wave Principle, which creates the same forms at all sizes of trend, with the added wrinkle that large fluctuations, at least in this data sample, occurred a bit more often than smaller ones relative to the time intervals between them.

Levy laws also govern birds' flying and landing patterns, drips from leaky faucets, the wanderings of ants, and fluctuations in cotton prices and heartbeats. Stanley is applying the behavioral similarities of complex sys-

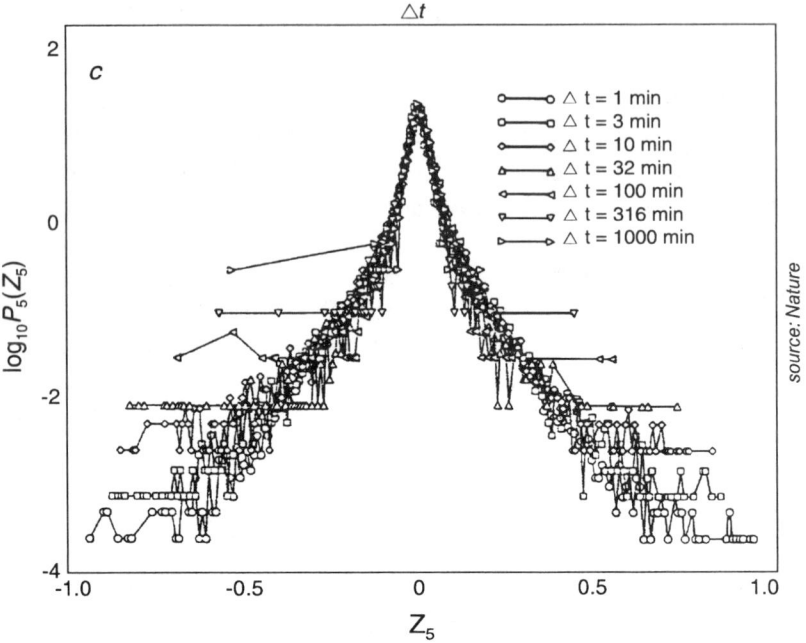

Consistent fractal fluctuation at varying time intervals in the S&P 500

Figure 2-16

tems to understanding landscape formation, traffic patterns, Alzheimer's disease and the behavior of neutron stars. Like fractals, power laws suffuse nature.

Quantity and Quality in Fractals and Power Laws

Fractals involve sizes, but specific sizes do not matter in describing or defining a fractal object. In the same way, power laws relate to sizes and frequencies, but the specific sizes and frequencies do not matter to the formulae. Quantitatively, what matters in each case is *relative* sizes and frequencies, i.e., *relationships*, not absolutes.

Qualitatively, what matters in fractals and power laws is *form*, not size. Trees are governed by form, not absolute branch size. Heartbeat is governed by pattern, not absolute frequency. The spirals of Nautilus seashells and the galaxies are governed by a single form, not their size. As we said in *Elliott Wave Principle*, "The patterns that Elliott discerned [in financial markets] are repetitive in *form* but not necessarily in time or amplitude." A fractal is not the only ubiquitous natural phenomenon whose essence is its form. The other is the spiral.

The Ubiquity of Spirals in Nature

Like fractals and power laws, spirals appear throughout nature. While Euclidean geometric forms (except perhaps for the ellipse) typically imply stasis, a spiral implies motion: growth and decay, expansion and contraction, progress and regress.[20] The logarithmic spiral, which depicts constant geometric expansion, is the quintessential expression of growth in the universe and is reflected in structures as diverse as pine cones, sunflowers, sea shells, whirlpools and hurricanes. It covers scales as small as the motion of atomic particles and as large as galaxies. The spiral is also one of biology's most ancient body forms. The exoskeletons of early sea animals developed Fibonacci-based spiral shapes that have persisted through to today, as you can see in Figures 2-25 and 2-27. A fossilized Lake Ivo fern is virtually identical to its present-day counterpart, as you can see in these two photographs from *The Smithsonian* (Figure 2-17). If you would like to see a counterpart to this form in fauna, hold up your arm so that your hand is at eye level, then make a fist (holding your thumb inside), and bend your wrist inward. Looking at the side view, do you see the fern? Figures 2-18 through 2-28 illustrate more of these forms.

Does the Wave Principle, which already incorporates two aspects shared by common patterns in nature, i.e., fractals and a power law, reflect spiral growth as well? The idealized depiction of the stock market's progression, as presented in Figure 1-4, is an excellent base from which to

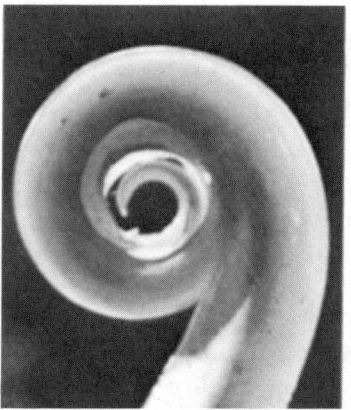 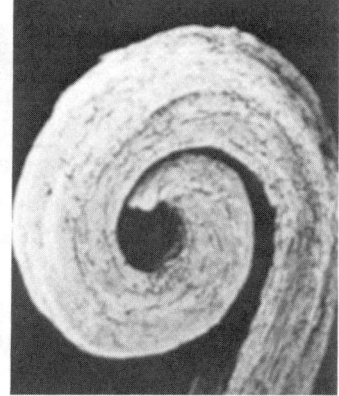

source: Smithsonian, Nov. 84

Lake Ivo fern, modern and fossilized

Figure 2-17

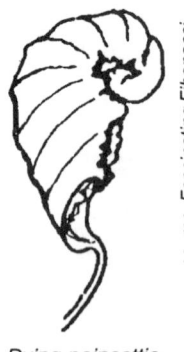

source: Fascinating Fibonacci

Dying poinsettia
leaf

Figure 2-18

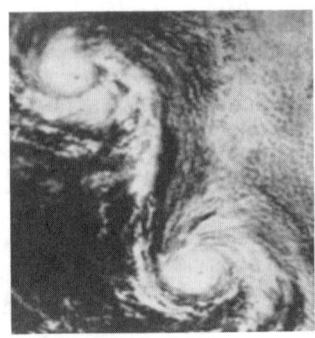

source: Omni Magazine

Hurricane

Figure 2-19

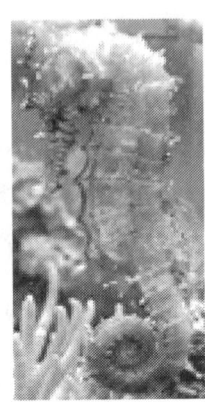

source: Jay Frase, http://home1.gte.net/frasej/

Sea horse

Figure 2-20

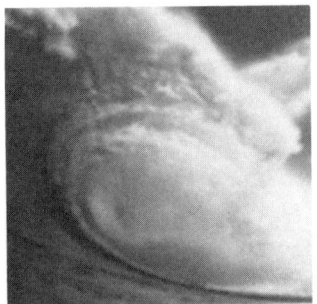

Ocean waves

Figure 2-21

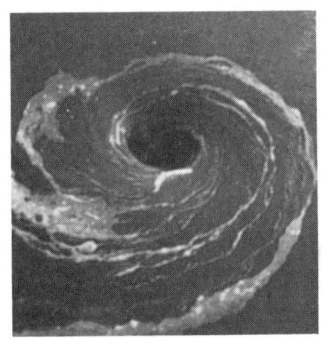

source: Omni Magazine

Whirlpool

Figure 2-22

source: D. Shechtman, Technion, Israel

Quasi-crystal under an electron microscope

Figure 2-23

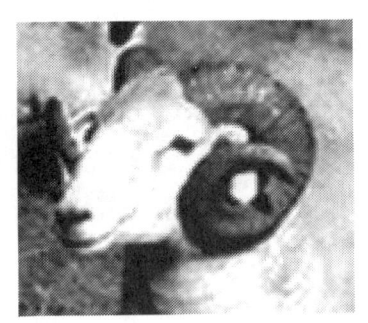

source: www.ansi.okstate.edu

Horn

Figure 2-24

source: Omni Magazine

Spirals in shells

Figure 2-25

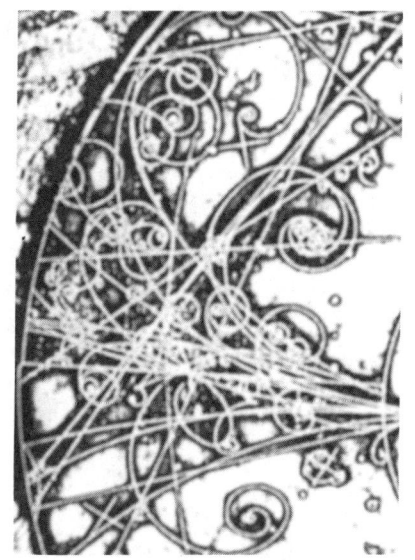

source: Nova-Adventures in Science

Atomic particles in bubble chamber

Figure 2-26

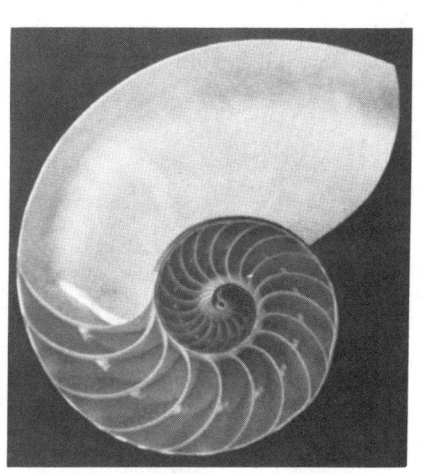

Nautilus

Figure 2-27

source: Hale Observatories

Spiraling galaxy

Figure 2-28

construct a logarithmic spiral, as Figure 2-29 illustrates. In this construction, the top of each successive wave of higher degree is the touch point of the exponential expansion. The further time extends, the larger the degrees of trend get, implying a geometric expansion in the size of the advances and retrenchments that form mankind's progress.

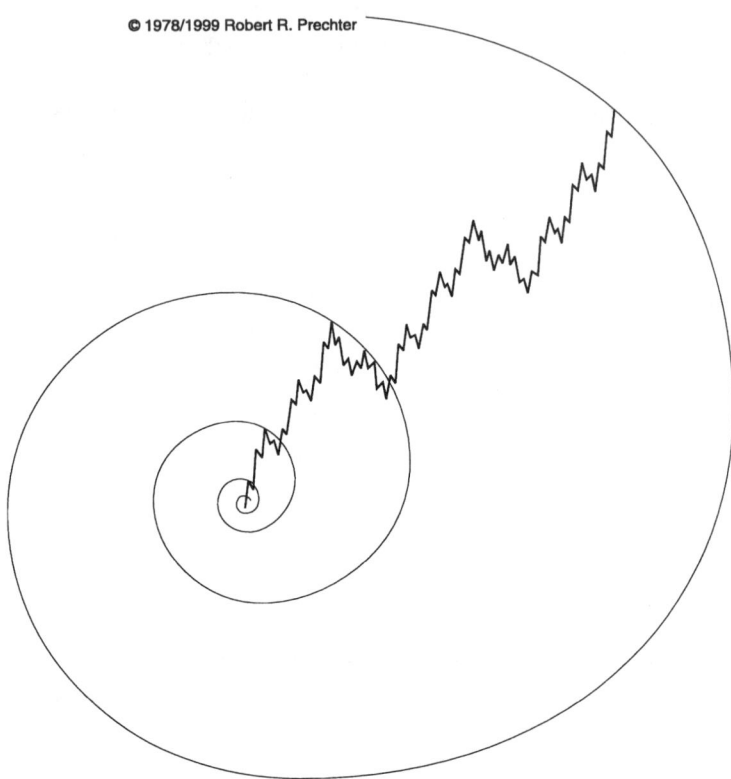

© 1978/1999 Robert R. Prechter

Elliott waves reflect spiral growth

Figure 2-29

The propagation of the *lowest* form of animal, bacteria, can be plotted as a logarithmic spiral. Figure 2-29 implies that the growth of the *highest* form of animal can also be plotted as a logarithmic spiral. While it may seem a wild concept that the progress of life, including human life, can be mapped as a logarithmic spiral, some recent scientific endeavors support this depiction, which was originally published in *Elliott Wave Principle* in

1978. For example, *Physics Reports* has just published a ground-breaking paper by Didier Sornette of the Department of Earth and Space Science and the Institute of Geophysics and Planetary Physics at the University of California at Los Angeles. "Discrete Scale Invariance and Complex Dimensions"[21] demonstrates log periodicity and complex dimensions in the stock market, which are exactly what Figure 2-29 implies. Two years ago, Sornette collaborated on a published study that specifically identifies the shape that results when such distributions, which are common in certain self-similar systems, are graphed. The report concludes, the "trajectory describing a discrete self-similar system [such as the stock market] in the complex coupling constant plane [such as a price graph] is a *spiral*."[22]

Scientists are finding the spiral shape in the natural processes of even broader aggregations such as ecologies. Here is an example, as described by *Newsweek*:

> Population biologists, for instance, were among the first to notice chaos. Lions and zebras, ferrets and prairie dogs — their numbers can career off into wild and seemingly random oscillations. Was this chaos? To find out, researchers sought strange attractors for these predator-prey systems — the fingerprint of chaos that shows the behavior of each population through time. Unfortunately, data on natural populations is lousy. Finding chaos requires several generations worth of clean data, and scientists don't have it. So chaoticians turned to lab and computer experiments. Researchers led by Oxford's [Robert] May recently built a computer model of parasites that lay eggs in insects. They input rules for how many parasites and hosts move to adjacent patches of grass each generation. Then they hit "go." When they mapped the relative abundances of hosts and parasites, they got diagrams resembling such emblems of chaos as intricate *spiral waves* and crystal lattices. "Simple interactions among species may lead...[to] chaotic patterns in space," says zoologist Anthony Ives of the University of Wisconsin, "where population booms and busts occur in a *seemingly random* pattern" — yet one that is actually a highly ordered lattice or spiral.[23] [see Figure 2-30.]

In other words, spiraling appears to be a fundamental aspect of growing systems that involve bipolarity, stress and fluctuation. This correlation is not only compatible with the Wave Principle's depiction of the human social experience but also with the fact that species fluctuations also apparently follow the Wave Principle, as Chapter 13 will demonstrate.

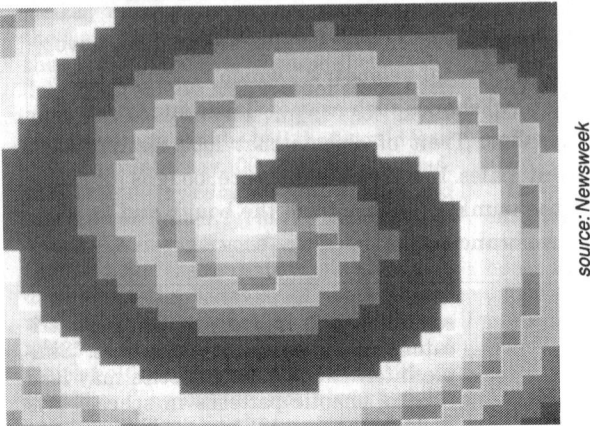

A mathematical simulation of a predator-prey balance in nature shows a spiral design

Figure 2-30

R.N. Elliott said sixty years ago that the phenomenon he described as the behavior of financial markets was a universal principle of nature. Scientific discoveries in the 1980s and 1990s are leading to the same conclusion. To put it summarily, it is no longer acceptable to label this aspect of the Wave Principle as grandiose or mystical; its general nature reflects discoveries of modern mainstream science. Now let us progress to some more pertinent specifics.

NOTES

1 Dunham, W. (1990). *Journey through genius.*

2 Goethe, J.W. (1790). "On the metamorphosis of plants."

3 Dauben, J.W. (1990). *Georg Cantor: his mathematics and philosophy of the infinite.*

4 For more on the pioneers in fractals, see *Classics on Fractals.* G.A. Edgar, ed. (1993), Addison-Wesley, Reading MA.

5 Hausdorff, F. (1919). "Dimension und äusseres mass." *Mathematische Annalen*, 79, pp. 157-179.

6 Elliott showed graphs of most of these activities in *The Wave Principle* (1938).

7 These sentences are collected from pp. 92, 147, 157, 183, 192, 217, 218, 228, 229 of *R.N. Elliott's Masterworks — The Definitive Collection* (1994), which includes *The wave principle* (1938), The *Financial World* articles (1939), "The basis of the wave principle" (1940) and *Nature's law* (1946). I have omitted ellipses and one-letter brackets for reading clarity.

8 Mandelbrot, B. (1988). *The fractal geometry of nature.*

9 Glazman, R. (1988, April). "Fractal features of sea surface...." *OE Reports.*

10 Briggs, J. and Peat, F.D. (1989). *Turbulent mirror*, p.110.

11 Gleick, J. (1985, December 29). "Unexpected order in chaos." *This World.*

12 Hanson, G. (1990, October 8). "A world that is graphically real." *Insight.*

13 Gutenberg, B. and Richter, C.F. (1949). *Seismicity of the earth.*

14 Zipf, G.K. (1949). *Human behavior and the principle of least action.*

15 Voss, R. (1992). "Evolution of long range fractal correlations and 1/f noise in DNA base sequences." *Phys. Lett.* 68:3805-3808.

16 Buchanan, M. (1997, November 8). "One law to rule them all." *New Scientist.*

17 Hotz, R. (1997, October). "A study in complexity." *Technology Review.*

18 *Ibid.*

19 Mantegna, R. and Stanley, H.E. (1995, July 6). "Scaling behaviour in the dynamics of an economic index." *Nature.*

20 As with nonlife and life (see near the end of Chapter 13), stasis and growth may not be that unrelated. There is an intimate connection between the governing ratio of the circle (*pi*, represented by π, which is 3.1416...) and

the governing ratio of the golden spiral (*phi*, represented by ϕ, which is 1.618034...). One formula illustrating the relationship between *pi* and *phi* is:

$$F_n \approx 100 \times \pi^2 \times \phi^{(n-15)},$$

where n represents the numerical position of the term in the sequence and F_n represents each term in the Fibonacci sequence. The number "1" is represented only once, so $F_1 \approx 1$, $F_2 \approx 2$, $F_3 \approx 3$, $F_4 \approx 5$, etc. (For more on *phi* and the Fibonacci sequence, see Chapter 3.)

21 Sornette, D. (1998). "Discrete scale invariance and complex dimensions." *Physics Report,* No. 297, pp. 239-270.

22 Saleur, H. and Sornette, D. (1996). "Complex exponents and log-periodic corrections in frustrated systems." *Journal de Physique I France* 6, No. 3, pp.327-355.

23 Begley, S., *et al.* (1992, May 25). "Finding order in chaos." *Newsweek.*

Chapter 3:

Robust Fractals and Fibonacci Mathematics

R.N. Elliott went *far* beyond the comparatively simple idea that financial prices form an indefinite fractal with an implied power law. His big achievements were in discovering *specific component patterns* within the overall form[1] as well as its connection to *Fibonacci mathematics*.[2] First we will explore pattern.

Types of Fractals

Until very recently, it has been generally presumed that there are two types of self-similar forms in nature: (1) *self-identical* fractals, whose parts are precisely the same as the whole, and (2) *indefinite fractals*, which are self-similar only in that they are similarly irregular at all scales.

Nature does produce fractals of the first type. When magnets, oils, crystals and water are at a critical state bordering on phase transition (i.e., between magnetic and nonmagnetic, a different cellular arrangement, a different molecular arrangement, and gas-liquid, respectively), the components are, except for size, "precisely, exactly, mathematically identical" to the whole.[3] In each case, the whole is not simply as irregular as its parts; it is *exactly the same form* as its parts, from the largest size component to the next and the next. Figures 2-8 through 2-10 illustrate this idea: The oil forms hexagons that make up larger hexagons; the snowflake is a precisely repeating hexagonal form; the rigidly repeating line pattern mimics the shape of a financial market.

Figures 2-14 and 2-15 are depictions of a seacoast and clouds, which are presumed to be fractals of the second type. The literature on natural fractals concludes that nature most commonly produces indefinite fractal

forms that are orderly only in the extent of their discontinuity at different scales and otherwise disorderly. Scientific descriptions of natural fractals detail no specific patterns composing such forms. Seacoasts are just "jagged lines," trees are composed simply of "branches," rivers but meander, and heartbeats and earthquakes are merely "events" that differ in frequency. Likewise, financial markets are considered to be self-similarly discontinuous in the relative sizes and frequencies of trend reversals yet otherwise randomly patterned. These conclusions may be due to a shortfall in empirical study rather than a scientific fact.

Robust Fractals: Elliott's Discovery of a Third Type of Self-Similarity

R.N. Elliott described for financial markets a third type of self-similarity. By meticulously studying the natural world of social man in the form of graphs of stock market prices, Elliott found that there are *specific patterns* to the stock market fractal that are nevertheless *highly variable* within a certain definable latitude. In other words, some aspects of their form are *constant* and others are *variable*. If this is true, then financial markets, and by extension, social systems in general, are not vague, indefinite fractals. Component patterns do not simply display *discontinuity* similar to that of larger patterns, but *they form, with a certain defined latitude, replicas of them*.

Elliott defined waves in terms of what makes them identical, thereby allowing for their variability in some aspects of detail within the scope of those definitions. He was even able to define some of the patterns' variable characteristics in probabilistic terms. Elliott's discovery of *degrees* in pattern formation, i.e., that a certain number of waves of one degree are required to make up a wave of the next higher degree, is vitally important because it links the building-block property of self-*identical* fractals to the Wave Principle, revealing an aspect of self-identity among waves that indefinite fractals do not possess.

The fact that both waves and (as we shall soon see) natural branching systems are fractals of *intermediate specificity* implies that nature uses this fractal style to pattern systems that require highly adaptive variability in order to flourish. Therefore, I think the best term for this variety of fractal is *robust* fractal.

Elliott's discovery of specific hierarchical patterning in the stock market is fundamental. Even fractals and power laws, which go to the essence

of form, are only a vague comment about that form. They do little to define the object. *If you can describe the pattern, you have the essence of the object.* The more meticulously you can describe the pattern, the closer you get to knowing what it is.

Although Elliott came to his conclusions fifty years before the new science of fractals blossomed, the very idea that financial markets comprise specific forms and identical (within the scope of their definitions) component forms remains a revolutionary observation because to this day, it has eluded other financial market researchers and chaos scientists. Elliott's work shows that the general relationship between sizes and frequencies of financial movements, currently considered a breakthrough discovery, is not the essence, but a by-product, of the fundamentals of financial market patterns.

The end of Chapter 2 commented that due to the new science of fractal geometry, the Wave Principle can no longer be considered fantastic on the grounds of the unlikelihood of self-similarity at different scales. There is good news pertaining to our current discussion as well. A group of scientists (see Arneodo, *et al.* in "The Robust Fractal Reappears" section later in this chapter) has very recently recognized that there is a type of fractal in nature whose self-similarity is intermediate between identical and indefinite. As far as I know, theirs is the only published study on the subject. Nevertheless, science is once again edging toward confirmation of another important aspect of the Wave Principle that heretofore, to skeptics, appeared to reflect either undue imprecision or undue complexity. In fact, it reflects reality. I believe that *robustness will prove to be the essence of fractals that matter most in nature.*

Describing in What Ways Waves Are Identical and in What Ways They Are Variable

The concept of a robust fractal is difficult to depict visually because a single illustration cannot convey both those aspects of an Elliott wave that are invariant and those that are variable, i.e., what its manifestations have in common and what they need not. We can draw the essence of an Elliott wave but not state the precise path that any manifestation of it will actually take. Elliott waves in reality always conform to a few simple rules of patterning, but vary considerably within that format. The advancing and declining patterns throughout Figure 1-4 are depicted as self-identical, like the forms in Figures 2-8 through 2-10, simply because there is no better way to con-

vey the essential idea. Presenting the full description of what actually happens requires verbal discussion and/or many illustrations.

Elliott described five elementary patterns in the stock market, which he called impulse, diagonal triangle, zigzag, flat and triangle. The first two occur in motive mode (i.e., when prices are moving in the direction of the trend of one larger degree, effecting the larger wave's progress), while the latter three occur in corrective mode (i.e., when prices are moving opposite the direction of the trend of one larger degree, punctuating its progress). Figure 3-1 summarizes these five patterns. In corrections, sometimes two of the patterns will occur side by side, interrupted by an intervening zigzag, as noted under the heading, "Double Three."

One Example of a Detailed Description of an Elliott Wave

This section should give you a flavor of Elliott's powers of observation as well as an idea of how robust fractals may be defined. He noted, for instance, the following characteristics of an impulse, the most common form of motive wave, as depicted in Figure 1-1 and in the top left of Figure 3-1. Do not bother to memorize these traits; the point is that the description is quite detailed.

> The impulse subdivides into five waves, which may be labeled 1, 2, 3, 4 and 5.
> Wave 2 never moves beyond the start of wave 1.
> Wave 3 is never the shortest wave.
> Wave 4 never moves beyond the end of wave 1.
> Waves 1, 3 and 5 each subdivide into five waves.
> Waves 2 and 4 each subdivide into a corrective pattern.
> Wave 3 always takes the form of an impulse.
> Wave 1 always takes the form of an impulse.[4]
> Wave 5 may be an impulse or a diagonal triangle (an Elliott wave that is defined elsewhere; see illustration in Figure 3-1).
> Typically, wave 1 or 3 or 5 is an extension, which means that it is substantially longer than each of the others and contains larger subdivisions than each of the others does.
> Wave 3 is most commonly the extended wave.
> Wave 1 is least commonly the extended wave.
> When wave 3 is extended, waves 1 and 5 tend toward equality of amplitude.

SUMMARY OF MOTIVE PATTERNS

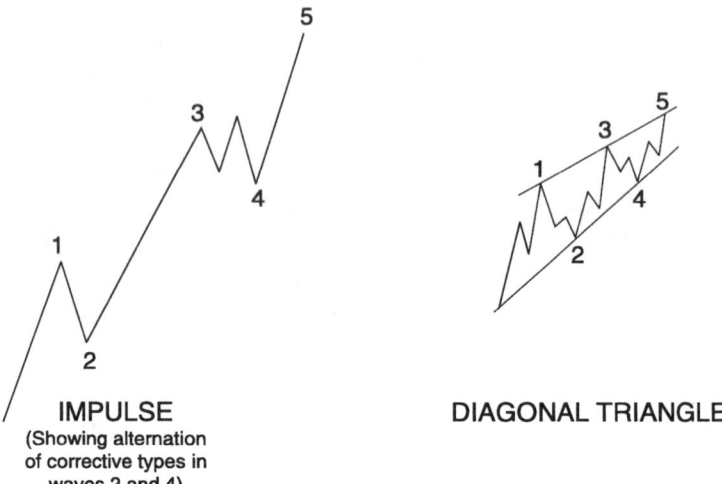

IMPULSE
(Showing alternation
of corrective types in
waves 2 and 4)

DIAGONAL TRIANGLE

SUMMARY OF CORRECTIVE PATTERNS

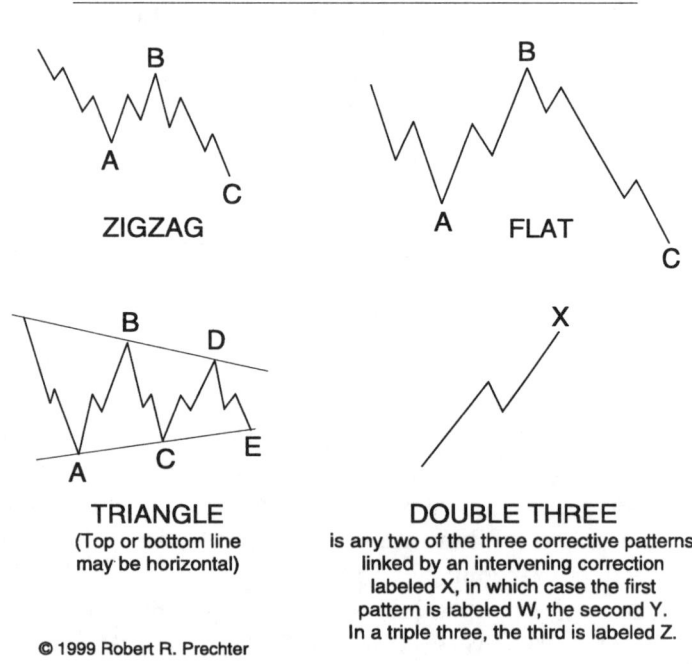

ZIGZAG

FLAT

TRIANGLE
(Top or bottom line
may be horizontal)

© 1999 Robert R. Prechter

DOUBLE THREE
is any two of the three corrective patterns
linked by an intervening correction
labeled X, in which case the first
pattern is labeled W, the second Y.
In a triple three, the third is labeled Z.

Figure 3-1

The center of wave 3 has the steepest slope of any equal period within the larger impulse.

Among the three basic types of corrective waves (see Figure 3-1), wave 4 will almost always be a different type than wave 2.

Wave 4 typically ends when it is between the starting and ending levels of subwave four of 3.

Wave 4 often divides the entire impulse into .618/.382 proportion.

Sometimes wave 5 does not exceed the level of the end of wave 3.

Wave 5 often ends when meeting or slightly exceeding a line drawn from the end of wave 3 that is parallel to the line connecting the ends of waves 2 and 4, on either arithmetic or semilog scale.

When wave 5 is extended, it is often 1.618 times as long as the net travel of waves 1 through 3.

When wave 1 is extended, it is often 1.618 times as long as the net travel of waves 3 through 5.

This list covers only the main rules and guidelines of form for this one Elliott wave. Go back to Chapter 2 and examine Figures 2-1 through 2-7. You will see that all of those illustrations incorporate these rules and guidelines.

Each of the five elementary patterns shown in Figure 3-1 has its own description as well as a short catalog of variations that are similarly delineated by differences in form. For instance, sometimes both boundary lines of a triangle slope toward each other, and sometimes either the top or bottom line is horizontal. As another example, sometimes wave B of a flat ends at the level of the start of wave A, and sometimes it ends beyond it. Elliott attached a name to each of these differences in form so that with his terms, we know immediately what form and variation we are talking about.

If Elliott was anything, he was meticulous. His description of waves, their positions within larger waves, and their relative frequency of occurrence have stood the test of sixty years' intensive application by some very dedicated practitioners,[5] with only minor modifications.[6] Additionally, I have quantified on sliding scales all of the patterns' variable features in the process of building our Elliott wave computer program, which I discuss in Chapter 4, and have formulated additional guidelines for discriminating among waves, some of which are referenced in Chapters 5 and 6.[7]

The essence of the Wave Principle is "5-3," but there is quite a bit more to know about it. There are reasons to believe that there is more to

know about the form of natural branching systems, and perhaps other natural fractals, as well. Before we make that connection, we have to investigate another aspect of waves.

The Fibonacci Sequence and Ratio

The Fibonacci sequence[8] is 1, 1, 2, 3, 5, 8, 13, 21, 34, 55, and so on. It begins with the number 1, and each new term from there is the sum of the previous two. The limit ratio between the terms is .618034..., an irrational number variously called the "golden mean" and "divine proportion," but in this century more succinctly *phi* (ϕ) after the architect Phidias, who designed the Parthenon. Both the Fibonacci sequence and the Fibonacci ratio appear ubiquitously in natural forms ranging from the geometry of the DNA molecule to the physiology of plants and animals, as we will see in this chapter and in Chapter 11. This book will not present a treatise on Fibonacci; you can find a pretty good one in Chapter 3 of *Elliott Wave Principle* and other sources.

In the past few years, science has taken a quantum leap in knowledge concerning the universal appearance and fundamental importance of Fibonacci mathematics. Chapters 10, 11, 12 and 21 will explore the wider scope of this new knowledge and its implications. For the time being, it might interest readers to know that some of the greatest intellects in Western thought, from Pythagoras to Isaac Newton, held a special reverence for the role of *phi* in nature.[9] (For more on this subject, see Chapter 3 of *Elliott Wave Principle*.) Some of history's greatest minds might have agreed with R.N. Elliott's rather incautious contention that *phi* is the secret of the universe,[10] but for now, let us simply explore how it relates to waves.

The Fibonacci Sequence in the Wave Principle

Elliott's publisher, renowned investment advisor Charles Collins, first realized that the Wave Principle is connected to the Fibonacci sequence, and communicated that fact to Elliott. After researching the subject to the small extent possible at the time, Elliott presented the final unifying conclusion of his theory in 1940,[11] explaining that the progress of waves has the same mathematical base as so many phenomena of life.[12]

The Fibonacci sequence governs the numbers of waves that form the movement of aggregate stock prices in an expansion upon the underlying 5-3 relationship. Figure 3-2 shows the progression. The simplest expres-

sion of a corrective wave is a straight-line decline. The simplest expression of a motive wave is a straight-line advance. A complete cycle is two lines. At the next degree of complexity, the corresponding numbers are 3, 5 and 8. This sequence continues to infinity.[13] We will now explore why this fact is important.

THE SUBDIVISION OF WAVES
REPRODUCES THE FIBONACCI SEQUENCE

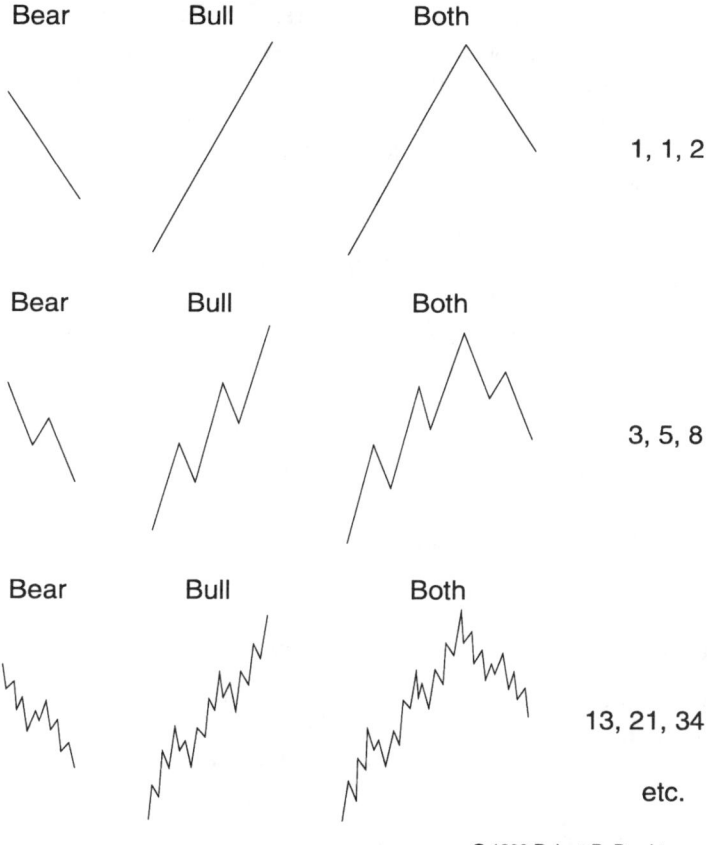

The subdivision of waves reproduces the Fibonacci sequence

Figure 3-2

The Fibonacci Sequence and Ratio in Plant Life

A grand connection between Fibonacci and life has been proposed from time to time. In the seventeenth century, mathematician Jakob Bernoulli, the father of probability analysis, was the first modern European to observe the importance of the Fibonacci ratio in nature. Early in the twentieth century, several publications reported on Fibonacci expressions in plant and animal physiology, including *The Curves of Life* by Theodore Cook (1914), *On Growth and Form* by Scottish zoologist D'Arcy Thompson (1917), *The Elements of Dynamic Symmetry* by Jay Hambidge (from articles published by the Yale University Press in 1919), and papers by Oxford professor A.H. Church on "Phyllotaxis in Relation to Mechanical Law."

There are many expressions of Fibonacci mathematics in plants, from leaf arrangements to branching tendencies to the numbers of petals in flowers. For instance, lilies have 3 petals, buttercups 5, delphiniums 8, marigolds 13, asters 21, and most daisies 34, 55 or 89. While flowers occasionally reveal non-Fibonacci numbers, says Professor Ian Stewart, "you don't find any other numbers anything like as often," and when you do, they often reflect the family of numbers called the Lucas sequence:[14] 1, 3, 4, 7, 11, 18, 29, etc., which is the Fibonacci phenomenon of additive growth starting with two different numbers, 1 and 3, instead of 1 and 2. Figure 3-3 is an idealization of a plant showing the number of its branches on various planes proceeding along the Fibonacci sequence as it climbs upward. Figure 3-4 is a photograph of the candy lily plant at the entrance to my driveway. From stem to tip, it subdivides 1, 2, 3, 5.[15] Its berries tend to have 21 kernels. Not all Fibonacci expression in plants is numerical. Figure 3-5 is a depiction of the baby's breath that came with the roses I bought for my wife recently. At every furcation, it branches into three stems that take the rough shape of an upwardly expanding cone. Can you spot how Fibonacci governs this form? If not, read endnote 16.[16] Stephane Douaday and Yves Couder of the Laboratoire de Physique Statistique and the Laboratoire de Physique in France explain that phyllotaxis, the Fibonacci-based structure of plants, is a self-organized growth process.[17] As we shall see, many (if not all) self-organized growth processes involve Fibonacci mathematics.

Fibonacci numbers appear in the tiniest first cells of a growing plant, called primordia, which grow outward from an apex along a spiral called a "generative spiral" that ultimately produces the plant. Two researchers, the Bravais brothers, found the mathematical rule that governs the spacing of the primordia along the generative spiral.[18] It turns out that the angles be-

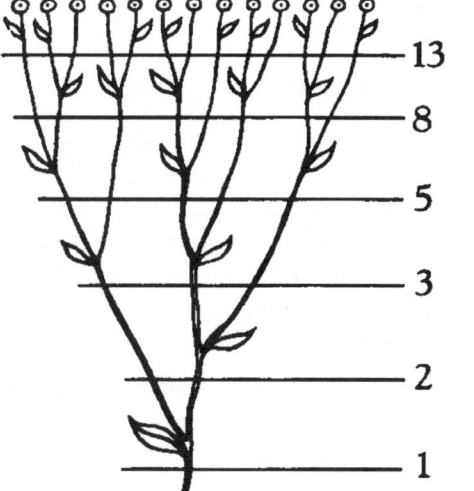

Sneezewort (*Achillea ptarmica*), with number of
stems at each horizontal level of development.
(Adapted with permission from E.H. Huntley,
The Divine Proportion.)

Figure 3-3

A candy lily branches 1, 2, 3, 5

Figure 3-4

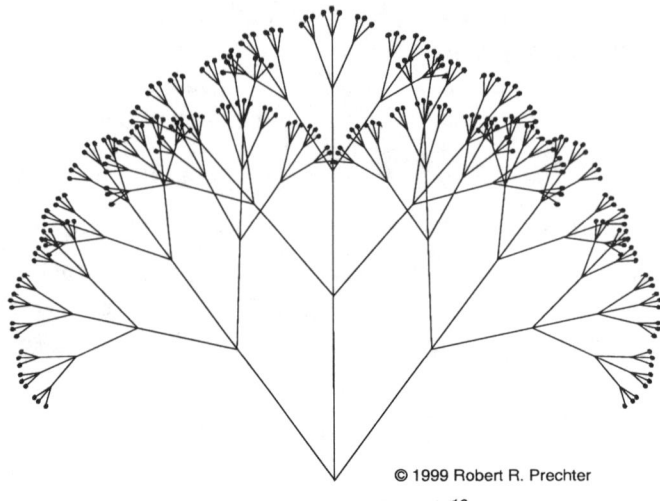

© 1999 Robert R. Prechter

Baby's breath exhibits phi[16]

Figure 3-5

tween the center of the apex and successive primordia is always the same, approximately 137.5 degrees. This angle is .382 (1 - ϕ and ϕ^2) of the full circle of 360 degrees and is called the golden angle. G. Van Iterson[19] in 1907 showed that this angle produces two families of interlocking Fibonacci spirals, one clockwise and the other counterclockwise (see Figures 3-9 through 3-11). In 1979, H. Vogel explained why: The golden angle is the only divergence angle at which seeds may pack without gaps, making it the most efficient method of packing and the only way to achieve full density in the seed head.[20,21]

Efficiency is not the only advantage that Fibonacci has for life forms. It is also the best sequence for robustness, which is to say, for providing the greatest latitude for variability and growth in an integer-based system. The reason is that the Fibonacci ratio has a unique property that sets it apart from all other irrational numbers. When using increasingly large whole numbers in fractions to approach limits, the differences between the result and the limit shrink more slowly for *phi* than for any other irrational number.[22] I infer from this fact that *phi* allows for more and longer growth in real-world entities, which must be counted in whole numbers, than any other limit.

To summarize the above paragraphs, nature uses Fibonacci for *efficiency* and *robustness* in plants, which are *self-organizing growth forms*. As this book progresses, we shall investigate the possibility that social man is participating in a self-organizing growth form whose progress is gov-

erned by Fibonacci mathematics because it allows the greatest efficiency and robustness.

Meticulous observers have related the Fibonacci sequence specifically to the growth and form of plants for some time. Now there is evidence that Fibonacci mathematics regulate *all* fractal branching systems.

Fibonacci in Diffusion-Limited Aggregations (Branching Systems)

In the early 1990s, five scientists from the Centre de Recherche Paul Pascal and the Ecole Normale Supeieure in France investigated the diffusion-limited aggregation model, which is a set that diffuses via smaller and smaller branches. Arneodo *et al.* state at the outset that it is "an open question whether or not some structural order is hidden in the apparently disordered DLA morphology."[23] To investigate the question, they use a wavelet transform microscope to examine "the intricate fractal geometry of large-mass off-lattice DLA clusters." (See Figure 3-6.) In the first linking (as far as I can discover) of the two concepts of fractals and Fibonacci since Elliott, they demonstrate that their research "reveals the existence of Fibonacci sequences in the internal 'extinct' region of these clusters."

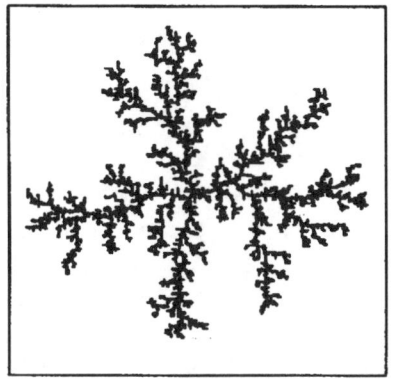

source: Growth Patterns in Physical Sciences and Biology

DLA cluster
Figure 3-6

These mathematics pertain to "apparently randomly branched fractals that bear a striking resemblance to the tenuous tree-like structures observed in viscous fingering, electrodeposition, bacterial growth and neuronal growth," which are "strikingly similar to trees, root systems, algae, blood vessels and the bronchial architecture," i.e., *the typical products of nature*. The study shows that these apparently random fractals are in fact *more orderly than previously realized*. Specifically, the authors find that the branching characteristics of off-lattice DLA clusters "proceed according to the *Fibonacci recursion law*," i.e., they branch in intervals to produce a 1-2-3-5-8-13-etc. progression in the number of branches. The authors of this study, then, have found the Fibonacci sequence in DLA clusters *in the same place that R.N. Elliott found the Fibonacci sequence in the Wave Principle*: in the increasing numbers of subdivisions as the phenomenon progresses.

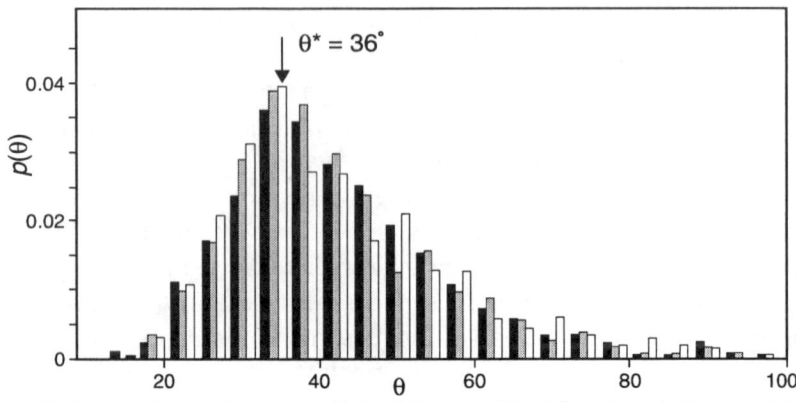

source: Growth Patterns in Physical Sciences and Biology

Histogram of screening angle values at the branching bifurcations in the wavelet transform representation of 4 off-lattice DLA clusters; three magnifications a^{-1} (black), $(2.2)\,a^{-1}$ (grey) and $(2.2)^2\,a^{-1}$ (clear) are shown, corresponding respectively to three successive generations of branching. A single maximum is observed for $\theta^* \sim 36°$.

Figure 3-7

The authors find even more evidence of Fibonacci. They have discovered that the most commonly occurring "screening angle" between bifurcating branches of these DLA clusters is 36 degrees, which holds *regardless of scale*. (See Figure 3-7.) This is the ruling angle of geometric phenomena that display Fibonacci properties, from the five-pointed star (see Figure 3-8) to Penrose tiles (see Figure 21-5). The authors elaborate:

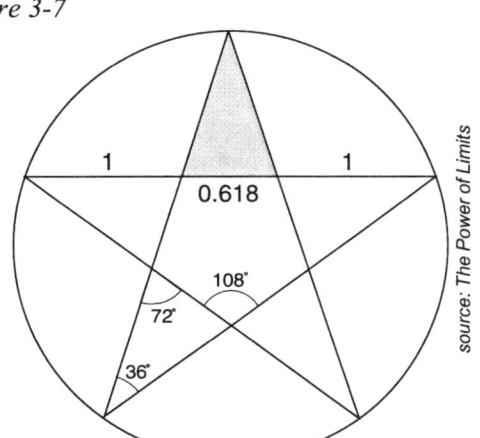

source: The Power of Limits

Fibonacci in the five-pointed star

Figure 3-8

The intimate relationship between regular pentagons and Fibonacci numbers and the golden mean $\phi = 2\cos(\pi/5) = 1.618...$ has been well known for a long time. The proportions of a pentagon approximate the proportions between adjacent Fibonacci numbers; the higher the numbers are, the more exact the approximation to the golden mean becomes. The angle defined by the sides of the star and the regular pentagons is $\theta = 36°$, while the ratio of their length is a Fibonacci ratio (F_{n+1}/F_n).

The authors conclude, "The existence of this symmetry *at all scales* is likely to be a clue to a structural hierarchical fractal ordering." Indeed, it is. In not a dissimilar way, Elliott found that the price lengths of certain waves are often related by .618, *at all scales*, revealing another, though perhaps less fundamental, Fibonacci aspect of waves.

There is another link between these two phenomena, though it is a bit amorphous conceptually. 36 degrees is 1/**5** of a semicircle, is the ruling angle of the **5**-pointed star, and is half the angle of the **pent**agon, whose 72-degree angles are 1/**5** of a circle. The average bifurcation angle, then, links the property of "fiveness" to DLA clusters just as Figure 1-1 displays the importance of "fiveness" to the Wave Principle. The formula for *phi* itself, which is $(\sqrt{5} - 1)/2$ or $(\sqrt{5} + 1)/2$ depending upon the inversion, is grounded upon the square root of **5**. Apparently, among all Fibonacci numbers, the number 5 has the most fundamental importance to *phi*. The reason may be its necessity in creating progress in the form of waves as explained in Chapter 1 under the heading, "Why 5-3?"

The authors announce that their "wavelet analysis provides the first numerical evidence for the existence of a 'Fibonaccian' quasi-fractal structural ordering in DLA clusters." This is terrific news because DLA structures occur in countless of nature's living forms and processes, one of which the Wave Principle purports to depict.

The Robust Fractal Reappears

In a brilliant concluding proposal, Arneodo, *et al.* determine from just this data that they are working with a type of fractal that scientists had not yet found, an intermediate form between perfect self-identity and vague, indefinite self-similarity:

> The intimate relationship between regular pentagons and Fibonacci numbers and the golden mean...has been well known for a long time.... The recent discovery of "quasi-crystals" [see Figure 2-23 and Chapter 21 —ed.] in solid state physics is a spectacular manifestation of this relationship. This new organization of atoms in solids, *intermediate between perfect order and disorder*, generalizes to the crystalline "forbidden" symmetries, the properties of incommensurate structures. *Similarly, there is room for "quasi-fractals" between the well-ordered fractal hierarchy of snowflakes and the disordered structure of chaotic or random aggregates.*"[24]

This is the same type of intermediately ordered fractal that R.N. Elliott described for the stock market. Of course, Elliott managed to detail many more aspects of that fractal, showing to a far greater degree how substantially its form is self-identical within a certain definable latitude of expression. As implied earlier, I prefer the term *robust* fractal to quasi-fractal since it has been established (to my satisfaction at least) that nature's processes of growth and expansion produce this type of fractal. Its connection to natural phenomena indicates that there is nothing quasi about it. I expect that it will eventually be found to be so common that other types of fractals should be called quasi.

To summarize, what we have here is a study that observes the Wave Principle's characteristics of fractality, fiveness and Fibonacci in a phenomenon (DLA clusters) that shares with the Wave Principle the fundamental aspect of robust self-similarity.

I will add that this is yet another study among many in the past twenty years that shows more order in apparently random processes than previously believed, which is what this book proposes about human social behavior. I would guess that more and greater such surprises are forthcoming in the sciences, both natural and social.

Arboration

The science of robust branching fractals is brand new. The literature has yet to settle on a noun for a branching fractal, a verb for its progress or an adjective for the property of being tree-like. ("Diffusion-limited aggregation" is rather a mouthful.) Taking a hint from Eugene Stanley of Boston University, who used the word "arborization" in one of his studies, I would like to suggest a nomenclature. Specifically to refer to the robust branching fractals common to nature (as opposed to self-identical or indefinite branching fractals), perhaps we can use the term *arbora*, a single one being an *arborum*. The branches themselves will be termed *arba*, one being an *arbum*. The verb *to arborate* will mean "to proceed in a robust branching fractal." The process will be called *arboration*. The adjective *arboral* will mean "having the properties of an arborum." As we shall soon see, waves and arbora have so much in common that they may be differing manifestations of the same underlying theme.

Degrees in Arboration and the Possibility of Other Specifics in Their Form

Recall that while indefinite fractals have infinite variability in their successive subdivisions, *waves* display an order in their relative sizes, as each manifestation has specific degrees of subdivision. Similarly, while trees, bronchial tubes and other arbora (see Figures 10-2 through 10-10) have branches of all sizes, each specific manifestation appears to have *degrees* of arboration. With respect to trees, there is the trunk, arms off the trunk, branches off the arms, twigs off the branches and leaf veins off the twigs. There is an order to the relative sizes in each manifestation of the branching process. One never sees branches that are, for instance, the same width as, or larger than, the trunk, just as one never sees an Elliott wave that is smaller than its components. In fact, there often appears to be a rough characteristic ratio between the size of each branch and its offshoots. This property appears to hold for the DLA model (see Figure 3-6) and all of nature's arbora. In this regard, arbora are very much like waves.

Whorls of seashells (see Figures 2-25, 2-27 and 3-12), which spiral according to Fibonacci mathematics, also display the phenomenon of degree, as each chamber and each whorl increases according to a ratio of the previous one. (Unlike waves and arbora, however, the relationships between them are mathematically rigid, producing an identical fractal.)

Once again, the very latest science may be uncovering this phenomenon. In just the past year, Sornette[25] has proposed that in most complex systems, the infinite number of scales that are present do not play an equivalent role. Rather, there are discrete levels in a global hierarchy. His work with Saleur on log periodicity (see Chapter 2) has led him to propose a mechanism for the natural emergence of discrete scale invariance (DSI) that applies to a host of examples. There is evidence of DSI in systems ranging from dust devils to cyclones in weather, from joints to plate boundaries in tectonics, from primary to quaternary structures in proteins, from molecules to systems in physiology, from neurons to hemispheres in the brain and from individual traders to national trading blocs in the global economy. DSI is a property of the examples of dwelling spaces (from rooms to cities) and knowledge blocks (from sentences to the internet) that I gave in Chapter 2. The Wave Principle is the only hypothesis that *from the start* proposed hierarchical degrees in the stock market's price structure.[26]

There may be more details to discover in DLA clusters and natural arbora. Taking a clue from waves, we might investigate whether arbora are composed of a limited number of specific component forms of arba. We

might ask whether they have common ratios of length, common ratios of width, a limited number of shapes, or rules for the specific number of arba that sprout. For now, I am content to observe that this shared property of DLA clusters and the Wave Principle suggests that one important characteristic of *all* robust fractals may be their development via specific degrees, just like their self-identical cousins.

To summarize all these findings, it appears that fractality, *phi*, the number 5 and the phenomenon of degree all appear to be factors in the morphology of robust fractals.

Fibonacci Spirals

The spiral is not only nature's premier growth/expansion form, but also one of biology's most fundamental. The DNA molecule, the code for life, is made up of two intertwining spirals. The .618 ratio between its width and cycle length (see Figure 11-1) makes it a Fibonacci-related spiral. Its form apparently carries forward into the final forms whose growth it governs. Daisies, pine cones and sun-

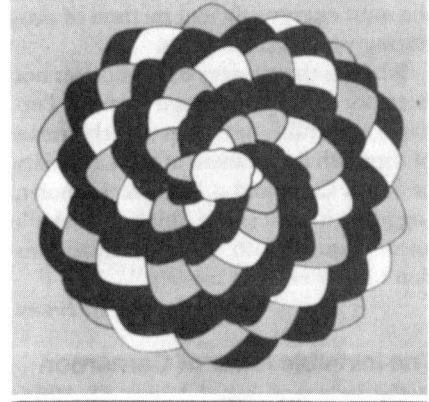

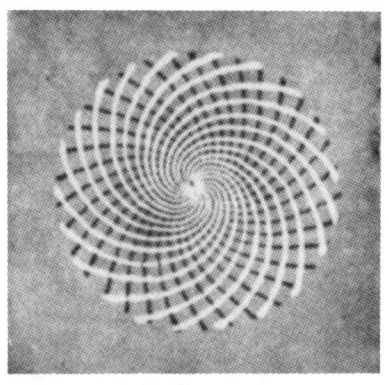

source: Mathematics

A SPIRALED FLOWER
The diagram above reveals the double spiraling of the daisy head. Two opposite sets of rotating spirals are formed by the arrangement of the individual florets in the head. They are also near-perfect equiangular spirals. There are 21 in the clockwise direction and 34 counterclockwise. This 21:34 ratio is composed of two adjacent terms in the mysterious Fibonacci sequence.

Fibonacci spirals in the daisy

Figure 3-9

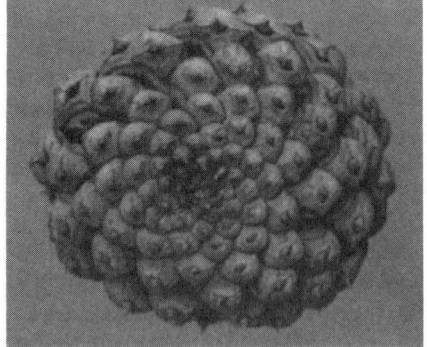

source: Science 86 Magazine, May 1986

Pine cone

Figure 3-10

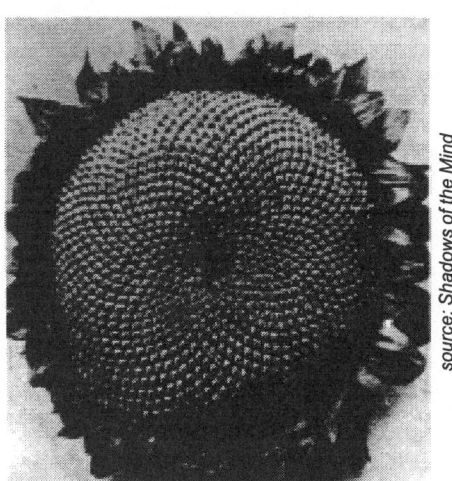

source: Shadows of the Mind

Fibonacci spirals in the seedhead of a sunflower

Figure 3-11

flowers provide famous examples, as spirals in one direction are composed of a Fibonacci number of seeds (or kernels), while spirals in the other direction are composed of the next Fibonacci number of seeds, and both sets of spirals exist simultaneously in one set of seeds, as shown in Figures 3-9 through 3-11. Many seashells grow in suc- cessive spirals, each of which is larger than its predecessor by the Fibonacci ratio (see Figures 2-27 and 3-12).

While a substantial portion of the form of these plants and animals is a Fibonacci spiral, for other species, the influence is less obvious. Architect György Doczi demonstrates a subtle golden-spiral correspondence between the style of growth of plants and animals. The sacrum in animals from frogs to humans, he says, is the center that corresponds to the apex of the generative spiral in plants. Out of each grow spiral-compatible forms that correspond to the divisions of the seashell (see Figure 3-12).

Figure [3-12] shows a man's hand, traced from an X-ray photo. ...The hand is a microcosm of the body. It grows out of the wrist as the spine grows out of the sacrum, and as wings grow out of a butterfly, *or as leaves and flowers grow out of their stems. ...The unity we share with plants* and animals is...[also] visible from the fact that our growth, like theirs, seems to unfold from a single center."[27]

Without belaboring the evidence, we can surmise that it is not just seashells that manifest Fibonacci-based spirals as a whole form, or heart muscles and ear canals (see Chapter 11) that manifest Fibonacci-related spirals in body parts. As Chapter 11 further demonstrates, all forms of life may have Fibonacci spiral aspects both in their parts and in their whole expression. The fact that the Wave Principle is Fibonacci-based and produces a logarithmic spiral (see Figure 2-29) connects it to the Fibonacci-spiral growth phenomena of life.[28] Next, I hope to show a unity among all these concepts.

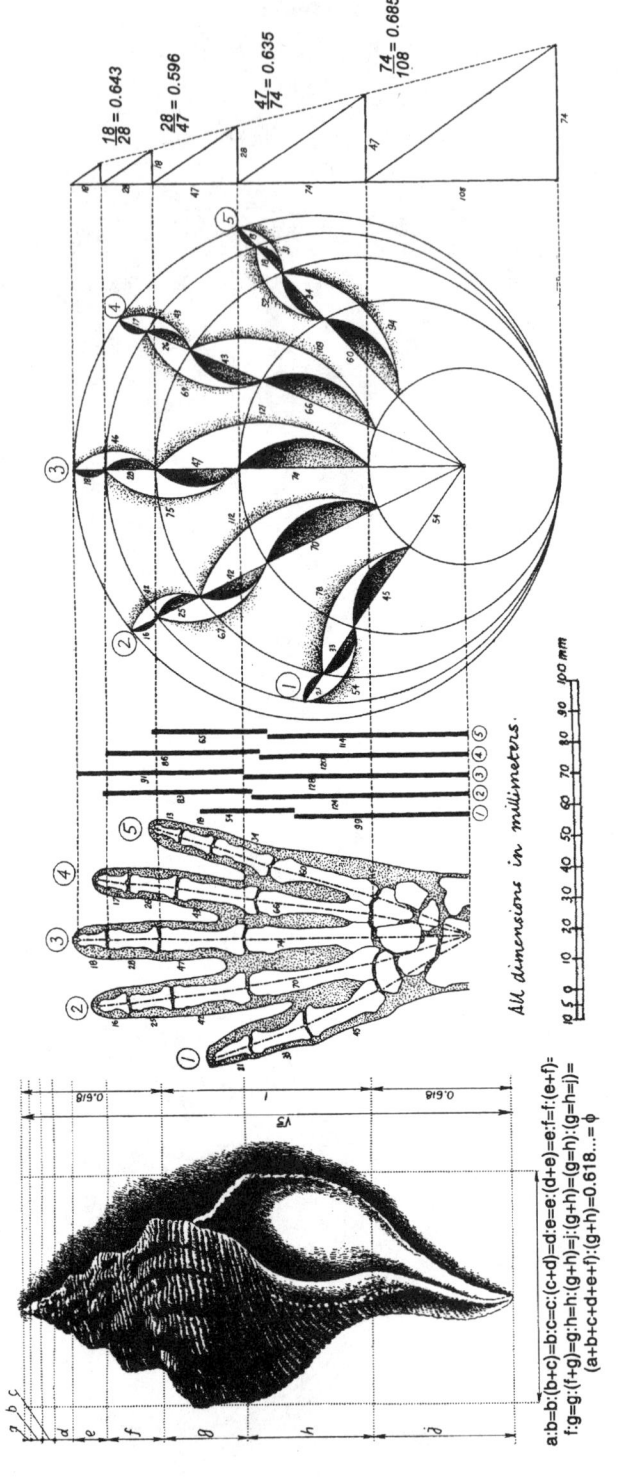

Natural Fibonacci Spirals Correspond to Natural Fibonacci Arbora in Both Plants and Animals

Figure 3-12

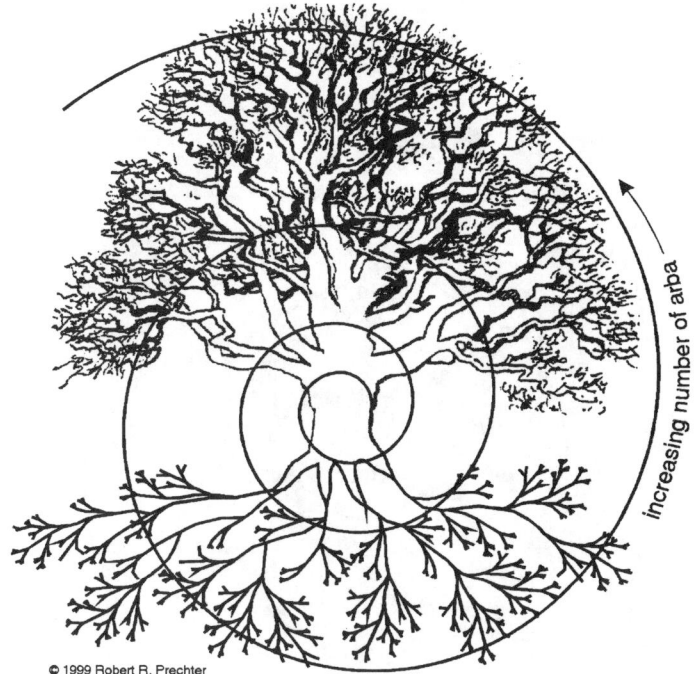

increasing number of arba

© 1999 Robert R. Prechter

Figure 3-13

increasing size of arba

© 1999 Robert R. Prechter

Figure 3-14

Nature's Developing Waves, Branching Arbora and Expanding Spirals — All the Same Thing?

Waves and arbora become *more complex*, and spirals *more expanded, as time proceeds*. These growth-related robust fractals reflect Fibonacci mathematics, robustness, fiveness and degree. In contrast, static fractals such as magnets, crystals and water in a critical state, and snowflakes (see Figures 2-8 and 2-9) *do not become more complex over time* and do not reflect Fibonacci mathematics. The difference appears to be that static fractals are phenomena of *space*, while robust fractals are growth patterns through *time*.

It could be that nature's developing waves, branching arbora and expanding spirals (and perhaps other robust fractals as well) share properties of robustness, degree, fiveness and Fibonacci because they are fundamentally all the same phenomenon. The only difference between them may be nature's manifestation or depiction, i.e., how the underlying process is "plotted" on reality's three-dimensional grid.

Waves reflect an expanding spiral, as shown in Figure 2-29. Arboration reflects an *expanding* spiral in terms of the *number* of arba and a *contracting* spiral in terms of the *size* of arba, as depicted in Figures 3-13 and 3-14.

Figures 3-15, 3-16 and 3-2 express the Fibonacci sequence in three different ways: as a *tree*,[29] a *spiral* and a *wave*.

The Fibonacci sequence as a tree

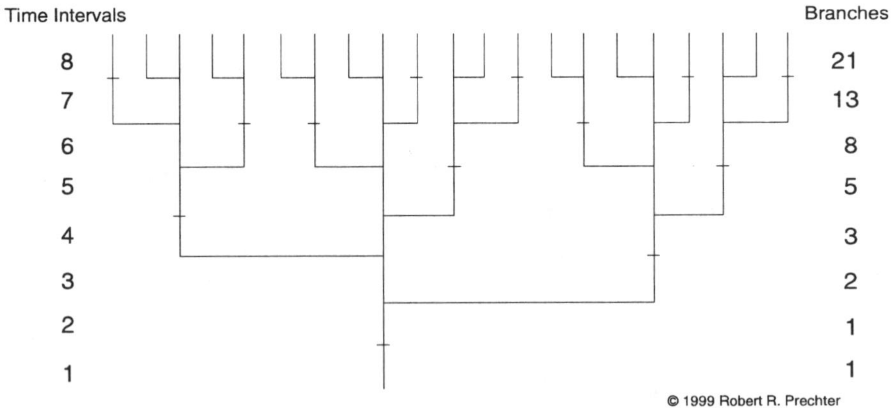

Time Intervals		Branches
8		21
7		13
6		8
5		5
4		3
3		2
2		1
1		1

© 1999 Robert R. Prechter

Figure 3-15

The Fibonacci sequence as a spiral

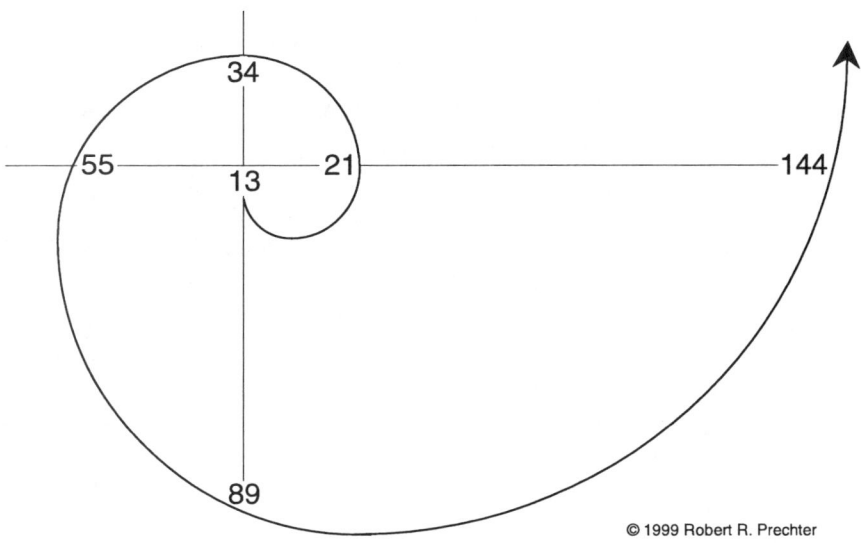

© 1999 Robert R. Prechter

Figure 3-16

Nature's Fibonacci-based growing forms have the same cross-repre-sentational property. Figure 3-12 shows how Fibonacci spirals and arbora are translated in plants and animals. We can see that in some sense, the *same thing* is going on, although the components of the spirals grow *larger* and the components of the arbora grow *smaller* while in each case making the entire form larger.

Natural *processes* express this cross-representational property as well. For example, evolution is a process that makes *waves, spirals and arbora.* Successful species branch out into subspecies, and so on, making arbora, as depicted in Figures 3-17 through 3-19, while the total number of species ebbs and flows in waves, as depicted in Figures 13-1 through 13-3. We can also depict the increasing number of species on earth as a spiral, as we did the Wave Principle in Figure 2-29 and the arbora in Figures 3-13 and 3-14, or we can extrapolate from population simulations such as depicted in Fig-ure 2-30.

Phylogeny of Reptiles
from 300 Million Years Ago to the Present

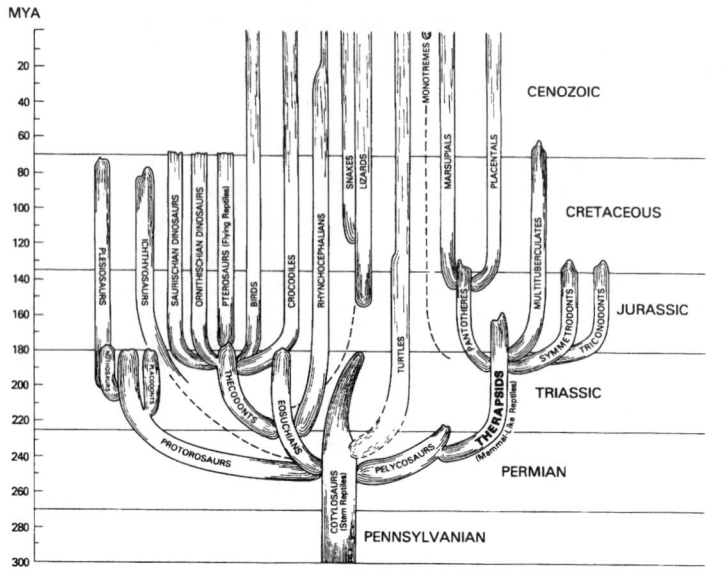

source: The Triune Brain in Evolution

Figure 3-17

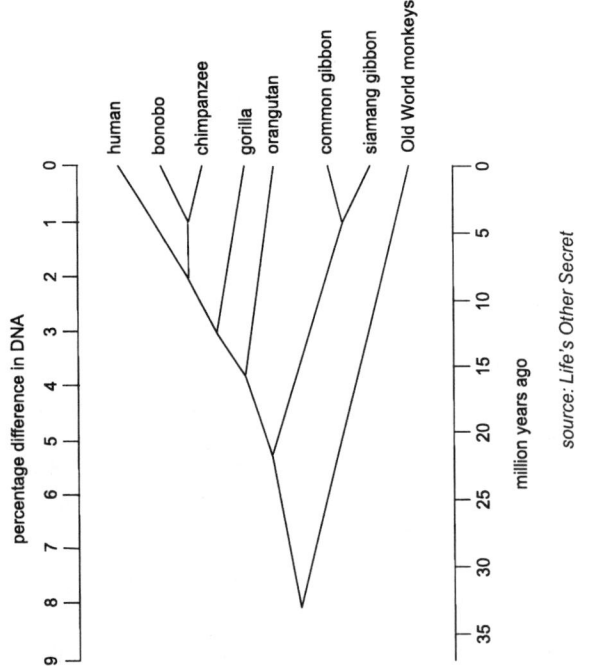

source: Life's Other Secret

Figure 3-18

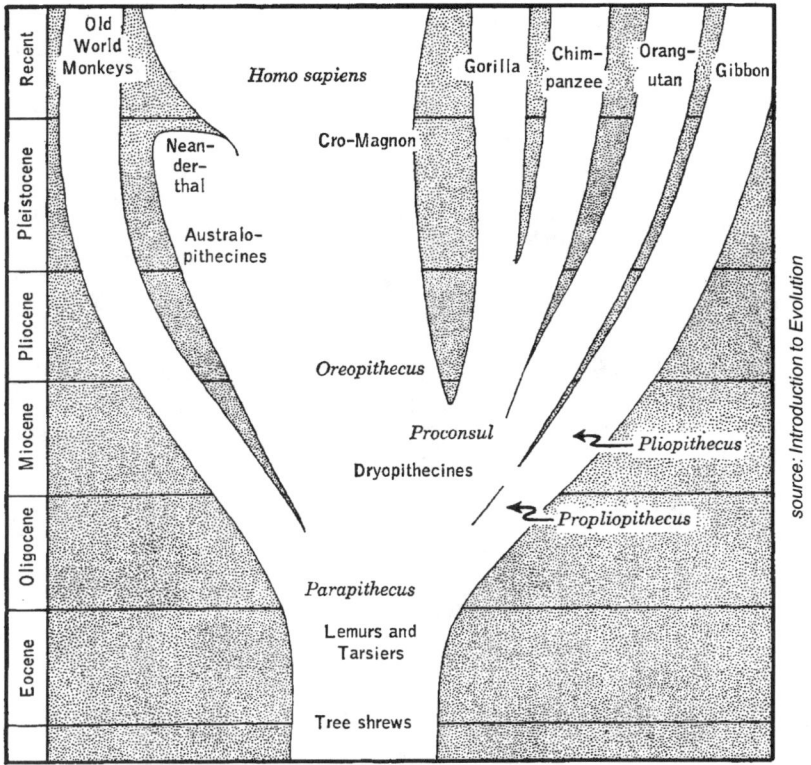

Figure 3-19

The propagation of language apparently makes both arbora and waves as well. Linguistic theory, whether by design, luck or sloppiness, closely relates two terms, *stammbaumtheorie* and *wellentheorie*, which translate into English as *family-tree theory* and *wave theory*, to describe the furcation of a parent language into branches and sub-branches via "waves of linguistic change."[30]

This transformation property may cover other types of fractals as well. For example, when is a topographic fractal (mountains, hills, hillocks, etc.) also an arborum? Answer: when water, snow or flowers fill the cracks. See Figure 3-20.

Figure 2-29 shows that a spiral can be superimposed upon a graph of the idealized wave form. It is also true that price trends can be graphed in such a way as to reveal not a line, but a spiral. Figure 3-21 shows the stock market's advance from 1942 to 1966, plotted by annual averages on a typical graph. We can plot the same data on a graph on which the X axis moves

source: Great Performance, Beaverton OR

Figure 3-20

incrementally clockwise, as shown in Figure 3-22. The resulting plot is a roughly-shaped outwardly-moving spiral. Figure 3-23 shows the stock market's decline from April 1930 to July 1932, plotted by monthly close on a typical graph. Figure 3-24 shows the same data graphed on a rotating axis, which produces a roughly-shaped inwardly-moving spiral. In other words, waves in the stock market may be conceived of as countless overlapping spirals of different sizes when time is graphed as a circle rather than a line. When economists say offhandedly that the economy "spirals" into depression, they are quite right. However, there is no reason to avoid saying (as to a man, they do) that it also spirals into advances.

There are two points of rest in our spiral depictions: the outer circle and the inner point. These points relate to Elliott waves, as they correspond conceptually to the peak moment at the end of wave 5 and the trough moment at the start of wave 1, respectively.

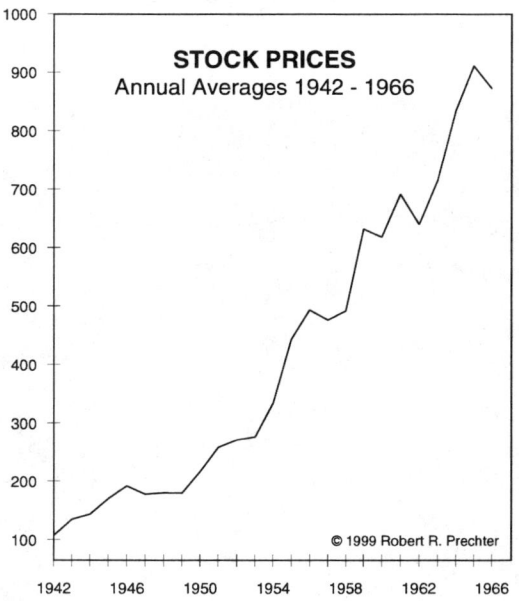

Figure 3-21

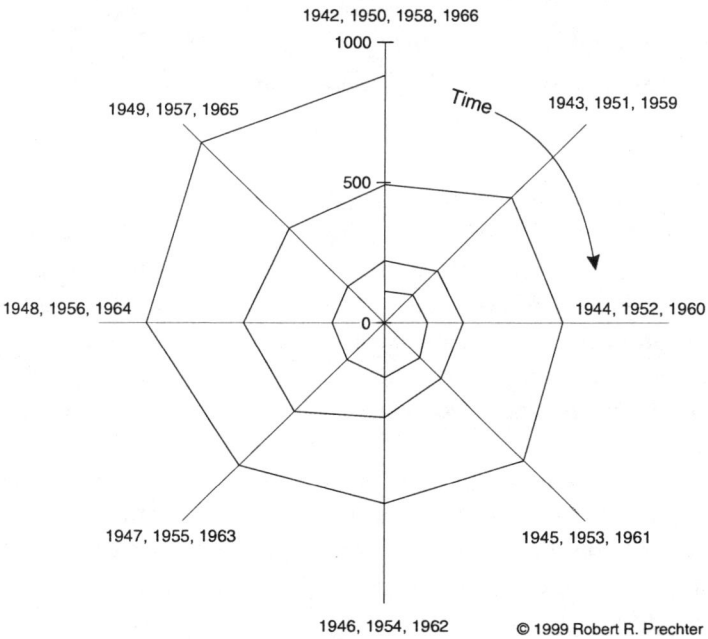

Figure 3-22

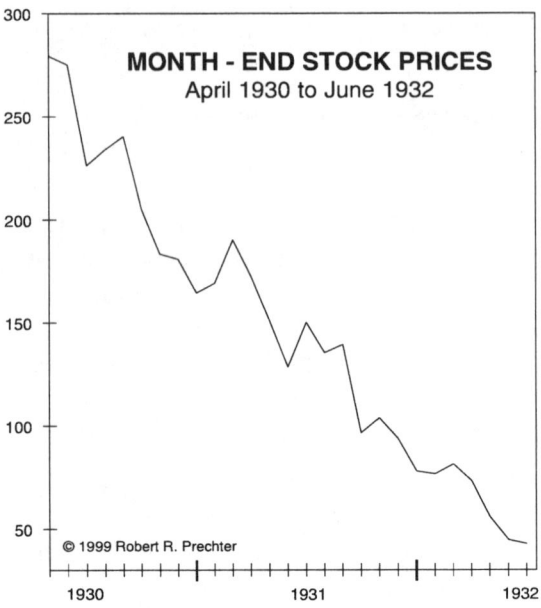

Figure 3-23

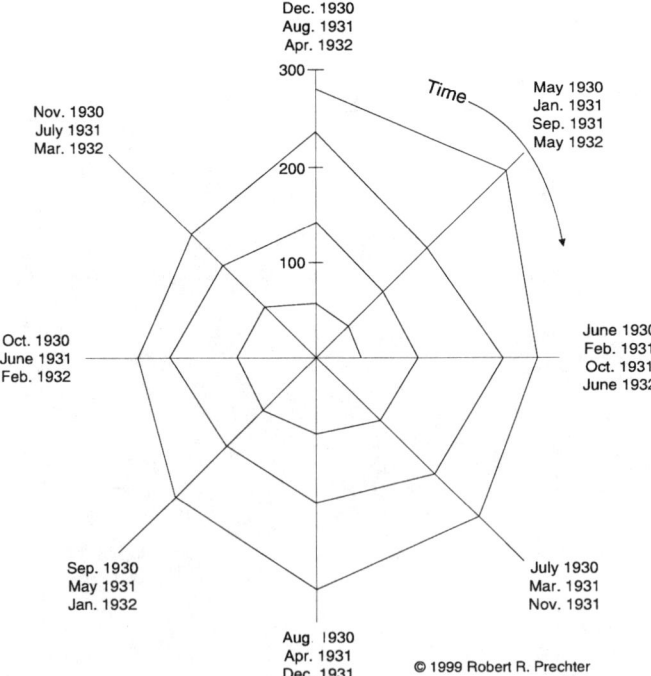

Figure 3-24

All these pictures resemble many natural expressions of growth and expansion — or recession and decay — from life forms to galaxies. In terms of their essence, then, there may be little difference among nature's progressing forms. The only difference may be the template upon which nature projects them. That, in turn, may depend upon whether time is accounted as a line (as in waves), an advancing disk (as in branches) or a circle (as in spirals). In the context of this interconnectedness, the idea of Elliott waves is not radical, but perhaps to be expected.

The Opposing Duality of Spirals, Waves and Arbora

I would like to make one last observation because it might be important, though I do not know why. A logarithmic spiral divides a plane in two, with the area inside the line and that outside each conforming to the spiral shape where they meet. All the space on the plane is involved in adapting to the spiral pattern. Waves are manifest as a jagged line dividing a plane, with the entirety of the two resulting areas joined as opposing shapes. Similarly, arbora are not just lines. They are actually a division of a plane in such a way as to fill an entire space with compatible branches *from two directions*. The dual nature of arboral systems is clearer when the arba are "fat," as in the photo of the embryo shown as Figure 3-25. Here,

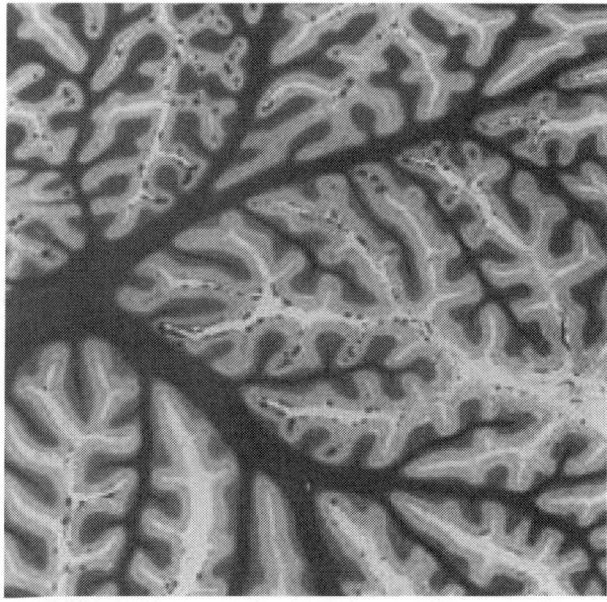

Arboral embryo

Figure 3-25

you can see the darker arboral system emanating from the left *and* the lighter arboral system emanating from the right, filling all the space. You can see the same effect when you hold up your hand and spread your fingers slightly apart. Space fills in the gaps with arba that are very much like the fingers themselves.

In other words, every phenomenon that arborates also makes the space around it arborate in response. Spirals, arbora and waves are simply a *division of plane-space that produces a like but opposing form* on both sides. I am not sure what this means, but it would surely delight the yin/yang philosophers in the Orient who taught centuries ago that reality derives from opposing duality.

A Connection to the Human Social Experience

The Wave Principle reveals that the human social experience follows a form that derives from the tension between the opposing dualities of progress and regress. Its ruling ratio is *phi*, the same number that governs nature's arbora and spirals, making it fundamental to nature's arrangements. In its broadest sense, then, the Wave Principle communicates the seemingly outrageous idea that the same law that shapes living creatures and galaxies is inherent in the mentation and activities of men *en masse*. We will explore the biological, perceptual and mentational origins of this phenomenon in Chapters 10 through 12.

As Chapter 16 later argues, the mass psychological fluctuations revealed by the stock market are not only *correlated* with mankind's actual progress and regress through history, but in fact *produce* them. What the Wave Principle ultimately says, then, is that mankind's progress, which results from his social nature, does not occur in a straight line, does not occur randomly, and does not occur cyclically. Rather, progress takes place in a Fibonacci-related arborating, spiraling or wave-fractal style that nature uses for all its robust forms. As the activity of social man has form, it is apparently no exception to the general law of order in the universe.

Professor Ian Stewart of Warwick University makes a case in his book, *Life's Other Secret*, that the cardinal code of life is mathematical, not biomechanical. He begs his readers, "We must turn at least some of our attention to life's other secret — the universal mathematical principles of growth and form that DNA exploits."[31] As the research throughout this book attests, it is exactly a "universal mathematical principle of growth and form" that the Wave Principle of human social behavior reflects. This is a tall claim, which it is the purpose of the rest of this book to verify.

NOTES

1 Elliott, R.N. (1938). *The wave principle.*

2 Elliott, R.N. (1940, October 1). "The basis of the wave principle."

3 Buchanan, M. (1997, November 8). "One law to rule them all." *New Scientist.*

4 There is one rare exception, which I pointed out in *Elliott Wave Principle.*

5 To read the original works of R.N. Elliott, Charles Collins, A. Hamilton Bolton, A.J. Frost and Robert Prechter, please see the list of sources at the end of this book.

6 For details on the few additions and corrections made by Frost and Prechter, see *Elliott Wave Principle.*

7 See also "Wave Personality" in Chapter 2 and "Ratio Analysis" in Chapter 4 of *Elliott Wave Principle.*

8 The sequence is named for the 13th century Pisan mathematician, Leonardo, son of Bonacci, or Fibonacci for short.

9 It has become fashionable in recent years to disparage the "simplistic, Newtonian" view of the universe as being "mechanical." Newton, however, may not have been entirely the Newtonian that his detractors would have us believe. When perhaps the greatest scientist of all time has the golden spiral carved on the headboard of his bed, you can bet, if the character of a man's life means anything, that he admired it for good reason.

10 It is also fashionable to dismiss as a mystical fixation the fascination that earlier scientists had for *phi.* Such dismissal would make sense if we were talking about Madame Blavatsky and Piazzi Smyth, but we are talking about people who rank among the few dozen greatest intellects of the ages. Dare we say they were fools in this regard, all of them?

11 Elliott, R.N. (1940, October 1). "The basis of the wave principle."

12 It is perhaps possible that R.N. Elliott was not the first person to observe a connection between Fibonacci numbers and financial markets. Harvard Emeritus Professor Barry Fell, whose book *Saga America* (1980) details the activities of North Americans around 300 B.C., made this observation:

> Mathematical notation in North America was revolutionized in the fifth century A.D., when the Nevada voyagers brought the newly invented Sanskrit system of decimal notation back from India. In this replica of a mathematical petroglyph from Massacre Lake, northwest Nevada, the annual crop report on maize is given in ancient Libyan script ... By far the

most sophisticated of the checkerboard patterns found at Nevada petroglyph sites are the grouping at the Whiskey Flat site..., [which] yield a sequence of numbers called by mathematicians the Fibonacci series.

Perhaps forecasting corn prices using Fibonacci ratios is not something new!

13 So far in this book, I have mentioned 1 overall form, 2 elementary patterns in motive mode, 3 elementary patterns in corrective mode, and 5 elementary patterns in all. This progression is a hint that the organization of the Wave Principle itself reflects the Fibonacci sequence. Figure 3-14 in *Elliott Wave Principle* depicts one such conceptual organization.

14 The Lucas sequence is named for 19th century French mathematician Edouard Lucas, who also coined the term "Fibonacci numbers."

15 It flowers at the number "5," which is where collective human behavior flowers under the Wave Principle. See Figure 18-6.

16 Each successive set of stems is approximately 2/3 of the length of the preceding set.

17 Douaday, S. and Couder, Y. (1993). "Phyllotaxis as a self-organized growth process." *Growth patterns in physical sciences and biology.*

18 Prusinkiewicz, P. and Lindenmayer, A. (1990). *The algorithmic beauty of plants.*

19 Thompson, D. (1917). *On growth and form.* p.857.

20 Vogel, H. (1979). "A better way to construct the sunflower head." *Mathematical Biosciences*, No. 44, pp. 145-174.

21 The main exception to this manifestation in plants is an angle that corresponds to the near-Fibonacci Lucas sequence, 1, 3, 4, 7, 11, 18, etc.

22 Khinchin, A. Ya. (1964). *Continued fractions*, p. 36.

23 Arneodo, A., *et al.* (1993). "Fibonacci sequences in diffusion-limited aggregation." *Growth patterns in physical sciences and biology.* All quotes in this section are from this source.

24 *Ibid.*

25 Sornette, D. (1997, October 15). "Generic mechanisms for hierarchies." *InterJournal Complex Systems*, No. 127. And (1998, June 30-July 3). "Discrete scale invariance in turbulence?" Proceedings of the 7th European Turbulence Conference. And "Discrete scale invariance and complex dimensions." *Physics Reports* No. 297, pp. 239-270. And Johansen, A. and Sornette, D. (1999). "Critical crashes." *Risk*, Vol. 12, No. 1.

26 Sornette proposes that there is a discrete set of laws and tools for each level in a DSI hierarchy. The Wave Principle does not imply such differences in the underlying psychology that produces waves of social mood. However, there are some differences in the rules and tools one employs to analyze the

stock market at different degrees. For example, below Minor degree, the relative size of each wave does not necessarily correspond to the relative size of its degree. The best overall labeling sometimes requires allowing Subminuette movements to be larger than Minuette ones. This never happens at larger degrees. Similarly, there are rare times that wave four will slightly overlap the price territory of wave one at Subminuette degree. Again, this never happens at larger degrees. This difference might simply be a function of the inaccuracy of stock averages in reflecting waves of social mood. Arboration, which appears generally to proceed according to the same law regardless of which degree is developing, has exceptions as well. For instance, the leaf on a tree, at the end of the arboration process, is different in construction from the branches.

27 Doczi, G. (1981). *The power of limits.*

28 **The Dearth of Data on *Phi* and Spirals**. Many scientists have an aversion to *phi*, perhaps because mystics have sometimes waxed eloquent over its properties. In many studies quoted later in Chapters 11 and 12 in which *phi* has obviously appeared, researchers do not even mention it. This is akin to finding that the ratio pertaining to a particular set of natural processes is 3.14 and not mentioning that it approximates *pi*. This aversion has led to a sad dearth of data about *phi* in nature, which forces me in this chapter to work with limited information, quoting architects instead of biologists. It is time for science to get over the fear of *phi*ing. When that fear is overcome, I believe we will see an explosion of *phi*-related research and discovery.

The same problem exists for natural spirals. I have seen no work dedicated to their assessment. Once again, this dearth of study forces me simply to make the observation that they are everywhere in nature. If the resulting vagueness bothers you, it does me, too. Unfortunately, until scientists tackle natural spirals as a field of study, we are stuck with little more than commenting on their repeated appearance.

29 Given this connection between waves and trees, perhaps when people say, "Wall Street is a jungle," they are more correct than they know.

30 (1976). *Webster's Third New International Dictionary.*

31 Stewart, I. (1998). *Life's other secret.*

PART II

VALIDATING THE WAVE PRINCIPLE BY ITS OWN OPERATION

Theoretical support for the Wave Principle continues later, in Part III. I could have arranged that section to follow Part I, but some readers at this point might require something concrete to justify their continuing investigation. Part II is dedicated to demonstrating the validity of the Wave Principle. Thereafter, we will venture further, and more solidly, into scientific support for it.

Chapter 4:

Modeling and Quantification
Support the Validity of the Wave Principle

A Simple Model Reflects Reality

In 1995, Michael Buettner of Elliott Wave International constructed a simple computer model of the Wave Principle without considering any actual market behavior. The model incorporates the three main rules as well as four guidelines of behavior for the impulse pattern, as follows:

(1) Wave two does not carry past the beginning of the preceding wave one.

(2) Wave three is not the shortest wave.

(3) Wave four does not enter the price range of wave one.

(4) Wave four usually has a form different from that of wave two. (This model uses a "zigzag" for wave two and a "flat" for wave four, which are their most common positions.)

(5) One motive wave is usually extended, and it is usually wave three. (Wave three is always extended in the model, which arbitrarily makes it equal to .618 times the summed lengths of waves one and five.)

(6) Waves five and one tend toward equality when wave three is extended. (The model makes them equal.)

(7) Waves are often related by Fibonacci ratios. (This model incorporates two common tendencies in having wave two retrace .618 of wave one and wave four retrace .236 of wave three.)

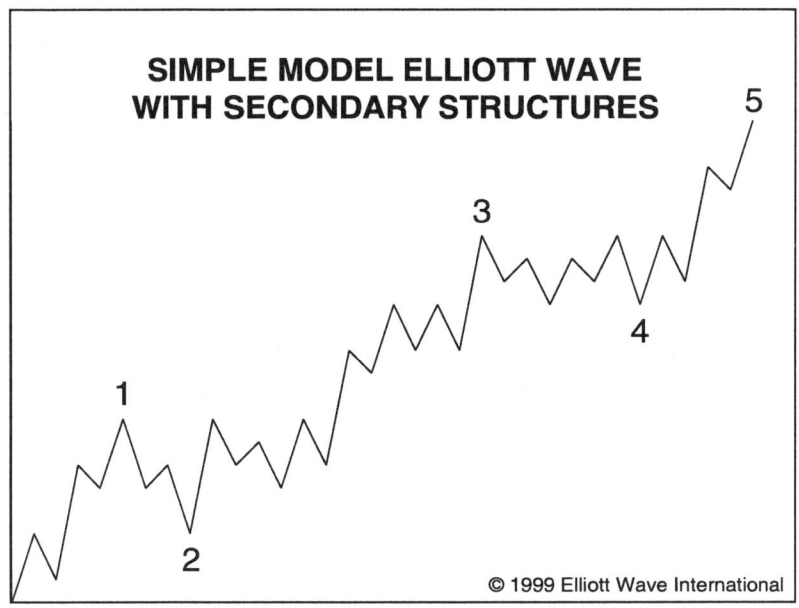

Figure 4-1

Figure 4-1 shows the picture created by the computer from this model. Figure 4-2 shows the same picture to five degrees of iteration. Below it is the actual plot of the Dow Jones Industrial Average from 1932. Understand that our model excludes numerous important subtleties among the Wave Principle's rules and guidelines and forces several rigidities not shared by the actual stock market. Nevertheless, as Buettner concludes, "The market model formulated in the 1930s, even when converted into a highly simplified mathematical idealization, reproduces to a remarkable degree the overall structure of the real market during the subsequent six decades."[1]

While it would be interesting to determine the fractal dimension of this model, it is an extreme simplification of the Wave Principle. A simulation incorporating all of the pattern variability that the Wave Principle is capable of modeling would provide a better match to the real-world behavior, which is what Elliott's definitions are designed to do. Perhaps our "expert system" computer program, discussed in the next section, will provide this opportunity.

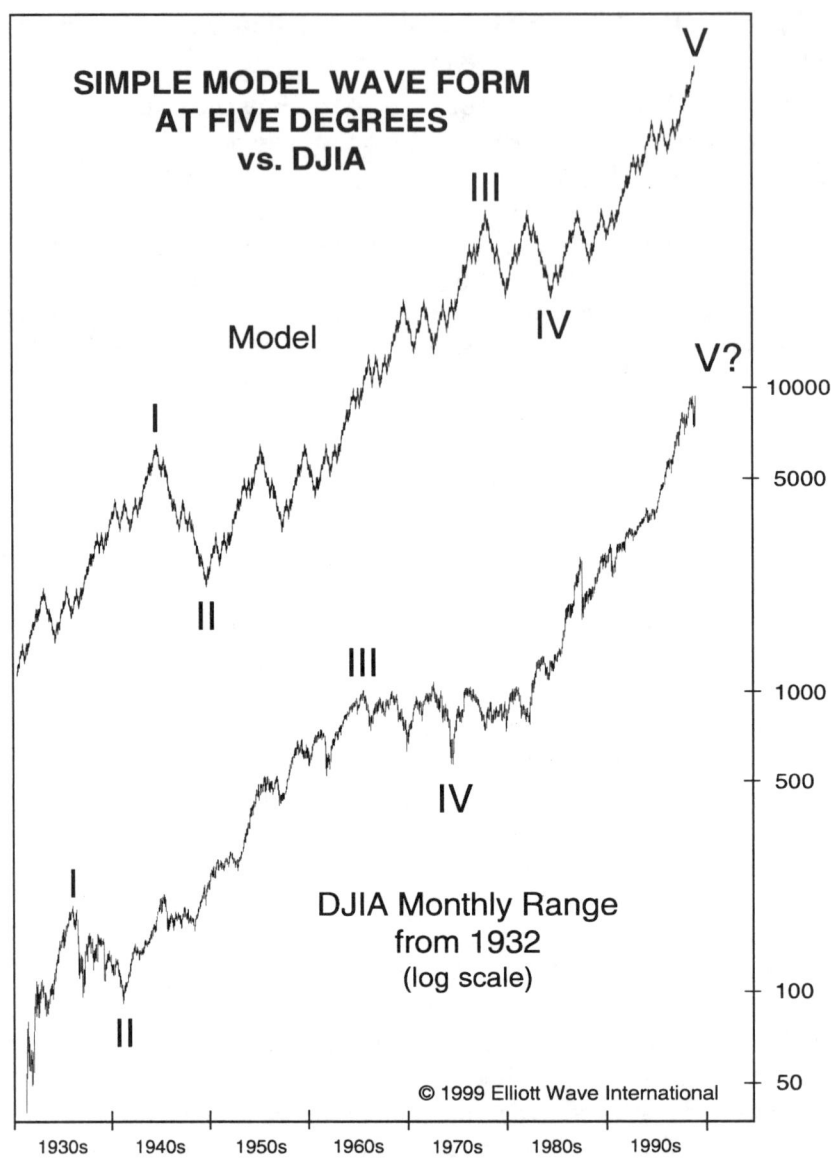

Figure 4-2

Computerization Reflects Objectivity, Consistency and Forecasting Value

Brock, Lakonishok and LeBaron have recently shown that two simple trend-following techniques can make money in markets. The authors conclude as follows:

> When work on nonlinearities in financial time series began, it was seen by many technical traders as justification for their work. They saw a clear connection between technical trading rules and nonlinearities. *For some rules, this connection is indisputable.* Rules that look for general patterns such as "head and shoulders" or more complicated figures are clearly attempting to find some kind of nonlinearity in these series.... We would like to emphasize that our analysis focuses on the simplest trading rules. Other *more elaborate rules may generate even larger differences between conditional returns.*[2]

So far, attempts to develop computer trading models based on fractals, chaos, power laws and so on have failed. As *The Economist* magazine put it in 1996, "Fund managers had hoped that chaos theory would lead them to finance's holy grail. It has delivered remarkably little."[3] The reason that attempts to date have failed is that they have no basis upon which to generate the elusive "more elaborate rules" to which the above study refers. They presume that the market is an indefinite fractal, as described at the start of Chapter 3, and proceed from there to nowhere. In contrast, the Wave Principle model provides a detailed set of rules of pattern formation that are derived from empirics and justified with a hypothesis.

To demonstrate the validity of that hypothesis, my firm, Elliott Wave International, is developing an "expert system" computer program called the Elliott Wave Analysis and Validation Expert System (EWAVES™). The program incorporates all the rules and guidelines currently believed to be valid for interpreting price action under the Wave Principle. To achieve this goal, I had to define each wave pattern *quantitatively.*

Since the market's precise position in the wave structure is always in question, and since one's interpretation of a pattern is only a probability until it is certifiably complete, the computer must be able to judge whether to label, for instance, an ongoing correction as a developing triangle or more likely something else, or whether to label an ongoing impulse as probably ending or not. It is one thing to draw an acceptable pattern called a "contracting triangle" and quite another to state exactly what is allowed

within its definition and what is not, and then to differentiate quantitatively between good triangles and unlikely triangles among those allowed.

Taken in its entirety, the labeling of all the waves that conforms best to ideal forms is the working model for the market's current position. Conformity is reevaluated with each new data point and changed whenever the ideal balance tips in favor of another labeling. This approach keeps the analysis and outlook adaptive to the developing pattern and bypasses the human flaw of stubbornness in the face of opposing information.

The task of quantification was not too difficult, but it was based upon my years of experience in viewing wave relationships, not statistical data on them. However, we had to start somewhere, as there was no way to generate statistics until we had defined the patterns we wanted to investigate. Now that the program is written, we can use it to *get* those statistics (for instance, a curve of common retracement percentages for each wave within a contracting triangle) and adjust our quantification parameters as they dictate.

The project began in the Artificial Intelligence Project Office at Lockheed Engineering Science Company in Houston, Texas. It was the only non-government project being handled by the company at the time. From there, the project was transferred, along with the head of the project, to our headquarters.

We utilized no "data fitting" in constructing the program. In other words, we did not fit the pattern, rules, guidelines or labels to any market's action. We simply quantified Elliott's rules and guidelines for pattern development, about 80% of which had been established by 1938. We tested the program in real markets for debugging purposes. It will run on any set of financial or other type of data. Our tests satisfy us that the program usually gives answers that are substantially the way we would analyze the data ourselves.

The first important fact about EWAVES is that it shows that the Wave Principle itself is an *objective* observation. Some critics have misrepresented the concept of the Wave Principle as a fantasy construct forced onto the market. Others have accused it of requiring subjective judgment. Both of these views are false. Objectivity in dealing with probabilities is not the same as subjectivity, and this computer program has now proved that the Wave Principle involves the former.

The next important fact about EWAVES is that it demonstrates the *consistency* of interpretation under the Wave Principle. In many cases, the

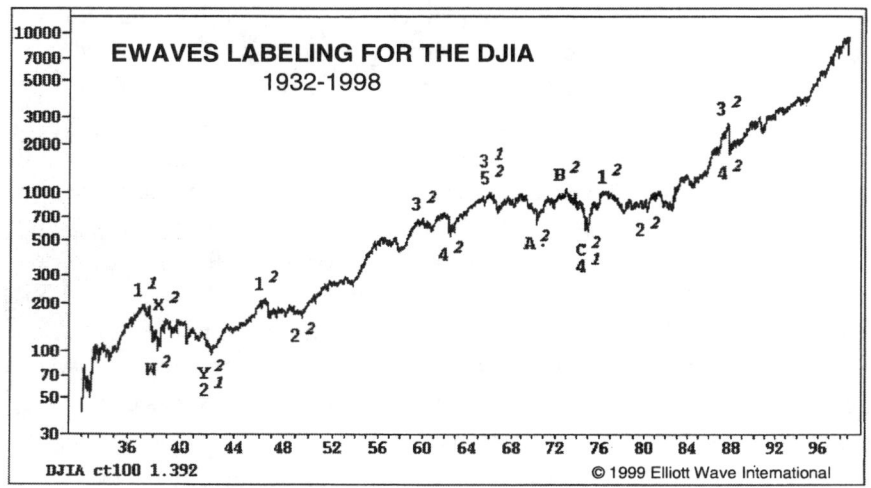

Figure 4-3

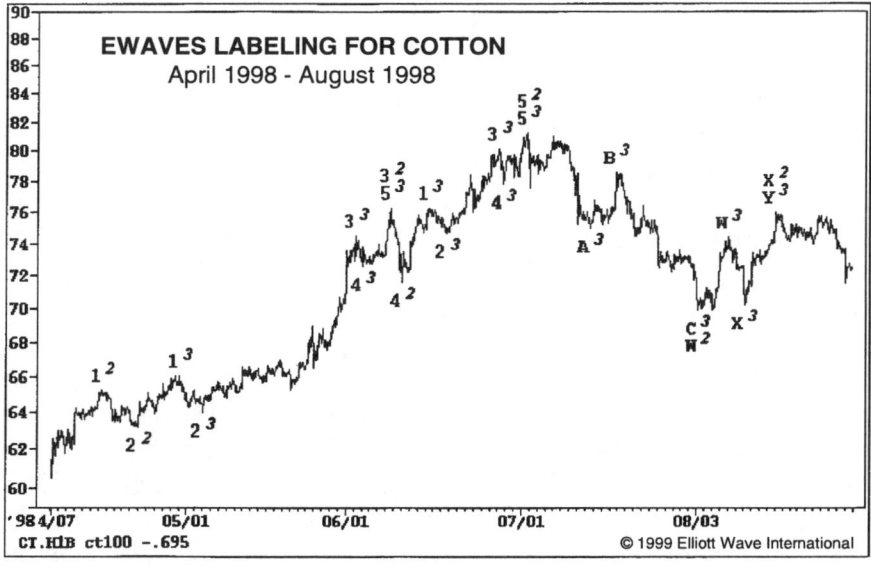

Figure 4-4

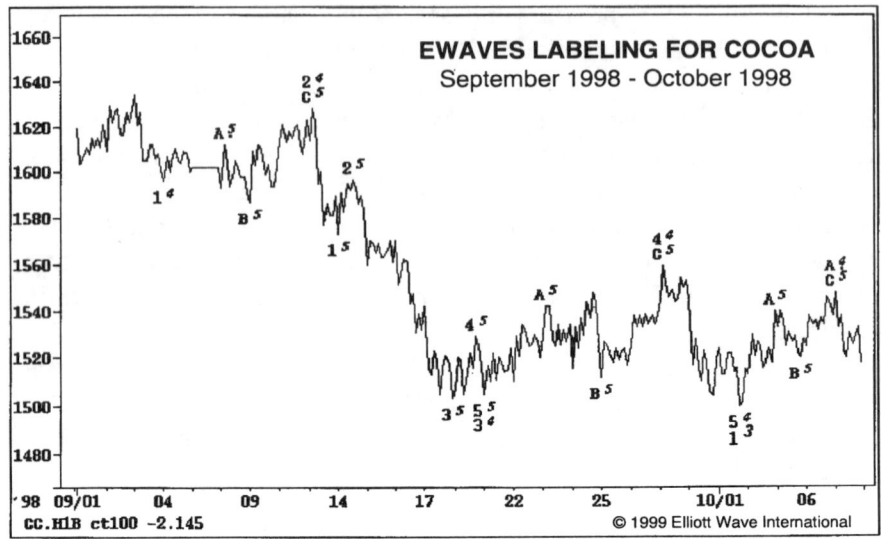

Figure 4-5

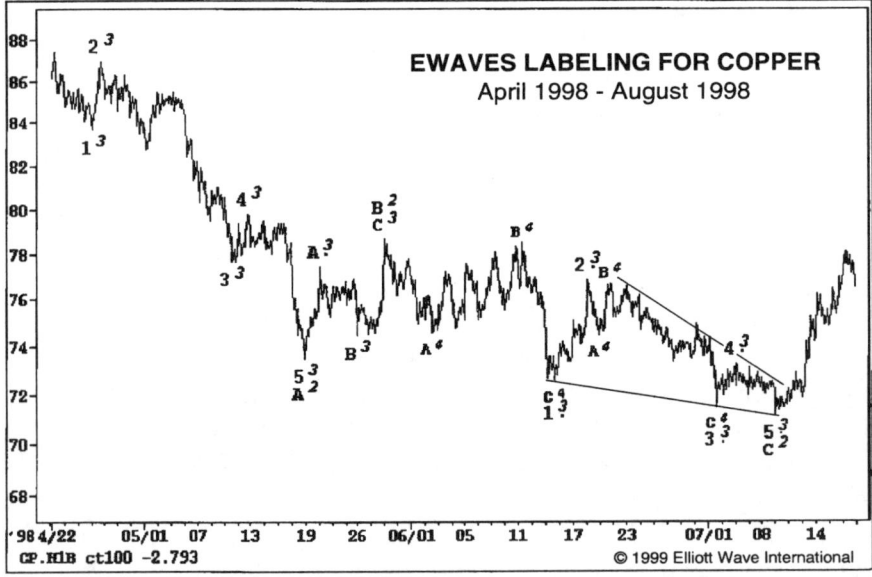

Figure 4-6

wave labeling that the program chooses in each instance as the most reflective of the rules and guidelines of the Wave Principle is the same as that chosen by a human expert. For example, its interpretation of the waves in the DJIA over the past 70 years, shown in Figure 4-3, is the same as that described in Chapter 5 via the analyses of Elliott, Bolton, Collins, Frost and Prechter that was summarized in Figure 4-2. In almost all cases, *one* labeling produced by the computer is the same as that chosen as best by a human expert. Figures 4-4 through 4-6 show additional examples. In no cases does EWAVES produce a labeling that a human would reject as impossible.

Another important aspect of EWAVES is that its operation is compatible with the larger theory of the Wave Principle. The program finds all the patterns so far described under the Wave Principle and is able to link them into a complex self-similar structure.

Finally, EWAVES is demonstrating a fairly reliable forecasting ability. For instance, it consistently and accurately called for rising DJIA prices from 1990 through today, and it accurately called for mostly lower prices in gold from 1996 to the present.

We have yet to quantify these forecasts to prove our point, but we are approaching that goal. Our plan is to develop a "signal" module that in essence would simplify EWAVES' conclusions into buy, sell and stop orders pertaining only to one or two degrees of trend. The program's output through this module would not be the Wave Principle and would provide far less information than a comprehensive wave interpretation, so any results would be a minimum expression of the forecasting value of the analytical engine of the program. Given our knowledge of real-world markets and the avoidance of false assumptions that have disappointed other programmers, we have reason to be optimistic.

The above paragraphs speak to the validity of the Wave Principle but hardly cover the value of the program. Practitioners of the Wave Principle, myself included, are often subjectively influenced, as all humans have their emotions and biases. This is not to support the false accusation that the Wave Principle *is* subjective or *requires* subjectivity. Nor does human subjectivity with respect to applying the Wave Principle make it different from any other approach. However, the fact that the Wave Principle can be computerized gives it an advantage over many other approaches. With an unemotional computer, interpreting price movements in markets is an entirely consistent exercise.

Equally important is EWAVES' volume advantage. The human mind can manipulate only a certain number of concepts at a time. EWAVES, on the other hand, simultaneously takes into account all patterns through several degrees when making its assessment of the best consistency score for labeling purposes. EWAVES lists (and can graph) *all* allowable wave counts and then rank them by accordance with ideal forms, producing an objective roster of outcomes ranked by probability.

Best of all for academic purposes, EWAVES is a wave analysis laboratory that can be used to test any question relating to the Wave Principle, including pattern frequency, characteristics, price targeting, etc., to help refine the Wave Principle through a more detailed empirical study. That is how we hope to use it to help launch this new science.

EWAVES identifies data series that do not reflect the Wave Principle and reports them as "uncountable." Undoubtedly, the program might at times produce a wave labeling for a series of random numbers, as the definition of random means numbers that can reflect anything, in this case including a wave sequence. (For more on this topic, see Chapter 19.) Nevertheless, if we have accurately computerized a valid concept, EWAVES' consistency score for random data would have to average significantly less than that for financial data. While we have yet to test such questions, at least we are developing the means to do so.

The computer history of the Wave Principle, as you can see by this discussion, is so new that it has barely begun. On the other hand, there is a fairly long history of application by people. The next two chapters examine some of that history as another indicator of the Wave Principle's validity.

NOTES

1　Buettner, M. (1995). "An evolutionary model of market growth: The *Elliott wave principle*." Unpublished paper.

2　Brock, W., *et al.* (1992, December). "Simple technical trading rules and the stochastic properties of stock returns." *Journal of Finance.*

3　"Chaos under a cloud." (1996, January 13). *The Economist.*

Chapter 5:

Forecasting Pattern on the Basis of Pattern

As L.F. Richardson pointed out, the length of a seacoast is dependent upon your method of measuring and your scale.[1] A ruler placed on a globe will give one answer; the same ruler applied to every indentation as one traverses the coast itself will give a vastly different one. Similarly, when people ask me where the stock market is going or even what its trend has been, I have to ask, "What degree are you talking about?" There can be multiple answers, as in, "The Minor trend is *down* within a *sideways* Intermediate trend within a *rising* Primary trend."

My colleagues and I spend our time assessing waves lasting minutes to those lasting centuries. For this chapter, I have chosen to chronicle forecasts that pertained to fairly long trends. There are several reasons for this decision. First, if I were to show only a few near-term predictions, readers would rightly assume that the results were due to luck. After all, with so much time within which to choose one's examples, a few would have to turn out right. Second, I want to relate the model shown in Chapter 4 to what practitioners expected along the way, from the first days of the Wave Principle's application. Third, fractals and complex systems are presumed to be unpredictable over any significant time, and I want to demonstrate the contrary before explaining in Chapter 20 why I disagree with that presumption. Finally, successful long-term forecasting is just plain impressive; no one but Elliott wave practitioners can do it.

One important test of a scientific hypothesis is its ability to predict outcomes. Although the Wave Principle hypothesis is difficult to quantify on the basis of predictability because it forecasts only *probabilistically* (see Chapter 20), there is nevertheless substantial evidence of its unique value. While reviewing the following excerpts, it is important that you

honestly consider the *utter uncertainty* that exists in real-time forecasting. Psychological experiments show that most people who review events in retrospect consider them to have been obviously implied at the time.[2] As Lee Simonson once said, "Any event, once it has occurred, can be made to appear inevitable by a competent historian."[3] That goes for all of us. "Fine," I always reply to protestations that previous trends were easy to predict, "then how do you forecast the *next* ten years?" Usually I do not get much of an answer. I think that after you read these statements and consider them in the proper light, you will agree that the authors' accuracy in describing the future is due to their knowing something useful.

Forecasting the DJIA over Half a Century

In *The Elliott Wave Principle — A Critical Appraisal*, Hamilton Bolton made this opening statement:

> As we have advanced through some of the most unpredictable economic climate imaginable, covering depression, major war, and postwar reconstruction and boom, I have noted how well Elliott's Wave Principle has fitted into the facts of life as they have developed.

The twists and turns of the plot of stock prices from 1932 to the present are history now, but before each one happened, the path that the DJIA was to take was considered utterly unpredictable or violently debatable. More accurately stated, the consensus at each major trend change was (and always is) *wrong*, for reasons to be discussed in Chapters 8 and 18. However, five people in succession applied a crude young science to forecasting the market's movement during that time with results that are unprecedented.[4]

As you read the excerpts that follow, notice that each analyst operated under the assumption of the Wave Principle. Each therefore consistently maintained the same essential conclusions regarding the wave position of the Dow Jones Industrial Average, namely: (1) 1932 marked the low of a *fourth* wave in a five-wave structure that began in the late 1700s. (2) The Dow required a *fifth* wave in that structure. (3) That fifth wave would itself subdivide into five waves of the next lower degree.

Locate the years 1942, 1953, 1960, 1966, 1970 and 1982 as marked in Figure 5-1. In each of those years, the foremost proponent of the Wave Principle at the time published the commentary that follows. To get a better feeling for the uncertainty of the outlook at the time, please take a piece of paper and cover the remainder of the graph forward from each date. Of course, even this exercise is inadequate to convey the full extent of the

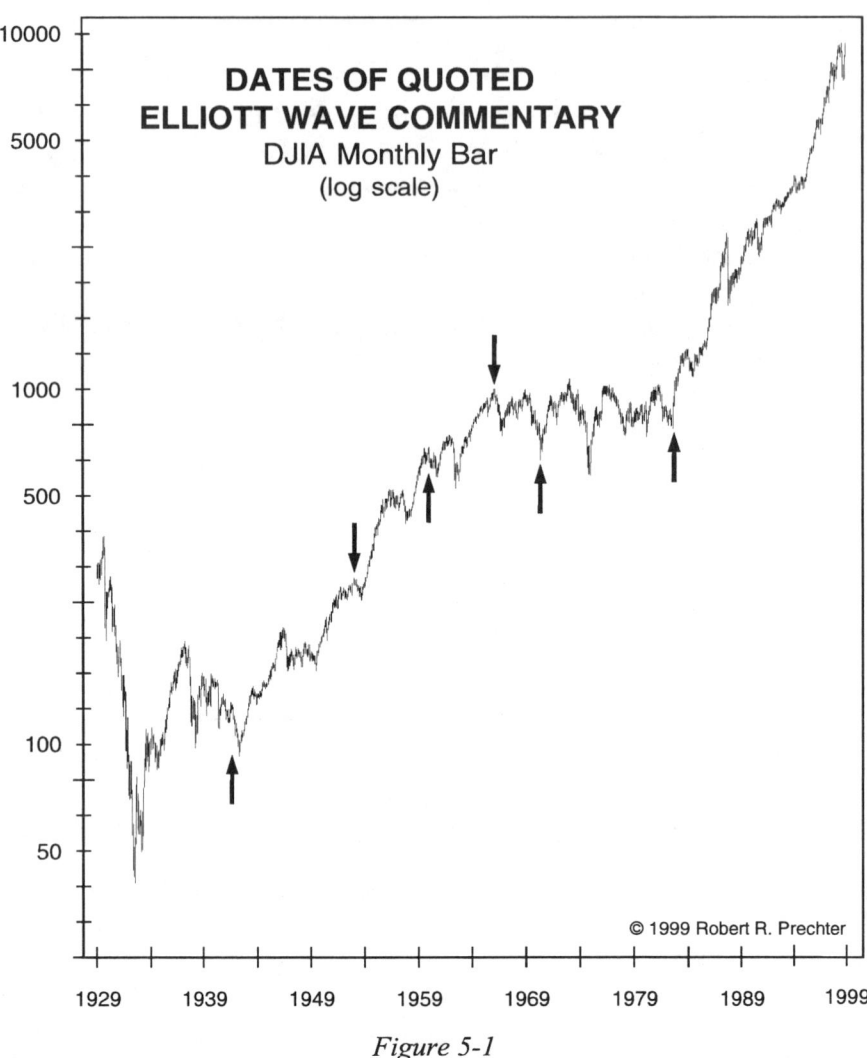

Figure 5-1

real-time uncertainty, as its very shape communicates something about the future that people did not know at the time.

Note: Wave notations were not standardized until very recently, so I have amended some of these presentations to maintain degree-label consistency. Also, some ellipses and minor edits are unmarked for ease of reading. For those interested, everything that each practitioner said about the long term outlook for stocks is reprinted in four volumes, as listed at the end of this book.

August 11 and 25, 1941

Ralph Nelson Elliott, recognizing the end of the wave (IV) corrective process (later labeled wave II of (V)) and forecasting the entire wave (V) advance:

The earliest available stock record is the Axe-Houghton Index, dating from 1854. The essential "change" characteristics of the long movement from 1854 to September 1929 are shown in the accompanying graph. The wave from 1857 to 1929 may be either Supercycle wave (I), (III) or (V), depending upon the nature and extent of development of the country before 1854.[5] There is reason to believe, however, that the period from 1857 to 1929 can be regarded as Supercycle wave (III). The market since 1929 has outlined the pattern of a gigantic thirteen-year triangle [Figure 5-2] of such tremendous scope that these defeatist years may well be grouped as Supercycle wave (IV) of an order dating back to as early as 1776. My observation has been that orthodox triangles appear only as the fourth wave of a [five-wave trend].[6]

Nature's inexorable law of proportion accounts for the recurrent 0.618 ratio of swing-by-swing comparison, [as you can see from] the following tabulation of important movements since April 1930:

The Cyclical Relativity of Market Trends

Wave No.	Dates From	To	Points From	To	Change			Ratio
R	April 1930	July 1932	296.0	40.5	255.5			
S	July 1932	March 1937	40.5	196.0	155.5	155.5/	255.5=	60.9%
T	March 1937	March 1938	196.0	97.0	99.0	99.0/	155.5=	63.6%
U	March 1938	Sept. 1939	97.0	158.0	61.0	61.0/	91.0=	61.6%
								Avg. 62.0%

These ratios and series have been controlling and limiting the extent and duration of price trends irrespective of wars, politics, production indices, the supply of money, general purchasing power, and other generally accepted methods of determining stock values. This feature proves that current events and politics have no influence on market movements.

Since the causes of this phenomenal market behavior originate in the relativity of the component cycles compressed within the triangular area, it is distinctly encouraging to be able to point out that the rapidly approaching apex of the triangle should mark the beginning of a relatively long period of increasing activity [i.e., price increase] in the stock market. Triangle wave E [shown as Ⓥ on the chart] is well advanced,

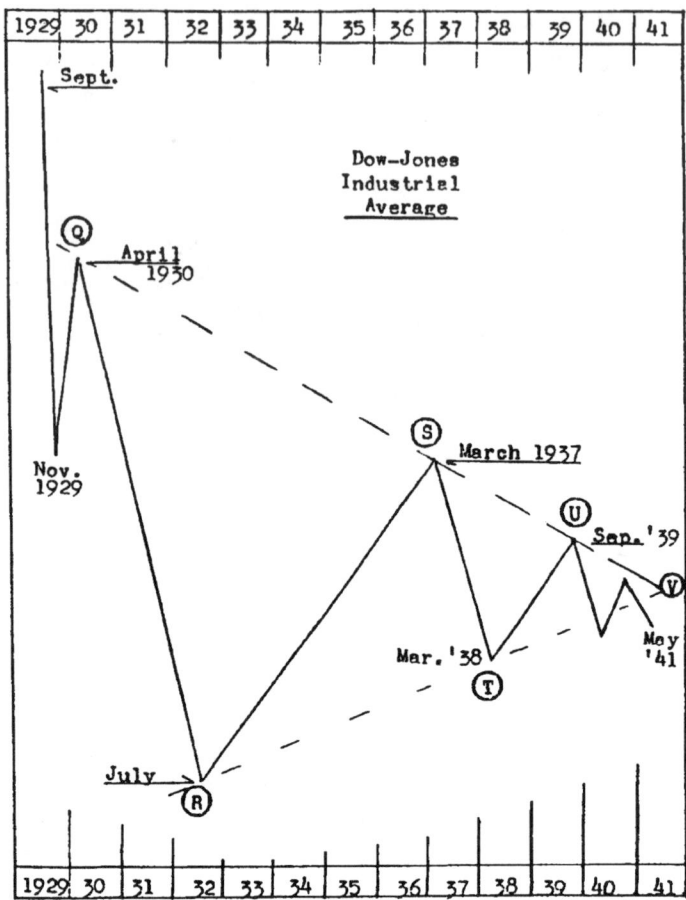

R.N. Elliott's wave interpretation from 1941

Figure 5-2

and **its termination,** within or without the area of the triangle, **should mark the final correction of the 13-year pattern of** *defeatism*. This termination will also mark the beginning of **a new Supercycle wave (V)** (composed of a series of cycles of lesser degree), **comparable in many respects with the long [advance] from 1857 to 1929.** Supercycle (V) is not expected to culminate until about 2012.[7] (See dashed line in the graph [Figure 5-3].) [8,9]

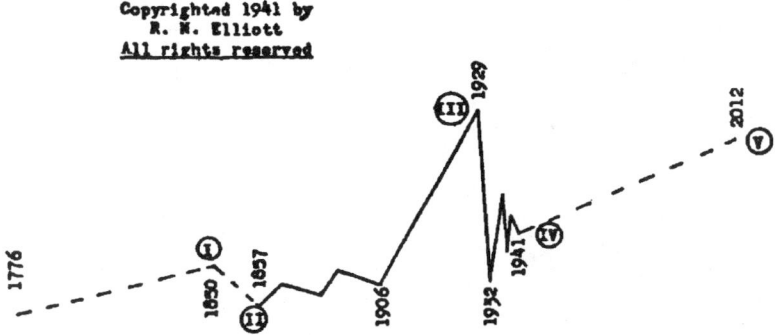

R.N. Elliott's interpretation of the long-term wave position
(not to scale or perspective)

Figure 5-3

[Note: The DJIA touched its low eight months later, in April 1942, during the darkest days of World War II. It has not looked back since.]

First Quarter, 1953

Arthur Hamilton Bolton, recognizing the position, and forecasting the extent, of wave III:

> The late R.N. Elliott in 1941 projected a pattern of future stock market behavior which has not varied in fundamentals from his original outline years ago. This last prediction, or hypothesis, is vitally important, because if Elliott is right, we will not see again probably in this century stock prices as low "in dollar price" as they were in 1942. Of course, inflation will take care of a great deal of that hypothesis anyway, but it does mean that **no major depression of the 1929-32 variety is in the cards in our lifetime** (although there may well be 1921s, 1896s, 1873s again within this span). Further, it is as well to keep the background in perspective; Elliott's projection was made at a time when deflation and not inflation was the current fear.
>
> The significance of Elliott's projection should now become more apparent.
>
> (1) Elliott's hypothesis calls for a series of bull markets from 1942 similar in degree to those between 1857 and 1929, in the pattern of 5 waves (3 up and 2 down in between), followed by 3 down (2 down and 1 up), all moving on to successively higher levels.
>
> (2) Wave ① of the first Cycle bull market was completed in 1946

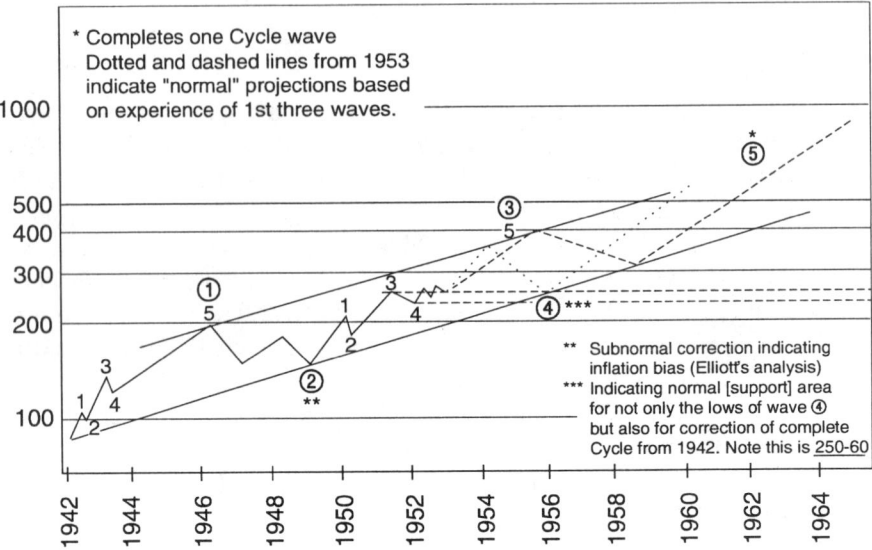

Figure 5-4

(Elliott's analysis [before his] death in 194[8]), and its correction (wave ②) was completed in June 1949.

(3) Because of both the time element (a third wave according to Elliott is never shorter in time than the first wave) and amplitude indicated, we must now still be in wave ③ of the 1942-? bull market (one Cycle wave).

(4) Following completion of wave ③ (not likely before 1954 because of time and amplitude elements), there should be a correction (wave ④) on the order of 1946-49, which, however, should not break the base line of the 1942-1949 lows, according to one of Elliott's tenets. (This is a normal expectation only and might in an extreme case be violated slightly.)

(5) Following wave ④, wave ⑤ should close out the first upward Cycle from 1942. Because of the time element again, **it looks like the 1960s before we face a correction to the whole rise from 1942 and anything approaching a major depression in stock prices.**[10]

[Note: Bolton's dashed line in Figure 5-4 called for a top near Dow 1000 by 1965.]

First Quarter, 1960

Hamilton Bolton, continued:

The ratio of 61.8 to 100 and 100 to 161.8 became a central part of Elliott's theories in regard to both *time* and *amplitude*. Thus, Elliott pointed out a number of other coincidences. For instance, the number of points from 1921 to 1926 (i.e., the first three waves) was 61.8% of the number of points of the last wave from 1926 to 1928 (the orthodox top). Likewise in the five waves up from 1932 to 1937. Again, the wave from the top in 1930 (297 DJIA) to the bottom in 1932 (40 DJIA) is 1.618 times the wave from 40 to 195 (1932 to 1937). Also, the decline from 1937 to 1938 was 61.8% of the advance from 1932-37 in DJIA points. Should the 1949 market to date adhere to this formula, then the advance from 1949 to 1956 (361 points in the DJIA) should be complete when 583 points (161.8% of the 361 points) have been added to the 1957 low of 416, or a total of **999 DJIA**. [See Figure 5-5.][11]

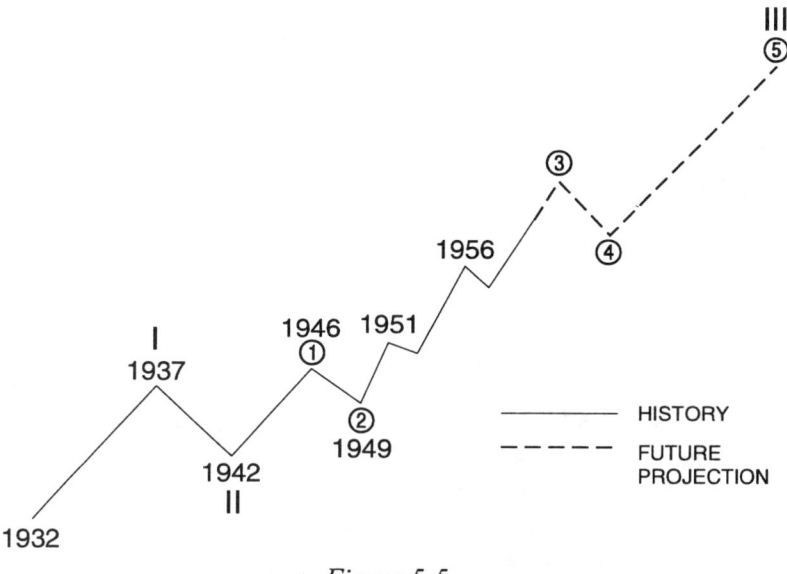

Figure 5-5

[Note: This was a perfect call not only for continuation of the bull market but for the level of its ultimate top. The daily closing high for the Dow in February 1966, thirteen years after the first quotation and six years after the second, was **995.14**. From that point, the stock market experienced its largest bear market since 1937-1942, exactly as forecast.]

First Quarter, 1966; published in April

Charles Joseph Collins, identifying the end of wave III and forecasting the extent of wave IV:

> In the count of Supercycle wave (V) from 1932, I find that two Cycle waves have been completed and a third may have completed in January 1966 or, if not (see subsequent discussion), then it is in the process of completion. These Cycle waves are illustrated in [Figure 5-6].
>
> Cycle wave III, beginning 1942, which is the wave of current interest, I break down as shown in [Figure 5-7]. Incidentally, the upward slant of Primary wave ④ between 1956 and 1962 carries inflationary implications.
>
> Primary wave ⑤ (1962-1966?) of Cycle wave III is shown in [Figure 5-8] by giving the monthly swings of the Dow Industrials. Since Intermediate wave (3) of this Primary wave extended, it would appear that **Intermediate wave (5), and thus Primary wave ⑤ as well as Cycle wave III, ended in January 1966,** as the market has subsequently developed a downthrust. (Those who might argue that such a downswing constitutes wave 2 of an extension of wave (5) are faced with Elliott's dictum that an extension can occur in any one of waves 1, 3 or 5, but

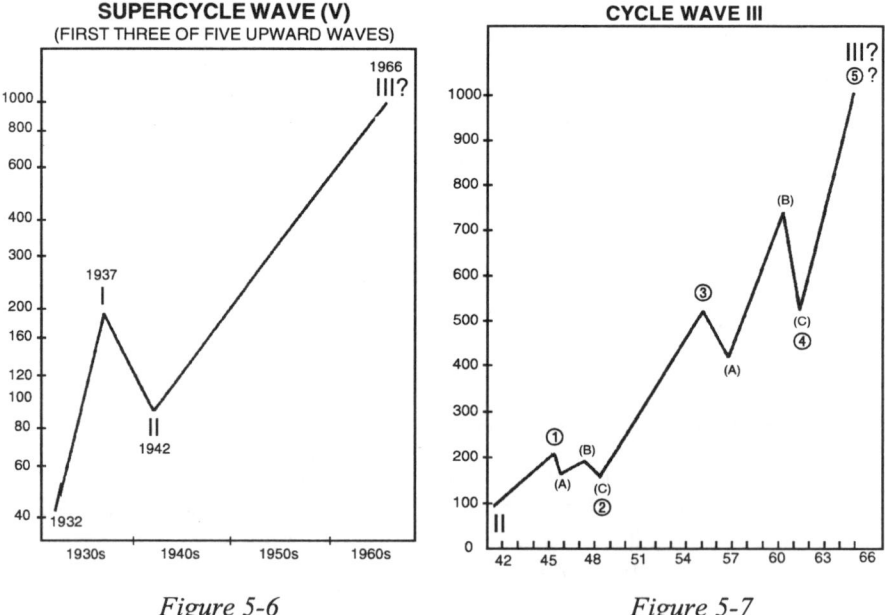

Figure 5-6   Figure 5-7

never in more than one. The extension in Intermediate wave (3), under Elliott's rule, would thus preclude an extension in Intermediate wave (5).)

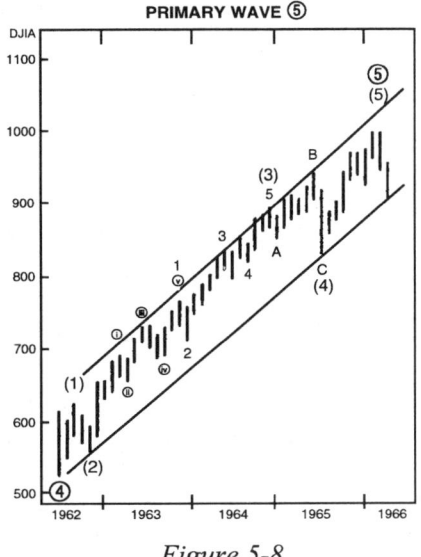

Figure 5-8

The third wave of Primary wave ⑤ extended, and Elliott states that an extension will be retraced twice. Such being the case, this would call for the "C" wave of Cycle wave IV to carry back at least to 770-710 on the Dow, in other words, to the approximate area within which the extension of Intermediate wave (3) began (see points 1 and 2 of [Figure 5-8]). The decline could carry further, however, under Elliott's rule that the correction of a wave should normally carry back to around the terminal point of the fourth wave of the five lesser waves that characterized the swing. The terminal point of the fourth Primary wave of Cycle wave III (see [wave ④ in Figure 5-7]) was established in 1962 at 524 on the Dow. **Purely as a speculation, might not the "A" wave of Cycle wave IV carry to the 770-710 area, the "C" wave to around the lower 524 point, with a sizable intervening "B" wave?**[12]

[Note: This was a perfect call of the Cycle degree top that had just occurred after 24 years of rise. It was also a perfect call of the extent of the first decline into the 1966 daily closing low, which was **744.31**, and a nearly perfect forecast of the ultimate low eight years later in 1974 at **577.60** basis daily closing figures.]

May 1970

Alfred John Frost, forecasting the low of wave IV:

A. Hamilton Bolton in May 1960 said, "Should the 1949 market to date adhere to the Fibonacci formula, then the advance from 1949 to 1956 (361 points in the DJIA) should be complete when 583 points (161.8% of the 361 points) have been added to the 1957 low of 416, or to

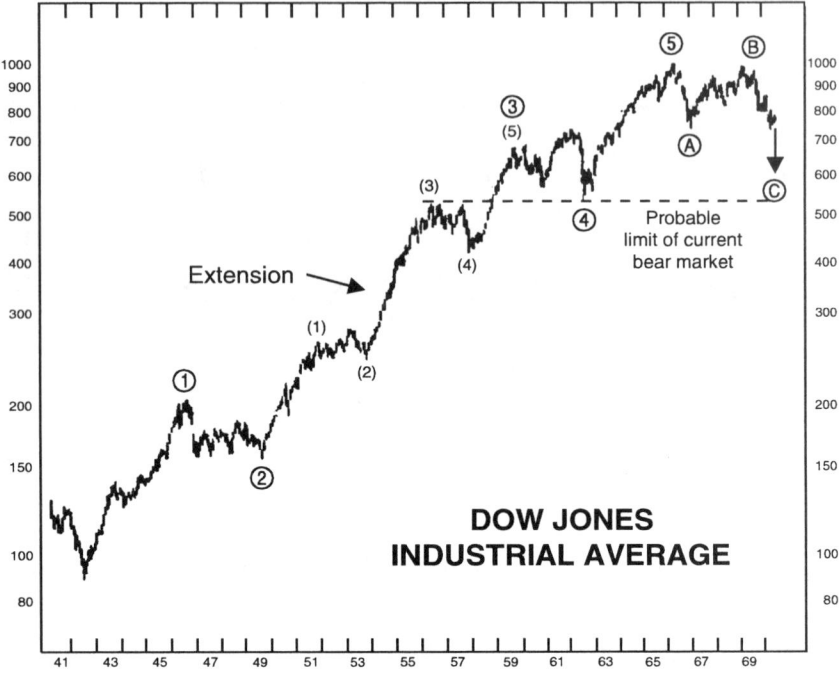

Figure 5-9

a total of 999 DJIA." This forecast was made almost six years before the great bull market peaked at approximately 1000 DJIA. Applying the same formula to determine the extent of the current bear market, we get a number of possibilities, each indicating that a severe market lies directly ahead. A drop of 61.8% from the recorded high of 1000 DJIA would bring the Dow back to 381, its 1929 high. This doesn't seem probable, [as] the current Cycle wave from 1966 should not overlap the 1929 high. Should the current C-wave from December 2, 1968 (DJIA 986) drop 414 points (161.8% of the 1966 A-wave decline of 256 points), **the market would bottom out at 572**. [See Figure 5-9.][13]

[Note: The low of the bear market occurred on December 9, 1974 with a daily close of 577.60 and a low hourly figure of **572.20**.]

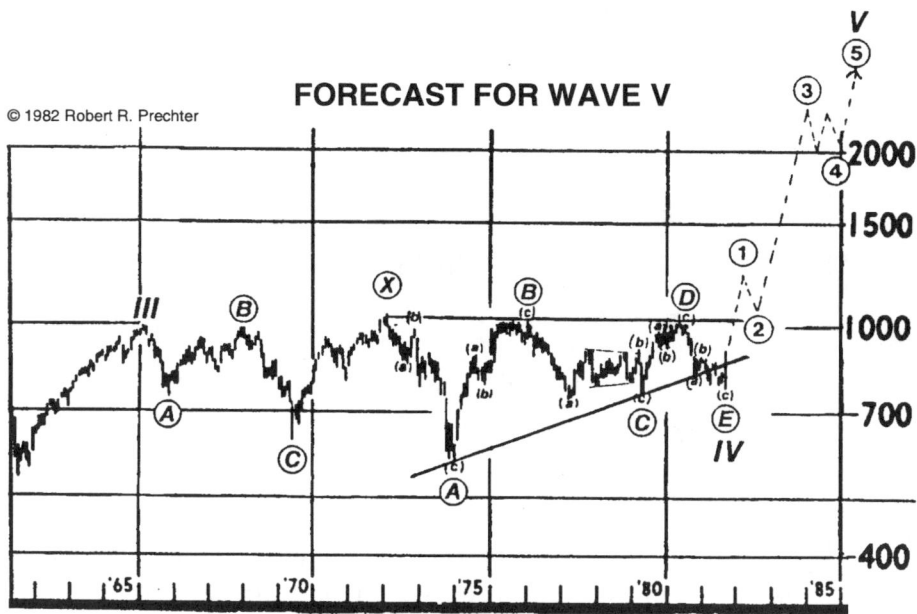

Figure 5-10

September 13, 1982

Robert Rougelot Prechter, Jr., identifying the onset of wave V and projecting its substantial extent:

This is a thrilling juncture for a wave analyst. For the first time since 1974, some incredibly large wave patterns may have been completed, patterns that have important implications for the next five to eight years. The technical name for wave IV by this count is a "double three," with the second "three" an ascending triangle. [See Figure 5-10.] **This wave count argues that the Cycle wave IV correction from 1966 ended last month (August 1982).** The lower boundary of the trend channel from 1942 was broken briefly at the termination of this pattern. A brief break of the long term trendline, I should note, was recognized as an occasional trait of fourth waves, as shown in *R.N. Elliott's Masterworks.*[14]

The task of wave analysis often requires stepping back and taking a look at the big picture and using the evidence of the historical patterns to judge the onset of a major change in trend. Cycle and Supercycle waves move in wide price bands and truly are the most important structures to take into account. [They indicate that] **a period of economic stability**

and soaring stock prices has just begun. One must conclude that a bull market beginning in August 1982 would ultimately carry out its full potential of five times its starting point, thus targeting 3885.[15]

[Note: In the midst of the most extreme stock market pessimism since 1942, Prechter identified the end of a 16-year period of net loss for the Dow a month after its end at 777 and projected a climb to what was perceived as an absurd level of nearly 4000.]

November 8, 1982

Robert Prechter, continued:

Surveying all the market's action over the past 200 years, it is comforting to know exactly where you are in the wave count. [See Figure 5-11.]

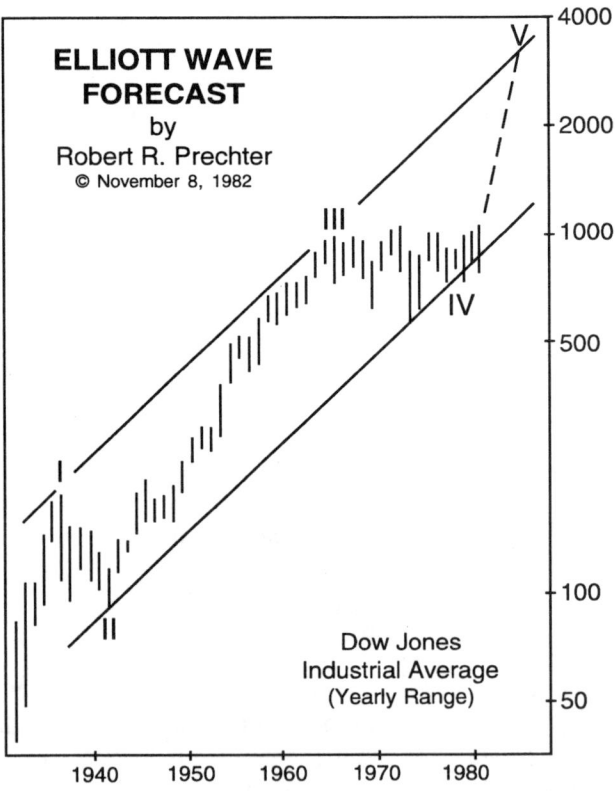

Figure 5-11

April 6, 1983

Robert Prechter, continued:

A normal fifth wave will carry, based on Elliott's channeling methods, to the upper channel line, which in this case cuts through the price action in the 3500-4000 range in the latter half of the 1980s. Elliott noted that when a fourth wave breaks the trend channel [as this one did in 1982], **the fifth will often have a throw-over, or a brief penetration through the same trend channel on the other [i.e., top] side**.

What might we conclude about the psychological aspects of wave V? As the last hurrah, it should be characterized, at its end, by an almost unbelievable institutional mania for stocks and a public mania for stock index futures, stock options, and options on futures. In my opinion, the long term sentiment gauges will give off major trend sell signals two or three years before the final top, and the market will just keep on going. In order for the Dow to reach the heights expected by the year 1987 or 1990, *and* in order to set up the U.S. stock market to experience the greatest crash in its history, which, according to the Wave Principle, is due to follow wave V, **investor mass psychology should reach manic proportions, with elements of 1929, 1968 and 1973 all operating together and, at the end, to an even greater extreme**.[16,17]

[Note: A financial mania is a rare event, occurring on average about once a century. This is the only prediction of a financial mania ever attempted. It has come to pass, as public and institutional desire to own corporate shares has been unprecedented. In fact, it is the greatest stock mania ever, as average U.S. stock valuation here in the second half of 1998 with respect to dividend yield and corporate book value is the highest in history by a substantial margin. Also as anticipated, the Dow has produced a "throw-over" of the upper channel line of the Supercycle advance and has met its upper channel line at Cycle degree (see Figures 5-12 and 18-5). The entire process has taken a decade longer and carried far further than originally imagined.]

Summary

No one has ever conducted market forecasting as a scientific experiment. Neither have Elliotters, so there is no data to quantify the value of these forecasts. Moreover, each of the practitioners cited above made errors along the way, an experience that is shared by everyone who attempts to forecast market prices. Nevertheless, to anyone but a random walker

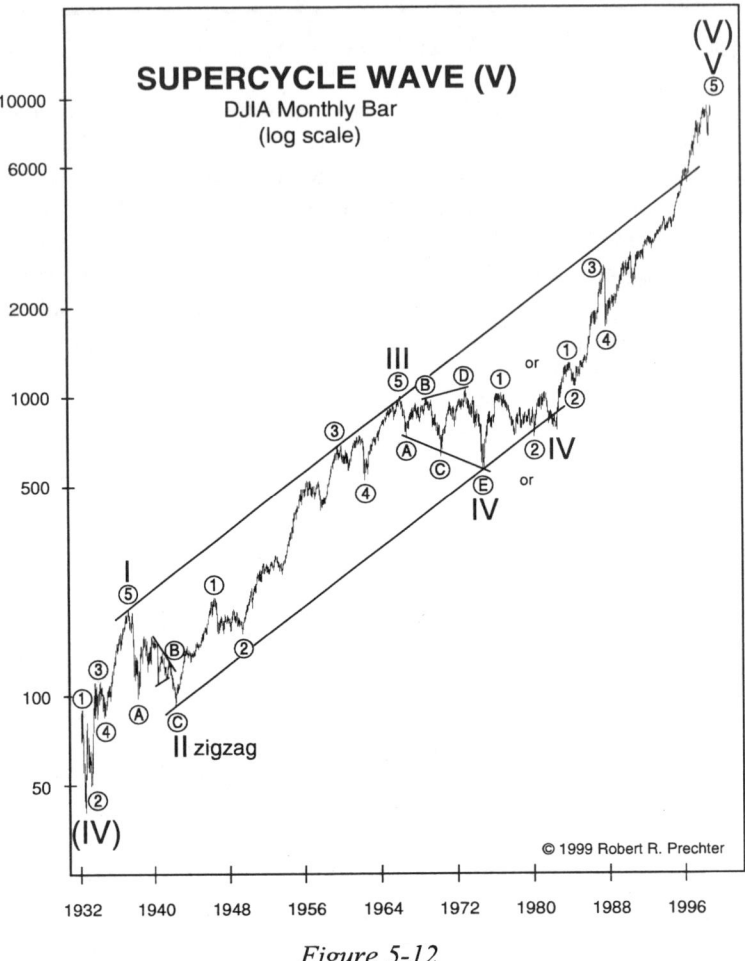

Figure 5-12

who blithely likens such commentary to coin-tossing (an invalid analogy), this is one powerful legacy, particularly when compared to the product of conventional methods, which we will explore in Chapter 19.

The three points that matter with respect to the above quotations are as follows: (1) No other approach to market forecasting has allowed anyone even to adopt a *perspective* such as these forecasts reflect. (2) No approach to market forecasting has produced a degree of *success* remotely approaching that cited above. (3) The outlook through these practitioners has maintained *consistency* throughout this sixty-year period, as each analyst held the same view of the ultimate path for prices and followed through accordingly. Only a valid theory of market behavior could do such things.

NOTES

1 Richardson, L.F. (1961). "The problem of contiguity." *General Systems Yearbook*, Vol. 6, pp. 139-187.

2 One experiment involved subjects forecasting the outcome of a supposed battle between the British and Africans in the 1800s. Those off-handedly informed of the "actual" outcome skewed their answers mightily toward what then became "obvious" from the details supplied, while those not so informed split their decisions 50/50. I regret to say that I do not have a reference for that study, so please enlighten me if you can and I will include it in the next edition.

3 Prochnow, H. (ed.) *The public speaker's treasure chest.*

4 To this list we might add the remarkable Edson Gould, who knew and used the Wave Principle but never said so. For details, see "A Biography of R.N. Elliott" in *R.N. Elliott's Masterworks.*

5 Data prior to 1854 was unavailable at that time.

6 Elliott accomplished this forecast with very limited data, encompassing only 1857 to 1942. He could not see the entire Grand Supercycle wave structure up to that time, which began in 1784 (see Figures 2-7 and 16-5). However, he could see the triangular nature of the corrective process from 1929, which shows up in PPI-adjusted "constant dollar" data (see Figure 16-3 inset and Figure 16-6). Triangles, he had already observed, appear only in the fourth wave position. From his intimate knowledge of how smaller patterns had linked together, then, he knew where the market was in its larger pattern despite having only a partial recording of it. Frost and I later attained the pertinent back data and validated his conclusion in *Elliott Wave Principle.*

7 Elliott's "2012" forecast was an offhand remark that meant, "it will be the same degree, and therefore about as long, as Supercycle wave (III)." 2012 is the year when their lengths would be exactly the same. He did not actually expect that precise a match. What he meant to convey was that he was predicting a *Supercycle* rise closer to *seven* decades rather than a Cycle degree rise closer to *one* decade or a Grand Supercycle closer to *twenty*. So far, the rise has lasted more than 5½ decades from 1942 and more than 6½ decades from 1932, putting it comfortably in the duration of a Supercycle degree advance.

8 Elliott, R.N. (1941, August 11). "Market apathy – cause and termination." (Educational bulletin*).*

9 Elliott, R.N. (1941, August 25). "Two cycles of American history." *Interpretive Letter* No. 17.

10 Bolton, A.H. (1953). "Elliott's wave principle." Supplement to *The Bolton-Tremblay Bank Credit Analyst.*

11 Bolton, A.H. (1960). "The *Elliott wave principle* — a critical appraisal." Supplement to *The Bolton-Tremblay Bank Credit Analyst.*

12 Collins, C.J. (1966). "The *Elliott wave principle* of stock market behavior." Supplement to *The Bolton-Tremblay Bank Credit Analyst.*

13 Frost, A.J. (1970). "The *Elliott wave principle* of stock market behavior." Supplement to *The Bolton-Tremblay Bank Credit Analyst.*

14 Elliott, R.N. (1938). *The wave principle.*

15 Prechter, R. (1982, September 13). "The long term wave pattern — nearing a resolution." *The Elliott Wave Theorist.*

16 Prechter, R. (1983, April 6). "A rising tide — the case for wave V in the Dow Jones Industrial Average." *The Elliott Wave Theorist.*

17 All of Prechter's comments from this time are reprinted in the Appendix to *Elliott Wave Principle.* The next logical question was and is, "If all goes according to expectations, what happens after wave V tops out?" This question was addressed well in advance, in 1978 in *Elliott Wave Principle,* in more detail in the April 6, 1983 report quoted here, and in even greater detail in the 1995 book, *At the Crest of the Tidal Wave.* I mention this because it is not just the great 20th century bull market that was in focus throughout the progression of comments cited throughout this section, *but its position in the even larger wave structure.*

Chapter 6:

Forecasting Price Extremes on the Basis of Typical Wave Relationships

As suggested by some of the commentary in Chapter 5, the Fibonacci ratio recurs in certain price relationships among waves. This fact provides a basis for creating guidelines applicable to very specific price forecasting. R.N. Elliott discovered several such relationships, and I have found a number of others. There is no point in cataloguing them in this book; for a list, see Chapter 4 of *Elliott Wave Principle*.

Bolton, Collins and Frost used this type of analysis to produce forecasts of pinpoint accuracy months or years in advance. The quoted excerpts from *The Elliott Wave Theorist* below present two detailed examples of applying wave ratio relationships to the forecasting puzzle. They relate actual situations in the two most important markets covered by the publication: the DJIA and U.S. Treasury bonds. These are striking examples because they went utterly contrary to majority opinion and preceded dramatic market action. You need not take the time to understand every nuance of these discussions. The point is to see that precise forecasting on this basis is possible.

Forecasting the DJIA Using Fibonacci Relationships

November 7, 1983

A break of Dow 1206 will virtually confirm that Primary ① has peaked and assure a continuation of the decline. If 1158 is broken, the next point of support is **1090**, which marks a .382 retracement of Primary ①. [See Figure 6-1.]

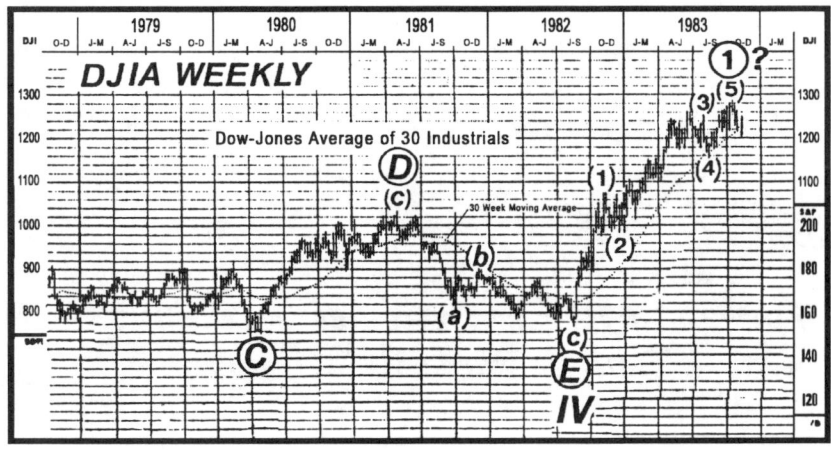

Figure 6-1

March 5, 1984

As the correction progresses, we should be able to get closer and closer to estimating where the final bottom will actually occur. Here are the calculations:

(1) Primary wave ② will retrace .382 of Primary wave ① at **1094.20**.
(2) Within the A-B-C decline, wave C will be .618 times as long as wave A at **1089.19**.

April 3, 1984

Already I am receiving in the mail Elliott-based arguments for an immediate collapse to Dow 200-500, a phenomenon that repeats every time the Dow falls 100 points or more. However, Primary wave ②, which is now in force, should bottom this year.

April 30, 1984

Primary wave ② has *not bottomed yet*. The stock market appears to be on the verge of a 100-point collapse, with a final intermediate term low expected in the May 30-June 4 time period. [See Figure 6-2, from the April 3 issue.]

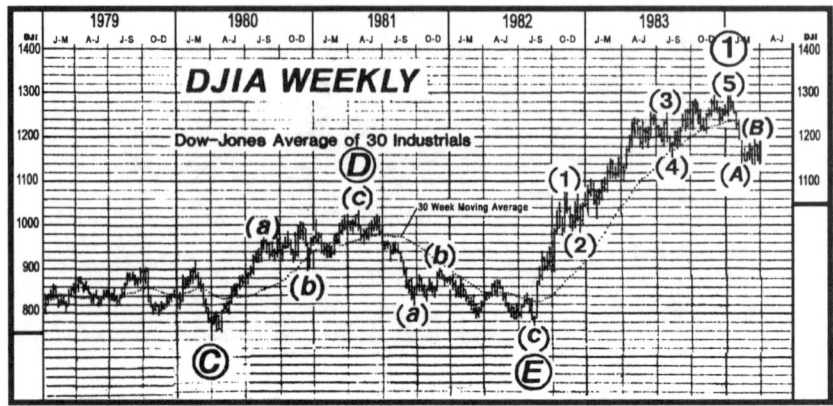

Figure 6-2

June 4, 1984

In terms of *price*, the downside target of 1090 was first computed *seven months ago*, in the November 7, 1983 issue. That basic target was reiterated in the March and April issues, with a "buy" strategy outlined (with minor variations) for the **1087-1099** area. The hourly low on May 30 was **1087.93**. The list of Fibonacci wave relationships now in place is so perfect as to be a compelling argument all by itself that a low is in the making [see Figure 6-3]:

(1) Wave (C) at 90.99 points, is .22 of a Dow point from being exactly .618 times as long as wave (A) at 146.88 points, a typical relationship in zigzags.

(2) Wave (B) at 35.27 points, is ½ point from being exactly .382 times as long as wave (C).

(3) Not only is wave (A) 1.618 times as long as wave (C), which is 2.618 times as long as wave (B), but the actual lengths are remarkably close to Fibonacci numbers: 146.88 points (Fibonacci 144), 90.99 points (Fibonacci 89), and 35.27 points (Fibonacci 34).

(4) Wave (A) lasted 5 weeks, wave (B) lasted 13 weeks, and wave (C) lasted 3 weeks, just as forecast in the May issue. The two impulse waves totaled 8 weeks. The entire correction lasted 21 weeks. Thus, the time lengths create the Fibonacci sequence, 3, 5, 8, 13, 21, re-

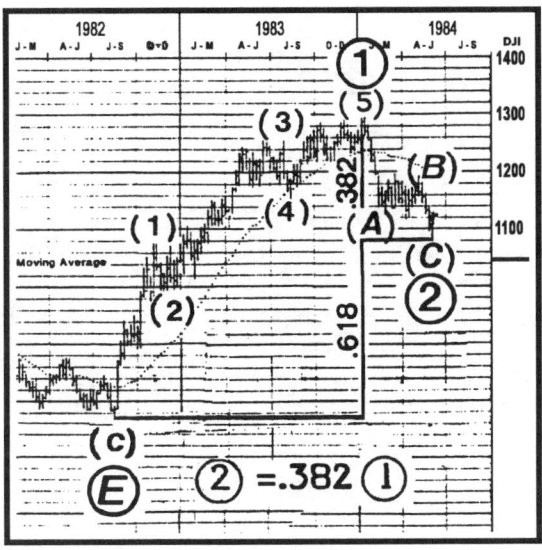

Figure 6-3

vealing that each time period, *as precisely defined by their Elliott Wave structures*, is related to each of the others by a Fibonacci ratio.

(5) Even the Minor moves are related precisely by Fibonacci ratios (see March and April issues).

July 11, 1984

The wave count from the June 15 low is not particularly bullish since it has not traced out a *clear* five waves up. The [price] parameters have not changed, however. The next cyclic lows of importance are due July 24-26.

July 24, 1984

Today's slight new closing low in the Dow at 1086.57 generated "sell signals" all over Wall Street. However, it appears to me that, just like the May 30 low and the June 15 low, this minor decline is actually providing another excellent opportunity to buy. The wave count is completing a *triple* zigzag from the January high and indicates a potential turn to the upside *within a few trading hours*. Taking in all the price action to the present, **Dow 1083 (+ or - 5)** is a very strong support level.

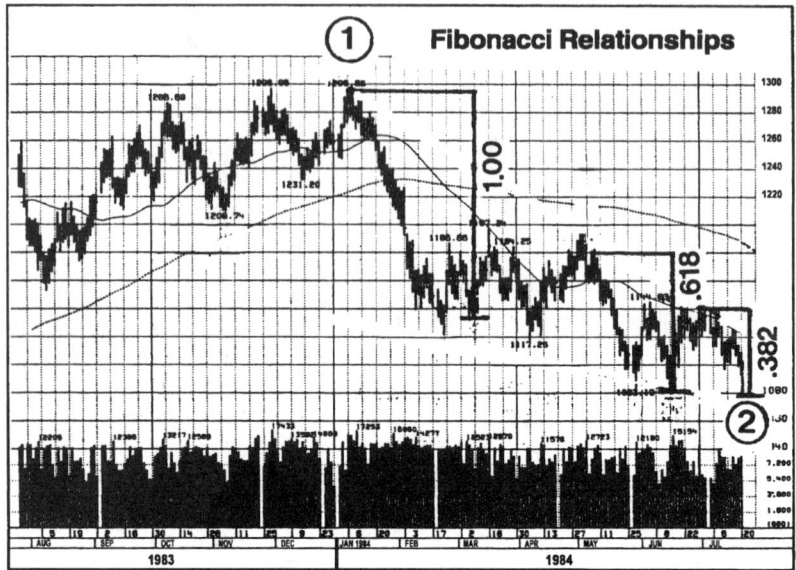

Figure 6-4

Based on typical Fibonacci relationships [see Figure 6-4, from the August 6 issue], I doubt that our stop at Dow 1070 hourly reading will be taken out.

August 6, 1984

The leap out of that bottom [at **1083.59** hourly reading on July 25, 1984], as if you hadn't heard, has been one for the record books and is powerful enough virtually to confirm that Primary wave ③ has begun. [See Figures 6-5 and 6-6.]

To contrast this approach with conventional wisdom, Chapter 11 of *At the Crest of the Tidal Wave* chronicles how historically unpopular a long-term bullish stock market opinion was at that time. The bond forecast recounted below concludes with a description of the consensus opinion of economists. It ties in with the discussions in Chapters 8 and 19.

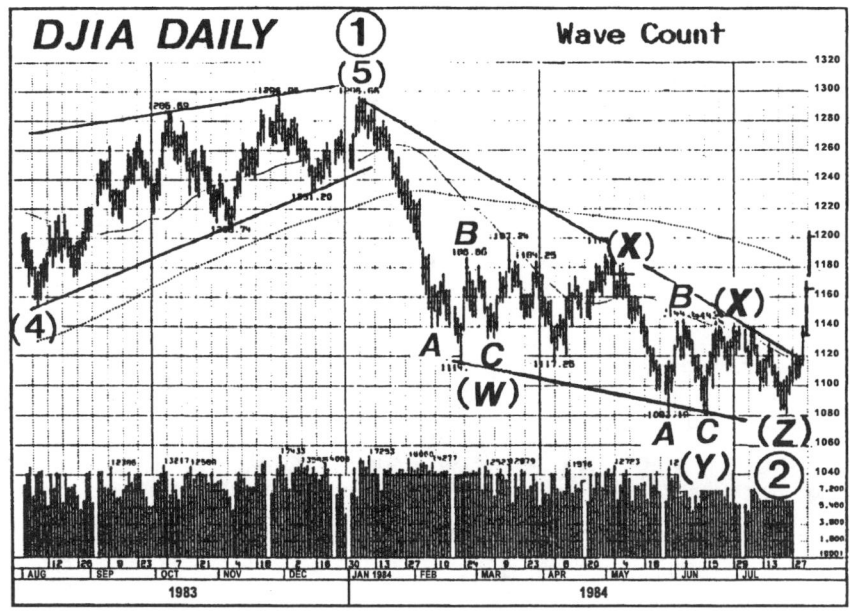

Figure 6-5

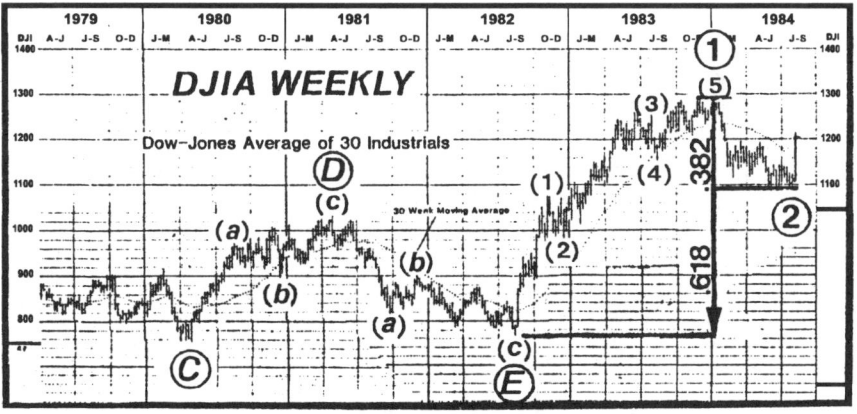

Figure 6-6

Forecasting Bond Prices Using Fibonacci Relationships

November 1983

Now it's time to attempt a more precise forecast for bond futures prices. Wave (a) in December futures dropped 11¾ points, so a wave (c) equivalent subtracted from the wave (b) peak at 73½ last month projects a downside target of 61¾. It is also the case that alternate waves within symmetrical triangles are usually related by .618. As it happens, wave B fell 32 points. 32 x .618 = 19¾ points, which should be a good estimate for the length of wave D. 19¾ points from the peak of wave C at 80 projects a downside target of *60¼*. Therefore, *the 60¼ - 61¾ area is the best point to be watching for the bottom of the current decline.* [See Figure 6-7.]

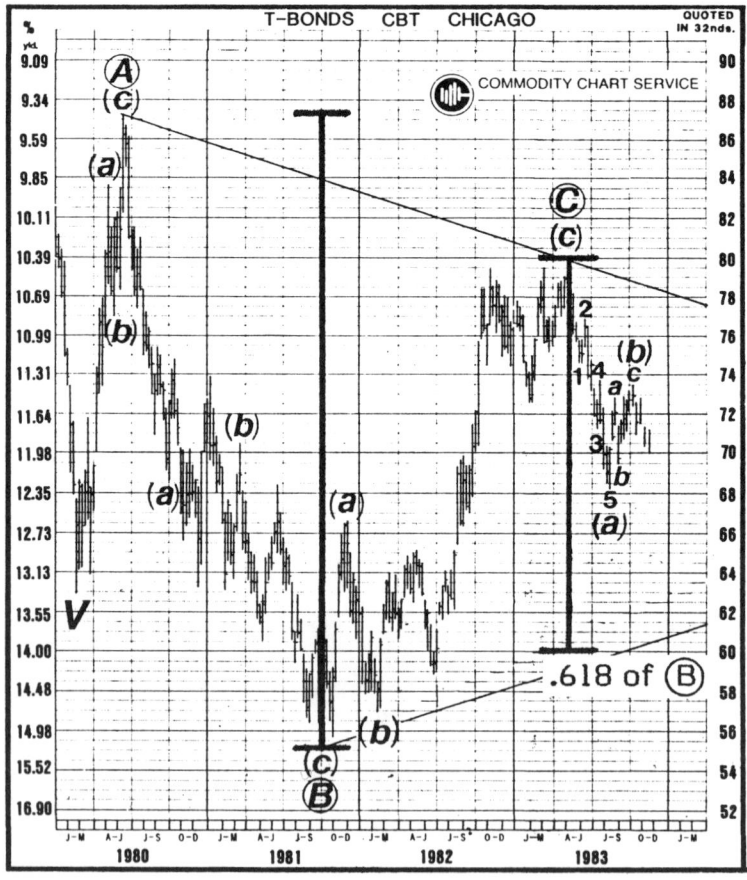

Figure 6-7

April 3, 1984 [after (b) ended in a triangle]

The ultimate downside target will probably occur near the point at which wave D is .618 times as long as wave B, which took place from June 1980 to September 1981 and traveled 32 points basis the weekly continuation chart. Thus, if wave D travels 19¾ points, the nearby contract should bottom at 60¼. In support of this target is the five-wave (a), which indicates that a zigzag decline is in force from the May 1983 highs. Within zigzags, waves "A" and "C" are typically of equal length. Basis the June contract, wave (a) fell 11 points. 11 points from the [slightly lower wave (b)] triangle peak at 70¾ projects 59¾, making the **60 zone (+ or - ¼)** a point of strong support and a potential target. As a final calculation, thrusts following triangles usually fall approximately the distance of the widest part of the triangle.[1] Based on [Figure 6-8], that distance is 10½ points, which subtracted from the triangle peak gives 60¼ as a target.

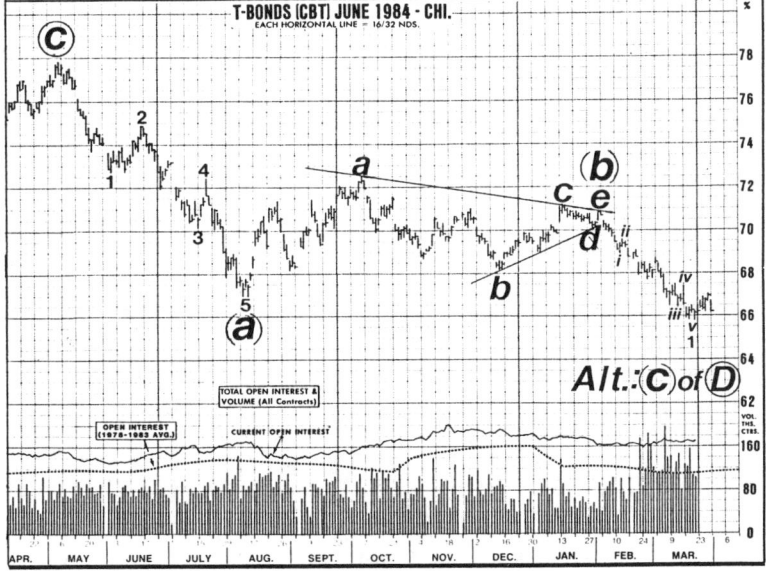

Figure 6-8

June 4, 1984

The most exciting event of 1984 is the apparent resolution of the one-year decline in bond prices. Investors were cautioned to hold off buying until bonds reached the **59¾-60¼** level. On May 30, the day that level was achieved, rumors about Continental Illinois Bank were flying, the 1100 level on the Dow was smashed in the morning on -650 ticks, and the June bond futures contract, amid panic selling, ticked briefly to as low as **59½**, just touching the triangle support line drawn on the chart last month. It stopped cold right there and closed at **59 31/32**, just 1/32 of a point from the exact center of our target zone. In the two and a half days following that low, bonds have rebounded two full points in a dramatic reversal. [See Figures 6-9 and 6-10.]

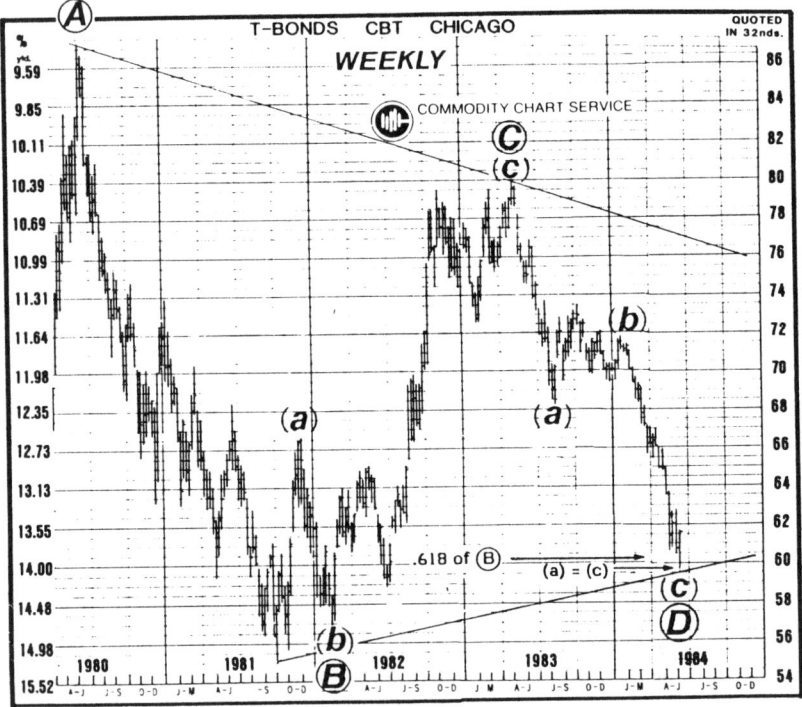

Figure 6-9

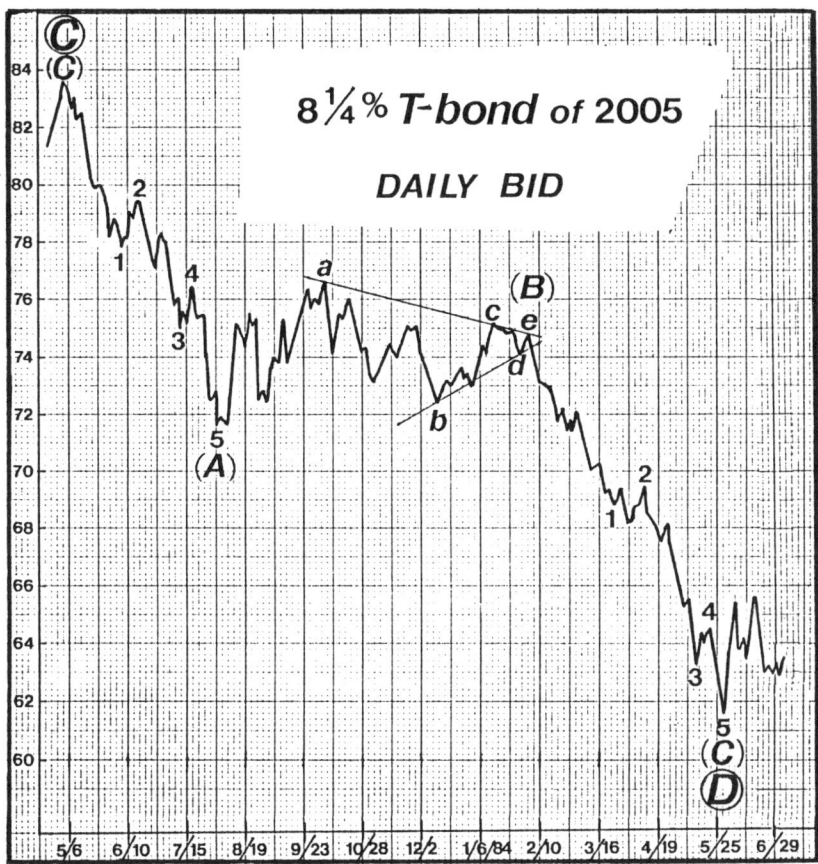

Figure 6-10

Are bonds truly making an important low? The technical evidence argues emphatically that they are. In reaching the Fibonacci support level, bonds traced out an impeccable wave pattern, with a five-wave (a), an a-b-c-d-e triangle (b), and a five-wave (c) from the May 1983 high.

The hourly chart shown [as Figure 6-11] illustrates how the Wave Principle operates even on the smallest level. Notice that all impulse waves are fives and all corrective waves are threes, as required. What's more, each of the Minor waves 1, 3 and 5 hit the lower channel line *precisely*, even though the powerful panic in wave iii of 3 broke the trendline briefly before snapping back into the channel. The channel itself has somewhat of a wedge shape, which is common in *ending* moves.

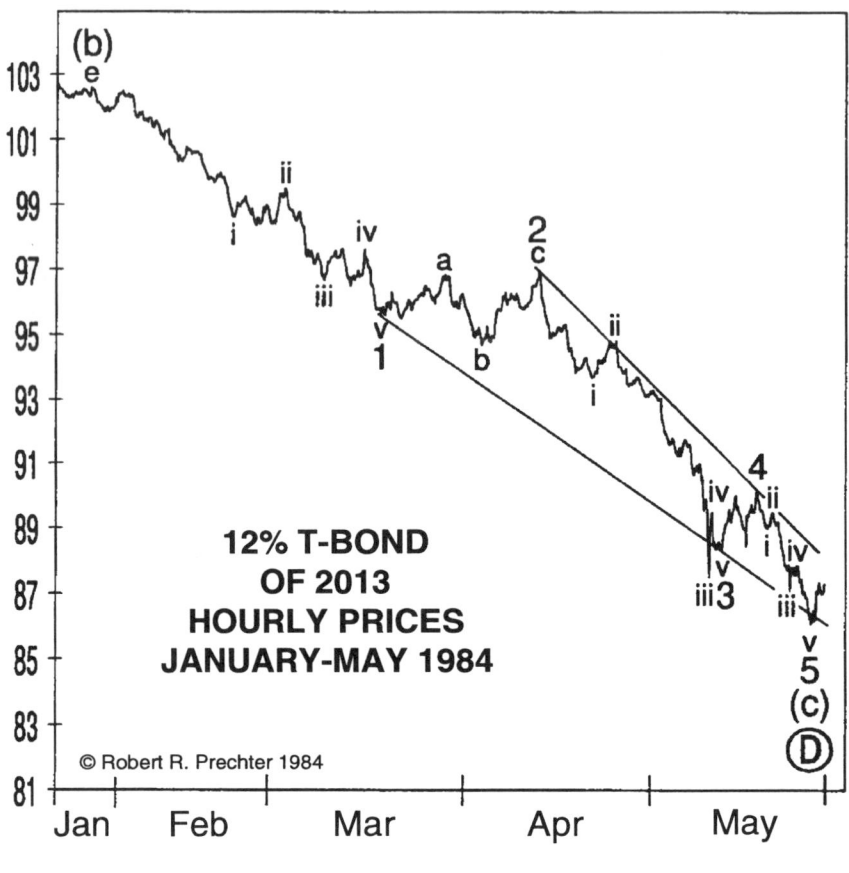

Figure 6-11

July 11, 1984

The background of investor psychology is very suggestive of an important bond market low. In fact, if this were the only measure I followed, it would appear that bonds are the buy of a lifetime. The news media, which all but ignored the rise in interest rates until May 1984, have been flooding the pages of the press with "higher interest rate" [meaning lower bond price] stories. Most of these came out, in typical fashion, *after* the May low, which was tested in June. During second waves, investors typically relive the fears that existed at the actual bottom while the *market* demonstrates an understanding, by holding above the previ-

ous low, that the worst has passed. The last five weeks have demon-strated this phenomenon vividly. On June 11, the WSJ headline read, "Fed Move to Tighten Credit is Expected During the Summer by Many Economists." On June 18, two full articles, including a front page fea-ture, focused on the prospects for higher interest rates: "Cooler Economy Seen Failing to Stem Further Rise in Interest Rates This Year" and "In-terest Rates Begin to Damp Economy; Many Analysts See Further Increases." On June 22, the WSJ featured an incredible *five-page* in-depth report entitled "World Debt in Crisis," complete with a picture of falling dominoes and quotes like these: from a congressman, "I don't think we're going to make it to the 1990s"; from a V.P. at Citicorp, "Let's be clear — nobody's debts are going to be repaid"; and from a former assistant Sec-retary of State for economic affairs, "We are living on borrowed time and borrowed money." On July 2, the WSJ reported, without saying so, that economists have panicked. Their forecasts for higher rates now extend halfway into next year! The headline read, "Higher Interest Rates Are Predicted for Rest of Year and Further Rises Are Seen for 1985's First Six Months." Says the article, *"Some say it would take a miracle for rates to fall."* The WSJ is not alone in taking the pulse of economists. *Financial World* magazine's June 27 poll listed the forecasts of 24 econo-mists against their beginning-of-year predictions. *Every single one of them* has raised his forecast in a linear-logic reaction to the rise in rates that has already occurred. They are using the same type of thinking that led them to a "lower interest rates ahead" conclusion a year ago, at the bottom [in rates, top in prices]. This overwhelming consensus based on fundamen-tal analysis is no guarantee that rates have peaked, but history shows that this type of analysis will rarely result in market profits. I prefer to bet on an overlooked theory that recognizes that market patterns repeat them-selves over and over again because people are people.

As further developments proved, that low marked the last buying op-portunity prior to the start of a historic advance in bond prices that has gone from 59½ to over 134 today, more than a 100% gain. Figure 6-12 shows the updated graph.

As the above excerpts show, wave ratio analysis, applied with knowl-edge of where such relationships are to be expected, forecasted the exact level of the 1984 lows in both stocks and bonds and then affirmed them as they occurred. In contrast, economists extended their gloomy bond market

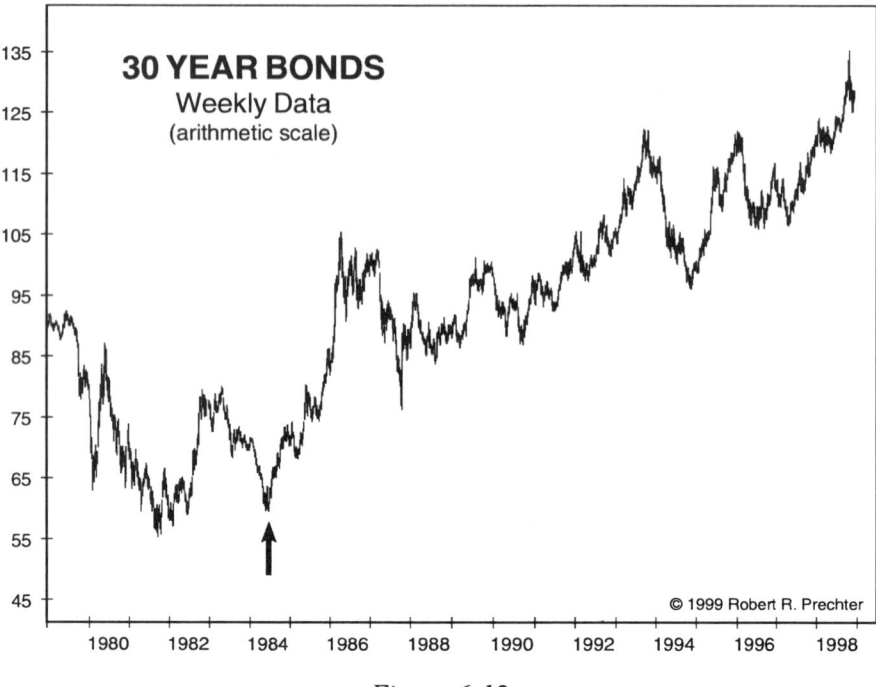

Figure 6-12

outlook to the stock market because of the belief that their forecasted higher interest rates would hurt the economy, which would hurt stocks. This conventional analysis provided exactly the wrong answer, while Elliott wave analysis accurately anticipated *and* recognized, via an *independent* analysis of each market, concurrent lows in both bond and stock prices.

Much More

Chapters 7 and 17 detail a few more long-term financial, economic, monetary and social forecasts that the Wave Principle has made possible. Chapters 4, 5 and 8 and the Appendix in *Elliott Wave Principle* present additional examples of stock market forecasting. The opening parts of Chapters 17, 18 and 19 in *At the Crest of the Tidal Wave* offer a condensed history of my forecasts for gold, the commodity index and collectibles. That book also presents current long-term forecasts for the monetary trend, gold, precious metals mining issues, the commodity index, copper, high-yield ("junk") bonds, high-grade bonds, real estate investment trusts, stock market breadth, mergers & acquisitions and the relative performance of

secondary stocks that so far have followed the expected scenarios, despite their dramatic divergence from the consensus outlook. Even if those scenarios go awry from here, their accuracy to date, which is beyond anything that conventional economics can offer, is an adequate demonstration of the Wave Principle's exceptional value. Expectations for the North American and European stock markets, real estate and the world economy, I remain convinced, are on the way to general fulfillment as well, notwithstanding any and all inaccuracies and errors that may occur with respect to postulated specifics.

I stated at the outset of this volume that my stance in this book is advocative. That word is not in the dictionary, but it should be. I intend it to mean that I have chosen to focus on validating the Wave Principle and on the unique accomplishments it makes possible. I am omitting a chronicle of my forecasting errors, while alerting you to the fact that there have been plenty of them, including looking for tops too early and too often in both stocks and bonds.

I plan to publish all of my commentary of past years along with a discussion of what I have learned from errors about both the principle and the limits of forecasting with it. The full record will serve those who wish to judge my errors or to hone their practice of the new science of socionomics by avoiding pitfalls that I did not. In the meantime, if you harbor any doubt as to the value of the Wave Principle *relative to any other extant approach*, Chapter 19 should disabuse you of that concern.

NOTES

1 The width of a contracting triangle is the distance between its boundary lines, measured vertically on the date of the triangle's inception.

Chapter 7

Relating Aspects of Market Behavior to Wave Degrees

Besides adding to and quantifying Elliott's rules and guidelines of wave pattern formation, I have spent a good deal of time relating indicators of market behavior to wave degrees. The fact that extremities in these indicators vary in accordance with degree is powerful evidence that wave degrees reflect something *real* in terms of human emotion and behavior. Chapter 14 will carry this theme much further. Herewith are four examples, involving (1) rate of price change, (2) investor psychology, (3) relative trading volume, and (4) the advance-decline disparity, or breadth.

Relating the Rate of Price Change to Wave Degree

One might expect that waves would exhibit power in relation to their degrees, and that is in fact the case. The amount of price change in aggregate stock prices over a specified duration reflects the power of a wave.

Figure 7-1 shows the DJIA plotted against a simple percentage difference between each month-end valuation and the one twelve months prior.[1] Observe that the *12-month rate of change in prices* for the S&P 500 index during the lift-off of each noted wave *is commensurate with the largest degree of the wave that has begun.* When an advance of Super-cycle degree began in 1932, the rate of change (ROC) quickly reached +146%. When smaller advances of Cycle degree began in 1942 and 1982, the ROC reached +51% and +53% respectively. When still smaller advances of Primary degree began, the ROC reached lesser peaks.

Declining waves show the same relativity in their extremes of speed. In the Supercycle degree decline that began in 1929, the ROC reached

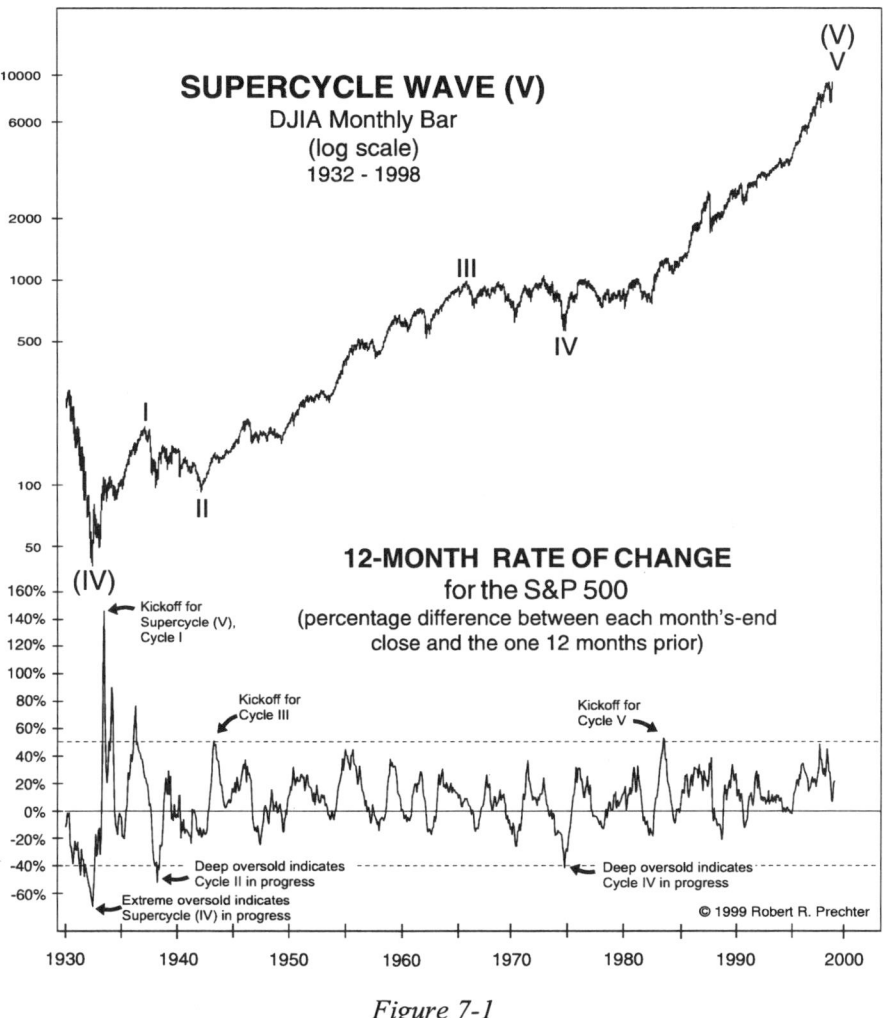

Figure 7-1

-70%. In the Cycle degree corrections that began in 1937 and 1966, the ROC reached -53% and -41% respectively. When still smaller declines of Primary degree began, the ROC reached lesser troughs. Although it is not shown on this graph, the Grand Supercycle corrective wave that began in the year 1720 had the greatest declining rate of change on record, as stock values in London fell 98% in two years.

To conclude, *waves appear to have quantifiable rate-of-change properties that reflect degree.* The higher the degree of the wave that has begun, the more extreme will be the initial speed of price movement.

I use a series of ROCs spanning 14 hours to 20 years to provide a profile of wave speed covering all degrees. These speed indicators are extremely helpful in assessing the progress of waves.

Relating Investor Psychology to Wave Degree

Aggregate dividend payout is a measure of the mental state of investors along the optimism-pessimism continuum. The greater their pessimism, the higher is the payout they demand to make up for perceived risk of capital loss. The greater their optimism, the lower is the payout they require to find stocks attractive, since they expect substantial capital gain.[2]

In Figure 7-2, observe that the *valuation of dividends* paid by the stocks in the Dow Jones Industrial Average at the end of each noted wave is *commensurate with the largest degree of the wave that has ended*. When an advance of Supercycle degree ended in September 1929, the annual dividend payout was 2.89% of the value of the index. When a smaller advance of Cycle degree ended in March 1937, the dividend payout was 3.63%.[3] The 1966 high was a *Cycle* degree top in nominal terms and *Grand Supercycle* degree top in constant-dollar terms. In a perfect compromise, its payout of 2.88% matched that of 1929's *Supercycle* high. When still

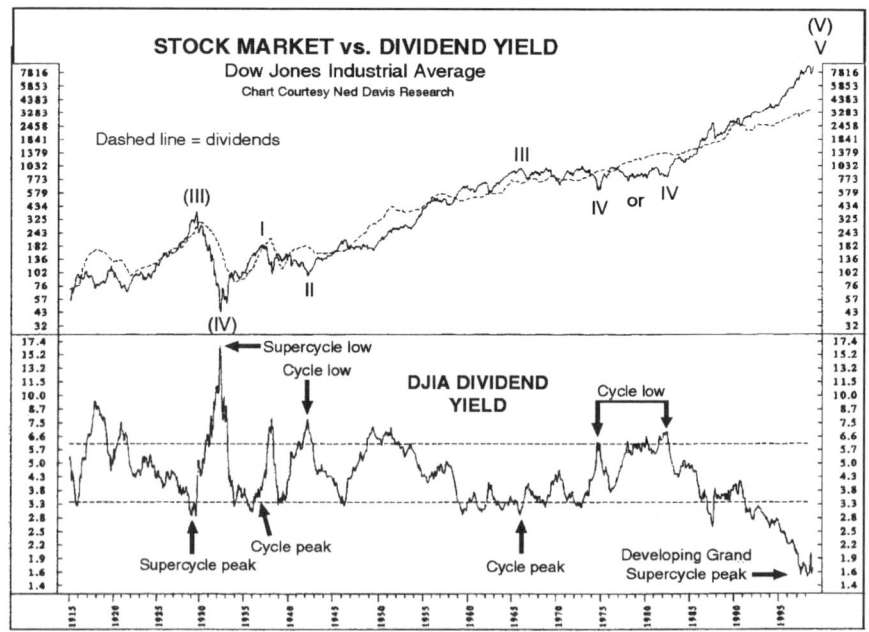

Figure 7-2

smaller advances of Primary degree ended, the dividend payout reached lesser peaks. The latest low reading of 1.51%[4] in May 1998 fits the interpretation, supported by the sixty years of forecasting presented in Chapter 5, that the market is approaching the end of a wave of Grand Supercycle degree.[5]

Declining waves show the same relativity in ending valuation. When a decline of Supercycle degree ended in July 1932, the payout was 17.35%. When corrections of Cycle degree ended in April 1942, December 1974, and August 1982, the dividend payout reached 7.93%, 6.56% and 7.12% respectively. When still smaller declines of Primary degree ended, valuation reached lesser troughs.[6]

Countless other indicators of investor sentiment reach extremes that relate to the degree of the wave that is ending. These include the ratio of trading volume in puts vs. calls, the ratio of open interest in puts vs. calls, futures premiums and discounts, and the ratio of the number of published books, advisory services, articles and magazine covers that reflect a bullish vs. bearish market opinion.

To conclude, *waves have quantifiable mass-sentiment properties that reflect degree.* The higher the degree of the wave that is ending, the more extreme will be the expression of social mood that produced both the sentiment reading and the wave itself.

Relating Trading Volume to Wave Degree

Now look at Figure 7-3, which is a graph of the dollar-valued trading volume in the stock market divided by the prevailing gross domestic product. This volume/GDP ratio is a measure of trading activity in the stock market compared to the value of the production of goods and services in the economy. It reflects the degree of national interest and activity in the stock market.

Observe that the *volume/GDP ratio* also reaches end-of-wave extremes *commensurate with the largest degree of the wave that is ending.* The larger the degree of an advancing wave, the higher the ratio. The Cycle degree tops of 1937 and 1966-1968 had ratios of 22% and 20% respectively. The Supercycle degree top of 1929 had a ratio of 135%. The currently developing top, which will be of Grand Supercycle degree, has already reached a ratio of 179%, the highest yet.

Declining waves show the inverse tendency. The larger the degree of the wave, the lesser is the volume/GDP ratio at some point late in its development.[7]

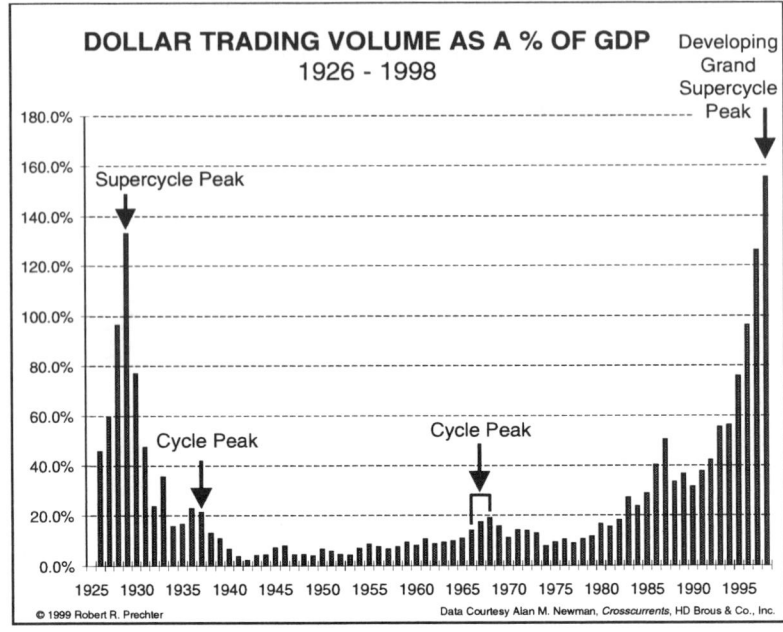

Figure 7-3

To conclude, *waves have quantifiable properties of relative volume that reflect degree.* The higher the degree of the wave that is ending, the more extreme will be the value of trading activity relative to the value of production.

Relating Breadth to Wave Number

The term "breadth" refers to the percentage of component segments of a market that are participating in its trend. In the overall stock market, for instance, such components include sectors, groups and individual stocks. *Every* advancing *fifth* wave, regardless of degree, has narrower breadth, i.e., a lower ratio of segment participation, than its corresponding *third* wave. This is just as true of Supercycle waves as Minor waves.

One measure of breadth is the cumulative sum of the ratios of the number of stocks up each day minus the number down, normalized for the total number of changed issues. This indicator is called the advance-decline line. If you study Figure 7-4, you will see that the a-d line's performance is better in any wave labeled with the number three than in the subsequent wave of the same degree labeled with the number five. The flat advance-decline line of the 1920s signaled the end of the entire advance from 1857.

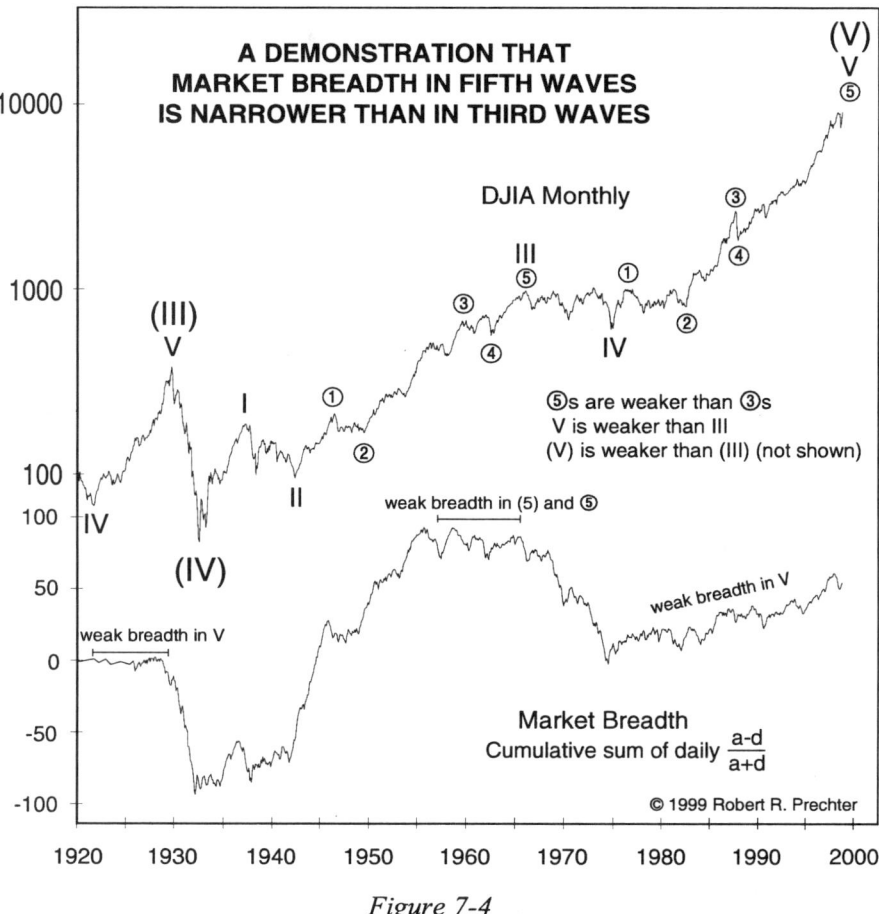

Figure 7-4

Similarly, the flat line in the mid-1960s signaled the end of the 1942-1966 bull market. The inability of this line in the past 24 years to surpass its 1966 high both reflects and supports the labeling that it has been a fifth wave, wave V.

Value in Forecasting

With quantifiable indicators of speed, mood, volume and breadth, we can validate or amend conclusions regarding the present position of the wave structure. For example, since the speed of liftoff has implications as to the degree of the wave that has begun, it implies a continuation of the trend until a movement of sufficient size has occurred. Also, since dividend valuation and volume extremes have implications as to the degree of

the wave that is ending, the next wave in the opposite direction will have to be of sufficient magnitude to reflect a change of that degree. In addition, expanding breadth precludes the possibility that a top is nigh.

Furthermore, each indicator helps to predict the others. For instance, extremes in valuation and relative volume can allow us to predict the relative extremity of the next major move in the ROC, and vice versa.

It is the case not only that each of these measures is a powerful indicator of the market's position but also that the market's outlook based upon an analysis of its wave structure is a powerful indicator of how each measure will behave. For example, once we label Cycle wave IV as over, we can expect the next peak reading in the ROC to reflect the power of a wave of Cycle degree. Similarly, once we call for a bull market that will register a Grand Supercycle high, we can expect dividend yield to fall below that of 1929's Supercycle high, and so on.

Forecasting with Indicators of Market-Related Behavior

These quantifiable aspects of waves not only allow for more reliable analysis and categorization but also increase our ability to forecast market behavior. This sentence is more than a claim. The following examples of actual forecasts demonstrate the value of this aspect of socionomics. They show both that the indicators are useful in forecasting waves and that a knowledge of waves is useful in forecasting the indicators. The following excerpts are reprinted from issues of *The Elliott Wave Theorist*. As you read through this commentary, consider that these indicators' intimacy with the very idea of the Wave Principle further validates it.

Forecasting with an Extremity of Sentiment

Elliott Wave Principle was published in 1978, with the Dow at 790. In that book, A.J. Frost and I were long-term bullish for many reasons, but one of them was the low valuation of dividends (i.e., the high dividend yield). As we said then,

> One of our objections to the "killer wave" occurring now or in 1979, as most cycle theorists suggest, is that the psychological state of the average investor does not seem poised for a shock of disappointment. Most important stock market collapses have come out of optimistic, high-valuation periods. Such conditions definitely do not prevail at this time, as eight years of a raging bear market have taught today's investor to be cautious, conservative and cynical.[8]

Take a look at Figure 7-2 and locate the high payout ratios of 1978 to 1982. This forecast called not only for rising stock prices but by implication, falling dividend yields. As you can see, both of these outlooks came to pass. The specific labeling of the advance as *wave V* of (V) implied that dividend yields would fall below any reading on the graph. That has happened as well.

My current analysis of the stock market with respect to dividend valuation should be evident from the notes on Figure 7-2. For details, see Chapter 10 of *At the Crest of the Tidal Wave*.

Forecasting Breadth

Taking for granted that the stock market would soar for years, *The Elliott Wave Theorist* a few months after the 1982 low turned its attention to forecasting the *relative quality* of the advance in terms of the average number of advances vs. declines on a daily basis.

November 29, 1982

Breadth measures almost always begin to show weakness during a fifth-wave advance when compared to the first through third waves. For this reason, I would expect a very broad market through wave ③, then increasing selectivity until the peak of wave ⑤, by which time the leaders in the Dow may be almost the only things going. For now, play any stocks you like. Later on, we may have to pick and choose more carefully.

April 6, 1983

Breadth during wave V should be unexceptional, if not outright poor relative to the spectacular breadth performance in the monolithic markets of the 1940s and 1950s, during wave III. Since it is an impulse wave, however, it will certainly be broader than anything we saw within wave IV from 1966 to 1982. ...A relatively poorly performing a-d line from 1982 to (I expect) 1987 will be a "sell signal" for the entire Supercycle from 1932. The lesson for now is, *don't use that underperformance as a reason to sell too early* and miss out on what promises to be one of the most profitable uplegs in the history of the stock market.

Figure 7-4 adds fifteen years of advance/decline data to the picture I had then, updating it to the present (December 1998). As you can see, Cycle wave V has indeed been weak relative to wave III, and Primary wave ⑤ has been weak relative to wave ③. Intermediate wave (5) (not shown)

has been weak relative to wave (3). All of these developments were exactly as forecast.

Forecasting with the Rate of Price Change

A year after the 1982 low came confirmation from the 12-month rate-of-change indicator that a rise of Cycle degree, *not* one either larger or smaller, had begun. Here is my real-time analysis of the event.

August 18, 1983

Indicators of stock market momentum almost always "announce" the beginning of a huge bull market. They do so by creating a tremendously overbought condition in the initial stage of advance. While this tendency is noticeable at all degrees of trend, the Annual Rate of Change for the S&P 500 is particularly useful in judging the strength of "kickoff" momentum in large waves of Cycle and Supercycle degree. This indicator is created by plotting the percentage difference between the average daily close for the S&P 500 in the current month and its reading for the same month a year earlier. The peak momentum reading is typically registered about one year after the start of the move, due to the construction of the indicator. What's important is the *level* the indicator reaches. As you can see [in Figure 7-5], *the level of "overbought" at the end of July 1983, approximately one year after the start of the current bull market, is the highest since May 1943, approximately one year after the start of Cycle wave III.* The fact that they each hit the *50%* level is a strong confirmation that they mark the beginning of waves of equivalent degree. In other words, August 1982 marked the start of something more than what has come to be regarded as the norm, a two-year bull market followed by a two-year bear. On the other hand, it has *not* indicated the start of a glorious "new era," either. If a wave of *Supercycle* degree were beginning, we would expect to see the kind of overbought reading generated in 1933, when the indicator hit 124%[9] one year after the start of wave (V) from 1932. There is now no chance that such a level can even be approached. Thus, the highest overbought condition in forty years signals to me that our Elliott Wave forecast for the launching of wave V is right on target.

Remember, this is just the setup phase. As I have argued since the early days of the current advance, the sentiment indicators should reach much more extreme levels than they ever saw in the 1970s. Put/call ratios and ten-day averages are valuable as far as they go, but they are best interpreted within the context of the broad sweep of market events.

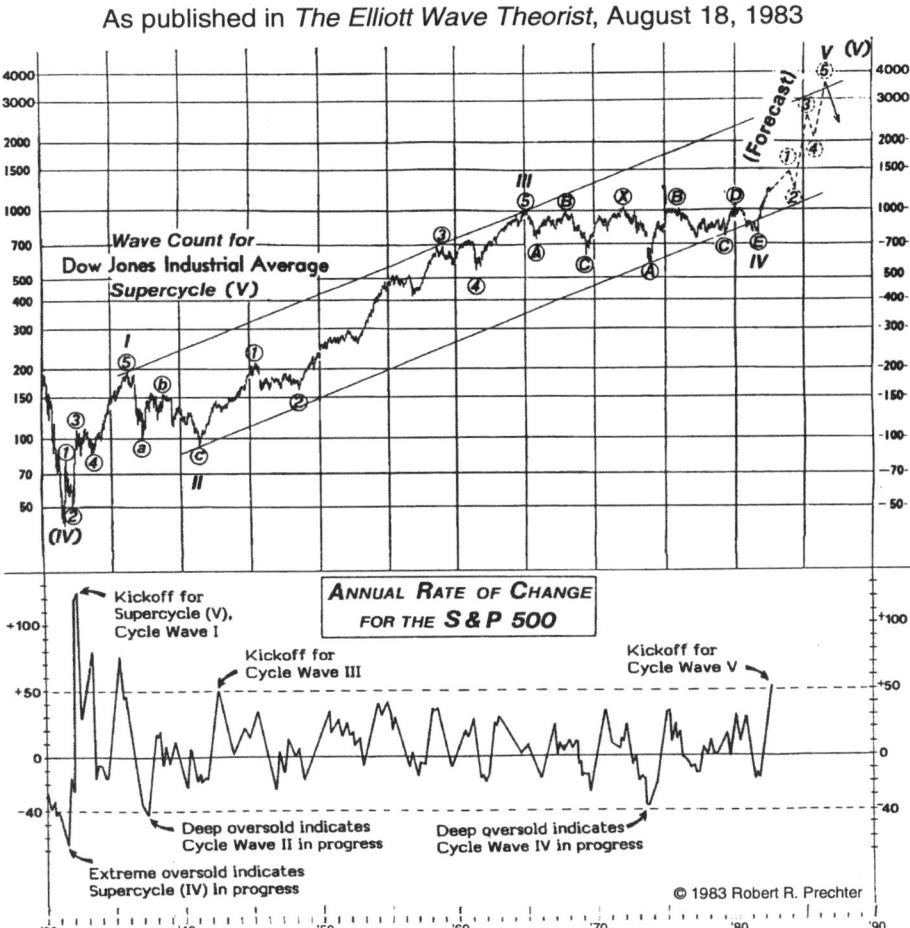

Figure 7-5

Take another look at the long-term Dow chart and ask yourself a few questions about some points that are considered common knowledge.

— Is the market really "more volatile" today than it has ever been in the past? No. A look at 1921-1946 throws that idea right out the window.

— Is the 1000 level a "high" level? For that matter, is 1200 a "high" level? Not any more! The long period spent going sideways since 1966 has put the Dow back at the lower end of its fifty-year uptrend channel in "current dollar" terms (and down to a point of very low valuation in "constant dollar" terms).

— Is the current bull market an "old" bull market that began in 1974 and therefore is "running out of time"? Hardly. Both in "constant dollar" terms and with reference to the 40-year uptrend, the Dow was more undervalued in 1982 than at the crash low in 1974.

— Is my Elliott-based expectation of a 400% gain in 5-8 years a wild one? It appears to be, when compared to recent history. But not when compared to 1921-1929, a 500% gain in 8 years, or 1932-1937, a 400% gain in 5 years.

— Can you always extrapolate current trends into the future? Definitely not. The one rule of the market is change.

— Is any cycle ever "just like the last one"? Not too often! In fact, Elliott formulated a rule about it, called the Rule of Alternation. Broadly interpreted, it instructs the investor to look for a different style of pattern as each new phase begins.

— Is recent market action "too strong," "overextended," "unprecedented," or even a "new era"? No, variations on today's theme have all happened before.

— Is the market a random walk or an erratic wild ride, whipping back and forth without form, trend or pattern? If so, it has "wandered" into long-lasting periods of clear trend, rhythmic cyclical repetition and impeccable Elliott Wave patterns.

At the very least, [Figure 7-5] helps you picture the market's action within the broad sweep of history, thus making next week's money supply report appear as irrelevant as it really is. Furthermore, it helps you visualize why a bull market that is larger than the 30%-80% gains of the upward swings of the last sixteen years is probable, while illustrating the *potential* for a bull market bigger than any in the last *fifty* years. So far, the market is behaving in such a way as to reinforce our original wave V forecast. As long as the market fulfills expectations, we can assume we're still on track.

———————————

At this point, I have explained the theory of the Wave Principle, connected it to fractals and spirals, showed that it can be quantified and modeled, related it to indicators of market behavior and demonstrated its utility in forecasting. Now we turn our attention to exploring its basis in biology, psychology and sociology.

NOTES

1   We chose a 12-month span for the ROC indicator to reflect the degrees being examined, but its exact span is arbitrary; an 11.9-month ROC would have a similar profile.

2   As a corollary phenomenon, the greater investors' pessimism, the more dividend payout *matters* to them, and the greater their optimism, the less relevant or necessary it is deemed. In today's market environment, dividends are actually considered a *detriment* to stock ownership, the theory being that it is better for management to put the money back into the company to make it grow faster. As far as I can determine, this attitude is unprecedented.

3   A year earlier, in March 1936, payout was briefly as low as 2.88% because companies were just recovering from the depression and temporarily had very low payouts that the market knew were about to increase.

4   The S&P 500 yields only 1.34% (July) the Dow Transports only .79% (March) and the NASDAQ over-the-counter index only .29 (December)!

5   For details, see my 1995 book, *At the Crest of the Tidal Wave.*

6   A quick comparison of both the dividend payouts and the ROC percentages suggests the possibility that the average maximum liftoff speed and psychological power exerted at each degree is not far away from a Fibonacci 2.618 multiple of that exerted at the next lower degree.

7   While the end of a declining wave often marks the low in the volume ratio, it sometimes reaches its nadir at the end of wave two *following* the larger correction, as it did in 1942, which was the low of wave II. This expression of apathy fits the description of "wave two" personality as described in Chapter 2 of *Elliott Wave Principle.*

8   Frost, A.J. and Prechter, R. (1978). *Elliott wave principle.*

9   This 124% calculation was based on monthly averages of daily closing figures, which is why it differs from the 146% figure generated when using month-end closes.

PART III

THE BASIS OF
THE WAVE PRINCIPLE
IN BIOLOGY, PSYCHOLOGY
AND SOCIOLOGY

The formal construction of the stock market's path implies a mechanism of impulsive cooperation on the part of market participants and therefore of society at large. Because aggregate stock price movement is intricately patterned, there must be primary causes of its behavior, forces that shape it. Part III argues that the primary mover of aggregate stock market prices is mass emotional change, which itself must be, and demonstrably is, independent of outside influence. The specifics of market action are determined by the naturally occurring direction, speed and extent of social mood changes.

If the Wave Principle were the only basis for making this claim, then proof would rest entirely upon demonstrating the validity of the Wave Principle. I believe the literature (including Chapters 5 through 7 of this book) has done a fair job of doing so. For many people, though, that is not enough to dispel skepticism. Is there any other basis to believe that mass emotional change is independent of social events and conditions? Are there biological and psychological sources of these emotional imperatives? Science provides insights that respond to this question in the affirmative.

Chapter 8:

Unconscious Herding Behavior as the Psychological Basis of the Wave Principle

The Triune Brain

Over a lifetime of work, Paul MacLean, former head of the Laboratory for Brain Evolution at the National Institute of Mental Health, has developed a mass of evidence that supports the concept of a "triune" brain, i.e., one that is divided into three basic parts. The primitive brain stem, called the basal ganglia, which we share with animal forms as low as reptiles, controls impulses essential to survival. The limbic system, which we share with mammals, controls emotions. The neocortex, which is significantly developed only in humans, is the seat of reason. Thus, we actually have three connected minds: primal, emotional and rational. Figure 8-1, from MacLean's book, *The Triune Brain in Evolution*, roughly shows their physical locations.

These three areas of the brain apparently followed an evolutionary path of development in that order, as evidenced by several observations. First, reptiles have a brain similar to humans' brain stem, mammals' brains have both that and a limbic system, and certain primates have both these and a significant neocortex. The fossil record reveals the same progression of appearance on earth for each of these groups of animals. Second, in humans, these three sections of the brain are stacked upon each other outward into the head as if the brain were a growing entity. An evolutionary progression explains this "piled-on" form. Third, the skull sizes of later and later hominids are larger and larger, accommodating this expansion. Larger brain size per se would be otherwise unnecessary, as absent evolution, all man would require relative to animals would be a more efficient

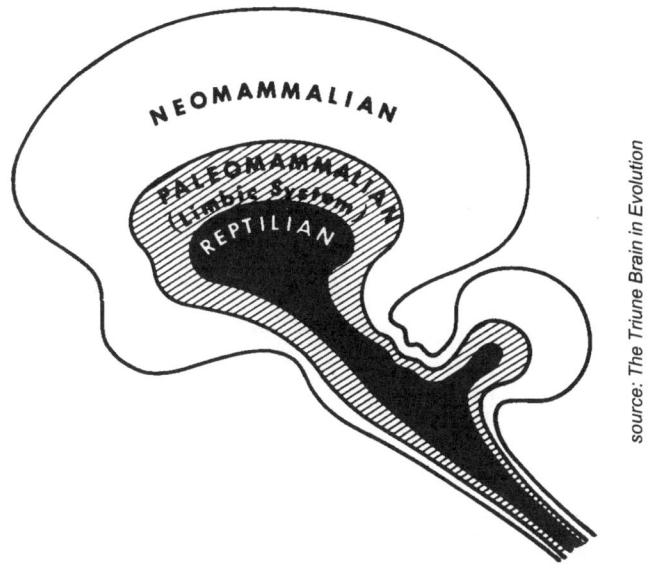

The three sections of the triune brain

Figure 8-1

and powerful mind. Evolution proceeds from forms already available. Fourth, in the human fetus, each portion of the brain develops in the above-described order, as cells of the neocortex organize directly from the cells of the lateral ventricle of the limbic system, which in turn sprouts from the reptilian complex.[1] This chain of events suggests that genetically encoded instructions for forming each more advanced portion of the brain joined an already existing list. Fifth, neural development in children is such that the lower areas of the brain *mature* in earlier years than the upper ones do.[2] This sequence of maturation gets the primitive neural necessities of survival out of the way before developing the higher mental functions. Finally, clinical tests, often in association with serious brain injuries, have produced a large body of evidence indicating that each portion of the triune brain handles functions and behaviors that are common to the animal ancestors that share it and which are absent in those that do not.

The "thinking" done by the brain stem and limbic system is primitive and pre-rational, exactly as in animals that rely upon them. The connection to evolution is important because it explains *why* man has a mind that includes unconscious, impulsive mentation.

The Impulsivity of the Basal Ganglia and Limbic System and Their Independence from the Neocortex

The neocortex is involved in the preservation of the individual by processing ideas using reason. It derives its information from the external world, and its convictions are malleable thereby. In contrast, the styles of mentation outside the cerebral cortex are unreasoning, impulsive and very rigid.

The basal ganglia control brain functions that are often termed instinctive: the desire for security, the reaction to fear, the desire to acquire, the desire for pleasure, fighting, fleeing, territorialism, migration, hoarding, grooming, choosing a mate, breeding, the establishment of social hierarchy and the selection of leaders. More pertinent to our discussion, this bunch of nerves also controls coordinated behavior such as *flocking, schooling* and *herding*. All these brain functions insure lifesaving or life-enhancing action under most circumstances and are fundamental to animal motivation. Due to our evolutionary background, they are integral to human motivation as well. "The limbic system," says MacLean, "underlies the *subjective experience of...emotional feelings* that guide behavior required for self-preservation and the preservation of the species."[3] In other words, it produces powerful emotions as a spur to further the objectives of the basal ganglia.

These two portions of the brain do not learn from new experience. For example, the limbic system houses the brain's pleasure center, which is activated by the neurotransmitter dopamine. In the 1950s, biologist James Olds[4] found that given a lever with which a rat could turn on the electric current that stimulated this portion of its brain, the animal would forgo every other activity — including eating and sleeping — to receive stimulation and would continue to work the lever until it died. Subsequent animal studies have demonstrated that profound pleasure has virtually no satiation point. A cat or monkey will press a bar 10,000 times an hour, for hours on end, to get such stimulation. Olds found that hungry rats were deterred from obtaining *food* if they had to cross a grid giving off 60 microamperes of electricity. To obtain *brain stimulation*, on the other hand, rats have crossed grids charged with 450 microamperes. "We couldn't go higher than that," Olds said, "the shock would knock them out." When they regained consciousness, the rats would resume their path toward the reward. Olds describes a colleague's project in which rats were given only one hour daily in which to eat or to stimulate their brains. After one rat starved

to death, the experimenters withdrew rats from the study once they dropped to 70 percent of their original body weight. John Cull, a San Antonio clinical psychologist, referring to human beings, says, "[this portion of] the brain doesn't make value judgments. It just says, 'I'm not getting enough dopamine.' And since there are a whole bunch of ways to make it, *we do whatever we have to do*."[5,6] This is impulsive, not reasoned, behavior. To differentiate this style of thinking from reason, I will use MacLean's term, *paleomentation*, to denote impulsive thought patterns derived from the primitive portions of the brain.

The emotional brain can be triggered by a walnut-sized structure called the amygdala. If the amygdala senses a threat, it reacts instantaneously, signaling crisis and setting off emotional alarms in the limbic system. In 1989, Dr. Joseph LeDoux, a psychologist at the Center for Neural Science at New York University, performed anatomically related studies at the Laboratory of Neurobiology at Cornell Medical Center and found neural pathways for emotional response that do not go through the cortex and which are faster than the cortex.[7] "The amygdala is just one synapse away from the thalamus, while the hippocampus is several additional synapses away," he explains. This physical difference produces "a difference of as much as 40 milliseconds...in the time it takes a sensory signal to reach the amygdala as compared with the hippocampus." LeDoux's research confirms that *emotion and corresponding reaction can occur both independently of, and prior to, thought*. Because paleomentation is quicker on the draw than the neocortex, emotions are often not reactions to considered *ideas* but immediate reactions to *perceptions* relayed by the senses. As LeDoux points out, "those extra milliseconds may be lifesaving. [However,] it's a very raw form of sensory information...it's a quick and dirty process; the cells are fast but not very precise."[8] Harvard psychologist Daniel Goleman, author of *Emotional Intelligence*, says succinctly, "Certain emotional reactions occur before the brain has even had time to fully register what it is that is causing the reaction; the emotion occurs before thought."[9] The result is *immediate responsive action* before the neocortex has time to mull over what is going on or what the consequences of the action will be. Suddenly endangered, we don't think first; we run like hell and then reflect on it later.

Because the goals of the limbic system in motivating behavior associated with self-preservation are so fundamental, it has the capacity to attach extremely compelling emotions to the impulses of the primitive brain. In

fulfilling this function, the limbic system holds four trump cards over the neocortex. First, as we have just seen, it is *faster* than the neocortex. Second, it regulates the *amplitude* of emotions as if it held the volume knob on a noise generator. Incredibly powerful emotions thereby *drown out* other signals, such as those from the rational cerebral cortex. Third, the limbic system is dissociated from the concept of time. Whatever it wants, it wants *now*. This dissociation disarms the neocortex, which plans in terms of achieving long-range values. Fourth, the limbic system has proved to be "*essential for a sense of personal identity and reality*."[10] People who have lost portions of that area in the brain lose the crucially important *feelings* attached to both their own identity and that of their environment. This is why the limbic system's feelings are taken so seriously by people and why challenges to them are typically met with fierce resistance, even if that challenge comes from reality itself. In a battle for the soul of a man in an emotionally charged situation, the limbic system usually wins. If you doubt its power and speed, try to envision how you would react if someone suddenly dumped a dozen writhing three-foot blacksnakes in your lap. Understanding that they are harmless, try to decide how long it would take you nevertheless to train yourself not to budge upon being surprised that way in the future.

There is not only a *physical* distinction between the neocortex and the primitive brain but a *functional dissociation* between them as well. The intellect of the neocortex and the emotional mentation of the limbic system are so independent that "the limbic system has the capacity to generate out-of-context, affective feelings of conviction that we attach to our beliefs *regardless of whether they are true or false*."[11] Epileptics experience storms of emotion that have nothing to do with the reality of the moment; it is just the limbic system firing in a frenzy. Epileptics also experience feelings of immense conviction about an "absolute truth" that is unconnected with any associated idea or thing whatsoever.[12] In normal people, too, feelings of certainty can be so overwhelming that they stand fast in the face of logic and contradiction. They can attach themselves to a political doctrine, a social plan, the verity of a religion, the surety of winning on the next spin of the roulette wheel, the presumed path of a financial market or any other idea.[13] This tendency is so powerful that Robert Thatcher, a neuroscientist at the University of South Florida College of Medicine in Tampa, says, "The limbic system is where we live, and the cortex is basically a slave to that."[14]

A soft version of that depiction, which appears to be a minimum state-ment of the facts, is that most people do live in the limbic system, particularly with respect to fields of knowledge and activity about which they lack ei-ther expertise or wisdom. Informed men may live substantially in the neocortex, but their choice of a field of expertise was probably induced by the limbic system in the first place. Regardless, in every case, the limbic system can still utterly overwhelm the neocortex when it perceives it must.

In effect, then, portions of the brain are "hardwired for certain emo-tional and physical patterns of reaction"[15] to insure survival of the species. Presumably, *herding* behavior, which derives from the same primitive por-tion of the brain, is similarly hardwired and impulsive. If so, how do these impulses join together to produce collective agreement in thought and ac-tion?

Herding Psychology and Financial Markets

As a primitive tool of survival, emotional impulses from the limbic sys-tem impel a desire among individuals to seek signals from others in matters of knowledge and behavior and therefore to align their feelings and convic-tions with those of the group. The desire to belong to and be accepted by the group is particularly powerful in intensely emotional social settings, when it can overwhelm the higher brain functions.

The less that reality intrudes on the thinking of a group, the stronger is its collective conformity. Dependence most easily substitutes for rigorous reasoning when knowledge is lacking or logic irrelevant. In a realm such as investing, where so few are knowledgeable, or in a realm such as fads and fashion, where logic is inappropriate and the whole point is to impress other people, the tendency toward dependence is pervasive. Trends in such activities are steered not by the rational decisions of individual minds but by the peculiar collective sensibilities of the herd.

In the 1920s, Cambridge economist A.C. Pigou connected coopera-tive social dynamics to booms and depression.[16] His idea is that individuals routinely correct their own errors of thought when operating alone but ab-dicate their responsibility to do so in matters that have strong social agreement, regardless of the egregiousness of the ideational error. In the realm of finance, as R.N. Elliott phrased it, Pigou maintained "that an error of optimism tends to create, throughout the community, a certain measure of psychological interdependence until it leads to crisis. Then the error of optimism dies and gives birth to an error of pessimism."[17] In Pigou's words,

Apart altogether from the financial ties by which different business-men are bound together, there exists among them a certain measure of *psychological interdependence*. A change of tone in one part of the business world diffuses itself, *in a quite unreasoning manner*, over other and wholly disconnected parts.[18]

"Wall Street" certainly shares aspects of a crowd, and there is abundant evidence that herding behavior exists among stock market participants. Myriad measures of market optimism and pessimism[19] show that in the aggregate, such sentiments among both the public and financial professionals wax and wane concurrently with the trend and level of the market. This tendency is not simply fairly common; it is ubiquitous. Most people get virtually all of their ideas about financial markets from other people, through newspapers, television, tipsters and analysts, without checking a thing. They think, "Who am I to check? These other people are supposed to be experts." Many people are emotionally dependent upon the ticker tape, which simply reports the aggregate short-term decision-making of others. This dependence is nearly universal, even among long-term investors. Financial markets induce a form of hypnosis in most people. Outwardly, they appear rational. Inside, their unconscious is in control. They are driven to follow the herd because they do not have firsthand knowledge adequate to form an independent conviction, which makes them seek wisdom in numbers. The unconscious says: You have too little basis upon which to exercise reason; *your only alternative is to assume that the herd knows where it's going*.

In 1987, Smith, Suchanek and Williams from the University of Arizona and Indiana University conducted sixty laboratory market simulations using as few as a dozen volunteers, typically economics students but also, in some experiments, professional businessmen. Despite giving all the participants the same perfect knowledge of coming dividend prospects and then an actual declared dividend at the end of the simulated trading day, which could vary more or less randomly but which would average a certain amount, *the subjects in these experiments repeatedly created a boom-and-bust market profile*. The extremity of that profile was a function of the participants' lack of experience in the speculative arena. Head research economist Vernon L. Smith came to this conclusion: "Experienced subjects frequently produce a market bubble, but the likelihood is smaller than for inexperienced subjects. When the same group returns for a third market, the bubble

disappears."[20] In the real world, "these bubbles and crashes would be a lot less likely if the same traders were in the market all the time,"[21] but novices are always entering the market.

While these experiments were conducted as if participants could actually possess true knowledge of coming events and so-called fundamental value, no such knowledge is available in the real world. The fact that participants create a boom-bust pattern *anyway* is overwhelming evidence of the power of the herding impulse.

It is not only novices who fall in line. It is a lesser-known fact that the vast majority of professionals herd just like the naïve majority. Figure 8-2 shows the percentage of cash held at institutions as it relates to the level of the S&P 500 Composite index. As you can see, the two data series move roughly together, showing that professional fund managers herd right along with the market just as the public does.

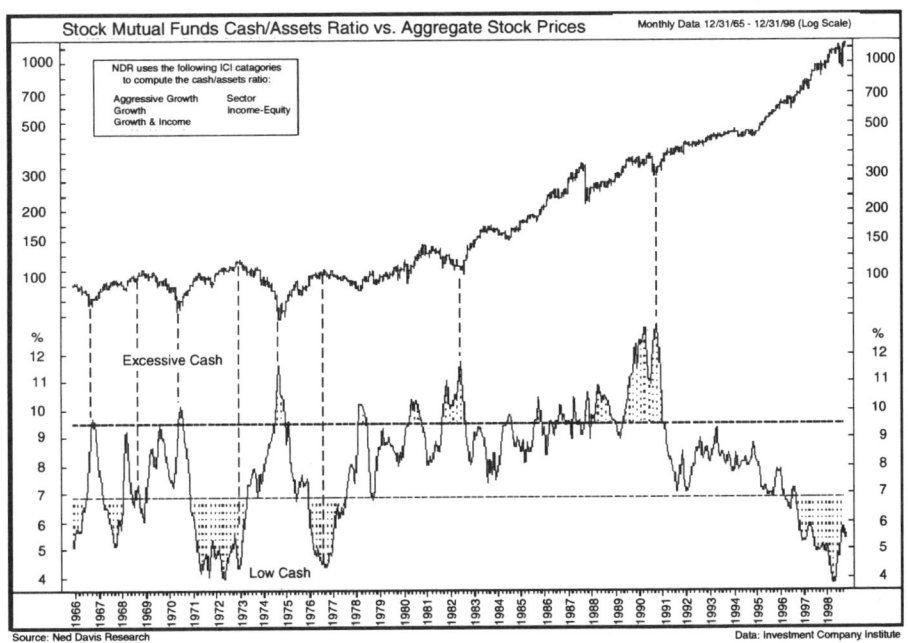

Figure 8-2

In the aggregate, apparent expressions of cold reason by professionals follow herding patterns as well. Finance professor Robert Olsen recently conducted a study of 4000 corporate earnings estimates by company analysts and reached this conclusion:

Experts' earnings predictions exhibit positive bias and disappointing accuracy. These shortcomings are usually attributed to some combination of incomplete knowledge, incompetence, and/or misrepresentation. This article suggests that the *human desire for consensus* leads to herding behavior among earnings forecasters.[22]

In that paper, Olsen shows that the greater the difficulty in forecasting earnings per share, which is a source of stress, *the more analysts' herding behavior increases*.[23] Equally important, as their herding behavior increases, the aggregate bias in their earnings estimates increases, and *the less accurate their aggregate estimates get*. This is a self-reinforcing system with failure the motivator of further failure.

The reason that forecasters' inaccuracy worsens with herding is that the net valuation of the stock market is the *result* of herding. To forecast on the basis of the current sentiments of the herd is to "forecast" the present mood, not future events. Success is simply a matter of whether the present mood maintains, which it usually does not. (For more on this point, see Chapter 18.)

How can seemingly rational professionals be so utterly seduced by the opinion of their peers to the effect that they will not only hold but also *change* opinions collectively? Recall that the neocortex is functionally dissociated from the limbic system. This means not only that feelings of conviction may attach to utterly contradictory ideas in different people, but that they can do so *in the same person at different times*. In other words, the *same brain* can support *opposite views* with equally intense emotion, depending upon the demands of survival perceived by its primitive components. This fact relates directly to the behavior of financial market participants, who can be flushed with confidence one day and in a state of utter panic the next. As Yale economist Robert Schiller puts it, "You would think enlightened people would not have firm opinions" about markets, "but they do, *and it changes all the time*."[24] In each case, they are fully capable of explaining their new conviction, all such utterances being simply (yet sometimes superficially brilliant) rationalizations obediently generated by the neocortex. As market analyst Paul Macrae Montgomery explains, "to the limbic system, the phrase 'net present value of future cash flows' is meaningless because its *only sense of time is now and only value is pleasure or relief from stress*."[25] To relieve that stress without suffering cognitive dissonance, the neocortex generates "reasons" for a person's action, justifying the attendant emotional imperative.

Throughout the herding process, whether the markets are real or simulated, and whether the participants are novices or professionals, the conviction of the *rightness* of stock valuation at each price level is powerful, emotional and impervious to argument. Gustave Le Bon, a pioneer in the study of crowd psychology, said a century ago, "It were as wise to oppose cyclones with discussion as the beliefs of crowds.... Time alone can act upon them."[26]

Falling into line with others for self-preservation involves not only the pursuit of positive values but also the avoidance of negative values, in which case the emotions reinforcing herding behavior are even stronger. Reptiles and birds harass strangers. A flock of poultry will peck to death any individual bird that has wounds or blemishes. Likewise, humans can be a threat to each other if there are perceived differences between them. It is an advantage to survival, then, to *avoid rejection by revealing your sameness*. D.C. Gajdusek researched a long-hidden Stone Age tribe that had never seen Western people and soon noticed that they mimicked his behavior; whenever he scratched his head or put his hand on his hip, the whole tribe did the same thing.[27] Says MacLean, "It has been suggested that *such imitation may have some protective value by signifying, 'I am like you.'*" He adds, "This form of behavior is phylogenetically *deeply ingrained*."[28] Thus, another advantage of herding behavior is the avoidance of seeming difference in order to defuse an excuse to attack.

This tendency toward mimicry is hardly confined to Stone Age tribes. Psychology professor Irving Janis of Yale University, after studying the dynamics of group decision making in the modern political setting, concluded, "In general, the greater the number of those in the decision maker's social network who are aware of the decision, the more powerful the incentive to avoid the social *disapproval* that might result from a reversal." What's more, "The greater the commitment to a prior decision, the greater the anticipated utilitarian losses, social disapproval and self-disapproval from failing to continue the present course of action and hence a greater degree of stress."[29]

That is why, in financial markets, when the best time to buy or sell is at hand, *even the person who thinks he should take action experiences a strong psychological pressure to refrain from doing so*. He thinks, if only half consciously, "When my neighbor or advisor or friend thinks it's a good idea, then I'll do it, too. If I do it now, and I'm wrong, they will all call me a dope, *and I'll be the only dope*. I'll be singled out for ridicule, which is not only agonizing but dangerous." Pressure from, and influence by, peers, then, is at least one reason why most people cannot bring them-

selves to change from a bullish to bearish orientation or vice versa if to do so would go against the ideas of their associates and contacts. It also explains why a market or other social trend can continue for a long, long time and why financial valuations can become so extreme as to appear outrageous to those who believe that people ought to base their decisions upon some calculable fundamental value.

The discomfort of being alone in one's convictions is so great that it involves physical reactions. "Emotional mentation," says MacLean, "represents the only form of psychological experience that, *by itself*, may induce pronounced autonomic activity" such as sweating, twitching, flushing, muscle tightening and hair standing on end. A person's reaction just *thinking* about taking an action apart from the herd can produce tenseness or even nausea. He knows from experience that anyone who shares a prevailing majority opinion on any subject, particularly one that is intensely attended by the emotions of the limbic system (such as politics, religion, wealth or sex), is treated with the respect due his obvious intelligence and morality. One who utters an opposing opinion is immediately punished by a chorus of deprecating smiles, cackles, mooing, snorting, nipping or outright hostility. It may sound funny, but if you are not used to verbal viciousness or rejection by the group, they are painful experiences, and most people cannot abide either.

Emotionally removed historians sometimes decry the lack of prescience among a population prior to a long-ago financial crisis or the lack of vocal critics in countries that are taken over by fascists, communists, inquisitors or witch-burners. Yet unless one is there, it is nearly impossible to imagine the social pressure to go along with the trend of the day. In many political and religious social settings, for example, "I am not like you" can mean death. The limbic system bluntly assumes that all expressions of "I am not like you" are infused with danger. Thus, herding and mimicking are preservative behavior. They are powerful because they are impelled, regardless of reasoning, by a primitive system of mentation that, however uninformed, is trying to save your life.

The evolutionary advantage of herding, the reason it is incorporated into our paleomentation, is probably that, for animals, it (1) increases the success of life-enhancing activities such as food gathering and preparation, (2) increases the odds of survival in case of attack by a predator, and (3) decreases the odds of being killed because of perceived strangeness. The resulting actions of herding prior to neocortextural mulling have saved many a life. Unfortunately for humans in modern times, there are important exceptions to that benefit. MacLean worries, "It is one thing to have the

anciently derived limbic system to assure us of the authenticity of such things as food or a mate, but where do we stand if we must depend on the mental emanations of this same system for belief in our ideas, concepts, and theories?"[30] As with so many useful paleomentational tools, herding behavior is counterproductive to success in the world of modern financial speculation. If a financial market is soaring or crashing, the limbic system senses an opportunity or a threat and orders you to join the herd so that your chances for success or survival will improve. The limbic system produces emotions that support those impulses, including hope, euphoria, cautiousness and panic. The actions thus impelled lead one inevitably to the *opposite* of survival and success, which is why the vast majority of people lose when they speculate.[31] In a great number of situations, hoping and herding can contribute to your well-being. Not in financial markets. In many cases, panicking and fleeing when others do cuts your risk. Not in financial markets. Paradoxically, then, it is not a confirmation of your correct posture when you look around and can comfortably say, "Everybody out there agrees with me." It is a warning. As John Spooner said, "If you sit in on a poker game and you don't see a sucker at the table, get up, because you're the sucker." The important point with respect to this aspect of financial markets is that *repeated failure usually does little to deter the behavior*. If repeated loss and agony cannot overcome the limbic system's impulses, then it certainly must have free rein in comparatively benign social settings.

Pointing both to long, persistent financial trends and to sudden giant changes in valuation, neither of which are ever generally anticipated, author J. Orlin Grabbe, straight to the point of this chapter, says, "It would seem that changing images of the future...are endogenous.... They are neither rational or irrational; they are pre-rational.[32] In other words, they are within men, not brought about by outside events. They are not irrational because they have a purpose, no matter how ill-applied in modern life. Yet neither are they rational, as they are within men's unconscious minds, i.e., their basal ganglia and limbic system, which are equipped to operate without and to override the conscious input of reason.

The Super-Organization of Crowds as Distinct from Their Individual Constituents

We have identified unconscious, impulsive mental processes in individual human beings that are involved in regulating behavior with respect to one's fellows in a social setting. Is it logical to expect such impulses to be patterned? When the unconscious mind operates, it could hardly do so ran-

domly, as that would mean no thought at all. *It must operate in patterns peculiar to it.* This is clearly the case in individuals, whose limbic systems produce the same patterns of behavior over and over. Can we link such patterns to the formation of a super-organic pattern such as the Wave Principle? There is evidence to support this hypothesis as well.

Gustave Le Bon said a hundred years ago, "The psychological crowd is a provisional being formed of heterogeneous elements, exactly as the cells which constitute a living body form by their reunion a new being which displays characteristics very different from those possessed by each of the cells singly."[33] Le Bon proposed a "law of the mental unity of crowds," whereby individuals cease to think independently and instead participate unconsciously in "a sort of collective mind."

Is this the outmoded view of a nineteenth-century empiricist who theorized a bit too glibly? Modern researchers are coming close to confirming his view. The November 1997 issue of *Physica A*, published by the European Physical Society, presents a study that specifically connects the stock market with the primitive mentation of animals, including their occasional collective mentation. Didier Sornette, along with Anders Johansen of the Niels Bohr Institute in Copenhagen, propose these relevant conclusions in their paper, "Large Financial Crashes":

"Stock markets are fascinating structures with analogies [to what is] arguably the most complex dynamical system found in the natural sciences, i.e., the human mind. Instead of the usual interpretation of the efficient market hypothesis in which traders extract and incorporate consciously (by their action) all information contained in market prices, we propose that the market as a whole can exhibit an "emergent" behavior not shared by any of its constituent[s]. In other words, *we have in mind the process of the emergence of intelligent behavior at a macroscopic scale that individuals at the microscopic scale have no idea of.* This process has been discussed in biology *for instance in animal populations* such as ant colonies or in connection with the emergence of consciousness."[34]

This postulation is utterly compatible with the Wave Principle. The behavior that a crowd as a whole exhibits is indeed "intelligent," being a mentation distinct from that experienced by each individual. However, it is not rational; it is impulsive, and that is why only students of crowd psychology, who have observed the difference between crowd behavior and individual behavior, have been comfortable with the very idea. When a herd "thinks," the result is not reason but an emotional interpersonal superorganic

dynamic that must be the source of waves. A person's *patterned psychological dynamics as they relate to the social environment* produce an unconscious impulse to herd, which in combination with like minds produces global patterns of interactive dynamics in a shared social setting. The resulting pattern of collective conduct apparently takes the form of the Wave Principle.

In general, social mood change need not necessarily involve every individual. A person is drawn in to the unconscious, unreasoning, psychologically interdependent social dynamic when he allows himself to be influenced primarily by the emotional state of others rather than by independent research, adequate knowledge and utter rationality. Most people are too busy and unmotivated to fulfill such a tall order. Even those committed to rationality find these requirements difficult to fulfill even in tailor-made situations and impossible to fulfill in all situations.

Even if one wishes to assert the utter rationality of some participants in society, their influence can matter only if most others share that rationality in weighing arguments *and* if the arguments of the rational participants are identical. This utopian situation never exists in real societies, where the sum of people's shared impulses overwhelms the power of logical yet often conflicting entreaties from various individuals. Indeed, those conflicts themselves provide an excuse for people to abandon the hard work of reason and succumb easily to commandeering by the basal ganglia and the limbic system. Regardless of the divergent thoughts and actions of any individual, then, the crowd will follow its characteristic patterns of behavior.

One way or the other, socially induced mood changes in most individuals are able to progress uninterrupted by intrusion from an independent cerebral cortex. That is why, *in the aggregate*, unless and until there evolves a change in the operation of the components of the human mind, human interpersonal dynamics will remain immutable.

NOTES

1 Larsen, W.J. (1997). *Human embryology.*

2 Wright, K. (1997, October). "Babies, bonds, and brains." *Discover*, p. 78.

3 MacLean, P. (1990). *The triune brain in evolution*, p. 247.

4 Nesmith, J. (1996, September 14). "The roots of personality..." *The Atlanta Journal-Constitution.*

5 *Ibid.*

6 Substance addiction triggers the same neurotransmitter and compels similarly focused and self-destructive behavior.

7 Ledoux, J.E.(1989). "Cognitive emotional interactions in the brain." *Cognition and Emotion*, Vol. 3, pp. 267-289.

8 Goleman, D. (1989, August 15). "Brain's design emerges as a key to emotions." *The New York Times.*

9 *Ibid.*

10 MacLean, P. (1990). *The triune brain in evolution*, p. 17.

11 *Ibid*, p. 569.

12 *Ibid*, pp. 453, 578.

13 We will explore some of these in Chapters 15 through 19.

14 Wright, K. (1997, October). "Babies, bonds and brains." *Discover,* p. 78.

15 Scuoteguazza, H. (1997, September/October). "Handling emotional intelligence." *The Objective American.*

16 Pigou, A.C. (1927). *Industrial fluctuations.*

17 From Charles J. Collins's foreword to *Elliott Wave Principle.*

18 Pigou, A.C. (1920). *The economics of welfare*, as quoted in Vittachi, N. and Faber, M. (1998). *Riding the millennial storm*, p. 112.

19 Among others, such measures include put and call volume ratios, cash holdings by institutions, index futures premiums, the activity of margined investors, and reports of market opinion from brokers, traders, newsletter writers and investors.

20 Smith, V.L., Suchanek, G.L. and Williams, A.W. (1988, September). "Bubbles, crashes, and endogenous expectations in experimental spot asset markets." *Econometrica*, Vol. 56, No. 5, p. 1149.

21 Bishop, J.E. (1987, November 17). "Stock market experiment suggests inevitability of booms and busts." *The Wall Street Journal,* p. 31.

Smith also notes in this article that when he imposes artificial trading curbs that limit downside movement during a session, it encourages people to generate a stronger-than-normal boom, which in turn makes the ensuing crash worse. Such mandated trading halts, which are in force today, are bound to make crashes worse from another perspective. When people are invested and know that with a bit more decline they will lose their option to exit and be

stuck with their shares, they panic even more than they would have otherwise. Potential new buyers will be reluctant to enter because they, too, might get stuck.

22 Olsen, R. (1996, July/August). "Implications of herding behavior..." *Financial Analysts Journal,* pp. 37-41.

23 Just about any source of stress can induce a herding response. MacLean humorously references the tendency of governments and universities to respond to tension by forming *ad hoc* committees.

24 Passell, P. (1989, August 25). "Dow and reason: distant cousins?" *The New York Times.*

25 Montgomery, P. (1991, September 19). Speech, "Stocks and the irrational: possible sub-cortical influences on contemporary equity market pricing." and (1992, September 13) Speech, "Capital markets and the irrational: possible non-cortical influences on the price structure of investments."

Paul Montgomery of Universal Economics was the first person to recognize the implications of Maclean's work with respect to investor impulsivity. *Market Analysis for the New Millennium* (New Classics Library, 2002) features his pioneering work on this topic.

26 Le Bon, G. (1895). *The crowd.*

27 Gajdusek, D.C. (1970). "Physiological and psychological characteristics of stone age man." *Symposium on Biological Bases of Human Behavior, Eng. Sci.* 33, pp. 26-33, 56-62.

28 MacLean, P. (1990). *The triune brain in evolution,* p.239.

29 Janis, I. (1972). *Victims of groupthink.*

30 MacLean, P. (1990). *The triune brain in evolution,* p. 453.

31 There is a myth, held by nearly all people outside of back-office employees of brokerage firms and the IRS, that many people do well in financial speculation. Actually, almost everyone loses at the game eventually. The head of a futures brokerage firm once confided to me that never in the firm's history had customers in the aggregate had a winning year. Even in the stock market, when the public or even most professionals win, it is a temporary, albeit sometimes prolonged, phenomenon. The next big bear market usually wipes them out if they live long enough, and if they do not, it wipes out their successors. This is true regardless of today's accepted wisdom that the stock market always goes to new highs eventually. Aside from the fact that this very conviction is false (Where was the Roman stock market during the Dark Ages?), what counts is *when people act,* and that is what ruins them.

32 Grabbe, J.O. (1995). *International financial markets.*

33 Le Bon, G. (1895). *The crowd.*

34 Sornette, D. and A. Johansen. (1997, November). "Large financial crashes." *Physica A.*

Chapter 9:

Theories and Observations Relating to Impulsivity and Herding

Encoded Behavioral Rules as a Possible Impetus for Herding

Many families of animals herd, flock, school and swarm, including fish, insects such as ants and bees, birds, many grazing mammals and apparently, humans. "There is something utterly awe-inspiring," says Ian Stewart, "...about [the] apparent unity of purpose [of] large groups of...social animals."[1] It is due, he argues, not to "instinct," but to mentally encoded *rules*. Paul MacLean observes that "reptiles are slaves to *routine, precedent and ritual*,"[2] strongly implying embedded behavioral rules. H. Hediger notes that the habits of a tree porcupine that he observed for seven years "were of almost clock-like regularity."[3] In other words, there may be no genetic code to "join a herd," but there may be a genetic code that imparts individual rules of behavior that *result* in herding.

The behavior of animals is mightily akin to that of units within systems that are programmed to follow certain simple rules. When Mark Tilden, in his Los Alamos laboratory, fed three rules into a robot, it behaved in a seemingly complex way that made it appear to be "thinking" about following sunlight around to maintain its solar power input.[4] Zoologist Fritz Vollrath[5] and Kate Douglas[6] have created "cyberspiders" that, with a short list of rules, construct all the webs made by actual spiders. These experiments show that the mental encoding of rules can account for why animals engage in apparently complex yet rigidly performed behavior. It seems a cogent explanation of why birds migrate and turtles swim to islands that have continental-drifted a thousand miles away. They are obviously not

working out their behavior on a slide rule or with a map. If three or four embedded mental rules could produce the course of action, then their mentation need not be that complex.

Inputting goals into a computer program can even cause sets of rules to evolve. Perhaps such rules evolved in the genetic code of plants and animals to further the goals of survival and reproduction. If so, it is likely that a few simple rules embedded in human genes and executed in the basal ganglia and limbic system originally to enhance the survival of all the organisms that preceded man through evolution are the source of human herding behavior.

Indeed, many human beings follow rules so slavishly that the response, "But we've always done it this way!" is often considered of self-evident weight in an argument over procedure. Says MacLean about human beings, "the stress generated by an actual or threatened change in routine is many times compounded when entire organizations are involved." In other words, rules that are shared by a human herd are all the more resistant to suggestions of change.

There are probably two types of rules, the hard-wired and the temporary-derivative. A hard-wired rule might be, "Go along with what most other people think, say or do." A temporary-derivative rule might be, "Most people agree that the stock market always goes up," or "we all know that country X is our enemy." Given the limbic system's role in asserting feelings as truth, initial evidence to the contrary of such learned rules would be (and typically is) perceived literally as unreal. This is why social trend changes always come as a surprise. To conclude, while generally a human does not consciously plan to herd or think he is herding, his unconscious mind may harbor *a few simple rules relating to the behavior of others* that tend to make him an unknowing participant in the herd.

Mental Contagion

One theory of the spread of ideas, which could be a mechanism employed by the herding impulse, is that ideas are units of cultural transmission having the property of self-replication, like a living thing that "propagates from brain to brain." Says Oxford zoologist Richard Dawkins, "When a craze, say for pogo sticks, paper darts, slinkies or jacks sweeps through a school, it follows a history just like a measles epidemic."[7] This mechanism is not related only to fads. Yale economist Robert Schiller uses the word

contagion to describe the psychological mechanism behind financial market trends. Attitudes about every imaginable thing sweep through the population.

Elaine Showalter, Avalon Foundation Professor of the Humanities at Princeton, offers a theory of social hysteria in terms of contagion. Her thesis is particularly important to our discussion because social hysteria is a pure case of *unreasoning emotion*, in this case aimed at inappropriate entities. Her book, *Hystories – Hysterical Epidemics and Modern Media*, chronicles the disease-like transmission of images that people incorporate mentally as if they were real, including alien abductions, satanic ritual abuse, recovered memories and multiple personality syndrome. Like the witch craze of the 1600s, all of these crazes have proved baseless, yet thousands of people insisted for quite awhile that they were real and dedicated immense energy to them. Social hysteria sometimes involves persecution of helpless victims who are demonized in socially transmitted paranoid visions, be they women (in the case of witches), fathers (in the case of recovered memories of child abuse), or people of other religions (such as Jews in Nazi Germany or Muslims in the Balkans). I would add that such demonization can include inanimate objects. In the early 1970s, people were obsessed with the evil of business conglomerates, and many deeply feared that the International Telephone and Telegraph company (ITT) would take over the world. In the 1980s and 1990s, there have been countless hysterical episodes over food, from Alar in apples to pesticide sprays to salmonella in chicken and eggs to cancer-causing meats to the evil of fats and oils, all of which have provided countless hours of discussion on TV talk shows. Today, people are beginning to panic over the coming "Y2K" disaster, which supposedly will bring the modern world to a screeching halt, just as people approaching the last millennium panicked over religious prophecies of the end of the world. Eventually, each incidence of social hysteria subsides, just as epidemics subside.

These observations pertain to our discussion in Chapter 8 of the *independence* of the limbic system and its ability to translate *emotions into images and images into perceived reality*. In the individual, these images are conjured to give the neocortex something to do, as otherwise the welling emotion of anxiety, for example, would have no referent. In the social context, images spread from one person to another, perhaps out of desire to join in group experience, a desire for attention, or perhaps simply by con-

tagion, any of which reasons reflects a *dependence* upon the thoughts and actions of others not unlike the dependence that investors display. Showalter regards hysteria as "a cultural symptom of anxiety and stress..requir[ing] at least three ingredients: physician-enthusiasts and theorists, unhappy, vulnerable patients and supportive cultural environments."[8] These prerequisites certainly fit the world of investing. As I argue in Chapter 14, though, it is unlikely that the sharing of cultural images is restricted to hysteria or the stock market and probable that it pertains to all social experience.

Mental contagion is an ugly idea to some people. Philosopher Daniel Dennett complains, "I'm not initially attracted to the idea of my brain as a sort of dung heap in which the larvae of other people's ideas renew themselves before sending out copies of themselves in an informational Diaspora."[9] Of course, one is not *attracted* to the idea, as independence is the hallmark of a rational man. However, it is folly to dismiss the idea of mental contagion, because ignorance of it is exactly how one becomes most susceptible to its expression in himself. It is a paradox (like so many truths) that one must recognize this aspect of one's mind in order even to attempt to rise above it and watch with a new understanding what is going on in society. That is what the Wave Principle makes possible.

Feedback as Characteristic of Financial Markets and Society

Like societies as a whole, financial markets are a quintessential example of systems whose results feed back into the system as new cause. As the most widely followed market index in the world, the Dow Jones Industrial Average not only *reflects* the pulse of investors, it *affects* the pulse of investors. Not only do investors' decisions make the Dow move in a direction, but the direction of the Dow often causes investors to make those very decisions. Every day, investors watch the same ticker tape, read the same newspapers, listen to the same financial television shows and watch the same market indices go up and down. Millions of people involved in the market absorb and reflect the same information, opinions and emotional expressions. It is almost as if the participants are in a town square, and an orator trying to whip up revolution is standing on a balcony, making the crowd's emotions wax and wane with each change in content, tone and volume. In the case of markets, however, the orator and crowd are mostly one and the same. Much of Wall Street's information, such as price level, direction, speed of price change and volume, is self-generated, and just like a mob, the financial community feeds off its own emotions. The reason is that every market decision is both *produced by* information and *produces*

information. Each transaction, while at once an *effect*, becomes part of the market and, by communicating transactional data to investors, joins the chain of *causes* of others' behavior. This process produces a feedback loop of information and impulsivity whose engine is the mass interaction of numerous basal ganglia and limbic systems and which is governed by man's unconscious social nature. Since he *has* such a nature, the process repeatedly generates the same forms.

Stock averages even allow the crowd to monitor itself, like fashion-conscious people watching each other at a shopping mall. In their function as monitors, averages such as the Dow Jones Industrial Average must be maintained as a standard. Let us explore this idea as it relates to the integrity of the DJIA. There is an oft-cited and not unreasonable objection to using the Dow in analysis or forecasting, which is that its components are not constant. For instance, Dow Jones & Co. replaces stocks in its averages from time to time, and occasionally one of the stocks splits. Either event changes the relative weightings of the individual issues in the average. Many people call such changes "distortions," implying that this stock average is a rubber yardstick.[10]

A spokesman for Dow Jones & Co. who maintains the Dow averages, admittedly a partisan on this issue, says, "The components may change with the times, but what the Dow represents remains constant."[11] The precision of the DJIA's long-term wave structures and price relationships over the years supports this view unequivocally. The constancy of the Dow is also revealed by its continually constructing long-term parallel trend channels according to Elliott's observation, for instance, in Figures 18-1 through 18-5. The constancy of the Dow is a necessity in accounting for the success of three specific forecasts recounted in Chapter 5. There are others on the record. For instance, even though Dow Jones & Co. substituted MMM for Anaconda in its premier average in 1976, the 1977-1978 decline still took the Dow exactly to a .618 retracement of the 1974-1976 advance, reaching a target I published in advance, as detailed in Chapter 4 of *Elliott Wave Principle*. Despite several splits and substitutions, the Dow's rise from 1974 nevertheless topped in 1987 within 0.07% of a level that made the 1974-1987 advance in percentage terms precisely equal to that of 1932-1937, fulfilling a wave relationship that A.J. Frost called for nine years in advance in *Elliott Wave Principle*.

Because of all this experience, it is clear to me that investors have a complex emotional relationship with the Dow *as such*, as an entity in itself, much as fans remain loyal to a sports team despite the continual replace-

ment of individual players. Professional investors' actions reflect this loyalty when they adjust their portfolios after a change in Dow (or S&P) components. They make such adjustments either to mimic what Dow Jones & Co. did or under the assumption that other people will do so. Each of these reasons conforms to the herding impulse.

Social Visioning as an Aspect of Herding

Why does a vast plurality of observers find extremely high or low financial market valuations utterly justifiable during their occurrence yet so obviously crazy in retrospect? That the majority (of money, actually, and therefore usually people) at the time of the extreme valuation believes it to be sensible is true by definition, or the pricing would not exist. Years later, historians look back at the time and cluck about how absurd prices were. Yet "every age," said Charles Mackay in 1852, "has its peculiar folly; some scheme, project or fantasy into which it plunges, spurred on either by love of gain, the necessity of excitement, or the mere force of imitation."[12]

Mackay uses the word "fantasy," as have a number of psychologists since. While *mood* definitely precedes action (see Chapter 16), it is not necessary that fantasy images precede that action. Herding people *feel* a certain way and can express themselves impulsively to reflect those feelings. They need not share any specific fantasy or image, just a mood. Nevertheless, the idea does *fit* the Wave Principle, so it may be that shared fantasy images are an *intermediate step* between mood change and resulting action.

Several social scientists have proposed models that involve people sharing a social vision that serves as a benchmark against which they judge the world. Unlike physical benchmarks, social visions *change*. Trends based upon subjective mental imagery undergo violent reversals when that imagery dissolves. The unconscious use of an inconstant benchmark explains why people may believe fully in a dream of perpetual prosperity one decade and succumb fully to a despairing nightmare of imminent doom the next. Their minds adapt to the group's changes in attitude as if reality itself had changed (and as a result, it usually does; see Chapter 16).

In 1952, Wilfred R. Bion presented a paper to the *International Journal of Psychoanalysis* on small-group dynamics. He characterized them as based upon primitive, shared unconscious fantasies, images or myths that come about as a way of relieving the pressure of, and evading the effort of, maintaining a rational, problem-solving orientation.[13] Psychologist Carl Jung,

many of whose ideas are controversial for good reason, nevertheless addressed the idea of human herding in terms that are not incompatible with this view. He proposed that all individuals inherit, both genetically and by cultural transmission, ideational forms, or "archetypes," that are "collective, universal and impersonal" and which together form a "collective unconscious" social mind that rules emotionally-charged social behavior.[14] Jung's "archetype" is essentially an unconsciously shared social dream, fantasy, image or myth.

Psychologist Lloyd deMause presents a case for a "psychogenic theory of history," whereby adults in groups first generate shared fantasies based upon childhood experience, then project them as images, and then act them out.[15] He cites as evidence the fact that social images in news photographs, cartoons, advertisements, political speeches, entertainment media and so on *precede* events that then appear to mimic those images. This theory is not incompatible with the Wave Principle. Socionomics is based upon the idea that social mood is responsible for the character of social action. Since mood is expressed immediately in countless ways other than buying or selling stock (see Chapter 14), expressions of the prevailing mood probably do include public visual images. These images would reflect mood quite immediately, before the public could mobilize itself enough to act in the economic and political arenas (see Chapter 16). However, I expect that the hypothesized connection of these images to childhood experience is derived from Freudian ideas, making that aspect of the theory highly conjectural. In light of the information in Chapter 8, I suggest that such images would necessarily coalesce around the concerns of the limbic system and therefore be *evolutionarily primitive* in their nature. The resulting images might appear to a psychologist as childlike, although children are not typically obsessed with wealth, death, survival or sex (which concerns shape many social images), and the limbic system is.

Regardless of any associated psychoanalytics, the essential idea of social visioning has had staying power, finding its way into such modern social words as "paradigm." Science historian Thomas Kuhn, for instance, defines this term as "the entire constellation of beliefs, values, techniques, and so on shared by the members of a given community."[16]

Swiss economist Eugene Bohler brings us closer to the subject of finance when he says, "The modern economy is as much a dream factory as Hollywood."[17] Terms such as "fantasy" and "social dream" might appear overdone to many readers. As a close observer of the public's view of the

stock market for many years, I find these terms utterly compatible with reality. What words better describe the results of a poll in late 1997 showing that *on average*, U.S. mutual fund investors expect their funds to gain *34% per year for the next ten years?*[18]

If social visioning is an intermediate step between social mood and social action, the dynamics of its manifestation would have to follow the Wave Principle, which governs its cause. It may well do exactly that. In 1965, B.W. Tuckman presented research on the developmental sequence of the psychological dynamics of small groups.[19] Expanding upon his observations in the 1980s, psychiatrist Philip Wells Shambaugh of the Harvard Medical School, an expert on small-group dynamics, observed a certain style of progress in the images that such groups share and made this report:

> The development of small groups, in its simplest form, proceeds in a series of five waves, alternatingly positive and negative. I began to wonder why such an undulation occurs and hypothesized that each stage of group development is patterned by an underlying shared fantasy. The first is the primordial paradise fantasy, the second, [a] negative phase, includes a number of competing fantasies, all marked by anger and hatred, the third [is marked] by the image of a Morean utopia, the fourth, again negative, is not often described but probably involves the decay of the utopian image, and the fifth, positive, is of a democratic group structure. If one accepts [Prechter's] thesis that the Elliott wave form is based on mass psychology, it makes sense. ...The homologizing between the fantasies of small and large groups [becomes] quite essential in this unexpected context.[20]

If social visioning occurs, and if it follows the Wave Principle, then people must share images and their associated feelings *all the time*, just as the Wave Principle is operating all the time. There is no reason to believe that people share images only at extremes in valuation or emotion, which only reflect their intensity. People often do share visions of boundless abundance or certain destruction, but these are the poles of the scale. In between, there are various degrees of optimism or pessimism and of uncertainty about the future, whose associated images would be correspondingly moderate. Pricing extremes in the stock market would reflect the power of social visions, and trend durations their persistence.

Habituation

Why is the mind so plastic with respect to financial valuation? Apparently, people adopt the recent past as normal no matter how unusual historically. Pathologist Frederick A. Hottes has a suggestion as to why:

> Sensory receptors experimentally have been shown to have the property of adaptation. Basically, if a continuous sensory stimulus is applied, the receptors respond at a very high pulse rate at first, then at a progressively lower rate until finally many of them no longer respond at all. Would the same response in the brain explain why the recent past is a stronger stimulus for behavior than older experiences/history books?[21]

Habituation is common in life forms as low as the sea-slug, whose six attendant neurons will eventually cease to cause a withdrawal of its gill when touched, as if it is getting used to the stimulation to the point that it is no longer stimulation. Humans' physical sensory apparati show the same diminution of response. If the brain reacts the same way, it would explain why people get used to new settings, whether physical or cultural, why they get bored with sameness in entertainment, and why they find new social events and trends shocking while accepting old social events and trends as normal.

University of South Florida College of Medicine's Dr. Robert Thatcher, founder and former director of the Applied Neuroscience Research Institute of the University of Maryland School of Medicine, suggests a mechanism for *long-term* habituation: periodic "waves" of nerve growth and brain restructuring.

> The new model of neural development holds that the primitive areas of the brain mature first; in the first three years of life, the regions in the cortex that govern our sensory and motor skills undergo the most dramatic restructuring, and these perceptual centers, along with instinctual ones such as the limbic system, will be strongly affected by early childhood experiences.
>
> But the frontal cortex, which governs planning and decision making, and the cerebellum, a center for motor skills, are also involved in emotional development. And those parts of the brain don't get rewired until a person is five to seven years old. What's more, another major restructuring of the brain occurs between ages nine and eleven, says Thatcher. Suddenly, the brain is looking less like a sculpture in stone and more like a work in progress.

Thatcher's readings of the EEGs of adolescents and adults have revealed that some reorganization of the brain may occur about every two years from birth to death. He proposes that these reorganizations happen in response to waves of nerve growth factor that sweep across the cerebral hemispheres in two-year cycles, revamping up to one-fifth of the brain's synaptic connections at the leading edge of the wave. The idea of the traveling waves is just a theory now — but it's a theory that's making more sense to more scientists.[22]

Such periodic restructuring would offer an adaptational advantage to survival. If a person's environment changes, his brain can adjust to it. This adaptability with reality as a reference may explain why one generation of people is utterly at home with farming, another with machines, another with electronics and another with computers.

Periodic waves of restructuring would explain why people fight *new* long-term social trends as abnormal while embracing *old* ones as normal. It takes time for brains to restructure themselves to fit the new social environment, which they invariably do, *as if it is a new environment in reality to which they must adjust to survive*. That is why each new level of financial prices, whether higher or lower, after some time is accepted as normal regardless of what might be considered historically reasonable value. As a result, few people are induced to sell at a market top or buy at a bottom.

The sliding response curve of habituation and the plasticity of waves of brain restructuring are marvelous adaptive mechanisms most of the time, but not in finance. As with the paleomentation of the limbic system, this otherwise very useful mental ability is counterproductive to successful financial speculation. By the time it becomes crucially important for people to recall the significance of a similar market environment or juncture in the past, they have forgotten it and have adjusted to the new one as if it were normality. Waves of brain restructuring might also account for why people are mostly oblivious to their own cycles of attitude. Incorporating the Wave Principle into one's thinking is an excellent way to be aware of one's own changes in attitude so that they do not mislead and also to anticipate social changes so that they are not a shock.

A Hypothesis of Dynamic Herding as a Function of a Fibonacci Bipolar Impulse to Imitate or Deviate

I would like to offer a hypothesis of the creation, maintenance and reversal of human social trends (whether involving the stock market, hair styles, musical preferences, skirt lengths, tie colors, or whatever). You may

be better served reading this section after reading Chapter 12, which presents the work of Lefebvre and Adams-Webber.

These psychologists posit and demonstrate that people's mental decision model is bipolar and that on average, people have a built-in bias, by a ratio of .618 to .382, toward the positive or optimistic end of the pole. One bipolar decision continuum might be, at one end, an impulse to *imitate* others, and at the other end, a capacity to *deviate* from the behavior of others. The research cited in Chapter 12 suggests that any such impulses would be biased toward imitation in a .618/.382 ratio.

Because imitation has the stronger tendency in this hypothesis, any initial random fluctuations in people's preferences in a neutral context would quickly lead to a slightly higher density of preference for one object or idea. That preference in turn would invoke the bias to imitate, which would increase that density and cause a trend toward agreement. Soon, that trend would culminate in a one-sided stance. After a state of preference was established in the majority of the population, individuals would deviate from time to time, but their number would usually be too small to attract enough imitation to change the group's orientation. Eventually, random impulses to deviate would, at some point, result suddenly in a large number of people deviating. If the imitation that then resulted were to involve enough people, a change in trend would occur. At the critical point, the change in overall orientation that establishes the new polarity would be very rapid.

While this model would work as described if imitation and deviation impulses were random, I believe that in the real world, they are not. Too long a time of consensus breeds reaction in people. Eventually, a long-standing condition of social agreement *fosters* deviation in many human beings. Therefore, to adjust the hypothesis slightly, I would contend that at some point, the neglected pole becomes attractively charged out of the desire for newness and the excitement of change, tipping the Fibonacci balance in its favor. Such a model might account for why voters slosh back and forth from conservatism to liberalism, generally reaching 62%/38% extremes before galloping in the other direction. This model might be termed the dynamic herding hypothesis.

In support of this possibility, one of Poulton's experiments cited in Chapter 12 asks subjects to rate the "lightness" of a gray sheet of paper against the poles of black and white.[23] Subjects tend very strongly to rate the paper at 62%, but 62% *of which pole* varied, producing data spikes at 38% and 62% of the white-black spectrum. Lefebvre offers this explanation:

For some subjects, the white sample played the role of the positive pole, and for others, the black one. The former marked 0.62 of the scale from point 0, and the latter from the point 100.[24]

The black/white dichotomy is quite reflective of the battle between liberals and conservatives in the political arena or bulls and bears in a financial market. Like the left-right spectrum in politics, the up-down spectrum in stock market belief is mostly a function of feeling, which is the realm of the limbic system.[25] In the former case, "left" and "right" are the poles of belief that alternate between positive (attractive) and negative (unattractive) in people's minds. In the latter case, "up" and "down" are the poles of belief that alternate between positive (probable) and negative (improbable). The recessive tendency to deviate triumphs when a majority adopts the previous negative pole as the positive one.

The Individual's Place in the Herd

The idea of patterned collective behavior is not easy for many people to accept because it appears *inhuman* in the sense that it does not reflect what *makes* people human — the rational faculty — while social action reflects impulses from an evolutionarily pre-human portion of the brain. Philosopher Friedrich Nietzsche bluntly stated the difference: "Madness is rare in individuals, but in groups, parties, nations and ages, *it is the rule.*"[26] Nevertheless, it is the impulsive mind that is essentially identical in almost every person. Our conscious minds make us human and different from each other, but it is our unconscious minds that make us the same.

Research shows that the power of the limbic system to override the neocortex varies a great deal among individuals. Some people find it difficult to control their emotions. Others, such as criminals, find it nearly impossible to resist their impulses.[27] The same fact may apply to herding behavior. For some people, imitation may be anathema. Others seem nearly incapable of independent rational exertion and soak up all their ideas from society. Everyone herds somewhat, and most people herd a lot. As lay philosopher Eric Hoffer said, "When people are free to do as they please, they usually imitate each other."[28]

Regardless of how rational some individuals in a financial market may be, *it is the most impulsive participants that wield absolute control over its trends*. Even if, say, only 30% of investors are prone to panic, that is quite

enough to precipitate one. When panic ensues, those less prone to panic know that if they do not act, they may be driven bankrupt by those who do. This knowledge creates a chain reaction as otherwise calm people succumb to the fear that the panic will ruin them. They capitulate because others are capitulating.

Alternatively, if, as I suspect, people run the gamut of panicability, then an initial panic by those most impulsive will draw in those next most disposed, which will increase the selling, which will trigger the next most disposed, and so on. The reverse is true in an uptrend with respect to confidence. As the trend extends and extends, less and less susceptible individuals succumb. Supporting this view is the illustrative fact that the great genius Isaac Newton was finally baited into the famous South Sea Bubble near its peak, losing the equivalent of a million 1998 dollars. His resulting loss caused him to remark, "I can measure the motions of bodies, but I cannot measure human folly." Now, with the Wave Principle, we have a basis for measuring that property and unraveling its mystery.

In the face of such impulses, our struggling neocortex has only two possible functions. The first is to eliminate conflict among the brain's parts by rationalizing, *ex post facto*, the decisions made by the limbic system. Gallons of ink and miles of transmission wires are wasted on this exercise daily. Brains engaged in this unconscious goal can reach a heated pitch. To anyone versed in the Wave Principle, the endless discussion and analysis of the news as it relates to the stock market appears fruitless and even bizarre. (For more on this topic, see Chapter 18.)

For the first time ever, the neocortex now has a second function. With knowledge of the Wave Principle, the neocortex may attack the problem of market analysis and social forecasting using reason. Understanding that financial market behavior is governed by the patterned unconscious, then, is precisely what, for the first time ever, allows analysis of it to be objective.

We can now postulate that paleomentational thought processes are the psychological motor of the trends and patterns of social mood that produce Elliott waves. How do we account for the fractal, Fibonacci-based, spiral-related pattern of Wave Principle dynamics? In Chapters 10 through 12, we will examine the biological origins of those aspects of nervous system behavior.

NOTES

1 Stewart, I. (1998). *Life's other secret.*

2 MacLean, P. (1990). *The triune brain in evolution*, p. 237.

3 Hediger, H. (1950). *Wild animals in captivity.*

4 The rules are: (1) If your solar cells are not generating more than X amount of power, spin at random and move 10 centimeters forward. (2) If they have been generating power above X for less than five seconds, move forward in a straight line at constant speed. (3) If they have been generating power above X for more than five seconds, stop.

5 Vollrath, F. (1992, March). "Spider webs and silks." *Scientific American*, pp. 52-58.

6 Douglas, K. (1996, August 10). "Arachnophilia." *New Scientist*, pp. 24-28.

7 Dawkins, R. (1993, December 15). "Is religion just a disease?" *The Daily Telegraph.*

8 Showalter, E. (1997). *Hystories – hysterical epidemics and modern media.*

9 Dennett, D. (1991). *Consciousness explained*, p. 202.

10 A presentation of this objection can be found in *Stock Market Logic*, by Norman Fosback (1976), The Institute for Econometric Research, Fort Lauderdale, pp. 282-284.

11 Reference unavailable.

12 Mackay, C. (1841). *Extraordinary popular delusions and the madness of crowds.*

13 Bion, W. (1952). "Group dynamics: a review." *International Journal of Psychoanalysis,* No. 33, pp. 235-247.

14 Jung, C. (1959). *The archetypes and the collective unconscious.*

15 deMause, L. (1982). *Foundations of psychohistory*, pp. 172-243.

16 Kuhn, T. (1962). *The structure of scientific revolutions*, (2nd ed. 1970).

17 Grabbe, J.O. (1995). *International financial markets.*

18 From a poll conducted by Montgomery Asset Management (San Francisco), released October 1997.

19 Tuckman, B.W. (1965). "Developmental sequence in small groups." *Psychology Bulletin* No. 63, pp. 384-399.

20 From a personal letter from P. Shambaugh to Robert R. Prechter, Jr., June 15, 1986.

21 From a personal letter from F.A. Hottes to R. Prechter, August 21, 1996.

22 Wright, K. (1997, October). "Babies, bonds, and brains," *Discover,* p. 78.

23 Poulton, E.C., *et al.* (1968). "Response bias in very first judgments of the reflectance of grays." *Perception and Psychophysics*, Vol. 3, pp. 112-114.

24 Lefebvre, V. "Sketch of reflexive game theory," from the proceedings of the Workshop on Multi-Reflexive Models of Agent Behavior conducted by the Army Research Laboratory.

25 See "The Extent of Impulsivity in Political Action" section in Chapter 16.

26 Nietzsche, F. (1886). *Beyond good & evil.*

27 Samenow, S. (1984). *Inside the criminal mind.*

28 Hoffer, E. (1955). *The passionate state of mind.*

Chapter 10:

Biological Connections to the Robust Fractal Aspect of the Wave Principle

Fractals in the Body

Why does the unconscious herding impulse produce a *robust fractal* pattern of social interaction? It might appear surprising if the brain were *not* associated with a robust fractal form of behavior. The human body, like much of nature, is a mass of robust fractals.

In 1992, researchers at Boston University, MIT and Harvard Medical School discovered that the fractal pattern in the nucleotide sequence of

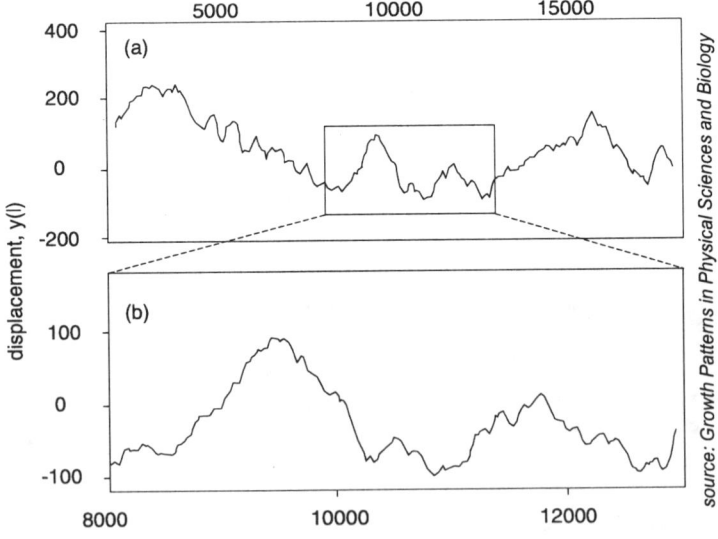

The DNA walk representation for the rat embryonic skeletal myosin heavy chain gene ($\alpha = 0.63$). (a) The entire sequence. (b) The magnification of the box within (a).

Figure 10-1

DNA links its parts over long stretches of the molecule in such a way as to produce "a remarkably long-range power law correlation."[1] Figure 10-1 shows both an *entire* sequence and a magnified *portion* of it. Their similarity is like that of the Elliott wave pattern at various degrees shown in Figures 2-1 through 2-7, suggesting at least the possibility that DNA is not an indefinite fractal but a patterned *robust* fractal.[2]

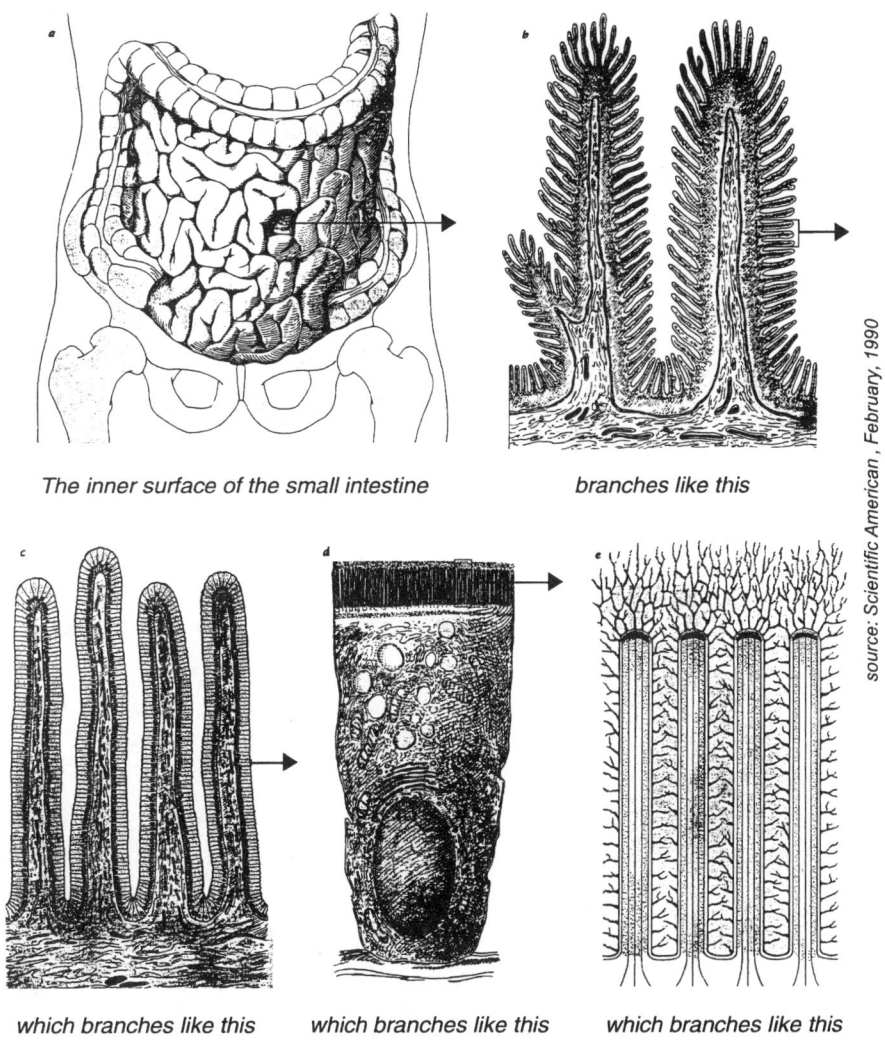

The inner surface of the small intestine   branches like this

source: Scientific American, February, 1990

which branches like this   which branches like this   which branches like this

Figure 10-2

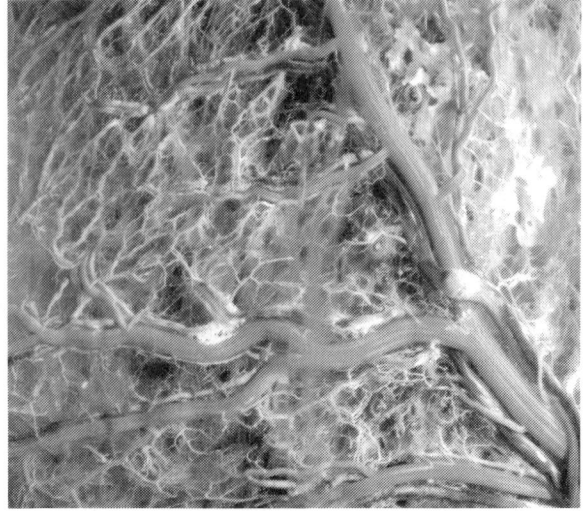

source: Fractals---The Pattern of Chaos

Blood vessels form an arborum

Figure 10-3

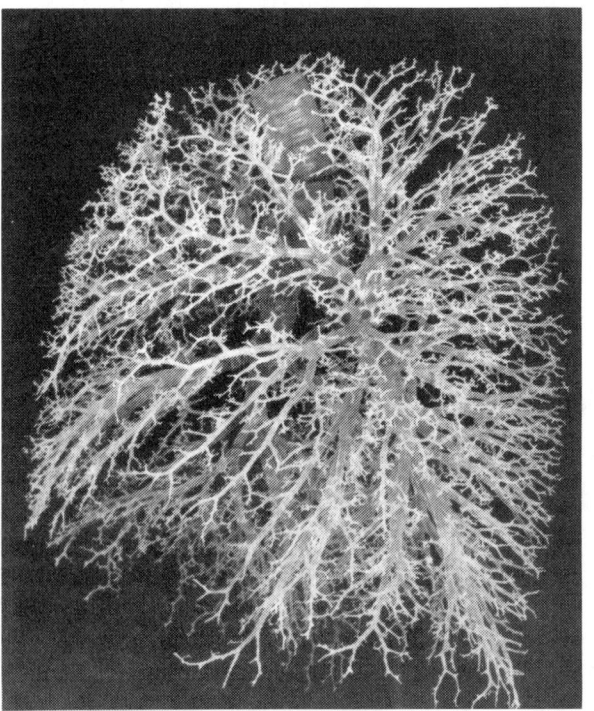

source: Lung Structure

Air passages in the lung form an arborum

Figure 10-4

The fractal aspect of DNA carries through to the forms it governs. For example, the circulatory system, the lungs, certain cardiac muscles, the surfaces of hemoglobin, the bile duct system, the urinary connecting tubes in the kidney, the placenta and the absorption surface of the small intestine are all fractal branching systems, or arbora. Figures 10-2 through 10-4 show examples.

Fractals in Nervous System Physiology

Well, guess what. The brain, and the forms to which it is directly connected, reflect this same design. An arborum suffuses the retina (see Figure 10-5), which is directly connected to the nervous system. Dr. Ary L. Goldberger of Harvard Medical School's Beth Israel Hospital made this observation in the February 1990 issue of *Scientific American*:

> Certain neurons, for instance, have a fractal-like structure. If one examines such neurons through a low-power microscope lens, one can discern asymmetric branches, called dendrites, connected to the cell bodies. At slightly higher magnification, one observes smaller branches on the larger ones. At even higher magnification, one sees another level of

The retina forms an arborum

Figure 10-5

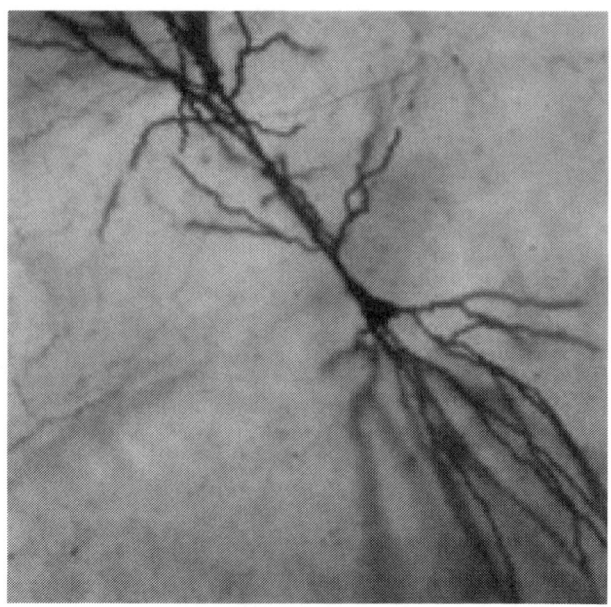

Neurons form arbora

Figure 10-6

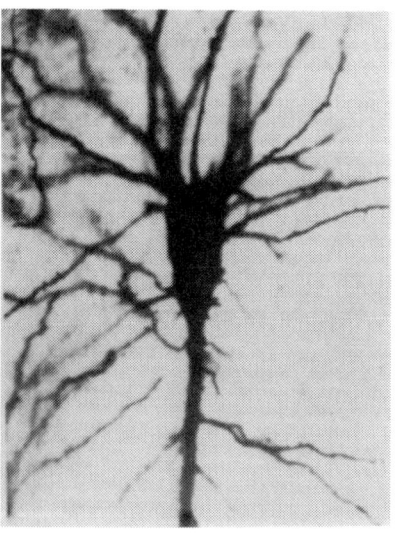

source: Journal of the American Medical Association

The giant pyramidal Betz cell of the motor cortex forms an arborum.

Figure 10-7

detail: branches on branches on branches.... If one saw two photographs of the dendrites at two different magnifications (without any other reference), one would have difficulty in deciding which photograph corresponded to which magnification.[3] [See Figure 10-6.]

Along with Dr. Lewis A. Lipsitz, also of Beth-Israel, Goldberger adds to the list of neurological arbora "the branching pattern of the Betz cells in the frontal cortex, spiny cells in the caudate, and anterior horn cells in the spinal cord."[4] (See Figure 10-7.) The same structures that we see at these micro scales occur at macro scales. The white tissues of the cerebellum, called the arbor vitae, or tree of life (see Figure 10-8), as well as the blood vessels in the brain (see Figure 10-9) arborate in a pattern not unlike that of a solitary oak tree (see Figure 10-10), which is apparently the way it has "grown" through evolution.

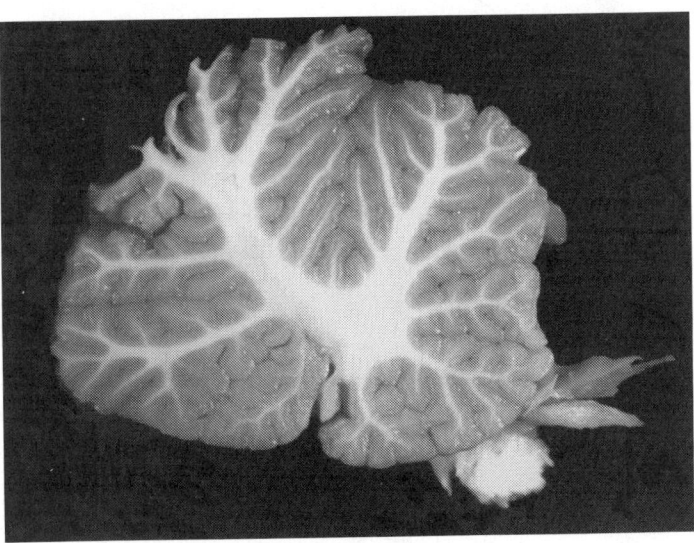

A sheep's cerebellum is an arborum

Figure 10-8

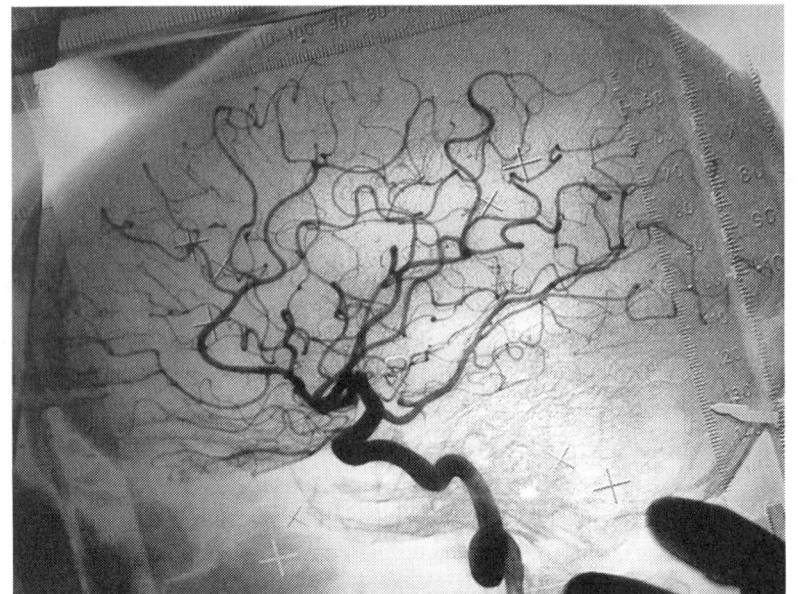

Blood vessels in the brain form an aborum
Figure 10-9

An oak tree is an arborum
Figure 10-10

Fractals in Nervous System Function

Iterated Systems president Michael Barnsley, who, with Dr. Alan Sloan, pioneered the development of fractal imaging systems for data compression software in the late 1980s, recently mused on PBS, "The most important fractal in the human body is the incredibly complex wiring circuit, the brain. We may never understand how our brains *work*, but if we do, I suspect that it will depend upon some application of fractal geometry."[5] Indeed it may, because it is not only the *structures* of the brain and nervous system that reveal fractals. Recent studies show that some of their impulsive *functions* do as well. For instance, the nervous system controls the human heartbeat. Researchers from Boston University and Harvard Medical School report that a healthy human heart beats irregularly. As reported by the *Dallas Morning News*,

> Plotting the time intervals [between beats] on a graph creates an interesting pattern. It's a complex, jagged line looking a little like a mountain range. The nature of the jagged pattern looks the same when it's graphed for a short time period – say minutes – or over a longer time, like 24 hours, corresponding to thousands of heartbeats. This similar structure persisting over different scales is what mathematicians call a fractal.[6]

Head researcher Dr. Ary Goldberger makes this observation:

> A fractal pattern in heartbeats implies some *long range correlations in nervous system activity*, since the involuntary (or "autonomic") nervous system regulates heartbeat. *And since the involuntary nervous system controls lots of things, the fractal pattern may appear elsewhere*, and in fact, the data that we have from other systems suggest that it applies more broadly to respiration, blood pressure control *and so forth*.[7]

Following up on that presumption, Dr. Jeffrey M. Hausdorff of Beth Israel Hospital, in cooperation with Harvard Medical School, has employed a special device to monitor striding patterns of healthy people. He finds that variations in stride display long-range self-similar correlations extending over hundreds of steps; in other words, their patterns are fractals. Echoing the conclusion of Dr. Goldberger's heartbeat study, he states, "each stride interval depends upon stride intervals at remote previous times."[8] This conclusion based upon the fractal nature of the nervous system's regulatory functions is exactly the same as that necessitated by the Wave Principle about financial markets: each movement depends upon movements in the past, both recent and remote. Our brains, then, "work" in accordance with fractal geometry, just as the Wave Principle does.

These studies reveal that fractals are crucial to the short- and long-range behavior and self-organization of man's nervous system. The Wave Principle reveals that fractals are crucial to the short- and long-range behavior and self-organization of man's social system. Is it farfetched to postulate a direct connection between the two?

Fractals as Tools of Efficiency, Efficacy and Robustness

Why does the body employ fractals? Three reasons appear to be efficiency, efficacy and robustness. As Goldberger explains with respect to other bodily systems,

> Fractal branches or folds greatly amplify the surface area available for absorption (as in the intestine), distribution or collection (by the blood vessels, bile ducts and bronchial tubes) and information processing (by the nerves).... Fractal structures, partly by virtue of their redundancy and irregularity, are robust and resistant to injury.[9]

Similarly, IBM physicist Richard Voss proposes that the fractal pattern in DNA might be involved in enhancing copying accuracy from one generation to the next.[10] I would postulate that DNA's fractal nature makes it active in ensuring the robustness of the species as well. Its copying "errors," which are commonly presumed to be random mistakes, are far more likely to be vital discontinuities, regulated fractally, that ensure adequate mutation to provide for the adaptability of the species to changing environments.

How do fractals contribute to the efficiency of human mentation? Fractals in the physical and functional aspects of the nervous system may help the brain *understand* fractals. It can certainly recognize clouds and trees and mountains in a flash. In contrast, it might take some time to teach a computer the difference between a cloud, a bird and an airplane. Then it might be confused by a blimp or a falling star. But the brain can usually tell the difference between the natural and the man-made in an instant. Perhaps it is able to recognize and deal with nature so intimately because of its parallelism with nature in both design and function. As Briggs and Peat summarize Nobel laureate Ilya Prigogine's view, "The brain is the nonlinear product of a nonlinear evolution on a nonlinear planet."[11] In 1990, Dr. Larry R. Vandervert proposed to the national convention of the American Psychological Association a chaotic/fractal dynamical unification model for psychology, in which he argues that the ability of the *mind* to understand fractals in the *world* may be a reflection of the fractal structure of the *brain.*[12]

Societies cluster for reasons of efficiency as well. People travel, congregate and settle in such a way as to produce a fractal cluster in the very organization of crowds, societies and cultures. Zipf discovered in 1949 that the distribution of the populations in towns cluster according to a power law.[13] Supporting that conclusion, Dr. Peter Grassberger of the University of Wuppertal in Germany demonstrates that epidemics spread throughout the population in a fractal pattern. That is to say, the distribution of people infected with a communicable disease within a small segment of the population looks much like the distribution throughout a larger segment.[14] This result is due to the fact that the social interaction of people produces a fractal, which is apparently the most efficient and robust arrangement for their interaction. Diseases, like computer viruses on the internet, occasionally take advantage of this efficient distribution system. The apparent value of fractals and power laws to social aggregations is consistent with the appearance of fractals in all kinds of social data, including financial market pricing data, as mentioned in Chapter 2.

The fractal nature of the *physiology* and *function* of the brain and mind is compatible with the fractal nature of its *product* in concert with like minds: the Wave Principle. Likewise, the primitive brain may impel mentational interdependence among humans in the pattern of the Wave Principle because this cooperative social fractal is valuable in terms of efficiency, efficacy and robustness. As Le Bon said in 1895, "Crowds are always unconscious, but this very unconsciousness is perhaps one of the secrets of their strength. In the natural world, beings exclusively governed by instinct accomplish acts whose marvelous complexity astounds us."[15]

Fractals as Necessary for Viability

The value of fractals in living forms may be even greater than efficiency, efficacy, robustness and other such utilitarian advantages to life; they may be necessary for life itself. Lipsitz and Goldberger have conducted studies demonstrating that *aging* coincides with a *reduction in the arboration of the nervous system* and that a reduction in the fractal irregularity of the heartbeat is a signal of an impending heart attack. In other words, health and vitality require fractal physiology and function. Prigogine says this about the brain:

The brain has to be largely irregular; if not, you have epilepsy. This shows that irregularity, chaos, leads to complex systems. It's not at all disorder. On the contrary, *I would say chaos is what makes life and intelligence possible.* The brain has been selected to become so unstable that the smallest effect can lead to the formation of order.[16]

In other words, perhaps not only the efficiency and adaptability of a complex system, but its very existence, depends upon its fractal patterns of irregularity.

As it happens, the life of a stock market uptrend also depends upon persistent fluctuation. Studies on trend-reaction frequency show that a paucity of reactions after a long uptrend is a reliable sign of an impending reversal.[17] As with an unnaturally smooth stride, heartbeat or brainwave, an unusually smooth rise in stocks is a precursor to the death of a bull market from old age or to a market heart attack or epileptic fit in the form of a crash. Apparently *what is true for individual life forms in this regard is true for super-organic social clusters as well.* They both depend upon fractals for health and perhaps even existence.

Conclusion

Fractals permeate individuals' nervous systems, the congregation of people, and their patterns of interaction. These facts are consistent with the discovery that these same people's minds, in combination with like minds, produce a fractal of collective mentation called the Wave Principle. Physiologist and Nobel laureate Sir Charles Sherrington calls the brain a self-organizing system that appears as "an enchanted loom, where millions of flashing shuttles weave a *dissolving pattern*, always a meaningful pattern [and] a shifting *harmony of sub-patterns*."[18] This description matches that of social behavior under the Wave Principle, where a harmony of sub-patterns weave together to form larger meaningful patterns that dissolve only to lead to the development of the next ephemeral pattern, all as a result of the self-organization of many individuals. To conclude, the brain may be disposed to participating in a fractal of collective sentiment because circumstantially, it, along with the rest of the human body's structures and functions, is of and for fractals in so many ways.

NOTES

1 Stanley, H.E., *et al.* (1993). "Fractal landscapes in physics and biology." *Growth patterns in physical sciences and biology.*

2 Goldberger, A., *et al.* (1990, February). "Chaos and fractals in human physiology." *Scientific American,* pp. 42-49.

3 *Ibid.*

4 Lipsitz, L. and Goldberger, A. (1992, April 1). "Loss of 'complexity' and aging." *Journal of the American Medical Association.*

5 Lesmoir-Gordon, N. (1994). "Fractals: the colors of infinity."

6 Siegfried, T. (1993, March 29). "Healthy hearts have complex rhythm." *The Dallas Morning News.*

7 *Ibid.*

8 Browne, M. (1997, April 15). "Variations in stride." *The New York Times.*

9 West and Goldberger point out in another article that branching in the lungs "approaches the more favorable ratio of surface to volume enjoyed by our evolutionary ancestors, the single-celled microbes." [ref: Goldberger, A., *et al.* (1990, February). "Chaos and fractals in human physiology." *Scientific American*, pp. 42-49.] Perhaps all of the body's fractal patterns are a method of reconstructing the environment of ancient life. For instance, the fractal nature of the absorption surface of the intestine might serve to approximate the surface/volume ratio of ancient unicellular microbes as well. Blood vessels likewise bring nutrients to all parts of the body as the sea did long ago to microbes. (Indeed, the body's regulation of salinity mimics the ancient environment of the sea. Our eyes are washed with a saline solution for the same reason.)

10 Voss, R. (1992, June). "Evolution of long range fractal correlations and 1-*F* noise in DNA-based sequences." *Physical Review Letters.*

11 Briggs, J. and Peat, D. (1989). *Turbulent mirror*, p. 166.

12 Vandervert, L. (1990, August 12). Presentations: "A chaotic/fractal dynamical unification model for psychology" and (1989, May) "Systems thinking and neurological positivism: further elucidations and implications."

13 Zipf, G.K. (1949). *Human behavior and the principle of least action.*

14 "The practical fractal."(1987, December 26). *The Economist.*

15 Le Bon, G. (1895). *The crowd.*

16 Prigogine, I. and Stengers, I. (1984). *Order out of chaos.*

17 Eliades, P. (1998, May 4). "Danger: bear may be crossing." *Barron's.*

18 Sherrington, C.S. (1940). *Man on his nature.*

Chapter 11:

Biological and Perceptual Connections to the Fibonacci Foundation of the Wave Principle

Fibonacci in the Body

Why does man's unconscious herding impulse produce a *Fibonacci*-based pattern of social interaction? Consider that the human body, like most plant and animal life forms, is a mass of Fibonacci expression, from micro to macro scales.

The DNA molecule, which is the data source for the developing human being, spirals in Fibonacci proportion. Given current best measurements, the length of one cycle is 34 angstroms, and its height is 20 angstroms, very nearly producing the Fibonacci ratio 34/21 (see Figure 11-1).[1] Fibonacci may be hidden more deeply in the structure of DNA. Stanley *et al.* note parenthetically in their power-law study, "The DNA walk representation for the rat embryonic skeletal myosin heavy chain gene [has a long range correlation of] *0.63*"[2] (see Figure 10-1), which once again is quite close to *phi*.[3]

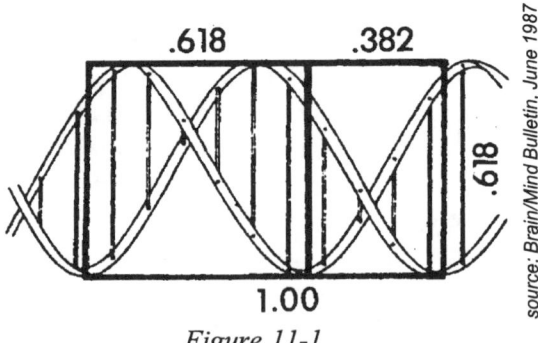

Figure 11-1

source: Brain/Mind Bulletin, June 1987

Biochemistry professor Guido Pincheira of the University of Chile argues that symmetry in DNA produces symmetry in the intermediate and final forms it governs. That symmetry, he says, includes Fibonacci expression.[4]

Fibonacci certainly does appear in the final form. One of the lowest forms of animal life, the starfish, mimics the Fibonacci-based five-pointed star shown in Figure 3-8. The highest form of life, man, also mimics this form when arms and legs are spread, as depicted in Figure 11-4.[5]

The golden section is found throughout the human body. The navel, which marks the source of life for a developing fetus, divides the average adult body into Fibonacci proportion. The neck divides the distance from navel to head into Fibonacci proportion (see Figure 11-2). Dr. Robert M. Ricketts of the University of Illinois in Chicago has produced an exhaustive description

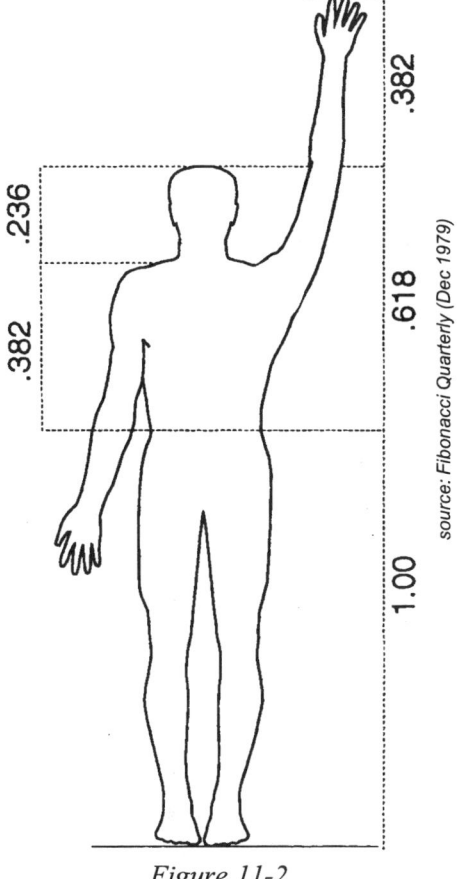

Figure 11-2

of Fibonacci relationships in the human head (see Figure 11-3).[6] Heart specialists confirm that the muscles of the left ventricle of the heart are made up of a series of spirals that repeatedly contract to a point that is approximately *62%* of the long axis from the aortic valve to the apex."[7] In the early 1960s, Drs. E.R. Weibel and D.M. Gomez meticulously measured the architecture of the lung and reported that the mean ratio of short to long tube lengths for the fifth through seventh generations of the bronchial tree is *0.62*, again the Fibonacci ratio.[8] Bruce West and Ary Goldberger have found that the diameters of the first seven generations of the bronchial tubes in the lung decrease in Fibonacci proportion.[9] Figure 11-4 is the famous drawing by Leonardo da Vinci pointing out the human body's Fibonacci proportions. Architect György Doczi summarizes the pervasive appearance of Fibonacci in the human body:

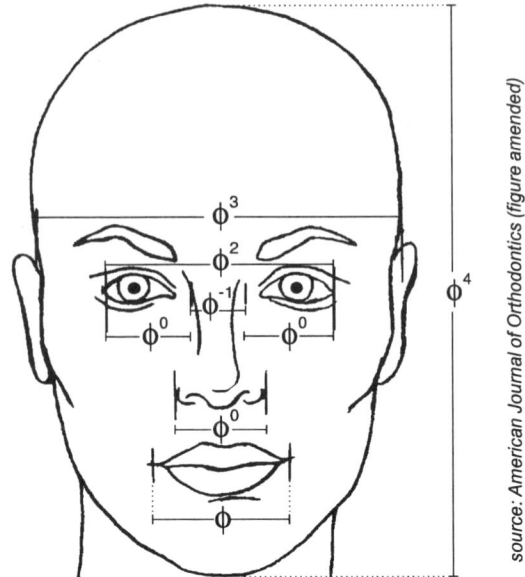

Figure 11-3

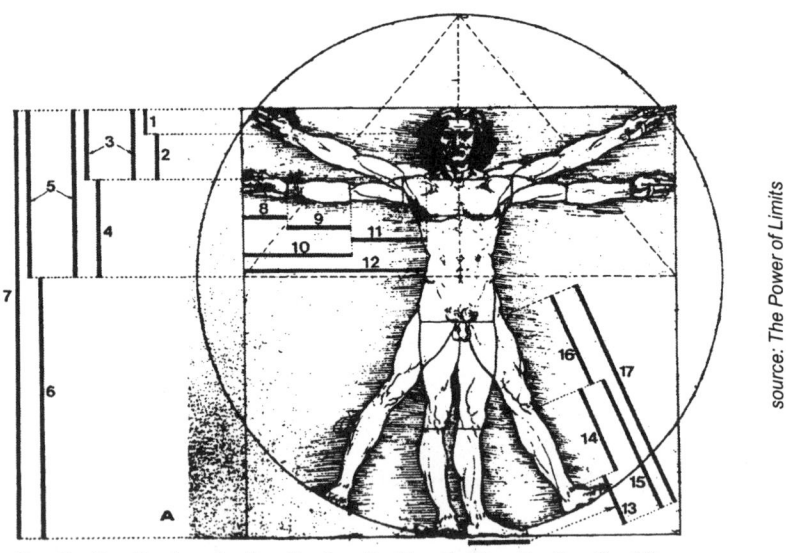

1 : 2 = 2 : 3 = 3 : 4 = 4 : 5 = 5 : 6 = 6 : 7 = 7 : 8 = 8 : 9 = 9 : 10 =
10 : 11 = 11 : 12 = 12 : 13 = 13 : 14 = 14 : 15 = 15 : 16 = 16 :17 = 0.618±

Leonardo da Vinci's depiction of Fibonacci relationships in the human body

Figure 11-4

All parts of the human body share the same proportional limitations. The length relationships of hand to arm to trunk...are shared...by
the relationships of head to neck, trunk, legs and feet. The entire human
bone structure fits neatly into three golden rectangles and a reciprocal,
the latter containing the head. We find an astonishing unity between the
proportional harmonies of the whole body and its diverse parts.[10]

From our most intimate genetic coding to our full body proportion,
we reflect the Fibonacci ratio. Is the brain so disposed as well? The answer
appears to be yes, both physiologically and functionally.

Fibonacci in the Physiology of the Brain and Nervous System

Oxford professor of mathematics Roger Penrose, who shared the Wolf
Prize for Physics in 1988 with cosmologist Stephen Hawking, presents this
discussion in his 1994 book, *Shadows of the Mind*:

The organization of mammalian microtubules is interesting from a
mathematical point of view. The number 13 might seem to have no particular mathematical significance, but this is not entirely so. It is one of
the famous Fibonacci numbers: 0, 1, 1, 2, 3, 5, 8, 13, 21, 34, 55, 89, 144,
... where each successive number is obtained as a sum of the previous
two. This might be fortuitous, but Fibonacci numbers are well known to
occur frequently (at a much larger scale) in biological systems. For example, in fir cones, sunflower heads, and palm tree trunks, one finds
spiral or helical arrangements involving the interpenetration of right-
handed and left-handed twists, where the number of rows for one handedness and the number for the other handedness are two successive
Fibonacci numbers. [See Figures 3-9 through 3-11.] (As one examines
the structures from one end to the other, one may find that a "shunt"
takes place, and the numbers then shift to an adjacent pair of successive
Fibonacci numbers.) Curiously, the skew hexagonal pattern of microtubules exhibits a very similar feature — generally of an even more precise
organization — and it is apparently found (at least normally) that this
pattern is made up of 5 right-handed and 8 left-handed helical arrangements, as depicted in [Figure 11-5]. In [Figure 11-6], I have tried to indicate how this structure might appear as actually "viewed" from within a
microtubule. The number 13 features here in its role as the sum: 5 + 8. It
is curious, also, that the double microtubules that frequently occur seem
normally to have a total of 21 columns of tubulin dimers forming the
outside boundary of the composite tube — the next Fibonacci number!

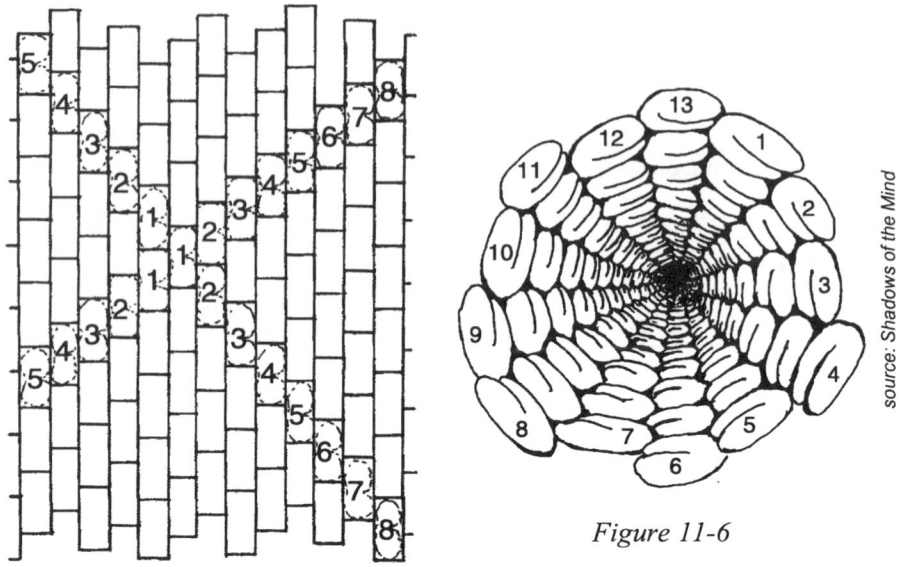

source: Shadows of the Mind

Figure 11-6

Figure 11-5

(However, one should not get carried away with such considerations; for example, the "9" that occurs in the bundles of microtubules in cilia and centrioles is *not* a Fibonacci number.)

Thus, the mammalian brain has an intricate Fibonacci expression in its microbiology.

Led by Stanley of Boston University, fifteen researchers from MIT, Harvard and elsewhere recently studied the physiology of neurons in the central nervous system with the goal of quantifying the arboration of the neurites, which are the arba of neurons. Taking the ganglion cells of a cat's retina as a model system, they find that the fractal dimension of the cells is "*1.68 + or - 0.15* using the box counting method and *1.66 + or - 0.08* using the correlation method."[11] Although the authors do not mention it, this is quite close to *phi*. Stanley *et al.* point out that this is the same as the fractal dimension for the diffusion limited aggregation (DLA) model, the generic model of diffusion through arboration (see Chapter 3). In other words, a fractal dimension of *phi* is apparently shared by all sorts of phenomena that grow according to a diffusion equation, specifically arbora such as the circulatory system, bronchial system, trees, bacteria, chemical reactions, and so forth, not the least of which is our very own brain's neurons.

Fibonacci in the Electrical Impulses of the Nervous System

It is not only the *physiology* of neurons and microtubules that reflects Fibonacci mathematics. Fibonacci appears to be expressed in the ratio of *electrical charges* within the cells of the body's nervous system. Here is a description of the electric charges of neurons from Coveney and Highfield:

> The membrane that cloaks each and every cell in the body is electrically charged because of a difference in numbers of electrically charged atoms — ions — inside and outside [of the cell].... Neurons, unlike other cells, are able to alter their electrical properties. When a signal is received from another neuron, the properties of the cell membrane change, allowing ions to travel across. Sodium ions flood in through large protein-based ion channels and the membrane potential changes rapidly *from -70 thousandths of a volt to +40 thousandths of a volt*. Although the local membrane properties change again to restore the status quo, this triggers similar changes in adjoining membrane so that a spike of electrical activity is sent out. This impulse, called an action potential, ripples along the length of the nerve.[12]

Although it does not seem to have been pointed out before, what this means is that the *peak negative charge* of the cells in each neuron is 70/110ths, or .636, and the *peak positive charge* is 40/110ths, or .364, of the entire range of its charge. These ratios are very close to the Fibonacci ratios, .618 and .382. While neuron potentials are variable from these values, the peak negative charge is always more than the peak positive charge. Given all the Fibonacci-related properties of the body, it might be prudent to investigate whether measurements of nerve cell electrical charges consistently, or on average, reflect the Fibonacci ratio.

Fibonacci as a Tool of Efficiency

Why do the brain and nervous system's innermost forms and functions exhibit Fibonacci proportions? It may be for the same reason that collective human interaction produces punctuated progress in the form of 5-3: Nature prefers the most efficient path. Quoting Penrose,

> Koruga (1974) has suggested that these Fibonacci numbers may provide advantages for the microtubule in its capacity as an "information processor." Indeed, Hameroff and his colleagues have argued, for more than a decade, that microtubules may play roles as cellular automata, where complicated signals could be transmitted and processed along the

tubes as waves of differing electric polarization states of the tubulins....
Koruga argues for a *special efficiency* in the case of a Fibonacci number-
related structure of the kind that is actually observed for microtubules.
There must indeed be some good reason for this kind of organization in
microtubules, since although there is some variation in the numbers that
apply to eukaryotic cells generally, 13 columns seems to be almost universal amongst mammalian microtubules.[13]

The Fibonacci-based style of *collective* human action that results from interactive mentation may also be a "special efficiency" of nature, just as its
inner structure and processes may be. In the case of the Wave Principle,
though, its goal is not the efficiency of an individual's biology but efficiency in the progress of the species.

Fibonacci Spirals in Neurology and Perception

Why does man's unconscious herding impulse produce a *spiral* pattern of social interaction, as revealed in Figure 2-29? The answer is that
spirals appear to be crucial to the functioning of our nervous system and
organs of perception, which at some level must be involved in the production of waves.

Like so many aspects of life, our
faculties of *perception* are replete
with spirals. As we all know from high
school biology, the cochlea of the inner ear is spiral shaped (see Figure
11-7). The sense of touch is also associated with spirals. According to an
article on a presentation by neurophysiologist Dr. Robert Thatcher,
"The receptive fields of the neurons
in our arms, legs and fingers wrap
around these surfaces in spiral bands,
similar to the sandal laces of a Roman soldier."[14]

Spiral cochlea of the ear

Figure 11-7

All physiologic sensors, including hearing, touch, taste, vision and
pain receptors, have not only spiral physiology, but also *response curves*
that are logarithmic. Hottes points out a possible larger connection:

Cellular action membrane potentials, which are important for muscles and the nervous system, have a voltage equal to the log of the ratio of the ion concentration outside the cell to that inside the cell. The brain and nervous system are made from the same type of cellular building units and look similar microscopically, *[so the response curve of] the central nervous system is probably also logarithmic.*[15]

The logarithmic-spiral nature of both the physiology and response curves of our faculties of perception apparently extends to our perception itself. Studies by E.L. Schwartz[16] show that when the brain receives spiral signals from curved surfaces on the retina, ear canal and so forth, it stores them as straight lines in a process called logarithmic conformal mapping.[17] This model of human perception, whereby the cerebral cortex translates the shapes of objects against a picture of the logarithmic spiral, offers a single answer to how the brain maintains size invariance, maintains rotational invariance, compresses information, perceives depth, perceives forms, perceives visual illusions and compares intersensory information.

What mathematical relationship do the curves on the retina have to the straight lines they represent both in reality and in the brain? A hint may come from Schwartz's estimate of the value of the parameter that characterizes the *difference* between the shape mapped on the retina and that in the brain, both in terms of magnification and deformation. Extrapolating the data from cats and monkeys, he has determined that the value of the parameter is *1.6 to 1.7.* Though he does not mention it, this is once again an expression of the Fibonacci ratio. From such data, Dr. Thatcher argues that the mind's processing and storage functions utilize as a standard against which objects are compared not just any spiral, but the *golden* spiral, whose radius increases by *phi* with each 90 degrees of rotation.

Thatcher further proposes that "Aesthetic feeling is the product of the complexity of an object and the degree of match of that object with the logarithmic spiral form in the brain." If this conclusion is true, it might explain why so many studies show that people consistently demonstrate a preference for Fibonacci proportions in objects and why so many artists throughout history, from ancient Egyptian and Greek architects to Leonardo da Vinci, have held a special fascination for Fibonacci relationships, consciously including them in their creations.

The link between all the forms and processes discussed in this Chapter is their Fibonacci component. Taken together, these studies indicate

that the Fibonacci-based *physiology* of animals' apparati of mentation and perception is intimately related to their Fibonacci-based *processes* of mentational impulse transmission and perception. If that is true, then perhaps we should be open to the idea that a *product* of impulsive mentation, i.e., the Wave Principle, has a Fibonacci-based form. The golden spiraling aspect of the Wave Principle (see Figure 2-29) is certainly compatible with the way the nervous system uses the spiraling physiology of the senses to translate reality into golden-spiral constructs and from there into mental perceptions. We might postulate at this point that when a number of individual human nervous systems interact in a social setting, individual differences, which are ruled primarily by the rational cerebral cortex, cancel out so that the collective net result is an unconscious Fibonacci-based spiraling and fractal progression of emotions and activity that reflects what all human nervous systems share in common: a set of Fibonacci-based spiraling and fractal structures and processes. Chapter 12 will bring these ideas to their culmination.

NOTES

1 According to Professor Guido Pincheira, when the researcher who measured these lengths in DNA was asked if he thought that with better measurements, the actual ratio of angstroms would be .618, he replied (off the record), "Of course!"

2 Stanley, H.E., *et al.* (1993). "Fractal landscapes in physics and biology." *Growth patterns in physical sciences and biology.*

3 The researchers calculated the correlation α of Figure 10-1 as follows: "We calculated a from the slope of double logarithmic plots of the mean square fluctuation $F(1)$ as a function of the linear distance 1 along the DNA chain for a broad range of representative genomic and cDNA sequences across the phylogenetic spectrum. In addition, we analyzed other sequences encoding a variety of other proteins as well as regulatory DNA sequences. We discovered that remarkably long-range correlations ($\alpha > 1/2$) are characteristic of intron-containing genes and non-transcribed genomic regulatory elements. In contrast, for cDNA sequences and genes without introns, we find that $\alpha \cong 1/2$ indicating no long-range correlations. Thus, the calculation of $F(1)$ for the DNA walk representation provides a new, quantitative method to distinguish genes with multiple introns from intron-less genes and cDNA based solely on their statistical properties. The finding of long-range correlations in intron-containing genes appears to be independent of the particular gene or the encoded protein — it is observed in genes as disparate as myosin heavy chain, beta globin and adenovirus. The functional (and structural) role of introns remains uncertain, and although our discovery does not resolve the "intron-late" vs. "intron-early" controversy about gene evolution, it does reveal intriguing fractal properties of genome organizations that need to be accounted for by any such theory." [ref: Stanley, *et al.*, "Fractal landscapes in physics and biology." *Growth patterns in physical sciences and biology.*]

4 Pincheira, G. (1997, November 27). Speech: "In the genome, symmetry seems to code symmetry."

5 If the head continues to grow through evolution, subsequent species may look even more like starfish (or Coneheads)!

6 Ricketts, R.M. (1982, May). "The biologic significance of the divine proportion and Fibonacci series." *American Journal of Orthodontics*, Vol. 81, No. 5, pp. 351-370.

7 My source is Dr. Glenn Freisen of Amarillo, Texas.

8 Weibel, E.R. (1962). "Architecture of the human lung." *Science*, No. 137 and (1963) *Morphometry of the human lung.*

9 West, B.J. and Goldberger, A.L. (1987, July/August). "Physiology in fractal dimensions." *American Scientist,* Vol. 75.

10 Doczi, G. (1981). *The power of limits.*

11 Stanley, H.E., *et al.* (1993). "Fractal landscapes in physics and biology." *Growth patterns in physical sciences and biology.*

12 Coveney, P. and Highfield R. (1995). *Frontiers of complexity,* p. 289.

13 Penrose, R. (1994). *Shadows of the mind.*

14 McIlvride, B. (1986, March 10-16). *MIU Review,* Vol. 1, No. 27.

15 Personal letter from F.A. Hottes to R. Prechter, August 21, 1996.

16 Schwartz, E.L. (1980). "Computational anatomy and functional architecture of striate cortex: a spatial mapping approach to perceptual coding." *Vision Res.,* Vol. 20, pp. 643-669. And (1980) "A quantitative model of the functional architecture of human striate cortex..." *Biol. Cybern.,* Vol. 37, pp. 63-76.

17 Experiments by Mario Markus of the Max Planck Institute for Molecular Physiology and Jack D. Cowan reveal that people experiencing hallucinations or who are under the influence of LSD often perceive spirals. Apparently, neurons' electrical impulses at such times bypass the brain's mapping function, thereby failing to translate the spirals into straight lines. [ref: Cowan, J.D. (1982). "Spontaneous symmetry breaking in large scale nervous activity." *International Journal of Quantum Chemistry,* No. 22, pp. 1059-1082.]

Chapter 12

Mentational Connections to the Fibonacci Foundation of the Wave Principle

A Fibonacci Influence in Individuals' Decision-Making Tendencies

Do our Fibonacci-structured neurons and microtubules and our Fibonacci-spiraled systems of perception and mental mapping in fact participate in Fibonacci patterns of mentation? Can we quantify what Smith, et. al (see endnote 8-18) term "endogenous expectations"? Perhaps the most rigorous work in this area has been performed by psychologists in a series of studies on choice. G.A. Kelly proposed in 1955 that every person evaluates the world around him using a system of bipolar constructs.[1] When judging others, for instance, one end of each pole represents a maximum positive trait and the other a maximum negative trait, such as honest/dishonest, strong/weak, etc. Kelly had assumed that average responses in value-neutral situations would be 0.50. He was wrong. Experiments show a human bent toward favor or optimism that results in a response ratio in value-neutral situations of 0.62, which is *phi*. Numerous binary-choice experiments have reproduced this finding, regardless of the type of constructs or the age, nationality or background of the subjects. To name just a few, the ratio of 62/38 results when choosing "and" over "but" to link character traits, when evaluating factors in the work environment, and in the frequency of cooperative choices in the prisoner's dilemma.[2]

Psychologist Vladimir Lefebvre of the School of Social Sciences at the University of California in Irvine and Jack Adams-Webber of Brock University corroborate these findings. When Lefebvre asks subjects to choose between two options about which they have no strong feelings and/ or little knowledge, answers tend to divide into Fibonacci proportion: 62%

to 38%. When he asks subjects to sort indistinguishable objects into two piles, they tend to divide them into a 62/38 ratio. When Adams-Webber asks subjects to evaluate their friends and acquaintances in terms of bipolar attributes, they choose the positive pole 62% of the time on average.[3] When he asks a subject to decide how many of his own attributes another shares, the average commonality assigned is 0.625.[4] When subjects are given scenarios that require a moral action and asked what percentage of people would take good actions vs. bad actions, their answers average 62%.[5] "When people say they feel 50/50 on a subject," Lefebvre says, "chances are it's more like 62/38."[6] If this is so, then *the Wave Principle may be a product not only of a herding impulse prompted by human interaction but also of a summation of a Fibonacci tendency in decision-making within individuals.*

Lefebvre concludes from these findings, "We may suppose that in a human being, there is a special algorithm for working with codes *independent of particular objects*."[7] This language fits MacLean's conclusion and LeDoux's confirmation (see Chapter 8) that the limbic system can produce emotions and attitudes that are independent of objective referents in the cortex.[8]

In pursuing the question of "whether we can quantify belief," Lefebvre has devised an ingenious quantitative model of the opinion function.[9] He proposes that human reflexion is multi-tiered, so that a person can have no image of himself, an image of himself, or an image of himself plus an image of himself imaging himself, and so on. A person can also have no image of another person, an image of another person, or an image of another person plus an image of the other person having an image of him, and so on. According to the bipolar model, each of these tiers of image can be either positive or negative. Lefebvre shows that when the tiers are combined, his model in neutral situations predicts imaging ratios between .6172 and .6180, depending upon the theoretical constraints employed. This prediction is consistent with the experiments that produce this ratio. His model also predicts the net results of judgments when the images of those being judged are skewed toward "good" or "bad." The mean result of these skewed tests, involving an equal number of good and bad images, is .618, showing that even in taking account objective data, subjects still skew their judgments positively, on average, by *phi*.

When subjects are asked to rate objects in between valueless poles, *phi* shows up in an even more interesting way. For instance, one might

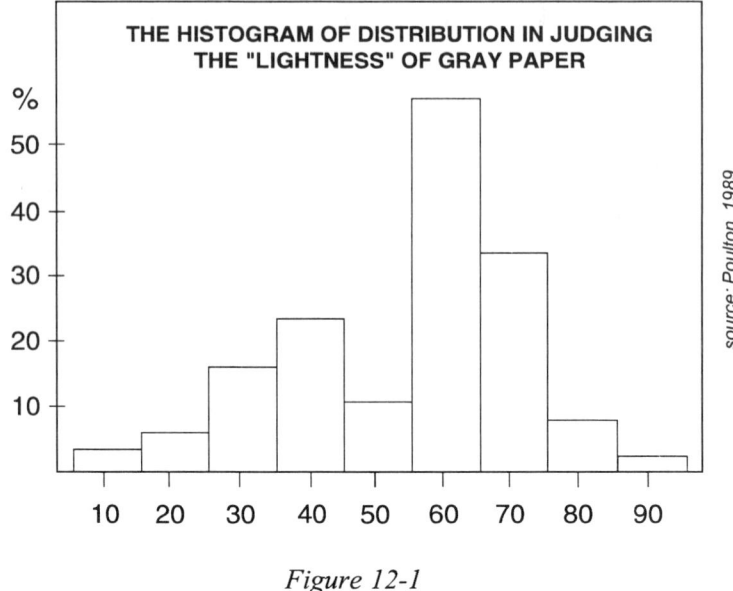

Figure 12-1

presume that if subjects were asked to evaluate the "lightness" of gray paper against solid white and solid black, that the results would produce a bell curve. In fact, however, subjects persistently avoid the middle of the spectrum and tend to mark it either 62% or 38% light.[10] (See Figure 12-1.)

Chapter 9 discusses the phenomenon of habituation, which is the process of becoming familiar. As it turns out, the very process of mental habituation skews people's positive judgment *in favor of the known* by *phi*.[11] When American subjects are asked to guess whether supposed (but actually fake) Chinese characters represent positive or negative attributes, they rate those characters to which they had previously been exposed a number of times as "positive" 63% of the time.[12] Lefebvre posits that when subjects have any excuse at all to do so, they create a bipolar mental construct weighted by the Fibonacci ratio. In this case, subjects divide the characters into two classes: "very well known" and "not very well known," *because that is the only difference between them that they can discern.* They then judge their positivity accordingly, assigning the "known" characters a positive value, on average at the 0.63 point along the scale, even though this aspect of the objects is irrelevant to the question they are attempting to answer. Simple familiarity, then, is enough to predetermine a positive evaluative skew. Chapter 8 discusses the tendency of animals and

people to favor individuals who are like themselves, in other words, familiar. This experiment shows that this bias is weighted by *phi*.

Fibonacci bipolar weighting is independent of the faculty of visual perception. When subjects first move an object a certain distance and then are blindfolded and asked to move the same object half that distance, they move it on average to a spot that is 0.615 of the original distance.[13] As Lefebvre concludes:

> The experiment demonstrated that the phenomenon of the golden section is related not to the primary processing of visual information, *but rather to the work of the central processor* operating with "generalized information."[14]

This is the same "central processor" that is involved in the production of Elliott waves.

If these statistics reveal something about human thought, they suggest that in many, perhaps all, individual humans, and certainly in an aggregate average, *opinion is predisposed to a 62/38 inclination*. With respect to each individual decision, the availability of pertinent data, the influence of prior experiences and/or learned biases can modify that ratio in any given instance. However, *phi is what the mind starts with*. It *defaults* to phi whenever parameters are unclear or information insufficient for an utterly objective assessment.

This is important data because it shows a Fibonacci decision-based mentation tendency in *individuals*. If individual mentation reflects *phi*, then it is less of a leap to accept that the Wave Principle, which also reflects *phi*, is one of its products. To narrow that step even further, we must be satisfied that *phi* appears in *group* mentation in the real world.

Fibonacci in Collective Mentation, Including the Stock Market

Does Fibonacci-patterned decision-making mentation in individuals result in a Fibonacci-patterned decision-making mentation in collectives? Data from the 1930s and the 1990s suggests that it does.

Lefebvre and Adams-Webber's experiments show unequivocally that the more individuals' decisions are summed, the smaller is the variance from *phi*. In other words, while individuals may vary somewhat in the *phi*-based bias of their bipolar decision-making, a large sum of such decisions reflects *phi* quite precisely. In a real-world social context, Lefebvre notes by example, the median voting margin in California ballot initiatives over

100 years is 62%. The same ratio holds true in a study of all referenda in America over a decade[15] as well as referenda in Switzerland from 1886 to 1978.[16]

In the early 1930s, before any such experiments were conducted or models proposed, stock market analyst Robert Rhea undertook a statistical study of bull and bear markets from 1896 to 1932. He knew nothing of Fibonacci, as his work in financial markets predated R.N. Elliott's discovery of the Fibonacci connection by eight years. Thankfully, he published the results despite, as he put it, seeing no immediate practical value for the data. Here is his summary:

> Bull markets were in progress 8143 days, while the remaining 4972 days were in bear markets. The relationship between these figures tends to show that bear markets run **61.1 percent** of the time required for bull periods.... The bull market['s]...net advance was 46.40 points. [It] was staged in four primary swings of 14.44, 17.33, 18.97 and 24.48 points respectively. The sum of these advances is 75.22. If the net advance, 46.40, is divided into the sum of advances, 75.22, the result is **1.621**. The total of secondary reactions retraced **62.1 percent** of the net advance.[17]

To generalize his findings, the stock market on average advances by **1s** and retreats by **.618s**, *in both price and time.*

Lefebvre and others' work showing that people have a natural tendency to make choices that are 61.8% *optimistic* and 38.2% *pessimistic* directly reflects Robert Rhea's data indicating that bull markets tend both to move prices and to endure 62% relative to bear markets' 38%. Bull markets and bear markets are the quintessential expressions of optimism and pessimism in an overall net-neutral environment for judgment. Moreover, they are created by a very large number of people, whose individual differences in decision-making style cancel each other out to leave a picture of pure Fibonacci expression, the same result produced in the aggregate in bipolar decision-making experiments. *As rational cogitation would never produce such mathematical consistency, this picture must come from the impulsive paleomentation of the limbic system, the part of the brain that induces herding.*

While Rhea's data need to be confirmed by more statistical studies, prospects for their confirmation appears bright. For example, in their 1996 study on log-periodic structures in stock market data, Sornette and Johansen investigate successive oscillation periods around the time of the 1987 crash and find that each period (t_n) equals a value (λ) to the power of the period's

place in the sequence (n), so that $t_n = \lambda^n$. They then state outright the significance of the Fibonacci ratio that they find for λ:

> The "Elliott wave" technique...describes the time series of a stock price as made of different "waves." These different waves are in relation with each other through the Fibonacci series, [whose numbers] converge to a constant (the so-called golden mean, 1.618), implying an approximate geometrical series of time scales in the underlying waves. [This idea is] *compatible with our above estimate for the ratio $\lambda \cong 1.5\text{-}1.7$.*[18]

This phenomenon of *time* is the same as the one that R.N. Elliott described for *price* swings in the 1930-1939 period as recounted in Chapter 5 (see Figure 5-2).

In the past three years, modern researchers have conducted experiments that further demonstrate Elliott's observation that *phi* and the stock market are connected. The October 1997 *New Scientist* reports on a study that concludes that the stock market's Hurst exponent,[19] which characterizes its fractal dimension, is *0.65*.[20] This number is quite close to the Fibonacci ratio. However, since that time, the figure for financial auction-market activity has gotten even closer. *Europhysics Letters* has just published the results of a market simulation study by European physicists Caldarelli, Marsili and Zhang. Although the simulation involves only a dozen or so subjects at a time trading a supposed currency relationship, the resulting price fluctuations mimic those in the stock market. Upon measuring the fractal persistence of those patterns, the authors come to this conclusion:

> The scaling behavior of the price "returns"...is very similar to that observed in a real economy. These distributions [of price differences] satisfy the scaling hypothesis...with an exponent of $H = 0.62$.[21]

The Hurst exponent of this group dynamic, then, is *0.62*. Although the authors do not mention the fact, this is the Fibonacci ratio. Recall from Chapter 11 that the fractal dimension of our neurons is *phi*. These two studies show that the fractal dimension of the stock market is related to *phi*. *The stock market, then, has the same fractal dimensional factor as our neurons, and both of them are the Fibonacci ratio.* This is powerful evidence that our neurophysiology is compatible with, and therefore intimately involved in, the generation of the Wave Principle.

Lefebvre explains why scientists are finding *phi* in every aspect of both average individual mentation and collective mentation:

The golden section results from the iterative process. ...Such a process must appear [in mentation] when two conditions are satisfied: (a) alternatives are polarized, that is, one alternative plays the role of the *positive pole* and the other one that of the *negative pole*; and (b) there is no criterion for the utilitarian preference of one alternative over the other.[22]

This description fits people's mental struggle with the stock market, it fits people's participation in social life in general, and it fits the Wave Principle.

It is particularly intriguing that the study by Caldarelli *et al.* purposely excludes all external input of news or "fundamentals." In other words, it purely records "all the infighting and ingenuity of the players in trying to outguess the others."[23] As Lefebvre's work anticipates, subjects in such a nonobjective environment default to *phi, which Elliott's model and the latest studies say is exactly the number to which they default in real-world financial markets.*

Phi Dimensionality as a Property Only of Robust Fractals

Clouds and mountains, which are indefinite fractals, have a Hurst exponent near 0.8. The studies cited in the previous section show that neurons (which grow as arbora) and the stock market (which grows as waves) have a Hurst exponent related to *phi*. These studies prompt me to suggest the hypothesis that fractal objects that manifest as arbora or waves, i.e., the fractal objects of growth and expansion, will have a Hurst exponent related to *phi*, setting them apart from other fractal objects, which will have other Hurst exponents. What this means is that *robust fractal objects split the difference between two Euclidean dimensions by .618*, while other fractal objects do not.

Putting the Fibonacci Data Together

Chapter 11 concludes that the Fibonacci-based biological structure of animals' apparati of perception and mentation are related to a Fibonacci-based logarithmic conformal mapping process that translates input from the senses into mental images via the golden spiral. At this point, we can add that in turn, all of these aspects appear to be involved in producing *a Fibonacci-based form of both individual and collective mentation.*

Now we come to the concluding point of the last three chapters. We know that both in their arboral form and in the range of their pulsating

electrical charges, our neurons have Fibonacci properties. We know that our spiraling apparati of perception and their paths of transmission via microtubules have Fibonacci properties. We know that our process of perception, i.e., the translation of reality into mental images via logarithmic conformal mapping, has Fibonacci properties. We know that our individual mentation, in the form of decision-making biases, has Fibonacci properties. We know that our collective interaction in a social setting has Fibonacci properties. We have the work of R.N. Elliott, who discovered, *before any of the above was known*, that the form of mankind's evaluation of his own productive enterprise (i.e., the stock market) has Fibonacci properties. Finally, we have my work and resulting contention, which will be explored in Part IV of this book, that the stock market is a direct recording of social mood change, which is the engine of social action, which in turn produces events that constitute history. This means that ultimately, the growth pattern of mankind has Fibonacci properties.

Throughout nature, countless animate forms and processes involved in growth and decay as well as inanimate forms involved in expansion and contraction are governed by *phi*. Given the findings of modern science here collected, it should no longer be considered speculative, much less mystical, to propose that mankind's pattern of progress through history is following this same law of nature. I would like to add that, given the chain of connection elucidated in this chapter, the natural and social sciences should nevermore be considered as distinctly different as traditionally thought.

NOTES

1 Kelly, G.A. (1955). *The psychology of personal constructs*, Vols. 1 and 2.

2 Osgood, C.E., and M.M. Richards (1973). *Language*, 49, pp. 380-412; Shalit, B. (1960). *British Journal of Psychology*, 71, pp. 39-42; Rapoport, A. and A.M. Chammah (1965). *Prisoner's dilemma*.

3 Adams-Webber, J. and Benjafield, J. (1973). "The relation between lexical marking and rating extremity in interpersonal judgment." *Canadian Journal of Behavioral Science*, Vol. 5, pp. 234-241.

4 Adams-Webber, J. (1997, Winter). "Self-reflexion in evaluating others." *American Journal of Psychology*, Vol. 110, No. 4, pp. 527-541.

5 McGraw, K.M. (1985). "Subjective probabilities and moral judgments." *Journal of Experimental and Biological Structures*, #10, pp. 501-518.

6 Washburn, J. (1993, March 31). "The human equation." *The Los Angeles Times*.

7 Lefebvre, V.A. (1987, October). "The fundamental structures of human reflexion." *The Journal of Social Biological Structure*, Vol. 10, pp. 129-175.

8 **More Evidence of Fibonacci in Human Relationships:** Even in the relationship between men and women we find the Fibonacci ratio. For instance, according to the U.S. Department of Labor, the (relatively) free market in the United States tends to pay women, on average, about 62% of the wages that it pays men for an hour of work. This is probably an expression of the difference between their proclivity for productivity. Feminists who deny differences of economic value between the sexes advocate male chauvinist conspiracy theories to explain the discrepancy. Without debating such theories, if they are true, its advocates must still concede that women let themselves be railroaded to that extent, which brings us back to the fact that there is a Fibonacci difference between the sexes of *some* type. Applying either theory, the productivity difference is a function of a difference in attitude either toward production or toward bullying by the other sex. The average earnings ratio, we must keep in mind, does not speak to either sex's *total* value, just its value in the productive context. Given the evidence in this book, we might expect to be surprised if the average difference in male and female attitudes and abilities were *not* phi.

9 Lefebvre, V.A. (1990). "The fundamental structure of human reflexion." In H. Wheeler, *The structure of human reflexion* (pp. 5-70). and Lefebvre, V.A., "A rational equation of attractive proportions," *Journal of Mathematical Psychology*, 36, 100-128.

10 Poulton, E.C., *et al.* (1968). "Response bias in very first judgments of the reflectance of grays." *Perception and Psychophysics*, Vol. 3, pp. 112-114.

11 Zajonc, R.B. (1968). "Attitudinal effects of mere exposure." *Journal of Personality and Social Psychology.* Monograph supplement, 9, No. 2, Part 2, pp. 1-32.

12 Lefebvre, V.A. (1997). *The cosmic subject.*

13 Bigava, Z.I. (1979). "A character of setting effects in various moving problems." In: Nadirashvili, S.A. (Ed.), *Voprosy Inzhenernoy I Socialnoy Psychologii (Problems of Human Factor and Social Psychology, in Russian)*, ii Tbilisi: Metsniereba.

14 Lefebvre, V.A. (1997). *The cosmic subject.*

15 Lefebvre, V.A. (1992). *A psychological theory of bipolarity and reflexivity.* and Lefebvre, V.A. (1997). *The cosmic subject.*

16 Butler, D. and Ranney, A. (1978). Referendums Washington, D.C., American Enterprise Institute for Public Policy Research.

17 Rhea, R. (1934). *The story of the averages.* (See discussion in Chapter 4 of *Elliott Wave Principle* by Frost and Prechter.)

18 Sornette, D., *et al.* (1996). "Stock market crashes, precursors and replicas." *Journal de Physique I France* 6, No.1, pp. 167-175.

19 The Hurst exponent (H), named for its developer, Harold Edwin Hurst [ref: Hurst, H.E., *et al.* (1951). *Long term storage: an experimental study*] is related to the fractal, or Hausdorff dimension (D) by the following formula, where E is the embedding Euclidean dimension (2 in the case of a plane, 3 in the case of a space): $D = E - H$. It may also be stated as $D = E + 1 - H$ if E is the *generating* Euclidean dimension (1 in the case of a line, 2 in the case of a plane). Thus, if the Hurst exponent of a line graph is .38, or ϕ^{-2}, then the fractal dimension is 1.62, or ϕ; if the Hurst exponent is .62, or ϕ^{-1}, then the fractal dimension is 1.38, or $1 + \phi^{-2}$. [source: Schroeder, M. (1991). *Fractals, chaos, power laws.*] Thus, if H is related to ϕ, so is D.

20 Brooks, M. (1997, October 18). "Boom to bust." *New Scientist.*

21 Caldarelli, G., *et al.* (1997). "A prototype model of stock exchange." *Europhysics Letters*, 40 (5), pp. 479-484.

22 Lefebvre, V.A. (1998, August 18-20). "Sketch of reflexive game theory," from the proceedings of *The Workshop on Multi-Reflexive Models of Agent Behavior* conducted by the Army Research Laboratory.

23 Caldarelli, G., *et al.* (1997, December 1). "A prototype model of stock exchange." *Europhysics Letters*, 40 (5), pp. 479-484.

Chapter 13:

From Long Waves to Rapid Vibration: The Motor of Life?

The Long-Term Transmission of Cultural Images

In Chapter 5, we saw that the Wave Principle operates over decades. In Chapter 9, we read theories of how ideas, images, hopes and fears propagate through a population. Can we tie these two facts together?

How is it that social wave structures develop over the *very long term*? After all, the people who were participating actively in society many decades ago certainly are not doing so today. How can something that people did years or decades or even centuries ago have anything whatsoever to do with what is going on in the society now? Before formulating an answer, I would like to present a paragraph from a newspaper column on the aftermath of a football game from sportswriter Mark Bradley that will illustrate my answer. In November 1984, the Florida Gators won the Southeastern Conference football championship for the first time in the fifty-year history of that university's participation in the SEC. Here is how Bradley described the scene:

> And when the scoreboard clock struck zero, five decades of frustration burst into five minutes of glorious joy. Gerald Wilkins, a reserve linebacker, sprinted to midfield, flung himself to the turf and writhed in ecstasy. Elaine Hall, the coach's wife, leaped to kiss Lomus Brown, the defensive tackle, on the cheek. On the chilled sideline, Alonzo Johnson bent at the waist and clutched his belly with his hands, trying to hold the moment inside. When he straightened up, it was clear he had failed: the rough, tough Florida linebacker was crying, weeping not only for the SEC championship the Gators had won, but for the fifty others they hadn't. Fittingly, it didn't come easy. To have waited fifty years and then won easily wouldn't have purged Gator souls the way Saturday's victory did.[1]

What on earth was going on here? These players were kids, nineteen or twenty years old. They had not even been alive for most of the previous games. They had been playing football at the university an average of only two years, so were unassociated with 96% of the previous seasons. The people in the stands, many of whom were students, could not have gone to every game for fifty years and cried over the losses. What happened?

Think about Bradley's phrase, "purged Gator souls." What had taken place was a cultural transmission of the experiences of the University of Florida's football team through fifty years to all the associated students, commentators, university officials, coaches, players and fans. Anyone who became involved with the university had been fully indoctrinated with the history of the team, undoubtedly in a matter of months. Each person readily incorporated and assimilated all of that information, and his limbic system processed it into a gut emotional feeling. *The sum total of those feelings erupted orgasmically at the end of the 1984 season with such energy and emotion that it was as if each participant had personally lost or witnessed the loss of every one of those championships until that year and had experienced the anguish that went with it.*

I think that in the same way, transmission of all kinds of cultural experiences and values takes place over the years, over the decades, and even over the centuries. How else can we account for the fact that some Southerners still resent Yankees for the Civil War or that some Muslims still resent Christians for the Crusades, events that took place over a century and nearly a millennium ago, respectively?

Social mood and experience has a memory. That is why waves continue to form at the highest observable degrees. Their antecedents provide the raw material for each new impulse and correction. Waves, then, represent a kind of forward-weighted summation of the human experience.

Waves In Evolution

Now let us expand the time horizon even further and investigate whether the Wave Principle governs not only the progress of *societies* but the overall progress of *all life on earth*. The September 1997 issue of *Nature* recounts a study by Per Bak, along with physicists Ricard Sole and Susanna Manrubia of the Polytechnic University of Catalonia in Barcelona and geologist Michael Benton of Bristol University, that concludes that the dynamics of species extinction have the same self-similar structure as earthquakes. "Massive extinctions happen far less frequently than tiny ones," reports the magazine, "but a graph showing the frequency of extinctions

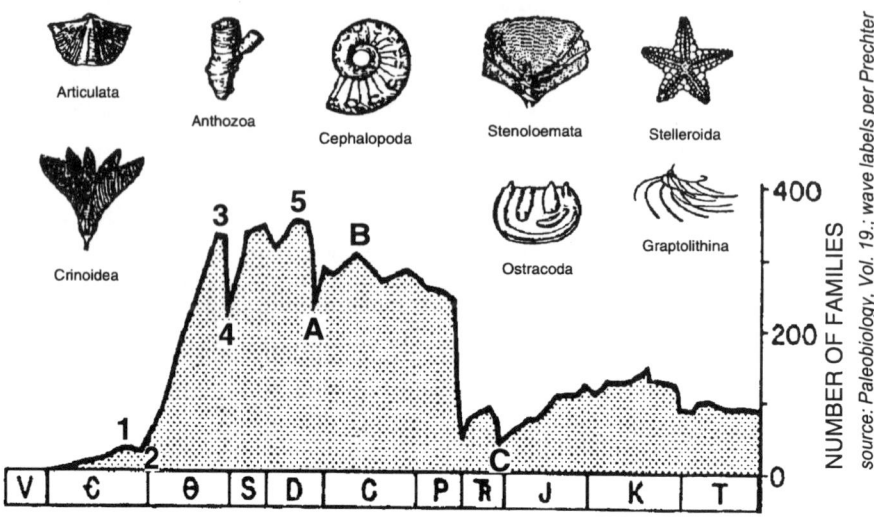

Figure 13-1

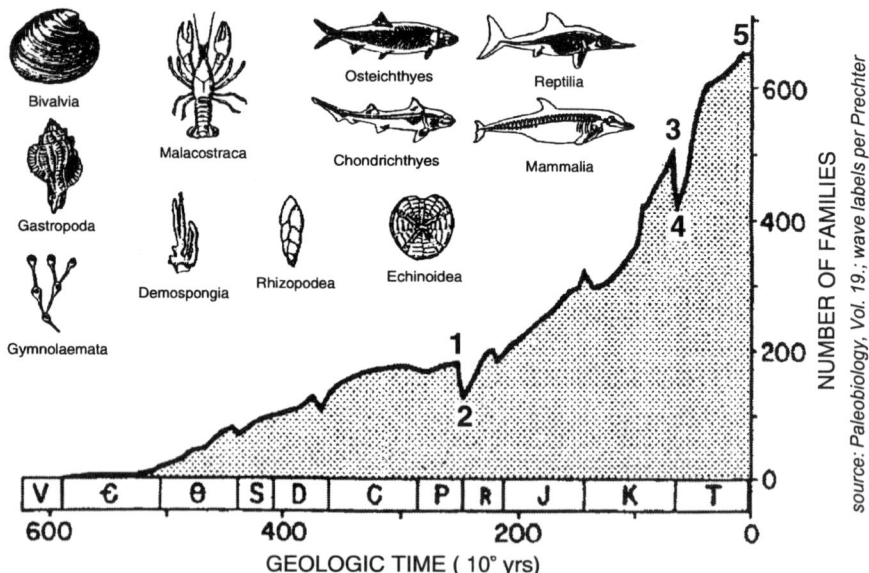

Figure 13-2

versus size closely follows a power law."[2] The researchers conclude from this fact that major extinctions can happen *without a catastrophic outside cause*.[3] In other words, evolution is a self-regulating complex dynamical system[4] that fluctuates in a fractal pattern, just as the stock market and human society in general.[5] What kind of fractal pattern of fluctuation does it produce?

Figure 13-1 is from J. John Sepkoski, Professor of Geophysical Science at the University of Chicago. It is his depiction of the estimated numbers of families of Paleozoic fauna that have existed through time. I have added wave numbers to his graph. As you can see, after five waves up, the number collapsed in three waves, with the requisite subdivisions in waves B and C. Of more interest to us, perhaps, is Figure 13-2, showing the estimated total number of families of *modern* fauna, which began to expand at the end of the Cambrian period. As you can see, it forms an excellent five-wave pattern as well. If you look closely, you can see that even the subdivisions have five waves. The occasional mass extinctions have simply been corrections in the wave-patterned progress of life on earth.

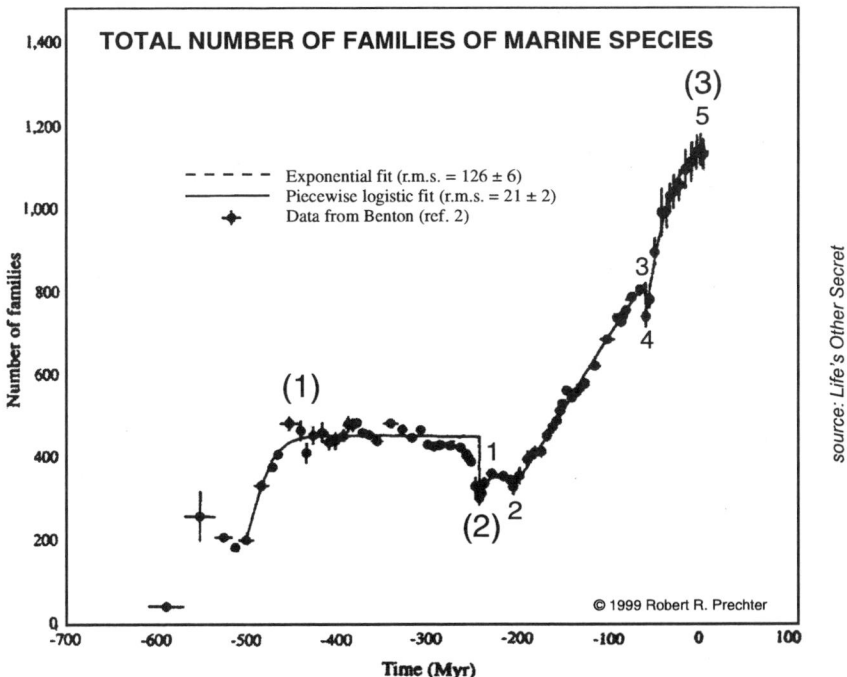

Figure 13-3

Figure 13-3 is a depiction of the total number of families of marine species throughout earth's biological era, as compiled by M.J. Benton. It shows a fair amount of detail that in turn reflects the Wave Principle. As you can see by the wave labels that I have applied to the graph, particularly the advance from 250 million years ago shows the classic five-wave form, complete with an extension in wave three.[6] From collective life's extreme micro-scales to its extreme macro-scales, there is the Wave Principle, time and again.

It is not that surprising to me that evolution develops according to the same principle that governs social systems. Societies and evolution share the essential traits of self-regulating complex dynamical systems. I contend that evolution *is* a social phenomenon, as it involves the constant intermingling of life forms. On this basis alone, I am inclined to postulate that the Wave Principle applies to *all* interactive systems of life, not just the human.

The Wave Principle in Individual Life Forms

The Wave Principle may be an even more fundamental aspect of life than that. There is evidence that it governs not only the progress of societal systems but of *individual* life forms as well. Chapters 2, 3, 10, 11 and 12 show that individual plants and animals are, or contain, fractals, golden spirals and many Fibonacci-related forms and processes. The Wave Principle *per se* is a bit more difficult to detect in individuals, but there are clues to its presence.

For instance, most animals have 5 major appendages, their overall form therefore being ruled by the same number that primarily governs the Wave Principle. The appendages of the human body reflect the Wave Principle's 5-3 progression. Of the 5 protrusions from the body, all but the head have 3 subdivisions. The final subdivisions (hands and feet) have 5 appendages. Each appendage, with two exceptions (the thumb and big toe), has 3 subdivisions. The entire structure is based upon a 5-3-5-3 alternation, just like the Wave Principle. It is as if the human body is expanding into space the way a wave advances on a graph.

There may be an expression of the Wave Principle in the development of individual plants. Germany's famous poet Johann Wolfgang von Goethe also considered himself a scientist. Whether he was a good one is a subject of controversy, but he certainly was a consummate observer with an eye for detail that rivaled R.N. Elliott's. Goethe was fascinated by nature's

constant display of creation, destruction and recreation and the possibility of finding "the ultimate secret of nature." To that end, he built a private botanical garden and closely studied the growth pattern of plants. His essay, "On the Metamorphosis of Plants," published in 1790, initiated the science of floral morphology, as well it should have. Two hundred years ago, Goethe's descriptions of plant morphology and adaptability included both their fractal aspects (see first paragraph below) and implications of evolution (see second paragraph). Pertinent to our discussion, we find that it also included a description of individual plant development that is nearly identical to a description of the Wave Principle (see third paragraph). The following is a summary of Goethe's conclusions:

> In a flash, he realized...that *all* the lateral outgrowths of the plant were simply variations of a single structure: the leaf. He saw that each organ, though outwardly changed from a similarity to a dissimilarity, had a virtual inner identity.

> Goethe saw in the changeableness of all the external characteristics of plants nothing but appearance; he drew the conclusion that...it might be possible to develop all plants from a single one. This small conceit was destined to transform the science of botany, indeed the whole concept of the world: with it came the idea of evolution. Metamorphosis was to become the key to the whole alphabet of nature. [Said Goethe,] "The plant forms around us are not predetermined, but are happily mobile and flexible, enabling them to adapt to the many conditions throughout the world, which influence them, and to be formed and re-formed with them."[7]

> Goethe also recognized that the process of development and refinement of form in plants worked through a threefold cycle of expansion and contraction. *The expansion of foliage was followed by a contraction into calyx and tracts; there followed a splendid expansion into petals of the corolla and a contraction into the meeting point of the stamen and stigma; finally there came a swelling into fruit followed by a contraction into seed. This six-step cycle completed, the essential plant was ready to start all over again.*[8]

That last paragraph is a stunning description to someone who knows the Wave Principle. It details *five waves* of progress in the form of *expansion-contraction-expansion-contraction-expansion*, which in turn is followed by a *larger contraction back to a starting point, from which the process repeats*. Even the nuances are compatible. The middle expansion into flowering is described as "splendid," which is exactly what I observed years

ago about the character of third waves. ("Third waves are wonders to behold." – Frost and Prechter, 1978) The final expansion is a "swelling into fruit," which is an excellent description of the social product of fifth waves, as shown in Figure 18-6, when society reaps, in the form of peace, abundance and goodwill, all its effort has sown during the advance. Then, the larger contraction, which follows the entire five-wave expansion, returns a portion of the plant to the starting point, just as a corrective wave returns social mood back to the starting point of a new five-wave sequence. Like the patterns in the stock market, the propagation of plants is not a cycle, but a wave to successive heights. The original plant remains intact, so the formation of new seed is much like the starting point *at a higher level* that occurs after a correction under the Wave Principle. The only apparent difference between the two processes is that the final contraction Goethe describes is a single event, whereas corrective Elliott waves subdivide into a three-wave contraction-expansion-contraction sequence.[9]

Might the same progression occur in animals, including humans? We already know from Chapters 2 and 10 that plants and animals share the presence of fractals, from Chapters 3 and 11 that plants and animals share the presence of spirals and Fibonacci mathematics. All these correlations indicate that the mathematics of the growth and form of plants and animals are not that different. Do humans also develop in five waves? Let us give it a try.

Highly speculative as it may be, I can describe human development the same way that Goethe described the development of plants. There are the first two years of growth, then a setback in the "terrible twos" (particularly in boys), a longer period of flowering in the child, the emotional setback of the early teens (particularly in girls), and the final maturation, both mentally and physically, the "swelling into fruit" of the adult, containing the seeds of the next generation. When that person has a child, the cycle begins again.

This five-wave pattern of progress and setback, which fits both plant and human life, admits the possibility that the Wave Principle governs not only the pattern of progress for living *aggregates* but also the pattern of progress for *individual life forms*, thus covering the entire spectrum of life. Indeed, Goethe concluded that he had outlined "the manifold specific phenomena in the magnificent garden of the universe back to *one simple general principle. ...The same law can be applied to everything living.*"[10] The purpose of this book is likewise to show that there is one simple general principle

that can be applied to everything living, and to describe it. I do not believe it to be coincidence that in its essence, *the description of the principle in each case is the same*. On this basis, I am inclined to postulate further that the Wave Principle governs the progress of *all* forms of life, not just societal systems.

The Implication of Continual Wave Subdivision

In the first part of this chapter, we examined the progression of waves over the very long term. Now we will examine the other end of the spectrum.

In Chapter 1, we saw that the Wave Principle operates over very *brief* times, as in Figure 2-1, which is a graph of every single incremental price change in the stock averages, the smallest scale of our data. In Chapters 10 and 11, we saw that our neurons have a fractal and Fibonacci-based construction and function. Can we tie these two facts together?

How is it that social wave structures develop over the *very short term*? In a 1987 speech, I provided this description of a five-minute trading pattern on the floor of the exchange:

> Let's say that there has been a bear market going on for a week. Now, to a pit trader, that's a major bear market: five straight trading days of declining prices, with small rallies along the way. It's already worn him out. One day, the traders are watching the tape, and it's kind of slow because volume has receded during the decline. Suddenly, the market seems to be stalled out. A couple of traders who have been there the longest, you know, the grizzled old guys that really know the game, who have been there for almost two whole years, are watching the tape from the back of the room, and they say, "buy me ten, buy me fifty, buy me a hundred." A few heads turn because these are pretty good-sized lots. Sure enough, the market starts to tick up a little bit. Then it stops again and starts to recede very slowly. Most people are saying, "Ah, it's the same old stuff, a rally and a decline; it's going to come back to new lows just like it's been doing for a week. Forget it." They take another bite of their sandwiches and keep half an eye on the board. This is the point of lethargy and conviction that marks a second wave. Soon they notice that the market isn't making a new low; it's holding at a higher bottom. Well, to traders, that's a fundamental news event. They start watching more closely, and all of a sudden, they get a bit excited, and one or two orders pop out. Then the floodgates open. They are screaming and yelling buy orders, and sure enough, prices are roaring up. It's a broad, powerful

third wave. It goes on for a full minute and a half but ends abruptly, and another reaction sets in. Guys who bought late have a small loss. It is the fourth wave's "surprising disappointment." Now, behind the scenes, over in the corner, there are some younger traders, who have been trading for only about a week and a half. They have been keeping an eye on this action, saying to themselves, "Man, look at that wild move! Look at the money we could have made just then! If I'd only been long! I tell you what, if this market starts up again *one more time*, I'm gonna buy. I'm getting ready." They're watching closely, eyes riveted on the board. Sure enough, the market starts up again. Those young guys start to yell in their orders: "Buy me one! Buy me one!" The market jumps to a new high. Orders from Merrill Lynch finally make it down to the floor, ending the flood as the fifth wave culminates. The old guys who started it all croak from the back, "Sell me ten, sell me fifty, sell me a hundred," and the five-wave move is over.

That chain of events is descriptive for a five-minute period, but it does not carry far enough. What about a five-*second* period? The compound construction of the Wave Principle implies, and perhaps demands, that the tiniest waves that we can plot in turn subdivide, and those in turn subdivide, and so on. Ultimately, it suggests that men's minds, in concert with others, must be *vibrating* in wave patterns between impulse and correction at the minutest scales of mental activity.

Is this implication sensible, or does it lead to an absurdity? We know that the nervous system both controls and is run by electrical impulses whose positive and negative charges appear to be in Fibonacci proportion. We know that these impulses travel via Fibonacci-organized microtubules as "*waves* of differing electric polarization states of the tubulins."[11] So the *electrical impulses* in the nervous system as well as the *physiological path they travel* in the form of *vibrating waves of polarization* are suffused with Fibonacci properties. Is it not possible that some of those waves at the minutest scale are also suffused with Fibonacci properties, i.e., that they vibrate in a 5-3 pattern that ultimately generates the Wave Principle? Perhaps this hypothesis could be stated more crisply, but at least there may be enough here to justify designing an experiment to test the idea of Fibonacci-patterned neurological vibration.

Since I have been speculating quite wildly, I might as well go all the way and suggest that infinitesimal Elliott waves of patterned electrical vibration may be the essence of consciousness, or perhaps even of animation.

If so, the Wave Principle may govern not only the *progress* of all forms of life but *the essence of life itself.*[12]

In Chapter 21, we shall investigate astronomer Andrei Linde's proposal that the entire universe is a robust fractal and psychologist Vladimir Lefebvre's observation that certain astronomic activity mimics an aspect of human mentation. In the context of his suggestion that different universes may have different physics, Linde asks,

> Does this mean that understanding all the properties of our region of the universe will require, besides a knowledge of physics, a deep investigation of *our own nature*, perhaps even *including the nature of our consciousness*? This conclusion would certainly be one of the most unexpected that one could draw from the recent developments in inflationary cosmology.[13]

The Wave Principle, which describes the social product of interactive unconscious mentation, is a crucial aspect of that proposed investigation. Since the Wave Principle influences collective animation (see Chapters 15 and 16) and, as we saw in this chapter, may even be the essence of individual animation, it is unquestionably a crucial aspect of the investigation into the essential nature of our mental function.

NOTES

1 Bradley, M. (1984, November 18). "At long last, Florida wins an SEC title." *The Atlanta Journal-Constitution.* Sentences are slightly rearranged.

2 Sole, R.V., *et al.* (1997, August 21). "Self-similarity of extinction statistics in the fossil record." *Nature,* Vol. 388, pp. 764-767.

3 The mechanism is as follows: Species that live on the lower end of the adaptability and viability scale die off. Upon occasion, after a number of marginal single species have died off, the number hovering at that lower end of the scale, particularly if they have a high degree of interdependence, is very large. A small environmental change can then result in many extinctions.

4 Such processes are said to display "punctuated equilibrium," a term coined in 1972 by Niles Eldredge of the American Museum of Natural History and Stephen Gould of Harvard to denote periods of stability interrupted by dramatic leaps or setbacks. However, equilibrium may not mean stasis. Land masses may be said to be at equilibrium in the absence of earthquakes, but as with evolution, the forces are never motionless. The stock market is always moving, to the point that it is difficult to designate any periods as "stable."

5 For the record, James W. Kirchner and Anne Weil of the University of California at Berkeley convincingly challenge Sole and Bak's findings with respect to the claim that extinctions follow a power law. [ref: *Nature.* (1998). No. 395, pp. 337-338. Published letter from James W. Kirchner and Anne Weil.] However this argument resolves, the graphs make my case that evolution follows the Wave Principle.

6 For a wave analyst, the implication of this pattern is obvious, though not comforting, as five waves up portends in the relatively near future the largest extinction since the one that occurred 300 to 250 million years ago. If this were a graph of the stock market, I would add that the slowing of upside rate of change in the past forty million years is a classic precursor of a reversal, which is strong support for the case that five waves are indeed ending.

7 Goethe, J.W. (1790)."On the metamorphosis of plants."

8 Tompkins, P. and Bird, C. (1973). *The secret life of plants.*

9 The fact that Goethe's description came from a man obsessed with empirics, coupled with the fact that (as far as I can tell) science has not expanded upon his description, suggests once again that intense empirical observation and inquiry of the type R.N. Elliott and Goethe practiced is a crucial, and perhaps neglected, aspect of modern science.

10   Goethe, J.W. (1790)."On the metamorphosis of plants."

11   Penrose, R. (1994). *Shadows of the mind.* (quoting Hameroff).

12   This idea recalls Eastern philosophical notions that existence *is* a tension between opposites. Perhaps we can suggest to these mystics that the opposites of yin and yang are not equal but related by *phi*, so that opposing values of .618 and .382 make the whole.

13   Linde, A. (1994, November). "The self-reproducing inflationary universe." *Scientific American.*

PART IV

AN INTRODUCTION TO
SOCIONOMICS

Part IV provides only an introduction to socionomics. I have written much more about it than is here. I hope that these chapters will present enough of a case to establish its central ideas. My next big project will be to write a more comprehensive book on the subject.

Chapter 14

Components of Mood

I hereby state at the outset of this short chapter that the ideas herein are not fully developed. It will, I expect, take another ten years to construct a full theory of the components, aspects, processes and structure of social mood. Waiting to resolve these questions would delay this book too much, so I beg your indulgence in these pages. Chapters 15 through 17 show the *results* of social mood trend so clearly that I think you will "get it" even if there is some vagueness in what it is we are "getting." I am still working on a hierarchy of terms and a more comprehensive explanation, but in the interests of getting some of these ideas out, I will present the following thoughts, which I would categorize as observational summaries at best, not yet a hypothesis.

Aspects of Social Polarity

R.N. Elliott said only that "human emotions...are rhythmical" and that their waves govern "all human activities, whether it is business, politics, or the pursuit of pleasure."[1] "Human emotions" is not a precise term. What does it really mean to say that the social mood trend is trending "up" or "down" at a particular degree? Specifically, what characteristics and emotions do waves reflect? What actual human feelings compose social mood?

There appears to be a social polarity that underlies all social interaction. We can refer to these opposites as "positive" and "negative," not simply to represent polarity but also to imply a value judgment with respect to the net social experience (though not to every aspect of it).

A good deal of empirical observation and historical investigation prompts the following list: A waxing positive social mood appears to

correlate with a collective increase in concord, inclusion, happiness, forbearance, confidence, supportiveness, adventurousness, ebullience, daring, friskiness, optimism, liberality, benevolence, sharpness of focus, practical thinking, a tendency to praise, a search for joy, an interest in love over sex, constructiveness, a desire to provide for oneself, a desire for togetherness, a desire for power over nature, feelings of homogeneity with others, clarity of thinking and emotion, embrace of effort, and feelings of alignment with others. A waxing negative social mood appears to correlate with a collective increase in discord, exclusion, unhappiness, anger, fear, opposition, protectionism, depression, defensiveness, somberness, pessimism, restriction, malevolence, dullness of focus, magical thinking, a tendency to criticize, a search for pleasure, an interest in sex over love, destructiveness, a desire for self-deprivation, a desire to separate from others, a desire for power over people, feelings of heterogeneity with others, fuzziness of thinking and emotion, avoidance of effort, and feelings of opposition toward others. The list below summarizes these polarities.

Positive mood/Negative mood

adventurousness/protectionism
alignment/opposition
benevolence/malevolence
clarity/fuzziness
concord/discord
confidence/fear
constructiveness/destructiveness
daring/defensiveness
desiring power over nature/desiring power over people
ebullience/depression
embrace of effort/avoidance of effort
forbearance/anger
friskiness/somberness
happiness/unhappiness
homogeneity/heterogeneity
inclusion/exclusion
interest in love/interest in sex
liberality/restriction
optimism/pessimism
practical thinking/magical thinking
search for joy/search for pleasure

self providence/self deprivation
sharpness of focus/dullness of focus
supportiveness/opposition
tendency to praise/tendency to criticize
togetherness/separatism

While I present these traits here in list form, I am certain that the correct depiction of these attributes and the things they cover is a tree. For instance, "clarity vs. fuzziness" has under it practical thinking vs. magical thinking styles as well as a preference for angular vs. rounded automobile styles. Similarly, "constructiveness vs. destructiveness" has under it stock market and business trends as well as trends in art and music. However, I have not fully developed this idea, which will require its own entire book, anyway. This chapter is just to give you the flavor of the two poles of social mood.

The tendencies listed above have concrete results. Here are a few examples:

(1) *Concord/Discord*: A rising mood leads to a substantial consensus in politics, culture and social vision; a falling mood leads to a divided, radical climate. After the social mood has risen for a number of years, the society tends to be peaceful; after it has fallen for a number of years, it tends to become involved in wars.

(2) *Inclusion/Exclusion*: A rising mood leads to feelings of social brotherhood and acceptance among races, religions and political territories, as well as toward animals, plants and proposed aliens. A falling mood leads to apartheid, religious animosity, cavalier cruelty, secession, independence movements and images of aliens as monsters.

(3) *Forbearance/Anger*: A rising mood leads to social expressions of acquiescence, apology and tolerance. A falling mood leads to social expressions of resistance, recrimination and intolerance.

(4) *Confidence/Fear*: A rising mood leads to speculation in the stock market and in business. A falling mood causes risk aversion in the stock market and business.

(5) *Embrace of effort/Avoidance of effort*: In a rising mood trend, people are disposed to expending effort, both mental, which elevates the use of reason, and physical, which elevates the ideal of fitness. In a falling mood trend, they are disposed to avoiding effort, which leads to magical thinking and physical laziness.

(6) *Practical thinking/Magical thinking*: Practical thinking manifests itself in philosophic defenses of reason, self-providence, individualism, peacemaking and a reverence for science. Magical thinking manifests itself in philosophic attacks on reason, self-abnegation, collectivism, witch hunts, war-making and a reverence for religion.

(7) *Constructiveness/Destructiveness*: The impulse to build shows up in the construction of record-breaking skyscraper buildings at social-mood peaks. At troughs, few buildings are built, and many of those already in place may be burned or bombed out of existence.

(8) *Desiring power over nature/Desiring power over people*: Desiring power over nature leads to a naturalistic mindset, political freedom and peaceful technological advances. Desiring power over people leads to a socialistic mindset, political repression and technological advances in warring.

The Wave Principle suggests that mankind has within its nature the seeds of social trend and social change. Men are animated by, or are animated to create, change. They desire it, or at least bring it about, even when it appears superficially that they would be better off if things stayed as they were. For example, adversity eventually breeds a desire to take responsibility, achieve and succeed, while prosperity eventually breeds irresponsibility, complacency and sloth, regardless of whether the change, considered rationally, would be a good thing.

Inclusion vs. Exclusion

To give you an idea of the far-reaching effects of a single polar continuum, let us examine just one of them: inclusion vs. exclusion. A waxing positive social mood accompanies increased inclusionary tendencies in every aspect of society, including the cultural, moral, religious, racial, economic, national, regional, social, financial and political. A waxing negative social mood accompanies increased exclusionary tendencies in every aspect of society. With that realization, you can predict increasing cooperation and acts of brotherhood in all those areas in bull markets and the opposite in bear markets.

For example, in bull markets, most people like similar styles of music; in bear markets, the dominant types are often very different. In bull markets, politics tends to be middle-of-the-road; in bear markets, radical positions gain acceptance, and the electorate becomes polarized. Free trade is encouraged in bull markets; protectionism is demanded in bear markets.

Racial harmony is promoted in bull markets, racial separation in bear markets.

Here are some concrete examples. Apartheid was made official South African policy in the 1940s at the end of the last Supercycle bear market (using PPI-adjusted prices; see Figure 15-2 or 16-6) near the peak of negative mood. It has been eliminated in the bull market of the 1990s near the peak of positive mood. A 1997 newspaper showed black and white African leaders, enemies for decades, clasping hands over their heads in the spirit of brotherhood. As another manifestation of exclusion and inclusion, religious wars were common in the Dark Ages and for awhile afterward, but have been a minor concern in the past eight centuries of rising long-term trend. Indeed, Catholic, Jewish and Arab leaders have all been apologizing, finding common ground and shaking hands publicly in the 1990s, an unprecedented spectacle. Similarly, nationalism was the political theme in the 1940s during a bear market; as this bull market has been peaking out, we have a new European Community with a unified currency, shadowy talk of a New World Order, and plans for the former Communist countries of Eastern Europe to join NATO. In the 1940s, the U.S. and Russia began a "cold war." In the 1990s, leaders of the U.S. and Russia, enemies for decades, clasped hands over their heads in the spirit of cooperation, reflecting the classic bull market sentiments of social inclusion.

The Correct Orientation toward Such Events

Each time one of these grand events occurs, whether viewed as good or evil, observers tend to see it as a turning point for mankind. Such observations are true, but because people think conventionally in terms of the direction of causality (see Chapters 18 and 19), it is a turning point in *precisely the opposite direction from what they assume it to be*. Conventional observers take each event "at face value" and assume that each positive event marks a turning point for the better and each negative event a turning point for the worse. However, every negative event mentioned in the above section indicated the approach a turning point for the better, while every positive event indicates the approach of a turning point for the worse. Lacking socionomics, conventional social observers are always entirely unprepared for the next chain of events. In contrast, observing what events reveal about extremes in social psychology prepares the socionomist for coming changes.

Some Cultural Expressions of Social Mood Trends

AREA OF CULTURE	RISING TRANSITION	PEAK POSITIVE MOOD	FALLING TRANSITION	PEAK NEGATIVE MOOD
CAMPUS TRENDS	Work hard, have fun	Positive-minded save-the-world social concern	Rebellious, angry social concern	From riots to sudden quiet
CREATIVITY	Positive mood creativity	Positive mood creative trend fully realized	Negative mood creativity; lack of creativity	Negative mood creative trend fully realized; destruction
DANCE	Partners together, tempo speeds up, partners separate	Partners apart, fast tempo	Partners come back together; tempos slow down	Partners together
FAMILY LIFE	Babies popular, family orientation, marriage	Trend reaches extreme	Children a negative value, divorce, "single" life preferred	Trend reaches extreme
FASHION (color)	Colors emerge	Bright colors dominate	Drabness emerges	Drab colors dominate
FASHION (covering)	Men's ties narrow	Bodies exposed, short skirts, bikinis for women, tight pants for men	Men's ties widen	Bodies covered; floor-length dresses, baggy pants
FASHION (style)	"Correctness" stressed	Flamboyant individuality for men and women	Anti-fashion fashions	Conservative dress returns
FITNESS/HEALTH	Healthy lifestyle, physical fitness practiced, encouraged	Body admired. Body-building peaks. Smoking, "junk" foods taboo	Fitness fanaticism wanes rapidly. Social concern replaces concern with self	"Working out" is out of fashion.
GOOD vs. EVIL	Bad guys vs. good guys (movies, pro wrestling). Heroes celebrated	Everybody's a good guy	There are no bad guys and no good guys. Heroes trashed	Everybody's a bad guy
JUDGMENTS	Answers are black and white	There is good in all	Who's to judge?	There is evil in all
MOVIES/TV/LITERATURE	"G" rated themes, adventure	Celebrate life; upbeat, entertaining themes	Social concern, symbolism, heaviness, anti-heroes	Horror, dead-end themes
NOSTALGIA	Nostalgia for black-and-white values	Focus on now	Nostalgia for mythical simpler times (back to the earth)	Focus on now
POETRY	Structured	Lyrical	Anarchic	Ugly

Table 14-1a

Some Cultural Expressions of Social Mood Trends *(cont'd)*

AREA OF CULTURE	RISING TRANSITION	PEAK POSITIVE MOOD	FALLING TRANSITION	PEAK NEGATIVE MOOD
POLITICIANS (perceptions of)	Strengths magnified, weaknesses overlooked, forgiven or denied	Politicians revered (Camelot, "Teflon")	Weaknesses magnified, strengths overlooked or denied	Politicians hated or deified
POLITICS	Relative stability	Desire to maintain status quo	Old styles fail	Radical parties and solutions
POP ART	Structured, traditional	Colorful, wild, "alive"	Anarchic --anything goes	Deliberately ugly, heavy, sedate
POP MUSIC (Arrangement)	Simplicity peaks, complexity returns		Complexity peaks, simplicity returns	
POP MUSIC (Image)	Dirty, happy	Clean, happy	Clean, angry	Dirty, angry
POP MUSIC (Lyrics)	Any non-negative theme OK	Joyous celebration and love songs	Anxious, socially conscious themes emerge	Songs of despair, hate, violence; also happy denial
POP MUSIC (Melody)	Melody emerges as a key ingredient	Lilting, complex, inventive melodies and harmony	Melody is eclipsed by various elements: rhythm, arrangement	Little melody or chord structure
POP MUSIC (Mood)	Upbeat, major keys	Upbeat, major and minor keys	Minor keys, downbeat, arty	Distorted sounds, atonality, dissonance
POP PHILOSOPHY	Achievement is possible and desirable	Love will save the world	Achievement is a waste of time	Hate and destruction will give the world what it deserves
RELIGION	Conservative religion but increasingly subdominant	Religious tolerance and inclusiveness	Religion is openly questioned and passionately reintroduced	Powerful fundamentalist religions and cults
SEXUAL IMAGES	"Masculine" men and "feminine" women	Heterosexual images peak	"Feminine" caring men; "masculine", liberated women	Focus on alternative sexual styles
SPORTS	Clean "good guy" sports		Rough "bad guy" sports	
STOCK MARKET (popular valuation of productive enterprise)	Rising	Topping	Falling or correcting	Bottoming
WAR	Old wars fought and concluded	Little conflict	More conflict; new wars begin	New wars begin or intensify

Table 14-1b

Anticipating the Character of Social Behavior

Once you incorporate these ideas, you can predict, probabilistically, many types of social behavior. You can test yourself on the following questions.

When would a society be more likely to have peaceful gatherings as opposed to hostile gatherings? In the 1940s, after over a decade of bear market, hundreds of thousands of men gathered in Europe and the Far East to kill each other. In 1996, after five decades of social mood rise, the United Nations managed, for the first time ever, a full attendance of world leaders for a friendly photograph. In 1967-1969, after over two decades of social mood rise, hundreds of thousands of people gathered in Monterey, California, Woodstock, New York and other locations for big parties known as music festivals. In 1970, after a year and a half of bear market, angry students gathered in huge numbers to protest the war in Vietnam. In August 1987, after five years of bull market, thousands of advocates of world peace convened in a "harmonic convergence" celebration.

When would a society be more likely to sport adventurous, frisky fashions as opposed to similar, conservative dress? Colorful clothes, short skirts, and diversity in appearance are typical of social mood peaks. Dull colors, long skirts and uniforms are common at social mood troughs.

When would a society progress toward free trade, and when would it restrict it? In the 1920s bull market, free trade was encouraged. In 1929, at the start of the bear market, Congress passed protectionist tariffs despite widespread knowledge that such policies are destructive.

When would a government be more likely to produce an atomic bomb (anger, fear, opposition, protectionism) and when would it be more likely to send a man to the moon (confidence, adventurousness, sharpness of focus)? The U.S. government dropped the first atomic bomb after 16 years of bear market (in constant-dollar terms); it put a man on the moon after 20 years of bull market.

When is a society more likely to develop science and technology and when is it more likely to focus on mysticism? The Commercial, Scientific, Industrial, Technological and Information Revolutions took place during positive social mood trends. The pace of religious conversions tends to be the greatest near the end of negative social mood trends.

I could go on for a hundred pages, but I trust you get the idea.

The table on the previous two pages shows a scattershot collection of observations along these lines that I made over thirteen years ago. This table is meant to be roughly representative, not precise or conclusive.

The social mood is always in flux at *all degrees of trend*, moving toward one of the polar opposites in every conceivable area, from hope for the future to fear of it, from a desire to speculate to a desire to conserve, from a preference for heroic symbols to a preference for antiheroes, from joy to cynicism, from a desire to build to a desire to destroy. There is so much more to say about how the historical characters of the arts, sciences, technology, religion and philosophy all parallel social mood trends, but that discussion will await a book dedicated to socionomics.

Aggregations and Their Interconnection

As implied in this book so far, society has *overall* mood trends. Statistics that reflect the society as whole, such as voting totals, the national economy, the society-wide popularity of different types of entertainment, etc., reflect that social mood. Within societies, there are countless *smaller* aggregations, each of which has its own waves. An aggregation that trades corn, copper, baseball cards or stocks has its own waves. Each city, state, political movement, religion and sport has its own waves. Smaller aggregations are embedded within larger ones. People can be members of several aggregations at once. The socionomist must obtain as much data as possible to isolate each phenomenon he studies, as each one has its own wave structure. An aggregation may be highly independent from or strongly influenced by the overall social mood, depending upon how widely shared their respective concerns are. Together, all the waves of all the aggregations weave the fabric of social life. Chapter 17 includes some examples of smaller aggregations. The next two chapters focus on the overall social mood and its influence with respect to what I consider the most accessible socionomic subjects.

NOTES

1 Elliott, R.N. (1938). *The wave principle*. Republished: (1994). *R.N. Elliott's Masterworks — The Definitive Collection*, p. 92.

Chapter 15:

Popular Cultural Trends as
Manifestations of Social Mood Trends[1]

If stock market trends reflect social mood trends, the emotions associated with those trends must have other manifestations. An examination of the major areas of social mood expression where data are available shows that they do, as popular cultural trends peak and trough coincidentally with the stock market in their joint reflection of the popular mood.

Any activity that quickly reflects changes in how people in general feel is a coincident indicator of social mood change. A person communicates his mood when he chooses a piece of music, decides what clothes to wear, buys a work of art, selects a movie, casts a vote, decides what sporting event to see, or chooses a book to read. Trends in music, movies, fashion, literature, television, popular philosophy, sports, dance, heroic images, commercial product styling, mores, gender-related ideals, family life, campus activities, religious activity, politics and poetry all reflect the prevailing mood, sometimes in subtle ways. The availability of numerous books, theaters, recordings, sports, fashions and political candidates is a requisite for the production of reliable data. The direction and extent of the relative popularity of various styles of these modes of expression reflect the direction and extremity of the dominant mood.

A record of these overall societal changes says nothing necessarily about how an individual or a specific group might feel or act but is an indication of the net mood of the society at large. For changes in mood to express themselves, *some* particularly susceptible people must undergo a *substantial* change in mood and/or *most* people must undergo *some* change in mood. I believe the mechanism is a function of both processes. As the mood dynamic progresses, those individuals whose state of mind is on the

cusp of change can be stirred to a new expression as a result of just a slight change in mood, which pushes them past the threshold. The further the swing in public mood carries, the larger will be the number of people stirred to the new expression.

While all avenues of cultural mood expression tend to ebb and flow in concert, we cannot expect *particular* forms of expression necessarily to lead the charge. Different media may be more dominant in the culture at different times. As an example, audio and video entertainment have a golden age at every social mood peak, but it does not show up as strongly in every subcategory. In the audio category, jazz music reached a pinnacle of popularity in the late 1930s at the top of wave I, rock music reached a pinnacle of popularity in the late 1960s at the top of wave III, and country music has reached a pinnacle of popularity in the 1990s as we approach the top of wave V. All three styles fall under the category of popular music. In the video category, films reached a quality peak in the late 1930s, television reached a quality peak in the 1960s, and computer games may be reaching a quality peak in the late 1990s. History repeats in *mood*, but not necessarily *mode*.

Noticeable changes in slower-moving mediums such as the movie industry more readily reveal changes in larger degrees of trend, such as Cycle. More sensitive mediums such as television change quickly enough to reflect changes in the Primary trends of popular mood. Intermediate trends are paralleled by current song hits, which can rush up and down the sales charts quickly as people change moods. Of course, *all* of these media of expression are influenced by mood changes of all degrees. The net impression communicated is a result of the mix and dominance of the forces in all these areas at any given moment.

The timing of the careers of dominant popular entertainers, whether movie stars, television stars or pop music stars, is closely aligned with the peaks and troughs in the stock market. At major social mood turning points, the dominant stars quickly fade into obscurity to be replaced by stars that reflect the newly emerging mood. For example, the Cycle degree social mood peak of 1966 coincided with a large number of long-running TV programs going off the air and the retirement of countless happy-mood pop music representatives. As Philip Norman said in *Shout*, in the matter of a single year, "the latter-day Mersey groups had all gone home to settle down as pork butchers and damp course engineers [construction workers]."[2] The next peak in December 1968 was the last gasp of the old trend, as shortly

thereafter, droves of formerly dominant stars and their venues became passe. Many broke up (as in pop groups), were canceled (as in TV shows), retired or died. This has been true at every major turn.

Sometimes trends rely on which wave is in force. For example, as a manifestation of fifth waves' attempt to relive the glories of the third wave, *nostalgia* becomes widespread. During wave V, fashions have reprised looks from the 1940s, 1950s and 1960s. The songs of the 1960s began flooding the airwaves in the 1980s as "oldies" became the most lucrative format in radio. Since then, there has hardly been a singer or group from the 1960s that has *not* returned to tour, record or appear on television. Elvis Presley, the Beatles, Frank Sinatra and even Benny Goodman have enjoyed adoring retrospectives. In TV land, the Nickelodeon channel has thrived running TV shows from the 1950s and 1960s. Old films have been colorized, restored and rereleased in theaters. The American Movie Classics channel has succeeded by running old black-and-white movies. Nostalgia is far less effective in powerful third waves and in bear markets because at such times people are far more interested in, or concerned with, the present than the past.

While analyses of such trends might appear important only to entertainment companies, they are relevant to almost every industry. It would help auto makers to know, for instance, that angular styles sell well in bull markets while rounded lines sell better in bear markets. Styling and color affect almost every product.

The biggest problem in proving the correlation that I propose in this chapter is a dearth of data. Unfortunately, there is today little demand and no central clearinghouse for such data. It will take a multi-year research project to gather and graph it all. Data unavailability is not the only problem. Given the limited introductory scope of this book, this chapter presents only a portion of what I know about the subject. My one small section on nuances in a single film genre provides just a glimpse of how close is the marriage between mood trends and the timing of related cultural events. For now, I hope that a few generalized examples and observations will suffice to convey the idea.

Depending upon which measures better illustrate the observed correlation, some of the foregoing graphs show the nominal DJIA, which is a dollars/shares ratio, others show the PPI-adjusted DJIA, which is a goods/shares ratio, and some show both. The PPI-adjusted measure is often loosely called the "constant-dollar" or "inflation-adjusted" Dow.

Trends in Hemlines

Harvard graduate Ralph Rotnem, a researcher at the Harris Upham brokerage firm, originated the so-called "hemline theory," which is the recognition that women's skirt lengths tend to rise and fall in tandem with the Dow Jones Industrial Average. Though this idea is often dismissed as frivolous, socionomics explains why there is a correlation. The trends of stock prices and women's hemlines are a function of social mood. When people feel bold and frisky, they buy stocks and wear more revealing clothes. When they feel threatened and conservative, they sell stocks and wear more concealing clothes. It is that simple.

Because skirt lengths have limits (the floor and the upper thigh respectively), the reaching of a limit implies the concurrence of an extreme positive or negative mood. As Figure 15-1 illustrates, hemlines were very low at the stock market bottom of 1921. They rose to miniskirt brevity in

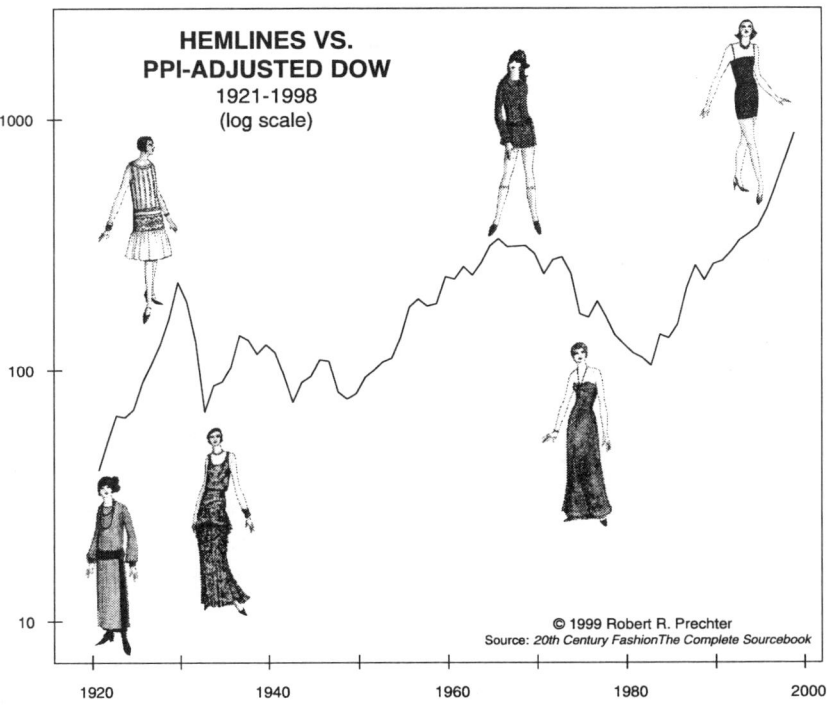

Figure 15-1

the late 1920s and late 1960s, peaking with stock prices both times. Hemlines plunged to maxiskirt floor-lengths in the 1930s and 1970s, bottoming with stock prices both times. Today, as we head into 1999, skirts worn by models and celebrities are extremely short (one runway featured what looked more like a wide belt), while those worn by the general public are just shy of 1968's minidress length.

Trends in Movies

The timing of the production and success of film genres is instructive as to social mood expression. Figure 15-2 plots the PPI-adjusted Dow-Jones Industrial Average marked with the acknowledged classics in two

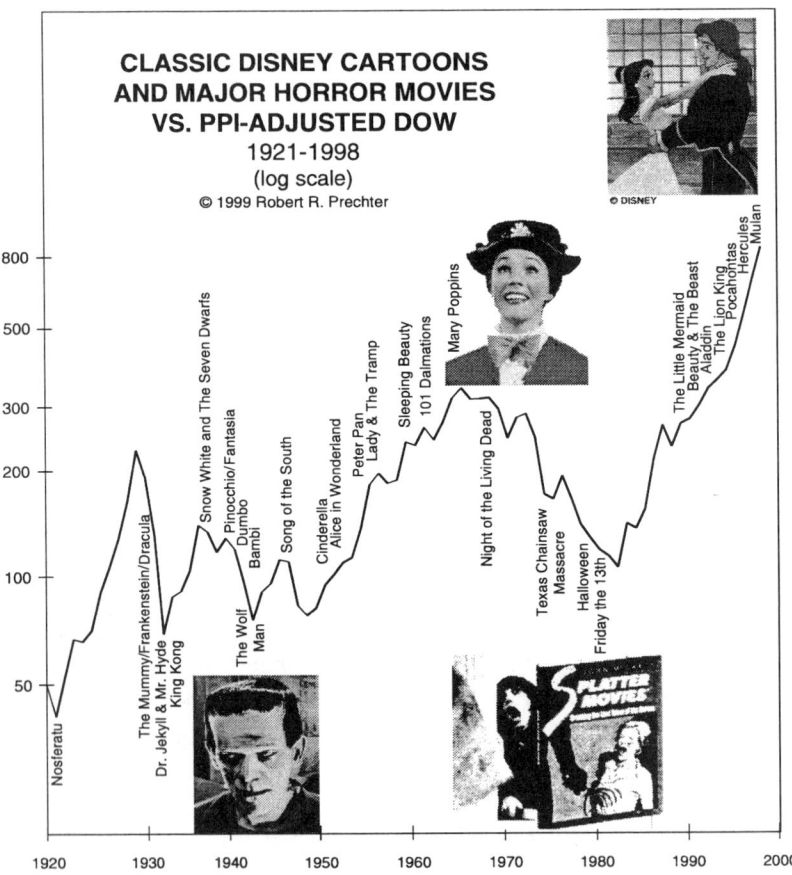

Figure 15-2

types of film entertainment: Disney cartoons and horror movies. If you are with me so far, you can probably guess in which direction of social mood trend each style of film has been innovative and popular.

The Walt Disney Company released its first feature-length cartoon in 1937, the year of the top of a roaring five-year bull market that accomplished the fastest 370% gain in U.S. stocks ever. As shown here by the titles listed on the top side of the graph, these films stayed popular for thirty years, culminating with the ultra-sunny *Mary Poppins* in 1964, and to a lesser degree, *The Jungle Book* in 1967. The end of this period of success was essentially coincident with the great stock market top of 1966. For the next sixteen years, as stock prices fell along with social mood, most people thought Disney's feature cartoons were silly and sentimental. Indeed, the studio's productivity fell by more than 50%. With the possible exception of *The Jungle Book*, not one cartoon film from this period is considered a classic. When the bull market returned in the 1980s and 1990s, so did feature-length Disney cartoons that have been both acknowledged classics and box-office blockbusters. In the last eleven years of bull market, Disney has produced ten feature cartoon films. In the briefest possible terms, Disney cartoons are bull market movies, reflecting the shared mood of both their creators and their viewers.

Now we will examine the other end of the spectrum, whose titles are listed on the bottom side of the graph. Horror movies descended upon the American scene in 1930-1933, the very years that the Dow Jones Industrials collapsed. Five classic horror films were all produced in less than three short years. *Frankenstein* and *Dracula* premiered in 1931. *Dr. Jekyll and Mr. Hyde* was released in 1932, the year of the great bear market bottom and the only year that a horror film actor (Frederick March, for that film) was ever granted an Oscar.[3] *The Mummy* and *King Kong* hit the screen in 1933, on the test of the low in stock prices and right at the trough of the Great Depression. These are the classic horror films of all time.[4] Ironically, Hollywood tried to introduce a new monster in 1935 during a bull market, but *Werewolf of London* was a flop. When film makers tried again in 1941, in the depths of a bear market, *The Wolf Man* was a hit. Producers made sequels to these films, featuring Frankenstein monsters, vampires, werewolves and undead mummies, for about a decade, into the bottom of wave II in 1942.

Shortly after the stock market bottom of 1942, films abandoned dark, foreboding horror in the most surefire way: by laughing at it. When Abbott

and Costello met Frankenstein in 1948, it showed that horror had lost its power. The cheesiness, mildness and comedy of the horror-based films of the ensuing bull market years and the limited extent of their innovation, influence and popularity stand in stark contrast to the films of the bear market years. For example, 1957's *I Was a Teenage Frankenstein*, released in the middle of an extended Cycle degree bull market, earned "the somewhat dubious distinction of being named one of the worst horror films ever made."[5]

When social mood reentered a major bear trend in 1966, so did groundbreaking horror movies. *Night of the Living Dead* debuted in 1968, the year after the last of that era's Disney cartoon classics. It was so influential that it spawned two sequels (both produced during the bear market), several derivations and two books. A breakthrough in gore entitled *The Texas Chainsaw Massacre* was released in 1974, as stocks made their nominal price lows.

In 1974, the year of the low for wave IV, horror-writer Stephen King burst upon the scene with his first novel, *Carrie*. His novels provided fodder for a number of horror-movie scripts, including the Hollywood slasher movie, *The Shining*, in 1977. At the darkest extreme of the trend, when PPI-adjusted prices were approaching bottom in 1978, the industry introduced so-called slice-and-dice films, or "splatter movies."[6] *Friday the 13th* and *Halloween* were so influential that they have spawned many sequels, none of which are rated by critics as highly as the originals. Not to be overly outdone, Broadway introduced the slasher play, *Sweeney Todd, the Demon Barber of Fleet Street*, in 1979, the same year that King's *Dead Zone* sat for six straight months on the *New York Times* bestseller list.[7]

Since 1982, and particularly since 1984, a bull market has been in force. Since that time, horror films have once again become increasingly derivative, muted or comic, just as in the years following 1942.

Nuances

All the subjects discussed in this chapter have countless coincidences of parallelism with social trends. While we do not want to get lost in the nuances of popular culture, a few observations should communicate the richness of the correlation. Here are a few examples relating to this one genre.

I observed years ago, and have often remarked, that the initial deterioration in the stock market during the fourth wave sets the stage for the

ultimate reversal (see "Wave Personality" in *Elliott Wave Principle*). Apparently, this is true across all manifestations of social mood, not just the stock market. For instance, the fourth-wave social-mood correction of one smaller degree immediately preceding the two major bear market periods illustrated in Figure 15-2 gave advance indications of the style of horror that would be produced in the ensuing bear market. In 1920 and 1921, at the bottom of the preceding Cycle degree bear market, *Dr. Jekyll and Mr. Hyde* with John Barrymore, and *Nosferatu*, the German vampire film that we all study in film class, presaged the monster movies of the 1930s and 1940s. In 1962, at the bottom of the preceding Primary degree bear market, *Psycho*, the famous Hitchcock knife-in-the-shower shocker, presaged the slasher movies of the 1970s.[8]

One pop record stands out in the annals of horror: "Monster Mash" by Bobby "Boris" Pickett. It became the #1 record in the country on October 20, 1962 and stayed there for two weeks. The exact date of the orthodox end of the three-year bear market labeled Primary wave ④ (see Figure 15-4) was October 23, 1962, another perfect coincidence of mood and expression. While this record echoed the old horror style, it was a comic treatment because mood in the larger trend was so elevated. The recording returned to the charts twice: in August 1970, right off the bottom of the deepest bear market in thirty years and again in May 1973 in the midst of the bear market of 1973-1974. (As that bear market deepened, the comic approach of "Monster Mash" became outmoded, and horror got serious again.)

Why was the Hammer Films company of England able to release a series of fairly successful horror films in that country from 1957 through 1974? The reason is that, unlike the soaring American stock market, the London stock market was in a mild bear market from 1959 to 1966. After a brief two-year rise, it joined with gusto the American downtrend from 1968 to 1974, suffering a decline nearly as deep as that of 1929-1932. Through the first half of the 1970s, as stocks and mood collapsed their hardest, Hammer released vampire films at five times the rate it did in the 1960s. As soon as the British stock market turned powerfully up in 1975, demand for Hammer's output fell so abruptly that the company folded. Was that the end of a nearly perfect social-mood parallelism? Perhaps not. Suddenly, after 23 years in which Hammer has languished as but a memory, advertising mogul Charles Saachi has purchased the name with the aim of transforming Hammer "from a debt-ridden relic into a global empire."[9]

Says an on-line site dedicated to vampires, "The future for Hammer looks promising for the first time in more than twenty years."[10]

The correlation between bear markets and horror holds before the days of movies. For example, America's master horror writer Edgar Allen Poe flourished in the Supercycle degree bear market of 1835 to 1842, during which time, according to *The World Book Encyclopedia*, "he produced several of his finest tales."[11] Poe died in 1847, "after five years of illness," five years that just happen to coincide with a rapid rise in social mood that began in 1842. That uptrend in public mood was not as well suited to his style, and the dissonance between them may have pressured his already weak constitution.

We may presume, with reverse wave analysis (see Chapter 17), that Shakespeare's *Macbeth*, the first modern slasher play, debuted in a bear market as well. The history of popular horror has traversed from plays to books to films, as once again, history repeats in mood but not necessarily mode.

The two books on horror movies that I have on my shelf (*Horror Movies* and *The Horror Film Handbook*) were published in 1974 and 1982, the exact years of the lows for stock prices in Cycle wave IV in nominal and PPI-adjusted prices respectively. Also on my shelf is a ten-volume set of books entitled, "The Works of Edgar Allen Poe," which I find was published in 1933, the bottom year of the depression. These are the times that people are interested in such topics, and the writers and publishers oblige.

Trends in Popular Music Expression

As a 78-rpm record collector put it in a *Wall Street Journal* article, music reflects "every fiber of life" in the U.S. Accordingly, its themes and tones have been virtually in lock step with social mood as reflected by the major trends in the Dow Jones Industrial Average. Figure 15-3 shows one major stock market cycle and the styles of music that were popular in the uptrend vs. the downtrend.

In the 1950s and early 1960s, as a great bull market was underway, major pop music stars were young and energetic, and their lyrical theme was, "I feel good and I love you." By the end of the decade, paisley-clad popsters in the Summer of Love sang in essence, "Oh, wow, I feel great and I love everybody." The excerpts below give you a flavor of the lyrics of hit songs near the peak:[12]

"Life, I love you! All is groovy." (1966)

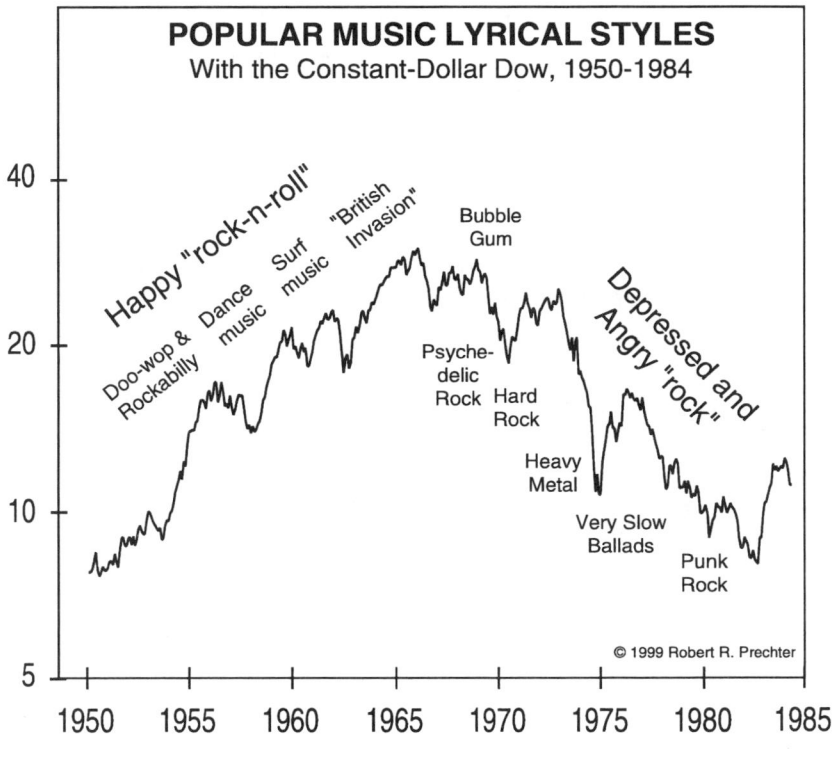

Figure 15-3

"'Scuse me while I kiss the sky." (1967)

"All you need is love. Love is all you need." (1967)

"If we unite, it will all turn out right. Every awareness seems to bring us together. When you're happy, every place feels like home. You'll be happier yet. It's wonderful!" (1967)

"I think it's wonderful that people are finally getting together. Reach out in the darkness and you will find a friend." (1968)

"Put a little love in your heart, and the world will be a better place for you and me; just wait and see." (1969)

After decades of general uptrend, stocks peaked in 1966 in the Dow and December 1968 in the Value Line Index. Coincident with that high was a peak in popular musical creativity, the product of which was manufactured and released into the following year. A music industry executive flatly told *The Wall Street Journal*, "Rock peaked in 1969."[13,14]

The reversal of trend at the peak of the bull market brought such a dramatic change in the character of the music from upbeat to downbeat themes and tone that a #1 song on the subject from 1971 lamented, "Something touched me deep inside the day the music died."[15] As the deepest bear market since the early 1940s got underway, pop music stars became socially concerned, world-weary, angry and cynical, and their lyrical theme changed to, "I'm depressed and you're no good." Here are some sample lyrics of the time:[16]

"When you're down and troubled, and you need a helping hand, and nothing, nothing is going right...I will be there to brighten up even your darkest night." (1970)

"I rode a tank, held a general's rank, when the blitzkreig raged and the bodies stank. I shouted out, 'Who killed the Kennedys?' when after all, it was you and me." (1970)

"Ticking away the moments that make up a dull day, you fritter and waste the hours in an offhand way. You run and run to catch up with the sun, but it's sinking. You're older, shorter of breath and one day closer to death." (1973)

"Day after day I'm more confused, so I look for a light through the pouring rain. I'm beginning to think that I'm wasting time. I want to get lost in your rock and roll and drift away." (1973)

"When I'm tired, I hide in my music, forget the day, and dream of a girl I used to know; I close my eyes and she slips away." (1976)

"All we are is dust in the wind." (1978)

At the end of the decade, punk rockers communicated in violent fashion an amorphous, tortured, "I'm in agony and I hate everybody."

With the advent of the bull market in 1982, punk rock abruptly disappeared and the old depressed lyrical mood waned. In the 1980s and 1990s, pop music has been mostly happy again, including even previously-perennially-depressed country music! There is a mix (after all, this is a weaker fifth wave, not a strong third), but world-weariness among pop stars is mostly gone, and many of its players and singers are once again young and energetic.

Speaking of young and energetic, a sickly-sweet musical style called "bubble gum" music, aimed at ten-to-fourteen year olds, enjoyed a brief heyday in the late 1960s with the Archies and the Ohio Express. This style abruptly disappeared after the 1968 stock market high. Twenty years later, in 1987-1989, bubble gum returned with big hits by Debbie Gibson and

Tiffany. After another long absence, the Spice Girls and Hanson have re-prised the genre in 1998. It has appeared at the end of each of three of the four longest stretches of economic expansion in U.S. history. (The fourth one lasted through 1944, when young bobby-soxers screamed for Frank Sinatra.) In other words, *each time economists have warbled, "this is the best of all possible worlds," teen songsters have warbled the same thing.*

The whole story of this period is not as simple as this brief discussion suggests. For instance, the 1970s also featured upbeat, airy pop tunes, and starting in 1975, "disco" dance music. There are two reasons for this diver-gence of trends. First, as listed in Chapter 14, bear market moods produce social *opposition* as opposed to *alignment*. In the bull market of the 1950s and 1960s, young people all listened mostly to the same music. The bear market, in contrast, sported two distinct trends, the depressed and angry one cited above and another that relentlessly pursued a sunny, singin'-in-the-rain outlook. Fans of each genre hated the other with a passion. The second reason is that from 1975 to 1982, though a bear market raged in PPI-adjusted terms, a bull market was picking up steam in nominal terms. This dichotomy fit the dichotomy in pop music. Once again, the complex-ity, depth and wonder of this subject is to be found in the details, which are too dense to present here. My 1985 essay, *Popular Culture and the Stock Market*, goes into more detail on the 1950-1985 period.[17]

Lyrical theme is not the only aspect of musical expression that is cor-related with social mood. It is easy to communicate lyrics in a print medium, which is why lyrical theme is the focus of this section. However, I consider it the least reliable aspect of pop music in communicating social mood. Melodic connotation, harmony, dissonance, noise content, artistic self-con-sciousness, the appearance and demeanor of the performers, implied benignity or violence, and the simplicity or complexity of notes, chord structure and arrangement appear to be even more reliably related to the trends of social mood than lyrics.[18] All of these things are quantifiable, and I hope to conduct proper studies on them someday.

Superstardom as a Reflection of Mass Emotional Release at a Social Mood Peak

When the social mood is overwhelmingly positive, people express ecstasy. One way they do it is to revere public figures. Young people are particularly prone to release ecstatic emotion by showering pop music per-

formers with adoration. Therefore, one manifestation of major degree ebullience is the excited and passionate idolization of pop musicians or singers by teenagers. Let us see how this idea has manifested itself this century.

There have been five major instances of crowd euphoria directed at pop music performers since the Supercycle low in 1932. Every one of them occurred in a bull market, and in particular, when a Primary or short Cycle degree advance was maturing. Figure 15-4 displays their positions within the wave structure.

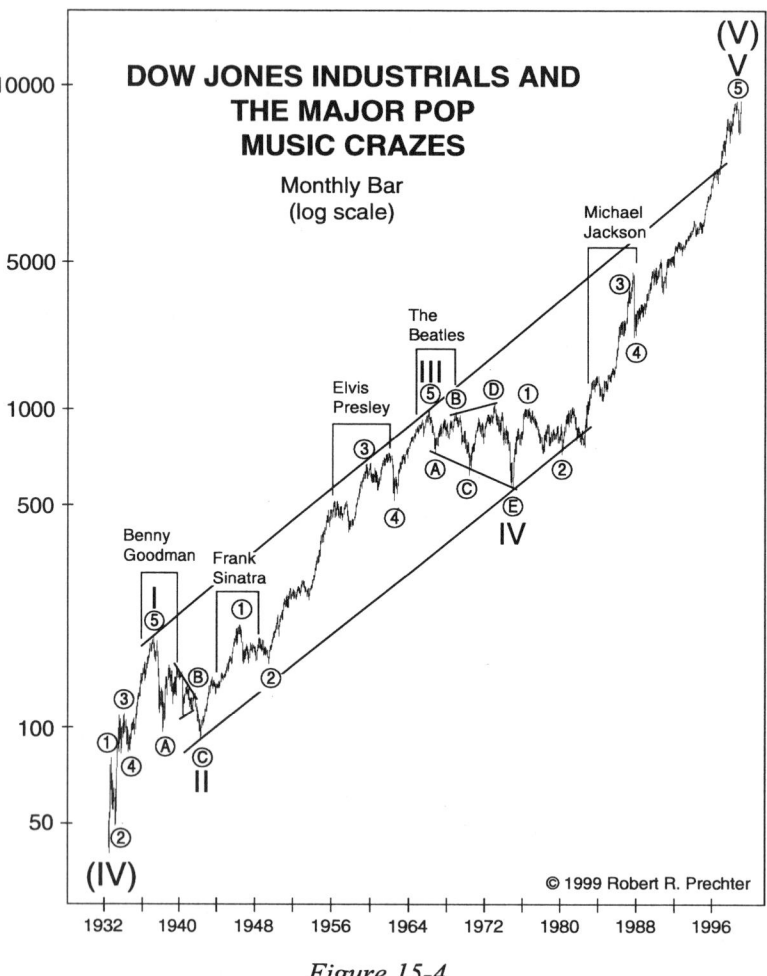

Figure 15-4

The first craze, which took place near the top of wave I, focused on Benny Goodman from 1935 to 1938. Goodman's "swing" music created such excitement that teenagers jammed concert halls and touched off riots. His moniker was the "King of Swing." The second craze was over Frank Sinatra in 1943-1946, near the top of wave ①. Teenaged girls known as Bobby Soxers suddenly swarmed and swooned over "The Voice." The third craze centered on Elvis Presley toward the end of wave ③ in the second half of the 1950s. His moniker was the "King of Rock 'n' Roll." The fourth craze surrounded The Beatles from 1963 to 1965, near the top of wave ⑤. They were dubbed "the Fab Four" and their music precipitated "Beatlemania." The fifth craze developed around Michael Jackson in the 1980s, in wave ③ of V. Jackson was crowned the "King of Pop." Here are some quotes that exemplify these social experiences and reflect their similarity:

1935-1938; peak year, 1937:

> The Goodman band became an overnight sensation at the Palomar Ballroom in Los Angeles in August 1935. [It] carried to unprecedented heights of success, reaching an apex in sheer popularity with the famous 1937 Paramount Theater engagement and the 1938 Carnegie Hall concert...[but] by 1938, the Goodman band had reached an artistic nadir, clearly reflected in its recordings.[19]

Note: This could just as well be a description of the rise into the peak and subsequent collapse in the stock market from 1935 to 1938.

1943-1949; peak year, 1944:

> Frank Sinatra's rise to become the most popular singer in the U.S. in 1944, accompanied by the loud screams of mostly female teenage fans, has often been compared with the outpourings of affection that accompanied the national appearances of Elvis Presley and the Beatles. ... The peak of the craze [was] probably the Columbus Day riot on October 12, 1944, when thousands of teens ran through Times Square after realizing that their compatriots inside the Paramount were staying for show after show (there were five a day) and they'd never get to see their hero.[20]

Note: This euphoric mayhem burst forth despite the raging of World War II. The bull market in social *mood* had to express itself regardless of social *events and conditions*, which were the result of the *preceding bear market* (see Chapter 16).

1955-1963; peak year, 1957:

It was the largest paying crowd ever to see an entertainer perform in Dallas (Elvis took home $18,000 out of a $30,000 gross), and from the moment Elvis appeared, waving to the crowd from the back of a Cadillac convertible as he circled the field, a kind of high-pitched, earsplitting, seismic wail went up, there were "screams of anguish" and "shrieks of ecstasy," the papers reported, that never wavered or stopped. The musicians couldn't hear a thing, apart from the crowd, said drummer D.J. Fontana. "All you could see was just thousands of bulbs going off. I thought, What's this guy done?"[21]

1963-1969; peak year, 1964:

According to Mark Lewisohn's survey of local newspaper coverage, "Beatles-inspired hysteria had definitely begun by the late spring [of 1963], some six months before it was brought to national attention by Fleet Street newspapers." Nonetheless, the national media's sudden saturation coverage could not help but amplify the underlying frenzy, creating a self-reinforcing process whose immediate effect was an absolutely tumultuous welcome at Heathrow Airport when the Beatles returned from a quick tour of Sweden on October 31. The Beatles themselves cited this event as the beginning of Beatlemania. The spectacle of many thousands of screaming fans jamming the airport made news across the land, and for the next three years photos of the Beatles' well-attended departures and arrivals at Heathrow were a staple of British media coverage. ...In each country, the scenes of uncontainable mass excitement were similar enough to have been scripted by a single invisible master of ceremonies: boisterous airport welcomes, clamoring crowds outside the Beatles' hotels, shrieking audiences at their shows, all magnified by virtually nonstop media coverage.[22]

Note the wonderful phrases, "self-reinforcing process" and "mass excitement similar enough *in each country* to have been scripted by a single invisible master."

1983-1991; peak years, 1983/1987:

Michael Jackson's popularity was such that one of his record albums produced both more hit singles and more sales than any other in history. Premiers of his music videos were treated as global media events. His Pepsi ads attracted more viewers than the TV shows that bracketed them. Viewers of the American Music Awards on television in January 1989 saw film

clips of Jackson's 1987-1988 world tour, held in stadiums. It attracted 4.4 million people, dwarfing every previous such event in terms of attendance and income. News clips showed cheering, screaming, sighing, crying, fainting, swooning, dancing, rioting teenagers, all over the world. An ecstatic English woman gushed, "It was just like this with the Beatles."[23]

Lesser idolizations along the way notwithstanding, these five clearly achieved the summit of fan adoration in the field of pop music. Why did it happen? Was it simply due to inordinate talent? If so, why have even better talents been less feted? Was it handsomeness? If so, why have more handsome singers failed? Some observers have come close to the answer. Writer Bill Holland said this in his discussion of the Sinatra phenomenon:

> Magnetism and charisma are still human mysteries. Why humans are riveted and mesmerized by watching, listening or being in the presence of certain persons is a phenomenon that has been studied by philosophers and scientists over centuries. It has never been explained. ...Somehow, through the mystery that personified itself every time [Sinatra] took to the stage, most of the time we, the audience, gladly gave ourselves to him because he carried us to *a certain emotional state* which we all recognize, desire and crave.[24]

George Harrison made this blunt comment about Beatlemania: "The world *used us as an excuse* to go crazy, and then they blamed it on us. But we were just in the middle."[25] Said Ringo Starr: "The problem with the Beatles is that *it didn't matter what we did*, we'd get the same applause."[26] As one contemporary performer said about the concertgoers of 1968 in general: "There were huge crowds everywhere, full of *mindless* adulation."[27] Says Robert Goldberg in explaining superstardom: "The more familiar you become, the more you are appropriated by your audience: *You cease to be a person* and become *a mirror in which fans read their own lives.*"[28] These descriptions reflect what happens in financial booms and swoons as well: Values and shares become meaningless as investors construct their own social fantasy to take their place. In other words, these performers not only appeared *in* a bull market, but their public personas *were* a bull market, driven by the mass cooperation of millions of limbic systems. *Each time it happened, it came at a similar point in the wave structure of a major advance in stocks*, when fear melted away and ebullience took its place. Simply put, these singers and musicians were the focal point for an outpouring of social ecstasy, which was clearly registering on the primary meter of social mood, the Dow Jones Industrial Average.

Such entertainers, because of their role in personifying social ecstasy, are the beneficiaries of more adulation than any other social figures of their day. The deaths or breakups of popular artists of this magnitude are widely and intensely mourned because people associate their intense memories of the joy of the bull market mood with the singers and musicians who best reflected and symbolized it.[29] The gratitude expressed toward the discoverer of a new technology or a cure for disease is nil compared to the gratitude showered upon these performers, the fondness of the memories associated with them and the agony experienced over their passing. Since positive social emotion is the engine of social productivity (see Chapter 16), perhaps that gratitude is not so ill-placed.

Do not presume that such reactions are only modern phenomena. This is timeless social behavior. The bull market of the 1830s, for instance, produced the same results with respect to the great pianists Chopin and Liszt, particularly the latter. Read Harold Schonberg's description of a typical Liszt concert:

> When Liszt played the piano, ladies flung their jewels on the stage instead of bouquets. They shrieked in ecstasy and sometimes fainted. Those who remained mobile made a mad rush to the stage to gaze upon the features of the divine man. They fought over the green gloves he had purposely left on the piano. One lady fished out the stub of cigar that Liszt had smoked. She carried it in her bosom to the day she died. Other ladies came away with priceless relics in the form of broken strings from the piano he had played. These *disjecta membra* were mounted in frames and worshipped. Liszt did not give mere concerts; they were saturnalia. The bemused Heine tells of a concert he attended at which two Hungarian countesses, contending for Liszt's snuffbox, threw each other on the ground and fought until they were exhausted. Heine once asked a medical man whose specialty was women to explain the nature of the hysteria that Liszt created. The physician, wrote Heine, "spoke of magnetism, galvanism and electricity; of contagion in a sultry hall filled with innumerable wax lights and some hundred perfumed and perspiring people...."[30]

Does this differ materially from a Sinatra concert in 1944, an Elvis concert in 1956, a Beatles concert in 1964 or Michael Jackson's world tour in 1987?[31]

"Contagion" is a key word in the good doctor's diagnosis, as we explored in Chapter 9 the idea of its role in the propagation of social mood.

"Magnetism" is the same word employed by Bill Holland in a 1998 article about Sinatra. Magnetism may be just a vague analogy implying attraction, but it specifically involves the alignment of numerous particles in the same direction, which is almost exactly what is going on socially with millions of limbic systems under these circumstances. Recall from Chapter 8 MacLean's observation that the limbic system can generate emotions that do not necessarily have a referent based in reality. What does the limbic system do with excess ecstasy? It bestows it upon the most popular attractive object that happens by. Charisma provides the excuse, and popularity allows unbound expression. No person would consider acting *alone* in the same way that he or she does at an ecstatic pop music concert (can you imagine being the only one wailing, weeping and screaming as others sit quietly?), but behavior is not bizarre when all others are doing the same thing. Dare we doubt that there were similar phenomena in ancient Roman, Greek and Egyptian times?

Data Required for Socionomic Study

Although the stock market will probably remain the single best indicator of social mood and mood change because of its precise measurement and long data history, socionomists should begin to detail, quantify, graph and study other cultural phenomena. A quantification of sporting event attendance figures, themes of popular entertainment, the number of notes and note changes in popular melodies, the lyrical content of popular songs, hemline lengths, tie widths, heel heights, the prominence of various colors in fashion and pop art, the angularity vs. roundness of automobile styling, average highway driving speed, sales of convertible cars, crime rates, religious activity, the construction of various architectural styles, and a host of other reflections of the popular mood, all weighted according to the volume of production and sales, would allow us to read charts of the public mood in the same way that we read charts of aggregate stock prices now. Any such data that followed the Wave Principle could be used to forecast trend changes in their own fields.

I believe that a plot of the net existence and dominance of these various popular cultural elements would produce charts closely paralleling those of aggregate stock prices. By comparing the evidence to stock price movement, we could test this empirical conclusion. If the data were indeed to show parallel trends, then we could use them in turn to forecast the stock market.

Coincident vs. Lagging Correlation

The trends in the stock market and such activities as described in this chapter are *coincident* because they reflect social mood trends *directly*. As positive mood waxes, many people buy stocks, watch Disney films, prefer music that expresses joy, and bestow their overflowing ecstasy upon pop stars. When the negative mood waxes, many people sell stocks, watch horror movies, prefer music that expresses dissatisfaction, and have little ecstasy to bestow.

In contrast, most trends that are deemed important to history, such as those economic and political, *lag* trends in social mood. The reason, I contend, is that while social mood trends are the cause of social action, the latter requires time to undertake.

The Greek philosopher Plato suggested a connection among cultural events 2400 years ago when he said, "When the mode of the music changes, the walls of the city shake." Or, according to another source, "When the modes of music change, the laws of the State always change with them." In other words, the trends of music and politics are connected. I propose that *all* cultural trends are so connected, via social mood. Chapter 16 will explore the more concrete results of social mood trends.

NOTES

1 Much of this chapter, along with parts of Chapters 14 and 16, was originally published in my 1985 paper, "Popular Culture and the Stock Market," some of which was excerpted in *Barron's*. [ref: Prechter, R. (1985, September 9). "Elvis, Frankenstein and Andy Warhol..." *Barron's*.] Ideas herein have since been appropriated at least twice without attribution.

2 Norman, P. (1981). *Shout: the true story of the Beatles.*

3 *Dr. Jekyll and Mr. Hyde* was produced three times this century: in 1920, 1932 and 1941, within one year of the three biggest stock market bottoms of that 21-year period.

4 The message of these monster movies appeared to be that people had an inhuman, horrible side to them. Hitler was placed in power in 1933 (an expression of the darkest public mood in decades) and fulfilled that vision. In discussing Fritz Lang's *M* (1931), "the first film to feature a serial [child molester/]killer as its protagonist," *The Atlanta Journal-Constitution* of October 7, 1997 said, "Even more chilling is the way Lang presages an encroaching horror that left thousands of children dead in Hitler's camps." Indeed, that is the chronology. Films reflect mood change concurrently and mood change results in action later (see Chapter 16).

5 Frank, A.G. (1974). *The movie treasury — horror movies.*

6 Different sources disagree slightly on the year-dates from some of these films. If you have a definitive source that proves any of these dates incorrect, please let me know.

7 King's horror output remained wildly popular through 1984, the last year of extreme social fear (see bond market discussion in Chapter 6). Since then, his style has softened, so he has remained popular, though much less so.

8 In constant-dollar terms, Supercycle wave (V) ended in 1966. Zombie movies became big immediately thereafter. The first zombie movie ever was *White Zombie*, released in 1932, at the low of Supercycle wave (IV). Once again, an event at the previous fourth wave low hinted at the trend to come after the end of the fifth wave.

9 Harlow, J. (1997, May 18). "Saatchi revives gory glory days of Hammer." *The Sunday Times* (London).

10 Web site: www.pathwaytodarkness.com

11 (1992). *The World Book Encyclopedia.*

12 (1) "59th Street Bridge Song (Feelin' Groovy)" by Paul Simon. (2) "Purple Haze" by Jimi Hendrix. (3) "All You Need Is Love" by Lennon/McCartney. (4) "It's Wonderful" by Cavaliere/Brigati. (5) "Reach Out in the Darkness" by Friend and Lover. (6) "Put a Little Love in Your Heart" by Jackie DeShannon.

13 Source unavailable.

14 Read this excerpt from *The Swing Era* about **1937**: "...For one fine moment in American musical history there was an alliance between national popular taste and a *creative music* called jazz...." This is exactly the way my generation feels about **1968** (+ and - one year): For one fine moment in American pop music history, there was an alliance between national popular taste and a creative music fusing blues, country, r&b, jazz, folk, latin, pop and classical influences, arranged and played with artistry and virtuosity. Each of these years is a Cycle degree top in the stock market.

15 MacLean, D. (1971). "American Pie."

16 (1) "You've Got a Friend" by James Taylor (1970). (2) "Time" by Mason/Waters/Wright/Gilmour (1970). (3) "Sympathy for the Devil" by Jagger/Richards (1973) (4) "Drift Away" by Mentor Williams (1973). (5) "More Than a Feeling" by Tom Scholz (1976). (6) "Dust in the Wind" by Walsh/Livgren (1978).

17 We hope to publish this essay as part of a book entitled *New Frontiers in Market Analysis* in the year 2000.

18 Prior to the 1970s bear market, there was never in American pop music an abrasive chordal relationship in a big-selling song like the G to C# progression in Black Sabbath's "Black Sabbath" or as much noise as there was in punk rock. The last time any music produced this much dissonance was Bartok's during the bear market of the 1930s.

19 Schuller, G. (1989). *The swing era.*

20 Ruhlmann, W. (1998, June 19). "Celebrating Sinatra." *Goldmine.*

21 Guralnick, P. (1994). *Last train to Memphis – the rise of Elvis Presley.*

22 Hertsgaard M. (1995). *A day in the life.*

23 Dick Clark Productions. (1989, January 30). *16th Annual American Music Awards.*

24 Holland, B. (1998, June 19). "The mystery of Frank Sinatra." *Goldmine.*

25 Smeaton, B. (1996). *The Beatles Anthology.* (Videotape series).

26 Gunderson, E. (1989, July 21). "Drumming up a super Starr tour." *USA Today,* p. D1.

27 Roeser, S. (1993, October 15). "Ginger Baker: anyone for polo?" (Comment from Steve Winwood, then with the band Blind Faith.) *Goldmine.*

28 Goldberg, R. (1995, November 20). "The fab four 25 years later." *The Wall Street Journal,* p. A12.

29 Upon his death, Frank Sinatra received 13 minutes of coverage on CBS Nightly News, far more than any other entertainer in the history of the program. Newspapers routinely featured the story in the top half of page

1.[ref: Holland, B. (1998, June 19). "The mystery of Frank Sinatra." *Goldmine*.] Elvis's death is mourned annually by millions, and he is periodically spotted alive and occasionally treated by the devout as a savior. John Lennon's death caused mass mourning and is still remembered in annual pilgrimages. His passing is often characterized as the death of a great cultural dream, as indeed it was. Michael Jackson may not be quite so idolized, as his popularity was in a fifth Cycle wave, which is usually a weak echo of the more powerful third wave, but it is unlikely that he will be forgotten.

30 Schonberg, H.C. (1987). *The great pianists from Mozart to the present.*

31 Liszt stayed nearly this popular through half of the wave (B) advance within the 1836-1859 bear market, then abruptly ceased doing paid concerts. He was revered throughout his life, and even as late as the 1870s, pianists wanted to "play like Liszt." Today, rockers are still trying to become the next Elvis or Beatles.

Chapter 16:

Historical Impulsion: Events that Result from Social Mood Trends

Le Bon surmised, "The memorable events of history are the visible effects of the invisible changes in human thought."[1] Indeed, major historic events that are often considered important to the future (i.e., economic activity, lawmaking, war) are not causes of change; they are the result of social mood changes that have already occurred. To put it succinctly, while the stock market is like a *thermometer* with respect to public mood, it is like a *barometer* with respect to public action.

The *primary* cause of each type of action is the same: social mood trends. The difference is in the time it takes to translate thoughts into results. The mechanics of this difference apply even to mood changes within individuals. For instance, a person whose ebullience crosses a particular threshold may decide on the same day to purchase a stock, wear a bright tie, build a house and expand his business. Results of the first two decisions can be fully realized in a matter of minutes. The results of the latter two decisions would take months to become fully realized. The first two would be recorded directly in cultural data. The latter two would show up later in data on activities that lag the initial impulse which produced them.

A reason that collective action in particular is a lagging indicator of aggregate mood change is that while an individual can initiate action immediately upon a mood change, a society requires a good deal of time for an extensive swing in mood to spread throughout the populace before it is positioned to initiate coordinated collective action. For instance, to motivate a body that represents the society to undertake an action such as creating a sweeping new law, electing a new regime or starting a war, the necessary

mood must have taken root throughout much of the society and reached extreme proportions. Then, just as with individual economic decisions, the ultimate manifestation must further await the mechanics of implementation.

If we were to plot very precisely statistics on the economy, war activity and election results, i.e., the products of social mood trends, they should produce plots that reflect, with a short time lag, the trends in the stock market. Let us examine some major areas of activity that the stock market, in its barometric function, foreshadows.

Economic Consequences of Social Mood Trends

Social mood trends have economic consequences. Men produce more goods and services when the dominant social mood trend is positive rather than negative. The reason for the lag between *mood* (as tracked by the stock market) and *result* is that it takes time for people to put their new-found energy to work and then to reap the fruits of its employment, or on the other hand to reverse one's forward momentum and witness the results.

If this is true, then economic trends should lag stock market trends. This is indeed an established fact, as the National Bureau of Economic Research in Cambridge has found that, year after year, the S&P Composite index of 500 stocks of major corporations is the single best indicator among the dozen that the Commerce Department uses to foreshadow broad economic trends.[2] In other words, no one has found a better advance indicator of the economy than the stock market. When we plot the history of recessions, depressions and economic booms against the stock market, we see this correlation at work. As we look at a few examples, notice that in each case, the economic change does not precede and cause mood change; it follows mood change. In fact, *the bigger the mood change, the bigger the effect.*

Figure 16-1 examines the big history-making stock market declines. As you can see, *the four largest declines in the stock market* over the past 250 years preceded *four of the largest depressions* in U.S. history, those of 1790-1794, 1840-1843, 1857-1858 and 1929-1933. The single largest stock drop (1929-1932) produced the single biggest depression. The multiple stock panics of 1795-1813 produced multiple depressions. The economic contractions of 1874-1879, 1884-1885, 1893-1894, 1896-1897, 1907-1908, 1920-1921 and lesser ones along the way all developed *after* downturns in stocks.

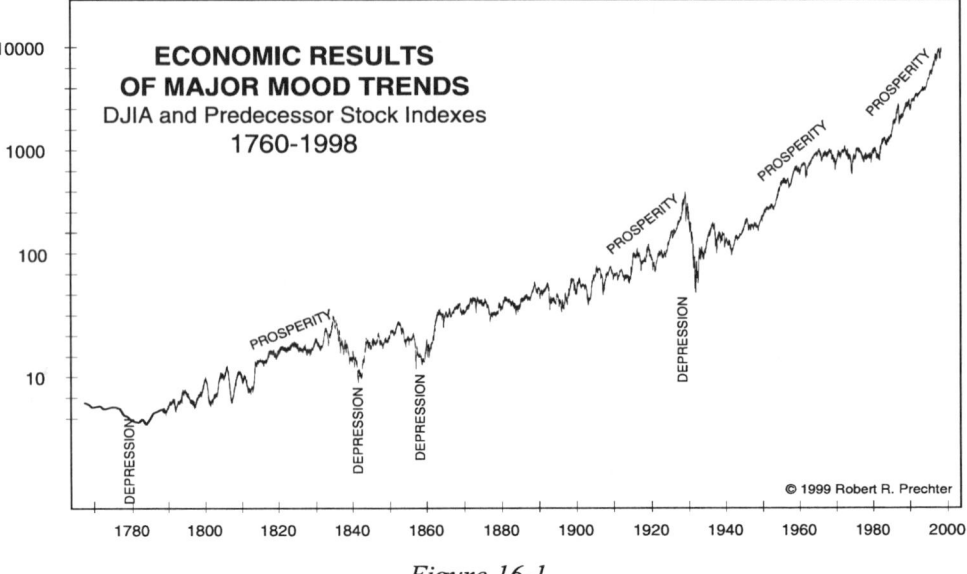

Figure 16-1

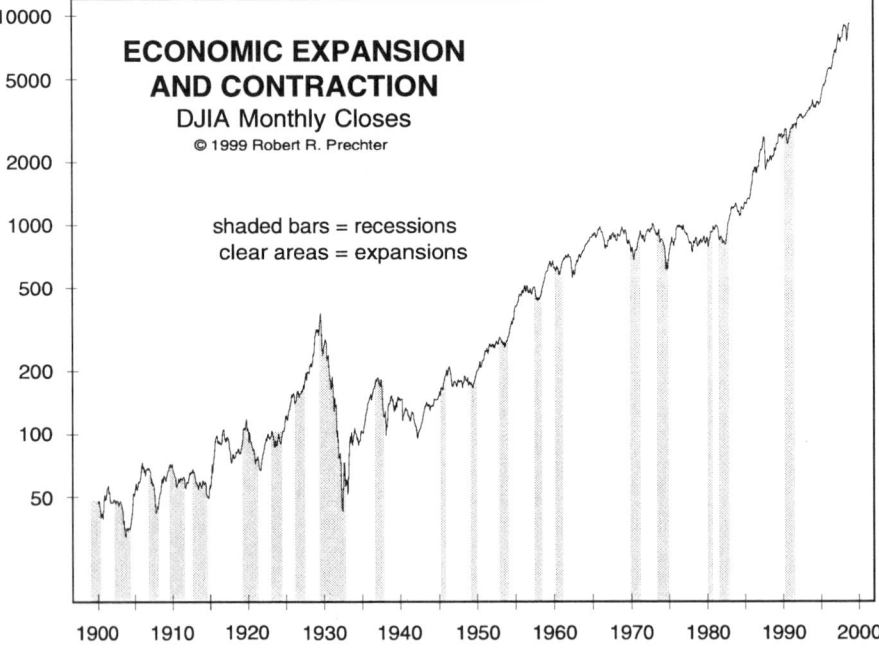

Figure 16-2

As you can see in Figure 16-2, every economic contraction in the 20th century also followed a stock market decline except for the recession of 1945. Every stock market decline did not produce a recession, but every *corrective wave* of at least Primary degree did, whether in wave A or C or both, as detailed in Figure 16-3. For example, in the corrections of 1937-1942 and 1959-1962, recessions occurred in the "A" waves but not in the "C" waves. In the corrections of 1946-1949, 1966-1970, 1976-1980 and 1987-1990 (as reflected by the Value Line Index per the inset), recessions occurred in the "C" waves but not in the "A" waves. There are even two relatively rare "E" waves of triangles on this graph: 1946-1949 (in PPI-adjusted prices; see inset and Figure 16-6) and 1973-1974, both of which produced recessions.[3] A socionomist, then, has the Wave Principle to make the stock market indicator of recession more accurate. Rather than saying simply that recessions often follow setbacks in the stock market, I have refined the indicator as follows: *A recession results from any negative mood trend (stock market correction) of Primary degree or higher,* typically af-

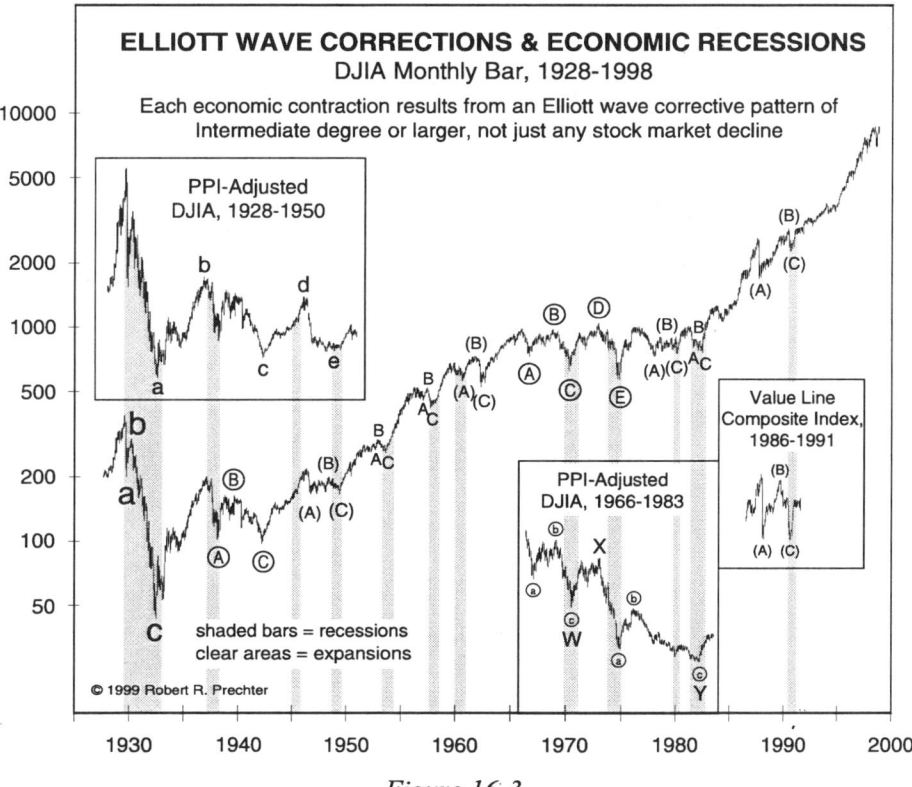

Figure 16-3

ter the start of at least one of its declining subwaves of one lower degree. Sometimes a recession occurs after the start of more than one subwave. This tendency is increasingly likely at Cycle and Supercycle degree and inevitable at Grand Supercycle degree and above.

Now take a closer look at *lesser* changes over the past five decades. In Figure 16-4, the yearly percentage change in real GDP is plotted against the 12-month rate of change in the S&P. Even in this crude rendition of annual data, one can see the *lagging* economic results of *leading* changes in mood. The stock market rose in 1954, and the economy expanded in 1955. The stock market fell in 1957, and the economy was weaker in 1958. The stock market soared in 1975, and the economy roared in 1976. Sometimes the nuances are telling. For example, the stock market's decline into *August* 1982 reflected lower energy levels among people, the result of which was less production into *November* 1982. The S&P topped in 1983 after the *fastest one-year rise* in forty years. This rapid change toward positive mood caused a higher energy and greater output, which peaked the following year, in 1984, at a 6.8% rate, *the highest annual output* of the past four decades. As mood continued to *wax, though at a lesser rate*, the economy

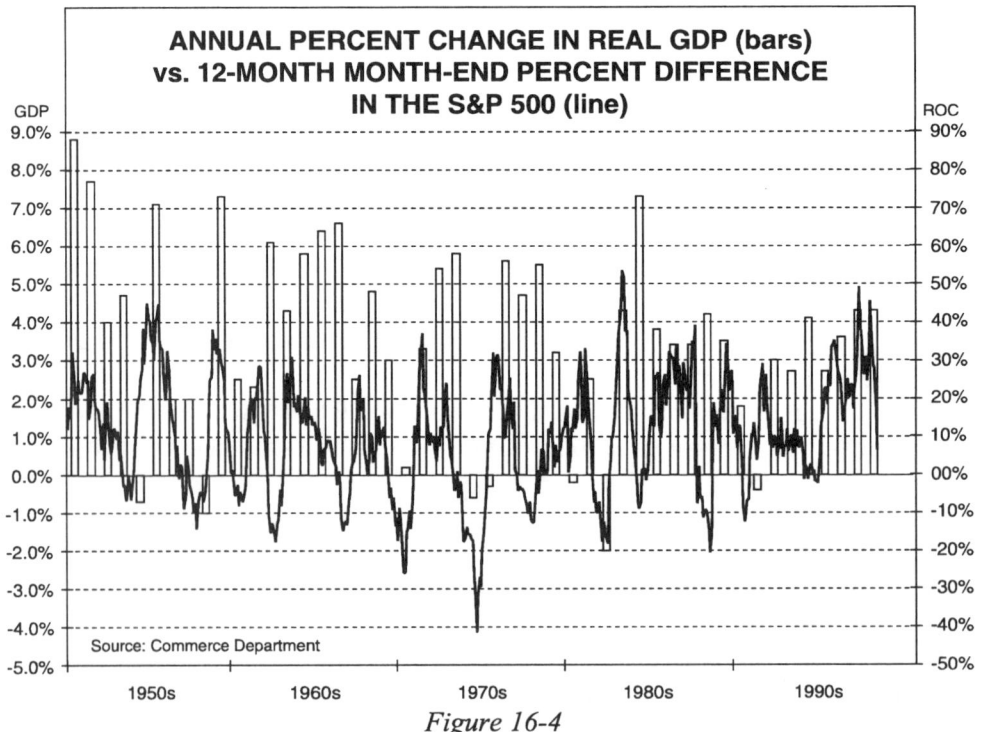

Figure 16-4

continued to *expand, though at a lesser rate.* The stock market, and there-fore mood, went into a "correction" from 1987 to 1990, as expressed most clearly in the Value Line stock index (see inset in Figure 16-3). The wax-ing negative mood finally produced a drop in productivity figures in 1991, the year *after* the correction ended.[4] Stocks rose to a new all-time high during the 1991 recession, leading the economy out of its slump.

The next major corrective pattern in the stock market will lead to the next recession, and if it is of large enough degree, to a depression. This train of causality is unceasing.

Supporting my thesis both of social mood causality *and* the direct-recording mechanism of the stock market is the inescapable observation that *the extent of expansion or contraction correlates with the degree of the preceding trend change in the stock market.*

Many economists brush off the tight correlation between stock mar-ket trends and economic trends by endlessly repeating the joke that "the stock market has called fifteen of the last ten recessions" or some such quip. This is myopia, and it is due to two things. The first reason is the lack of knowledge of the Wave Principle. One must know what corrective *pat-terns* are in order to observe the right correlation between those patterns and economic activity. Second, a bureau has established an "official" defi-nition of a recession, which requires meeting a certain arbitrary threshold of contraction. If the economic statistics do not fit into that formula, then it is not considered a recession. However, *all* changes in the economy are relevant to investigating their correlation to the trends in the stock market. Sometimes the larger uptrend in mood is so powerful that a decline in stock prices produces only a brief contraction or just a *slowdown* in productive gains. The result is still recessive, but not a "recession." Like the intensity of social mood itself, the *effects* of social mood are a function not only of the size of mood change but also of its *position within the overall wave structure*, which injects nuances into the study.

As a final comment, I would add that any method that calls fifteen out of the last ten recessions is immeasurably more successful than any econo-mist on record and infinitely more successful than economists in the aggregate (see Chapter 19). It is unfathomable that serious professionals can poke fun at such a record. Moreover, when we take the Wave Principle into account, corrective patterns have announced *every* recession this cen-tury but one (1945).[5]

Stock market trends also predicate trends in corporate earnings, as shown in Figure 19-3. I have more work to do to show how closely stocks and economic output track each other, but I believe there is enough evi-

dence here to establish my hypothesis of the social mood causality of economic trends. We will now examine some *political* effects of social mood.

Peace

The latter portions of major bull markets are always relatively peaceful times. For instance, the latter bull market periods of 1815-1835, 1875-1892, 1921-1929, 1954-1965 and 1982 to today have been almost entirely free of U.S. war involvement.

Major advances in mood invariably produce overtures of reconciliation and treaty. In 1928-1929, at the top of Supercycle wave (III), President Hoover pursued the Kellogg-Briand peace pact and presided over a contraction in U.S. armed forces. Lesser degree social mood peaks bring lesser expressions of peace. For example, in January-February 1966, right at the top of Cycle wave III, President Johnson pushed a "peace offensive" in Vietnam, which soon melted into an escalation of the war as the ensuing bear market unfolded. On January 23, 1973, days after an all-time high in the DJIA that held for ten years, President Nixon concluded a peace agreement that ended the Vietnam War. In 1987, as the stock market reached a zenith, the Soviet Union pulled out of Afghanistan, which it had engaged in war at the stock market bottom in 1982. At the same time, President Reagan, who had been referring to the Soviet Union as the Evil Empire, reached a major missile ban agreement with the Soviets in mid-September, a few weeks from the high. (It was signed as a treaty on December 8, a lagging result of the previous mood trend.)

In the late 1990s, we are approaching the top of wave (V), which will also mark a Grand Supercycle degree top, the largest in over 2½ centuries. Coextensively, during this time there have been almost too many peace initiatives to count. Olive branches have been offered in the political, religious, racial and social realms worldwide, many of which have addressed grievances and soothed conflicts that have existed for centuries. Here is a partial list: the Prime Minister of Israel and the Chairman of the Palestine Liberation Organization, enemies (symbolically speaking) for millennia, executed a historic peacekeeping handshake for the press; 117 nations signed the North American Free Trade Agreement (NAFTA) and the General Agreement on Tariffs and Trade (GATT); after decades of violence, the Irish Republican Army ceased military operations in Northern Ireland, and the English and Irish Prime Ministers signed a peace treaty; the Catholic Church entered into an accord with the Jewish state in which the Vatican and Israel, enemies symbolically for nearly 2000 years, officially recog-

nized one another for the first time; Russia, Ukraine and the U.S., after 40 years of mutual nuclear threat, promised in a treaty to stop aiming warheads at each other; China and Russia, enemies for decades, signed a peace pact vowing not to use force against one another; Presidents Clinton and Yeltsin met in a summit that was described as a "virtual lovefest" by *USA Today*; Yeltsin stated flatly in a speech at the Library of Congress: "We will never fight the United States";[6] France invited Germany to parade its soldiers down the Champs-Elysees in Paris on France's biggest national holiday in a symbol of postwar reconciliation; a European Union was consummated following 1500 years of repeated conflict in the region.[7] Some elements of this list are depicted in Figure 18-6. This multi-year pageant of apology, concession and agreement and the concurrent wonderful atmosphere of international peace and cooperation are consistent with my Elliott wave case that an uptrend of *Grand* Supercycle degree is ending.

War

Major mood retrenchment produces war, as humans finally express their collective negative mood extreme with representative collective action. As with economic output, the size of a war is almost always related to the size of the bear market that induces it. Figure 16-5 is a depiction of the U.S. stock market (spliced to the English one prior to 1789) for the past 300 years. As you can see, the three biggest wars involving North Americans followed the three largest stock market declines. The Revolutionary War began near the end of the 64-year bear market in British stock prices that began in 1720. The Civil War followed the 24-year bear market of 74% that ended in 1859. World War II began six years after the 89% collapse in stock prices that bottomed in 1932 and during a 50% drop into 1942.

The Revolutionary War was arguably an English war that resulted from England's bear market, and the lack of an efficient technology for transporting troops across the Atlantic Ocean kept casualties relatively low. Regardless, it is the case that all wars involving United States soldiers have typically produced American casualties in proportion to the size of the mood retrenchment that led to the war. Some statistics are remarkably reflective of this tendency. In World War I[8] and the Vietnam War, which accompanied or immediately followed corrections of *Cycle* degree, deaths among U.S. military personnel totaled 53,402 and 47,378 respectively. In the Civil War and World War II, which accompanied or immediately fol-

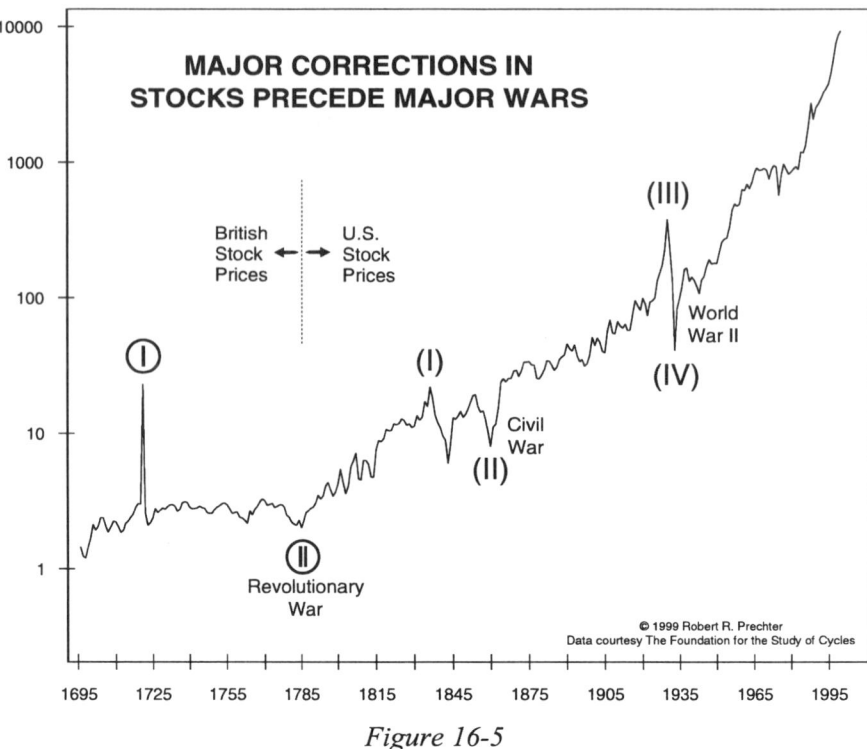

Figure 16-5

lowed corrections of *Supercycle* degree (one degree larger), deaths caused directly by war activity totaled 294,900[9,10] (including Confederates) and 291,557 respectively. In the wars that accompanied or immediately followed corrections of *Primary* degree, such as the Bay of Pigs fiasco and the Gulf War, only a few U.S. military personnel died.[11]

The Importance of Wave Labels to Bellicose Action

I must mention something here that is rather technical but which is too important to relegate to an endnote. Conflict results from a contraction in mood, but the appearance of conflict is *not* strictly a function of the size of the contraction. *It is a function both of its size and its position in the wave structure.* To predict conflict, then, one must know the Wave Principle. The most intense conflicts, such as wars, are not associated with all large bear markets but *typically occur during or immediately after the largest C waves in corrective processes of Primary degree and higher.* A waves, regardless of extent, rarely result in war.

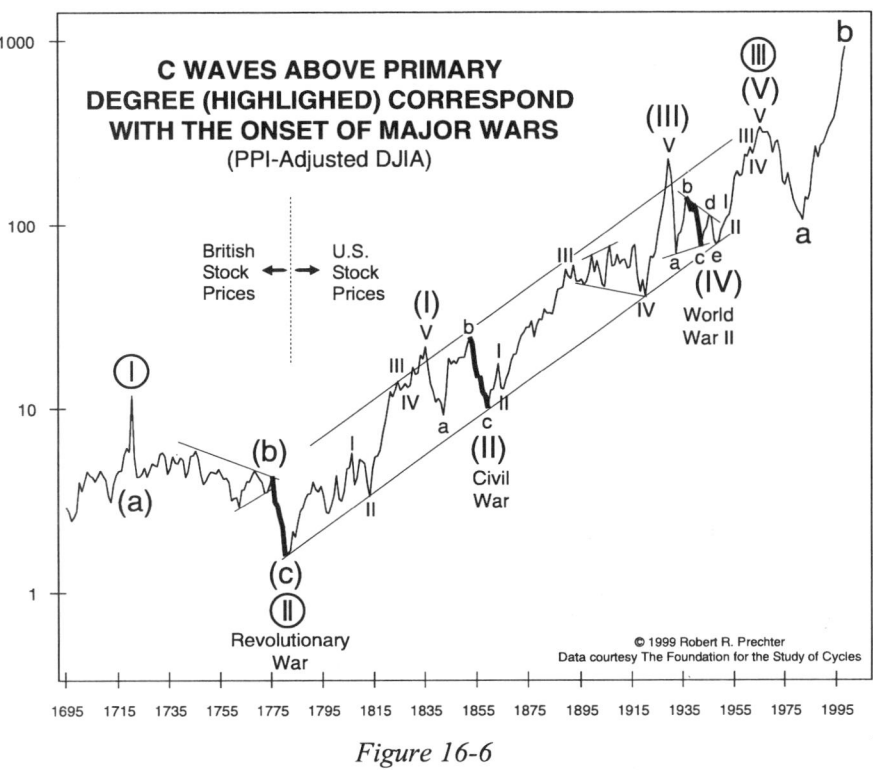

Figure 16-6

Figure 16-6 is the same graph as Figure 16-5 except that it is adjusted for changes in the Producer Price Index, which allows us to see some different nuances in the 20th century. I have labeled all pertinent A-B-C corrections and overlaid a thick, dark line over the C waves. As you can see, the huge A wave crashes in mood of 1720-1722, 1835-1842 and 1929-1932, despite their monstrous severity, *did not produce wars*. The C waves that followed each of them *did*.

Let us go through each of these three bear markets to see the development of events. When the last Grand Supercycle bear market began in 1720 with a devastating two-year stock market collapse for wave **(a)**, no major war followed. The Revolutionary War broke out in the *late* 1700s during wave **(c)** of the (a)-(b)-(c) corrective process. When Supercycle wave (II) began in 1835 with a seven-year collapse for wave **a**, no war occurred. The Civil War began in 1861, two years after the end of wave **c**. When Supercycle wave (IV) began in 1929 with a record-breaking three-year collapse for wave **a**, no war followed. World War II began in 1938, one year after

the start of wave **c** of (IV). (All of these declines were "C" waves in nominal terms as well, the only difference being that the last one was wave Ⓒ of II, as shown in Figure 5-12.)

Even the smaller bear markets exhibit these characteristics. (The following three examples are not illustrated.) The War of 1812 did not break out with the panic of 1807 in wave Ⓐ but during the *second* declining phase, in wave Ⓒ. The Spanish-American War did not take place in wave Ⓐ of IV in 1890, but in 1898, two years after the end of wave Ⓒ of IV. World War I did not begin with the panic of 1907, but during the *second* declining phase of the corrective pattern from 1910 to 1914. The Vietnam War, which began uncharacteristically early with regard to Elliott wave patterns,[12] nevertheless reached its greatest intensity and saw its strongest domestic opposition (in the form of "May Day"1970 campus riots, which resulted in the shooting of students at Kent State University at the month of the stock market low) during Primary wave Ⓒ of IV (refer to Figure 16-3). The Gulf War did not break out after the 1987 crash, which was wave (A) in the Value Line index (see inset in Figure 16-3), but in January 1991, right after the end of wave (C) in October 1990. Like the record for recessions, the record for wars has one exception. The Mexican War, a brief encounter in 1848, took place near the top of wave b within a 24-year bear market. The Vietnam War is at least a partial exception. Overall, this evidence indicates *that wars are almost always the product of "C" waves in a corrective process* of at least Primary degree, not merely any severe decline in stock prices and social mood.[13]

Apparently society handles the first retrenchment in social mood, no matter how severe. "A" waves surprise optimistic people, who are unprepared and unwilling to wage war. After the monstrous crash of 1720-1722, in fact, not only was there no significant war, but major powers arranged a "détente" (partly to deal with the debt under which so many of them labored). It is the second drop that makes a sufficient number of increasingly stressed people angry enough to attack others militarily.[14] "C" waves are apparently the "last straw" psychologically for those who suffered once in the "A" wave. This proposed psychological sequence appears to explain the social result even though, to complicate matters, what are labeled "C" waves in some stock indexes may be labeled "wave two" of the new advance in others. The Civil War fits a "wave two" labeling in both plots, and World War II attended such labeling in the nominal DJIA (see Figure 16-5).

The Importance of Wave Position to Social Acts of Construction and Destruction

Advance-decline statistics in the stock market during third waves and "C" waves show broad participation by a great number of *stocks* (see discussion in Chapter 7). Likewise, in third waves and "C" waves, a broad cross section of the *populace* is apparently influenced or affected by the social mood trend. The ethic of achievement that is rooted throughout a society in a third wave up induces the fulfillment of *constructive* social goals, such as the interstate highway system and the space program that were executed in the U.S. during wave III (or the Great Pyramid of Egypt or the roads and aqueducts of the Roman empire undoubtedly as well). On the other hand, the wide spread of anger, fear and deprivation throughout a society in a "C" wave decline induces the fulfillment of *destructive* social goals through actions such as waging war.

War between nations is not the only consequence of large C waves down in mood. Bear markets of sufficient size appear to bring about a desire to slaughter groups of successful people. In 1793-1794, radical Frenchmen guillotined countless members of high society. In the 1930s, Stalin slaughtered Ukrainians. In the 1940s, Nazis slaughtered Jews. In the 1970s, Communists in Cambodia and China slaughtered the affluent. In 1998, after their country's financial collapse, Indonesians went on a rampage and slaughtered Chinese merchants.

Such undertakings, particularly when sponsored by the state as most of them are, require immense cooperation. It might be postulated that major "C" wave declines are times when *destructive social goals are achieved with wide cooperation*, just as third waves on the upside are times when *constructive social goals are achieved with wide cooperation*.

I include this section because it makes the larger point that *a rigorous practice of socionomics depends upon an understanding of the details of the Wave Principle*. While elsewhere this book meticulously avoids discussing Elliott wave nuances to keep from bogging you down in detail, it is important to understand their utmost importance.

Nuclear Testing as a Function of Worldwide Social Mood

If you take the time to read the history of wars, you will find that the statements and events that lead to tensions that lead to conflict and then to escalation often quite faithfully reflect mood changes recorded by the DJIA. For example, the Mexican War resulted from tensions that began in 1835,

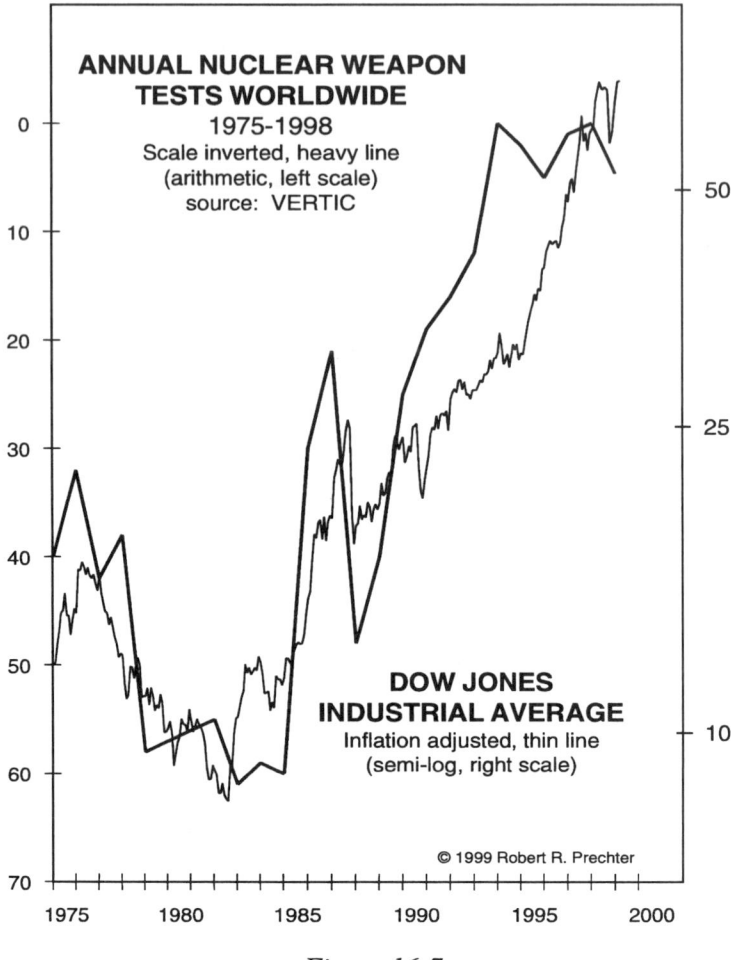

Figure 16-7

the year the bear market started. The Civil War resulted from tensions that built throughout the bear market of 1835-1859.

While we do not have graphs of warlike thinking or preparation to show how well they would correlate with the smaller ebbs and flows of social mood, we do have one that comes close. Figure 16-7 is a graph of the number of annual worldwide nuclear weapons tests in the past twenty years plotted against the DJIA. Note the extreme parallelism. This relationship makes the point that smaller waves of mood change result in responses that are sometimes far more subtle than warring, *but they take place nevertheless*.

Figure 16-8

Political Freedom as a Function of Worldwide Social Mood

Figure 16-8 is a graph of worldwide political freedom over the past 200 years plotted against U.S. stock prices.[15] Note the general parallelism. This relationship suggests that advancing waves tend to lead to political freedom, while retrenchments tend to lead to political repression. As social mood becomes more positive, more territory moves from dictatorship to representative government. As social mood becomes more negative, more territory falls to dictators. For example, communists took over Russia at the social mood low of 1917. Fascists took over Germany at the social mood low of 1933. Russia took over Eastern Europe over the course of the 1946-1949 bear market, which ended the 20-year-long Supercycle wave

IV corrective pattern in constant-dollar terms (see Figure 16-6). Mao took over China right at the end of wave e of the pattern, in 1949. Pol Pot took over Cambodia in 1975, immediately after the low of Cycle wave IV. In contrast, the Communists voluntarily *relinquished* power over Russia and Eastern Europe at the social mood high of 1989.[16]

Electoral Consequences of Social Mood Trends

The social psychology that accompanies a bull or bear market is the main determinant not only of how voters select a president but also of how they perceive his performance. Correlation with the stock market, consumer confidence, economic performance and other measures suggests that social mood is by far the main determinant of presidential popularity.

What a leader does is mostly acausal with respect to the public's opinion of him. There are two reasons for this fact. First, his actions, despite their endless analysis in the press, do little to affect his popularity. Second, his popularity is dependent upon a social mood and economy over which he can exercise no countertrend influence. If you are new to these ideas, they may be hard to swallow. Aren't some presidents fools or rogues and others statesmen? Don't some presidents affect the economy for good or ill? As to the first question, the answer is, certainly there are presidents of high or low character and ability. However, that does not affect their popularity. For example, President John Kennedy blew the only military conflict in which he engaged the country, attacked the steel industry out of pique to no result, and continually committed adultery. He is revered. Why? Because the country was in a state of euphoria for all but a few months of his term, euphoria that morphed three months later into Beatlemania. As to the second question, the answer is, certainly presidential actions affect the economy. However, the president is not the one who is in control of his social efficacy. For example, the laissez-faire and low-tax policies of President Ronald Reagan helped spur the economy in the early 1980s, but they did not help spur the economy in those ways in 1979 *because he was not elected in 1976*. Social mood called the shots on when it was time for a change. When most of the population wanted lesser taxes and regulation, they got it.

First we will examine the electoral fortunes of some U.S. political figureheads both at extremes in social mood trends as well as in more moderate times. As we shall see, social mood determines their perceived efficacy, legacy and fate.

Near lows of major bear markets, incumbent presidents have suffered their greatest defeats. Apparently, the populace blames the rapid mood change toward the negative and its associated events (such as economic contraction) on the incumbent, so voters overwhelmingly reject him and the party he represents.

For example, Martin Van Buren was ousted by a landslide in 1840 near the low of wave **a** of (II); Herbert Hoover was ousted by a landslide in 1932 at the low of wave (IV), Jimmy Carter was ousted by a landslide in 1980 near the low of wave ② in nominal terms and a major low in constant-dollar terms. An interesting victim of dramatic market change to the downside was Richard Nixon. He was elected by a landslide in 1972, two months before the price *peak* of wave IV in nominal terms, then had to resign his office amidst a barrage of social hatred two months before the price *low* of wave IV less than two years later. Figure 16-9 shows the timing of these events. (See Figures 16-5, 16-6 and 5-12 for wave labels.)[17]

The extent of the political reversal is related to the degree of the bear market. The most dramatic defeats of incumbent U.S. presidents have occurred near lows within Supercycle degree bear markets. Lesser ones have occurred near lows within Cycle degree bear markets.

The larger the degree of the market reversal, the longer the party newly elected at its end holds power afterward, since that party is credited with causing the turnaround. After the Supercycle wave (II) low of 1859 when a Democrat had been in office, Republicans won six elections in a row. After the equivalent Supercycle wave (IV) low of 1932 when a Republican had been in office, Democrats won five elections in a row. (For wave labels, see Figure 16-5.) The one-degree-smaller Cycle low of 1828 gave Democrats a comparatively lesser three elections in a row, just as the similar lows of 1896, 1920 and 1980 (see Figure 16-6) each gave Republicans three elections in a row. The key determinant is *not* the politics of the party, but which one is blamed for the preceding downward social mood trend.

The *second* election in a new bull market produces a landslide in favor of the party, and typically the candidate, already in power. In 1832, a landslide retained Andrew Jackson in office. In 1864, a landslide retained Abraham Lincoln in office. In 1924, a landslide retained Calvin Coolidge in office. In 1936, a landslide retained Franklin Roosevelt in office. In 1956, an electoral landslide retained Dwight Eisenhower in office. In 1984, a landslide retained Ronald Reagan in office. Every one of these was a retention in a new bull market.

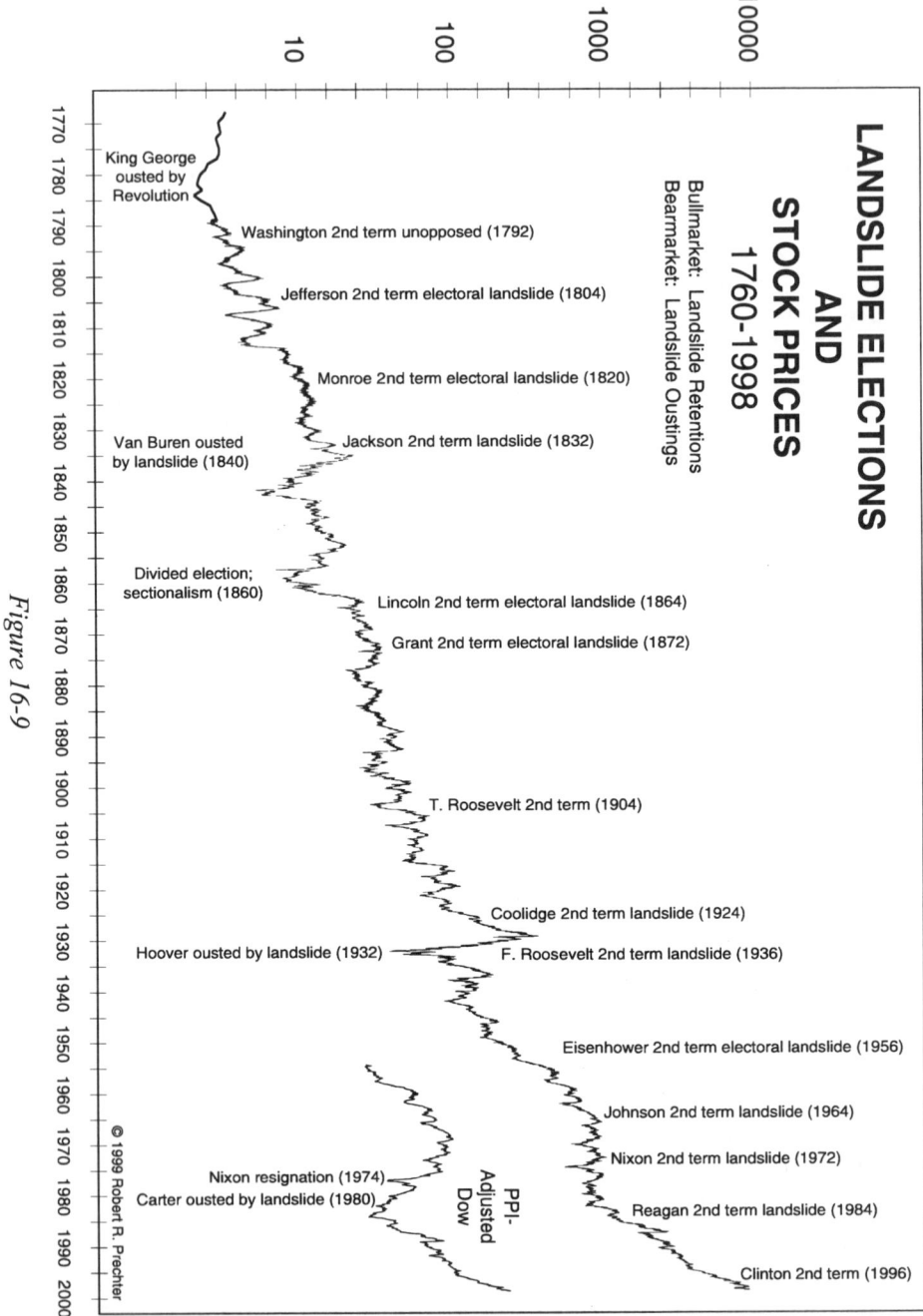

Figure 16-9

LANDSLIDE ELECTIONS
AND
STOCK PRICES
1760-1998

Bullmarket: Landslide Retentions
Bearmarket: Landslide Oustings

King George ousted by Revolution

Washington 2nd term unopposed (1792)

Jefferson 2nd term electoral landslide (1804)

Monroe 2nd term electoral landslide (1820)

Van Buren ousted by landslide (1840)

Jackson 2nd term landslide (1832)

Divided election; sectionalism (1860)

Lincoln 2nd term electoral landslide (1864)

Grant 2nd term electoral landslide (1872)

T. Roosevelt 2nd term (1904)

Coolidge 2nd term landslide (1924)

Hoover ousted by landslide (1932)

F. Roosevelt 2nd term landslide (1936)

Eisenhower 2nd term electoral landslide (1956)

Johnson 2nd term landslide (1964)

Nixon 2nd term landslide (1972)

Nixon resignation (1974)

Carter ousted by landslide (1980)

Reagan 2nd term landslide (1984)

Clinton 2nd term (1996)

PPI-Adjusted Dow

© 1999 Robert R. Prechter

In each developing fifth wave of Cycle degree, that candidate's *party* also won a third election. In 1836, within one year of the peak of wave V of (I), Martin Van Buren was elected by a substantial margin (though smaller than his predecessor, since the peak had occurred a year earlier), securing a third consecutive term for the Democratic party. In 1928, within one year of the peak of wave V of (III), Calvin Coolidge wisely declined to run (he would have won the election but lost the respect of history), and Herbert Hoover was elected by a substantial margin (a landslide, since the uptrend was still in force), securing a third consecutive term for the Republican party. In 1988, in wave V of (V), George Bush was elected by a substantial margin (though smaller than his predecessor, since a temporary peak had occurred a year earlier), securing a third term in a row for the Republican party. These examples show that fifth waves of *Cycle* degree to date have guaranteed *two* additional elections to the recently elected party, usually by large margins. Fifth waves of *Primary* degree appear to guarantee one additional election.

Presidents are also retained by landslides in elections that take place near major stock market tops. Grant won a landslide in 1872. In 1964, Lyndon Johnson, who had presided since Kennedy's death, won in a landslide. In 1972, Nixon won reelection in a landslide.

The implication is clear: In the first case, nervous voters want society to "stay the course" in its new-found good fortune. In the second case, they want to maintain the euphoria that they feel at a social mood peak. In both cases, they think that reelecting a president or maintaining a political party will have the desired effect. The cause-and-effect relationship, however, is in the opposite direction.

Nuances

Once again, I will explore nuance briefly, just to communicate how closely history repeats at similar times in the wave structure. As one example, Cycle degree fifth waves have produced a remarkably similar sequence of elections and background conditions in the past two hundred years. Wave V of (I) occurred from 1828 to 1835. Republican Andrew Jackson was elected by a large margin (178 to 83 electoral votes), was retained in office by a landslide victory (219 to 49), enjoyed an endearing nickname, "Old Hickory," and presided during a debt-fueled speculative boom in stocks and land. He was succeeded by a member of the same party. Wave V of (III) occurred from 1921 to 1929. Republican Warren

Harding was elected by a large margin (404 to 127); Calvin Coolidge took over when Harding died in office, was retained in office by a landslide victory (382 to 136 and a margin of 1.9:1 in popular vote, the largest ever), enjoyed an endearing nickname, "Silent Cal," and presided during a debt-fueled speculative boom in stocks and land. He was succeeded by a member of the same party. The liftoff portion of wave V of (V) occurred from 1982 to 1987. Republican Ronald Reagan was elected by a large margin (489 to 49), was retained in office by a landslide victory (525 to 13), enjoyed an endearing nickname, "The Great Communicator," and presided during a debt-fueled speculative boom in stocks and land. He was succeeded by a member of the same party. 1988 was the first time that a sitting Vice President was elected since 1836 and the first time that the Republicans had won three in a row since 1928, each of those being near the previous fifth wave peaks of Cycle degree.

If an uptrend in social mood persists for a long time, it eventually becomes taken for granted. Then voters' patterns change because *they no longer assume that they must keep a particular person or party in power to maintain what they now regard as normal conditions.* However, they change exactly in a way that reflects their increasing ebullience and confidence as the positive mood reaches extremes. A typical result is the election of politicians more willing to express social feelings of abundance by supporting or initiating social programs. For instance, after electing the conservative Eisenhower twice during the initial phase of a long bull market, the public voted in a moderate Kennedy and then a liberal Johnson near the top. Similarly in the 1980s, after electing the conservative Reagan twice during the initial phase of the bull market, the public voted in a moderate Bush and then a liberal Clinton.

Given that Cycle wave V of (V) is ending a much larger *Grand* Supercycle, a second president, Bill Clinton, has enjoyed the benefits of an extension of wave V's debt-fueled uptrend in stocks and land. As befits the relative weakness of a fifth wave of a fifth wave, the quality of the luster is off substantially. He did not win his second term in a landslide, and his nickname is a far less endearing "Slick Willie." (To see my comments and forecast regarding President Clinton's fortunes, see Chapter 17.)

There may be a connection between fifth waves of Supercycle degree as well. 1998 has marked the first year since 1928, near the end of wave V of (III), that each of three consecutive elections has produced Republican domination of both houses of Congress.

Even Near-Term Trends in Mood and Politics are Correlated

Major trends, then, are quite clear in their electoral influence. What about trends that last mere months? Join me on a roller coaster ride with President George Bush.

The *Time* magazine cover of August 1989 read, "How Bush Decides: He's smarter than Reagan, less driven than Carter and savvy like Nixon"! Gallup polls of January 1990 showed that Bush sported a phenomenal approval rating of 80% at the end of his first year in office compared to Reagan's 40%, Carter's 55%, and Nixon's 61%. The only higher first-year approval rating recorded was in 1961 when President Kennedy enjoyed the euphoria of all-time stock market highs after the extended Primary wave ③ of the 1950s. *The Wall Street Journal* on April 20 called Bush "a man for the season" who "wins praise" and "rides a huge current of political popularity." On May 1, a political cartoon showed Bush rejoicing that the U.S. had turned "into a one-party system!"

A *single quarter* made a tremendous difference. When the Dow slid 21% from mid-July to mid-October 1990, the Value Line index fell nearly to its 1987 low and the Dow Transports finished a collapse of 47%, the press no longer regarded Bush as a political genius. In October and November, they bombed him with derisive headlines and comments such as, "Bush May Have Lost 1992 Already," "From Sizzle to Fizzle," "Bush Faces a GOP Revolt," "The Bush Blueprint Bombs," "The Carterization of Bush," "Is Bush Presidency Headed for Doom?," and "a quagmire of indecision and ineptitude which could take him the rest of the Presidency to dig out." The direct effect of the social mood change on the perception of national leaders extended around the world:

1) England's Margaret Thatcher resigned under pressure after serving for eleven years, the longest term for a British Prime Minister this century.

2) The Prime Minister of Singapore, the longest serving democratically elected head of state, resigned.

3) The President of France, according to headlines of the time, was "fighting to stay in power" as his administration fell apart.

4) The President of Brazil's political honeymoon came "to an abrupt end eight months after he came to power," said *The Wall Street Journal*.[18]

Just four months after the press unleashed its blizzard of derision, the Dow had soared back at 3000. George Bush's approval rating soared right

with it, to 91%, the highest in the history of the records. The media loved him again.

Now the most popular president ever, George Bush was considered unbeatable in the 1992 elections. Prominent Democrats refused to run, so a pack of relative unknowns took to the hustings. You may recall the end of the story. For the rest of 1991, corporate earnings, as a result of the bear market in mood that ended in 1990, plummeted in their sharpest drop since the 1940s. The unemployment rate, which was near 5% when Bush took office, jumped to nearly 8% (see Figure 16-10). Both of these measures of economic well-being were recovering in late 1992, but too sluggishly to cheer the now-disillusioned public. Just eighteen months after his record-setting approval rating, Bush lost the election.

Did this fantastic roller-coaster ride reflect *anything* but social mood? It is absurd to think otherwise. George Bush, as an *individual*, did not in three months metamorphose from a genius to a buffoon, then five months later from a buffoon to the greatest president ever, then in the next eighteen months to a pitiable loser. His change of mind on taxes, for instance, would have been hailed as "statesmanlike" in an uptrend. His handling of the Gulf War, seen first as brilliant as stocks soared, was later found wanting after stocks languished for a year and the economy slowed. At no time did Bush's essential character or moderate, pragmatic political philosophy

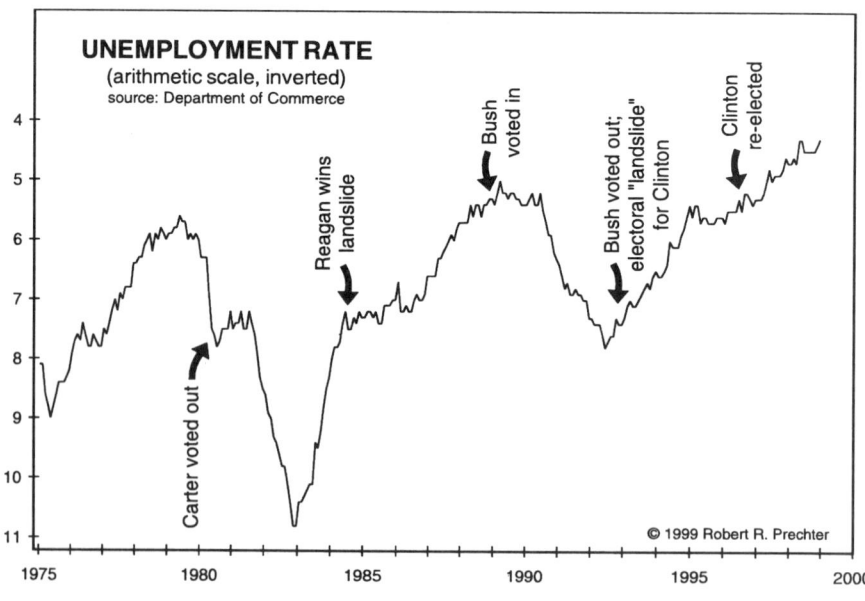

Figure 16-10

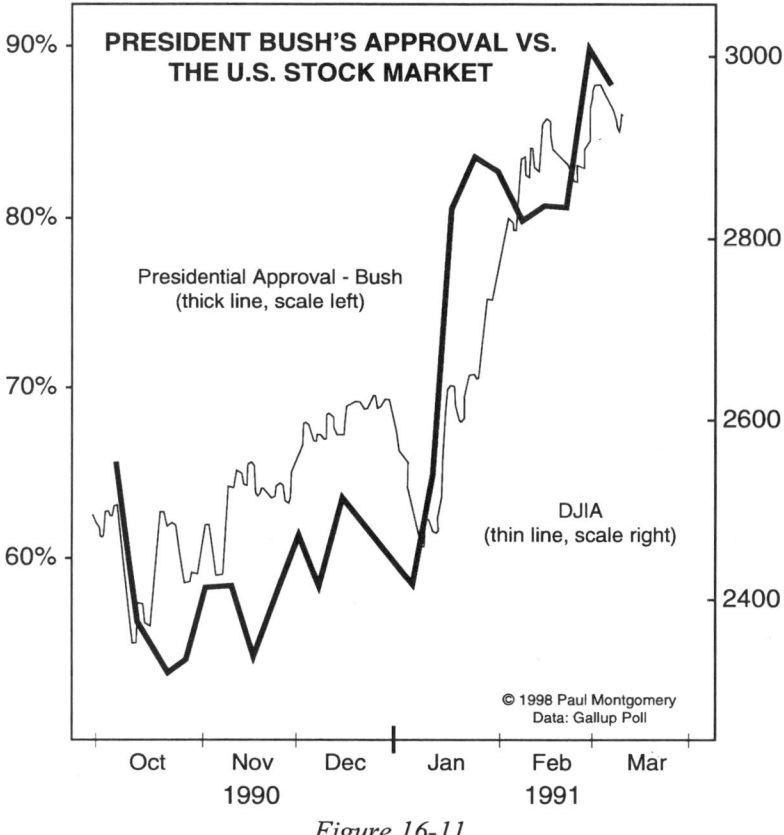

Figure 16-11

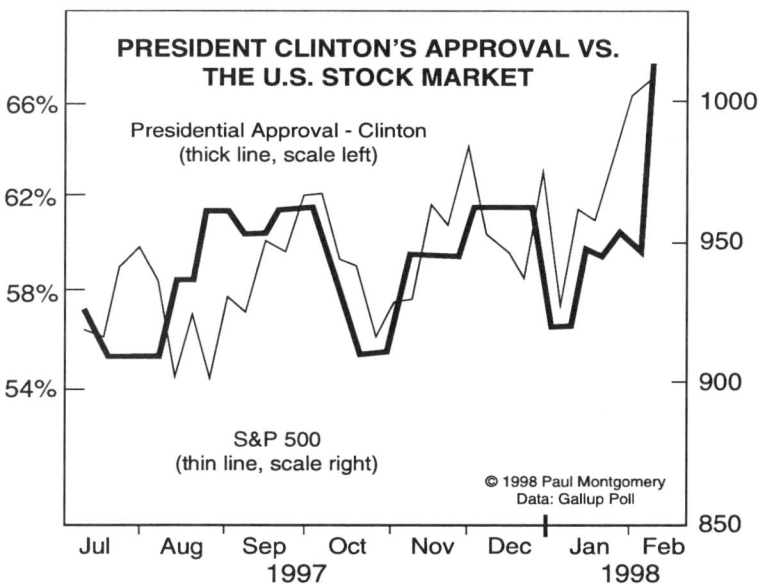

Figure 16-12

change. At each turning point in the wave structure, it was not Bush, but the focus and perception of him, that changed.

We have the records for Bill Clinton as well, and they show the same ebbs and flows with stocks and the economy as did those for George Bush. For some details, see Chapter 17. Analyst Paul Montgomery presented two charts (Figures 16-11 and 16-12) of President Bush's and Clinton's popularity vs. the Dow Jones Industrial Average, each over an eight-month period. These periods included intensely emotional events, the Gulf War and a sex scandal, respectively. As you can see, even such visceral subjects and war, sex and scandal cannot be shown to have a claim on the people's view of the president. Only their aggregate and *independent* mood, as reflected by the trends in the DJIA and its results as reflected by economic statistics, unquestionably does.

There are times when these lines diverge, but when they do, it is always in the direction of the lagging economic statistics. It is never due to the president's actions *apart* from those.

Herding and Leader Selection: Two Results of a Single Cause: Social Mood, Which Follows the Wave Principle

Dr. Paul MacLean concludes from his research, "The reptilian brain in mammals plays a crucial role in...selecting leaders."[19] This is the same portion of the brain that produces the herding impulse. While one might surmise that even in the most primitive portion of the brain, apparently different functions such as mood, herding and judging leaders might be distinct from each other, Figures 16-11 and 16-12 show that this is not the case. I conclude from this parallelism that the latter two operate as a *single impulse*, apparently directed by fluctuations in mood. The connection of social mood specifically to *the* leader is further evident upon observing that voters always associate their feelings primarily with the president, not Congress. If the president during a stock market collapse is of one party while Congress is dominated by the other party, the president's party gets the blame. During the 1929-1932 crash, for instance, Democrats controlled Congress and even passed the Smoot-Hawley tariffs, which many economists warned were economically dangerous, yet the president's party, the Republicans, paid the price. Opposition Congresses bedevil(ed) both Nixon and Clinton, but the president in both cases has received the credit or blame for social moods. Obviously there is little rational thought attached to the very visceral connection among mood, herding and the assessment of leaders. Certainly, however much there is cannot dent the collective expression of the reptilian complex.

In January 1998, *USA Today* summed up the influence of a persistent positive social mood trend on the image of the leader when it said, "President Clinton is the most resilient survivor of scandal in modern American history."[20] The "Teflon coating" that has allowed scandalous allegations of all kinds to slide off his back is simply the sheen of a positive social mood deep in people's minds, which is reflected in rising stock prices. Many observers see Clinton's new all-time highs in popularity amidst countless scandals as a paradox. Montgomery lucidly explains that it is not:

> It constitutes a paradox only if one expects our [collective] opinions regarding our leaders to be rational. As neuroscience, much less casual observation, makes clear, the feelings we have for our leaders are the product not of our highest, but rather our lowest, cortical processes.[21]

Montgomery makes another observation, which summarizes how the lowest cortical processes operate:

> President Bush's popularity as measured by the Gallup Poll moved in an exquisitely precise Elliott wave pattern and followed perfect Fibonacci proportions.[22]

Obviously, if the stock market follows the Wave Principle, and if the public perception of the leader mirrors the stock market, then the public perception of the leader follows the Wave Principle.

The Extent of Impulsivity in Political Action

To produce the results we have examined in this section, it is not necessary that all people vote impulsively. In fact, many do follow a political philosophy. Vote totals over the past two centuries suggest that perhaps 1/3 of the populace consistently votes toward one end of the left-right spectrum and 1/3 votes toward the other, while 1/3 is mostly rudderless, voting with the current mood rather than by consistent thought. However, even those who are consistently left or right tend to fluctuate in the *intensity* of that orientation, thus also participating in cycles of social expression.

The left-right spectrum itself is utterly prerational, as it mostly represents (1) the survival impulse among producers to keep the means of their sustenance vs. the survival impulse among nonproducers and their sympathizers to appropriate it, and (2) the impulse among some people to direct others' behavior vs. the impulse among others to do as they please. Only the up-down spectrum, between individual liberty and authoritarianism, has differences that may be regarded as philosophical.

The Inevitability of Change in the Mechanics of Events when Social Mood Changes

Each Elliott wave pattern has implications both for its own development and for coming events that it causes. The more one works with the Wave Principle and studies history as it relates to similar pattern junctures, the more one is able to forecast specific developments outside the market (see Chapter 17). Yet it is important to understand that events always fall into place to reflect the trend of the market, and thus of social mood, *whether we can describe them in advance or not.*

As an example, when Frost and I originally forecasted the great bull market of the 1980s, we had no idea where the vehicles for speculation would come from. Five years later, in 1983, *The Elliott Wave Theorist* pointed out a number of emerging conditions associated with the bull market:

> With sentiment, momentum, wave characteristics and social phenomena all supporting our original forecast, can we say that the environment on Wall Street is conducive to developing a full blown speculative mania? In 1978, an Elliott analyst had no way of knowing just what the mechanisms for a wild speculation would be. "Where is the 10% margin that made the 1920s possible?" was a common rebuttal. Well, to be honest, we didn't know. But now look! The entire structure is being built as if it were planned. Options on hundreds of stocks (and now stock indexes) allow the speculator to deal in thousands of shares of stock for a fraction of their value. Futures contracts on stock indexes, which promise to deliver nothing, have been created for the most part as speculative vehicles with huge leverage. Options *on* futures carry the possibilities one step further. And it's not stopping there. Major financial newspapers are calling for the end of any margin requirements on stocks whatsoever. "Look-back" options are making a debut. S&Ls are leaping into the stock brokerage business, sending flyers to little old ladies. And New York City banks are already constructing kiosks for quote machines so that depositors can stop off at lunch and punch out their favorite stocks. Options exchanges are creating new and specialized speculative instruments — guess the CPI and win a bundle! In other words, the financial arena is becoming the *place to be*. And, as if by magic, the media are geometrically increasing coverage of financial news. Financial News Network is now broadcasting 12 hours a day, bringing up-to-the-minute quotations on stocks and commodities via satellite and cable into millions of homes.[23]

At the same time, services that rate analysts and fund managers were just coming into being, and the mutual fund industry began its greatest expansion in history.

Not only did these market-related factors develop, but economic conditions improved in response to the rise. Interest rates declined, inflation receded, employment grew, unemployment fell, production expanded, and a business-friendly political environment predominated. In essence (and also in many specifics; see Chapter 17), *those conditions were forecasted years ahead of time by the simple prediction that wave V in stocks lay ahead.*

Forecasting such specifics is an immense challenge because major social mood changes bring about unbelievably radical social changes. For instance, in 1929, with the Dow at 381, who could have said specifically that in ten years, war and holocaust would begin in Europe, that in twelve years, Japanese aircraft would attack Pearl Harbor, and that within twenty years, the most populous country in the world, as well as half of Europe, would be taken over by Communists? The *character*, or *tenor*, of each of these actions was utterly consistent with the developing wave structure at the time. Specifics, however, cannot be forecasted at the outset, only surmised. As social trends develop, we can anticipate more and more specifics and formulate plans in time to take advantage of blossoming developments or to avoid the trouble spots.

The Occasional Imposition of Structural Rigidity

In some cases, extremes in mood cause actions that impose structural rigidity on a society. The effects of such institutionalization continue for a long period because it takes time to play out the consequences of the rigidity imposed at the extreme point of mass mood. Once a restrictive political policy is put in place, it can most definitely affect such things as economic output. For instance, the imposition of a mild rigidity in the form of wage and price controls or a substantial rigidity such as communism or fascism has always served to dampen a country's economic progress thereafter regardless of a later upswing in mood.

As an extreme example, the collective mood in Germany in July 1932 was so negative that its expression produced Adolf Hitler's peak of popularity, exactly concurrent with the month of the low in stocks. Although the underlying public mood as reflected by stock prices was changing toward the less negative from July 1932 forward, and although Hitler's popularity

was accordingly waning, he remained just popular enough to be granted the reins of power. The consequences of the social action taken just after the social-mood low took thirteen years to play out because the representatives of the negative popular mood gained such great political power. The collective mood in the United States also reached a negative extreme in 1932-1933. One manifestation of that mood extremity was the increased enrollment in and disruptive activity by the Communist Party in the U.S. In contrast to the German experience, however, the most extreme political forces never achieved political control, so the improving mood was allowed to express itself in the years that followed.

Policies are relevant, but they are not the *fundamental* cause of conditions. Governments institute policies in response to the prevailing (or sometimes the immediately preceding) social mood trend, so it is the public's mood that is ultimately responsible for the change. Furthermore, it is a change in the trend of mood that ultimately causes authorities to ditch the policy or people to ditch the authorities.

History and the Socionomic Hypothesis

All of history flows from the fact that men have a nature, that this nature includes unconscious patterns of interaction, and that these patterns produce results in human social action. Humanity might have produced a history without the unconscious herding impulse. However, it would not have produced the passionate, collective history that we do have, with its wars, treaties, construction, destruction, migrations, governments, religions, societies and cultures. Elliott waves, to state it directly, are the first cause of history. Since waves are governed by mathematics, history has a mathematical basis. Since waves are governed by *Fibonacci* mathematics, then the mathematics with which nature is most intimate are behind the tenor and events of history.

The mathematics of robust fractal geometry (see Chapter 3) also account for both the repetitiveness and uniqueness of history. The Wave Principle provides a scientific explanation for the observation, "History repeats in the generalities but not in the details." Because fundamental Elliott wave patterns are limited in number while their manifestations have substantial variability, and because the continual expansion of degree imparts uniqueness to every wave, interactive human mentation and behavior, which produce history, are continually repeated, but not precisely. Once again, empirics and hypothesis are compatible.

NOTES

1 Le Bon, G. (1895). *The crowd.*

2 Malabre, A.L. (1987, February 23). "The stock market and the business cycle." *The Wall Street Journal.*

3 Elliotters should note that W, Y, and Z are used to label certain other types of corrections.

4 The 1991 recession, which followed this three-year Primary degree bear market, also precipitated the Gulf War and induced Hollywood to award five Oscars, including best picture, to *Silence of the Lambs*, a film about a brutal cannibalistic serial killer.

5 Even this one might be seen as the lagging result of the bear market that ended in 1942, but that seems too substantial a time lag to assert definite causality.

6 Nichols, B. (1994, September 28). "Warm fuzzy summit." *USA Today.*

7 Update: In July 1999, Christians traversed the path of the Crusades, this time as a gesture of religious reconciliation. In May 2002, after the Dow rallied back above 10,000, Russia entered into a formal alliance with NATO.

8 Overall, World War I was a larger war than the associated bear market appears to have warranted. However, it was clearly preceded by a long bear market environment of increasing social frustration. The stock average in 1914 was little higher than it was in 1889, a full 25 years earlier. During that time, stock indexes had three major setbacks of 40% to 60%.

9 Another 284,000 died of disease indirectly caused by the war, making the total of Civil War-related deaths 578,900.

10 Price, William H. (1961). *The Civil War handbook.*

11 The Korean War of 1950-1953 is not so easily categorized by degree. It immediately followed the last low (wave e) in the *Supercycle* degree triangle pattern in constant-dollar terms (see Figure 16-6), which was a low only of *Primary* degree in nominal terms (see Figure 5-12 or 15-4). Accordingly, the total number of U.S. deaths, from both battle and other causes, at 54,246, was between the numbers associated with each degree exclusively.

12 The fact that the Vietnam War took place during a bear market that was simultaneously wave (a) in constant-dollar terms (see Figure 16-6) and which included two advances back to the level of the prior bull market's high in nominal terms may bear upon why it was unpopular. Much of the society was still in a socially positive mood, and simply did not feel like fighting.

13 Notice in Figure 16-6 that the current wave position implies wave c directly ahead. While this decline, should it unfold, could be dangerous in

terms of war potential, it is unlikely to produce a "World War III" type worldwide conflict. The reason is that the approaching wave c is not the *largest* wave c due in the pattern. It is expected to be only wave c of (a) of a larger (a)-(b)-(c) flat correction or (a)-(b)-(c)-(d)-(e) triangle. This wave labeling will soon bring the constant-dollar DJIA back to the same position as the nominal DJIA, which now faces the start of wave (a). For more on this topic, see Chapter 5 of *At the Crest of the Tidal Wave.*

14 People's anger shows up in countless ways. For example, while labor-management relations are harmonious in bull markets, they are acrimonious in bear markets, precipitating disputes and strikes. Even the U.S. homicide rate has quite well paralleled major PPI-adjusted stock trends in data from 1960 to the present.

15 Actually, this graph should probably be constructed as a percentage of worldwide population, as the number of countries could, depending upon circumstances, be meaningless.

16 In extremely rare cases, political repression at a social mood low leads to a war that the repressors lose, a prime example being the Revolutionary War.

17 Landslide oustings at major "A" wave lows appear inevitable, as the populace is shocked by the dramatic social mood change toward the negative. "C" wave elections are less predictable, often because by then social conditions are so unstable. The election of 1860, near the end of wave c of (II), reflected extremely negative sentiment. It certainly saw the ousting of the previous president, Buchanan, but the vote was close precisely because the political scene was so divided that the nation was not voting as a whole (the winner, Lincoln, wasn't even on the ballot in ten states), but by section (North vs. South), thus hardly reflecting contentment with the status quo. Social conditions during wave c of (IV) in constant-dollar prices were clearly chaotic as well, as World War II raged. The public image of Franklin Roosevelt had already benefitted from the greatest momentum kickoff of the century (see Figure 7-1) and the gains made thereafter. He then benefitted from the calendar. Had his third election taken place in 1942 near the low of wave II, he may have lost, even with a war in progress. However, he had the good fortune that elections were scheduled two years on either side of the low, both during stock market rallies.

18 Kamm, T. (1990, November 16). "Brazil's president, after eight months, finds roar of crowd is now against him." *The Wall Street Journal.*

19 MacLean, P.D. (1990). *The triune brain in evolution.*

20 Page, S. (1998, January 22). "President's resilience faces biggest test." *USA Today.*

21 Montgomery, P.M. (1998, February 4). *Universal Economics.*

22 Montgomery, P.M. (1991, March 15). "Neurophysiology, presidents and the stock market, part III." *Universal Economics.*

23 Prechter, R.R. (1983, August 18). "The superbull market of the '80s: has the last wild ride really begun?" *The Elliott Wave Theorist,* Special Report.

Chapter 17

Forecasting Success Supports the Validity of Socionomics

Chapters 5 through 7 showed that the Wave Principle is unique in providing a basis for forecasting markets. This chapter, to the extent possible for this extremely young science, aims to demonstrate a broader application of socionomics to social forecasting.

If mass mood change is the cause of coming social events, then evidence of mood change or coming mood change is the single most important area of discovery for those who wish to peek into the future of social events. The practical value of the Wave Principle is that it provides, for the first time ever, a context for disciplined market analysis, economic analysis and social analysis. A proper identification of the patterns imparts an immense amount of knowledge about society's position within its behavioral continuum and therefore about its probable ensuing path.

As implied in this book so far, there are two types of socionomic forecasting:

(1) predicting trends in social phenomena based upon waves within the phenomena themselves, and

(2) predicting economic, political, social, cultural and other trends based upon the wave position of indicators of overall social mood such as the stock market.

Aside from an initial orientation, the rest of this chapter presents actual socionomic forecasts issued over the past two decades. I have examples of both type one and type two forecasts and end with examples of applying them to individual experiences in the social realm. Please take the time to

reflect on their uniqueness. It is not a matter of, say, half of economists calling for an up quarter and the socionomist happens to be on the lucky side. Each of these forecasts has a character that only socionomics makes possible.

Waves in Social Phenomena Other than Financial

Chapters 5 and 6 give several examples of the first type of forecasting as applied to financial markets. Yet that is not the only realm in which it can be applied. Before reviewing past predictions, let us look at one example of waves in other social phenomena.

Take a close look at Figure 17-1, which is the per capita consumption of cigarettes in the United States throughout this century. As you can see, this data traced out a fairly classic Elliott wave advance over nine decades. Writers discussing this graph attempt all sorts of guesses about the reasons for both the advancing trend and the reversal, noting such supposedly causal events as "World War II." We all know that cigarettes were popular in World War II, but is that a *reason* they were popular? The reversal in 1963 appears even more mysterious. The Center for Disease Control and Prevention and the National Cancer Institute report, for example, that over the

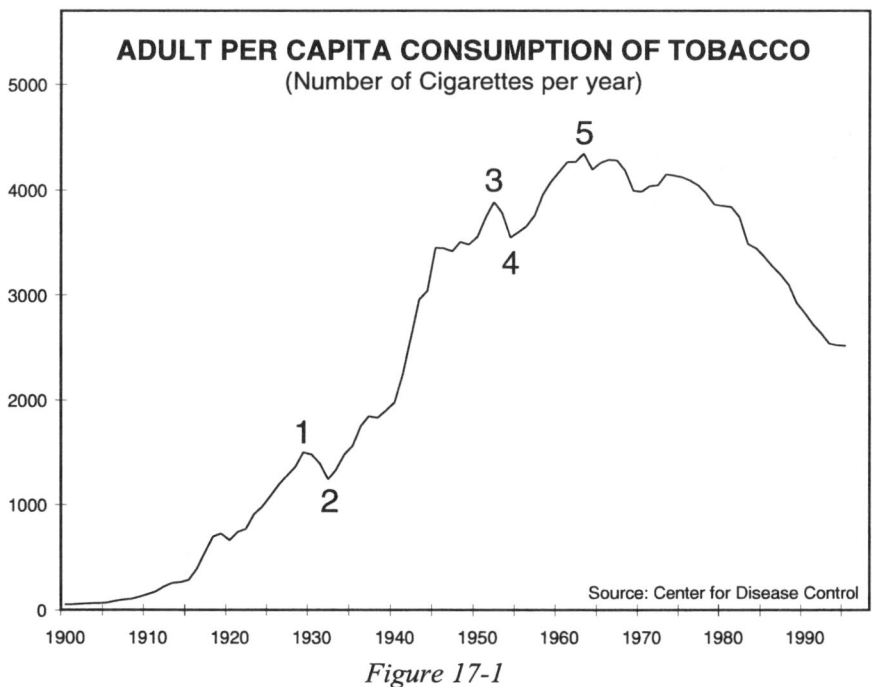

Figure 17-1

twenty-two years up to the time of the report in August 1995, smoking among black teenagers dropped dramatically from 26% to 4.4%. Says the director of the Office on Smoking and Health at the CDC, "It's a public health success story that we can't take credit for because we didn't do it. We can't [even] explain it."[1] Feeling compelled nevertheless to do so, people interviewed for the article go on to cite six retrospectively-conjured "theories" of why it happened, every one of which demands its own explanation.

A socionomist can go directly to the heart of the matter. Smoking is a social phenomenon. As such, its popularity has followed the Wave Principle. In the two dozen years after the peak came the Surgeon General's report, a broadcast ad ban, the beginning of a "nonsmokers' rights" movement and higher federal cigarette taxes. Of course, these are presumed to be causes of the change in attitude, but actually, they are results. Every trend carries within it the seeds of its own demise. Surgeons General would not have bothered to look into the health aspects of cigarettes if over 40% of adult Americans weren't smoking them. The government never could have gotten away with an ad ban or tax hikes without public support. The nonsmokers' rights campaign was a backlash reaction to widespread smoking. Decades prior to the Surgeon General's report, it was widely reported that cigarettes probably caused lung cancer. In the 1940s, they were called "coffin nails," in the 1950s "cancer sticks." When I was a kid in the 1960s, everyone knew that smoking was harmful, but it still looked cool. In the 1970s, I heard the term "death sticks," essentially the same slang term used thirty years earlier. Medical knowledge did not stop the uptrend. What did stop the uptrend? Five waves, that's what, complete with equally-sized waves 2 and 4, an extended wave 3, suggestion of the proper subdivisions within waves 1 and 3 even in this crude data, and a slowing upside rate of change in wave 5. The bear market that ensued is replete with incidents of social reaction toward cigarettes. To many teenagers, smoking is not even cool any more. It is not really accurate to say that such differences in action and attitude caused the trend change; they *are* the trend change.

At this point, the downtrend has lasted 34 years, which is .618 of the approximately 55-year long uptrend, and per capita consumption has fallen by about 2/5. At least one cigarette company has taken an aggressive pro-freedom stance in its advertising in reaction to what it sees as the harsh puritanism of the anti-smoking zealots. A socionomist, then, should be on the lookout for signs of a reversal.

This is an example of a nonfinancial social trend that could have been forecast, not one that was. Since the very idea of attempting to perform such forecasting occurred to me only a few years ago, and since normally

we would have to make a determined effort to seek out such fairly obscure data, and since long-term forecasts take time to play out, I have only two examples of attempts at such forecasting for which there has been time enough for at least a partial resolution. The first was made by a novice.

PREDICTING SOCIAL TRENDS BASED UPON WAVES WITHIN THE PROCESS

A Forecast of the U.S. Savings Rate

Here is a social forecast made on October 18, 1990 by Robert E. Burt, an *Elliott Wave Theorist* subscriber, who sent in the following commentary along with the graph shown in Figure 17-2:

> Enclosed is a *Wall Street Journal* clipping you may not have noticed. The chart shows the U.S. savings rate since 1970. What struck me was how it is a nearly classic example of the first four steps in a five-step long-term downtrend. I have included a blowup with my [wave] numbers drawn in. ...If one assumes wave 5 falls as far from the recent high as wave 1, then one has a...savings rate of 0.6%, occurring some time in late 1992 or early 1993. If one notes that the bottom of wave 3 is almost

Figure 17-2

twice as much below the top as wave 1, a case can be made for an even more catastrophic *negative* savings rate of around -3.1% at that time.[2]

Figure 17-3 would show the same graph updated through today, except that the ensuing downtrend so upset the government that the keepers of the figures (perhaps justifiably) changed the formula to include money-market funds, which pushed the ratio to higher levels. Regardless of this change in scale and some resulting differences in the curve, you can see that not only did Mr. Burt's general expectation for a new low come to pass, but so did his specific call for a drop to minus 3.1%, which is about where Figure 17-3 would show the current rate to be had statisticians maintained the old formula. The forecast took longer to play out than expected because wave 3 in this data lasted an additional two years.[3]

The uniqueness of this forecast in calling for a trend reversal is its most remarkable feature. The savings rate had just soared from 1% to 5% in less than two years, yet the forecast did not extrapolate; it called for a downturn to *new lows*. It would be very surprising if any conventional economist said anything like it at the time.

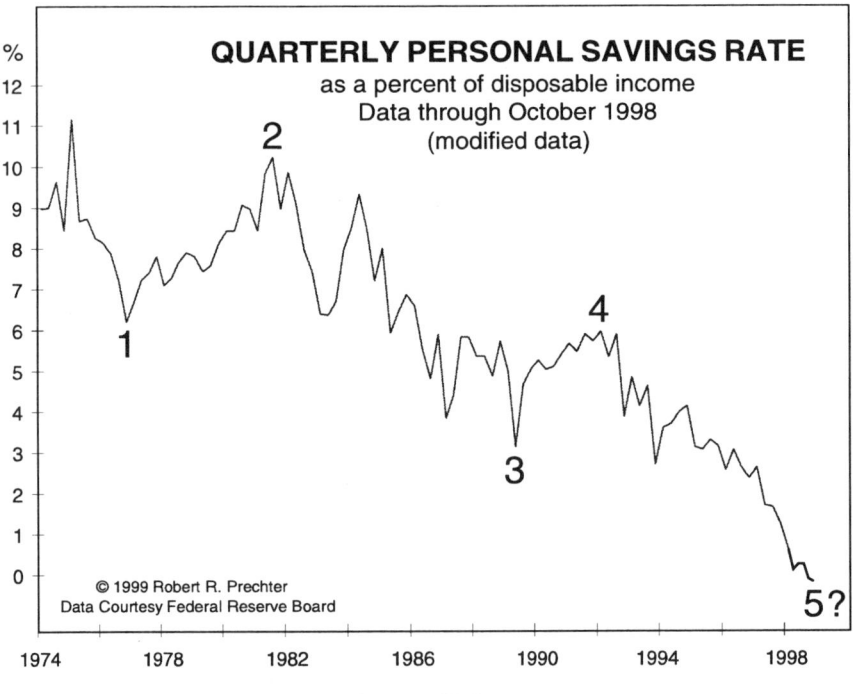

Figure 17-3

A Forecast for Baseball

I have found parallel trends between many different types of social activities and the stock market. Predicting some social trends might appear frivolous, but to the industry involved, correctly anticipating trend changes would be worth millions of dollars.

Immediately following the 1992 baseball season, *The Elliott Wave Theorist* published an analysis and forecast for the fortunes of that great American game, along with practical advice for collectors, players and team owners. The following quotes are excerpted from issues of *The Elliott Wave Theorist* published on the dates listed:

October 30, 1992

> **A Top in Baseball?** The first World Series game was held in 1903. This year was the Fibonacci 89th World Series. The *emotion* surrounding the 88th and 89th World Series games was huge. The 1991 series was widely described as "the best World Series ever." It brought together two "worst-to-first" teams, a battle of underdogs (who are always popular). Fans were chanting and "tomahawk chopping" like college fraternity lunatics. The games attracted a high 24.0 share of TV viewers. The teams were greeted by throngs totaling nearly a million people at post-series hometown parades. The 1992 series was similarly emotional, particularly in Canada, as the Toronto Blue Jays took on the symbolism of national pride. Indeed, the Atlanta Braves were the only team ever to have been magically groomed for such a setting by a decade of billing as "America's Team." It was the first nationalistic World Series ever.[4]
>
> *There is reason to believe that baseball players' salaries, as well as baseball cards and other memorabilia, have just made a "spike top" along with fans' emotions.*
>
> You may recall that our "Popular Culture" Special Report of 1985 concluded that baseball is a bull market sport.... When the first World Series was played in October 1903, the Dow was making a low at 43. It was never lower during another World Series, enjoying an 89-year net uptrend. If stocks are topping in a major way as the Wave Principle argues, so is the uptrend in baseball's popularity. In the past few years, Hollywood has idolized baseball in *Field of Dreams*, *The Babe* and *A League of Their Own*. The widespread popularity of such sentiment toward a subject often coincides with a peak in interest among the population.

Could baseball be in for a 55-year period of decline in public favor? Signs of a turn are there. *If you're an investor, take profits on baseball cards. If you're a player, sign a long-term contract. If you're an owner, sell your club.* Kids will soon be trading in their bats for helmets (or hockey pucks, soccer balls, or equipment for a more violent sport yet to come). If you're a real fan, you'll still find yourself griping about baseball some time in the 1990s.

Result: A few months later came these dramatic reports of a sudden change of fortune for the prices of baseball cards and their manufacturers' stocks, both of which collapsed:

THE WALL STREET JOURNAL
January 27, 1993

New York – Baseball-card stocks were hit by news that market leader Topps Co. will report its first quarterly loss in more than a decade.

Topps – which experienced strong insider selling last year – sank 31%, to $8.50 from $12.25, on seven times its usual volume.

The announcement sent shares of several companies in the sports-memorabilia business south yesterday. Among them was Marvel Entertainment Group, the comic-book giant that purchased card manufacturer Fleer Corp. last September. Shares of Marvel, which according to analysts gets roughly half its revenue from Fleer, slid $3.25, or 11.5%, to $24.875 on five times its normal volume.

"The speculative bubble has burst in the new cards," said....

ROCKY MOUNTAIN NEWS
April 7, 1993

SPORTS TRADING CARDS: Market has started to fall apart

The market is crumbling. Manufacturers are laying off employees as their stock tumbles and they cut back on production. Retailers are going out of business. Prices on goods are slashed. Card collecting exploded in popularity in the 1980s and turned into a highly profitable business. Card brands increased from one in the 1970s to 40. Then came the crash of '92-93. Pro Set filed for Chapter 11 bankruptcy. Topps, the trading card leader, lost 30% of its stock value in one day after it reported an expected quarterly loss.

January 29, 1993

[Elliott Wave International's] Pete Kendall has just obtained the data
on baseball attendance during this century. As you can see by [Figure 17-
4], the figures appear to have traced out an exceptional Elliott Wave,
ending with the 1992 season. Notice that the 1981 strike brought attendance back to the preceding fourth wave, just as it was scheduled to do.
When the data is plotted on semilog scale (not shown), the entire rise
from the World War I low in 1916 forms a wedge, which has bearish
implications. At minimum, then, baseball faces its *largest percentage
drop in attendance since it became the national sport*. At junctures such
as this, it is even appropriate to consider that it may fall far enough out of
favor in coming years to cease *being* the premier national sport.

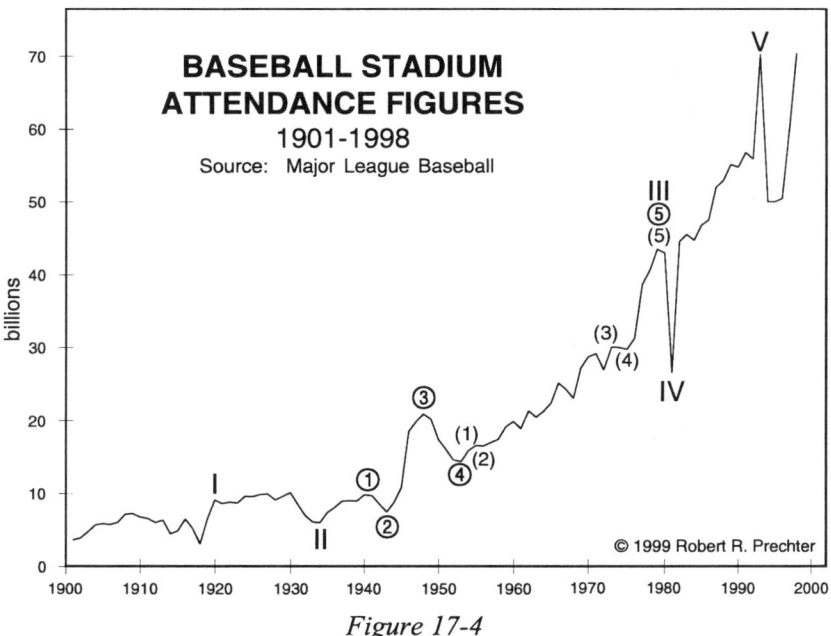

Figure 17-4

Result: 1993 was another record-attendance year, as fans bought season
tickets on the strength of their overwhelming enjoyment of the previous
two years. In 1994, baseball players called a strike. It closed down the
season, causing the largest drop in attendance since the beginning of baseball in arithmetic (but not quite in percentage) terms. In 1994, there was no
World Series for the first time ever. Fans' bitterness extended the low turnout into 1995. The following article revealed the immense pressure on the
trading-card industry resulting from this change in fortunes:

USA TODAY
March 23, 1995
Strike is 'another nail' in trading cards' coffin

In limbo because of the major league players' strike, the baseball trading-card business faces a grim question: How low can it go? Not much lower, says Steve Myland, a wholesaler in Phoenix: "The strike has had a profound effect. The industry is collapsing." Joe Bosley, a dealer in Reisterstown, Md., says sales of baseball cards issued in recent years are down 90%: "It's another nail in the coffin." Myland estimates 20-30% of card retailers have folded since the strike began, as have four card publications. Topps says its production is at its lowest level in 30 years. Upper Deck says it cut back by 75%.

Was it luck that the players' strike happened after our forecast? It might have been. However, there are two reasons to think otherwise. First, it is definitely incorrect to presume that the strike was an "outside cause" that struck the baseball industry out of nowhere. I would argue that the strike, which was called by players making multiple millions of dollars who thought they were worth even more, was a consequence of baseball's affluence, which in turn was a consequence of its popularity. The entire event was internal to baseball and its fortunes, and it occurred right after one could identify five waves up in the attendance figures. Since then, the popularity of baseball has waxed again in tandem with the continuation of the bull market in stocks. However, it still significantly lags its pinnacle of 1991-1993 in terms of emotion, trading card values, television viewership and stadium attendance per team.

In 1996, despite record home-run statistics and a World Series match-up of the American and National leagues' most popular franchises, attendance was still off 14% from that of 1993, while television ratings for the World Series showed the third lowest percentage viewership ever. In 1997, attendance again remained moderate. In 1998, home-run statistics of several players set all-time records (record home runs are a bull market phenomenon, but that's another topic), two new teams were added to the leagues (another consequence of affluence typical of tops), the country felt as affluent as ever, stocks made new all-time highs, the economy was in the seventh year of an expansion, and America liked baseball again. This resurgence in the sport's achievements and popularity is a direct reflection of the resumption of the bull market in stocks after 1994. Despite all that, the 1998 World Series attracted the lowest television viewership *ever*. The two new teams added to the total turnout, which matched the peak of 1993, but turnout per team has yet to exceed that peak.

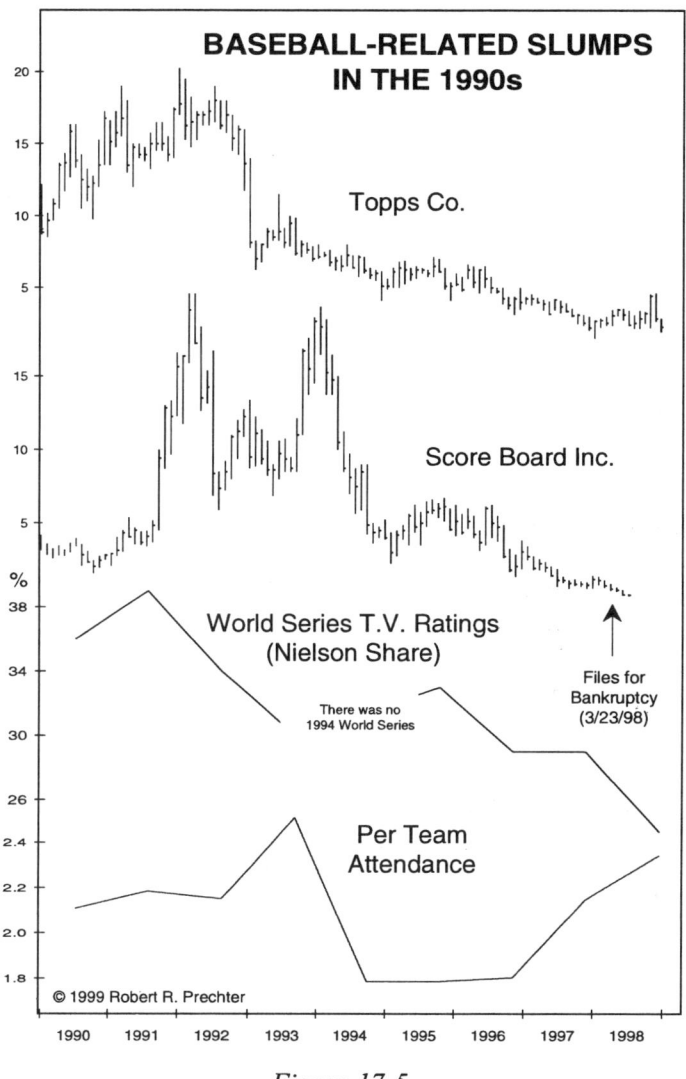

Figure 17-5

Most forecasters would simply extrapolate the multi-decade uptrend into the future. Maybe the uptrend will continue; there is no *guarantee* that wave 5 has ended; it could subdivide and last decades longer. However, if my thesis is correct that baseball is a bull market sport, and if my wave interpretation is correct that a Grand Supercycle bull market is nearing its end, then baseball's fortunes are due for a reversal on that basis (see next section for a discussion of this type of forecasting) as well as all those

listed above. Time will tell, but at least you can see that my forecast for a multi-year decline in the popularity and fortunes of baseball is actually that, not a description of present conditions tagged with the title of a forecast.

PREDICTING DEPENDENT SOCIAL TRENDS FROM WAVES IN THE STOCK MARKET

I noticed the relationship between the stock market's trends and subsequent social events in the 1970s but did not realize how intimate the relationship was to both popular culture and social history until the 1980s. That is why, to date, we have very little of this type of socionomic forecasting on record. However, what is on the record has an even more accurate history than Elliotters' financial market forecasting. I have made few socionomic forecasts of this type that have *not* worked out, at least in a general sense.

Forecasting a Macroeconomic Trend

The first three years of the 1980s contained the most months of officially recognized economic contraction since the Great Depression bottomed out in March 1933. Stocks' advance on powerful upside momentum in August-October 1982 signaled the start of the recovery. On November 8, precisely at the end of the contraction, *The Elliott Wave Theorist* changed its front page summary from RECESSION IN PROGRESS to RECOVERY BEGINNING, stating flatly, "The stock market has given a powerful signal: the current very deep recession is ending." The January 10, 1983 issue announced RECOVERY UNDERWAY, which was then amended to ECONOMIC BOOM on March 7. This forecast was based on one thing: an understanding of the *degree* of the upturn in the stock market. The start of a bull market of Cycle degree implied a long period of economic expansion. What indeed began the very next month was the longest uninterrupted economic expansion since 1961-1969.

This forecast also maintained historical consistency with the developing long-term wave structure shown in Chapter 5. For example, because the expected bull market was specifically to be Cycle wave V of Supercycle wave (V), it would be the cousin to Cycle wave V of Supercycle wave (III), i.e., the 1920s. That is why in April 1983, when *The Elliott Wave Theorist* reiterated that "a period of economic stability has just begun," it added that its onset had a "parallel with late 1921."[5]

As for the ultimate *end* of the new long-term expansion, the December 1985 issue explained that my approach toward identifying it would be the same:

> We should keep the ultimate probability of an economic crash and financial calamity in mind, but it is still *too early* to prepare for it. Legions of super bears have warned of impending monetary collapse, imminent full-scale banking crises, and so forth for years. Although they continue to warn that such events could occur "out of the blue," "at any time," and "without warning," *history shows that a substantial decline in the stock market has always provided an early warning to such conditions. As long as the stock market is trending upward, there is no reason to harbor such fears.*[6]

Conventional economists, in contrast, had no means by which to predict a long expansion, much less comment on its position within the multi-decade trends of the U.S. economy.

Forecasting Macroeconomic Nuance

Fifth waves are weaker than third waves, both in terms of their intramarket ("technical") performance and their extramarket ("fundamental") results. This simple truth has immense value in applied forecasting. Chapter 7 presented some useful intramarket comparisons. This section covers some extramarket comparisons.

The idea that there is a difference in quality between the macroeconomic trends that manifest from a *third* wave and those that manifest from a *fifth* wave has been a part of the Wave Principle for twenty years. Our 1978 book, *Elliott Wave Principle,* described third waves as "wonders to behold" as they deliver on the promise of rising stocks with "increasingly favorable fundamentals." In contrast, "the fifth of the fifth [wave] will lack the dynamism that preceded it." This description is useful because contrasting periods of economic performance can confirm or contradict a wave interpretation. However, it can also be the basis for *forecasting the quality of economic trends.* For example, by labeling the March 1942 to February 1966 bull market wave III, Frost and I in 1978 established the extramarket vitality of the 1950s and early 1960s as a standard that the forecasted wave V bull market would not surpass. *The Elliott Wave Theorist* reiterated the expected relationship between the two periods with this description in the August 1983 report on the upcoming "superbull market":

This fifth wave will be built more on unfounded hopes than on soundly improving fundamentals such as the U.S. experienced in the 1950s and early 1960s. And since this fifth wave, wave V, is a fifth within a larger fifth, wave (V) from 1789, the phenomenon should be magnified by the time the peak is reached.[7]

This is an unusually specific forecast. The very idea of commenting on the relative strength of a projected multi-year recovery is so unusual that no economist has ever attempted anything of the kind. Once you understand that economic trends fit the overall Elliott Wave structure, you can understand how I could presume to do it. How has this prediction fared?

Observe from Figure 15-4 that each of the two great post-Depression expansions accompanied a bull market in stocks that has lasted 24 years, from 1942 to 1966 in the first instance and from 1974 so far through now (1998) in the second. The percentage gain in the DJIA over the course of the latter has been *55% greater* (so far) than over that of the former. On that basis alone, one might assume that wave V should have produced a stronger economy than wave III. On the contrary, the progress and foundation of wave V have failed to measure up to those of wave III to a glaring extent, exactly as forecast. Figures 17-6 contrasts the economic strength of wave III vs. wave V through June 1998. Figure 17-7 highlights the difference in GDP between the latter half of both waves. Combining the GDP and Industrial Production figures, we may generalize that the economic power of wave V has been 62% of that of wave III.

To grasp the full measure of the underlying weakness of wave V's "fundamentals," one must look beyond economic figures to the corporate, household and government balance sheets that underlie production. Figure 17-8 shows the glaring contrast between waves III and V in eight such measures. Add to these the remarkable fact that at the end of wave III, the U.S was a net *creditor,* while today, near the end of wave V, the U.S. is a *debtor* of unprecedented scope, owing a record $1.3 trillion more to foreigners than it is owed.

The forecast included this phrase: "The phenomenon should be magnified by the time the peak is reached." In other words, the economic expansion would wane even further as wave ⑤ of V progressed and further as wave (5) of ⑤ progressed. True to expectation, the economic expansion has slackened further in the latter stages of wave V. Real GDP growth has been 21% *less* so far in the 1990s during wave ⑤ than in the 1980s during wave ③.

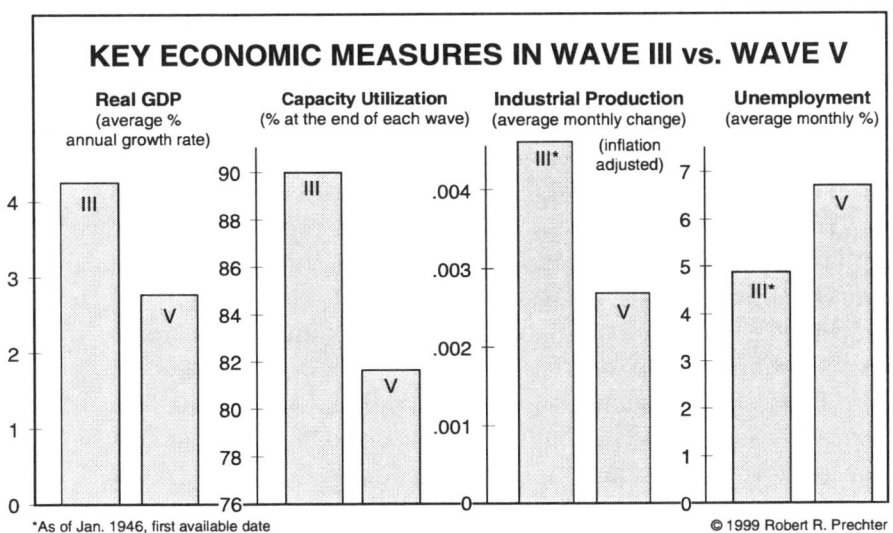

Figure 17-6

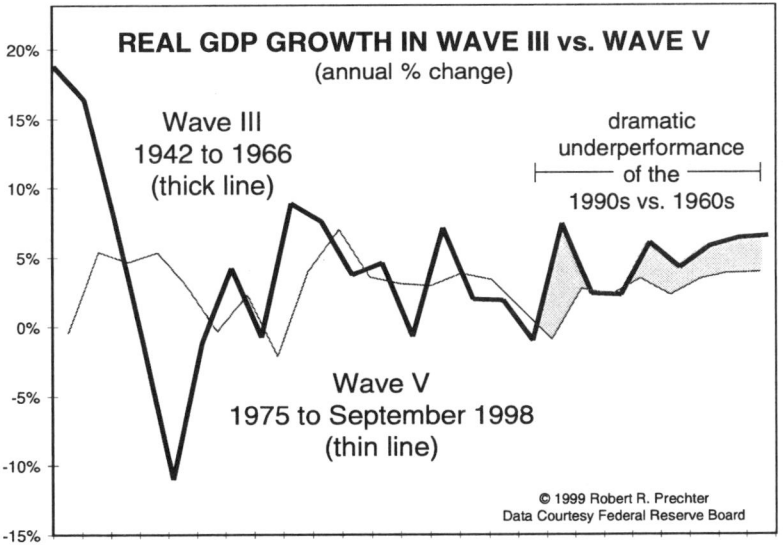

Figure 17-7

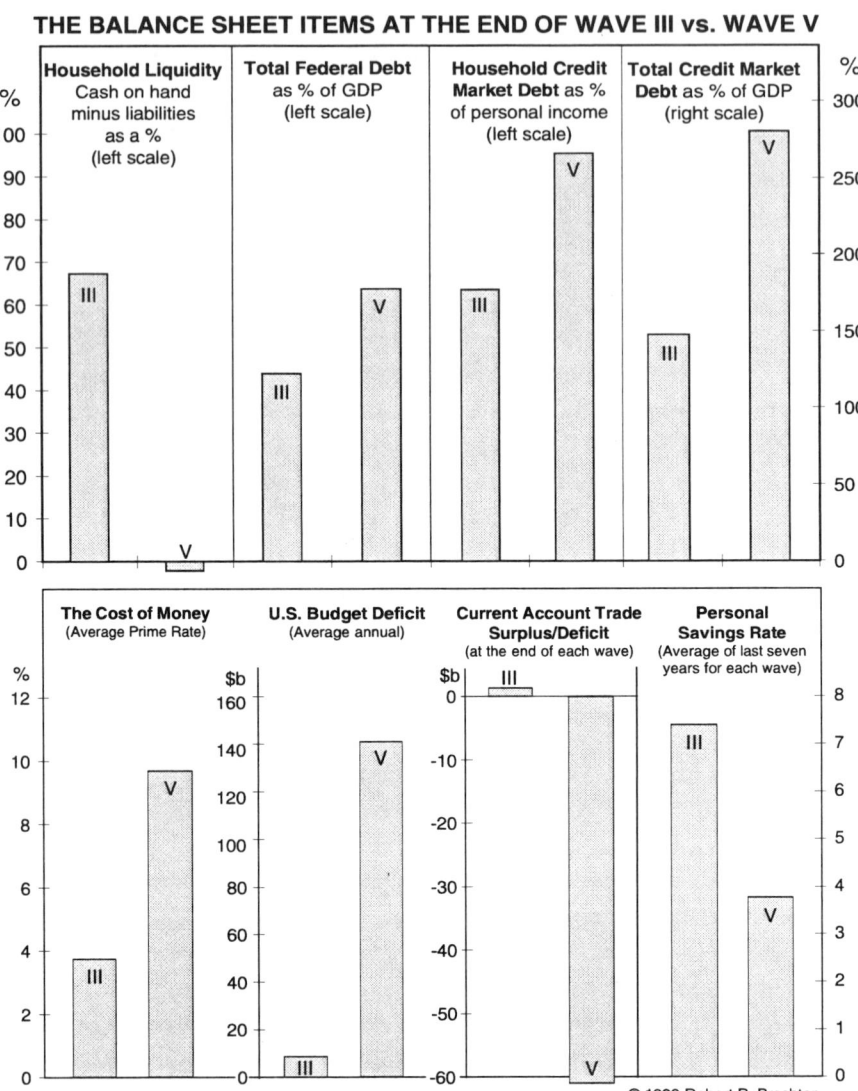

Figure 17-8

The juxtaposition of sky-high expectations (as represented by the highest stock market dividend valuation of all time) and the actual persistent slowing of economic growth is a revelation about the immense strength of social optimism near a fifth wave peak as compared to its inability to produce commensurate real results.

An objective contrast of the quality of the macroeconomic and fiscal aspects of waves III and V shows that wave V has been a weaker performance in terms of *every relevant measure*. Yet probably because background conditions since 1982 have been so much better than those in the *1970s*, conventional observers miss this very important long-term distinction. In contrast, the Wave Principle provides the basis for a profound insight regarding the relative character of the economic environment of the 1980s and 1990s. What's more, it is available not only as a useful latter-day observation (which even today is utterly lacking in current conventional economic discourse) but as a *prediction*, made fifteen years ago.[8]

Forecasting a Specific Monetary Trend

The spiraling inflation of the 1970s finally culminated in January 1980. In its final year, dozens of experts, including economics professors, congressmen, senators, cabinet members, scientists, institute spokesmen and even the president of the United States, specifically predicted that gasoline would reach $2 to $3 a gallon, both inevitably and soon.[9]

Such luminaries, needless to say, are usually unqualified in any predictive methodology to forecast commodity prices, yet such facts never seem to impose an impediment to issuing unqualified opinions. Had these particular forecasters expressed precisely the opposite sentiments, they would have been correct. It is now twenty years later, and gasoline still has not reached those forecasted prices. In fact, the inflation-adjusted cost of gasoline today is the lowest in decades. The true meaning of this blizzard of prognostications calling for higher prices is that they reflected the extremity of the emotional trend and therefore signaled the *end* of the rise in gasoline prices.

One forecaster did take a different view, right in the heat of the intense panic over inflation. As far as we know, there is not a single comparable commentary from that time. This is a remarkable fact given that there are thousands of forecasters of monetary trends.

In December 1979, *The Elliott Wave Theorist* spelled out its expectations for the major sea change that was at hand. *Commodities* (now *Futures*) magazine published my comments in its January 1980 issue. Here is an excerpt:

The incredible conjunction of "fives" in different markets [gold, silver, interest rates, bonds, and commodities] all seem to point to the same conclusion: *The world is about to begin a phase of general disinflation* [i.e., decelerating inflation]. As I see it, a pattern of several disinflationary years leading to a deflationary trend later on would be a perfect scenario for the Elliott outlook for stocks. A gradual disinflation would create an optimistic mood in the country and lead to the conclusion that we may have finally licked the inflation problem. This sentiment would support a bull market in stocks for several years until the snowballing forces of deflation began to take over. At that point, a major deflationary crash would be impossible to avert, and the Grand Supercycle correction would be underway.

As you can see in Figure 17-9 and 18-3, the inflationary trend that had accelerated for 13 years ended abruptly that very month. Indeed, the above paragraph spelled out ahead of time, just weeks before the reversal of trend, the experience of the past nineteen years. It may also spell out the next experience as well, but that remains to be seen.

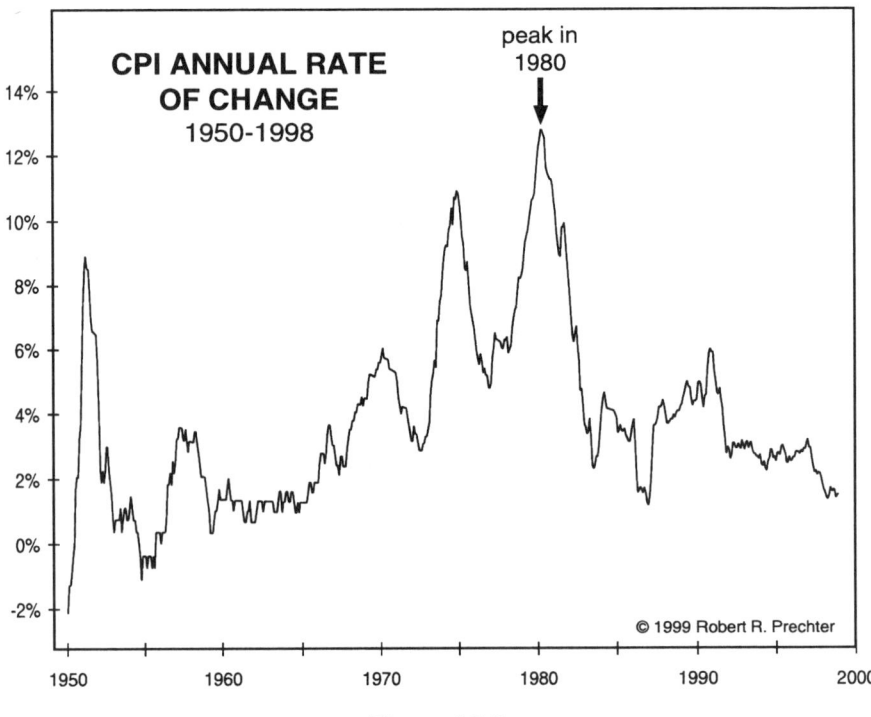

Figure 17-9

There were additional nuances to this forecast that you are welcome to review in Chapter 14 of *At the Crest*, which also attempts to forecast the next macro-monetary event. As with the economic outlook, monetary forces are part of the Elliott wave continuum, so the termination of each phase always has inescapable implications concerning the next one.

Forecasting Peace

Given the Elliott wave outlook in 1982 for a Cycle degree bull market, which portended an increasingly gentle social atmosphere, *The Elliott Wave Theorist* made this assertion on October 6, 1982:

> The confirmed status of the long-term trend of the stock market has tremendous implications. It means[, for instance], *no international war for at least ten years*.

That forecast was both comforting and accurate.

Forecasting the Fortunes of National Leaders

Watching the precision with which the level of presidential popularity had tracked the Dow and its rate of change, I began attempting to anticipate the fortunes of presidents of the United States. Below are excerpted summaries of my three forecasts to date, followed by the outcome.

Ronald Reagan

January 5, 1987

> Politically speaking, President Reagan will almost certainly survive the Iran "Contra"versy. His "Teflon" (a slick surface) coating, to which the press continually refers and off of which all potential difficulties slid until 1986's fourth wave correction, is simply the popular goodwill provided by a bull market. (Contrast that to what bear market presidents Hoover, Nixon and Carter experienced.) Given the Elliott Wave outlook for the stock market going into 1988, the Teflon will undoubtedly return, and President Reagan (assuming he lives through his term) will eventually exit as the most loved president in U.S. history.

Result: Reagan survived the controversy. His exit in January 1989 coincided with the top quarter in 1980s GDP growth, which was the lagging byproduct of the 1980s bull market. The last sentence above was hyperbolic, but when Reagan finally rode into the sunset, the headline in the (admittedly partisan) *Wall Street Journal* in a December 1989 article cred-

iting him with the death of communism read, "Man of the Decade? Man of the Century!" Reagan is easily the most revered president since Kennedy and the most respected since Roosevelt.

George Bush

Chapter 16 recounts the extremely high public approval ratings that George Bush enjoyed in his first year of office. Nevertheless, with Republicans having upon his election won 21 of the 34 presidential elections (a Fibonacci 61.8%) since it first fielded a candidate in 1856, it was apparently time for the GOP to find itself on the losing side of the ratio.

July 27 and September 28, 1990:

EWT is already on record as forecasting a collapse in George Bush's popularity from the highest ratings ever for a President to a level that will ensure the impossibility of his reelection in 1992. Over the remainder of his term, look for a persistent, unrelenting change in the general assessment of his performance, which increasingly will be seen as inadequate, and eventually as downright lousy. There are only 2 1/3 years until the next election. Bush's approval rating remains at historically high levels. Regardless, I am more than willing to retain this radical forecast.

July 31, 1992

...George Bush will lose the election, as predicted by *The Elliott Wave Theorist* when he sported a 89% (91% according to one poll) popularity rating just one year ago.[10] At this juncture, with Bush's approval rating at 34% (having declined from one Fibonacci number to another), it appears that Bill Clinton, the Doonesbury candidate, will win in November.

October 30, 1992

As late as last July, 69% of portfolio managers polled by *Barron's* predicted a Bush victory, only 9% a Clinton victory (22% called for Perot). Regardless of the outcome of Tuesday's vote, EWT's forecast on this issue illustrates the value of the Wave Principle particularly well. Three years ago, and even six months ago, there was literally no one in print predicting a loss or even a close race for George Bush in the 1992 presidential election. Top-level Democrats, you may recall, refused even to run, because George Bush was believed to be unbeatable. That's the main reason why Governor Bill Clinton finds himself with a strong shot at the White House.

Forecasting like this can be worth quite a bit if you place bets with Ladbroke's in London. But it could mean everything to the right politician. Clinton has numerous negatives (earning the nickname, "Slick Willie"), but a top-name Democrat running from the start with confidence would have been a shoo-in.

With the S&P having rallied in the past three weeks almost back to its all time high, Bush could still beat Clinton, but if he does, he'll wish he hadn't. Richard Nixon won the 1972 election at a nearly identical market juncture, and two years later, he was forced by scandal to resign.

Result: George Bush had taken office at the high quarter in the S&P's earnings per share. He exited a few quarters past the end of the biggest drop in earnings since the 1940s, which was a consequence of the three-year bear market (as reflected by the Value Line index; see Figure 16-3) from 1987 to 1990. Bush, the most popular president *ever* a year and a half earlier, lost the election. The winner was the man who ten out of eleven portfolio managers predicted would lose and who *The Elliott Wave Theorist* predicted "will win in November."

Bill Clinton

December 2, 1994

The Nixonian parallel is playing out closely. The guideline of alternation dictates the difference this time around. While it was the liberal press that exploited Nixon's weaknesses, today it is the conservative press that is exploiting Bill Clinton's weaknesses. Even after the massive Democratic party defeat [in 1994], however, almost no one entertains the idea that Clinton might not make it to 1996. Yet, pressures will soon build that could force Clinton out of office. The main social forces keeping the Clintons' various scams and affairs from full disclosure have been the cooperation of mostly sympathetic media (which in the U.S. have ignored the stories that make headlines in Europe), and a still mostly benevolent public mood as reflected by a high Dow Jones Industrial Average.

September 1, 1995

As for the political arena, though only sixteen months remain in the presidential term, *The Elliott Wave Theorist* remains on record forecasting the removal from office of President Clinton, probably by impeachment or resignation, but at least by vote, as a result of these same forces. Public heroes are of their times, and their images become vulnerable when the wind changes.

December 1, 1995

After the correction had ended in late 1994, Clinton's approval rating was down near 40%, and even some Democrats were publicly denouncing his policies. In February, *The Wall Street Journal* noted that the presidency was in "free fall." Since then, however, Clinton has charged back with a Teflon coat that would make Ronald Reagan envious. His approval rating is at 52%, an 18-month high. The social mood controls the image of the social leader. In this case, the mood is sky-high, and his image is the recipient of its benefits. When the bear market begins, all of this will change, and the atmosphere will become like that of 1973 when the American Civil Liberties Union was running ads explaining "How To Impeach President Nixon." When the trend turns down, the White House press corps will become as thirsty for blood as it was in 1973 and 1974.

July 28, 1996

As one headline noted, "Character Bullets Are Bouncing Off Clinton." ...As outrageous as our outlook sounds today with Clinton leading Dole in the polls by an all-time record amount as recently as May (a gap that historically no challenger has been able to close), we still expect that the bear market in public mood will change President Clinton's Teflon to Velcro and cause his downfall, probably before the November election.

November 1, 1996

The Elliott Wave Theorist inaccurately forecast four years ago that a falling stock market would make Clinton an unpopular president. We were wrong about Clinton because we were wrong about the stock market. ...This situation is a replay of 1972, when an incumbent, supported by a social euphoria reflected by all-time highs in the Dow Jones Industrial Average, won in a landslide. He was then hounded out of office less than two years later. The public's lack of interest in Whitewater, the travel office scandal, Filegate, campaign finance violations, Bimbogate, Vince Foster's death, etc., has a flustered Dole asking, "Where is the outrage in America?" Pundits assure us that "character is a dead issue" in 1996, which it is, for now. A recent NBC poll says that 73% of Americans feel it is more important for a President to understand their problems ("feel their pain") than to be of high moral and ethical character....Dole can console himself with the fact that he won't be in the White House when the market turns down and the public's outrage is unleashed. When that happens, there will be an acute interest in the Clintons' dirty laundry.

...We are so near the crest of this historic bull market that we also predict that Clinton will be forced out of office. The degree of the bear market further suggests that the scandal that will oust him will dwarf anything in the history of U.S. presidential politics. One of his terms may not be in office; it may be in jail.

January 31, 1997

According to a Gallup poll, Bill Clinton is the most admired man in the country. His approval rating has risen past 60%, its highest level ever. *USA Today* celebrated his inauguration by publishing an entire section on the President's upcoming term. As one would expect with the Dow so close to its all-time high, most Americans are satisfied with their lives and optimistic about their children's futures. Clinton keeps saying he will model his second term on that of Theodore Roosevelt. We think the analogy could turn out to be more accurate than he realizes. Roosevelt's second term was rocked by the crash of 1907. While Roosevelt served his term out, Clinton will find it much harder to do so, as negative social moods are a natural chemical for ripening scandals, and the taste for them.

January 30, 1998

What are the odds that any president will be forced from office? Out of [41 previous] U.S. presidents, only Richard Nixon was forced from office, placing 40-to-1 odds on any such expectation. Yet even before Clinton was elected, our working analogy for whoever did win the office was the presidency of Richard Nixon....The Nixonian analogy has been working out even more closely than we imagined. Like Nixon, Clinton survived and then thrived in his first term by deftly riding a wave of positive mass emotion. Nixon's approval rating topped out at 67% within a month of his second inauguration in January 1973, when the Dow hit a record high of 1,051.69. Clinton's Gallup poll rating hit a high of 62%, also within days of his second inauguration. From the January 1973 high, the market began a two-year fall of 45%, and scandal slowly engulfed the Nixon White House. The first year of Clinton's second term was far better than Nixon's, although near the lows of last April's correction, an AP story did make the first reference to a "Watergate echo," noting "similarities" linking "Washington's atmosphere in the spring of 1997 to the spring of 1973." For the most part, however, it was smooth sailing by a "brilliant politician." Last summer's Whitewater hearings lacked the drama and public fascination of the Watergate hearings in the

summer of 1973 because the stock market was still trending upward. Key to our fledgling social science is that Clinton's perceived dexterity in avoiding outrage last year paralleled the market's run to record highs on August 6 (DJIA) and December 5 (S&P) 1997, driving Clinton's popularity to another high in September....The problem Clinton faces in this regard is that the public's mood has enjoyed a rocket ship ride since 1994, and its outlook on stocks (34% per year for the next decade, according to polls) reflects that fact that Americans expect their mood and speculative fortunes to continue waxing at historical-record speed. Anything less will disappoint. Anything less, we would add, is inevitable. The critical factor for Clinton is therefore not if, but when it happens. Andrew Jackson survived personal scandals as he negotiated his way through Cycle wave V of (I) in the 1830s, a cousin of today's Cycle wave V of (V). It was his successor, Martin van Buren, who rode the downwave and suffered deep unpopularity as a result. Clinton could survive politically if the bull market were to continue through his term. However, we see that as so unlikely that we stick with our original forecast for the ultimate outcome.

Naturally, many observers feared that market weakness would *result* from the situation: "An escalating scandal could trap stocks," says one article; "Clinton's Problems Could Bring Damage to Markets," says another. These efforts to gauge stocks' prospects based on the president's popularity are misguided. The market will do what it will, and social events will follow. The latest scandal's heat is a *result* of five months of corrective psychology. The causality is actually the inverse of the way these newspaper comments read. In fact, as the ink dried on them, the market began a rally, revealing once again that *it* is in charge, not the scandal. If the market soars again, the public is likely to retain a positive image of Clinton no matter what investigators uncover. If the stock market suffers a significant setback, it will reflect a social mood change toward dissatisfaction, and the strongest pillar of support for the president will give way.

July 31, 1998

Yesterday, *USA Today* called Monica Lewinsky's immunity deal on Tuesday a *"seismic shift"* in the legal and political pressure on the White House. We would apply the same term to what is happening in the stock market. Like the stock market, the Clinton team has used every stall tactic in the book. Their fortunes are linked, and both have run out of time.

Result: President Clinton has become the second U.S. president in history to be impeached. His behavioral history had provided the information necessary to identify his area of vulnerability. Then, all it took to trigger this fallout was a 20% drop in the DJIA (from July 20 to October 8) and a 30% drop in the average stock, as represented by the Value Line index. As far as I am concerned, this outcome is sufficient to demonstrate the value of an insight provided by the socionomic approach.

Even the weekly sequence of events has reflected the sociological dynamic. Clinton avoided political trouble for years until the 1998 stock market setback, which was the biggest since 1990. Congress finally acted on *October 8*, the exact day of the bottom in stock prices, voting 258 to 176 in favor of an impeachment inquiry. This set machinery in motion that could not be stopped, so despite the subsequent full recovery of the blue chip averages to previous highs, Congress finally impeached Clinton on Saturday, December 19, but with dramatically waning enthusiasm. The voting margins on the four articles of impeachment were 228/221/205/148 to 206/212/229/285, averaging 200.5 to 233. The voting averages on the two articles that passed were 224.5 to 209, much less than the voting margin of October 8. This difference reflects the waning of negative mood forces as reflected by the stock rally. As of December 20, the S&P Composite index has made a new all-time high, *and Clinton's popularity has reached 73%, also an all-time high.* In other words, despite everything else, *the stock market and the economy are in complete control of his public image.* Knowledge about his flawed character and behavior count for nothing against that background. Paul Gigot asks in *The Wall Street Journal*, "Why is lying less offensive in the 1990s than it was in the 1970s?"[11]

Virginia Postrel asks in *Reason,* "How is it that Bill Clinton is holding at about 60 percent support in public opinion polls — a lot better than he has done in a presidential election — while the political establishment sees him as an utter disgrace? It has been the year's great mystery."[12] Contrast the 1973-1974 bear market with the 1990s bull market, and you will see the answer to these mysteries.

It cannot be stressed strongly enough that the popularity of leaders, whether Reagan, Bush, Clinton or ones to come, is a direct reflection of social mood, which is governed independently and unconsciously by co-operating limbic systems. Character, morality, policies and events are meaningless to this portion of the brain. It does not reason; it generates feeling. It is fortunate for socionomics that the Clinton saga is so dramatic, as it demonstrates clearly that sociometers such as stock prices and presidential popularity move together even when events that conventional reasoning would assume are contrary to those trends are of historic proportion.

The main point with respect to socionomics is not whether the social image of these various public figures is *true,* but its *timing. Secretly immoral or incompetent public figures are protected by bull market psychology regardless of the facts, and truly upstanding or talented public figures are ravaged by an emerging bear regardless of the facts.*

A Forecast for Basketball

In the middle of the 1996-1997 basketball season, Peter Kendall of Elliott Wave International wrote a detailed socionomic study of the 100-year history of professional basketball and forecasted a dramatic reversal for the fortunes of the profession. Said Kendall:

> This examination of [basketball's] history shows the dominant influence of social mood on an American sport. The game's structure, rules and fortunes have developed in a manner that is totally consistent with the ebb and flow of the bull market in stocks.[13]

The 1997-1998 season and climax were euphoric, rivaling baseball's of 1991. "We were allowed up to Olympus,"[14] said *The Wall Street Journal* about Michael Jordan's performance in the final game.

Just a few months since that time, as I prepare this book, a major portion of the 1998-1999 season has been canceled. This action is the result of a strike that developed as a consequence of the social mood retrenchment (as reflected by the stock market decline) that ended in October. The cancelation is a first-time event in the half-century history of the

National Basketball Association. It is costing players, retailers, arenas and cities millions of dollars per missed game. This reversal is not unlike a crash from the pinnacle in a financial market. In December, the women's American Basketball League, which was formed in 1996, folded. Team owners who read Kendall's report had one full season to sell out gracefully before the debacle. Owners of Nike stock, which Kendall specifically cited as a short sale, had two months to sell, as the stock topped at 75 in February 1997 and has since fallen to 30. "How," asks the *Atlanta Journal & Constitution*, "could a business that brings in $2 billion [per year] have reached the point of self-destruction?"[15] The answer is, because it reached a pinnacle.

Whether this reversal in basketball's fortunes is the start of the long decline that Kendall envisions remains to be seen. Once again, however, the socionomic approach appears to have provided a most interesting insight into a unique situation.

APPLYING SOCIONOMICS TO INDIVIDUAL EXPERIENCES IN THE SOCIAL REALM

Individuals who become the focus of public adoration can survive the inevitable cooling of public acclaim if they understand that the immediate maintenance of their fame and social efficacy rests less on their actions than on public attitudes. Napoleon said quite accurately, "While my star is rising, nothing can stop me; while my star is falling, nothing can save me."[16] I do not know why he came to that conclusion, but a public person can reach it much easier if he knows about the Wave Principle.

Anticipating the Peak in a Public Persona from its Waves

Financial gurus are a social phenomenon like pop stars, which makes their fates somewhat forecastable. My knowledge that person and persona are different saved me from taking too seriously the market guru "round trip" that I experienced in the 1980s. I knew exactly what was happening at the time and even plotted the path and position of my "star." Figure 17-10 shows the monthly total of active subscriptions to *The Elliott Wave Theorist* in the 1980s. As wave 5 of the advance began to slow, I knew that the end of the ride was near. One day in September 1987, about twenty reporters with notepads and cameras crowded into a small hotel room in New York City to hear what the guru had to say. Although anyone else in that position would have used that scene as an opportunity for massive public-

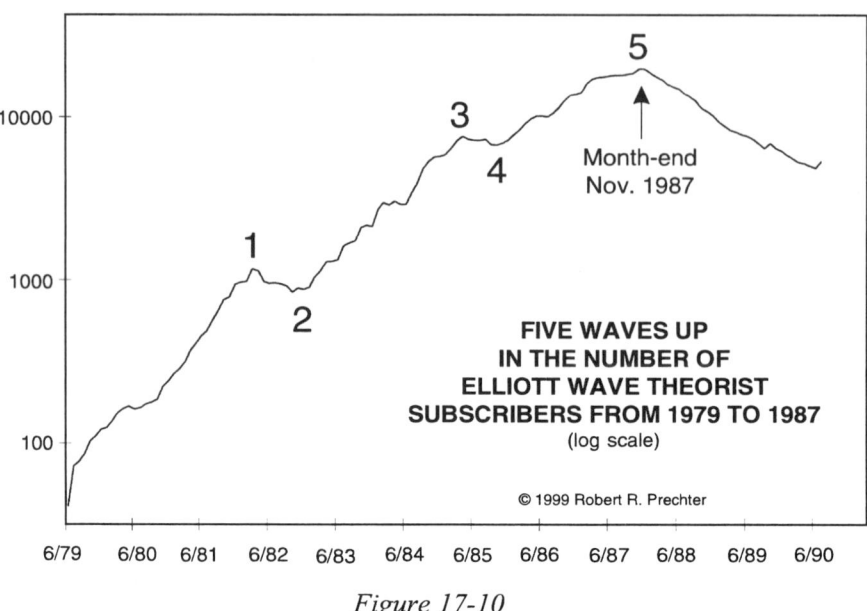

Figure 17-10

ity, I decided to do the opposite. I gave worthless, noncommittal answers to every question, and soon the room was empty. I didn't want my persona to have to fall from an even higher plane than it had already achieved. Yet that still was not quite the peak. Less than a month later, after being bullish since the 1984 low, I turned bearish on October 5, 1987, at the top of a rally less than 90 points from that year's high. Many papers, including *The New York Times,* reported the change. In October and November, reporters called ceaselessly and even parked their vans out on my street. Several people reported to me a rumor that Air Force One had landed on a nearby highway. These events were even stronger evidence of a top in my persona's fortunes. My subscriptions continued to reach new all-time highs through November.

In the midst of this frenzy, I foreshadowed the change with this comment to *USA Today*, published October 9: "There will be times when people will focus in on my 70 percent record for good calls...and there will come a time that people will focus on the bad calls. "[17]

Hoping to back out of the situation with the least personal damage, I suggested a new guru, Elaine Garzarelli, in my November 2 issue.[18] Upon plotting the first downtick on the graph in January 1988, I immediately ceased booking new speeches and media appearances, honoring only commitments for that year that were already made.

Sure enough, despite the fact that 1988 was one of my best forecasting years,[19] some members of the media had had enough of Prechter and began to attack the persona that their colleagues had overinflated. Some media people decided that my sell recommendation of October 5, which was the highest-level sell of any monitored advisor, was not good enough. According to them, I should have specifically predicted 900 points down in two weeks, and anything short of that was failure. The star fell, as it was destined to do, being a product of social mood and focus, which are as fleeting as limbic whims. Garzarelli became the new temporary hero. These waves seemed to anticipate my success in application as well, because shortly thereafter, I entered a long period of relatively poor forecasting.[20]

Calling Reversals for Public Icons on the Basis of Extreme Events

Even though one may not have charts of superstars' waves handy, sometimes events are so extreme as to serve as a top signal. However, just because someone receives an award does not mean that his persona is peaking, and just because he is the subject of a negative article does not mean that his persona is bottoming. To serve as such a signal, an event must truly be an extreme social assessment of value.

I have made two forecasts on this basis. In 1992, Elaine Garzarelli's image was so attractive that she began appearing on television in panty hose commercials. On January 31, 1992, I presented the following assessment of her persona:

> Based on the typical progression, I would conclude that 1992 will witness the peak in her heroic public image, and the media will begin to shift focus toward some of her errors. It is the same natural flow of social psychology that produces bull and bear markets.

Within a few months, the press savaged her money management results, and her firm let her go.

Chapter 15 discussed the wave positioning of pop music superstars. Michael Jackson enjoyed a long superstardom, which led to an extreme event that signaled the reversal of his persona. Here is my assessment from March 29, 1991:

> It would be reasonable to assume that the astounding value of the contract that Mr. Jackson signed with Sony on March 19, as noted in the article that follows, is a sign of a peak in his valuation.

USA TODAY
March 21, 1991

Jackson hits billion-dollar note

Michael Jackson and Sony signed a partnership deal Tuesday that Sony says is worth a potential $1 billion to him.

"A national treasure" is how Columbia chairmen Jon Peters and Peter Guber describe Jackson.

The planet's top star gained unprecedented success, first with 1982's *Thriller*, which sold 40 million copies to become history's best seller, then with 1987's *Bad* (25 million copies). [21]

Within a year of that event, Jackson's image began slipping. Reviews of his records became mixed to critical, and his sister ridiculed him in public. That was wave A down. Then came a wave B bounce, when Jackson performed for the Super Bowl halftime show in January 1993. By the end of that year, his image was collapsing in a powerful wave C. The list of indignities that year is stunning. He was accused of child molestation. An estranged sibling and fired former employees (paid to appear on tabloid TV shows) were alleging conduct suggestive of guilt. He was hospitalized with a drug problem. He had to cancel the remainder of a world tour. Two major companies terminated their commercial relationships with him. He was sued for millions by promoters for cutting short his tour. He was sued for millions by two songwriters who claimed he stole their material. A high profile university reneged on giving him a prestigious award. Police ordered pictures of his genitals to verify testimony, and it was rumored that they were being peddled to publications. Certainly his behavior in those months, good or bad, had not *changed*; it was the public's *focus* that changed. Moreover, whether Jackson actually committed wrongdoing that warrants the collapse of his image is irrelevant to the dynamic. Unlike most, the following newspaper comments actually stated his situation quite accurately:

The self-proclaimed king of pop has enjoyed a lucrative reign, but that kingdom is eroding and in danger of collapse. In rushing to exploit dubious evidence of wrongdoing (Jackson reading *Child* magazine, for instance), the media seem oblivious to the concept of presumed innocence. Is this rush to judgment fair? Probably not, but you can't expect restraint when the stakes are so high and the drama so gripping. A be-

loved musical hero of children is a confessed drug addict and suspected child molester. A global icon may retreat from view forever. Guilty or not, Jackson is a tragedy unfolding. If the boy's story holds up, if a jury convicts him, we'll witness a fall from grace as indelible as Richard Nixon's. Both involve admired men empowered by the trust of millions. No Hollywood scandal compares.[22]

Experiences of mass rejection are never easy for celebrated people. Nevertheless, as a result of understanding the Wave Principle and preparing for the change, I suffered a lot less psychological pain than other former market "gurus." So if you plan to be famous, plot your persona's progress and pay attention to the waves. If you know what is really going on, you will not end up bitter or dead at a young age or pine away your life wishing for a return to former glory. What's more, if you play your cards exactly right, you might be able to engineer a retirement from the fray at the top and be remembered in your peak state forever.[23]

Elliott Wave International has a number of other social forecasts pending. They cover everything from the success of professional basketball to the exercise craze, both of which we expect to reverse trend significantly in coming years. Perhaps we will investigate these areas of social experiences in a number of years to see how they work out.

NOTES

1 "Call it a miracle, or call it a mystery, but black youths shunning tobacco." (1995, August 13). *The Atlanta Journal-Constitution.*

2 Personal letter from R.E. Burt to R. Prechter, October 18, 1990.

3 Either that, or wave 4 is a flat correction. It is actually a too-common aspect of forecasts made by Elliotters that our time targets are too near in the future. I have many times been fooled by how much longer it takes for trends to play out than I anticipate.

4 The November 1, 1991 issue of *The Elliott Wave Theorist* included these additional descriptive words:

> Listen to baseball analyst Don Sutton, being interviewed before Game 3 of the NL playoffs:
>
> *Reporter*: "You normally see these kinds of crowds at college football games in the Southeast. It's hard to believe this is baseball and to see this sort of enthusiasm."
>
> *Sutton*: "Most of the time when people are really revved up and into it, it's from a negative standpoint and not from a positive standpoint. In 28 years of being around baseball, it has been the most remarkable phenomenon I've seen in baseball."
>
> The "tomahawk chop," the "Indian war chant" and "homer hankies" were continually displayed in unison by tens of thousands of people at a time. 40 year olds acted like 20 year olds. Drums beat for weeks, game or no game. People showed up hours early at the ballpark to soak up the supercharged atmosphere of the crowd. These upbeat social rituals directly involved hundreds of thousands of people. Millions were involved indirectly via television. Victory celebrations in Atlanta and Minneapolis (despite sleet) attracted 760,000 people. The victory parade in Atlanta, with floats and 16 bands, attracted the largest crowd ever to flood downtown for any event. As one observer said on TV prior to a game, "It's the Woodstock of sports."

5 Prechter, R.R. (1983, April 6). "A rising tide." *The Elliott Wave Theorist*, Special Report. For the full text, see the Appendix to *Elliott Wave Principle*.

6 As it turned out, I did harbor such fears prematurely. After correctly anticipating the economic contraction of 1990-1991, which followed on the heels of the 1987-1990 bear market (as best reflected by the Value Line index; see inset in Figure 16-3), I ignored rising stock prices thereafter and did not call for the expansion that ensued. This is obviously a psychological failure on my part but not on the part of the approach, which evidenced its continuing validity against my opinion!

7 Prechter, R. (1983, August, 18). "The superbull market of the '80s: has the last wild ride really begun?" *The Elliott Wave Theorist,* Special Report.

8 The multi-decade economic underperformance of the 1980s and 1990s vs. that of the 1950s and 1960s has important implications about the severity of the *next* economic contraction. Further, the underperformance of the rate of the economic expansion since 1932 as compared to that from 1857 to 1929 has even more important implications. For details on both these differences and the resulting outlook, see Chapters 9, 12 and 13 of *At The Crest of the Tidal Wave.*

9 (1986, September 9). *Daily News Digest,* Vol.12, No.45. This publication produced a great list of dire quotes from such personages as Kenneth Arrow, Professor of Economics, Stanford University; Representative John Dingel, D-MI, Chairman, Subcommittee on Energy and Power; James Schlesinger, Secretary of Energy; President Jimmy Carter; Marshall Loeb, *Time* magazine; Leonard Silk, *The New York Times*; Senator Howard Metzenbaum, D-OH; Senator Dale Bumpers, D-AR; and Carter Henderson in the *Bulletin of Atomic Scientists.*

10 This all-time record high approval rating for a president of the United States in the late summer of 1991 coincided with what may have been the most euphorically emotional baseball season ever, as described earlier in this chapter.

11 Gigot, P.A. (1998, August 14). "Woodward and Bernstein lose their fastball." *The Wall Street Journal.*

12 Postrel, V. (1998, December). "The two faces of Bill Clinton." *Reason*, p. 4.

13 Kendall, P. (1996, December 16). "Basketball and the bull market." a Special Report of *The Elliott Wave Theorist.*

14 "Too Good." (1998, June 16). *The Wall Street Journal.*

15 Denberg, J. (1998, December 9). "A League's Fiscal Rift." *The Atlanta Journal-Constitution*, p. E1.

16 Ludwig, E. (1926). *Napoleon.*

17 Shaw, R. and Landis, D. (1987, October 9). "Prechter flees Wall St. for Georgia hills." *USA Today.*

18 The November 2, 1987 issue of *The Elliott Wave Theorist* said this:

> **Garzarelli for Guru**: It has come to light that New York analyst Elaine Garzarelli was blamed by some clients for causing the October 16 crash because she sent out bearish warnings the previous week.... Elaine clearly is bright, she has put in the time and effort to know what she is talking about, and she has the guts to say so. Elaine has my vote for Nu Guru.

That was a pretty good call. The media took to Ms. Garzarelli and focused only on her successes for the next 4½ years.

19 According to the newsletter rating service, *Commodity Traders' Consumer Report*, EWT was the second-best performer in stock market timing that year among all monitored publications.

20 On December 31, 1992, I published an analysis of one larger trend of the popularity of the Wave Principle in terms of my professional efforts, which contains a prediction yet to be fulfilled.[ref: "An application of the wave principle to business." *The Elliott Wave Theorist* special report.]

21 Gunderson, E. (1991, March 21). "Jackson hits billion dollar note." *USA Today*.

22 Gunderson, E. (1993, November 19). "Jackson faces the man in the mirror." *USA Today*.

23 Upon extremely rare occasions, when society is particularly sensitive to their achievements or they themselves are particularly sensitive to the social mood, very talented people have enjoyed comebacks that carry them back to or beyond previous extremes of public glory. However, the path to that position is rarely the same as it was the first time.

Chapter 18:

Thinking Socionomically

Renowned financier Bernard Baruch, who was as close to markets as anyone, saw a connection between economic trends and the herding impulse of animals. He also understood the crucial importance of that knowledge to a correct social analysis:

> All economic movements, by their very nature, are motivated by crowd psychology. Without due recognition of crowd-thinking...our theories of economics leave much to be desired....It has always seemed to me that the periodic madnesses which afflict mankind must reflect some deeply rooted trait in human nature — a trait akin to the force that motivates the migration of birds or the rush of lemmings to the sea.... It is a force wholly impalpable...*yet, knowledge of it is necessary to right judgments on passing events.*[1]

The Irrelevance of Outside Cause to the Self-Organization of Complex Systems, Including Social Systems

Let us revisit the fact, discussed in Chapter 13, that extinctions follow a power law. As Per Bak and his colleagues have discovered, catastrophic events such as asteroids striking the earth are unnecessary to the solution of why there are mass extinctions from time to time. The dynamics of evolution themselves are such that mass extinctions can, and probably do, happen simply as part of the operation of the system. Computer simulations bear out the results of an endogenous dynamic. Bak and Kim Sneppen, when they were at the Brookhaven National Laboratory in the early 1990s, developed an evolutionary model using the basics of Darwin's theory. They found that species, simply interacting with each other, evolved and became extinct in the model according to a power law; there were many small

changes, fewer medium-sized ones, and a few huge ones, just as in actual evolution. They did not program asteroid impacts into the computer. Says Bak, "A huge extinction doesn't necessarily imply a corresponding catastrophic cause."[2] This is a wonderful sentence because what Bak means is that there is no corresponding *outside* cause, which is what I have been saying about finance and macroeconomics for years. Bak and Kan Chen of Simon Fraser University (British Columbia) say as much about the economy in the January 1991 issue of *Scientific American*:

> Conventional models assume the existence of a strongly stable equilibrium position for the economy, whereby large aggregate fluctuations can result only from external shocks that simultaneously affect many different sectors in the same way. Yet it is often difficult to identify the reasons for such large-scale fluctuations as the depression of the 1930s. If, on the other hand, the economy is a self-organized critical system, *more or less periodic large-scale fluctuations are to be expected even in the absence of any common jolts across sectors.*[3]

Two studies in particular have destroyed the idea that outside causality is necessary to explain financial markets. Chapter 8 reported on a stock market simulation study from 1987 using a few dozen people at a time that "repeatedly created a boom-and-bust market profile." Chapter 12 reported on the latest stock market simulation study by European physicists Caldarelli, Marsili and Zhang, in which a limited number of participants bet on a currency relationship with "no real information input." Their aim was to observe financial market psychology "in the absence of external factors." Here is what they find with respect to causality:

> In spite of the simplicity of our model and of the strategies of the single participants, and the *outright exclusion of economic external factors*, we...find a market which behaves surprisingly realistically. These results suggest that a stock market can be considered as a self-organized critical system: The system reaches dynamically an equilibrium state characterized by fluctuations of any size, *without the need of* any parameter fine tuning or *external driving.*[4]

Says Marsili, "The understanding that we got is that the statistics of price histories in financial markets can be understood as *the result of the internal interaction, and not the fundamental interaction with the external world.*"[5] Adds Tony Chapman in reviewing the study, "*The outside world has no influence*, something that might surprise real traders who rely heavily on news from the economic world outside their trading floor."[6] In reviewing

this model, the October 1997 *New Scientist* says the same thing about the stock market that Bak says about earthquakes, extinctions and economic contractions: "You don't need a crisis to trigger a financial crash."[7]

There is far more to the process than these tentative comments imply. It is not just the catastrophes that need no outside cause but the *entire process*. As a team member put it, "Our ultra-simplified model has *all* the major characteristics of a real market: bull runs, crashes and mini-crashes."[8]

This phenomenon applies to companies as well, whose structure is social and whose products' success depends upon aggregate human desires. A research team including Stanley and Michael Salinger of Boston University's School of Management has studied fluctuations in corporate success and setback. *New Scientist* states, "The group's results show a *universal pattern of growth* that holds for firms of all types, *whatever business they are in*."[9] This sentence is nearly identical to a hundred I have written over the years. Its sentiment permeates the literature on the Wave Principle.

The Impossibility of Outside Cause with Respect to Social Systems

The studies cited above are important because they show that no outside causes of financial market and macroeconomic behavior are *necessary*. To the extent possible, this book explains something even more important: why there *are not*, and *cannot be*, outside causes of financial, economic and social behavior. Think about it. When dealing with social events, what is an "external shock"? What is an "outside cause"? Other than the proverbial asteroid striking the earth, which presumably might disrupt the NYSE for a couple of days, or the massive earthquake or destructive hurricane that we already know does not affect financial market behavior in any noticeable way, there is in fact, in the social context, *no such thing as an outside force or cause*. Every "external shock" ever referenced in finance is in fact an *internal event*. Trends in the stock market, interest rates, the trade balance, government spending, the money supply and economic performance are all ultimately products of collective human mentation. Human minds create these trends and change both them and their apparent interrelationships as well. It is men who change interest rates, trade goods, create earnings and all the rest. All social events, whether a rise in interest rates, a drop in the stock market, or even a war, are the result of collective human mentation. To suggest that such things are outside the social phenomenon under study is to presume that people do not communicate (consciously or otherwise) with each other from one aspect of their social lives to another.

This is not only an unproven assumption but an absurd one. All financial events, indeed all social movements, are part and parcel of the interactive flux of human cooperation. All such forces are intimately commingled all the time. Yet to the conventional analyst, each is as detached a cause as a cue stick striking a billiard ball. It is this error that so profoundly undermines the conventional approach. As we have seen throughout this book, the Wave Principle shapes the trends in markets, economics, politics, cultural trends, the personas of social heroes and even evolution, implying a universal pattern of growth and decay for all social phenomena.[10] It is time to abandon the idea of outside causality for social mood and action.

The most extreme example that I can think of that could be argued as constituting an outside event that would affect societies is an epidemic or pandemic. After all, they kill thousands or millions of people. How could they fail to be an important social factor affecting mood?

The fact is that epidemics and pandemics seem to hit populations during major negative social mood trends. Perhaps it happens that way because people's psychological constitutions are weaker during bear markets. Perhaps it is because people's personal behavior, whether involving hygiene (as in the time of the plague or in recent years with respect to hypodermic needles used to inject drugs) or sexual promiscuity, is more conducive to spreading disease during social mood retrenchments. Perhaps it is because social mood retrenchment brings economic contraction, which makes people less able to afford the creature comforts that ward off disease and more apt to crowd into smaller, more affordable spaces. Whatever the reason, when we study pandemics of the Dark Ages or the Spanish influenza epidemic that broke out during the bear market of 1917 (which year also saw intense fighting in World War I and the Communist coup in Russia), there always appears to be a bear market in force, and the extent of the epidemic tends to correlate with the size of the setback in mood.[11]

R.N. Elliott observed that markets often travel within parallel trend channels.[12] Take a look at Figures 18-1 though 18-5 and observe how some of the most volatile markets in history, which operated in extremely diverse economic and social conditions, nevertheless traveled paths that reflect this fundamental aspect of collective behavior. These channels contain prices regardless of wars, energy crises, speeches, assassinations, Watergates, Peanutgates, Travelgates, Zippergates, jawboning or the weather. Financial markets, it appears, often know exactly where they are, where they have been, and at least in some respects, where they are going. The events of economics, politics and history must mean nothing to them. Conventional views of social causality, chaos, randomness and unpredictability

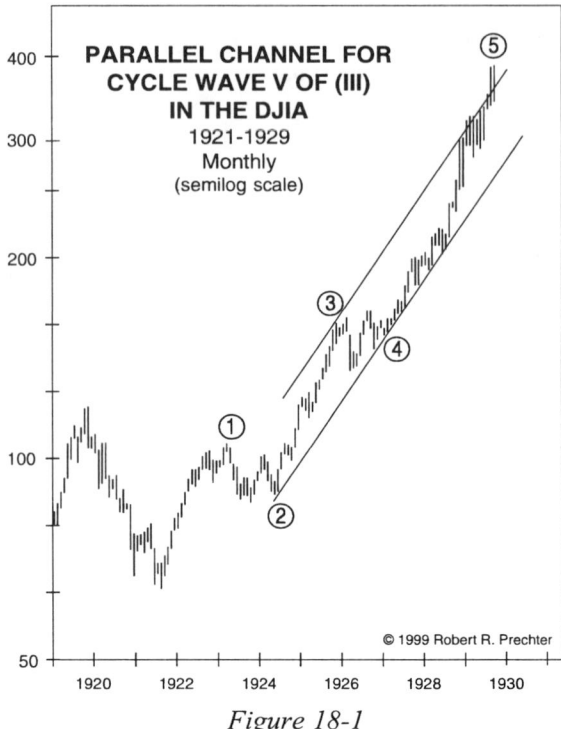

Figure 18-1

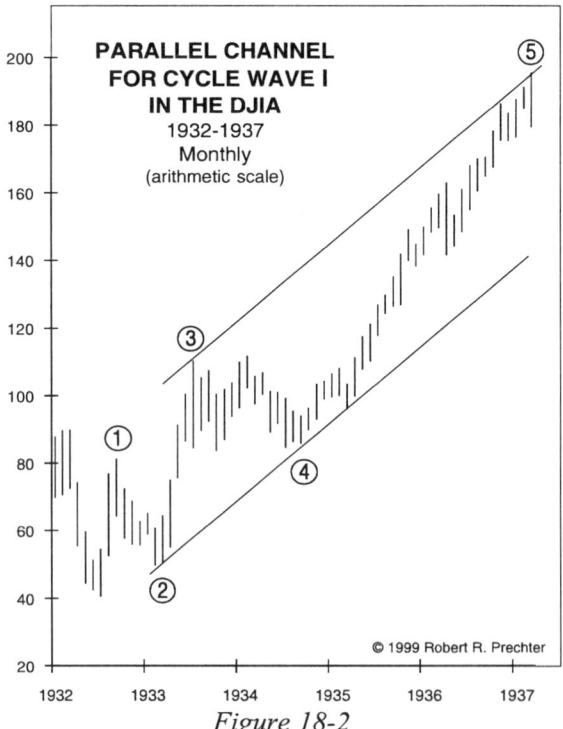

Figure 18-2

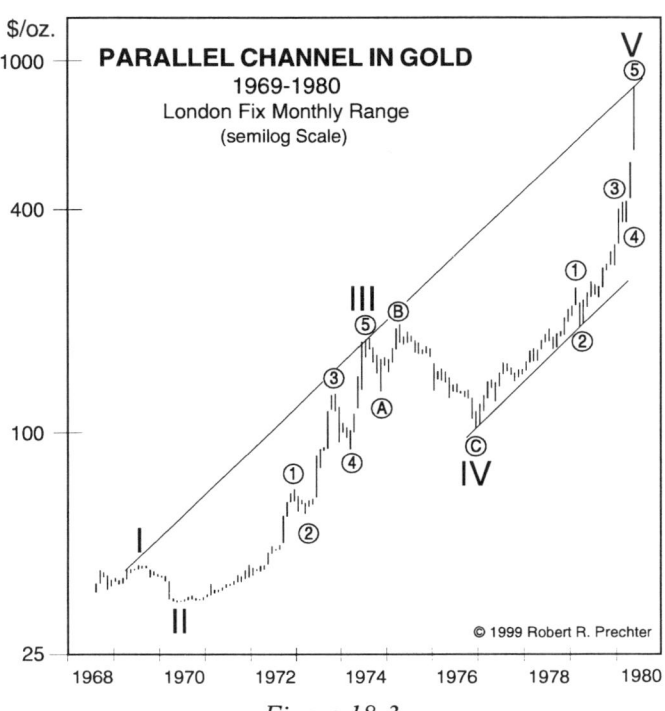

Figure 18-3

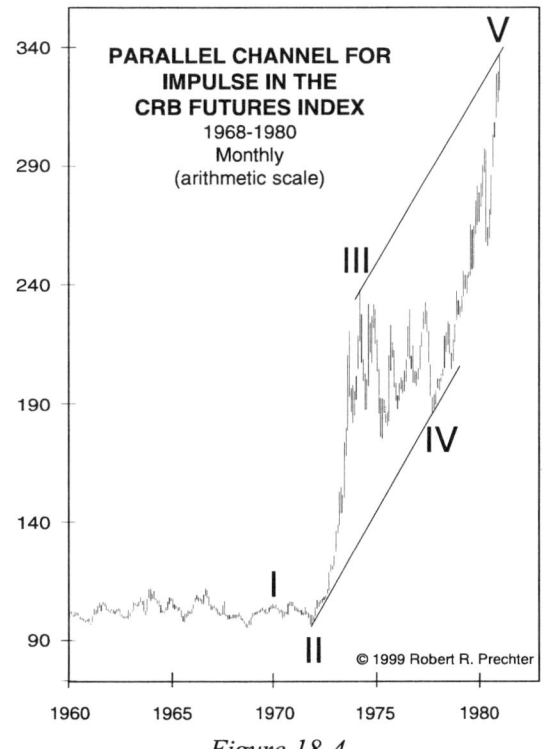

Figure 18-4

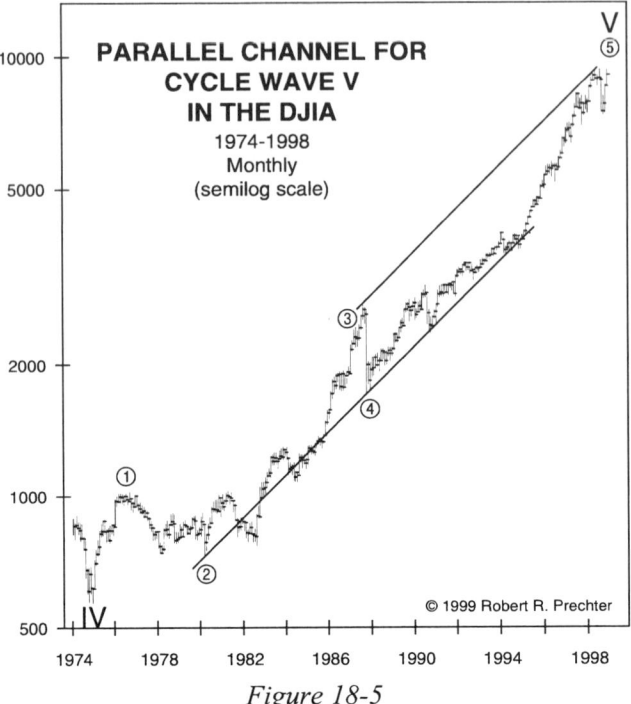

Figure 18-5

(see Chapters 19 and 20) are incompatible with this observation. The Wave Principle, on the other hand, subsumes it.

For over twenty years and throughout this book, I have argued that economics and politics are acausal to financial and system behavior. The reason is not only that outside causality is unnecessary, as modern studies are proving. It is because outside causality is *impossible* because financial markets are patterned according to the Wave Principle.

The Direction of Social Causality

If social mood is patterned, it cannot be the result of random social events, and there is no basis upon which to suggest that it is somehow the result of social events that are themselves perfectly patterned to produce the Wave Principle, which would require utter event determinism. Yet Chapter 16 shows an intimate connection between social events and mood. Therefore, the only possible direction of causality is the opposite of that popularly assumed. To summarize what I call the socionomic insight, social events do not shape social mood; social mood shapes social events. Mass psychological fluctuations are not simply correlated with mankind's

actual progress and regress through history, but in fact are their engine. Collective mood shapes the character of social interaction, and thus of resulting actions and events.

The evidence of this insight is continually available. Just the past few months provide several dramatic examples. The financial collapse in Indonesia in October 1997 led to riots in April 1998 and the ousting of a previous popular ruler, Suharto, who had been president for 32 years. The financial collapse in South Korea beginning in October 1997, which brought its stock market to an 11-year low, led to massive labor strikes in April 1998. The collapse in the Russian stock market, the ruble and its government bonds in 1998, has led to "a profound political crisis." Financial uptrend precedes social euphoria, and financial downtrend precedes social crisis.

The Uselessness of News Even to the Clairvoyant

Champions of news causality truly have a fundamental problem, which is that no investor really knows the implication of any piece of news. This fact is hidden by the ease with which financial news writers can retrospectively pull out from the plethora of news on any given day a story that appears to justify whatever market movement occurred. The reverse order of things is not so accommodating. If you could construct a time-machine mailbox that would generate *The New York Times* a full day early but with news about the stock market omitted, you would be just as unable to forecast the next day's market action as if you had nothing at all to read. Riots, peace pacts, summits, earthquakes, destructive hurricanes, price changes in commodities, assassinations, triumphs of statesmanship and political scandals — nothing of this sort has more than a momentary effect on the stock market, much less any predictive value. This week, an economics writer for *The Atlanta Journal-Constitution* said quite accurately, "If history is any guide, the stock market could go either way today in the wake of the U.S. air strikes against Afghanistan and Sudan."[13] Correct! Kudos for an economic writer who bothered to look at the record before opining. (Now go back to Chapter 16 and review how reliably the market, as a meter of the social mood that triggers such events, tends to fall *prior* to military activity.)

In August, *The Atlanta Journal-Constitution* ran an article that reviewed a 42-year history of surprise news and the stock market entitled, "Identifying Sell-off Trigger Difficult."[14] That is to say, it is difficult *even in retrospect* to make any connection between dramatic surprise events and what the market does. The biggest decline in the period studied was

the 1987 crash, about which the article quite accurately says, *"Scholars still debate the reasons why."* Imagine scholars endlessly debating about things that history proves have no validity! That is what so many scholars do because their ideas of financial market causality, rationality and efficiency are all wrong, yet they see no alternative.

Once you understand that news is not causal, you realize that even if you got it in advance, you could not forecast the stock market. Once you understand that news has no forecasting value, you recognize that there is no valid news-related explanation for the market's behavior on Black Monday, last Tuesday or next Thursday, either, or on any market day at all, or any week, month, year, decade or century. Though these facts are counterintuitive, it does not take a dedicated market student long to observe the acausality of news to the stock market. A socionomist observes, and more important, *understands*, the reverse causality. As R.N. Elliott said, "At best, news is the tardy recognition of forces that have already been at work for some time and is startling only to those unaware of the trend."[15]

Reasoning from Conditions to Markets – in Advance

The belief that news affects the market is the lowest and most common level of misunderstanding. There is a higher level of misunderstanding, which at least pays tribute to the *fact* that the market moves ahead of events. Technicians assert that the reason earnings lag stock prices is that smart investors anticipate, or "discount," the future, in other words, guess the future correctly.

While this position is a time-honored and valiant attempt to explain why events lag stock prices, I believe it is false. The idea that the mass of investors possess near-omniscience about the economic future is difficult to defend. It does not explain why in 1928 the market foresaw nothing but blue sky, in 1929 very suddenly foresaw depression, and in early 1930 anticipated a recovery that never happened. One might try to make a case that smart investors sell stocks when they get a whiff of trouble in their own businesses. If the economy typically turned before or even coincidentally with stocks, this argument might be plausible. But stocks lead the economy, normally by months. Then there is the problem that when you ask investors what they think, they express no inkling of coming economic changes. At the start of a bull trend, the vast majority is bearish, while at the start of a bear trend, it is bullish. Their erroneous convictions often reach an extreme by the end of wave 2 or B of the new trend, right at the worst time.

Because markets are patterned, the concept of near-perfect collective forecasting *must* be false. Otherwise, future events would have to be patterned according to the Wave Principle, and the collective would have to anticipate each nuance perfectly. This is an untenable position.

The truth is that the stock market does not see into the future, as the discounting concept suggests; it reflects instantaneously the *causes* of the future. Optimistic people expand their businesses; depressed people contract their businesses. The results show up later as an apparently "discounted" future. The actions of human beings spurred on by an increasingly ebullient or pessimistic social mood cause earnings to rise or fall. Rising earnings are the fruits of a bull market, and falling earnings are the result of a bear. The same thing is true of political action. Politicians do not turn the tide of a bull or bear market by enacting or abandoning policies. The mass emotional environment, as reflected by the market, forces them at some critical point to act.

Socionomics Reverses the Thinking Process Relating Markets and Events

While knowledge of current events and extramarket conditions has almost no value in predicting the stock market, knowledge about the position of the market can help predict changes in outside conditions. The Wave Principle provides a basis for speculating upon upcoming changes in market trends and therefore the events that result from the social psychology that the trend changes represent. This ability provides an opportunity to prepare for the coming character of events, and sometimes even actual events, before they are realized. It is worth knowing, for instance, that banks were closed by government decree in 1933 shortly after the low of Supercycle wave (IV) and that most of the banks in the country closed in 1857 as well, at the end of Supercycle wave (II). It is unlikely, therefore, that with regard to bank health, the next bear market of Supercycle or larger degree will fail to produce similar results. Most analysts work the other way around. For example, they wait until they have observed widespread bank failures and then declare their bearish meaning for the stock market, which is precisely the opposite of their true implication. With the Wave Principle, we have a tool that allows us to use the pattern of social mood objectively and properly rather than let *it* bend *us* to its design.

A conventional analyst asks, "What will the Fed's actions do for, or to, the stock and bond markets? The socionomist asks, "What will stock

and bond market action do for (or to) the reputation of the Fed?" A conventional analyst sees a country's prime minister as standing "at the helm of the economy."[16] The socionomist sees social mood, and thus the market, and thus the economy, as standing at the helm of the prime minister's reputation. A conventional analyst asks how bills in Congress will affect the stock market. The socionomist asks what the stock market says about the kinds of bills that will be introduced and whether they will be passed. A conventional analyst points out that an election was *divisive*. The socionomist says it was *divided*. A conventional analyst says that the outbreak of war will make people fearful and angry. The socionomist says that angry and fearful people are prone to engaging in war. A conventional analyst asks how a federal government tax surplus will help the country. The socionomist asks when it is in the wave progression of social mood that budget surpluses typically occur and forecasts the surplus. A conventional analyst asks what the impact of revised corporate earnings estimates will be on the stock market. The socionomist watches the trend of stock prices and predicts in what direction analysts will revise their earnings estimates. Let us explore some concrete examples of this reversal of roles.

Throughout the 1950s, people built bomb shelters. They were responding to events that had *already happened*, in essence preparing for 1945 a decade late. In 1994, the Smithsonian Institution placed a bomb shelter in its collection as a relic. Observers, conventional analysts all, hailed it as reflecting the beginning of a new era of peace for mankind. What is the true importance of that occurrence as a reflection of social mood? It reflects a complacency common to developing major social mood tops. It suggests to a socionomist that the long-term positive mood trend is nearing an extreme and that worries about warfare will probably soon begin waxing again. Conventional thinkers waste time building shelters when they are unnecessary and then have no shelters when they need them the most. Socionomists do the opposite.

Here is another example. Major market uptrends eventually bring into fashion the recurring belief that market timing is passé and useless, if not counterproductive: "All one needs is good stock selection. Just stay in good stocks, and you will make money *and* be safe." When have we seen this sentiment widely expressed? Answer: 1928, 1968 and 1998. Few made this case in June 1984. No one made this case in December 1974. No one said this in 1932, 1942, 1859 or 1842. What socionomic conclusion can you draw when this opinion is pervasive? *It is a symptom of complacency*

about the trend of the overall market, a complacency that people express only very late in uptrends. Now contemplate the kind of irony that we continually observe when thinking socionomically. *It is precisely the position of the stock market in its overall trend that induces people to say that the position of the stock market in its overall trend is irrelevant.* At the bottom of a bear market, *timing* becomes the new philosophy, which assumes its place on the pedestal just when it is actually time to concentrate on holding and selecting stocks.[17] Socionomists can observe and profit from such irony in the marketplace every day; conventional analysts produce irony every day without knowing it.

The Media as Reflectors of Consensus Mood

Socionomics shows why the media must always be wrong in the aggregate when reporting predictions about major social trends. Reporters usually are nonprofessional in the fields they cover, so the feelings of reporters in general mirror those of the public. Reporters often contact financial analysts who express their own feelings about markets, thus reflecting society's consensus feelings. A bullish analyst rarely gets a forum at a major market bottom, and a bear rarely gets one at a major market top. The media's *choice of times to quote* certain professionals typically shows those professionals retrospectively in their worst light.

James Stack of Investech undertook the tedious job of culling market-related articles going all the way back to the 1920s.[18] The resulting chronicle is a tragicomedy of never-ending wrongness. As John Rothchild sums up Stack's conclusions, "When they are predicting anything that involves money, economists, prominent investors and the reporters who quote them haven't been wrong on occasion; *they've been unerringly errant.*"[19] Paul Montgomery of *Universal Economics* and Ned Davis of *Ned Davis Research* have studied the timing of the covers of major news magazines, finding that whenever one of them takes a stand on the stock market, it is invariably an important turn in the other direction that typically lasts years.[20,21,22]

I have noted a sister phenomenon. When trends reach extremes, reporters no longer require the services of financial professionals to express an opinion; the continuation of the trend is so obvious to them that they become convinced that anyone can do it, and they take on the forecasting themselves. Error at such times is guaranteed.

Forecasting Implications of Extremes in the Character of Events

Though events are the result of social mood, even they have some predictive value when they reach extremes. Of course, that value is precisely the opposite of what is typically assumed (see Chapter 19). Baron von Rothschild encapsulated this truth when he said about investing, "Buy when blood is running in the streets." In other words, when things look darkest, it must be a low in mood and therefore a low in stock and bond prices. Here is an example. On November 12, 1857, right at the low of wave (c) of a 22-year bear market of Supercycle degree, a headline in the *Boston Globe* read, "Energy Crisis Looms — World To Go Dark — Whale Blubber Scarce." A few weeks earlier, in October, *Harper's Weekly* made this statement:

> It is a gloomy moment in the history of our country. Not in the lifetime of most men has there been so much grave and deep apprehension; never has the future seemed so incalculable as at this time. The domestic economic situation is in chaos. Our dollar is weak throughout the world. Prices are so high as to be impossible. The political cauldron seethes and bubbles with uncertainty. Russia hangs, as usual, like a cloud, dark and silent, upon the horizon. It is a solemn moment. Of our troubles no man can see the end.[23]

Perhaps no man could "see the end," but it was directly at hand. That month marked a low in stock prices and economic performance that was never breached and from which stock prices soared 3.5 times in value in six years and 47.6 times in 72 years.

The converse is also true. In 1928, the happy character of events and conditions reflected an extreme of positive social sentiment that hinted at a reversal. Similarly, in 1965, after 23 years of bull market, the United States had no war, no shortages, undisputed world power, cheap energy, a happy populace and a productive economy. The spirit of abundance and invincibility was so great that Congress and President Lyndon Johnson initiated the greatest expansion of government-sponsored social programs in history, including Medicare, the Voting Rights Act, Head Start, the Elementary and Secondary Education Act and the Housing and Urban Development Act. The government had launched The Great Society. Was it time to be optimistic or pessimistic?

In 1979, after 13 years of bear market, the U.S. had "uncontrollable" inflation, labor unrest and violence, slipping world power, shortages, ex-

pensive energy, stifling regulation, confiscatory taxes and had even lost a war for the first time ever. The Roper organization reported that for the first time in the history of its poll dating back to 1959, Americans rated the future as less promising than the present. President Jimmy Carter lectured the country on its "crisis of confidence." Was it time to be pessimistic or optimistic?

Extremes in conditions at Supercycle degree are even more dramatic. Political events were *scary and dangerous* in the Supercycle degree bear market (in constant-dollar terms) of the 1930s and 1940s. They included totalitarian takeovers of vast territory, war on an unprecedented scale, state-directed murders of forty million people, countless atrocities, the invention and deployment of atomic bombs and the annihilation of cities. These events reflected the negative social psychology of a Supercycle degree bear market. *That period also accompanied one of the greatest stock market lift-offs of all time.*

As you can see, an extreme character of social events implies nearness of a trend change in the opposite direction. In this way, social events, when their character is extreme, can be a contributory tool to socionomic forecasting.

Shall we apply this concept to today's environment as we enter 1999? The character of today's social events is as bright as any time in history. Look around and witness how a Supercycle upswing in mood has produced events during this decade that are so positive as to have been previously unimaginable. Officials have pronounced the forty-year-long Cold War officially over; the U.S.S.R. has freed Eastern Europe, creating what *The Wall Street Journal* called "a period of euphoria unequaled in the postwar era"; China appears to be on the long-term road to adopting capitalism and freedom; U.S. political leaders have promised a perpetually balanced Federal budget by constitutional amendment; the U.S. won its first war in 46 years; South Africa ended apartheid three and a half centuries after the Dutch arrival in South Africa and 45 years after its adoption as official government policy; and countless political and religious leaders have reached conciliation after decades, centuries and in some cases millennia of animosity, as listed in the "Peace" section of Chapter 16.

The response of today's conventional analysts to these conditions is as optimistic as it was in the late 1920s. For example, State Department Policy Planner Francis Fukuyama, in his widely praised *New York Times* bestselling book, declares "the end of history as such" because political risks have been obliterated by the global triumph of Western liberal de-

mocracy.[24] World officials agree, expressing joy that a new golden age of world peace and prosperity has begun. The public agrees; as a result of all this truly wonderful news, the Consumer Confidence statistic in 1998 approached its highest levels of the past 25 years. The vast majority of citizens, public and private, including all conventional futurists, economists and political analysts, are bullish on the stock market, the economy and the future as far as the imagination can project. However, you, as a reader of this book, have the basis for a more reliable perspective.

Understanding that "bullish" means that things will improve and "bearish" means that things will deteriorate, *are the events described above bullish or bearish?* Events of recent years, as chronicled above, are the *opposite* of the social spectacle of the 1930s and 1940s. Figure 18-6 details the colossal difference in political tone between the results of the Supercycle wave (IV) *bear* market and the results of the Supercycle wave (V) *bull* market. The photographs on the following pages communicate the difference in human terms.

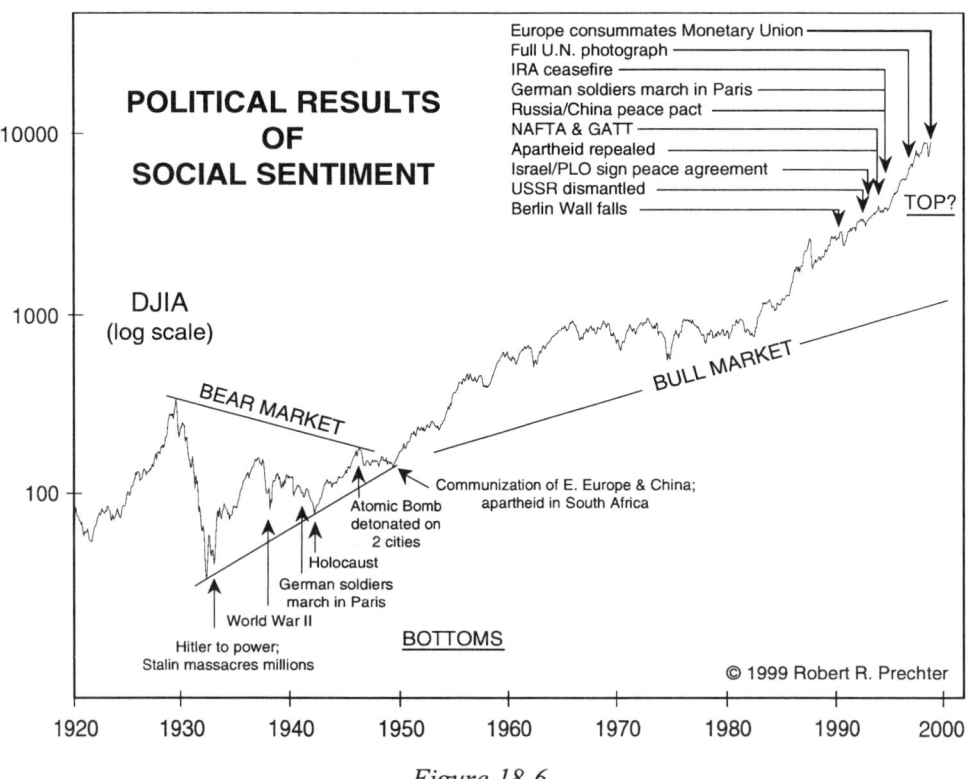

Figure 18-6

*As perverse as it may seem, these photos represent an extreme in negative social mood
and therefore a time to become increasingly optimistic*

source: Collier's Photographic History of World War II

Hitler enters Danzig, September 1939

source: The Manhattan Project

Atomic Bomb, July 1945

source: Inside the Vicious Heart

Buchenwald, 1945

As perverse as it may seem, these photos represent an extreme in positive social mood and therefore time to become increasingly pessimistic

Peacemaking handshake between
Prime Minister Rabin of Israel and PLO President Arafat

source: The Atlanta Journal-Constitution, 9/93

Historic day for South Africa
End of an era: Races equal under new constitution

source: David Brauchli, AP, 11/18/93

UK and Ireland plan for peace

source: Financial Times, 12/16/93

Pacts mark 'historic' day
BREAKTHROUGH IN RUSSIA All is warmth

source: Associated Press, Jan 1994

'no more war'
Jordan, Israel agree to seek permanent peace

source: USA Today, 7/26/94

A picture-perfect U.N.: 185 leaders side by side

source: Associated Press, 10/23/95

Are the latest events, deeply welcome as they are otherwise, consistent with events that accompany a social-mood bottom or top? Given your answer, should we anticipate an acceleration or long continuance of the trend we have enjoyed or begin anticipating a reversal?

If your answer is the same as mine, then you disagree with (to the nearest percent) *100%* of economists, who conclude that these events have created "favorable fundamentals" that are bullish for the indefinite future. According to *The Wall Street Journal*, 55 out of 55 economists polled in July 1998 say that the odds of a "recession or that the stock market will enter a bearish phase are slim."[25] Adds *The New York Times* on August 15, "not a single Blue Chip economist sees a recession."[26] *Business Week* magazine's August 31, 1998 issue features a cover story on the 21st century economy. A team of reporters and editors "examined every aspect of the economy" and have concluded that "all elements are in place for an era of long-term growth."[27] This conclusion would have been visionary in the fourth quarter of 1974 or 1982, when no conventional economist said it. Should a socionomist change his opinion because every conventional economist and futurist in the country disagrees with it? Chapter 19's discussion of economists' aggregate track record answers that question emphatically. The answer is no, whether our statement of probability (not certainty) turns out right in this particular instance or not.

Events look so good at a major top and so bad at a major bottom that few can envision any trend but a continuation, if not acceleration, of the one that brought them there. The point of this section is to communicate that *that very fact* implies an increased probability of change.

Keep in mind that event extremes are *relative*. Just because times are good does not mean that it must be a top. Similarly, just because times are bad does not mean that it must be a bottom. Both the Renaissance and the Dark Ages lasted a long time. The key, as always, is a proper perspective provided by the wave structure.

Predicting the Popularity of Socionomics Itself

A socionomist even has the advantage of being able to anticipate changes in the public's perception of his own value and the validity of his work. The reason is that social mood trends correlate with the waxing and waning of interest in such things as the very notion of cycles and waves of social mood. In uptrends, social cycles themselves are increasingly ignored, derided or declared dead as people credit policy makers with the power that brought about the uptrend. At tops, this sentiment is pervasive. For

example, in September 1929, the president of the New York Stock Exchange, echoing the sentiments of bank presidents, economists and government officials, said, "It is obvious that we are through with business cycles as we have known them."[28] In 1991, a professor of political economy speaks for his entire profession in saying, "There are very few ideas in macroeconomics that serious economists agree on, but doubting the existence of the Kondratieff [cycle] is one of them."[29] In July 1998, an MIT professor declares that "this expansion will run forever" because we have "policy levers" to "keep the current expansion going."[30] At such times, the idea of social cycles is anathema to conventional thought.

In contrast, when negative social mood waxes and financial and economic changes become volatile, cycles become *de rigueur* as people search for causes of the dramatic events that caught them off guard. One such period was 1929 to 1949. R.N. Elliott was inspired to do his work by the 1929-1932 collapse, publishing books in 1938 and 1946. Nikolai Kondratieff sent his paper, "Long Economic Cycles," to Harvard in 1935. Harvard economics professor Joseph Shumpeter expanded upon the Kondratieff cycle (which he called "the single most important tool in economic forecasting") in his 1939 book, *Business Cycles*.[31] Edward R. Dewey started the Foundation for the Study of Cycles in the 1940s after the U.S. government asked him to explain the causes of the 1929 crash. He and Edwin F. Dakin finished *Cycles: the Science of Prediction* in 1945.[32,33]

Over the years, membership in the Foundation for the Study of Cycles fell when the stock market went up and rose when it corrected. In the 1960s' uptrend, cycles were again passé and interest waned. In the corrective period of the 1970s, both the foundation and the Kondratieff cycle returned to prominence. Books such as *Cycles – The Mysterious Forces that Trigger Events* by Dewey (1971), *The Kondratieff Wave* by Shuman and Rosenau (1972) and *Cycles* by Dick Stoken (1978) were strong sellers, and cycle-oriented financial newsletters flourished. In the 1990s, cycles are once again considered relics of the past. With that background, you should not be surprised to learn that in 1997 and 1998, after 15 years of relentless bull market, the Foundation for the Study of Cycles ceased issuing publications after over half a century of operation.[34]

Why does interest in this subject fluctuate? The answer is that people equate uptrends with predictability and downtrends with unpredictability. The *Harper's Weekly* quote from 1857 includes the phrase, "never has the future seemed so incalculable as at this time." Translation: "The market has been falling for several years." The media constantly characterize market setbacks as injecting "uncertainty" into a picture of the future that

presumably was previously as clear as crystal. I am not exaggerating when I say that this foible is timeless. Just this month, after a three-month decline in the Dow and a six-month decline in the Value Line index, *The Wall Street Journal* says, "The prevailing sentiment among investors these days appears to be confusion. And confusion is costly after so many years of *predictability*."[35] Translation: "After going up for years, the market has trended down for several months." If uptrends are so predictable, then why didn't these same investors know that one had ended in April/July and another had already begun six days before the article appeared? The timeless conceit that uptrends are predictable explains why people ignore cycles in uptrends and embrace them in downtrends.

Today, after decades of advance, virtually no one is interested in cycles of human behavior. Once again, the majority believes that the market and the economy are "predictable" and the uptrend will persist because policy makers have engineered social retrenchments out of existence. This belief is a luxury of a neocortex that is not threatened by a limbic system in fear of, or desiring to escape blame for, a serious economic setback. Of course, the extremity of today's bemusement toward the outmoded idea of social cycles is yet another signal of an approaching major social mood reversal and the beginning of a trend back towards a general interest in patterns of social behavior. I hope this book contributes to that trend.[36]

Reverse Forecasting: Inducing Waves from Past Social Events6

If society's actions are patterned over five minutes, five hours, five days, five weeks, five years and five decades, as the graphs in this book indicate, they might be patterned over five centuries and five millennia. Indeed, it is my contention that all of history can be understood from the standpoint of waves, and in fact *only* from that standpoint.

Because waves manifest themselves in events, we now have a basis for delving into the past, where no stock market prices have been charted, and using social events and conditions to induce the position of waves. Figure 18-7 is one possible categorization of the historical trends of Western culture since Roman times. We have market price data from the year 1690 forward, but the waves prior to 1690 in this depiction are constructed on the basis of social trends and events. The few notes on the illustration hint at the reasons behind my wave labels. In my opinion, Elliott wave patterns can be induced back to the start of the Bronze Age. This kind of analysis can provide a panoramic view of the past, and by implication, of the future as well. There is obviously much more to say on this subject as well, but that will wait for another time.

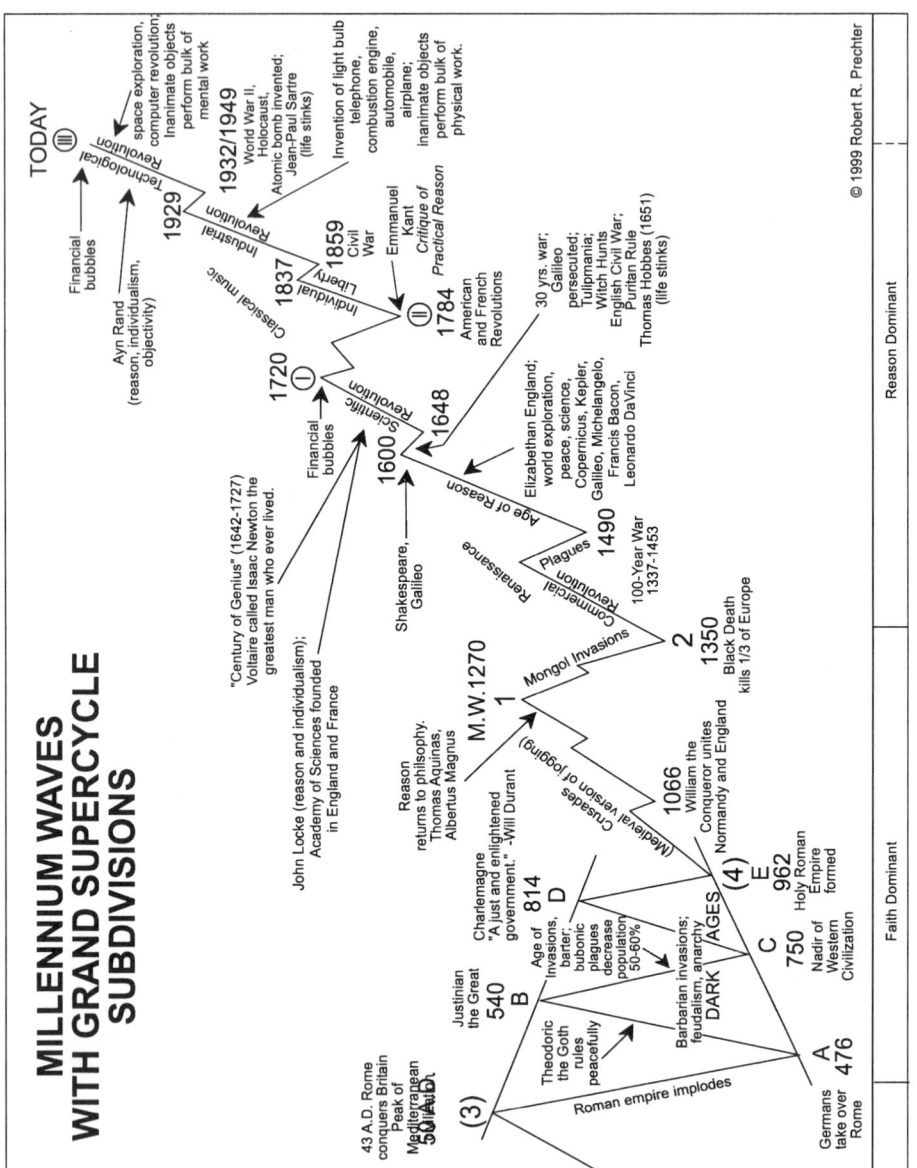

Figure 18-7

NOTES

1 From Baruch's foreword to Mackay's *Extraordinary popular delusions and the madness of crowds.*

2 Bak, P. and Chen, K. (1991, January). "Self-organized criticality." *Scientific American*, pp. 46-53.

3 *Ibid.*

4 Caldarelli, G., *et al.* (1997, December 1). "A prototype model of stock exchange." *Europhysics Letters*, 40 (5), pp. 479-484.

5 *Ibid.*

6 Chapman, T. (1998, January-February). "Speculative trading: physicists' forays into finance." *Europhysics News.*

7 Brooks, M. (1997, October 18). "Boom to bust." *New Scientist.*

8 *Ibid.*

9 Buchanan, M. (1997, November 8). "One law to rule them all." *New Scientist.*

10 The invalidity of outside event causality may apply to more than the social sciences. Formological causality may apply to physical sciences as well, certainly biology.

11 AIDS might appear to be an exception, as this slow-moving epidemic has remained in force during the bull market years of the 1980s and 1990s. However, in PPI-adjusted Elliott wave terms (see Figure 16-6), a bear market pattern of Grand Supercycle degree began in 1966. The advance since 1982 is just subwave b. Moreover, during this advance, the epidemic has waned significantly, as AIDS today is no longer in the top ten causes of death in the United States, the rate halving in 1997 alone. [ref: Kim, L. (1998, October 8). "Fewer lives lost to AIDS." *The Atlanta Journal-Constitution*, p. A1.]

12 Sometimes channels manifest themselves on arithmetic scale, sometimes on semilog scale. They most commonly involve a line that connects the ends of waves two and four. New note: Wave ⑤ within Figure 18-5 also travels within a parallel trend channel. For an illustration, see "A Confluence of Fives" from July 1999 in *View from the Top* (New Classics Library, 2002), Figure 4.

13 Walker, T. (1998, August 21). "Impact of air strikes on stocks uncertain." *The Atlanta Journal-Constitution*, p. E1.

14 Walker, T. (1998, August, 6). "Identifying sell-off trigger difficult." *The Atlanta Journal-Constitution*, p. F3.

15 Elliott, R.N. (1946). *Nature's law.*

16 Sakarui, J. (1998, July 10). "Japan goes with veteran at helm of wayward economy." *The Atlanta Journal-Constitution.*

17 On October 6, 1982, with the Dow in the 900s, *The Elliott Wave Theorist* said, "This bull market should be the first 'buy-and-hold' market since the 1960s. The experience of the last 16 years has turned us all into traders, and it's a habit that will have to be abandoned."

18 James Stack, Investech Research, Whitefish MT.

19 Rothchild, J. (1998). *The bear book.*

20 Davis, N. (1992). "Being right or making money." *Ned Davis Research Inc.*

21 Montgomery, P. (1986, March 8). "Volcker part III: The Godfather." And (1990, October 11). "Magazine covers and real estate." *Universal Economics.*

22 Montgomery, P. (1995, April 6). Presentations. "The logical primacy of immaterial mental states in the price structure of investments...." And (1996, May 17). "Economic theory and technical analysis...."

23 "The lesson of the day." (1857, October 10). *Harper's Weekly.*

24 Fukuyama, F. (1992). *The end of history and the last man.*

25 Ford, C.M. (1998, July 7). "Survey sees brunt of Asian crisis hitting U.S. soon." *The Wall Street Journal,* p. A2.

26 Nasar, S. (1998, August 15). "Cloudy blue skies." *The New York Times.*

27 "The 21st century economy." (1998, August). *Business Week.*

28 Source unavailable.

29 Angrist, S.W. (1991, August 8). "Believers in one wave theory see U.S. in deep trough soon." *The Wall Street Journal.* (quoting Allen Meltzer, professor of political economy and public policy at Carnegie-Mellon University.)

30 Dornbush, R. (1998, July 30). "Growth forever." *The Wall Street Journal.*

31 Schumpeter, J. (1939). *Business cycles.*

32 Dewey, E. and Dakin, E. (1945). *Cycles: the science of prediction.*

33 The key here is popularity. Both Kondratieff's original study and Spengler's book, *Decline of the West,* were published in 1926, but it was in the 1930s and 1940s that their views became food for discussion.

34 Update: Following a power struggle amongst Board members involving multiple accusations of misconduct, the Foundation for the Study of Cycles dissolved in October 1999, a single quarter prior to the peaks of the major stock averages.

35 Ip, G. (1998, October 14). "Risk and uncertainty wreak havoc on stocks." *The Wall Street Journal*, p. C1.

36 In classic socionomic irony, the Wave Principle is likely to become better accepted just as it becomes particularly difficult to apply, in a Grand Supercycle corrective process.

PART V

FURTHER AFIELD

Chapter 19:

Problems with Conventional Approaches to Financial Markets, and Their Solution in Socionomics

As in Chapter 18, I deliberately use contemporary citations of conventional financial and economic thinking throughout this chapter to show that all one need do is open the newspaper on any given week to find examples of it. Most examples are from the second half of 1998 and were culled pretty much as I wrote the book.

Random Walk; Efficient Market Hypothesis

For years, some theoreticians[1,2,3] have argued that stock price movements are random. Their assertion under the Efficient Market Hypothesis is that all investors make informed and rational decisions, weighing more or less identically the meaning of various events and conditions that affect markets and immediately adjusting investment values accordingly. Since no one can predict random outside forces, markets fluctuate randomly. Statisticians have run tests on financial market prices to demonstrate that they follow a "random walk" and are therefore unpredictable. "For two decades," said *Fortune* magazine in 1988, "finance professors have taught EMH as if it were as indisputable as the laws of gravity."[4]

Go back to Chapter 4 and review the simple computer-generated model that Elliott Wave International designed to create a simulated market based upon the Wave Principle. Clearly every single movement in the model is utterly determined; after all, a simple formula produces it. Did you know, however, that the standard statistical methods of assessing the presence of determinism would find that the results of our model were *random*? How is this error possible? Stephen R. Cunningham, Assistant Professor in the Department of Economics at the University of Connecticut provides an

answer. His research paper in the *Review of Financial Economics* reaches this stunning conclusion:

> Neither the Samuelson-Fama tests for efficient markets nor the popularly-used augmented Dickey-Fuller (1979) test for unit roots *can successfully discriminate between a fully deterministic time series, generated from a nonlinear (chaotic) process, and a random walk.* A researcher applying these methods to a simple nonlinear price process would be misled into believing that such a series is a random walk.[5]

This fact proves that the champions of EMH and random walk do not know, despite their claims, that markets are random. The failure of EMH researchers' statistical applications successfully to determine randomness in utterly determined chaotic data series invalidates the empirical basis of their work. This book, I hope, invalidates the theoretical basis of it, the idea that aggregate financial market behavior is based upon the efficient, rational processing (error #1) of extramarket information (error #2).

Standard-bearers for random walk smugly joke of producing random data series that look so much like stock charts that they fool people into thinking they *are* stock charts, as if this proves something. The *definition* of the word random is that the data can look like anything, so why shouldn't some of them look like stock charts? Similar charts of random data and stock prices no more prove that stock prices are random than they prove random data are stock prices. If randomly generated dots on a scale happened to produce music, it would hardly prove that music is random. In technical terms, as Paul Montgomery points out, such assertions commit the logical error of "affirming the consequent."[6]

A champion of random walk, still plying his axioms in the very latest issue of Bloomberg's *Personal Finance* magazine, uses this common argument in favor of market randomness: "More than 90 percent of professional mutual fund managers were outperformed by the S&P 500. If it were that easy to earn excess returns by exploiting the predictable patterns in the market, we should be able to find a substantial number of professionals who are able to do so."[7] This is nonsense, for several reasons. (1) In the past decade, most of the money in the stock market has been handled by professionals. To demand that professionals outperform themselves is to demand the negation of a tautology. (2) Using the S&P, one of the best-performing investments among all stock indexes, bonds and commodities in the entire world over the past 16 years, as a benchmark for money managers to *exceed* is an inverted straw-man argument. (3) To demand that

professional investors beat a bull market is to create a negative-sum game and then insist that the majority win at it. Every manager has to have some cash, and every manager pays commissions. By definition, it is impossible for the majority to beat a bull market. Even random walkers must reject this cute ruse. It is quite certain that if we were to isolate a bear market period in which many money managers beat the market simply because many of them held some cash, random walk proponents would not then declare such performance as evidence against their model. (4) Beating the market is a false standard. To be consistent, random walkers should also insist that portfolio managers beat the market on the short side in bear markets. After all, market prices are simply ratios, making direction irrelevant. Carried to its extreme, their benchmark demands no less than constant outperformance in every market fluctuation, which is absurd. The only valid question is whether a manager makes enough money to make investing with him a good idea relative to what you would do as an individual. (5) Nonrandomness hardly means that earning excess returns should be "that easy." This is a blanket substitution of one idea for another. Chapter 8 explains why it is anything but easy. (6) If professionals are operating under false premises, the patterns they perceive would be inconstant and therefore inadequate for reliable forecasting. In this case, their failures would not prove randomness, but epistemological error. (7) The argument presents a false dichotomy, an "either-or" that is not necessary. Random walk is a possible answer to the more general question of why few people do well at investing but hardly a necessary one. Impulsive herding behavior would explain why most people do not perform brilliantly in financial markets. It also happens to be the actual reason.

As A.J. Frost and I said in our 1978 book, "the Elliott Wave Principle challenges the Random Walk Theory at every turn."[8] As the Wave Principle reveals, the overall pattern of stock price movement is nonrandom and indeed so formally constructed that price fluctuation cannot (as argued in Chapter 18) be the result of reasoned decisions by well-informed individuals dealing continually with new information, as is commonly assumed. It is my contention after closely observing the market and its participants for twenty years that few investment and trading decisions are based on reason, logic and knowledge gained from comprehensive research. Rather than tell my own stories or repeat the classic cases described by Charles Mackay in his indispensable tome, *Extraordinary Popular Delusions and the Madness of Crowds*, I will let Rita Koselka, writing recently for *Forbes,* describe what goes on in an everyday auction market like those in finance:

Lured by free food and wine, I went with some female former Harvard Business School classmates to attend what Sotheby's, the big auction house, advertised as a mock auction. Sipping our chardonnay, we were herded into the auditorium with several hundred other invitees— all business school graduates, each of us [with] $40,000 in fake credit. We proceeded to behave in ways that threw scant credit on our M.B.A.s. A blue-glaze Oriental vase sold for well beyond our supposed $40,000 limit.

The final item up for bid was tea for eight with Sotheby's president, Diana Brooks. But this time we were bidding real money. Figuring I could find some friends to chip in, I thrust my paddle in the air at $600. A quick nod of acknowledgment from auctioneer Hildesley and then I was forgotten. The tea sold at $1,200 to a zealous young woman two rows ahead. She had a determined air about her that said, No matter what you bid, I'll top it.

The one business lesson I came away with may not be the one Sotheby's intended: I've learned it's nearly impossible to behave rationally at an auction, so written bids left with the auctioneer in advance are the only way to go. (If the top bid at auction is less than your written bid, you'll pay the lower price.) Unless you are a lot more disciplined than most folk, stay away from the auction room.[9]

The above description of people's behavior in such environments is far closer to reality than academic models based on investor rationality, fully disseminated knowledge and random outside impetus. Emotions rule most of the players in an auction crowd; the more naïve and/or impulsive some of players are, the less rational is the bidding.

Such behavior is the focus of a newly developing area of scientific study called behavioral finance, whose champions have been conducting experiments that demonstrate the validity of technical (i.e., market behavioral) analysis and the invalidity of EMH. One example is the paper, "Simple Technical Trading Rules and the Stochastic Properties of Stock Returns" by William A. Brock, Josef Lakonishok and Blake LeBaron, published in the *Journal of Finance* in 1992.[10] It shows that two simple technical trading methods based upon moving averages and trendlines generate returns in excess of those predicted by models presuming randomness. Both of these tools rely on the almost embarrassingly simple fact that *markets trend*, but even that is a challenge to EMH.

What is the status of the rational man in a trending market or emotional auction? When herding stock market investors have the bit in their mouths, rational individuals are powerless to stop the stampede. In fact, *they often have no choice but to take the trend into account* regardless of how they would otherwise value stocks.

Might the rare nonherding professional fund manager rise above this dynamic? In most cases, he cannot. His choice is this: He can raise cash in a bull market and buy stocks in a bear market, which would be prudent investing, or he can stay in business. That is his choice. If he acts counter to the market's trend, then his customers leave in droves. They place their funds with managers whose policies reflect their feelings. Any mutual fund manager whose personal opinion counters that of the majority will tell you how frustrating it is to be in this trap. Rationality, to most managers, means getting rich giving customers what they want, not losing most of them with prudent investing. Regardless of the market outlook of any specific fund manager, then, the herding majority remains in complete control of the bulk of professionally managed money.

Why is EMH so popular? There appear to be two reasons. First, the isolation of many academics from the real world of finance explains why they are not immediately uncomfortable with the idea. As a writer for the *International Herald Tribune* put it in 1995 with well chosen words, "If you believe that markets and investing live in the chilly climes of abstract thought, you probably haven't spent too long tracking your investments through the ups and downs of raging, irrational bull runs or the weird, depressing illogic of a bear phase."[11] The second reason that EMH is popular stems from the fact that, like most people, academics lose money in markets. Less like most people, however, academics are quite sure that they are highly intelligent and adequately informed. They think, "If someone as smart as I, thinking logically, consistently loses money when I invest, then markets must surely be random." Sure, chuckle if you will. Then read this comment from an academic economist:

> I have personally tried to invest money, my client's money and my own, in every single anomaly and predictive device that academics [mistake #1] have dreamed up, and *I have yet to make a nickel* on any of these supposed market inefficiencies [mistake #2]. If there's nothing investors [here is the extrapolation to everyone else] can exploit in a systematic way, time in and time out [must it be *always?*], then it is very hard to say that information is not being properly incorporated into stock prices."[12]

Perhaps this conclusion would explain his failure if that were our only information, but how does it explain the monstrous, persistent success of futures trader Paul Tudor Jones? Obviously, it does not. Socionomics accounts for both of their experiences. Most people cannot escape the impulses of their limbic systems. A rare few can.

As I have vowed to refrain from blunt criticism in this book, I am indebted to James B. Rogers, adjunct professor of security analysis at Columbia Business School and an outrageously successful investor, for his summary judgment, "The random-walk theory is absurd,"[13] and to Yale economics professor Robert Schiller for his incautious outburst, "The efficient-market hypothesis is the most remarkable error in the history of economic theory."[14] A.J. Frost and I take some pride in having flatly denied the validity of the theory in our book as early as 1978.

Despite Schiller's passionate statement, truly the most remarkable error in economics and sociology is not EMH but its underlying bedrock belief in event causality, which is shared by nearly everyone. That is what this book is designed to correct.

Weak EMH

EMH started to run into problems when academics began pointing out patterns of market behavior. In 1985, for example, DeBondt and Thaler reported that stocks that underperformed the market for several years tended to outperform the market for several years thereafter.[15]

The study begins with data from 1933, which mask a flaw in it. In the half-dozen years prior to that time, weak stocks got weaker, and many ended up as wallpaper. Buying relative losers in those years resulted in disaster. Over the past fifteen years since 1983, a bit before the study was published, the market has produced the same apparent anomaly: Stocks that have outperformed for awhile have tended to keep outperforming, and vice versa. The reason for this difference is that the 1920s and 1982 to now are fifth waves, when breadth is weak (see Chapter 7) and investors narrow their focus to a decreasing list of big winners. The results of this study, then, are not a consistent fact but a function of the labels of the waves. They are also a function of the fairly persistent upward direction of the market, as the period of the study encompassed most of the Supercycle wave (V) bull market, skewing the results.[16] In most bear markets, by contrast, underperforming stocks just get weaker. Regardless of this data bias, this study does suggest inefficiency and/or nonrationality via persistence in market-related behavioral trends.

The authors' hypothesis is that investors occasionally "overreact" to news about companies. In other words, *they assume outside causality, the bedrock of EMH, as a starting point*. However, because company news lags stock prices, it is impossible that investors "react" to any such thing. If they do not react, then they cannot overreact.

Although this study has spawned a fair amount of follow-up work, its results are explicable as simply a function of directional waves: Any study looking for stocks that have gone one direction for a set length of time is bound to include many that are near the end of wave patterns. So during market environments when investors are willing to shift from sector to sector and stock to stock (which is most of the time), previously weak stocks will outperform for awhile and previous strong stocks will underperform for awhile. In this context, rational efficiency and the modification of it are irrelevant concepts. The good news here, though, is that researchers are at least *pointing out*, via statistics, that at least sometimes, markets trend in a way that contraindicates EMH.

There are times when markets are extremely volatile, and it is those times that are particularly difficult to sweep under the rug of rational efficiency. For example, William A. Brock of the Social Systems Research Institute of the University of Wisconsin states flatly, "In my opinion, *no satisfactory explanation* has been found [for] the most recent crash,...Black Monday, October 19, 1987."[17] In other words, there was no event or change in outside conditions to justify the violence of the change in people's rational decision making on that day (actually over a two-week period starting October 6). This is true, of course,[18] and damning to EMH. As another professor says, "The [1987] crash makes us realize that prices are not *entirely* efficient."[19]

All these professors are brave souls and deserve credit for challenging EMH orthodoxy. However, as Chapter 20 discusses in more detail, there remains no reason whatsoever to assert that the market is nonrational only briefly and occasionally, when it is volatile or falling or in a short-term trend, and rational the rest of the time, when it is calm or rising or engaged in a long-term trend. These are simply presumptions, and they derive from no science of which I am aware. All such views are simply accommodations of the Efficient Market Hypothesis, or at least its underlying presumption that market participants primarily "react" to outside events and news in the first place, which they do not.

On the belief that sometimes markets are inefficient, some analysts spend immense time searching for "pockets of inefficiency" in the market

that the EMH dynamic has presumably yet to incorporate, which means essentially, "important information that others don't know yet." Even if such events *were* causal, the effort expended to find those elusive pockets would be a waste of time because most investors behave otherwise than rationally. As I argued in Chapter 16, social actualities are the *product* of social mood, so in terms of overall market trends, there is no such thing as valuable event-related information in the conventional sense.[20] The social mood that led to any such events has already been and gone.

Tautological Rationality

Perhaps the nth degree of dependence upon the rationality model has just been published in an article in the *Financial Analysts Journal*. It argues that *buying because prices are rising* is rational, so "rational behavior by individual investors can cause a market bubble," which is defined as "some self-reinforcing, self-perpetuating mechanism that prevents successive security prices from being random."[21] This stance essentially defines nonrationality out of existence. If this theory is correct, then market crashes are rational, too, and so is selling when they occur. Would anyone like to take the affirmative side of that one? The fact is that buying *only* because prices have been rising is *not* rational because rising prices mean that the market is that much closer to a top. For the same reason, selling *only* because prices have been falling is not rational, either.

The Idea of Intrinsic Value

For rationality to be the driving force behind markets, EMH must assume that the objects of financial speculation have an *intrinsic value*. However, value is not inherent in objects; the term value pertains only when human beings *desire* something. Human desire, particularly for investments, where the lure of gain and the fear of loss are so potent, is hardly constant. This fact pertains particularly to investment prices, which are governed almost entirely by the shifting mental states of those bidding and asking in an auction market. If all it took to discern the value of an investment were to compute it on a calculator, then investments would hardly fluctuate as dramatically as they do.

The stock market bestows greatly divergent values upon various real things at different times, the most important of these being (1) dividends, (2) the value of corporate assets, and (3) the yield on high-grade bonds. When it comes down to valuing stock certificates apart from their appre-

ciation potential, these are the only values that matter. An investor trades his money for a quarterly payment called a *dividend* plus the guarantee that if the company had to, it could *liquidate* and divide up the proceeds among shareholders, and he takes this action in lieu of lending his money out at *interest* to a solid, healthy debtor. In just this century, the Dow Jones Industrial Average has yielded as little as 1.5% in dividends and as much as 17.4%. It has been valued as high as 5.6 times corporate book value (which is the value of assets on the firm's balance sheet) and as little as 0.5 times. It has yielded as much as 4.9 times as much as Treasury bonds and as little as 0.25 times as much.[22] These huge differences are due to one thing: people's opinion about the *capital gain potential* of stocks, i.e., the extent to which they are bullish or bearish. Therefore, such valuations are a direct measure of investors' optimism or pessimism. These mental attitudes do not pay enough attention to intrinsic value to give it the time of day.

Figure 19-1 shows the bond yield/stock yield ratio for Japanese investments over the past fifty years. In 1968, they were just about equal. In 1998, thirty years later, they are again just about equal. But look what

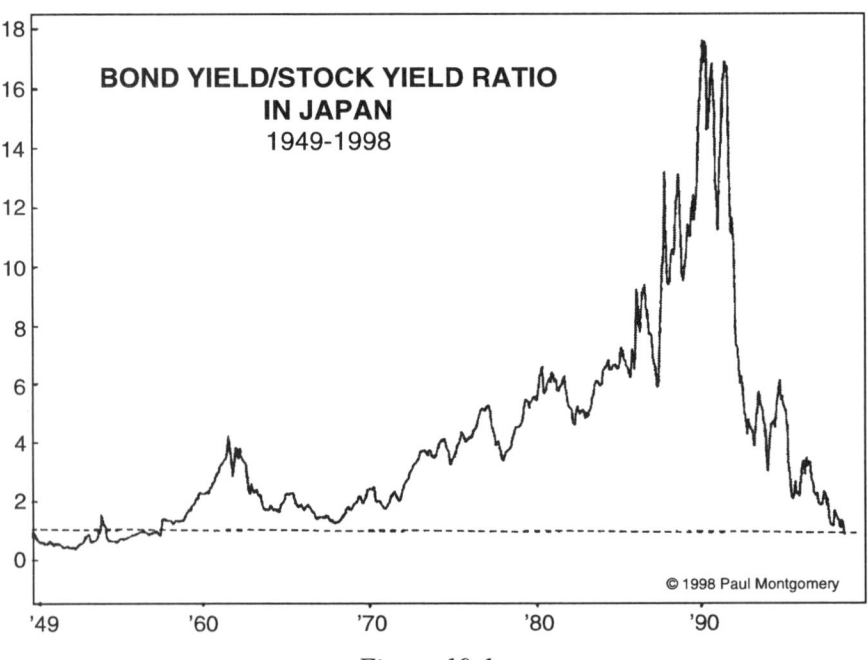

Figure 19-1

happened in between! The relative desire to own corporate shares over debt expanded by *18 times* and then contracted just as much. No valuation model that includes interest rates takes this difference into account because it is precisely interest rates that are factored out in the ratio. There is no way that changes in earnings can explain it unless one asserts that earnings changes compel irrational behavior. The difference is no small adjustment; it is the meat of the bull and bear markets that occurred over this period. As Paul Montgomery puts it, this ratio records changes in "amorphous states of mind" that make a mockery of the idea of intrinsic value.

How does one explain by way of "fundamental value" that baseball cards sold for one price in 1991 and one-tenth of that price in 1993? How does one account for the fact that President John Kennedy's rocking chair sold for $453,000 in May 1996 and less than two years later, in March 1998, sold for $23,000, $1/20^{th}$ as much? Obviously these objects, like corporate shares, have no specific intrinsic value.

Some theoreticians construct models of what stocks "should" be worth. Obviously, there is no such thing. Even if the premise of such models were valid, the relentless uncertainly about facts *relating to value* coupled with the ever-present uncertainty about what the naive majority may do *without regard for value* is plenty enough to destroy the utility of attempting to invest with respect to "intrinsic value."

The "Too Popular" Theory and the "Self-Fulfilling Prophecy" Theory

One of the arguments used by random walkers, fundamental analysts, "contrarians" and others is that analysis of price patterns in markets cannot work because "people learn." If patterns work, goes the argument, then they will quickly become popular, at which time they will no longer work. There is no point in singling out price patterns as unworkable on this basis; if people learn to an extent that makes this objection valid, then *no* method can work, including whatever analysis the proponent of this theory proposes.

Does this mean that random walk defenders have a point? No. The very thought of the majority of investors actually learning the Wave Principle or any comprehensive approach to market analysis before investing is absurd. They would all have to quit their jobs to become market experts, in which case there would be no economy to support financial markets. So the objection is moot on a practical basis. It is invalid in theory as well. As LeDoux's laboratory work shows, rats whose cortexes have been removed

can develop fears related to specific stimuli, but unlike rats with cortexes, they cannot learn to abandon them when the relationship between stimulus and result is dismantled.[23] This experiment proves that *the limbic system cannot learn.* This, along with the limbic system's immense power, is the reason that social patterns are immutable. Knowledge of any valid approach to market analysis, even among a substantial number of people, is not a cure for the continuance of patterns.

The above-cited objection further relies on the falsehood that knowing a market method is the same as knowing where the market is going. All analytical methods are tools only for *probabilistic* forecasting (see Chapter 20), leaving most investors chronically uncertain about the future no matter what their approach. This situation gives the limbic system all the room it needs in most people's psyches to operate exactly as it pleases.

The "too popular" objection has also been disproved by events. A national financial magazine dated October 1977 made this obligatory comment: "Over the last few years, the Wave Principle has gathered too much of a following and, therefore, it has less value today. Almost invariably, you can write off a technique when it gets too much of a following."[24] How does that statement look in light of the decade that followed, when the idea of the Wave Principle spread worldwide and had its greatest period of popularity ever?[25]

Finally and fundamentally, *the very claim that a market method can become popular enough to ruin itself reveals the reason why the claim is invalid,* as belief in this idea reflects the human trait of skepticism. When I have a period of good forecasting, some people say, "You have been right so long that you are due for a fall." When I have had a period of poor forecasting, the same people say, "See? It doesn't work." They do not remain consistent and tell me I am now ready for a period of brilliance. Whether I have been right or wrong, they are skeptical. So the mere fact that people ask the question, "If you or Elliott wave become too popular, won't that destroy the theory?" provides the answer to the question: Skepticism will not allow it to become "too popular."

Now let us examine the other side of this coin. In several cases after a successful forecast based upon the Wave Principle has come to pass, critics charge that the method itself has no value; it was simply that once a particular successful forecast had been disseminated, it became a "self-fulfilling prophecy;" people made it happen. This idea is absurd on several levels. First, the only way that one's forecast becomes widely dissemi-

nated is if he or she has been quite successful for awhile in the first place. Obviously *those* forecasts could not have been self-fulfilling prophecies. Second, if a popular analyst's forecasts did become self-fulfilling prophecies, then he would never fail thereafter, would he? Each new prediction would be taken as gospel and then fulfilled accordingly, forever. Obviously, subsequent forecasting errors disprove this theory. Third, consider the absurdity of even a single such event. If everyone knew that the Dow would bottom at 1087, why would anyone sell at 1100 or 1088? Wouldn't everyone buy more? If so, from whom would they buy? Finally, this hypothesis ignores the fact that forecasts are widely disseminated every day. Obviously all of them are not fulfilled; indeed most are proved utterly wrong. When does self-fulfillment come into play according to this theory? Only when one works. Now the claim is revealed as tautological.

Here we reach the fun part. The "self-fulfilling prophecy" theory is the *opposite* conclusion from the *same premise* that produces the "if it gets too popular, it won't work" theory. Both arguments begin with the idea that forecasts based upon a particular method might become popular. Then one concludes that therefore it cannot work, and the other concludes that therefore it will work perfectly! Each argument is nothing more than a quick *ad hoc* rationalization by people who believe that probabilistically accurate, objectively determined social forecasting is impossible.

Why are such bogus theories popular? A socionomist knows that the limbic system impels the neocortex to come up with reasons to avoid conflict with one's emotions. These two theories are classic examples, and I have little doubt that there are individuals who at different times have uttered them both.

The Wave Principle is a description of a fundamental aspect of the nature of human behavior. In order for society to continue going through wave patterns, it must be part of human nature to believe that theories of determined mass psychology are indefensible and not worth examining. People must be primed to accept bullish arguments at tops and bearish arguments at bottoms. This means that they have to be ever open to rationalization via bogus theories of market behavior. How else will they generate the patterns that fear, greed and hope forever produce?

Macroeconomic Formulae: Man as Machine

Economists devise today's macroeconomic formulations under the presumption that people react to outside stimuli like billiard balls following physical laws. Unlike physics formulae, though, the concepts represented

by the variables in these equations are often imprecise. Many that are considered precise are not because they ignore the varying mental states of people. Often, the equations do not relate very well to the real world. The combination of vague definitions, improper assumptions and detached impracticality prompted Nobel prize winner Wassily Leontief of the Institute for Economic Analysis at New York University to say this in 1982:

> Year after year, economic theorists continue to produce scores of mathematical models and to explore in great detail their formal properties; and the econometricians fit algebraic functions of all possible shapes to essentially the same sets of data *without being able to advance, in any perceptible way, a systematic understanding of the structure and the operation of a real economic system.*[26]

In 1986, William Niskanen Jr. of the Cato Institute was more succinct: "Macroeconomic theory is in absolute shambles."[27]

The biggest flaw in macroeconomic formulations is their underlying assumption that the "billiard ball" has a fixed mental state. However, the mental states of people vary, so their "reaction" to a "cause" will be different at different times. For example, an increase in the money supply might lead to lower interest rates in some cases and higher interest rates in others, depending upon what people discern to be the meaning, if any, of the event. Because mental states change, the attempt to define a constant relationship is futile. This is certainly true in the stock market. In some stock market environments, rising bond prices are considered bullish; in others, bearish. In each case, there is always an apparently airtight logical argument in favor of the relationship. For instance, the conflicting arguments regarding stock and bond trends, offered depending upon the season, are: (1) Bonds compete with stocks for the investor's dollar, so when one market rises, the other falls. (2) Higher bonds mean lower interest rates, which helps the economy and makes speculative borrowing easier, so when one market rises, the other one rises. While each of these arguments appears true from time to time, that means the other is false. There is no macroeconomic formula that can express a *consistent* relationship.

A single discussion should concretize this point. Governments long operated under the assumption that the higher the tax rates they impose upon citizens, the higher their revenues will be. (Revenue = fixed social product x tax rate.) This would indeed be a consistent relationship if society were a physical system. However, people are not machines. Sometimes people increase their productive efforts when tax rates are high; indeed, that has been happening in recent decades in the U.S., as both parents of

most families now must work to make up for the real income shortfall that high taxes have produced. At other times, people slow their productive efforts when most of their product is confiscated. This is one reason why communism fails. Thus, given a certain social mindset, higher tax rates can lead to *lower* revenues. In this case, *the end result is the opposite of the intended result*. Economist Arthur Laffer explained this phenomenon in 1980. He thereby proposed a different macroeconomic formula that relates tax rates to government income. The Laffer curve claims that one particular rate of taxation will return the greatest revenue to the government. If the rate is lower or higher than that, revenue will be less. (Revenue = predictably variable social product x tax rate.) This formula, too, relies on the assumption that society is a physical system like a machine that can be overburdened to such a degree that it slows down. Like its predecessor, it sounds sensible and could be applied with consistent results *if people were automatons*. However, suppose that this formula is accepted by a government that is taxing citizens above the supposed ideal level for maximum revenues. To achieve a goal of greater revenues, it lowers tax rates. Revenues rise. It works! Then after a few years, people begin to understand that lower taxes made them more prosperous. They agitate for further reductions in tax rates and elect politicians who will accommodate them. Taxes are lowered further. Government revenues fall. People begin to resent even the lowered tax rates as an impediment to their prosperity. Taxes are slashed; government revenue shrinks. *The end result is the opposite of the intended result.* Whether this would actually happen in any particular circumstance is perhaps debatable, but it *could* happen, and that is the difference between social and physical systems.

Coveney and Highfield are damning in their assessment of the formulae that have so long been taught in the typical undergraduate course in economics:

> It has taken economists a long time to recognize the inherent complexity of their subject. For decades, the central dogma of economics revolved around stale equilibrium principles in a manner entirely analogous to the application of equilibrium thermodynamics.... Many economists have sought to shoehorn all economics into theories whose merits are their mathematical simplicity and elegance rather than their ability to say anything about the way real-world economies work....Classical equilibrium-based concepts have been infecting the minds of generations of science and economics students with the dogma that the behavior of a complex system can be deduced by simply summing its component parts.[28]

I would disagree on only two points: First, economists for the most part have *not* recognized the error in their premises; only a few have. Second, the old economic theories are not elegant; they are ugly. In contrast, we have a truly elegant law in the Wave Principle, which is the bedrock principle of sociology and finance, and therefore ultimately of macroeconomics. The science of macroeconomics must drop the mathematics of physics and adopt the mathematics of sociology. Minds are not billiard balls or machines or computers; they are *minds*.

The "Potent Directors" Presumption

Virtually all conventional financial analysts and economists accept assumptions about certain men's ability to control the social future, be they presidents, treasury secretaries or central bankers. Last month, an article from *The Washington Post* entitled, "Key Players Control Money Supply," tells us that the Bank of International Settlements "helps keep the banking system steady in turbulent times...protects the world financial system...[and] focuses on *ensuring* that [a local] crisis doesn't threaten the world's intricate [banking] system."[29] The BIS, says the article, has "secret conversations that can shape the course of the global economy." This type of belief permeates practical economic discourse. It persists despite failure after failure of officials to control money, interest rates, commodity prices, retail prices, stock markets, and economic growth and contraction. The fact is that central banking authorities *never* reverse a financial spiral, in either direction. They participate in (and typically encourage) them in uptrends and flail uselessly at them in downtrends. As I type this sentence, I am looking at this headline in *The Wall Street Journal*: "Why the World Bank Failed To Anticipate Indonesia's Deep Crisis." The article opens with this salvo:

> The World Bank considered Indonesia's rise from poverty its greatest triumph. A shattering economic reversal is returning as many as half of its 200 million people to destitution. In some villages, they are unable to afford food...banks are on the ropes...[it's a] historic setback, in the words of the World Bank's top official here.[30]

How could the supposed generator of Indonesia's boom not only find itself unable to stop the collapse but be utterly oblivious to the fact that something untoward was developing? The subhead of the article explains all you need to know: "[It Got] 'Caught Up In [the] Enthusiasm'." Yes, bankers are human, too, and they, like most people, get swept up in the

waves of optimism and pessimism so fully that they do not even realize that they are of, not above, the waves.

The Federal Reserve Board is believed to have godlike powers to propel or rein in economic growth in the United States by manipulating interest rates. Almost no economist disputes this "obvious" fact. Even distinguished scientists, who would never accept a casual assumption in their own fields, take this one for granted.[31] Yet consider: If central banks actually could regulate their economies, then the wild history of interest rates and economic behavior in the 20th century would not have taken place. Did the Fed manage the economy into the Great Depression? Did the Fed engineer the double-digit interest rates of the 1970s and early 1980s? Did the central bank in Japan program that country's debt crisis and developing depression of the 1990s? If a central bank's power to lower interest rates can turn an economy around, why did the U.S. crash into depression in the 1930s despite an aggressive lowering of the discount rate from 6% to 1.5% by 1931? Why is Japan still in recession after eight years of persistently lower discount rates from 6% to 0.5%? Neither policy designed to reverse these trends of deflation, bear market and economic contraction worked.

In truth, the Fed is not even in charge of interest rates. It is not the commander of the market but a puppet. If it were otherwise, then the federal funds rate would not have soared to 19.1% in 1981. Instead, the Fed would have kept rates at 4%, and the market would have dutifully followed. (If you believe *that*, I have a bridge to sell you.) So, anticipating the Fed's decisions on the discount rate as if a drama were unfolding is a waste of time and emotion. There is no need to monitor the look on members' faces for hints of their decisions. There is no need to hold one's breath when listening to the chairman announce the board's decision. A socionomist monitoring the T-bill rate can predict with fair accuracy what the Fed will do. No one monitoring the Fed's decisions can predict what T-bill rates will do.

Since 1913, when the Federal Reserve system was created to "maintain stability," the dollar has lost *94%* of its value,[32] an unconscionable appropriation of wealth. In recent days, newspapers have been reporting on the utter failure of the International Monetary Fund (IMF) to stave off financial collapse in Russia. It did succeed in one thing: It quickly blew over a hundred billion dollars in the attempt. Such is the utility of financial "policy."

Why do people fail to notice that authorities have no beneficial power? One important reason is that most of the time, *times are good*. It is easy

then to presume that the authorities are doing their jobs just fine. It is only when markets fall, interest rates soar or economies implode that the truth is revealed, and such times are comparatively brief. Perhaps that is why examples of failure simply invoke rationalization. Economists can always cite supposed causes of the "aberrant" behavior. The 1930s? "The Fed was young then and didn't know what it was doing." 1974 and 1980? "The politicians messed things up and the Fed finally fixed them." Japan? "Its bank is not as smart as our Fed; it didn't make the right moves." Asians? "What do they know about macroeconomic management?" The rationalization is endless. Three weeks after the report of the latest World Bank debacle, the same newspaper published an editorial by an MIT economist who steadfastly maintains the conventional presumptions. Referring to the economic expansion of the past seven-to-eight (depending upon which statistics you use) years, he says, "This expansion will run forever. We will not see a recession for years to come,...as we have the *tools* to keep the current expansion going. *Policy levers [and] our policy team...*will keep it from happening."[33] Echoes the celebrated director of the Economic Forecasting Center at Georgia State University, "Another depression would require a degree of *policy stupidity* that would *never happen again.*"[34]

Today we are also told that authorities can change the course of the stock market:

> It is known as the "plunge protection team," an emergency council of America's top financial officials that operates with its own special staff in the shadows of the U.S. Treasury....The purpose of the group, known officially as the Working Group on Financial Markets, is to avoid repeating the near-catastrophe of October 19, 1987....The permanent members include the chairman of the Federal Reserve, Alan Greenspan, and the heads of the Securities and Exchange Commission and the Commodity Futures Trading Commission....Decisions are made in conjunction with the National Economic Council at the White House, and the powerful governor of the New York Federal Reserve Bank. They have each other's telephone numbers at all times and are plugged into a sophisticated "market surveillance" system that helps them to anticipate trouble.... Each agency has a confidential crisis plan. At the SEC, this is known as the Red Book, or more properly, the Executive Directory for Market Contingencies. The team relies on "circuit breakers" to ensure an orderly fall in the markets, with intermittent halts in trading. It can extend open lines of credit, inject money into the system and cut interest rates....There is also speculation that it might intervene directly in the stock market, buying shares and futures contracts to prop up the indexes.[35]

That article appeared on September 2, 1998. Three weeks later, on September 24, came this assessment from *The Wall Street Journal* about the same team's attempts to deal with the financial crisis in Asia:

With little notice, President Clinton summoned his top advisers to the Oval Office on Labor Day for a late-night huddle on the spreading global financial crisis....His anxiety about the adequacy of the U.S. response had been building for weeks. From vacation on Martha's Vineyard, Mass., he had phoned Treasury Secretary Robert Rubin, fly-fishing in Alaska, almost daily. On his trip to Moscow, he hectored top aides for new ideas. He and his political soulmate, British Prime Minister Tony Blair, talked about convening an emergency meeting of world leaders. ...Mr. Clinton wanted bold solutions as big as the problem. But Mr. Rubin wanted to be cautious; he worried that a meeting of world leaders would create unrealistic expectations.

The year-long financial firestorm may be turning into a Vietnam for Washington's "best and brightest" economic minds....Through hubris, political clumsiness and the unintended consequences of well-meant policies, the Clinton administration and its allies at the International Monetary Fund have, so far, failed to contain what President Clinton now calls "the worst financial crisis in half a century."

The power of the United States, in many ways mightier than ever, seems no match for international flows of money unleashed, in part, at the urging of the U.S. itself....It will be years before the world can fully understand what went wrong and whether different policies might have staved off some of the pain.[36]

The article is incorrect in saying that it will take years to understand what went wrong. Every sentence in the above excerpt screams out the absurdity of the project. The only question remaining is, How many years will it take before economists admit that such posturing does little more than provide a false hope that is viciously destructive to anyone who adopts it? It certainly has yet to happen, as faith in such things as "plunge protection teams" still abounds.

Is there any science to support my position? Thanks to recent research, there is. Experiments show that financial markets without central authorities behave no differently from those with them. Recall the financial market simulation model produced by Caldarelli, Marsili and Zhang, discussed in Chapters 12 and 18, which mimics the stock market with only a few participants and no outside information. The authors state, "Our model does not implement the many corrections [sic] which are taken in similar cases

by central authorities in a real market."[37] Intentionally or not, this study shows that *actions of central authorities are irrelevant to whatever is essential to market behavior.* Such actions, therefore, are apparently not corrective of anything noticeable, so they are of no fundamental consequence.

Government agencies in particular not only do not, but *cannot*, affect such trends. The reason is that government does not act; it reacts. Moreover, it is always the *last* institution to react, because it is the ultimate crowd, every decision being made by committee as a result of pressure from a majority of voters. For example, the securities laws of 1934 were passed to prevent the crash that had already occurred and the depression that had already bottomed. Indeed, it was a lagging indicator that the bottom had passed. Similarly, the Monetary Control Act passed in December 1980 was designed to deal with the runaway inflation that had raged for a decade and had ended nearly a year before. Again, the passage of the act was a lagging indicator that the period of accelerating inflation was over. As you can see, any seeming successes of such government policies are reverse-causal. Both apparent social-policy stupidity and apparent social-policy brilliance are *results* of socionomic cycles, not causes.

People today almost unanimously believe that government, the IMF, the World Bank, the Japanese central bank and the Federal Reserve system have potent and magic powers to shape macroeconomic forces. The cause of this error is once again the belief in extramarket causality. In fact, it is the interaction of millions of people that sets interest rates and regulates the economy. The power of financial "authorities" to manage markets and economies is like the power of the Wizard of Oz: smoke and bluster. Faith in these wizards is little different from pre-civilized people's accordance of similar powers to witch doctors. Like the ministrations of a witch doctor, the typical result of "policy," if there is any result at all (after all, policy is a social phenomenon, too), is to make things worse. Complexity theory recognizes nature's processes of *self organization*. It is a short step to realize that *society operates the same way.* That is why free societies are more successful and productive than controlled ones. They self organize far more efficiently than any human directors could make them do. Just like the Communists who could never figure out who was directing the industrial success of the United States, conventional analysts keep trying to identify the "directors" that make everything in the markets and the economy happen, but the only actual director is the behavioral dynamic that governs human interaction. Every attempt at control, whether by com-

munists, fascists, socialists or central bankers, can only misdirect energy
and resources, thereby impeding the efficiency of the self-organizing process. So macroeconomic policies are not merely impotent, they are
counterproductive.

In sum, mechanics and "tools" are of no assistance unless you are
tinkering with a machine, and human society is not a machine. Harboring
an illusion of being in control of the waves is a guarantee of getting caught
up in them. This is yet another illusion that socionomics has the power to
eliminate.

Presumed Mechanical Determinants of Market Movements

A variant of the approach that assumes society is a machine is the idea
that the stock market is a machine. If it is running properly, the implied
idea seems to go, then prices rise. If prices *fall*, the machine is broken. The
trick, then, is to identify the weak cogs every now and then and fix them.
The crash of 1987 was such a storm of mass emotion that it caused "market
as machine" theorists to work overtime explaining the drop and figuring
out how to "fix" the system. The theory that gained the most credence was
that the crash was caused by so-called portfolio insurance computer programs, which in essence sold stocks as the market went lower. This process
presumably fed upon itself. Unfortunately for the theory, it does not explain very well why markets around the world crashed simultaneously or
why the decline stopped.[38] It is at an utter loss to explain why many indexes around the world that had *no* computer trading fell *further* than the
DJIA. It also ignores the fact that throughout 1986 and 1987, market observers in an equally serious tone had continually explained why a stock
market crash was impossible because of "the safeguards that are in place,"[39]
safeguards such as portfolio insurance. In 1988, I had a lot of fun putting
up a chart of the crash and then asking the audience how many felt that it
would not have happened, or would have been mitigated, had there been
no program trading. Usually half or more of the attendees would raise their
hands. Then I would tell them the answer was unequivocally "no," and by
the way, did I mention that this was a picture of the *1929* crash?

Inconvenient facts have no bearing on strongly held beliefs of mechanistic causality, as demonstrated in July by a major editorial in *The Wall
Street Journal*. Addressing portfolio insurance and a few other mechanical
aspects of the market, two finance professors of the highest caliber, reporting on the opinion of "the nation's leading academic scholars," explain,

"Sources of structural fragility [in the market] have been substantially, *if not totally*, corrected, [making] a repeat of the hair-raising events of 1987 highly unlikely."[40] In response to this presumption, I would say that to this day in evolutionary history, the emotional fragility of the human limbic system remains uncorrected. Until neocortexes evolve enough to dominate their primitive antecedents, the market shall ever rise, fall and occasionally crash.

Linear Extrapolation: "Predicting" the Present

Trend extrapolation is the crudest form of technical analysis, and it is employed by nearly all conventional analysts, though they rarely realize it. Mainstream social and economic forecasting has forever been a practice of extrapolating present and recent conditions and trends into the future. More specifically, apparent predictions are simply (1) descriptions of present conditions (2) multiplied by an unconsciously calculated summation of multiple forward-weighted moving averages of the trends of those conditions. Obviously, in a *changing* world, this approach is doomed to fail. Because of this practice, both economists and futurists in general have always been notoriously optimistic at tops and pessimistic at bottoms, producing highly inaccurate forecasts of coming events. Now we know why. Because the forecasters have no reliable basis upon which actually to attempt a forecast, the prevailing social mood has full rein to affect the tone of their conclusions. The stronger the mood, the stronger their conviction, the more inventive their rationalizations, and the more extreme and confident their extrapolation. This means that the closer the social mood gets to the point of change, the greater will be conventional forecasters' conviction that it will *not* change, and the further into the future will be their extrapolation. (See the classic example from July 1984 in the bond market section of Chapter 6.)

This convention is demonstrated almost daily in the financial press. A new 1998 book that is "must" reading for stock market watchers contains the statement, "I predict that we are *soon going to see* the greatest economic boom in our history."[41] This would have been a useful forecast, in fact it would have been an *actual* forecast whether it had turned out right or not, back in 1982. Today, it is simply a description of what has happened in the past sixteen years, multiplied and extrapolated into the pervasive social dream of the moment. A recent favorite headline of mine, from *The Wall Street Journal*, is "Economists Forecast Mild Inflation of 2.5% Yearly Through 2008."[42] Is there *any basis whatsoever* for this decade-long year-

by-year forecast? Obviously not. Like all such "forecasts," it is simply a statement of present conditions tempered by recent trends. It is a "prediction" of the present.

This wholly psychological phenomenon applies to virtually all people in all social fields. For instance, after Tiger Woods won the 1997 Masters tournament, a sports reporter explained how prior to the event he had been skeptical of Jack Nicklaus's opinion of Tiger Woods' abilities, but now he was declaring Nicklaus's opinion "an understatement," as there was no one to beat Woods over the next 30 tournaments.[43] Countless sports writers echoed this sentiment. To date, Woods has yet to win another tournament. The point is not that the forecasters were wrong twice. The point is that at neither time did they make a forecast, at least not with any tools that allow one to do so. They were simply describing the latest achievements of the man. Their *claim* that they were forecasting does not change that fact. Nor does the same claim do so for economists.

The natural, unconscious way of anticipating reality is to observe it over time and assume that trends will continue in the same way as they have in the past. While this approach is applicable to physics, it is improper to apply it to social trends. By succumbing to the natural tendency to extrapolate, forecasters become part of each wave rather than rise above it.

There is a greater irony. The very fact that people extrapolate trends in this manner, particularly when their fellow men support them by agreeing, is what creates extremes in social sentiment. Thus, the phenomenon that *produces* the turning points in social behavior is precisely the one that *masks* them.

Futurists in all social fields must abandon the practice of extrapolation and adopt a method of identifying sociological *patterns* and their concomitant indications of social trend *change*. Anyone can recognize, with the appropriate data, the state of the economy and its recent trend, which is the most that today's economists do. Without the proper tools, however, no one can anticipate changes in either. Anticipation is the reason for being in the economics profession. To know (even in probabilistic terms) in the midst of a recession whether that recession is ending or about to slip deeper into depression is worth a king's ransom. To know that the peak or trough of a major economic trend is nigh is of inestimable value to nearly everyone. To identify months after the fact that a turn has occurred is comparatively useless. After an upturn, the bargains are gone. After a downturn, your junk bonds are impossible to sell, business buyers have disappeared, and liquidity has dried up in the real estate market.

Conventional Reasoning from Event Causality

Conventional analysts study *extramarket* data, that is, events, conditions and processes outside the marketplace, which are deemed to be the factors, or "fundamentals,"[44] that drive the market. For example, people generally assume that the stock market is driven by interest rates, the economy, politics, corporate earnings and the Fed.

While a conventional analyst will insist that some event or other market (earnings, the economy, oil prices, debt levels, interest rates, liquidity, etc.) caused a movement in the stock market, if you ask him to *predict* the stock market on the same basis, he cannot give you an answer unless he predicts what the presumed causal factor will do. We have uncovered a secret, which is that conventional analysts must *predict their own indicators*. It is not good enough to say, for instance, that stocks will go up as long as earnings increase. You must predict earnings to arrive at a payoff. To do that, you need an indicator of earnings. And so on; the chain is endless. Furthermore, a conventional analyst cannot adjust for error. If earnings fall and stocks are going up, or if interest rates fall and stocks fall with them (as has been the case in Japan for the past half-decade), he has no basis upon which to modify his stance. He just stays wrong.

The belief in outside causality is so ingrained that people use its language to impart nonsense. One writer in August noticed that the stock market has risen 500 points "every time another woman comes forward telling [about] the President."[45] Rather than consider therefore that the bull market has been unrelated to the president's sex life, he opines that sex scandals must be *bullish*. He simply cannot imagine abandoning the false idea of news causality. A recent newspaper quotes an economist at a major brokerage firm who thinks he is giving a reason why the economy will continue to expand. He says, "The fundamentals that support the domestic economy remain good to excellent,"[46] fundamentals such as rising incomes, an abundance of jobs and the availability of credit. This is not an isolated *faux pas*, but a generic utterance. Can you see that this analysis is a tautology? A good economy *is* rising incomes, abundant jobs and expanding credit. He is actually saying, "The fundamentals that support the fundamentals..." or "the domestic economy that supports the domestic economy...." Describing the economy's current condition says nothing about the future, yet economists continually speak as if it does.

The error of belief in outside causality is not confined to economists. Even physicists who discover the impotence of this presumption cannot let

go of it. For example, although Caldarelli, Marsili and Zhang demonstrate that a small group of traders can mimic the actual stock market without a single outside causal element, they still cling to the old myths. "By no means," they say, "can one conclude that our model captures all the relevant aspects of a real market....In a true economy, there are external driving factors, such as politics, natural disasters, human psychology, etc."[47] The first sentence is careful science; the latter sentence is pure assumption. It is also inaccurate to include "human psychology," which is not an external factor but the essence of what the researchers have studied. This leaves natural disasters, which have zero effect on the stock market (try to pick out one on a chart of the averages) and politics. To boil down their only presumed external factor, then, it is politics. Despite the dramatic implications of their study, the authors maintain the assumption that "authorities" can "correct" markets in the "real" world, as revealed by the quote cited earlier in this chapter. That hard-nosed scientists include these unsupported examples of outside event causality shows how deeply the underlying presumption is held.

The Faddishness and Unreliability of Purported Economic and Financial Relationships

This section undertakes a cursory review of the role that conventional economic discourse has played in influencing investors' views of what data is helpful in stock market forecasting. It should give you an idea of how lacking is a coherent framework from which to reason.

Throughout most of the 1980s, stock market watchers waited in fear of the weekly money supply report. It was widely and firmly believed that this figure would determine the course of stock prices. When that fixation died, the bond market became the key. Every tick in bonds was scrutinized for foreknowledge of the next short-term move in stocks. Later came the insistence that the near-term trend of the U.S. dollar held the answer to where stocks would go. In every case, economists had ready detailed explanations of the causal relationship involved. Investors *abandoned* each focus as readily as they assumed it, the *difference being the lack of any explanation for doing so and the lack of any notice that there wasn't one.*

How did each of these points of focus fare as keys to market behavior? The popular argument concerning the money supply was that a "high" figure is bearish because it might result in higher interest rates, which are bad for stocks. The only thing contradicting this conventional wisdom is the fact that the money supply roared throughout the 1980s bull market,

and when the increases finally slowed, the market crashed. In other words, the correlation was the opposite of what popular economic wisdom supposed.

The "bond market indicator" became very popular by the mid-1980s on the theory that since declining interest rates are bullish for stocks and vice versa, and since everyone knows this, then every movement in U.S. T-bond futures prices would translate into a movement in the same direction in the stock market. In other words, a rise in bond prices means a drop in interest rates, which means less competition for stocks, which means stocks go up. The daily and weekly trends of stocks and bonds began to diverge about the time this relationship was popularized. They became almost entirely disconnected for months during mid-1987, when the most money was being bet on their prior lock-step relationship. Soon, daily commentators forgot about the whole idea.

The dollar's value was the next point of focus. The dollar had risen from 1979 to 1985. It was first viewed as a welcome event, evidence that inflation might be slowing and the U.S. was becoming strong again in the eyes of the world. Then economists said the dollar was "too high" because its value was supposedly hurting exports. Stock market followers initially welcomed the decline in the price of the dollar that began in 1985. That trend was dramatic and persistent as well, so it created full-blown worry by early 1987 that it had gone "too far," and what was worse, there had been little change in exports. All this hand wringing amounted to naught. Throughout this time and despite huge oscillations in the price of the dollar relative to other currencies, the DJIA continued to advance as if nothing about the dollar mattered to it. This was in fact the case. Eventually, people stopped watching the dollar, too. (But like all these points of focus, it will return.)

What do these fixations have in common? First, they reveal a desire among investors to have one simple indicator of the future course of stock prices. Second, not one of them is an indicator derived from market activity itself; each one is from outside the market and simply presumed to have an impact upon it. Third, all have apparently logical explanations. Fourth, intense scrutiny of each one of these "key figures" was in fact counterproductive to a correct assessment of the trend of the stock market. All served to keep investors' eyes off the ball. Finally, each new key-relationship claim appeared at first blush to sound reasonable, but it was never connected to enough, or any, history. Indeed, none of them was the least bit investigated, as in each case, a brief glance at a graph would have instantly debunked the claim. Nobody, it seems, ever bothered to look.

One reason why no one investigates these purported financial and economic relationships is that their purpose is to be tools not of understanding but of rationalization. Each time, knowing too much would destroy the utility of the tool. It is easier for the neocortex to rationalize when it does not know or think too much. That is why one day in a bull market, it can be found engaged in explaining why a *rise* in the Nikkei is bullish for U.S. stocks ("It is a vote of confidence that the Japanese recession will not deepen and so will not spread to the United States"), and the next day it can be found engaged in explaining why a *drop* in the Nikkei is bullish for U.S. stocks ("That money will have to flee to a strong market"). The same available duality of meaning holds for *all* of the above-mentioned "relationships." Here is an example: "A falling dollar is good because it makes our exports more affordable" and "A rising dollar is good because a strong currency reflects a strong economy." Can you do it with the "money supply" indicator?

Two Detailed Examples: Corporate Earnings and the National Trade Balance

I could choose to detail examples of supposed causal relationships that you would quickly accept as bogus ideas. Instead, I shall deliberately investigate two ideas that most people hold very strongly and which they have held for many years. If we can debunk these two time-honored certainties, we can easily debunk the next one that comes along.

Corporate Earnings

As I write this paragraph, today's newspaper sports this headline in the business section: "Determining What Will Move Market Not Difficult — But Forecasting Its Direction Is Harder." The "easy" part is no surprise, since virtually everyone in finance agrees: "Earnings are the primary sources of stock price movement, which accounts for Wall Street's preoccupation with next month's earnings reports...."[48]

Is the indicator valid? Are stocks *driven* by corporate earnings? In June 1991, *The Wall Street Journal* reported on a study by Goldman Sachs's Barrie Wigmore, who found that "only 35% of stock price growth [in the 1980s] can be attributed to earnings and interest rates." Wigmore concludes that all the rest is due simply to *changing social attitudes toward holding stocks*. (Actually *all* of it is due to changing social attitudes, and earnings

are their *product*.) Says the Journal, "[This] may have just blown a hole through this most cherished of Wall Street convictions."[49] This study shows that *even in retrospect*, the "fundamentals" that most analysts are relying upon have little relationship to stock price movement.[50]

What about simply the *trend* of earnings vs. the stock market? Well, since 1932, corporate profits have been down in 19 years. The Dow *rose* in 14 of those years. In 1973-74, the Dow *fell* 46% while earnings *rose* 47%. 12-month earnings peaked at the bear market low. Earnings do *not* drive stocks. As Figure 19-2 illustrates and as Arthur Merrill showed years ago,[51] earnings *lag* stock trends. As shown in Chapter 16, the economy lags stock trends. It is therefore *impossible* for earnings or the economy to drive stocks. Forecasting the stock market is indeed impossible when the supposedly easy part is a wrong premise.

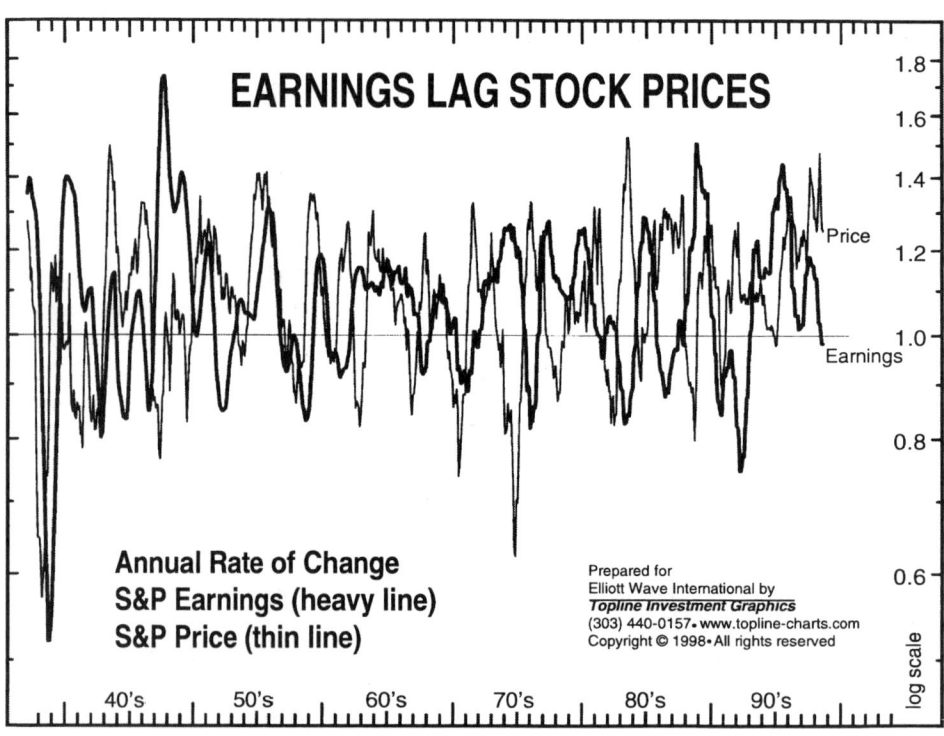

Figure 19-2

Trade Figures

In 1988, investors became "fixated" and "riveted," according to *The Wall Street Journal*, upon the monthly reported U.S. balance of trade with foreign nations. As with the other figures cited previously and now temporarily abandoned, this one appears to act as a simple indicator of stock prices. It is derived from outside the market. It has an apparently logical explanation: trade deficits (a negative value of U.S. exports minus imports) are bad for our country's "balance of payments," so they are bad for the

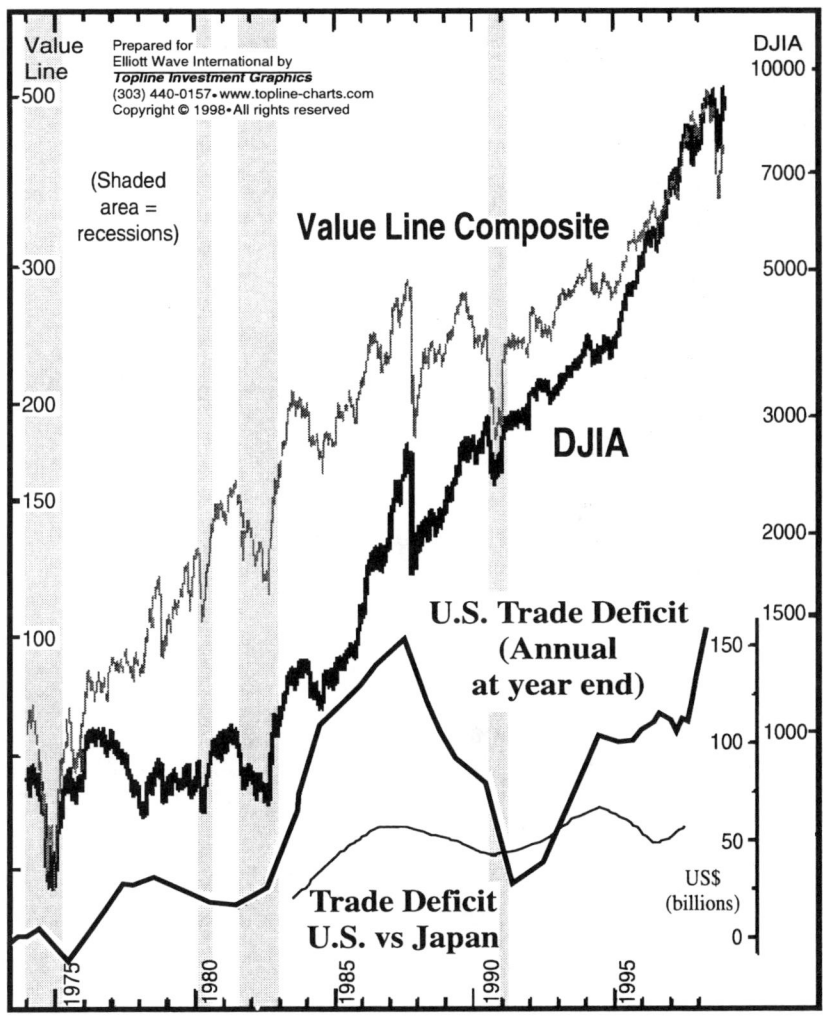

Figure 19-3

country, so they are bad for stocks. There is only one problem: The facts are once again in direct opposition to the assumption.

Figure 19-3 reveals that in fact the trade gap has followed the rises and falls of the U.S. stock market and economy very closely, *but in precisely the opposite way that economists assume.* The bigger has been the deficit, the *stronger* have been the stock market and the economy, and vice versa. Despite countless reports that "the trade deficit is slowing economic growth," statistics reveal the opposite experience for decades. A cursory perusal of Figure 19-3 reveals that the monthly trade deficit has expanded throughout most of the 1975-1998 bull market. Had the devil approached you in 1975 and given you the next 23 years of trade balance figures in exchange for your soul, you would have sold short right then and gone bankrupt ten times over as a result. The only periods that you would have been bullish (1978-1982 and 1987-1991), you would have made nothing.

As for the economy, the recessions of 1980 and 1982 followed a narrowing trade deficit. The next time the deficit began to narrow, in late 1987, it again led three years later to a recession, as the deficit shrank all the while. Those who followed the observations of economists and expanded their businesses in 1979 or 1989 on economists' predictions that the newly shrinking trade deficit was bullish got caught in *both* recessions.

In both cases, when the trade deficit began expanding again, so did the economy. Yet in 1994, the federal government, spurred on by economists, became apoplectic over the persistent trade gap and even risked a trade war over it. If the administration had somehow managed to force a further reduction in the trade gap, it would have derailed the economic recovery that came with its renewed expansion, reaping the opposite results that economists promised.

Today this erroneous theme remains alive and well. The Associated Press recently told us, "The Asian currency crisis hit America full force in March, pushing the month's trade deficit to a record."[52] What is the implication? "Analysts predict this year's overall deficit will easily be the *worst in history*," "worst" implying that it is a bad thing for the economy, despite 24 years of the reverse correlation. An economics writer for *The Atlanta Journal-Constitution* tells us, "The soaring trade deficit presents clear evidence that Asia's mess is starting to lap onto U.S. shores."[53] At any time the deficit was soaring during the preceding 24 years of a generally rising trend, did it present "clear evidence" of an Asian mess? No, because *Asia was not in a mess; it was booming. The supposed connection to any crisis in Asia does not exist.* As I write this paragraph, the figures for August

have just been released. Concomitant with the new all-time high in stocks in July and the continued economic expansion, trade figures hit an all-time record deficit, showing that the trends remain in lock step. Needless to say, the chief economist at a "Washington think tank" says, "We have a lot of bad months ahead of us on trade...it wouldn't take a lot to push us into a recession."[54] If his forecast is for "bad months," i.e., higher deficits, then he should not be predicting a recession. If he expects a recession, then he should forecast a narrowing trade deficit. At least the writer of the AJC article admits this much: "It's hard to comprehend the story because the facts are so jumbled." The facts are *not* jumbled. It is the thinking that is jumbled because the wrong premise is unceasingly at war with the facts. The correct premise is that when the U.S. economy is strong, its citizens buy more goods from abroad, while citizens of other countries, most of which have a higher savings rate, save a portion of the money they receive rather than spend it. The trade balance does not cause economic trends; it results from them. This situation may change, but that is how it has transpired for at least the past few decades.[55]

A further irony of conventional assertion, after two dozen years of wrong-headed consternation over the rising trade deficit, is that when the U.S. economy contracts again (as it surely will), these same writers and analysts will be saying, "See, we told you that the big deficit was bad! Look what finally happened." Those of us watching the graph, however, will probably be observing a *shrinking* deficit along with the next contraction. We can further assume, until the relationship changes, that as the economy continues to shrink, the trade deficit will continue to shrink right along with it. Conventional analysts, meanwhile, will be saying that the new trend is bullish. Those who believe it will get caught in the developing economic downdraft for the same reason they were too cautious all the way up: a belief that the relationship of the trade balance to economic health is the opposite of what it actually is, both in causality and implication.

That the purported relationship between such data and the trend of the stock market does not exist is invaluable knowledge for avoiding losses and for allowing the implementation of effective investment strategy, not only for the long term but also for the short term. For example, Dave Allman on the Elliott Wave Short-Term Update on May 16, 1988, the night before a monthly trade figure was to be reported, ignored the fact that an announcement was due and listed three Elliott-wave calculations indicating a short term high "within five points of Dow 2025" and added, "the [short-

term] cycle high we've been tracking is due now." The trade figure reported before the next morning's opening was, according to one televised economist, "unbelievably good." The high Dow print that morning was 2023, as trade-report watchers bought stocks on the "good news" of a lower figure while those who had bought the previous day celebrated because they had "guessed right." The rally ended in thirty minutes. In the next two days, the Dow plummeted 100 points to a new low for the month. The point is not who was right on the market in this instance but who was wasting his time and who had his eyes on what mattered. The "key numbers" watchers had their eyes on the magician's flashy assistant instead of the magician himself, and they got fooled.

Although news followers pay the price for being lazy, they aren't short of explanations when the market moves contrary to the presumably logical way. They simply invent a new premise! When the market underwent the mysterious drop described above, some after-the-fact explanation was necessary. (Had it gone up, the explanation would be obvious.) They therefore offered the idea that the report of a narrower trade deficit may have generated "inflation fears," which caused the market to drop. By logical extension, shouldn't big deficits have stirred *deflation* fears from mid-1982 through mid-1987, when the trade deficit rose persistently? Yet that was a period during which the money supply soared 170%. Also, why was the U.S. dollar rallying if the market had inflation fears? Like the supposed bearish indication of a growing trade deficit, this new explanation was all rationalization, sans evidence or integration.

The multitude who stay up nights trying to guess these various figures and explain their meaning haven't done any correlative research. They have countless theories but no data. In contrast to such varying obsessions, a socionomist focuses primarily on the patterns and psychology of the market, not on the background.

The Conflict Between Reality and False Premise

Even though most economists use the stock market as a leading economic indicator, they habitually present arguments reasoned in the other direction because they cannot imagine the proper chain of causality to be true. Conventional analysts try to reason from economics and political policy, which they call "the fundamentals," to mood (i.e., stock prices). This approach is backward, which is why it consistently fails at the most critical times. The so-called fundamentals are the caboose on the train.

This approach appears successfully predictive occasionally when the train is on a long straightaway. Then the trends are the same. Those in the caboose, however, are unequipped to predict a coming curve in the track that will change the direction of the locomotive. However, those up ahead observing the direction of the locomotive can tell you quite reliably what the caboose will do. This is why an economist cannot predict the stock market, but a stock market observer can do quite well at predicting the economy.

The actual direction of cause and effect does not stop economists from continuing to assert its opposite. Six months after the stock and currency collapses in Thailand, the Associated Press on December 8, 1997 said, "The permanent closure of insolvent finance companies is expected to leave 5000 to 10,000 workers unemployed, rattle the already battered stock market and spark a further drop in Thailand's currency, the baht, which has lost more than 40% of its value against the dollar."[56] Observe that the stock market and currency collapsed *first*, precipitating the failure of companies and unemployment. Despite this chronology, experts interviewed by the press cannot help presuming that those events will be causal of stock market trends. If that were so, why did stocks bottom nearly a year before unemployment hit its peak for the Great Depression in 1933? Why didn't the highest number of business failures and workers unemployed in nearly a century then "rattle an already battered stock market"? The *Washington Post* likewise said on May 28, "...the latest display of labor unrest threatens to plunge South Korea into a new financial crisis."[57] However, there was no "labor unrest" or any other social crisis preceding the latest financial crisis, was there? Indeed, that country's social mood in the summer of 1997 was confident, ebullient, even downright giddy. But overwhelming contradiction is no deterrent to conventional analysts, where an erroneous underlying assumption stubbornly governs all commentary.

This foible is not new. Garfield Drew[58] and John Train[59] describe how investors of the late 1940s braced for a "typical postwar depression" that the majority of economists predicted would follow World War II. It never came. Nor should it have. A financial crisis in the 1850s *preceded* the Civil War. A financial crisis in the 1930s *preceded* World War II. While a deep recession did follow World War I, which is one of two apparent precedents that economists were using, the usual chronology is evident there as well in that before the war started, the stock market had been falling for two years, it was below its peak of eight years previous, and the economy had been in recession for an unprecedented four years out of five.

While there is no tradition of postwar economic contraction, there is a very consistent precedent of prewar bear market. Because these facts do not fit the conventional prescription, they are ignored as meaningless.

Conventional Analysts Cannot Avoid Using Trend Extrapolation

Is there an internal logical flaw in using extramarket events for market forecasting? I think so.

If someone is bullish on stocks because interest rates have recently fallen, you are justified in asking, "How do you know that interest rates did not stop falling today, in which case stocks are about to decline?" He might respond, "well, the latest economic report shows a flat trend, which supports lower interest rates," in which case you are justified in asking, "How do you know that the economy didn't just turn up?" At some point, he must respond that he will wait for a change of some kind, a report of a stronger economy or a rate rise by the Fed. Then you can ask, "How do you know that the economic report you are waiting for will not reflect the *only* economic uptick or that the Fed will not raise rates *once* and then start lowering them again with the result that you will have sold your stocks at the bottom?" If he answers that he doesn't know, then he remains stuck with no basis for a forecast. If he continues to provide more causal indicators of his causal indicators, the chain is endless. Both of these answers are dead ends. His only way out of this dilemma is finally to provide a prediction based upon trend extrapolation. More often than not, an analyst pressed into this corner simply says that he sees no evidence of a change in trend for his supposed cause, an answer that relies on the fact that trends persist. The presumably trending cause (in this case the economy) will affect the trend of the next cause (in this case Fed policy), which will then affect a market (i.e., interest rates) that will affect the one he actually wants to predict (i.e., stocks).

Since the conventional analyst cannot avoid employing trend extrapolation at some point, might we ask him, "Isn't it far easier merely to extrapolate the trend of the market that you actually want to predict?" Instead of saying, "the trend of the economy is flat, which trend should continue, so the Fed should continue to lower interest rates, so stocks should continue to rise until the economic trend changes," he could simply say, "the trend of stocks is up until *that* trend changes." That way, he not only saves trouble but also avoids the pitfall of requiring his whole chain of causality to maintain itself. Because history shows numerous exceptions

for each supposed relationship, each step removed from the market he wishes to forecast further weakens his market conclusion. In contrast, trend extrapolation works with equal effect and lack thereof with the market he is trying to forecast in the first place.

Conventional analysts would do far better to trash all of their supposed indicators and just trend-follow the market with a single moving average, like Dick Fabian[60] does. The chain of argument with a moving average trend indicator, as with Elliott wave analysis, is direct and finite. Indicators such as these speak to the future, and that's that.

Conventional Attempts Are Counterproductive to Anticipating the Future

I hope this book changes some economists' methods forever. Entrenched conventional economists may attack the thesis of this book. If they do so in a scholarly way, fine. If they disparage socionomics without much in the way of argument, it will be helpful for you to understand what legs they do not have to stand on.

Business Week summarized the state of modern economics in 1982 when it said, "[With] a dismal performance...economists revealed most clearly...the extent to which their profession lags intellectually."[61] Evidence of the failure of conventional forecasting methods is more than pervasively anecdotal. According to *The Wall Street Journal*, a study of its own surveys since 1982 of the country's top economists reveals that in the aggregate, these acknowledged experts predicted accurately the *direction* (forget the extent) of interest rates *only 22% of the time*, which is less than half the success rate that would be produced purely by *guessing*.[62] Conventional methods of economic prediction, then, produce worse than worthless results; they are typically *misleading*. As Paul Montgomery says bluntly, "Economic theory obviously fails abjectly at predicting interest rates over any time frame whatsoever."[63]

What about forecasting corporate earnings and stock prices? It is widely known by longtime market watchers (and shown statistically as well; see the study cited in Chapter 8) that both earnings estimates and buy/sell recommendations from brokerage-house "fundamental" analysts relentlessly lag stocks' price curves. The higher a stock goes, the more analysts in the aggregate adjust their earning estimates upward, so the more they insist on buying it. After a stock tops out, "strong buy" changes to "buy" when the stock is down 35%, then to "hold" when the stock is down 50%, then to

"sell" at the bottom, when earnings estimates are finally revised downward. The lowest earnings reports and estimates come *after* the stock price recovers because as we have seen, earnings lag stock prices.

This persistent failure rate is not lost on economists. Most just play it safe by predicting growth all the time. *Business Week* said in 1996, "Over the past 25 years, economic forecasters have missed four of the past five recessions."[64] London's *Financial Times* likens economics to the businesses of "astrologers and quack doctors," whose clients nevertheless "continue to listen to them with extraordinary credulousness."[65]

Everyone knows *that* economists are almost always wrong. Now we need to understand *why* they are almost always wrong. In 1995, the London Economics consultancy analyzed predictions made by the U.K.'s top 34 economic forecasting groups, "including all the most quoted forecasters, [such as] the Treasury, the National Institute and the London Business School, [who use] elaborate econometric models of the economy."[66] John Kay, a professor of economics at the London Business School, reported on this study for the *Financial Times*. His cogent comments both describe the problem and hint at its cause. Read this description carefully:

> It is a conventional joke that there are as many different opinions about the future of the economy as there are economists. The truth is quite the opposite. Economic forecasters do not speak with discordant voices; they all say more or less the same thing at the same time; the degree of agreement is astounding. The differences between forecasts are trivial relative to the differences between all forecasts and what happens, [as] *what they say is almost always wrong.* It is clear from the analysis that there is a consensus forecast, which most forecasters cluster around to such a degree that it is barely worth distinguishing between one estimate and another. Yet the consensus forecast failed to predict *any* of the most important developments in the economy over the past seven years — the strength and resilience of the 1980s consumer spending boom, the depth and persistence of the 1990s recession, or the dramatic and continuing decline in inflation since 1991. Nor have the past four years been worse than usual for the forecasting profession. They did no better in the 1980s. And it is always safer to be wrong in a crowd. In large organisations, it is often more important to be wrong for the right reasons than to be correct. Even when they are proved wrong, forecasters see it as important to maintain the consensus in retrospect. For example, banks maintain as an article of faith that the depth of the recent recession and the magnitude of the property market collapse could not have been pre-

dicted. Looking more carefully at the figures in the tables, [we find that] the consensus forecast is easy to calculate, since it can be derived by taking the average of the present and the past. Yet the fundamental weakness in this approach is that it is incapable of identifying structural changes in the economy.[67]

These comments fit the thesis of this book. The relentless act of *herding*, which is due to fathomless feelings of *uncertainty*, which in turn is due to the application of methods that *do not work*, keeps the profession of economics in a perpetual fog. Chapters 10 and 11 of *At the Crest of the Tidal Wave* elaborate on the psychology behind conventional forecasting, revealing in more detail why it produces worse than random results.

Based upon their record, economists have no authority to complain about errors in the track record of practitioners of the Wave Principle. The pertinent question is, "*compared to what?*" Any approach that is *not persistently wrong* about future changes in trends and events is better than conventional methods. Any approach that has a rationale behind it is better, too. Socionomics wins on both counts.[68]

This is not to say that there are not legitimate gripes about how we fledgling socionomists conduct our craft. A crucial requirement of reliable forecasting is a thorough understanding of the limits of one's model. Although we are learning fast, we do not have those limits nailed down yet. Many Elliott wave practitioners are nonrigorous, sometimes too credulous, and often try to extract more from the principle than it will provide. Elliotters suffer from the same paleomentational impulses as economists, and sometimes it colors our predictions to the point of counter-productivity. Some of these problems result from the fact that socionomics is so new that there is no consistent line of inquiry, no cadre of supporters and no body of work to buttress our efforts. By necessity, practitioners of this new science are mavericks. We do, however, start with a stronger base because our premises are true. That is the reason for the great difference between our results and others'.

Why Does the Conventional Approach Remain So Entrenched?

If news is not the motor of market trends, and if outside forces are not causal to social mood and action, why do people assume that they are? There are two main reasons for the persistence of these myths.

As shown in Chapter 16 and discussed in Chapter 18, *economic and political news is not unrelated to the stock market; it lags the stock market.*

One can be fooled by the proximity of market behavior and extramarket events because of a single important technical fact: *the market trends, and so does the news that results from the social mood change that propels it*, so the two are often going in the same direction. When conventional forecasters appear right, it is merely a reflection of the sociological fact that there *are* social trends. Economists' forecasts lag those trends, but for as long as the trend continues *past* the time that they first discern it, they can appear correct. The correlation between markets and news that does exist fools people into believing that there is empirical support for their apparently natural assumption that events are the causal factor. It also occasionally rewards economists and investors for their assumption about news, often for extended periods. Occasional reward is all it takes to reinforce the belief. Experiments show that lab rats will work much harder pushing a lever for an occasional randomly generated reward than a regularly predictable one.[69] In this situation at least, the same tendency appears to apply to people.

The second reason for the persistence of the belief in event causality is that it is so effortless. In Chapter 21, we explore astronomer Andrei Linde's theory that parts of the universe inflate exponentially in a self-replicating fractal, a process he calls "chaotic inflation." Linde muses on the long dominance of the "big bang" theory, saying, "One of the main reasons for the popularity of the old big bang scenario is that imagining the universe as a balloon expanding out in all directions is relatively easy. It is much harder to grasp the structure of an eternally self-replicating fractal universe."[70] I think that the "outside cause" paradigm has a firm hold on people's minds for the same reason. Like the expanding balloon analogy of the big bang, it is easy to imagine by simply extrapolating from physics.

Linde adds, "Once we began relaxing these [big bang] assumptions, we immediately found that inflation is not an exotic phenomenon invoked by theorists for solving their problems. It is a general regime that occurs in a wide class of theories of elementary particles." Similarly, when we delve into our subject, we find that the "general regime" of the Wave Principle "occurs in a wide class of theories" involving growth and life, while outside causality is more applicable to the behavior of billiard balls and balloons.

I assert that the matter is not simply that the purported causal relationships of macroeconomics are extremely complex or that they change at inopportune times but that in a fundamental sense, *there aren't any*. Markets follow the Wave Principle no matter what, and that is the only cause that is consistent. Once you can demonstrate to yourself that the stock mar-

ket has a life of its own, you will begin to feel, as rightly you should, that it is the guys peering at and poring over each new statistic relating to the course of the economy or each new political nuance who are the real "tea leaves and entrails" bunch when it comes to anticipating the next move in the stock market. Conventional analysis is not a sound, reasonable approach; it is nonsense. It does not analyze the fundamental; it analyzes the extraneous.

"Economic forecasting," goes the old joke, "is like trying to drive a car blindfolded and following directions given by a person who is looking out the back window." With socionomics, we are no longer looking out the back window; we are facing forward. With the Wave Principle, we are no longer driving blind. We can see enough about the road ahead to negotiate the car.

NOTES

1 Cootner, P.H. (1964). *The random character of stock market prices*.

2 Firth, M. (1977). *The valuation of shares and the efficient-markets theory*.

3 Malkiel, B.G. (1985). *A random walk down wall street*.

4 Hector, G. (1988, October 10). "What makes stock prices move?" *Fortune*.

5 Cunningham, S. (1993, Fall). "Unit root testing: a critique from chaos theory." *Review of Financial Economics*.

6 Montgomery, P. (1996, May 17). Presentation. "Economic theory and technical analysis."

7 Malkiel, B. (1998, July/August). "Still on a random walk." *Bloomberg's Personal Finance*.

8 Frost, A.J. and Prechter, R.R. (1978). *Elliott wave principle — key to market behavior*.

9 Koselka, R. (1996, June 3). "The madness of well-heeled crowds". *Forbes*.

10 Brock, W.A., *et al.* (1992, December). "Simple technical trading rules and the stochastic properties of stock returns." *The Journal of Finance*, Vol. 47, No. 5.

11 Baker, M. (1995, October 7-8). "Investing: rhyme or reason?" *International Herald Tribune*, p. 6.

12 Malkiel, B. (1998, July/August). "Still on a random walk." *Bloomberg's Personal Finance* (quoting Richard Roll).

13 Klein, E. (1986, November). "Psychology meets the stock market." *Columbia*.

14 Donnelly, B. (1987, October 23). "Efficient-market theorists are puzzled by recent gyrations in stock market." *The Wall Street Journal*.

15 DeBondt, W. and Thaler, R. (July, 1985). "Does the stock market overreact?" *The Journal of Finance*, Vol. XL, No. 3, pp. 793-808.

16 It is very common for academic studies to have enough evidence to discover apparently constant market relationships such as this at just about the time they are ready to fail. The relationships are often valid, but only in context of the Wave Principle.

17 Brock, W.A. (1991). "Causality, chaos, explanation and prediction in economics and finance." *Social Systems Research Institute*, No. 387.

18 It is true despite some very inventive commentary from *The Wall Street Journal* that tried to blame it on a few words from the mouth of a government official, as if that were a rare event.

19 Hector, G. (1988, October 10). "What makes stock prices move?" *Fortune.*

20 Chapter 18 discussed the counter-intuitive exception.

21 Treynor, J. (1998, March/April). "Bulls, bears, and market bubbles." *Financial Analysts Journal.*

22 These ratios are derived from data provided by the Federal Reserve Bank of St. Louis (PO Box 442, St. Louis, MO 63166) and Ned Davis Research (2100 Riveredge Parkway, Atlanta GA 30238).

23 Goleman, D. (1989, August, 15). "Brain's design emerges as a key to emotions." *The New York Times.*

24 Kulkosky, E. (1977, October 15). "The Elliott wave's surprising message to investors." *Financial World.*

25 The Principle itself is probably on an Elliott wave of acceptance: three steps forward and two steps back.

26 Leontief, Wassily (1982, July 9). Letter to the editor. *Science.*

27 Brock, D. (1986, June 30). "Seeing the economy's future with a shattered crystal ball." *Insight.*

28 Coveney, P. and Highfield, R. (1995). *Frontiers of complexity,* p. 335.

29 Berry, J.M. (1998, July 6). "Key players control money supply." *The Washington Post.*

30 Brauchli, M.W. (1998, July 14). "Why the world bank failed to anticipate Indonesia's deep crisis." *The Wall Street Journal.*

31 For example, Harvard biologist Edward O. Wilson, who convincingly postulates a direct connection between genetics and culture in his book *Consilience,* nevertheless graciously accepts unchallenged the promise that "In the United Stated, the Federal Reserve Board now has enough knowledge and legal power to regulate the flow of money and prevent — we trust! — the economy from spinning into catastrophic inflations and depressions," irrespective of genetics, culture and six thousand years of economic history.

32 "Stand still, little lambs, and be shorn!" (1998, March). *Economic Education Bulletin.* American Enterprise Institute, Great Barrington, MA.

33 Dornbush, R. (1998, July 30). "Growth forever." *The Wall Street Journal.*

34 Ratajczak, D. (1998, August 30). "Global economy requires action." *The Atlanta Journal-Constitution.*

35 Evans-Pritchard, A. (1998, September 2). "'Plunge team' ready to spring into action." *Electronic Telegraph* (internet).

36 Wessel, D. and Davis, B. (1998, September 24). "How global crisis grew despite efforts of a crack U.S. team." *The Wall Street Journal.*

37 Caldarelli, G., *et al.* (1997, December 1). "A prototype model of stock exchange." *Europhysics Letters*.

38 Actually, many will whisper that the Fed bought S&P futures the day of the low, October 20. Had they not, we are then to presume according to the computer-causality model, the decline would have continued to zero.

39 This phrasing is from a January 1987 report from the Chase Manahattan Bank of London.

40 Litton, R.E. and Santomero, A.M. (1998, July 28). "Why a market correction won't replay 1987." *The Wall Street Journal*.

41 Dent, H.S. (1998). *The roaring 2000s*, p. 94.

42 "Economists forecast mild inflation of 2.5% yearly through 2008." (1998, May 26). *The Wall Street Journal*.

43 Sheeley, G. (1997, 14 April). "Runaway Tiger: Woods wins Masters by record 12 shots with 18-under total." *The Atlanta Journal-Constitution,* p. D1.

44 It is perturbing that conventional analysts have appropriated this word, as the actual *fundamentals* of market behavior are the unconscious forces that guide men in social mentation, the Elliott wave patterns that they produce, and at a deeper level the Fibonacci formology of nature's growth patterns.

45 Acker, L. (1998, August). "Why so bearish?" *3F Forecasts*.

46 "Economy surging behind spending." (1998, June 27). *The Atlanta Journal-Constitution*.

47 Caldarelli, G., *et al.* (1997). "A prototype model of stock exchange." *Europhysics Letters*, 40 (5), pp. 479-484.

48 Walker, T. (1998, June 21). "Determining what will move market not difficult — but forecasting its direction is harder." *The Atlanta Journal-Constitution*.

49 Lowenstein, R. (1991, June 6). "Goldman study of stocks' rise in '80s poses a big riddle." *The Wall Street Journal*, p. C1.

50 This is particularly evident in the 1980s and 1990s because the stock market has been in a *fifth* wave, whose product is weaker than that in a third wave (see discussion in Chapter 17).

51 Reference unavailable.

52 "Trade deficit soars to $13 billion." (1998, May 20). *The Atlanta Journal-Constitution*.

53 Geewax, M. (1998, June 21). "U.S. could become entwined in downturn." *The Atlanta Journal-Constitution*.

54 "Trade deficit hits record." (1998, October 21). *The Atlanta Journal Constitution*.

55 The full explanation is more complex. One of the many exports of the U.S. during its recent decades of economic strength has been dollars. Other countries' banks believe that this indefinable nonentity is a store of value, so they stock it as "reserves." One day, when U.S. economic soundness appears questionable, this socially shared mental image will dissolve, and many dollars will be desperately repatriated.

56 Horn, R. (1997, December 8). "Thailand starting big financial over-haul." *The Atlanta Journal-Constitution*, p. A12.

57 Jordan, M. (1998, May 28). "S. Koreans walk off their jobs...." *The Washington Post*.

58 Drew, G. (1955). *New methods for profit in the stock market.*

59 Train, J. (1994). *The money masters.*

60 Fabian Investment Resources, Huntington Beach, CA.

61 "A dismal performance." (1982, January 18). *Business Week*, p. 124.

62 Harman, T. (1993, July 6). "Economists look for moderate growth in second half...." *The Wall Street Journal*, p. A2.

63 Montgomery, P. (1998, February 4). *Universal Economics.*

64 Mandel, M.J. (1996, September 30). "Especially dismal at down-turns" *Business Week*, pp. 88-89.

65 Kay, J. (1995, September 29). "Cracks in the crystal ball." *Financial Times*.

66 *Ibid.*

67 *Ibid.* These sentences are substantially rearranged; I have omitted ellipses for reading clarity.

68 A rare few economists do pay homage to what matters at a fundamental level. Clarence B. Carson says, "It is necessary to keep in mind throughout the study of economics the enduring nature of things. Only thus can we discover or be aware of the *principles*, the operation of cause and effect, *the order that underlies and endures* through change." [ref: Carson, C., (1990). *Basic economics.*]

69 Source unavailable.

70 Linde, A. (1994, November). "The self-reproducing inflationary universe." *Scientific American*.

Chapter 20:

Some Key Fundamentals of Socionomics

Financial Man is Not the Same as Economic Man

It is universally presumed that the primary law of *economics*, i.e., that price is a function of supply and demand, also rules *finance*. However, human behavior with respect to prices of investments is, in a crucial way, the *opposite* of that with respect to prices of goods and services. When the price of a good or service rises, *fewer* people buy it, and when its price falls, *more* people buy it. This response allows pricing to keep supply and demand in balance. In contrast, when the price of an investment rises, *more* people buy it, and when its price falls, *fewer* people buy it. This behavior is not an occasional financial market anomaly; it always happens. Look back at Figure 7-3, the graph of the dollar-valued trading volume in the U.S. stock market divided by the prevailing gross domestic product. As you can see, volume expands as stock prices rise and contracts as they fall. In economic matters, rising prices *repel* buyers; in investment matters, rising prices *attract* buyers. This difference is not incidental; it is fundamental.

Many market theorists argue that the law of supply and demand operates in finance but is simply "suspended" for periods of time because people "overreact" and "rationalize" with "elaborate arguments" why they should pay up for investments.[1] The difference between any such idea and what happens in markets for goods and services is irreconcilable by conventional economic theory. People never act in any such way with respect to goods and services. Most investors can quickly rationalize selling an investment because its price is falling or buying it because its price is rising, but there is not a soul who desperately rationalizes doing with less bread because the price is falling or who drives his car twice as much because the price of gasoline has doubled. In economic behavior, the law of supply and

demand does not lie dormant *ever*. It is like the law of gravity; it works *all* the time. It cannot "fail to apply," even temporarily. Prices are the balance beam from which the scales of supply and demand hang. Changes in buying patterns are virtually instantaneous in responding to price changes for bread, cars, TVs and shoes.

In the same way, investment behavior has *its* iron law: the Wave Principle. This law governs unconscious, impulsive, collective herding behavior, while the law of supply and demand governs conscious, logical, individual economic decision-making. The former law governs prices for intangible values, whether associated with tangible goods or not; the latter law governs prices for utilitarian tangibles.[2] Attempting to apply the law of supply and demand to investment markets is akin to attempting to apply the laws of physics to falling in love. They do not pertain.

The law of supply and demand always produces *practical* behavior in the realm of economics. The Wave Principle (despite its apparent value for life and progress *per se*) produces *impractical* behavior in the realm of finance. In the *product* marketplace, the rational goal of survival leads to price stability and objectivity. In the *investment* marketplace, prerational impulses of survival lead to wild overvaluation and undervaluation. Time and again, observers, particularly those who understand the iron law of economics, complain that the stock market's action appears unreasonable. That observation is wholly correct. The decision to buy into rising prices and sell into falling prices is not governed by the reasoning neocortex but by the unconscious herding impulse, which generates inappropriate behavior in the financial realm as part of a generalized attempt to enhance the odds of survival. It is baffling only to those who insist that "supply and demand" rule finance.

It is not that reasonableness in finance is utterly absent; we are not talking about irrationality. People who invest in markets know through cold reason that they value their own lives and prosperity. Those who buy in bull markets are following the very reasonable desire to *enhance their sustenance*, while those who sell in bear markets are following the very reasonable desire to *survive*. Unfortunately, the portion of the brain that generates unconscious urges directs their behavior in this regard. The primitive mechanism employed is so inappropriate to the situation that instead of enhanced success, it produces guaranteed failure.

Because these desires *per se* are rational, they work just fine in the world of goods and services. In the product marketplace, the consumer

wants prices lower while the producer wants them higher, and for the same fundamental reasons: survival and self sustenance. The process of mediating these identical goals between polarized dealers produces an objective, natural balance expressed as price.

In the world of investments, however, the consumer (who buys it) and the producer (who creates and wants to sell more of it) *both want prices higher*. Rather than become excited to buy as prices *fall*, as consumers of goods and services do, investors become excited to buy as prices *rise*. Since desire and hope are entirely on the side of price rise, only fear and despair can be on the side of price decline. Thus, when prices fall, investors are pressured past endurance to sell. Both of these impulses are contrary to the way consumers behave with respect to goods and services.

The dynamics of the Wave Principle underlie financial markets and lead to nonobjective valuation. Individual investors who desire to be objective in financial speculation face the inescapable requirement of understanding that fact and its implications.

Direction, Volatility and Duration Do Not Determine the Source of Sociological Motive

Robert Schiller polled individual and institutional investors about why they sold stocks on October 19, 1987. Most of them admitted candidly that "they sold because others were selling,"[3] i.e., they were herding. It is welcome to have research telling us that the crash of 1987 was a "psychological event." However, no one ever thinks to poll investors about why they had *bought* stocks relentlessly throughout the preceding year. If any pollster did ask, *the truth would be exactly the same*, but he would find little honesty about that fact because in *rising* markets, people have plenty of time to let their neocortexes formulate all kinds of rationalizations for herding action. Panic is a faster-acting emotion than hope, and the neocortex is often stumped in coming up with an explanation for it. One of my favorite quotes in this regard, undoubtedly rushed out near press time, is this one from *The Wall Street Journal*: "The U.S. dollar continued to decline yesterday despite economic news that could have been bullish for the currency if traders' mood weren't so bearish."[4]

Market commentators often blame a declining trend on herding, but they virtually never ascribe a *rising* trend to herding. This convention is displayed so often that all one need do is read the papers for a few days to find an example. On June 2, 1998, the Dow Jones News Service quoted a

brokerage firm's director of investment strategy after a few weeks of price decline in a broad list of technology stocks as follows: "The herd mentality is *taking over*." That is to say, herd mentality had nothing to do with the multi-year buying binge on all-time record volume producing all-time record valuation for technology stocks; *that*, we are to presume, was all fueled by the rational decision-making of independently minded individuals. On June 15, 1998, the morning after the intraday low of a correction in that index, *USA Today*, parroting economists, repeated, "the drop is based more on psychology than fundamentals."[5] A mere six trading days after that assessment was published, the NDX rocketed to a new all-time high. Once again, no experts claimed that that *rise* was due to psychology. As always, they found adequate "fundamentals" to explain the leap.

Direction is even presumed to affect the efficacy of fundamental indicators. Read this from October 9 of this year:

> Just 18 months ago in the midst of the steadily rising bull market, Wall Street's top strategists could start their computers, plug in the latest numbers for inflation, interest rates, dividends and corporate earnings, and come up with a reasonably plausible prediction of where the stock market was headed.
>
> But, my, how times have changed. Global financial markets are ricocheting. The usual relationships are gone. Stocks can't be counted on to move up as interest rates go down. The psychology of fear has become a big and changing factor, one that can't be plugged into economics-based models. No wonder the models are not much comfort any more.[6]

That is to say, psychology never interferes with these rational models of cause and effect when prices *rise*; it only happens when they fall. As you might guess, quick willingness to blame psychology only for declines is related to people's tendency, discussed in Chapter 18, to equate downtrends with unpredictability and uptrends with predictability. Of course, that the forecasts generated by the above-referenced models were any good on the upside is a myth; people simply felt comfortable and did not need to explain away all the errors. The market decline caused discomfort, evidence being that the above assessment was written on the exact day of the low following a three-month 20% decline in the S&P Composite index and a six-month 30% decline in the broader stock averages. (The limbic system is not only in charge of stock price trends; it is in charge of the timing of psychologically forced rationalization about them.)

The question is whether it is valid to assert, as it continually is, that psychology plays a part only in the crowd's stock-*selling* behavior and not

its stock-*purchasing* behavior. The problem with the stance that advances are rational and declines are emotional is that market direction is simply a function of how the ratio of two assets is expressed. For example, one can plot stocks in terms of dollars or dollars in terms of stocks, or dollars in terms of yen or yen in terms of dollars. Stock prices express the value of stocks in terms of dollars (dollars per share), but they could just as well be inverted to show the value of dollars in terms of stocks (shares per dollar). Some of the graphs in this book depict the inflation-adjusted Dow, which expresses the value of stocks in terms of a pile of certain goods (goods per share). In each case, an uptrend in one expression of the ratio is a down-trend in the other. People are simply allowed a perpetual choice of whether to hold stocks or dollars, either of which can rise or fall in value with respect to the other. This means that *the engine of motivation for each direction cannot be different.* It is either rationality or herding behavior or some kind of mix, *all the time.*

A century ago, upon noticing that professional students of psychology made the same essential error in assigning only "bad" behavior to the herd mentality, Le Bon asserted the duality of crowd behavior:

> Without a doubt criminal crowds exist, but virtuous and heroic crowds, and crowds of many other kinds, are also to be met with. The crimes of crowds only constitute a particular phase of their psychology. The mental constitution of crowds is not to be learnt merely by a study of their crimes, any more than that of an individual by a mere description of his vices.[7]

The same is true of markets; one cannot understand herding behavior by studying only market crashes. He must study advances as well.

The direction of some markets does determine, for most people, *which* impulsive emotion is involved. This is particularly true for stock prices, in which most people are betting on the upside. That is why uptrends look different from downtrends on a stock market graph. Hope is the fuel for advances in stocks and fear the fuel for declines. Hope, fear and compla-cency express themselves differently. Hope tends to build slowly, while fear often crystallizes swiftly. Nevertheless, they are both still *emotions* and so derive from the same motivational engine.

In some markets, such as those for commodities, the price direction of these emotions is inverted. Commodity charts look different from stock index charts because their most violent movements, generated by fear (of drought, shortage, war, etc.) occur near tops instead of bottoms, and their

lazier meanderings, generated by optimism, occur in mature downtrends instead of mature uptrends.

In some markets, direction has no such relationship because the two sides are equally opposed emotionally. For instance, a falling price of the U.S. dollar vs. the Japanese yen depicts, at the same time, an uptrend to a Japanese investor and a downtrend to a U.S. investor.

Regardless of which direction a market is trending, *all of its governing emotions are generated by the herding impulse.* In the most fundamental sense, the direction of prices does not change people's minds or their behavior. Their unconscious still follows the herd, expressing the form of the Wave Principle.

Neither does volatility determine the source of motive. As this book attests, there are many reasons to conclude that paleomentation rules even when financial markets appear calm and/or "reasonably valued," which times are merely transitional states along the emotional continuum. Herding and flocking animals are often calm for long periods when grazing or resting in a quiet field. When one begins to run or fly, however, panic throughout the group is a hairsbreadth away from being triggered. Similarly in the stock market, the reversal of a trend is due when just one extra change of mind is required to tip the balance. When that person makes his decision, the trend reverses, and the dynamic is played out in the other direction.

The duration of a trend is likewise irrelevant to the source of the market's motive. Some professors go way out on a limb to declare that *upon occasion*, and *in the short run*, financial markets become emotional rather than rational. One says, for instance, "In the *short run* (anything from a day to a few months), emotions and other biases may lead us to make a decision that may not be based on rationality."[8] The authors of the market simulation experiment discussed in previous chapters issue a similar explanation for the immutable patterns they have uncovered. Like governments after a crash, they attribute the results to technically oriented speculators as distinct from fundamentally oriented long-term investors: "Th[e results] suggest that the statistics we observe in real markets is mainly due to the interaction among 'speculators' trading on *technical* grounds, regardless of economic *fundamentals.*"[9] Elliott dispensed with this idea sixty years ago when he showed that markets are fractals. Mandelbrot again dispensed with this idea over a decade ago when he said about near and long-term market fluctuations, "the mechanisms don't seem to be differ-

ent." The idea that "investors" trade rationally on external economic fundamentals while "speculators" trade emotionally on internal psychology is to assign a different motive to someone trading long term vs. someone trading short term. My own observations suggest no difference whatsoever other than time frame. When the public commits to investing "long term" after years of bull market, it is a purely psychological phenomenon that is analogous to a speculator committing to a rally a day or two before the top. As Chapters 5, 6, 16 and 18 attest, outside factors do not drive market behavior at *any* degree of trend.

We must recognize that rising markets have the same causal origin as falling ones, calm ones the same as volatile ones, and long-term ones the same as short-term ones. The Wave Principle reveals unequivocally that a structural dynamic, probably impelled by paleomentation, is in control of the aggregate stock market trend and level, and therefore social mood, *at all times.*

The Inapplicability of the Concept of Nonlinearity to Formological Systems

"Chaos" denotes physical processes that superficially appear random because of their immense variability of result but which in fact are patterned in hidden ways that adhere to mathematical formulae. Chaos theory made a great breakthrough in finding order in presumably random processes. Though utterly determined, chaotic processes are not predictable past a short time because the slightest variation in initial conditions changes the outcome.

"Complexity" denotes dynamical systems that generate paths of evolution. Complexity theory claims to have found only a vague order in self-organizing systems, one that is based upon structural influences but not fully determined. Complex systems are therefore presumed to be just as unpredictable as chaotic systems.

Both chaos and complexity are considered to be "nonlinear," which means that output is not proportional to input. In my opinion, it is incorrect to describe financial markets as nonlinear phenomena. The very concepts of linearity and nonlinearity depend upon the idea of cause and effect generated by "input" affecting the system. In a linear system, the same cause always produces the same effect, while in a nonlinear system, the same cause can have very different effects, such as the snowflake that finally causes the avalanche. However, financial market movements *cannot* result

from a chain of incremental causes that trigger a reaction *because they follow the Wave Principle*. If the cause of a market's process is its form, then in a sense, the system *is linear*, or perhaps better said, *direct*. When the stock market completes a fifth wave, it retreats in corresponding degree. There is never an essential difference in result. This conclusion pertains to every system that progresses in waves. The concept of nonlinearity in such systems is therefore not paramount and may not even apply.

For all systems that follow the Wave Principle, then, and perhaps for all systems that are robust fractals, the idea of nonlinearity may turn out to be an interim concept. It falsely presumes linear event causality *and* deduces unpredictability of result when in fact, (1) the results are not unpredictable, and (2) there is a direct cause to explain them. Such systems are not linear or nonlinear, as events are irrelevant. Such systems are *formological*, which means that they proceed relentlessly according to form. I propose the term *formological system* for such phenomena.

The November 1997 *New Scientist* suggests that some scientists may be edging toward this way of thinking:

> For hundreds of years, science has proceeded on the notion that things can always be understood – and can only be understood – by breaking them down into smaller pieces and by coming to know those pieces completely. Systems in critical states – and they seem to be plentiful – flout this principle.[10]

What the author means is that the structure of systems in critical states (see Chapter 3) is not dependent upon the properties of their parts and the directional causality of events perpetrated by those parts but upon a *form* that wells up within or imposes itself upon the system. The Wave Principle shows that *form*, not atomistic cause and effect, determines all social systems and perhaps all living systems. Chapter 21 further explores this theme.

The False Presumption of Unpredictability for Complex Systems

Belief in the inherent unpredictability of complex systems is entrenched. Part I of this book argues that there is far more order than currently believed in formological systems such as robust fractals, including waves and arbora. The following discussion shows how radical this idea is.

After obliterating the idea of randomness as fundamental to nature, chaos and complexity theorists quickly reenshrined it when they found that they were not immediately able to forecast specifics of the outcomes of

their processes. Paul Davies, in *The Cosmic Blueprint*, states this conclusion succinctly:

> Typically, errors in ordinary dynamical systems grow in proportion to time (i.e., linearly). By contrast, in a chaotic system, the errors grow at an escalating rate; in fact, they grow exponentially with time. *The randomness of chaotic motion is therefore fundamental*, not merely the result of our ignorance. Gathering more information about the system will not eliminate it. *In other words, all power of prediction is lost.*[11]

The April 1997 *New Scientist* reiterates what complexity theorists currently believe: Even though we know that complex phenomena follow power laws, "it is *impossible to predict even roughly* the size of the next step"[12] in *any* system that follows a power law, be it earthquakes, bird flight or the stock market.

Chaotic systems, say scientists, are inherently unpredictable due to the "butterfly effect" (a phrase coined by MIT meteorology professor Edward Lorenz), which is the idea that small changes in "initial conditions" will result in massive changes later. For instance, a butterfly flapping its wings over Bolivia affects air currents, and if you do not take the butterfly into account, you cannot predict the weather in Siberia.

Articles, books and programs on social forecasting parrot the idea, erroneously applying it to formological systems as if it is a principle. Michael Barnsley on PBS says, "The thing that has come out of the Mandelbrot set...is that even in a utopian world, in practice you may not be able to predict the future; it can be deterministic in principle but not in practice."[13]

Edgar E. Peters, who in 1989 presented the idea of fractals in financial markets to *The Financial Analysts' Journal*, challenging EMH, nevertheless makes this assertion in the March-April 1991 issue:

> The further out in time we go, the less reliable our forecasts are. Th[is] point is particularly important. It means that, as with the weather, accurate, long-range economic forecasting is not feasible from a practical standpoint. Even if we were able to determine the equations of motion underlying the S&P 500, we would still not be able to forecast beyond a short time frame....[14]

The Fortune Sellers, by William Sherden asserts, "Complex systems have no natural laws governing their behavior at either their microlevel (individual humans) or their macrolevel (the economy); thus, complex systems cannot be scientifically predicted."[15] The *Dick Davis Digest*, summarizing

the conclusions of several writers on the subject, states flatly, "The bottom line in applying chaology to financial markets is that forecasting is a waste of time; the chaotic nature of chains of events make predictions impossible."[16] John Liscio in *Barron's* says, "Any prediction that extends more than a month or so into the future is simply destined to fail."[17] "Simply" is exactly how this position is reasoned, as it first assumes the wrong causality (that events cause events) and then proclaims failure as therefore inevitable.

Fancy as it sounds, this idea, which permeates complexity discourse, is not new. Alfred Marshal, an English economist and John Maynard Keynes' teacher, noted in his 1890 book, *Principles of Economics*, that economic phenomena "do not lend themselves easily to mathematical expression." Philosopher Karl Popper said in 1957, "There is no doubt that the analysis of any concrete social situation is made extremely difficult by its complexity."[18] These long-running presumptions are valid only when one restricts his formulae to those applicable to physics and further presumes, as people still do today, that there are no mathematics distinctly applicable to social interaction. This long-standing error is understandable, as there has been little basis to assume otherwise until now. However, this does not excuse the arrogance and expressions of utter certainty that are typical of some modern proponents of this view.

The view expressed by these various quotations is wrong. To be sure, if one applies tools applicable to systems of linear causality to attempt to predict outcomes of formological systems, the result will be failure. The proper prediction of such systems is not in this approach. The key to predicting formological systems is in their *patterns*. I cannot reconcile the above view of market behavior, the "butterfly effect" view, with any experience I have had forecasting with the Wave Principle. What "errors" are they talking about? What randomness? What events? Randomness, events and error have nothing to do with the path of the stock market, much less are they fundamental.

In fact, there is not a shred of evidence that errors in forecasting the stock market escalate over time. Though two of the preceding quotations claim that predictions within "a short time frame" that extend only "a month or so" are reasonably expected to be accurate, there is no indication that any analyst depending upon event causality can predict the stock market over a month or so or even over a day or so or a minute or so. Because forecasting the stock market on this basis is *equally* impossible over all durations, the premise of event causality and chaotic error amplification must be false.

When applying the Wave Principle, the length of time into the future *per se* has nothing at all to do with forecasting accuracy. The fundamental determinant of forecasting accuracy is the *clarity of form*. The important question is, at what degrees have the developing patterns provided enough information to generate useful probabilities? Those are the degrees at which prediction will be the most reliable and accurate, whether they anticipate developments going out days or centuries.

In fact, contrary to all current views on the subject, it is the *long-term social trends*, the ones that chaos scientists say are impossible to predict, that are in fact *easier* to predict. Chapters 5 and 17 provide evidence of this fact. The reason that long-term trends are easier to forecast is that there are much more data to apply in one's analysis of form (such as breadth, volume, sentiment and behavioral statistics in markets, as described in Chapter 7) as well as a higher component of accuracy in the sociometer that one is using (for instance, aggregate stock prices).

The philosopher Kierkegaard, who correctly posited that progress is not smooth, was nevertheless similarly pessimistic about predictability. "In life, only sudden decisions, leaps or jerks can lead to progress. Something decisive occurs always only by a jerk, by a sudden turn *which neither can be predicted from its antecedents nor is determined by them.*"[19] The fact of the Wave Principle (1) affirms Kierkegaard's observation about progress and regress but (2) negates his assumptions about their unpredictability and (3) clarifies what antecedents do and do not determine the subsequent sudden turn.

Prigogine said resignedly in 1990, "I can never come up with an absolute theory of the stock market or of traffic flow because I can't read your soul."[20] The Wave Principle qualifies as an absolute theory of the stock market because it allows us to view, and to a great degree read, the soul of collective man.

Sherden adds this presumable *coup de grace* reason against economic predictability: "Complex systems are so highly interconnected with numerous positive and negative feedback loops that they often have counterintuitive cause-and-effect results."[21] Here are both the *reason* that herding takes place (feedback) and a correct observation that the typical outcome is *counterintuitive* to the neocortex's cause-and-effect presumption that actions and events cause actions and events. Despite the author's presumption, these observations do *not* speak to predictability, and they *are* compatible with the Wave Principle.

James Gleick said in a 1985 article, "Mandelbrot's mimicking of stock market and river charts *does not help in predicting* particular rallies and

floods."[22] That is true, because he has mimicked only one very rough aspect of the stock market and flooding patterns: their fractal irregularity. He has not even considered, much less discovered, that they might exhibit forms.

The Wave Principle makes obsolete the idea that there is some kind of principle of inherent unpredictability in all complex systems. It presents a leap in scientific knowledge and value: Forecasting is possible in any system that displays the Wave Principle.

The Probabilistic Nature of Scientific Social Forecasting

An article entitled "Chaos" contrasts two long-standing views of the predictability of nature:

> The French mathematician Pierre Simon de Laplace [in 1776] proposed that the laws of nature imply strict determinism and complete predictability, although imperfections in observations make the introduction of probabilistic theory necessary. Poincare [in 1903] foreshadowed the contemporary view that arbitrarily small uncertainties in the state of a system may be amplified in time and so predictions of the distant future cannot be made.[23]

The Wave Principle says that both of these views are wrong, at least as they apply to nature's social trends, which are neither completely predictable nor utterly unpredictable in the distant future ("in the distant future" meaning, in modern expressions of this sentiment, "of any useful duration"). In fact, they are *highly* predictable in both *general* and *probabilistic* terms and *somewhat* predictable in *specific* terms. What is more, these facts pertain *regardless of the time scale*, as clarity of pattern is the prime determinant of predictability.

The Wave Principle guarantees reliable forecasting only of *probabilities*. It allows us to predict some aspects of the future and not others. For example, early in a new social mood trend, we can forecast society's coming *character* changes but not necessarily specific events. We can forecast that a major rising impulse wave will bring an increase in goodwill and productivity. The specific decisions that each man makes and the specific social actions and events that result depend upon countless details and are therefore chaotic. As the trend progresses, however, we can watch for signs to indicate such specifics and actually anticipate some of them quite well, as demonstrated in Chapter 17.

When predicting wave forms themselves, a comparatively difficult task, we might be able to anticipate, for instance, a five-wave advance of a certain relative size and duration, as various Elliotters did in the excerpts presented in Chapter 5. However, there is no known way to anticipate whether that advance will have an extended first, third, or fifth wave, or no extension at all or whether the movement will adhere to a parallel channel or whether an impulse will end with a diagonal triangle. (Figures 2-1 through 2-7 display the diversity of appearance in impulses.) Still, we do have immense knowledge of probabilities, as you can see from all the guidelines for impulses cited in Chapter 3. The good news is that such questions often do not matter. If we anticipate a five-wave structure, often all that is required is to observe its progress and decide when it is over. Given the fractal nature of the move, the fifth wave will subdivide into five smaller waves, and so on, providing a solid basis for making that decision.

Some people who come in contact with the Wave Principle dismiss it when they find out it cannot predict the future perfectly. This is like a blind man foregoing surgery to bring about sight in one eye because he would prefer to have sight in both. The probabilistic aspect of social forecasting is simply what is available; it is the reality of the situation, and nothing will change it. A search for the proverbial "holy grail" in finance or any other social science is as futile as the name implies.

It should not be too hard to get over this hurdle. In 1927, Werner Heisenberg discovered that subatomic particles' position and timing could be predicted only in terms of probability. If we must be satisfied with the fact that these *physical events* can be foretold only probabilistically, should we really gripe that predicting *social events* has the same restriction? We all accept that there are specific laws governing cloud formation, earthquakes and plant growth. We also accept that the *product* of these laws is immensely complex and variable, and predictable only in probabilistic terms. The same thing is true about human social mood and the history that it generates. So at times, we will know more than most people by understanding these laws, *and* we will often be able to anticipate the *character* of the next trend in social mood, *and* we will have a few very important, even crucial, insights about coming events, *but* there is no way we will know everything, or even most things, about the specific product of those laws. Similarly, we might be able to predict the conditions that will produce a jungle or a desert, and we might even be able to guess quite a few particulars thereof, but we cannot predict the future of every plant or the

shifting of every sand dune. This degree of forecasting ability with the Wave Principle reflects what Yale professor of applied physics Roderick V. Jensen, in contrast to most of his colleagues, says is true of all chaotic systems:

> Chaotic dynamical systems are also like football games. Even with the largest imaginable digital computer, you could not predict the outcome with certainty.... Because of the complexity and unpredictability of chaos, direct numerical simulations of football games and turbulent flows are likely to remain impractical with even the largest supercomputers. *However, we can nevertheless compute reliable odds or probabilities for the outcomes of these processes.*[24]

Very recent work by Sornette and Johansen, published just months ago, supports this view. These authors call the stock market "a dynamical out-of-equilibrium...complex system," the same system that the legion of writers cited earlier say cannot be predicted at all. Yet they come to a rare conclusion:

> Crashes have their origin in the collective "crowd" behavior of many interacting agents.... The underlying cause of [a] crash must be searched years before it is in the progressive accelerating ascent of market price[s].... The origin of crashes is...constructed progressively by the market as a whole. The main point of this paper is that the market anticipates the crash in a subtle self-organized and cooperative fashion, *hence releasing precursory "fingerprints" observable in the stock market prices.*[25]

In other words, there is an element of predictability in markets not despite their complexity but because of it.[26] This conclusion is along the lines of Coveney and Highfield's hesitant observation that "work... [involving]...evolutionary and nonlinear principles...provides all-important evidence that the complex behavior of financial markets *is* predictable to some extent."[27]

I see no reason why this view should be so tentatively advanced. Nature's laws generally produce predictable results, yet most scientists currently believe that complexity (1) is controlled by laws and (2) produces utterly unpredictable results. I believe that this view must be modified. Systems that follow patterns are in fact highly predictable, within limits and in terms of probabilities. Ultimately, then, we can say that *laws of formological systems* lead to *utterly predictable results* within the confines of *probability statements*. That is how I view the Wave Principle, and its successful application in that light bears out that view.

Indeed, does it make sense that scientists quickly and emphatically posit randomness in any process for which we have yet to discover a law that applies? The word "universe" means "one order." So many assumptions of randomness have been disproved over the centuries and particularly over the past two decades that perhaps we would do better to begin with the opposite assumption. That is what Elliott did in his first published words about the stock market:

> No truth meets more general acceptance than that the universe is ruled by law. Without law, it is self-evident there would be chaos, and where chaos is, nothing is.... Very extensive research in connection with...human activities indicates that practically all developments which result from our social-economic processes follow a law that causes them to repeat themselves in similar and constantly recurring serials of waves or impulses of definite number and pattern.... The stock market illustrates the wave impulse common to social-economic activity.... It has its law, just as is true of other things throughout the universe.[28]

To put it in modern terms, there is no "butterfly effect" in social mood. There is no hurricane or earthquake effect. There is no peace or war effect. There is no exogenous effect, period. Social mood is formological, not reactive. On the other hand, minute details of the tangible actions that *result* from social mood are nearly infinitely variable and may indeed be subject to a butterfly effect. For instance, the precise outcome of a negative social mood manifestation such as war may depend upon whether there is a fog over the English Channel or whether the leader of one side is visited by a pneumonia bacterium.

The Value of Forecasting with the Wave Principle

With the caveat of immense specific variability within the known aspects of the Wave Principle, it is still the case that the practical value of all we know about it is immense. The first fantastic value that the Wave Principle provides is an amazing *perspective*, as you can see in Chapter 5. The second value is an occasionally remarkable *accuracy*, as you can see in Chapter 6. The third great value is that it provides a basis for assessing the past and analyzing the present in a *consistent context*, to which all the predictive literature on the subject attests. Finally, the Wave Principle indicates in advance the relative *magnitude* of the next period of social progress or regress. With all these gifts, we have a basis for informed, truly rational decision-making with regard to anticipating the tenor of future events. Its very nature forces us to look at the big picture, elevating our perceptions

above the cacophony of daily news and providing the opportunity to make sense of the great social trend changes and the dramatic events that accompany them. As a result, the Wave Principle provides a basis for achieving a great sense of calm about the future, which no longer appears as a black cloud of unknowable chaos (sometimes just a grey cloud of partly knowable chaos).

The *general results* of social mood, i.e., economic trends, political trends, peace and war, etc., are fairly easy to predict, as they follow what has already occurred in social mood. Predicting social mood trends themselves, and their immediate reflectors such as stock index trends, fashion and entertainment trends, etc., is more difficult, but the Wave Principle at least provides a basis for doing so. With knowledge of how the patterns unfold, to the extent of our ability, effort and emotional detachment, we can enjoy success even at that daunting task.

Because the Wave Principle describes patterns of collective behavior, the accuracy of any resulting forecast depends upon (1) the reliability of the investing crowd's behavioral patterns and (2) the ability of an analyst to identify the relevant ones properly. In fact, the patterns, while varied, are more than reliable; within the bounds of their definitions, they are inviolate, a characteristic that makes wave analysis incalculably superior to other methods. An analyst's ability to identify the relevant patterns, interpret them properly and anticipate the ones to follow is another matter. *That* task is exceedingly difficult. Nevertheless, even on that score, the Wave Principle provides some advantages that most forecasting methods lack. For instance, it provides a method of conceiving and then ranking alternative scenarios. Perhaps most important, the Wave Principle provides a built-in mechanism for changing one's mind. The ultimate determinant of the objective analyst's opinion is the *market itself*, not a presumption about outside causes. This approach provides an objective basis for staying in tune with the developing trends and for changing one's opinion when necessary.

Social forecasting is an ability that has deftly eluded man throughout his existence and indeed has been considered as impossible as a perpetual-motion machine. The Wave Principle changes all that. Because of it, we finally have a way to forecast much about our social future, not with magic or revelation or astrology or sorcery or voodoo or mindless linear extrapolation, but with science.

Coveney and Highfield assert, quite generously given the state of conventional economics, that "economics straddles the divide between science

and the humanities." With the Wave Principle, economics is now science, and with socionomics, even the humanities are tools of science.

The Role of Percepts in Forming an Accurate Concept of Human Social Behavior

Some critics quickly presume that the Wave Principle is "based on" a mathematical model. Others presume it was "derived from" a grand analogy to nature's processes. Both of these assumptions are utterly false. If either were true, then the risk of preconception, and thus of theory shaping observation, would be real. But the patterns were uncovered empirically with no preconceived notions whatsoever along either of those lines, which fact the literature proves unequivocally. Thus, the discovery of the Wave Principle *began* with percepts and it can be *reduced* to percepts. At bottom, we can point and say, "*Look.*"

This fact is diametrically opposed to most of what passes for macro-economic analysis, which too often advances formulas and theories irrespective of observation. For instance, in literally hundreds of instances, the media have reported an economist saying (usually when the stock market is down for a few weeks) that "the wide and widening U.S. trade deficit is bad for the economy and bearish for the market." It sounds logical at first blush, but look again at Figure 19-3. What do you *see*? You see that the trend of the trade deficit has waxed and waned in *precisely the opposite way* from what the theory presumes. *So what are you going to believe, a logical assertion, or your eyes?*

On this crucial question rests your chance for success. In the case of the trade deficit, the wrong answer *is* logical. If so, how can it be wrong? It can be wrong if the premise behind the logic is false. In this case, that is a fact that one can discern simply by looking. Your eyes come first.

What do you think happens when you show that graph to someone who believes otherwise? He evades it. He does not comment. He will not accept that trees are green if he thinks they should be blue. Paradox stymies him instead of igniting his mind to inquire. As Stephen M. Goldfeld once noted, "An economist is someone who sees something working in practice and asks whether it would work in principle."[29] More accurately, a conventional economist is often someone who sees something working in practice yet rejects its validity because it does not fit his model. As financier Mike Epstein jokes, "To an economist, real life is a special case."

Even if a conventional sociologist cannot see why something is true, he *must* place his perceptions of reality above his conceptions. Suppose an economist were confronted with the question of what would be the result of action by political forces to reduce the trade deficit by forcibly curbing imports or subsidizing exports with tax money. If he believes his eyes, he would conclude, even if he does not know why, that such actions might damage both the markets and the economy. Indeed, they would. So percepts can be valuable to economists in heading off political catastrophe, even if the mechanisms are not immediately clear. The great value in according importance to percepts is that they force you to examine and reshape your concepts until they conform to reality.[30]

It is on the question of perception vs. presumption that your assessment of the Wave Principle will depend. You have no choice if you are a scientist, but that does not mean it is easy. As the great A. Hamilton Bolton remarked about wave analysis, "The hardest thing is to believe what you see."[31]

While percepts are the bedrock of understanding aggregate financial behavior, the Wave Principle has a grand conceptual model as well, which was developed from those percepts. That is the essence of science, and we in this fledgling field are doing our inadequate best to perform it.

The Compatibility of Socionomics with Good Science

Socionomics has all four qualities that a science should possess. *Parsimony*: Human social mood follows the Wave Principle, which is succinctly represented in Figure 1-4. *Generality*: Socionomics subsumes all the social sciences as well as the character of the humanities. *Consilience*: Socionomics is compatible with, and derives from, the natural sciences. *Predictiveness*: Socionomics allows for better social prediction than any extant method.

Still lacking is the establishment of a *demonstrable, direct causal chain* linking the Fibonacci aspects of biology to those of sociology. We have only the strong hints of their consistency, as detailed in Chapters 3, 11 and 12. Furthering this understanding is the province of natural scientists.

The Necessity and Goodness of Waves

Some people react to the Wave Principle with annoyance because it challenges the idea that men, through government or some other agency, can control collective behavior and the social future. They are sure that the

government can "engineer" a recovery; they are certain that the central bank can "fine-tune" the money supply; they hope that cash infusions will "jump-start" a foreign economy. All of these beliefs are false.

However, the truth is actually more comforting. No, we cannot direct our social future, but the wild ride that we experience as a species is characteristic of systems that survive, grow and prosper. Ilya Prigogine won a Nobel Prize for discovering a most amazing fact: that ordered complexity and life *necessarily* arise in open systems. Entropy is not an antagonist in this arrangement but a partner, as the system takes in energy and exports entropy to the larger environment. The structures that dissipate entropy "are created by and thrive in a far-from-equilibrium, high-energy, unstable, even volatile environments,"[32] such as the stock market, such as society, such as life on earth. Says Michael Hutchison in *Megabrain*,

> Prigogine's vision of a universe of dissipative structures replaces the mechanistic view of a cosmos of "things" with a cosmos of *"process"*...[that is] unpredictable, self-organizing and evolutionary...*characterized by a series of leaps and bounds, or discontinuities*, rather than a gradual, incremental progression.... Prigogine's ideas...demonstrate that *periods of instability, perturbation, upheaval, collapse and chaos* are not to be seen as absolute evils *but instead as absolute necessities*, as phases through which every structure must pass *in order to evolve to higher levels of complexity....*[33]

This is an excellent description of both the style of progress under the Wave Principle and its message for mankind. It means that the type of behavior that the Wave Principle describes as the engine of the human social experience is both *necessary* and *good*, whether we happen to like its current expression or not. "Civilization," said Elliott, "rests upon change."[34] Philosophers from Lao Tzu and Heraclitus to Nietzsche and Goethe have celebrated opposing forces, strife, struggle, and cycles of creation and annihilation, all of which are different terms for the same underlying succession of change that is the secret engine of natural progress. The Wave Principle says that these philosophers' vague perceptions were correct. Even more valuable, it gives us a visual depiction of the form and progression of those opposing forces so that such philosophers' perceptions and sentiments no longer have to be vague.

Measured, recurring corrections of social trends are part of the natural robust fractal order of things. They have a purpose and are good, or they would not exist. Because human progress takes place in a "three steps for-

ward, two steps back" manner, it is clear that the "two steps back" are required to put psychology and motivation in a condition to support the next geometric rise in material, social, cultural and intellectual progress. As implied in Chapter 13, corrections may be part of the mechanism of life itself. The very ultimate success of life may depend upon the occasional weeding out of those not intelligent enough to prepare, strong enough to fight, benevolent enough to avoid participating in the destruction of others, or unlucky enough to be in the wrong place at the wrong time. Yet, although we now know for a fact that the preservation and flourishing of living systems requires setbacks and calamities, the Wave Principle further communicates that such setbacks are only *partial* and that *the long-term trend is ever upward*. This knowledge is a welcome comfort in difficult times.

The Goodness of Socionomics

Socionomics allows us to understand and purge from our minds dangerous conceptual errors. An example is the idea that war creates prosperity. Now, if you really stop to think about it (ten seconds should suffice), you might conclude that any activity that destroys thousands or millions of lives and obliterates billions of dollars worth of property would actually be destroying prosperity, not creating it. In fact, that is exactly what war does. Unfortunately, the erroneous premise of event causality is so entrenched in economists' and historians' minds that the vast majority of them agree that war "stimulates the economy." How do they come to such a bizarre, even evil, conclusion? Simple: During wars, the downtrend in social mood that caused the war typically reverses, and production tends to rise along with the new uptrend. Economists presume that this chronology means causality. *Post hoc ergo propter hoc.*

Here is an actual and typical summary of prevailing economic wisdom: "World War I provided a quick fix to the economy.... If there ever was a great war for the economy, it was World War II.... The Vietnam War was at first positive in its economic effect...but impacted adversely on inflation...."[35] These are the views of an economic historian at The American University from an article entitled, "Is War Good For the Economy?" Having read statements like these countless times, I know that such notions are nearly unanimous among economists.

With the science of socionomics, we can understand that war is simply a social act that follows and expresses a negative social mood. It comes long after the onset of a major corrective wave because it takes that long

for people to become angry enough to want to go to war and then arrange actually to wage one. The uptrend in mood that follows and the economic expansion that results are natural and unrelated to whether war actually breaks out. To put it in value-related terms, war is the result of negatives, not the cause of positives.

The value and goodness of this knowledge are immense. On the one hand, you have a socionomist who advises, "War is the result of a negative social psychology, which is why it occurs near the end of bear markets. I counsel you in such environments to watch potential enemies closely, particularly those whose societies have succumbed most thoroughly to the forces of the negative social mood. I also counsel you to beware the domestic impulse to wage war and do what you can to divert it. After all, war is *a bad thing* that should be avoided if it can be." On the other hand, you have a conventional economist who advises, "The economy tends to pick up during or after wars, so war must create economic expansion. If you want to pull this country out of recession, use every means, secret and overt, to insinuate your nation into a war. After all, net-net, war is *a good thing* that should be used to advantage." Who would you rather have advising your nation's leader or advising a rival country's leader when its economy is weak?

As related in Chapter 16, Adolf Hitler assumed the reins of power in 1933 as a result of the most extremely negative social sentiment in nearly a century. Stock markets around the world soared from that point forward, never seeing the level of those lows again. Following conventional assumptions and logic, an economist is forced to conclude that Adolf Hitler was *a good thing* for stocks and the world economy. A socionomist says that Hitler was put in power as a result of the most negative social psychology since 1859, which was *a bad thing*. Which explanation makes sense? Which explanation is *good*?

Determinism or Free Will?

It has been proposed that the novelty and diversity of nature are such that nature can be viewed as *self*-determined, as if it had free will.[36] It appears more accurate to say that nature's growth patterns are robust but deterministic, conforming without digression to waves, branches, spirals, or some other like expression of an underlying (apparently Fibonacci-based) fundamental form. The robustness of these patterns produces immense diversity. That diversity is (at least presently) unpredictable in terms of precisely forecasting all, or even many, specific attributes of the particu-

lars. Still, unpredictability is not the same as saying that nature has a free will to do what it likes.

It is similarly clear that *collective systems do not possess or exercise free will.* Referring to the expansions and failures of publicly traded companies, *New Scientist* says that Eugene Stanley "has found power laws...even in systems in which the units have 'free will.'"[37] Quotation marks notwithstanding, if a system follows a power law, it is unlikely to be exercising free will. The dynamics of *aggregations* such as corporations, governments and societies are primarily determined by herding, which is impulsive and impelled by paleomentation. Certainly individuals at the head of such enterprises exercise great influence, but who chooses to put those particular individuals in such positions? The group does. They are appointed by boards, elected by voters or emerge as popular heroes. Their apparent power is actually a reflection of their ability to satisfy collectives of employees, customers or voters. This observation is compatible with Stanley's results; groups and societies are what the Wave Principle addresses. As the product of collectives dependent upon the public, corporate histories are exactly where we would expect power laws and the Wave Principle to show up. The Wave Principle form shows that a collective system is, like nature overall, robust but deterministic.

An individual man, on the other hand, does have the faculty of decision-making, conscious choice and an independent will to act in many, perhaps even most, matters. Free choice is a gift of the independent neocortex,[38] which can mull, consider and choose. Philosophically, there is no other rational position possible, as a full determinist has no business trying to convince anyone of anything. If he believes all thoughts are determined, then so are his and mine, so what is the point of discussion? The very presentation of his argument negates the argument.

The capabilities of a man's independent conscious mind include the potential to understand, recognize and to some degree mitigate or overcome some of the impulsive forces of his unconscious mind. While the Wave Principle structurally restricts the number of possible outcomes of *social* trends, it leaves the individual free, if he understands that the structure exists, to work to avoid to some degree his own tragic and/or comic unwitting participation in those trends. Indeed, he can sometimes profit from them. How can you succeed at this task?

As Francis Bacon explained, "Nature cannot be ordered about, except by obeying her." The tenor of the social future is like a law of physics; it

cannot be ordered about. But you *can* manipulate your place in that future if you understand the forces at work. Knowledge of the Wave Principle dynamic is the only reliable basis upon which you can rise above the crowd and think, and act, independently of it. If you have the mental fortitude to do so, you can act independently of prevailing social illusions and resist being swept along by the social pressure to conform that they exert. Indeed, you can take advantage of the patterns of human sociology not only to survive but also to prosper. You can put yourself in a position to observe the crowd and thereby avoid or even profit from its excesses rather than become a part of it.

Unfortunately, independence is excruciatingly difficult for most people to assert in socially charged situations because the effects of the patterns are so pervasive and the power of the unconscious so strong. Hope, fear, denial and inertia are all part of the process. It is work to exercise and train your neocortex to overcome these influences and act independently. The number of consistently successful traders and investors is infinitesimally small compared to the total number of participants in markets. Indeed, after creating a valid method for market analysis, the main secret that successful professional traders (who are exceptionally rare people) learn through constant repetition of experience is how to resist or ignore emotional input from their limbic systems so as to allow their reason to prevail. This takes much time and practice, and even then, there is no guarantee that one's constitution can continuously take the heat.

Nevertheless, each person must do it to the extent possible. Living in harmony with social trends can make the difference between a happy, successful life and one in which time is spent futilely fighting the underlying tide. Failing to prepare for the next major trend can mean losing the opportunity of a lifetime, or it can be ruinous, and not only financially, but at times physically as well. At crucial turning points, an individual can act independently of the social flux if he has the knowledge and the will to do so. The rest of the time, he can hop aboard social trends and harness their power to his advantage. As the Easterners say, "Follow the way." As the Westerners say, "Don't fight the tape." In order to heed these nuggets of advice, however, it is necessary to know what is the Way, and which way the tape. There is no better method for answering that question than the Wave Principle.

NOTES

1 Pugsley, J. (1995). "Anthology of essential articles." *John Pugsley's Journal*.

2 Fad products such as art, fashion clothes, baseball cards, Pet Rocks, Cabbage Patch Kids, Beanie Babies, President Kennedy's golf clubs, etc., may be tangible, but they are not utilitarian. They satisfy intangible desires, thus fluctuate in price according to the Wave Principle rather than the law of supply and demand. Some such products can actually become viewed as investments, not goods, at which time they typically soar in price and then collapse.

3 Laderman, J. and Pennar, K. (1988, October 17). "Did the crash make a dent?" *Business Week*, p. 88.

4 I don't have the date, just the clipping. As the comment is so generic, I have not gone to the trouble to pinpoint this reference.

5 Rynecki, D. (1998, June 15). "Bull markets susceptible to anxieties." *USA Today*.

6 Henry, D. (1998, October 9). "High stakes guessing game: markets defy easy answers." *USA Today*.

7 Le Bon, G. (1895). *The crowd*.

8 Shomali, H.B. (1995, Winter/Spring). "Technical versus fundamental analysis: a view from academe." *MTA Journal*.

9 Caldarelli, G., *et al.* (1997). "A prototype model of stock exchange." *Europhysics Letters*, 40 (5), pp. 479-484.

10 Buchanan, M. (1997, November). "One law to rule them all." *New Scientist*.

11 Davies, P. (1988). *The cosmic blueprint — new discoveries in nature's creative ability to order the universe*.

12 Casti, J. (1997, April 19). "Flight over wall street." *New Scientist*.

13 Lesmoir-Gordon, N. (Producer). (1994). "Fractals: the colors of infinity."

14 Peters, E.E. (1991, March/April). "A chaotic attractor for the S&P 500." *Financial Analysts Journal*.

15 Sherden, W. (1998). *The fortune sellers*.

16 Davis, D. (1990, April 23). "Butterfly flap: chaology says no to market timing." *Dick Davis Digest*, Vol. 8, No. 190.

17 Liscio, J. (1998, March 2). "The seer syndrome." *Barron's*.

18 Popper, K.R. (1957). *The poverty of historicism*.

19 Reference unavailable.

20 Tindol, R. (1989, December 11). "Vanguard of a new approach to physical sciences." *On Campus*.

21 Sherden, W. (1998). *The fortune sellers*.

22 Gleick, J. (1985, December 8)."The man who reshaped geometry." *The New York Times*.

23 Crutchfield, J.P., *et al.* (1986, December). "Chaos." *Scientific American*, pp. 46-57.

24 Jensen, R.V. (1987, March-April). "Classical chaos." *American Scientist*, Vol. 75.

25 Sornette, D. and Johansen, A. (1997, November 1). "Large financial crashes." *Physica A – Statistical and Theoretical Physics*. This study cites *Elliott Wave Principle* as a source.

26 *Business Week* ran an article in its November 2, 1992 issue with this headline: "Chaos hits wall street — the theory, that is; an arcane market system is making waves." Well, this is cutesy, but perhaps in a few years, it will be inverted to read, "Waves are making over chaos theory."

27 Coveney, P. and Highfield, R. (1995). *Frontiers of complexity*.

28 Elliott, R.N. (1938). *The wave principle*.

29 Goldfeld, S.M. (1984, November). "Modeling the banking firm." *Journal of Money, Credit and Banking*, p. 611.

30 Let me provide an example in an unrelated area. A member of my family suffered from terrible migraines as a child. After studying the literature, we began looking for possible "triggers." To that end, we kept a diary of everything the child did, looking for triggers in food, sleep, stress, etc. The search appeared fruitless, as we found nothing preceding the migraines that correlated with them. Would the child have to eliminate *every* food and activity that preceded the migraines? That might be the answer of a conventional analyst who knows that outside cause must precede internal result. One day when reviewing the diary, I saw a consistent correlation between the migraines and events that happened *afterward*. Now, according to the conventional premise, any such correlation would be impossible. How could an event following a migraine trigger it? I had a choice. I could take the percept seriously or insist that it be coincidence because it did not appear to fit the model. Because I took the better route, this percept led me to the correct concept and therefore to a solution. I noticed that the events following migraines always involved some kind of responsibility on the part of the child. Ultimately, I realized that the trigger for each migraine was the child's realization that directly ahead lay a stressful situation. Coming down with a migraine was a way to escape it. The child's *fears* preceded the migraines, but *events* followed them. This realization led us to a happy resolution to the crisis.

31 Bolton, A.H. (1960). *The Elliott wave principle—a critical appraisal*.

32 Hutchinson, M. (1987). *Megabrain*.

33 *Ibid.*

34 Elliott, R.N. (1940). "The basis of the wave principle." Republished: (1994). *R.N. Elliott's Masterworks — The Definitive Collection*, p.192.

35 DiBacco, T. (1990, August 24). "Is war good for the economy?" *Fort Myers News-Press.*

36 Jantsch, E. (1980). *The self-organizing universe.*

37 Buchanan, M. (1997, November 8). "One law to rule them all." *New Scientist.*

38 One of the areas of the brain responsible for some aspects of free will "appears to be located within or at least close to the anterior cingulate sulcus, on the inside of a fold of the cerebral cortex." [ref: Wilson, E. (1998). *Consilience*, p. 108]

Chapter 21:

The Kitchen Sink: Linking Physics to the Human Social Experience, A Principle Behind Ordered Complexity, Hints of Robust Fractals in the Heavens, the Fibonacci Foundation of Robust Forms, and Phimation as an Opposing Principle to Entropy

At the risk of going overboard, I will nevertheless take one more step. Put succinctly, I believe that we can link the Wave Principle to all of nature in a grand underlying theme.

The Wave Principle in Nonliving Processes?

Scientists see so much in the way of shared mathematics and behavior in living and nonliving systems that they are beginning to question whether there is that big a dividing line between life and nonlife; the continuum is smoother than they thought.[1] The Belousov-Zhabotinski (BZ) chemical reaction pulses like life. It also produces spiral waves that resemble the muscles in the heart and the electrical activity within our brains. Fire is animated, consumes organic material, and exudes waste. Water self-organizes into crystals when it is frozen, and silicone oil self-organizes into cells when it is heated, much in the way that the cells of slime molds self-organize into a super-organism when challenged for food or in the way that conditions on earth a few billion years ago appear to have been conducive to the self-organization of amino acids that are the foundation of life. Like

living entities, inanimate entities produce spirals (galaxies and hurricane clouds) and arbora (river systems and chemical deposits). Can they produce Elliott waves as well?

Figure 21-1 shows the absorbance by cement slurry of each wavelength of infrared light, a property that is important for timing the hardening of cement for oil-well drilling operations. Why such a relationship should have *fluctuations* in it I have no idea, but those fluctuations do produce a pattern that I can label as Elliott waves. Wave 4 even falls to the territory of wave four of 3, following typical wave behavior. The entire plot even channels well on semilog scale (not shown). Whether this actually *is* an Elliott wave, as opposed to random data that happen to mimic one, I hesitate at this time to say.

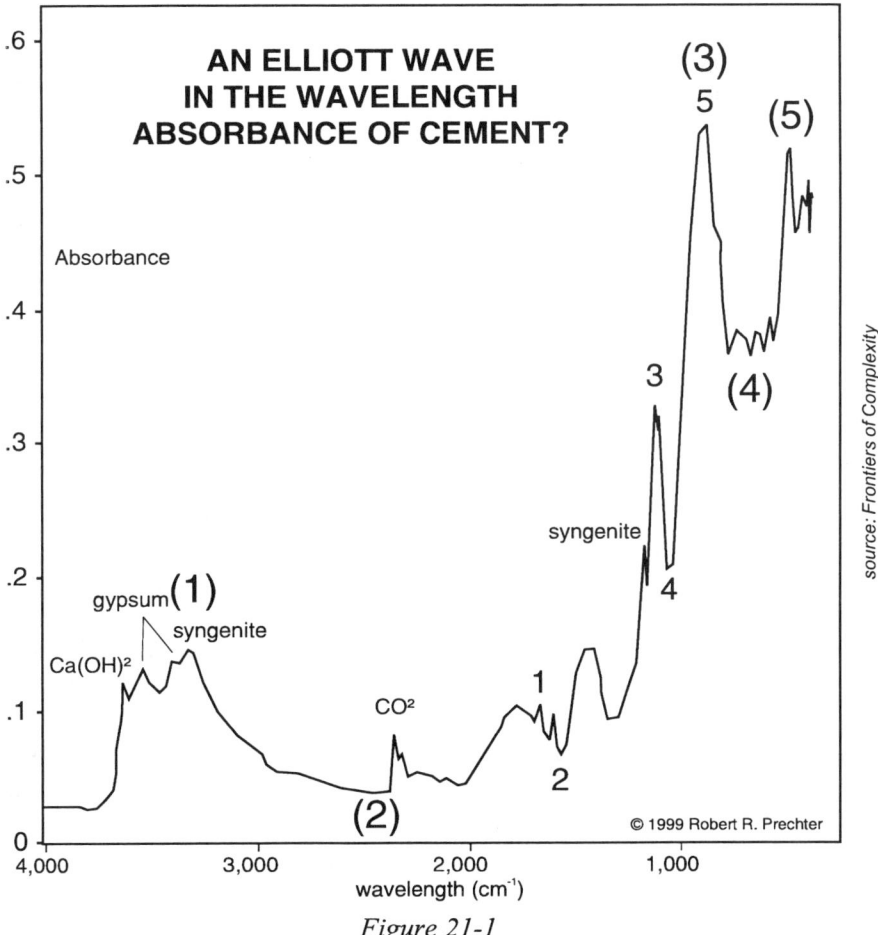

Figure 21-1

If inanimate processes such as this do produce waves, they would not be expected to compound for as long a time as waves of life. They would form what we call in commodity markets "contained waves,"[2] which need not build to ever loftier heights. The difference between commodity markets and the stock market is that stock market valuation reflects a phenomenon of persistent growth, while commodity prices need not.[3] The same difference undoubtedly applies to natural processes of life in general vs. natural processes of nonlife, which is why waves of the two would be expected to differ in this way. If Bak's sandpile (see below) were fed grain by grain forever, it would be an *unnatural* nonliving process that mimics life in its aspect of receiving a continuous input of energy. As a result, it would undoubtedly manufacture larger and larger avalanches the higher the pile extends, just as social man is doing.

On the slim evidence of Figure 21-1, I am hesitant to make one more suggestion, but will do so anyway. As postulated in Chapters 3 and 12, Fibonacci mathematics may come into play when nature constructs arbora, waves or spirals, whether living or not. It is also possible that the Wave Principle governs all kinds of self-organized dynamical systems that display fluctuation, i.e., active collectives of all types, whether they are living or not. To find out whether it does, we should investigate sandpiles, as well as rainfall, flooding and earthquake patterns, to see if they not only share with animate processes the properties of fractals, power laws, criticality and self-organization, but progress in Elliott waves as well.[4]

A Chain of Relationship From Physics to the Human Social Experience

"You can't extrapolate from physics or chemistry to human behavior," says Belgian theoretical chemist Ilya Prigogine, "but it is interesting to see the things they have in common mathematically."[5] It is particularly interesting to see what certain inanimate physical processes have in common with collective human mentation. For example, in studying sand piles, Bak and Chen found a phenomenon that I would characterize as very like herding behavior. Their machine dropped single grains of sand at regular intervals. A pile shaped roughly like a cone quickly developed. Then, at seemingly unpredictable times, a single grain added to the pile produced a slide of many grains down the side of the cone. As sand was added, the cone continued to grow. Landslides continued, and their sizes varied. Upon occasion, a particularly large slide occurred. Here is their summary of this behavior:

At criticality, the size of the landslide does not depend on the size or the number of new grains added. It depends on the holistic behavior of all the grains acting together. *The global behavior of the total pile transcends the behavior of the individual grains within it.* At criticality, every grain is interacting in complex ways with all its neighbors. *The motion of one grain on the slope can induce motion in thousands of others.*[6]

I would emphasize one implication in the above description. It is not only at criticality that the behavior of the sand pile is dependent upon the holistic behavior of all the grains acting together. It is just as true when sand grains hold each other up when the system is stable. Such interdependence holds true *all the time.* As I argued in Chapter 20, the ceaselessness of human interdependence and common influence persists whether the herd is excited and active or not. As it is with sand piles in this regard, so it is with plate tectonics, evolution and human social interaction.

Can we form a *chain of connection* linking physics and chemistry along a continuum all the way up to collective human mentation and activity? Stanley *et al.* relate the DLA model (see Chapter 3) to the underlying physical determinants of neuron growth (see Chapter 12):

The key point is that the growth follows rules that faithfully represent the solution of the equations for a diffusion-limited process, including the presence of stochastic noise. It has recently become established that the resulting clusters accurately describe a class of growth phenomena in which the diffusion equation or Laplace equation $\Delta^2 x = 0$ controls the essential physics. Thus growth phenomena governed by *chemical* gradients (in which case x is the concentration), by *electrical* gradients (x is an electrical potential), or by a *difference in viscosity* between the inside and outside of the pattern (x is the pressure) all are believed to be described by the DLA model. It is known that growing neurons respond to *chemical gradients* and *electric fields*, and it is also known that there is a *difference in viscosity* between the neuronal cytoplasm and the surrounding intercellular matrix. For this reason, it is not implausible that DLA might represent a zeroth order description of neuron growth.[7,8]

Since both the DLA model and neuron growth are suffused with Fibonacci properties, there must be Fibonacci-related forces hidden in the underlying physical processes of neuron formation. Hints of these forces may be found in Figure 2-26, which reveals a logarithmic spiral in the activity of sub-

atomic particles, in Figure 2-23, which reveals a Fibonacci spiral embedded in the quasi-crystal, and in Figure 21-1, which depicts a possible Fibonacci-based Elliott wave in the infrared absorbance of cement slurry. For the most part, it is only those natural processes related to growth/decay and expansion/contraction that appear to manifest Fibonacci properties. We may surmise, then, that Fibonacci-related forces hidden in physics exert themselves particularly when called upon to generate or regulate *expanding or growing forms, including all life forms.*

We know that fundamental patterns of nature relating to growth or expansion, in forms as diverse as galaxies, DNA, and the paths of subatomic particles, have Fibonacci properties. We know that chemistry, fluid dynamics and electricity are involved in shaping our neurons, which have Fibonacci properties. By linking these observations to the studies cited in Chapters 10 through 12, we have less to muse about *extrapolating* from physics and chemistry to human behavior and more to link them *directly.* Taken together, all the studies and conclusions cited in Chapters 2, 3, 10, 11, 12 and here do nothing less than connect, via *phi*, the *physics* and *chemistry* within the mind to its *biology* to its *perception* to its *mentation* to its *behavior*, both individually and collectively. If chemistry, electricity and fluid viscosity are responsible for forming and energizing neurons, and if neurons are responsible for carrying thought, and if human thought processes produce patterns of decision-making, and if decision-making produces the Wave Principle, and if all of them share Fibonacci properties, then we have established a chain of relationship from the behavior of elementary matter and energy all the way up to collective human mentation and, as we saw in Chapters 15 and 16, from there to its manifestation in human interaction and thus ultimately to the very path of human social progress.

One may speculate, though not assert, that as chemistry, fluid physics and electricity serve to organize and energize microstructures in the nervous system, their Fibonacci properties may actually *influence* the development of Fibonacci-related forms in those structures, which in turn may influence the development of Fibonacci-related processes within the neurology of living entities, which in turn influence their style of mentation, which in turn influence their product. Thus, we might speculate that there is a chain of influence deriving from the minutest forms of matter all the way up to the cultural progress of man.

While such a chain of causality is an attractive explanation for nature's larger structures and perhaps correct, I would leave open the possibility that virtually everything that grows or expands in nature has Fibonacci properties more because of a formological imperative that permeates everything that progresses rather than because of a linear chain of influence. Unfortunately, this type of thinking has little science behind it. It does have some philosophy behind it, but as we are coming to the end of this book, we will leave such speculations for another time.

A Principle Behind Ordered Complexity

How does the simplicity of 5-3 wave alternation give rise to the complexity of the human social experience? As scientists have been discovering lately, that is, generally speaking, the way that the universe works. Here is a pertinent section from a 1996 article in *The New York Times*:

> Last week in the journal *Nature*, scientists at the University of Texas and the University of Santiago in Chile described a remarkable experiment in which they tapped into nature's self-organizing flow. Jiggling a layer of sand at just the right rhythm caused patterns of circular peaks and craters to emerge. *Sometimes these vibrating structures — dubbed oscillons — joined to form larger patterns, which came together to form still more intricate designs.* The photographs of this naturally arising order call to mind the process of subatomic particles combining to form atoms, and atoms to form molecules and crystals – science's Great Chain of Being.
>
> It is hard not to let the imagination run wild. Could real particles – the quarks and leptons of particle physics – be created from the jostlings of some kind of incredibly tiny subatomic sand? With the right rhythms, could scientists jostle their sandboxes so that the "molecules" combined to form cells, and the cells joined with other cells to produce some weird artificial life?
>
> These are the kinds of speculative leaps you sometimes hear when hanging out with complexity theorists. But behind the fantasies is a serious, sober effort to understand one of science's most engaging mysteries: how order emerges in the world. Experiments like the one described in *Nature* show that masses of identical tokens (like the sand grains), *each capable of interacting only with its immediate neighbors*, can spontaneously generate intricate patterns. Then these patterns become tokens in another game, consorting with one another to form the next level in an intricate hierarchy. Simplicity gives rise to complexity.

Instead of grains of sand, think of neurons in a brain, each communicating only with its neighbors and yet generating the far-reaching patterns of thought. Or think of traders buying and selling, each of these purely selfish exchanges giving rise to the blind, overarching forces of the marketplace, Adam Smith's invisible hand. In all these examples, there is no need of a Grand Conductor, looking down from above and orchestrating the flow. The order bubbles up from below, as though something universal were going on.

Is there a parallel between sand grains cooperating to form oscillons and quarks cooperating to form the particles that form the atoms that form jaguars? Stuart Kauffman...[of] Sante Fe Institute believes that the laws we already know are not enough to understand these great towers of complexity. *Something extra is needed - a grand principle that would explain how order inexorably arises in the world.* In his view, it is not by chance that molecules in the primal sea came together to form the first self-reproducing cell, the grandparent of us all. *The chemistry was guided by yet-to-be-discovered laws of self-organization, laws that are as fundamental and irreducible as those of physics.*[9]

I believe that we have a piece of that "grand principle." The Wave Principle may not explain *how* ordered complexity arises in the world, but it certainly depicts at least one form of its progress. This chapter explores the idea that it operates "as though something universal were going on."

In Chapter 2, we noted the ubiquity of fractals, spirals and power laws in both animate and inanimate objects and systems. In 1970, Leo Kadanoff, then at Brown University, expressed an emerging realization that countless systems from magnetic to atomic to biologic can reach "critical states." He said that physical systems show "a kind of universal organization in which details of the original system get obliterated."[10] *What interacts doesn't matter. The simple fact of interconnection brings order and self-similarity all the way through the system.* This property is shared by both *animate and inanimate* systems. How far does this tendency permeate the universe?

Fractals and Degrees in the Heavens

Astronomers began realizing in the 1950s that the universe is patterned in a certain way. Stars cluster as constellations, constellations as galaxies, galaxies as superclusters. In the late 1980s, astronomers discovered a "super-supercluster."[11] Though the term was not in use at the time, it has become increasingly clear that the heavens are arranged as a fractal.

Is this an infinitely variable fractal, like a seacoast? No, there appear to be *distinct relative sizes to which we can attach names*, such as star, constellation, galaxy, cluster, supercluster and super-supercluster. In other words, the arrangement of matter in space may have the characteristic of specific *degrees*, just like arbora and the Wave Principle. Indeed, it is curious that the names chosen by astronomers are not unlike Elliott's nomenclature of degree: minor, intermediate, primary, cycle, supercycle, and grand supercycle. The astronomical arrangement of matter, it seems, has, in this regard, more in common with the robust fractals of waves and arbora than with the apparently indistinct relative scaling of seacoasts, clouds and mountains. Is there a more specific connection to robust fractals?

Arbora and Waves in the Heavens

In the past four years, two astrophysical theorists, armed with up-to-date observations of the universe, have proposed models that reflect not only fractals but waves as well. Stanford physicist Andrei Linde, in the November 1994 issue of *Scientific American*, proposes a "*self-reproducing inflationary universe* in which the universe is "a self-generating... growing...fractal that sprouts other inflationary universes." He says that the result "appears to be both chaotic and homogenous, expanding and stationary." Linde says that his model solves six of the main problems with the "big bang" theory, including the flatness of space, the size of the universe, the timing and speed of the expansion, and the uniformity of matter distribution. Linde adds that along with gravitational waves, density perturbations, which affect the distribution of matter in the universe, imprint upon the microwave background radiation in such a way as to be consistent with the "ripples in space," the "perturbations in temperature of the background radiation," found by the Cosmic Background Explorer (COBE) satellite. Now comes the interesting part from our point of view:

> One can visualize quantum fluctuations of the scalar field in an inflationary universe as *waves*. They first moved in all possible directions and then froze on top of one another. In some parts of the universe...these newly frozen waves increased the scalar field. Those rare domains where the field jumps high enough begin exponentially expanding....If the universe contains at least one inflationary domain of a sufficiently large size, it begins unceasingly producing new inflationary domains... producing a fractal-like pattern of universes....The total number of inflationary bubbles on our "cosmic tree" grows exponentially in time [and] indefinitely far away from the trunk of the tree (see Figure 21-2).[12]

Figure 21-2

Needless to say, a *self-generating growing fractal* that appears *both chaotic and homogenous, expanding and stationary* is equally a description of human progress according to the Wave Principle. The idea that it is based on *waves* makes the two concepts even more compatible.

Says Linde, "One can interpret each peak as a new 'big bang' that creates an inflationary 'universe.'" In the same way, under the Wave Principle, one can interpret each new peak in a wave, or each new trough, as a "big bang" that creates a new social "universe" of experience. That is why there are eras in human society, for instance, the roaring 'twenties, the depressed 'thirties, the warring 'forties, the conservative 'fifties, the exuberant 'sixties, the schizophrenic 'seventies, the bootstrap 'eighties and the speculative 'nineties. Each is its own temporary universe that leads at a sudden point of change to the next one.

Linde is not alone in the character of his ideas. The January 9, 1997 issue of *Nature* reports that astronomer Jaan Einsasto of the Tartu Observatory in Estonia, in cooperation with astronomers from other nations, has evidence that superclusters of galaxies are distributed not randomly, as astronomers have assumed, but in a sort of cosmic crystal on a "three-dimensional chessboard." If so, says the team, then it could only have happened if there is "*some hitherto unknown process that produces regular structure at large scales.*"[13] Could this presumed law of physics, this unknown ordering process, govern at *all* scales and pertain not only to the

universe itself but to countless processes within it? If so, it would be mightily compatible with the principle of waves discussed in this book. In fact, that is precisely the term that these astronomers use. Here is a report by *The New York Times*:

> Suspicions that there might be a pattern to these superclusters began to arise in the late 1980s. Looking out along a narrow line of sight in what is called a "pencil beam" survey, astronomers found that galaxies seemed to be bunched periodically, *as though stellar matter were somehow congealing on the crests of waves.*[14]

We are coming closer to an ordering principle in the distribution of matter in the universe. So far, we have evidence of *robustness, degree, arboration and waves*, four main aspects of the Wave Principle. Can we find the main determinant, *Fibonacci*?

Fibonacci in the Heavens

If Linde's description of the universe is accurate, then the universe is a branching structure. That branching structure could be an arborum. As shown in Chapter 3, arbora reflect *phi* both in the multiplication of their arba and in the most common angle of furcation, 36 degrees.

Behind Einasto's description of the arrangement of superclusters as being like "a cosmic crystal" lies the possibility that their arrangement may actually be like a *quasi*-crystal. In the early 1980s, Daniel Shechtman of Technion in Haifa, Israel, discovered a type of crystal that contains spiral arrangements and is governed by Fibonacci mathematics. Initially believed impossible, the quasi-crystal has been verified by photographs made with an electron microscope (see Figure 2-23). The quasi-crystal exhibits "five-fold symmetry," which means that a single rotation of the crystal exposed to an X-ray produces a symmetrical scattering pattern five times.

While these are pure speculations, there is some concrete evidence of Fibonacci mathematics at work in our solar system. The September/October 1989 issue of *Cycles* magazine reports that the solar sunspot cycle of 10.88 years is skewed in time so that the average time from maximum to minimum sunspot activity is 6.80 years and the average time from there back to maximum activity is 4.08 years.[15] The ratios of each phase to the whole cycle are .625 and .375, which are 5/8 and 3/8, ratios of Fibonacci numbers.[16]

While there is considerable latitude in the ratios (.547, .656, .724 and .536), it is also the case that the average mean ratios of the distances of adjacent planets among the first six planets from the sun, excluding the Mars/Jupiter relationship, is .615, the Fibonacci ratio. The Mars/Jupiter separation is so great as to imply by this numerology that there is a missing planet between them. That is where the asteroids are located. The Titius-Bode Law, developed in 1766, recognized these relationships and correctly predicted the position of the next planet, Uranus.

In 1986, *The New York Times* printed a picture of the ten-mile-long nucleus of Halley's comet.[17] An alert subscriber of mine[18] noted its skewed appearance, measured its two lengths and found that they are in Fibonacci relationship, as shown in Figure 21-3.

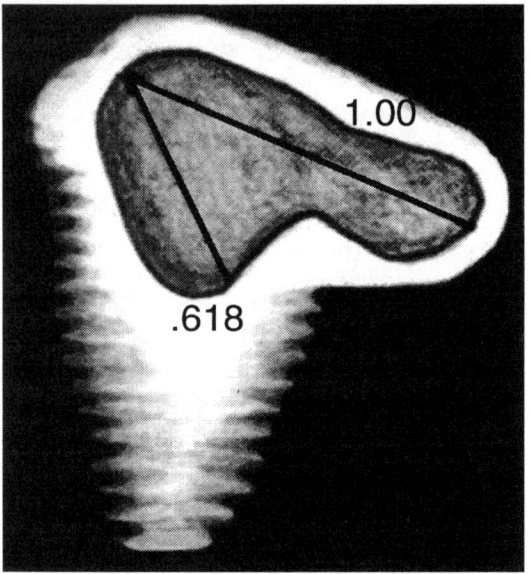

The phi *proportion in the nucleus of Halley's Comet*

Figure 21-3

The opposing polarities of the magnetism of solar wind may produce a "warped heliocentric current sheet" that serves as a boundary between the positive and negative sectors of the magnetic field. J.M. Wilcox and associates, in *Science* magazine, describe this sheet as a logarithmic spiral structure, as reproduced in Figure 21-4.[19]

source: Cycles Magazine, May/June 1983, Vol. 34, #4, p.107

Logarithmic spirals in the heliocentric current sheet

Figure 21-4

A Hint of the Universe in the Mind

If, as Prigogine and Vandervert assert (see Chapter 10), the mind is fractal and chaotic because the universe is fractal and chaotic, then the human brain and mind share fundamental aspects of form with the universe.[20] There is at least one aspect of astronomic behavior that reflects not just Fibonacci, but a specific expression of it that mimics the Fibonacci-weighted bipolar constructs of human mentation discussed in Chapter 12. The X-ray source MXB 1730-335, called the Rapid Burster, emits radiation in a quasi-periodicity. Dr. Lefebvre and Yuri N. Efremov of the Sternberg Astronomical Institute at Moscow State University have just reported that the two sets of overlapping frequencies produced by this irregular oscillation are related by *phi* both in terms of the frequency of the burst and the interval between them. Says their paper, "In sets of observations which give this ratio with a standard error equal to or less than 0.02, its average value is 1.61."[21] Both these and other astronomers have noted that the frequency system governing the output of the Rapid Burster appears at the beginning of the burst to "know how large the burst is going to be,"[22] much as a person must know at the beginning of a sentence what the entire sentence structure will be. Given the relationship of this phenomenon to

Lefebvre's work with bipolar mental constructs (see Chapter 12), he and Efremov conclude that this finding "opens the possibility of *an intrinsic similarity between the RB activity and human cognition.*" In Chapter 12, I linked the *phi*-based physical structure of neurons to *phi*-related electrical charges to the *phi*-based apparati and dynamics of perception to the *phi*-based product of mentation. Apparently, this link may carry to the behavior of the Rapid Burster.

All of these observations might be coincidence. However, the coincidences are piling up. Given the context of our discussion, these are far more than curiosities; they may pertain to the essence of universal arrangement. How universal is Fibonacci to compound arrangement?

Fibonacci as Fundamental to Robust Compounding and Subdividing Forms

Paul Steinhardt, a theorist at the University of Pennsylvania, along with several colleagues, postulates that the structure of a quasi-crystal is based upon the mathematics of "tiling," which involves the fitting together of geometric shapes to fill space. Roger Penrose has recently demonstrated that a plane can be completely covered using two specific types of rhombus-shaped tiles (see Figure 21-5). He found the astonishing fact that no pattern of tiles is ever exactly repeated, which means that patterns made by

source: Bull. Inst. Math. & its Appl., Vol.10

Figure 21-5

these two tiles are infinitely robust. *Infinite robustness within a process involving rigid restriction* is a property shared by arbora and Elliott waves, both of which are governed by Fibonacci. What governs Penrose's quasi-periodic tiling pattern? It turns out that both the *areas* of the tiles and therefore the *numbers* of the tiles in any given (large) area, are in *Fibonacci proportion*, the same proportion that governs both the numbers and sizes of motive vs. corrective Elliott waves. In addition, the *angles* of the rhombi are single, double, triple and quadruple multiples of 36 degrees, the ruling angle of the Fibonacci-based five-pointed star and of the DLA model of arboration discussed in Chapter 3.[23] This means that you can slide the 36 degree angle of one of Penrose's tiles into the nooks of the average arborum.

Hans C. von Baeyer points out in *Discover* magazine that the Penrose tiling scheme is very like the Fibonacci sequence itself in that it contains no repeating patterns and is generated by two simple rules.[24] It appears that when nature produces patterns with infinite variance, whether animate or inanimate, it utilizes, and probably must utilize, Fibonacci mathematics to do so. In other words, Penrose's tiles suggest that *phi* is a fundamental property of forms that are self-identical in some ways yet infinitely variable in others, i.e., robust forms.

Penrose's tiles support the applicability of the Fibonacci sequence to processes of structured yet infinitely variable *partitioning* and its inverse, structured yet infinitely variable *building*. Of course, the Wave Principle first suggested this idea, as Fibonacci governs both the partitioning of waves into components and the building of waves into larger and larger structures. This compatibility between Penrose tiles and Elliott waves suggests that the Fibonacci sequence is a mathematical principle that pertains not only generally to natural processes of growth and decay but also specifically to robust partitioned expansion.

The Universe and the Wave Principle

Taken together, these observations and theories make a tentative case that the universe produces *fractal waves of growth* that are governed by *Fibonacci*. What kind of wave system has fractal waves of growth governed by Fibonacci? Answer: the one described in this book. The Einasto team's description of the universe as a latticework structure governing a fractal arrangement of matter congealing on the crests of waves is very like R.N. Elliott's description of the stock market, which is a latticework structure governing a fractal arrangement of collective mentational changes and

trends that congeal in waves. The Lefebvre team's description of the Rapid Burster as representative of a Fibonacci aspect of human cognition supports R.N. Elliott's contention that collective human mentation follows a principle that is found throughout the universe. Is it reaching to propose that some fundamental Fibonacci form that underlies all robust fractals is at work in both cases, and probably in countless others? Says *The New York Times*,

> The Einasto study, involving a much wider sweep of the sky than the pencil-beam surveys, is harder to explain away. Maybe, back in the beginning, the dice were loaded. *As the universe was unfolding, some unknown ordering principle might have been at work.*[27]

If so, what is the nature of this "unknown ordering principle"?

The Fundamentality of Form

When Frost and I wrote *Elliott Wave Principle* in 1978, the first word in the book that we italicized was the word *form*. Waves are variable in terms of extent and duration, but they never terminate until they complete a certain *form*. The discovery of the Wave Principle is a tremendous breakthrough for many reasons, not the least of which is that it reveals the importance of form in human life. The apparent fundamentality of form prompted several writers in the 1920s to develop and expand upon a theory of "morphogenetic fields," which supposedly account for the development of physical forms in nature.[28] In 1981, Rupert Sheldrake, in *A New Science of Life*, argued that such fields actively transmit a memory from foregoing entities to new entities that are influenced by a field of the same "probability structure."[29] Regardless of whether such ideas are valid, it is easy to understand some men's *passion* to account for the importance of form. Central to morphogenetic hypotheses is the true (in my opinion) observation that *there is something of paramount importance in form as such.*

The importance of form in the universe has received too little attention from scientists. One reason why science has gravitated away from detailed descriptions of forms may be the intricacy and therefore the required observational meticulousness of the task. Says Jochen Bockmuhl, leader of the Nature/Science section of the laboratory at the Goetheanum in Dornach, Switzerland, "A science [that] would approach concrete realities demands a faculty of observation which is *at home on several levels* and requires constant practice."[30] Descriptions so developed do not begin conveniently with mathematics; they end with them. One way to discover

mathematical properties of nature, it seems to me, is with the most detailed empirically derived description one can create. That is how R.N. Elliott proceeded, and it led him to understand the underlying mathematics of financial markets. This approach also led Mandelbrot to understand the commonality of mathematics in fractals. Even in these fields, however, who on earth has studied minutely the patterns of lightning, rivers, blood vessels or coastlines as closely as R.N. Elliott studied the patterns in stock averages[31] or Goethe the patterns of plants?[32] The useful results of such undertakings should lead scientists to view such painstaking observation at least as a value, if not a fundamental one to science.

To find much serious thought about forms, we have to go all the way back to ancient Greece. Pythagoras saw the universe as a product of an underlying, ubiquitous mathematical order. Plato postulated archetypal forms that serve as generative *uber*models for less perfect and more variable forms that appear in nature. Aristotle saw form as a property that exists within, and determines the shape of, each individual entity.[33] These views are typically seen as opposing each other. While each of these men would probably argue well into the night about their differences, I think that *all* of them are correct: Order in the universe reflects the order of mathematics; growth in the universe is based upon a Fibonacci *uber*form that is ubiquitous and mathematically orderly; each entity deriving from that form contains within it the causal and variable instructions for its particular manifestation, which includes environmental adaptability.

Goethe, who may have discovered the Wave Principle in the progress of plant growth (see Chapter 13), also had something to say about the genesis and fundamental nature of form, as summarized in this description:

> Seeing that every part of the plant is a metamorphosis of the archetypal "leaf" organ, Goethe came to the conception of an *archetypal* plant, or *Ur-pflanze*, a supersensible force...which possesses within itself the capacity to take on manifold forms, and which at a particular time takes on that form which is best suited to the conditions of the external environing world.[34]

Goethe asserted that the sequence of development reflecting the Wave Principle that he described in plants "applied to everything living." Chapter 3 postulates that the primary patterns of natural growth and expansion — spirals, arbora and waves — are actually different expressions of a single underlying phenomenon of form, which is based upon *phi*. As Goethe's "archetypal plant" might behave somewhat like Linde's concept of the en-

tire universe, as shown in Figure 21-2, *we should not neglect to consider and pursue the possibility that this* phi-*based principle may apply to everything growing, whether alive or not.*

The Engine of Formation: *Phimation* Against Entropy

If any of this is true, how does it come about? The second law of thermodynamics states that heat always dissipates into the environment, ultimately making any closed system (one that has no outside source of energy) heat-homologous and therefore dead. Entropy is the unavoidable winding-down of energy differentials. Open systems (which enjoy an input of energy) are a different matter. As energy flows into an open system, complex systems come into being, grow and thrive. Prigogine argues that the immense dissipation of entropy propels the formation of expanding structures and systems from the cosmological to the living and even propels the evolution of laws of nature to accompany the evolving systems. (Earlier in time, he argues, there were no laws of planetary motion or biology, as there were no planets or life.) Because robust fractals are so common in such systems and so similar, there is probably a law of formative development that governs them. I would bet that if there is a *first* law of growing, expanding or striving structures, including (if Linde is correct) even the universe itself, its governing ratio is *phi*.

Perhaps we can speculate, with inspiration from Prigogine's elegant explanation of how order arises from chaos, that there may be some kind of universal *force* or *field* that impels what is essentially a *striving against entropy*. This formative law is governed by Fibonacci mathematics, which is why manifest forms of growth and expansion are as well. (If it is a force, its persistence would account for the increasing order and complexity of related systems. If it is a field, it must have the same positive relationship to *time* that a gravitational field has to *mass*, which would also account for the increasing order and complexity of related systems.) Fibonacci formation, or, for want of a better expression, *phimation*, then, may be *an opposing principle to entropy*. It is the yin of growth and progress that opposes the yang of dissolution and decay. From it would flow all the lesser laws that govern its expression in terms of robust structures such as spirals, arbora, waves and whatever other forms it may subsume. One could hardly depict the concept of a measured, regulated striving against entropy more elegantly than with an Elliott wave, as shown in Figure 1-5. The opposition of entropy and phimation, I contend, is the grand underlying theme of nature.

If it is not already blatantly evident, I will state here that these rumina-
tions derive from the furthest frontiers of my understanding and are far
from socionomics, the only field in which I claim expertise. That will not
stop me, however, from continuing.

A Principle of Universality

The Principle of Universality so far is only a hoped-for goal of being
able to model and understand all complex systems with one formulation. If
such a principle exists, it will unite the sciences and place many of the
processes of the universe under a single name. The "unknown ordering
principle" for which scientists are searching would have to pertain to far
more than "just" the ordering of the stars in the universe, the pulsing of the
sun or the arrangement of the planets in our solar system. It would have to
pertain to everything from subatomic particle behavior to the structure of
DNA to the essence of life to collective human behavior to the pattern of
the cosmos, the very processes shown in this book to be related. *New Scientist* sums up the view required to embrace universality:

> From earthquakes to evolution, the notion of universality lies be-
> hind theories that are adding an extra dimension to our understanding of
> the world. But the consequences of the idea may ultimately be far more
> profound. For hundreds of years, science has proceeded on the notion
> that things can always be understood — and can only be understood —
> by breaking them down into smaller pieces and by coming to know those
> pieces completely. Systems in critical states — and they seem to be plen-
> tiful — flout this principle. Important aspects of behavior have little to
> do with the detailed properties of their component parts. Organization in
> a magnet, a company or an ecosystem isn't down to the particles, people
> or organisms that make it up.... "Without universality," says James
> Crutchfield, a physicist at the University of California at Berkeley, "each
> and every complex system would be a discipline to itself, and the very
> enterprise of science would be doomed from the start." With it, there
> seems to be a basis for a true "theory of collectives" of all sorts.[35]

To sum up today's scientific view, then, there is a basis for saying that
there may exist a principle of collectives that underlies the self-organization of all self-organizing things, at all scales. This book says we have
more than hope for that principle; *we have one aspect of the principle itself*, a structural principle that combines Fibonacci and growth in a marriage
called the Wave Principle, which in turn may be a manifestation, like arbora

and other robust fractals, of a more fundamental principle of collectives that may be termed phimation. Look back at Chapter 13 and observe again that evolution follows the Wave Principle. Look back at Chapter 5 and observe again that the stock market follows the Wave Principle. Recall Chapters 10 through 12 and consider that the brain and mind have fractal and Fibonacci properties, the key aspects of the Wave Principle. Reread in Chapter 13 the description of individual life forms following the Wave Principle. Go back to Chapters 15 and 16 and observe again that social action and all of history are products of the Wave Principle. Look back at Figure 21-1 and recall that even inanimate processes might follow the Wave Principle. The Wave Principle is connected to every phenomenon discussed in this book, uniting them all. As early as 1940, R.N. Elliott had seen enough about his discovery of a structure behind "the various moods of human behavior" to assert that it had as its cause "the immutable natural law...of change... that governs all things."[36] In 1946, he titled the Wave Principle "Nature's Law." He was not overstating the case. If there is a principle of universality for collective action, or of progress against entropy, this may be it. At the very least, I believe, it is a manifestation of it.

NOTES

1 One difference between objects and growth processes may be that when dealing with objects, we can say that for every action there is an equal reaction; within growth processes, we may be entitled to say that for every action there is a .618 reaction!

2 See Chapter 6 of *Elliott Wave Principle.*

3 In times of fiat money, commodity prices do, however, inversely reflect the phenomenon of persistent decay in the value of the purchasing medium, which allows their waves to compound over many decades.

4 Here is an idea for two experiments. Treat earthquakes as corrections. That makes the impulsive component a measure of stress. Plot stasis as a continuing *uptrend in stress*, steady over time, and earthquakes as reactions. After two (or four, in an extension) reactions of approximately equal size, is the next one larger? After two (or four) of those, is the next one larger still? If so, we can begin to predict earthquakes. If not, fine. Earthquakes are not living growth patterns, so there is no compelling reason to insist that waves must be there. As a second experiment more closely related to an animated growing system, plot each added sand grain in Bak's sandpile as an uptrend in growth, and sandslides as corrections. Does the overall process create an Elliott wave?

5 Tindol, R. (1990, December 11). "Vanguard of a new approach to physical sciences." *On Campus.*

6 Bak, P. and Chen, K. (1991, January). "Self-organized criticality." *Scientific American*, pp. 46-53.

7 Stanley, H.E., *et al.* (1993). "Fractal landscapes in physics and biology." *Growth patterns in physical sciences and biology,* p.134.

8 In the authors' expressions of the equation, they use the letter ϕ to represent the variable. Since it has no Fibonacci denotation in this context, I have replaced it with x.

9 Johnson, G. (1996, September 8). "From grains of sand: a world of order." *The New York Times.*

10 Domb, E. and Green, M. (1971). "Critical behavior: universality and scaling." *Critical Phenomena*, Vol. 5, p. 100. Also, private communication.

11 Peratt, A.L. (1990, January/February). "Not with a bang." *The Sciences.*

12 Linde, A. (1994, November). "The self-reproducing inflationary universe." *Scientific American.*

13 Einasto, J., *et al.* (1997, January 9). "A 120-Mpc periodicity in the three-dimensional distribution of galaxy superclusters." *Nature.*

14 Johnson, G. (1997, January 19). "The real star wars: between order and chaos." *The New York Times*, p. 4.

15 Collins, C.J. (1989, September/October). "The effect of sunspot activity on the stock market." *Cycles.*

16 Thanks to EWT reader K. M. Manning for this insight.

17 (1986, November 1). *The New York Times*, p. 1

18 P. Kendrick of Falmouth, Maine.

19 Wilcox, J.M. (1980). "Origin of the warped heliospheric current sheet." *Science*, Vol. 209, pp. 603-605.

20 It may not be a new idea that the mind and the universe are reflections of each other. In ancient Egypt, the pharaoh Tutankhamen rested his head upon a curved alabaster pedestal. On each side was a figurine, one representing the guardian of the easternmost reach of the universe, the other the guardian of the westernmost. In the eyes of that culture, the mind of the pharaoh *was* the universe.

21 Lefebvre, V. and Efremov, Y. "Possible analogues of cognitive processes in the patterns of X-ray variability of the rapid burster" Astrophysical archive on the Internet (1998).

22 Kawai, N., *et al.* (1990). "Spectral evolution of type II bursts from the Rapid Burster." *Astronomical Society of Japan,* No. 42, pp. 115-133.

23 In viewing Penrose's pattern, one gets the distinct impression of a three-dimensional quality as if the pattern were a pile of regular and skewed cubes. Is the third dimension somehow a product of Fibonacci mathematics?

24 Von Baeyer, H.C. (1990, February). "Impossible crystals." *Discover.*

25 Johnson, G. (1997, January 19). "The real star wars: between order and chaos." *The New York Times*, p. 4.

26 For a history of these theories, see Rupert Sheldrake's book, *A New Science of Life.*

27 Sheldrake, R. (1981). *A new science of life.*

28 Bockemuhl, J. and Suchantke, A. (1995). "The morphic movements of plants as expressions of the temporal body." *The metamorphosis of plants.*

29 This time-consuming task was facilitated by the fact that Elliott was physically debilitated for half a dozen years by a disease that nearly killed him. He was forced to cease his previous substantial mobility, which apparently gave him immense time for quiet contemplation and study. For details of his life, see the biography in *R.N. Elliott's Masterworks.*

30 The rarity of Goethe's feat and approach is in keeping with the centuries-long direction of science away from studying forms and toward

studying components. Andreas Suchantke informs us that "Goethe's discovery of the metamorphosis of plants has, until very recently, provoked no new research of any depth. ...Science has followed a path of development so different from Goethe's methods that bridging the gap thus opened up is now well-nigh impossible." [ref: Bockemuhl, J. and Suchantke, A. "The metamorphosis of plants as an expression of juvenilisation in the process of evolution" and "The leaf: 'the true proteus'," from *The metamorphosis of plants.*] For those interested, this short book is an excellent series of treatises on the formative motions of plants.

31   These summaries are my interpretation of descriptions from only one source. If they are inaccurate in any way, please let me know.

32   Tompkins, P. and Bird, C. (1973). *The secret life of plants.*

33   Buchanan, M. (1997, November 8). "One law to rule them all." *New Scientist.*

34   Elliott, R.N. (1940, October 1). "The basis of the wave principle."

If you would like to learn more about various aspects of the Wave Principle as listed below, please read the publications cited hereafter.

More on socionomics:
Pioneering Studies in Socionomics (due in 2002)
Website (currently in development): **www.socionomics.org**

Details of the patterns, their application, and Fibonacci mathematics:
Elliott Wave Principle

Original exposition by, and a biography of, the Wave Principle's
discoverer: ***R.N. Elliott's Masterworks***

History of the principle's application:
R.N. Elliott's Market Letters
The Complete Elliott Wave Writings of A. Hamilton Bolton
The Elliott Wave Writings of A.J. Frost and Richard Russell

Related studies of the 1970s, 1980s and 1990s:
Market Analysis for the New Millennium

Financial and economic outlook for the 2000s and beyond:
At the Crest of the Tidal Wave
View from the Top of the Grand Supercycle
Conquer the Crash

Ongoing application to U.S. stock, U.S. bond, gold and silver markets:
The Elliott Wave Theorist
The Elliott Wave Financial Forecast

Ongoing application to all other markets:
(Request list from Elliott Wave International)

All books and periodicals listed above are available from
Elliott Wave International, Inc.

Mailing address: **P.O. Box 1618, Gainesville, GA 30503**
Phone: **800-336-1618, 770-536-0309**
Fax: **770-536-2514**
E-mail address for products: ***customerservice@elliottwave.com***
E-mail address for comments: ***bb@elliottwave.com***
Web site: ***www.elliottwave.com***

Sources

"16th annual American music awards." (1989, January 30). Dick Clark Productions, Burbank, CA.

"A dismal performance." (1982, January 18). *Business Week*, p. 124.

Abzug, Robert H. (1985). *Inside the vicious heart: Americans and the liberation of Nazi concentration camps*. New York: Oxford University Press.

Acker, Larry. (1998, August). "Why so bearish?" *3F Forecasts*. Vol. 12, No. 8.

Adams-Webber, J. and Benjafield, J. (1973). "The relation between lexical marking and rating extremity in interpersonal judgment." *Canadian journal of behavioral science*, Vol. 5, pp. 234-241.

Adams-Webber, Jack. (1997, Winter). "Self-reflexion in evaluating others." *American Journal of Psychology*, Vol. 1110, No. 4. pp. 527-541.

Ahuja, Anjana. (1998, June 29). "The nature of numbers." *The London Times*.

Alexander, Garth and Smith, David. (1998, September 27). "Fund crash took world economy to brink of collapse." *The London Times*.

Angrist, Stanley W. (1991, August 8) "Believers in one wave theory see U.S. in deep trough soon." *The Wall Street Journal*.

Arneodo, A., Argoul, R. Bacry, E., Muzy, J.F. and Tabbard, M. (1993). "Fibonacci sequences in diffusion-limited aggregation." *Growth Patterns in Physical Sciences and Biology*, edited by Juan Manuel Garcia-Ruiz, Enrique Louis, Paul Meakin and Leonard M. Sander. New York: Plenum Press.

Bak, Per and Chen, Kan. (1991, January) "Self-organized criticality." *Scientific American,* pp. 46-53.

Baker, Martin. (1995, October 7-8). "Investing: rhyme or reason?" *International Herald Tribune,* p. 6.

Ball, R. and Bartov, E. (1996, June). "How naïve is the stock market's use of earnings information?" *Journal of Accounting and Economics*, Vol. 21, No. 3.

Begley, Sharon, Service, Robert and Underhill, William. (1992, May 25). "Finding order in chaos." *Newsweek*.

Bell, E.T. (1936). *Men of mathematics*. New York: Simon & Schuster.

Bergamini, David and the editors of *Life*. (1963). *Mathematics*. New York: Time-Life Books.

Berreby, David. (1993, March). "Chaos hits Wall street." *Discover Magazine*.

Berry, John M. (1998, July 6). "Key players control money supply." *The Washington Post*.

Bigava, Z.I. (1979). "A character of setting effects in various moving problems." In: Nadirashvili, S.A. (Ed.), Voprosy Inzhenernoy I Socialnoy Psychologii (Problems of Human Factor and Social Psychology, in Russian), ii Tbilisi: Metsniereba.

Bion, Wilfred. (1952). "Group dynamics: a review." *International Journal of Psycho-analysis,* No. 33, pp. 235-247.

Bisher, Furman. (1984, November 17). "The Gator grail, the hallowed hall." *The Atlanta Journal-Constitution*.

Bishop, Jerry E. (1987, November 17). "Stock market experiment suggests inevitability of booms and busts." *The Wall Street Journal*.

Bockemuhl, Jochen and Suchantke, Andreas. (1995). *The metamorphosis of plants*. Capetown, South Africa: Novalis Press.

Bolton, Arthur Hamilton. (1953). "Elliott's wave principle." Supplement to *The Bolton-Tremblay Bank Credit Analyst*. Republished (1994). *The Complete Elliott Wave Writings of A. Hamilton Bolton*. Prechter, Jr., Robert Rougelot. (Ed.). Gainesville, GA: New Classics Library.

Bolton, Arthur Hamilton. (1960). "The Elliott wave principle — a critical appraisal." Supplement to *The Bolton-Tremblay Bank Credit Analyst*. Republished: (1994). *The Complete Elliott Wave Writings of A. Hamilton Bolton*. Prechter, Jr., Robert Rougelot. (Ed.). Gainesville, GA: New Classics Library.

Bradley, Mark. (1984, November 18). "At long last, Florida wins an SEC title." *The Atlanta Journal-Constitution*.

Brauchli, Marcus W. (1998, July 14). "Why the world bank failed to anticipate Indonesia's deep crisis." *The Wall Street Journal*.

Briggs, John and Peat, F. David. (1989). *Turbulent mirror*. New York: Harper & Row.

Briggs, John. (1992). *Fractals — the pattern of chaos*. New York: Simon & Schuster.

Brock, David. (1986, June 30). "Seeing the economy's future with a shattered crystal ball." *Insight*.

Brock, William A. (1991). "Causality, chaos, explanation and prediction in economics and finance." *Social Systems Research Institute,* No. 387, a publication of the University of Wisconsin – Madison.

Brock, William A., Lakonishok, Josef and LeBaron, Blake. (1992, December). "Simple technical trading rules and the stochastic properties of stock returns." *Journal of Finance,* Vol. 47, No. 5.

Brooks, Michael. (1997, October 18). "Boom to bust." *New Scientist*.

Browne, Malcolm W. (1997, April 15). "Variations in stride." *The New York Times*.

Browne, Malcolm W. (1989, September 9). "A new solid that matters." *Toronto Globe and Mail*.

Buchanan, Mark. (1997, November 8). "One law to rule them all." *New Scientist*.

Buettner, Michael. (1995). "An evolutionary model of market growth: the Elliott wave principle." Unpublished paper.

Butler, D. and Ranney, A. (1978). Referendums Washington, D.C., American Enterprise Institute for Public Policy Research.

Caldarelli, G., Marsili, M. and Zhang, Y.C. (1997, December 1). "A prototype model of stock exchange." *Europhysics Letters*, Vol. 40, No. 5, pp. 479-484.

"Call it a miracle, or call it a mystery, but black youths shunning tobacco." (1995, November 20). *The Wall Street Journal*.

Carson, Clarence B. (1990, December). *Basic economics*. Foundation for Economic Education.

Casti, John. (1995). *Complexification*. New York: Harper.

Casti, John. (1997, April 19). "Flight over wall street." *New Scientist Magazine*.

"Chaos under a cloud." (1996, January 13). *The Economist*.

Chapman, Toby. (1998, January-February). "Speculative trading: physicists' forays into finance." *Europhysics News*.

Church, A.H. (1904). "Phyllotaxis in relation to mechanical law." London: Williams & Norgate.

Collier, P.F. (1985). *Collier's photographic history of world war II*. New York: Bonanza Books. (reprint from original 1946, NY: P.F. Collier, Inc.)

Collins, Charles J. (1989, September/ October). "The effect of sunspot activity on the stock market." *Cycles*.

Collins, Charles J. (1966). "The Elliott wave principle of stock market behavior." Supplement to *The Bolton-Tremblay Bank Credit Analyst*. Republished: (1994). *The Complete Elliott Wave Writings of A. Hamilton Bolton*. Prechter, Jr., Robert Rougelot. (Ed.). Gainesville, GA: New Classics Library.

Cook, Theodore. (1914). *The curves of life*. London: Archibald Constable.

Cootner, P.H. (1964). *The random character of stock market prices*. Cambridge, MA: MIT Press.

Coveney, Peter and Highfield, Roger. (1995). *Frontiers of complexity*. New York: Ballantine Books.

Cowan, J.D. (1982). "Spontaneous symmetry breaking in large scale nervous activity." *International Journal of Quantum Chemistry*, No. 22, pp. 1059-1082.

Crutchfield, James P., Farmer, J. Doyne, Packard, Norman H. and Shaw, Robert S. (1986, December). "Chaos." *Scientific American*, pp. 46-57.

Cunningham, Steven R. (1993, Fall). "Unit root testing: a critique from chaos theory." *Review of Financial Economics*, Vol. III, No. 1.

Dacosta, N.C.A. (1994, September). "Overreaction in the Brazilian stock-market." *Journal of Banking and Finance*, Vol. 18, No. 4.

Dauben, Joseph W. (1990). *Georg Cantor: his mathematics and philosophy of the infinite*. Princeton University Press.

Davies, Paul. (1988). *The cosmic blueprint — new discoveries in nature's creative ability to order the universe*. New York: Simon & Schuster.

Davis, Dick. (1990, April 23). "Butterfly flap: chaology says no to market timing." *Dick Davis Digest*, Vol. 8, No. 190.

Davis, Nathan E. (1992). "Being right or making money." *Ned Davis Research Inc.*

Dawkins, Richard. (1993, December 15). "Is religion just a disease?" *The Daily Telegraph*.

Dawson, Chester. (1998, July 4). "Japan: time's right for tax cuts" *The Atlanta Journal-Constitution*.

DeBondt, Werner F.M. and Thaler, Richard. (1985, July). "Does the stock market overreact?" *The Journal of Finance*, Vol. XL, No. 3.

DeMause L. (1982). *Foundations of psychohistory*, pp.172-243.

Denberg, Jeffrey. (1998, December 9). "A league's fiscal rift." *The Atlanta Journal-Constitution*, p.E1.

Dennett, Daniel. (1991). *Consciousness explained*. London: Allen Lane. p.202.

Dent, Harry S. (1998.) *The roaring 2000s*. New York: Simon & Schuster.

Dewey, Edward R. and Dakin, Edwin F. (1945). *Cycles: the science of prediction*. The Foundation for the Study of Cycles.

DiBacco, Thomas. (1990, August 24). "Is war good for the economy?" *Fort Myers News-Press*.

Dissanaike, Gishan. (1994, December). "On the computation of returns in tests of the stock market overreaction hypothesis." *Journal of Banking and Finance*.

Doczi, György. (1981.) *The power of limits*. Boulder, CO: Shambhala Publications.

Domb, Eds C. and Green, M. (1971). "Critical behavior: universality and scaling." *Critical Phenomena*, Vol. 5 p.100. Academic Press. Also, private communication.

Donnelly, Barbara. (1987, October 23)."Efficient-market theorists are puzzled by recent gyrations in the stock market." *The Wall Street Journal*.

Dornbush, Rudi. (1998, July 30). "Growth forever." *The Wall Street Journal*.

Douady, Stephane and Couder, Yves. (1993). "Phyllotaxis as a self-organized growth process." *Growth patterns in physical sciences and biology*. Garcia-Ruiz, Juan Manuel, editor, *et al*. New York: Plenum Press.

Douglas, Kate. (1996, August 10). "Arachnophilia." *New Scientist*, pp. 24-28.

Drew, Garfield. (1955). *New methods for profit in the stock market*. Republished 1966. VT: Fraser Publishing Co.

Dunham, William. (1990). *Journey through genius: the great theorems of mathematics*. New York: John Wiley & Sons.

"Economists forecast mild inflation of 2.5% yearly through 2008." (1998, May 26). *The Wall Street Journal*.

"Economy surging behind spending." (1998, June 27). *The Atlanta Journal-Constitution*.

"Edgar Peters' fractal market hypothesis: a new market theory." (1994, May 31). *Derivative Risk Analyst*.

Edgar, G.A. (ed.) (1993). *Classics on fractals*. Reading MA: Addison-Wesley.

Einsasto, J., Einasto, M., Gottlober, S., Muller, V., Saar, V., Starobinsky, A.A., Tago, E., Tucker, D., Andernach, H., and Frisch, P. (1997, January 9). "A 120-Mpc periodicity in the three-dimensional distribution of galaxy superclusters." *Nature*.

Eliades, P. (1998, May 4). "Danger: bear may be crossing." *Barron's*.

Elliott, Ralph Nelson. (1938). *The wave principle*. Republished: (1994). *R.N. Elliott's Masterworks — The Definitive Collection*. Prechter, Jr., Robert Rougelot. (Ed.). Gainesville, GA: New Classics Library.

Elliott, Ralph Nelson. (1940, October 1). "The basis of the wave principle." Republished: (1994). *R.N. Elliott's Masterworks — The Definitive Collection*. Prechter, Jr., Robert Rougelot. (Ed.). Gainesville, GA: New Classics Library.

Elliott, Ralph Nelson. (1941, August 11). "Market apathy – cause and termination." Educational Bulletin. Republished: (1993). *R.N. Elliott's Market Letters (1938-1946)*. Prechter, Jr., Robert Rougelot. (Ed.). Gainesville, GA: New Classics Library. Also (1994) *R.N. Elliott's Masterworks — The Definitive Collection*. Prechter, Jr., Robert Rougelot. (Ed.). Gainesville, GA: New Classics Library.

Elliott, Ralph Nelson. (1941, August 25). "Two cycles of American history." Interpretive Letter No. 17. Republished: (1993). *R.N. Elliott's Market Letters (1938-1946)*. Also (1994) *R.N. Elliott's Masterworks — The Definitive Collection*. Prechter, Jr., Robert Rougelot. (Ed.). Gainesville, GA: New Classics Library.

Elliott, R.N. (1946). *Nature's law: the secret of the universe*. Republished: (1994). *R.N. Elliott's Masterworks — The Definitive Collection*. Prechter, Jr., Robert Rougelot. (Ed.). Gainesville, GA: New Classics Library.

Elson, Lawrence M. and Kapit, Wynn (1992). *Anatomy coloring book*. New York: Harper Collins.

Engel, Stefan. (1962). *Lung structure*. Springfield, IL: Charles C. Thomas.

Evans-Pritchard, Ambrose. (1998, September 2). "'Plunge team' ready to spring into action." *Electronic Telegraph* (internet).

Fell, Barry. (1980). *Saga America*. New York: Times Books, pp. 327, 330.

Firth, M. (1977). *The valuation of shares and the efficient-markets theory*. London: The Macmillan Press Ltd.

Ford, Constance M. (1998, July 7). "Survey sees brunt of Asian crisis hitting U.S. soon." *The Wall Street Journal*, p. A2.

Frank, Alan G. (1974). *The movie treasury — horror movies*. London: Octopus Books.

Fraser, James L. (1984, June 6). "Unpopular independent action." *The Contrary Investor*.

"Frontiers of finance." (1993, October 9). *The Economist*.

Frost, Alfred John, and Robert Rougelot Prechter, Jr. (1978). *Elliott wave principle — key to market behavior*. Gainesville, GA: New Classics Library.

Frost, Alfred John. (1970). "The Elliott wave principle of stock market behavior." Supplement to *The Bolton-Tremblay Bank Credit Analyst*. Republished: (1996). *The Elliott Wave Writings of A.J. Frost and Richard Russell*. Prechter, Jr., Robert Rougelot. (Ed.). Gainesville, GA: New Classics Library.

Fukuyama, Francis. (1992). *The end of history and the last man*. New York: Avon Books.

Fund, John H. (1994, June 14). "Welfare: putting people first." *The Wall Street Journal*.

Gajdusek, D.C. (1970). "Physiological and psychological characteristics of stone age man," *Symposium on Biological Bases of Human Behavior, Eng. Sci.* 33, pp. 26-33, 56-62.

Gauquelin, Michel. (1970). *The scientific basis of astrology*. p. 23-24. (from French astronomer Paul Couderc's *la Relativité*, p. 28). New York: Stein & Day.

Geewax, Marilyn. (1998, June 21). "U.S. could become entwined in downturn." *The Atlanta Journal-Constitution*.

Gigot, Paul A. (1998, August 14). "Woodward and Bernstein lose their fastball." *The Wall Street Journal*.

Glazman, R.E. (1988, April). "Fractal features of sea surface manifested in microwave remote sensing signatures." *OE Reports*.

Gleick, James. (1985, December 29). "Unexpected order in chaos." *This World*.

Gleick, James. (1985, December 8). "The man who reshaped geometry." *The New York Times*.

Goerner, S.J. (1992). "Chaos as tip of an iceberg: the big picture of physics' revolution in understanding the order-producing universe." Paper presented to the Chaos Network Conference.

Goethe, J.W. (1790). "On the metamorphosis of plants."

Goldberg, Robert. (1995, November 20). "The fab four 25 years later." *The Wall Street Journal*.

Goldberger, Ary L., Rigney, David R. and West, Bruce J. (1990, February). "Chaos and fractals in human physiology." *Scientific American*, pp. 42-49.

Goldfeld, Stephen M. (1984, November). "Modeling the banking firm." *Journal of Money, Credit and Banking*, p. 611.

Goleman, Daniel. (1989, August 15). "Brain's design emerges as a key to emotions." *The New York Times*.

Goleman, Daniel. (1995). *Emotional intelligence*. New York: Bantam Books.

Grabbe, J. Orlin. (1995). *International financial markets*. New York: Prentice Hall.

Gunaratne, P.S.M. and Yonesawa, Y. (1997, August). "Return reversals in the Tokyo stock exchange: a test of stock market overreaction." *Japan and the World Economy*.

Gunderson, Edna. (1989, July 21). "Drumming up a super Starr tour." *USA Today*.

Gunderson, Edna. (1991, March 21). "Jackson hits billion dollar note." *USA Today*.

Gunderson, Edna. (1993, November 19). "Jackson faces the man in the mirror." *USA Today*.

Guralnick, Peter (1994). *Last train to Memphis – the rise of Elvis Presley*. Boston: Little-Brown.

Gutenberg, B. and Richter, C.F. (1949). *Seismicity of the earth*. Princeton, NJ: Princeton University Press.

Guyton, Arthur C. (1991). *Textbook of medical physiology*. (8th ed.). W.B. Saunders.

Hambidge, Jay. (1919). *The elements of dynamic*. Yale University Press.

Hanson, Gayle. (1990, October 8). "A world that is graphically real." *Insight.*

Harlow, John. (1997, May 18). "Saatchi revives gory glory days of Hammer." *The Sunday Times* (London).

Harman, Tom. (1993, July 6). "Economists look for moderate growth in second half but warn creation of jobs will remain sluggish." *The Wall Street Journal*, p. A2.

Hausdorff, Felix. (1919). "Dimension und äusseres mass." *Mathematische Annalen*, 79, pp. 157-179.

Hausdorff, Jeffrey M., Mitchell, Susan L., Firtion, Renee, Peng, C.K., Cudkowicz, Merit E., Wei, Jeanne Y., and Goldberger, Ary L. (1997). "Altered fractal dynamics of gait: reduced stride-interval correlations with aging and Huntington's disease." American Physiological Society. 0161-7567/97.

Hausdorff, Jeffrey M., Peng, C.K., Wei, Jeanne Y. and Goldberger, Ary L. (1996). "Fractal analysis of human walking rhythm."

Hawkins, Gerald S. and White, John B. (1965). *Stonehenge decoded.* New York: Delta Books.

Hector, Gary. (1988, October 10). "What makes stock prices move?" *Fortune.*

Hediger, Heini. (1950). *Wild animals in captivity.* London: Butterworth.

Henry, David. (1998, October 9). "High stakes guessing game: markets defy easy answers." *USA Today.*

Hertsgaard, Mark (1995). *A day in the life.* New York: Delacorte Press.

Hoffer, E. (1955). *The passionate state of mind.* Buccaneer Books.

Holland, Bill. (1998, June 19). "The mystery of Frank Sinatra." *Goldmine.*

Horn, Robert. (1997, December 8). "Thailand starting big financial overhaul." *The Atlanta Journal-Constitution*, p. A12.

Hotz, Robert Lee. (1997, October). "A study in complexity." *MIT Technology Review.*

Hurst, H., Black, R. and Simaika, Y. (1951). *Long-term storage: an experimental study.* London: Constable.

Hutchison, Michael. (1987). *Megabrain.* New York: Ballantine Books.

Ip, Greg. (1998, October 14). "Risk and uncertainty wreak havoc on stocks." *The Wall Street Journal.*

Janis, Irving L. (1972). *Victims of groupthink.* Boston: Houghton Mifflin.

Jantsch, Erich (1980). *The self-organizing universe.* Oxford: Pergamon.

Jensen, Roderick V. (1987, March-April). "Classical chaos." *American Scientist*, Vol. 75.

Johansen, Anders and Sornette, Didier. (1999). "Critical crashes." *Risk*, Vol. 12, No. 1

Johnson, George. (1996, September 8). "From grains of sand: a world of order." *The New York Times.*

Johnson, George. (1997, January 19). "The real star wars: between order and chaos." *The New York Times*, p. 4.

Johnson, W.A. (1986, September 17). "Remember warnings of $3/gallon gas?" *Daily News Digest.*

Jordan, Mary. (1998, May 28). "S. Koreans walk off their jobs: workers protest growing layoffs." *The Washington Post.*

Jung, Carl. (1959). *The archetypes and the collective unconscious.* (2nd edition, 1981) Princeton University Press.

Kamm, Thomas. (1990, November 16). "Brazil's president, after eight months, finds roar of crowd is now against him." *The Wall Street Journal.*

Kawai, N. *et al.* (1990). "Spectral evolution of type II bursts from the rapid burster." *Astronomical Society of Japan* No. 42, pp. 115-133.

Kay, John. (1995, September 29). "Cracks in the crystal ball." *Financial Times.*

Kelly, G.A. (1955). *The psychology of personal constructs.* New York: Norton.

Kendall, Peter. (1996, December 16). "Basketball and the bull market." *The Elliott Wave Theorist* special report.

Khinchin, A. Ya. (1964.) *Continued fractions.* University of Chicago Press, p. 36

Kim, James. (1998, July 24). "Traders seize PC power." *USA Today.*

Kim, Lillian Lee. (1998, October 8). "Fewer lives lost to AIDS." *The Atlanta Journal-Constitution.*

Klein, Easy. (1986, November). "Psychology meets the stock market." *Columbia.*

Knott, Ron. (1997, October 18). "The Lucas numbers." www.mcs.surrey.ac.uk/Personal / R.Knott/Fibonacci/lucasNbs.html.

Koselka, Rita. (1996, June 30). "The madness of well-heeled crowds." *Forbes Magazine.*

Kuhn, Thomas. (1970.) *The structure of scientific revolutions,* (2nd ed.) University of Chicago Press. (Original 1962)

Kulkosky, Edward. (1977, October 15). "The Elliott wave's surprising message to investors." *Financial World.*

Laderman, Jeffrey and Pennar, Karen. (1988, October 17). "Did the crash make a dent?" *Business Week.*

Larsen, William J. (1997). *Human Embryology.* New York: Churchill Livingstone.

Le Bon, Gustave. (1895). *The crowd.* (France). Republished 1960. New York: Viking Press.

Lefebvre, Vladimir. (1992). "A rational equation of attractive proportions." *Journal of Mathematical Psychology,* 36, 100-128.

Lefebvre, V.A. (1987, October). "The fundamental structures of human reflexion." *The Journal of Social Biological Structure,* Vol. 10, pp. 129-175.

Lefebvre, Vladimir. (1990). *The fundamental structures of human reflexion.* Peter Lang Publishing.

Lefebvre, Vladimir. (1992). *A psychological theory of bipolarity and reflexivity.* Lewinston, NY: The Edwin Mellen Press.

Lefebvre, Vladimir. (1997). *The cosmic subject.* Moscow: Russian Academy of Sciences Institute of Psychology Press.

Lefebvre Vladimir. (1998, August 18-20). "Sketch of reflexive game theory." Workshop on Multi-Reflexive Models of Agent Behavior. Army Research Laboratory, Los Alamos, NM.

Lefebvre, Vladimir and Efremov, Yuri N., (1998). "Possible analogues of cognitive processes in the patterns of X-ray variability of the rapid burster." Astrophysical archive on the Internet.

Leontief, Wassily. (1982, July 9). "Academic Economics." (Letter to the Editor) *Science,* Vol. 217, No. 4555.

Lesmoir-Gordon, Nigel (producer). (1994). "Fractals: the colors of infinity." Gordon Films (distributed by Films for the Humanities, Princeton NJ).

Liang, Y.G. and Mullineaux, D.J. (1994, Spring). "Overreaction and reverse anticipation 2 related puzzles." *Journal of Financial Research,* Vol. 17, No. 1.

Linde, Andrei. (1994, November). "The self-reproducing inflationary universe." *Scientific American.*

Lipsitz, Lewis and Goldberger, Ary L. (1992, April 1). "Loss of 'complexity' and aging – potential applications of fractals and chaos theory to senescence." *Journal of the American Medical Association,* Vol 267, No. 13.

Liscio, John. (1998, March 2). "The seer syndrome." *Barron's.*

Litton, Robert E. and Santomero, Anthony M. (1998, July 28). "Why a market correction won't replay 1987." *The Wall Street Journal.*

Lowenstein, Roger. (1991, June 6). "Goldman study of stocks' rise in 80s poses a big riddle." *The Wall Street Journal.*

Ludwig, Emil. (1926). *Napoleon.* New York: Garden City Publishing.

Mackay, Charles. (1841). *Extraordinary popular delusions and the madness of crowds.* (London.) Reprinted 1980, Three Rivers Press.

MacLean, Paul D. (1990). *The triune brain in evolution: role in paleocerebral functions.* New York: Plenum Press.

Malabre, Jr. Alfred L. (1987, February 23). "The stock market and the business cycle." *The Wall Street Journal.*

Malkiel, Burton. (1985.) *A random walk down wall street,* 4th ed. New York: Norton.

Malkiel, Burton. (1998, July/August). "Still on a random walk." *Bloomberg Personal Finance.*

Mandel, Michael J. (1996, September 30). "Especially dismal at downturns." *Business Week.*

Mandelbrot, Benoit. (1988). *The fractal geometry of nature.* New York: W.H. Freeman.

Mantegna, Rosario N. and Stanley, H. Eugene. (1995, July 6). "Scaling behaviour in the dynamics of an economic index." *Nature,* Vol 376.

Marshal, Alfred. (1890). *Principles of economics.* New York: MacMillan & Co.

McGraw, K.M. (1985). "Subjective probabilities and moral judgments." *Journal of Experimental and Biological Structures,* Vol. 10, pp. 501-518.

McIlvride, B. (1986, March 10-16). "Dr. Robert Thatcher, leading neurophysiologist, visits MIU." *MIU Review,* Vol. 1, No. 27.

McKaig, Angie. (1996-1998). Website *Pathway to darkness,* www.pathway todarkness.com, Toronto, Canada.

Miller, Rich. (1998, February 2). "Economists: Asian storm about to hit U.S." *USA Today.*

Montgomery, Paul Macrae. (1986, March 8). "Volcker part III: The godfather." *Universal Economics.*

Montgomery, Paul Macrae. (1990, October 11). "Magazine covers and real estate." *Universal Economics.*

Montgomery, Paul Macrae. (1991, March 15). "Neurophysiology, presidents and the stock market, part III." *Universal Economics.*

Montgomery, Paul Macrae. (1991, March 19). *Universal Economics.* (untitled market commentary published and broadcast to clients.)

Montgomery, Paul Macrae. (1991, September 19). "Stocks and the irrational: possible sub-cortical influences on contemporary equity market pricing." Presentation to Grant's Fall Conference, Chicago, Illinois.

Montgomery, Paul Macrae. (1992, September 13). "Capital markets and the irrational: possible non-cortical influences on the price structure of investments." Presentation to the Elliott Wave International conference, Buford, Georgia.

Montgomery, Paul Macrae. (1995, April 6). "The logical primacy of immaterial mental states in the price structure of investments: or how to outperfom the markets in 10 easy minutes a week." Presentation to *Straw Hats in the Winter: An Overview of Behavioral Finance,* Cincinnati, Ohio.

Montgomery, Paul Macrae. (1996, May 17). "Economic theory and technical analysis: the unscientific nature of the 'rational' approach, versus the rational nature of the 'unscientific' approach." Presentation to the 21st Annual Market Technicians Association Seminar, Marco Island, Florida.

Montgomery, Paul Macrae. (1998, February 4). *Universal Economics.* (untitled market commentary published and broadcast to clients.)

Moody, Paul Amos. (1962.) *Introduction to evolution.* (2nd Ed.) New York: Harper & Row.

Nasar, Sylvia. (1998, August 15). "Cloudy blue skies." *The New York Times.*

Nesmith, J. (1996, September 14). "The roots of personality: researchers are zeroing in on the biological and genetic foundations that determine who we are." *The Atlanta Journal-Constitution.*

Neuharth, Al. (1998, July 31). "'Ryan' movie misses the cause of WWII." *USA Today.*

Nichols, Bill. (1994, September 28). "Warm fuzzy summit." *USA Today.*

Nietzsche, F. (1886). *Beyond good & evil.* (Translated by Walter Kaufmann, 1989). Vintage Books.

Norman, Philip. (1981). *Shout: the true story of the Beatles.* New York: Simon & Schuster.

Ogburn, Charlton. (1984). *The mysterious William Shakespeare.* McLean, VA: EPM Publications.

Oglesby, Christy. (1998, August 18). "State unable to judge effect of welfare shift." *The Atlanta Journal-Constitution.*

Olsen, R. (1996, July/August). "Implications of herding behavior for earnings estimation, risk assessment, and stock returns." *Financial Analysts Journal.*

Osgood, C.E., and Richards, M.M. (1973). *Language,* Vol. 49, pp. 380-412.

Page, Susan. (1998, January 22). "President's resilience faces biggest test." *USA Today.*

Passell, Peter. (1989, August 25). "Dow and reason: distant cousins?" *The New York Times.*

Penrose, Roger. (1994.) *Shadows of the mind – a search for the missing science of consciousness.* Oxford University Press.

Peratt, Anthony L. (1990, January/February). "Not with a bang." *The Sciences.*

Peters, Edgar E. (1991, March/April). "A chaotic attractor for the S&P 500." *Financial Analysts Journal.*

Pigou, Arthur C. (1920). *The economics of welfare.* London: F. Cass.

Pigou, Arthur C. (1927). *Industrial fluctuations.* London: F. Cass.

Pincheira, G. (1997, November 27). "In the genome, symmetry seems to code symmetry." Presentation to the International Conference on the Unity of the Sciences, Washington, DC.

Planck, Max. (1949). *Scientific autobiography and other papers.* New York: Philosophical Library. (translated by F. Gaynor). pp. 33-34.

Popper, Karl R. (1957). *The poverty of historicism.* Boston: Beacon Press.

Postrel, Virginia. (1998, December). "The two faces of Bill Clinton." *Reason,* p. 4.

Poulton, E.C., Simmonds, D.C.V. and Warren, R.M. (1968). "Response bias in very first judgments of the reflectance of grays: numerical versus linear estimates." *Perception and Psychophysics,* Vol. 3, pp. 112-114.

Prechter, Jr., Robert R. (1982, September 13). "The long term wave pattern — nearing a resolution." *The Elliott Wave Theorist.* Republished: (1996) *Elliott wave principle — key to market behavior.*

Prechter, Jr., Robert R. (1983, April 6). "A rising tide — the case for wave V in the Dow Jones industrial average." *The Elliott Wave Theorist* special report. Republished: (1996) *Elliott wave principle — key to market behavior.*

Prechter, Jr., Robert R. (1983, August 18). "The superbull market of the '80s: has the last wild ride really begun?" *The Elliott Wave Theorist* special report. Republished: (1996) *Elliott wave principle — key to market behavior.*

Prechter, Jr., Robert R. (1985, September 9). "Elvis, Frankenstein and Andy Warhol: using pop culture to forecast the stock market." *Barron's.*

Prechter, Jr. Robert R. (1985, December 31). "1986: Another bull market for stocks." *The Elliott Wave Theorist* special report.

Prechter, Jr., Robert R. (1986, May). "The fractal design of social progress." Presentation given to the Market Technicians Association, Boston.

Prechter, Jr. Robert R. (1992, December 31). "An application of the wave principle to business." *The Elliott Wave Theorist* special report.

Price, William H. (1961). *The civil war handbook.* Fairfax, VA: Prince Lithograph Co.

Prigogine, I. and Stengers, I. (1984). *Order out of chaos.* New York: Bantam Books.

Prochnow, Herbert. (ed.). (1986). *The Public Speakers Treasure Chest.* New York: Harper & Row.

Prusinkiewicz, P. and Lindenmayer, A. (1990). *The algorithmic beauty of plants.* Springer-Verlag.

Pugsley, John (1995). "Anthology of essential articles." *John Pugsley's Journal.* Phoenix Communications.

Raghaven, Anita and Pacelle, Mitchell. (1998, September 24). "A hedge fund falters, and big banks agree to ante up $3.5 billion." *The Wall Street Journal.*

Rapoport, A. and Chammah, A.M. (1965). *Prisoner's dilemma.* University of Michigan Press.

Ratajczak, Donald. (1998, August 30). "Global economy requires action." *The Atlanta Journal-Constitution.*

"Reducing the health consequences of smoking: 25 years of progress." (1989). A report of the Surgeon General. DHHS Publication No. (CDC) 87-8411.

Rhea, Robert A. (1934). *Story of the averages: a retrospective study of the forecasting value of Dow's theory as applied to the daily movements of the Dow-Jones industrial & railroad stock averages.* Republished January 1990. Omnigraphi.

Richardson, L.F. (1961). "The problem of contiguity: an appendix of statistics of deadly quarrels." *General Systems Yearbook*, Vol. 6, pp. 139-187.

Ricketts, Robert M. (1982, May). "The biologic significance of the divine proportion and Fibonacci series." *American Journal of Orthodontics*, St. Louis, Vol. 81, No. 5, pp. 351-370.

Roeser, Steve. (1993, October 15). "Ginger Baker: anyone for polo?" *Goldmine.*

Rothchild, John. (1998). *The bear book: survive and profit in ferocious markets.* New York: John Wiley & Sons, Inc.

Ruhlmann, William. (1998, June 19). "Celebrating Sinatra." *Goldmine.*

Rynecki, David. (1998, June 15). "Bull markets susceptible to anxieties." *USA Today.*

Sakarui, Joji. (1998, July 10). "Japan goes with veteran at helm of wayward economy." *The Atlanta Journal-Constitution.*

Saleur, H. and Sornette, D. (1996). "Complex exponents and log-periodic corrections in frustrated systems." *Journal de Physique I France* 6, No. 3, pp. 327-355.

Samenow, Stanton E. (1984.) *Inside the criminal mind.* New York: Times Books

"Savings rate cut in 1990s." (1990, October 15). *The Wall Street Journal.*

Savit, Robert. (1990, August). "Chaos and economics." *New Scientist.*

Saxon, Edward, Utt, Kenneth and Bozman, Ron (producers), and Demme, Jonathon (director). (1991). *Silence of the lambs* (film). Orion Pictures.

Scholl, Jaye. (1998, September 28). "The big fizzle." *Barron's.*

Schonberg, H.C. (1987). *The great pianists from Mozart to the present.* New York: Simon & Schuster.

Schroeder, Manfred. (1991). *Fractals, chaos, power laws: minutes from an infinite paradise.* New York: W.H. Freeman & Co.

Schuller, Gunther. (1989). *The swing era.* Oxford University Press.

Schumpeter, Joseph. (1939). *Business cycles.* New York: McGraw-Hill.

Schwartz, E.L. (1980). "A quantitative model of the functional architecture of human striate cortex with application to visual illusion and cortical texture analysis." *Biol. Cybern.*, Vol. 37, pp. 63-76.

Schwartz, E.L. (1980). "Computational anatomy and functional architecture of striate cortex: a spatial mapping approach to perceptual coding." *Vision Res.*, Vol. 20, pp. 645-669.

Scism, Leslie and Browning, E.S. (1998, August 6). "In the battle of the stock-market gurus, bulls win a round." *The Wall Street Journal*, p. C1.

Scuoteguazza, Henry C. (1997, September/October). "Handling emotional intelligence." *The Objective American.*

Seagle, Gene Jay. (1993, October). "Time and tide." *MTA Newsletter.*

Sepkoski, Jr., J. John. (1993). "Phanerozoic taxonomic diversity." *Paleobiology*, Vol. 19.

Shalit, B. (1960). *British journal of psychology*, 71, pp. 39-42.

Shambaugh, Philip Wells. (n.d.) "The cultural theory of small group development." *Group Psychodynamics — New Paradigms and New Perspectives.* Chicago: Year Book Medical Publishers.

Shaw, Russell and Landis, David. (1987, October 9). "Prechter flees wall st. for Georgia hills." *USA Today.*

Sheeley, G. (1997, April 14). "Runaway Tiger: Woods wins Masters by record 12 shots with 18-under total." *The Atlanta Journal-Constitution.*

Sheldrake, Rupert. (1981). *A new science of life.* St. Martin's Press.

Sherden, William. (1998). *The fortune sellers.* New York: John Wiley & Sons.

Sherrington, C.S. (1940). *Man on his nature.* Cambridge University Press.

Shomali, Hamid B. (1994/1995, Winter/Spring). "Technical versus fundamental analysis: a view from academe." *MTA Journal.*

Showalter, Elaine. (1997). *Hystories: hysterical epidemics and modern media.* New York: Columbia University Press.

Siegfried, Tom. (1992, August 31). "Fractal patterns within DNA may encode mysteries of life." *The Dallas Morning News.*

Siegfried, Tom. (1993, March 29). "Healthy hearts have complex rhythm." *The Dallas Morning News.*

Smeaton, Bob. (1996). *The Beatles anthology* (Videotape). Hollywood, CA: Capitol Records.

Smith, Vernon L., Suchanek, Gerry L. and Williams, Arlington W. (1988, September). "Bubbles, crashes, and endogenous expectations in experimental spot asset markets." *Econometrica*, Vol. 56, No. 5, p. 1149.

Sole, R.V., Manrubia, S.C., Benton, M. and Bak, P. (1997, August 21). "Self-similarity of extinction statistics in the fossil record." *Nature*, Vol. 388, pp. 764-767.

Sornette, Didier, Johansen, Anders, and Bouchaud, Jean-Philippe. (1996). "Stock market crashes, precursors and replicas." *Journal de Physiques I France* 6, No. 1, pp. 167-175.

Sornette, Didier, and Johansen, Anders. (1997, November 1). "Large financial crashes." *Physica A – Statistical and Theoretical Physics*, edited by Capel, H.W., Mulder, B., Stanley, H.E., and Tsallis, C. Vol. 245, Nos. 3-4.

Sornette, Didier. (1997, October 15) "Generic mechanisms for hierarchies." *InterJournal Complex Systems* No. 127.

Sornette, Didier. (1998, June 30-July 3). "Discrete scale invariance in turbulence?" Proceedings of the 7th European Turbulence Conference.

Sornette, Didier. "Discrete scale invariance and complex dimensions." *Physics Reports* No. 297, pp. 239-270.

"Stand still, little lambs, to be shorn." (1998, March). *Economic Education Bulletin*. American Enterprise Institute, Great Barrington, MA.

Stanley, H.E., Buldyrev, S.V., Caserta, F., Daccord, G., Eldred, W., Goldberger, A., Hausman, R.E., Havlin, S., Larralde, H., Nittmann, J., Peng, C.K., Sciortino, F., Simons, M., Trunfio, P., and Weiss, G.H. (1993). "Fractal landscapes in physics and biology." *Growth patterns in physical sciences and biology*. New York: Plenum Press.

Stein, R. Conrad. (1993). *The Manhattan project*. Chicago: Children's Press.

Stewart, Ian. (1998). *Life's other secret*. New York: John Wiley & Sons.

Stokes, William Lee. (1966). *Essentials of earth history*. (2nd ed.) New Jersey: Prentice-Hall.

"Tech stocks are hurt by uncertainty over Asia." (1998, June 2). *The Atlanta Journal-Constitution*.

"The 21st century economy." (1998, August). *Business Week.*

"The lesson of the day." (1857, October 10). *Harper's Weekly*.

"The mathematics of markets: a survey of the frontiers of finance." (1993, October 9). *The Economist*.

"The practical fractal." (1987, December 26). *The Economist*.

The World Book Encyclopedia. (1992). Chicago: World Book.

Thompson, D'Arcy. (1917). *On growth and form*. Cambridge University Press.

Tindol, Robert. (1989, December 11). "Vanguard of a new approach to physical sciences." *On Campus* (University of Texas staff publication).

Tompkins, Peter and Bird, Christopher. (1973). *The secret life of plants*. New York: Harper & Row.

"Too Good." (1998, June 16). *The Wall Street Journal*. (editorial).

Toon, John. (1988, April/May). "New technology uses fractals to transmit images." *Tech Topics*, publication of the Georgia Tech Alumni Association.

"Trade deficit hits record." (1998, October 21). *The Atlanta Journal-Constitution*.

"Trade deficit soars to $13 billion." (1998, May 20). *The Atlanta Journal-Constitution*.

Train, John. (1994). *Money masters*. New York: Harper Collins.

Treynor, Jack. (1998, March/April). "Bulls, bears, and market bubbles." *Financial Analysts Journal*.

Tuckman, B.W. (1965). "Developmental sequence in small groups." *Psychology Bulletin*, No. 63, pp. 115-133.

Vandervert, Larry R. (1990). "Systems thinking and neurological positivism: further elucidations and implications." *Systems Research,* 7, 1/17.

Vicsek, Tamás. (1993). "The fractal nature of common patterns." *Growth Patterns in Physical Sciences and Biology.* Garcia-Ruiz, Juan Manuel, editor, *et al.* New York: Plenum Press.

Vittachi, Nury and Mark Faber. (1998). *Riding the millennial storm: Marc Faber's path to profit in the financial crisis.* New York: John Wiley & Sons, p. 112.

Vogel, H. (1979). "A better way to construct the sunflower head." *Mathematical Biosciences* #44, pp. 145-174.

Vollrath, Fritz. (1992, March). "Spider webs and silks." *Scientific American,* pp. 52-58.

Von Baeyer, Hans C. (1990, February). "Impossible crystals." *Discover.*

Voss, Richard. (1992, June). "Evolution of long range fractal correlations and $1/f$ noise in DNA-based sequences." *Physical Review Letters,* 68:3805-3808.

Walker, Tom. (1998, August 1). "Stocks conclude week on sour note." *The Atlanta Journal-Constitution.*

Walker, Tom. (1998, August 21). "Impact of air strikes on stocks uncertain." *The Atlanta Journal-Constitution.*

Walker, Tom. (1998, August 6). "Identifying sell-off trigger difficult." *The Atlanta Journal-Constitution.*

Walker, Tom. (1998, June 21). "Determining what will move market not difficult – but forecasting its direction is harder." *The Atlanta Journal-Constitution.*

Walters, Charles. (1993, June). "An interview with P.Q. Wall, analyst." *Acres, USA.*

Washburn, Jim. (1993, March 31). "The human equation." *The Los Angeles Times.*

Webster's Third New International Dictionary, 1976.

Weibel, E.R. (1962). "Architecture of the human lung." *Science,* No. 137.

Weibel, E.R. (1963). *Morphometry of the human lung.* Academic Press.

Weiss, Gary. (1992, November 2). "Chaos hits wall street – the theory, that is." *Business Week.*

Wessel, David and Davis, Bob. (1998, September 24). "How global crisis grew despite efforts of a crack U.S. team." *The Wall Street Journal,* p. A1.

West, Bruce J. and Goldberger, Ary L. (1987, July/August). "Physiology in fractal dimensions." *American Scientist,* Vol. 75.

Wilcox, J.M. (1980). "Origin of the warped heliospheric current sheet." *Science,* Vol. 209, pp. 603-605.

Wilson, Edward O. (1998). *Consilience: the unity of knowledge.* New York: Alfred A. Knopf.

Winter, Douglas E. (1986). *Stephen King: the art of darkness.* New York: Signet Books.

Witten, T.A. and Sander, L.M. (1981). *Phys. Rev. Lett.* 47, 1400. (1983). *Phys. Rev.* B 27, 5686; Sander, L.M. (1986). *Nature* 332, 789; Recent work on the dynamics of DLA growth is described in Schwarzer, S. Lee, J., Havlin, Stanley, H.E. and Meakin, P. (1991). *Phys. Rev.* A 43, 1134-1137 and refs. therein. A "void channel" model for DLA structure is described in Lee, J. Havlin. S. and Stanley, H.E. (1992). *Phys. Rev.* A 45, 1035.

Wright, K. (1997, October). "Babies, bonds, and brains." *Discover,* p. 78.

Zajonc, R.B. (1968). "Attitudinal effects of mere exposure." *Journal of Personality and Social Psychology.* monograph supplement, 9, No. 2, Part 2, 1-32.

Zipf, G.K. (1949). *Human behavior and the principle of least action.* Reading, PA: Addison-Wesley.

Index